MICROECONOMICS

MICROECONOMICS

FOURTH EDITION

PAUL WONNACOTT / RONALD WONNACOTT
UNIVERSITY OF MARYLAND
UNIVERSITY OF WESTERN ONTARIO

JOHN WILEY & SONS
NEW YORK / CHICHESTER / BRISBANE / TORONTO / SINGAPORE

Acquisitions Editor: John Woods
Cover Illustrator: Jana Brenning
Cover Calligrapher: Stuart David
Text Designer: Madelyn Lesure
Developmental Editors: Barbara Heaney and Georgene Gallagher
Managing Editor: Joan Kalkut
Copy editing Supervisor: Gilda Stahl; Copy editor: Betty Pessagno
Production Manager: Joe Ford; Production: Hudson River Studio
Photo Research: John Wiley Photo Research Department

Library of Congress Cataloging in Publication Data:

Wonnacott, Paul.
[Economics. Selections]
Microeconomics / Paul Wonnacott, Ronald Wonnacott. — 4th ed.
p. cm.
Selections from authors' Economics, 4th ed., 1990.
Rev. ed. of: An introduction to microeconomics. 3rd ed. 1986.
Companion to: Macroeconomics. 4th ed. 1990.
Includes bibliographical references.
ISBN 0-471-50838-1
1. Microeconomics. I. Wonnacott, Ronald J. II. Wonnacott, Paul. Introduction to microeconomics. III. Wonnacott, Paul. Macroeconomics. IV. Title.
HB172.W6925 1990 89-24760
338.5—dc20 CIP

Printed in the United States of America

10 9 8 7 6 5 4 3 2

ABOUT THE AUTHORS

Ronald J. Wonnacott received his Ph.D. in economics from Harvard in 1959, and has taught at that university, the University of Western Ontario, and the University of Minnesota. He has written widely on the subject of U.S.-Canadian trade and on the economics of customs unions and free trade areas—much of this with his brother Paul. Their joint book, *Free Trade between the United States and Canada: The Potential Economic Effects* (Harvard University Press, 1967) was one of the studies that led to a twenty-year debate in Canada and to the recent Free Trade Agreement between the United States and Canada. Ron Wonnacott has also co-authored books on statistics and econometrics with a third brother, Tom (also published by John Wiley). He is a past president of the Canadian Economics Association and a Fellow of the Royal Society of Canada. He shares an enthusiasm for tennis and skiing with Paul. He loves the music of Mozart, and is a member of the Honourable Company of Edinburgh Golfers.

Paul Wonnacott studied history as an undergraduate at the University of Western Ontario. He then switched to his second and greatest academic love—economics—receiving his Ph.D. from Princeton. He was on the faculty of Columbia University before taking his present post at the University of Maryland. He has written extensively on international economics. In joint work with brother Ron on the theory of customs unions, the two authors emphasize the gains achieved when a trading partner reduces its barriers to imports. Paul Wonnacott has a keen interest in economic policy. While with the Council of Economic Advisers, he participated in work which led to the decision to adopt flexible exchange rates in the early 1970s. He has also served on the staffs of the Canadian Royal Commission on Banking and Finance, the Federal Reserve Board, and the U.S. Treasury. He is currently on leave from the University of Maryland, serving as the economic adviser to the Undersecretary of State.

To
Doug
Debi
Rob
Cathy
Brandon
Jason

PREFACE

TO THE INSTRUCTOR

The fourth edition of *Microeconomics* represents the most comprehensive revision to date. The extensive revisions build on and refine the framework of earlier editions. Details on "What's New" in this edition are provided in the next section.

This book, and its companion volume on macroeconomics, were inspired by two major questions that arose in our teaching—and by our uneasiness regarding the answers.

For microeconomics, the principal question was the following: Does the introductory study of microeonomics lack coherence? To the student, does microeconomics tend to become just one thing after another—a guided tour through the economist's workshop, introducing as many polished pieces of analytic machinery as possible for later use in more advanced courses? In our view, there is little point in concentrating on analytic techniques for their own sake, when the time could instead be spent applying basic economic theory to interesting policy issues. Even for those students who continue in economics, we doubt that it is useful to focus heavily on analytic techniques. True, such a focus gives students some headstart in their later courses, but it also increases the risk that they will be bored by repetition and will miss some of the forest while concentrating on the trees. Therefore, we follow a simple rule of thumb: In introducing analytic concepts, we focus on those most useful in studying policy issues.

We have attempted to make microeconomics more interesting and understandable by organizing our discussion around two continuing themes: **efficiency** and **equity.** Efficiency is the focus of attention in Parts III and IV, and equity in Part V. Throughout the microeconomic chapters, students are shown how policy changes can affect efficiency and redistribute real income. In many instances there can be tension between the goals of efficiency and equity—the "big tradeoff" in the words of Arthur Okun. While we provide numerous illustrations where efficiency and equity can be in conflict, we also provide examples where there is no conflict. For example, less discrimination in the labor market is not only equitable, but also efficient (Ch. 24).

For macroeconomics (covered in a companion volume, *Macroeconomics*), the principal question was this: After studying introductory economics, are students able to understand public controversies over such topics as the level of government spending and taxation, the rising national debt, and monetary policy? Are we training our students to understand the front pages of the newspaper? For many years, the introductory course was aimed at teaching students how policy should be run, that is, at providing a cookbook of "right" answers. While many books express more doubts and qualifications than was the case a decade ago, we have altered the focus of the course even more by building up to the seven controversial questions in the companion volume:

- How can inflation exist at the same time as a high rate of unemployment?
- In the face of an unemployment-inflation dilemma, what options do policymakers have?
- How does the economy adjust to inflation, and what complications does inflation present to the policymaker?
- Why have productivity and growth been disappointing since 1973?
- Is fiscal or monetary policy the key to aggregate demand?
- Should the authorities attempt to "fine tune" aggregate demand?
- Should exchange rates be fixed or flexible? What complications do international transactions introduce into monetary and fiscal policies?

These, then, are the first two objectives of our book:

1. To provide coherence and interest to microeconomics by focusing on the two major themes of efficiency and equity.

2. To provide an understanding of the major, controversial policy questions.

THE FOURTH EDITION: WHAT'S NEW?

The biggest single innovation in the fourth edition is a new recurring theme: LIVING IN A GLOBAL ECONOMY. This new theme was inspired by the increasingly close ties between the United States and the international economy. In 1950 exports plus imports of goods and services were equal to only 9.3% of U.S. gross national product; less than 10% of our economy was tied directly to international trade. By 1970 the figure had grown to 12.7%, and by 1988, to 23.3%. With the relaxation of capital controls and improvements in communications, financial ties have grown even stronger. Furthermore, major new economic policy issues have arisen in international relations—such as the protection of the environment.

Topics under the general heading of LIVING IN A GLOBAL ECONOMY include:

- Why **office rents** vary among the major financial and economic centers, such as London, Tokyo, Hong Kong, and New York. (This illustrates the concepts of demand and supply in Ch. 4, pp. 58–59.)

■ The recent **free trade agreement between the United States and Canada** (Ch. 3, pp. 43–44)—a topic in which we have had a personal interest since the 1960s, when Harvard published our book, *Free Trade Between the United States and Canada: The Potential Economic Effects.*

■ The move toward **privatization** of government-owned enterprises in a number of countries, such as the United Kingdom. (This section, in Ch. 5, pp. 77–78, includes our favorite quotation: Sir John Egan's observation that Prime Minister Margaret Thatcher "has never liked owning car companies. She barely puts up with owning the police.")

■ The **foreign elasticity of demand** for U.S. goods, and why low short-run elasticities mean that the trade balance adjusts only slowly to a change in exchange rates (Ch. 6, p. 138).

■ The **stock market crash** of 1987: What was happening in Tokyo, Hong Kong, and London? (Ch. 8, pp. 169–170).

■ The **world's largest firm**—Nippon Telegraph and Telephone (Ch. 12, p. 252).

■ **Foreign investment** in the United States (Ch. 23).

■ **Poverty rates** in selected foreign nations (Ch. 25).

Other important changes include:

■ **Full color,** used for a functional purpose. Costs and supply are shown in red, while demand is shown in blue. Green—the color of money—is often used to represent dollar values.

■ A complete rewriting of the **introductory chapters on microeconomic theory** (Chs. 6–10) in response to numerous suggestions by users. As part of the revisions, both long-run and short-run costs for all types of firms are described in Chapter 9, before we turn to specific markets in which firms may be operating (perfect competition in Chs. 10–11, monopoly in Ch. 12, and so on).

■ A drawing together of **farm problems** into a single chapter (Ch. 15). Here we go beyond the traditional discussion of unstable prices to include contemporary issues: the international subsidy war and the heavy burden of debt faced by some farmers.

■ An explanation of the three-step procedure used by the U.S. government in deciding whether to permit a **merger** (pp. 253–254). This passage addresses many important issues which antitrust authorities did not adequately consider in the past. We also present a new diagram (Fig. 14-1, p. 248) that illustrates a tradeoff that often must be faced: Larger size permits a greater exercise of market power but can allow firms to capture greater economies of scale.

■ A recasting of the diagram and an explanation of a **discriminating monopoly** to illustrate how the monopolist charges a higher price in the less elastic market (pp. 208–209).

■ A complete reorganization of Chapter 13 on markets **between perfect competition and monopoly.** The chapter now begins with monopolistic competition—the market closest to perfect competition—and then moves to oligopoly. Finally, a new section at the end of the chapter describes game theory. Instructors may choose to place heavy emphasis on game theory, or they may skip this topic *without any loss of continuity.*

■ An expansion of the chapter on pollution into a chapter on the quality of life. It now includes **safety** and **health** regulations (pp. 290–293).

■ Addition to the chapter on trade policy of topics such as the arguments for **strategic protection** and for attempts to "engineer" a comparative advantage. This chapter also includes recent developments such as the "super 301" cases initiated against Japan, Brazil, and India in 1989.

SLOW, ORDERLY EXPOSITION

One of our major objectives has been to explain important ideas as simply as possible, in slow, orderly steps. In some cases, this has meant the use of a specific illustration as a way of introducing an abstract idea. For example, once students have been shown a specific illustration of a Pareto improvement (Box 11-2, p. 179), we have found that they can understand the idea of a Pareto optimum—a topic which some authors have judged too difficult to include, or have presented in a way that is too demanding for students to follow.

In other cases, the desire to proceed in slow, orderly steps has meant the addition of detail. For example, in the companion volume, our introduction to the concepts of aggregate demand and aggregate supply is more detailed (and, in our opinion, much more precise) than that of most competing books.

In summary, we have made the slow, methodical development of theory one of our principal goals. Students have responded favorably to our organization and writing style.

SUPPLEMENTS

There are five supplements available to users of *Economics,* Fourth Edition. They are also available to users of this text:

1. **Study Guide,** which includes:
   - A statement of the purpose of each chapter.
   - A list of learning objectives.
   - A detailed summary highlighting the important ideas covered.
   - Exercises in matching important terms and their definitions.
   - True-False practice exam-type questions.
   - Multiple-Choice practice exam-type questions.
   - Numerical and graphical exercises.
2. **Instructor's Resource Guide,** which includes for each chapter:
   - Learning objectives.

- Teaching Hints.
- Lecture outline, also available on disk with **Lecture Maker** lecture customizing software for IBM PCs.
- Answers to end-of-chapter problems.
- Transparency masters of text art not part of transparency package.

In some chapters there is supplementary material that can be used to expand your lectures into topics not covered in the text.

3. **Test Bank.** Expanded for this edition, this includes about 2,000 multiple-choice and true-false questions. It is available in computerized format for the IBM and Macintosh computers.
4. **Transparencies.** Approximately 100 two-color transparencies will be available to adopters.
5. **Software.** Developed by Charles Staelin of Smith College, this software includes a number of innovative graphical, numerical, and other types of exercises to reinforce fundamental macro and micro concepts.

TO THE STUDENT

Economics is like the music of Mozart. On one level, it holds great simplicity: Its basic ideas can be quickly grasped by those who first encounter it. On another level, below the surface there are fascinating subtleties that remain a challenge—even to those who spend a lifetime in its study. We therefore hold out this promise: In this introductory study, you will learn a great deal about how the economy works—the basic principles governing economic life that must be recognized by those in government and business who make policy decisions. At the same time, we can also promise that you won't be able to master it all. You should be left with an appreciation of the difficult and challenging problems of economics that remain unsolved.

Perhaps some day you will contribute to their solution.

HOW TO USE THIS BOOK

Our objective has been to make the basic propositions of economics as easy as possible to grasp. As you encounter each new topic, essential terms are printed in **boldface** and are followed by definitions set apart from the main text. These key terms should be studied carefully during the first reading and during later review. (A glossary is provided at the end of the book, defining terms used in this text as well as other common economics terms that you may encounter in class or in readings.) The basic ideas of each chapter are summarized in the Key Points at the end of the chapter; new concepts introduced in the chapter are also listed.

When you read a chapter for the first time, concentrate on the main text. Don't worry about the boxes. They are set aside from the text to keep the main text as simple and straightforward as possible. The boxes fall into two broad categories: First are the boxes that provide interesting and occasionally amusing asides, for example, Kurt Vonnegut's tale in Box 24-2 (p. 437) of the Handicapper-General whose aim is to ensure that people will not only start out equal but also finish that way. Second are the boxes that present detailed theoretical explanations that are not needed to grasp the main ideas in the text. If you want to glance at the boxes that are fun and easy to read, fine. But when you first read a chapter, don't worry about those that contain more difficult material. On the first reading, you may also skip appendixes and starred (*) footnotes; these also tend to be more difficult and are not essential to the thread of the main story. Come back to them after you have mastered the basic ideas.

Economics is not a spectator sport. You cannot learn just from observation; you must work at it. When you have finished reading a chapter, work on the problems listed at the end; they are designed to reinforce your understanding of important concepts. [The starred (*) problems either are based on material in a box, or they are more difficult questions designed to provide a challenge to students who want to do more advanced work.] Because each chapter builds on preceding ones, and because the solution to some of the problems depends on those that come before, remember this important rule: Don't fall behind. In this regard, economics is similar to mathematics. If you don't keep up, you won't understand what's going on in class. To help you keep up, we recommend the *Study Guide* (fourth edition) which is designed specially to assist you in working through each chapter. It should be available in your bookstore.

Bon voyage!

ACKNOWLEDGMENTS

During the work on this fourth edition, we have accumulated many debts. First and foremost, our thanks go to John Woods, who had overall responsibility for the development of the book and supplements. He has tirelessly contributed to the final product in ways too numerous to list. For editorial assistance, we thank Georgene Gallagher, Barbara Heaney, Gilda Stahl, and Betty Pessagno. The unstinting work of Joe Ford, Ed and Lorraine Burke, and Joan Kalkut kept production of the book on schedule. We thank Maddy Lesure for an outstandingly attractive design of the text, and Ron Blue for his imaginative layout of the *Study Guide.*

We are particularly indebted to teachers and scholars who have advised us or reviewed the book in its many drafts, and have provided a wealth of suggestions. To all, we extend our thanks.

David Able
Mankato State University

Jack Adams
University of Arkansas

Morris Adelman
M.I.T.

Lyndell Avery
Penn Valley Community College

Charles A. Berry
University of Cincinnati

Benjamin Blankenship
U.S. Department of Agriculture

Ake Blomqvist
University of Western Ontario

Frank Brechling
University of Maryland

Gerold Bregor
University of South Carolina

Charles R. Britton
University of Arkansas

Mario Cantu
Northern Virginia Community College

John Cochran
Arizona State University

John M. Cooper
Moorhead State University

Harvey Cutler
Colorado State University

Padma Desai
Columbia University

Donald Ellickson
University of Wisconsin, Eau Claire

Paul Farnham
Georgia State University

Rudy Fichtenbaum
Wright State University

Richard Freeman
Harvard University

Bernard Gaucy
Hollins College

Howard Gilbert
South Dakota State University

Allen Goodman
Wayne State University

Gordon Green
Bureau of the Census

Loren Guffey
University of Central Arkansas

Ralph Gunderson
University of Wisconsin, Oshkosh

George Hoffer
Virginia Commonwealth University

Ig Horstmann
University of Western Ontario

Sheng Hu
Purdue University

Richard H. Keehn
University of Wisconsin, Parkside

David Laidler
University of Western Ontario

William Lastrapes
Louisiana State University

Edward Montgomery
Michigan State University

Peter Morgan
University of Western Ontario

Mark Morlock
California State University, Chico

N.R. Vasudeva Murthy
Creighton University

Wallace Oates
University of Maryland

John Palmer
University of Western Ontario

Dwight Perkins
Harvard University

Wayne Plumly, Jr.
Valdosta State College

Robert Puth
University of New Hampshire

Charles Register
University of Baltimore

Judy Roberts
California State University

Kenneth G. Scalet
York College of Pennsylvania

Robert Schwab
University of Maryland

William Schworm
University of British Columbia

Alden Shiers
California Polytechnic State University

Calvin Siebert
University of Iowa

Andre Simmons
University of Nevada

Timothy Smeeding
University of Utah

Rebecca M. Summary
Southeast Missouri State University

Robert W. Thomas
Iowa State University

Ralph Townsend
University of Maine

John Vahaly
University of Louisville

Paul Weinstein
University of Maryland

John Whalley
University of Western Ontario

C. G. Williams
University of South Carolina

Mark E. Wohar
University of Nebraska

BRIEF CONTENTS

CONTENTS

Part IV ECONOMIC EFFICIENCY: Issues of Our Time

MICROECONOMICS

PART I

BASIC ECONOMIC CONCEPTS

Alfred Marshall, the great teacher and scholar of a century ago, described economics as the "study of mankind in the ordinary business of life." Within this broad description, economics deals with many specific questions. To list but a few:

- Why is it so difficult to get a job at some times and so easy at others?
- Why did our nation produce so much more in 1989 than in 1939?
- What determines the relative prices of goods? Why is water cheap, even though it is necessary to life itself? Why are diamonds expensive, even though they are an unessential luxury?
- How do business executives decide which goods to produce?

Those are some of the questions that you will encounter in this book.

CHAPTER 1
ECONOMIC PROBLEMS AND ECONOMIC GOALS

Economy is the art of making the most out of life.
GEORGE BERNARD SHAW

Some years ago, a Japanese mass-circulation newspaper, the *Mainichi,* conducted a survey of 4,000 people, asking them what they thought of first when they heard the word *takai* (high). "Mount Fuji," said 12%. The overwhelming majority—88%—said, "Prices." In the United States, only two presidents have failed in their bids for reelection in the past 75 years. In 1932, Herbert Hoover was defeated by Franklin D. Roosevelt. At that time, the economy was approaching the low point of the Great Depression; more than one worker in five was out of a job. Roosevelt promised hope. In 1980, Jimmy Carter lost to Ronald Reagan. In that year, the increase in the average level of prices—that is, the inflation rate—was 12.4%. Those two elections showed how much the American public cares about the problems of unemployment and inflation. With the rare exception of the individual who inherits great wealth, most of us are concerned with the jobs available to us and with the purchasing power of the incomes we earn.

Economics is a study of problems, such as inflation and unemployment. It is also a study of success.

ECONOMIC PROGRESS

From the vantage point of our comfortable homes of the late twentieth century, it is easy for us to forget how many people, through history, have been losers in the struggle to make a living. Unvarnished economic history is the story of deprivation, of 80-hour weeks, of child labor—and of starvation. However, it is also the story of the slow climb of civilization toward the goal of relative affluence, where the general public as well as the fortunate few can have a degree of material well-being and leisure.

One of the most notable features of the U.S. economy has been its growth. Although there have been interruptions and setbacks, economic progress has been remarkable. Figure 1-1 shows one of the standard measures of success—the increase in total production per person.[1] The average American now produces more than twice as much as the average American in 1945 and about six times as much as the average American at the turn of the century. Furthermore, the higher output is produced with less effort: The average number of hours worked by those in manufacturing has declined about 25% during this century (Fig. 1-1). Thus economic progress in the United States has been reflected both in an increase in the goods and

[1]The measure of output in this diagram is *gross national product,* or GNP for short. This concept will be explained in Chapter 6.

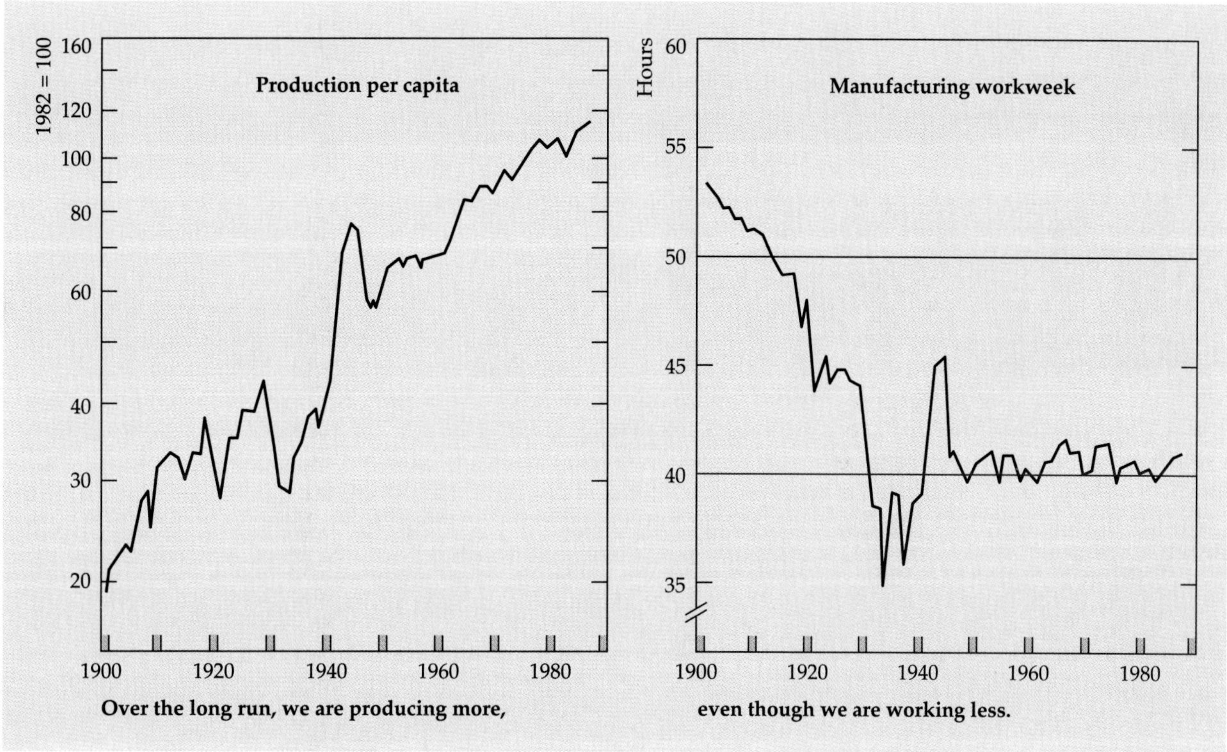

FIGURE 1-1 Production per person and hours worked.
(Source: Board of Governors of the Federal Reserve, *1988 Historical Chart Book.*)

services that we produce and enjoy, and in a greater amount of leisure time. (However, not everyone enjoys more leisure. A 1988 poll by Louis Harris indicated that professional people average 52.2 hours per week and that people in small businesses work 57.3 hours.)

A similar tale of success has occurred in many other countries. In the period from 1960 to 1987, national output grew at an average annual rate of 3.8% in France, 3.0% in Germany, 3.6% in Italy, 3.2% in the United States, and 4.2% in Canada. Nor has growth been confined to the countries of Europe and North America. Particularly notable has been the growth of the Japanese economy. From the ashes of the Second World War, Japan has emerged as one of the leading nations in the world. As a result of a rapid growth averaging 6.7% per year between 1960 and 1987, Japan now ranks with Switzerland, the United States, Norway, and Canada as one of the highest income countries in the world. Other stories of success have come from the middle-income areas of East Asia, such as South Korea, Hong Kong, and Singapore. Figure 1-2 shows the growth rates in a number of countries and continents.

ECONOMIC PROBLEMS

Although rapid growth has occurred in many countries, it has been neither universal nor automatic. In a number of the poorest countries, the standard of living remains abysmally low, with an average income per person of less than $200 *per year.* The World Bank—an international institution whose major purpose is to lend to the low-income countries—estimates that, between 1965 and 1986, output per person rose at an average annual rate of only 1.25% in the 30 poorest countries (excluding China). The record is even bleaker in 10 of these countries, where population has outrun the

(*a*) Industrial countries.

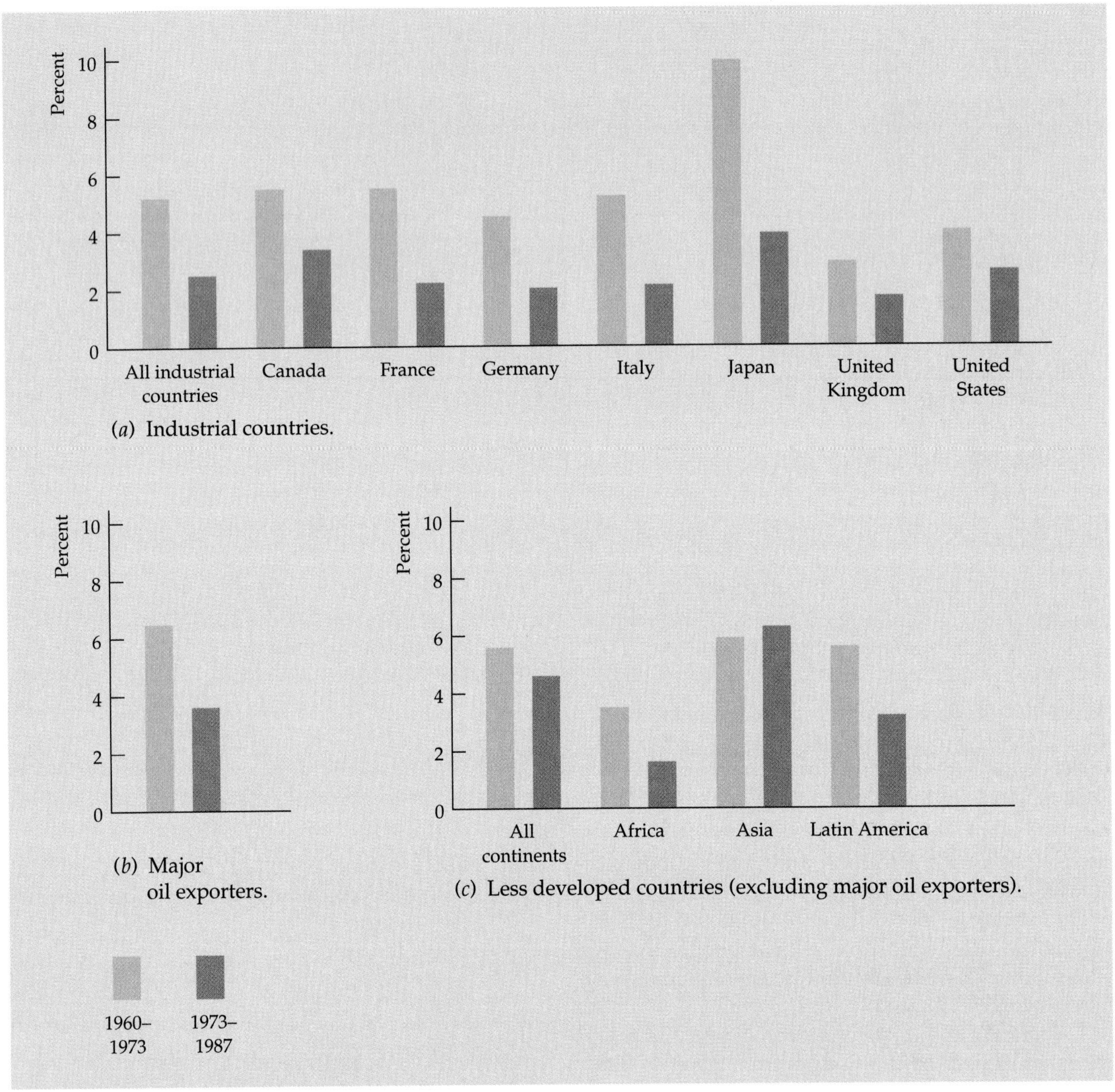

(*b*) Major oil exporters.

(*c*) Less developed countries (excluding major oil exporters).

FIGURE 1-2 Annual rates of increase in output, 1960–1987.

Output has grown rapidly in many countries, particularly Japan. Note that for most countries, growth slowed down after 1973—with the rapidly developing economies of Asia being an exception. The slower growth may be traced in part to the disruptions caused by the rapid increase in the price of oil. (Source: World Bank, *World Development Report*, various issues.)

increase in production and output per person has actually declined.[2]

In both rich countries and poor, substantial economic problems remain. Even in the relatively prosperous United States, we may wonder:

- Why are some people unable to find work when so much needs to be done?
- Why do pockets of poverty remain in an affluent society?
- Why have prices marched upward?
- Are we really producing the right things? Should we produce more housing and fewer cars? Or more subways and fewer office buildings?
- Why is pollution such a problem? What should be done about it?

ECONOMIC POLICY

Why? and *What should be done?* are the two key questions in economics. The ultimate objective of economics is to *develop policies to deal with our problems*. However, before we can formulate policies, we must first make every effort to understand how the economy has worked in the past and how it works today. Otherwise, well-intentioned policies may go astray and lead to unforeseen and unfortunate consequences.

When economic policies are studied, the center of attention is often the policies of the government—policies such as taxation, government spending programs, and the regulation of particular industries such as electric power. However, the policies of private businesses are also important. How can they best organize production in order to make goods at the lowest possible cost? What prices does a business charge if it wants to maximize profits? When should a supermarket increase the stocks of goods in its warehouse?

THE CONTROVERSIAL ROLE OF GOVERNMENT

For more than 200 years, economics has been dominated by a controversy over the proper role of government. In what circumstances should government take an active role? When is it best for government to leave decisions to the private participants in the economy? On this topic, the giants of economics have repeatedly met to do battle.

In 1776, Scottish scholar **Adam Smith** published his pathbreaking book, *An Inquiry into the Nature and Causes of the Wealth of Nations*.[3] Modern economics may be dated from that historic year, which was also notable for the Declaration of Independence. Smith's message was clear: Private markets should be liberated from the tyranny of government control. In pursuit of their private interests, individual producers will make the goods that consumers want. It is not, said Smith, "from the benevolence of the butcher, the brewer, or the baker that we expect our dinner, but from their regard to their own interest." There is an "invisible hand," he wrote, that causes the producer to promote the interests of society. Indeed, "by pursuing his own interest he frequently promotes that of the society more effectually than when he really intends to promote it." In general, said Smith, the government should be cautious about interfering with the operations of the private market. According to Smith, the best policy is generally one of **laissez faire**—leave it alone. Government intervention usually makes things worse. For example, government imposition of a tariff is generally harmful. (A *tariff*, or *duty*, is a tax on a foreign-produced good as it enters the country.) Even though a tariff generally helps domestic producers who are thereby given an advantage over foreign producers, the country as a whole loses. Specifically, a tariff increases the cost of goods available to consumers, and this cost to consumers generally outweighs the benefits to producers. Smith's work has been refined and modified during the past 200 years, but many of his laissez-faire conclusions have stood the test of time. For example, there is still a very strong economic argument against high tariffs on imported goods. In recent decades, one of the principal areas of international cooperation has been the negotiation of lower tariffs.

---

[2]World Bank, *World Development Report 1988* (Washington, D.C., 1988), pp. 222–223.

[3]Available in the Modern Library edition (New York: Random House, 1937). Smith's book is commonly referred to as *The Wealth of Nations*.

During the Great Depression of the 1930s—a century and a half after the appearance of the *Wealth of Nations*—the laissez-faire tradition in economics came under attack. In 1936, **John Maynard Keynes** published his *General Theory of Employment, Interest and Money* (also known, more simply, as the *General Theory*). In this book, Keynes (which rhymes with Danes) argued that the government has the duty to intervene in the economy to put the unemployed back to work. Of the several ways in which this could be done, one stood out in its simplicity. By building public works, such as roads, post offices, and dams, the government could provide jobs directly and thus provide a cure for the depression.

With his proposals for a more active role for government, Keynes drew the ire of many business executives. They feared that, as a result of his recommendations, the government would become larger and private enterprise would gradually be pushed out of the picture. But Keynes did not foresee this result. He believed that, by providing jobs, the government could remove the explosive frustrations caused by the mass unemployment of the 1930s, and could make it possible for Western political and economic institutions to survive. His objective was to modify our economic system and make it better. Unlike Karl Marx, he was not trying to destroy it. (For a brief introduction to the revolutionary ideas of Marx, see Box 1–1.)[4]

Thus Smith and Keynes took apparently contradictory positions—Smith arguing for less govenment and Keynes for more.[5] It is possible, of

[4]Throughout this book, the boxes present illustrative and supplementary materials. They can be omitted without losing the main thread of the discussion.

[5]Conflicting views over the proper role of government may be found in the works of two retired professors: the University of Chicago's Milton Friedman (who argues for less government) and Harvard's John Kenneth Galbraith (who argues for more). See John Kenneth Galbraith, *The Affluent Society* (Boston: Houghton Mifflin, 1958) and Milton Friedman and Rose Friedman, *Free to Choose* (New York: Harcourt Brace Jovanovich, 1980). We recommend that if you read one of these books, you also read the other. Each puts forth a convincing case. Nevertheless, they are flatly contradictory .

BOX 1–1 Karl Marx

The main text refers to two towering economists—Adam Smith and John Maynard Keynes. In the formation of the intellectual heritage of most American economists, Smith and Keynes have played leading roles. If, however, we consider the intellectual heritage of the world as a whole, Karl Marx is probably the most influential economist of all. The current economic systems in a number of countries—most notably the Soviet Union and China—were founded on Marx's theories.

Many business executives viewed Keynes as a revolutionary because he openly attacked accepted opinion and proposed fundamental changes in economic policy. But by revolutionary standards, Keynes pales beside Marx. The Marxist call to revolution was shrill and direct: "Workers of the world, unite! You have nothing to lose but your chains."

Why did they have nothing to lose? Because, said Marx, workers are responsible for the production of all goods. Labor is the sole source of value. But workers get only part of the fruits of their labor. A large—and in Marx's view, unjustified—share goes to the exploiting class of capitalists. (Capitalists are the owners of factories, machinery, and other equipment.) Marx believed that, by taking up arms and overthrowing capitalism, workers could end exploitation and obtain their rightful rewards.

On our main topic—the role of government—Marx was strangely ambivalent. Who would own the factories and machines once the communist revolution had eliminated the capitalist class? Ownership by the state was the obvious solution; in fact, this has been the path taken by countries such as the Soviet Union. The revolution has led to state ownership of the means of production. Yet, Marx also believed that the revolution would eventually lead to the "withering away" of the state. However, there has been no perceptible sign of this withering away in Marxist societies.

course, that each was right. Perhaps the government should do more in some respects and less in others. Economic analysis does not lead inevitably to either an activist or a passive position on the part of the government. The economist's rallying cry should not be, "Do something." Rather, it should be, "Think first."

ECONOMIC GOALS

The ultimate goal of economics is to develop better policies to minimize our problems and to maximize the benefits from our daily toil. More specifically, economists focus on a number of major goals:

1. *A low rate of unemployment.* People willing to work should be able to find jobs reasonably quickly. Widespread unemployment is demoralizing, and it represents an economic waste. Society foregoes the goods and services that the unemployed could have produced.

2. *Price stability.* It is desirable to avoid rapid increases—or decreases—in the average level of prices.

3. *Efficiency.* When we work, we want to get as much as we reasonably can out of our productive efforts.

4. *An equitable distribution of income.* When many live in affluence, no group of citizens should suffer stark poverty.

5. *Growth.* Continuing growth, which would make possible an even higher standard of living in the future, is generally considered an important objective.

The list is far from complete. Not only do we want to produce more, but we also want to do so without the degradation of our environment; the **reduction of pollution** is important. **Economic freedom**—the right of people to choose their own occupations, to enter contracts, and to spend their incomes as they please—is a desirable goal. So, too, is **economic security**—freedom from the fear that chronic illness or other catastrophe will place an individual or a family in a desperate financial situation.

The achievement of our economic goals provides the principal focus of this book. As a background for later chapters, let us look at the major goals in more detail.

1. A LOW RATE OF UNEMPLOYMENT

The importance of full employment was illustrated most clearly during the **Great Depression** of the 1930s, when the United States and many other countries conspicuously failed to achieve it. During the sharp contraction from 1929 to 1933, total output in the United States fell almost one-third, and spending for new buildings, machinery, and equipment declined by almost 80%. As the economy slid downward, more and more workers were thrown out of jobs. By 1933, one-quarter of the labor force was unemployed (Fig. 1-3). Long lines of the jobless gathered at factory gates in the hope of work; disappointment was their common fate. Nor was the problem quickly solved. The downward slide into the depths of the depression went on for more than three years, and the road back to a high level of employment was even longer. It was not until the beginning of the 1940s, when American industry began working around the clock to produce weapons, that many of the unemployed were able to find jobs. There was not a single year during the whole decade 1931–1940 that unemployment averaged less than 14% of the labor force.

A ***depression*** exists when there is a very high rate of unemployment over a long period of time.

Something had clearly gone wrong—disastrously wrong. Large-scale unemployment represents tremendous waste; time lost in involuntary idleness is gone forever. The costs of unemployment go beyond the loss of output: Unemployment also involves the dashing of hopes. Those unable to find work suffer frustration and a sense of worthlessness, and they lose skills as they remain idle.

The term **unemployed** is reserved for those who are willing and able to work but are unable to find jobs. Thus, those of you who are full-time college students are not included among the unemployed. Your immediate task is to get an education, not a job. Similarly, the 70-year-old retiree is not included in the statistics of the unemployed, nor are those in prisons or mental institutions, since they are not available for jobs.

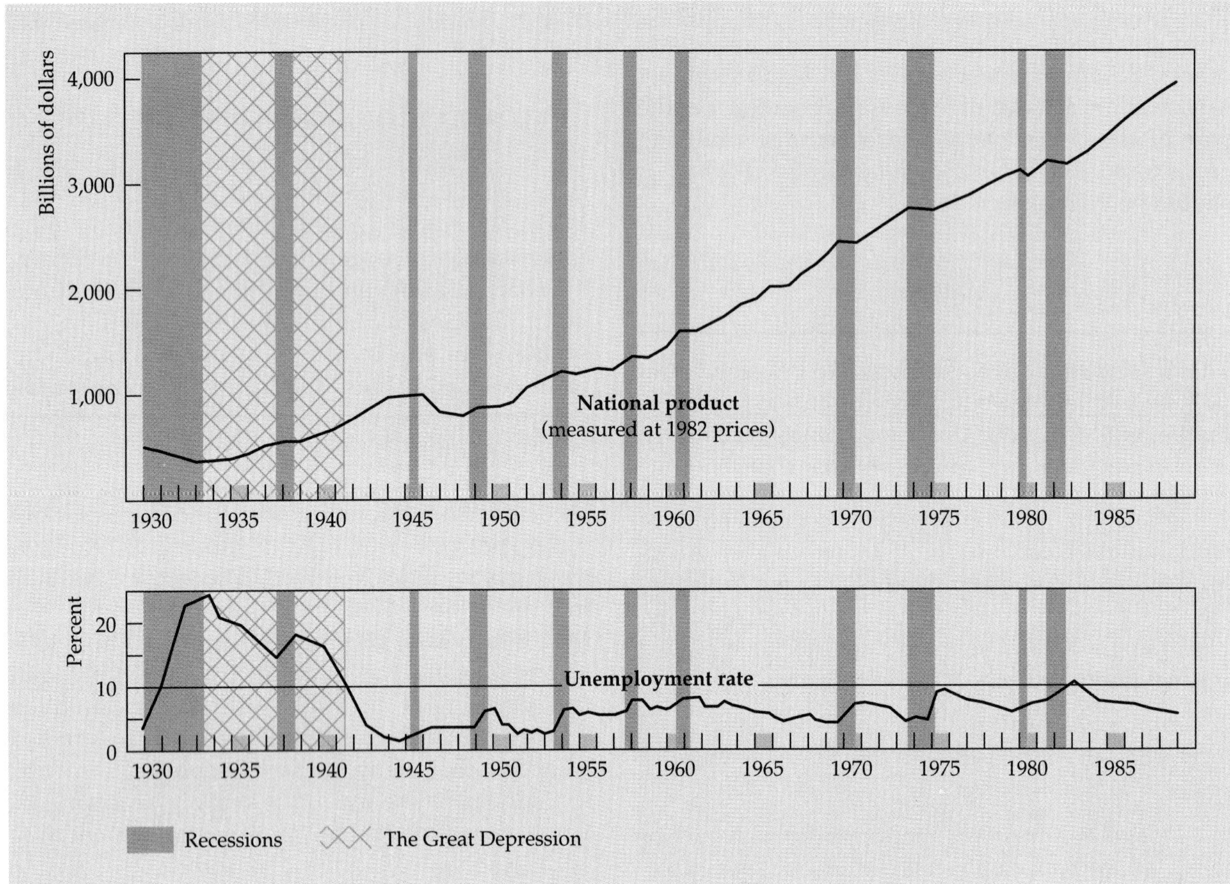

FIGURE 1-3 Output and unemployment in the United States, 1929–1988.

During the Great Depression, output fell and the unemployment rate rose sharply to 25%. In recent decades, the unemployment rate has been much lower.

A person is ***unemployed*** if he or she is available and looking for work but has not found it.

At the end of the Second World War, the Great Depression was still a fresh memory. The public, the politician, and the economist shared a common determination that a repeat of the 1930s could not be permitted. This determination was reflected in the **Employment Act of 1946,** which declared:

> It is the continuing responsibility of the Federal Government to use all practical means. . . to promote maximum employment, production, and purchasing power.

Since the end of the Second World War, we have been successful in avoiding a depression; there has been no repetition of the high unemployment rates of the 1930s. However, the past four decades have not been an unbroken story of success. From time to time, there have been downturns in the economy—much more moderate, it is true, than the slide of 1929 to 1933, but downward movements nonetheless. These more moderate declines, or **recessions,** have been accompanied by an increase in the unemployment rate. In December 1982, during the worst recession of the past four decades, the unemployment rate rose to a peak of 10.6%. Although we have been successful in avoiding big depressions, the problem of periodic recessions has not been solved.

A ***recession*** is a decline in total output, income, employment, and trade, usually lasting 6 months to a year, and marked by widespread contractions in many sectors of the economy. (The decline is not confined to just one or two industries, such as steel or aircraft.)

2. STABILITY OF THE AVERAGE PRICE LEVEL

Unemployment caused the downfall of Herbert Hoover in 1932. **Inflation** was a significant reason for the defeat of Jimmy Carter in 1980.

Inflation is an increase in the average level of prices.
Deflation is a fall in the average level of prices.

Observe in Figure 1-4 how the average of prices paid by consumers has risen through most of our recent history, with the period 1920–1933 being a notable exception. Prices rose most rapidly during and after World War I and for a brief period after World War II. Between 1973 and 1981, inflation was unusually severe for peacetime periods. (Details on how to draw and interpret diagrams may be found in the appendix to this chapter and in the *Study Guide* that accompanies this text.)

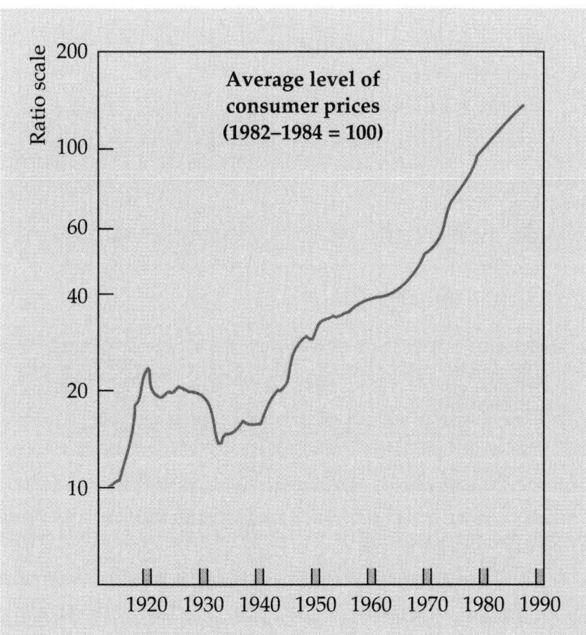

FIGURE 1-4 Consumer prices.

Occasionally prices have fallen—for example, during the early 1930s. In recent decades, however, the trend of prices has been clearly upward. In 1974, and again in 1979 and 1980, the United States suffered from "double-digit" inflation—a rise in the average level of prices by more than 10% per year.

Whereas unemployment represents sheer waste—society loses the goods that might have been produced by those out of work—the problem with inflation is less obvious. When a price rises, there is both a winner and a loser. The loser is the buyer who has to pay more. However, there is a benefit to the seller, who gets more. On balance, it is not clear whether the society is better or worse off.

It is true, of course, that there is much resentment of inflation, but perhaps at least some of this resentment reflects a peculiarity of human nature. When people find the goods they *sell* rising in price, they see the increase as perfectly right, normal, and justified. On the other hand, when they find the goods they *buy* rising in price, they often view the increase as evidence of the seller's greed. When the price of wheat rises, farmers see themselves at last getting a reasonable return from their toil. When the price of oil increases, the oil companies argue that they are getting no more than the return necessary to finance the search for more oil. When the price of books rises, authors feel they are getting no more than a "just" return for their creative efforts, and book publishers insist they are being no more than adequately compensated for their risks. However, when the farmer, the oil company, the author, and the book publisher find that the prices of the goods they *buy* have increased, they believe they have been cheated by inflation. We may all be the victims of an illusion—the illusion that each of us can and should have a rise in the price of what we sell, but that the price of what we buy should remain stable. For the economy as a whole, this is not possible.

This two-sided nature of price increases—a gain to the seller but a loss to the buyer—means that it is difficult to evaluate the dangers of inflation. Indeed, there has been considerable controversy as to whether a low rate of inflation (say, 1% or 2% per annum) is dangerous, or whether, on the contrary, it may actually be beneficial to society. Some say that a small rate of inflation makes it easier for the economy to adjust to changes and to maintain a high level of employment.

When inflation gets beyond a moderate rate,

however, there is widespread agreement that it becomes a menace. It becomes more than a mere transfer of money from the buyer to the seller; it interferes with the production and exchange of goods. This has most clearly been the situation during very rapid inflations, when economic activity was severely disrupted. **Hyperinflation**—that is, a skyrocketing of prices at annual rates of 1,000% or more—occurs most commonly during or soon after a military conflict, when government spending shoots upward—for example, in the South during the civil war, in Germany during the early 1920s, and in China during its civil war in the late 1940s. A hyperinflation means that money rapidly loses its ability to buy goods. People are anxious to spend money as quickly as possible while they can still get something for it.

Clearly, hyperinflation of 1,000% or more per year is an extreme example. However, lower rates of inflation, amounting to 10% or less per year, can also have serious consequences:

1. Inflation hurts people living on fixed incomes and people who have saved fixed amounts of money for their retirement or for "a rainy day" (future illness or accident). The couple who put aside $1,000 in 1960 for their retirement suffered a rude shock: In 1989, $1,000 bought no more than $250 bought in 1960.

2. Inflation can cause business mistakes. For good decisions, businesses need an accurate picture of what is going on. When prices are rising rapidly, the picture becomes obscured and out of focus. Decision makers cannot see clearly. (For example, business accounting is done in dollar terms. When there is rapid inflation, some businesses may report profits when, on a more accurate calculation, they might actually be suffering losses. Consequently, inflation can temporarily hide problems.) Our economy is complex, and it depends on a continuous flow of accurate information. *Prices are an important link in the information chain.* For example, a high price should provide a signal to producers that consumers are especially anxious to get more of a particular product. But in a severe inflation, producers find it difficult to know whether this is the message, or whether the price of their product is rising simply because all prices are rising. In brief, *a severe inflation obscures the message carried by prices.*

Here, it is important to distinguish between a rise in the **average level of prices** (inflation) and a change in **relative** prices. Even if the average level of prices were perfectly stable (that is, no inflation existed), some *individual* prices would still change as conditions changed in specific markets. For example, new inventions have cut the cost of producing computers, and as a result computer companies have been able to cut prices sharply. At the same time, energy prices (for oil, gasoline, electricity, etc.) have risen during the past 20 years, particularly in 1973 and 1979. The resulting fall in the price of computers relative to the price of oil has performed a useful function. It has encouraged businesses to use more of the relatively cheap computers in their operations and to conserve on the relatively expensive oil. (This is not, of course, to deny that the rise in the price of oil was painful, particularly to those living in the colder areas of the country.)

3. EFFICIENCY

This illustration—of how businesses use more computers when they become cheaper—is one example of economic **efficiency.**

In an economy, both the unemployment rate and the inflation rate may be very low, but performance may still be poor. For example, fully employed workers may be engaged in a lot of wasted motion, and the goods being produced may not be those that are needed most. In this case, the economy is inefficient.

> *Efficiency* is the goal of getting the most out of our productive efforts.

Under this broad definition, two types of efficiency can be distinguished: **technological efficiency** and **allocative efficiency.**

To illustrate *technological efficiency* (also known as *technical* efficiency), consider two bicycle manufacturers. One uses a certain number of workers and machines to produce 1,000 bicycles. The other uses the same number of workers and machines to produce 1,200 bicycles. The second manufacturer is not a magician but simply a better manager. The second manufacturer is technologically efficient, whereas the first is inefficient. Technological inefficiency exists when more output can be produced with the existing machines and workers, working at a reasonable pace. (Technological efficiency does not require a sweatshop.) Because technological inefficiency involves wasted motion and sloppy management, better management is the solution.

Allocative efficiency, on the other hand, occurs when the *best combination of goods* is produced with the *lowest cost combination of inputs.* How much food should we produce? How many houses? Suppose we produce only food and do so in a technologically efficient way, with no wasted motion. We will still not have achieved the goal of allocative efficiency because consumers want both food and housing.

Thus allocative efficiency involves the choice of the best combination of outputs. It also involves using the best (lowest cost) combination of inputs. Consider the earlier illustration. The cost of computers is coming down, while the cost of imported oil has risen. If businesses fail to adjust—and fail to conserve oil and to use computers more—there is allocative inefficiency.

Relative prices perform a key role in encouraging allocative efficiency. As we have noted, the decrease in the price of computers encourages businesses to use more computers and less of other, relatively more expensive inputs. While it is undesirable to have large changes in the *average* level of prices (inflation or deflation), changes in *relative* prices may perform a very useful function, encouraging businesses and consumers to conserve on scarce goods and to use cheaper alternatives instead.

4. AN EQUITABLE DISTRIBUTION OF INCOME

Ours is an affluent society, yet many people remain so poor they have difficulty buying the basic necessities of life, such as food, clothing, and shelter. In the midst of plenty, some live in dire need. Should some people have so much while others have so little?

When the question is put this way, the compelling answer must surely be no. Compassion requires that assistance be given to those crushed by illness and to those born and raised in cruel deprivation.

Our sense of equity, or justice, is offended by extreme differences. Thus most people think of *equity* as a move toward *equality.* But not all the way. The two words are far from synonymous. While there is widespread agreement that the least fortunate should be helped, there is no consensus that the objective of society should be an equal income for all. Some individuals are willing to work overtime; it is generally recognized as both just and desirable for them to have a higher income as a consequence. Otherwise, why should they work longer hours? Similarly, it is generally considered right for the hardworking to have a larger share of the nation's income pie, since they have contributed more to the production of the pie in the first place.

There is no agreement on how far we should go toward complete equality of incomes. The best division (or distribution) of income is ill defined. Therefore much of the discussion of income distribution has been focused on narrower questions, such as: What is happening to those at the bottom of the ladder? What is happening to the families who live in poverty?

Poverty is difficult to define in precise dollar terms. For one thing, not everyone's needs are the same. The sickly have the greatest need for medical care. Large families have the most compelling need for food and clothing. There is no simple, single measure of the "poverty line," below which families may be judged to be poor. Reasonable standards may, however, be established by taking into consideration such obvious complications as the number of individuals in a family. The poverty standards defined by the U.S. government in 1988 are shown in Table 1-1.

There are two ways of raising people above the

TABLE 1-1 Poverty Standards, 1988

Size of Family	*Poverty Line*
One person	$6,000
Two persons	7,690
Three persons	9,420
Four persons	12,075
Five persons	14,290

According to U.S. government standards, families are poor if their incomes fall below these figures. For example, a four-person family is poor if it has an income of less than $12,075.

poverty line. The first is to increase the size of overall national income. As income rises throughout the economy, the incomes of those at the lower end will also generally rise. In the words of President John Kennedy, "A rising tide lifts all boats."

A second way to reduce poverty is to increase the share of the nation's income going to the poorest people. Thus poverty may be combated by a **redistribution of income.** For example, the well-to-do may be taxed in order to finance government programs aimed at helping the poor. A number of government programs have attempted to raise the share of the nation's income going to the poorest families.

During the 1950s and 1960s, progress was made toward that goal. Between 1950 and 1969, the share of the poorest 20% of families rose from 4.5% to 5.6% of total income. Furthermore, a rising tide was lifting all boats. Because of the vigorous expansion of the economy, average family income rose about 40%—even after adjusting for inflation. The rising tide of income, together with the larger percentage going to the poor, combined to raise the incomes of the poorest fifth by more than 70% (again, after adjusting for inflation). Thus the poorest of 1969 were much better off than the poorest of 1950. Nevertheless, they were still very poor by the overall standards of society.

Figure 1-5 shows the steady decline in the percentage of the population living in poverty during the 1960s, from 22.1% to 12.1%. After a brief reversal during the recession of 1970, the downward trend continued, reaching a low of 11.1% in 1973. Until 1978 there was little change, but between 1978 and 1983, the rate increased to 15.2%. Since 1983, the rate has again declined, although it remains above the lows of the 1970s. We are still far short of the objective of eliminating poverty. Why is this task so difficult? One reason is unemployment; many of the poor are unemployed. The poverty rate increased between 1978 and 1983 when the economy was in recession and the unemployment rate was increasing. Both poverty and unemployment decreased during the long expansion after 1983.

Unemployment has not been the only reason for poverty. Although the unemployment rate was no higher in 1981 than in 1976, the percentage of the population living in poverty was substantially higher (14.0% compared with 11.8%). Poverty is a perplexing problem.

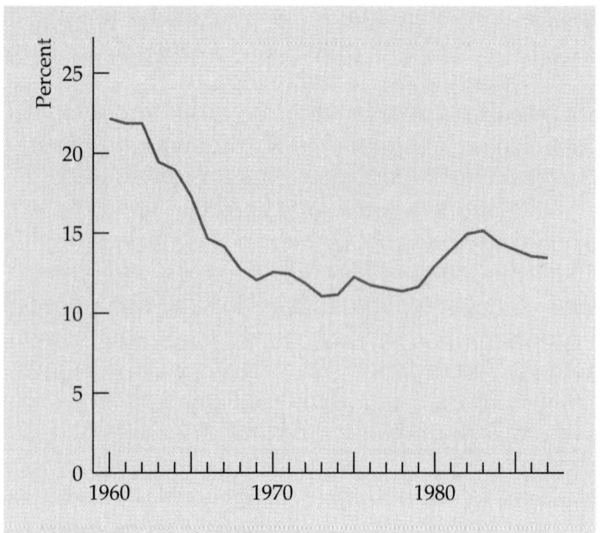

FIGURE 1-5 The percentage of the population living in poverty.

During the long expansion of the 1960s there was a substantial decline in the percentage of the population living in poverty. After 1979, the percentage living in poverty increased. (Source: *Annual Report of the President, 1989,* p. 342.)

5. GROWTH

In an economy with large-scale unemployment, output can be increased by putting the unemployed back to work. Slack in the economy can be reduced, and productive capacity can be used more fully. Once the economy approaches its capacity, however, additional increases in output require an increase in the productive capacity itself. Capacity can be raised either by an addition to the available resources (for example, an increase in the number of factories and machines) or an improvement in technology (that is, the invention of new, more productive machines or new ways of organizing production). When economists speak of growth, they typically mean an *increase in the productive capacity* of the economy that results from technological improvement and additional factories, machines, or other resources.

The advantages of growth are obvious. If the

economy grows, our incomes will be higher in the future. We and our children will have higher standards of material comfort. Moreover, some of the rising production can be used to benefit the poor without reducing the incomes of the rich.

Emphasis on growth as an economic objective has changed substantially over the years. During the Kennedy administration in the early 1960s, growth became a prominent national goal, both because of its economic advantages and the importance of "keeping ahead of the Russians." During the late 1960s and early 1970s, doubts began to develop. While the advantages of growth are obvious, it comes at a cost. If we are to grow more rapidly, more of our current efforts will have to be directed toward the production of machines and away from the production of consumption goods. In the future, of course, as the new machines begin operating, they will turn out more consumption goods—more clothing, furniture, or cars. Thus current policies to stimulate growth will make possible higher consumption in the future. For the moment, however, consumption will be lower. Thus, in order to evaluate a high-growth policy, we have to compare the advantage of higher *future* consumption with the sacrifice of lower *current* consumption.

Seen in this light, it is not clear that the faster the rate of growth, the better. Future generations should be considered, but so should the present one.

Even if we were concerned solely with the welfare of coming generations, it would not be so clear that the more growth, the better. Very rapid rates of growth may harm the environment. If our primary objective is to produce more steel and more automobiles, we may pay too little heed to the belching smoke of the steel mills or to the effect of the automobile on the quality of the air we breathe. Thus during the 1970s there was less emphasis on growth than there had been during the early 1960s and more emphasis on other goals, such as the preservation of the environment.

During the Reagan administration, the pendulum swung back toward growth as an objective. Vigorous growth was again seen as a way of dealing with many economic problems, including poverty. Kennedy's remark—"A rising tide lifts all boats"—again became popular in Washington. (In rebuttal, Herbert Stein observed: "Unfortunately, that is not true. A rising tide does not lift the boats that are under water.... Many kinds of poverty will not be significantly relieved by faster growth.")[6]

INTERRELATIONS AMONG ECONOMIC GOALS

The achievement of one goal may help in the achievement of others. As already noted, growth may make it easier to reduce the problem of poverty. Additional income may be provided to the poor out of the growth in total income, without reducing the income of those at the top. Thus social conflicts over the share of income may be reduced if the size of the nation's total income is increasing.

Similarly, the poverty problem is easier to solve if the unemployment rate is kept low, so that large numbers of unemployed do not swell the ranks of the poor. When goals are **complementary** like this (that is, when achieving one helps to achieve the other), economic policymaking is relatively easy. By attacking on a broad front and striving for several goals, we can increase our chances of achieving each.

Unfortunately, however, economic goals are not always complementary. In some cases, they are in conflict. For example, when unemployment is reduced, inflation generally gets worse. There is a reason for this phenomenon. Heavy purchasing by the public tends to reduce unemployment, but it also tends to increase inflation. It reduces unemployment because, as the public buys more cars, unemployed workers get jobs again in the auto factories; when families buy more homes, construction workers find it easier to find jobs. At the same time, heavy purchasing tends to increase inflation because producers are more likely to raise their prices if buyers are clamoring for their products. Such **conflicts among goals** test the wisdom of policymakers. They feel torn in deciding which objective to pursue.

---

[6]Herbert Stein, "Economic Policy, Conservatively Speaking," *Public Opinion*, February 1981, p. 4. (Stein was chairman of the Council of Economic Advisers from 1972 to 1974.)

A PREVIEW

These, then, are the five major objectives of economic policy: *high employment, price stability, efficiency, an equitable distribution of income,* and *growth.* The first two goals are related to the stability of the economy. If the economy is unstable, moving along like a roller coaster, its performance will be very unsatisfactory. As it heads downhill into recession, large numbers of people will be thrown out of work. Then, as it heads upward into a runaway boom, prices will soar as the public scrambles to buy the available goods. The first two goals may, therefore, be viewed as two aspects of a single objective: that of achieving an **equilibrium** with stable prices and a low unemployment rate. This will be the major topic in Parts II–V (Chapters 6 through 19) of this book.

Equilibrium is the first of the three main "E's" of economics. The second E—**efficiency**—will be studied in Parts VI–VIII (Chapters 20 through 34). Are we getting the most out of our productive efforts? When does the free market—where buyers and sellers come together without government interference—encourage efficiency? When the free market does not encourage efficiency, what (if anything) should be done?

Part IX (Chapters 35 through 40) deals primarily with the third E—**equity.** If the government takes a laissez-faire attitude, how much income will go to the workers? To the owners of land? To others? How do labor unions affect the incomes of their members? How can the government improve the lot of the poor?

The final major objective—growth—cuts across a number of other major topics and thus appears periodically throughout the book. However, before we get into the meat of the three issues of equilibrium, efficiency, and equity, we must first set the stage with some of the basic concepts and tools of economics. To that task we now turn in Chapters 2 through 5.

KEY POINTS

1. During the twentieth century, substantial economic progress has been made in the United States and many other countries. We are producing much more, even though we spend less time at work than did our grandparents.

2. Nevertheless, substantial economic problems remain: problems such as poverty in the less developed countries and at home, high rates of unemployment, and inflation.

3. One of the things that economists study is how to deal with problems, either through private action or through government policies.

4. In the history of economic thought, the role of government has been controversial. Adam Smith in 1776 called for the liberation of markets from the tyranny of government control. By 1936, John Maynard Keynes was appealing to the government to accept its responsibilities and to undertake public works in order to get the economy out of the depression.

5. Important economic goals include:

(a) An equilibrium with high employment and price stability.

(b) Efficiency. *Allocative efficiency* involves the production of the right combination of goods, using the lowest cost combination of inputs. *Technological efficiency* occurs when people produce the maximum quantity of output with a given quantity of inputs, while working at a reasonable pace.

(c) Equity in the distribution of income.

(d) A satisfactory rate of growth.

6. Large changes in the *average* level of prices are undesirable. However, changes in *relative* prices may be desirable as a way of encouraging people to conserve scarce goods and to use more plentiful, cheaper alternatives instead.

7. Goals are complementary if the achievement of one helps in the achievement of the other. For example, a reduction in unemployment also generally reduces poverty. However, goals may be in conflict. An increase in spending works to reduce unemployment, but it can also increase the rate of inflation.

KEY CONCEPTS

laissez faire
depression
recession
unemployment
inflation
deflation
hyperinflation
average level of prices
relative prices
allocative efficiency
technological efficiency
poverty
equal distribution of income
equitable distribution of income
redistribution of income
growth
complementary goals
conflicting goals

PROBLEMS

1-1. According to Smith's "invisible hand," we are able to obtain meat, not because of the butcher's benevolence, but because of his self-interest. Why is it in the butcher's self-interest to provide us with meat? What does the butcher get in return?

1-2. Suppose another depression were to occur like the depression of the 1930s. How would it affect you? (Thinking about this question provided a major motivation for a generation of economists. They were appalled at the prospect and determined to play a role in preventing a repetition of the Great Depression.)

1-3. The section on an equitable distribution of income reflects two views regarding the proper approach to poverty:

(a) The important thing is to meet the basic needs of the poor—that is, to provide at least a minimum income for the purchase of food, shelter, and other necessities.

(b) The important thing is to reduce inequality—that is, to reduce the gap between the rich and the poor.

These two views are not the same. For example, if there is rapid growth in the economy, objective (a) may be accomplished without any progress being made toward (b). Which is the more important objective? Why? Do you feel strongly about your choice? Why?

1-4. In Figure 1-1, observe that the strong downward trend in the length of the workweek ended about 1950. Before that date, part of the gains of the average worker came in the form of shorter hours. Since 1950, practically all the gains have consisted of higher wages and fringe benefits. Can you provide any reason why the workweek leveled out in 1950?

1-5. Explain how an upswing in purchases by the public will affect (a) unemployment and (b) inflation. Does this result illustrate economic goals that are complementary or conflicting?

APPENDIX
DIAGRAMS USED IN ECONOMICS

Chapter 1 contains diagrams that illustrate important points, such as the increase in production per person since 1900 (Fig. 1-1) and the fact that economic growth slowed down after 1973 (Fig. 1-2). In the study of economics, diagrams are used frequently—as you may see by flipping through this book. A picture is often worth a thousand words. Diagrams can fix important ideas in our minds. They present information in a vivid and eye-catching way. Unfortunately, they can also mislead. The first and lasting impression may be the wrong impression. This appendix explains some of the major types of diagrams used in economics and some of the ways in which diagrams may be used to impress or mislead rather than inform.

Three major types of diagrams will be considered:

1. Diagrams that present and compare two facts.
2. Diagrams that show how something changes through time. For example, Figure 1-4 illustrates how the average level of prices has usually risen but has sometimes fallen.
3. Diagrams that show how two variables are related—for example, how an increase in family income (variable 1) results in an increase in spending (variable 2).

1. A SIMPLE COMPARISON OF TWO FACTS

The simplest type of diagram brings together two facts for comparison. Often, the best method of presenting two facts—and the least likely to mislead—is to use a *bar chart* like the one shown back in Figure 1-2. In the top left corner, the first bar shows that the average rate of increase in output in industrial countries was 5.2% per year between 1960 and 1973, while the next bar shows that the rate was only 2.5% between 1973 and 1987. By comparing the heights of the bars, we immediately see how the rate has changed.

THINGS TO WATCH

Even such a simple diagram may carry a misleading message. There are several "tricks" which an unscrupulous writer can use to fool the reader.

Suppose, for example, that someone wants to present the performance of a country or a corporation in the most favorable light. Consider an example—a country whose steel production rose from 10 million tons in 1980 to 20 million tons in 1990.

Figure 1-6 is a bar chart illustrating this comparison in the simplest, most straightforward way. Glancing at the height of the two bars in this diagram, the reader gets the correct impression—steel production has doubled.

This is a very good performance but not a spectacular one. Suppose someone wants to make things look even better. Two easy ways of doing so—without actually lying—are illustrated in Figure 1-7.

The left panel is designed to mislead because part of the diagram is omitted. The heights of the bars are measured from 5 million tons rather than

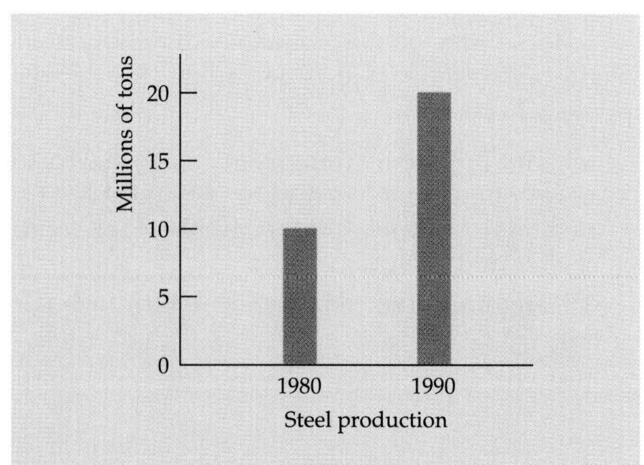

FIGURE 1-6 A simple bar chart.

The simplest bar chart provides a comparison of two numbers, in this case the production of steel in two years. We see correctly that steel production has doubled.

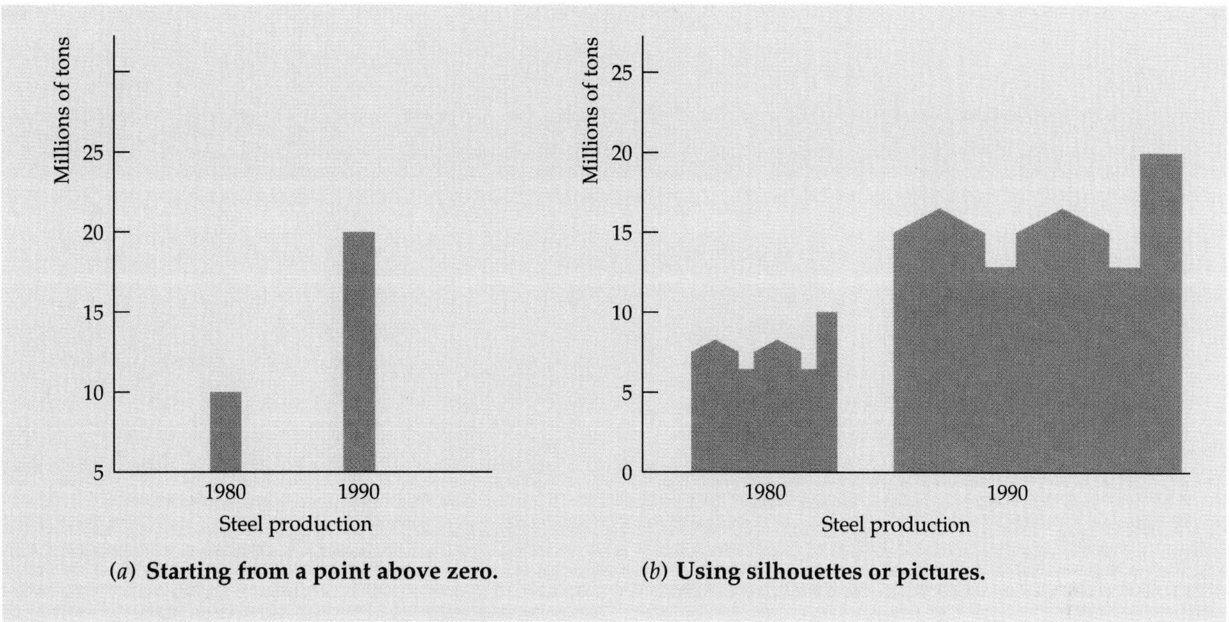

FIGURE 1-7 Variations on the simple bar chart.

Readers may be misled by variations on the simple bar chart. Both of the above panels present the same information as in Figure 1-6. In the left panel, the vertical axis begins with 5 million tons, rather than zero. In the right panel, pictures are used, rather than bars. In each case, the reader may be left with the erroneous impression that steel production has more than doubled.

zero. Thus the 1990 bar is three times as high as the 1980 bar, and the unwary reader may be left with the wrong impression—that steel production is three times as high, whereas in fact it is only twice as high. This, then, is the first thing to watch out for: Do the numbers on the vertical axis start from zero? If not, the diagram may give the wrong impression.

The right panel shows another way in which the reader may be fooled. The bars of Figure 1-6 are replaced with something more interesting— pictures of steel mills. Because production has doubled, the steel mill on the right is twice as high as that on the left. But notice how this picture gives the wrong impression. The mill on the right is not only twice as high. It is also twice as wide, and we can visualize it as being twice as deep, too. Therefore, it isn't just twice as large as the mill on the left; it is many times as large. Thus the casual reader may again be left with the wrong impression—that steel output has increased manyfold, when in fact it has only doubled. This, then, is the second reason to be wary: Look carefully and skeptically at diagrams that use silhouettes or pictures. Do they leave you with an exaggerated impression of the changes that have actually occurred?

Figure 1-8 illustrates a third way to mislead readers.[7] In both panels, the facts are correct regarding the average price of common stock in the United States. (Each share of common stock represents part ownership of a company.) The left panel shows that, between 1929 and 1953, the average price of stocks did not change at all. The right panel shows facts that are equally true. Between 1932 and 1953—almost the same period of comparison—stock prices increased *six fold*. How can *both* of these panels be correct? The answer: Between 1929 and 1932, the most spectacular stock market

[7]For more detail on how readers may be misled, see the sprightly book by Darrell Huff, *How to Lie with Statistics* (New York: W.W. Norton, 1954).

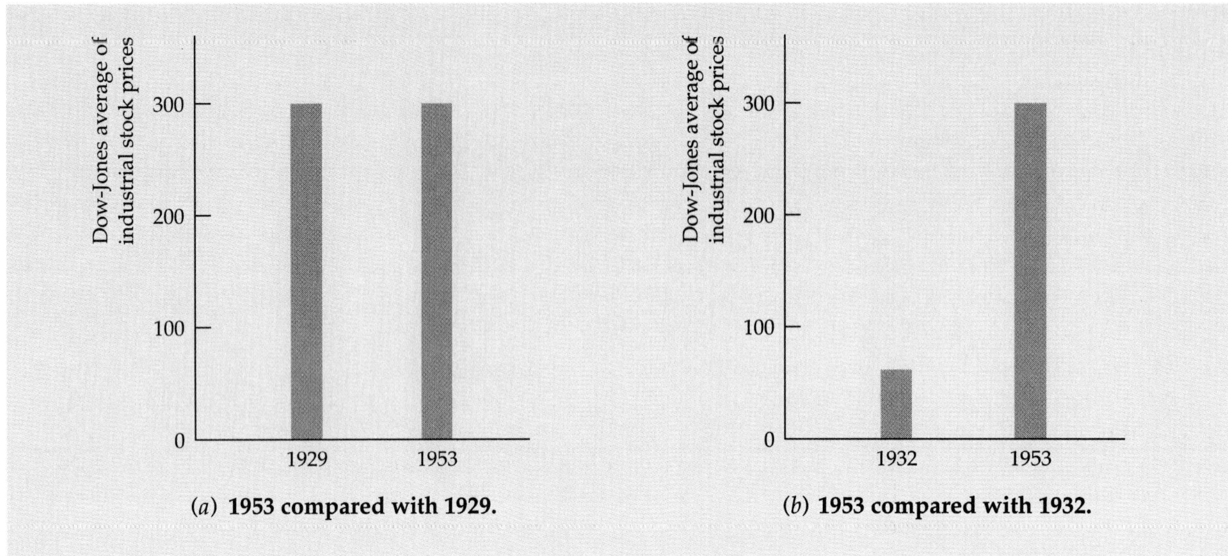

FIGURE 1-8 Comparisons depend on the times chosen.

Comparisons may change even when seemingly minor changes are made in the dates. In 1953, stock prices were no higher on average than in 1929 (left panel). However, they were six times as high in 1953 as they had been in 1932.

collapse in American history occurred, with stocks losing five-sixths of their value.

Notice the contrast between the two panels. The left one implies that not much can be gained by entering the stock market. The right panel gives exactly the opposite impression: The stock market is the place to get rich. Thus, an author can give two completely different messages, depending on the choice of the initial "base" year (1929 or 1932). So beware. In any diagram showing how something has changed over time, ask yourself: Has the author slanted the results by selecting years designed to mislead?

2. TIME SERIES: HOW SOMETHING CHANGES THROUGH TIME

That last problem can be avoided by providing more information to the reader with a **time series** diagram, showing stock prices *every* year, not just a beginning and final year. Even better is to show stock prices every month. With a more detailed figure, the reader can see a much more complete story, including both the collapse of 1929–1932 and the way in which stock prices have risen since 1932.

A *time series* diagram shows how something (such as the price of stocks, the output of steel, or the unemployment rate) has changed through time.

However, even when we provide a detailed time series, a number of issues remain. Here are some of the most important.

SHOULD WE MEASURE FROM ZERO?

In discussing a simple comparison between two facts, we seem to have settled the question of how we should measure up the vertical axis of a diagram. To start at any figure other than zero can be misleading—as in Figure 1-7*a*, when steel production was measured up from a starting point of 5 million tons.

Once we provide the detailed information of a time series, we should reopen the question of how to measure along the vertical axis. The problem is that we now have two conflicting considerations.

We would like to start from zero to avoid misleading the reader. On the other hand, starting from some other point may make the details of a diagram much easier to see.

This is illustrated in Figure 1-9, which shows the rate of unemployment in each year from 1978 to 1988. In the left panel, the unemployment rate is measured vertically, starting from zero. This gives us the best picture of how the overall unemployment rate compares in any two years we might like to choose (for example, 1979 and 1982). Contrast this with the right panel, where the measurement of unemployment starts above zero. Like Figure 1-7*a*, this panel can be misleading. For example, it might leave the impression that the unemployment rate tripled between 1979 and 1982, whereas in fact it increased by far less (approximately from 6% to 10%).

However, the right panel has a major compensating advantage. It provides a much clearer picture of how the unemployment rate *changes* from year to year; the year-to-year differences are much more conspicuous. These year-to-year changes are very important, as they are one measure of fluctuations in the economy. Consequently, the right-hand diagram can be more informative.

If panel *b* is chosen, readers must be warned that we have not started from zero. One way is to leave a gap in the vertical bars to show that something has been left out. Another way, also shown in panel b, is to leave a gap in the vertical axis itself.

HOW SHOULD GROWTH BE ILLUSTRATED?

Some time series—such as a nation's population—have a strong tendency to grow through time. If we measure in the normal way along the vertical axis, the curve becomes steeper through time, as shown in the left panel of Figure 1-10. There is nothing necessarily wrong with this presentation; the increase in the population between 1970 and 1980 (23 million) was in fact much greater than the increase between 1870 and 1880 (10 million).

However, there are two related problems with this figure. First, the numbers in the early years—

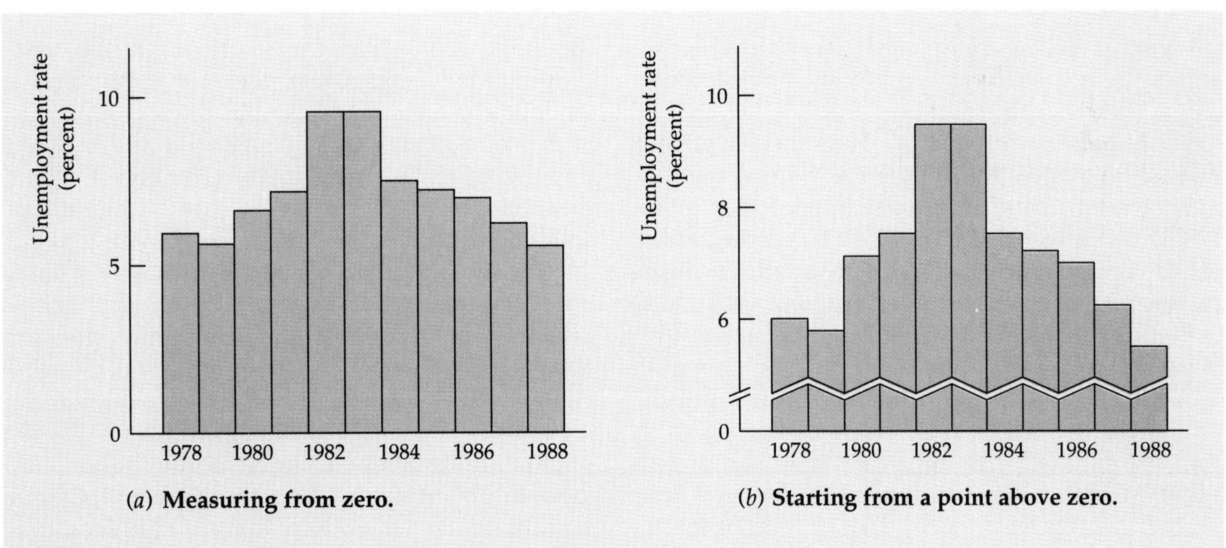

FIGURE 1-9 A time series: The unemployment rate, 1978–1988.

The reader is provided much more information with a time series showing every year or every month rather than just two years. In this diagram, there is an advantage in starting the vertical measurement above zero. Observe that the detailed year-to-year changes stand out more clearly in the right panel than in the left. To warn the reader that something has been left out, a gap is left in the vertical bars.

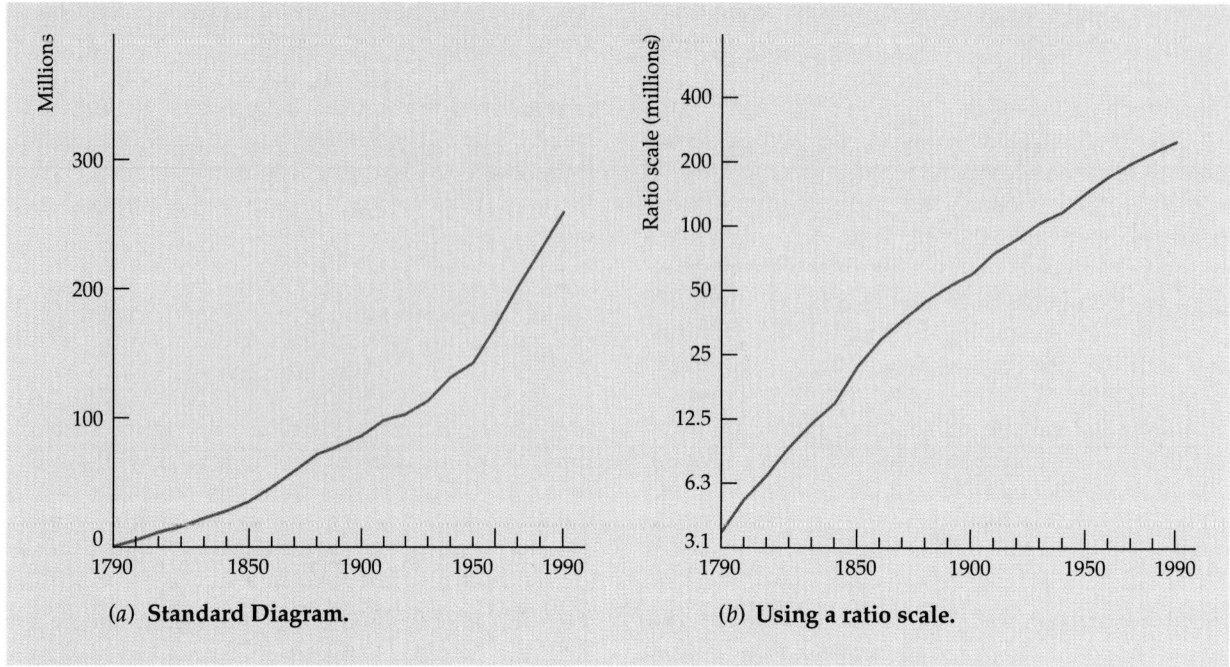

FIGURE 1-10 Population of the United States, 1790–1990.
A ratio scale allows us to identify the period when the rate of population growth was most rapid. It occurred when the slope of the curve in the right panel was steepest.

before, say, 1820—are so small that details can scarcely be seen. Second, we may be interested not just in the absolute numbers but in the *rate* at which population is growing. Thus the 10 million increase in population in the 1870s represents a much greater rate of increase (2.3% per year) than the 23 million increase of the 1970s (1.1% per year).

To highlight the rate of growth, a **ratio** or **logarithmic** scale is used on the vertical axis in panel *b* of Figure 1-10. On such a scale, equal *percentage* changes show up as equal distances. For example, the vertical distance from 50 million to 100 million (an increase of 100%) is the same as the distance from 100 million to 200 million (also an increase of 100%). In such a diagram, if something grows at a *constant rate* (for example, by 2% per year), it traces out a *straight line.* By looking for the steepest sections of the time series, we can identify the periods when population has grown at the most rapid rate. (Similarly, back in Fig. 1-4, which is also drawn on a ratio scale, the steepest parts of the curve show when the most rapid rates of inflation occurred.)

A ratio scale is appropriate for a time series—like population—that grows. However, it is inappropriate for a series that does not have a strong tendency to grow. For example, there is no reason to expect a greater and greater percentage of the population to be living in poverty, and it would therefore be inappropriate to use a logarithmic scale in a figure showing the poverty rate.

Finally, note that, when a logarithmic scale is used, the question of whether the vertical axis is measured from zero becomes irrelevant, since zero *cannot* appear on such a diagram. By looking at Figure 1-10*b*, we can see why. Each time we go up 1 centimeter (one notch on the vertical axis), the population doubles—from 50 to 100 million, and then to 200 million. We can make exactly the same statement the other way around: Each time we go down a centimeter, the population falls by half—from 50 million to 25 million, then 12.5 million, and so on. No matter how far we extend the diagram downward, each additional centimeter will reduce the population by one-half. Therefore the vertical axis can *never* reach zero on such a diagram.

REAL OR MONETARY MEASURES?

People often complain that the federal government is getting too big. Suppose we wanted to look at the size of the government. How would we do so?

The most obvious way is to look at the amount the government spends. Measured in dollars, the growth of government spending has been truly stupendous over the past half century (Fig. 1-11). There are, however, several shortcomings to this simple measure.

The first has to do with prices, which have risen substantially during the past half century. Inflation means that, even if the government had remained exactly the same size—building the same number of roads, keeping the same number of soldiers in the army—it would have spent many more dollars; its expenditures in dollar or **nominal** terms would have gone up rapidly. In order to eliminate the effects of inflation, government statisticians calculate what government expenditures *would have been if prices had not gone up*—that is, if prices had remained at the level existing in a single year. Such a measure of government expenditures—in **constant-dollar** or **real** terms—is shown in panel *a* of Figure 1-12. Observe how much more slowly government expenditures have grown when the effects of inflation are eliminated. Chapter 6 will provide details on how real expenditures are calculated.

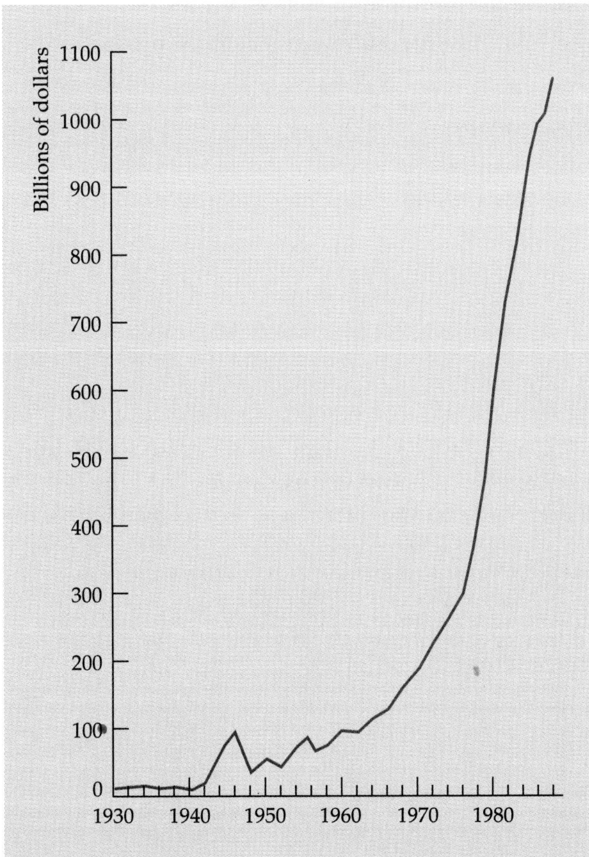

FIGURE 1-11 Federal government expenditures, measured in dollars.

As measured by the number of dollars spent, the size of the federal government has expanded very rapidly.

RELATIVE MEASURES

Even when measured in real terms, government expenditures have risen substantially. Does this, in itself, mean that the government is too big? The answer is, not necessarily. One reason is that, as the government has grown, so has the overall economy. Thus we may ask the question: Has the government grown *relative to the economy?* (As in Fig. 1-1, the size of the economy is measured by gross national product, or GNP.) In Figure 1-12, panel *b*, observe that government expenditures have not grown much relative to the economy (that is, as a percentage of GNP) in recent decades.

In passing, we note that, even if government spending is rising relative to the size of the overall economy, this does not, in itself, mean that the government is "too big;" nor would a downward trend necessarily mean that the government was "too small." During the 1930s, government spending was rising relative to the size of the economy, yet defense spending was still too low to meet the growing threat from Hitler. On the other hand, as we come to an accommodation with the Soviet Union, it may be clear that we can reduce military spending in relative safety.

3. RELATIONSHIPS BETWEEN VARIABLES

Frequently, economists want to keep track of the relationship between two variables. Table 1-2 provides an illustration—the relationship between the incomes of households and their expenditures for the basic necessities (housing, food, and clothing).

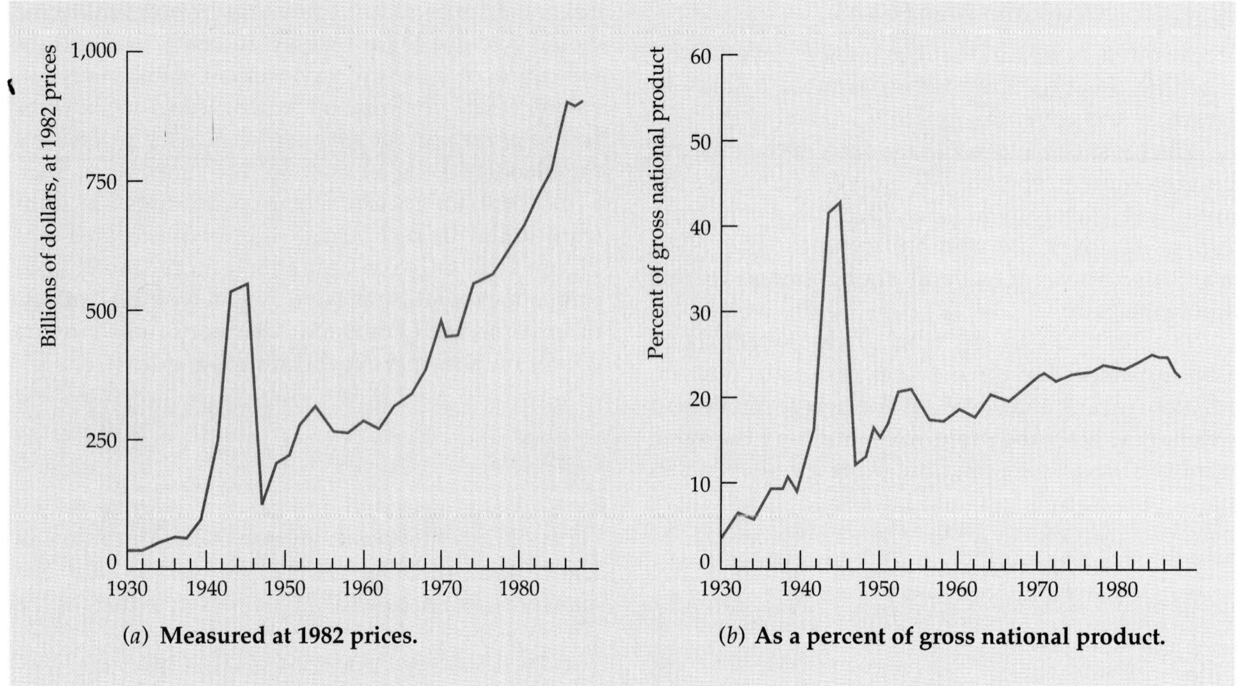

FIGURE 1-12 Federal government expenditures: Alternative presentations.
When the effects of inflation are removed in the left panel, the growth of government spending is much less spectacular than in Figure 1-11. The right panel shows that the size of the federal government has grown relatively slowly as a fraction of gross national product.

The top row (row *A*) indicates that the American family with an income of $10,000 spends $7,000 on the basic necessities. Similarly, row *B* shows that a family with an income of $20,000 spends $11,000 on these basics.

The data in Table 1-2 may be graphed as Figure 1-13, where income is measured along the horizontal axis and expenditures for basics up the vertical axis. (The lower left corner, labeled "0," is the **origin**—that is, the starting point from which both income and basic expenditures are measured.) To plot the data in row *A* of the table, we measure $10,000 in income along the horizontal axis and $7,000 in spending for basics up the vertical axis. This gives us point *A* in the diagram. Similarly, points *B*, *C*, and *D* represent corresponding rows *B*, *C*, and *D* in Table 1-2.

One question that can be addressed with such a diagram is how expenditures on the basics change as income increases. For example, as in-

TABLE 1-2 Household Income and Expenditures for Basics

Family	*(1) Household Income (after taxes)*	*(2) Expenditures for Basics*
A	$10,000	$7,000
B	20,000	11,000
C	30,000	14,500
D	40,000	17,500

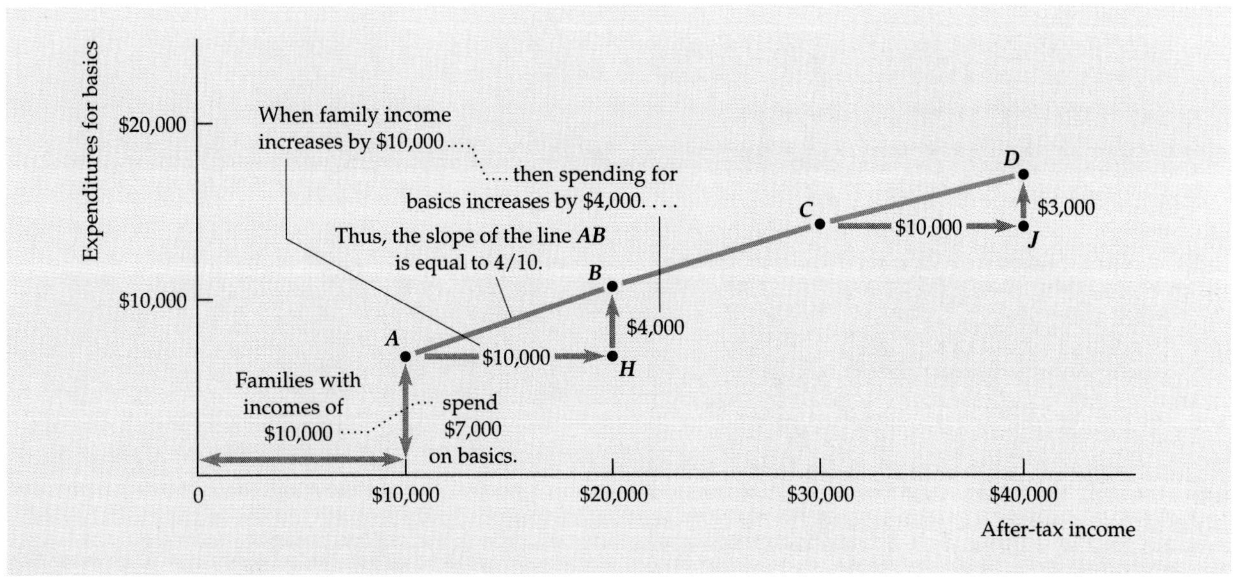

FIGURE 1-13 How expenditures for basics are related to income.

As family income increases (along the horizontal axis), the family's expenditures for the basics increase (as measured up the vertical axis). The *slope* of the line between any two points—such as *A* and *B*—shows how strongly expenditures for basics respond (*HB*) to an increase in income (*AH*).

come increases from $10,000 at point *A* to $20,000 at point *B*, basic expenditures rise from $7,000 to $11,000; that is, expenditures on the basics rise by $4,000 in response to the $10,000 increase in income.

This relation can be illustrated by drawing a line between points *A* and *B*, and looking at its **slope**—slope being defined as the *vertical change* or *rise* (*HB*) *divided by the horizontal change* or *run* (*AH*). In this example, the slope is $4,000/$10,000 = 4/10. As incomes increase from point *A* to point *B*, families spend 40% of the increase on the basics.

Observe in this diagram that the slope becomes smaller as incomes increase and we go further to the right. Whereas the slope is 4/10 between *A* and *B*, it is only $3,000/$10,000, or 3/10, between C and *D*. This smaller slope makes sense. Families with high incomes already have good houses, food, and clothing. When their income goes up another $10,000, they don't spend much more on the basics; they have other things to do with their income.

Nevertheless, no matter how far to the right this diagram is extended, the line joining any two points will always slope *upward*—that is, the slope is always *positive*. The reason is that, as people's incomes rise, they are always willing to pay somewhat more in order to get better houses, food, and clothing.

In some relationships, however, there may be a downward-sloping curve. Figure 1-14 illustrates the situation facing a company producing a small business aircraft. The costs facing such a company are high: It has the expense of designing the aircraft, and it requires an expensive plant for production. If the firm produces only a few units each year (say, 10 aircraft, measured along the horizontal axis), it will operate at point *A*. It will be unable to charge a price high enough to cover its costs, and it will therefore suffer a loss—that is, its profit

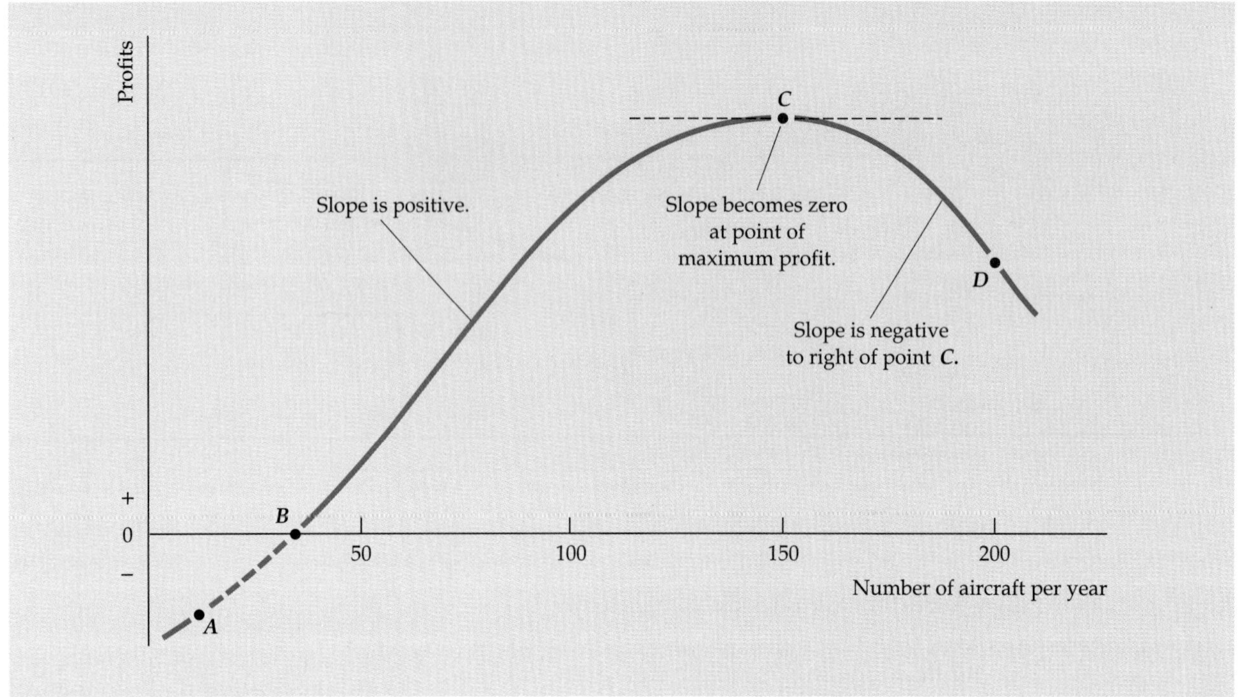

FIGURE 1-14 Output and profits.

If the firm produces only a few planes, it cannot cover its costs. It suffers losses. (Profits are negative.) As production increases, its losses shrink as it approaches point *B*. Then, to the right of *B*, the firm begins to make profits. As long as output is less than 150 units, the profits curve has a *positive* slope; that is, it slopes upward. Profits reach a peak at point C and thereafter begin to decline. Thus to the right of C the curve has a *negative* slope. At the point where the curve reaches its peak, it is horizontal. The slope is zero.

(measured along the vertical axis) will be negative. As it sells more, its revenues will rise, and it will begin to make profits to the right of point *B*.

Profits do not rise indefinitely. If the company were to produce a large number of planes—say, 200—it would have to slash prices in order to sell them. This would reduce its profits. Thus the profit curve at first slopes upward, reaches a peak at *C*, and then slopes downward.

Point *C* is very significant for the firm. At this point, the firm *maximizes its profits*. The curve ceases to slope upward and is just about to slope downward; the slope is just about to switch from being positive to becoming negative. Thus, at the point of maximum profit, the slope of the curve is *zero*.

CHAPTER 2
SCARCITY AND CHOICE
The Economic Problem

Economics studies human behaviour as a relationship between ends and scarce means.
LIONEL ROBBINS

When Neil Armstrong stepped on the moon in 1969, the space program achieved its most spectacular success. Now, 20 years later, Carl Sagan, the noted Cornell astronomer and author of the best-selling *Cosmos,* has proposed a new space adventure. He has urged that a space ship be sent to Mars with a U. S. and Soviet crew. The time has come, he believes, for human eyes to look directly at that mysterious planet.

Sagan's proposal has met with skepticism. The reason is cost. The U.S. share of such a project would be huge—perhaps as much as $100 billion. How could we pay for it? Through additional taxes that would require the public to give up income in order to finance the space program? Through cutbacks in other spending by the federal government—for roads, social security, or defense? Sagan's proposal has run directly into the central **economic problem.** We must make **choices.** We cannot have everything we want, because:

1. Our material **wants** are virtually **unlimited.**
2. Economic **resources** are **scarce.**

If we use our productive capacity to send a spaceship with human passengers to Mars, we will have less for other things.

The economic problem is the need to make choices among the options permitted by our scarce resources.

Economics is the study of how scarce resources are allocated to satisfy alternative, competing human wants.

To *economize* is to achieve a specific benefit at the lowest cost in terms of the resources used.

UNLIMITED WANTS. . .

Consider, first, our wants. If we can survive in a simple one-bedroom bungalow, why do we aspire to much larger homes filled with gadgets? Why do our material wants never seem to be satisfied? Material wants arise for two reasons. First, each of us has basic biological needs: the need for food, shelter, and clothing. But there is also a second reason. Clearly, we are prepared to work more than is required to meet our minimum needs. We want more than the basic diet of vegetables and water needed to sustain life. We want more than the minimum clothing needed to protect us from the cold. In other words, we want not only the essential goods and services that make life possible, but also some of the nonessentials that make life pleasant. Of course, the two basic reasons for material wants cannot be sharply separated. When we sit down to a gourmet meal at a restaurant, we are getting the food essential for satisfying our biological requirements. But we are getting something more. When we savor exotic foods in a comfortable and stylish atmosphere, we are also getting luxuries. Such nonessentials are sufficiently pleasant that we are willing to work to obtain them.

The range of consumer wants is exceedingly broad. We want **goods,** such as houses, cars, shoes, and tennis rackets. Similarly, we want **services,** such as medical care and transportation. When we get what we want, it may whet our appetites for something more. We may become dissatisfied with the old lawnmower and want a self-propelled one instead. After we buy a house, we may wish to replace the carpets and drapes. Furthermore, as new products are introduced, we may want them too. We want video recorders, home computers, and a host of other products never dreamed of by earlier generations. Even though it is conceivable that, some day, we will say, "Enough," that day seems far away. Our material wants show no sign of being completely satisfied.

. . . AND SCARCE RESOURCES

Not all wants can be satisfied because of the second fundamental fact. Although our productive capacity is large, it is not without limit. There are only so many workers in the labor force, only a given amount of land, and only a certain number of machines and factories. In other words, our resources are limited.

Resources are the basic inputs used in the production of goods and services. Therefore, they are also frequently known as **factors of production.** They can be categorized under three main headings: land, capital, and labor.

1. Land. Economists use this term in a broad sense, to include not only the land cultivated by farmers and the land in cities used as building lots, but also the other gifts of nature that come with the land. Thus the minerals that are found under the soil, and the water and sunlight that fall on the soil, are all part of the land resource.

2. Capital. This term refers to buildings, equipment, and inventories of materials (such as steel) to be used in the productive process. An automobile factory is "capital," and so are the machines in the plant and the steel with which automobiles will be built. In contrast to land, which has been *given* to us by nature, capital has been *produced* at some time in the past. It may have been the distant past; the factory may have been built 25 years ago. Or it may have been the recent past; the steel may have been manufactured last month. The process of producing and accumulating capital is known as **investment.**

Unlike *consumer goods* (such as shoes, cars, or food), *capital goods* or investment goods (such as tractors, factories, or machinery in the factories) are not produced to satisfy human wants directly. Rather, they are intended for use in the production of other goods. Capital produced now will satisfy wants only indirectly and at a later time, when it is used in the production of consumer goods. The production of capital therefore means that someone is *willing to wait.* When a machine is produced rather than a car, the choice is made to forego the car now in order to produce the machine, thus making it possible to produce more cars or other goods in the future. Capital formation therefore involves a choice between consumption *now* and more consumption *in the future.*

One point of terminology should be emphasized here. Unless otherwise specified, economists use the term "capital" to mean **real capital,** not financial capital. In previous paragraphs, we've been referring to real capital—the factories and machinery used to produce other goods. On the other hand, **financial capital** consists of financial assets such as common stocks, bonds, or bank deposits. Such assets are important. The holder of a stock or bond, for example, has a form of wealth that is likely to produce income in the future, in the form of dividends on the stock or interest on the bond. But, while an individual might consider 100 shares of General Motors stock as part of his or her "capital," they are not capital in the economic sense. They are not a resource with which goods and services can be produced.

Similarly, when economists talk of investment, they generally mean **real investment**—the accumulation of machines and other real capital—and not financial investment, such as the purchase of a government bond.

3. Labor. This term refers to the human resource—the physical and mental talents that people apply to the production of goods and services. The construction worker provides labor, and so does the college professor or the physician. The professor produces educational services, and the doctor produces medical services.[1]

One particular human resource deserves special emphasis: **entrepreneurial ability.** Entrepreneur is a French word that means "someone who undertakes." More specifically, it means someone who

a. *Organizes production,* bringing together the factors of production—land, labor, and capital—to make goods and services.

b. *Makes business decisions,* figuring out what goods to produce and how to produce them.

c. *Takes risk,* knowing that there is no guarantee that business decisions will turn out to be correct.

d. *Innovates,* introducing new products, new technology, and new ways of organizing business.

In order to be successful, an entrepreneur needs to be aware of changes in the economy. Is the market for adding machines declining, while that of computers is expanding? If so, the successful entrepreneur will not build a new assembly line for adding machines but will instead consider the production of computers. Some entrepreneurs are spectacularly successful. For example, Steve Jobs and Steve Wozniak set up Apple Computer while they were still in their twenties. Their mushrooming sales helped to make the microcomputer a common household appliance—and made them multimillionaires in the process. Other entrepreneurs are engaged in much more prosaic, everyday enterprises. The teenager who offers to cut a neighbor's lawn for $10 is an entrepreneur. So is the college student who has a business typing other students' papers. The key questions facing an entrepreneur are these: Are people willing to pay for what I can produce? Can I sell the good or service for a price high enough to cover costs and have some profit left over?

Because entrepreneurs are the ones who undertake the production of new goods, they play a strategic role in determining the dynamism and growth of the economy.

SCARCITY AND CHOICE: THE PRODUCTION POSSIBILITIES CURVE

With unlimited wants and limited resources, we face the fundamental economic problem of **scarcity.** We cannot have everything we want; we must make *choices.*

The problem of scarcity—and the need to make choices—can be illustrated with a **production possibilities curve** (PPC). This curve shows what can be produced with our existing resources (land, labor, and capital) and with our existing technology. Although our resources are limited and our capacity to produce is likewise limited, we have an option as to what goods and services we produce. We may produce fewer cars and more aircraft or less wheat and more corn.

In an economy with thousands of products, the choices before us are complex. In order to reduce this complexity, consider a very basic economy with only two goods (cotton clothing and wheat) where a decision to produce more food (wheat) will leave us able to produce less clothing.

The options open to us are illustrated in the hypothetical production possibilities curve in Figure 2-1. Consider first an extreme example, in which all our resources are directed toward the production of food. In this case, illustrated by option *A*, we would produce 20 million tons of food but no clothing. This clearly does not repre-

[1] The preceding paragraphs have presented the traditional division of the factors of production into the categories of land, labor, and capital. While this traditional division is still popular, present-day economists do not universally subscribe to it. In particular, some economists now talk of "human capital." This term may be defined as the education and training that add to the productivity of labor. Human capital has two of the important characteristics of physical capital: (1) it requires a willingness to wait during the training period, when the trainee does not produce goods or services; and (2) it results in an increase in the productive capacity of the economy, since a trained worker can produce more than an untrained one.

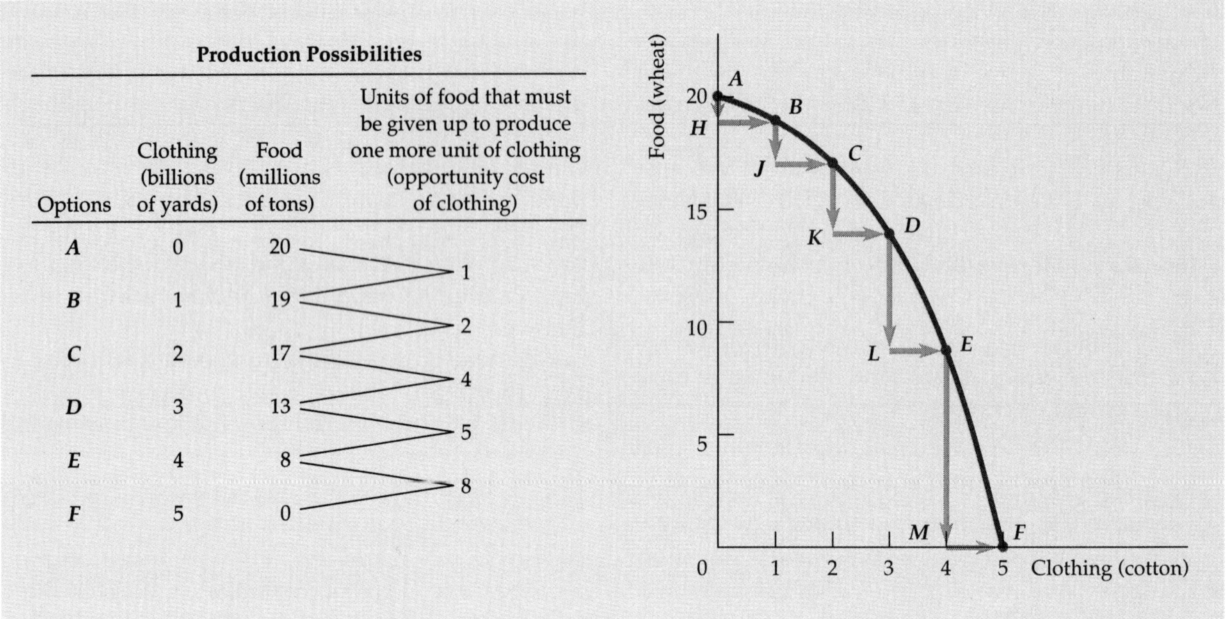

Production Possibilities

Options	Clothing (billions of yards)	Food (millions of tons)	Units of food that must be given up to produce one more unit of clothing (opportunity cost of clothing)
A	0	20	
B	1	19	1
C	2	17	2
D	3	13	4
E	4	8	5
F	5	0	8

FIGURE 2–1 The production possibilities curve.

The curve shows the combinations of two goods that can be produced with limited resources of land, labor and capital.

sent a desirable composition of output. Although we would be well fed, we would be running around naked. However, no claim has been made that the points on the production possibilities curve are necessarily *desirable;* the only claim is that they are *possible.* And point *A* is possible.

At the other extreme, if we produced nothing but clothing, we would make 5 billion yards, as illustrated by point *F.* Again, this is a possible outcome but not a desirable one. We would be well dressed as we faced starvation.

THE SHAPE OF THE PRODUCTION POSSIBILITIES CURVE: INCREASING OPPORTUNITY COSTS

More reasonable cases are those in which we produce some quantities of each good. Consider how the economy might move from point *A* toward point *F.* At point *A*, nothing is produced but food. It is grown on all types of arable land throughout the nation. In order to begin the production of clothing, cotton would be planted in the areas that were comparatively best suited for cotton production—those in Alabama and Mississippi. From these lands, we would get a lot of cotton, while giving up just a small amount of food that might have been grown there. This is illustrated in the move from point *A* to point *B* on the production possibilities curve. Only one unit of food is given up in order to produce the first unit of clothing.

As more cotton is produced, however, land must be used that is somewhat less suited to its production. As a result, the second unit of clothing does not come quite so easily. To produce it, more than one unit of food must be given up. This is illustrated in the move from point *B* to point *C.* As clothing production is increased by one more unit (from one unit to two), food production falls by two units (from 19 to 17). The **opportunity cost** of the second unit of clothing—the food we have to give up to acquire it—is thus greater than the opportunity cost of the first unit.

Further increases in the production of clothing come at higher and higher opportunity costs in terms of food foregone. As we move to the third unit of clothing (from point *C* to *D*), we must start planting cotton in the corn belt of Iowa. A lot of food must be given up to produce that third unit of clothing. Finally, in the last move from point *E* to point *F*, all our resources are switched into the production of clothing. The last unit of clothing comes at an extremely high opportunity cost in terms of food. Wheat production is stopped on the farms of North Dakota and Minnesota, which are no good at all for producing cotton. The wheat lands remain idle, and the farmers of North Dakota and Minnesota migrate further south, where they can make only minor contributions to cotton production. Thus the last unit of clothing (the move from point *E* to *F*) comes at a very high cost of eight units of food.

The ***opportunity cost*** of a product is the alternative that is given up to produce that product. In the illustration, the opportunity cost of a unit of clothing is the food that is given up when that unit of clothing is produced.

Therefore the *increasing opportunity cost of cotton is a reflection of the specialized characteristics of resources*. Resources are not completely adaptable to alternative uses. The lands of Minnesota and Mississippi are not equally well suited to the production of cotton and wheat. Thus the opportunity cost of cotton rises as its production is increased.

As a result of increasing opportunity cost, the production possibilities curve in Figure 2-1 *bows outward*. Technically, this curve is described as *concave to the origin*. The arrows in this figure illustrate why. The horizontal increases in clothing production—from point *H* to *B*, from *J* to *C*, from *K* to *D*, and so on—are each one unit. The resulting reductions in food production—measured vertically from *A* to *H*, *B* to *J*, *C* to *K*, and so on—become larger and larger, making the curve increasingly steep as we move to the right.

While opportunity costs generally increase, as shown in Figure 2-1, it is not logically necessary that they must do so. In some cases, it is possible for opportunity costs to be constant. For example, beef cattle and dairy cattle can graze on similar land; it is possible that the resources used to raise beef are equally suited for dairy cattle. Thus the opportunity cost of beef in terms of milk may be constant. If so, a production possibilities curve drawn with milk on one axis and beef on the other would be a straight line.

THE PRODUCTION POSSIBILITIES CURVE IS A FRONTIER

The production possibilities curve in Figure 2-1 illustrates what an economy is capable of producing. It shows the *maximum* possible combined output of the two goods. In practice, actual production can fall short of our capabilities. Obviously, if there is large-scale unemployment, labor resources are being wasted. The same is true if workers are employed but are wasting their time on the job. In either case, the result is a point like *U*, inside the production possibilities curve in Figure 2-2. Beginning at such a point, it is possible to produce more food *and* more clothing (and move to point *D*) by getting those who are wasting their time or are

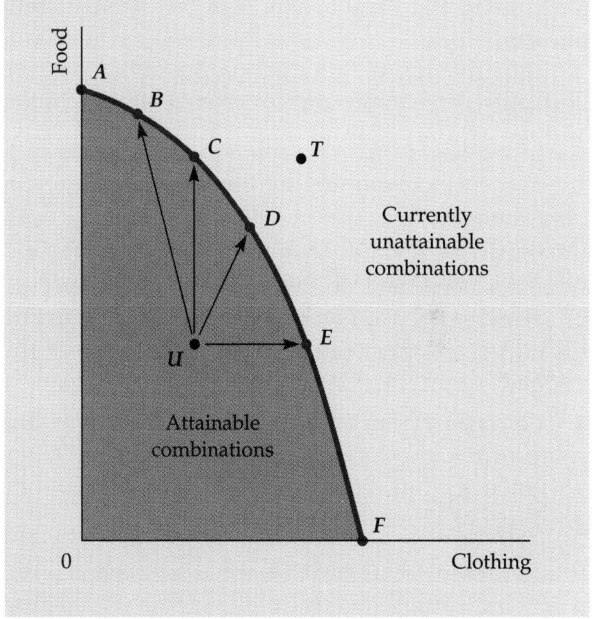

FIGURE 2-2 Unemployment and the production possibilities curve.

Point *U* represents a position of large-scale unemployment. If people are put back to work, the economy can be moved to point *D*, with more food *and* more clothing.

With its limited resources, the society can choose any point along the production possibilities curve, or any point within it. Points in the shaded area within the curve are undesirable; the society could do better by moving out to the curve. Points beyond the curve are unattainable with the resources currently at our disposal.

unemployed back to work. (With full employment, we alternatively could choose any other point on the production possibilities curve, such as *B*, *C*, or *E*.)

Thus, although the production possibilities curve represents options open to the society, it does not include all conceivable options. The attainable options include not only the points on the curve, but also all points in the shaded area inside the curve.

The production possibilities curve therefore traces out a *frontier* or *boundary* of the options open to us. We can pick a point on the frontier if we don't waste resources and maintain a high level of employment. Or we can end up inside the curve if we use resources in a wasteful way or mismanage the economy into a depression. But points such as *T* outside the curve are currently unattainable. We cannot reach them with our present quantities of land, labor, and capital, and with our present technology.

In summary, the production possibilities curve illustrates three important concepts: scarcity, choice, and opportunity cost.

1. *Scarcity* is illustrated by the fact that combinations outside the curve cannot be attained. Even though we might want such combinations, we cannot have them with the resources available to us.
2. Because we cannot have combinations outside the curve, we must settle for a *choice* of one of the attainable combinations outlined by the PPC.
3. *Opportunity cost* is illustrated by the downward slope of the production possibilities curve. When we reallocate our resources to produce more of one good, we produce less of another.

GROWTH: THE OUTWARD SHIFT OF THE PRODUCTION POSSIBILITIES CURVE

As time passes, a point such as *T* (Fig. 2-2) may come within our grasp as our productive capacity increases and the economy grows. There are three main sources of growth:

1. Technological improvement, representing new and better methods of producing goods.
2. An increase in the quantity of capital.
3. An increase in the number of workers, and in their skills and educational levels.

Consider a technological improvement. Suppose a new type of fertilizer is developed that substantially increases the output of our land, whether cotton or wheat is being grown. Then we will be able to produce more wheat and more cotton. The production possibilities curve will shift out to the new curve (PPC_2) shown in Figure 2-3.

> ***Growth*** is defined as an increase in the productive capacity of the nation. It is illustrated by an outward movement of the production possibilities curve.

Although the new fertilizer illustrated in Figure 2-3 increases our ability to produce *both* wheat and cotton, other types of technological improvement may increase our ability to produce only *one* of them. For example, the development of

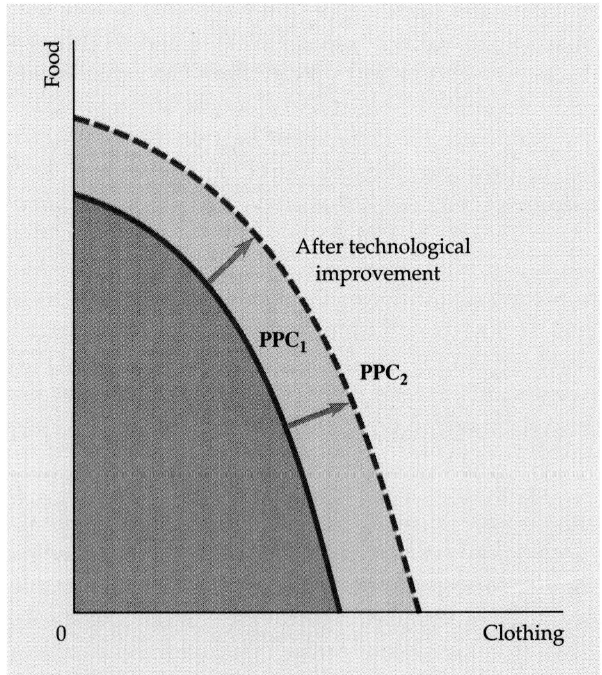

FIGURE 2-3 Technological improvement.

As a result of the development of a new fertilizer, productive capabilities increase. The production possibilities curve moves outward.

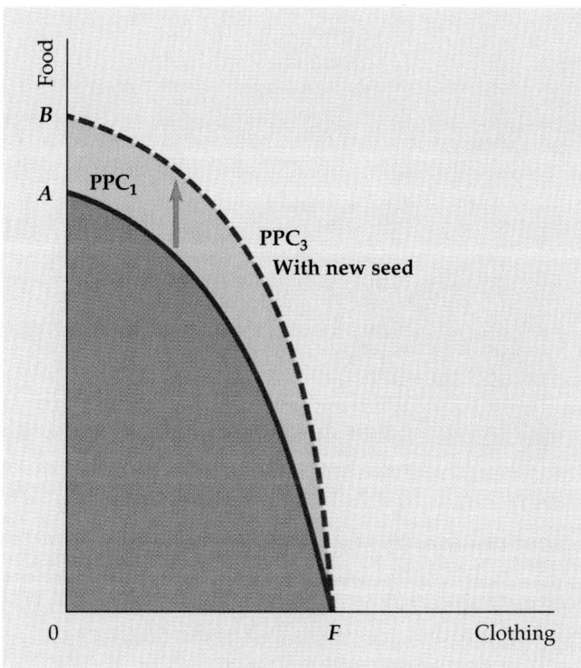

FIGURE 2-4 Technological improvement in a single good.

When a new, improved strain of wheat is developed, the production possibilities curve moves out to PPC_3.

a new disease-resistant strain of wheat will increase our ability to produce wheat but not cotton. In this case, illustrated in Figure 2-4, nothing will happen to the place where the production possibilities curve meets the axis for clothing. If we direct all our resources to the production of clothing, we can still produce no more than is shown by point *F*. However, if we direct all our resources to wheat, we can produce more; the other end of the PPC moves upward along the food axis, from *A* to *B*. The development of the new strain of wheat therefore causes the PPC to move upward, from PPC_1 to PPC_3.

GROWTH: THE CHOICE BETWEEN CONSUMER GOODS AND CAPITAL GOODS

As an alternative to technological change, consider the second source of growth listed above: an increase in the quantity of capital. The capital we have today is limited. However, capital itself can be produced. The quantity of capital we will have in the year 2020 will be determined in large part by how much of our resources we choose to devote this year and in coming years to producing capital, rather than consumer goods.

In order to study this choice, we must look at a different production possibilities curve—not one showing food and clothing, but rather, one showing the choice between the production of *capital goods* (such as machines and factories) and the production of *consumer goods* (such as food, clothing, and television sets).

In Figure 2-5, two hypothetical countries are compared. Starting in 1990, these two countries face the same initial production possibilities curve (PPC_{1990}). The citizens of country *A* (on the left) believe in living for the moment. They produce mostly consumption goods and very few capital goods, at point *C*. As a result, their capital stock will not be much greater in 2020 than it is today, so their PPC will shift out very little. In contrast, the citizens of country *B* (on the right) keep down the production of consumer goods in order to build more capital goods, at point *F*. By the year 2020, their productive capacity will be greatly increased, as shown by the large outward movement of the PPC. Because they have given up so much consumption today, their income and ability to consume will be much greater in the future. Thus any society faces a choice: How much consumption should it sacrifice now in order to be able to consume more in the future?

AN INTRODUCTION TO ECONOMIC THEORY: THE NEED TO SIMPLIFY

The production possibilities curve is the first piece of theoretical equipment the beginning economics student typically encounters. There will be many more. At this early stage, it is appropriate to address directly a problem that often bothers both beginning and advanced students. The production possibilities curve, like many other theoretical tools that will be introduced in later chapters, represents a gross simplification of the real world. When the PPC is drawn, it is assumed that only two types of

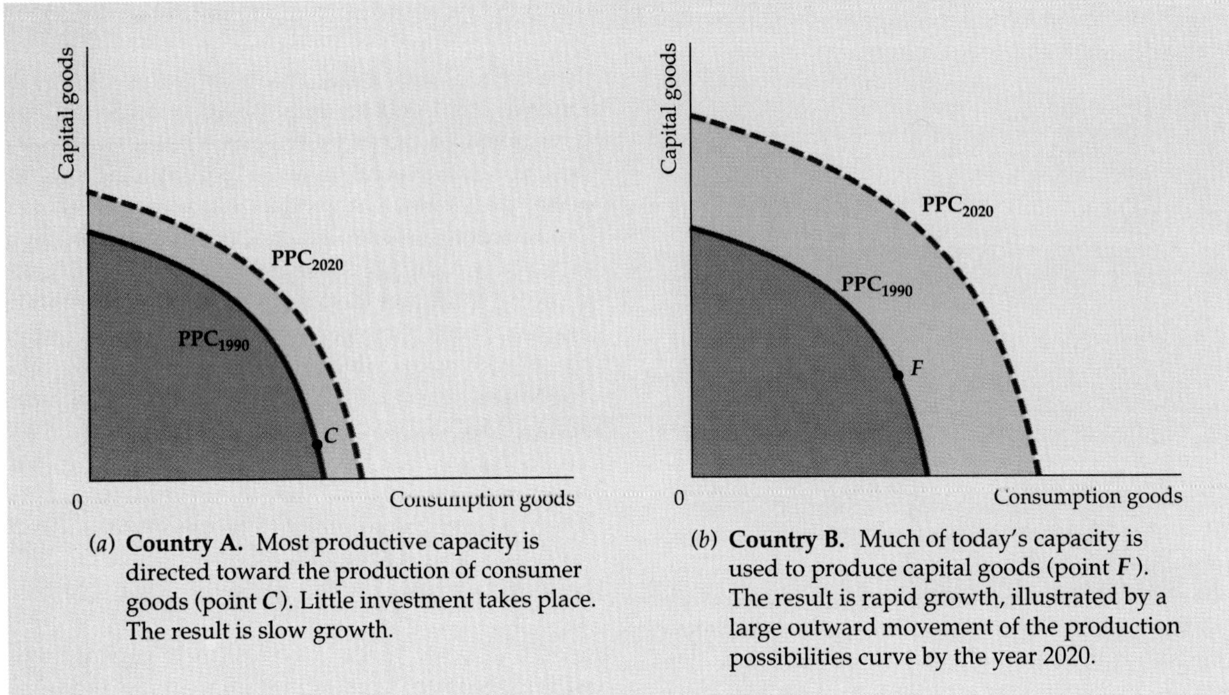

(*a*) **Country A.** Most productive capacity is directed toward the production of consumer goods (point *C*). Little investment takes place. The result is slow growth.

(*b*) **Country B.** Much of today's capacity is used to produce capital goods (point *F*). The result is rapid growth, illustrated by a large outward movement of the production possibilities curve by the year 2020.

FIGURE 2-5 Capital formation now helps to determine future productive capacity.

This figure illustrates the choice between consumer goods and capital goods. The country on the left consumes most of its current output and does not invest very much in new capital equipment. It therefore grows slowly. In contrast, the country on the right is willing to direct a large fraction of its current production into investment. It grows rapidly as a result.

goods can be produced—food and clothing, or consumer goods and capital goods. Diagrams are limited to two alternatives because the printed page has only two dimensions. Yet obviously, there are thousands of goods produced in the modern economy. This raises a question: With our simple approach, can we say anything of relevance to the real world?

THEORY NECESSARILY MEANS SIMPLIFICATION

If we wished to describe the real world in detail, we could go on without end. A complete description would be useless as a guide to private behavior or public policy; it would be too complex. In a sense, theory is like a map. A road map is necessarily incomplete. In many ways, it is not very accurate, and, indeed, it is downright wrong. Towns and villages are not round circles. Roads of various qualities do not really come in different colors. If a road map were more realistic, it would be less useful for its intended purpose. If it tried to show every house and every tree, it would be an incomprehensible jumble of detail. A road map is useful precisely because it is a simplification that shows in stark outline the various roads that may be traveled. Similarly, the objective of economic theory is to draw in stark outline the important relationships among producers and consumers.

When details are left out of a road map, it becomes more useful as a guide for the auto traveler. However, it becomes less useful for other purposes. A road map is a poor guide for airplane pilots, who instead need a map with the height of mountains marked clearly. A road map is also a poor guide for sales managers, who need a map showing regional sales targets and staff assignments. The way in which a map is constructed depends on its intended use. Various maps are "true," but they do not represent the "whole truth." An important question for a map user thus becomes: Do I have the best map for my purpose?

The same generalization holds for economic theory. If we wish to study long-run growth, we may use quite different theoretical tools from those we would use to study short-term fluctuations. If we want to study the consequences of price controls on the housing market, we may use different tools from those we would choose to investigate the economic consequences of a cut in the defense budget. Just as in the case of the map, the "best" theory cannot be identified unless we know the purposes for which it is to be used.

The production possibilities curve is a theoretical tool whose purpose is to illustrate the concept of scarcity. *If* we begin on the PPC, with our resources fully employed, then we can come to a significant conclusion: To produce more of one good, we will have to cut back on the production of some other good or service. The "if" clause is important. It tells us that when we consider points along the PPC, we are making an assumption—that resources are fully utilized. When the "if" clause is violated—that is, when the economy begins with large-scale unemployment—then we reach quite a different conclusion: The economy *can* produce more consumer goods and more capital goods at the same time. Thus the "if" clause acts as a label on our theoretical road map. It makes clear the assumptions we are making and tells us when the map can be used.

For the novice and old hand alike, it is essential to recognize and remember such "if" clauses. We must pay attention to the set of assumptions underlying any theory that we use. If we don't, we may use the wrong theory and make serious policy mistakes—just as the pilot who uses the wrong map may fly a plane into the nearest mountain top.

THE DISTINCTION BETWEEN POSITIVE AND NORMATIVE ECONOMICS

The uses of theory are many, but they may be divided into two main families. **Positive or descriptive** economics aims at understanding how the economy works. It is directed toward explaining the world as *it is,* and how various forces can cause it to change. In contrast, **normative** economics deals with the way the world (or some small segment of it) **ought to be.**

A debate over a *positive* statement can often be settled by looking at the facts. For example, the following is a positive statement: "U.S. steel production last year was 100 million tons." By looking up the statistics, we can find out whether this was true. A more complicated positive statement is: "There are millions of barrels of oil in the rocks of Colorado." With a geological study, we can discover whether this claim is likely to be so. A third positive statement is this: "If a ton of dynamite is exploded 100 feet below the surface, 1,000 barrels of oil will be released from the rocks." By experimentation, we can discover whether this is generally true.

A *normative* statement is more complex: for example, "We ought to extract large quantities of oil from the Colorado rocks." Facts are relevant here. If there is no oil in the rocks of Colorado (a positive conclusion), then the normative statement that we ought to extract oil must be rejected for the very simple reason that it cannot be done. However, facts alone will seldom settle a dispute over a normative statement, since it is based on something more—on a view regarding appropriate goals or ethical values. A normative statement involves a value judgment, a judgment about what ought to be. It is possible for well-informed individuals to disagree over normative statements, even when they agree completely regarding the facts. For example, they may agree that, in fact, a large quantity of oil is locked in the rocks of Colorado. Nevertheless, they may disagree whether it should be extracted. Perhaps these differences may develop over the relative importance of a plentiful supply of heating oil as compared with the environmental damage that might accompany the extraction of oil.

Although some positive statements may be

easily settled by looking at the facts, others may be much more difficult to judge. This is particularly true of statements making claims about causation. They may be quite controversial because the facts are not easily untangled. For example: "If there is no growth in the money stock next year, then inflation will fall to zero"; or, "If income tax rates are increased by 1%, government revenues will increase by $20 billion next year"; or, "Rent controls have little effect on the number of apartments offered for rent."

In evaluating such statements, economists and other social scientists have two major disadvantages as compared with natural scientists. First, experiments are difficult or impossible in many instances. Society is not the plaything of economists. They do not have the power to conduct an experiment in which one large city is subjected to rent control while a similar city is not, simply to estimate the effects of rent control. Nevertheless, economists do have factual evidence to study. By looking at situations in which rent controls have actually been imposed by the government, they may be able to estimate the effects of those controls. Moreover, in special situations, economic experiments *are* possible, particularly when the government is eager to know the results. For example, experiments have been undertaken to determine whether people work less when they are provided with a minimum income by the government. (The results will be reported in Chapter 39.)

The second disadvantage is that the social sciences deal with the behavior of people, and behavior can change. Suppose we estimate corporate profits next year to be $200 billion. We might carelessly conclude that, if the profits tax is raised by 10%, the government will receive an additional $20 billion in revenues. But this is not necessarily so. With a higher tax rate, businesses may behave differently, in order to reduce the taxes they have to pay. Furthermore, even if we have evidence on how businesses have responded to a 10% tax increase in the past, we cannot be certain that they will respond the same way in the future. As time passes, they may become more imaginative in finding ways to avoid taxes. The possibility that people will learn and change has been one of the most interesting areas of research in economics in recent years.

In contrast, physical scientists study a relatively stable and unchanging universe. Gravity works the same today as it did in Newton's time.

KEY POINTS

1. *Scarcity* is a fundamental economic problem. Because wants are virtually unlimited and resources are scarce, we must make *choices.*

2. The choices open to society are illustrated by the *production possibilities curve.* This illustrates the concept of the *opportunity cost* of a good *A,* which is the amount of another good *B* that must be sacrificed to produce *A.*

3. Not all resources are identical. For example, the land of Mississippi is different from the land of Minnesota. As a consequence, opportunity cost generally increases as more of a good is produced. For example, as more cotton is produced, more and more wheat must be given up for each additional unit of cotton. As a result, the production possibilities curve normally bows outward.

4. The production possibilities curve is a frontier, representing the choices open to society—*if* there is full utilization of land, labor, and capital. If there is large-scale unemployment, then production occurs at a point within this frontier.

5. The economy can grow and the production possibilities curve can move outward if

- **(a)** Technology improves.
- **(b)** The capital stock grows.
- **(c)** And/or the labor force grows.

6. By giving up consumer goods at present, we can produce more capital goods and thus have a growing economy. The production of capital goods (investment) therefore represents a choice of more future production instead of present consumption.

7. Like other theoretical concepts, the production possibilities curve represents a simplification. Because the world is so complex, theory cannot reflect the "whole truth." Nevertheless, a theory—like a road map—can be valuable if it is used correctly. In order to determine the appropriate uses of a theory, it is important to identify the assumptions on which the theory was developed. As theories are developed in this book, it will be essential to pay attention to the assumptions underlying each.

KEY CONCEPTS

scarcity
goods
services
resources
the economic problem
economics
factors of production
land
labor
capital
investment
entrepreneur
production possibilities curve
opportunity cost
growth
positive economics
normative economics

PROBLEMS

2-1. "Wants aren't insatiable. The economic wants of David Rockefeller have been satisfied. There is no prospect that he will spend all his money before he dies. His consumption is not limited by his income." Do you agree? Does your answer raise problems for the main theme of this chapter, that wants cannot all be satisfied with the goods and services produced from our limited resources? Why or why not?

2-2. "The more capital goods we produce, the more the U.S. economy will grow, and the more we and our children will be able to consume in the future. Therefore, the government should encourage capital formation." Do you agree or disagree? Why? Can any case be made on the other side?

2-3. Is your answer to Problem 2-2 an example of "positive" or "normative" economics? Why?

CHAPTER 3
SPECIALIZATION, EXCHANGE, AND MONEY

Money... is not of the wheels of trade: it is the oil which renders the motion of the wheels smooth and easy.

DAVID HUME

The early French colony at Quebec was a forbidding place in winter, with temperatures often falling to 20° below zero. Keeping warm was the first problem. Getting supplies from France was a close second. During the winter, the St. Lawrence River was clogged with ice.

Of the many things the colony lacked, money was one. Not only did ships have difficulty sailing up the river, but even when they did come, they had little currency; the colony's sponsors in France were reluctant to send money. The colonists found that barter—for example, the trade of a bushel of wheat for a bag of salt—was very cumbersome; even in a simple economy, money was essential. What could they do? They hit upon an ingenious solution. They used playing cards as money. The man with an ace in his pocket often had a smile on his face.

In the modern economy, as in the early colonies, money plays a central role. Over the decades, production has become increasingly specialized with the development of new machinery and equipment. **Specialization** contributes to efficiency; often, workers can produce more by specializing. But **specialization necessitates exchange.** A farmer who produces only beef wants to exchange some of that beef for clothing, cars, medical services, and a whole list of other products.

This chapter will

- Describe the two types of exchange:
  1. barter.
  2. exchange with money.
- Explain why exchange using money is so much simpler than barter.
- Provide more detail on how people can gain from specialization and exchange.

EXCHANGE: THE BARTER ECONOMY

In a **barter** system, no money is used: One good or service is exchanged directly for another. The farmer specializing in beef must find a hungry barber and thus get a haircut, or find a hungry tailor and thus exchange meat for a suit of clothes, or find a hungry doctor and thus obtain medical treatment. A simple barter transaction is illustrated in Figure 3-1. In a barter economy, there are dozens of such bilateral (two-way) transactions: between the farmer and the tailor; between the farmer and the doctor; between the doctor and the tailor; and so on.

Barter can be very inefficient. Farmers may spend half their time producing beef and the other

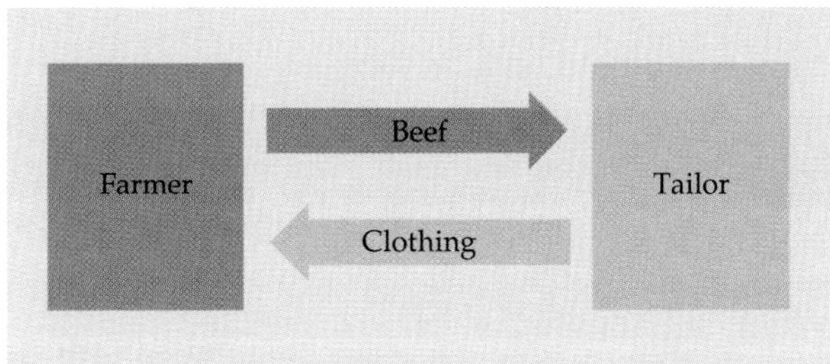

FIGURE 3-1 Barter.

With barter, no money is used. The farmer exchanges beef directly for clothing. Transactions involve only two parties—in this case, the farmer and the tailor.

half searching for someone willing to make the right trade. Barter requires a **coincidence of wants:** Each of those engaged in barter must have a product that the other wants. The farmer not only must find someone who wants beef, but that someone must also be able to provide something in exchange that the farmer wants. Furthermore, with barter, there is a problem of **indivisibility.** A suit of clothes—or an automobile, or a house—should be bought all at once, and not in pieces. To illustrate, suppose that a beef farmer who wants a suit of clothes has been lucky enough to find a tailor who wants meat and is willing to make a trade. The suit of clothes may be worth 100 pounds of beef, and the farmer may be quite willing to give up this amount. The problem is that the tailor may not be *that* hungry and perhaps only wants 50 pounds of beef. In a barter economy, what is the farmer to do? Get only the jacket from this tailor and set out to find another hungry tailor in order to obtain a pair of pants? If the farmer does so, what are the chances that the pants will match?

EXCHANGE WITH MONEY

With money, exchange is much easier. It is no longer necessary for wants to coincide. In order to get a suit of clothing, the farmer need not find a hungry tailor, but only someone willing to buy the beef. The farmer can then take the money from the sale of the beef and buy a suit of clothes. Money represents **general purchasing power**—that is, it can be used to buy *any* of the goods and services offered for sale. Therefore, complex transactions among many parties are possible with money. Figure 3-2 presents a simple illustration with three parties. Actual transactions in a monetary economy may be very complex, with dozens or even hundreds of participants.

Note how money solves the problem of indivisibility. The farmer can sell the whole carcass of beef for money and use the proceeds to buy a complete set of clothes. It doesn't matter how much beef the tailor wants.

In the simple barter economy, there is no clear distinction between seller and buyer, or between producer and consumer. When bartering beef for clothing, the farmer is at the same time both the seller (of beef) and the buyer (of clothing). In contrast, in a monetary economy, there is a *clear distinction between seller and buyer.* In the beef market, the farmer is the seller; the tailor is the buyer. The farmer is the producer; the tailor is the consumer.

THE CIRCULAR FLOW OF EXPENDITURES AND INCOME

The distinction between the producer and the consumer in a money economy is illustrated in Figure 3-3. Producers—or businesses—are in the right-hand box; consumers—or households—in the left. Transactions between the two groups are illustrated in the loops. The top loops show consumer expenditures for goods and services. Beef, clothing, and a host of other products are bought with money.

The lower loops show transactions in economic resources. In a complex exchange economy, not only are consumer goods bought and sold for money; so, too, are resources. In order to be able to buy food and other goods, households must have money income. They acquire money by providing the labor and other resources which are the inputs of the business sector. For example, workers provide their labor in exchange for wages and salaries, and owners of land provide their property in exchange for rents.

Figure 3-3 is simplified. For example, it does not include government or foreign purchases of goods and services, which are very important. Remember the purpose of simplification discussed in Chapter 2: to show in sharp outline the relationships on which we want to concentrate. Figure 3-3 shows the circular flow of payments—that is, how businesses use the receipts from sales to pay their

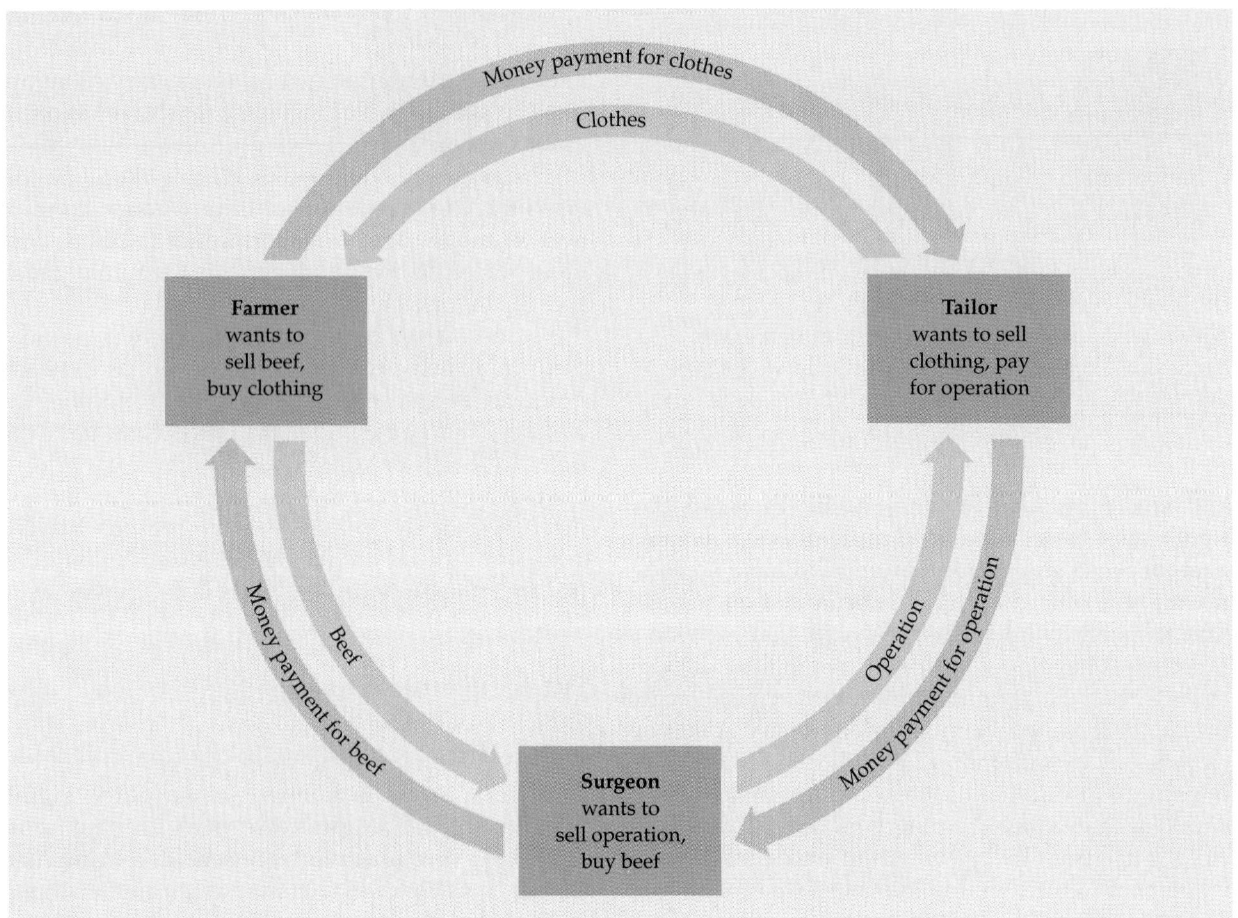

FIGURE 3-2 Multilateral transactions in a money economy.

In a money economy, multilateral transactions among many participants are possible. The farmer gets clothing from the tailor, even though the tailor does not want to buy the farmer's beef. Flows of money are shown in green.

wages, salaries, and other costs of production, while households use their income receipts from wages, salaries, and so on, to buy consumer goods.

THE MONETARY SYSTEM

Because barter is so inefficient, there is a natural tendency for something to become accepted as money. One example was the early colony at Quebec, where playing cards were used as money.

The powerful tendency for money to appear may also be illustrated by the prisoner-of-war camp of World War II.[1] Economic relations in such a camp were primitive and the range of goods was very limited. However, some things were available: rations supplied by the German captors and the Red Cross parcels that arrived periodically. Each person received a parcel containing a variety of items such as cheese, jam, margarine, and cigarettes. Nonsmokers who received cigarettes were eager to trade them for other items. Thus the basis was established for exchange.

[1]This illustration is based on R. A. Radford, "The Economic Organization of a POW Camp," *Economica* (November 1945), pp. 189–201.

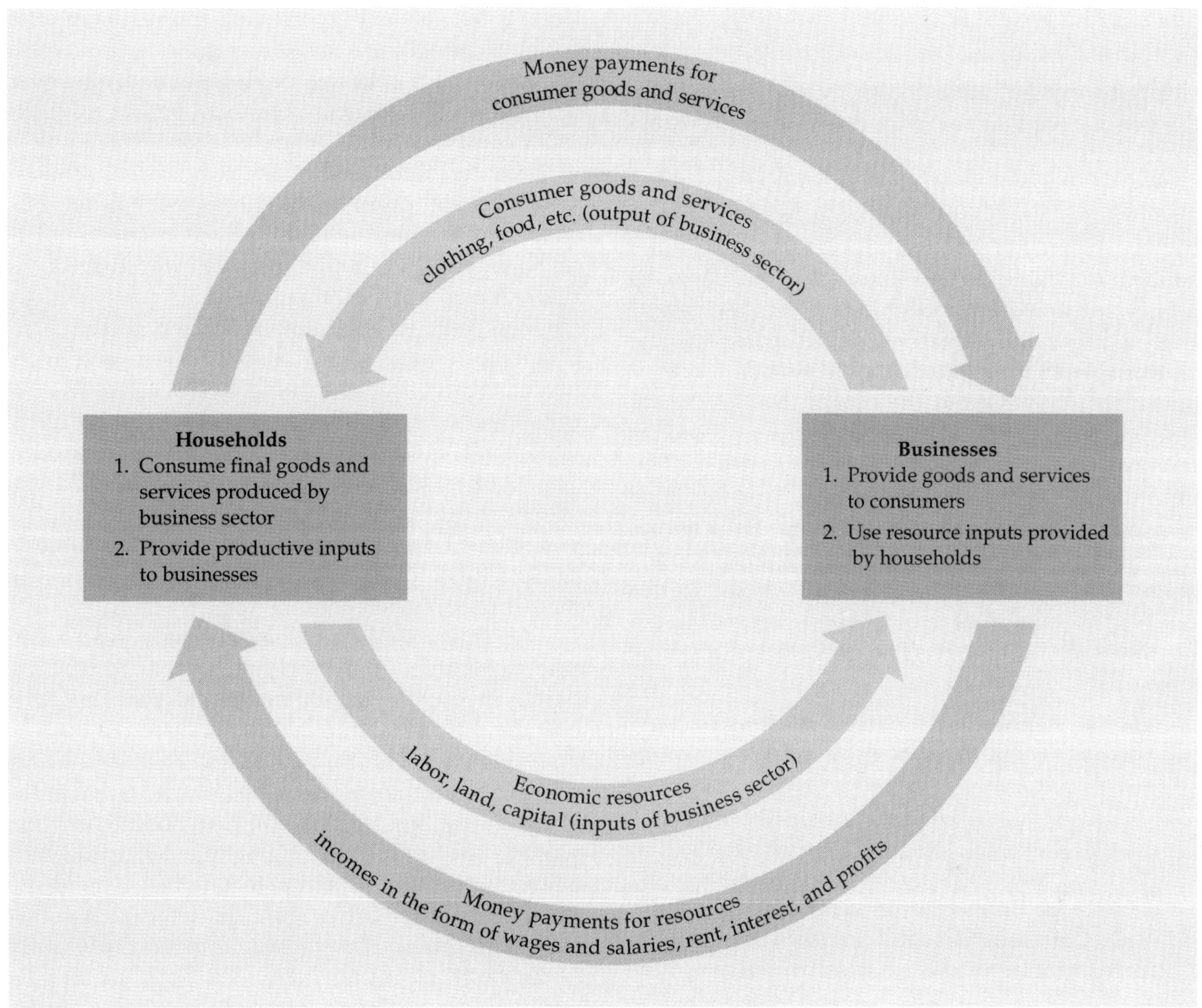

FIGURE 3-3 The flow of goods, services, resources, and money payments in a simple economy.

Monetary payments are shown in the outer loop. These pay for the flow of goods and services and resources shown in the inner loop.

At first, trading was rough and ready, with no clear picture of the relative values of the various items. In one instance, a prisoner started walking around the camp with only a can of cheese and five cigarettes, and returned with a complete Red Cross parcel. He did so by buying goods where they were cheap and selling them where they were expensive. As time went by, the relative prices of various goods became more stable, and all prices came to be quoted in terms of cigarettes. For example, a can of cheese was worth twenty cigarettes. Not only did cigarettes become the measuring rod for quoting prices, but they were also used as the common **medium of exchange**—that is, cigarettes were the item used to buy goods. Cigarettes became the money of the POW camp. This was a natural evolution; there was no government to decree that cigarettes were money, and no authority to enforce that choice. At other times and in other societies, other items have been used as money—items as diverse as beads, porpoise teeth, rice, salt, wampum, stones, and even woodpecker scalps.

MONETARY PROBLEMS IN THE POW CAMP

Cigarette money made the primitive economy of the prisoner-of-war camp more efficient. But problems occurred, including problems quite similar to those of more advanced monetary systems. Distinctions among various brands of cigarettes became blurred. Although all cigarettes were not equally desirable to smokers, all were equal as money. In paying for beef or other items, a cigarette was a cigarette. What was the consequence? Smokers held back the desirable brands for their personal use and spent the others. The less desirable cigarettes therefore were the ones used as money; the "good" cigarettes were smoked. This example illustrates **Gresham's law**. This law, first enunciated by Elizabethan financier Sir Thomas Gresham (1519–1579), is popularly and loosely abbreviated: "Bad money drives out good." In this case, "bad" cigarettes drove "good" cigarettes out of circulation as money. (The good cigarettes were smoked instead.)

> ***Gresham's law:*** If there are two types of money whose values in exchange are equal while their values in another use (like consumption) are different, the more valuable item will be retained for its other use while the less valuable item will continue to circulate as money. Thus the "bad" (less valuable) money drives the "good" (more valuable) money out of circulation.

The tendency of the prisoners to treat every cigarette as equal to every other cigarette caused another monetary problem. As a cigarette was a cigarette, prisoners often pulled out a few strands of tobacco before passing a cigarette along. This development corresponds precisely to a problem that has occurred whenever gold coins have circulated: People have "clipped" coins by chipping off bits of gold. Furthermore, the cigarette currency became debased: Some enterprising prisoners rolled cigarettes from pipe tobacco or broke down cigarettes and rerolled them, reducing the amount of tobacco in each. Similarly, governments have from time to time given in to the temptation to debase gold coins by melting them down and reissuing them with a smaller gold content. (Private entrepreneurs have had a strong incentive to do the same, but they have been discouraged throughout history by severe punishments for counterfeiters.)

It was not clipping or debasement, however, that led to the greatest monetary problems in the POW camp. As long as there was a balanced inflow of both cigarettes and other goods, the exchange system of the camp worked reasonably well. But, from time to time, the weekly Red Cross issue of 25 or 50 cigarettes per prisoner was interrupted. As the existing stock of cigarettes was consumed by smokers, cigarettes became more and more scarce. Desperate smokers had to offer more and more to get cigarettes; their value skyrocketed. To put the same point another way: Other goods were now exchanged for fewer and fewer cigarettes. A can of cheese that previously sold for 20 cigarettes dropped in value to 15, 10, or even fewer cigarettes. Thus there was deflation—a decline in the prices of other goods, measured in terms of money (cigarettes).

As cigarettes became increasingly scarce and prices continued to fall, prisoners began to revert to barter in exchanging other goods. Smokers who had the few remaining cigarettes were reluctant to give them up to make purchases. Then, from time to time, thousands of cigarettes would arrive at the camp during a brief period. Prices soared; in other words, the value of cigarettes fell. Prisoners became reluctant to accept cigarettes in payment for other goods. Once again, barter became common. Thus *the monetary system worked smoothly only as long as a reasonable balance was kept between the quantity of money (cigarettes) and the quantity of other goods.*

Two characteristics of a good monetary system may be drawn out of this story of the "cigarette standard:"

1. A smoothly operating monetary system should be made up of money whose value is **uniform.** Nonuniform money will set Gresham's law into operation, with "bad" money driving "good" money out of circulation. In the United States, the Federal Reserve System issues our paper currency and is responsible for assuring that money is uniform. One dollar bill is as good as another. It doesn't matter whether the $1 bill I have in my pocket is crisp and new, or whether it is tattered and soiled. The Federal Reserve will replace it with a new bill of equal value when it becomes excessively worn. This uniformity in the value of each dollar bill obviously adds to the ease of exchange—and it means that Gresham's law does not operate in our modern economy.

2. A second important characteristic of a good monetary system is that there be the **proper quantity of money,** neither too much nor too little. In the United States, the responsibility for controlling the quantity of money also lies with the Federal Reserve. This important topic will be studied in Part III of this book.

COMPARATIVE ADVANTAGE: A REASON TO SPECIALIZE

The beginning of this chapter described three key elements in the development of an economy. People **specialize.** For example, the farmer concentrates on producing beef. Specialization then requires **exchange.** The farmer exchanges beef to get other goods and services. Finally, **money** makes specialization and exchange run smoothly. However, money doesn't explain why specialization and exchange are advantageous in the first place. Why are specialization and exchange efficient? Why do they increase the goods and services we enjoy, and thus provide the propellant that drives the wheels of commerce?

One answer is provided by the **principle of comparative advantage.** To understand this principle, it is useful to look first at the simpler concept of **absolute advantage.**

A good is often made in the place that is best suited for its production: steel near the coal mines of Pennsylvania, corn in the fertile fields of Iowa, bananas in the tropical lands of Central America, coffee in the cool highlands of Colombia, and so on. In technical terms, there is some tendency for a good to be produced in the area that has an *absolute advantage* in its production.

> A country (or region or individual) has an ***absolute advantage*** in the production of a good if it can produce that good with fewer resources (less land, labor, and capital) than can other countries (or regions or individuals).

To illustrate how this principle applies to specialization between individuals, consider the case of the lawyer and the professional gardener. The lawyer is better at drawing up legal documents and the gardener generally is better at gardening, so it is in the interest of each to specialize in the occupation in which he or she has an absolute advantage.

The truth is often more complicated than this, however. By looking at the complications, we will be led to the idea of comparative advantage. Suppose a certain lawyer is better at gardening than the gardener; she's faster and more effective—in short, she has a "greener thumb." She has an absolute advantage in both the law and gardening. If absolute advantage were the key, she would practice law and do her own gardening as well. Does this necessarily happen? The answer is no. Unless this lawyer positively enjoys gardening as a recreation, she will leave the gardening to the professional. Why? Even though the lawyer, being an excellent gardener, can do as much gardening in 1 hour (let us say) as the gardener could in 2, she will be better off to stick to law and hire the gardener to work on the flowers and shrubbery. Why? In 1 hour's work, the lawyer can draw up a will, for which she charges $100. The gardener's time, in contrast, is worth only $10 per hour. By spending the hour on the law rather than on gardening, the lawyer comes out ahead. She earns $100 and can hire the gardener for $20 to put in 2 hours to get the gardening done. By sticking to law for that 1 hour, the lawyer gains $80, which she can then use to buy more goods and services. To sum up: Because of specialization and exchange, she ends up with more goods and services. (This principle is explained in more detail in Box 3-1.)

The gardener also gains through specialization and exchange. Although he has to work 10 hours in order to earn the $100 needed to hire the lawyer to draw up his will, at least he gets a will. If he spent that 10 hours instead trying to draw up a will himself, he might end up with no will at all, or "half a will"—a piece of paper that might or might not be valid, because the only law he would know would be whatever he might be able to pick up in that brief 10 hours. Thus by specialization and exchange, the gardener gets a better will than he could acquire by producing it himself.

BOX 3–1 *Illustration of Comparative Advantage*

A. Assume the following:

1. In 1 hour, the lawyer can plant 20 flowers.
2. In 1 hour, the gardener can plant 10 flowers. (Therefore the lawyer has the ***absolute advantage*** in gardening.)
3. The lawyer's time, in the practice of law, is worth $100 per hour.
4. The gardener's time, in gardening, is worth $10 per hour.

B. *Question:*

How should the lawyer have 20 flowers planted?

Option 1: Do it herself, spending 1 hour.

Cost: She gives up the $100 she could have earned by practicing law for that hour.

Option 2: Stick to the law, and hire the gardener to plant the 20 flowers.

Cost: Two hours of gardener's time at $10 per hour, making a total of $20.

C. ***Decision:*** Choose option 2.

Spend the available hour practicing law, earning $100.

Hire the gardener to do the planting for $20.

Net advantage over option 1: The difference of $80 that can be spent on other goods.

D. *Conclusion:* The lawyer has the *comparative advantage* in law. By specializing in this and exchanging, she ends up with $80 more goods and services. This is her incentive to specialize.

This example leads to two important conclusions:

1. There are *mutual benefits* from specialization and exchange. The lawyer gains by specializing and hiring someone else to do the gardening. The gardener likewise gains by specializing and hiring someone else to provide legal services.

2. Absolute advantage is *not* necessary for mutually beneficial specialization. The lawyer has an absolute advantage in both gardening and law; the gardener has an absolute disadvantage in both. The lawyer specializes in the law where she has a *comparative advantage.* In gardening, she is only twice as productive as the gardener, but in law she is many, many times as productive.

British economist **David Ricardo** enunciated the principle of comparative advantage in the early nineteenth century to illustrate how countries gain from international trade. But comparative advantage provides a general explanation of the advantages of specialization; it is just as relevant to domestic as to international trade. Nevertheless, it is customary to follow Ricardo and consider this principle as part of the study of international economics. We will follow the custom, and put off our detailed analysis of comparative advantage to Chapter 33 on international trade.

Comparative advantage, then, provides one reason for specialization and exchange. But there is a second fundamental reason.

ECONOMIES OF SCALE: ANOTHER REASON TO SPECIALIZE

Consider two small cities that are identical in all respects. Suppose that the citizens of these cities want both bicycles and lawnmowers but that neither city has any advantage in the production of either good. Will each city then produce its own, without any trade existing between the two? Probably not. It is likely that one city will specialize in bicycles, and the other in lawnmowers. Why?

The answer is **economies of scale.** To understand what this term means, first assume that there is no specialization. Each city directs half its productive resources into the manufacture of bicycles and half into the manufacture of lawnmowers, thus producing 1,000 bicycles and 1,000 lawnmowers. But if either city specializes by directing all its productive resources toward the manufacture of bicycles, it can acquire specialized machinery and produce 2,500 bicycles. Similarly, if the other city directs all its productive resources toward the manufacture of lawnmowers, it can produce 2,500. Note that each city, by doubling all inputs into the production of a single item, can more than double its output of that item from 1,000 to 2,500 units. Thus economies of scale exist.

> ***Economies of scale*** exist if an increase of x% in the quantity of every input causes the quantity of output to increase by more than x%. (For example, if all inputs are doubled, then output more than doubles.)

Even though neither city has any initial advantage in the production of either product, both can gain by specialization. Before specialization, their combined output was 2,000 bicycles and 2,000 lawnmowers. After specialization, they together make 2,500 bicycles and 2,500 lawnmowers.

While Ricardo's theory of comparative advantage dates back to the early nineteenth century, the explanation of economies of scale goes back even further, to Adam Smith's *Wealth of Nations* (1776). In Smith's first chapter, "Of the Division of Labour," there is a famous description of pin-making:

> A workman not educated to this business . . . could scarce, perhaps, . . . make one pin in a day, and certainly not twenty. But in the way in which this business is now carried on, not only the whole work is a peculiar trade, but it is divided into a number of branches. . . . One man draws out the wire, another straightens it, a third cuts it, a fourth points it, a fifth grinds it at the top for receiving the head. . . . Ten persons, therefore, could make among them upwards of forty-eight thousand pins in a day. Each person, therefore, . . . might be considered as making four thousand and eight hundred pins in a day.[2]

What is the reason for the gain that comes from the division of pin-making into a number of separate steps? Certainly, it is not that some individuals are particularly suited to drawing the wire, whereas others have a particular gift for straightening it. On the contrary, if two individuals are employed, it matters little which activity each is assigned. Adam Smith's "production line" is efficient because of economies of scale which depend on

1. The introduction of specialized machinery.
2. Specialization of the labor force on that machinery.

Modern corporations also derive economies of scale from a third major source:

3. Specialized research and development, which make possible the development of new equipment and technology.

In the modern world, economies of scale provide the second important reason for specialization and exchange—along with comparative advantage. Economies of scale help to explain why the manufacturers of automobiles and mainframe computers are few in number and large in size. It is partly because of economies of scale that the automobile industry is concentrated in the Detroit area, with Michigan shipping cars to other areas in exchange for a host of other products.

However, economies of scale explain much more than the trade among the regions, states, and cities *within* a country. They also are an important explanation of trade *between* countries. For example, economies of scale in the production of large passenger aircraft go on long after the U.S. market is met. Thus Boeing achieves a major advantage by producing aircraft for the world market. There are gains to the aircraft buyers, too. For example, Australians can buy a Boeing 747 for a small fraction of what it would cost to manufacture a comparable airplane in Australia.

LIVING IN A GLOBAL ECONOMY

ECONOMIES OF SCALE AND THE U.S.-CANADIAN FREE TRADE AGREEMENT

Even the huge U.S. market is not large enough for some producers to capture all the economies of scale—for example, the manufacturers of aircraft and mainframe computers. But it is large enough for the producers of many other goods, such as automobiles. In fact, U.S. auto firms can offer a

[2]Adam Smith, *An Inquiry into the Nature and Causes of the Wealth of Nations* (Modern Library edition, New York: Random House, 1937), pp. 4–5.

wide variety of models and still produce most of them at the high volume needed to gain substantially all the economies of scale. Thus these producers can achieve low cost and at the same time provide a wide choice of models to consumers.

The United States is unique, however, because it is such a large economy. Smaller economies—like Canada's—cannot produce a wide range of cars and at the same time achieve the high-volume output necessary to achieve low cost. Thus in producing cars, Canada has a choice among three options.

1. It can produce a variety of models, each at a small scale and therefore at high cost, for the domestic Canadian market. This option would provide car buyers with a choice among models, but at high cost.

2. It can produce a small number of models, each at high volume, for the domestic market. This alternative would provide the advantage of low cost, but consumers would not have much choice.

3. It can gain both advantages (high-volume, low-cost production and a wide variety of models) by engaging in international trade. Produce only a few models in Canada, at high volume and low cost. Export many of these cars, in exchange for a variety of imported models.

Historically, up to the early 1960s, Canadian automotive policy was based on the first choice. But the twin advantages of the third option are clear and can come about only through international trade. In order to gain these advantages, Canada entered a special agreement with the United States in 1965, allowing tariff-free passage of cars both ways across the border.

The favorable experience with the auto agreement encouraged the two nations to negotiate a broad free trade agreement, which came into effect at the beginning of 1989. Under this comprehensive agreement, tariffs between the two countries on all goods will be phased out by 1998. In addition, the agreement provides for freer trade in services (such as banking services) and in energy, and for greater freedom of investment across the border.

For Canada, economies of scale provide the main advantage of the free trade agreement. Canadian businesses are now in the process of reorganization, cutting down the number of products and models they produce, but increasing the output of each. Much of the output from the longer production runs is destined for the U.S. market.

The agreement also promises gains for the United States. Northeastern states will find it easier to purchase inexpensive hydroelectric power from Quebec. U.S. firms will have freer access to the Canadian market; Canada will be phasing out tariffs that are generally two or three times as high as U.S. tariffs. The Canadian market will become even more important for U.S. exporters. Before the free trade agreement, Canada already was the largest market for U.S. exports. Indeed, a single Canadian province (Ontario) bought more U.S. exports than did Japan.

In this chapter, the advantages of specialization and exchange have been studied. Exchange takes place in markets; how markets operate will be the subject of the next chapter.

KEY POINTS

1. By specializing, people become more productive. But specialization requires exchange. Specialization and exchange make the economy more efficient; that is, we end up with more goods and services as a consequence.

2. The most primitive form of exchange is barter. Its disadvantage is that it requires a coincidence of wants. Producers waste a lot of time searching for the right trade.

3. Exchange is much easier and more efficient with money. Thus money has developed even in the absence of government action—as happened in the prisoner-of-war camp.

4. In the prisoner-of-war camp, some cigarettes were more desirable than others. The desirable cigarettes were smoked, leaving the less desirable cigarettes to circulate as money. This illustrated Gresham's law: "Bad money drives out good." In the modern U.S. economy, the Federal Reserve provides the currency, with every dollar bill worth the same as every other one; there is no "bad" money to drive "good" money out of circulation.

5. There are two major reasons why specialization and exchange increase efficiency, and thus increase the quantity of goods and services we can acquire. (a) Comparative advantage and (b) economies of scale.

6. Our example of *comparative advantage* is the lawyer who is better than the gardener at both the law and gardening. Even so, she does not do her gardening herself, because she has an even greater advantage in the law. She can gain by specializing in law (her comparative advantage) and hiring the gardener to do the gardening.

7. Economies of scale exist if an increase of x% in the quantity of every input causes the quantity of output to increase by more than x%.

KEY CONCEPTS

specialization
exchange
barter
coincidence of wants
indivisibility
general purchasing power
medium of exchange
Gresham's law
debasement of the currency
absolute advantage
comparative advantage
economies of scale

PROBLEMS

3-1. (a) Among the goods the United States exports are commercial aircraft, computers, and agricultural products such as soybeans and wheat. Why are these goods exported?

(b) Imports include automobiles, television sets, oil, and agricultural products such as coffee and bananas. Why are these goods imported?

(c) The United States exports some agricultural products and imports others. Why? The United States exports many aircraft, but it also imports some. Why are we both exporters and importers of aircraft? The United States and Canada export large numbers of cars to one another. Why?

3-2. Suppose that one individual at your college is outstanding, being the best teacher and a superb administrator. If you were the college president, would you ask this individual to teach or to become the administrative vice-president? Why?

3-3. Most jobs are more specialized than they were 100 years ago. Why? What are the advantages of greater specialization? Are there any disadvantages?

3-4. Draw a production possibilities curve (PPC) for the lawyer mentioned on p. 41 and in Box 3-1, putting the number of wills drawn up in a week on one axis and flowers planted on the other. (Assume that the lawyer works 40 hours per week.) How does the shape of this PPC differ from that in Chapter 2?

* **3-5.** Draw the production possibilities curve of one of the two identical cities described in the section on economies of scale. Which way does the curve bend? Does the opportunity cost of bicycles increase or decrease as more bicycles are produced?

---

*Problems marked with asterisks are more difficult than the others. They are designed to provide a challenge to students who want to do more advanced work.

CHAPTER 4

DEMAND AND SUPPLY: The Market Mechanism

Do you know,
Considering the market, there are more
Poems produced than any other thing?
No wonder poets sometimes have to seem
So much more business-like than business men.
Their wares are so much harder to get rid of.
ROBERT FROST, *NEW HAMPSHIRE*

Although some countries are much richer than others, the resources of every country are limited. Choices must be made. Moreover, every economy is specialized to some degree. In every economy, therefore, some mechanism is needed to answer the fundamental questions raised by specialization and by the need to make choices:

- **What** goods and services will be produced? Which of the options on the production possibilities curve will be chosen?
- **How** will these goods and services be produced? For example, will cars be produced by relatively few workers using a great deal of machinery, or by many workers using relatively little capital equipment?
- **For whom** will the goods and services be produced? Once goods are produced, who will consume them?

DECISIONS BY PRIVATE MARKETS AND BY THE GOVERNMENT

There are two principal mechanisms by which the three questions above can be answered. First, answers can be provided by Adam Smith's "invisible hand." If people are left alone to make their own transactions, then the butcher and baker will provide the beef and bread for our dinner. In other words, answers may be provided by transactions among individuals and corporations in the **market.**

In a ***market,*** an item is bought and sold. When transactions between buyers and sellers take place with little or no government interference, then a ***private*** or ***free*** market exists.

The government provides the second method for determining what goods and services will be produced, how they will be produced, and for whom.

Conceivably, a nation might depend almost exclusively on private markets to make the three fundamental decisions. The government might be confined to a very limited role, providing defense, police, the courts, roads, and little else. At the other extreme, the government might try to decide almost everything, specifying what is to be produced and using a system of rationing and allocations to decide who gets the products. But the real world is one of compromise. In every actual economy, there is some *mixture* of markets and government decision-making.

However, reliance on the market varies substantially among countries. By international standards, the U.S. government plays a restricted role; most choices are made in private markets. In the United States, most factories, machinery, and other forms of capital are owned by private individuals and corporations. The U.S. government owns only a limited amount of capital—for example, the power plants of the Tennessee Valley Authority—and undertakes less than 5% of the nation's overall investment. In most other countries, government enterprises undertake between 10% and 25% of investment. In many foreign countries, the government owns the telephone system, railroads, and all the major electric power plants—and in some cases, even factories that produce steel, automobiles, and other goods.

At the other end of the spectrum from the United States are centrally planned economies such as those in the Soviet Union and Eastern Europe, where the government owns most of the capital. In these countries governments decide what is to be produced with this capital. For example, the Soviet Union has a central planning agency that issues detailed directives to the various sectors of the economy to produce specific quantities of goods. It would be a mistake, however, to conclude that government planning is all-pervasive. Markets for goods exist in the Soviet Union, as in other centrally planned economies. Moreover, the Soviet Union is currently engaged in experiments to reduce the influence of the government and place more reliance on markets.

A ***capitalist*** or ***free enterprise economy*** is one in which most capital is privately owned, and decisions are made primarily through the price system (that is, in markets).

A ***centrally planned economy*** is one in which the government owns most of the capital and makes many of the economic decisions.

Because of their importance in the United States, private markets will be our initial concern. Later chapters will deal with the economic role of the government.

HOW PRIVATE MARKETS OPERATE

In most markets, the buyer and the seller come face to face. When you buy clothes, you go to the store selling them; when you buy groceries, you physically enter the supermarket. However, physical proximity is not required to make a market. For example, in a typical stock market transaction, someone in Georgia puts in a call to his broker to buy 100 shares of IBM common stock. About the same time, someone in Pennsylvania calls her broker to sell 100 shares. The transaction takes place on the floor of the New York Stock Exchange, where representatives of the two brokerage houses meet. The buyer and the seller of the stock do not leave their respective homes in Georgia and Pennsylvania.

Some markets are quite simple. For example, a barbershop is a market, since haircuts are bought and sold there. The transaction is obvious and straightforward; the service of haircutting is produced on the spot. In other cases, markets are much more complex. Even the simplest everyday activity may be the culmination of a complicated series of market transactions.

As you sat at breakfast this morning drinking a cup of coffee, you were using products from distant areas. The coffee itself was probably produced in Brazil. The brew was made with water that perhaps had been delivered in pipes manufactured in Pennsylvania and purified with chemicals produced in Delaware. The sugar for the coffee may have been produced in Louisiana or the Caribbean.

Perhaps you used artificial cream made from soybeans grown in Missouri. Possibly, your coffee was poured into a cup made in New York State and stirred with a spoon manufactured in Taiwan from Japanese stainless steel which used Canadian nickel in its production. All this was for one cup of coffee. Imagine the far more complex story of where a computer or car originates!

In such a complicated economy, something is needed to keep things straight, to bring order out of potential chaos. **Prices** bring order by performing two important, interrelated functions:

1. Prices provide **information.**
2. Prices provide **incentives.**

To illustrate, suppose we start with an example of chaos, with too much coffee in New York and none in New Jersey. Coffee lovers in New Jersey would clamor for coffee, even at very high prices. The high price is a signal, providing *information* to coffee owners that there are eager buyers in New Jersey. It also provides them with an *incentive* to send coffee from New York to New Jersey. In any market, the price provides the focus for interactions between buyers and sellers.

PERFECT AND IMPERFECT COMPETITION

Some markets are dominated by a few large firms; other markets have thousands of sellers. The "big three" automobile manufacturers (General Motors, Ford, and Chrysler) make most of the cars sold in the United States, with the rest provided by foreign firms. Such an industry, which is dominated by a few sellers, is an **oligopoly.** Some markets are even more concentrated. For example, there is just one supplier of local telephone services to homes in your area; the telephone company therefore has a **monopoly** on local service. On the other hand, there are thousands of wheat producers.

A ***monopoly*** exists when there is only *one seller.* An ***oligopoly*** exists when a *few sellers* dominate a market.

The number of participants in a market has a significant effect on how the price is determined. In the wheat market, where there are thousands of buyers and thousands of sellers, no individual farmer produces more than a tiny fraction of the total supply. No single farmer can affect the price of wheat. For each farmer, the price is given; the individual farmer's decision is limited to the amount of wheat to sell. Similarly, millers realize that they are each buying only a small fraction of the wheat supplied. They realize that they cannot, as individuals, affect the price of wheat. Each miller's decision is limited to the amount of wheat to be bought at the existing market price. In such a **perfectly competitive** market, *there is no pricing decision* for the individual seller and the individual buyer to make. Each buyer and seller is a **price taker.**

When there are so many buyers and sellers that no single buyer or seller has any influence over the price, the result is ***perfect competition*** (sometimes shortened simply to *competition*).

In contrast, individual producers in an oligopolistic or a monopolistic market know that they have some control over price. For example, IBM sets the prices of its computers. That does not mean, of course, that it can set *any* price it wants and still be assured of making a profit. It can offer to sell at a high price, in which case it will sell only a few computers. Or it can charge a lower price, in which case it will sell more.

A *buyer* may also be large enough to influence price. General Motors is a large enough purchaser of steel to be able to bargain with the steel companies over the price of steel. When individual buyers or sellers can influence price, **imperfect competition** exists.

Imperfect competition exists when any buyer or any seller is able to influence the price. Such a buyer or seller is said to have ***market power.***

Note that the term *competition* is used differently in economics and in business. Don't try to tell someone from Chrysler that the automobile market isn't competitive; Chrysler is very much aware of the competition from General Motors, Ford, and the Japanese. Yet, according to the economist's definition, the automobile industry is far *less* competitive than the wheat industry.

An *industry* refers to all the producers of a good or service. For example, we may speak of the automobile industry, the wheat industry, or the accounting industry. Note that the term *industry* can refer to *any* good or service; it need not be manufactured.

A *firm* is a business organization that produces goods and/or services. A *plant* is an establishment at a single location used in the production of a good or service—for example, a factory, mine, farm, or store. Some firms, such as General Motors, have many plants. Others have only one—for example, the local independent drug store.

Because price is determined by impersonal forces in a perfectly competitive market, the competitive market is simplest and will therefore be considered first. The perfectly competitive market is also given priority because competitive markets generally operate more efficiently than imperfect markets, as we will eventually show in Chapters 25 and 26.

DEMAND AND SUPPLY

In a perfectly competitive market, price is determined by demand and supply.

DEMAND

Consider, as an example, the market for apples, in which there are many buyers and many sellers, with none having any control over the price. For the buyer, a high price acts as a deterrent. The higher the price, the fewer apples buyers purchase. Why is this so? As the price of apples rises, consumers switch to oranges or grapefruit, or they simply cut down on their total consumption of fruit. Conversely, the lower the price, the more apples are bought. A lower price brings new purchasers into the market, and each purchaser tends to buy more. The response of buyers to various possible prices is illustrated in the **demand curve** in Figure 4-1. Points *A*, *B*, *C*, and *D* correspond to

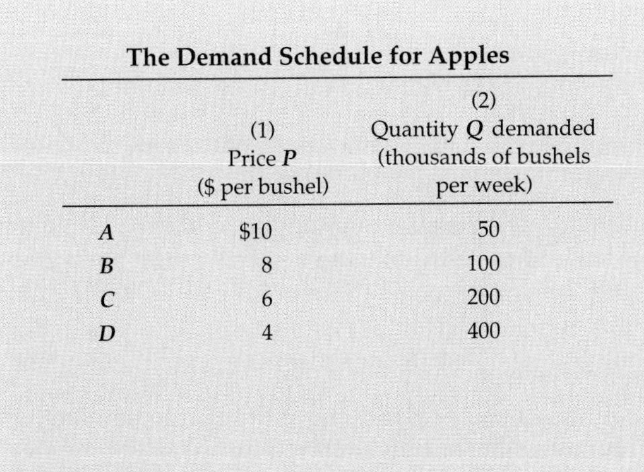

The Demand Schedule for Apples

	(1) Price *P* ($ per bushel)	(2) Quantity *Q* demanded (thousands of bushels per week)
A	$10	50
B	8	100
C	6	200
D	4	400

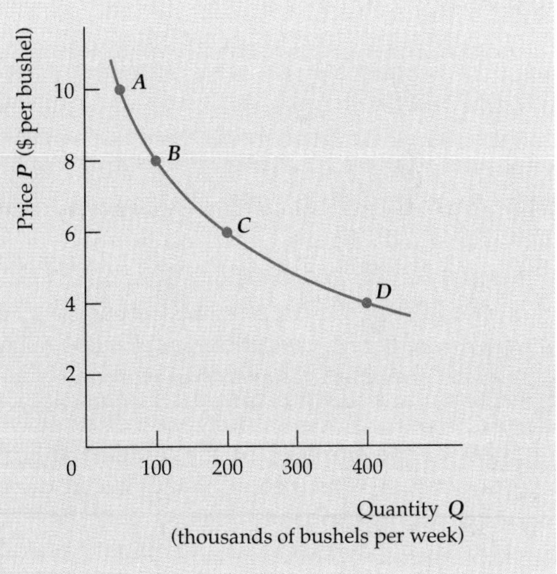

FIGURE 4-1 The demand curve.

At each of the possible prices specified, there is a certain quantity of apples that people would be willing and able to buy. This information is shown in two ways: in tabular form and as a diagram. On the vertical axis, the possible prices are shown. In each case, the quantity of apples that would be bought is measured along the horizontal axis. Since people are more willing to buy at a low price than at a high price, the demand curve slopes downward to the right. Demand curves are shown throughout this book in blue.

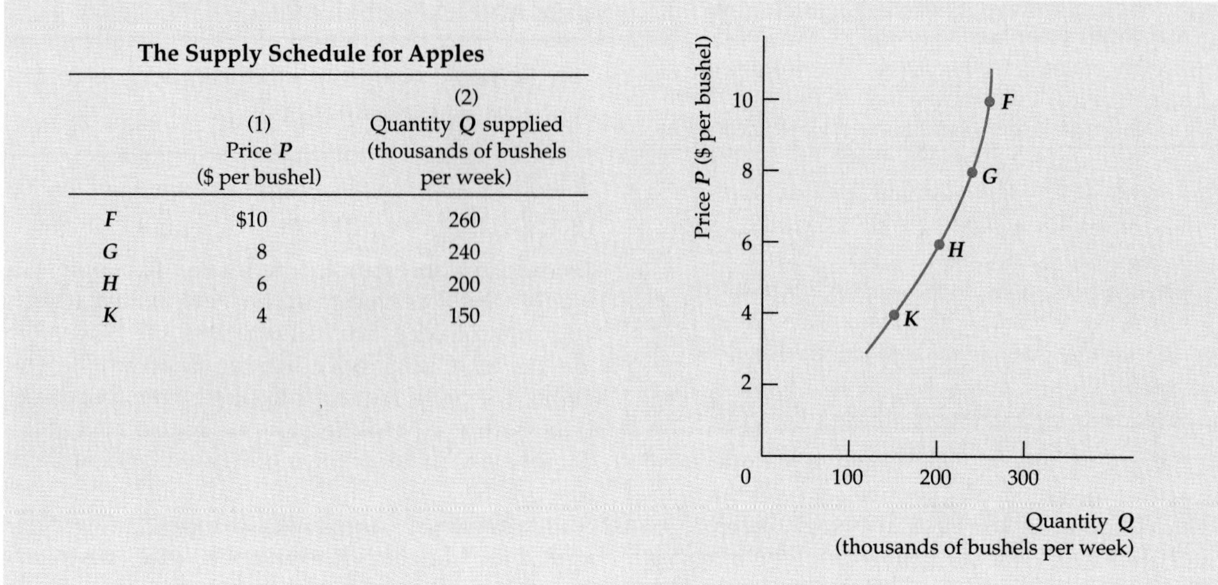

The Supply Schedule for Apples

	(1) Price P ($ per bushel)	(2) Quantity Q supplied (thousands of bushels per week)
F	$10	260
G	8	240
H	6	200
K	4	150

FIGURE 4-2 The supply curve for apples.

For each of the possible prices specified, the supply schedule indicates how many units the sellers would be willing to sell. This information is illustrated graphically in this figure, which shows how the supply curve slopes upward to the right. At a high price, suppliers will be encouraged to step up production and offer more apples for sale. Supply curves are shown throughout this book in red.

rows *A*, *B*, *C*, and *D* in the **demand schedule** shown beside the figure.

A ***demand curve*** or a ***demand schedule*** shows the quantities of a good or service which buyers would be willing and able to purchase at various market prices.

It should be emphasized that a demand curve reflects not just what people want, but also *what they are willing and able to pay for.*

The demand curve or demand schedule applies to a *specific population* and to a *specific time period.* Clearly, the number of apples demanded during a month will exceed the number demanded during a week, and the number demanded by the people of Virginia will be less than the number demanded in the whole United States. In a general discussion of theoretical issues, the population and time framework are not always stated explicitly, but it nevertheless should be understood that a demand curve applies to a specific time and population.

SUPPLY

Whereas the demand curve illustrates how buyers behave, the supply curve illustrates how sellers behave; it shows how much they would be willing to sell at various prices. Needless to say, buyers and sellers look at high prices in a different light. A high price discourages buyers and causes them to switch to alternative products, but a high price encourages suppliers to produce and sell more of the good. Thus, the higher the price, the higher the quantity supplied. This is shown in the **supply curve** in Figure 4-2. As in the case of the demand curve, the points on the supply curve (*F*, *G*, *H*, and *K*) are drawn from the numbers in the corresponding rows of the **supply schedule** beside the figure.

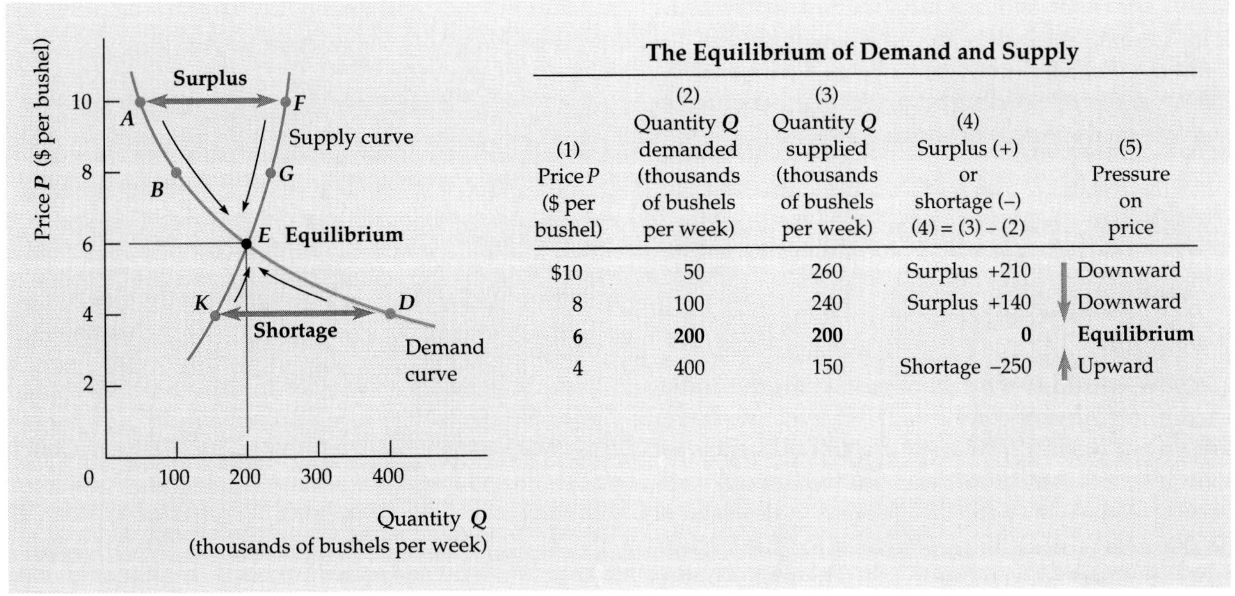

The Equilibrium of Demand and Supply

(1) Price P ($ per bushel)	(2) Quantity Q demanded (thousands of bushels per week)	(3) Quantity Q supplied (thousands of bushels per week)	(4) Surplus (+) or shortage (–) (4) = (3) – (2)	(5) Pressure on price
$10	50	260	Surplus +210	Downward
8	100	240	Surplus +140	Downward
6	**200**	**200**	**0**	**Equilibrium**
4	400	150	Shortage –250	Upward

FIGURE 4-3 How demand and supply determine equilibrium price and quantity.

Equilibrium exists at point *E*, where the quantity demanded equals the quantity supplied. At any higher price, the quantity supplied exceeds the quantity demanded. Because of the pressure of unsold stocks, competition among sellers causes the price to be bid down to the equilibrium of $6. Similarly, at a price less than the $6 equilibrium, forces are set in motion which raise the price. Because the quantity demanded exceeds the quantity supplied, eager buyers clamor for more apples and bid the price up to the equilibrium at $6.

A ***supply curve*** or a ***supply schedule*** shows the quantities of a good or service that sellers would be willing and able to sell at various market prices.

THE EQUILIBRIUM OF DEMAND AND SUPPLY

The demand and supply curves may now be brought together in Figure 4-3. The **market equilibrium** occurs at point *E*, where the demand and supply curves intersect. At this equilibrium, the price is $6 per bushel, and sales are 200,000 bushels per week.

An ***equilibrium*** is a situation in which there is no tendency to change.

To see why *E* is the equilibrium, consider what happens if the market price is initially at some other level. Suppose, for example, that the initial price is $10, which is above the equilibrium price. What happens? Purchasers buy only 50,000 bushels (shown by point *A* in Figure 4-3), while sellers want to sell 260,000 bushels (point *F*). Therefore, there is a large **surplus** of 210,000 bushels. Some sellers are disappointed: They sell much less than they wish at the price of $10. Unsold apples begin to pile up. In order to get them moving, sellers now begin to accept a lower price. The price starts to come down—to $9, then $8. Still there is a surplus, or an excess of the quantity supplied over the quantity demanded. The price continues to fall. It does not stop falling until it reaches $6, the equilibrium. At this price, buyers purchase 200,000 bushels, which is just the amount the sellers want to sell; in other words, the "market is cleared." Both buyers and sellers are now satisfied with the quantity of their purchases or sales at the existing market price of $6. Therefore, there is no further pressure on the price to change.

A ***surplus*** exists when the quantity supplied exceeds the quantity demanded. (The price is above the equilibrium.)

Now consider what happens when the initial price is below the equilibrium, at, say, $4. Eager buyers are willing to purchase 400,000 bushels (at point D), yet producers are willing to sell only 150,000 bushels (at point K). There is a **shortage** of 250,000 bushels. As buyers clamor for the limited supplies, the price is bid upward. The price continues to rise until it reaches $6, the equilibrium where there is no longer any shortage because the quantity demanded is equal to the quantity supplied. At point E, and only at point E, will the price be stable.

A ***shortage*** exists when the quantity demanded exceeds the quantity supplied. (The price is below the equilibrium.)

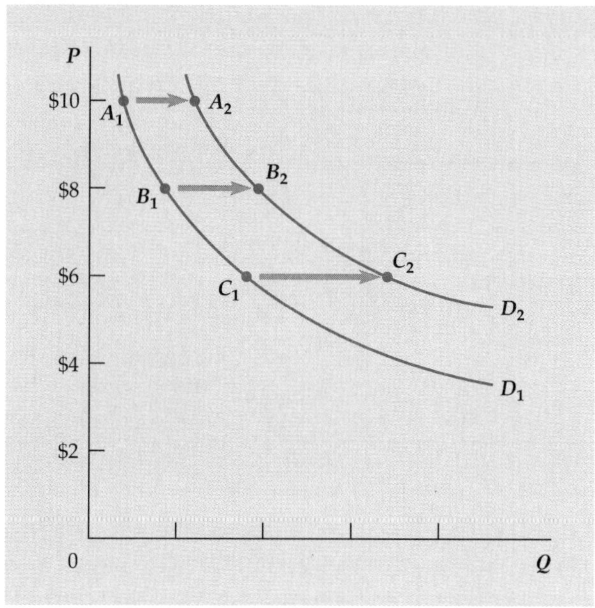

FIGURE 4-4 A change in the demand for apples.
When incomes rise, there is an increase in the number of apples that people want to buy at any particular price. At a price of $10, for example, the quantity of apples demanded increases from point A_1 to A_2. At other prices, the increase in incomes also causes an increase in the number of apples demanded. Thus, the whole demand curve shifts to the right, from D_1 to D_2.

SHIFTS IN THE DEMAND CURVE

The quantity of a product that buyers want to purchase depends on the price. As we have seen, the demand curve illustrates this relationship between price and the quantity demanded. But the quantity that people want to purchase also depends on other influences. For example, if incomes rise, people will want to buy more apples—and more of a whole host of other products, too.

The purpose of a demand curve is to show how the quantity demanded is affected by price, **and by price alone.** When we ask how much people want to buy at various prices, it is important that our answer not be disturbed by other influences. In other words, when we draw a demand curve for a good, we must *hold constant incomes and everything else that can affect the quantity demanded,* with the sole exception of the price of the good. We make the **ceteris paribus** assumption—that all other things remain unchanged. (*Ceteris* is the same Latin word that appears in *et cetera,* which literally means "and other things." *Paribus* means "equal" or "unchanged.")

Of course, as time passes, other things do *not* remain constant. Through time, for example, incomes generally rise. When that happens, there is an increase in the quantity of apples demanded. The whole demand curve shifts to the right, as illustrated in Figure 4-4. Since *economists use the term "demand" to mean the whole demand curve or demand schedule,* we may speak of this rightward shift in the curve more simply as an *increase in demand.*

DEMAND SHIFTERS

A shift in the demand curve—that is, a change in demand—may be caused by a change in any one of a whole host of other things. Some of the most important are income, prices of related goods, and tastes.

1. *Income.* When incomes rise, people are able to buy more. And people do in fact buy more of the typical or **normal good.** For such a good, the number of units demanded at each price increases as incomes rise. Thus the demand curve shifts to the right with rising incomes, as illustrated in Figure 4-4.

Not all goods are normal, however. As incomes rise, people may buy *less* of a good. For example, they may demand less margarine, since they are now able to afford butter. Or they may stop buying day-old bread since they can afford fresh bread instead. When the increase in income causes a leftward shift of the demand curve, the item is an **inferior good.**

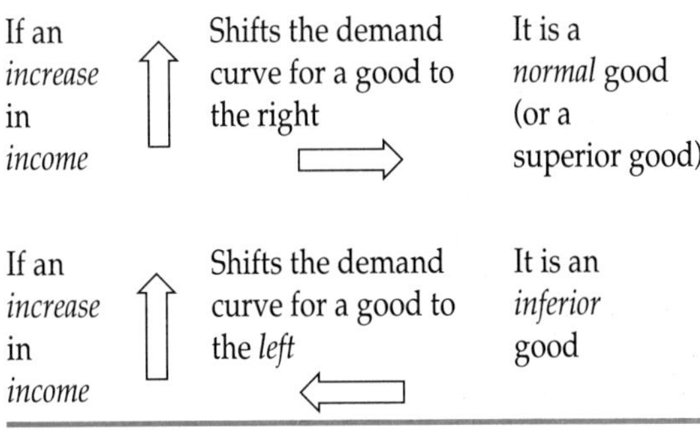

2. *Prices of Related Goods.* A rise in the price of one good can cause a shift in the demand curve for another good.

For example, if the price of oranges were to double while the price of apples remained the same, buyers would be encouraged to buy apples instead of oranges. Thus a rise in the price of oranges causes a rightward shift in the demand curve for apples. Goods such as apples and oranges—which satisfy similar needs or desires—are **substitutes.** Other examples are tea and coffee, butter and margarine, bus and train tickets, or heating oil and insulating materials.

For **complements** or **complementary goods,** exactly the opposite relationship holds. In contrast to substitutes—which are used *instead of* each other—complements are used *together,* as a package. For example, gasoline and automobiles are complementary goods. If the price of gasoline spirals upward, people become less eager to own automobiles. The demand curve for cars therefore shifts to the left. So it is with other complements, such as tennis rackets and tennis balls, or formal clothing rentals and tickets to a formal dance.

Finally, many goods are basically *unrelated,* in the sense that a rise in the price of one has no significant effect on the demand curve of the others. Thus bus tickets and butter are unrelated, as are coffee and cameras.

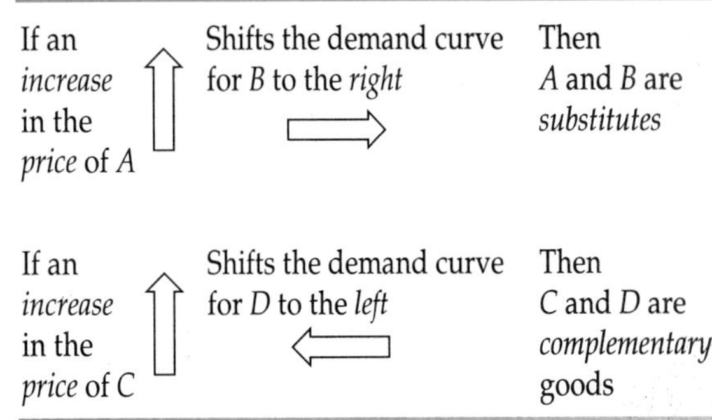

3. *Tastes.* Tastes change over time. Because of increased interest in physical fitness, more people are jogging. This activity increases the demand for running shoes. Tastes, and therefore demand, are quite volatile for some products, particularly for fads like video games.

This list covers some of the most important demand shifters, but it is far from complete. To see how it might be extended, consider the following questions:

1. If the weather changes, how will the change affect the demand for skiing equipment? For snow tires?

2. If people expect cars to be priced $2,000 higher next year, what effect will this expected increase have on the demand for cars this year?

3. As more and more families get video cassette recorders, and thereby become able to skip through the commercials with the fast scan button, how will this affect the demand by companies buying television ads? (A. C. Neilsen, a firm that rates TV shows as a service for advertisers, has found that, when people watch taped shows, half of them do in fact "zap" the commercials.)

WHAT IS PRODUCED: THE RESPONSE TO A CHANGE IN TASTES

At the beginning of this chapter, three basic questions were listed. To see how the market mechanism can help to answer the first of these—"*What* will be produced?"—consider what happens when there is a change in tastes. Suppose, for example, that people develop a desire to drink more tea and less coffee. This change in tastes is illustrated by a rightward shift in the demand curve for tea and a leftward shift in the demand curve for coffee.

As the demand for tea increases, the price is bid up by eager buyers. With a higher price, growers in Sri Lanka and elsewhere are encouraged to plant more tea. At the new equilibrium, shown as point E_2 in Figure 4-5, the price of tea is higher than it was originally (at E_1), and the consumers buy a larger quantity of tea. In the coffee market, the results are the opposite. At the new equilibrium (F_2), the price is lower and a smaller quantity is bought.

Thus, competitive market forces cause producers to "dance to the consumers' tune." In response to a change in consumer tastes, prices change. Tea producers are given an incentive to step up production, and coffee production is discouraged.

SHIFTS IN SUPPLY

While the market encourages producers to "dance to the consumers' tune," the opposite is also true. As we will now see, consumers also "dance to the producers' tune." The market involves a complex

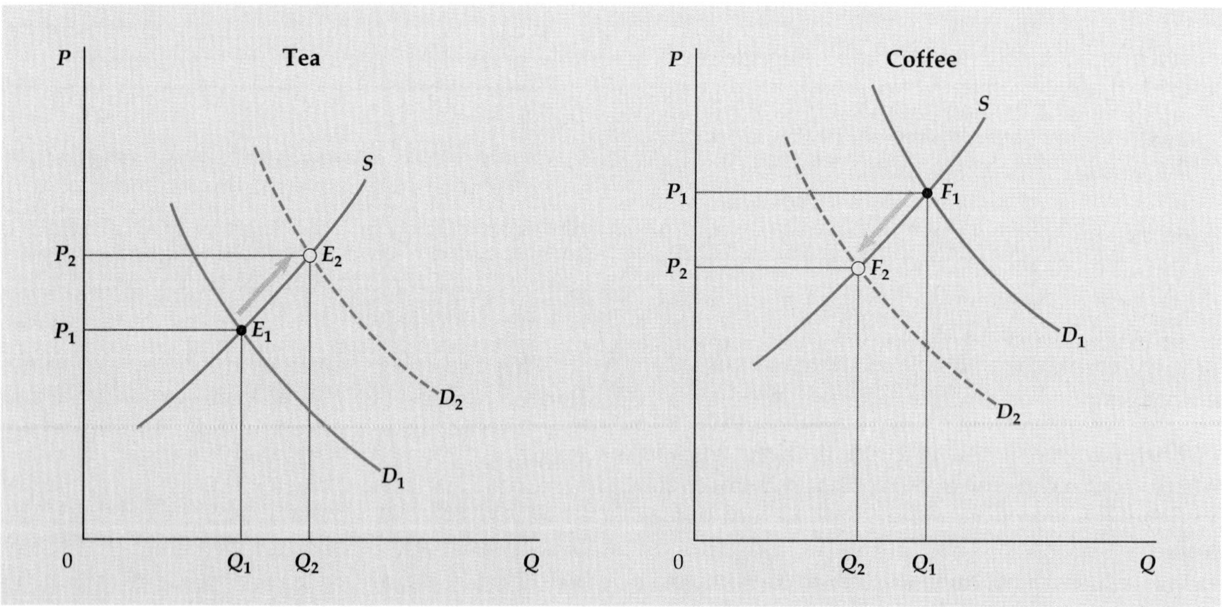

FIGURE 4-5 A change in tastes.
A change in tastes causes the demand for tea to increase and the demand for coffee to decrease. As a result, more tea is bought, at a higher price. Less coffee is bought, and the price of coffee falls.

interaction: Sellers respond to the desires of buyers, and buyers respond to the willingness of producers to sell.

Just as the demand curve reflects the desires of buyers, so the supply curve illustrates the willingness of producers to sell. In an important respect, the two curves are similar. The objective of each is to show **how the quantity is affected by the price of the good, and by this price alone.** Thus, when we draw the supply curve, once again we make the *ceteris paribus* assumption. Everything except the price of the good itself is held constant.

SUPPLY SHIFTERS

As in the case of demand, the other things that affect supply can change through time, causing the supply curve to shift. Some of these other things are the following:

1. *The Cost of Inputs.* For example, if the price of fertilizer goes up, farmers will be less willing to produce wheat at the previously prevailing price. The supply curve will shift to the left.

2. *Technology.* Suppose there is an improvement in technology that causes costs of production to fall. With lower costs, producers will be willing to supply more at any particular price. The supply curve will shift to the right.

3. *Weather.* This is particularly important for agricultural products. For example, a drought will cause a decrease in the supply of wheat (that is, a leftward shift in the supply curve), and a freeze in Florida will cause a decrease in the supply of oranges.

4. *The Prices of Related Goods.* Just as items can be substitutes or complements in consumption, so they can be substitutes or complements in production.

We saw earlier that substitutes in consumption are goods that can be consumed as *alternatives* to one another, satisfying the same wants—for example, apples and oranges. Similarly, **substitutes in production** are goods that can be produced as *alternatives* to one another, using the same factors of production. Thus, corn and soybeans are substitutes in production; they can be grown on similar land. If the price of corn increases, farmers are encouraged to switch their lands out of the production of soybeans and into the production of corn. The amount of soybeans they are willing to supply at any given price decreases; the supply curve for soybeans shifts to the left.

Earlier, we also observed that complements in consumption are used *together*—for example, gasoline and automobiles. Similarly, **complements in production** or **joint products** are produced together, as a package. Beef and hides provide an example. When more cattle are slaughtered for beef, more hides are produced in the process. An increase in the price of beef causes an increase in beef production, which in turn causes an increase in the production of hides—that is, a rightward shift of the supply curve of hides.

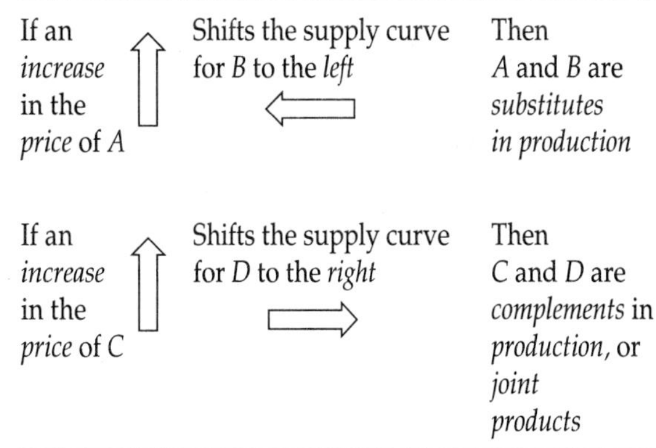

THE RESPONSE TO A SHIFT IN THE SUPPLY CURVE

To illustrate how "consumers dance to the producers' tune," suppose there is a frost in Brazil, which wipes out part of the coffee crop. As a result, the supply curve shifts to the left, as illustrated in Figure 4-6. With less coffee available, the price is bid upward. At the new equilibrium (G_2), the price is higher and the quantity sold is smaller.

How do consumers respond to the change in supply? Because of the higher price of coffee, consumers are discouraged from buying. For example, some may decide to drink coffee only once a day, rather than twice. Anyone who is willing and able to pay the high price will get coffee; those who are unwilling or unable to pay the price will not get it. Thus *the high price acts as a way of allocating the limited supply among buyers.* The coffee goes only to buyers who are sufficiently eager to be willing to pay the high price, and sufficiently affluent to be able to afford it.

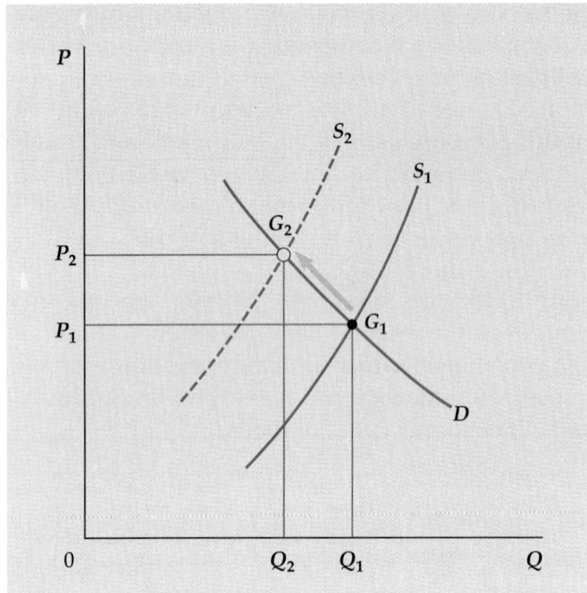

FIGURE 4-6 A shift in supply.

A freeze in Brazil causes a leftward shift in the supply curve of coffee. The result is a movement of the equilibrium along the demand curve from G_1 to G_2. At the new equilibrium, there is a higher price, and a smaller quantity is sold.

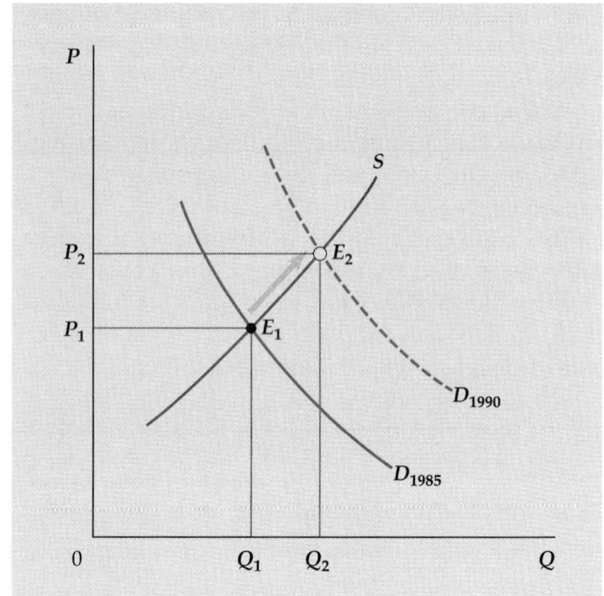

FIGURE 4-7 A shift in the demand for tea.

This diagram, based on the left panel of Figure 4-5, shows that there is an increase in the quantity of tea supplied as the equilibrium moves from E_1 to E_2. However, supply does not change, since the supply curve does not move.

SHIFTS IN A CURVE AND MOVEMENTS ALONG A CURVE

Because the term *supply* applies to a supply schedule or a supply curve, a change in supply means a *shift* in the entire curve. Such a shift took place in Figure 4-6 as a result of a freeze in Brazil.

In this figure, observe that the demand curve has not moved. However, as the supply curve shifts and the price consequently changes, there is a movement *along* the demand curve from G_1 to G_2. At the second point, less is bought than at the original point. The quantity of coffee demanded is less at G_2 than at G_1.

The distinction between *a shift in a curve* and a *movement along a curve* should be emphasized. What can we say about the move from G_1 to G_2?

1. It is correct to say that "supply has decreased." Why? Because the entire supply curve has shifted to the left.

2. It is *not* correct to say that "demand has decreased." Why? Because the demand curve has not moved.

3. It is, however, correct to say that "the quantity demanded has decreased." Why? Because a smaller quantity is demanded at G_2 than at G_1.

A similar distinction should be made when the demand curve shifts. This is shown in Figure 4-7, based on the left panel of Figure 4-5, where the demand for tea increases because of a change in tastes. The rightward movement of the demand curve causes the equilibrium to move *along* the *supply* curve, from E_1 to E_2. It is *not* correct to say that supply increases, since the supply curve does not move. However, the *quantity supplied* does increase as the price rises. Quantity Q_2 is greater than Q_1.

THE INTERCONNECTED QUESTIONS OF WHAT, HOW, AND FOR WHOM

We have explored how two tunes are played. Demand is the tune played by consumers, and supply is the tune played by producers. Each group dances to the tune played by the other.

If we now want to go beyond the question of *what* will be produced to the other questions—*how?* and *for whom?*—we must recognize that the world is even more complex. More than two tunes are being played. In fact, there is a whole orchestra, with the tune played on any one instrument related to the tunes played on all the others.

The major segments of the economy are illustrated in Figure 4-8, which adds detail to Figure 3-3 (in Chapter 3). The **product markets** for apples, coffee, bread, housing, and so forth, are represented by the upper box; these are the markets studied thus far. The box at the bottom indicates that there are similar **markets for factors of production,** with their own demands and supplies. For example, to produce wheat, farmers need land; they create a

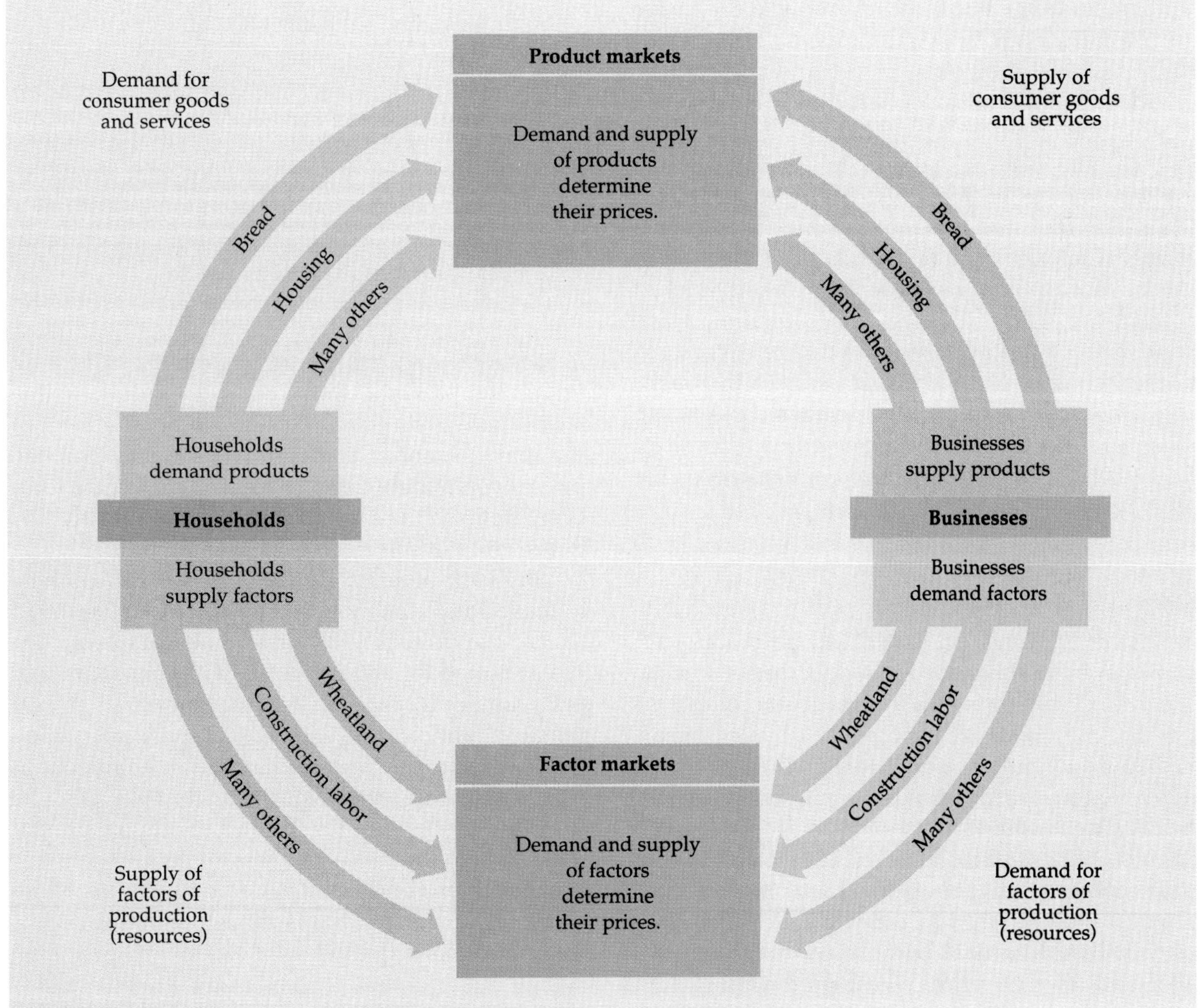

FIGURE 4-8 Markets answer the basic questions of what, how, and for whom.

The product markets (top box) are most important in determining *what* is produced, and the factor markets (lower box) in determining *how* goods are produced and *for whom.* However, there are many interrelationships among the two boxes. For example, incomes change in response to changing demand and supply conditions in the lower box, and these changing incomes in turn influence the demand for products in the upper box.

demand for land. At the same time, those with land are willing to sell or rent it if the price is attractive; they create a supply of land.

To answer the question "*What* will be produced?" we begin by looking at the top box, where the demand and supply for products come together. If there is a large demand for bread, producers will respond by producing a lot. But eventually it is necessary to look at the lower box, too, where the demand and supply for the factors of production come together. Why are the factor markets relevant? Because the demand and supply in the upper box are influenced by what happens in the factor markets in the lower box.

For example, consider what happened when oil was discovered in Alaska several decades ago. To build the pipeline needed to get the oil out, workers had to be hired. As a consequence, the demand for construction labor in Alaska increased sharply. The price of labor (that is, the wage rate) in Alaska shot up, and construction workers flocked in from the lower 48 states. The spiraling wage payments in Alaska (lower box) had repercussions on the demands for goods and services in Alaska (upper box). For example, the demand for Alaskan housing in the upper box increased as a result of the higher earnings of construction workers in the lower box.

HOW? AND FOR WHOM?

To answer the question "*What* will be produced?" we began by looking at the product markets in the upper box of Figure 4-8. To answer the questions *how?* and *for whom?* we look first at the lower box.

The factor prices established in the lower box help to determine *how* goods are produced. During the Black Death of 1348–1350 and subsequent plagues, an estimated quarter to a third of the Western European population died. As a consequence, labor supply was reduced and wages rose sharply, by 30 to 40%. Because of the scarcity of labor and its high price, wheat producers had an incentive to farm their lands with less labor. Wheat was produced in a different way, with a different combination of labor and land. In those days, as today, the market mechanism helped to determine how the society conserved its scarce supply of a factor—in this case, labor.

The answer to the question "*For whom* is the nation's output produced?" depends on incomes, which are determined by the interplay of supply and demand in factor markets (lower box in Figure 4-8). For example, the supply of doctors is small compared with the demand for doctors. The price of medical "labor" is therefore high; doctors generally have high incomes. On the other hand, unskilled labor is in large supply and is therefore cheap. Consequently, the unskilled worker receives a low income and is able to buy only a small share of the nation's output.

LIVING IN A GLOBAL ECONOMY

RENTING AN OFFICE IN TOKYO, LONDON, OR HONG KONG

While Japan is rich, the Japanese are not.

CLYDE PRESTOWITZ[1]

In real estate, so the saying goes, three things are important: location, location, and location. Prime office space is similar in design and quality in all of the major financial capitals of the world. But the price it commands depends very much on the location. Demand and supply can differ greatly between cities, resulting in quite different rents.

Buoyant demand and limited supply combine to make Tokyo the most expensive city in the world to rent an office. In 1988, office space in downtown Tokyo rented for an average of $175 per square foot per year. For a space 12' × 9', that meant an annual rental of almost $19,000. Not surprisingly, many junior executives found themselves cramped in offices that were little bigger than closets.

New York was far behind, with an annual rental of "only" $45 per square foot. That was cheaper than London ($155), Paris ($70), or Hong Kong ($65). Hong Kong is in surprising company, for it is often classified as a less developed area.

[1]*Trading Places: How We Allowed Japan to Take the Lead* (New York: Basic Books, 1988), p. 311. Prestowitz was counselor for Japanese Affairs, U.S. Department of Commerce.

How can offices be so expensive then? One reason is the short supply of land: Hong Kong has 5.5 million people crowded in an area about 20 miles square. Another reason is the booming economy. Hong Kong is one of the best places to do business in all of East Asia, and firms are willing to pay the high rents.

THE MARKET MECHANISM: A PRELIMINARY EVALUATION

Some see private enterprise as a predatory target to be shot, others as a cow to be milked; but few are those who see it as a sturdy horse pulling the wagon.

WINSTON CHURCHILL

There are thousands of markets in the United States and millions of interconnections among the markets. Changes in market conditions are reflected in changes in prices. As we have seen, prices provide information to market participants; they provide them with incentives to respond to changing conditions; and they bring order out of a potentially chaotic situation.

STRENGTHS OF THE MARKET

In some ways, the market mechanism works very well. Specifically:

1. The market *gives producers an incentive to produce the goods that consumers want.* If people want more tea, the price of tea is bid up, and producers are encouraged to produce more.

2. The market *provides an incentive to acquire useful skills.* For example, the high fees that doctors charge give students an incentive to undertake the long, difficult, and expensive training necessary to become a physician.

3. The market *encourages consumers to use scarce goods carefully.* For example, when the coffee crop is partially destroyed by bad weather, the price is driven up and people use coffee sparingly. Those who are relatively indifferent are encouraged to switch to tea. Even those who feel they must have coffee are motivated to conserve. With the high price of coffee, they are careful not to brew three cups when they intend to use only two.

4. Similarly, the price system *encourages producers to conserve scarce resources.* In the pasturelands of Texas, land is plentiful and cheap; it is used to raise cattle. In contrast, in Japan land is relatively scarce and expensive; cattle don't "run the range" over huge acreages of land the way they do in the United States.

5. The market involves a *high degree of economic freedom.* Nobody forces people to do business with specific individuals or firms. People are not directed into specific lines of work by government officials; they are free to choose their own occupations. Moreover, if people save, they are free to use their savings to set themselves up in their own independent businesses.

6. Markets provide *information on local conditions.* For example, if an unusual amount of hay-producing land in a specific county is plowed up to grow corn, then the price of hay in that county will tend to rise. The higher price of hay will signal farmers that they should put some of the land in this county back into hay. No government agency can hope to keep up-to-date and detailed information on the millions of localized markets like this one, each with its own conditions. Note the amount of information that is relevant, even for this simple decision on whether hay or corn should be planted: the quality of the land, particularly its relative productivity in hay and corn; the number of cattle and horses that eat hay; the cost of fertilizer for hay and for corn; the cost of seed for each; and so on and on.

In evaluating how well a market works, we should keep in mind the most important question of all: *compared to what?* Even a poor market may work better than the alternatives. Thus, one of the strongest arguments for the market parallels Winston Churchill's case for democracy: It may not work very well, but it does work better than the alternatives that have been tried from time to time.

THE ALTERNATIVE OF PRICE CONTROLS: SOME PROBLEMS

Consider what happens if the government tries to keep a price down by setting a *price ceiling.* Specifically, suppose it sets the price at P_1, below the equilibrium at E in Figure 4-9. The result is a shortage AB. Eager buyers have trouble finding the

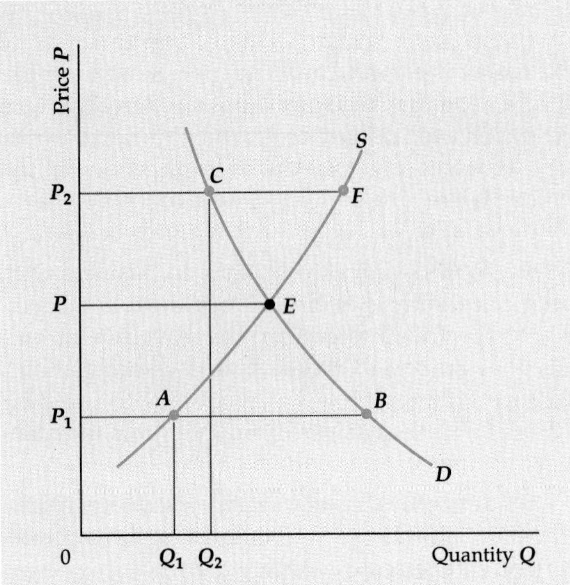

FIGURE 4-9 Price-setting by government.

If the government sets a price ceiling at P_1 to keep the price below the equilibrium at E, the result is a shortage AB. Observe that consumers end up with less; the quantity supplied at A is less than at equilibrium E.

On the other hand, if the government sets a price floor at P_2, the result is a surplus. The government can keep the price at P_2 if it is willing to buy the surplus CF. Again the public ends up with less—at C—than it would get at equilibrium E. Thus, when the government sets the price, consumers get a smaller quantity, *whether the price is set above or below its equilibrium.*

good. Thus, when the United States had a ceiling on gasoline prices in 1979, drivers had to wait in long lines at gas stations. Obviously, they wasted time—not to mention the gasoline they wasted while waiting in line.

Moreover, as a result of price controls, goods may disappear from regular distribution channels and flow instead into illegal **black markets.** In this case, the scarce goods go to those willing to break the law. Furthermore, the public may end up paying more for black market goods than it would pay in a free market. Black marketeers charge higher prices because they want compensation for the risks and because they have to use informal, inefficient marketing arrangements.

A ***black market*** is one in which sales take place at a price above the legal maximum.

Price controls can create other problems. For example, in its desire to prevent labor unrest, the Polish government kept bread fixed at a low price—so low that it was less than the price of the grain that went into making the bread. Therefore it was cheaper for farmers to feed their livestock bread rather than grain. When they did so, the labor and other resources that had been used to make grain into bread were wasted.

THE MARKET MECHANISM: LIMITATIONS AND PROBLEMS

Although the market has impressive strengths, it is also the target of substantial criticisms:

1. While the market provides a high degree of freedom for participants in the economy, *it may give the weak and the helpless little more than the freedom to starve.* In a market, producers do not respond solely to the needs of consumers. Rather, they respond to the desires of consumers that are backed up with cash. Thus under a system of *laissez faire,* the pets of the rich may have better meals and better health care than the children of the poor.

2. Markets *simply won't work* in some parts of the economy. When there is a military threat, individuals cannot provide their own defense. An individual who buys a rifle has no hope of standing against a foreign power. Defense is provided by the government, with organized military forces. The police and the judicial system are other services that can best be provided by the government. No matter how well the market works in general, people can't be permitted to "buy" a judge. (Even though the government provides the judicial system, a problem may still arise. See Box 4–1.)

3. In a system of laissez faire, *prices are not always the result of impersonal market forces.* In many markets, one or more participants have the power to influence price. *The monopolist or oligopolist may restrict production* in order to keep the price high, as we will see in detail in later chapters.

4. Activities by private consumers or producers may have undesirable *side effects.* Nobody owns the

BOX 4–1 *What's the Price of Justice?*

The bizarre case of Pennzoil vs Texaco raised a troubling question: What's the price of justice? According to press reports, one month after Pennzoil lodged a $15 billion suit against Texaco in 1984, Pennzoil's lead lawyer gave $10,000 to Judge Anthony Farris of the district court of Harris County, Texas, to help the judge finance his reelection campaign. When Texaco's lawyers found out, they expressed their shock and moved that Farris be disqualified. The motion was denied by a judge who offered a quaint explanation: if judges had to step aside for the mere appearance of impropriety, it would play havoc with the system. Texaco's lawyers decided they had to do something. They raised the bid, distributing $72,700 in campaign contributions to seven justices of the Texas Supreme Court who were expected to make a final ruling in the case—including three who weren't even running for reelection. Was this enough? Hardly. Texaco's lawyers were cheapskates. Pennzoil's lawyers responded with $315,000, including contributions to four justices who weren't running. One of the supreme court justices was so appalled that he resigned to campaign for reform.

Texans are not alone in wondering whether money is undermining the integrity of their judicial system. Although Texas is one of just a handful of states that still elect all their judges, most states—39, to be exact—have elections for at least some judges. At one time, judicial elections were inexpensive. But with televison and highly paid campaign consultants, some contests have become very costly.

And what of the Pennzoil-Texaco case? Pennzoil's suit was based on the complaint that Texaco had taken over Getty Oil in spite of Getty's prior commitment to sell out to Pennzoil. The jury awarded Pennzoil $10.5 billion, plus interest—much more than the total value of Getty. The award drove Texaco temporarily into bankruptcy while a settlement was being worked out.

Sources: "Pennzoil and the Judge," *The Washington Post,* July 30, 1987: William P. Barrett, "The Best Justice Money Can Buy," *Forbes,* June 1, 1987; and Sheila Kaplan, "What Price Justice? Oh, About $10,000," *The Washington Post,* May 17, 1987.

air or the rivers. Consequently, in the absence of government restraints, manufacturers may use them as garbage dumps, harming those downwind or downstream. The market provides no incentive to limit such negative side effects.

5. An unregulated system of private enterprise *may be quite unstable,* with periods of inflationary boom giving way to sharp recessions. Economic instability was a particularly severe problem in the early 1930s, when the economies of many countries collapsed into a deep depression. (On this and some other occasions, instability in the economy was compounded by ill-advised policies by the government.)

6. In a system of laissez faire, businesses may do an excellent job of satisfying consumer wants as expressed in the marketplace. But should the businesses be given high marks if they have *created the wants in the first place by advertising?* In the words of retired Harvard Professor John Kenneth Galbraith, "It involves an exercise of imagination to suppose that the taste so expressed originates with the consumer."[2] In this case, the producer is sovereign, not the consumer. According to Galbraith, the consumer is a puppet, manipulated by producers with the aid of Madison Avenue's bag of advertising tricks. Many of the wants that producers create and then satisfy are trivial: for example, the demands for automobile chrome and junk food.

Without arguing the merits of each and every product, defenders of the market system question Galbraith's point. In part, their defense of the market is based on the question "Compared with what?" If market demands are dismissed, who then is to decide which products are "meritorious" and which are not? Government officials? Should not people be permitted the freedom to make their

[2]John Kenneth Galbraith, "Economics as a System of Belief," *American Economic Review* (May 1970): 474. See also Galbraith, *The New Industrial State* (Boston: Houghton Mifflin, 1967).

own mistakes? And why should we assume that created wants are without merit? After all, we are not born with a taste for art or good music. Our taste for good music is created when we listen to it. Galbraith certainly would not suggest that symphony orchestras are without merit, simply because they statisfy the desire for good music which they have created. But who then is to decide which created wants are socially desirable?

If these criticisms of the market are taken far enough, they can be made into a case for replacing the market with an alternative system. Those favoring centrally controlled economies lay particular emphasis on points 1, 5, and 6 in their argument that the market should be replaced with government direction of the economy.

However, these criticisms are also often made by those who seek to reform, rather than replace, the market system. The recent economic history of Western Europe, North America, and many other parts of the globe has to a significant extent been written by such reformers. If the market does not provide a living for the weak and the helpless, then its outcome should be modified by private and public assistance programs. If monopolies have excessive market power, they can be broken up or their market power restrained by the government. If the production of a good creates pollution or other undesirable side effects, such side effects can be limited by taxation or controls. So say the reformers.

Although the market is a vital mechanism, it has sufficient weaknesses and limitations to provide the government with a major economic role. This role will be the subject of the next chapter.

KEY POINTS

1. Every economy has limited resources and involves specialization and exchange. In every economy, a mechanism is needed to answer three fundamental questions:

- **(a)** What will be produced?
- **(b)** How will it be produced?
- **(c)** For whom will it be produced?

2. The two principal mechanisms for answering these questions are the government and private markets.

In the real world, all countries rely on a *mixture* of markets and government actions. However, the mixture differs among countries. The United States places a relatively heavy reliance on the market. In centrally planned countries such as the USSR and other nations in Eastern Europe, the government has much more pervasive influence.

3. *Prices* play a key role in markets, providing information and incentives to buyers and sellers.

4. Markets vary substantially, with some being dominated by one or a few producers, whereas others have many producers and consumers. A market is *perfectly competitive* if there are many buyers and many sellers, with no single buyer or seller having any influence over the price.

5. In a perfectly competitive market, equilibrium price and quantity are established by the intersection of the demand and supply curves.

6. In drawing both the demand and supply curves, the *ceteris paribus* assumption is made—that "other things" do not change. Everything that can affect the quantity demanded or supplied—with the sole exception of price—is held constant when a demand or supply curve is constructed.

7. If any of these "other things"—such as consumer incomes or the prices of other goods—do change, the demand or supply curve will shift.

8. *What* the economy produces is determined primarily in the market for goods and services in the upper box of Figure 4-8. On the other hand, *how* and *for whom* are determined primarily in the factor markets (the lower box). However, there are numerous interactions among markets. The answer to each of the three questions depends on what happens in both the upper and lower boxes.

9. A substantial case can be made for the market system because it encourages firms to produce what people demand, and because it encourages the careful use of scarce goods and resources. Nevertheless, the market also has significant weaknesses, which provide the government with an important economic role.

KEY CONCEPTS

market	market power	*ceteris paribus*
capitalist economy	industry	demand shifter
free enterprise	firm	normal good
central planning	plant	inferior good
mixed economy	demand	substitutes
monopoly	supply	complements
oligopoly	equilibrium	supply shifter
perfect competition	surplus	joint products
imperfect competition	shortage	black market

PROBLEMS

4-1. Figure 4-6 illustrates the effect of a Brazilian freeze on the coffee market. How might the resulting change in the price of coffee affect the tea market? Explain with the help of a diagram showing the demand and supply for tea.

4-2. The relatively high incomes of doctors give students an incentive to study medicine. Other than the expected income and costs of training, what important factors affect career decisions?

4-3. It is often said that "the market has no ethics. It is impersonal." But individual participants in the market do have ethical values, and these values may be backed up with social pressures. Suppose that, in a certain society, it is considered not quite proper to be associated with a distillery. With the help of demand and supply diagrams, explain how this view will affect:

(a) The demand and/or supply of labor in the alcohol industry.

(b) The willingness of people to invest their funds in the alcohol industry, and the profitability of that industry.

4-4. Suppose that social sanctions are backed up by law and that people caught selling marijuana are given stiff jail sentences. How will this affect the demand and supply of marijuana? The price of marijuana? The quantity sold? The incomes of those selling marijuana?

* **4-5.** In distinguishing between substitutes and complements, the text lists a number of simple examples. Tea and coffee are substitutes, whereas cars and gasoline are complements.

It is worth looking more closely at one example, however, that may not seem quite so simple: heating oil and insulation. How would you correct or rebut the following erroneous argument:

> "Heating oil and insulation are complements, not substitutes, because they are used together. In Alaska, they use a lot of heating oil and a lot of insulation. In California, they don't use much of either."

*Problems marked with asterisks are more difficult than the others. They are designed to provide a challenge for students who want to do more advanced work.

Try to answer this question without looking at the following hints. But if you have difficulty, consider these hints:

(a) Think about the market for heating oil and insulation in a single city, say, St. Louis. When the price of heating oil goes up in St. Louis, do you think that this causes the demand curve for insulation to shift to the right or to the left? Does this make insulation a complement or substitute for heating oil, according to the definitions in the text?

(b) Are natural gas and oil substitutes or complements? Suppose the incorrect statement in quotation marks above had mentioned heating oil and natural gas rather than heating oil and insulation.

(c) If we accept the erroneous statement shown above in quotation marks, can't we argue in a similar manner that there are no such things as substitutes? For example, wouldn't we also accept the following incorrect conclusion: "In California, more apples and more oranges are sold than in Alaska. Therefore, apples and oranges are used together. They are complements, not substitutes." Do you see that this statement is incorrect, because it departs from the standard assumption that "other things remain unchanged?" In identifying complements and substitutes, we must not switch from one location and population (Alaska) to another (California); we must look at a single set of people (the St. Louis example in part a). Do you see why economists emphasize the assumption that "other things remain unchanged" (*ceteris paribus*)?

CHAPTER 5
THE ECONOMIC ROLE OF GOVERNMENT

Government does not go beyond its sphere in attempting to make life livable. . . .
OLIVER WENDELL HOLMES

When Franklin Delano Roosevelt became president in 1933, the nation was mired in the Great Depression. Roosevelt believed that the government had the responsibility to do something to alleviate the widespread economic misery. He summarized his view: "As new . . . problems arise beyond the power of men and women to meet as individuals, it becomes the responsibility of the Government itself to find new remedies." Quite a different opinion was expressed by President Ronald Reagan in 1980. Government, said Reagan, "is not the solution to our problem. Government *is* the problem."

Government affects the economy in four ways, by

- Spending.
- Taxation.
- Regulation.
- Operating public enterprises, such as power plants.

Chapter 4 pointed out that public enterprise is quite limited in the United States; it is much less important here than in other countries. Accordingly, this chapter will concentrate on the other three ways in which the government affects the U.S. economy—spending, taxation, and regulation. A final section of the chapter describes the changing attitudes toward public enterprises in Britain and a number of other countries.

The government's decisions to spend, tax, regulate, or establish public enterprises all help to answer the questions highlighted in Chapter 4: *What* goods and services will be produced? *How?* and *For whom?*

1. *Spending.* When the government pays social security pensions to retirees, it influences *who* gets society's output; the recipient of a pension is able to buy more goods and services. When the government builds roads or buys aircraft, it affects *what* is produced. When the government spends money for agricultural research, it influences *how* food will be produced.

2. *Taxes.* When the government collects taxes, it influences *who* gets society's output. When you pay taxes, you have less left to buy goods and services. Taxes also affect *what* is produced. For example, the tax on gasoline is much higher in Europe than in the United States. That is one reason why European cars are smaller, on average, than U.S. cars. Finally, the tax system may also influence *how* goods are produced. For example, by changing tax laws, the government can encourage businesses to use more machinery.

3. *Regulation.* Governmental regulations also influence what, how, and for whom goods and services are produced. For example, the government prohibits some pesticides and requires seat belts in cars. It thereby affects *what* is produced. By requiring producers of steel to limit their emissions of smoke, the government influences *how* goods are produced. It also regulates some prices—for example, some city governments impose rent ceilings so that people with low and moderate incomes can afford to keep their apartments. Such ceilings affect *who* gets the output of society. More of the present tenants stay, and fewer apartments are available for newcomers and young people.

In the private market, people have an option of buying or not buying products such as television sets and cars. In contrast, government activities generally involve compulsion. Taxes *must* be paid; people are not allowed to opt out of the system when the time comes to pay income taxes. Similarly, government regulations are enforced by compulsion; car manufacturers *must* install safety equipment. Compulsion sometimes exists even in a government spending program. Young people *must* go to school—although their parents do have the option of choosing a private school rather than one run by the government.

Having presented a broad overview, we now look at government spending, taxation, and regulation in more detail.

GOVERNMENT EXPENDITURES

During the nineteenth and early twentieth centuries, government expenditures covered little more than the expenses of the army and navy, a few public works, and the salaries of a small number of government officials. Except for wartime periods when spending skyrocketed to pay for munitions, weapons, and personnel, government spending was small. As late as 1929, all levels of government—federal, state, and local—together spent less than $11 billion a year. Of this total, about three-quarters was spent at the state and local levels. Highway maintenance and education were typical government programs. This does not mean, however, that a rigid policy of laissez faire was followed. Even during the nineteenth century, governments at both the state and local levels participated in some important sectors of the economy. For example, governments helped railroads and canal systems to expand.

With the depression of the 1930s, a major increase in government activity began. Distress and unemployment were widespread, and the government became more active. During the decade 1929–1939, federal government spending increased from $3 billion to $9 billion. Part of the increase was specifically aimed at providing jobs through new agencies, such as the Civilian Conservation Corps (CCC). Then, when the United States entered the Second World War in 1941, the government undertook huge spending to pay for military equipment and personnel. By 1944, defense amounted to more than 40% of gross national product (GNP).

When the war ended in 1945, the nation demobilized and government spending fell by more than 50%. Expenditures never fell to the low levels of 1929, however, because the government had taken on new peacetime responsibilities. For example, during the 1930s it began the *social security* system, whose principal function is the payment of pensions to retired people. More recently, the government has introduced *medicare* to provide medical assistance to the elderly, and *medicaid* to provide such assistance to the needy. Expenditures for weapons and other military purposes have also remained high for the past four decades.

GOVERNMENT PURCHASES VERSUS TRANSFERS

Government expenditures may be classified into two major categories:

- **Purchases of goods and services.**
- **Transfer payments.**

Government ***purchases*** of goods include items such as paper, computers, and aircraft. The government purchases services when it hires schoolteachers, police officers, and employees for government departments. When the government purchases goods and services, *it makes a direct claim on the productive capacity of the nation.* For example, when the government orders a computer, the manufacturer uses glass, plastic, copper, silicon chips, machines, and labor to make the computer. Similarly, the purchase of services involves a claim on productive resources. The police officer hired by the government must spend time on the beat and thus becomes unavailable for work in the private sector.

Government ***transfer payments,*** on the other hand, are payments *for which the recipient does not provide any good or service in return.* Transfer payments include social security and medicare benefits for the elderly and welfare payments such as medicaid. Of the transfer payments, social security and medicare are by far the largest, accounting for 28% of total federal government expenditures in 1988.

A ***transfer payment*** is a payment by the government to an individual, for which the individual does not provide a good or service in return. Social security benefits, unemployment compensation, and welfare payments are examples of transfers.

When the government purchases goods or services, it makes a claim on the productive capacity of the economy. For example, when it buys computers, labor and materials have to be used to produce those computers. In contrast, transfer payments represent no direct claim by the government on the productive capacity of the nation. It is true, of course, that when the government collects social security taxes from workers and pays benefits to retirees, the pattern of consumer spending is affected. The old have more to spend and workers have less.

The left panel of Figure 5-1 shows total government expenditures, including transfers. The right panel shows government purchases of goods and services; that is, it excludes transfers. These are the expenditures that make a direct claim on the productive resources of the economy. In each panel,

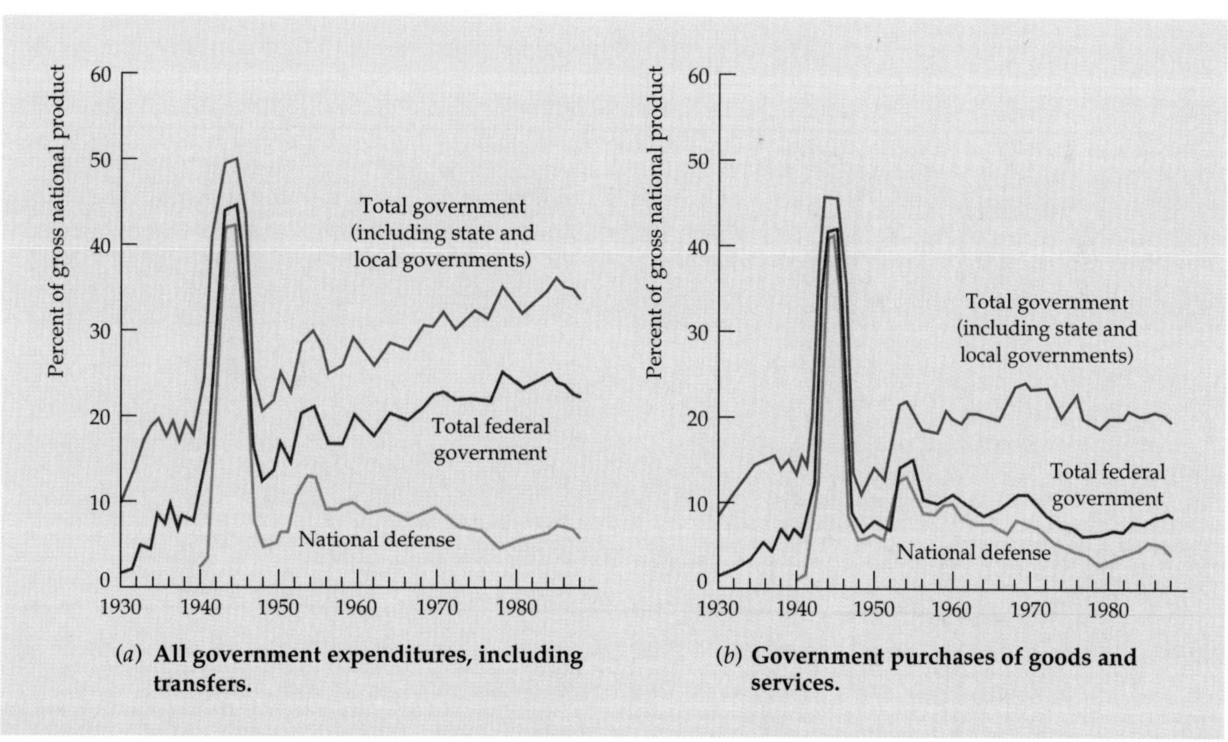

FIGURE 5-1 Government expenditures, 1930–1988 (as percentage of gross national product).

The left panel shows how total government expenditures, including expenditures on goods and services and the amounts redistributed in the form of transfers, have grown as a percentage of gross national product. The right panel shows only the expenditures for goods and services. As a percentage of GNP, these expenditures have not changed much over the past three decades.

expenditures are shown as a percentage of the overall size of the economy, as measured by gross national product or GNP. (Chapter 6 will explain in detail how GNP is measured.) Observe that as a percentage of GNP, government purchases of goods and services are approximately what they were three decades ago (right panel). Purchases by state and local governments have gone up, but these increases have been approximately matched by the declining percentage for the federal government. In 1988, federal government purchases of goods and services were only two-thirds as large as the combined purchases of state and local governments.

The two panels give two quite different impressions of the size of government. If we look only at purchases of goods and services in the right panel, then the percentage of national product going to the government has been quite stable over the past three and a half decades. If, on the other hand, we include transfers and look at total government expenditures in the left panel, the government's percentage is increasing. In brief, the government is not directly claiming a larger and larger share of the nation's product for itself (right panel). It *is*, however, claiming a larger share when account is taken of what it *redistributes* in the form of social security and other transfer payments.

EXPENDITURES OF THE FEDERAL GOVERNMENT

Figure 5-2 shows expenditures of the federal goverment in more detail. Notice how much defense expenditures have changed through the years. In the 1960s, they ran between 7% and 10% of GNP. By 1979, they fell below 5%. During the 1980s, they rose above 6%.

This figure also shows the increase in social security and medicare expenditures through the years. The combined social security and medicare program surpassed defense expenditures in 1976 to

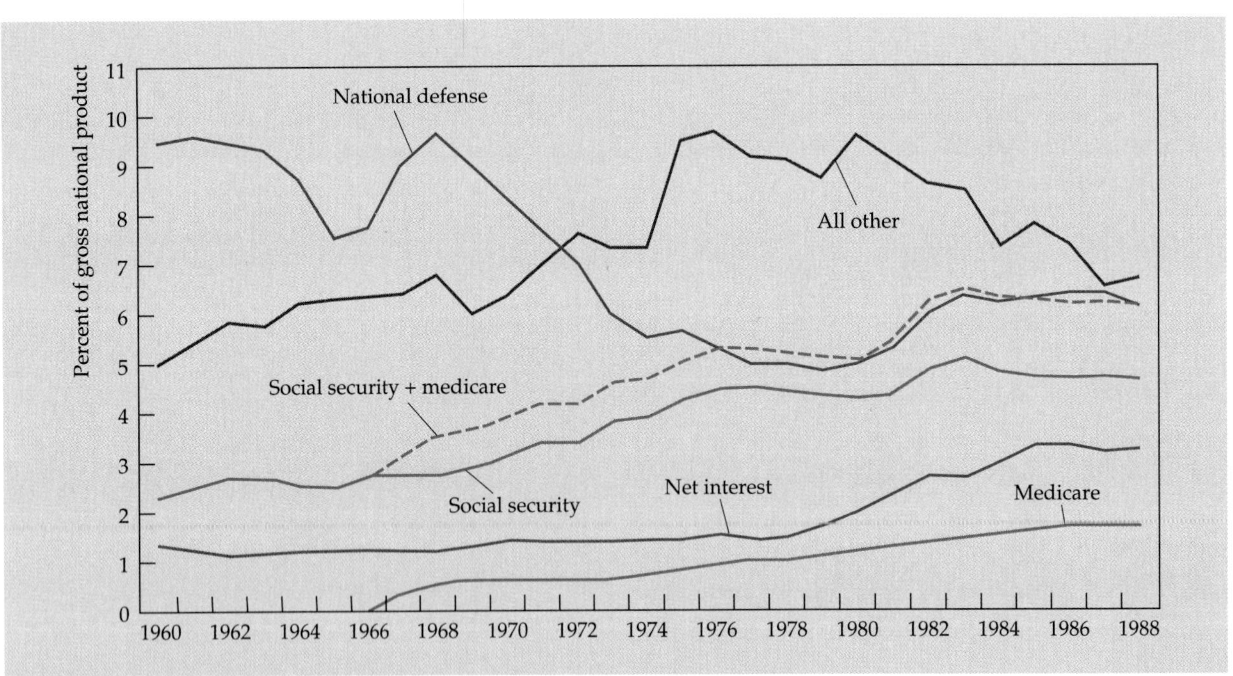

FIGURE 5-2 Federal government expenditures, 1960–1988 (as percentage of gross national product).

Federal government expenditures for interest, social security, and medicare have increased rapidly.

become the largest single spending category. Interest payments have also been rising rapidly, from a little over 1% of GNP in the early 1960s to more than 3% by the late 1980s. There are two reasons for this rapid increase in interest payments: (1) interest rates rose; and (2) the government's debt, on which interest must be paid, grew rapidly during the 1980s.

TAX REVENUES

Figure 5-3 presents a breakdown of the revenues of the federal government. The ***personal income tax*** provides the greatest share of revenues. This tax is levied on taxable personal income—that is, on the incomes of individuals and families after the subtraction of various exemptions and deductions.

For a married couple with two children, the income tax was levied at the rates shown in Table 5-1 in 1989. Because of exemptions and deductions, such a couple did not have to pay tax on the first $13,200 of income. The *average tax rate* (col. 3) is simply the total tax divided by income. Observe that, as income rises, the percentage of income paid in tax also rises. Therefore, the income tax is **progressive.** Note, however, that at very high incomes, the progressivity practically disappears and the tax is approximately **proportional,** between 27% and 28%.

TABLE 5-1 Federal Income Tax, 1989†

(1) *Income*	(2) *Tax*	(3) *Average Tax Rate* (3) = (2) ÷ (1)	(4) *Marginal Tax Rate (tax on additional income)*
$10,000	0	0	0
$20,000	$1,020	5.1%	15%
$50,000	$6,280	12.6%	28%
$100,000	$20,878	20.9%	33%
$200,000	$53,878	26.9%	33%
$250,000	$68,544	27.4%	28%
$500,000	$138,544	27.7%	28%
$1,000,000	$278,544	27.9%	28%

†For a married couple with two children, filing jointly and claiming the standard deduction.

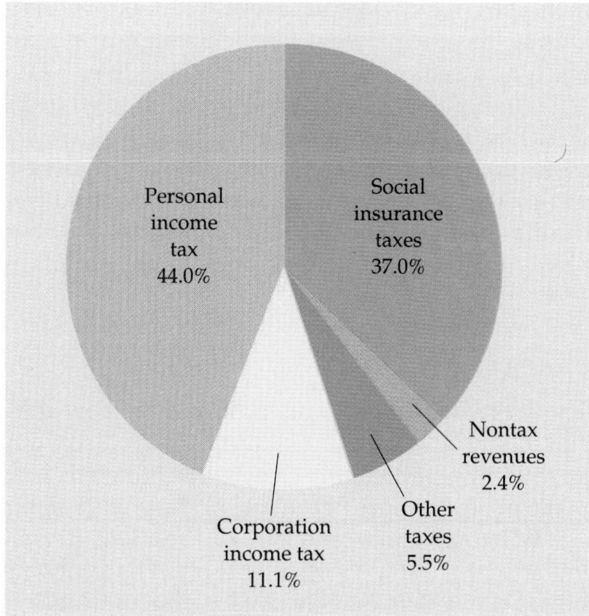

FIGURE 5-3 Federal government receipts, 1990 (projected).

The personal income tax is the largest single source of revenue for the federal government. Social insurance taxes—mainly for social security—are in second place.

> If a tax takes a larger percentage of income as income rises, the tax is ***progressive.***
>
> If a tax takes a smaller percentage of income as income rises, the tax is ***regressive.***
>
> If a tax takes a constant percentage of income, the tax is ***proportional.***

The ***marginal tax rate*** is shown in the last column; it is the tax rate on *additional* income. For example, at an income of $20,000, a couple is in the 15% marginal tax bracket and accordingly pays 15¢ tax on each additional dollar of income. The marginal tax rate increases to 28% and then to 33%.

The last column shows something peculiar. As income rises to $250,000, the marginal tax rate comes *down* again to 28%. This peculiarity is explained by the political compromises that led to the Tax Reform Act of 1986. The Congress and the administration wanted to advertise that they were cutting the *maximum* tax rate to 28%. This is in a sense true: The *average* tax rate (col. 3) does not rise above 28%. However, the marginal rate does rise above 28%—to 33% over a range.

Although the personal income tax remains the largest single component of federal government revenues, social insurance taxes (to pay for social security and unemployment insurance) have risen rapidly, from 16% of total federal revenues in 1960 to 37% in 1988. Social security contributions, or taxes, are paid to finance old-age pensions and payments to the families of contributors who die or are disabled. In 1989, the tax stood at 15.02% of wages and salaries up to a maximum income of $48,000; half the tax is collected from the employer and half from the employee. In order to finance the rapid increase in social security payouts, the social security tax has been increased repeatedly. It was 6% in 1960, 9.6% in 1970, and 12.25% in 1980. The maximum income subject to tax has also been rising.

The social security tax is ***regressive.*** While it is collected at a flat percentage on incomes up to a limit of $48,000 in 1989, any additional income is exempt from the tax. Thus the tax constitutes a higher percentage of the income of an individual making $48,000 per year than of someone making three times that much, who gets most income free of this tax. Nevertheless, if we look at the social security system *as a whole*—both taxes and benefits—we find that it favors lower income people. They receive bigger benefits, compared to the taxes they have paid, than do high-income people. While lower income people pay a disproportionate share of the social security tax, they receive an even larger share of the benefits.

The tax on corporate income (profits) constitutes the third most important source of federal revenue. In recent decades, the corporate income tax has become less important as a source of revenue—falling from about 25% of total federal revenues in the 1950s to about 11% in 1988.

Minor amounts of revenues are brought in by other taxes, such as excise taxes—on items such as cigarettes, alcoholic beverages, and gasoline—and customs duties imposed on goods imported into the United States. The government also has small receipts from nontax sources, such as fees paid by users of some government services.

EXPENDITURES, REVENUES, AND DEFICITS

When the government's revenues fall short of its expenditures, its budget is in ***deficit.*** In order to pay for the shortfall, the government has to borrow the difference. When it does so, its outstanding *debt* increases.

> If a government's revenues exceed its expenditures, it has a budget ***surplus.***
>
> If a government's revenues fall short of its expenditures, it has a budget ***deficit.***
>
> If a government's revenues equal its expenditures, its budget is ***balanced.*** (The term *balanced budget* is often used loosely to mean that the budget is either in balance or in surplus; that is, revenues are at least as great as expenditures.)
>
> The government's ***debt*** is the amount it owes. The debt increases when the government runs a deficit and borrows.

In the past quarter century, the U.S. government has run a deficit every year except 1969. During the early 1980s, the deficits grew rapidly, reaching a peak of 6.3% of GNP in 1983 (Fig. 5-4).

Large government deficits pushed up the size of the national debt from $909 billion in 1980 to more than $3 trillion in 1990. The large deficits were especially surprising because they occurred during the presidency of Ronald Reagan, who had vigorously attacked deficits prior to his election in 1980.

REAGANOMICS

The large deficits are one indication of how difficult it is to develop and execute an overall economic strategy—particularly when the objective is to make major changes in the role of the government.

When he came into office, President Reagan intended to change policy sharply. His economic program—which quickly was given the label of "Reaganomics"—included the following objectives:

1. Increase defense expenditures.
2. Restrain and, where possible, reduce other expenditures by the federal government.

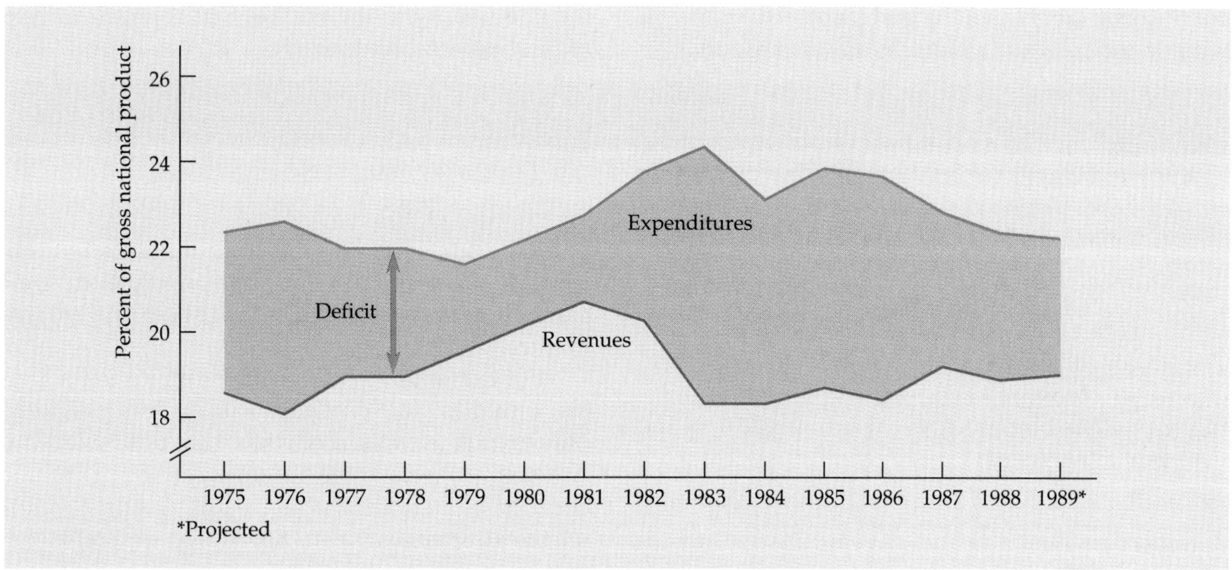

FIGURE 5-4 The federal budget: Expenditures, receipts, and deficits (as percentages of gross national product).

Over the past decade, expenditures of the federal government have been substantially higher than projected revenues, resulting in budget deficits.

3. Reduce government regulation.
4. Cut tax rates.

These policies were based on a philosophy of what the government should and should not do. In President Reagan's view, the major responsibilities of the government were to provide protection from external enemies and to provide the basis for an orderly society. He believed that government had gone far beyond its appropriate role. One of his objectives, said Reagan, was to "get the government off the backs of the people."

President Reagan achieved some of his objectives. The tax law enacted in 1981 provided for cuts in tax rates over the period from 1981 to 1984. Defense expenditures were increased, both in dollar terms and as a percentage of national product. But other expenditures were much more difficult to cut than expected, even though some programs were slashed. The early hopes of the Reagan administration—that the budget could be balanced by 1984—were dashed. In fact, deficits ballooned.

The high deficits meant that the national debt grew rapidly. As a result, interest on the debt also grew rapidly. The high interest expenditures will make it even more difficult to balance the budget in the future.

THE EARLY BUSH ADMINISTRATION

The large deficits severely limited President George Bush's options when he entered the White House in 1989. He had a number of goals that were not easily reconciled:

- Additional government spending on children, the homeless, and education, as a way of building a "kinder, gentler nation."
- No new taxes, in line with his unequivocal campaign promise.
- A reduction and elimination of the budget deficit by the early 1990s.

To help reduce the deficit, the president suggested broad categories on which spending was to be cut back, but he did not identify specific programs. Congress was invited to join in the politically difficult process of picking the actual programs to be cut. It seems likely that the budgetary situation will remain difficult throughout his administration.

PRINCIPLES OF TAXATION

The art of taxation consists of plucking the goose so as to obtain the largest amount of feathers with the least possible amount of hissing.

JEAN BAPTISTE COLBERT
SEVENTEENTH-CENTURY FRENCH STATESMAN

The major objective of taxation is to raise revenues—to obtain feathers without too much hissing. But other objectives are also important in the design of a tax system.

1. NEUTRALITY

In many ways, the market system works admirably. Adam Smith's invisible hand provides the consuming public with a vast flow of goods and services. As a starting point, therefore, a tax system should be designed to be *neutral.* That is, it should disturb market forces as little as possible, unless there is a good reason to the contrary.

For the sake of illustration, consider a far-fetched example. Suppose that blue cars were taxed at 10% and green cars not at all. This tax would clearly not be neutral between blue and green cars. People would have an incentive to buy green cars; blue cars would practically disappear from the market. A tax that introduces such a distortion would make no sense.

While this illustration is trivial, actual taxes do introduce distortions. For example, several centuries ago, houses in parts of Europe were taxed according to the number of windows. As a result, houses were built with fewer windows. To a lesser degree, the current property tax introduces a perverse incentive. If you have your house repaired, the government's evaluation of your house (the assessed value) may be raised and your taxes increased as a consequence. Therefore property taxes encourage you to let your property deteriorate.

The problem is that every tax provides an incentive to do something to avoid it. As long as taxes must be collected, complete neutrality is impossible. The objective of the tax system must therefore be more modest: to aim toward neutrality. As a starting point in the design of a tax system, the disturbance to the market that comes from taxation should be minimized.

2. NONNEUTRALITY: MEETING SOCIAL OBJECTIVES BY TAX INCENTIVES

There is, however, an important modification that must be made to the neutrality principle. In some cases, it may be desirable to disturb the private market.

For example, the government might tax polluting activities, so that firms will do less polluting. The market is disturbed but in a desirable way. Another example is the tax on cigarettes, which, in addition to its prime objective of raising revenue for the government, also discourages cigarette consumption.

3. EQUITY

Taxation represents coercion; taxes are collected by force if necessary. Therefore it is important that taxes both be fair and give the appearance of being fair. There are, however, two different principles for judging fairness.

The Benefit Principle. This principle recognizes that the purpose of taxation is to pay for government services. Therefore, let those who gain the most from government services pay the most.

If this principle is adopted, then a question arises: Why not simply set prices for government services which people can voluntarily pay if they want the services? In other words, why not charge a price for a government service, just as General Motors charges for cars? This approach may work—for example, for a toll road from which drivers can be excluded if they do not pay. But it will not work for public goods that benefit people even if they do not pay—for example, police, disease control programs, and air traffic control. Everyone will enjoy them, but no one will offer to pay for them. It is the function of the government to determine whether such programs are worthwhile. Once the decision is made to go ahead, people must be required to support the program through taxes. If the **benefit principle** of taxation is followed, the government estimates how much various individuals and groups benefit, and sets taxes accordingly.

Ability to Pay. If the government sets taxes according to the benefit principle, it does not redistribute income. The people who are taxed also get benefits from government programs. If the government wishes to redistribute income, it can set taxes according to the ***ability to pay.*** The basic measures of the ability to pay are income and wealth.

> If taxes are imposed according to the ***benefit*** principle, people pay taxes in proportion to the benefits they receive from government spending.
>
> If taxes are imposed according to the ***ability to pay*** principle, higher taxes are paid by those with greater ability to pay, as measured by income and/or wealth.

If the government were to levy a progressive income tax and an inheritance tax, and at the same time provide assistance to those at the bottom of the economic ladder, it would substantially redistribute income from the rich to the poor. But the world is not so simple. The government levies many other taxes as well, and some of these are proportional or even regressive. Overall, high-income groups pay only a slightly higher percentage of their incomes in taxes than do low-income groups.[1] It is on the expenditure side that the government has its greatest effect in redistributing income. We have already noted that the social security system as a whole favors lower income people. Even though they pay more than a proportionate share of social security taxes, they get an even larger share of benefits.

4. SIMPLICITY

To anyone who has spent the first two lovely weekends of April sweating over an income tax form, simplicity of the tax system is devoutly to be desired. Of course, we live in a complex world, and the tax code must to some degree reflect this complexity. But, as a result of decades of tinkering, the U.S. income tax has become ridiculously complicated. Indeed, it has become so complicated that the Internal Revenue Service (IRS) itself gives incorrect answers to taxpayer inquiries about one-third of the time. Mortimer Caplin, a former commissioner of the IRS, found that the tax code had grown so "horrendously complex" that he turned to an accounting firm to prepare his own return. So did Wilbur Mills, the ex-chairman of the House Ways and Means Committee—a committee that is largely responsible for writing the tax laws. (However, Donald Alexander, another former IRS chief, prepares his own tax return, since he thinks that those who write and enforce the law "should have to undergo the ordeal to see what it's like.")

A number of proposals have been made to simplify the tax system. Some people have flippantly suggested an ultra-simple, two-line tax form:

line 1: What did you make last year? $___.

line 2: Send it in.

THE TAX REFORM ACT OF 1986

Widespread dissatisfaction with the existing tax system led to the Tax Reform Act of 1986. This act had broad bipartisan support, including the president and congressional leaders such as Senator William Bradley and Congressman Dan Rostenkowski.

The Tax Reform Act had two major features:

1. It plugged or restricted a number of *loopholes* that had allowed people to avoid taxes on some of their income. For example, the investment tax credit—which had given businesses a tax break as a reward for investing—was eliminated. Tax advantages for owners of real estate were reduced. Capital gains (that is, gains on the sales of stocks, bonds, or other assets) are now taxed at the same rate as earned income, rather than at the lower, preferential rates that existed before 1986.

2. It cut tax rates. For example, the average tax for individuals with incomes less than $10,000 was cut

---

[1] It is surprisingly difficult to tell who pays some of the taxes. For example, do corporate taxes come out of the pockets of the owners of corporations, who on average have higher incomes than the general public? Or are they passed on to the general public, in the form of higher prices? This issue is studied in detail by Joseph Pechman, *Who Paid the Taxes, 1965-85?* (Washington, D.C.: Brookings Institution, 1985).

by more than half. Toward the upper end of the income scale, the highest marginal tax rate on personal income was reduced from 50% to 33%. The tax rate on corporate profits was cut from 46% to 34%.

The closing of loopholes (point #1) means that more income is now taxed. As a result, it is possible to reduce tax rates (point #2) while still maintaining total revenues. The objective of the 1986 act was to reform taxes and make them fairer; it was not designed to raise or lower the total amount the government was taking from the public.

The tax system not only became fairer; it also moved in the direction of neutrality. Because loopholes were restricted and tax rates reduced, people now have less incentive to look for special ways to avoid taxes. They have less incentive to look for tax gimmicks when they make investments, and more incentive to focus on profitability instead. In this way, tax reform has contributed to the efficiency of the economy.

In addition to increasing fairness and neutrality, the proponents of the 1986 legislation at first hoped to achieve a third goal, also—to make the tax system simpler. However, very early in the debate, Congress recognized that, whatever the virtues of the proposed reform, it would not simplify taxes. The word "simplification" was quietly dropped from the title of the bill. But two objectives out of three is not bad. In the tax reform debate, Congress turned in a distinguished performance.

GOVERNMENT REGULATION

The government's budget, amounting to hundreds of billions of dollars, has a substantial effect on the types of goods produced and on who gets these goods. In addition, the government affects the economy through its regulatory agencies, such as the Environmental Protection Agency (EPA) which controls pollution. The cost of *administering* such agencies—which amounts to only 2% to 3% of the federal government's budget—is an inadequate measure of their importance. The cost to businesses of *complying* with these regulations is far higher. For example, it costs a steel mill much more to install pollution-control devices than it costs the EPA to administer the regulations. The gains to the public—in the form of cleaner air—are likewise much greater than the small amounts that appear in the federal budget.

During the past century, a number of steps have been taken to limit the most flagrant abuses of private business. In 1890, the Sherman Act declared business mergers that create monopolies to be illegal. Then the Federal Trade Commission (FTC) was established in 1914 in the belief that monopolies should be prevented before the fact, rather than punished after they are created.

Regulation goes far beyond the control of monopoly. For example, the Food and Drug Administration (FDA) determines the effectiveness and safety of drugs before they are permitted on the market. The financial shenanigans of the 1920s—which contributed to the collapse into the depression—led in 1933 to the establishment of the Securities and Exchange Commission (SEC) to regulate financial markets. The SEC requires corporations to disclose information about their finances. Banks are extensively regulated by the Federal Reserve System, the Federal Deposit Insurance Corporation, the Comptroller of the Currency, and state regulatory agencies. The Federal Aviation Administration (FAA) sets and enforces safety standards for aircraft.

In the 1960s and 1970s, there was an upswing in regulatory activity, with the addition of such agencies as the Equal Employment Opportunity Commission (EEOC), the Environmental Protection Agency (EPA), the Commodity Futures Trading Commission (CFTC), and the Occupational Safety and Health Administration (OSHA).

In many areas, regulation is relatively uncontroversial. For example, few people complain when the Federal Aviation Administration enforces safety standards for the airlines. Similarly, there is widespread support for government regulation aimed at keeping unsafe drugs off the market. The FDA drew particular praise because it had blocked the distribution of thalidomide, a drug to relieve nausea that caused birth defects when it was used in Europe.

However, doubts set in after the flurry of regulatory activity of the 1960s and 1970s. In particular, there were growing concerns that some government regulations were working at cross purposes. For example, the Justice Department and the FTC were charged with the responsibility of reducing monopoly abuse and increasing competition in the U.S. economy. But, at the same time, the Civil Aeronautics Board (CAB) was *limiting* competition among airlines. In order to fly a new route in competition with existing carriers, an airline needed approval of the CAB, and the CAB regularly turned down such requests. In addition, banking regulation set the interest rate that banks could offer to depositors, and limited competition between banks and other financial institutions. During the Carter and Reagan administrations, major steps were taken to reduce regulation of banks and airlines. At the end of 1984, the CAB went out of business.

Under the Reagan administration, with its desire to reduce the regulatory hassles faced by business, enforcement of safety and environmental regulations became less vigorous. Particularly with respect to the environment, the policies of the administration stirred controversy. The EPA became a demoralized agency, touched by scandal. Critics of the administration pointed out that the EPA performed an essential function. Without it, there would be nothing in the competitive market system to give businesses any strong incentive to restrain pollution.

What is needed is a sense of balance. The private market mechanism has substantial defects. For example, corporations cannot on their own be counted on to pay sufficient attention to limiting pollution. But government agencies also have defects; they are not run by superhumans capable of solving all our problems. Furthermore, government regulation can be costly. While we use government agencies to deal with major defects in the market, we should be prepared to live with minor failures, where the cure may be worse than the defects themselves.[2]

Regulation in the public interest is made particularly difficult because of the political clout of producers. When regulations are being developed, the affected industry makes its views known forcefully. But the views of consumers are diffuse and often underrepresented. In an extensive study of regulatory agencies, the Senate Government Operations Committee concluded that the public is outnumbered and outspent by industry in regulatory proceedings. The committee chairman observed that regulatory hearings "can be likened to the biblical battle of David and Goliath—except that David rarely wins." This conclusion should come as no surprise. For decades, an irreverent definition has circulated in Washington: A sick industry is one that cannot capture control of its regulatory agency.

The heavy influence of producers is not simply the result of a conspiracy of wealth. Rather, it is an intrinsic feature of a highly specialized economy. Each of us has a major, narrow, special interest as a producer, and each of us has a minor interest in a wide range of industries whose goods we consume. We are much more likely to react when our particular industry is affected by government policy; we are much less likely to express our diffuse interest as consumers. The political clout of producers is primarily the result of modern technology and a high degree of specialization; it is not primarily a result of our particular system. It exists in a wide variety of political-economic systems, including those of Britain, France, Germany, Japan, and the Soviet Union.

THE ROLE OF THE GOVERNMENT

With government budgets reaching hundreds of billions of dollars, and with an extensive list of government regulations, the U.S. economy is clearly a substantial distance away from a pure market system of laissez faire. What principles and objectives guide the government when it intervenes?

In part, government intervention is based on deep social attitudes that are often difficult to explain. Thirty years ago, Americans could look askance at government-financed, "socialized" medicine in Britain. Yet at the same time they could consider British education "undemocratic" because many well-to-do Britons sent their children to privately financed elementary and secondary schools. The British, on the other hand, were proud of their educational system and were puzzled by what they considered a quaint, emotional American objection

---

[2]The government does not, however, always exercise common sense. Many bizarre laws are on the books. For example, it is illegal in Seattle to carry a concealed weapon more than 6 feet long. An ordinance in Danville, Pennsylvania, requires that "fire hydrants must be checked one hour before fires." Sault Ste. Marie had a law against spitting into the wind. In Washington, D.C., it was illegal to punch a bull in the nose. These examples are taken from Laurence J. Peter, *Why Things Go Wrong* (New York: Morrow, 1984) and Barbara Seuling, *You Can't Eat Peanuts in Church and Other Little-Known Laws* (New York: Doubleday, 1975).

to public financing of medical care. During the past three decades, the gap between the two societies has narrowed, with increasing governmental involvement in medicine in the United States and a decline in the importance of privately financed education in Britain.

The government intervenes in the economy for many reasons; it is hard to summarize them all. We will look at five of the main ones.

1. PROVIDING WHAT THE PRIVATE MARKET CANNOT

Consider defense expenditures. For obvious political reasons, defense cannot be left to the private market. The prospect of private armies marching around the country is too painful to contemplate. But there also is an impelling economic reason why defense is a responsibility of the government.

The difference between defense and an average good is the following. If I buy food at the store, I get to eat it; if I buy a movie ticket, I get to see the film; if I buy a car, I get to drive it. But defense is different. If I want a larger, better equipped army, my offer to purchase a rifle for the army will not add in any measurable way to my own security. My neighbor, and the average person in Alaska, Michigan, or Texas, will benefit as much from the extra rifle as I do. In other words, the benefit from defense expenditures *goes broadly to all citizens; it does not go specifically to the individual who pays.* If defense is to be provided, it must be financed by the government.

Such goods—where the benefit goes to the public regardless of who pays—are sometimes known as **public goods.**

2. DEALING WITH EXTERNALITIES

An ***externality*** is a side effect—good or bad—of production or consumption. For example, when individuals are immunized against an infectious disease, they receive a substantial benefit; they are assured that they won't get the disease. But there is an ***external benefit*** as well, because others gain too; they are assured that the inoculated individuals will not catch the disease and pass it along to them. Similarly, there is an external benefit when people have their houses painted. The neighborhood becomes more attractive.

An ***external cost*** occurs when a factory pollutes the air. The cost is borne by those who breathe the polluted air. Similarly, someone who drives an unsafe car imposes an external cost. He may kill not only himself, but others too.

An ***externality*** is a side effect of production or consumption. Persons or businesses other than the producer or consumer are affected. An externality may be either positive (for example, vaccinations) or negative (for example, pollution).

Because of the effects on others, the government may wish to encourage activities that create external benefits and to discourage those with external costs. It can do so with any of its three major tools: expenditures, regulations, or taxes. The government spends money for public health programs, for the immunization of the young. In many states, regulations require the inspection of automobiles, to keep cars with poor brakes off the highways. And some states impose higher taxes on leaded than on unleaded gasoline in order to reduce pollution.

3. ENCOURAGING THE USE OF MERIT GOODS

Government intervention may also be based on the view that people are not in all cases the best judges of what is good for them. According to this view, the government should encourage ***merit goods***—those that are deemed particularly desirable—and discourage the consumption of harmful products. People's inability to pick the "right" goods may be the result of short-sightedness, ignorance, or addiction.

In some cases, the government attempts merely to correct ignorance in areas where the public may have difficulty determining (or facing?) the facts. The requirement of a health warning on cigarette packages is an example. In other instances, the government goes further, to outright prohibition, as in the case of heroin and other hard drugs.

The government intervenes relatively sparingly to tell adults what they should or should not consume. (Children are another matter, however; they are not allowed to reject the "merit" good, education.) However, substantial government direction does occur in welfare programs, presumably on the ground that those who get themselves into financial difficulties are least likely to make wise consumption decisions. Thus part of the assistance to the poor consists of food stamps and housing programs rather than outright grants of money. In this way, the government attempts to direct consumption toward housing and milk for the children, rather than (perhaps) toward liquor for an alcoholic parent.

4. HELPING THE POOR

The market provides the goods and services desired by those with the money to buy, but it provides little for the poor. In order to help the impoverished and move toward a more humane society, government programs have been established to provide assistance for old people, the handicapped, and the needy.

5. PROMOTING ECONOMIC STABILITY

Finally, if we go back to the beginning of the upswing in government activity—to the depression of the thirties—we find that the primary motivation was not to affect the kinds of products made in the economy, nor specifically to aid the poor. Rather, the problem was the quantity of production. With unemployment rates running over 15% of the labor force year after year, the problem was to produce more, because more of almost anything would help put people back to work. Since the dark days of the 1930s, the government has been held responsible for maintaining a reasonably stable economy, with a low rate of unemployment.

LIVING IN A GLOBAL ECONOMY

THE PRIVATIZATION OF PUBLIC ENTERPRISE

In the half century from 1929 to 1979, governments in many countries undertook new responsibilities. The general trend was toward more government—more government spending, more taxation, more regulation, and more government enterprises. This trend has been broken in the past decade. In the United States, the Reagan administration pushed through a cut in income tax rates. A number of countries have begun a process of *privatization*, selling their government enterprises to private owners.

Britain has been a leader in privatization since the election of the Conservative government under Margaret Thatcher in 1979. During her first term (1979–1983), the most important part of the privatization program was the sale of 600,000 units of government-owned housing to the tenants for a total of £4.5 billion (approximately $6 billion, or an average of $10,000 per unit). Since 1983, housing sales have continued, but the sales of government corporations have become even more important. The British government has sold its interests in British Aerospace, British Airways, British Gas, British Telecom, Rolls Royce, and the Jaguar/Rover automotive group, to name some of the more significant. Sir John Egan, chairman of Jaguar, observed that "The Prime Minister [Margaret Thatcher] has never liked owning car companies. She barely puts up with owning the police."

In its privatization program, the British government had a number of objectives.

1. The government ***raised funds*** by selling enterprises—over £400 million in 1980–1981 and £5.1 billion in 1987–1988. However, receipts from the sale of enterprises did not represent a net gain to the government. Until 1987, almost all the firms offered for sale were profitable. Thus the government was giving up a flow of future profits.

2. The government hoped and expected that there would be a ***gain in efficiency.*** Freed from the heavy hand of government supervision and spurred on by the profit motive, private firms would have an incentive to adopt more productive methods. The government therefore hoped that the nation would reap a long-term gain, in terms of a greater output of goods and services.

3. The government hoped to increase the ***mobility of the labor force*** by selling government-owned housing to the tenants. Workers living in such housing had traditionally been discouraged from moving to take new employment opportunities. Once they left government-subsidized housing, they might have great difficulty finding comparable housing elsewhere because of long waiting lists. When the government sold the houses to the tenants, the new owners were free to sell them and move to new job opportunities.

4. The government was eager to promote an ***ethic of ownership and enterprise.*** In the words of one member of the Thatcher government:

> Our aim is to build upon our property-owning democracy and to establish a people's capital market, to bring capitalism to the place of work, to the high street and even to the home. . . . These policies also increase personal independence and freedom, and by establishing a new breed of owner, have an important effect on attitudes. They tend to break down the division between owners and earners.[3]

It is not surprising that privatization has been a subject of intense ideological debate. Proponents of "people's capitalism" urge the government on. Opponents are concentrated in the Labour Party and labor unions. They argue that privatization is disruptive; it costs the government future revenues when profitable enterprises are sold; and it leads privatized firms in the telecommunications and airline industries to "skim cream." That is, they introduce new services only in profitable locations and shirk their responsibility to provide services to the more remote and less affluent regions. So say the critics.

[3]John Moore, financial secretary of the Treasury, as quoted in Raymond Vernon, ed., *The Promise of Privatization* (New York: Council on Foreign Relations, 1988), p. 41.

Substantial steps toward privatization have also been taken in a few other countries: Bangladesh, Chile, and France. Other countries are planning major privatization programs, including New Zealand, the Philippines, and Turkey. More limited divestitures have occurred in Ecuador, Italy, Mexico, and Senegal. Critics insist that privatization is more talk than action. Nevertheless, Raymond Vernon of Harvard University concludes that "the sheer number and diversity of the countries involved suggest that the movement is more than a rash of children's crusades."[4] Vernon points out that attitudes shifted abruptly in favor of privatization in many countries during the early 1980s. Even the Chinese and Soviet governments seem to be moving away from tight and comprehensive control of their enterprises.

[4]Vernon, *The Promise of Privatization*, p. 1.

KEY POINTS

1. The government affects the economy through expenditures, taxation, regulation, and publicly owned enterprises.

2. Except for the period of demobilization after World War II, total government spending (including transfers) has been on an upward trend as a percentage of gross national product (GNP). If, however, only purchases of goods and services are counted, the government's share of GNP has been quite stable over the past three decades. State and local governments have grown, while federal government purchases of goods and services have declined as a percentage of GNP.

3. Federal transfer payments have risen rapidly as a percentage of GNP. Social security is the largest transfer program.

4. Personal income taxes and social security taxes are the two main sources of revenue for the federal government, with corporate income taxes coming in a distant third.

5. Federal government revenues have fallen far short of expenditures. As a result, the federal government has run large deficits, running as high as 6.3% of GNP in 1983.

6. Government regulatory agencies are active in many areas, regulating monopoly and protecting the public from misleading advertising, unsafe drugs, and pollution.

7. The primary reasons for government intervention in the economy are to:

> **(a)** Provide public goods that cannot be supplied by the market because individuals have no incentive to buy them. Individuals get the benefits regardless of who pays.
>
> **(b)** Deal with externalities, such as pollution.
>
> **(c)** Encourage the use of merit goods and discourage or prohibit harmful products.
>
> **(d)** Help the poor.
>
> **(e)** Help stabilize the economy.

8. A number of objectives are important in the design of a tax system:

> **(a)** In general, neutrality is a desirable objective.
>
> **(b)** In some cases, however, the government should alter market signals by taxation. For example, a tax can be used to discourage pollution.
>
> **(c)** Taxes should be reasonably simple and easily understood.
>
> **(d)** Taxes should be fair. There are two ways of judging fairness: the benefit principle and ability to pay.

KEY CONCEPTS

purchase of goods and services	regressive tax	benefit principle
transfer payment	proportional tax	ability-to-pay principle
income tax	deficit	public good
average tax rate	surplus	merit good
marginal tax rate	balanced budget	externality
progressive tax	tax neutrality	privatization

PROBLEMS

5-1. "That government governs best which governs least." Do you agree? Why or why not? Does the government perform more functions than it should? If so, what activities would you like it to reduce or stop altogether? Are there any additional functions that the government should undertake? If so, which ones? How should they be paid for?

5-2. "State and local governments are closer to the people than the federal government. Therefore, they should be given some of the functions of the federal government." Are there federal functions that might be turned over to the states and localities? Do you think they should be turned over? Why or why not? Are there federal functions that the states are incapable of handling?

5-3. The government engages in research. For example, the government has agricultural experimental stations, and during the Second World War, the government developed the atomic bomb through the Manhattan Project. Why do you think the government engages in these two types of research, while leaving most research to private business? Does the government have any major advantages in undertaking research? Any major disadvantages?

PART II

THE FOUNDATIONS OF MICROECONOMICS

The Consumer and the Firm

This book's companion volume provides a broad overview of the **macroeconomic** "forest"—that is, overall magnitudes such as GNP and the average level of prices. The rest of this book will focus on the **microeconomic** "trees"—that is, the detailed relationships among various industries and groups in the economy.

Specifically, the rest of the book provides answers to the *central microeconomic questions* introduced in Chapter 4:

- *What* is produced?
- *How* is it produced?
- *For whom* is it produced?

Part 2 sets the stage. In Chapters 6–9, the curtain goes up on the two main sets of characters in microeconomics:

- Consumers who demand products.
- Producers who supply them.

The study of microeconomics begins by picking up the demand and supply curves of Chapter 4. A brief review of those curves is provided in the next two pages under the heading "Remember?" If you don't remember, we recommend that you reread Chapter 4.

Remember?

DEMAND. . .

The quantity of apples demanded depends on the price of apples . . .

. . . and other influences, such as a change in the price of oranges or bananas, or an increase in consumer income.

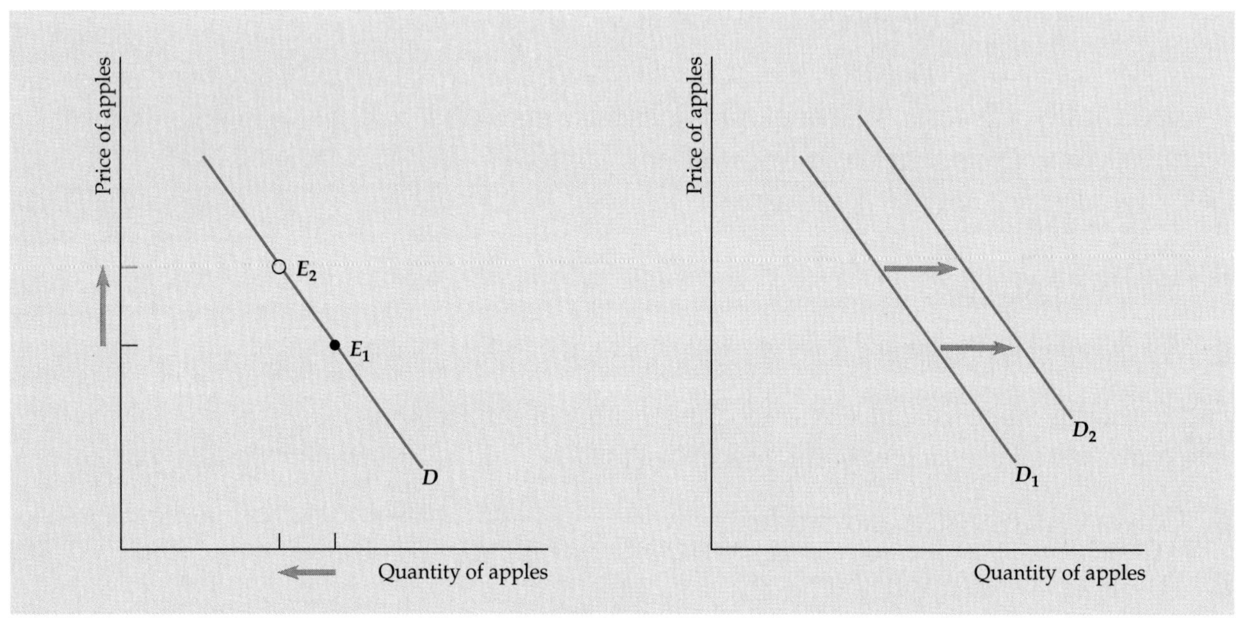

In this panel, observe that, as the price of apples rises, the quantity demanded becomes smaller. Such a movement along a given demand curve is described as a "decrease in the quantity demanded."

In this panel, note that if one of the other influences changes, the demand curve shifts. For example, if income rises, the demand curve shifts from D_1 to D_2. This rightward shift is described as an "increase in demand." (For a few products—the inferior goods—an increase in income causes the demand curve to shift to the left.)

SUPPLY. . .

The quantity of apples supplied depends on the price of apples . . .

. . . and other influences, like the weather, the price of fertilizer and other inputs, changing technology, and the prices of alternative outputs like wheat.

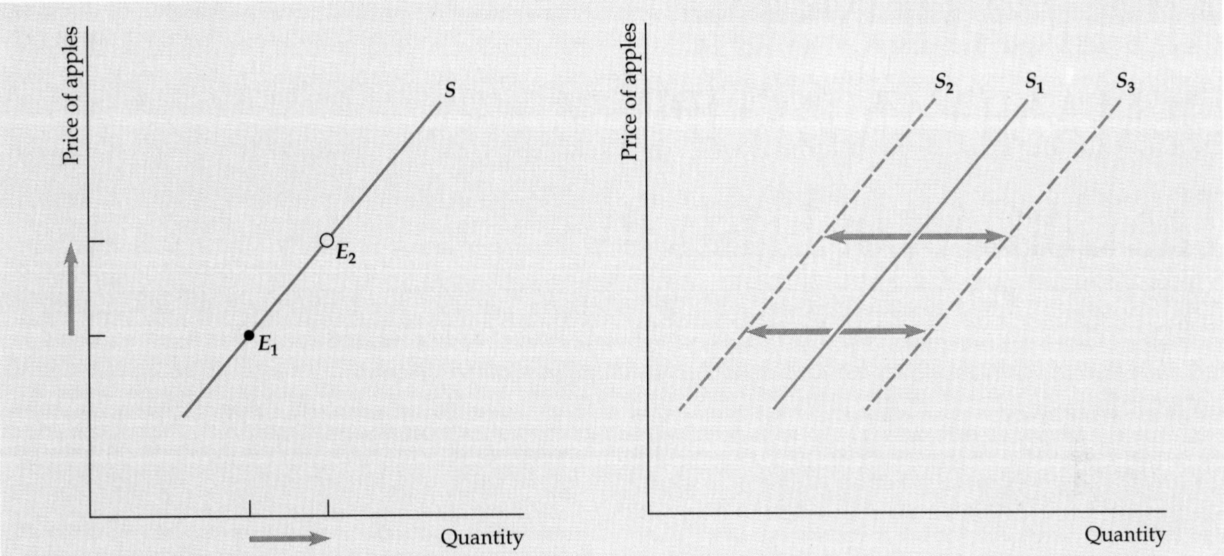

In this panel, observe that, as the price of apples rises, the quantity supplied becomes larger. Such a movement along a given supply curve is described as an "increase in the quantity supplied."

In this panel, observe that if one of these other influences changes, the supply curve shifts. For example, if the price of fertilizer rises, the supply curve shifts from S_1 to S_2.

SUPPLY AND DEMAND TOGETHER DETERMINE PRICE

Note: Neither curve shifts as long as other influences on supply and demand do not change ("other things equal"). However, . . .

. . . suppose that other influences do change. For example, suppose that consumer income rises, so that demand shifts from D_1 to D_2. Then equilibrium moves form E_1 to E_2 (with more sold at a higher price).

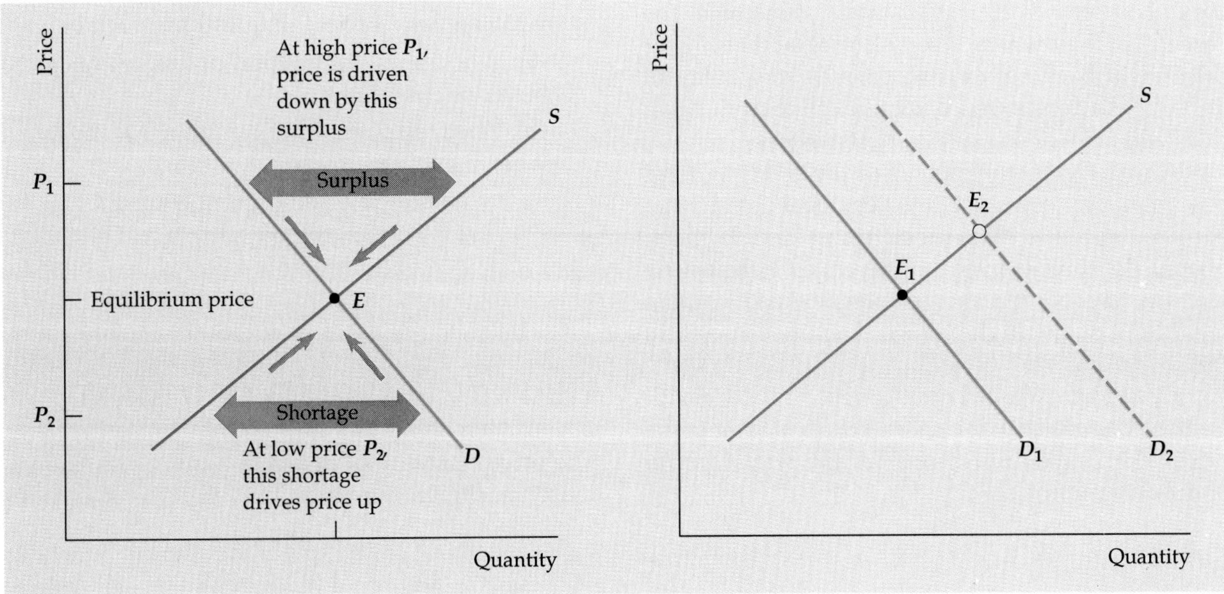

CHAPTER 6
APPLICATIONS OF DEMAND AND SUPPLY
The Concept of Elasticity

We might as reasonably dispute whether it is the upper or the under blade of a pair of scissors that cuts a piece of paper, as whether the value is governed by utility [demand] or cost of production [supply].

ALFRED MARSHALL
PRINCIPLES OF ECONOMICS

Suppose that you are the manager of Fenway Park, the home of the Boston Red Sox. You have been selling tickets for $8 each, but because of the huge salaries you are paying two star players, you are losing money. The owners who hired you may be millionaires, but they want something done to stop the losses. Specifically, they suggest that you raise the price of tickets to $10. This suggestion bothers you, particularly when it leaks out to the newspapers. Not only do sportswriters denounce the "greed" of the owners. They also argue that higher prices will backfire, causing fans to stay away in droves. As a consequence, total revenue from ticket sales will fall—or so say the sportswriters.

Who is right—the owners or the sportswriters? You cannot be sure. The answer depends on what happens to ticket sales when prices rise. If many people do stay away, your revenues will indeed fall. On the other hand, if people keep coming regardless of the higher price, your revenues will rise.

Thus, to answer the question, you must consider how *responsive* your sales are to a change in price. That is, you must consider the *price elasticity* of the demand for tickets.

This chapter will

- Explain the concept of price elasticity of demand.
- Show how total revenue depends on price elasticity.
- Explain the similar concept of price elasticity of supply.
- Show how elasticities are important for answering a wide variety of questions, such as
    - **(a)** Who bears the burden of a sales tax—the buyer or the seller?
    - **(b)** What happens to government revenues when a tax is increased?
    - **(c)** What are the effects of rent control?
- Explain a number of other elasticity concepts, such as income elasticity.

THE PRICE ELASTICITY OF DEMAND

The **price elasticity of demand**—sometimes known, more simply, as the *elasticity of demand*—measures how strongly buyers respond to a change in price. Specifically, the price elasticity of demand E_d is defined as

$$E_d = \frac{\text{percentage change in quantity demanded}}{\text{percentage change in price}} \qquad (6\text{-}1)$$

EXAMPLES

Some price increases cause a sharp reduction in purchases; others have little effect. For example, when the price of cars increases by 1%, car buyers respond strongly; they reduce their purchases about 2%. The price elasticity of demand for cars can therefore be calculated as

$$\frac{-2\%}{1\%} = -2$$

On the other hand, when the price of gasoline goes up by 1%, buyers respond much more weakly. Most drivers stay on the road, and their purchases of gasoline fall only a little—about 0.2% during the first few months. (Over a period of years, they respond somewhat more strongly, since they gradually replace their cars with more fuel-efficient models.) Thus the short-run price elasticity of demand for gasoline can be calculated as

$$\frac{-0.2\%}{1\%} = -0.2$$

Buyers of cars thus respond more strongly to a change in price than do buyers of gasoline.

Dropping the Minus Sign. To avoid confusion when comparing elasticities, economists sometimes drop the negative sign and report only the *absolute value* of elasticity. When they do so, they can state unambiguously that the elasticity of demand for cars (2.0) is higher than the elasticity of demand for gasoline (0.2). Note how awkward it is to make a comparison when the negative signs are retained: is –2.0 higher or lower than –0.2?

For simplicity, and to avoid confusion, we will drop the minus signs in the elasticity measurements presented in the following section. There is not much cost in doing so. Price elasticities of demand are always negative; when the price changes, the quantity demanded moves in the opposite direction. Thus the elasticity formula (6-1) always gives a negative number. We should remember that the price elasticity of demand is negative, whether or not the minus sign is reported.

Elastic and Inelastic Demand. Demand curves may be divided into three categories, depending on the absolute value of the elasticity:

If $|E_d| > 1$, the demand curve is ***elastic.*** The percentage change in quantity demanded is greater than the percentage change in price.

If $|E_d| < 1$, the demand curve is ***inelastic.*** The percentage change in quantity demanded is less than the percentage change in price.

If $|E_d| = 1$, the demand curve has ***unitary elasticity.*** The percentage change in quantity demanded equals the percentage change in price.

The two vertical lines | | mean absolute value; that is, the negative sign is dropped.

CALCULATING ELASTICITY

Note that elasticity is defined in terms of *percentage* changes, not changes in the number of units. If we simply used the number of units, our calculation would be arbitrarily affected by the unit chosen. For example, the change from \$2 to \$4 is two units, if prices are measured in dollars. But measured in cents, the same change from \$2 to \$4 is 200 units. Similarly, the change in quantity would depend on whether we were measuring in bushels or tons. By using percentages, we avoid such problems. A change from \$2 to \$4 represents the same percentage, whether we measure in dollars or cents.

The Beginning-point Problem. An annoying problem remains. A change from \$2 to \$4 can be considered either 100% (if we start from \$2 and double it to \$4) or 50% (if we begin at \$4 and cut it in half, to \$2). This means that, if we calculate elasticity in a simple way, our results depend on which point we start from. For example, consider demand between points *A* and *B* in Figure 6-1, where

	Quantity	*Price*
A	40	\$4
B	60	\$2

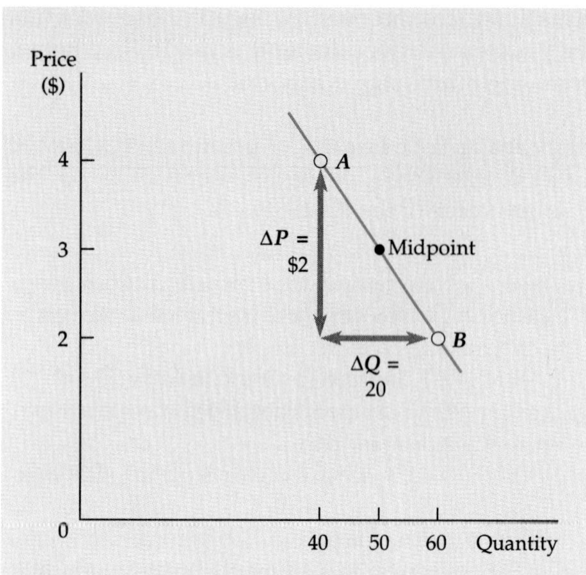

FIGURE 6-1 Elasticity of demand: The midpoint calculation.

Suppose we want to calculate the elasticity of the demand curve between *A* and *B*. If we start from *A* and use this as the basis for calculation, we find an elasticity of 1.00. Alternatively, if we start from *B*, we calculate an elasticity of 0.33.

Our measurement of elasticity should *not* depend on the starting point. This problem can be solved by avoiding either end and by using the middle point instead. This gives an elasticity of 0.60, as calculated in the text.

If we begin at point *A* and move to *B*, quantity *Q* increases by 50% (from 40 to 60), whereas price *P* falls by 50% (from $4 to $2). This gives the following calculation:

$$E_d = \frac{\text{percentage change in } Q}{\text{percentage change in } P} = \frac{50\%}{50\%} = 1$$

If we begin at *B*, however, we calculate the decrease in quantity at 33.3% (from 60 to 40), while price increases by 100% (from $2 to $4). This gives us

$$E_d = \frac{33.3\%}{100\%} = 0.333$$

This result is unsatisfactory; the measure of elasticity between *A* and *B* should not depend on the starting point.

The most straightforward solution to this problem is to avoid either end of the demand curve and use the *average* or *middle point* instead.[1] In the **midpoint formula** for elasticity, we use the *average* quantity and *average* price:

$$E_d = \frac{\Delta Q, \text{ as \% of the average of the two quantities}}{\Delta P, \text{ as \% of the average of the two prices}} \qquad (6\text{-}2)$$

where the Greek letter Δ means "change in."

For the section of the demand curve between *A* and *B* in Figure 6-1, the change in quantity = 20 and the average quantity = 50 [that is, (40 + 60)/2]; thus, the numerator is 40% [that is, (20/50) × 100%]. The change in price = $2 and the average price = $3 [that is, ($4 + $2)/2]; thus, the denominator is 66.7% [that is, ($2/$3) × 100%]. Applying the midpoint formula, we get:

$$E_d = \frac{40\%}{66.7\%} = 0.60$$

The Elasticity of Demand: What Happens to Total Revenue? To see why the concept of elasticity is important, consider two examples—one from agriculture and another from manufacturing.

There isn't a farmer in the country who complains when he has a good crop. But the more thoughtful ones may be concerned if everyone else has a good crop, too. The reason is simple: When a bumper crop is thrown on the market, the price falls, and that can hurt farmers more than they gain from the increase in quantity. Paradoxically, farmers may receive less revenue from a large crop than

[1]An alternative solution is to look at short segments of the demand curve, in which case the starting point becomes unimportant. The percentage difference between $2.00 and $2.01 is about the same, regardless of which of these prices is used as the base.

Students who have taken calculus will recognize that this method can be taken to the limit, where the length approaches zero. When this is done, elasticity can be measured at a *point* on the demand curve. One reason why economists use calculus is to avoid irksome difficulties such as the beginning-point problem.

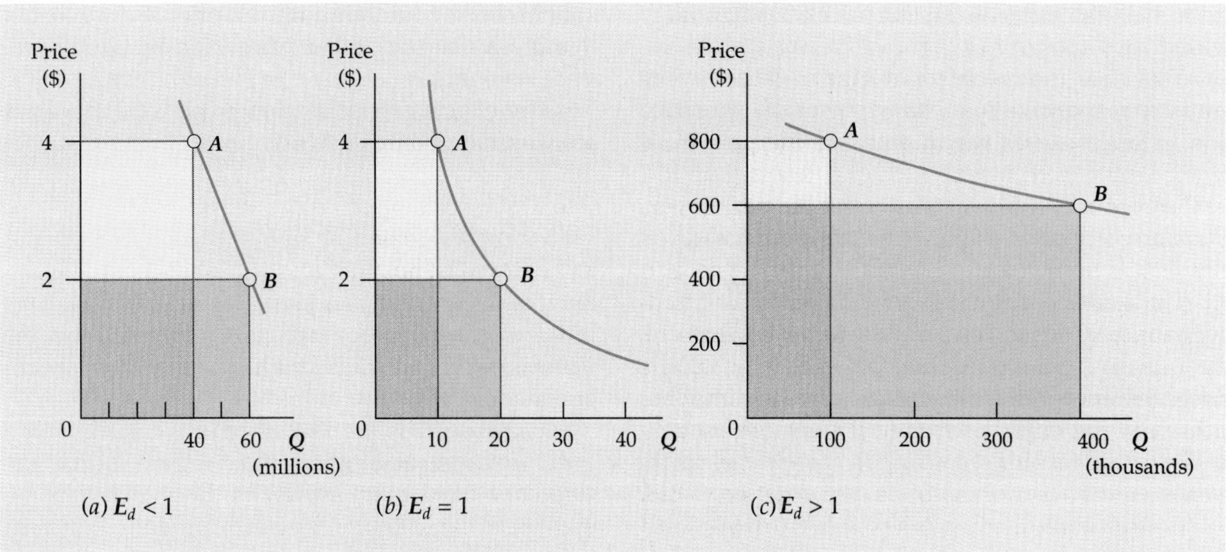

FIGURE 6-2 Elasticity of demand and total revenue.

The elasticity of demand falls into three categories, depending on what happens to the total revenue of sellers. If a fall in price causes a fall in total revenue, demand is inelastic (left panel). If a fall in price causes a rise in total revenue, quantity is responding strongly; the demand is elastic (right panel). If the increase in quantity is barely sufficient to compensate for the lower price, total revenue is constant and elasticity of demand is one (center panel).

a small one. Although each individual farmer has an incentive to "make hay while the sun shines," farmers as a whole may be worse off if the crop is large.

This possibility is illustrated in panel *a* of Figure 6-2. In this hypothetical example, the initial position is *A*. Farmers sell 40 million bushels at a price of $4. This gives them total revenue of $160 million—that is, the price of $4 times the quantity of 40 million. This total revenue is illustrated by the size of the yellow plus green rectangle below and to the left of point *A*. The base of this rectangle measures quantity *Q*, whereas the height measures price *P*. Thus the area of the rectangle—its base *Q* times its height *P*—is a measure of the **total revenue,** $P \times Q$.

Total revenue is measured by the $P \times Q$ rectangle below and to the left of a point on the demand curve.

Now suppose that, with a bumper crop of 60 million bushels, the price collapses all the way to $2. The new total revenue is the $P \times Q$ rectangle below and to the left of point *B*: $2 × 60 million = $120 million. In this illustration, the total revenue of farmers falls from $160 million to $120 million when they produce more. The increase in quantity is too small to compensate farmers for the lower price.

In this case, demand is *inelastic*—that is, the absolute value of the elasticity is less than 1. (This is the same demand as shown in Figure 6-1. As already noted, its elasticity is 0.6 in the range between *A* and *B*.)

The second example is taken from the early history of the automobile. At the beginning of the twentieth century, the automobile was a plaything of the rich. Henry Ford was determined to change this situation. He mass-produced his model T and cut prices, gambling that the increase in sales would more than compensate for the lower price. He was right. As he cut prices, his revenues soared.

This case is illustrated in Figure 6-2*c*. Buyers are very responsive to a change in price. A reduction in price causes the quantity to increase by a much larger percentage, with the result that the total revenue rectangle ($P \times Q$) becomes larger. Demand is *elastic*—that is, the absolute value of elasticity is more than 1.

The center panel of Figure 6-2 shows the intermediate, borderline case in which the increase in the quantity demanded just balances the fall in price. Whenever the price falls, the quantity increases by the same percentage. This is just enough to leave total revenue constant. In this case, elasticity is 1.

In each case, as consumers move down along the demand curve, two conflicting forces are working on total revenue:

1. The increase in quantity works to increase revenue.

2. The fall in price works to depress revenue.

If demand is elastic, the percentage increase in quantity is greater than the percentage fall in price. Thus the increase in quantity more than compensates for the fall in price, and total revenue increases.

If demand is inelastic, the percentage increase in quantity is less than the percentage fall in price. The fall in price overwhelms the effect of the increasing quantity, and total revenue falls.

If demand has an elasticity of 1, quantity and price change by the same percentage. They just offset one another; total revenue does not change.

Elasticity, then, helps to explain the Fenway Park puzzle with which the chapter opened. The owner assumed that the demand was inelastic and that a rise in price would increase revenues. The sportswriters were arguing the opposite—that demand was elastic and a price increase would reduce revenues.

The effects of a price change on total revenues are summarized in Table 6-1.

ELASTICITY AND SLOPE

In Figure 6-2, the most elastic demand curve (panel *c*), is flatter than the least elastic (panel *a*). This raises a question: Can we judge elasticity by the flatness of the curve? Is "high elasticity" just another way of saying "low slope"?

The answer is *no*. The slope of a curve is not a good measure of elasticity. The reason is that the slope of a curve is measured by the *absolute* change in price divided by the *absolute* change in quantity. In contrast, *percentage* changes are used to measure elasticity.

Two specific examples in Figure 6-3 demonstrate why flatness and elasticity are not the same. Panel *a* shows a demand curve with a constant total revenue of $50 at every point. As already noted, this curve has a constant elasticity of 1 throughout its range. But it does not have a constant slope; it becomes flatter as quantity increases.

The second example is a straight-line demand (Fig. 6-3*b*). It has a constant slope, but its elasticity changes, becoming lower as we move down along it. The calculations in Table 6-2 show that elasticity is 2 in the range between *A* and *B*, whereas elasticity is only 0.5 in the range between *B* and *C*.[2]

[2]If you have trouble remembering that elasticity falls as we move downward to the right along a straight-line demand, here's a tip. As we move to the right and *Q* becomes larger, any specific increase in *Q* represents a smaller and smaller *percentage* increase. Thus, the elasticity gets smaller and smaller.

TABLE 6-1 Elasticity and Total Revenue

If demand is	*That is*	*This means that*	*Therefore, when price falls, total revenue:*
elastic	$\lvert E_d \rvert > 1$	% change in Q > % change in P	rises
of unitary elasticity	$\lvert E_d \rvert = 1$	% change in Q = % change in P	doesn't change
inelastic	$\lvert E_d \rvert < 1$	% change in Q < % change in P	falls

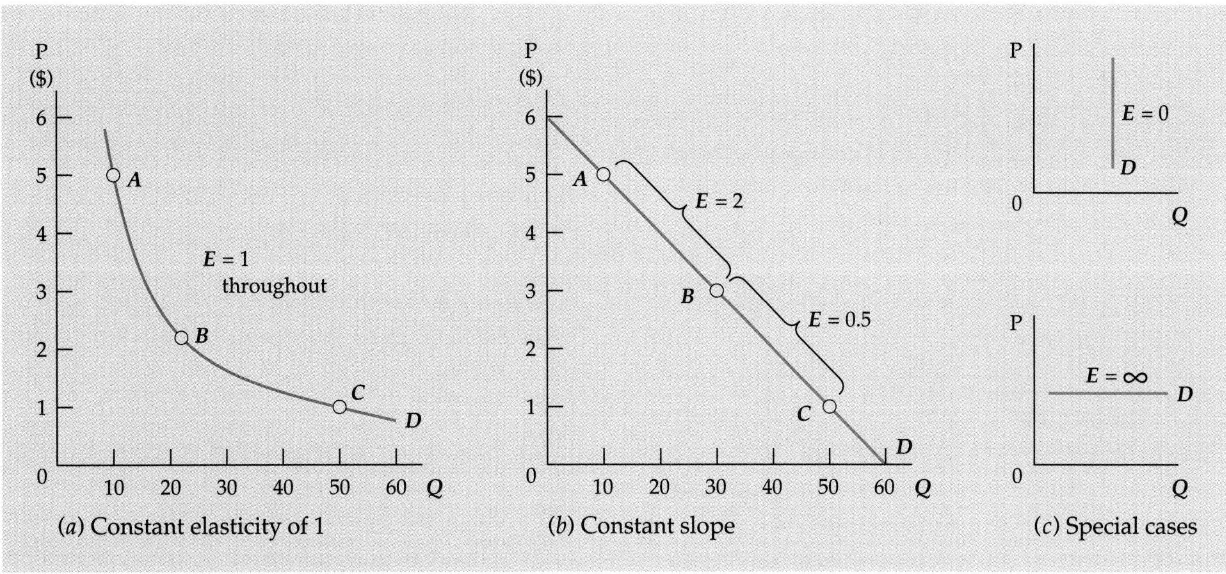

FIGURE 6-3 Elasticity and flatness are not the same.
The curve on the left has a constant elasticity of 1 throughout. But it consistently gets flatter as we move to the right. The straight-line demand in panel *b* has a changing elasticity, in spite of its constant slope. Two special cases are shown in panel *c:* a vertical demand curve, with an elasticity of zero; and a horizontal demand curve, with an infinite elasticity.

Thus constant slope does not mean constant elasticity, nor does constant elasticity mean constant slope.

All is not lost, however. There is one generalization we can make about slope and elasticity. If we compare two demand curves *that pass through the same point,* then the flatter one is more elastic. For example, point *A* is in exactly the same position in the first two panels of Figure 6-3. In each case, $P = \$5$ and $Q = 10$. At this point, the demand curve in panel *b* is flatter than the demand curve in panel *a*, and it also has a higher elasticity.

Finally, panel *c* of Figure 6-3 shows two extreme cases:

1. If demand is *vertical,* quantity is completely unresponsive to a change in price. No matter what happens to price, the change in quantity is zero.

TABLE 6-2 Calculating Price Elasticity along a Straight-line Demand (using midpoint formula)

Fig. 6-3b, Point:	*(1)* Q	*(2)* ΔQ	*(3)* *Average Q*	*(4)* $\frac{\Delta Q}{Q}$ *(4) = (2) ÷ (3)*	*(5)* P	*(6)* $\lvert\Delta P\rvert$	*(7)* *Average P*	*(8)* $\frac{\lvert\Delta P\rvert}{P}$ *(8) = (6) ÷ (7)*	*(9)* *∣Elasticity∣* *(9) = (4) ÷ (8)*
A	10				$5				
		20	20	1.0		$2	$4	0.5	2
B	30				$3				
		20	40	0.5		$2	$2	1.0	0.5
C	50				$1				

Thus the numerator in the elasticity formula is zero, and elasticity is therefore zero.

2. The other extreme is a *horizontal* demand. In this case, price does not change. Thus, the denominator of the elasticity formula is zero, and elasticity is *infinite.* This horizontal demand is spoken of as being *infinitely elastic* or *perfectly elastic.*

WHAT DETERMINES ELASTICITY OF DEMAND?

Why is the demand for some products highly elastic, while the demand for others is inelastic?

1. *Substitutability.* Items that have good substitutes generally have a more elastic demand than those that do not. For example, sugar has reasonably close substitutes, such as corn syrup or honey. In contrast, salt does not have such good substitutes. The elasticity of demand is higher for sugar than for salt. In particular, manufacturers of soft drinks shift from sugar to corn syrup when the price of sugar rises.

Because of the importance of substitutes, the elasticity of demand is lower for a product if we define it broadly than if we define it narrowly. For example, the elasticity of demand for Chevrolet cars is high, because Fords, Chryslers, and Toyotas are very good substitutes. However, the demand for all cars as a group is much lower, because there is no close substitute for the automobile. Similarly, the demand for beef is much more elastic than the demand for all food (Table 6-3). Chicken and pork are reasonably good substitutes for beef, but there is no substitute for food as a whole.

2. *Necessities Versus Luxuries.* Essentials such as food generally have an inelastic demand because purchasers feel they can scarcely do without them. Note the problem faced by farmers. They produce something—food—that is essential for survival. Therefore its elasticity of demand is low, and farmers can accordingly be penalized with lower revenues when they produce a bumper crop.

Luxuries generally have a more elastic demand. For example, luxuries such as foreign vacations have an elastic demand because purchasers can stop buying them if their prices rise. When the value of the dollar soared in terms of other currencies in the mid-1980s, foreign travel became cheap and Americans flocked abroad.

TABLE 6-3 Estimated Price Elasticities of Demand in the United States

Elasticity very low (below 0.5)
Salt
Coffee
Gasoline (in the short run)
All food (taken as a single good)
Elasticity low (0.5 to 0.8)
Gasoline (in the long run)
Cigarettes
Elasticity about 1
Beef
Housing
China and tableware
Elasticity high (1.2 to 2.0)
Furniture
Electricity
Elasticity very high (above 2.0)
Millinery
Foreign travel

Source: A number of studies, including H. S. Houthakker and Lester D. Taylor, *Consumer Demand in the United States* (Cambridge, Mass.: Harvard University Press, 1966).

3. *Percentage of Income.* Big items in a budget generally have a more elastic demand than small items. To cite an extreme example, the demand for houses is more elastic than the demand for toothpicks. Purchasers may spend a week trying to negotiate a price reduction of 1% on a new house. But they won't even notice a 20% drop in the price of toothpicks. Thus, for small items, consumers are insensitive to price.

4. *Time.* The elasticity of demand generally increases with time. One example has already been cited near the beginning of the chapter. If the price of gasoline rises, there is very little immediate effect on the quantity that people buy. The typical car may be driven less, but not much less; most drivers are not going to stay off the road just to save gasoline. It takes some time for drivers to switch to smaller cars, and longer yet for the auto companies to design and build more fuel-efficient models. But when they do, the public's purchases of gasoline are further reduced. Thus, quantity responds more in the long run than in the short.

There can be exceptions to this general rule, particularly for durable goods such as cars. Suppose the price of cars rises. In this case, the quantity demanded may fall sharply and quickly. The reason is that most drivers can keep their old cars longer; they can stay out of the market for a while when the price rises. However, as time passes, the old cars wear out, and drivers feel compelled to buy replacements. Thus the demand for cars is less elastic over a period of one or two years than it is over a very short period of a month or two.

THE PRICE ELASTICITY OF SUPPLY

Just as elasticity of demand describes the responsiveness of buyers to a change in price, so elasticity of supply describes the responsiveness of sellers. The **price elasticity of supply, E_S,** is defined as

$$E_S = \frac{\text{percentage change in quantity supplied}}{\text{percentage change in price}} \qquad (6\text{-}3)$$

Supply is elastic if producers respond strongly to price changes, or inelastic if they respond relatively weakly. Specifically:

If $E_S > 1$, the supply curve is ***elastic.*** The percentage change in quantity supplied is greater than the percentage change in price.

If $E_S = 1$, the supply curve has ***unitary elasticity.*** The percentage change in quantity supplied equals the percentage change in price.

If $E_S < 1$, the supply curve is ***inelastic.*** The percentage change in quantity supplied is less than the percentage change in price.

Note that, as the price increases, so does the quantity that suppliers offer for sale. Thus, total revenue ($P \times Q$) goes up, whether or not the supply curve is elastic. Elasticity of supply is therefore quite unlike elasticity of demand in an important respect. We cannot tell whether supply is elastic by investigating whether total revenue increases in response to a change in price.

There is, however, a simple way to determine whether supply is elastic. If supply has an elasticity of 1, quantity increases by the same percentage or fraction as does price. Thus the supply curve traces out a straight line from the origin, as illustrated in Figure 6-4*b*. (Note that the slope does not have to

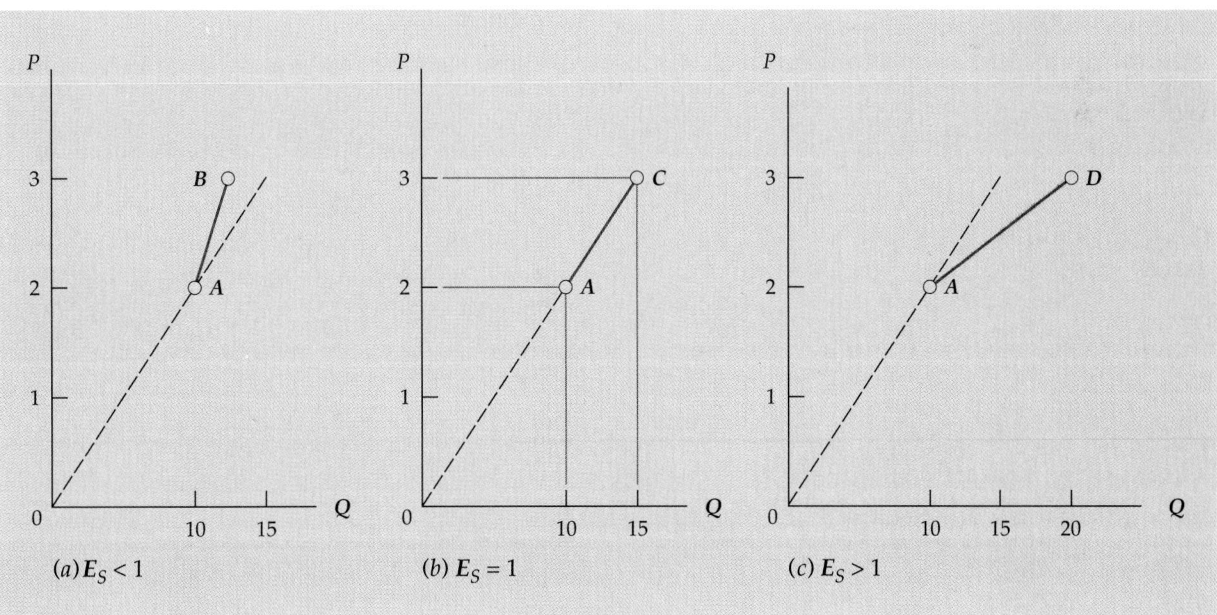

FIGURE 6-4 Elasticity of supply.

In the center panel, a supply curve with an elasticity of 1 is a straight line going through the origin. An increase of 50% in price causes the same 50% increase in the quantity supplied. If the response of quantity is stronger, elasticity is greater than 1 (right panel). If the response is weaker, elasticity is less than 1 (left panel).

be 45°; *any* straight line from the origin has an elasticity of 1.) If supply is steeper than a straight line through the origin, then quantity changes by a smaller percentage than price; supply is inelastic (panel *a*). On the other hand, if supply is flatter than a line through the origin, it is elastic (panel *c*). Thus, to tell if supply is elastic, we can use a simple test: draw a straight line through the origin to the supply curve. Is the supply curve flatter than this straight line? If so, it is elastic.

WHAT DETERMINES ELASTICITY OF SUPPLY?

Several things influence elasticity of supply.

1. *Time.* When the price of a good increases, producers may want to sell a lot more, but they may have to expand their capacity to do so. This may take time. Thus quantity may respond more strongly, and elasticity accordingly may be higher, as time passes.

This idea was emphasized almost a century ago by Alfred Marshall, Cambridge University's great economist and teacher. Marshall distinguished three time periods:

(a) The *momentary* or *immediate* effect, before producers have had a chance to respond at all.

(b) The *short-run* effect, when firms can increase output, using their existing plant and equipment.

(c) The *long-run* effect, after existing firms have been able to add new capacity, and new firms have been able to enter.

Marshall applied this distinction to the market for fresh fish. Suppose demand suddenly rises from D_1 to D_2 in Figure 6-5*a*. On the first day, the quantity supplied is not influenced at all by price. Whatever has been caught (Q_1) is put on the market, regardless of price. The immediate supply S is completely inelastic, and the shift in demand causes a sharp rise in price to P_2.

In the days that follow, the higher price induces fishing boat captains to increase the size of their crews and to fish somewhat longer hours. The quantity of fish caught and offered for sale increases. Thus supply becomes more elastic in panel *b*, and price settles down somewhat to P_3. But this is not the long-run equilibrium. As more time passes, new boats can be built and even more fish caught. In the long run, then, supply is even more elastic, as shown in panel *c*. The result is a further moderation of price, to P_4.

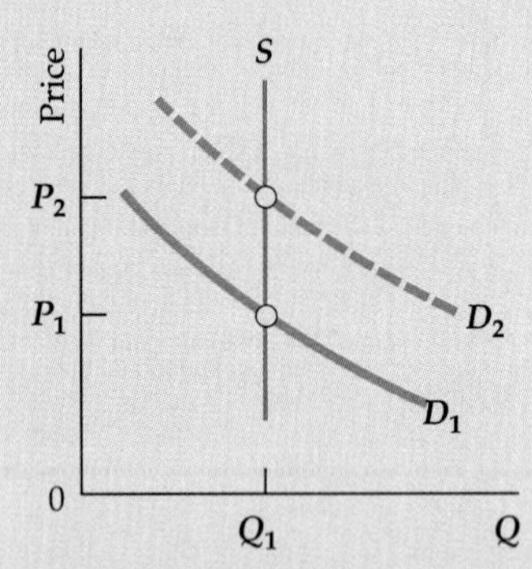

(*a*) **Immediate effect.**
On the first day, supply is completely inelastic. Thus, the shift in demand from D_1 to D_2 results in a very large price increase, to P_2.

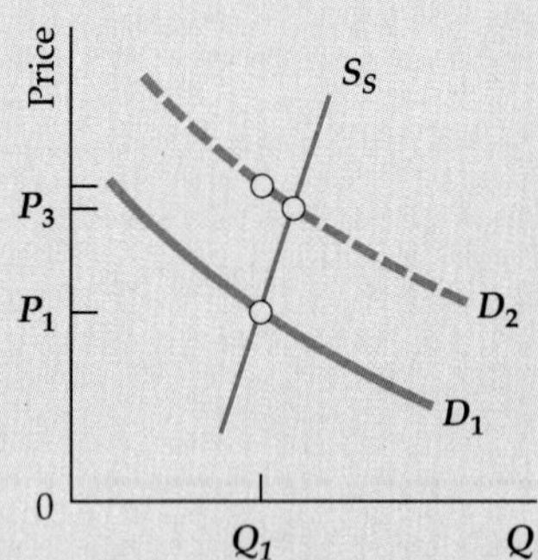

(*b*) **Short-run effect.**
Supply now has some elasticity, since the catch of fish can be increased by hiring larger crews and using existing boats more heavily. Thus, the price rise is moderated to P_3.

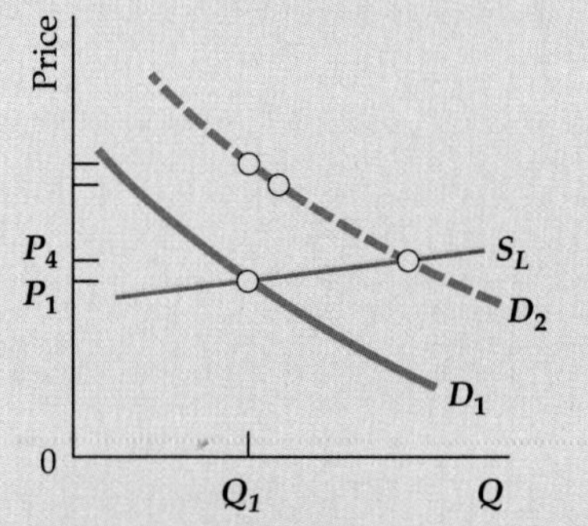

(*c*) **Long-run effect.**
Supply now has even greater elasticity, since there is now time for new boats to be built. As a result, more fish are sold and the price settles down further to P_4.

FIGURE 6-5 How the elasticity of supply changes over time.

2. *Substitutes or Complements in Production.* Does an item have a close *substitute in production?* That is, can the labor, land, and equipment used to produce it be readily switched into the production of another good? If so, quantity will generally respond strongly to price, and the elasticity of supply will be high. Thus the elasticity of supply is greater for an individual grain—such as rye—than for all grains taken together. The reason is that, in the face of a fall in the price of rye, a farmer is able to reduce the quantity grown by shifting production into a substitute grain like wheat or barley. This ability of producers to respond to a change in price works to make the supply of rye elastic.

On the other hand, if the price of all grain falls, a farmer will have much more difficulty shifting out of grain production because there are no close substitute activities. It would be very expensive to move into a less closely related activity, such as dairy farming, because of the high costs of new capital equipment. Because farmers are less able to respond, the elasticity of supply is smaller for all grains as a group than it is for a single grain. In short, products like rye with a close substitute in production have a more elastic supply than goods without a close substitute.

In contrast with substitutes—such as rye and wheat—other goods may be *complements in production,* or *joint products.* When you produce one, you get the other—for example, beef and hides. Most of the value of a steer is in the meat and relatively little in the hide. Therefore, the decision to butcher a steer is strongly influenced by the price of beef, but very little by the price of hides. Once the steer has been butchered, the relatively unimportant hide will be sold regardless of the price. In other words, the supply of hides is inelastic because hides are a relatively unimportant joint product.

3. *The Feasibility and Cost of Storage.* Goods that rot quickly must be put on the market regardless of price; their elasticity of supply is low. In Marshall's day, when refrigeration was inadequate, it was not feasible to store fish from day to day. This made his example particularly striking. Today, with better and cheaper refrigeration, the elasticity of the fish supply is not zero even for a single day. In the face of a collapse in price, suppliers have the option of withdrawing some of their catch and putting the extra fish on ice for a day or two.

SIGNIFICANCE OF ELASTICITY

A number of examples will illustrate just how much the concept of elasticity can enrich demand-and-supply analysis.

INCIDENCE OF A TAX: WHO PAYS?

Governments collect **excise taxes** on a number of specific products, such as gasoline, cigarettes, and alcoholic beverages. When the government imposes a tax of, say, $1, we might guess that the tax will simply be passed along to the buyer, who will pay $1 more. However, this is not generally the case. The question of **incidence**—who actually pays—is one of the more interesting and important tax questions for governments, whether at the federal, state, or local level.

> An ***excise tax*** is a tax on a specific product, such as gasoline or cigarettes.
>
> The ***incidence of a tax*** is the division of the burden. Who actually pays the tax?

To shed light on this question, consider the supply and demand for a good shown in Figure 6-6*a*. The initial equilibrium before the tax is at E_1, with 6 million units sold at a price of $2. Suppose now that the government imposes a tax of $1 per unit, which it collects from sellers. Who actually bears the burden of this tax?

The effect of the tax is to shift the supply curve upward by the full $1, from S_1 to S_2. To see why, consider any point on the supply curve—say, 8 million units. Point *A* on the supply curve S_1 shows that, before the tax, sellers would not offer these 8 million units for sale unless they received $2.50 per unit. This means that *after* the tax, they will not be willing to offer 8 million units unless they receive $3.50, at point *B*—enough to pay the government the $1 tax and still have the same $2.50 left. Thus point *B* is on the new, after-tax supply curve S_2. No matter what point we consider on S_1, the corresponding point on S_2 is $1 higher. The entire supply curve therefore shifts upward by the amount of the tax. But this does not necessarily mean that the equilibrium price will increase by $1.

On the contrary, observe what happens when

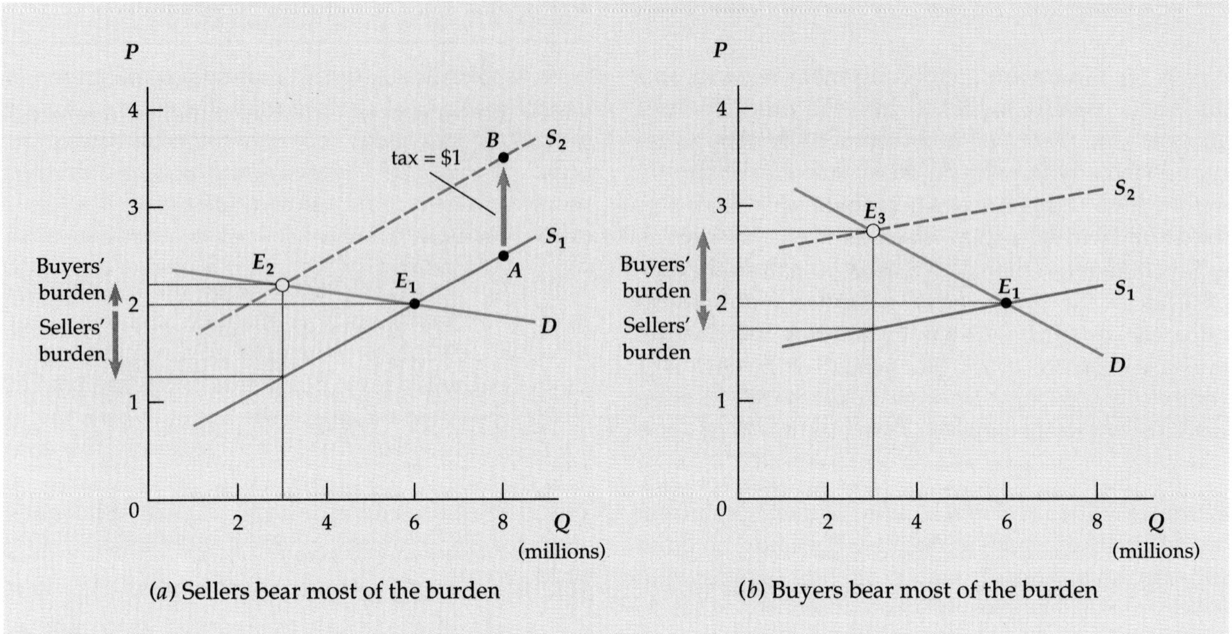

FIGURE 6-6 Elasticity and the incidence of a tax.
If the demand curve is more elastic than the supply curve, then sellers bear more of the tax burden than buyers, as shown in the left panel. But if the demand curve is less elastic than supply, buyers will be stuck with the greater burden—as illustrated in the right panel.

the \$1 tax is imposed in Figure 6-6*a*. The upward shift of the supply curve causes the equilibrium to move from E_1 to E_2. The price that consumers pay goes up 25¢, from \$2.00 to \$2.25. Thus, consumers bear only 25¢ of the burden of the tax. Sellers bear the remaining 75¢. It is true that their selling price rises by 25¢, from \$2.00 to \$2.25. But \$1.00 of this total must go to the government, so sellers get only \$1.25 after tax—or 75¢ less than the \$2.00 they originally got in the no-tax situation at E_1. The two arrows along the vertical axis illustrate how the \$1 tax is split up into the 25¢ burden on buyers and the 75¢ burden on sellers.

Buyers bear a smaller share of the burden in this case because they are more responsive to changes in price than are sellers. Demand is more elastic than supply. However, in panel *b* the reverse is true. Here, sellers are more responsive to a change in price; supply is more elastic than demand. As a result, sellers bear the lighter burden; most of the tax is *shifted forward* to the buyer.

These conclusions can best be understood if we think of two groups in a market—one buying and the other selling. Suppose one group—it doesn't matter which—takes the view: "We aren't keen to stay in the market. If the price moves against us, we can back away. In responding to price changes, we're flexible, sensitive, *elastic*." Suppose the other group feels: "We have no choice; we must stay in the market. Even if price moves against us, we can't back away. We're inflexible, unresponsive, *inelastic*." Not surprisingly, this second group will bear most of the burden of a tax and, in other situations as well, will be in the more vulnerable position.

ELASTICITY AND TAX REVENUE

Elasticity not only determines who bears the burden of a tax, but also affects the amount of revenue the government collects.

When the federal government increases the tax on gasoline, drivers have little choice but to pay. Their only alternative is to drive less. But suppose

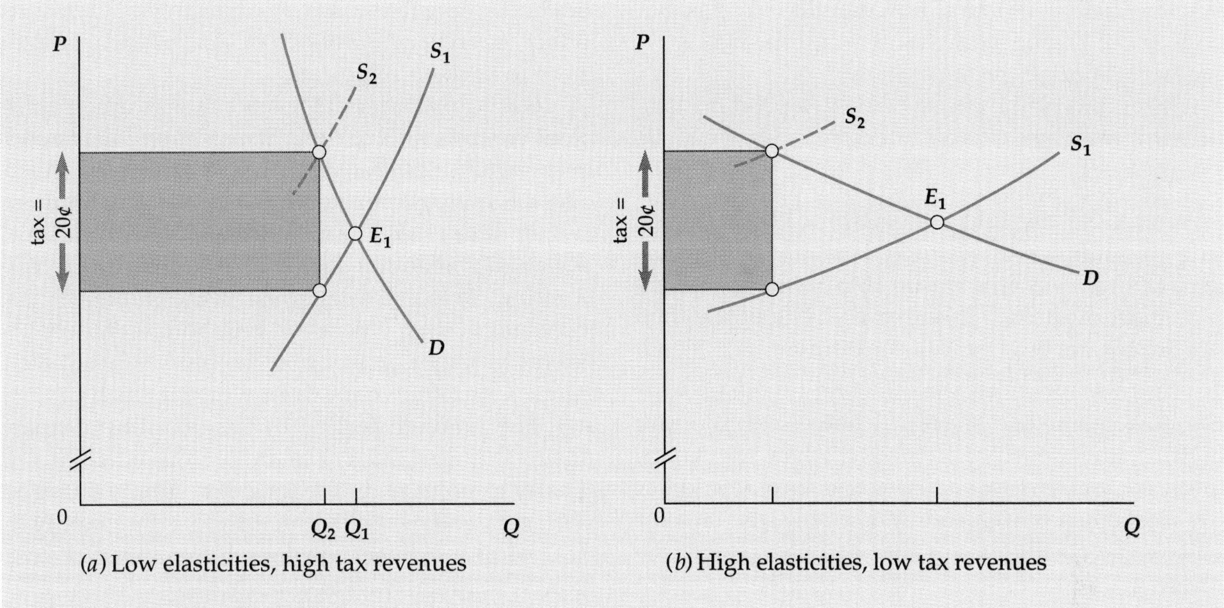

FIGURE 6-7 Tax collections depend on elasticities.

(*a*) In the United States
For the whole United States, elasticities of demand and supply of gasoline are low. A tax therefore causes a relatively small change in quantity.

(*b*) In D.C.
For D.C. or a small state, elasticities of demand and supply are much larger. If D.C. alone increases its gasoline tax, quantities may fall sharply, and tax revenues as a result may be disappointing.

that the District of Columbia (D.C.) increases the gasoline tax. Unless Maryland and Virginia follow suit, most motorists do have an alternative. They can avoid the higher D.C. tax by filling up in the neighboring states. The elasticity of demand for gasoline in the United States as a whole is low. But in D.C. it is high, because gasoline bought in Maryland or Virginia is a close substitute.

Figure 6-7 shows why this is important. Panel *a* illustrates what happens when the federal government imposes a tax of, say, 20¢ a gallon. Both demand and supply are quite inelastic. In the face of the tax, quantity falls only a little, and government revenues are high. (Revenues are equal to the shaded area, which is the quantity Q_2 sold times the tax of 20¢.)

When the D.C. government imposes a tax, however, the quantity sold in D.C. may decrease sharply because both demand and supply are highly elastic, as illustrated in panel *b*. Demand for D.C. gas is very elastic because drivers can buy gas in neighboring states. Supply elasticity is also high because sellers can close down their D.C. stations and set up operations just across the border in Maryland or Virginia. The result is that the government's tax revenues may be quite disappointing, as illustrated by the small shaded area in Figure 6-7*b*.

In fact, when the D.C. government raised the tax on gasoline from 10¢ to 18¢ several years ago, they learned how high elasticities could be. Gas sales fell sharply, and revenues were much lower than predicted. Within a few months, ten gas stations in the District closed down, and the D.C. government repealed the tax increase.

In summary, the effects of a tax depend on elasticity in two ways:

1. The *incidence of a tax* depends on the *relative* elasticities of demand and supply. Those on the side with the lower elasticity bear the larger burden. If supply is less elastic than demand, sellers bear most of the tax. If demand is less elastic than supply, buyers bear most of the burden.

2. The *revenues* from a tax depend on the elasticities of demand and supply. If both elasticities are high, quantity will fall sharply when the tax is imposed, and this will depress revenues. The lower the elasticities of demand and supply, the smaller will be the decline in quantity and the greater the revenue.

Consequently, when governments tax individual products, they generally pick items with low elasticities of demand, such as cigarettes and alcoholic beverages. (Low elasticities are only one reason to pick cigarettes and alcohol. Legislators generally face less political opposition when they raise such "sin taxes.")

Elasticities are also the key to understanding the effects of many other policies. Consider, for example, the effects of rent control laws.

RENT CONTROL

A number of cities—such as Paris, Vienna, and New York—have extensive experience with rent controls. Controls are popular with tenants, who want affordable housing. But like many other quick fixes, their long-term effects can be unpleasant. To understand why, we will use the distinction between the inelastic short-run supply and the much more elastic long-run supply.

Figure 6-8*a* illustrates what happens when rent control is imposed. The maximum rent that owners can legally charge is set at R_1, below the equilibrium rent R_E. In the short run, the number of apartments is approximately fixed, as shown by short-run supply S_S. At the low controlled rent R_1, there is a shortage of *AB* units, and it is difficult to find an apartment. When a renter moves out, there is a scramble to get the vacant apartment. This basic effect of rent control—that apartments become hard to find—is important.

Even greater shortages develop as time passes. Rent controls reduce the construction of new apartment buildings because they reduce the rental income owners can hope to receive. Furthermore, owners may let their buildings deteriorate and eventually abandon them. The results can be devastating. Swedish economist Assar Lindbeck has concluded that, "next to bombing, rent control seems in many cases to be the most efficient technique so far known for destroying cities."[3]

The gradual decline in the quantity of apartments is illustrated by the move from *B* to *F*, *G*, and finally to point *H* on the long-run supply curve S_L. This curve shows the ultimate effect on quantity (at *H*) after apartment owners have adjusted completely to the new level of rents (R_1).

In the short run, most tenants benefit from the controls. They pay a lower price, and they get almost the same amount of housing at *B* as at the free-market equilibrium *E*. Over the long run, however, it is doubtful that renters benefit on average. While they still pay a lower price, they have less housing at *H* than at *E*. It is exceedingly difficult for newcomers to find a place to live.

Once the problems are recognized, it may already be too late to eliminate rent controls without severe pain. Just as the major gains to tenants come in the first few years of rent control, so the major penalties to tenants come in the first few years of decontrol, for reasons shown in Figure 6-8*b*. Once point *H* has been reached, the stock of housing has been reduced. There is a new short-run supply curve (S_2), which reflects the new, smaller stock of housing. If rent control is suddenly ended, even a sizable increase in price will not cause much increase in the number of apartments in the short run. That is, the short-run supply is inelastic because new buildings cannot be constructed quickly. Thus a sudden abolition of controls can lead to a very sharp jump in rents. In fact, rents can jump all the way up to R_2 (point *K*), far

[3]Assar Lindbeck, *The Political Economy of the New Left* (New York: Harper and Row, 1971), p. 39.

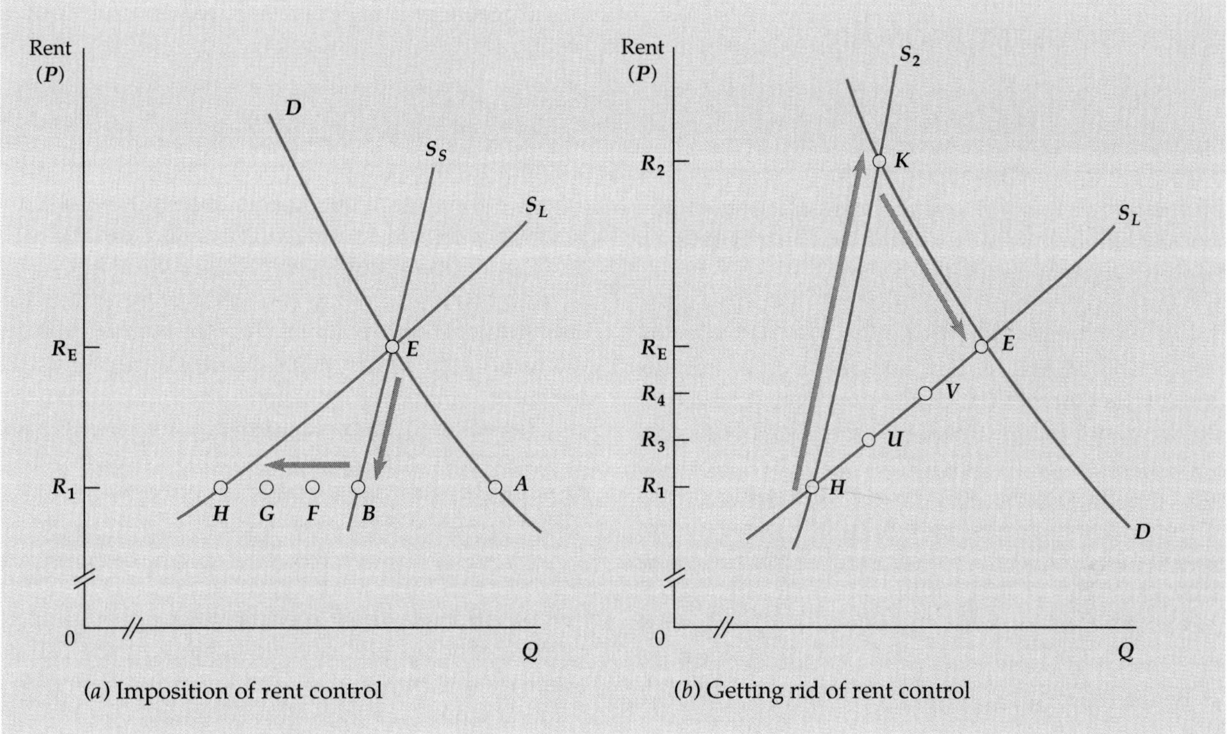

(*a*) Imposition of rent control

(*b*) Getting rid of rent control

FIGURE 6-8 Effects of rent control.

Panel *a* shows the effects of putting a ceiling of R_1 on rents. In the short run, there is a shortage of *AB*, and apartments are hard to find. As time passes, new construction declines and old buildings are abandoned. The shortage becomes more severe, eventually increasing to distance *AH*, with point *H* being on the long-run supply curve. Panel *b* shows what happens if rent controls are suddenly eliminated. Rents shoot up to R_2. It is only as new buildings are constructed that the rents subside to the long-run equilibrium *E*. (This figure builds on the distinction between short-run and long-run supply shown earlier in Fig. 6-5.)

above the initial free-market rent of R_E. Any politician who supports decontrol may have to face a group of enraged tenant voters. It is only as time passes, and new buildings are constructed, that rents move gradually back down from *K* toward the long-run equilibrium at *E*.

One way to avoid the worst of the adjustment problem is to remove controls gradually. By slowly increasing permissible rents, the jump to *K* can be avoided. If the rent ceiling is gradually increased from R_1 to R_E, the stock of housing will have time to increase. For example, if the rent ceiling is raised first to R_3, the stock of housing will gradually adjust to point *U* on the long-run supply curve. Then the ceiling can be raised to R_4, causing an increase in the housing stock to *V*. Finally, if the ceiling is raised to R_E, the housing stock will adjust to its long-run equilibrium at *E*. Controls can then be abolished without an upward jump in rents. A number of economists have suggested that rent controls be phased out in this gradual manner.[4]

[4]For example, Anthony Downs, *Rental Housing in the 1980s* (Washington, D.C.: Brookings Institution, 1983), p. 9. Downs recommends that the phasing out of controls be combined with rent subsidies for the poor.

LIVING IN A GLOBAL ECONOMY

THE ELASTICITY OF FOREIGN DEMAND FOR U.S. GOODS

In the late 1980s, financial analysts around the world held their breath: Would the roller coaster in foreign exchange markets continue?

In the early part of the decade, the price of the dollar had soared as foreigners rushed to buy cheap U.S. bonds, stocks, and real estate. For example, the price of the dollar rose from 220 yen in 1981 to more than 260 yen by early 1985. The soaring dollar made it difficult for American firms to sell abroad, because their goods were being priced out of world markets. In 1981, a U.S. good worth $100 sold for 22,000 yen; by early 1985, the same $100 item cost 26,000 yen in Japan (that is, 100 × 260 yen). U.S. exports stagnated, while imports soared. By 1985, the U.S. trade deficit—the excess of imports over exports—had shot up to $127 billion.

Then a sharp reversal took place in foreign exchange markets. The dollar began to move rapidly downward. By late 1987, it had slid below 125 yen—less than 50% of its peak in early 1985!

Consequently, U.S. goods became a bargain again. That same $100 product could now be sold in Japan for 12,500 yen. U.S. exports began to recover. But a question held the financial markets in suspense: Would U.S. exports recover fast enough to prevent further large U.S. trade deficits? How responsive would foreign demand be to cheaper U.S. goods? How elastic was the foreign demand for U.S. exports?

We noted earlier that elasticities are generally higher in the long run than in the short term. Nowhere is this principle more true than in international markets. It takes time to adjust to a change in price: foreigners may take time to become accustomed to U.S. products (low short-run elasticity of demand), and new distribution channels in foreign countries may be expensive and time consuming to establish (low short-run elasticity of supply). As a result, the upswing in U.S. exports was painfully slow in coming. The U.S. trade deficit in 1988 was $120 billion—only 5% less than in 1985.

Price elasticities are just as important in the world economy as they are within the United States.

OTHER ELASTICITY MEASURES

Prices play a strategic role in the market system, providing signals and incentives to buyers and sellers. In microeconomics, one of the central questions is how buyers respond to a change in price. The strength of their response is, of course, exactly what the price elasticity of demand is designed to measure.

Buyers also respond to other influences, such as income. To measure the strength of this response, economists also use an elasticity concept.

INCOME ELASTICITY OF DEMAND

Just as price elasticity measures how the quantity demanded responds to price changes, so income elasticity measures how the quantity demanded responds to income changes. Formally,

$$\text{Income elasticity of demand} = \frac{\text{percentage change in quantity demanded}}{\text{percentage change in income}} \qquad (6\text{-}4)$$

Notice how similar the definition of **income elasticity of demand** is to that of price elasticity presented earlier (Eq. 6-1).

The U.S. auto market provides an example of a high income elasticity of demand. Various estimates place this elasticity between $2^1/_2$ and 3. In other words, there is an increase of $2^1/_2$ to 3% in the quantity of autos purchased in response to a 1% increase in income. On the other hand, the income elasticity of gasoline is about 1 and that of tobacco is considerably less (about 0.5). Thus the demand for tobacco is "income inelastic"; when income rises, tobacco purchases rise by a smaller percentage.

Recall that income is a "demand shifter"; when income rises, the demand curve generally shifts to the right. The income elasticity of demand measures the magnitude of that shift. In the case of automobiles, the shift is important, whereas in the case of tobacco it is far less so. For a small category of goods—**inferior goods**—an increase in income shifts the demand curve to the *left*. Purchases decline as income rises. In such cases, the income elasticity of demand is negative.

For an ***inferior good***, the income elasticity of demand is negative. An increase in income causes a decrease in the quantity demanded.

For a ***normal good***, the income elasticity of demand is positive. An increase in income causes an increase in the quantity demanded.

Because the income elasticity can be either positive or negative, it is *important not to drop the minus sign for an inferior good.* In contrast, the price elasticity of demand can be counted on to be negative, and the sign is sometimes dropped. A reader will know without being told that a rise in price causes a decline in the quantity demanded.

CROSS ELASTICITY OF DEMAND

The quantity of a good demanded depends not only on its own price, but also on the prices of other goods. For example, the demand for cars depends on the price of gasoline. The strength of this effect is measured by the **cross elasticity of demand** (which is also sometimes known as the cross-price elasticity of demand). Formally,

$$\text{Cross elasticity of demand, } E_{xy} = \frac{\text{percentage change in quantity of } X \text{ demanded}}{\text{percentage change in the price of } Y} \tag{6-5}$$

As in the case of income elasticity, it is important to report whether the cross elasticity is positive or negative. If it is positive, an increase in the price of Y causes an *increase* in the quantity of X demanded, and the goods are **substitutes.** For example, beef and pork are substitutes: A 1% increase in the price of pork causes the quantity of beef demanded to increase by about 0.3%. That is, it causes the demand curve for beef to shift to the right by 0.3%. A 1% increase in the price of butter causes the quantity of margarine demanded to increase by about 0.8%. Thus butter and margarine are even closer substitutes than beef and pork.

On the other hand, if cross elasticity is negative, an increase in the price of Y causes a *decrease* in the quantity of X demanded. The goods are **complements.** When you buy one, you also tend to buy the other. Thus, for example, tennis rackets and tennis balls are complements. When the price of rackets (Y) increases, people buy fewer rackets and play less. The demand for tennis balls (X) is reduced; that is, it shifts to the left. The cross elasticity shown in Equation 6-5 is negative and measures the magnitude of this shift.

In summary, the sign of the *income elasticity* determines whether goods are normal goods (+) or inferior goods (–). The sign of the *cross elasticity* determines whether goods are substitutes (+) or complements (–). In each case, the numerical value of the elasticity measures the strength of the effect. Finally, when the simple term *elasticity* is used, it means *price* elasticity.

KEY POINTS

1. Price elasticity of demand measures the responsiveness of quantity demanded to price; the more responsive, the more elastic. Similarly, elasticity of supply measures the responsiveness of quantity supplied to price.

2. The price elasticities of demand and supply are calculated using *percentage* changes in price and quantity, not absolute changes.

3. Over a segment of a demand curve, percentage calculations are different depending on which end is chosen as the starting point. Elasticity should not depend on this arbitrary choice. To avoid this problem, calculations are based on the *midpoint* or *average* of the two ends.

4. Price elasticity of demand determines what happens to total revenue as price changes. If demand is elastic, a fall in price will raise revenues ($P \times Q$). If demand is inelastic, a fall in price will lower revenues. Finally, if demand has an elasticity of 1, total revenues will not be affected by a change in price.

5. The flatness of a demand or supply curve is not a measure of its elasticity. Nevertheless, if two curves pass through *the same point,* the flatter curve is the more elastic.

6. Price elasticity of demand depends on a number of characteristics. Specifically, elasticity of demand tends to be high

(a) If the good is a luxury rather than a necessity.

(b) If the good is a large rather than a small percentage of the consumers' total expenditures.

(c) If the good has close substitutes.

(d) If the time period is long.

7. Price elasticity of supply tends to be high

(a) If the time period is long.

(b) If the good has close substitutes in production—that is, if the productive factors can easily be switched to other products.

(c) If the good can easily be stored.

8. The incidence of a tax depends on the relative elasticities of demand and supply. Those on the side of the market with the higher elasticity are willing to back away from the market; they can't be stuck with much of the burden. Those on the side with the lower elasticity bear the larger burden. If supply is less elastic than demand, sellers bear most of the tax. If demand is less elastic than supply, buyers bear most of the burden.

9. The *revenues* from a tax depend on the elasticities of demand and supply. If both elasticities are high, quantity will decrease sharply when the tax is imposed, and this decrease will depress revenues. The lower the elasticities of demand and supply, the smaller will be the decline in quantity and the greater the revenues.

10. Because elasticities of supply are higher in the long run than in the short run, most of the adverse effects of rent controls come only with the passage of time. The number of apartments gradually declines if rents are kept artificially low.

11. Just as price elasticity of demand measures the responsiveness of the quantity demanded to a change in price, so the income elasticity of demand measures the responsiveness of the quantity demanded to a change in income.

12. Elasticities can be just as important in international trade as in the domestic economy. Since 1985, low short-run elasticities have meant that U.S. exports responded only slowly when the price of the U.S. dollar began to fall in terms of foreign currencies.

KEY CONCEPTS

price elasticity of demand
midpoint or average calculation
total revenue as a $P \times Q$ rectangle
price elasticity of supply
short-run elasticity
long-run elasticity
incidence of an excise tax
income elasticity of demand
cross elasticity of demand

PROBLEMS

6-1. Several years ago, a *New York Times* editorial stated that a 50% increase in the price of gasoline would lower consumption by an estimated 10%. Does this imply anything about the elasticity of supply? Of demand? If so, what?

6-2. Fill in the blanks. In the figure shown below:

Curve with greatest elasticity is _______
Next greatest elasticity is _______
Next greatest is _______
Lowest elasticity is _______
Unit elasticity is _______

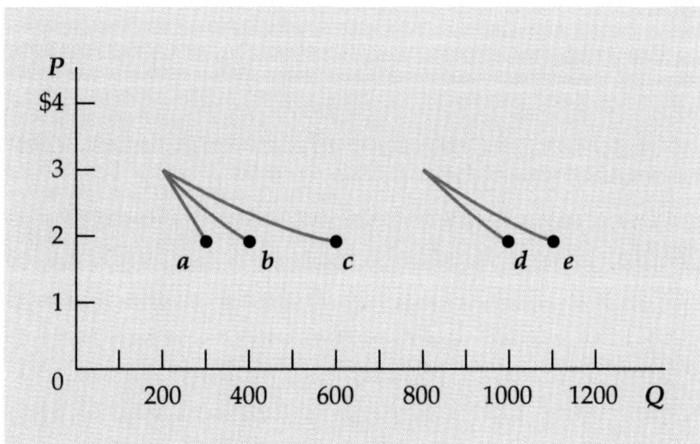

6-3. **(a)** Why didn't we define elasticity much more simply, as just the flatness of a curve; that is, elasticity = (the change in Q) ÷ (the change in P)?

(b) "Flatness is a poor measure because it depends on the arbitrary scale in which P (or Q) is measured." Is this statement true or false? Explain why.

6-4. Using the midpoint formula, calculate the elasticity of the section *AB* in the demand curve shown here. Do the same for the section *CE*. Consider the following statement: "Since *AB* and *CE* have the same flatness, but different elasticity, this shows once again that flatness does not necessarily reflect elasticity." Is this statement true or false?

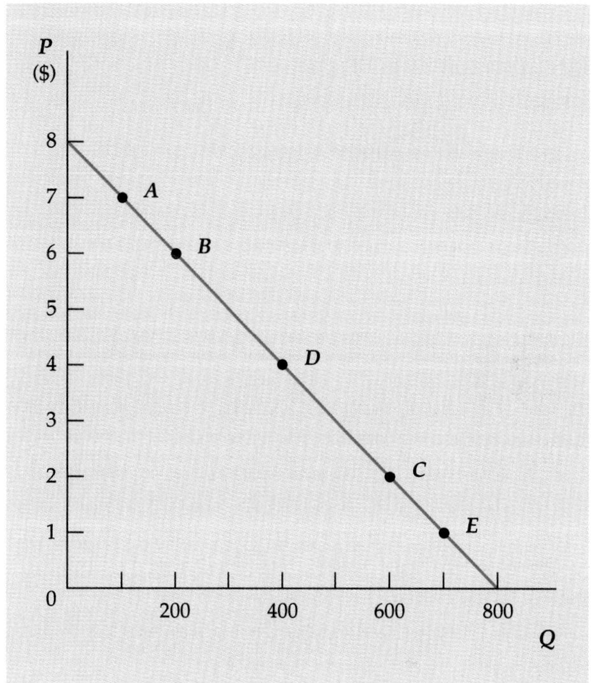

6-5. The quantity of salt demanded responds very little to a change in price. Does it respond to anything else—such as income—or is it practically fixed?

6-6. "Heating oil for homes has a greater elasticity in the long run than in the short." Do you agree? Explain.

6-7. Would you expect the income elasticity of food to be higher or lower than that of restaurant meals? Explain.

CHAPTER 7
DEMAND AND UTILITY

When you have nothing else to wear
But cloth of gold and satins rare
For cloth of gold you cease to care
GILBERT AND SULLIVAN,
THE GONDOLIERS

In the *Wealth of Nations,* Adam Smith posed the famous *paradox of value.* He observed that water is one of the most useful commodities in the world; we would die without it. Yet its price is low. In contrast, diamonds are quite unnecessary; people can easily live without them. Yet their price is high. Is the economic world upside down?

This chapter will provide an answer to Adam Smith's puzzle. It will also explain:

- How the overall market demand curve for a product—such as movie tickets or shoes—can be derived from the demands of individual consumers.
- How demand depends on the satisfaction or utility that a product provides.
- How consumers can make the best choice among the many products offered for sale.
- How consumers are concerned not only with the monetary cost of products, but also with the time they spend to buy or use products.

MARKET DEMAND AS THE SUM OF INDIVIDUAL DEMANDS

Behind the **market demand** for a good or service lie the demands of **individual consumers.** Of course, not all people are alike. Some are rich; others are poor. Some love the movies; others find them a bore. But in spite of different tastes, their individual demands can be added to find the market demand. Figure 7-1 shows how. To keep things simple, two individuals represent the millions of consumers in the economy. Ann Johnson's demand (panel *a*) shows how many movie tickets she is willing and able to buy per month at various prices. Note that Bill Kelly's demand (panel *b*) is quite different; he won't go at all if the price rises above $5. At any given price, the quantities demanded by each consumer are added horizontally to find the corresponding point on the market demand in panel *c*. For example, at a price of $3, Ann demands seven movie tickets, while Bill demands six. Thus the total number of tickets demanded at $3 is the sum of 6 + 7 = 13. Of course, in a community with thousands of people, thousands of individual demand curves would have to be added horizontally to get the market demand curve.

Observe that individual demand curves are labeled with a small *d* in the panels on the left, to distinguish them from the market demand with a capital *D* in the panel on the right.

DIMINISHING MARGINAL UTILITY

Why do the individual demand curves slope downward? Why would Ann and Bill go to the movies more often at a lower price?

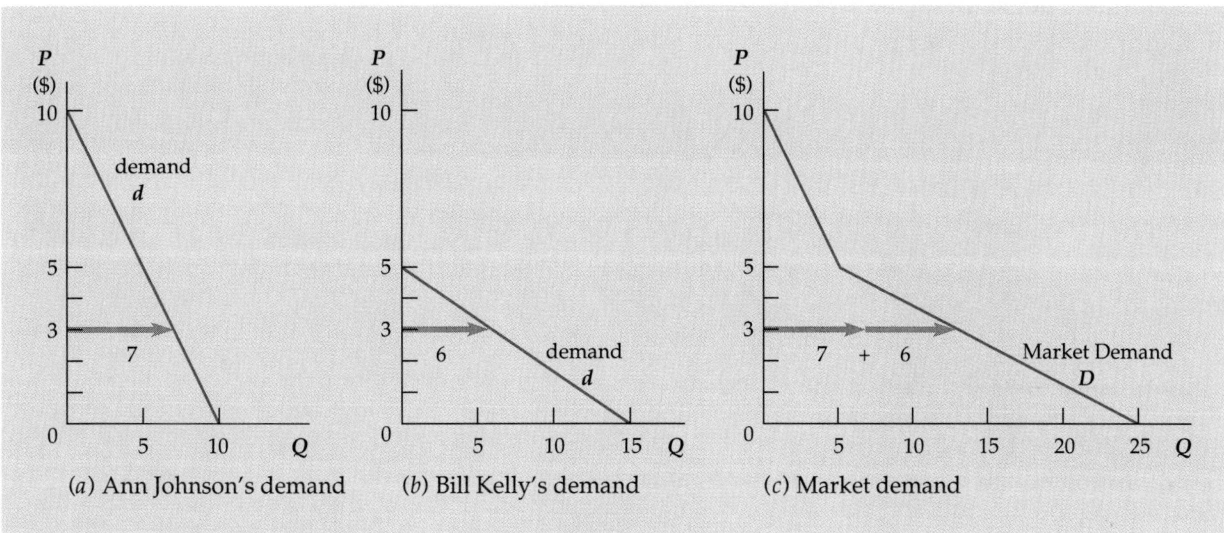

FIGURE 7-1 Adding individual demand curves to get market demand.
To find the quantity demanded at each price, horizontally add the quantities demanded by all individual consumers. For example, at a price of $3, add the 7 units demanded by Ann Johnson to the 6 demanded by Bill Kelly, to get the 13 units demanded in total.

Part of the answer has already been offered earlier in Chapter 4. When the price of a good falls, it becomes cheaper compared to other items. Consumers therefore *switch* away from the other items and buy more of the lower priced item instead. For example, when the price of chicken falls, people eat more chicken and less beef and fish.

Economists have also searched for more detailed answers. Over a century ago, English economist William Stanley Jevons suggested looking at an individual's total food consumption as the sum of 10 equal parts:

> If his food be reduced by the last part, he will suffer but little; if a second tenth part be deficient, he will feel the want distinctly; the subtraction of the third part will be decidedly injurious; with every subsequent subtraction. . . his sufferings will be more serious until he will be on the verge of starvation.[1]

While Jevons was not quite as lyrical as Gilbert and Sullivan with their "cloth of gold and satins rare," he did hit upon an important idea. The less food people have, the more highly they value it. Or, to restate the same point, the more they have, the less highly they value another unit. The satisfaction or **utility** provided by each additional unit becomes smaller and smaller. Jevons thus put forward the **law of diminishing marginal utility.**

> The ***marginal utility*** of a good or service is the increase in satisfaction that an individual receives from consuming one additional unit of that good or service.
>
> The ***law of diminishing marginal utility*** states that the marginal utility of a good or service will decline as more units of that good or service are consumed.

Unfortunately, we must be careful with this "law." There can be exceptions. A second ski lesson, for example, may provide more utility than the first—fewer bruises and more fun. But as more and more lessons are purchased, marginal utility eventually must decline. The hundredth lesson during the season will provide less satisfaction than the ninety-ninth.

The term *marginal* should be emphasized because it plays such a central role in economics. *Marginal* utility is the *extra* or *added* utility from

---

[1]Jevons, *Theory of Political Economy* (1871).

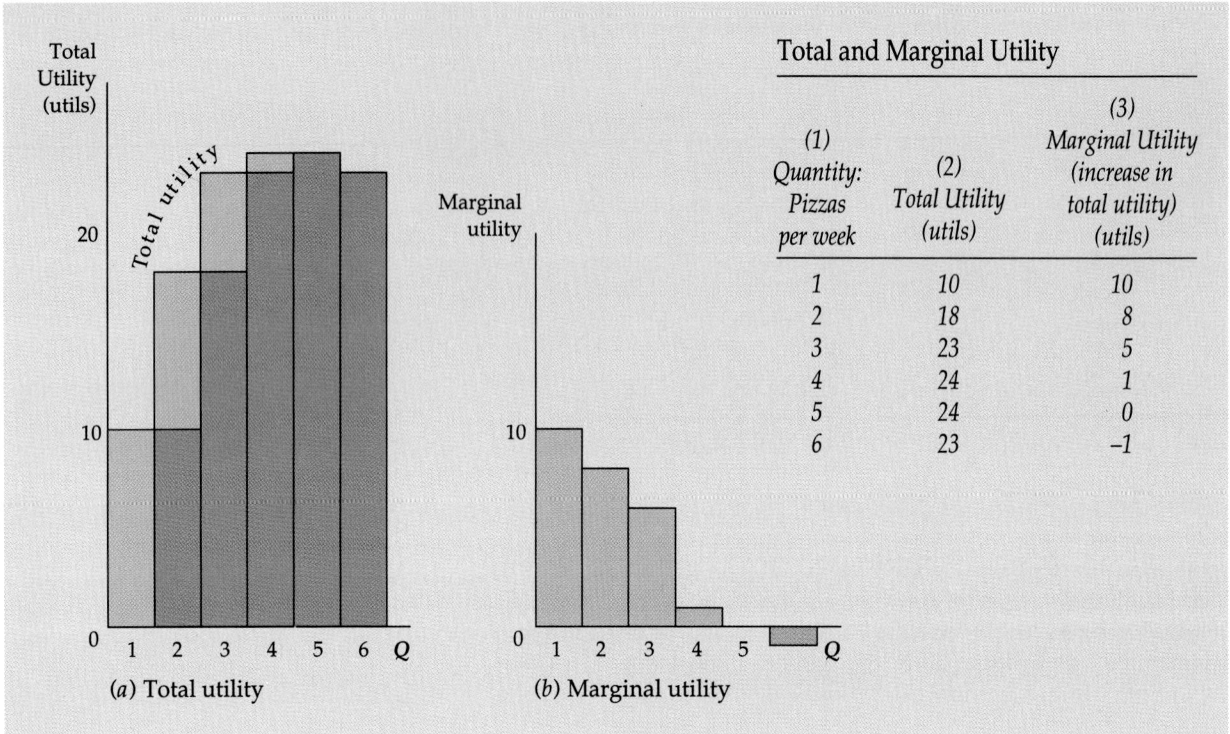

Total and Marginal Utility

(1) Quantity: Pizzas per week	(2) Total Utility (utils)	(3) Marginal Utility (increase in total utility) (utils)
1	10	10
2	18	8
3	23	5
4	24	1
5	24	0
6	23	–1

FIGURE 7-2 Total and marginal utility.

This figure illustrates the numbers shown in the table. Marginal utility represents the increase in total utility when one more unit is consumed. Thus, the marginal utility blocks in panel *b* are the same as the blue stairsteps in panel *a* that show how total utility increases.

consuming one more unit, as illustrated in the example in Figure 7-2 and the accompanying table. The "stairsteps" in panel *a* show how total utility increases as more is consumed. For example, when consumption increases from two to three pizzas per week, total utility increases from 18 to 23 units or "utils." (The term *util* is sometimes used to mean "unit of utility.") Thus the marginal utility of the third pizza is the blue upward step of 5, from 18 to 23 utils. These marginal utility stairsteps in panel *a* are reproduced as the marginal utility bars in panel *b*. The stairsteps become smaller as the number of pizzas increases in panel *a;* this means diminishing marginal utility in panel *b*.

As long as each additional pizza provides some marginal utility, total utility increases. In some situations, however, a consumer has too much of a product—so much that an additional unit provides no benefit and is a nuisance instead. In that case (unit 6 in Fig. 7-2), the marginal utility is negative (panel *b*), which causes total utility to start downward (panel *a*).

MARGINAL UTILITY AND THE DEMAND CURVE

The downward-sloping demand curve illustrates the idea of diminishing marginal utility. Let's look again at Ann Johnson's demand for movies, originally shown in Figure 7-1 and repeated in more detail in Figure 7-3*a*. Consider the third movie per month. She would be willing to pay a maximum of $7 to see it. Thus $7 is a monetary measure of the

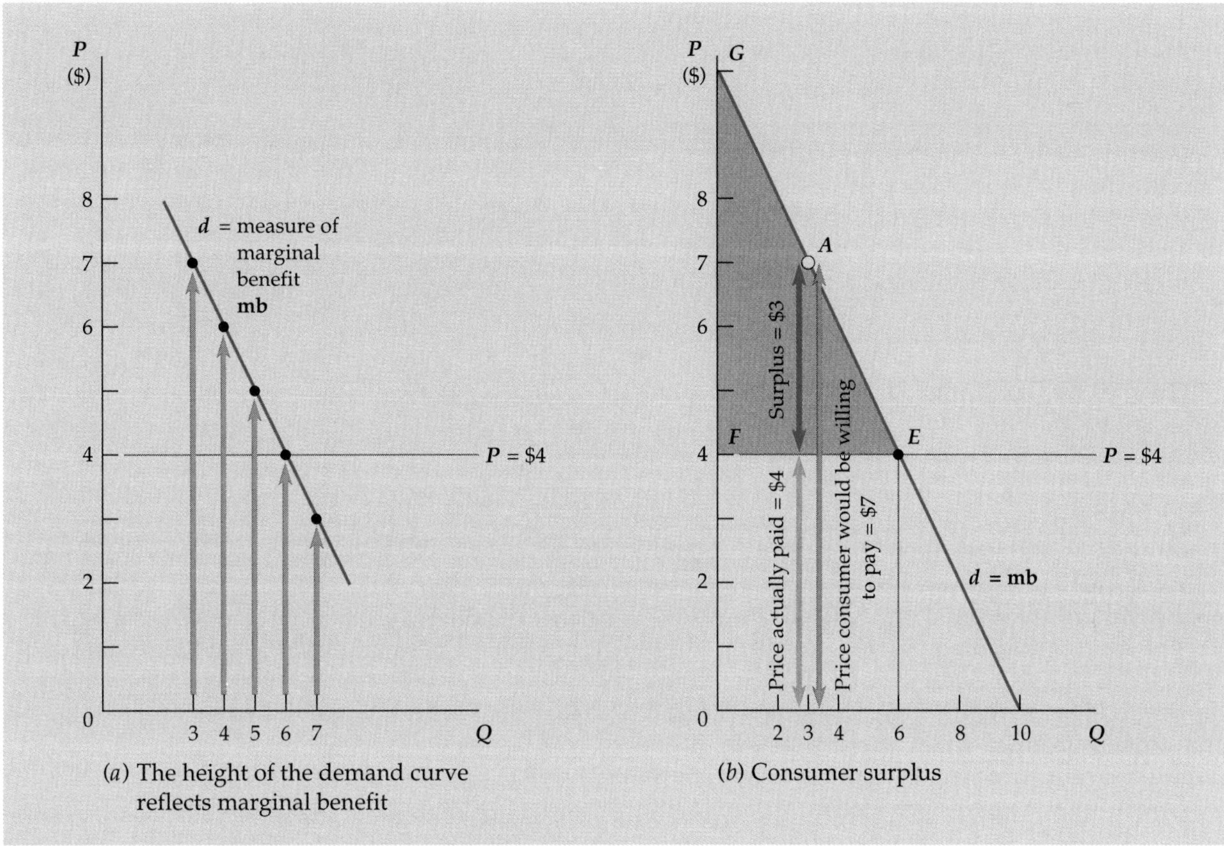

FIGURE 7-3 The demand curve and consumer surplus.

Willingness to pay—as shown by the height of a point on the demand curve—is a monetary measure of the marginal benefit which the consumer receives from that unit of the good.

In panel *b*, observe that the consumer would have been willing to pay as much as $7 for the third unit, at point *A*. But its price is only $4. Therefore, the consumer gains a surplus of $3 on this unit, shown by the blue arrow. The total surplus on all units purchased is measured by the light blue triangular area *EFG*.

utility it provides her. However, she gets less enjoyment or utility from the fourth movie; she is willing to pay only $6 to see it. Thus, $6 is a monetary measure of the marginal utility or marginal benefit provided by the fourth movie, and so on.

Essential idea for future chapters: When we see an individual demand curve, we can envisage a set of vertical arrows running up to it, as illustrated in Figure 7-3a. The height of each arrow is a monetary measure of the marginal utility or the marginal benefit provided by that unit.

CONSUMER SURPLUS

At a price of $4, Ann is willing to buy six tickets. But she is *barely* willing to buy the sixth ticket; it is scarcely worth its price of $4.

However, consider one of the earlier units, say, the third. If necessary, she would have been willing to pay $7 for it. But actually, she has to pay only the box-office price of $4. Thus, she reaps a surplus of $3 on this unit—that is, the difference between the $7 price she would have been willing to pay and the $4 price she actually pays. There are similar surpluses on all other units to the left of unit 6—large surpluses on the first few units and a much smaller surplus of only $1 on the fifth unit. The total **consumer surplus** is equal to the blue triangular area in Figure 7-3*b*.

> ***Consumer surplus*** on a unit purchased is the difference between the maximum amount the consumer would be willing to pay for that unit and the market price that actually is paid. Consumer surplus is measured by the triangular area below the demand curve and above the market price.

Observe that consumer surplus is not the same as the utility provided by the good. The marginal benefit provided by the third unit is measured by the height of the demand curve—that is, $7. Consumer surplus is only the $3 *difference* between the $7 marginal benefit and the $4 price actually paid. In Figure 7-3*b*, it is illustrated by the blue arrow from the $4 price line up to the demand curve.

The idea of consumer surplus, introduced by the famous British economist and teacher Alfred Marshall (1842-1924), illustrates how people can gain from purchases of movie tickets—or hamburgers, or cars, or a host of other products. Suppliers may gain, too; the production of films may be very profitable and may provide high incomes to actors and technical workers. Thus, when one group (consumers) gains, this does *not* mean that some other group (producers) must lose. The marketplace is *not* a "zero sum game," in which one group loses what another gains. Instead, both consumers and producers can gain through specialization and exchange which add to the general prosperity.

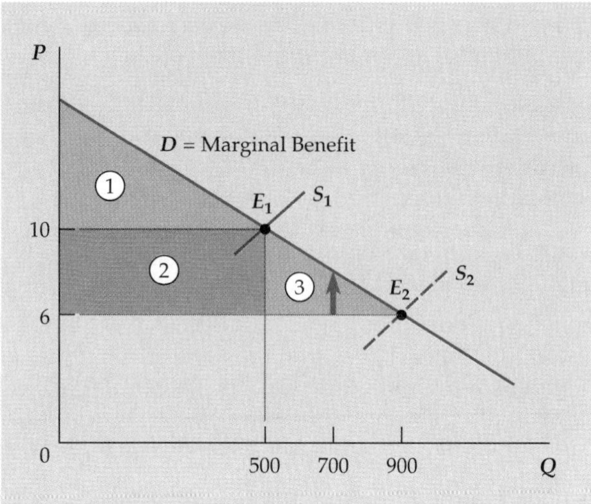

FIGURE 7-4 Increase in consumer surplus as price falls.

When the price falls, consumers are better off. In this diagram, they pay $4 less for each of the first 500 units, for a total gain of $2,000 (area 2). They also gain area 3 on the additional 400 units bought when the price falls from $10 (at E_1) to $6 (at E_2).

CHANGES IN CONSUMER SURPLUS

When the price of a good falls, consumers are clearly better off. The increase in consumer surplus is a measure of how much. In Figure 7-4, the initial equilibrium between supply and market demand is at point E_1, with consumers buying 500 units at a price of $10. Consumers enjoy an initial surplus equal to triangle 1. Now suppose that the equilibrium moves to E_2 as a result of a rightward shift in the supply curve. The price drops from $10 to $6, with consumers now buying 900 units. Now their consumer surplus is the larger triangle 1 + 2 + 3, for a net gain of areas 2 + 3.

When examined in more detail, the increase in consumer surplus can be regarded as follows. Consumers save $4 per unit on each of the first 500 units, or a total gain of $2,000 as shown by shaded area 2. But they also reap a surplus on the additional 400 units that they now buy at the lower price. For example, the surplus on unit 700 is illustrated by the blue arrow that measures the difference between the $8 the consumer would have been willing to pay for that unit and the $6 price actually paid. The gain from all 400 additional units is therefore equal to blue area 3. Thus, when the price falls from $10 to $6, the total gain to consumers is equal to areas 2 + 3.

> **Essential idea for future chapters: If the market price falls, the gain to consumers is shown by the horizontal area between the old and new price and to the left of the demand curve. This is the increase in consumer surplus. If the price increases, consumers lose this amount.**

THE PARADOX OF VALUE

The distinction between total utility and marginal utility helps to solve the puzzle posed by Adam Smith in the *Wealth of Nations*. How can the price of diamonds, which are quite unnecessary, be so high, when the price of water is so low?

To explain this **paradox of value,** we must consider both demand and supply. The price of water is low because it is so plentiful; a huge quantity can be supplied at a very low price. Because it is cheap, people consume a large quantity, even using it in ways that provide very little satisfaction, such as washing the car or watering the lawn. Thus its low price means a low *marginal* utility for the last unit bought by consumers, illustrated by the arrow *BE* in Figure 7-5.

On the other hand, diamonds sell at a high price because they are very scarce and costly to produce; they can be supplied only at a high price. Consequently, they are bought only by the most eager people; the only buyers are people whose marginal utility is high enough to justify the high price. Therefore, the high price of diamonds means that, *at the margin*—where we look at only the last unit consumed—diamonds are more valuable than water.

This is only part of the story. The total utility of water includes the utility not only of the last glass we use, but also of every other glass. The ones that

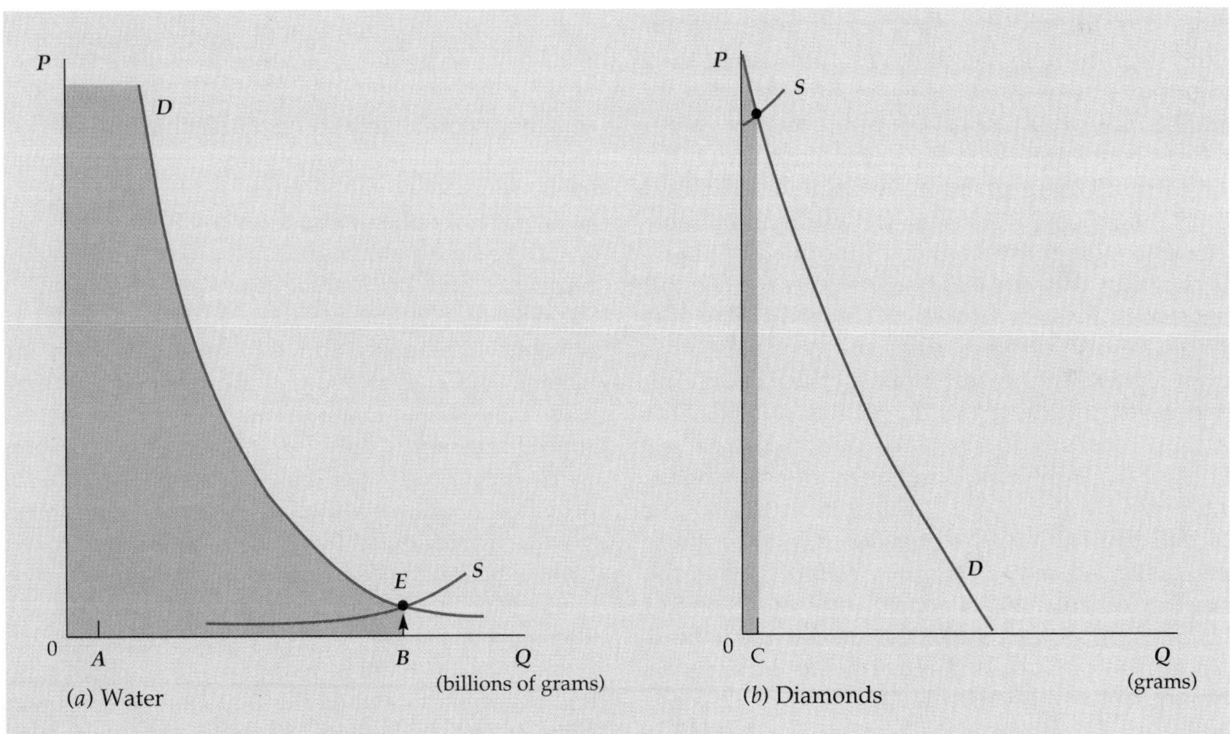

FIGURE 7-5 The Paradox of Value.

Market prices are determined by demand and supply. Because of the plentiful supply of water, its price is low. Even though the first few units provide enormous utility (at *A*), consumers also use it in less important ways—for example, to wash the car. Its marginal utility is low, as shown by the arrow at *B*, even though its total utility is very large indeed. For diamonds the story is the opposite—a high marginal utility, but a much smaller total utility.

keep us from dying of thirst have a very high utility indeed. In fact, the marginal utility of one of those first units of water, say *A*, is so high that we don't have enough room at the top of the diagram to show it. In other words, the total benefit from water—the shaded area in panel *a*—is so large that there isn't room to show it in full. Compare this to the relatively small total benefit from diamonds—the shaded area in panel *b*. Thus we conclude that, overall, water is much more valuable than diamonds, even though its price is lower—that is, even though its value *at the margin* is less. The paradox of value is resolved.

THE CONSUMER'S CHOICE AMONG GOODS: THE OPTIMAL PURCHASE RULE[2]

Consumers have limited incomes; they cannot have everything they want. They must make choices among the wide range of products for sale—movies, hamburgers, books, shoes, and so on.

With all these products available, how does a consumer choose? Consider the example in Table 7-1, where the consumer has an income of $10 and is choosing between hamburgers priced at $2 and paperback mystery novels priced at $4. At these prices, what purchases does the consumer rank most highly? The highest ranking choice is the item that gives the most for the money—that is, the highest marginal utility (MU) or satisfaction per dollar. This is the first hamburger, which provides 12 "utils" for a price of $2, or 6 utils per dollar. The second hamburger gives the second highest utility per dollar, namely, 5 utils per dollar. (This is the number of utils, 10, divided by the price of $2.) Hamburger #3 and mystery #1 are tied for third place; each provides 4 utils per dollar. Next comes Hamburger #4, tied with mystery #2 at 3 utils per dollar.

These rankings are summarized in Table 7-1, part B. The consumer goes as far down this list as income allows. This is to line 3, where the total expenditure of $10 exhausts the income of $10. The best choice the consumer can make is to buy 3 hamburgers and 1 mystery.

Note that, when the consumer is making the best, utility-maximizing choice, the MU/*P* ratio is the same for the last unit of both goods (4 utils per dollar). In general, where the consumer is faced with many goods, the consumer makes the best choice by following the **optimal purchase rule:**

$$\frac{MU_1}{P_1} = \frac{MU_2}{P_2} = \frac{MU_3}{P_3} = \text{MU of last \$1 spent on any other product} \qquad (7\text{-}1)$$

where

MU_1 is the marginal utility of the first good,

P_1 is the price of the first good, and so on.

In other words, maximum attainable satisfaction requires that the marginal utility of the last dollar spent on good #1 be the same as the marginal utility of the last dollar spent on every other good.

To see why, suppose that the consumer makes a mistake and stops somewhere else in Table 7-1. Suppose that the individual erroneously decides to buy one hamburger and two mysteries with the income of $10. Observe that the optimal purchase rule (Eq. 7-1) is violated. The MU/*P* ratio for the second mystery is only 3; the second mystery provides only 3 utils per dollar. But the hamburger provides 6 utils per dollar. Because hamburgers provide more utility per dollar, the consumer can make a better choice by switching away from mysteries and by buying more hamburgers instead. Specifically, the best decision is to buy one fewer mystery and use the $4 to buy two more hamburgers. Observe that, when this is done, the consumer gains 18 utils from the additional hamburgers (that is, 10 utils for the second plus 8 utils for the third), while giving up only 12 utils when the second book is foregone.

Thus, when expenditures are rearranged to satisfy Equation 7-1, there is a net gain of 6 units of utility (18 for the two additional hamburgers minus 12 for the book foregone). Once the condi-

[2]Note to instructors: This section may be skipped if you cover the appendix. The indifference curves in the appendix provide an alternative way of explaining the consumer's choice among goods.

TABLE 7-1 Maximizing Utility (consumer with income of $10)

A. Calculating marginal utility per dollar

	Hamburgers (price P = $2)		*Mystery novels (price = $4)*	
	Marginal Utility (MU) (utils)	*Marginal Utility per dollar (MU/P)*	*Marginal Utility (Utils)*	*Marginal Utility per dollar (MU/P)*
Unit #				
1	12	6	16	4 ←
2	10	5	12	3
3	8	4 ←	8	2
4	6	3	4	1
5	4	2	2	0.5

B. Ranking of purchases

Rank of Hamburgers (H) and Mystery Novels (M)	*Cumulative expenditure*
1. Hamburger #1, at 6 utils per dollar	1H @ $2 = $2
2. H #2, at 5 utils per dollar	2H @ $2 = $4
3. H #3 and Mystery #1, tied at 4 utils per dollar	3H @ $2 + 1M @ $4 = $10
4. H #4 and M #2, tied at 3 utils per dollar	4H @ $2 + 2M @ $4 = $16

The consumer buys three hamburgers and one mystery novel, using the total income of $10 and equating the MU/*P* ratio of hamburgers and novels.

tions of Equation 7-1 are met—with three hamburgers and one book—the consumer is picking the best package of goods; no improvement can be made by a further rearrangement of purchases. (Try it. Within the budget constraint of $10, the consumer cannot pick any combination that yields more utility than the three hamburgers and one book.)

As an alternative to the optimal purchase rule (Eq. 7-1), there is another way to explain the consumer's choice among goods. This alternative uses *indifference curves,* which dispense with the idea of measurable "utils" of utility. It turns out that measurable "utils" are not really needed to explain how a consumer behaves. In fact, modern microeconomics is built on indifference curves instead. Indifference curves have only one disadvantage: students generally find them more difficult than Equation 7-1. They are therefore placed in the appendix at the end of this chapter.

EXTENSIONS OF DEMAND THEORY

Time is Money

BEN FRANKLIN

In deciding whether to buy a product, the consumer considers the utility the product will yield and its cost. Cost is a broad concept, covering more than just the purchase price. Other costs include:

- *Transactions costs.* These are the costs, in addition to the purchase price, incurred when *buying* the good.
- The *costs of using* a product, including the time involved in using it.

TRANSACTIONS COSTS

To illustrate transactions costs, suppose that, after studying the profit prospects of International Business Machines, you buy 100 shares of IBM stock from a "discount" broker. In addition to the cost of the stock itself, you incur two transactions costs:

1. *The commission* charged by the broker. Discount brokers provide one and only one service: buying or selling stocks. For this service, they charge a fee or commission. They do not give advice or provide information on companies. Thus you also face a second cost.

2. *Search cost,* also called information cost. This is the cost of collecting information needed to make an informed decision. This cost includes not only the time you spend in your study of IBM, but also any out-of-pocket expenses you may incur. For example, you may subscribe to publications that provide information on corporations.

You may decide to go to a full-service broker, who will charge more than a discount broker but will offer information and advice on which stocks to buy. In this case, the commission covers not only the cost of actually executing the transaction, but also some of the search costs.

It's not just stockbrokers who are in the information business. Real estate agents also provide information to both buyers and sellers. They give buyers information about houses that are available. They provide sellers with advice on pricing a home and information on who the buyers are.

If you're selling a house, should you go to a real estate agent—to whom you will have to pay a commission if the house is sold—or should you place an ad in the paper and try to sell the house on your own? You will usually fare better by going to an agent; agents are in the business of making contacts with potential buyers. Specialization in marketing may be just as important as specialization in other skills, such as law or medicine.

Nevertheless, you should beware. Whenever you deal with people who provide information or advice, it's important to ask: Is the information or advice really in *your* interest, or are the agents being influenced—consciously or subconsciously—by quite different interests of their own? For example, is the real estate agent suggesting that you set a low price on your home in order to make it easy to sell? Will the doctor who advises you to have an operation actually do the operation, receiving a fee? (Getting a "second opinion" is generally wise. Even in cases where there is no conflict of interest, a second opinion can provide additional information.) Doesn't the stockbroker have an interest in getting you to buy so that he or she can earn commissions?

How Do Search Costs Influence Market Price? The greater the information of consumers and the more willing they are to bear search costs by seeking alternative sellers, the less dealers will be able to charge higher prices than their competitors do. Thus search reduces the average price the public pays, as well as the variation in prices. Moreover, the percentage variation in price will be less for large ticket items like cars—where it pays the public to search intensively—than for small-ticket items where it's not worth the trouble. A grocer may therefore be able to raise the price of salt by 10% without anyone noticing. But a car dealer who tries to charge 10% more than the competition will soon be out of business.

Search efforts provide several benefits. Individuals who search generally purchase products that better satisfy their requirements. Moreover, the benefits go beyond the individual. The more information the public has, the less likely it is that a poor product will survive in the marketplace. In addition, high-priced firms are under pressure to cut prices in order to retain their customers. Prices therefore tend to be lower. Of course, if all these things happen, it becomes less necessary for an individual to incur large search costs. There will be less risk of being overcharged or of ending up with a shoddy product. Thus, paradoxically, the more searching the public does, the less any individual buyer needs to search.

Time represents a major part of search costs—for example, the time a consumer spends shopping at various car dealers.

TIME COSTS IN CONSUMPTION

Time can be important not only in searching for products, but also in using them.

Examples abound. One reason car buyers are

concerned about reliability is that they don't want to waste a lot of time driving the car back and forth to the dealer for repair. Time may also be an important consideration in other purchases. For example, a day-long bus trip from Buffalo to Boston may cost less than an airline ticket. But most people don't take the bus because it takes more time. Moreover, people with high incomes—whose time is valuable—incur higher time costs in traveling by bus. The poor may take a bus; the rich fly.

Time cost helps to explain consumption patterns, not only within the United States but also among countries. In North America we buy costly home appliances: They save valuable time. In poorer countries, the laundry is more likely to be done by hand.

KEY POINTS

1. Market demand is the sum of individual demands.

2. As a consumer consumes more of a product, its marginal utility eventually declines.

3. The downward-sloping demand curve reflects declining marginal utility.

4. The height of the demand curve gives a monetary measure of the marginal utility or marginal benefit of the good to the buyer. When you see a demand curve, you should visualize the vertical marginal benefit arrows beneath it.

5. The total utility derived from a product—such as water—exceeds the total amount ($P \times Q$) that consumers spend for it. The excess of utility over the price paid is *consumer surplus,* which is measured by the triangle below the demand curve and above the price.

6. When price falls, consumer surplus increases by the horizontal area to the left of the demand curve and between the old and the new price.

7. Water provides much more total utility than diamonds. However, water has a much lower price, and therefore the consumer continues to purchase additional units until its marginal utility is low. Water has not only high-priority uses, such as drinking, but also lower priority uses, such as watering the lawn.

8. The consumer is most eager to spend money on the item with the highest MU/P ratio; this gives the most for the money. The product with the next highest MU/P ratio is the next best purchase, and so on.

9. In equilibrium, the consumer's MU/P ratio is equal for all products purchased.

KEY CONCEPTS

individual demand	diminishing marginal utility	transactions cost
market demand	consumer surplus	search costs
marginal utility	paradox of value	time costs

PROBLEMS

7-1. Suppose each of three individuals has unit elasticity of demand for a particular good. Without drawing any diagrams, can you guess what the elasticity of the total market demand for this good will be?

Now draw diagrams showing each of the individual demands and how the market demand is constructed. How does the slope of market demand compare with the slope of the individual demands? Is market demand therefore more elastic? Explain why or why not.

7-2. Using your own example, explain why marginal utility must eventually fall.

7-3. Can you think of anything for which your marginal utility rises over a range?

7-4. Redo Table 7-1 on the assumption that the price of mystery novels is $2, not $4. With an income of $10, how many hamburgers and mysteries will the consumer buy? What happens to this individual's demand for mysteries as the price falls from $4 to $2? Next, suppose that the consumer's income rises to $12, while the price of mysteries and hamburgers each remain at $2. What will this individual buy now?

7-5. "Food is clearly more important than entertainment. Therefore, people will spend more on food than on entertainment." Explain why this conclusion is not necessarily correct.

7-6. Suppose that you think your MU/*P* ratio is higher for movies than for food. What can you do to improve your situation?

* **7-7.** Suppose that a new publication appears, which provides detail on prices and the quality of products in local stores. What is likely to happen to the elasticity of demand facing individual retailers as a result? Why?

* **7-8.** When you buy a car, who do you think gains more—you or the car manufacturer? Why? (Be careful! This is a difficult question.)

APPENDIX

THE THEORY OF CONSUMER CHOICE

Indifference Curves

In this appendix, we develop an important principle that was introduced in Chapter 2 and reiterated in this chapter: Consumers must *choose between alternatives.* To illustrate, consider an individual consumer. Suppose for simplicity that the individual is consuming only two goods, food and clothing. To analyze the decision the consumer faces, we introduce the concept of an **indifference curve,** shown in Figure 7-6 and the accompanying table.

To illustrate this concept, suppose that the individual begins at point *A*, where three units of clothing and two units of food are consumed. Then, to draw the indifference curve through *A*, we ask the consumer the following question: "What other combinations of clothing and food would leave you equally well off?"

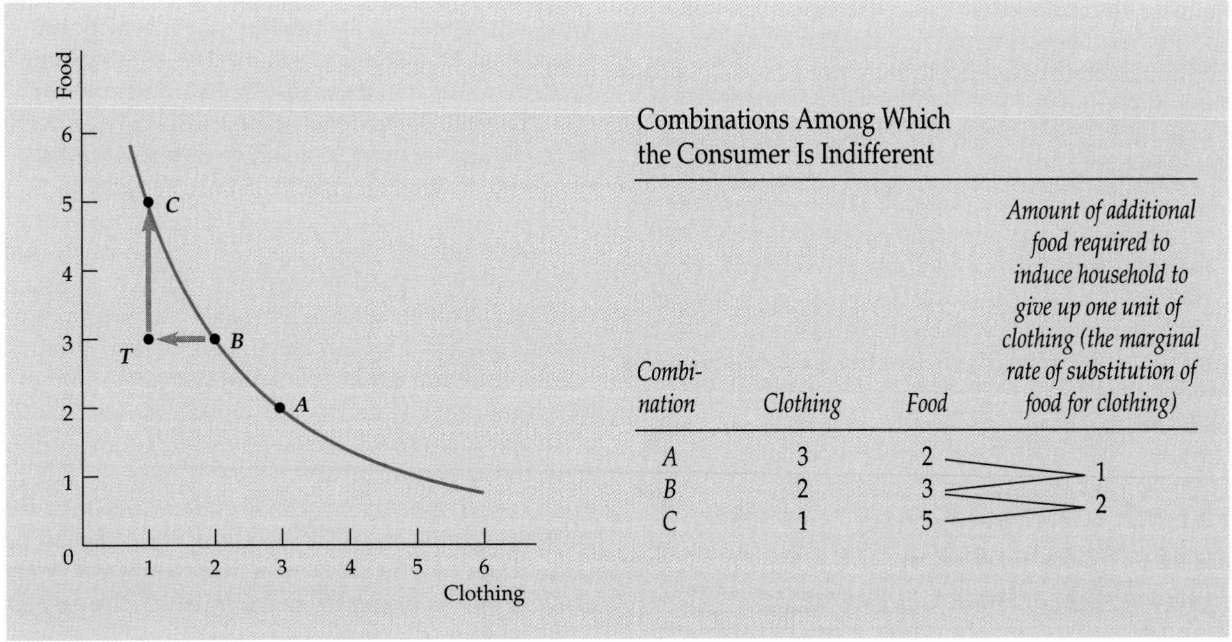

Combinations Among Which the Consumer Is Indifferent

Combination	*Clothing*	*Food*	*Amount of additional food required to induce household to give up one unit of clothing (the marginal rate of substitution of food for clothing)*
A	3	2	
			1
B	2	3	
			2
C	1	5	

FIGURE 7-6 An indifference curve.

An indifference curve joins all points where the individual has the same level of utility or satisfaction. The individual is "indifferent" among the various points on an indifference curve.

The individual may inform us that he or she would be equally satisfied at point *B*, with two units of clothing and three units of food. In other words, if the individual starting at *A* were asked to give up one unit of clothing in return for one more unit of food, the individual would respond that he or she didn't care whether or not such a change took place. The individual is indifferent between points *A* and *B*.

On an ***indifference curve,*** each point represents the same level of satisfaction or utility. An individual is indifferent among the various points on the indifference curve.

Now let us continue the experiment, asking the individual under what conditions he or she would be willing to give up one more unit of clothing. In moving upward and to the left from point *B*, the individual recognizes that he or she is getting short of clothing and already has a lot of food. The individual states a willingness to give up another unit of scarce clothing, but only in return for a large amount (two units) of food. Consequently, point *C*, representing one unit of clothing and five of food, is on the same indifference curve as *A* and *B*. Because the individual is increasingly reluctant to give up clothing as he or she has less and less, the indifference curve generally has the bowed shape shown.

(Although indifference curves are usually bowed, this need not always be the case. For example, a two-car family might be indifferent among the choices of (*A*) two Chevs, no Ford; (*B*) one Chev, one Ford; or (C) no Chevs, two Fords. Then, with Chevs on one axis and Fords on the other, the indifference curve joining points *A*, *B*, and *C* is a straight line. The reason is that this particular family considers the two cars to be *perfect substitutes* for each other.)

THE MARGINAL RATE OF SUBSTITUTION: THE SLOPE OF THE INDIFFERENCE CURVE

In moving from *B* to *C* in Figure 7-6, notice that the slope of the indifference curve is 2. (To be precise, it is –2, but we ignore the negative signs in this appendix.) The slope has an important economic meaning. It is the amount of food ($TC = 2$) that is required to compensate for the loss of one unit of clothing ($BT = 1$)—that is, it is the **marginal rate of substitution of food for clothing.**

The marginal rate of substitution (MRS) of food for clothing is the amount of food required to compensate for the loss of one unit of clothing, while leaving the consumer equally well off. Geometrically, it is the slope of the indifference curve (with the negative sign ignored).

Because it takes two units of food to compensate for one unit of clothing, the marginal utility of one unit of clothing is twice as high as the marginal utility of one unit of food in the range *BC*. Thus the slope of the indifference curve represents the *ratio* of the marginal utilities of the two goods.

$$\text{MRS} = \frac{\text{MU}_{\text{clothing}}}{\text{MU}_{\text{food}}} = 2$$

THE INDIFFERENCE MAP

The indifference curve in Figure 7-6 is reproduced as u_1 in Figure 7-7. Instead of starting at point *A*, the consumer might have started at another point, such as *F* or *G*; there is an indifference curve that passes through each of these points as well. In other words, there is a whole family of indifference curves which form the *indifference map* in Figure 7-7.

Although all points on a single indifference curve represent the same level of utility or satisfaction, points on another indifference curve represent a different level of satisfaction. Observe that, at point *G*, the consumer has more clothing and more food than at *F*. Thus the individual prefers *G* to *F*. Because other points on u_3—such as *H*—are equivalent to *G*, they must also be preferred to *F* and to every other point on u_2. Therefore indifference curve u_3 represents a higher level of satisfaction or utility than u_2. The farther the indifference curve is away from the origin (to the northeast), the greater the level of satisfaction.

Incidentally, this figure illustrates how three variables can be shown in a diagram with only two dimensions. The three variables are the quantity of food, the quantity of clothing, and the individual's utility. We can visualize this system of indifference

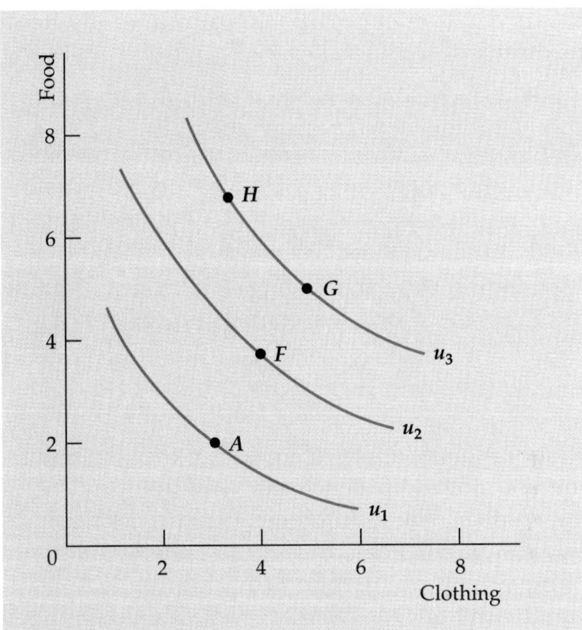

FIGURE 7-7 An indifference map.

An individual has a whole set of indifference curves, each curve representing a different level of utility. Thus u_2 represents a higher level of utility than u_1, and u_3 a still higher level.

curves as mapping out a utility hill, with each curve representing a contour line showing points with equal utility, just as a geographer's contour line shows points of equal height above sea level. A geographer's contour lines do not cross, and the indifference curves of an individual do not cross either.

Moving from the origin to the northeast, the consumer goes up the utility hill to higher and higher levels of satisfaction. One advantage of the indifference curve, as compared to the marginal utility approach, is that we don't have to measure *how* high up the hill the individual is. All we need to know is how various packages are ranked. That is, we need to know that *G* is above *F;* we don't need to know how much above. Thus the indifference curve discards the idea of measurable marginal utility. However, it retains an important feature of marginal utility theory. Even though we no longer talk about the number of "utils" a product yields, the idea of *relative* marginal utilities is retained in the indifference curve. The marginal rate of substitution—that is, the slope of the indifference curve—represents the ratio of the marginal utilities of the two goods.

THE BUDGET LIMITATION

As we have seen, the indifference map reflects the individual's *desires;* the individual prefers *G* to *F* in Figure 7-7 and is indifferent between *H* and *G*. However, the individual's behavior depends not only on *wants,* but also on *ability* to buy.

What the individual is able to buy depends on three things: money income, the price of food, and the price of clothing. If the individual's income is \$100, while the price of food is \$10 per unit and clothing is \$20, the various options open to the individual are illustrated by the **budget line** *KL* in Figure 7-8.

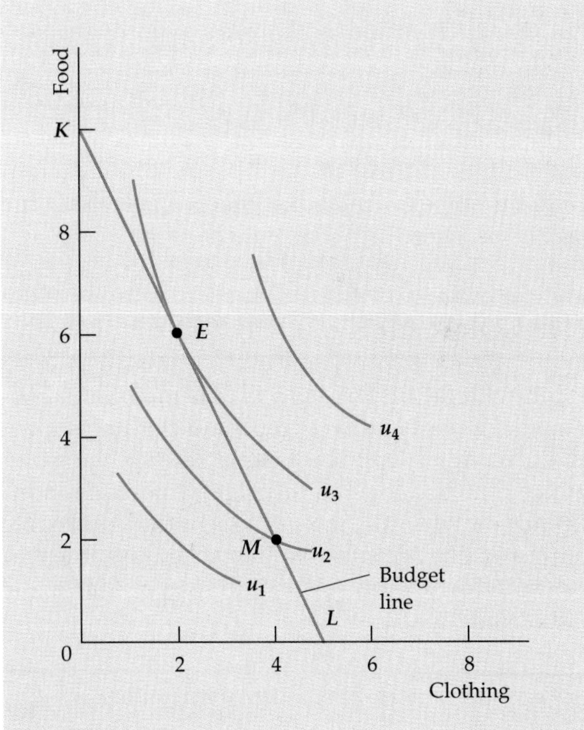

FIGURE 7-8 The equilibrium of an individual with a budget limit.

KL represents the household's budget limit. Each point on this line represents a combination of food and clothing that can be purchased, and that just barely exhausts the income. To achieve equilibrium with the highest level of satisfaction, the individual moves along the budget line to the point *E* of tangency with the highest achievable indifference curve.

The ***budget line***—sometimes called an *income line* or *price line*—shows the various combinations of goods that can be purchased by an individual with a given money income and facing a given set of prices.

If the whole $100 is spent on food at $10 per unit, the individual can buy 10 units, as shown by point *K*. At the other extreme, if the individual spends the whole income of $100 on clothing at $20 per unit, five units can be bought, as shown by point *L*. Similarly, it can be shown that any other point on the straight line *KL* will exactly exhaust the budget of $100. (As an exercise, show that this is true for point *M*.)

The slope of the budget line between *K* and *L* is:

$$\frac{\text{Vertical distance } OK}{\text{Horizontal distance } OL} = \frac{10}{5} = 2$$

But this is the same as the price ratio of the two goods; that is:

$$\frac{P_{\text{clothing}}}{P_{\text{food}}} = \frac{\$20}{\$10} = 2$$

Thus the slope of the budget line is *equal to the price ratio of the two goods.*

THE CONSUMER'S EQUILIBRIUM

Faced with the budget limit *KL*, the individual purchases the combination of food and clothing shown at *E*, moving along the budget line to the point where that line touches the highest possible indifference curve, in this case u_3. Any other affordable purchase, like *M*, is less attractive because it leaves the individual on a lower indifference curve—u_2 rather than u_3.

A consumer maximizes satisfaction or utility by moving along the budget line to the highest attainable indifference curve. This is achieved at a point of tangency such as *E* in Figure 7-8

A point of tangency, of course, is a point where the slope of the indifference curve (MRS = the ratio of the marginal utilities of the two goods) is equal to the slope of the budget line (the ratio of the prices of the two goods). Thus we can confirm Equation 7-1 on page 388. The consumer reaches a maximum of satisfaction when:

Slope of indifference curve = slope of budget line

That is:

$$\frac{MU_{\text{clothing}}}{MU_{\text{food}}} = \frac{P_{\text{clothing}}}{P_{\text{food}}}$$

Rearranging this, and letting 1 represent clothing and 2 represent food, we confirm Equation 7-1:

$$\frac{MU_1}{P_1} = \frac{MU_2}{P_2}$$

In conclusion, we reemphasize that the budget line and the indifference map are independent of one another. The indifference map shows the individual's preferences; in defining the indifference map, we pay no attention to what the individual can actually afford. What the individual can afford is shown by the budget line. When the indifference map and the budget line are brought together, the choice of the consumer is determined.

DERIVING A DEMAND CURVE FROM AN INDIFFERENCE MAP

The indifference curve/budget line analysis is used in Figure 7-9*a* to show how the consumer responds to a fall in the price of clothing. When clothing was originally priced at $20 per unit, we have seen that the budget line was *KL* and the equilibrium was E_1—both reproduced from the previous figure. Now suppose that the price of clothing falls to $10 while the price of food remains unchanged. Because the price ratio has changed, the slope of the budget line changes. Specifically, the budget line rotates from *KL* to *KR*. If all $100 is spent on clothing, the consumer can now buy 10 units at point *R*. But because the price of food does not change, the new budget line still ends at point *K*, as before. Faced with the new budget line *KR*, the consumer again searches for his or her highest achievable indifference curve, finding it at the point of tangency E_2.

These two points of equilibrium, E_1 and E_2, can be used to derive two points on the demand curve of the individual. To do so, we must broaden the coverage of the indifference curve, which initially dealt with the individual's evaluation of only two

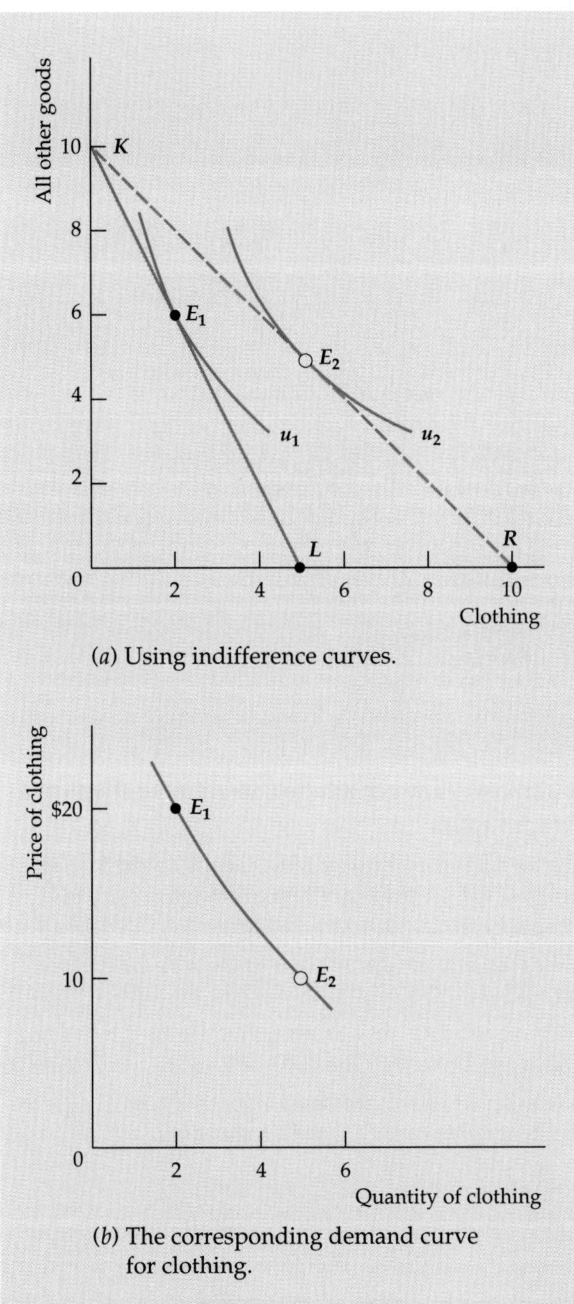

FIGURE 7-9 The effect of a fall in the price of clothing. As the price of clothing falls from \$20 to \$10, the budget line rotates counterclockwise from *KL* to *KR*. As a result, the quantity of clothing purchased increases from two to five units. In panel *b*, exactly this same information about price and quantity is shown; again the consumer moves from point E_1 to E_2. In panel *b* these points define the consumer's demand curve.

goods, food and clothing. The demand curve, on the other hand, illustrates the eagerness to obtain a good, such as clothing, by giving up money. Money, in turn, represents general purchasing power, which could be used to buy any other good or service. Thus, in Figure 7-9*a*, the broad, general alternative of all other goods and services is shown on the vertical axis, replacing the specific alternative of food shown earlier in Figure 7-8.

Observe how the two points on the demand curve in panel *b* of Figure 7-9 correspond to the two points on the indifference curves in panel *a*. At E_1, two units are bought at a price of \$20 per unit; at E_2, five units are bought at \$10. The individual's demand curve can therefore be derived from his or her indifference map plus the budget line, which rotates as the price of the good changes.

THE RESULTS OF A PRICE CHANGE: SUBSTITUTION AND INCOME EFFECTS

When the price of clothing falls, *ceteris paribus*, the household buys more clothing, for two reasons. First, clothing becomes cheaper compared to other goods. Consequently, the consumer *switches* from other goods to clothing. This is called the *substitution effect*. Second, when the price of clothing falls, the purchasing power of the consumer's money income increases. The consumer can buy more of everything—including clothing. The increase in clothing purchases is called the *income effect*.

This distinction is illustrated in Figure 7-10, which shows how the increase in clothing purchases from Q_1 to Q_2 can be broken down into substitution and income effects. To look at the effects of substitution alone, we keep the consumer on the original indifference curve u_1. This means that **real income** is held constant. At the same time, we allow the slope of the price line to change to reflect the lower price of clothing. Thus we find a new price line *ST* parallel to *KR*—thereby reflecting the new price—but tangent to the original indifference curve u_1 at point *V*. The **substitution effect** is the quantity change Q_1Q_3 associated with the move from E_1 to *V*.

The consumer does not actually move from E_1 to *V*, but from E_1 to E_2. The rest of the move—from *V* to E_2—represents the **income effect.** Observe that a shift in the price line from *ST* to *KR* results from a change in real income alone; that is, it involves no change in relative prices, since the slopes of ST and KR are the same.

A consumer's ***real income*** remains *constant* whenever the consumer remains on the same indifference curve.

The ***substitution effect*** is the change in the quantity purchased which would occur as a result of a change only in relative prices, with real income held constant. In Figure 7-10, it is the distance from Q_1 to Q_3.

The ***income effect*** is the change in the quantity purchased which would occur as a result of a change only in real income. In Figure 7-10, it is the distance from Q_3 to Q_2.

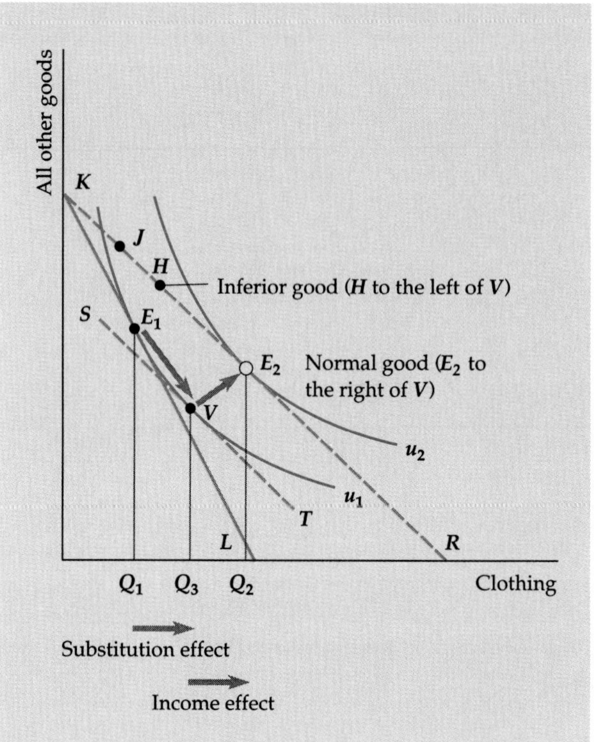

FIGURE 7-10 The substitution and income effects of a price reduction.

With the fall in the price of clothing, there is a move from equilibrium E_1 to E_2, which can be broken down into two parts:

1. The move from E_1 to V illustrates the *substitution effect* by holding real income constant. (V is on the same indifference curve as E_1.)

2. The move from V to E_2 shows the income effect by holding relative prices constant. (The slopes at V and E_2 are the same.)

Note: both effects are measured along the Q axis. Q_1Q_3 is the substitution effect, and Q_3Q_2 the income effect.

When the price of clothing falls, the shape of the indifference curve guarantees that the substitution effect will lead an individual to buy more clothing and less of other goods. That is, point V must be to the southeast of E_1 in Figure 7-10.

It is not, however, certain whether the income effect is positive or negative. For the vast majority of goods—the *normal goods*—the income effect is positive. As income increases, the individual buys more of the good and E_2 is to the right of V in Figure 7-10. But for *inferior goods,* the income effect is negative; an increase in income alone *reduces* the quantity purchased. In this case, an indifference curve touches budget line KR at a point such as H, to the left of V. (To illustrate this possibility, erase u_2 and draw in this other indifference curve, ensuring that it is tangent to KR at H.)

Economists have been fascinated with the logical possibility that the income effect might not only be negative, but also sufficiently strong to more than offset the substitution effect. In this case, an indifference curve would be tangent to KR at a point such as J, to the left of E_1. Then the reduction in the price of the good would lead to a move from E_1 to J and a *reduction* in the purchase of that good. Such an outcome is extremely rare, if it happens at all. One example has been attributed to Victorian economist Robert Giffen, involving the purchase of potatoes in a very poor economy. In such a special case, a decrease in the price of the basic staple—potatoes—might so increase people's real income and their purchases of meat and other expensive foods that they would buy fewer potatoes. Notice that such a peculiar good—a so-called *Giffen* good—would have a strange demand curve. It would slope downward and *to the left.*

CHAPTER 8
BUSINESS ORGANIZATIONS
Proprietorships, Partnerships, and Corporations

Business is a game—the greatest game in the world if *you know how to play it*
THOMAS J. WATSON, SR., OF IBM

The demand for a consumer good depends on the choices of millions of single individuals and families. The supply side is more complex. Some goods are supplied by single individuals—for example, the wheat produced by an individual farmer—but most are produced by groups of people working within business corporations. Some corporations are quite small—for example, the local firm selling heating oil to homeowners. Others are much larger and more complex—huge corporations such as General Motors, Boeing, or AT&T.

This chapter will

- Outline the main types of business organization.
- Summarize the objectives that businesses pursue.
- Explain how a business gets the funds to finance expansion.
- Explain the motivations of the buyers and sellers of stocks and bonds, and some of the reasons why stock prices fluctuate.

This chapter provides background for the next five chapters, which will explain the decisions firms must make as they produce and sell their products.

BUSINESS ORGANIZATIONS

There are three types of business organization: the **sole proprietorship,** the **partnership,** and the **corporation.** The sole proprietorship and the partnership are the most common forms of very small business, although even a one-person business may be a corporation. At the other end of the spectrum, large businesses are almost exclusively corporations. The large size of many corporations is reflected in Figure 8-1. Although the largest number of businesses are proprietorships, by far the largest share of business is conducted by corporations.

SOLE PROPRIETORSHIPS AND PARTNERSHIPS: THEIR ADVANTAGES AND DISADVANTAGES

A sole proprietorship is the easiest form of business to establish. If I decide to make pottery in my basement, or design computer software in a spare bedroom, I may do so. I can begin tomorrow, without going through legal and organizational hassles. A sole proprietorship has advantages for someone who wants to experiment with a new line of work;

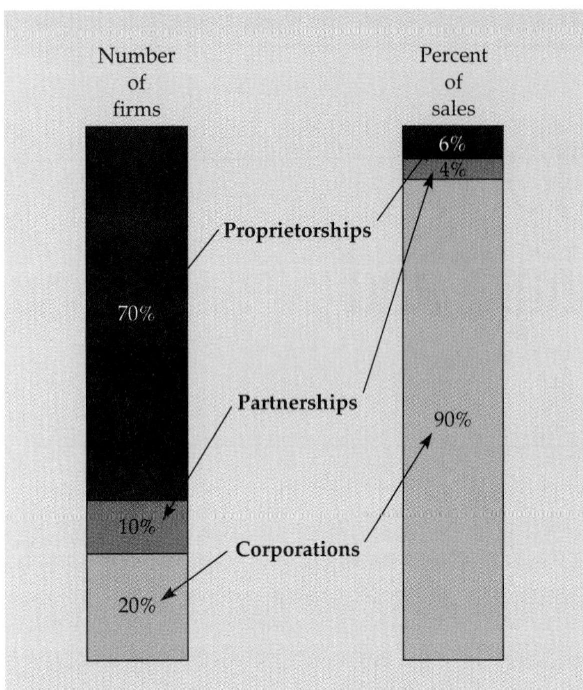

FIGURE 8-1 Proprietorships, partnerships, and corporations, 1988.

Most of the businesses in the United States are sole proprietorships. But many corporations are large, and corporations do about 90% of the business. (*Source: Statistical Abstract of the United States.*)

this may explain why so many sole proprietorships go out of business quickly.

The sole proprietorship is flexible and uncomplicated. The proprietor buys needed materials, hires help, and undertakes to pay the bills. The profits of the business belong to the owner and are shared by no one—except the government, which collects income taxes when the owner declares the profits as part of his or her personal income.

The sole proprietorship has disadvantages, however. The most obvious drawback is that there are limits to how much one individual can manage. Consider a typical small enterprise, the gasoline station. In this sort of business, a single owner has problems. While help can be hired to operate the pumps, it is better to have someone around who is "in charge." Yet one individual would find it a crushing burden to be always on hand during the long hours when a gas station is open. The obvious solution is to take on a partner who will be jointly responsible.

Some partnerships are made up of just two people; others include dozens of partners. In a typical partnership, each partner agrees to provide some fraction of the work as well as some of the financing. In return, each partner receives an agreed share of the profits or suffers an agreed share of the loss. Again, the partnership is easily established; a simple oral agreement will do. This casual method is not recommended, however, for it is a way to lose both business and friends. A formal partnership agreement, drawn up by a lawyer, can prevent grief.

Both the sole proprietorship and the partnership are simple and flexible, but they share the following major disadvantages:

1. A proprietor has **unlimited liability** for all the debts of the business. This means that, if the business runs into difficulty, the owner can lose more than his or her initial investment. Personal assets may be lost in order to pay *creditors*—that is, those to whom the business owes money. For example, a farmer's land may be auctioned off to pay debts to a bank or an implement dealer.

In the standard type of partnership, partners similarly have unlimited liability; they can lose their personal assets as well as the money they originally put into the business. Furthermore, a partnership entails a particular form of risk: *Each partner is liable for the obligations undertaken by the other partner or partners,* and each partner runs the risk of being left "holding the bag" if the other partners are unable to meet their shares of the obligations of the partnership.

2. There is a problem of *continuity.* When a single proprietor dies, the business may also die, although an heir may take over the shop or farm and continue to run it. Continuity can be even more awkward in a partnership. When a partner dies, the original partnership automatically ends, and a new partnership must be formed. A new partnership agreement is likewise necessary whenever a new partner is admitted. This is not surprising. After all, each of the partners will be liable for the acts of the new partner.

3. Finally, there is the problem of *financing growth.* A partnership or proprietorship has a number of financial sources: the personal wealth of the owner or owners; the profits made by the business which can be plowed back into it to purchase new equipment or buildings; the mortgaging of property; and borrowing from banks, suppliers, friends, and relatives. Proprietorships and partnerships, however, may have difficulty borrowing the money needed for expansion. Because of the risk that the business will be unable to repay, banks are reluctant to lend large amounts to a struggling new enterprise.

It may also be difficult to bring in new owners to help with the financing. It is true that a carrot, in the form of a share of the profits, can be dangled in front of potential investors. But with the carrot comes a stick. In gaining the right to a share of the profits, a new partner also undertakes unlimited liability for the debts of the business. Consequently, outside investors will be reluctant to share in the partnership unless they have carefully investigated it and have developed an exceptionally high degree of confidence in the partners. This may make it very hard for a partnership to get the financing needed for expansion.

THE CORPORATION

Corporation: *An ingenious device for obtaining individual profit without individual responsibility.*

AMBROSE BIERCE, *THE DEVIL'S DICTIONARY*

The major advantage of the corporate form of organization is that it **limits the liability** of its owners: All they can lose is the amount they have invested. When people buy **shares** of the **common stock** of a business, they acquire partial ownership of the business without facing the danger of unlimited liability. If the business goes bankrupt and is unable to pay its debts, the owners lose the purchase price of their shares but not their personal property. By reducing the risks of investors, the corporate form of business makes it feasible to tap a wide pool of investment funds. Thus the corporation is the form of business most suited to rapid growth with the use of outside funds.

Each ***share of common stock*** represents a fraction of the *ownership* (that is, a fraction of the *equity*) of a corporation.

Because of the limited liability, a corporation's creditors cannot lay claim to the owners' personal property if the corporation fails, although the creditors can claim the assets of the corporation itself. Corporations must inform those with whom they do business of this limited liability. In the United States, they do so by adding "Inc." or "Incorporated" to their corporate title. The British have traditionally added "Ltd." or "Limited" to the title of their corporations, although the official designation was changed to "Public Limited Company," or "PLC," in 1980. The French and Spanish use a more colorful warning: Corporations' titles are followed by the letters S.A.—for *Societe Anonyme*, or *Sociedad Anonima* (anonymous society).

When the corporate form of business was introduced in Great Britain some centuries ago, corporation charters were awarded only rarely, by special grants of the king and parliament. These corporations were granted substantial privileges. Some were given special rights to conduct business in the British colonies—the East India Company, for example. During the nineteenth century, however, a major revolution occurred in business and legal thinking, and the modern corporation emerged. General incorporation laws were passed, granting anyone the right to form a corporation. The formation of a corporation is generally a straightforward and uncomplicated legal procedure, although there are a few significant exceptions—such as banking, where government regulation is important. Some states, such as Delaware, have adopted liberal incorporation laws to encourage businesses to incorporate there.

In addition to limited liability, the corporation offers the advantage of continuity. In law, the corporation is a fictitious "legal person." When stockholders die, the corporation survives. The shares of the deceased are inherited by their heirs, and the corporation's organization is not disturbed. The heirs need not be concerned about accepting the shares, because they are not liable for the corporation's debts. Furthermore, the corporation survives if some of the stockholders want to get out of the business. These stockholders can sell their shares to anyone willing to buy, and the company need not be reorganized.

A Disadvantage: Double Taxation of Dividends. A corporation offers major advantages: limited liability and continuity. But there is also a disadvantage: Corporate profits are *taxed twice* if they are paid out as dividends to stockholders. In contrast, the profits of a proprietorship or a partnership are taxed only once, as the personal income of the proprietor or partners.

Consider an example of how corporate profits are taxed. A corporation with 1 million shares outstanding makes pretax profits of $10 million, or $10 per share. These profits are subject to the corporation tax, which might amount to, say, $3 million, or $3 per share. (The corporation income tax rate is 34% for all profits above $75,000 per year, but the effective rate is less than 34% because of detailed provisions of the tax law.) This leaves $7 million in after-tax profits, or $7 per share. Of this $7, the corporation might retain $5 for expansion of the business and pay out the remaining $2 per share as dividends to the shareholders. In turn, the shareholders must include the dividends of $2 per share as part of their personal income and pay personal income tax on them. Thus dividend income is taxed twice: first, when it is earned as part of the total profits of the corporation, and, second, when it is paid out in dividends and becomes the personal income of the shareholder who receives it.

The *double taxation of dividends* has long been a subject of controversy. Critics point out that (1) corporations are encouraged to grow bigger, because the profits retained for expansion are taxed only once, whereas profits going into dividends are taxed twice, and (2) businesses are encouraged to expand by borrowing rather than by issuing more stock, because interest is taxed more lightly than dividends. The interest paid on debt is treated as a business cost. Consequently, revenues used to pay interest are not counted as profits; they are taxed only once, as the income of the person who receives the interest. When taxes encourage businesses to go deeply into debt, they make the economic system more unstable; businesses face high interest costs and are more likely to go bankrupt.

One way to deal with these criticisms would be to allow businesses to treat dividends in the same way as interest—as a business cost. Dividends would no longer be taxed twice. The loss in tax revenues might be made up by raising the tax rate on profits retained by the corporation.

Defenders of the present tax system respond that this cure would be worse than the disease. The higher tax rate on retained profits would reduce the profits that businesses have left to finance expansion. Thus, it would weaken their ability to grow and survive in a highly competitive world economy.

The advantages and disadvantages of corporations and partnerships are summarized in Table 8-1.

HYBRID ORGANIZATIONS: HAVING YOUR CAKE AND EATING IT, TOO

Two intermediate organizations—a subchapter S corporation and a limited partnership—permit their owners to enjoy a major advantage of the standard corporation while avoiding one of its major disadvantages. Specifically, these intermediate organizations allow owners to avoid double taxation, while at the same time providing them with the protection of limited liability.

A *subchapter S corporation* is treated in the federal tax code as if it were a partnership. Rather than being subject to the federal corporate tax, its profits are treated as if they were the personal income of the individual owners and are taxed as such. Thus the owners avoid the double taxation of corporate dividends, while still enjoying the limited liability of a standard corporation. This special treatment is, however, limited to small organizations; a subchapter S corporation can have no more than 35 stockholders.

A *limited partnership* likewise avoids the double taxation of the standard corporation; the partnership's profits are taxed as the personal income of the owners and are not subject to the corporate profits tax. The limited partnership has rather complicated provisions regarding liability. There are two classes of owners—the *general partners,* who run the firm and who are personally responsible for its debts, and the *limited partners,* who are passive investors and who enjoy limited liability.

Businesses found the tax advantages of limited partnerships increasingly attractive as a result of the tax reform act of 1986, which substantially reduced personal income taxes while at the same time closing many of the loopholes in the corporate profits tax. A number of corporations reorganized as "master" limited partnerships (MLPs). Unlike traditional limited partnerships, such master limited partnerships operate much as corporations do,

TABLE 8-1 Types of Business Organizations: Their Advantages and Disadvantages

Type of Firm	*Advantages*	*Disadvantages*
Individual Proprietorship	1. Easy to establish 2. Simple organization; owner makes the decisions 3. Earnings taxed only once, as personal income of owner	1. Unlimited liability; owner's personal assets are at risk 2. Limited ability to raise funds for expansion 3. Business generally terminates with death of owner (although it may be taken over by an heir)
Partnership	1. Permits management responsibilities to be shared by several owners 2. Earnings taxed only once, as personal income of partners	1. Unlimited liability; owners' personal assets are at risk 2. More complicated than individual proprietorship; danger of conflict among partners 3. Less able than corporations to raise funds 4. Business must be terminated or reorganized with death of any partner
Corporation	1. Limited liability for owners 2. Company is not terminated with death of owners 3. Corporations are generally more able to raise funds for expansion 4. Much larger, more complex organizations are possible than with other two types	1. Dividends are taxed twice, once as corporate income, and once as personal income of stockholder 2. Management can be complicated; managers may pay little attention to interests of stockholders

issuing shares that can be traded on stock exchanges and getting into traditional corporate fields such as hotel chains, health care, motion pictures, and cable television. In 1981, only three such MLPs were formed; in the tax reform year of 1986, 38 were established. The U.S. Treasury has become concerned with the loss of tax revenues and is considering tightening up the partnership law.

HOW A CORPORATION FINANCES EXPANSION

The corporation can obtain funds for expansion in the same way as a proprietorship or partnership—that is, by borrowing from banks or plowing profits back into the business. A large corporation has additional options. It can issue common stock, bonds, or other securities.

COMMON STOCK

When the corporation sells additional shares of common stock, it takes on new part-owners, because each share represents a fraction of the ownership of the corporation. As a part-owner, the purchaser of common stock receives not only a share of any dividends paid by the corporation, but also the right to vote for the corporation's directors who, in turn, choose the corporate executives and set the corporation's policies. (On the question of who actually controls a corporation, see Box 8-1.)

BONDS

Rather than take on new owners by issuing additional common stock, the corporation may raise funds by issuing bonds, which is a way of borrowing. A bond represents the debt of the corporation; it is an IOU that the corporation is obliged to repay, whether or not it is making profits. If the corporation doesn't pay, it can be sued by the bondholder.

A bond is a long-term form of debt which does not fall due for repayment until 10, 15, or more years from the time it was initially sold (issued) by the corporation. Bonds usually come in large denominations—for example, $100,000. The original buyer normally pays the corporation a sum equal to the face value of the bond. In effect, the original buyer is lending $100,000 to the corporation. In return for the $100,000, the corporation is committed to make two sets of payments to the bondholder:

1. Interest payments that must be made during the life of the bond. If the interest rate is, say, 11% per annum on a bond with a $100,000 face value, the interest payment is $11,000 per year. For most

BOX 8-1 Who Controls the Corporation?

Because stockholders elect the board of directors, who in turn choose management, it might seem at first glance that the corporation is run in the interests of the stockholders. However, things are not necessarily that simple. If a company's stock is spread among a large number of shareholders, it may, in practice, be run by a group of insiders made up of the directors and senior management. Many stockholders do not go to the annual stockholders' meeting; it is not worth the time and effort to show up.

The separation of ownership and control of corporations was pointed out as early as 1932 by A. A. Berle and Gardner C. Means in their *Modern Corporation and Private Property*. Berle and Means found that the stockholding of the 200 largest corporations was very diffuse. For 88 of them, no single family or group of business associates owned as much as 10% of the stock. A later study indicated that, by 1963, ownership was spread even more thinly. What was true of 88 of the 200 largest corporations in the earlier period was by then true of 169. Thus the separation between ownership and control apparently is becoming wider, increasing the chance that the interest of executives will be given greater weight than the interests of the stockholder-owners.

Recent research has emphasized the general problem of **principals** (in this case, stockholders) who employ **agents** (corporate executives) to act on their behalf. The agents may pursue their own goals instead; they may, for example, hire incompetent friends or relatives.

This does not mean that the management is free to do anything it pleases. If things go badly, a group of dissident stockholders may ask other stockholders to give them their **proxies**—that is, the right to vote on their behalf at the annual meeting. If the dissident group gets enough proxies, it can vote the management out. Furthermore, if the company is badly run, the price of its stock is likely to be depressed. An outsider may then buy the company by offering stockholders a higher price, hoping to reap a big gain by installing new, more vigorous management. There has been a rash of such buyouts in recent years.

Note that it is not just corporations that are run by "agents" whose interests may differ from the "principals." The same is likely to be the case in *any* big organization, including government. Presidents and prime ministers, who act as agents for the voting public, may pursue their own agendas rather than the public interest—whatever that may be. Indeed, the fear that government leaders would pursue their own goals, at the expense of the public, was the major reason why the U.S. Constitution provided for a division of powers between the president, congress, and the courts.

Why not avoid such "agent" problems by having smaller organizations in which "principals" can manage and protect their own interests directly? The answer is, big organizations may be efficient, enjoying economies of scale. A small corporation with a few hundred employees may be easy to manage, but it cannot produce low-cost cars.

bonds, interest payments are made semiannually—in this case, $5,500 every six months.

2. A payment of the $100,000 **face value,** or **principal,** when the date of maturity arrives. That is, the corporation must repay the amount of the loan at maturity.

Since a bond commits the corporation to make the payments of interest and principal, it provides the purchaser an assured, steady income—provided the corporation avoids bankruptcy. Common stock, on the other hand, involves a substantial risk. During periods of difficulty, the corporation may reduce or eliminate the dividend, and the market price of the stock may plummet. In more dire circumstances, if the corporation goes bankrupt and its remaining assets are sold, bondholders are paid in full before stockholders get a nickel. Thus bonds provide more safety than stocks. But if the company hits the jackpot, the stockholder, not the bondholder, will reap the large rewards. The stockholder will be able to look forward to rising dividends, but the bondholder will get no more than the interest and principal specified in the bond contract.

Bonds are not the only type of debt which a corporation can issue. It may also issue *notes,* which are similar to bonds except that they have only a few years to maturity. *Commercial paper* is even shorter term, being normally issued for just a few months. With the rapid development of financial markets in recent decades, more corporations have been able to raise funds by issuing notes or paper. Corporations often issue commercial paper rather than borrow from banks, because the interest rate on paper is generally lower.

As a general rule, the original purchasers may resell all types of securities—common stocks, bonds, notes, and commercial paper.

FINANCIAL MARKETS

In some ways, the markets for stocks and bonds are similar to the markets for wheat or shoes or automobiles. For example, an increase in the demand for General Motors stock will tend to bid its price up, just as an increase in the demand for shoes will tend to bid their price up. Nevertheless, in one very important way, the market for stocks and bonds is quite different. When you buy a pair of shoes or a car, you can examine the available merchandise and make a reasonably good judgment as to its quality. But when you buy a common stock, you are, in effect, buying a future prospect—something that is clearly intangible and difficult to judge in an informed and balanced way. Similarly, when you buy a bond, you are buying a set of promises made by the bond issuer to pay interest and principal on schedule.

Because average investors can experience much difficulty evaluating the prospects of a corporation, a strong case can be made for regulations that require the disclosure of information by firms issuing securities. In the United States, such regulations are enforced by the Securities and Exchange Commission (SEC). Before offering securities to the public, companies are required to issue a **prospectus,** which is a formal statement of the current position and the future prospects of the corporation.

THE OBJECTIVES OF BUYERS OF SECURITIES

In spite of disclosure requirements, purchasers of securities face an uncertain future. Because of the risks they face, they do not simply choose the bond that has the highest interest rate; they also consider the likelihood that the company will actually repay. Indeed, purchasers of securities have three objectives to balance: return, risk, and liquidity.

Return is the annual yield, measured as a percentage of the cost of the security. For example, if a bond is purchased for $10,000 and it pays interest of $1,200 per year, then it yields 12%.

Risk is the chance that something will go wrong. For example, the company may go bankrupt, and the bondholder may lose both interest and principal. Risk can be reduced in a number of ways: by buying bonds rather than stocks, by buying "blue chip" securities of large, stable corporations, and by *diversification.* By holding the stocks of a number of companies in different industries, stockholders can diversify and thus reduce the risk that the value of their portfolios will collapse.

Finally, **liquidity** reflects the ability of the owner to sell an asset on short notice, at a stable and predictable price, and with little cost and bother. A bank account is highly liquid, since it may be withdrawn at any time for its full dollar value. At the other end of the spectrum, real estate or paintings are very illiquid. If you have to sell your home on short notice, you may have to accept a price that is much lower than you could get with a lengthier selling effort.

Although investors look for a combination of high return, low risk, and high liquidity, they do not all weigh the three objectives equally. Some—particularly those with steady incomes who are saving for the distant future—do not consider liquidity important, whereas others (perhaps those with children about to enter college) want to keep liquid investments on which they can draw in the near future. Different investors may have quite different attitudes toward risk.

THE OBJECTIVES OF ISSUERS OF SECURITIES

A company that is raising funds also has three objectives to balance: to obtain funds in such a way as to *achieve a high return* for the corporation's stockholders; *to avoid the risk* facing the company; and *to assure the availability* of money when it is needed.

A corporation balances risk and return when it chooses whether to issue stocks or bonds. In contrast with the view from the buyer's side, the view of the corporation selling securities is that *bonds* have a *higher risk* than common stock. If the corporation sells bonds, interest payments must be made no matter how badly the company may be doing. On the other hand, the company can cut dividends in the event of a downturn in business.

Although it is safer for a corporation to issue stock, there is a disadvantage: Additional stock involves taking on new part-owners. If the company does well, the original stockholders must share their rising profits with the new stockholders. In contrast, consider what happens if the corporation raises funds by selling bonds instead—that is, if the corporation increases its **leverage.** After the required payment of interest on the bonds, any large profits go only to the original stockholders. Thus the more highly leveraged a corporation is, the greater is the uncertainty for its owners. Their potential return is large, but so is the risk of bankruptcy. (The appendix to this chapter describes how companies keep their accounts, and explains the concept of net worth in more detail.)

Leverage is the ratio of debt to net worth. If this ratio is large, the corporation is *highly leveraged*.

The ***net worth*** of a corporation is the difference between its assets and liabilities. It is a measure of the stockholders' ownership or *equity* in the company.

In addition to balancing risk and return, corporations have one final objective when issuing securities: to make sure funds are available when they are needed. As a general rule, it is not advisable to finance a new factory with short-term borrowing. It is unwise to have to keep repaying a short-term debt and borrowing money again each year to finance a factory over, say, a 20-year lifetime. In some of those years, funds may not be available to borrowers, or they may be available only at a very high interest rate. New factories should therefore be financed by long-term borrowing, by the issue of additional stock, or by retained profits.

In order to ensure the availability of money for unpredictable requirements that can arise, a corporation may arrange a **line of credit** at a bank. A line of credit is a commitment by a bank to lend up to a specified limit at the request of the company.

THE BOND MARKET

Because security buyers balance risk and return, risky securities generally must have higher yields, or nobody will buy them. This is reflected in the bond market yields shown in Figure 8-2. Observe that the highest grade corporate bonds, classified Aaa by Moody's Investors' Service, have lower yields than the riskier corporate bonds, classified Baa. (In judging the quality of bonds, investors' services consider such factors as leverage and the stability of a corporation's earnings.) In turn, U.S. government bonds, which are free from risk of default, have lower yields than even the highest grade corporate bonds.

Note also that the gaps between these three sets of bonds—U.S. government, corporate Aaa, and corporate Baa—are not constant. The gap between corporate Aaa and Baa yields shot up most conspicuously during the early 1930s. As the economy collapsed into the depression, bankruptcies mounted and many shaky firms went under. The risks associated with the holding of low-grade

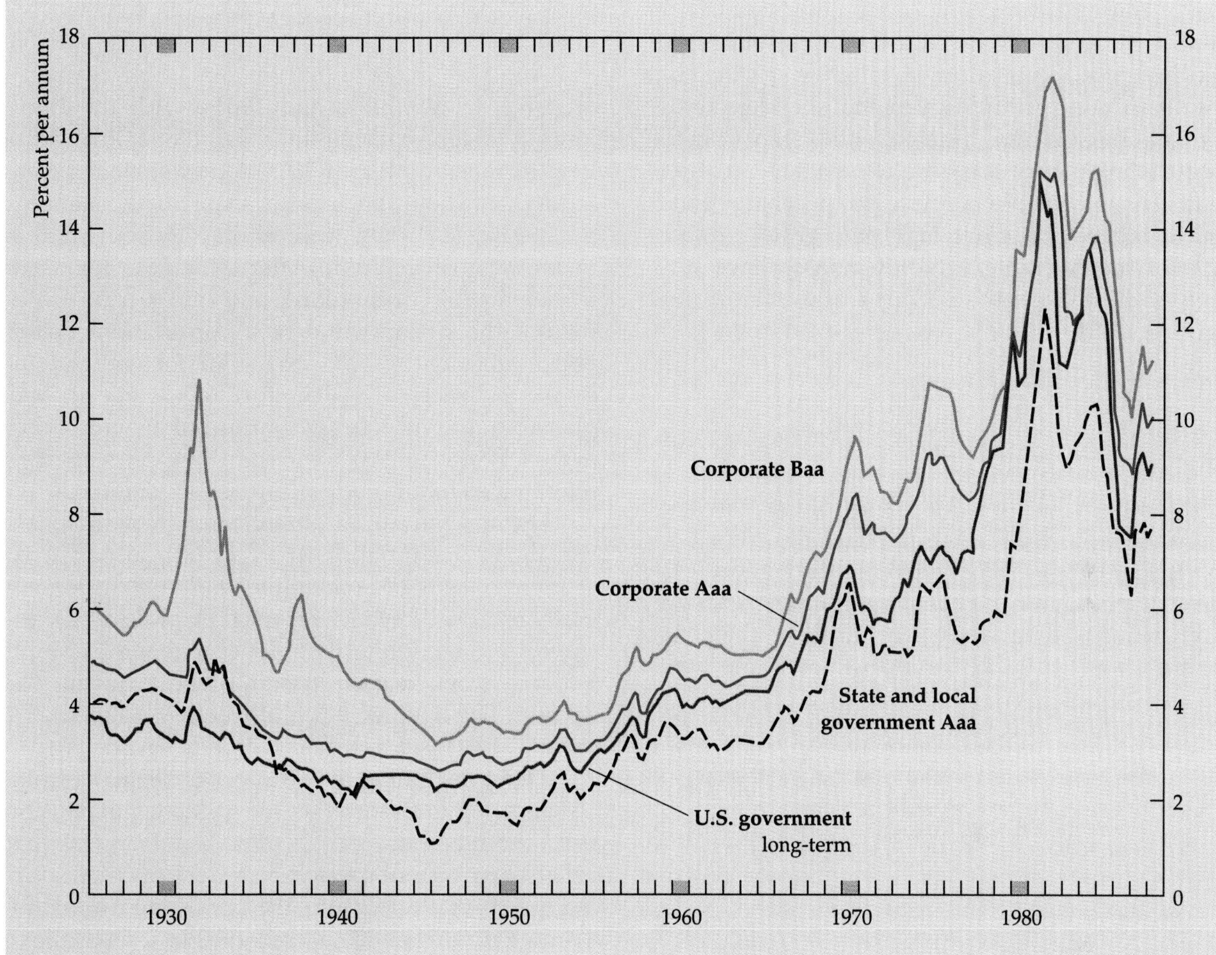

FIGURE 8-2 Long-term bond yields.

The differences between yields on different securities reflect primarily differences in risk. (A notable exception is the low yield on state and local government securities, which reflects their tax-exempt status.) The rising trend of all interest rates between 1965 and 1981 was caused primarily by a rise in the rate of inflation.

corporate bonds rose; consequently, their yields also rose compared to the yields on high-grade bonds. **Risk premiums** also increased during the recessions of 1974 and 1982, when the gap between the yields on corporate Aaa and corporate Baa bonds widened. The gap between risk-free U.S. government bonds and corporate Aaa bonds also widened.

A *risk premium* is the difference between the yields on two grades of bonds because of differences in their risk.

Taxes are another reason for differences in bond yields. Bondholders generally have to pay income taxes on the interest they receive. Interest on state and local government bonds, however, is exempt from the federal income tax, and from some state income taxes as well. Because of the tax advantage, states and localities can find buyers for their bonds even though they offer low interest rates. Thus the difference in tax treatment explains why yields on state and local government bonds are lower than those on other bonds.

A notable feature in the bond market was the

sharp upward movement of all interest rates between 1965 and 1981. An important reason for this rise was the acceleration of inflation during that period. When inflation is high, bondholders recognize that interest and principal will be repaid in the future when money is less valuable than it is at present. They therefore hesitate to purchase bonds unless interest rates are high enough to compensate for the declining value of money. Since 1981, the rate of inflation has declined, and interest rates have receded.

THE STOCK MARKET

Corporate stocks are bought and sold on the stock exchanges, the most famous being the New York Stock Exchange. Stockbrokers throughout the country maintain close contact with the exchanges, buying and selling stocks on behalf of their customers.

A ***broker*** acts as a representative of a buyer or seller, offering to buy or sell on behalf of clients.

Prices fluctuate on the stock exchanges in response to changes in demand and supply. Stock purchasers are interested in such things as the current and expected future profits of the corporation. Thus stock prices may rise rapidly during periods of prosperity.

In the 1920s, the desire to "get rich quick" in the stock market became a national mania. With stocks rising, many investors learned that individuals, too, could use leverage to increase their potential gains; they borrowed large sums to buy stocks in the expectation that their prices would rise. Then came the Great Crash of 1929. The Dow-Jones average of 30 major industrial stocks fell from 381 in 1929 to 41 in 1932 (Fig. 8-3). Many investors were wiped out. The stocks of the best corporations in America shared in the disaster. From a price of $396 in early September 1929, General Electric fell to $168 in late November and to $34 by 1932. Similarly, General Motors dropped from $72 to $36 to $8, and AT&T from $304 to $197 to $70.[1]

Another major upswing in stock averages occurred in the 1950s and 1960s, with the Dow-Jones average reaching 1,000 by 1966. During the long expansion of the 1960s, common stocks were attractive. They promised a share in the nation's prosperity, and they were widely looked on as a hedge against inflation. After all, stocks represent ownership of corporations, and in a period of inflation, the dollar value of a corporation's plant and equipment should rise with the general increase in prices. This comforting viewpoint was plausible, but it was not borne out by unfolding events. From its 1966 high, the Dow-Jones average retreated as inflationary pressures accelerated.

During the 1970s, stock market participants concluded that inflation was very unhealthy for the economy; signs of accelerating inflation were generally followed by declines in stock prices. As measured by the popular Dow-Jones average in Figure 8-3, the stock market went nowhere during the decade: The average price of stocks was about the same in 1980 as it had been a decade earlier.

Then, beginning in 1982, stocks began a strong advance. One reason was the vigorous expansion from the recession of 1981–1982. Another was that inflation was under much better control than during the 1970s. At any rate, the Dow-Jones industrial average rose from 800 in mid-1982 to a peak above 2,700 in the summer of 1987. By that time, many holders of stocks were becoming nervous. A sharp reaction soon came. In a panicky selloff on October 19, the Dow-Jones average plunged 23%—a sharper fall than had occurred in any single day in 1929. Over $500 billion in stock values evaporated, but the underlying economy was much stronger than it had been in 1929. A moderate, healthy growth continued into 1988, in contrast to the economic collapse that followed the stock market crash of 1929.

[1]For some of the drama of the collapse, see Frederick Lewis Allen, *The Lords of Creation* (New York: Harper, 1935), Chapter 13, or John Kenneth Galbraith, *The Great Crash, 1929* (Boston: Houghton Mifflin, 1961).

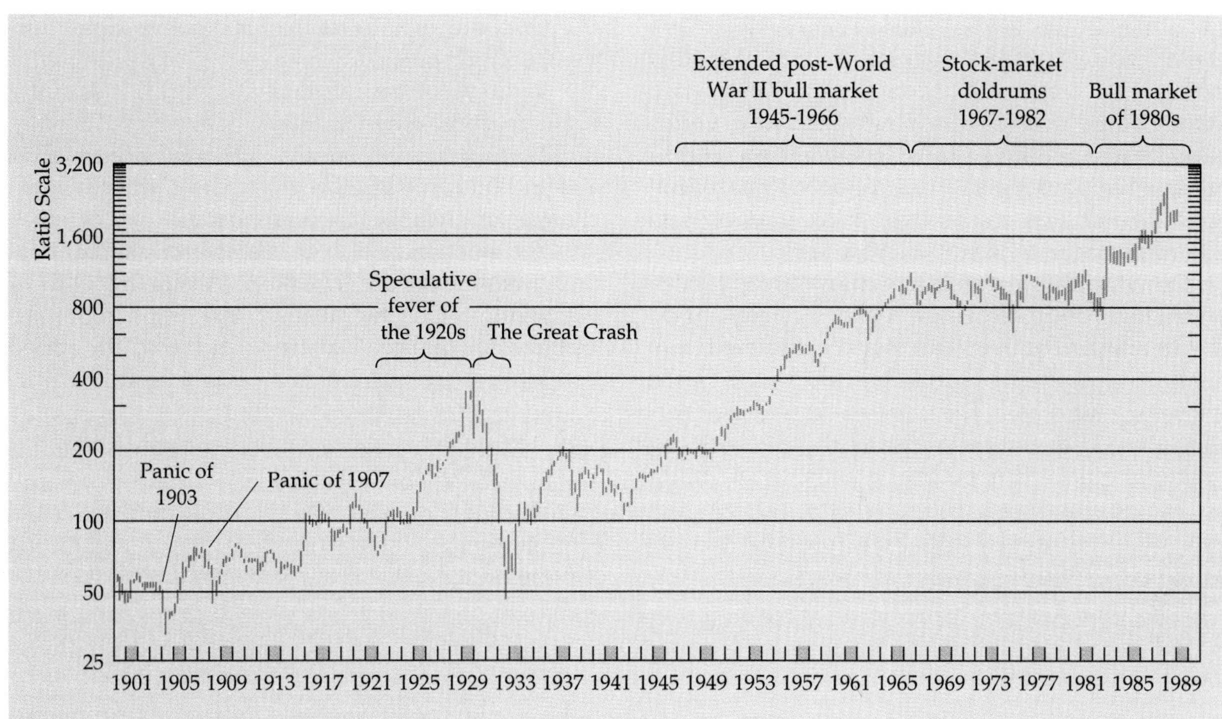

FIGURE 8-3 The Dow-Jones industrial stock average, 1900–1989.

The biggest swing in stock prices, in percentage terms, took place during the rising "bull" market of the 1920s, the collapsing "bear" market of 1929–1932, and the subsequent recovery of 1932–1936. In the first two decades after World War II (1945–1966), average stock prices rose about sixfold. But between 1966 and 1982, there was no further gain; on average, stock prices were lower in 1982 than in 1966. Beginning in 1982, a strong upward movement occurred, raising the average price of stocks to an all-time high in the summer of 1987. (Note: The vertical axis is drawn with a ratio or logarithmic scale. As explained in the appendix to Chapter 1, equal vertical distances represent equal percentage changes. For example, the distance from 100 to 200 is the same as the distance from 200 to 400.)

LIVING IN A GLOBAL ECONOMY

WHAT'S HAPPENING IN TOKYO, HONG KONG, AND LONDON?

In the week preceding Black Monday, October 19, 1987, signs of nervousness accumulated in New York and other major financial centers. By the beginning of that week, the Dow-Jones average had already dropped more than 200 points from its August high of 2,700. Between Wednesday (October 14) and Friday (October 16) it slipped another 200 points before the markets closed for a weekend of nervous reflection.

By the time New York traders woke for breakfast on Monday morning, they had some troubling news. Because of the international time difference, Far Eastern and European stock markets open before New York. In fact, when the stock exchange opens on Monday morning in Tokyo, it is only 7:00 P.M. on the previous evening in New York, and the

Tokyo market has already closed before New York opens. The news from Tokyo was bad: the Monday market had fallen 4%. From Hong Kong—two hours behind Tokyo—the news was worse: The market had gone into a tailspin toward the end of the day. London, which was still open, was in full retreat. Financiers reached for their phones, and sell orders began to pile up in New York.

Downward pressures had thus already been established before the market opened in New York. The downward movement quickly gathered momentum, with the market falling 200 points in the first hour and a half. There was a respite, as "bargain hunters" began buying stock. But the ensuing weakness quickly turned into a panic as orders to sell were dumped into the collapsing market. The scene on the stock exchange floor was surreal, with glassy-eyed brokers staring in stunned disbelief as the index dropped more than 500 points (23%) during the single day.

As news spread around the world, it set off a chain reaction when markets opened on Tuesday. In Tokyo, prices fell almost 15%; in Sydney, 25%; and in London, 15%. In Hong Kong, the stock exchange simply kept its doors closed.

The stock market had become an international one. Musing on the wreckage, Wolfgang Otto of Frankfurt's Commerzbank observed that the global stock market "is here to stay. But," he added in warning, "the price of it is greater volatility."[2]

[2]As quoted in *Business Week,* November 2, 1987, p. 54.

KEY POINTS

1. There are three forms of business organization: the sole proprietorship, the partnership, and the corporation.

2. Sole proprietorships and partnerships are simple and flexible. On the other hand, corporations also have advantages: (a) limited liability and (b) automatic continuity, even if one or more of the owners should die.

3. A corporation can obtain financing by issuing (selling) common stock. All three types of businesses may raise funds by borrowing. Large corporations, however, find it easier than sole proprietorships or partnerships to borrow. They may do so by issuing bonds, notes, or commercial paper.

4. The purchaser of securities balances three objectives: *high return, low risk,* and *high liquidity.*

5. A company that issues new securities also tries to find the best balance among three objectives: (1) to make the *return* of the corporation's stockholders as high as possible, (2) to avoid *risk,* and (3) to assure the *availability* of money when needed.

6. In general, bonds are less risky than common stocks for buyers of securities. However, it is riskier for corporations to issue bonds or other debt than it is to issue new stock, since interest on the debt is a legal obligation. If the corporation doesn't pay interest, it may be forced into bankruptcy. However, the corporation can cut dividends on its stock.

7. When corporations increase their debts, they thereby increase their leverage; that is, they increase their ratio of debt to net worth. While this raises their potential gain, it also increases their risk of bankruptcy, since they must make interest and principal payments no matter how bad business is.

8. Because stocks and bonds represent claims to future profits or interest payments, an evaluation of the issuer's prospects is extremely important for anyone buying a security. To help protect the purchaser, the Securities and Exchange Commission (SEC) requires corporations to make relevant information available to the public.

KEY CONCEPTS

sole proprietorship
partnership
limited liability
corporation
common stock
equity (ownership)
double taxation of dividends
principal (or face value) of a bond
yield (or return)
risk
liquidity
leverage
prospectus
line of credit
risk premium

PROBLEMS

8-1. In your view, what is the best form of business organization for

- **(a)** A farm?
- **(b)** A gasoline station?
- **(c)** A pharmacy?
- **(d)** A law firm?
- **(e)** A manufacturer of steel?

In each case, explain your choice.

8-2. Figure 8-1 indicates that the typical U.S. corporation is larger than the typical partnership. Can you explain why?

8-3. Even though many corporations are large, a corporation may be very small, with only one owner. For example, a small building contractor may set up a corporation. Can you explain why?

8-4. Suppose you are an investment adviser and a 50-year-old person comes to you for advice on how to invest $100,000 for retirement. What advice would you give? What advice would you give to a young couple who want to temporarily invest $20,000 which they expect to use for a downpayment on a home two years from now?

8-5. If a corporation increases its leverage, what are the advantages and/or disadvantages for:

- **(a)** The owner of a share of the corporation's stock?
- **(b)** The owner of a bond of the corporation?

***8-6.** The text describes a tax advantage that sole proprietorships and partnerships can have over corporations. In your own words, explain this advantage, using a numerical example.

APPENDIX

BUSINESS ACCOUNTING: The Balance Sheet and the Income Statement

Business accounts are an important tool for helping management keep track of how well the company is doing and what it is worth. They are also a valuable source of information for potential buyers of the company's stock or bonds. In addition, businesses are required to keep accounts for tax purposes.

There are two major types of business accounts:

1. The **balance sheet,** which gives a picture of the company's financial status at a *point* in time—for example, at the close of business on December 31 of last year.
2. The **income statement**—also called the **profit and loss statement**—which summarizes the company's transactions over a *period* of time, such as a year.

The income statement records the *flow* of payments into and out of a company over a period of time. It is like a record of the amount of water that has flowed into and out of Lake Michigan during a year. The balance sheet, on the other hand, measures the situation at a specific point in time. It is like a measure of the *stock* of water in Lake Michigan today at noon.

THE BALANCE SHEET

The balance sheet shows (1) the **assets** which a company owns, (2) the **liabilities** which it owes, and (3) the value of the **ownership** of the stockholders. Assets must be exactly equal to the total of liabilities plus ownership. To use a simple illustration: If you have a car worth \$7,000 (an asset), for which you still owe \$4,000 to the bank (your debt or liability), then \$3,000 is the value of your ownership in the car.

The same fundamental equation also holds for a corporation:

Assets = **liabilities** (what is owed) + **net worth** (the value of ownership)

Assets are listed on the left side of the balance sheet, whereas liabilities and net worth are listed on the right. Because of the fundamental equation, the two sides must add to the same total. **The balance sheet must balance.**

The ***net worth*** of a corporation—the amount the stockholders own—is equal to the assets minus the liabilities of the corporation.

TABLE 8-2 Balance Sheet of AT&T, Dec. 31, 1987 (simplified; millions of dollars)

Assets			*Liabilities and Net Worth*		
1. Current assets		$14,970	5. Current liabilities		$10,575
(a) Cash	$2,785		(a) Accounts payable	$4,680	
(b) Receivables	7,689		(b) Payroll	2,332	
(c) Inventories	3,157		(c) Other	3,563	
(d) Other	1,339		6. Long-term debt		7,243
2. Property, plant and equipment		20,681	7. Other liabilities		6,153
3. Other assets		2,775	**8. Total liabilities**		**23,971**
			9. Net worth (4 - 8)		**14,455**
			(a) Paid-in capital	9,679	
			(b) Retained earnings	4,776	
4. Total assets (items 1 + 2 + 3)		**38,426**	**10. Total liabilities and net worth (8 + 9)**		**38,426**

Source: AT&T, *Annual Report, 1987.*

As an example, consider Table 8-2, which shows the balance sheet of American Telephone and Telegraph (AT&T).

THE LEFT-HAND SIDE: ASSETS

AT&T has sizable assets in the form of cash (bank accounts) and accounts receivable—for example, the value of long-distance telephone services that customers have used but have not yet paid for. AT&T has sizable inventories of materials and parts, and major assets in the form of land, plant (buildings), and equipment.

THE RIGHT-HAND SIDE: LIABILITIES AND NET WORTH

AT&T has a number of short-term liabilities: amounts which AT&T has not yet paid for the electronic parts and other items it has bought from suppliers (accounts payable); wages, salaries, and benefits not yet paid for work already performed (payroll); and other short-term liabilities. In addition, at the end of 1987, AT&T had an outstanding long-term debt of more than $7 billion. (If debt matures within one year, it is short term; if it matures in more than one year, it is long term.)

At the end of 1987, AT&T's total assets were $38,426 million, and its liabilities were $23,971 million. The net worth—the ownership of all stockholders—was therefore $14,455 million. Of this total, $9,679 had been paid in by stockholders purchasing shares from the company. The rest ($4,776 million) represented retained earnings—that is, profits made over the years that had been plowed back into the business.[3]

[3]"Retained earnings" may sound like a pool of funds which the corporation has readily available. However, this is generally not the case. Most retained earnings are not held in the form of cash; most are used to buy machinery or other items.

Suppose that, in the first year of its operation, a corporation earns $1,000 and retains it all. (It pays no dividend.) The $1,000 may be used to buy a new machine. Then, as a result, the following changes occur in the balance sheet:

	Change in		
Assets		*Net worth*	
Machinery	+$1,000	Retained earnings	+$1,000

The retained earnings have not been held in the form of idle cash; they have been put to work to buy machinery. The machinery shows up on the asset side. When the retained earnings are included in net worth, the balance sheet balances.

At the end of 1987, there were about 109 million shares of AT&T common stock outstanding. (AT&T is the most widely held U.S. stock.) Each share represented an equity, or **book value,** of $13.30—that is, $14.5 billion in net worth divided by 109 million shares.

The ***book value*** of a stock is its net worth per share. It is calculated by dividing the total net worth of the company by the number of shares outstanding.

If you are thinking about buying common stock of a company, its book value should interest you. If it has a high book value, you will be buying ownership of a lot of assets. However, *don't get carried away by a high book value.* If the assets happen to be machinery and equipment that can be used only to produce buggy whips or other items for which there is no demand, the high book value may not be worth very much; the assets may not earn much income in the future. On the other hand, the stock of a profitable corporation may sell for substantially more than its book value, particularly during a stock-market boom. During the summer of 1987, the stocks making up the Dow-Jones industrial average sold for more than twice their book value. (AT&T sold as high as $35.88, or about 2.7 times book value.)

TABLE 8-3 Income Statement of AT&T, 1987 (millions of dollars)

1. Revenues		$37,074
(a) Sales of services	$19,659	
(b) Sales of products	10,206	
(c) Rental revenues	3,733	
(d) Other	3,476	
2. Less: Costs		33,898
(a) Costs, excluding items below	15,980	
(b) Depreciation	3,724	
(c) Selling and administrative costs	11,107	
(d) Research and development	2,453	
(e) Interest	634	
3. Income (profit) before taxes (1 - 2)		3,176
4. Less: Income taxes		1,132
5. Net income (net profit) (3-4)		2,044
(a) Dividends	1,320	
(b) Retained earnings	720	

Source: AT&T, *Annual Report, 1987.*

THE INCOME STATEMENT

Whereas the balance sheet shows the assets, liabilities, and net worth of a corporation at a point in time, the income statement shows what has happened *during a period of time*—for example, during a calendar year. AT&T's income statement for 1987 is shown in Table 8-3.

During 1987, AT&T had $37.1 billion in revenues, more than half of which came from long-distance telephone services. Costs of $33.9 billion must be subtracted from revenues to calculate before-tax profit of $3.2 billion. Corporate income taxes were $1.1 billion, leaving an after-tax profit of $2.0 billion, or $1.85 per share. Of this after-tax profit, $1.3 billion was paid in dividends to stockholders, and $720 million was retained by the company. Observe that the retained earnings in Table 8-2 are substantially greater than those shown in Table 8-3. The reason is as follows: The income statement in Table 8-3 shows only the retained earnings during the one year, 1987. In contrast, the balance sheet in Table 8-2 shows all retained earnings accumulated over the entire lifetime of the company. (Actually, it's not quite as simple as that, because major changes were made in AT&T's balance sheet when it was split up, with the regional telephone companies becoming independent corporations.)

CHAPTER 9
THE COSTS OF PRODUCTION

Which of you, intending to build a tower, sitteth not down first, and counteth the cost?
LUKE 14:28

Businesses make profits by selling at a price that exceeds cost. Therefore, two of the major concerns of business executives are: (1) what price can they get, and (2) how can they keep costs down, while still maintaining or improving quality?

The following chapters (10-13) will show how price depends on the type of market in which a business operates. Does the business have many competitors, or does it have the market to itself? But first, in this chapter we will investigate the costs of production.

THE SHORT RUN AND THE LONG RUN

Like consumers, business firms have choices to make. One of the most important has to do with the way in which goods are produced: what *combination of inputs* will a firm use in the productive process? For example, will an automobile manufacturer be able to produce most cheaply by using a highly automated assembly line, with a great deal of equipment and only a few workers? Will the wheat farmer use a lot of fertilizer on each acre or produce the wheat using more land and less fertilizer?

The freedom of action of a business is, however, severely limited in the short run. For example, the way in which General Motors makes cars this year is determined largely by decisions already made in the past. General Motors already has in place the robots, stamping machines, and factories that it will use in this year's production runs; it is now too late to order new machines or build new factories. In the short run, its decisions are limited: How many cars will it produce, and how many workers will it employ on the production line to make these cars? Over the longer run, of course, GM has much more freedom. If it is making decisions on what it will be doing five or ten years from now, it will have time to expand its capital by building new factories or buying new equipment. Or it can contract its capital by deciding not to replace obsolete plant or equipment.

Thus economists make a distinction between the **short run** and the **long run.** In the short run, one or more inputs are fixed. For example, GM has only a fixed quantity of plant and equipment, and a farmer has only a fixed quantity of land. In the long run, a firm can pick from a full menu of choices. It can choose to produce in a **capital-intensive** manner—with many machines and few workers—or in a **labor-intensive** manner, with many workers and few machines.

The ***short run*** is the period when one or more inputs are fixed.

The ***long run*** is the period when the firm is able to change the quantities of all inputs, including capital and land.

The first part of this chapter will deal with costs in the short run. This will provide background for the later part of the chapter, which considers the long run when choices may be made regarding the best combination of labor and capital.

The short run is not defined as any specific number of weeks, months, or years. Rather, it is the time period when plant, equipment, or other input is fixed, *whatever* that period might be. In some industries, the short run may last many years. For example, it takes a decade or more to design and construct a large electric power plant. In other industries, the short run may be just a matter of days. For example, a college entrepreneur can quickly buy a small computer and thus acquire the capital equipment to set up business typing term papers. Furthermore, the short run may be briefer for an expanding firm than for a contracting firm. An expanding firm may be able to acquire new equipment quickly, whereas a contracting firm may be able to reduce its capital stock only slowly. There may be no market in which it can sell its used machinery, and its capital stock may take years to wear out.

COSTS IN THE SHORT RUN

In the short run, output can be raised by increasing the quantities of variable inputs, such as labor, raw materials, and parts and supplies bought from other businesses. Because some inputs (plant and equipment) are fixed in the short run, whereas others are variable, a firm's total costs may be divided into two components: (1) **fixed costs** and (2) **variable costs.**

1. *Fixed costs* or *overhead costs.* Fixed costs (FC) are the costs that do not change as output changes. They are incurred *even if no output is produced at all.* For example, even if no output is produced, the firm will still have to pay *interest* on the funds it has borrowed to buy equipment or to construct buildings. Factories and equipment will *depreciate* even if they stand unused, and firms will still have to buy *insurance* against fire and other risks.

Table 9-1 shows the short-run costs of a hypothetical manufacturer of shoes. Note that fixed costs (col. 2) remain constant at $35, regardless of the quantity of output q (col. 1).

TABLE 9-1 Short-Run Costs of a Hypothetical Firm Producing Shoes

(1) Quantity Produced (pairs) q	(2) Fixed Cost FC	(3) Variable Cost VC	(4) Total Cost TC = FC + VC (4) = (3) + (2)	(5) Marginal Cost MC = change in total cost	(6) Average Total Cost ATC = TC ÷ q (6) = (4) ÷ (1)	(7) Average Fixed Cost AFC = FC ÷ q (7) = (2) ÷ (1)	(8) Average Variable Cost AVC = VC ÷ q (8) = (3) ÷ (1)
0	$35	0	$ 35				
				$ 59 – $ 35 = $24			
1	35	$ 24	59		$59	$35	$24
				75 – 59 = 16			
2	35	40	75		37.50	17.50	20
				95 – 75 = 20			
3	35	60	95		31.67	11.67	20
				120 – 95 = 25			
4	35	85	120		30	8.75	21.25
				150 – 120 = 30			
5	35	115	150		30	7	23
				190 – 150 = 40			
6	35	155	190		31.67	5.83	25.83
				245 – 190 = 55			
7	35	210	245		35	5	30

2. *Variable costs.* On the other hand, variable costs (VC) do increase as output increases, since the firm uses more variable inputs such as labor, raw materials, and electricity.

> ***Fixed costs*** (FC) are those costs that do *not* change as output changes.
>
> ***Variable costs*** (VC) are those costs that *do* change as output changes.

Total cost is calculated by adding variable and fixed costs. Suppose, for example, that output is seven units and variable costs are $210 (Table 9-1, col. 3). When this sum is added to fixed costs of $35, we find the total cost of producing seven units of output: $245 (col. 4).

> ***Total cost*** (TC) is the sum of fixed and variable costs:
>
> TC = FC + VC

MARGINAL COST

One of the decisions that businesses face is: "Should we expand our production?" **Marginal cost** (MC)—that is, the *additional* cost as output increases by one unit—plays a key role in this decision.

> ***Marginal cost*** (MC) is the increase in total cost when one additional unit is produced.

Marginal cost is calculated in column 5 of Table 9-1. For example, as the firm's output increases from six to seven units, its total cost in column 4 increases from $190 to $245, or by $55. Thus, the marginal cost of the seventh pair of shoes is $55. Similarly, the marginal cost of the sixth unit is calculated as $190 – $150 = $40.[1]

AVERAGE TOTAL COST

The firm may also be interested in its cost *per unit* of output. At an output of five units, the per-unit cost or **average total cost** (ATC) is simply the $150 in total costs divided by the five units, or $30 per unit. Similarly, average total cost can be calculated at any other output by dividing total cost by the number of units. This is done in column 6 of Table 9-1.

> ***Average total cost*** (ATC), also known as *average cost* (AC), is total cost divided by the number of units produced.

We have already seen that total cost can be broken down into fixed cost and variable cost. Similarly, average cost can be broken down into its two components:

Average cost = average fixed cost + average variable cost

Average fixed cost (AFC) is fixed cost divided by output. In the example presented in Table 9-1, fixed cost is $35. Thus, at an output of five units, we see (col. 7) that the firm's average fixed cost is $35 ÷ 5 = $7. Similarly, average variable cost (AVC) is variable cost divided by output. At an output of five units, the firm's variable cost is $115. Therefore, its average variable cost (col. 8) is $115 ÷ 5 = $23.

> ***Average fixed cost*** (AFC) is fixed cost divided by output.
>
> ***Average variable cost*** (AVC) is variable cost divided by output.
>
> ***Average total cost*** (ATC) is the sum of these two:
>
> ATC = AFC + AVC

GRAPHICAL PRESENTATION

The various costs given in Table 9-1 are reproduced in Figure 9-1. In panel *a*, the lowest arrow shows fixed cost; this cost remains constant at $35 regardless of output. To this fixed cost, we add the variable cost to get the total cost. For example, at an output of five units, variable cost is $115, as shown by the long arrow. The important concept of mar-

[1] Sometimes a firm makes decisions in batches, rather than one unit at a time. For example, a small drug firm might want to decide whether to increase production by 1,000 bottles of aspirin, from, say, 200,000 bottles to 201,000. If the additional costs are $200, then the marginal cost over this range is 20¢ per bottle—that is, $200 ÷ 1,000.

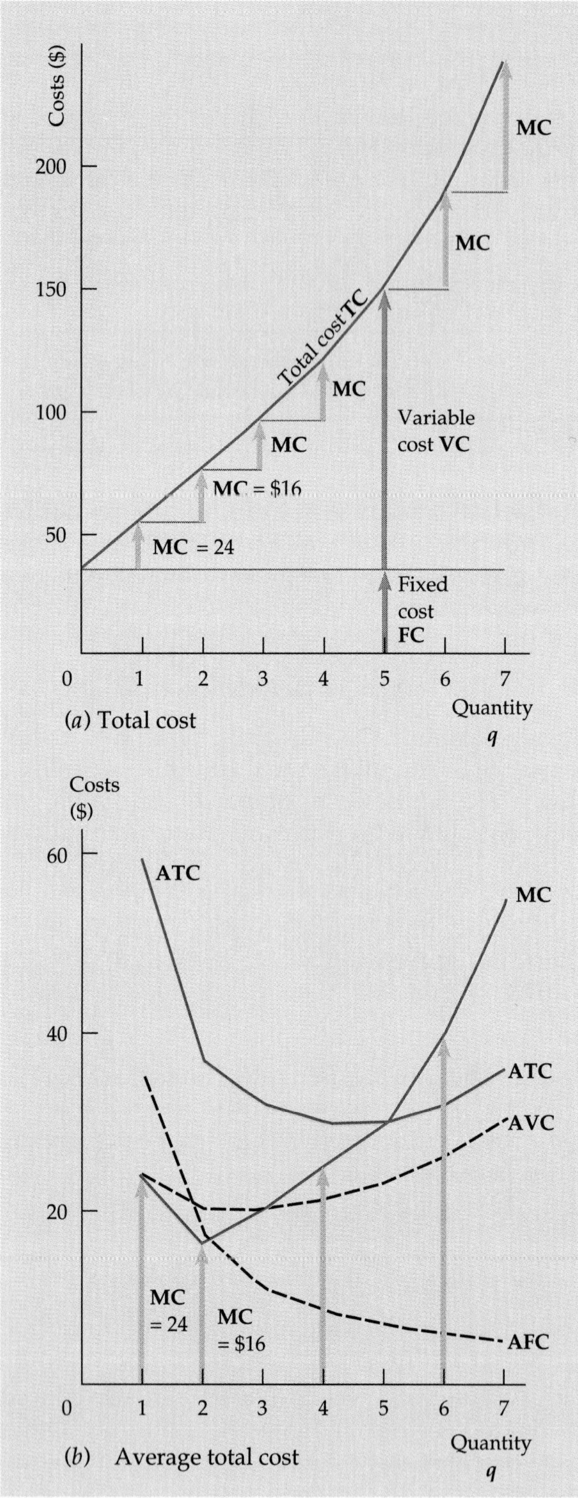

ginal cost (MC) is illustrated with the red arrows; MC shows how total cost increases as each successive unit of production is added.

Panel *b* illustrates average total costs. Its vertical scale is stretched out, compared to panel *a,* in order to make it easier to read. Note that average total cost at first falls, and then eventually rises. Average variable cost also traces out a U shape. In contrast, average fixed cost (AFC) falls continuously as output increases. It must. After all, fixed cost—$35, in this case—is being spread out over more and more units as output increases.

Note that panel *a* shows total cost and its components, whereas panel *b* shows the various average cost curves. Marginal cost, which will play a key role in future chapters, is shown in both panels. For example, the marginal cost of the second unit is $16; that's how much total cost increases in panel *a* when the second unit is produced. In panel *b,* the marginal cost curve is constructed by extracting the MC arrows from the upper diagram and graphing them. (The MC arrows are longer on the lower diagram, since the vertical axis is stretched.)

THE RELATIONSHIP BETWEEN AVERAGE AND MARGINAL COSTS

In Figure 9-1*b,* observe that, whenever marginal cost is below the average cost curve, the average curve is falling. This *must* be so; the low marginal cost drags down the average. When the marginal cost is above the average cost, it pulls the average up; the average cost curve rises. Finally, when the marginal cost equals the average cost—as it does

FIGURE 9-1 Short-run costs.

This figure illustrates the short-run costs of the firm in Table 9-1.

In panel *a,* total cost is the sum of fixed cost and variable cost. Marginal cost indicates how much total cost is increasing, and is shown by the set of red arrows in panel *a* or in panel *b.* In panel *b,* average total cost is the total cost divided by the number of units produced.

for the fifth unit—then marginal cost has a neutral effect. It neither pulls the average up nor drags it down. Average cost is flat; it has reached its lowest point. Thus *the marginal cost curve cuts through the lowest point on the average total cost curve.* (The same is true of average variable cost: MC cuts through its lowest point, too.)

This relationship between average and marginal is a general one; it applies to more than cost curves. For example, if you have an average grade of 80 on your first two chemistry exams, a lower grade of 65 on your third exam will drag your average down to 75 (that is, 80 + 80 + 65, divided by 3). On the other hand, if you come through with a high grade of 95 on that third, "marginal" exam, you will pull your average up. Finally, if your third exam is 80, this will leave your average score unchanged at 80. Box 9-1 shows how the relationship between marginal and average also holds in baseball.

THE SHORT-RUN PRODUCTION FUNCTION

Costs of production depend on (1) the amount of inputs used in the productive process, and (2) the prices of these inputs.

BOX 9–1 *Why a Firm's Costs Are Like a Baseball Player's Average*

Late in the 1980 season, Kansas City's George Brett had the best chance to hit the magic .400 (40 hits in each 100 times at bat) since the Boston Red Sox' Ted Williams did it with .406 in 1941. The numbers in the diagram show Brett's batting performance during one week in September. In the first three games against Chicago and Detroit he batted a disappointing .250 (one hit in each four times at bat). Since this marginal performance (shown in green) was below his average in the .380s, it pulled his average down. But in the next three games, his fortunes improved: He batted .500 or better. Since this marginal performance was above his average, it pulled his average up.

Did Brett go on to hit .400? Although the last three games shown here started him off on a hitting streak that carried him over .400 for a week in late September, he couldn't maintain the pace. He had a number of games where he got only one hit for four trips to the plate—or only .250 for the day. His lower marginal hitting dragged his overall average back down. He finished the season with .390. To repeat: A low marginal performance drags the average down; a high marginal performance pulls the average up.

So too with marginal and average costs—as we have already seen in Figure 9-1b. Until marginal cost and average cost reach their point of intersection at 5 units of output, marginal cost is below average cost and is therefore pulling average cost down. As output expands beyond five units and marginal cost soars above average cost, average cost is pulled upward.

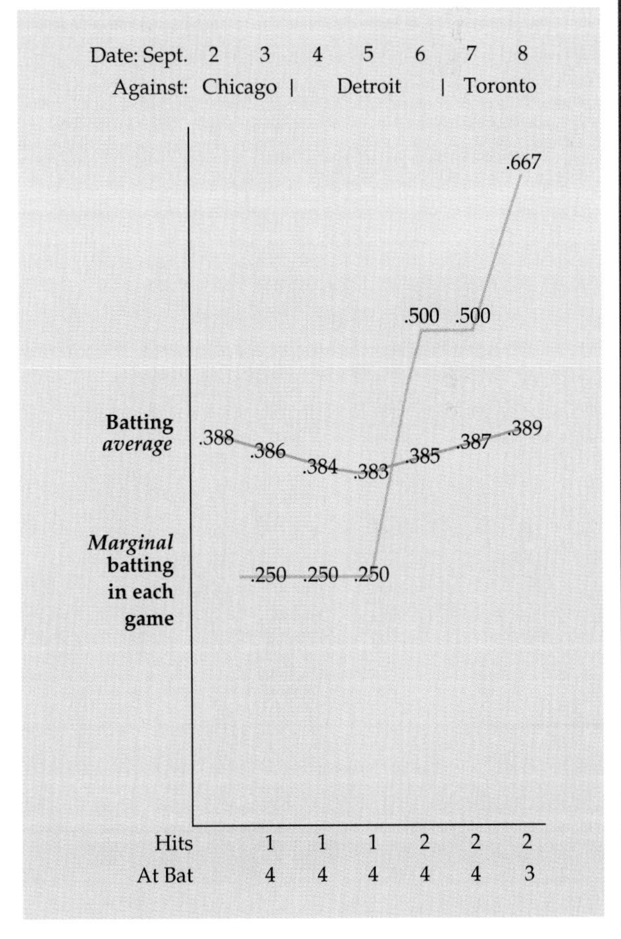

The first of these points—the relationship between the quantity of inputs and the amount of output—is summed up in the **production function.** Specifically, the production function shows how the quantity of output changes as the quantities of inputs are changed. In the long-run production function, the quantities of *all* inputs can be changed. (An illustration will be provided in Appendix 9-A.) However, in the short run, some factors—such as plant and equipment—are fixed in quantity. Thus, the short-run production function shows how output changes as the quantities of labor and other variable inputs change, while the quantities of other inputs—such as plant and equipment—are fixed.

The ***production function*** shows how the quantity of output changes as the quantities of inputs change. In the production function, both output and inputs are measured in physical units (rather than dollars).

The ***short-run production function*** shows how output changes as the quantities of labor and other variable inputs change, while the quantities of other inputs—plant, equipment, and land—are fixed.

TOTAL, AVERAGE, AND MARGINAL PRODUCT

The first three columns of Table 9-2 provide a simple, hypothetical example of a short-run production function for a bicycle factory that has only one variable factor of production, labor. The first column shows the number of units of labor; the second shows the fixed quantity of capital input; and the third shows the amount of output associated with each quantity of labor input. For example, if the firm employs three workers (col. 1), its *total product* (TP) is 18 bicycles per week (col. 3). To emphasize that total product is being measured in physical terms rather than dollars, it is sometimes called total *physical* product (TPP).

From the total product, we can calculate *marginal product* (MP) and *average product* (AP). The marginal product of labor is shown in column 4; it is the *change* in output as one more unit of labor is added. For example, when the labor input increases from three to four units, output increases from 18 to 21 bicycles. The MP of the fourth unit of labor is therefore three bicycles. Average product is shown in column 5; it is the total product divided by the number of units of labor input.

TABLE 9-2 Short-run Production Function of Hypothetical Firm Making Bicycles

(1) Units of Labor L	*(2) Units of Capital* K	*(3) Total Product* TP	*(4) Marginal Product of Labor* MP (4) = Δ (3)	*(5) Average Product of Labor* AP (5) = (3) ÷ (1)	*(6) Wage per Worker* W	*(7) Marginal Cost* MC (7) = (6) ÷ (4)
0	1	0				
			5			
1	1	5		5	$300	$60†
			7			
2	1	12		6	300	42.86
			6			
3	1	18		6	300	50
			3			
4	1	21		5.25	300	100
			2			
5	1	23		4.6	300	150
			1			
6	1	24		4	300	300
			0			
7	1	24		3.43	300	
			−1			
8	1	23		2.88	300	

†MC is $60 not just for the first bicycle, but for each of the first five bicycles produced by the first worker.

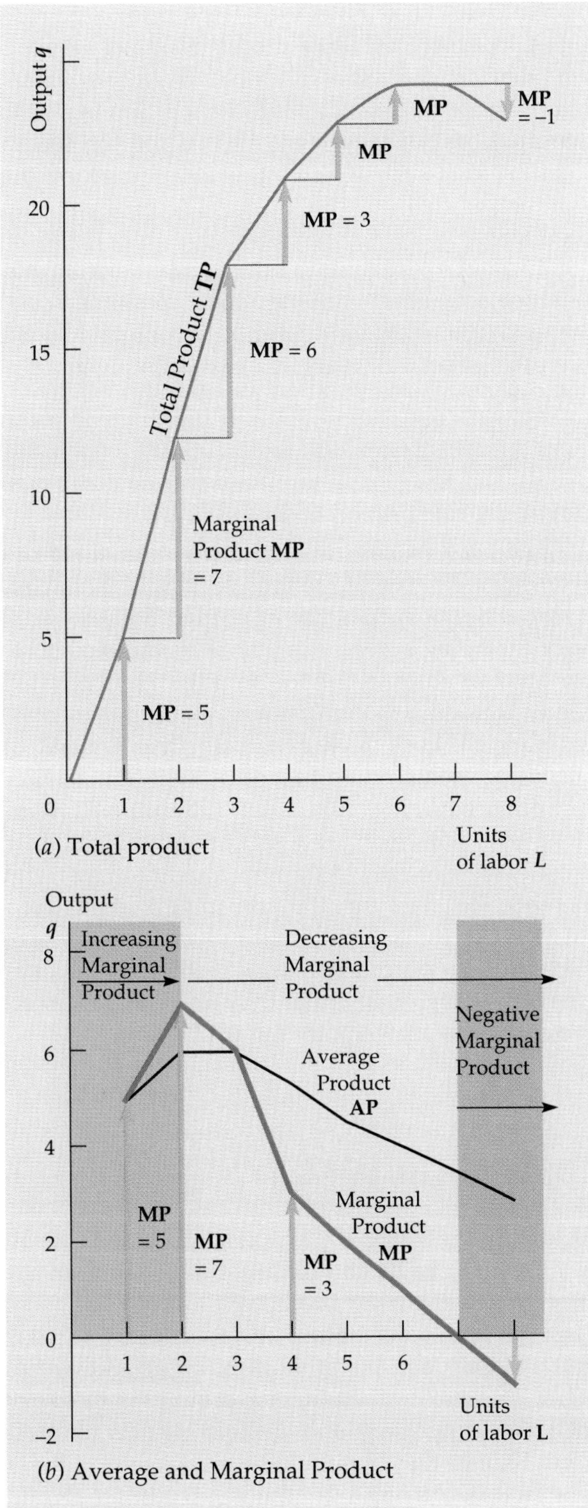

The ***marginal product*** (MP) of an input is the increase in the quantity of output when one more unit of the input is added, with the amount of all other inputs held constant.

Figure 9-2 displays the numbers in the first five columns of Table 9-2 graphically. In panel *b*, we again see that when a marginal measure is above the average, the average is rising; when the marginal is below the average, the average is falling; and when the marginal equals the average, the average is flat. However, there is one notable difference between Figure 9-2*b* and Figure 9-1*b*. The average cost curve of Figure 9-1*b* traced out a U shape; the average product (AP) curve of Figure 9-2*b* is an inverted U. Thus, the AP curve is flat at its *top*, not at its bottom; the MP curve cuts through the peak of the average product curve, when three workers are employed. The earlier conclusion can therefore be sharpened up: a marginal curve cuts through either the lowest *or* the highest point of an average curve.

THE LAW OF DIMINISHING RETURNS

Observe in Figure 9-2*b* that, although the marginal product of the second worker is above the first, the addition of the third, fourth, and fifth workers results in smaller and smaller additions to output. This is in keeping with the **law of eventually diminishing returns,** sometimes known more simply as the law of diminishing returns.

The *law of eventually diminishing returns:* If more units of one input (such as labor) are added while all other inputs (such as capital) are held constant, the marginal product of the variable input (labor) must eventually decline.

FIGURE 9-2 Total and marginal product curves.
In panel *a*, marginal product measures how much total product changes when one more unit of labor is used. Panel *b* illustrates the average and marginal product of labor of the hypothetical firm shown in Table 9-2.

To explain this law, consider more closely the bicycle firm with a given stock of capital. As the firm initially hires more labor, each additional worker increases the firm's output by a substantial amount. Indeed, it is possible that the marginal product of the second worker is above that of the first, as shown in Figure 9-2*b*. The reason is that the plant may be designed for several workers, so that a single worker would waste a lot of time walking from one machine to another. But ultimately, as the firm hires more workers and its fixed capital equipment is operated closer and closer to capacity, an additional worker will add only a small amount to the firm's output. All the new employee can do is work on odd jobs or wait for one of the machines to be free. In other words, there is a decrease in the marginal product of labor. One can envision a situation in which there are so many workers that some get in the way and actually hamper production. In this case, the marginal product would be negative, as shown when the eighth worker is added in Figure 9-2*b*.

This law is easily confirmed in agriculture. As more workers are added to a constant amount of land—say, 100 acres—the marginal product of labor *must* eventually fall. If it did not, then the entire world could be fed from this single farm—or, for that matter, from your back garden.

In Part 5 of this book, we will see that the law of diminishing returns is a key to explaining wages and other income payments. For now it is important because it explains why marginal costs must ultimately rise.

MARGINAL PRODUCT AND MARGINAL COST

At the beginning of the previous section on the short-run production function, we noted that costs of production depend on the amount of inputs used in the productive process, and the prices of these inputs. Having dealt with the amounts of inputs in the production function, we find it a short step to bring the prices of inputs into the calculations in order to find costs. In the last column of Table 9-2, marginal cost is calculated on the assumption that the cost of hiring a worker is $300 per week.

Note that the first worker has a marginal product of five bicycles. Since it costs $300 per week to hire that worker (shown in col. 6), the marginal cost of those five bicycles is $60 each. Similarly, the marginal cost of bicycles is $100 when the fourth worker is added—that is, the $300 wage of the worker divided by the three additional bicycles produced.

Thus we establish a significant relationship between marginal product and marginal cost. Because the marginal product eventually must decrease, short-run marginal cost must eventually increase.

THE U-SHAPED AVERAGE COST CURVE

We can now explain in detail why the short-run average cost curve of the typical firm is U-shaped. It slopes downward at the beginning because fixed costs are being spread over more units; fixed costs per unit of output decline rapidly, as illustrated earlier in Figure 9-1*b*. However, as output increases, marginal cost must eventually rise. Indeed, if output is increased to the place where machines and other equipment are being fully utilized, marginal cost will rise very high and will certainly exceed average cost. As a result, average cost will increase. To sum up: the spreading out of fixed costs works toward an initial reduction in average costs. But, as output increases further, rising marginal costs eventually take over and pull the average cost curve upward, giving it a U shape.

COSTS IN THE LONG RUN

Although the quantity of capital is fixed in the short run, it can be changed in the long run. In the long run, there are no fixed costs; all costs can vary. The firm has to decide not only how much labor it will use, but also the amount of plant and equipment. This presents business executives with one of their most important and challenging sets of questions: Should they acquire new machines and build new factories in order to expand output? Or should they contract by deciding not to replace old capital as it wears out and becomes obsolete?

Consider a small bicycle company that has been producing a low output of 100 units per week. Its small capital stock initially limits it to the short-run average cost curve SAC_1 in Figure 9-3 (where the *S* stands for short-run). Suppose that this firm now wants to expand from 100 units to a larger output, say, 140 per week. It could do so by hiring more labor while continuing to use its present small stock of capital. In other words, it could continue to operate on SAC_1 and the corresponding short-run marginal cost curve SMC_1. But if it does, it will face high average costs—at *d*—and an even higher marginal cost at *c*.

For the long run, this approach to producing goods doesn't make sense. The firm has the option of buying more equipment. By providing workers with more equipment, the firm will be able to cut its average costs. In other words, the firm can make the *long-run* decision to expand its capital. Once it has acquired the new capital, it will operate on a new short-run average cost curve SAC_2. (Each short-run AC curve applies to a specific amount of capital. When the firm's stock of capital changes, so does its short-run AC curve and the corresponding MC curve.) Note how successful this approach is. Since it is now operating on SAC_2 rather than SAC_1, the firm's average cost of producing 140 units is *e* rather than *d*.

If the firm expects to produce any output greater than 120 bicycles per week, the larger quantity of capital is better; it will mean lower average costs. That is, for any output exceeding 120, SAC_2 lies below SAC_1. But if it expects to produce anything less than 120 units, the firm will do better to stick with the smaller, initial quantity of capital, because in this range SAC_2 lies *above* SAC_1. The reason is that a large capital stock means high fixed costs. If very little output is produced, the high fixed cost will be spread over a small number of units; average cost will be high. Unused capacity is expensive.

In summary, then, a firm with a low initial capital stock follows SAC_1 as it expands output. But when output expands beyond 120 units per week, the firm should acquire more capital and move to SAC_2. The lowest average cost it can achieve in the long run—when it can choose between either of the two sets of capital stock—is given by the heavy curve in Figure 9-3.

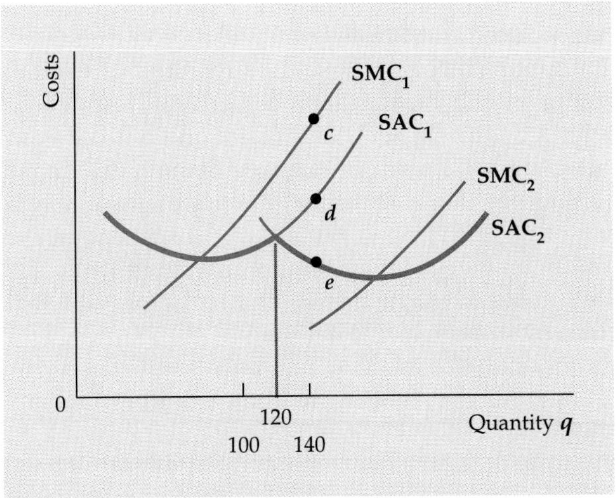

FIGURE 9-3 Costs in the short run and the long run.
SAC_1 shows short-run average cost with a given fixed capital stock 1. If the firm wishes to produce more than 120 units in the long run—say 140—it can reduce its average cost by expanding its capital stock and moving to short-run average cost SAC_2. This reduces its average cost from *d* to *e*.

THE ENVELOPE CURVE AND THE BEST COMBINATION OF INPUTS

In Figure 9-4, we reproduce SAC_1 and SAC_2 and add two more cost curves SAC_3 and SAC_4 that apply when the capital stock is even larger. If the firm making a long-run decision wishes to produce output q_3, it chooses the plant and equipment required to operate on short-run curve SAC_3 and operates at point *H*. This is the lowest possible average cost at which the firm can produce q_3. Alternatively, if it wishes to produce q_4, it chooses the plant and equipment required for SAC_4 and operates at point *J*—the lowest average cost at which it can produce q_4. Similarly, to produce quantity q_2 in the lowest cost way, the firm chooses the quantity of plant and equipment SAC_2 and operates at point *G*. If we join all points like *G*, *H*, and *J*, the result is the heavy **long-run average cost curve** (LAC). This is sometimes called an *envelope curve* because it encloses all the short-run SAC curves from below. (While it now seems quite easy

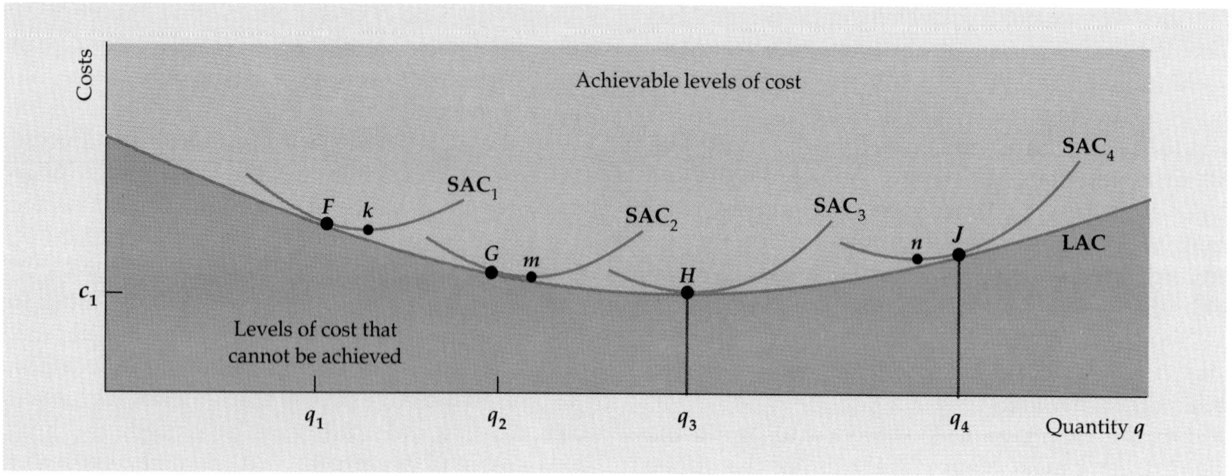

FIGURE 9-4 The long-run envelope cost curve.

The SAC curves are the short-run average cost curves that apply if capital stock is fixed at various levels, 1, 2, 3, etc. LAC is the long-run average cost curve that encloses all of them from below. The envelope curve LAC is useful when the firm is planning for the long run, when it is free to select any quantity of capital. For example, to produce q_3, it would select capital stock 3, operating on SAC_3 at point *H* and keeping its average cost down to the lowest possible level—that is, the height of *H*. Similarly, to produce q_4, it would select capital stock 4, operating on SAC_4 at point *J* and keeping its cost down to the lowest possible level for that output.

to draw this curve, the economist who introduced the idea had difficulty, as explained in Box 9-2.)

The envelope curve thus provides the answer to a key question facing the producer: In the long run, what is the lowest cost combination of labor and capital inputs? The best quantity of capital depends on the desired quantity of output. For example, if the firm wants to produce output q_4, it picks the quantity of capital that corresponds to SAC_4 and hires the quantity of labor needed to produce at point *J*. (Appendix 9-B provides more detail on the optimum choice of inputs.)

To draw the smooth envelope curve LAC shown in Figure 9-4, we assume that the firm can choose from many quantities of capital in the long run. You can visualize many intermediate SAC curves in Figure 9-4. Nevertheless, capital may be somewhat "lumpy." For example, a firm can't acquire half a machine. The "lumpy" case was illustrated in Figure 9-3: The firm could either stick with the initial capital stock (one machine) or move to SAC_2 by adding a second machine. If capital is "lumpy," the envelope curve will be scalloped, like the heavy curve in Figure 9-3.

We emphasize that LAC shows the *lowest* average cost at which each output (such as q_3 or q_4) can be produced in the long run, when producers have the opportunity to adjust their quantity of capital. Points in the brown area below LAC cannot be achieved with present technology and with present factor prices. Points in the area above LAC could be chosen, but a technically efficient firm rejects any such point in favor of a lower cost point on the LAC. However, it may temporarily produce in the area above LAC in the short run, before it has a chance to adjust its capital stock.

ECONOMIES OF SCALE

Observe that, to the left of *H* in Figure 9-4, long-run average cost falls as output increases. The question arises: How can that be? How can the cost per unit fall when output is increased from, say, 100 units to 200?

The answer lies in **economies of scale.** Recall from Chapter 3 that economies of scale exist if an x% increase in the quantity of *all* inputs results in

BOX 9–2 *If You Have Had Trouble Drawing Curves in Economics, You Are Not Alone*

The discerning reader will notice in Figure 9-4 that LAC touches the lowest short-run curve (SAC_3) at its minimum point. But it doesn't touch any other SAC curve at its minimum. For example, it touches SAC_1 slightly to the left of its minimum point *k*.

This problem is so subtle that it was missed by Jacob Viner, the economist who first developed the idea of the envelope curve. He asked his draftsman to draw an envelope curve to pass through the minimum point on each SAC curve. His draftsman knew that this couldn't be done, and said so. Viner insisted. The draftsman thereupon presented him with a long-run curve that went through the minimum points on each SAC. But it clearly wasn't an envelope curve. (To confirm this, sketch a curve through the minimum points such as *k*, *m*, and *n*, and you will see that it is not the envelope curve LAC at all.) Viner permitted the erroneous diagram to appear in his article, complaining that his obstinate draftsman "saw some mathematical objection. . . which I could not succeed in understanding."[†]

There was a sequel. In the 1930s, Viner criticized Keynes' new theory of unemployment and income. On his arrival in North America, Keynes was asked to name the world's greatest living economist. He reportedly replied that modesty prevented him from naming the greatest, but the second greatest was surely Viner's draftsman.

[†]Jacob Viner, "Cost Curves and Supply Curves," 1931, reprinted in George J. Stigler and Kenneth E. Boulding, *Readings in Price Theory* (Homewood, Ill.: Richard D. Irwin, 1952), p. 214.

an increase of more than x% in the quantity of output.

The way in which economies of scale lead to decreasing average costs may be illustrated with an example. Suppose that a firm faces fixed input prices. That is, it won't bid up the wage rate, regardless of how many workers it hires; nor will it bid up the price of steel or machinery, no matter how much it buys. Then, an increase of, say, 100% in the quantity of all inputs raises total costs by the same 100%. (Twice as many inputs are used, at constant prices.) With economies of scale, however, output rises by more than 100%. With total costs rising more slowly than output, average cost per unit falls. Thus we come to an important conclusion: If input prices are constant, economies of scale mean falling long-run average costs.[2]

In turn, another question arises: Why should economies of scale exist? A number of reasons can be cited. Greater output may make greater specialization possible, and workers may become adept at specialized tasks—like the workers in Adam Smith's pin factory (Chapter 3). It also means that more highly specialized machinery can be used in assembly-line operations. Furthermore, with greater output, a firm may be better able to use its talent. If a production line supervisor is able to direct 20 workers but is in charge of only 10, output and the number of workers employed can be doubled without requiring another supervisor. Similarly, the firm's executives may be able to handle more work and responsibility; as the firm grows and output increases, new managers are initially not required. Therefore there is less management cost for each unit of output, and average costs tend to fall.

With all these reasons for economies of scale, why are there ever **diseconomies of scale,** where LAC turns up (as it does to the right of output q_3 in Fig. 9-4)? The supervisor example provides a clue. Suppose output and employment, which have already doubled, now increase by another five times. In addition to the original supervisor, five new supervisors must now be hired. Thus far, it seems that average cost need not change, since there has been the same proportionate increase in both output and costs. But another person may now be required just to coordinate activities among the six supervisors. Thus as a company grows, new

[2]However, if a firm bids up the price of inputs, its average cost may rise even though there are economies of scale.

tiers of management may have to be created. Eventually, a point is reached where management becomes too costly and unwieldy, and decision making becomes too cumbersome and slow. There are just too many people between the vice president who makes the final production decisions and the workers on the line who carry them out. Consequently, average costs increase. Thus it is not only the short-run cost curve that is U shaped, but also the long-run cost curve. (But the long-run curve is much wider and more gently sloping.)

Diseconomies of scale exist if an $x\%$ increase in the quantity of *all* inputs causes the quantity of output to increase by less than $x\%$. (For example, if all inputs increase by 100%, output increases by less than 100%.)

There are *constant returns to scale* if an $x\%$ increase in the quantity of *all* inputs causes the quantity of output to increase by the same $x\%$.

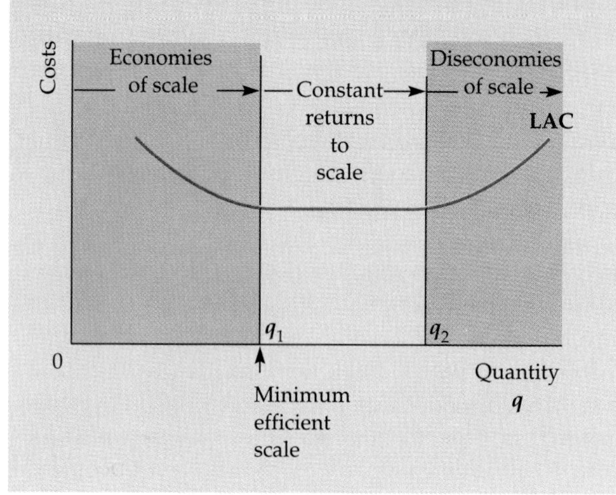

FIGURE 9-5 Minimum efficient scale.

For some firms, the envelope curve flattens out, and there are constant returns over a range—illustrated here as the range from q_1 to q_2. Output q_1 represents the *minimum efficient scale.*

The point at which decision making becomes unwieldy generally occurs much earlier in agriculture than in industry. Consequently, point *H*, where LAC begins to rise, is encountered at a relatively small output. One reason is that, on a relatively small farm the owner-operator has the opportunity and incentive to make crucial decisions with great speed. When the sun shines, the farmer makes hay. When crops are ripe, the farmer drops secondary activities and works very hard to harvest the crop. On the other hand, if the farm were part of a huge company, the crop could be lost by the time a decision worked its way through several echelons of management.

THE RANGE OF CONSTANT RETURNS AND MINIMUM EFFICIENT SCALE

Although diseconomies of scale and higher average costs set in at an early stage in agriculture, they come at a much larger output in most manufacturing firms. This is one of the reasons for the existence and continued growth of large corporations like IBM and Boeing.

It is also possible that there may be constant returns to scale and a horizontal long-run cost curve over a considerable range, as illustrated in Figure 9-5. In this case, firms with quite different sizes may have similar costs and may compete on a relatively even footing. For example, General Motors is much larger than Ford, which in turn is much larger than Chrysler, but their costs of producing a car are not greatly different. (Actually, the three firms are organized differently, with GM producing more of its own parts and the other two buying a much larger percentage of their parts from outside suppliers. As a consequence, the relative costs of the three companies shifted as conditions changed in the market for parts. GM used to have a significant cost advantage, but the advantage shifted to Ford in the 1980s, when parts produced in-house became more expensive than parts purchased from outside.)

If returns to scale are constant over a wide range, as illustrated in Figure 9-5, companies are in a good position to compete once they have reached the **minimum efficient scale** at which long-run average cost levels out. But they can have a very tough time if they remain stuck far to the left. For example, even though Ford and Chrysler are in a relatively good position to compete with GM, American Motors was too small. It suffered a string of losses before it was taken over by Chrysler in 1987.

The ***minimum efficient scale*** is the output or scale at which average total cost reaches its minimum.

In some industries even a huge corporation may not have exhausted all the advantages of size. Large commercial airplanes are one: Boeing could produce aircraft more cheaply if it produced twice as many. In such an industry, there is a strong tendency for small competitors to be driven out. The Western world has only three major producers of large passenger aircraft—Boeing, McDonnell-Douglas, and Airbus of Europe. Indeed, it is quite possible that Boeing would be the only survivor in the absence of two factors aiding its competitors: (1) product differentiation (aircraft are somewhat different, and airlines have different needs), and (2) government subsidies to Airbus. Product differentiation also explains the existence of a number of firms that produce planes for specialized markets, such as twin-engine turboprops designed for small airports.

Finally, it is important to recognize that, in the phrase "minimum efficient size," the term *efficient* is used in a very specific way: it *applies to costs only.* The minimum efficient scale is the output at which *costs* reach a minimum, but this output is not necessarily the most efficient in terms of the overall operation of the economy. Perhaps Boeing could produce planes more cheaply if it doubled its output. If it did so, however, our economy would not become more efficient. We would be producing more planes than the airlines could put to good use. To study the overall efficiency of the economy, we will have to look beyond the cost side to consider demand, too.

ECONOMIES OF SCALE AND DIMINISHING RETURNS

A firm can enjoy "economies of scale" and *at the same time* face the "law of diminishing returns." Since economies of scale mean falling costs and diminishing returns mean rising costs, we might well wonder: how is this possible? The answer is that the law of diminishing returns is a short-run concept that applies if only one input (labor) changes, whereas economies of scale is a long-run concept that applies when *all* factors are variable.

Figure 9-6 illustrates how the same firm can face both economies of scale and diminishing returns. *In the short run,* as more labor is applied to the given capital stock, marginal costs rise, as shown by arrow *f*. These rising costs are a reflection of diminishing returns. However, as capital increases *in the long run,* costs fall as the firm moves down along LAC (arrow *e*). There are economies of scale.

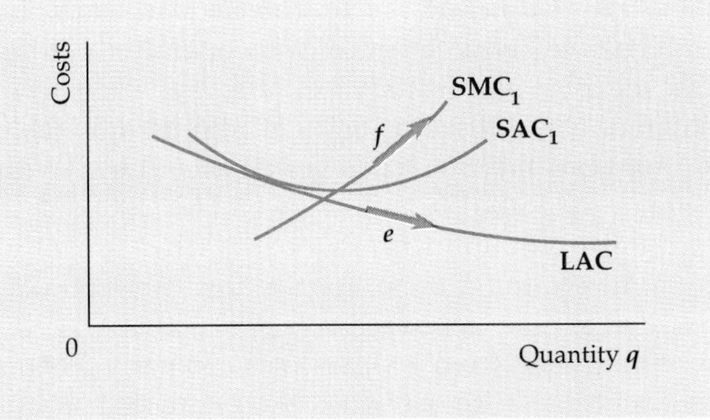

FIGURE 9-6 How a firm can face both economies of scale and diminishing returns.

This firm faces diminishing returns, as shown by arrow *f*. Its marginal cost curve SMC_1 rises in the short run, so long as its capital stock is fixed at level 1. For this firm, there are also economies of scale, as shown by arrow *e*; its long-run average cost LAC falls as it is able to increase its use of *all* factors.

THE ECONOMIST'S CONCEPT OF COST: OPPORTUNITY COST

In studying costs, economists start with the idea that resources are scarce and have alternative uses. The labor and capital employed in the manufacture of bicycles are not available to produce food, clothing, or housing. To an economist, the *alternatives foregone* represent the true costs of producing a good or service. In economics, "cost" means **opportunity cost.**

The ***opportunity cost*** of an input is the return that it could earn in its best alternative use.

Opportunity costs are not identical to the accounting costs faced by a business. To understand the distinction, let us consider an example. Suppose you have a friend who operates a store, and she asks you to study her business. The breakdown of her accounting costs in column *a* of Table 9-3 suggests that she has a good thing going. With revenue of $500,000 and costs of $420,000, she is earning an accounting profit of $80,000.

When you dig more deeply, however, you discover that she could earn a $50,000 salary by accepting a job from an insurance company. This is an *implicit cost* (or *imputed cost*) because it is not paid out of pocket. But we must include it, as we have done in column *b*, or we would not have an adequate picture of the true economic costs in operating this business—that is, the cost of all the resources used, including her own time. In addition, we would not be able to judge whether she is doing as well in this business as she could in another activity, namely, working for the insurance company.

In Table 9-3, opportunity costs include *both* the explicit, out-of-pocket costs and the implicit costs. The explicit, out-of-pocket costs are opportunity costs; for example, the $30,000 in rent is the going price for using the store. If your friend does not use the store, some other retailer will. Similarly, $40,000 is the going price for labor; it represents what her employees could earn in alternative jobs. The implicit costs, such as the $50,000 salary that she has to forego in order to run her store, are also opportunity costs.

Opportunity cost indicates *how much an input must be paid to keep it in its present use.* For example, your friend must earn $50,000—her opportunity cost—or she will have an incentive to shift out of her present activity into the higher return insurance business. (Incidentally, your friend may have strong nonmonetary preferences for running her own store, such as the freedom to be her own boss. In such circumstances, she might be willing to stay in retailing even if she didn't cover her full $50,000 opportunity cost. Although such nonmonetary motives may be important, we ignore them in the simplified story presented here.)

You also discover that your friend has other opportunity costs that must be included in column *b*. For example, she has some of her own funds tied up in this business. What would be her best alternative use of these funds? She indicates that she would lend out part, getting $8,000 in interest. She would use the rest to buy part-ownership of a company in which she could expect a $12,000 profit. This last item—the opportunity cost of capital—is called **normal profit.**

We emphasize that whenever we draw a cost curve in this book, we include not only explicit out-of-pocket accounting costs, but also implicit costs such as normal profit.

TABLE 9-3 Measurement of Costs and Profits (thousands of dollars)

(a) By accountants			*(b) By economists*		
Total Revenue		$500	Total Revenue		$500
Costs (out-of-pocket)			Explicit (out-of-pocket) costs		
Labor	$40		Labor	$40	
Materials	350		Materials	350	
Rent	30		Rent	30	
	420	420			
			Implicit costs (income foregone)		
			Owner's salary	50	
			Interest	8	
			Normal profit	12	
			Total costs	490	490
Accounting profit		$80	Economic (above-normal) profit		$10

Therefore, in our example, costs are the full \$490,000 shown in column *b* of Table 9-3. This broad definition means that costs tell us how much all the resources employed by the firm could be earning elsewhere. Since her \$500,000 of revenues exceed this \$490,000 cost, she has earned **above-normal profit** or **economic profit** of \$10,000. To an economist, the word *profit* means *above-normal* profit unless otherwise stated. It is the \$10,000 above-normal profit that allows you to judge that your friend does indeed have a good thing going. Her business not only provides her an appropriate \$50,000 income for her own time and an appropriate return for the capital she has invested, but also an additional \$10,000. If the existing firms in an industry are making such above-normal profits, other enterpreneurs have an incentive to move into this business, as we will see in detail in the next chapter.

Now suppose that salaries in other jobs increase. Specifically, suppose the insurance company increases its offer to your friend from \$50,000 to \$65,000. When column *b* is accordingly recalculated, the \$10,000 of above-normal profit becomes an economic loss of \$5,000. Even though your friend still earns an income from her business, she is no longer able to earn as much as in her best alternative activity. As long as she views this alternative line of work as equally interesting, she has an incentive to move.

Thus *economic profit* (or loss) *provides a signal, indicating whether resources are being attracted to* (or repelled from) *an activity.*

Economic profit is above-normal profit, that is, profit after all costs, including the opportunity cost of capital, have been taken into account. In other words, economic profit is any profit over and above the normal profit needed to keep capital in the industry.

LIVING IN A GLOBAL ECONOMY

THE QUEST FOR LOWER COSTS

In this chapter, we have considered some of the important decisions a firm must make in its search for lower costs. For example, how much capital should it acquire in the long run?

Thus far, however, input prices have been taken as given. Another way in which a firm can reduce its costs is by searching for cheaper sources for its inputs. A firm's purchasing department may therefore play a very important role, looking for low-cost suppliers of machinery, materials, and other inputs.

One way to obtain low-cost inputs is to move to the place where they are located. Thus, in the eighteenth and nineteenth centuries, farmers were drawn to the low-cost land in the American West. In the late nineteenth and early twentieth centuries, the steel industry concentrated in Pennsylvania, where it had access to low-cost, plentiful coal. A few decades later, textile firms migrated from New England to the South, attracted by low wages.

The search for lower cost inputs can cross national boundaries. Thus the low-cost land of the Western states beckoned not only farmers in Eastern states, but also the tired and the poor of Europe. The search for low-cost oil drew the major oil companies to the Middle East, Venezuela, and Nigeria. Now, in the search for low wage rates, U.S. auto firms are having some of their cars and parts produced in Korea and Mexico.

Such moves have created controversy. Corporations have been criticized for their willingness to move production abroad, since American workers can lose jobs. Nevertheless, a strong case can be made that the international search for lower costs is on balance beneficial for the United States. It adds to the efficiency of the world economy—as will be explained in detail in Chapter 19. Most obviously, consumers gain when they can buy inexpensive goods produced with low-cost foreign inputs.

Furthermore, although adjustments can be very painful, they can leave even the initial losers in an improved situation. For example, New England has traditionally been one of the chief losers as footloose industries headed for the South or overseas. Yet, during the 1980s, New England was very successful in replacing the lost jobs with even higher paying jobs in computers and other expanding industries.

KEY POINTS

1. In the long run, there are no fixed costs. In the long run, the producer can choose any combination of capital and labor.

2. In the short run, however, the stock of capital cannot be changed; capital costs represent a *fixed* or overhead cost.

3. Total costs = fixed costs + variable costs

4. Marginal cost = the change in total cost when one more unit is produced. The marginal cost curve cuts through the lowest point on the average cost curve.

5. The production function shows how the quantity of output changes as the quantities of inputs change. The *short-run* production function shows how output changes as the quantities of labor and other variable inputs change, while the quantities of other inputs—plant, equipment, and land—are fixed.

6. The law of eventually diminishing marginal returns states that, as more and more of one factor (for example, labor) is employed while all other factors remain constant, the marginal product of the variable factor (labor) must eventually decline.

7. Marginal cost depends on marginal product. The law of eventually diminishing returns means that marginal cost must eventually rise.

8. In the long run, when all factors are variable, the firm can pick the lowest cost way of producing a specific quantity by choosing a point on the envelope curve.

9. Economies of scale exist when an $x\%$ increase in all inputs causes output to rise by more than $x\%$. Diseconomies of scale occur when an $x\%$ increase in all inputs causes output to rise by less than x%.

10. Even in the presence of economies of scale, a firm may nevertheless face diminishing returns. Economies of scale mean that average cost falls in the long run, when *all* factors of production are increased in the same proportion. Diminishing returns mean that marginal cost rises in the short run when only *one* factor of production is increased.

11. By cost, economists mean "opportunity" cost. Thus, economists include not only the explicit accounting costs, but also implicit costs, such as the normal profit on capital invested in the enterprise.

12. After all such opportunity costs have been covered, any remaining economic profit (that is, above-normal profit) provides an indication of how much more resources are earning in this activity than in the next best alternative. If present firms are making such a profit, resources are attracted to this industry. On the other hand, if present firms are not covering their opportunity costs—that is, if they are suffering an economic loss—then resources are encouraged to move out.

KEY CONCEPTS

short run
long run
fixed cost
variable cost
total cost
marginal cost
average cost

production function
marginal product
diminishing returns
envelope curve
economies of scale
diseconomies of scale
constant returns to scale

minimum efficient scale
economic *versus* accounting definitions of cost
implicit costs
opportunity cost
economic profit

PROBLEMS

9-1. "In the long run, all costs are variable." Do you agree? For example, might the expenses for machinery be a variable cost?

9-2. Suppose that the firm in Table 9-1 had fixed costs of $500 rather than $35, while variable costs remained the same. Recalculate Table 9-1.

> **(a)** Do higher fixed costs change marginal costs? Why or why not?
>
> **(b)** Does the output at which average cost reaches a minimum increase, decrease, or remain the same? Why?

9-3. MC cuts the lowest point on the ATC curve. Explain why it also cuts the lowest point on the average variable cost curve.

9-4. For each of the following, explain whether you agree or disagree, and why:

> **(a)** Whenever MC is rising, average total cost must be rising.
>
> **(b)** Whenever MC is rising, average variable cost must be rising.
>
> **(c)** Whenever MC is above average total cost, average total cost must be rising.
>
> **(d)** Whenever MC is above average variable cost, average variable cost must be rising.
>
> **(e)** Whenever MC is above average fixed cost, average fixed cost must be rising.
>
> **(f)** Whenever ATC is above MC, MC must be rising.

9-5. In Box 9-1, observe that George Brett was batting .388 on September 2. Suppose that he had two hits in five times at bat (that is, he batted .400) in every game from September 2 to the end of the season. Would he have ended up with an average of .400 for the whole season? Why or why not?

9-6. In Table 9-2, observe that the marginal product of labor begins to decline when the third worker is added. Now suppose that the firm has two units of capital rather than only one. Will the marginal product of labor still begin to decline when the third worker is added? Or will it begin to decline at some other point—for example, when the second worker is added or when the sixth worker is added? Why?

9-7. " 'Diminishing returns' mean 'rising costs,' while 'economies of scale' mean 'falling costs.' Therefore, a firm cannot be facing both diminishing returns and economies of scale." Do you agree? Why or why not?

9-8. Explain why economists include normal profit as a "cost." If above-normal profit exists, what does this tell us?

9-9. Suppose a farmer in Kansas provides a statement of his costs to his income tax accountant; are there any opportunity costs he may miss? Explain.

APPENDIX 9-A
THE LONG-RUN PRODUCTION FUNCTION

In the long run, the firm can change the quantity of all its inputs. Table 9-4 gives an example of a **long-run production function** with two dimensions, which show what happens when the quantities of labor and capital are changed. From left to right, the quantity of labor increases. In the upward direction, the quantity of capital increases. Each number in the table indicates the maximum output that the firm can produce with various specific combinations of inputs. For example, if the firm uses three units of capital (*K*) and five units of labor (*L*), it can produce 39 units of output. (For the moment, ignore the fact that some numbers in Table 9-4 are shown in color. The reason for this color coding will be explained in Appendix 9-B.)

Table 9-4 is the long-run production function of the firm whose short-run production function was shown earlier in Table 9-2. Note that column 3 of that earlier table now appears in Table 9-4 as the bottom row, showing output for various quantities of labor when there is 1 unit of capital. In fact, the long-run production function is made up of a whole set of rows, with each representing a different short-run production function. Once the firm chooses how much capital it will use, it is confined in the short run to operate along the corresponding row of this table. For example, if it were to choose six units of capital, then it would be confined in the short run to the top line of the production function. In the long run, it can move anywhere in Table 9-4.

This long-run production function can be used to illustrate economies of scale. Consider what happens when *both* inputs are increased by the same percentage. Suppose that the firm begins with one unit of capital and one unit of labor. It produces five units of output. Now, if it doubles its labor force from one to two workers, and also doubles its capital from one to two units, its output more than doubles, from 5 to 19. Then, if it increases each input by an additional 50%—from two units to three—output again increases by a greater proportion, from 19 units to 30. Since its output increases by a greater percent than its inputs, it enjoys economies of scale.

TABLE 9-4 A Hypothetical Firm's Production Function

This simplified long-run production function shows the number of units of output a firm can produce with various combinations of inputs. For example, if the firm uses 2 units of labor and 1 unit of capital, the second box in the bottom row indicates that it can produce 12 units of output.

Units of Capital (K)						
6	24	35	42	47	51	54
5	23	32	39	44	48	51
4	20	28	35	40	44	47
3	17	24	30	35	39	42
2	14	19	24	28	32	35
→ 1	5	12	18	21	23	24
	1	2	3	4	5	6
	Units of Labor (L)					

The same firm is subject to the law of eventually diminishing returns, however. Consider what happens when only *one* input—labor—is increased while the quantity of capital is fixed at, say, one unit. The firm is therefore confined to the bottom row in the production function. As it increases the input of labor, it does indeed encounter diminishing returns. As it increases the input of labor, the second worker has a marginal product of seven units (that is, 12 – 5), while the third worker has a marginal product of only six units (18 – 12). This confirms the point made in Figure 9-6: A firm may face both economies of scale *and* diminishing returns.

APPENDIX 9-B

FINDING THE MINIMUM COST FOR EACH QUANTITY OF OUTPUT

The long-run production function in Appendix 9-A can be used to address the questions raised at the beginning of the chapter: What combination of inputs will a firm use? For example, will it use a great deal of capital and only a small amount of labor? Or will it use many workers and only a little quantity of capital? Observe that this is a long-run decision, since it is only in the long run that the firm's capital can be changed.

This appendix explains how the firm picks the best combination of inputs. When it does so, it gets its average cost down to a point on the envelope curve shown in Figure 9-4.

GRAPHING THE PRODUCTION FUNCTION: EQUAL-OUTPUT CURVES

To calculate the lowest cost method of producing the desired output—say, 24 units—the first step is to graph the production function in Table 9-4. Note that several input combinations in that table yield 24 units. These appear in color and are reproduced to form the "output = 24" curve in Figure 9-7. Similarly, a curve representing "output = 35" is also extracted from Table 9-4. These equal-output curves—often called *isoquants*—are similar to the indifference (or equal-utility) curves in Figure 7-7. Just as the indifference map in that earlier diagram showed a whole family of indifference curves, each representing a higher level of utility as the household moved northeast from the origin, so the production function provides a whole set of equal-output curves that also forms a hill. As the firm moves to the northeast, using more inputs, it reaches higher output levels.

In one respect, however, the equal-output curves of the producer contain more information than the indifference curves of the consumer: Each equal-output curve represents a *specific quantity* of output. For example, the two curves in Figure 9-7 show output of 24 and 35 units. On the other hand, all we know about indifference curves is whether they represent "higher" or "lower" levels of satisfaction. We don't know how many "units of utility" they represent.

GRAPHING THE PRICES OF INPUTS: EQUAL-COST LINES

Minimizing cost requires not only the equal-output curves, but also information on the prices of inputs. How is this graphed? If the price of labor is $20 per unit and the price of capital is $30, then the straight

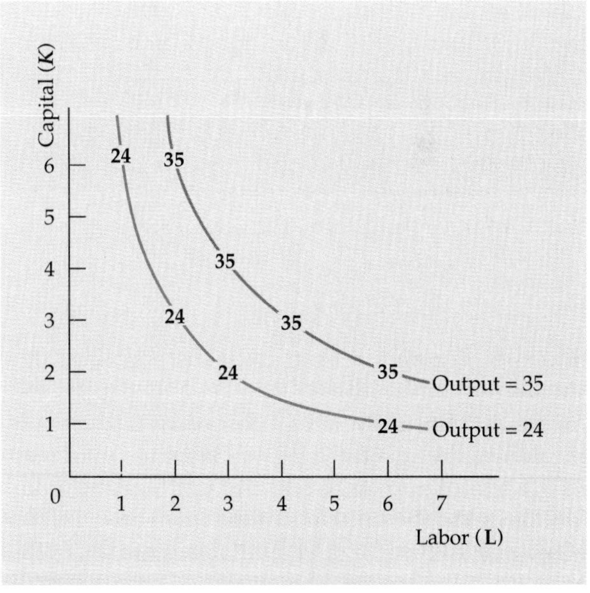

FIGURE 9-7 Equal-output curves.

To graph the production function, we extract the colored numbers from Table 9-4 and draw equal-output curves. For example, each of the input combinations that yields an output of 24 units in Table 9-4 is graphed in this diagram and connected to become the "output = 24" curve.

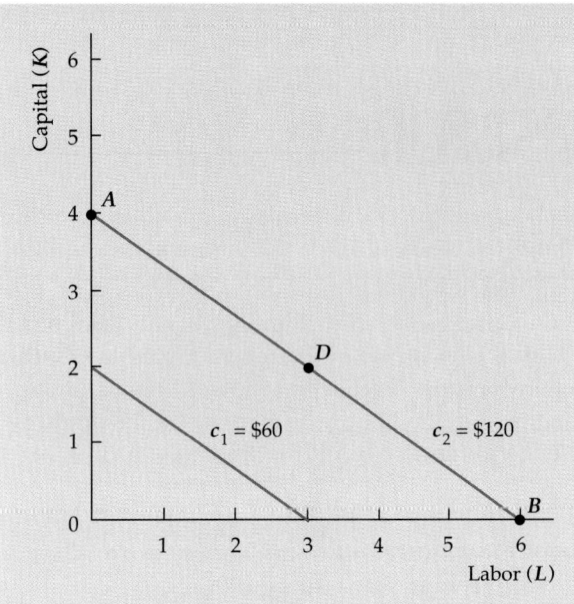

FIGURE 9-8 Equal-cost lines.

If the price of labor is $20 per unit and the price of capital is $30, then c_2 is the equal–cost line that shows all combinations of these two inputs that can be purchased for $120. For example, combination *D* of three units of labor and two of capital costs 3($20) + 2($30) = $120; similarly, combination *B* costs 6($20) + 0($30) = $120. Parallel line c_1 is also an equal cost line, but it shows all input combinations that would cost $60. There is a whole family of similar parallel lines, each representing a different cost. If the price of labor relative to capital changes, then there is a whole new family of parallel lines with a different slope.

line c_2 in Figure 9-8 is an *equal–cost line.* This line shows all combinations of labor and capital that can be purchased for a total cost of $120. For example, this is the cost the firm will incur at *A* if it buys four units of capital at $30 per unit and no labor. Similarly, combination *D* comprising three units of labor and two units of capital also costs $120; that is, 3 × $20 + 2 × $30. Likewise, c_1 represents the input combinations that would cost the firm $60. You can visualize a whole family of parallel lines showing successively higher costs for the firm as it moves to the northeast.

MINIMIZING COSTS FOR A SPECIFIC QUANTITY OF OUTPUT

Figure 9-9 brings the previous two diagrams together. Curves q_1 and q_2 are from the firm's production function in Figure 9-7, while the solid green lines are equal–cost lines similar to those in Figure 9-8. If the firm wishes to produce 24 units of output, it will do so at the lowest cost by using the input combination shown by E_2 (two units of capital and three of labor). That is:

The firm selects the point on the equal-output curve that is tangent to an equal-cost curve.

Any other way of producing this same output is rejected because it would be more costly. For example, the firm does not use input combination E_4 because it lies on higher cost line c_4.

Similarly, if the firm wishes to produce 35 units of output, it selects tangency point E_5, once again determining the best combination of labor and capital to produce that quantity of output.

Thus for each output, such as q = 24, it is able to select the lowest cost combination of inputs. It is able to answer the question: "How much capital and labor should it use to produce 24 units of output?" When it does so, it picks the best SAC curve in Figure 9-4 for 24 units of output, and it picks a point on the long-run envelope curve. It can do the same for every other output, thus deriving the whole long-run average cost curve.

THE EFFECT OF A CHANGE IN THE PRICES OF INPUTS

If the relative price of labor and capital changes, there is a new family of equal–cost lines with a different slope. For example, if the price of capital rises from $30 to $60 while the price of labor is unchanged, you can confirm that flatter line c_3 is now the new $120 equal–cost line. You can visualize the whole family of new equal-cost lines parallel to it. Thus:

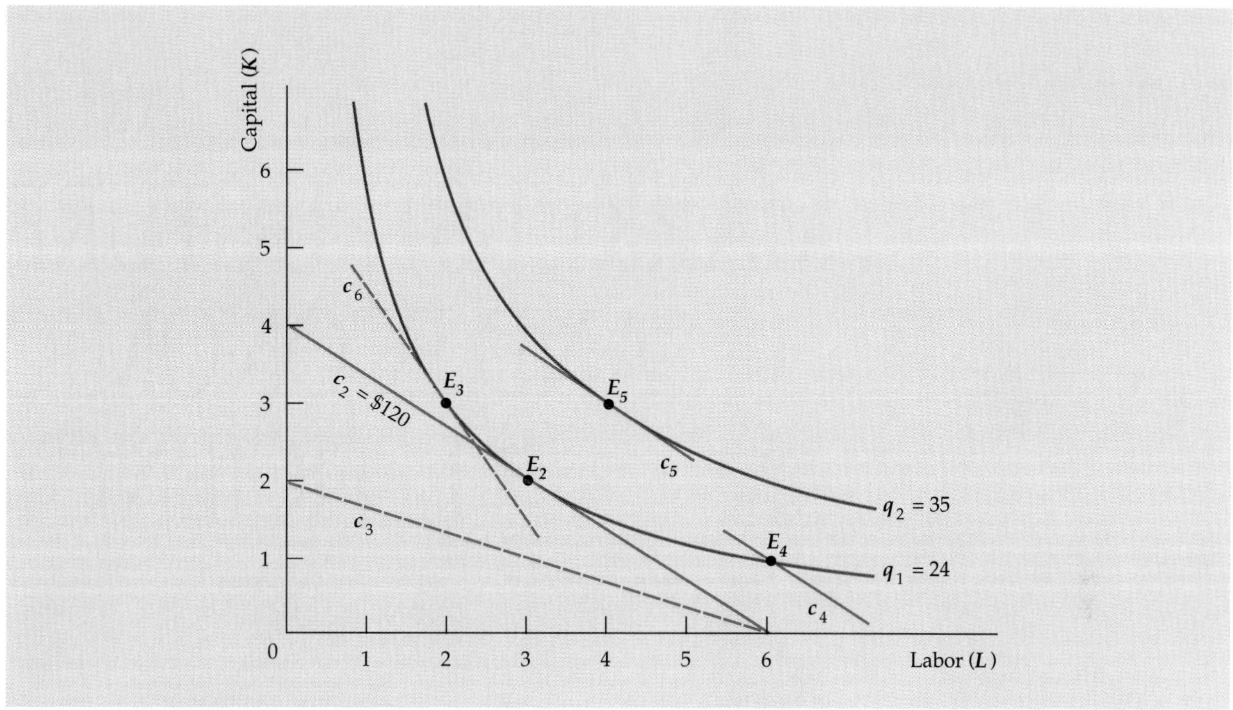

FIGURE 9-9 Minimizing cost: A point of tangency.
The lowest cost way of producing 24 units of output is to select the point where the "output = 24" curve is tangent to an equal–cost line. This is at E_2, using 3 units of labor and 2 units of capital. Similarly, to produce 35 units of output at the lowest possible cost, the firm selects tangency point E_5.

The slope of the family of equal-cost lines depends on the relative price of the firm's inputs.

Thus an equal-cost line for the firm is similar to a budget line for the consumer. In either case, the slope depends on the relative price of the items being purchased.

Now suppose that capital has become *less* (rather than more) expensive relative to labor, and the equal–cost lines have therefore become steeper. Specifically, suppose the new set of equal–cost lines is c_6 and the family of lines parallel to it. To produce 24 units of output, the firm no longer uses input combination E_2. Instead it shifts to E_3, the point of tangency with one of its new equal-cost lines. This type of shift to the northwest will also occur along q_2 and all the other equal–output lines. Thus the firm moves northwest, substituting an input that has become relatively less expensive (capital) for the one that has become relatively more expensive (labor).

PROBLEM

9-10. With capital at $30 and labor at $20, how much less is the cost incurred by the firm that operates at E_2 rather than E_4 in Figure 9-9?

PART III

MARKET STRUCTURE AND ECONOMIC EFFICIENCY

Part 3 will address one of the central issues of economics, namely, *allocative efficiency:*

- Is the right combination of outputs being produced, using the right combination of inputs?

The answer depends on the structure of markets.

- Markets may be perfectly competitive, with individual producers and sellers being unable to influence market price. If so, Adam Smith's invisible hand will be at work. In the pursuit of profit, firms will generally serve the interests of society, providing an efficient outcome (as explained in Chapters 10 and 11).

- Markets may be imperfect, with individual producers having the power to influence price. If so, Adam Smith's invisible hand will fail. In the pursuit of profit, a firm will generally produce less than the efficient, socially desirable amount (Chapters 12 and 13).

Thus Part 3 will show how the pursuit of private profit and the interests of society sometimes coincide and sometimes conflict.

This part of the book will lay the basis for the policy issues addressed in Part 4. If the private market fails to provide an outcome that is efficient, what—if anything—should the government do about it?

CHAPTER 10
SUPPLY IN A PERFECTLY COMPETITIVE MARKET

Business is never so healthy as when, like a chicken, it must do a certain amount of scratching for what it gets.

HENRY FORD

If markets are perfectly competitive—with many buyers and many sellers—Adam Smith's invisible hand will generally be at work. In the pursuit of private profit, firms will generally serve the interests of society. Chapter 11 will explain how. In the present chapter, we set the stage by addressing a question faced by a perfectly competitive firm: How much does it produce?

PERFECT COMPETITION AS A LIMITING CASE

In practice, firms vary considerably in their ability to influence price. A huge corporation like Boeing can have substantial influence over the price of its product. Other firms, like the local gas station, have very little influence. Although the station may be in a particularly strategic location, and as a result may be able to charge a few cents more than its competition, it cannot charge 25¢ more per gallon without losing its customers.

Perfect competition may be regarded as a limiting case in which individual producers and buyers have no influence at all over price. Economists have identified a number of characteristics of perfect competition:

1. There are a *large number of buyers* and a *large number of sellers.*

2. Each buyer and each seller is a *price taker;* none has any influence over price.

3. The product is *standardized* or *homogeneous.* No firm has an advantage in terms of design or quality of product, or location at which the product is sold.

4. Each buyer and each seller has *perfect information* about prices and product. There are no ignorant buyers who might go to a higher priced firm, giving that firm some freedom to charge high prices.

5. There is *freedom of entry* and *exit.* Firms face not only the actual competition of many producers of the same product, but also potential competition from new producers who will enter the market if the price rises. If the price falls, firms are free to leave the industry.

Historically, farm products have provided the classic examples of perfect competition. There are many producers and many buyers of wheat; no single producer or consumer has any influence over price; each grade of wheat is a standardized product; daily and hourly price quotations are available to buyers and sellers; and it is relatively easy for farmers to start or stop producing wheat.

It is true that, in recent decades, price supports and other government programs mean that the prices and quantities of many crops are no longer set by impersonal market forces. In this chapter, we will ignore this complication and simply study what happens in the absence of government intervention.

Of course, we are unlikely to meet all the characteristics of perfect competition in the real world. For example, some farmers pay little attention to price quotations. But as long as many farmers do watch prices, the quantity supplied may respond to price in a way that is very close to that suggested by the theory of perfect competition. Perfect competition may be regarded as a limiting case. Some markets closely approximate the perfectly competitive ideal; others—such as the market for cars or aircraft—are quite different. Individual producers of cars or aircraft do have an ability to set the price of their output.

PERFECT COMPETITION: DEMAND AS SEEN BY AN INDIVIDUAL PRODUCER

The chapter on demand and utility (Chapter 7) showed how the market demand curve can be derived by a horizontal summing of the demands of individual buyers. This idea is repeated in Figure 10-1. The demands of the various flour mills that purchase wheat are shown on the left. These individual demand curves slope downward; when the price falls, each miller wants to buy more. When these demands are added horizontally, they give the market demand shown in the center panel.

There is yet another type of individual demand curve—the demand curve as seen by the individual *seller.* This is shown at the right, with Smitz and Svenson representing the thousands of farmers. In a perfectly competitive market, the price is set by the impersonal forces of demand and supply. Once price has been set at, say, $4 per bushel, the individual farmer can sell any quantity at that price—whether 100 bushels or 10,000. The farmer has no need to cut the price in order to sell more; no matter how much the individual farmer dumps on the market, it will be a mere drop in the bucket and will not depress the price. Nor can any individual farmer push up the price by withholding wheat. If the farmer tries to get a higher price—$4.10, for example—there will be no takers; buyers will turn to the many other farmers willing to sell

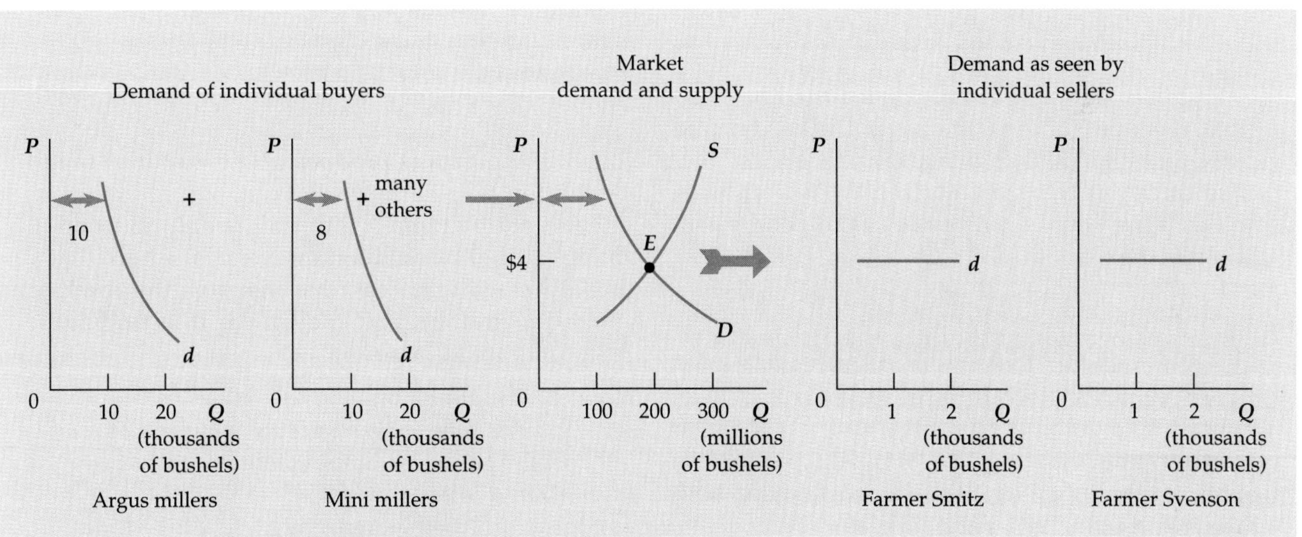

FIGURE 10-1 Demand curves of individual buyers and sellers.

As the price falls, each individual buyer will be more eager and will increase the quantity demanded. Thus the demand curves of individual buyers slope downward to the right, as illustrated by the demand of the two millers shown on the left. In contrast, the demand curve that the individual seller faces is perfectly horizontal in a competitive market, as shown on the right. The individual seller cannot charge a higher price without losing all sales, and there is no need to cut price below the market price in order to sell more.

at the going price of $4.00. As a result, the demand curve as seen by the individual producer is horizontal, as illustrated in Figure 10-1.

Thus, in a perfectly competitive market:

The demand of an individual *buyer* slopes downward to the right.

The demand facing an individual *seller* is horizontal.

MARGINAL REVENUE

Because the price is given for the individual firm selling in a perfectly competitive market, each additional unit sold will increase the firm's total revenue by an amount equal to the price. Consider, for example, a perfectly competitive firm that faces a price of $4, with Svenson's farm in Figure 10-1 being an example. If this farm sells one bushel, it will have revenue of $4; if it sells two bushels, it will have revenue of $8. Each time it sells one more bushel, its total revenue will rise by $4. Its **marginal revenue** is therefore equal to the $4 price.

Marginal revenue (MR) is the increase in total revenue when one more unit is sold.

For the perfectly competitive firm, the marginal revenue curve is the same as the demand curve that it faces. Both demand and marginal revenue trace out the same horizontal line, with the height being equal to the price of the good established in the marketplace.

PROFIT MAXIMIZATION: MARGINAL REVENUE = MARGINAL COST

To determine how much a firm will produce in order to maximize profits, we must know both marginal revenue and marginal cost.

Figure 10-2 illustrates a perfectly competitive firm facing a price and marginal revenue of $40, as illustrated by the horizontal line P = MR = d. The best output for this firm is six units, at F, where marginal cost MC equals marginal revenue MR. A decision to produce a greater output, say seven, will be a mistake, since the $55 marginal cost of producing that seventh unit exceeds the $40 of additional revenue that it brings in. On the other hand, if the firm is producing less, say four units, expansion will be in its interest. Why? The marginal cost of adding a fifth unit is only $30, and it brings in $40 of additional revenues. At six units, however, marginal cost has risen to the level of marginal revenue, and the firm is in equilibrium. Its profits are a maximum.

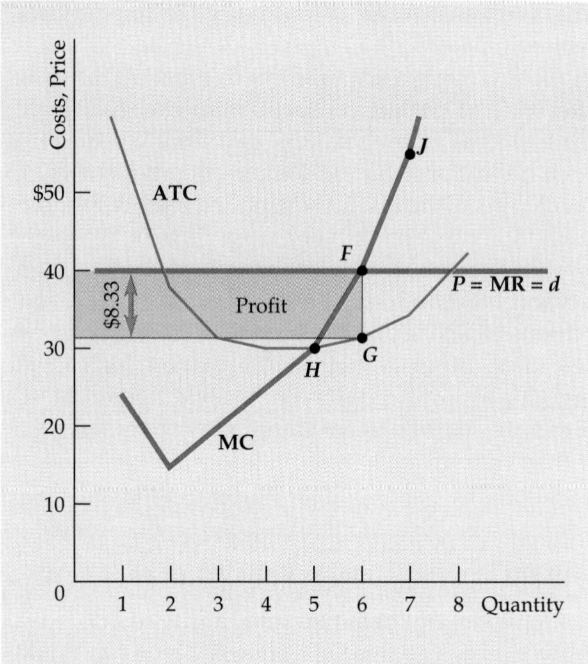

FIGURE 10-2 Profit maximization for a perfectly competitive firm.

The firm maximizes profits by choosing output where P = MC. When the price is $40, this is at an output of six units. Profits are illustrated by the shaded blue area, which equals the $8.33 profit per unit times the six units produced. (*Note:* This shows the same firm as Table 10-1.)

Any firm, whether in a perfectly or imperfectly competitive market, maximizes profits by producing where

$$MC = MR$$

The decision to expand, contract, or maintain current production depends on what is happening *at the margin.*

For a perfectly competitive firm, MR = Price P

Therefore, a perfectly competitive firm maximizes profits where

$$MC = MR = P$$

This principle can be confirmed in Table 10-1. The first four columns list the firm's costs. (This is the same hypothetical shoe firm whose costs were first shown in Table 9-1.) Column 5 shows how the firm's total revenue increases by $40 each time output is expanded by one unit, giving the constant marginal revenue of $40 in column 6. Profits are calculated in the last column as total revenue minus total cost. The firm's maximum profit is $50, which is realized at an output of six units. The arrow on the right marks this as the output the firm will produce. (Profit is also $50 when five units are produced. In cases like this one, economists assume that the firm produces the larger number.) Note that, at this profit-maximizing output of six, marginal cost in column 3 is equal to the marginal revenue of $40 in column 6. This confirms our conclusion that the firm maximizes profit when its marginal cost is equal to marginal revenue.

If the firm is producing more than the equilibrium quantity, the excess of marginal cost over marginal revenue will drag profits down. For example, if the firm adds a seventh unit, marginal cost is $55 whereas marginal revenue is only $40. The difference of $15 is reflected in profits, which decrease by the same $15, from $50 to $35.

In Figure 10-2, total profit is shown by the blue area. This profit area of $50 is equal to the number of units (six) times the per-unit profit of $8.33. This per-unit profit can be found by subtracting the average total cost ($31.67, in col. 4, Table 10-1) from the average revenue ($40, in col. 6).

An alternative view of profit maximization is presented in Box 10-1.

SHORT-RUN SUPPLY OF A PERFECTLY COMPETITIVE FIRM

The firm facing a $40 price responds by producing six units. What does it do if the price rises to $55?

To answer this question, visualize the horizontal price line shifting up to a new price of $55 in Figure 10-2. This new price line once again represents marginal revenue. The firm will respond by increasing its production to seven units, moving to point *J* where MC again equals MR. Alternatively,

TABLE 10-1 Profit Maximization by a Hypothetical Shoe Firm Facing a Price of $40

(1) *Quantity of output* *q*	(2) *Total cost* *TC*	(3) *Marginal cost* *MC*	(4) *Average total cost ATC* *(4) = (2) ÷ (1)*	(5) *Total revenue* *TR*	(6) *Marginal Revenue MR = Average Revenue AR = Price P*	(7) *Profit or loss* *(7) = (5) – (2)*
0	35			0		–35
		24			40	
1	59		59	40		–19
		16			40	
2	75		37.50	80		5
		20			40	
3	95		31.67	120		25
		25			40	
4	120		30	160		40
		30			40	
5	150		30	200		50
		40			40	
6	190		31.67	240		50 ←
		55			40	
7	245		35	280		35
		85			40	
8	330		41.25	320		–10

suppose that the price falls to $30. Output will now be cut back to five units at *H*, where MC once again equals MR.

Notice that, in showing how much output the firm will supply at various prices, we are defining the firm's supply curve. As price rises, the firm follows its marginal cost curve upward; as price falls, it follows its marginal cost curve down. Thus the MC curve defines the supply curve of the individual firm—subject to one important qualification.

BOX 10–1 *Another View of Profit Maximization: Total Revenue and Total Cost*

Graphing a firm's marginal revenue and marginal cost curves in Figure 10-2 is not the only way we can illustrate how it maximizes its profit. We can alternatively graph its *total* revenue and *total* cost curves in the figure shown here.

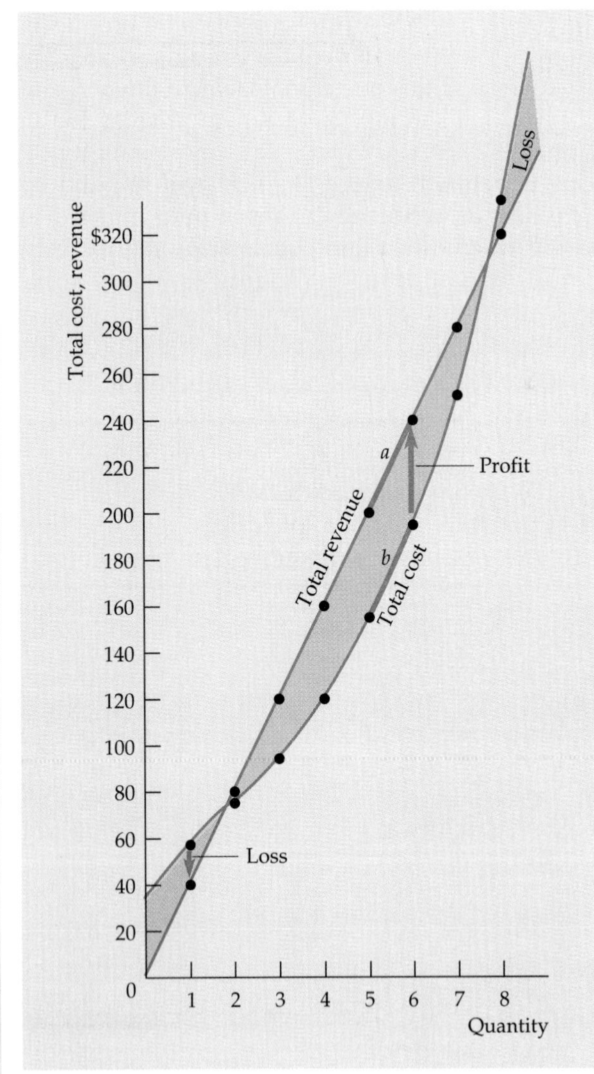

Specifically, we first plot the firm's red total cost curve, taken from Table 10-1. Next, the firm's total revenue is plotted as the straight line from the origin. Because the firm faces a given price of $40, total revenue is $40 when one unit is sold, $80 when two are sold, $120 when three are sold, and so on. Note that the slope of this line is equal to the price and to the marginal revenue.

Initially, if the firm produces only one unit of output, it operates at a loss of $19 shown by the red arrow. Its total cost of $59 exceeds its total revenue of $40. However, as it increases output, it moves upward to the right out of the red loss area into the blue profit range, where total revenue has risen above total cost. Finally, at eight units or more of output, total cost rises above total revenue, and the firm again operates at a loss.

Where in the range between two and seven units of output does the firm maximize profits? The answer is at six units, the output where its profit (the vertical distance between the total revenue and total cost curves) is greatest.†

When profit is maximized—at the sixth unit—the slopes of the total revenue and total cost curves are the same. Specifically, the slope of segment *a* equals the slope of segment *b*. We have already seen that the slope of the total revenue line is marginal revenue. Likewise, the slope of the total cost curve measures marginal cost.‡

Thus when the firm picks its maximum profit, it is picking the place where the total revenue and the total cost curves have the same slope. In doing so, it is equating MR and MC—just as it did when it maximized profits in Figure 10-2.

†Again, profits are the same at five units, and we again follow the convention, assuming that the larger output is sold. We also assume that the firm can't produce a fraction of a unit; for example, it can't produce 5 1/2 units.

‡Readers familiar with calculus will see why it is a valuable tool in economics. Marginal cost is simply the first derivative (slope) of the total cost curve.

THE SHUTDOWN POINT

The qualification is that the firm may not produce anything at all. If it does produce, MC does indeed determine the quantity supplied. However, if the price falls low enough, the firm will shut down. Therefore the next important question is: How far can the price fall before the firm closes down and stops producing altogether?

This question is addressed in Figure 10-3 and corresponding Table 10-2, which show the problem the firm faces as the price declines. By the time price has fallen to $30, the firm finds that its profits have disappeared. It picks the best point, at *H*, where its MC equals the MR of $30. (This best point is also shown by the arrow in col. 9 of Table 10-2.) At this point, however, the price is no higher than average cost; profits have fallen to zero. The best the firm can do is *break even.*

> The ***break-even point*** is the lowest point on the average total cost curve. When the price is at this height, the firm makes zero economic profits.

It might seem that this is the lowest price at which the firm would be willing to produce. Any lower price will result in losses. However, in the short run, the firm *cannot escape losses by shutting down.* The reason is that it has fixed costs; it has expenses even if it produces nothing. The difficult

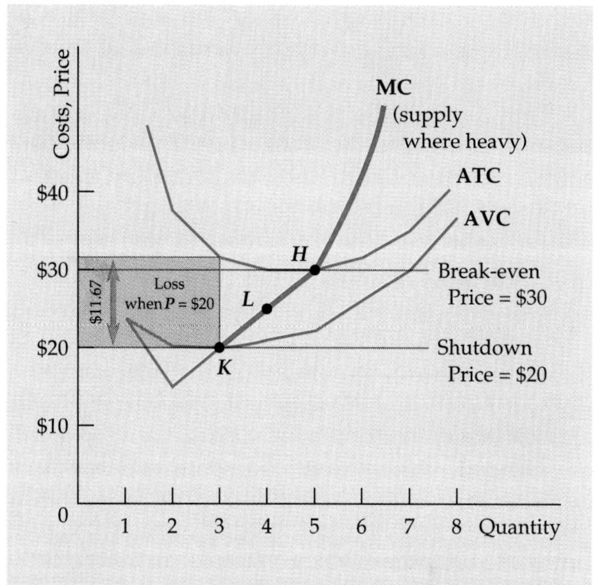

FIGURE 10-3 Producing at a loss in the short run.
If the price is below $30, the firm suffers a loss. The firm minimizes this loss by producing where $P = MC$, as long as price is at or above the $20 which will cover average variable cost. If the price is even lower, the firm cannot cover its AVC and will shut down.

Thus the MC curve represents the short-run supply curve of the individual firm, provided that the price is at or above the minimum point on the AVC curve. The short-run supply is therefore the heavy portion of the MC curve above the point where it intersects the AVC curve.

TABLE 10-2 Minimizing Loss as Price Falls

(1)	(2)	(3)	(4)	(5)	(6)	(7)	(8)	(9)	(10)	(11)	(12)	(13)
							Best Output (shown by arrow) if:					
							Price = $30 = MR		*Price = $25 = MR*		*Price = $20 = MR*	
Quantity q	*Fixed Cost FC*	*Variable Cost VC*	*Total Cost TC*	*Marginal Cost MC*	*Average Total Cost ATC*	*Average Variable Cost AVC*	*Total Revenue TR*	*Profit (+) or Loss (–) TR – TC*	*Total Revenue TR*	*Profit (+) or Loss (–) TR – TC*	*Total Revenue TR*	*Profit (+) or loss (–) TR – TC*
1	35	24	59	24	59	24	30	–29	25	–34	20	–39
2	35	40	75	16	37.50	20	60	–15	50	–25	40	–35
3	35	60	95	**20**	31.67	20	90	–5	75	–20	60	–35 ←
4	35	85	120	**25**	30	21	120	0	100	–20 ←	80	–40
5	35	115	150	**30**	30	28	150	0 ←	125	–25	100	–50
6	35	155	190	40	31.67	26	180	–10	150	–40	120	–70

question then becomes: how can the firm minimize losses? By shutting down, or by continuing to produce?

Suppose that the price falls to $25. MC equals MR at *L*, at an output of four units. This is the best point to produce—if the firm produces anything at all. Should it do so?

The answer is yes. If it produces four units, its total costs will be $120 (Table 10-2), and its total revenue $100 (column 10); it will accordingly suffer a loss of $20. But this loss is less than the fixed cost of $35, which will be the amount it will lose if it shuts down. If it shuts down, it will have nothing to sell, and its revenues will be zero.

There is another way of looking at the firm's decision to produce four units. If it does so, it will have to pay out $85 in variable costs. Total revenues of $100 exceed these variable costs. The $100 in revenues will more than justify the decision to produce. The $15 by which revenues exceed variable costs will reduce losses; the $15 can be used to pay part of the fixed costs. Losses will be only $20 when four units are produced, compared to the $35 that the firm will suffer if it shuts down.

Thus as long as the firm is at least covering its variable costs, it continues to produce. That remains true as long as the price in Figure 10-3 is above the **shutdown point,** *K*, which is the minimum point on the average variable cost curve. If the price reaches this level—$20—then the loss reaches $35, as calculated in the last column of Table 10-2 and illustrated by the red rectangle in Figure 10-3. At this point, the loss from producing is the same as the $35 loss in fixed costs that the firm suffers if it shuts down. The firm is indifferent as to whether it shuts down or continues to produce. At any lower price, it would shut down; its losses from producing would exceed the $35 loss of fixed costs if it shut down.

The ***shutdown point*** is the minimum point on the average variable cost curve, where the MC curve cuts the AVC curve. If the price is below this point, the firm produces nothing.

Thus the firm's supply curve corresponds to its MC curve, *provided that* the price is above the minimum point on the AVC.

A firm's ***short-run supply curve*** is that part of its marginal cost curve MC that lies above its average variable cost curve AVC.

The key point in this chapter is this:

A perfectly competitive firm's supply curve reflects marginal cost. The height of the supply curve is equal to the firm's marginal cost.

THE SHORT-RUN MARKET SUPPLY CURVE

Chapter 7 showed how the market demand curve *D* is the horizontal sum of the demand curves *d* of individual consumers. Similarly, the short-run market supply curve *S* can be drawn by horizontally summing the short-run supply curves *s* of the individual producers. (As before, lower case letters represent the individual participants, whereas capital letters represent the whole market demand or supply.)

This horizontal summation is illustrated in Figure 10-4, where two firms are taken as representative of the innumerable producers in a competitive market. The dashed horizontal section at the bottom of each individual supply curve is at the shutdown price; the firm would be unwilling to supply anything at a lower price.

SUPPLY IN THE LONG RUN

In the long run, cost and supply conditions are different from those of the short run in several ways:

1. In the long run, there are no fixed costs. All costs are variable. For example, costs for equipment—in the form of depreciation and maintenance costs—are fixed in the short run. As equipment wears out, however, a decision has to be made whether or not to replace it. At this point, the firm has a choice; equipment costs are variable.

2. Because the firm can change the quantity of plant and equipment in the long run, the long-run average total cost curve is much flatter and wider than a short-run average total cost curve. Specif-

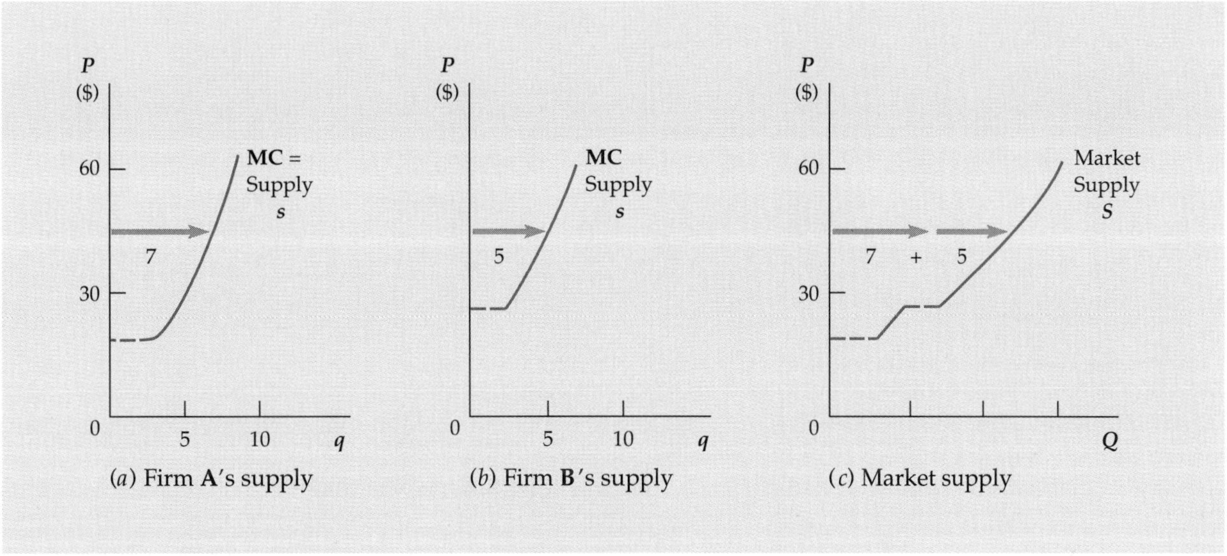

FIGURE 10-4 Adding individual supply curves to get short-run market supply.
By adding horizontally the amounts that each firm is willing to produce at a given price, we can find the corresponding point on the short-run market supply curve.

For simplicity, this figure shows only two firms, which are representative of the many firms in a perfectly competitive market.

ically, the long-run average total cost curve is the envelope curve of all the possible short-run ATC curves—as illustrated in Figure 9-4 in the previous chapter.

3. In the long run, new firms *enter* industries where the existing firms are earning above-normal profits.

4. In the long run, firms *leave* an industry if they are not earning at least a normal profit—that is, if they are suffering an economic loss. (Recall from the previous chapter that the economist's definition of costs includes normal profit.) As old equipment wears out, firms can leave the industry rather than replace the equipment. A firm with an economic loss can be held in an industry only by fixed costs, as illustrated earlier in Figure 10-3. In the long run, however, there are no fixed costs to hold losing firms.

THE IMPORTANCE OF ENTRY AND EXIT

Figure 10-5 illustrates how the entry of new firms affects supply. Initially, with 300 similar firms in the industry, each supplying ten units at price P_1 in panel *a*, there are 3,000 units supplied to the market in panel *b*. Indeed, at any price such as P_1, the quantity supplied to the market is found by horizontally multiplying the supply *s* of the individual firm in panel *a* by 300. In other words, to derive the industry's supply curve S_{300}, we repeat the procedure already shown in Figure 10-4; we horizontally sum the supply curves of all the individual firms.

If 100 similar new firms enter, increasing the number to 400, then 4,000 units are supplied at price P_1; the supply curve shifts from S_{300} to S_{400}. On the other hand, if 100 firms leave, the supply curve shifts to the left, from S_{300} to S_{200}.

Entry and exit are the keys to understanding the long-run equilibrium of a competitive industry. They ensure that, in the long run, firms in a perfectly competitive industry make normal profits, but no more. In brief, the reason is this: When price is sufficiently high to create above-normal profits, new firms enter. As a result, the quantity offered for sale increases. The price is consequently bid down, thus working to eliminate above-normal profits. Alternatively, if price is too low to provide

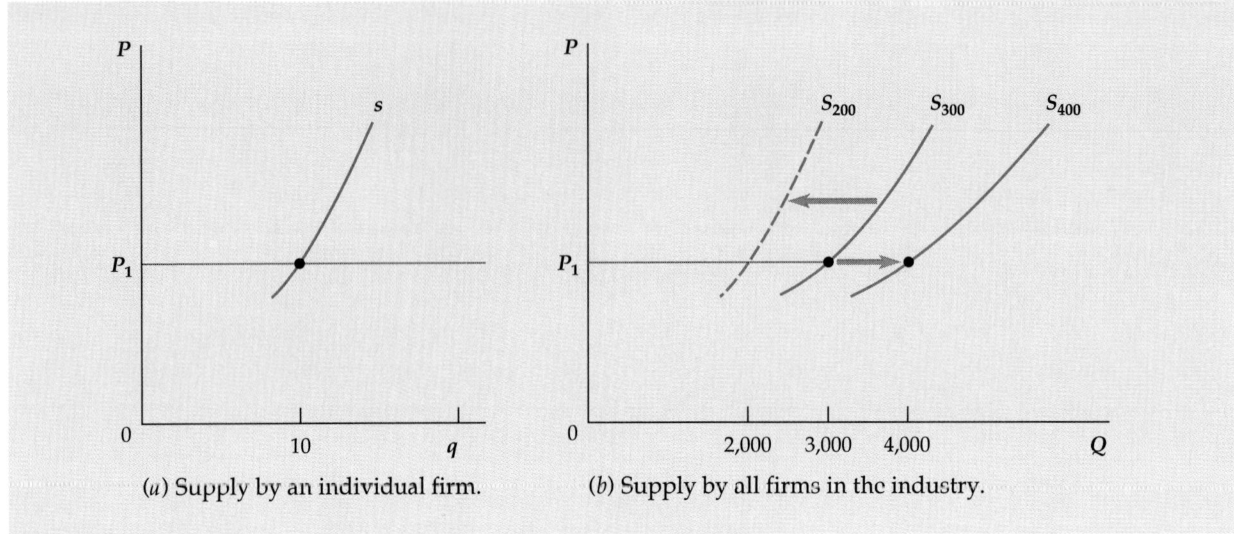

FIGURE 10-5 Supply curve shifts as new firms enter or old firms leave.
If 100 new firms enter, the industry's supply curve shifts rightward, from S_{300} to S_{400}. If 100 firms leave the industry, the supply curve shifts leftward, from S_{300} to S_{200}.

normal profits, firms leave. This reduces the quantity supplied. As a result, the price is bid up until firms are earning normal profits.

To explain this in detail, we distinguish two possibilities.

CASE 1: PERFECTLY ELASTIC LONG-RUN SUPPLY

In the first case, every input is uniform or *homogeneous*. All land is identical, all entrepreneurs are equally skillful, all workers have the same talents, and so on. In addition, the industry is not very large in the economy. As a result, the industry does not bid up the prices of its inputs when it expands; expansion of the industry causes no change in input prices. In brief, new entrants can obtain the same quality of inputs as existing firms, and inputs are available at stable prices. In these circumstances, the long-run supply curve will be horizontal.

Figure 10-6 illustrates why. Panel *a* shows an individual firm; the right panel shows the demand and supply for the whole industry. In this example, initially there are 1,000 identical firms. For each, the short-run supply curve *s* coincides with the short-run marginal cost curve SMC. For the market as a whole, the short-run supply curve is found by adding 1,000 such individual supply curves horizontally. This gives the short-run market supply curve S_{1000} in panel *b*.

At first, the industry is in equilibrium at E_1 (panel *b*). For some time, price has been stable at P_1 and output stable at 5,000 units. Each of the 1,000 firms produces an output of five units, as shown in panel *a*. Each of these firms is making only a normal profit, producing at *H*, which is the lowest point on its short-run average total cost curve SAC and also the lowest point on its long-run average total cost curve LAC.

At *H*, the individual firm breaks even; P_1 is just sufficient to cover the firm's average cost. Because existing firms are earning no above-normal (economic) profit, there is no incentive for new firms to enter. *H* is a long-run equilibrium for the firm (panel *a*), and E_1 is the corresponding long-run equilibrium for the industry (panel *b*).

Now consider what happens if demand increases to D_2 (panel *b*). *In the short run*, before the amount of capital and the number of firms can change, the higher demand causes a rise in price to P_2, with the industry moving up the short-run supply curve S_{1000} to new equilibrium E_2. In the face of

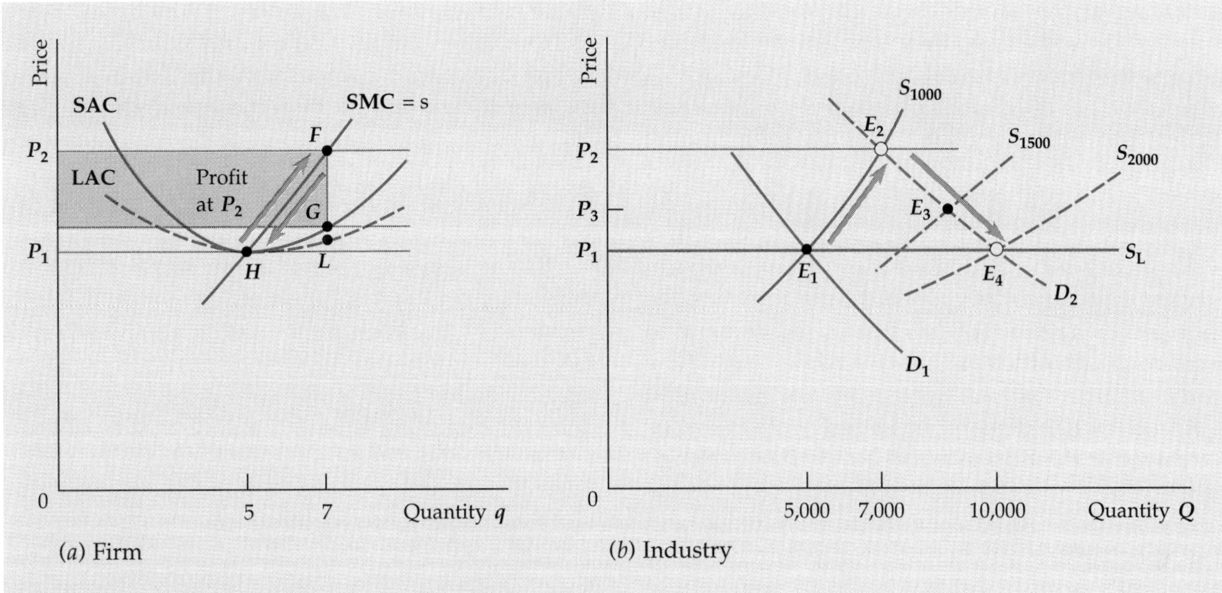

FIGURE 10-6 Long-run adjustment to an increase in demand.
In this diagram, both the firm and the industry are initially in equilibrium at price P_1. The firm in panel *a* is at *H*, producing five units. The industry is in equilibrium at E_1, with 5,000 units sold. There are 1,000 firms like the one in the left panel.

Now suppose that demand increases from D_1 to D_2 in the right panel. In the short run, the price rises to P_2, and firms make profits shown by the shaded area. New firms enter, shifting supply to the right in panel *b*. The price falls. In the long run, the price drops all the way back to P_1 at new equilibrium E_4. The individual firm in panel *a* moves back to *H*; it no longer makes profits, and there is no further incentive for new firms to enter. Therefore E_4 is a long-run equilibrium for the industry, and *H* is the corresponding equilibrium for the firm.

the higher price, each firm in the left panel moves up its short-run supply curve to *F*, where it makes a short-run profit equal to the shaded blue area. That is, it makes a profit of *FG* on each of the seven units it produces. This is above-normal profit, since normal profit is included in calculating the average cost curve.

This profit attracts new entrants, who want to "get in on a good thing." As new firms come in, the short-run supply curve of the industry shifts to the right (panel *b*). By the time the number of firms has increased to 1,500, the short-run supply curve is S_{1500}, and the equilibrium has moved to E_3. However, the resulting price P_3 is still high enough to provide above-normal profits, and new firms continue to enter.

The process of entry will continue until price falls to P_1 and above-normal profit is eliminated. In panel *b*, observe that this does not happen until the number of firms has increased to 2,000, and the new supply S_{2000} intersects demand at E_4. With the price now back to P_1, each firm in panel *a* has reacted by moving back down its supply curve from point *F* to zero-profit point *H*. At the new long-run equilibrium E_4 (panel *b*), 10,000 units are sold, with each of the 2,000 firms producing five units.

We can now construct the long-run supply curve S_L in panel *b* by joining points of long-run equilibrium like E_1 and E_4. Unlike short-run supply curves S_{1000}, S_{1500}, and S_{2000}—each of which is drawn on the assumption of a specific number of firms—supply curve S_L applies to the long run when there is time for the number of firms to change. Observe that this long-run supply curve S_L is horizontal (perfectly elastic); in the long run, price doesn't rise at all as a result of an increase in demand. The reason is that the higher demand can be satisfied by new firms entering the industry, producing at the same cost as the existing firms. They can do so because they have access to inputs of the same quality, at stable prices.

Efficient Scale in the Long Run. Whenever the market is in long-run equilibrium at a point on S_L (panel *b*), the individual firm produces at *H* (panel *a*), which is the lowest point not only on the short-run average cost curve SAC, but also on the long-run average cost curve LAC. That is, the firm has the appropriate amount of plant and equipment to produce at its efficient scale. Why is that? Why won't a firm expand, increasing its plant and equipment when demand increases?

Suppose the firm in panel *a* has already decided to expand in an attempt to hold on to a market of seven units. By adding additional plant and equipment, it can reduce its average cost for those seven units from *G* (on SAC) to *L*, a point on its long-run average cost curve LAC. But observe that point *L* is above P_1, the price at which new competitors can enter the market and sell the product. In the face of such competition, the firm will suffer losses if it stays at *L*. It therefore cuts back; as plant and equipment become obsolete or worn out, they are not replaced. The firm moves back to its most efficient size at *H*, the lowest point on its long-run average cost curve.

There is one qualification. In some industries, there may be no single most efficient size; the LAC curve may be horizontal over a range when it reaches its minimum. In such circumstances, a firm may indeed expand and stay at a larger size when demand increases. Where the LAC curves of individual firms are horizontal, firms of various sizes can coexist, and we cannot tell how many firms will exist in long-run equilibrium.

A Fall in Demand. A similar argument applies if demand declines from D_1 to D_3 in Figure 10-7. The

FIGURE 10-7 Long-run adjustment to a decrease in demand.

In this diagram, the initial equilibrium is the same as in Figure 10-6. Now, however, demand decreases from D_1 to D_3 in panel *b*. In the short run, the price falls to P_4, and each firm in panel *a* suffers a loss because the price is too low to cover its average cost. Some firms leave the industry, shifting the supply curve to the left in panel *b*. The price recovers. In the long run, the price moves all the way back to P_1 at the new long-run equilibrium E_6. Each of the remaining firms moves back to *H* in panel *a* and no longer suffers losses. Consequently, there is no further pressure for firms to leave.

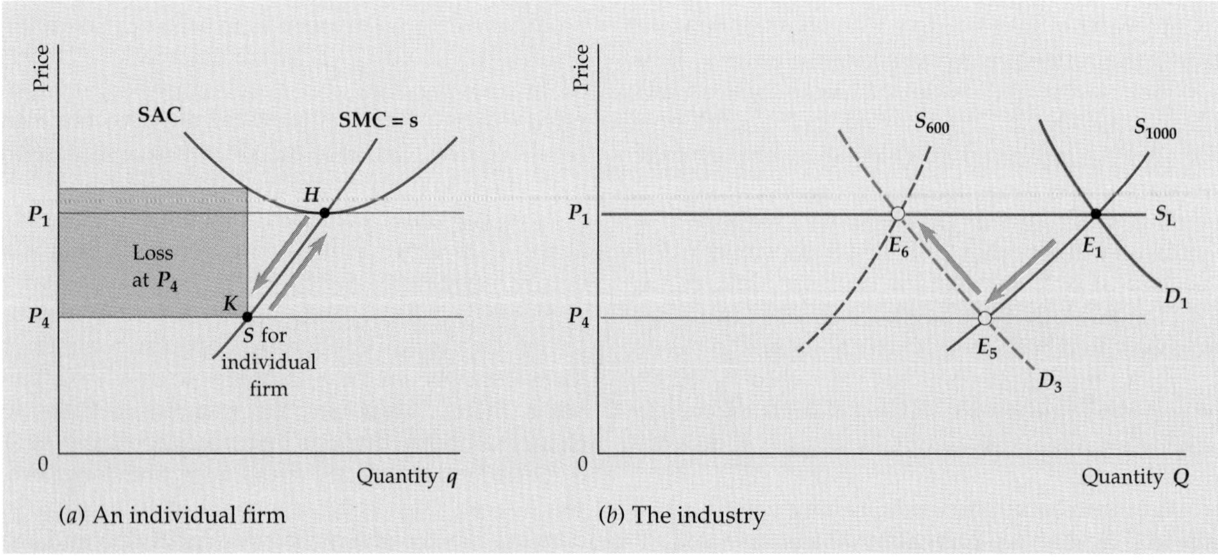

industry in panel *b* moves to a new short-run equilibrium E_5, with price depressed to P_4. In response to the lower price, each individual firm in panel *a* moves down its short-run supply curve from *H* to *K*. Each firm suffers losses because the price is now less than average cost. As their old equipment wears out, firms decide not to replace it; in the long run they prefer to leave the industry altogether. As a consequence, the supply curve in panel *b* shifts to the left. This continues until the industry reaches a new equilibrium at E_6, with only 600 firms. Price has gone back up to P_1, and each individual firm in panel *a* has responded by moving back up to *H*. At this point, the firm no longer suffers a loss; therefore firms have no further incentive to leave. Again we see that the long-run industry supply S_L, defined by joining the long-run equilibrium points such as E_1 and E_6, is horizontal.

CASE 2: A RISING LONG-RUN SUPPLY CURVE

A horizontal long-run supply curve is a special case. Even in the long run, the supply curves of many industries slope upward to the right. This happens if costs rise as new firms enter, either because these firms bid up the prices of inputs or because they have to use inputs of lower quality. For example, new wheat growers may find that the highest quality land is already being used by existing producers; the only land still available may be less productive.

Such a case is illustrated in Figure 10-8. As before, an increase in demand from D_1 to D_2 in the right panel causes a move to a new short-run equilibrium at E_2. At high price P_2, profits of existing

FIGURE 10-8 Long-run adjustment with a rising supply curve.

In this diagram, factors of production are not uniform in quality; some land is more suitable than other land for growing wheat. When demand increases from D_1 to D_2 in panel *b*, the price rises to P_2 in the short run. The profits of existing farms attract new entrants. As the number of farms increases from 100 to 150, the short-run industry supply moves from S_{100} to S_{150}. As a result, price declines from P_2 to P_3. However, it does not fall all the way back down to P_1 because the new entrants must use land that is less suitable for growing wheat; thus they face higher costs. In the long run, the competition for the best land will bid its rent upward, causing the cost curves of the initial firms in panel *a* to shift upward from *V* to *W*. Thus excess profits of the original firms on the best land disappear, as these profits are transformed into payments to land and other specialized factors of production.

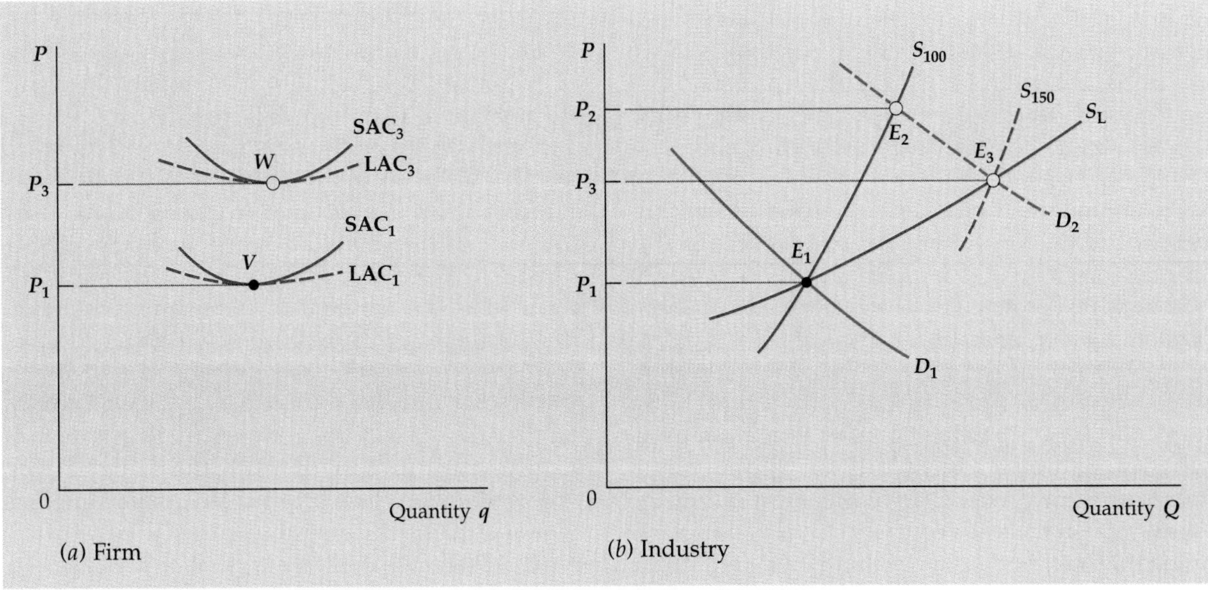

firms encourage new entrants. As in case 1, the new entrants increase supply, which brings the price down from P_2—but in this case, not all the way down to P_1. Instead price only falls to P_3. At that point, a new firm producing on the best land that is left—relatively poor land on which costs of production are relatively high—is just able to cover its costs at W in panel *a*. Because any additional firm would have to use even poorer land, it would have even higher costs. Thus there is no further incentive for firms to enter and E_3 is the new long-run equilibrium. The long-run supply curve S_L, constructed by joining long-run equilibrium points such as E_1 and E_3, slopes upward. It is more elastic than the short-run supply curves S_{100} and S_{150} but not perfectly elastic.

As the price of wheat increases and wheat farming is extended to less productive land, it is not just new firms that will face a cost of W (panel *a*). The costs of the original farmers will also rise to this level, as their long-run cost curve moves up from LAC_1 to LAC_3. Their costs will rise because their land will become more valuable. Rents on this original land will be bid up. New farmers will be willing to pay a higher rent to get this land, since their alternative would be to move to less productive land. When this land is sold, it will go for a higher price; the land will be more valuable because of the rise in the price of wheat.

We can confirm that competition in the market for land will push the average costs of an original wheat farm all the way up to the point where they again equal the price, at W in panel *a*. The reason is straightforward. If the average costs of a farm remained below price P_3, the farmer using this land would reap an above-normal profit. Other farmers would be eager to get such land, and competition would bid up its rent or selling price until such above-normal profits disappeared. Thus competition for the most desirable land will mean that farmers' profits will disappear as rents or prices of land increase; profits will be transformed into higher payments for land.

Note that we must be careful when interpreting a cost curve such as LAC_3 in Figure 10-8*a*. At W, the firm is producing at its minimum average cost. However, this does not mean that a decrease in price would drive this farm out of the wheat industry. On the contrary, if this is one of the original farms, there is a cushion in its costs. If the price of wheat falls, rents on this land will fall; costs will follow prices back down to point V if demand shifts back to D_1 in panel *b*.

THE REALLOCATION OF RESOURCES: THE ROLE OF PROFITS

Profits promote economic efficiency, encouraging entrepreneurs to redeploy resources in response to changes in consumer demand. For example, when consumers demand greater quantities of a product, they bid up the price. The resulting short-run profits (Fig. 10-6) encourage entrepreneurs to enter the industry, increasing output in response to consumer demand.

Similarly, if demand for a product falls, price declines and businesses suffer short-term losses. The losses drive some producers out of the industry. In response to the decline in demand, less is produced. Some of the labor and capital in this industry are shifted elsewhere in the economy, where demand is stronger and where the resources can be put to better use. Again, as demand changes, prices and profits respond, providing a powerful incentive for firms to produce the goods and services the public wants.

THE GAINS TO PRODUCERS FROM A HIGHER PRICE

When the price of a product rises, producers benefit. Figure 10-9 illustrates how much they gain when the price rises from \$500 to \$700.

At the lower price, firms produce at E_1 on their supply curve; 30 units are sold. When the price increases to \$700, output goes up to 50 units, at E_2. For each of the initial 30 units, producers get an additional \$200 when the price rises. This provides a gain of $\$200 \times 30 = \$6,000$, as illustrated by area 1.

There is also a gain on the additional 20 units. Consider one of these, say, unit #40. The marginal cost of that unit is measured by the height of the supply curve S—in this case, \$600. (Recall that the supply curve is derived from the marginal cost curves of the producing firms, as explained in Figs. 10-3 and 10-4.) Because the marginal cost of unit #40 is \$600, while it fetches a price of \$700, the pro-

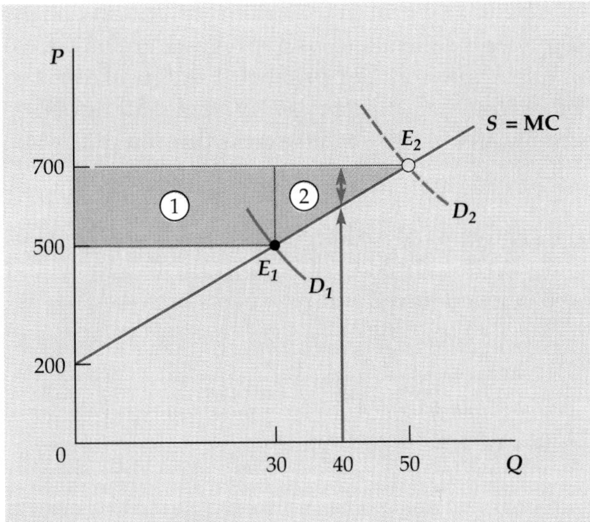

FIGURE 10-9 The gain to producers when price rises.
When the price rises from $500 to $700, producers gain. On each of the initial 30 units, they gain $200, as shown by area 1. On additional units produced, they gain the difference between the price and the marginal cost. For example, on the fortieth unit, the price is $700, while the marginal cost is $600. Thus producers gain $100 on that unit. The gain on all such additional units is area 2, giving a total gain to producers of areas 1 + 2 when the price increases from $500 to $700.

ducer gains $100 on that unit, as indicated by the blue arrow. Similar gains are made because price exceeds the marginal cost of other units as output increases from 30 to 50, giving a gain of triangular area 2. Thus, producers gain by areas 1 + 2 when price increases from $500 to $700.

Essential idea for future chapters: If price rises, the gain to producers may be estimated as the horizontal area to the left of the supply curve between the old and the new prices.[1] If market price falls, producers are worse off by a similar amount.

Such gains go to somebody on the production side, but the recipients may be quite different in the short and the long run. In the short run, firms already in the industry capture the gain in the form of profits. In the long run, new firms enter and bid up the price of land or other specialized factors of production. Specialized factors of production may include labor with a particular skill. For example, as demand increases and the price of auto repairs goes up, service stations find that they must pay higher wages to attract and keep skilled mechanics.

[1]This gain is sometimes spoken of as an increase in *producer surplus.* It is analogous to the increase in consumer surplus when the price falls.

REPRISE: THE BURDEN OF A TAX

It is now possible to investigate the effects of an excise tax in detail. Figure 10-10 provides an elaboration of the idea presented earlier in Figure 6-6.

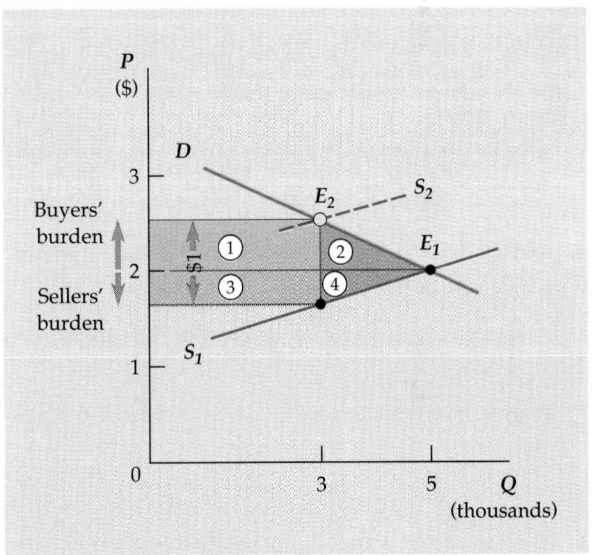

FIGURE 10-10 The excess burden of a tax.
Except in an extreme case where either the demand or supply curve is horizontal, a tax will fall partly on consumers and partly on producers. In this example, the $1 tax shifts the supply curve from S_1 to S_2, and equilibrium from E_1 to E_2. Since price increases from $2 to $2.60, the reduction in consumer surplus is equal to area 1 + 2. The price received by producers, net of tax, falls from $2 to $1.60, and producers therefore lose area 3 + 4. Thus consumers and producers together are worse off by area 1 + 2 + 3 + 4. The government's tax collections amount only to rectangle 1 + 3—that is, the tax of $1 times the 3,000 units sold. The losses to buyers and sellers together therefore exceed the amount of tax collection by area 2 + 4, which represents the excess burden of the tax. It is a net loss to society.

Once again, the arrows on the vertical axis illustrate how the burden of a $1 tax is divided. In the example in Figure 10-10, the buyer pays 60¢ more and the producer gets 40¢ less. However, the total burden on buyers and sellers depends not only on the change in the price that each faces, but also on the number of units bought and sold.

In Figure 10-10, the number of units decreases from 5,000 to 3,000 as a result of the tax. The total burden on buyers is area 1 + 2—that is, the decrease in consumers' surplus when the price they pay increases. The price to producers goes down, which inflicts a burden on them equal to area 3 + 4.

Observe that the total burden to buyers and sellers together—area 1 + 2 + 3 + 4—exceeds the amount that the government collects in taxes. By collecting $1 in tax on each of the 3,000 units sold, the government gets revenues of $3,000—that is, area 1 + 3.

The $3,000 that goes out of the pockets of the buyers and sellers and into the government's treasury is known as the **primary burden** of the tax. The additional burden on buyers and sellers—namely, area 2 + 4—is the **excess burden** of the tax. It does not "go" to anybody. It is a net loss in economic efficiency as a result of the tax, which results when buyers cut back their purchases by 2,000 units. In the absence of a tax, consumers would have enjoyed area 2 and producers area 4.

The ***primary burden*** of a tax is the amount paid by the taxpayers to the government.

The ***excess burden*** of a tax is the loss in economic efficiency that results when people change their behavior in response to the tax. (In this case, they reduce the quantity consumed.)

KEY POINTS

1. An individual producer in a perfectly competitive market has no influence over price. Hence the demand curve facing each individual producer is perfectly elastic.

2. In a perfectly competitive market, a firm's marginal revenue MR = price *P*.

3. A firm maximizes profits by picking the output where

$$MC = MR$$

4. The short-run supply of a perfectly competitive firm is the portion of its marginal cost curve MC that lies above its average variable cost curve AVC.

5. If existing firms are making an above-normal profit, new firms will be attracted into an industry. If existing firms are operating at a loss, some will leave.

6. An industry's long-run supply is more elastic than its short-run supply. One important reason is that, in response to a higher price, new firms enter. As a result, industry output increases.

7. If new firms can enter an industry without bidding up the prices of inputs, long-run supply is completely elastic. But if input prices are bid up as new firms enter, long-run supply is not completely elastic; it slopes upward.

8. A price increase provides a gain to producers equal to the area to the left of the supply curve, and between the old and the new price (areas 1 + 2 in Fig. 10-9).

KEY CONCEPTS

freedom of entry and exit
marginal revenue
profit maximization
 where MR = MC
break-even point
shutdown point
short-run supply curve
primary burden of a tax
excess burden of a tax

PROBLEMS

10-1. Suppose marginal cost is \$50 whereas marginal revenue is \$90. Should the firm expand production? What happens to profit if it produces one more unit?

10-2. Recalculate Table 10-1 and find the profit-maximizing output if the firm's price is \$55. What is the profit at this output?

10-3. Return to Table 10-1 and find the profit-maximizing output if the firm's price is \$50. What happens to output as the price increases from \$40 to \$50? Why?

10-4. Suppose that the fixed cost of the firm in Table 10-1 were \$70 rather than \$35.

> **(a)** Recalculate the table.
>
> **(b)** What happens to ATC? To MC? To the output of the firm? To profit?
>
> **(c)** Does the output at which ATC reaches a minimum increase, decrease, or remain the same. Why?
>
> **(d)** Calculate average variable cost AVC. Does the output at which AVC reaches a minimum increase, decrease, or remain the same. Why?
>
> **(e)** If your answers were different for (c) and (d), explain why.
>
> **(f)** At what price will this firm shut down? How does this compare with the shutdown price in Figure 10-3?

10-5. To understand the problem of operating at a point like *L* in Figure 10-3, suppose that you have inherited a house in another city which you want to rent. You have to pay \$200 a month of fixed costs, such as taxes and exterior painting, whether or not it is rented. You also have to pay variable costs averaging \$100 per month for extra repairs and interior decorating if you do rent it. If you can get only \$150 per month in rent, should you rent it or not? Explain why.

10-6. (a) Consider a firm operating at the lowest point on its SAC and LAC curves (for example, point *H* in Fig. 10-6*a*). Does its short-run supply extend below this point? If so, how far? Why?

> **(b)** Suppose price falls below this point. Explain how the firm, with the benefit of hindsight, would view its original decision to enter this industry. What would its output be in the short run and in the long run? What does this suggest about the relative elasticities of short-run supply and long-run supply?

10-7. Suppose that Figure 10-6 represents the costs and supply of an agricultural product.

> **(a)** What happens to the rent on land used by this industry as demand increases? Why?
>
> **(b)** Suppose you have to guess what this product is. Is it more likely to be corn or cranberries? Why?

CHAPTER 11
PERFECT COMPETITION AND ECONOMIC EFFICIENCY

Under perfect competition, the business dodoes, dinosaurs and great ground sloths are in for a bad time—as they should be.

R. H. BORK AND W. S. BOWMAN, JR.

In Chapter 7, we examined how consumers in a perfectly competitive market respond to the price they face. In Chapter 10, we studied how producers on the other side of such a market respond. In this chapter, these two sides are brought together in order to *describe* how a perfectly competitive market operates. This will then be used to *evaluate its performance* from the point of view of society as a whole. Does a perfectly competitive market force producers to be efficient, as the above quote suggests? How well does it deliver the goods and services the public wants?

This chapter shows that, if two important assumptions are satisfied, a perfectly competitive market does provide an efficient result, with neither too much nor too little output being produced. Future chapters will illustrate why other market structures typically do not result in allocative efficiency. For example, the next chapter will show that monopoly is generally not efficient, because too little output is produced.

TWO IMPORTANT ASSUMPTIONS

Thus far, no distinction has been made between the *private benefit* a good provides to those who buy it, and the benefit it provides to society as a whole—its *social benefit*. Often the two are the same. For example, when someone buys beefsteak, the only benefit that goes to society is the benefit received by that individual. There is no additional benefit to anyone else. However, private and social benefit don't always coincide in this way. For example, if your neighbors hire a gardener, they receive a benefit; but there is also an additional benefit that goes to you.

For now, however, this complication will be ignored. It is assumed that the purchaser is the only one who benefits from the good; that is, the benefit received by the purchaser represents the total benefit to society. Thus

Assumption 1. Social benefit is the same as the private benefit of the purchaser. More precisely, the marginal benefit of a good to society as a whole—which we will call MB_S—is the same as MB, its marginal benefit to those who buy it. Either can be measured by the height of the market demand curve.

$$MB_S = \text{MB to consumers} \qquad (11\text{-}1)$$

A similar assumption is made about cost.

Assumption 2. The cost of a good to society is the same as the private cost incurred by producers of this good. More precisely, the marginal cost of a good to society as a whole—which we will call MC_S—is the same as MC, its marginal cost to producers. Either is shown by the height of the market supply curve.

$$MC_S = \text{MC to producers} \qquad (11\text{-}2)$$

For example, the cost to society of producing wheat is generally just the cost incurred by wheat farmers. However, there are again exceptions. The cost to society of paper may not only be the private cost incurred by the firms producing it, but also the cost to those people living downstream who suffer if these firms dump polluting wastes into the river.

Exceptions to these two assumptions are important and will be the focus of attention in Chapters 16, 17, and 18. Until then, however, the analysis will be limited to perfectly competitive markets in the large number of cases in which these two assumptions are valid.

HOW A PERFECTLY COMPETITIVE MARKET WORKS

Figures 11-1 and 11-2 illustrate the decisions of many consumers and many producers in a perfectly competitive market. In the middle panel of Figure 11-1, note that supply and demand are equal at an equilibrium output of 100 units and a $10 price. At this equilibrium, the quantity purchased by each consumer is shown in the panels on the left, whereas the quantity sold by each producer is shown in the panels on the right. (As always, we use only a few consumers and producers to represent the very large number of participants in this market.)

In Figure 11-1, the central panel showing *S* and *D* is so important that it is reproduced in Figure 11-2. Panel *a* of Figure 11-2 shows what's happen-

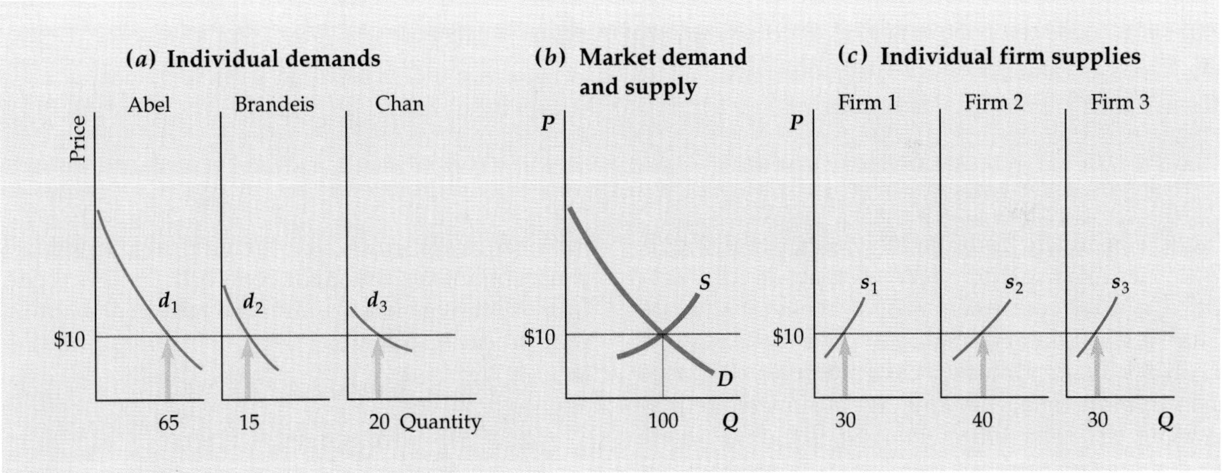

FIGURE 11-1 Individual consumers and producers in a perfectly competitive market.

In panel *b*, market demand *D* is the sum of the individual demands in panel *a*, whereas market supply *S* is the sum of the supplies of individual firms in panel *c*. The perfectly competitive solution, where *S* and *D* intersect, is at a price of $10 and an output of 100 units. The bars in panel *a* show how each consumer continues to purchase until marginal benefit MB equals the $10 price; the bars in panel *c* show how each firm produces to the point where its marginal cost MC is equal to this $10 price. Because each consumer's MB is therefore equal to each producer's MC, any change in production or consumption will result in an efficiency loss.

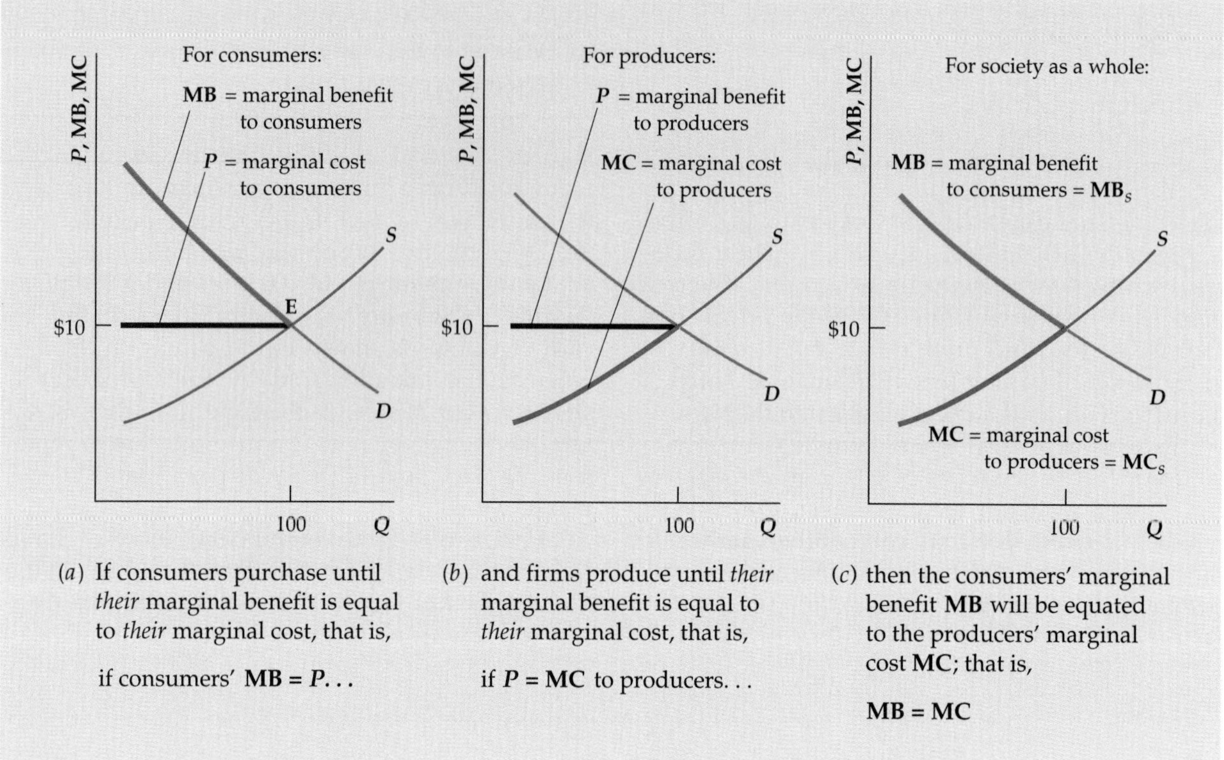

FIGURE 11-2 The competitive market: the equalization of marginal benefit and marginal cost leading to an efficient output.
This is an elaboration of panel *b* in Figure 11-1.

ing to consumers, as originally described in Figure 7-3. The demand curve tells us that, faced with a price of $10, consumers will purchase 100 units. That is, consumers facing a $10 price move to point *E* on the demand curve. Let's interpret that decision in more detail. As long as consumers are purchasing less than 100 units, their marginal benefit (given by the height of the demand curve) will be greater then their marginal cost of another unit (given by the $10 price *P*). Hence it will be in their interest to buy another unit, and continue to do so up to point *E where their marginal benefit MB becomes equal to their marginal cost P.*

$$\textit{For consumers: } \text{MB} = P \qquad (11\text{-}3)$$

Panel *b* shows what is happening to producers, as originally described in Figure 10-2. Producing firms make the decision that is best for *them* by continuing to produce and sell this good until *their marginal benefit equals their marginal cost.* In perfect competition, the marginal benefit that they obtain from selling one more unit is the price *P*. Therefore, they produce 100 units.

$$\textit{For producers: } P = \text{MC} \qquad (11\text{-}4)$$

From these two equations, it follows that

$$\text{Consumers' MB} = \text{MC to producers} \qquad (11\text{-}5)$$

as shown in panel *c* of Figure 11-2. Finally, recall the two key assumptions introduced earlier in Equations (11-1) and (11-2). Because of these two assumptions, the equation above becomes:

$$\text{MB}_S = \text{MC}_S \qquad (11\text{-}6)$$

That is, the marginal benefit to society equals the marginal cost to society. This is the condition that provides an efficient outcome for society as a whole, as we will confirm in the next section.

The efficient outcome for society is where

$$MB_S = MC_S$$

This occurs in perfect competition if social benefits are the same as benefits to consumers and social costs are the same as costs to producers.

To sum up thus far: Under perfect competition, with consumers making *their* best decision by equating *their* marginal benefit and marginal cost in panel *a,* and producers making *their* best decision by equating *their* marginal benefit and marginal cost in panel *b,* the result in panel *c* is an efficient output for society as a whole.

This conclusion is so important in economics that it is emphasized in Box 11-1 and will now be illustrated with two examples.

DEMONSTRATING WHY PERFECT COMPETITION IS EFFICIENT

It has just been shown that if Assumptions 1 and 2 hold, perfect competition equates the marginal benefit to society MB_S and the marginal cost to society MC_S. It can now be demonstrated that when $MB_S = MC_S$, the outcome is efficient.

The market supply and demand curves from panel *c* of Figure 11-2 are reproduced in Figure 11-3. Now suppose that output is expanded beyond the perfectly competitive quantity of 100 units where marginal benefit to society equals marginal cost to society. Specifically, in panel *a,* suppose the quantity is 140 units. This outcome is inefficient, as we can see by considering any one of the additional units of output beyond 100—unit *c,* for example. The benefit it provides to society is shown by the gray arrow, the height of the demand curve. However, its cost is even greater, as shown by both this gray arrow and the red arrow above it—that is, the height of the supply curve. Thus the marginal cost of this unit exceeds the benefit it provides; there is a net loss to society shown by the red arrow. The sum of all similar losses on all the excess units of output in the range between 100 and 140 is shown by the red triangle. This represents the efficiency loss that results from producing too much. This idea is important. Even though food, for example, may be inherently very good—

BOX 11–1 Conditions That Result in an Efficient Solution

Since MB and MC represent marginal private benefits and costs, and MB_S and MC_S represent marginal social benefits and costs, then:

If social and private benefits are the same,	$MB_S = MB$	(11-1)
and if consumers in a perfectly competitive market act in their own self-interest by purchasing up to the point where their marginal benefit equals price	$MB = P$	(11-3)
and if producers in a perfectly competitive market act in their own self-interest by producing up to the point where their marginal cost equals price,	$P = MC$	(11-4)
and if private and social costs are the same,	$MC = MC_S$	(11-2)
then Adam Smith's "invisible hand" works; the pursuit of private interest by both consumers and producers yields a result that is in the interest of society as a whole	$MB_S = MC_S$	(11-6)

That is, there is an efficient solution.

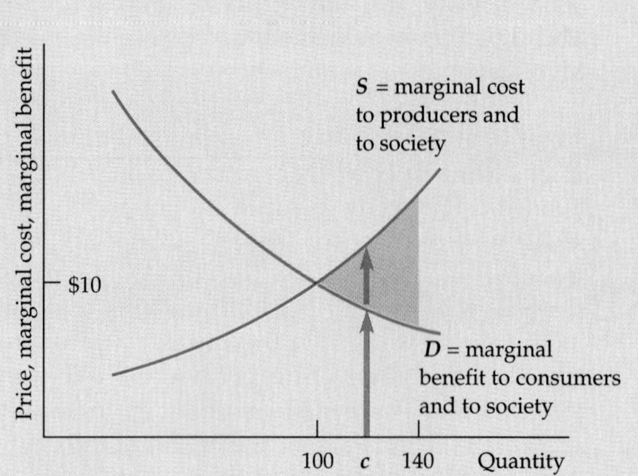

(*a*) **Too much.** Output is 140, which is greater than the perfectly competitive equilibrium of 100 where marginal benefit to society is equal to marginal cost to society. On each of these 40 additional units there is an efficiency loss because marginal cost (the height of the supply curve) exceeds marginal benefit (the height of the demand curve). The total efficiency loss from all such units of excess output is the red triangle.

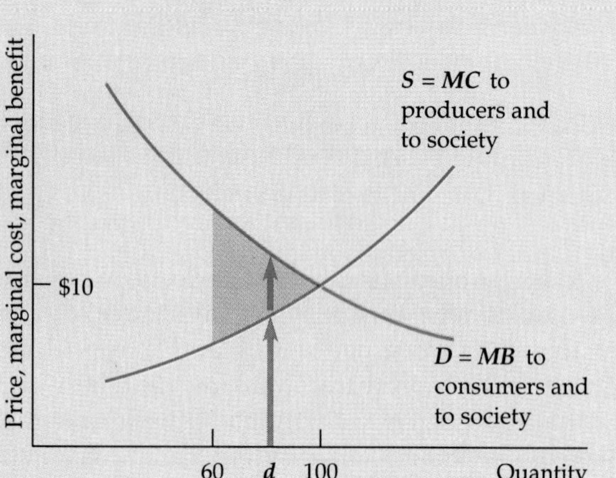

(*b*) **Too little.** Output is restricted to only 60 units, less than the competitive level of 100. On each of these 40 units foregone, marginal benefit (the height of the demand curve) would have exceeded marginal cost (the height of the supply curve). There is therefore an efficiency loss because these potentially beneficial units are not produced. This loss is shown as the red triangle.

FIGURE 11-3 Inefficient quantities of output.

and, indeed, essential to life itself—it is possible to produce too much.

On the other hand, suppose that for some reason output is less than 100 units—say, the 60 units shown in panel *b*. This outcome is also inefficient; to see why, consider one of the units that is no longer produced, say *d*. Its cost would have been the gray arrow under the supply curve, and its benefit the gray arrow *plus* the red arrow under the demand curve. Thus, the net benefit to society of producing it would have been the red arrow—that is, the amount by which benefits to consumers exceed costs of production. Or to put the same point another way, society incurs the loss of this red arrow because this potentially beneficial unit is not produced. The sum of all such losses through the range of restricted output from 100 down to 60 is the red triangle. This is the efficiency loss that results from producing too little. An example is the rent control program described earlier in Chapter 6, which leads to a reduced output of housing units and therefore an efficiency loss.

Thus the perfectly competitive output of 100 units is the efficient output, where marginal benefit and marginal cost to society are equal. There is an efficiency loss if either more or less is produced.

This idea of an efficiency loss—sometimes called a *deadweight loss*—is a central concept in the study of microeconomics. You should therefore master Figure 11-3 before proceeding. In particular:

Idea Essential for Future Chapters: An efficiency loss—or deadweight loss—occurs whenever there is a move away from the output where the marginal benefit to society is equal to the marginal cost to society. Such an efficiency loss from producing too much or too little can be shown graphically by red triangles, such as those in Figure 11-3.

Finally, as an alternative demonstration of why efficiency occurs at the perfectly competitive output—where marginal benefit and cost to society are equal—return to Figure 11-1, where we first illustrated the perfectly competitive market. Suppose you are an all-powerful bureaucrat or czar and think you can do better than this perfectly competitive solution. Specifically, suppose that you arbitrarily order that, instead of the equilibrium quantity of 100 units, 40 more units are to be produced. Try as you like, you cannot avoid a social loss on those additional units. On the one hand, they must cost more than $10 to produce. Regardless of the firms you select to produce them in panel *c*, those firms will have to move to the right, *up* their supply curves to a higher marginal cost. At the same time, those additional units will be consumed by individuals in panel *a* who value them at less than $10. No matter who gets to consume these units, those individuals will move to the right, *down* their demand curves to a lower marginal benefit. Because the cost of each additional unit is greater than $10, and the benefit it provides is less than $10, there is a net social loss—that is, an efficiency loss. You thought you could do better; in fact, you did worse.

A further discussion of efficiency is provided in Box 11-2 and in the appendix at the end of this chapter.

FREE ENTRY AND ECONOMIC EFFICIENCY

For perfect competition to exist, one of the key requirements is free entry. If this condition is not met, inefficiency may result.

INEFFICIENCY BECAUSE FREE ENTRY IS BLOCKED

Suppose that the third firm in Figure 11-1 has been blocked out of this market for some reason; for example, suppose it's a firm that needs a government license, and it has been turned down. Because its supply s_3 no longer exists, total market supply in the center panel is less—that is, it lies to the left of *S*. You can visualize (or sketch in) this new supply curve. Note that the equilibrium output where this new supply intersects *D* is less than

BOX 11–2 Pareto and the Elimination of Deadweight Loss

With a small amount of extra effort and imagination, we can increase our understanding of the important idea of efficiency.

A change that will make one individual better off without hurting anyone else is called a **Pareto-improvement,** after Italian economist Vilfredo Pareto (1848–1923), who originated the idea. If all such Pareto-improvements have been made, the result is a **Pareto-optimum.** This is exactly what economists mean by an efficient solution. It means that all deadweight losses have been eliminated—that is, all possible Pareto-improvements have been made. It is no longer possible to make any individual better off without making somebody else worse off.

The idea of a Pareto-improvement can be illustrated by referring back to Figure 11-1. Suppose that initially Brandeis gets one less unit than we have shown there (namely, 14 units), whereas Chan gets one more (21 units). A Pareto-improvement is now possible because Chan can be made better off without hurting anyone else—that is, without hurting Brandeis, the only other person involved. Here's how. Let Chan sell that one unit to Brandeis for $10. Chan benefits from this transaction. Because he values his twentieth unit at $10, he values his twenty-first unit—the one he is giving up—at less than $10; so he benefits when he receives $10 for it. At the same time, Brandeis has not been hurt because he values the unit he receives—his fifteenth—at exactly the same $10 that he pays for it.

This Pareto-improvement is possible because initially all producers and consumers did not value their last unit equally. With this transaction, however, we have reached the perfectly competitive solution in Figure 11-1, where all consumers and producers *do* value their last unit equally, at $10. That is, the marginal benefit MB for every consumer is now equal to the MB for every other consumer, and is also equal to the marginal cost MC for every producer. Consequently, any further Pareto-improvement is impossible. Therefore this perfectly competitive solution is Pareto-optimal, that is, efficient.

the efficient output level of 100, and a triangular efficiency loss therefore results. Potentially beneficial units of output are not produced because this third firm is unable to enter this market and produce them.

LIVING IN A GLOBAL ECONOMY

FREER ENTRY INTO THE LONDON FINANCIAL MARKET

Several years ago, the British government decided to relax regulations in the financial markets. In the "Big Bang" of 1986, it abruptly swept many regulations aside, including barriers restricting foreign firms operating in London. Many banks and other financial institutions from New York, Tokyo, and the world's other financial centers seized the opportunity. The resulting intense competition quickly drove down the fees for financial services, such as buying or selling stocks or bonds. Although this industry may still not precisely follow the perfectly competitive model, opening up the entry of new firms has made it far more competitive and efficient.

In terms of Figure 11-1*b*, the pre-1986 supply was well to the left of *S* because of government regulations that restricted foreign firms. Price was high, and an inefficiently low quantity of services was provided. When regulations were relaxed and the output of foreign firms consequently increased, the supply curve shifted to the right toward *S*. Prices fell and quantity increased toward the efficient amount where *S* and *D* intersect.

OTHER TYPES OF EFFICIENCY

Thus far, this chapter has shown only how perfectly competitive markets can provide *allocative efficiency,* that is, the *right combination of goods.* This follows because each good is produced at the intersection of supply and demand (for example, 100 units in Fig. 11-3). Therefore there is neither too much nor too little production of any good.

Let us now consider how well perfect competition measures up in terms of *technological* and *dynamic* efficiency.

TECHNOLOGICAL, OR TECHNICAL, EFFICIENCY

Technological, or technical, efficiency means avoiding outright waste. Thus a restaurant is technically inefficient if it produces a standard meal using the same amount of capital but twice as much labor as other restaurants. A construction firm is technically inefficient if it destroys its machinery because it fails to keep it oiled. In brief, technical inefficiency exists if there is poor management and unnecessarily high costs. To illustrate in panel *a* of Figure 11-4, technical inefficiency raises the firm's average cost curve up to AC_2, compared with the average cost curve AC_1 of a technically efficient firm.

Perfect competition works toward technical efficiency as well as allocative efficiency. If a firm is inefficient and is therefore producing at a high-cost point such as *F*, it won't be able to survive in competition with technically efficient firms that produce with average costs at *G*. Thus, inefficient firms tend to go the way of the dinosaurs—to be driven out of business by their existing competitors or by new firms with lower costs. (Note how perfect competition puts pressure on firms to produce at the lowest point on their average cost curves. We also saw this pressure in our earlier example in Fig. 10-6, where the firms that survive in the long run produce at the lowest point *H*.)

In contrast to the firm in perfect competition, a monopoly firm may be protected from the pressures of competition. If it has a stranglehold on a market—because of a patent, for example—it can survive even if management is sloppy; it doesn't have to worry about facing new competitors. But even though monopoly does not *have* to achieve technical efficiency, it still has an incentive to do so; greater technical efficiency means greater profits. Therefore, in later chapters we will generally show monopoly firms producing on their technically efficient average cost curves.

DYNAMIC EFFICIENCY

Dynamic efficiency exists when changes are occurring at the best rate—for example, when new technology is being developed and adopted at the best rate. Although a competitive market gets high marks for promoting allocative efficiency and technical efficiency, its superiority is less clear in terms of dynamic efficiency.

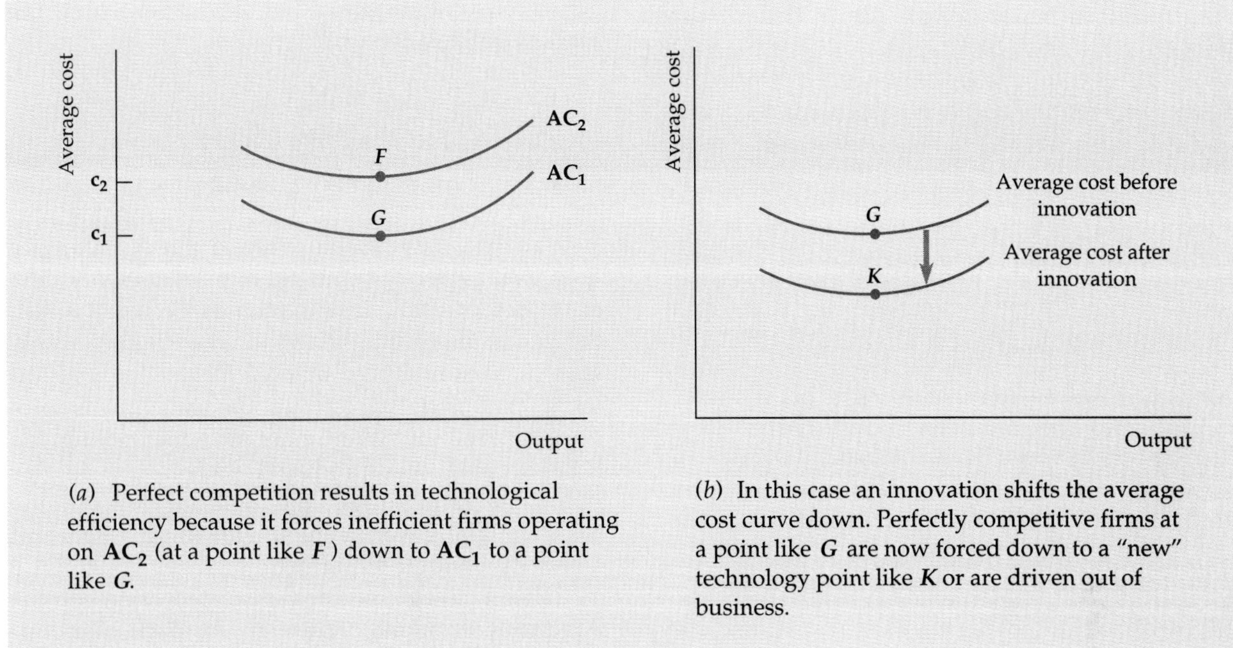

(*a*) Perfect competition results in technological efficiency because it forces inefficient firms operating on $\mathbf{AC_2}$ (at a point like *F*) down to $\mathbf{AC_1}$ to a point like *G*.

(*b*) In this case an innovation shifts the average cost curve down. Perfectly competitive firms at a point like *G* are now forced down to a "new" technology point like *K* or are driven out of business.

FIGURE 11-4 How perfect competition promotes technical and dynamic efficiency.

In some ways, perfect competition does indeed promote dynamic efficiency. Suppose, for example, that a new process or new invention has been discovered that reduces costs. This new technology shifts the average cost curve down as shown in panel *b* of Figure 11-4. Firms that do not lower their costs by adapting to this new technology will be left producing at a point such as *G*, at a disadvantage in competing with firms using the new technology and producing at a point such as *K*. Thus firms that ignore new technology and are consequently unable to compete will also go the way of the dinosaurs. We conclude that, by forcing firms to *adopt* new technology, perfect competition generates dynamic efficiency.

However, let's go one step further and ask the question: What sort of market does the best job of *creating* new technology in the first place? There is considerable debate over this question, with many contending that, in this respect, perfect competition is not necessarily best. It is easier for a large, monopolistic firm to finance the research necessary for many innovations. Furthermore, a large firm has more incentive to engage in research, since it is large enough to reap many of the gains. In contrast, no individual farmer has much incentive to try to develop a new strain of wheat; most of the gains would go to other farmers. (It is this lack of incentive for individual farmers that has led the government into supporting agricultural research.)

In conclusion, the competitive market scores high in two of the three aspects of efficiency—including allocative efficiency, which will be our focus in the next few chapters.

REPRISE: HOW THE COMPETITIVE MARKET DETERMINES WHO WILL PRODUCE AND WHO WILL CONSUME

Figure 11-5 shows how a competitive market answers two key questions: Who will produce a good, and who will consume it? Panel *a* shows how demand and supply determine the equilibrium quantity and $15 price.

Panel *b* illustrates how the $15 price acts as a barrier that determines who will consume this

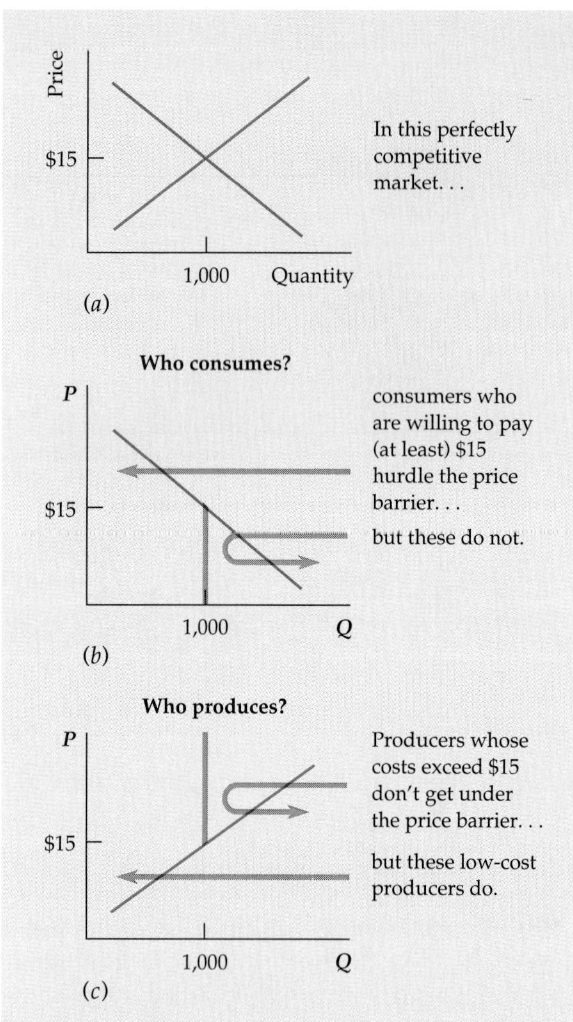

FIGURE 11-5 Price as a barrier that screens buyers and sellers in a competitive market.

good. Those who value it at $15 a unit or more will buy it; those who place less value on it won't buy it. In panel *c*, this same price also acts as a barrier, blocking out all high-cost producers who are unable to sell it for $15. Thus a perfectly competitive price screens out unenthusiastic buyers and high-cost sellers; both groups are excluded from the market because of one simple criterion—they are unwilling or unable to meet the market price. Thus the answer of a perfectly competitive market to the question: "Which firms will produce a good?" is "Those that can do so least expensively." Its answer to the question "Which individuals will get to consume the good?" is "Those who place the highest dollar value on it."

PREVIEW: PROBLEMS WITH THE COMPETITIVE MARKET

This analysis has thus far painted a rosy picture of how well perfectly competitive markets work. The examples of inefficient outcomes occurred when the government intervened to overrule the workings of a competitive market. When the government czar dictated output, too much was produced. When the government set a rent ceiling, too little housing was produced. Indeed, up to this point, the analysis has had a strong laissez faire message: The government should leave the market alone, its wonders to perform.

This message gives a distorted view of the American economy, however. In particular, our conclusion that a perfectly competitive market is efficient depends on the four basic conditions listed in Table 11-1, and they are often violated. Table 11-1 shows how they may be violated and lists the chapters that deal with each case. When these conditions are violated, a laissez faire economy will operate inefficiently. Government intervention may make the economy work more efficiently, not less. Furthermore, *even when all four conditions are met,* the outcome will not necessarily be quite as good as this chapter has suggested thus far, as we will now see.

RESERVATIONS ABOUT THE PERFECTLY COMPETITIVE OUTCOME

1. THIS OUTCOME DEPENDS ON THE DISTRIBUTION OF INCOME

Let's return again to Figure 11-1. Suppose that Abel has a higher income than Brandeis and for this reason he has greater demand for this good. (Remember, demand depends both on desire for the product and ability to pay. With his higher income, Abel has a greater ability to pay.) Figure 11-6 is a reproduction of Figure 11-1, with only the one change shown in the shaded area: The incomes of Abel and Brandeis are reversed. Brandeis now has the high income and hence high demand, whereas

TABLE 11-1 How the Four Basic Conditions That Lead to Efficiency Can Be Violated

	Condition	Will be violated if:	Considered in Chapter(s):
(11-1)	$MB_S = MB$	There are benefits to others than purchasers; for example, neighbors enjoy a well-kept garden.	18
(11-2)	$MC = MC_S$	There is pollution or other costs not borne by producers.	16, 17
(11-3)	$MB = P$	A single buyer has some influence over price. This may occur if there are only a few buyers.	22
(11-4)	$P = MC$	A single seller has some influence over price. This may occur if there are only a few sellers.	12, 13, 22

Abel has the low income and low demand, as shown in the first two panels in this diagram. Since nothing else need change, the rest of Figure 11-6 is the same as before.[1] In this diagram, just as in Figure 11-1, a perfectly competitive market yields an efficient solution. However, it is a quite different solution. There is no way that economists can be certain about which of the two solutions is better; all we can say is that both are efficient.

Abel and Brandeis, of course, will each have a clear opinion about which is better. Abel prefers Figure 11-1, where he gets most of this good (65

[1]With the switch in incomes, market price need not be exactly the same $10 as shown in Figure 11-1, but this detail is unimportant and does not affect the conclusion.

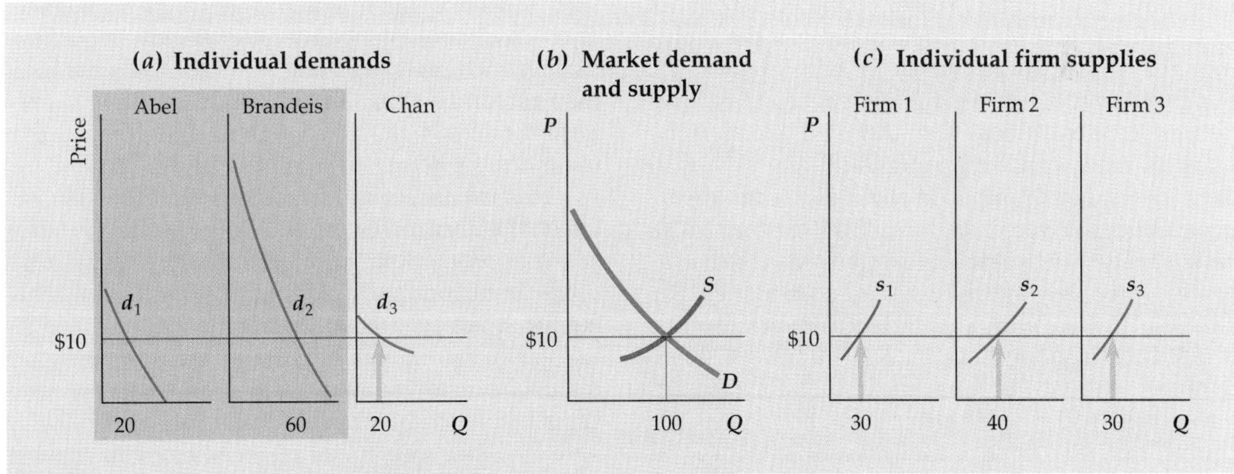

FIGURE 11-6 Another efficient, perfectly competitive solution.

This figure is similar to Figure 11-1, except that Brandeis now has a greater income and demand than Abel, and consequently consumes the greater quantity (60 units). This diagram also shows a perfectly competitive solution just like the one in Figure 11-1. Both solutions are efficient, but which is better? An economist can't judge, because in the move from Figure 11-1 to this figure it is impossible to compare Brandeis' utility gain with Abel's utility loss.

units), whereas Brandeis prefers Figure 11-6, where *he* gets the lion's share. However, from the point of view of society as a whole, there is no way to judge. True, if it were possible to meter the heads of these two individuals and conclude that, in moving from Figure 11-1 to Figure 11-6, Brandeis's gain in satisfaction or utility exceeded Abel's loss, the pattern in Figure 11-6 could be judged superior. This cannot be done, however, for *there is no way of comparing the utility or satisfaction one person gets from a good with the utility someone else gets.*

In summary, for each possible distribution of income, there is a different perfectly competitive solution. Each of these solutions is efficient, but it is not possible to demonstrate that one is better than the rest. The question of how income should be distributed is one that economists alone cannot answer, although Chapter 24 will shed more light on it.

2. THE MORAL HAZARD PROBLEM

Insurance is a valuable service that is bought and sold. Even if the market for insurance were perfectly competitive—and often it is not—a problem of **moral hazard** would remain. The behavior of buyers may change once they acquire insurance. For example, once they get fire and theft insurance, they may no longer be so careful to lock their doors or take fire precautions. Consequently, more buildings may burn down, which is a loss to society. Similarly, when drivers get insurance, they may become careless. Even here, however, competitive markets may work in a rough-and-ready way to limit losses. For example, in the typical auto insurance policy, drivers still have two reasons to be careful. First, any deductible clause means that to some degree they are risking their own money. For example, drivers with a $200 deductible clause run a risk because they have to pay the first $200 of damages. Second, drivers know that their insurance rates will rise if they have accidents. (Of course, they also have a third reason: They may be killed.)

Some of the clearest cases of inefficiency occur when the government offers insurance. For example, the government offers storm insurance without tying the premiums closely to risks. As a result, people have an incentive to build cottages too close to the ocean. Inefficiency results because the government provides coverage for mistakes that would not otherwise have been made.

> ***Moral hazard*** occurs when people who are insured become less careful in protecting themselves against risk.

3. BUYERS OR SELLERS MAY BE MISLED BY PRICE SIGNALS

In a perfectly competitive market, the price acts as a signal to which producers and consumers react. But what happens if they misinterpret this signal, and get the wrong message? Specifically, what happens if they are shortsighted and overreact to the current price?

It has, for example, been suggested that such an overreaction by farmers may cause cycles in the production of hogs and other animals. Suppose that, after a period of stability, the supply falls as a result of disease, and the price shoots up. Seeing this high price, farmers are induced to expand hog production. When these hogs come to market at a later date, the result will be an oversupply and the price will fall. In turn this depressed price will induce farmers to switch out of hog production. This shift will create a scarcity in the next period, which will lead once again to an abnormally high price. Thus an initial disturbance may set off a price fluctuation with price high one year, low the next, high the next, and so on. The cycle may continue if producers misread the price signals and erroneously use today's price to make production decisions.

This instability is partly due to the time lag between the decision to produce hogs and their delivery to the market. Similarly, delays may cause cycles in output and price fluctuations in the market for wheat and beef. Wheat must be planted in the fall or spring for harvest in the summer, and the decision to breed cattle is often made several years before the beef is eventually sold.

Note that such cycles are most likely to occur if farmers are shortsighted, and pay too much attention to current price. Once they take a longer perspective, the market may become more stable. However, as long as they do overreact to current price, even a perfectly competitive market may follow a cyclical pattern. When that happens, it does not work well, as we will confirm in the next section.

SPECULATION AND PRICE INSTABILITY

A cycle of fluctuating prices may be broken in several ways. First, after perhaps two or three sharp changes in price, more and more farmers may recognize what is happening and accordingly stop making the erroneous assumption that today's price provides a good prediction of tomorrow's price. As farmers do this, the price cycle is moderated. Second, others in the economy—speculators—may recognize what is happening and take action.

SPECULATION AS A STABILIZING INFLUENCE

The public often views speculators as gamblers whose profits or losses have little or no effect on the general well-being. However, the actions of speculators may benefit the economy as a whole, as we will now show. (The next section will demonstrate how speculation may damage the economy.)

To illustrate how speculation works, suppose that price in a hog cycle was high last year and is accordingly low this year. Now a number of people realize: "This has happened before. This is that hog cycle again. Because price is low this year a lot of farmers will be getting out of hogs. Next year pork will be scarce and the price will go way up again. Let's buy some of this year's cheap pork, refrigerate it, and sell it next year."

> ***Speculation*** is the purchase of an item in the hope of making a profit from a rise in its price, or the sale of an item in the expectation that its price will fall.

From the viewpoint of society as a whole, is such stabilizing speculation beneficial? The answer is yes. To see why, consider what happens when speculators buy pork this year when its price is low, and then sell it next year when its price is high.

For the speculator, this venture will be profitable—if the costs of storage, and so on, are not too high—because it puts into practice the advice any stockbroker will give: Buy low and sell high. The remarkable thing is that this action benefits not only those who undertake it, but also society as a whole because it moderates the price cycle. Why? The speculators' purchase of pork when it is cheap creates an additional demand that prevents its price from falling quite so far. When the speculators sell pork later at a high price, this creates an additional supply that prevents the price from rising quite so far. Thus, the cycle is moderated by speculation.

Panel *a* of Figure 11-7 shows the demand curve for pork. In the absence of speculation, initial equilibrium is at E_1, with low price P_1 because of high output Q_1. Panel *b* shows the same demand curve for next year but with lower production Q_2. In the absence of speculation, equilibrium is at E_2 and the price is a high P_2.

Now suppose that speculators enter the market. This year in panel *a*, they buy $Q_1'Q_1$ units when the price is low, store them, and sell them next year when the price is high. This year their purchases reduce the available supply from Q_1 to Q_1'. Therefore, price is raised from P_1 to P_1'. Next year, their sales increase the supply from Q_2 to Q_2', thereby lowering the price from P_2 to P_2'. Note that the cyclical swing in price may be almost eliminated. In Figure 11-7, speculation changes price in the two years to P_1' and P_2', and there is very little difference between these two prices. The only reason why there is a difference at all is that speculators have to earn a return to cover their storage and interest costs—and to compensate them for the risk they run if they guess wrong, and the price in the second year falls instead of rises.

The speculation in Figure 11-7 not only provides an adequate return for speculators, but it is also beneficial for society as a whole. True, reduced consumption this year takes away benefits from the public now, as shown by the red area in panel *a* of Figure 11-7. To confirm this loss, note that since typical unit *j* is no longer consumed, its marginal benefit to consumers is eliminated; this loss is shown by the red arrow. The total loss is the total red area because all such benefits are eliminated in the range $Q_1'Q_1$. However, this year's loss to consumers in panel *a* will be more than offset by an even greater blue increase in benefit to consumers next year in panel *b*.

The reason for this difference is that, in this year of plenty when there is a glut, the public is losing units that it doesn't value highly because its appetite is already reasonably satisfied. But next year when there is a scarcity, a "relatively hungry" public will be getting back these units when they

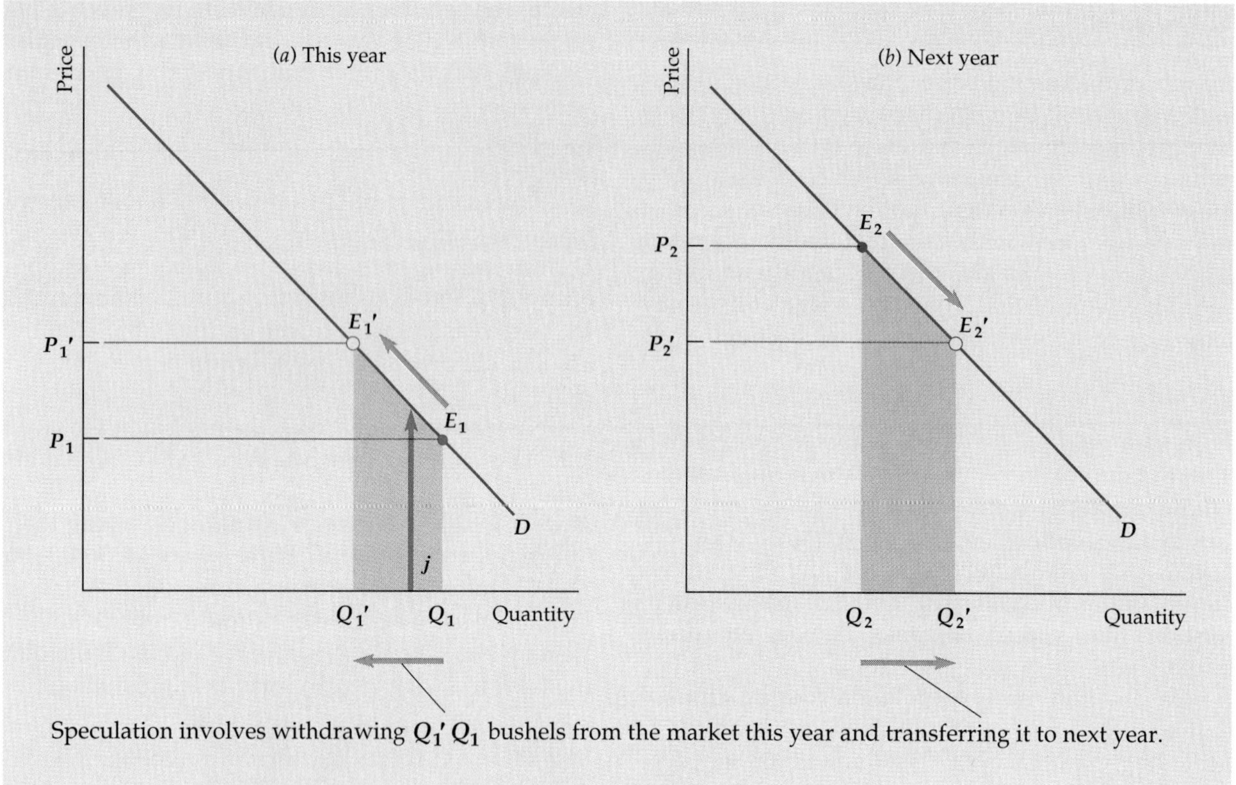

FIGURE 11-7 How speculation may have the beneficial effect of stabilizing price.

Without speculation, equilibrium this year is at E_1 and next year at E_2. Successful speculation reduces the available supply on the market this year from Q_1 to Q_1' and transfers it to next year, thus increasing the supply by this same amount, from Q_2 to Q_2'. This raises the price this year and lowers it next year until the two are almost equal. The beneficial effect of speculation is the difference between the blue gain from increased consumption next year and the smaller red loss from decreased consumption this year.

do have a high value. The difference between the red and blue areas therefore indicates the net benefit to society from this speculation.

In short, when speculators succeed in making a profit by "buying low and selling high," they reduce the fluctuation in price. They also reduce the fluctuation in the quantity consumed. Without speculation, different quantities—Q_1 and Q_2—would be consumed each year; with speculation, roughly the same quantities are consumed—Q_1' and Q_2'. By ironing out the fluctuation in quantities—that is, by moving some of this good from a year of glut to a year of scarcity—speculation provides a benefit to society.

This conclusion—that there is a benefit from eliminating a price cycle—also means that there is a loss from having a price cycle in the first place. A pattern of stable prices would be better for society. This then leads us to our second major reservation about a perfectly competitive market: It may lead to unstable prices if there is a failure in the timing and signaling mechanism as, for example, occurs in a hog cycle. If speculators do not iron out this unstable price pattern, the public loses.

SPECULATION AS A DESTABILIZING INFLUENCE

Speculators emerge as heroes thus far, but only because it has been assumed that they can predict the future correctly. However, they may guess wrong, and if they do, their actions can result in a loss both to themselves and to society. For example, suppose they purchase and store pork this year on the expectation that there will be a greater shortage and higher price next year, and they are wrong; there is a glut and lower prices instead. In this case, speculators lose because the pork they hold falls in price. Moreover, society as a whole also loses, because speculators move some of today's supply into next year's period of plenty, when pork is valued even less. Thus the individual success of speculators *and* their potential benefit to society depend on their ability to predict the future.

Finally, there is another possible cost of speculation to society. Although the speculators described thus far operate in a perfectly competitive way, suppose they do not. In this case, the outcome may be very different—and very costly—as the following story illustrates.

THE HUNT BROTHERS: DOWN AT HEEL, WITH LESS THAN A BILLION DOLLARS LEFT

H. L. Hunt believed he had a "genius gene" that he passed on to his sons. He died in 1974 before he could find out how wrong he was. Bunker and several of H. L.'s other sons lost billions of dollars in the 1980s. One of these billions was lost in silver speculation. A great deal can be learned from this story of personal disaster.

To set the stage, note that on rare occasions, speculators may try to **corner a market,** that is, buy enough of the good to become the dominant holder, and thus acquire the power to set a higher price. To see why this sort of anticompetitive speculation is quite different from perfectly competitive speculation, note that the perfectly competitive speculators who buy today to sell next year are *hoping* for a future shortage and higher price. On the other hand, speculators who try to corner a market may be trying to *create* a future shortage and higher price. If they can succeed in buying up most of the existing quantity, they can then drive up the price by, say, cutting their sales in half. In this case, there is an efficiency loss; society loses because of the artificially created shortage.

Even if the speculator doesn't succeed in cornering the market, heavy purchases or sales may be damaging for society because of the price swings that result. In the example provided by Bunker Hunt and his brothers, their heavy purchases of silver contributed to the rise in its price from less than $10 an ounce in 1979 to a record level of more than $50 in January 1980. By that time, the Hunt group held an estimated *one-sixth* of the Western world's stock of silver. Improbable though it might seem—and although the Hunts still had a long way to go—it appeared they might be trying to corner the world market in silver. (One investigator was not so sure; he wondered whether they were just playing a game of monopoly with real money.) In any case, their adventure turned into disaster. The silver market turned down, in part because of the slack demand caused by the 1980 recession. A wave of selling drove the price of silver back down below $10 an ounce; it was in this price collapse that the Hunts lost an estimated $1 billion. Moreover, this disaster was followed by others. Thus by 1987, the brothers who had been worth over $5 billion in 1982 were down to their last billion. Then in October 1988, Bunker Hunt and one of his brothers filed for protection under the U.S. bankruptcy law, surely the largest personal filing in American history.

In assessing the damages from their silver speculation, no one pretended that such price gyrations were beneficial to the economy as a whole. Indeed, they dislocated industries that use silver, such as photography, for example. Thus we conclude that this type of speculation is costly to society, *whether or not* the speculator actually succeeds in cornering the market.

KEY POINTS

1. For society as a whole, the output where marginal social cost is equal to marginal social benefit provides allocative efficiency.

2. If social costs are the same as private costs and social benefits the same as private benefits, a perfectly competitive market results in an efficient output. In these circumstances, perfect competition eliminates deadweight loss; it allocates resources efficiently.

3. Perfect competition also encourages technological efficiency by putting pressure on firms to operate on their lowest possible average cost curves.

4. Perfectly competitive firms need not be the best at introducing new innovations. Large firms have more financial strength and more incentive to develop new products, and thus may be better able to promote dynamic efficiency. However, perfectly competitive firms do have a strong incentive to adopt new innovations, once they exist.

5. For each distribution of income, there is a different perfectly competitive result. Economics cannot tell us clearly which one is best.

6. One problem with a perfectly competitive market is that its price signals may be misread, and price may fluctuate as a result. An example is the hog cycle that occurs where producers erroneously assume that price this year is a good indication of what price will be next year.

7. Speculation may be beneficial in a perfectly competitive market if it reduces price fluctuations. Competitive speculators, if successful in buying low and selling high, will tend to stabilize price. The actions of unsuccessful speculators will not stabilize price, nor will they be beneficial to society.

KEY CONCEPTS

private versus social benefit
private versus social cost
allocative efficiency
efficiency loss (deadweight loss)
technological, or technical, efficiency
dynamic efficiency
moral hazard
misleading market signals
speculation
when speculation is efficient
cornering a market

PROBLEMS

11-1. By showing what happens to individual consumers and producers in panels *a* and *c* in Figure 11-1, confirm that a reduction of output to below 100 units must result in an efficiency loss.

11-2. "A perfectly competitive price that all buyers and sellers take as given is the key link in orchestrating production and consumption in an efficient way." Do you agree? If so, illustrate. If not, explain why not.

11-3. According to Adam Smith, the pursuit of private gain generally leads to public benefit. Under what circumstances is this not true?

11-4. Suppose that all existing firms in a perfectly competitive industry are all producing in panel *a* of Figure 11-4 at technologically inefficient point *F*, with price also at this level. Show how they will be driven out of business by technologically efficient new entrants producing at *G*. In your answer, address the following questions: Is there initially a profit to be made by new entrants producing at *G*? Why? Do new firms therefore enter? What does this do to industry supply? What then happens to industry price? Can the old firms at *F* remain in business?

11-5. "If speculators guess wrong, they lose and so does society." Using a diagram like Figure 11-7, show why this statement is correct. In your answer, assume that speculators buy a good in one year but that, in the next year when they sell it, it is even more plentiful and cheap.

11-6. What moral hazards, if any, can arise in

- **(a)** Fire insurance?
- **(b)** Storm insurance?
- **(c)** Health insurance?
- **(d)** Life insurance?

Are there any cases in which insurance would reduce the chance of an unfavorable outcome?

APPENDIX

ILLUSTRATING THE EFFICIENCY OF PERFECT COMPETITION WITH INDIFFERENCE CURVES

This chapter has shown that perfect competition results in efficiency—provided social and private benefits are the same and social and private costs are equal. To illustrate this point, demand and supply curves were used. The same conclusion can be shown in an alternative way, using the indifference curves explained in the appendix to Chapter 7 and the production possibilities curve (PPC) introduced in Chapter 2.

Figure 11-8 illustrates how producers maximize their income. Suppose that they are initially at point *A* on their production possibilities curve, making 500 units of clothing and 1,300 units of food. Suppose also that the prices of food and clothing are both $10 per unit. Then producers' income totals $18,000—that is, ($10 × 500) + ($10 × 1,300). Producers are now on the $18,000 income line L_1, whose slope reflects the relative prices of the two goods, just like the slope of the equal–cost lines in Figure 9-8. Just as there was a whole family of equal–cost lines in that earlier diagram, we can visualize a whole set of parallel equal–income lines such as L_1 and L_2 in Figure 11-8, each indicating successively higher income levels as producers move to the northeast. The objective of producers is to reach the highest one possible. For example, producers operating at point *A* on the $18,000 income line can do better by moving along the PPC to point *E*, which is on the $20,000 income line. (At *E*, they produce 1,000 units of each good for a total income of $20,000.) This is the best they can do—it is the highest income line they can reach.

Producers maximize their income by producing at the point on the production possibilities curve that is tangent to the highest attainable income line.

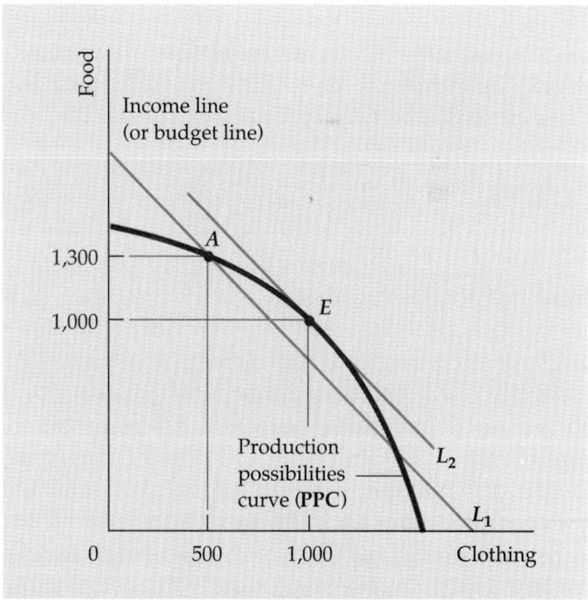

FIGURE 11-8 How producers maximize their incomes.
The line representing producers' income goes through point *A* at which production initially takes place. The slope of this line depends on the relative prices of the two goods. Producers attain the highest income line by moving to tangency point *E*, where the slope of the production possibilities curve is the same as the slope of the income line.

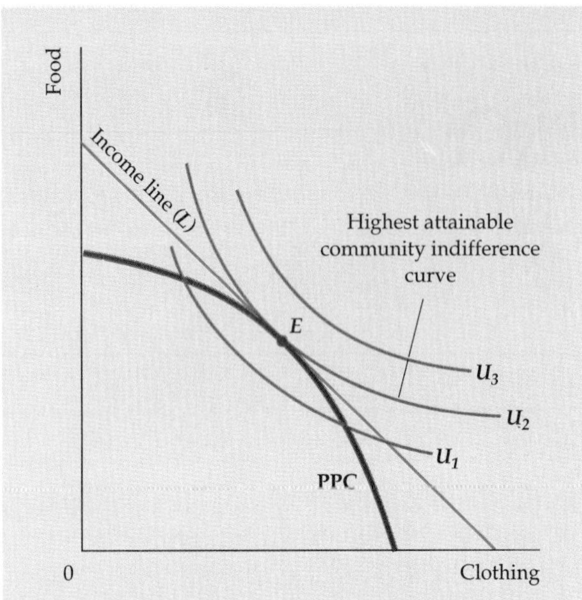

FIGURE 11-9 The competitive equilibrium.

The competitive equilibrium occurs at *E*. Producers pick the point where the PPC is tangent to the highest attainable income line. Consumers pick the point where the income line is tangent to the highest attainable indifference curve. At this point *E*, the production possibilities curve and the indifference curve are tangent. The maximum level of utility U_2 is achieved, given the productive capacity of the economy as shown by the PPC.

In Figure 11-9, we put this theory of producer behavior together with our earlier theory of consumer behavior, in which we described consumer preferences with a set of indifference curves. In a perfectly competitive economy, in which every producer and every consumer takes prices as given, equilibrium is at *E* in Figure 11-9. On the one hand, producers maximize their income by selecting point *E* on the production possibilities curve because this point is tangent to the highest attainable income line *L*. At the same time, consumers maximize their utility by also selecting point *E*—because this is the point of tangency between their highest attainable indifference curve U_2 and the income line *L*. Thus the community as a whole achieves an efficient solution, because at *E* it is producing the combination of food and clothing that lifts it to its highest attainable level of utility U_2. Given the community's ability to produce, as shown by its PPC, there is no way it can reach a higher level of satisfaction than U_2. For example, it's not possible to reach U_3.

This, then, is our alternative illustration of the proposition established in Figure 11-2: A competitive economy leads to an efficient solution.[2]

It should be emphasized again that this efficient solution results from producers on the one hand, and consumers on the other, responding independently to the competitive market prices reflected in the slope of the income line *L*.[3] This in turn raises the final question: Why does the competitive market generate the relative prices shown

[2]It may seem that there must be a catch somewhere. According to this analysis, there seems to be a unique efficient solution at *E*—and we have already seen in Figure 11-6 that there is not: For each income distribution there is a different efficient solution. This puzzle is resolved by noting that in Figure 11-9 we have drawn a set of indifference curves for the *community as a whole,* rather than for an individual household. There are problems in defining such a community indifference system; there is no simple way of "adding up" the preferences of all the individuals in the nation. For example, consider the simple extreme case of a two-person economy. If I have all the income, my preferences are the ones that count; if you have all the income, it is your preferences that count. In other words, a community's preferences depend on who has the income. Hence there is no unique community indifference system; the community's indifference map can change every time a change occurs in the distribution of income. Nor, as a consequence, is there any unique efficient equilibrium; the equilibrium depends on how the nation's income is distributed. This is exactly the conclusion reached earlier.

[3]To illustrate what can go wrong if producers do not act as perfect competitors, suppose that the producers of clothing form a monopoly and restrict the supply of clothing. In other words, the economy moves to the left of *E* in Figure 11-9, and it is no longer possible to reach indifference curve U_2. Consequently, the nation's utility is less than a maximum, that is, less than U_2.

by *L*? To answer this question, suppose that initially the relative prices are different; specifically, suppose that they are shown by line L_1 in Figure 11-10. (The lower slope of L_1 reflects a lower relative price of clothing.) Facing these relative prices, producers maximize their income by producing at *A*, the point of tangency between the PPC and income line L_1. But consumers try to consume at *B*, the point of tangency between income line L_1 and indifference curve U_3. However, they are in fact unable to reach point *B*, since the economy is incapable of producing this combination of food and clothing. (*B* is outside the PPC.) As a consequence, markets are out of equilibrium. The quantity C_B of clothing demanded by consumers exceeds the quantity C_A supplied by producers; the price of clothing consequently rises. At the same time, the quantity F_B of food demanded is less than the quantity F_A supplied; the price of food falls. As the relative prices of food and clothing change, the slope of the income line changes. Specifically, the income line rotates from L_1 toward *L*. In response, producers move from *A* toward *E*, while consumers move from *B* toward *E*. This movement continues until the income line actually becomes *L* and producers and consumers have moved all the way to *E*. Only then are demand and supply brought into equilibrium. Thus the equilibrium prices are indeed those reflected in line *L*.

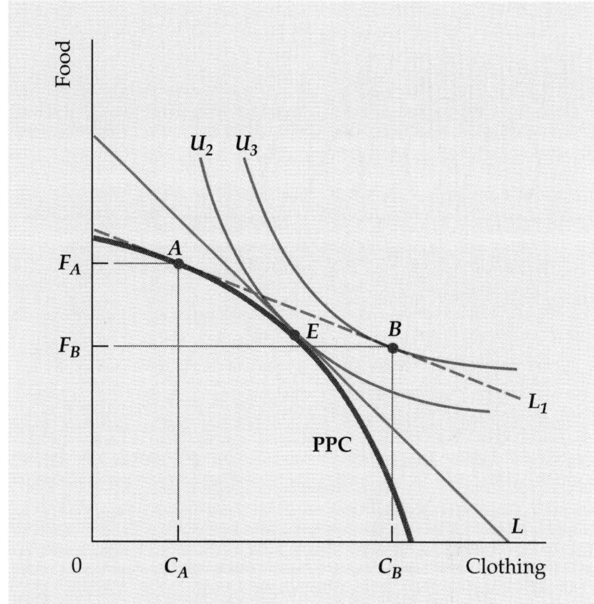

FIGURE 11-10 How markets adjust from an initial point of disequilibrium.

If the relative price of clothing is originally below its equilibrium—that is, if prices are those reflected in L_1 rather than *L*—producers will want to produce at *A* and consumers will want to consume at *B*. As a result, there will be a shortage of clothing equal to $C_B - C_A$ and a surplus of food equal to $F_A - F_B$. Consequently, the price of clothing will rise and the price of food will fall until these prices reach their equilibrium values, reflected in the slope of the income line *L*.

CHAPTER 12
MONOPOLY

The monopolists, by keeping the market constantly understocked. . . sell their commodities much above the natural price.

ADAM SMITH, *WEALTH OF NATIONS*

At one end of the market spectrum there is perfect competition, with many sellers. At the other end there is monopoly, with only one seller. (The term monopoly comes from the Greek words *monos* meaning "single" and *polein* meaning "to sell.") Chapter 11 showed that, under certain conditions, perfect competition is efficient. This chapter will demonstrate that monopoly is not. A case can therefore be made for government intervention in the marketplace. But in what way should the government intervene?

To begin, consider the conditions that lead to monopoly.

WHAT CAUSES MONOPOLY?

There are four major reasons why there may be only one firm selling a good:

1. *Monopoly may be based on control over an input or technique.* A firm may control something essential that no other firm can acquire. One example is the ownership of a necessary resource; for example, Alcoa's control over bauxite supplies allowed it to monopolize the sale of aluminum before World War II. Another example is the ownership of a *patent*, which allows the inventor exclusive control over a new product or process for a period of 17 years. (Patents are designed to encourage expenditure on research by allowing the inventor to reap a substantial reward.) When an existing firm owns an essential patent or exclusive control over a resource, new firms might like to enter the industry but they cannot; the industry remains monopolized.

2. *Legal monopoly.* It is sometimes illegal for more than one company to sell a product. For example, a private bus company is sometimes given the exclusive right to service a community.

3. *Monopoly resulting from mergers.* If permitted by law, several producers may merge into a single firm in order to charge a higher price and increase their profits. However, once these firms have merged to create a monopoly, it may not be easy to maintain. New firms may be attracted by the high price.

4. *Natural monopoly.* A natural monopoly exists when economies of scale are so important that one firm can produce the total output of the industry at lower cost than could two or more firms. An example is the local telephone service. It obviously costs less to string one set of telephone wires down a street than two.

The prevalence of monopoly depends partly on how narrowly a market is defined. When the jumbo jet was first introduced, Boeing had a temporary monopoly; other companies had not yet developed their jumbos to compete with the 747. However, Boeing did not have a monopoly in the broader market for airliners, since it still had to compete with McDonnell-Douglas and other firms in the sale of smaller aircraft. As another illustration, the local gas company has a monopoly in providing natural gas, but not in the broader market of heating homes where it must compete with firms supplying oil and electricity. Indeed, in the very broadest sense, every producer competes with every other producer for the consumer's dollar. If you buy a new television, you may help to pay for it by turning down your thermostat and thus reducing your gas bill. Therefore, in a very broad sense, the gas company is in competition even with the producer of televisions.

If markets are defined in a reasonably limited way, however, significant areas of monopoly exist—in local water service, local gas service, and local electrical service, to name a few. Nonetheless, the importance of monopoly should not be overstated. *Oligopoly*—where the industry is dominated by a few sellers—is much more important in the U.S. economy. Some of the largest industries in our economy are oligopolies, including automobiles, aircraft, heavy construction equipment, and large electrical generators. Long-distance telephone service, which used to be the monopoly of AT&T, is now an oligopoly.

Although oligopoly occurs more frequently than monopoly, it is appropriate to consider monopoly first, because monopoly is logically at the other extreme to perfect competition. When this study of monopoly is complete, the stage will be set for a study of markets between monopoly and perfect competition in Chapter 13.

NATURAL MONOPOLY: WHEN ECONOMIES OF SCALE LEAD TO A SINGLE FIRM

The cost conditions that lead to natural monopoly are shown in panel *b* of Figure 12-1 and are contrasted with cost conditions that do not in panel *a*. The two products are assumed to have identical demand curves in order to highlight the difference in their costs—the central issue in explaining natural monopoly.

In the industry shown in panel *a*, a typical firm's minimum efficient scale—that is, the output where its long-run average cost curve AC reaches a minimum—is only 10 units of output. Since this is

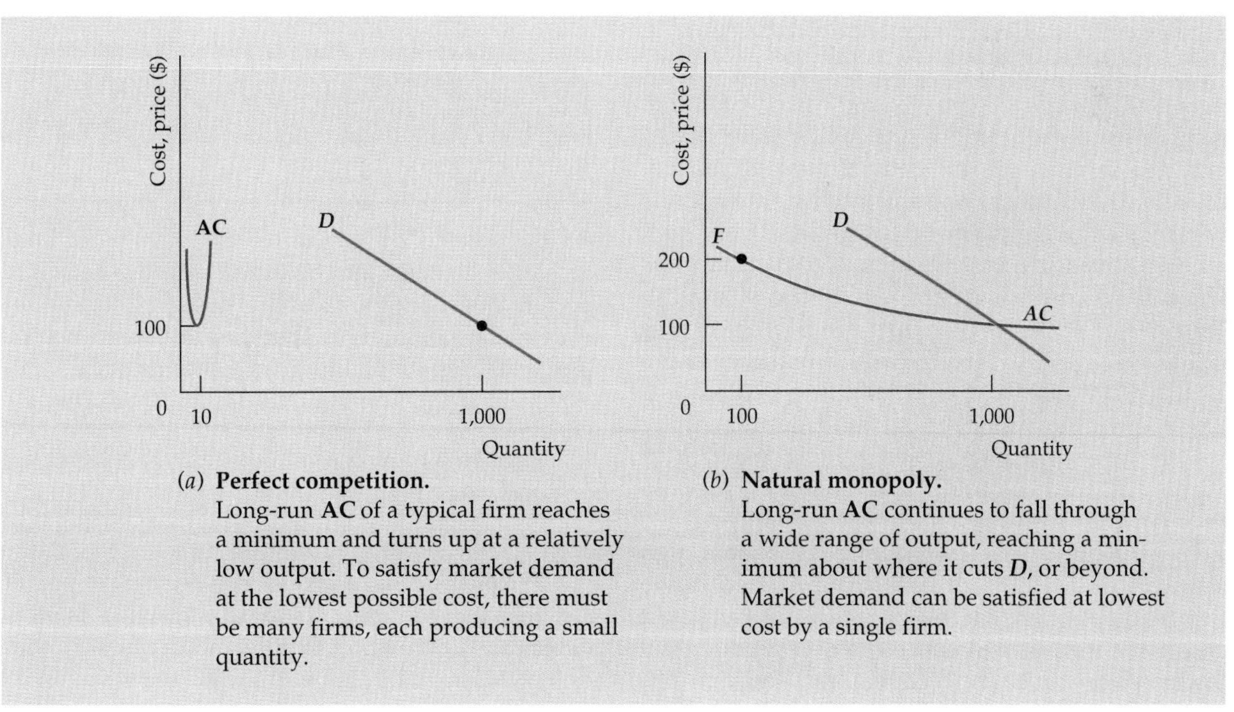

(*a*) **Perfect competition.** Long-run **AC** of a typical firm reaches a minimum and turns up at a relatively low output. To satisfy market demand at the lowest possible cost, there must be many firms, each producing a small quantity.

(*b*) **Natural monopoly.** Long-run **AC** continues to fall through a wide range of output, reaching a minimum about where it cuts ***D***, or beyond. Market demand can be satisfied at lowest cost by a single firm.

FIGURE 12-1 How cost conditions can lead to natural monopoly.

only a very small portion of the total market, total demand cannot be satisfied by one firm operating at its minimum cost. Instead, the least costly way of servicing this market is to have many small firms producing just 10 units each. If a firm tries to produce at higher volume, say, 20 units, it will incur a relatively high cost that will leave it unable to compete with smaller, lower cost firms. With many small firms surviving, the result is perfect competition.

In panel *b*, AC reaches the same minimum value of $100, but only when a much larger volume of output is produced. Unlike the AC curve in panel *a* that reaches a minimum and turns up at a very small volume, AC in panel *b* continues downward. The minimum efficient scale doesn't occur until about 1,000 units of output. Thus the least expensive way of servicing the market is with one firm. This industry is a **natural monopoly.**

> ***Natural monopoly*** occurs when the average cost of a single firm falls over such an extended range of output that one firm can produce the total quantity sold at a lower average cost than could two or more firms.

Why might costs continue to fall through much or all of the range needed to satisfy total market demand? The answer may be high fixed cost, that is, high overhead. Local electric, telephone, water, and gas services are all natural monopolies, because the fixed cost in running electric or telephone wires, or in laying water or gas pipes, is very high relative to variable cost. To illustrate what happens when fixed costs dominate, set fixed cost back in Table 9-1 at $1,000, rather than just $35, and recalculate average cost. Note how AC continues to fall as this $1,000 of fixed overhead is spread over a larger and larger number of units of output.

To verify that the cost curve in panel *b* in Figure 12-1 leads naturally to a monopoly, suppose that initially a few firms are each producing 100 units at point *F*. This low volume results in a high average cost of $200 for each firm. An aggressive firm will discover that, by increasing its output, it can lower its cost and hence offer its product at a lower price than its competitors. Thus it can squeeze them out of business. In such a case of natural monopoly, competition tends to drive all firms but one out of the market. Small firms, with their relatively high costs, simply cannot compete with the single large firm operating at lower average cost.

Consumers obviously benefit from the low price during the period of competition when the industry is being "shaken down" and the number of firms reduced. However, this favorable situation for the consumer is likely to disappear once the successful firm has eliminated all its competitors and has emerged as a monopoly. It now does not have to worry much about the entry of new competitors. With its high volume—and therefore low cost—the monopoly can greet any new entrants with whatever price cutting is necessary to drive them into bankruptcy. With little fear of present or future competition, the monopoly is then free to raise its price. As a result, consumers of this product are at the mercy of the monopolist, except insofar as they are prepared to cut back their purchases in the face of a higher price—or insofar as the government regulates price. The question is: If the monopoly is free of regulation, how high will it set its price? Before we answer this question, we need to make one more distinction between perfect competition and monopoly.

THE DIFFERENCE IN THE DEMAND FACING A PERFECT COMPETITOR AND A MONOPOLIST

To analyse this difference we first review in detail an earlier conclusion: The individual firm selling in perfect competition faces a horizontal (infinitely elastic) demand curve. Therefore it has no **market power,** that is, no ability to influence its price.

> The ***market power*** of a firm is its ability to influence its price, and thereby its profit.

To confirm that a farmer has no market power, suppose that the price of a bushel of wheat is $4, as determined by market supply and demand in panel *b* of Figure 12-2. Panel *a* shows the response of the individual farmer to this price. He produces 2,000 units, where MC = *P*. He takes the $4 market

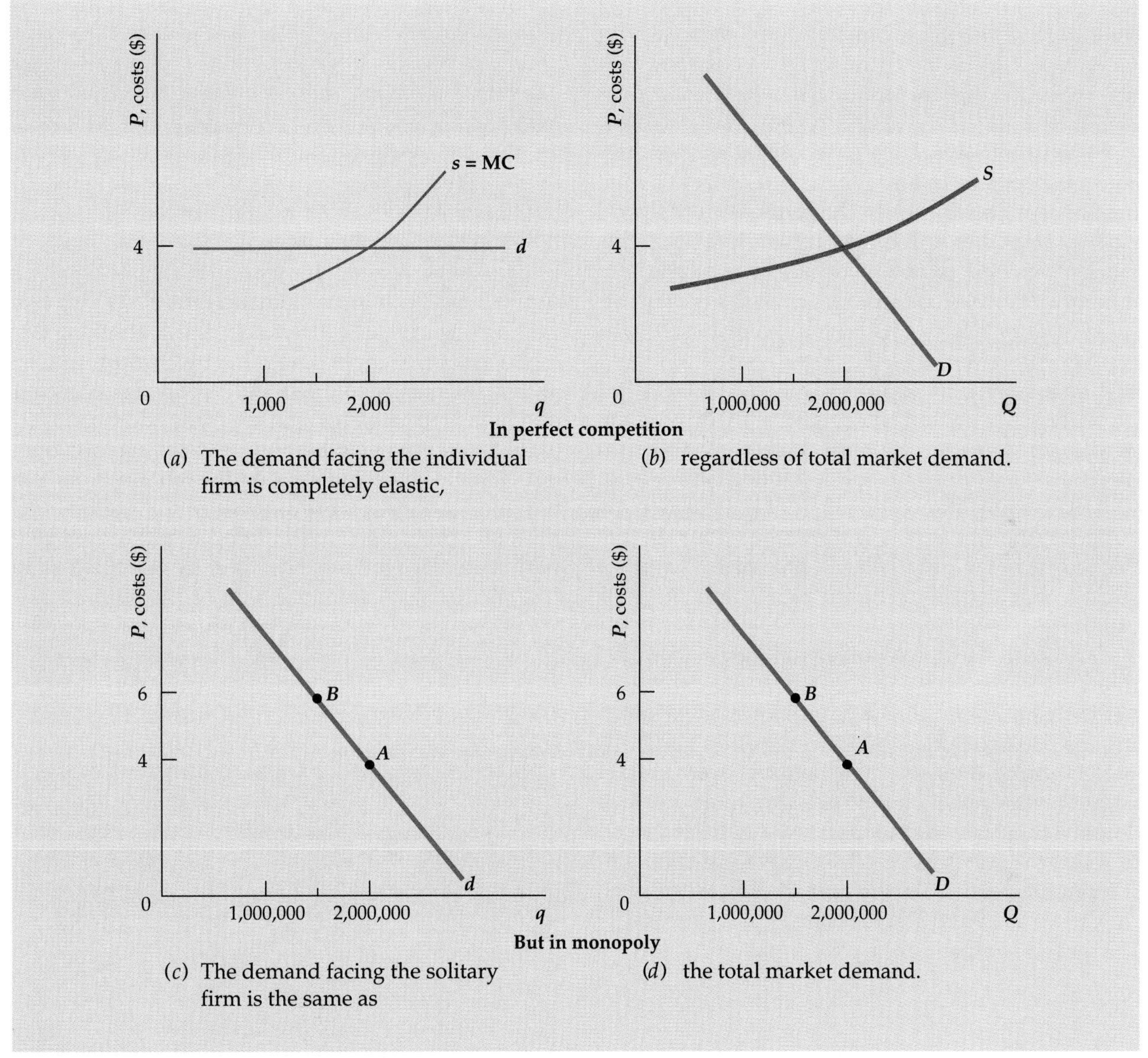

In perfect competition

(*a*) The demand facing the individual firm is completely elastic,

(*b*) regardless of total market demand.

But in monopoly

(*c*) The demand facing the solitary firm is the same as

(*d*) the total market demand.

FIGURE 12-2 The difference in the demand facing the monopolist and the perfect competitor.

On the left, the demand facing an individual firm is marked with a small *d*. Market demand is shown on the right with a capital *D*.

price as given. If he quotes a higher price—say, $4.10—the completely elastic demand indicates that he won't be able to sell *any* units. He can't make the higher price stick. Alternatively, if he tries to raise market price by reducing his output and making this good scarce, that won't work either. Specifically, suppose he cuts his output in half, from 2,000 to 1,000 units. This will reduce market supply in panel *b*, shifting *S* to the left, but by such a trivial amount—only 1,000 units—that this action won't even be noticed in the market. If you try to draw the new supply curve, you will find that you are essentially just drawing a line over the old supply *S*. The market price, as determined in panel *b*, will therefore remain the same. The farmer has tried to raise the price, but this attempt to exercise market power has failed miserably. As an individual seller, he has no influence whatsoever over price.

The situation facing a monopoly is quite different, as shown in panels *c* and *d*. In panel *d*, total market demand is exactly the same as in the competitive case above. The only difference is that this market demand is now satisfied by a single monopoly firm. In other words, *the demand facing the individual firm in panel c is exactly the same as the total market demand in panel d.*

As a result, the monopoly can indeed affect price. To see why, suppose that it is initially selling at a $4 price. Because it is the only seller, this firm alone is supplying all the 2 million units sold, shown at point *A* in both panel *c* and panel *d*. Now suppose the monopoly raises the price to $6. Because it is the only seller, it can make this price stick, although sales will fall from 2 million to 1.5 million.

In short, the monopoly firm has market demand within its grasp. It can move along the market demand curve from a point like *A* to *B*, selecting the one that suits it best. On the other hand, the perfect competitor has no control over market price. Instead, the individual firm faces its own completely elastic demand curve, and all it can do is select the *quantity* to sell. Whereas the monopolist can raise the price, the perfect competitor must take price as given. The monopolist is a *price maker;* the perfect competitor is a *price taker.*

WHAT PRICE DOES THE MONOPOLIST SELECT?

As we saw in Chapter 10, *any* firm—whether a monopolist or perfect competitor—maximizes profit by selecting the output at which its marginal cost MC equals its marginal revenue MR. In that earlier chapter we also saw that *marginal revenue for the perfectly competitive firm is the given market price at which it sells.* In our present example, marginal revenue for the perfectly competitive firm in panel *a* of Figure 12-2 is the $4 selling price. No matter how many units the firm sells, its revenue will increase by $4 if it sells one more. In other words, its marginal revenue schedule is identical to its completely elastic demand curve. *However, for the monopolist, marginal revenue is not equal to the selling price, and the marginal revenue curve is different from the demand curve.*

WHAT IS THE MARGINAL REVENUE OF A MONOPOLIST?

Suppose the monopoly firm in Figure 12-3 moves from *B* to *C* along its demand curve. At *B* it was selling one unit at $50, but now at *C* it is selling two units at a price of $45 each. In other words, at *C* its average revenue *AR* is $45. What is its marginal revenue for that second unit? What additional revenue does it receive because it is selling two units rather than one? To calculate the answer, note that the monopoly's total revenue from selling one unit was $50 but when it sells two, its total revenue is $90. Thus its revenue has risen by $40. This is its *marginal revenue* from the sale of the second unit. Note that the firm's marginal revenue of $40 is less

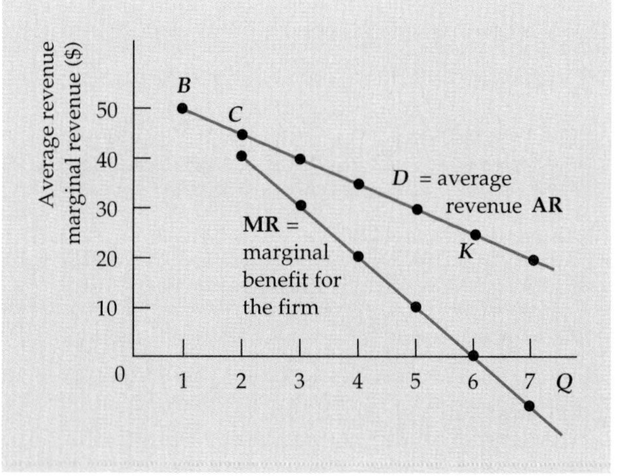

FIGURE 12-3 Why a monopolist's demand (AR) and marginal revenue (MR) differ.

Numbers are drawn from Table 12-1. At point *B*, the monopoly sells one unit for $50. At point *C*, it sells two units for $45 each, for a total revenue of $90. The sale of the second unit increases its total revenue by $90 – $50 = $40, which is its marginal revenue. Another way to calculate this is to note that the monopoly receives a $45 price on the sale of the second unit, but from this amount it must deduct the $5 "loss" on the first unit because it is getting only $45 for it rather than the original $50.

than the $45 price. This point is worth emphasizing:

For a monopolist, marginal revenue MR is less than price *P*.

Table 12-1 shows the monopolist's marginal revenue at each output. Total revenue is given in column 3, whereas column 4 shows how this total revenue changes for each successive unit sold. This marginal revenue schedule MR is graphed in Figure 12-3. Note how the monopoly's marginal revenue curve lies below its demand curve.

The demand and marginal revenue curves now become the stepping stones needed to answer the following question: How high does a profit-maximizing monopoly set its price?

MONOPOLY OUTPUT AND PRICE

Like any other firm, the monopoly maximizes profit by equating marginal cost MC with marginal revenue MR. An illustration is provided in panel *a* of Figure 12-4, where the monopolist's *D* and MR curves are shown, along with its MC and AC curves. The monopoly selects output Q_1 where MC and MR intersect. This is the output that maximizes its profit. If the firm selects any other output—whether greater or smaller—its profit will be less. For example, the firm would make a mistake not to produce unit Q_2, since that unit adds more to its revenues (at *W*) than it adds to its cost (at *T*).

A monopolist—like a perfect competitor—maximizes profit by selecting output where

Marginal cost MC = marginal revenue MR

However, for the monopolist—unlike the perfect competitor—MR is less than price.

With its output thus determined at Q_1, what price does the firm then charge? In other words, what is the maximum price the monopoly can charge and still sell quantity Q_1? The answer is given by the demand curve, which indicates at point *E* that the firm can charge a price as high as P_1 and still sell those Q_1 units. This choice by the monopolist of output Q_1 and price P_1 is often referred to as its selection of the *profit-maximizing point (E) on its demand curve*.

A monopoly, like any other firm, must address another important question: Should it be in business at all? For the firm shown in this diagram, the answer is yes. In selling Q_1 units, it makes an *above-normal* or *monopoly profit* of *EV* on each unit. This is the difference between the price it gets for selling each unit—the height of *E* on the demand curve—and its average cost of producing each unit, that is, the height of *V* on the AC curve. The monopoly will remain in business as long as it can cover its

TABLE 12-1 How Marginal Revenue for a Monopoly Is Derived from Its Demand (Average Revenue) Information

Demand			
(1) Quantity (Q)	*(2) Price P (average revenue)*	*(3) Total Revenue (P × Q)*	*(4) Marginal Revenue (MR)*
1	$50	$ 50	
2	45	90	(90 – 50) = $40
3	40	120	(120 – 90) = 30
4	35	140	(140 – 120) = 20
5	30	150	(150 – 140) = 10
6	25	150	(150 – 150) = 0
7	20	140	(140 – 150) = –10

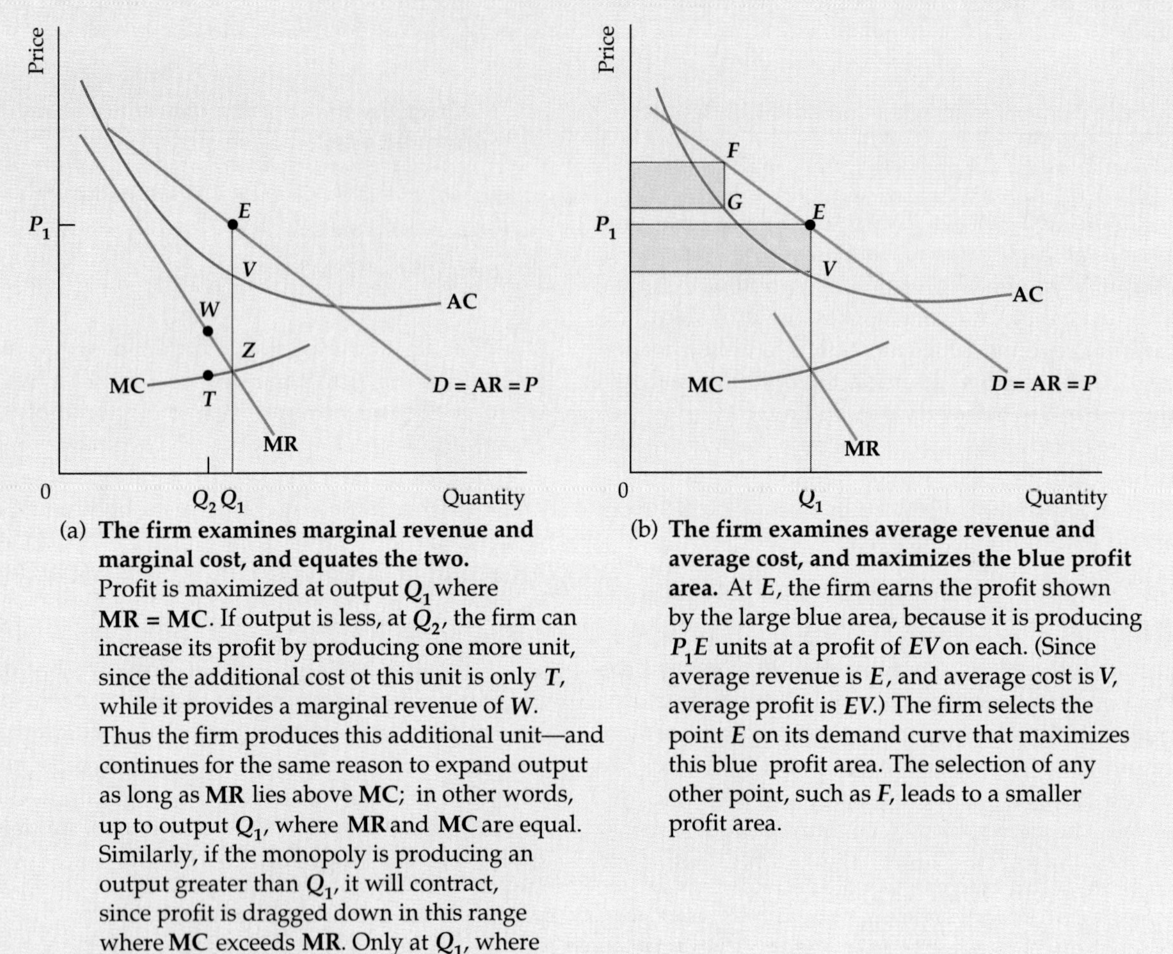

(a) **The firm examines marginal revenue and marginal cost, and equates the two.** Profit is maximized at output Q_1 where **MR** = **MC**. If output is less, at Q_2, the firm can increase its profit by producing one more unit, since the additional cost ot this unit is only *T*, while it provides a marginal revenue of *W*. Thus the firm produces this additional unit—and continues for the same reason to expand output as long as **MR** lies above **MC**; in other words, up to output Q_1, where **MR** and **MC** are equal. Similarly, if the monopoly is producing an output greater than Q_1, it will contract, since profit is dragged down in this range where **MC** exceeds **MR**. Only at Q_1, where **MC** = **MR**, is there no incentive to expand or contract.

(b) **The firm examines average revenue and average cost, and maximizes the blue profit area.** At *E*, the firm earns the profit shown by the large blue area, because it is producing P_1E units at a profit of *EV* on each. (Since average revenue is *E*, and average cost is *V*, average profit is *EV*.) The firm selects the point *E* on its demand curve that maximizes this blue profit area. The selection of any other point, such as *F*, leads to a smaller profit area.

FIGURE 12-4 Two equivalent views of the profit-maximizing equilibrium of a monopoly.

costs, including a normal profit—that is, as long as its selling price *E* is at least as high as its average cost *V*. (Recall from Chapter 8 that the average cost curve includes normal profit.) However, if the demand curve lies below the average cost curve throughout its entire range, it is not possible for the monopoly to cover its costs, and it will leave this business in the long run.

If distance *EV* is the firm's profit per unit, what is its total profit? The answer is the large shaded area in panel *b* of Figure 12-4—that is, the per-unit profit *EV* times P_1E, the number of units sold. This area is shaded in blue to represent above-normal profit, in contrast to losses, which will appear later in red.

These two panels show in two equivalent ways how the monopoly firm maximizes profit. In panel *a*, it equates MC and MR. Alternatively, in panel *b*, it arrives at the same output Q_1 by selecting the point *E* on its demand curve that maximizes the shaded profit area. That is, it selects the point *E* that creates a larger profit rectangle than would be created by selecting *any* other point on its demand curve, such as *F*.

We will use these two approaches interchangeably. For now, we concentrate on the MC = MR approach in panel *a*. Later, we will use the approach in panel *b* because it clearly shows the profits which the firm is attempting to maximize. Moreover, panel *b* demonstrates both conditions that a firm must satisfy: It ensures (1) that the marginal condition MC = MR is met and (2) that the firm is operating at a profit—or, more precisely, that the firm is not operating at a loss that would drive it out of business in the long run.

The two ways a monopolist maximizes profit are also illustrated by the firm shown in Table 12-2. In columns 4 and 5 it maximizes profit by selecting the output of four units where MR = MC. In column 7, it selects exactly that same output by maximizing its profit directly.

PROFIT MAXIMIZATION FOR A MONOPOLIST: TWO REMAINING CLARIFICATIONS

A Monopolist Produces Where Demand Is Elastic. Although a monopoly can quote the price at which it will sell, it still does not have complete freedom in the marketplace. It can only sell what consumers will buy. In other words, it is only free to select a point on its demand curve.

Whatever point a monopoly firm does select will certainly be on the elastic portion of its demand curve. This conclusion can be derived from the following chain of reasoning. In Figure 12-4 the firm's equilibrium is where MR = MC. Because its MC is positive, its MR must also be positive. This means that its total revenue TR must increase as its price falls and output increases; that is, its demand must be elastic (as shown back in Figure 6-2). Thus the monopolist does indeed select a point on the elastic portion of its demand curve.

Table 12-2 provides a simple illustration. The monopoly will select between 1 and 5 units of output, where its demand is elastic. (As its output increases and price falls, its total revenue in column 6 increases.) It won't sell where demand is inelastic, at say, seven units of output, because the seventh would reduce its total revenue from \$150 to \$140. It makes no sense at all to sell that seventh unit when it costs something to produce but does not increase the firm's revenue.

A monopolist does not have a supply curve. Although there is a demand curve in Figure 12-4, there is no

TABLE 12-2 Two Methods of Profit Maximization for the Monopolist

Demand						
(1) Quantity Q from Table 12-1	*(2) Price P from Table 12-1*	*(3) Total Cost TC*	*(4) Marginal Cost MC*	*(5) Marginal Revenue MR [col 4 in Table 12-1]*	*(6) Total Revenue TR (1) × (2) [col 3 in Table 12-1]*	*(7) Profit = TR – TC (6) – (3)*
1	\$50	60			50	50 – 60 = –10
2	45	70	(70 – 60) = 10	40	90	90 – 70 = 20
3	40	85	(85 – 70) = 15	30	120	120 – 85 = 35
4	35	105	(105 – 85) = 20 ⇔	20	140	140 – 105 = 35 ⇐
5	30	130	(130 – 105) = 25	10	150	150 – 130 = 20
6	25	160	(160 – 130) = 30	0	150	150 – 160 = –10
7	20	195	(195 – 160) = 35	–10	140	140 – 195 = –55

Columns 1, 2, 5, and 6 here are columns 1, 2, 4, and 3 in Table 12-1. Column 3 shows total cost, while column 4 shows how this total cost changes for each successive unit sold; that is, column 4 is marginal cost MC. The monopolist maximizes profit at four units of output by either (a) equating marginal cost and marginal revenue, as shown by the red arrow, or (b) maximizing profit directly by comparing total revenue and total cost, as shown by the black arrow.

TABLE 12-3 Types of Markets

Type	*Characteristics*	*Is There a Supply Curve?*	*Is There a Demand Curve?*	*How Is Price Determined?*
Perfect competition	Many buyers and sellers, with no single market participant affecting price	Yes	Yes	By intersection of demand and supply curves
Monopoly	One seller, many buyers	No	Yes	By seller, facing market demand
Monopsony	One buyer, many sellers	Yes	No	By buyer, facing market supply
More complex cases	Few buyers, few sellers	No	No	In complex manner

supply curve. How is this to be explained? Recall the type of question that a supply curve answers. If the price were given at, say $10, how many units would suppliers be willing to sell? This is a question that is relevant in a perfectly competitive market. But it is not relevant for a monopoly because the monopoly firm does not take price as given. Instead it sets price. Therefore there is no supply curve. The first two rows of Table 12-3 compare the "many-sellers" case of perfect competition where there is a supply curve with the "single-seller" case of monopoly where there is not.

Of course, on the other side of the market, a similar complication can arise. For your future reference, the third row of this table shows the "single-*buyer*" case of monopsony, where there is no *demand* curve. The reason is that a demand curve exists only if there is a large number of buyers—with every individual buyer addressing a question such as: "At a given price of $10, how many units will I buy?" But a single monopsony firm does not take the price as given; it sets the price. For example, the only employing firm in a small town will be a monopsonist in the labor market; it will be able to set the wage rate it will pay. In such cases, there is no demand curve.

With this description of monopoly now in hand, it is appropriate to consider how efficient monopoly will be from the point of view of society as a whole.

IS MONOPOLY EFFICIENT?

No one can argue that a monopolist is impelled by "an invisible hand" to serve the public interest.

R. H. TAWNEY

How well do monopolistic firms perform in the three categories of efficiency: *technological* efficiency, *dynamic* efficiency, and *allocative* efficiency?

A monopoly may be *technologically* inefficient; the firm may not be operating on its lowest possible cost curve. Because it has no competition, a monopoly may be careless in its cost controls, and resources may be wasted as a consequence. In drawing our diagrams, we have been ignoring this kind of inefficiency. However, in doing so we should not forget: *Technological* inefficiency in monopoly industries may impose a cost on society.

The relationship between monopoly and *dynamic* efficiency is less clear. As noted in the previous chapter, large, profitable monopolistic firms may have greater financial capacity and incentive to engage in research and development than smaller, perfectly competitive firms. This research and development may lead to new techniques of production that will lower the firm's cost curves. Or it may lead to distinctive new products. For example, when AT&T was still a monopoly, its Bell Labs developed the transistor, which made the vacuum tube obsolete and opened up the enormously important field of solid-state electronics. (Chapter 28 will deal with the dynamic effects of large firms in more detail.)

Finally, consider the central concept of efficiency studied by economists: *allocative* efficiency—or just "efficiency," for short. As we saw in the previous chapter, a good is being produced efficiently if its marginal social cost is equal to its marginal social benefit. To simplify our task, we continue the assumptions of the last chapter—that the marginal social cost MC_s = MC to the producer and that the marginal social benefit MB_s = MB to consumers. The MB to consumers—and therefore to society as a whole—is measured by the height of the demand curve shown in Figure 12-5. The marginal cost to society is MC, the marginal cost of this good to the only firm producing it. Since society's marginal cost intersects society's marginal benefit at *R*, the efficient quantity of output is Q_1.

This is not the output that the monopoly produces, however. Instead, as we have seen, it produces the smaller and therefore inefficient output Q_2, where MC = MR. The reason that it produces too little is that the firm equates marginal cost MC not with the marginal benefit to *society* (the height of the D curve) but instead with MR, the marginal benefit to the *firm* itself. Thus Adam Smith's invisible hand fails. The pursuit of benefit by an individual firm does *not* result in the best output for society.

The efficiency loss that results because monopoly produces too little (Q_2 rather than Q_1) appears as the red triangle. Note its similarity to the triangle in Figure 11-3*b*, which also showed the efficiency loss from too little output.

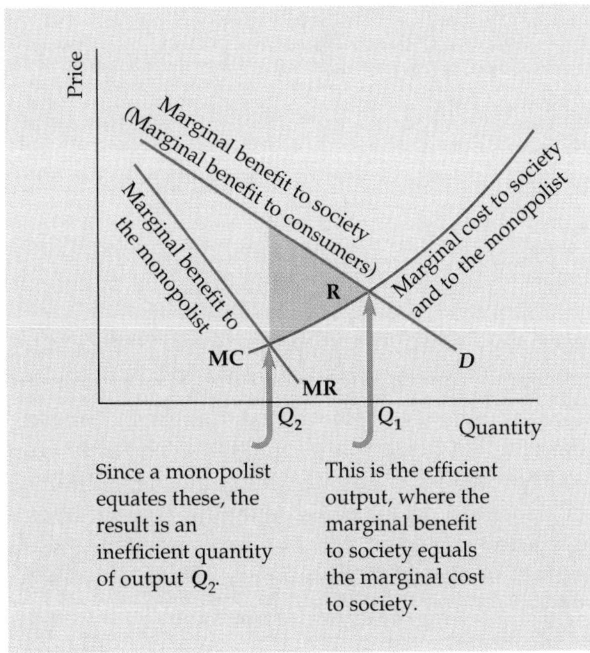

FIGURE 12-5 Monopoly results in allocative inefficiency: The invisible hand goes astray.

Monopoly results in output Q_2, which is less than the efficient output Q_1. Each of the units of reduced output between Q_1 and Q_2 would offer a higher marginal benefit to society (shown by the height of the *D* curve) than its marginal cost to society. It would therefore be beneficial to produce these units, and the efficiency loss from monopoly occurs because these potentially beneficial units are not produced. This loss is shown by the red triangle.

MONOPOLY RESULTING FROM A MERGER

As a specific example of how monopoly can reduce efficiency, consider what happens if a group of perfectly competitive firms merge to form a monopoly.

Figure 12-6*a* illustrates a perfectly competitive industry with output Q_1. Chapter 11 showed in detail why this perfectly competitive output is efficient. At output Q_1, supply—reflecting marginal costs to firms and to society—is equal to demand, reflecting marginal benefits to consumers and to society.

Now suppose in panel *b* that these small firms merge in order to form a monopoly and raise price. Furthermore, suppose that the merger leaves costs and demand unchanged. In other words, the cost and demand curves for the monopoly in panel *b* are *exactly the same* as the cost and demand curves that existed under perfect competition in panel *a*. What price and quantity does the monopoly firm select in order to maximize its profits?

The firm follows the monopolist's standard strategy, calculating its marginal revenue curve MR from its demand curve *D*. It then reduces output from Q_1 to Q_2, where MC = MR, and raises price from P_1 to P_2. In other words, it selects point E_M on the demand curve. The reduction in output from Q_1 to Q_2 means that too little is being pro-

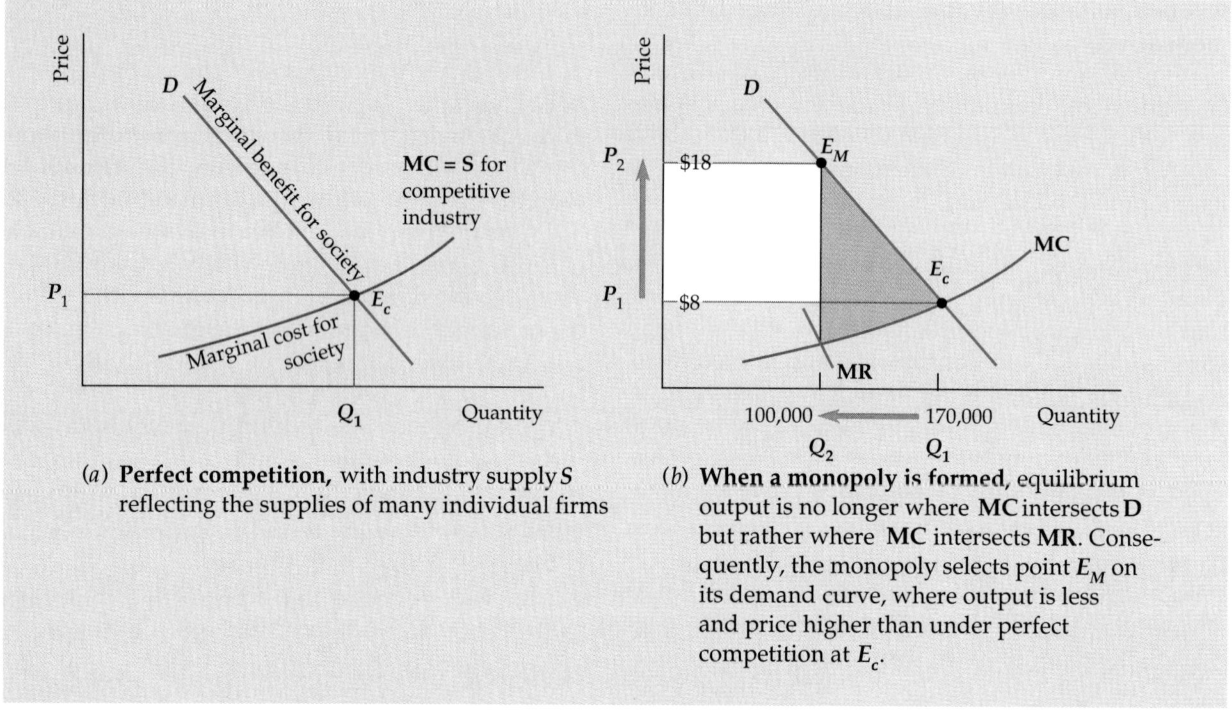

(*a*) **Perfect competition,** with industry supply *S* reflecting the supplies of many individual firms

(*b*) **When a monopoly is formed,** equilibrium output is no longer where **MC** intersects **D** but rather where **MC** intersects **MR**. Consequently, the monopoly selects point E_M on its demand curve, where output is less and price higher than under perfect competition at E_c.

FIGURE 12-6 When a perfectly competitive industry (panel *a*) is monopolized (panel *b*), the result is a red efficiency loss and a white transfer of income.

duced, creating the triangular red efficiency loss in panel *b*.

The monopolist's policy of restricting output is designed to make the good scarce so that its price can be raised. For producers who form a monopoly, it is this ability to raise price that provides them with an opportunity for profit that wasn't available to them when they were perfect competitors.

This type of blatantly monopolistic merger is outlawed by antitrust laws. However, the government itself has established marketing agencies for products such as milk, in order to help restrict output and raise price, and thus help farmers gain some of the advantages of monopoly.

An important objective of such a marketing agency is to transfer income from consumers to farmers and thus raise farm income. The transfers that result from monopoly, or from monopoly-like marketing boards, are now worth considering in detail.

THE TRANSFER EFFECT OF MONOPOLY

If only efficiency is considered, then the clear judgment is that society is harmed if a perfectly competitive industry is monopolized (Fig. 12-6). Although this conclusion is generally correct, it's not absolutely airtight, for two reasons. One is described in Box 12-1; the other arises because of the transfers associated with monopoly.

Consider what happens when a perfectly competitive industry is monopolized. Consumers suffer while the monopolized producers benefit. In Figure 12-6*b*, the price that consumers pay and producers receive rises by $10. With 100,000 units still being purchased, there is a transfer from consumers to producers equal to the $1 million white rectangle (100,000 units times $10 a unit).

This white area cancels out in dollar terms; the monopolized producers gain the $1 million while consumers lose it. However, it may not cancel out in terms of satisfaction. That is, the gain in satisfac-

BOX 12–1 The Theory of the Second Best

The conclusion that the monopolization of an industry results in inefficiency—that is, a misallocation of resources—is generally correct but not always.

To understand why, consider industry X in an economy where all other industries are perfectly competitive. If X is monopolized, not enough of X's output is produced. There is allocative inefficiency because too few of the nation's resources are going into the production of X. This is the standard conclusion.

Suppose, however, that all other industries are themselves monopolized but X is perfectly competitive. In this case, there will be too little output of all the other goods; in other words, there will be too much X. What happens if industry X is now monopolized? This will reduce its output, moving it in the right direction by bringing it back closer into line with the other industries. Thus the allocation of the nation's resources may actually be *improved*.

This is known as the **problem of the second best.** The first best economy is one in which all industries behave in a competitive way. If one industry is then monopolized, the economy becomes less efficient. However, in a second best world—one in which some industries are *already* monopolized—it is unclear whether monopoly in yet another industry will make the economy more or less efficient. There is no simple answer to this question; the theory of the second best is quite complex.

> The ***theory of the second best*** is the theory of how to get the best results in remaining markets when one or more markets have monopoly or other imperfections about which nothing can be done.

A second best argument is sometimes made in support of government policies to monopolize an agricultural industry—that is, raise price by restricting output. Since the rest of the economy is pervaded by monopoly, so the argument goes, monopolizing agriculture may improve the nation's resource allocation. By and large, economists remain unimpressed with this argument and continue to recommend that we aim at the "first best" solution by reducing the influence of monopoly wherever it may be found. Hence the theory of the second best is introduced here, not as a reason for encouraging monopoly in any specific sector, but rather as a warning that the economic world is seldom as simple as we might hope.

---

tion to producers who receive this extra $1 million may conceivably be greater than the reduction in satisfaction to consumers who lose it. For example, suppose that the item is something like the grapes from which champagne is made; the farmers who produce the grapes get together to set up a marketing board that raises the price. The consumers of champagne are so wealthy they hardly notice the increase in price. However, if the farmers who produce the grapes have low incomes, they may get great satisfaction from the additional $1 million they receive. In this case, most people would conclude that the act of transferring income can provide a net benefit. Moreover, it is conceivable that such a benefit might offset the red efficiency loss that arises because output declines from Q_1 to Q_2. In this case, one could argue that the monopolization of the industry would be desirable.

While this argument is logically possible, it is also somewhat strained; we have picked a very special case. Normally, a transfer from consumers to the owners of a monopoly would be judged inequitable, with consumers losing more satisfaction than the wealthier monopoly owners would gain. In this case, the transfer would add a further reason—along with inefficiency—to support the conclusion that the monopolization of the industry results in a net loss to society.[1] Note that this prob-

[1]Any full evaluation of monopoly involves examining several other issues as well. For example, to the degree that firms hire lawyers to help them establish or strengthen a monopoly position, then it's reasonable to argue that, from society's point of view, these legal resources are being wasted. See Anne Krueger, "The Political Economy of the Rent-Seeking Society," *American Economic Review*, June 1974, pp. 291–303; and Richard Posner, "The Social Costs of Monopoly and Regulation," *Journal of Political Economy*, August 1975, pp. 807–828.

lem of whether the $1 million is of equal benefit to buyers and sellers arises in evaluating almost every economic policy, whether it is controlling monopoly price, limiting pollution, or opening trade with foreign countries. Most policies result in a change in some market price, and hence a transfer of income between buyers and sellers. Thus any normative conclusion on whether or not the policy is desirable requires a reasonable working assumption about how people compare in their valuation of income.[2] Anyone unprepared to make such an assumption is restricted to positive economics—to an analysis of economic events, and institutions, without any judgment on whether or not they have been beneficial to the community as a whole.

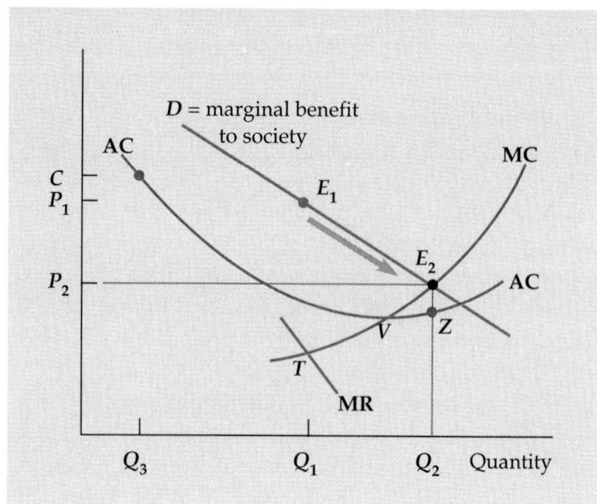

FIGURE 12-7 Natural monopoly: Regulating price rather than breaking up the firm.

Without price regulation, the monopoly produces at E_1, where MR = MC. If the government sets a maximum price of P_2, the firm is pushed down its demand curve to point E_2. Its output increases from Q_1 to the efficient Q_2 where the marginal benefit to *society* D is equal to MC. The efficiency gain is the elimination of the original "triangle" of monopoly inefficiency E_1E_2T.

GOVERNMENT POLICIES TO CONTROL MONOPOLY

In formulating policies to protect the public from monopoly, the government should begin with the question: Is the industry in question a natural monopoly or not? Suppose it is not; suppose the monopoly is the result of mergers of efficient, competitive firms. In this case, we've just seen that there is a strong argument for preventing monopolization, or if it has occurred, for breaking it up. To achieve this objective, antitrust laws have been passed. They will be considered in Chapter 14.

The balance of this chapter will concentrate on the other case, where the industry is a natural monopoly. Because of economies of scale, the average cost curve AC for a firm keeps falling over a wide range of output, as illustrated in Figure 12-7. The least expensive way for market demand to be satisfied is by one large producer. Breaking the monopoly up into a number of smaller firms would raise costs. There is no need for more than one set of electrical wires running down a street, nor for more than one set of gas lines. Graphically, breaking up the natural monopoly in Figure 12-7 into a number of small firms, each with output Q_3, would raise average cost to C; the benefits from economies of scale would be lost. In the case shown here, everyone would lose. The monopoly would lose its monopoly profit. Moreover, consumers would also be damaged. Even if the new, perhaps highly competitive firms were to earn no economic profit, they would still have to sell at a high price C just to cover their high costs—and that price would be higher than the price P_1 that consumers were paying before the monopoly was broken up.

Thus breaking up a natural monopoly is no solution at all. Indeed, breaking up the firm is a move in the wrong direction because it will raise costs. A more promising policy is to get the firm to *expand* from E_1 down its demand curve to the efficient point E_2, where the marginal benefit to consumers (and to society) is equal to the marginal cost to the firm (and to society).

How can the government get the monopoly to do this? The answer is: Set the maximum price that the firm can charge at P_2, the price at which its MC curve intersects the demand curve. This is called **marginal cost pricing.**

[2]The same issue arises in macroeconomics. During any period in which the nation's per capita income increases, most Americans benefit, but a few are hurt. Any judgment that such an income increase has been of benefit to the nation overall involves a reasonable assumption about how people compare in their valuation of income.

Marginal cost pricing is setting price at the level where MC intersects the demand curve.

Since the monopoly is now prohibited from raising price, it is forced to act like a perfectly competitive firm, taking price P_2 as given. Like the perfectly competitive firm, it will produce to point E_2, where its MC curve rises to the level of its given price P_2. Because E_2 is the efficient output where MC intersects demand, this policy has eliminated the original efficiency loss caused by monopoly. (That original efficiency loss was triangle TE_1E_2, because the monopoly chose equilibrium E_1 rather than the efficient equilibrium E_2.)

Note that, in forcing the move to the efficient point E_2, the government has *not* broken up this natural monopoly. It has simply removed *the monopoly's market power*—that is, the power of the monopoly to set a high price. In practice, there are two ways the government can do this:

1. It may take over and operate the monopolized activity, setting the price of its output at P_2. This is generally the case with water services.

2. Alternatively, the government may let the monopoly continue as a privately owned firm but will set up a regulatory agency to control its price. This agency then dictates price P_2. This is generally the way that the government sets the price that electric companies can charge.

Consider how well marginal cost pricing solves the monopoly abuse of producing too little at too high a price. The monopoly is forced to reduce its price, and consequently it sells more. That is, its output increases. In addition, its monopoly profit is reduced. Because the firm initially maximized profit at E_1, any other point on the demand curve—specifically, E_2—results in less profit. However, its profit is not necessarily eliminated; in Figure 12-7, a per-unit profit of E_2Z remains.

Unfortunately, dealing with monopoly is seldom so easy in practice. Although marginal cost pricing still allows a profit in the example shown in Figure 12-7, in other circumstances it may lead to a loss. In such cases, marginal cost pricing is not a satisfactory policy, since it would drive the firm out of business. Such a monopoly requires some other form of regulation. This difficult case is dealt with in Box 12-2.

BOX 12–2 Unfortunately, Dealing with Natural Monopoly Is Often Not So Simple

In Figure 12-7, average cost reached a minimum and turned up at point *V before* it reached the demand curve; that is, it turned up to the left of the demand curve. Figure 12-8 presents an even clearer case of natural monopoly, where the average cost curve AC continues to fall until *after* it has crossed the demand curve. In this instance, the regulation of monopoly price presents special problems.

To see why, suppose the government tries to apply the policy of marginal cost pricing that worked so well in Figure 12-7. It again tries to drive the monopoly firm down its demand curve from its original profit-maximizing equilibrium E_1 to the efficient point E_2, where marginal cost intersects demand. As before, suppose it attempts to do so by regulating price at P_2. This policy will not work because the price P_2 is not high enough to cover average cost at *G*. The firm's per unit loss is GE_2, and its total loss is the red area. Eventually, the firm will be driven out of business—a worse outcome than at the original E_1. In this case, marginal cost pricing is a failure.

A different approach is required. To improve on the free-market outcome at E_1, the government has three main options.

1. AVERAGE COST PRICING

The lowest price the government can set without eventually forcing the firm out of business is P_3, which will result in a new equilibrium at E_3. Here price is barely high enough to cover average cost; the firm just breaks even. This policy is called *average cost pricing*. Once again, the regulatory agency takes away the monopoly's power to select a point on its demand curve; the agency makes the decision on the appropriate point and makes it stick by regulating price.

Average cost pricing is setting price at the level where AC intersects the demand curve.

In theory, break-even price P_3 should be easy for the

BOX 12–2 *Unfortunately, Dealing with Natural Monopoly Is Often Not So Simple (continued)*

regulatory agency to find. If the firm is earning an (above-normal) profit—as it would, for example at E_1—price is too high; it should therefore be lowered. If the firm is operating at a loss, at a point like E_2, price is too low; it should therefore be raised. This simple rule of thumb will bring the regulators to P_3, the price that just covers costs, including a fair return on the capital the owners have invested. In practice, however, it is very difficult to determine P_3, largely because of problems in defining (1) a fair percentage return to capital and (2) the amount of capital invested. (These problems are examined in the appendix.)

Finally, the effect of average cost pricing on efficiency is shown in panel *b* of Figure 12-8. If it were possible to move the monopoly all the way down its demand curve from E_1 to E_2, the result would be the now familiar "triangular" efficiency gain shown as areas 4 + 5. However, average cost pricing allows us to move this firm only part way, from E_1 to E_3. Therefore the gain is limited to area 4.

We conclude that since this policy of average cost pricing increases monopoly output from Q_1 to Q_3, it results in a *gain in allocative efficiency*. (Remember that unless we state otherwise, the word *efficiency* means "allocative efficiency.") Unfortunately, however, this policy (and any of the others described in this box or in Figure 12-7) may lead to a loss in technical efficiency. That is, the firm may not operate on its lowest possible cost curve. After all, why should the firm in Figure 12-8 strive hard to lower its costs, when a reduction in costs will cause the regulatory agency to correspondingly lower price? Why shouldn't the firm's executives be allowed generous expense accounts, since such costs are simply passed on to consumers in the form of higher prices? No matter what the firm does, it isn't allowed to make an above-normal profit; so why should it tightly control its costs? (At best, the firm can earn an above-normal profit only temporarily, between the date it reduces its costs and the date the regulatory agency gets around to reducing its price.) Consequently, price regulation will increase overall efficiency only if the increase in allocative efficiency outweighs any loss in technical efficiency.

2. GOVERNMENT SUBSIDY PLUS MARGINAL COST PRICING

Another option is to force the firm in panel *a* of Figure 12-8 all the way down its demand curve from E_1 to efficient point E_2 by marginal cost pricing, while at the same time paying the firm whatever lump-sum subsidy is necessary to cover its loss. In other words, a regulated price of P_2 drives the firm down its demand curve to point E_2 (thus capturing the entire possible efficiency gain 4 + 5), whereas a subsidy equal to the red area in panel *a* keeps the firm in business.

Although this policy may be attractive in theory, it raises such serious problems in practice that it is seldom used. It is difficult for the public to understand why a government committed to controlling the market power of monopoly should end up subsidizing it. The point that the government is also regulating price—and thus eliminating the profit of the monopoly—is difficult to explain to the public. Moreover, the policy of taking money out of the monopolist's pocket with one hand (the regulated price) while putting it back with the other (the subsidy) may strike the public as being inconsistent, even though it is not. In addition, the general problem in price regulation reappears here. As long as the government is committed to subsidizing the costs of a monopolist, how can those costs be controlled? A firm may be very successful in holding costs down as long as it has to meet the test of the marketplace where failure means bankruptcy, but it may be far less successful in controlling its costs if it knows it will receive a subsidy for any loss it incurs.

3. GOVERNMENT OWNERSHIP

The political problems in granting a subsidy are less severe if the government owns the monopoly, which it can then operate at efficient point E_2, charging the public P_2. Again, taxpayers must subsidize the loss that results. Government-owned mass transit systems are often cited as examples; government subsidies cover more than half the costs of the typical large urban public transportation system.

To conclude, we reemphasize that the same problem arises here as with the other policies discussed in this box. As long as the firm's management receives whatever subsidy is necessary to cover its costs, it has inadequate incentive to keep costs down. There is a good reason why this problem may become serious in a public enterprise. Even in a private enterprise, the owners (stockholders) may have problems controlling an inefficient management. However, in a public enterprise this is even more difficult because of the layers of government bureaucracy separating the managers of the enterprise from its owners—in this case, the taxpayers. (The problems of a bureaucracy are examined further in Chapter 18.)

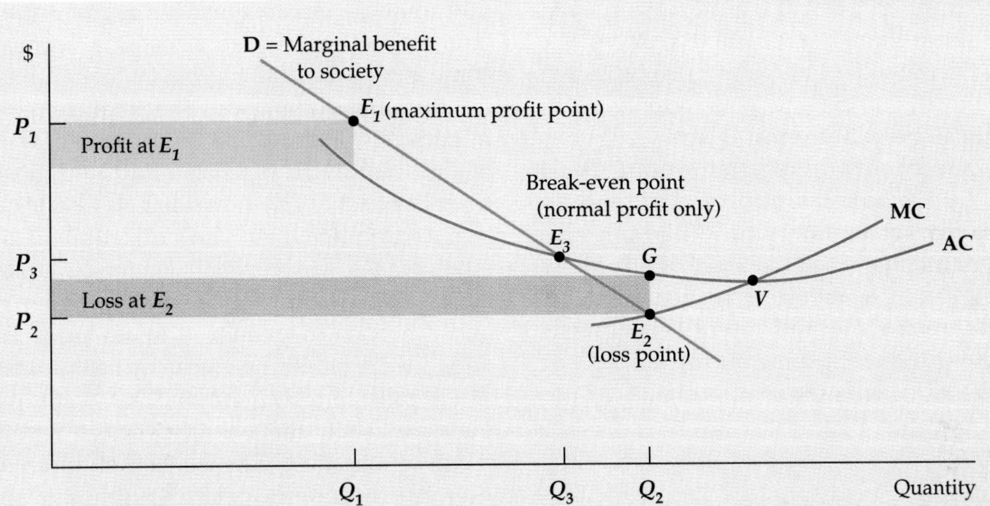

(*a*) **Average cost pricing.** An unrestricted monopoly would maximize profit by selecting point E_1 on its demand curve. The profit it would earn is shown by the blue area. Average cost pricing pushes the monopoly down its demand curve to E_3, by setting a price ceiling at P_3. At this point the firm just breaks even, earning only the normal profit necessary to keep it in business.

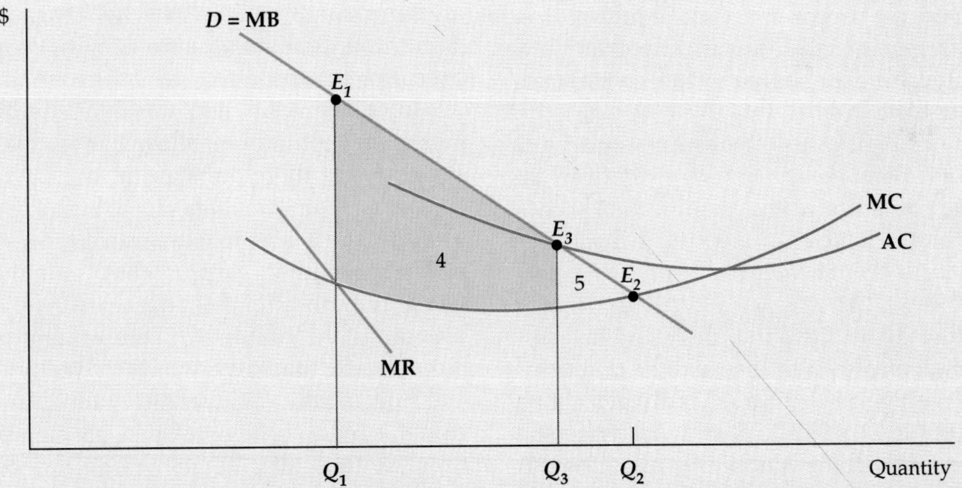

(*b*) **Efficiency gains that are achieved (4), and those that are not (5).** If it were feasible to push the monopoly firm all the way down its demand curve from E_1 to E_2, then there would be an efficiency gain 4 + 5. But since the firm can be pushed down only to E_3, the efficiency gain is limited to area 4.

FIGURE 12-8 Regulating monopoly price: The difficult case.

Finally, the example in Figure 12-7 presents a puzzle. A government price ceiling increases efficiency here, but in other circumstances a government price ceiling—such as the ceiling on rents described earlier—*reduces* efficiency. How is this possible? The answer: The ceiling on rents moved an industry *away* from an efficient competitive equilibrium. On the other hand, the price ceiling in Figure 12-7 moves an inefficient monopoly at E_1 *towards* an efficient equilibrium at E_2.

Clearly, government intervention can be a powerful tool, because it can move a market away from its free-market equilibrium. Although this move can be damaging if the free market is initially competitive, it can be beneficial if the free market is initially monopolized. For this reason, economists oppose price regulation in some circumstances but favor it in others.

PRICE DISCRIMINATION: LETTING A MONOPOLIST ACT LIKE A MONOPOLIST—IN SPADES

The argument so far is that a monopolist should not be allowed the freedom to set a high price. However, this general rule has an interesting exception which can be illustrated in the special case of the only dentist in a small town.

In panel *a* of Figure 12-9, the demand curve *D* shows the total demand for her services from all patients in the community. The diagram also shows her average costs, which, as always, include her opportunity costs—the income she could earn elsewhere.

If she must quote the same price for her services to all patients, she will not stay in this community: The average cost curve *AC* is always above the demand curve *D*, regardless of what price she picks. Consequently, there is no single price she can select that will cover her costs. The best she can do is to select a point like *E* on the demand curve, setting her fee at P_1 and selling quantity Q_1. However, she still suffers a loss. Specifically, her total loss, compared with what she could earn elsewhere, is the red area: that is, *Q* units sold at a loss of CP_1 on each.

Under such circumstances, this community loses its dentist. But isn't there some other way she could be allowed to charge for her services so that she could earn a higher income and be convinced to stay after all? The answer is yes. Indeed, she can charge more in a way that will not only increase her earnings but leave a net benefit to the community as well. Here's how: by *discriminating* among patients, selling her services at a higher price to some than to others.

Specifically, suppose the total demand shown in panel *a* of Figure 12-9 is made up of the demand of the wealthy in panel *b*, and the demand of the poor in panel *c*. These two panels also show P_1, her best single price if she can't discriminate. But if she *is* allowed to discriminate, her best strategy is to charge the wealthy in panel *b* a higher price P_W, and the poor in panel *c* a lower price P_P. To see why, first consider her wealthy customers in panel *b*. At price P_1, the demand by these patients is inelastic. Thus she can earn more revenue from them by charging them a higher price. (At price P_W, her revenue is price P_W times quantity Q_W, which is area 3 + 6. This is greater than her revenue of 6 + 7 if she charges P_1.) In contrast, the demand of her low-income patients in panel *c* is highly *elastic* at price P_1, and she can earn more from them by charging them a *lower* price. (Revenue 8 + 9 is greater than 8 + 5.) Thus by charging different prices, the dentist can earn a higher total revenue from *both* groups.

In this special case, the dentist's higher earnings from both groups allow her to cover her average cost and therefore stay in town. An important reason is that, by charging a higher price to the wealthy, she is able to extract from them area 3, *part* of the consumer surplus they gain because she stays. But despite this, the wealthy—as well, of course, as the poor—still receive a consumer surplus benefit that they would have lost if she had left. Specifically, the wealthy gain 2, and the poor gain 4 + 5 + 1. (The consumer surplus from a dentist's services may be very large indeed. An individual faced with a severe toothache may be *willing to pay* far more than the price actually charged.)

The conclusion in this case is that price discrimination is justified because it benefits everyone concerned. However, even when price discrimination is desirable, it may not be possible. To make different prices stick, the discriminating monopolist must be able to divide the market, preventing individuals who can buy at the low price from

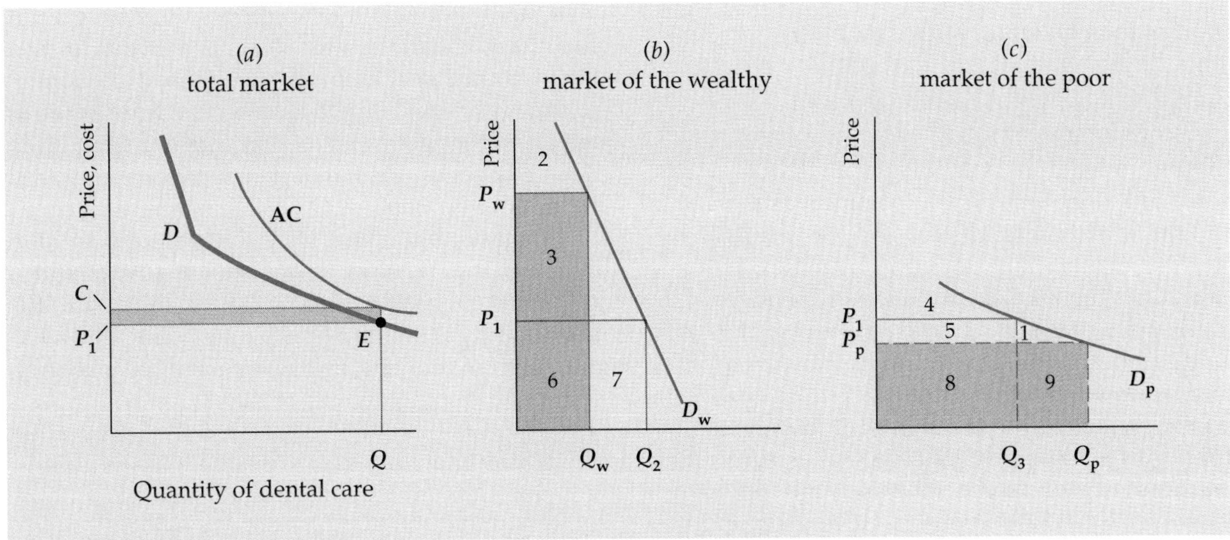

FIGURE 12-9 When price discrimination by a monopoly may be justified.
If the dentist can charge only one price, she will leave town, because the demand D always lies below AC. Any point such as E that she might select on D would thus leave her operating at a loss, shown by the red area. On the other hand, she will stay if she is allowed to earn a profit by discriminating, charging a higher fee P_W to the wealthy and a lower fee P_P to the poor. Although this is a special case, it shows that if a monopoly is able to discriminate, it can increase its revenue by charging a higher price in the less elastic market than in the more elastic market.

turning around and selling to those who are charged the higher price. In our example, the dentist is able to divide the market: A poor patient who is able to buy a dental bridge at a bargain price obviously cannot turn around and sell it to a rich friend. On the other hand, a bus company may not be able to divide its adult market, charging some customers $10 and others $20. The reason is that those who are able to buy cheap $10 tickets may sell them to the others for a price like $15 which benefits both groups. (However, the bus company *can* divide its market between adults and children, since an adult can't buy a cheap ticket from a child and use it on a bus. The company may also give a discount to senior citizens, because they are also relatively easy to identify, and those who are not 65 usually don't want to pretend that they are.)

Finally, it should be reemphasized that price discrimination by the monopolist in Figure 12-9 is desirable because D *does not overlap* AC and the dentist would leave otherwise. However, price discrimination cannot be similarly justified in the normal case of monopoly which we will concentrate on hereafter—namely, the case in which D does overlap AC and the monopolist can therefore at least cover costs by quoting a single price. In that case, price discrimination is sometimes justified and sometimes not. One of the justified cases is charging a higher highway toll during rush hours to reduce congestion. An unjustified case occurs when a large nationwide firm, challenged by emerging new competitors in a region, lowers its price in this region to drive them out of business.

However, when we talk about regional price discrimination, we must be careful. If a higher price in a distant region is due to *higher costs,* such as the extra freight and insurance costs that have to be paid on longer shipments, then economists avoid the term *discrimination.* Instead price discrimination is a difference in price that does *not* reflect differences in costs.

LIVING IN A GLOBAL ECONOMY

THE WORLD'S LARGEST FIRM

Nippon Telegraph and Telephone (NTT) is the dominant firm in Japanese communications. It is also the world's largest firm. By 1988, the total value of its outstanding stock was over $295 *billion*—more than the total value of the eight largest U.S. companies, or *all the companies listed on the West German stock market.* In a world in which many U.S. companies would be happy to see their stock selling for, say, 20 times earnings, NTT was selling for 250 times earnings. (Noncomparable accounting practices explain some of this large difference. Moreover by 1989, Nippon stock had come down from its previous high level as the corporation was touched by scandal.)

Until 1985, NTT had a complete monopoly over Japanese internal telecommunications. Although it now faces several competing firms, they have a difficult task ahead, because NTT is proving to be a tough competitor. Its huge size gives it economies of scale, and its ability to offer a very wide range of telephone services and equipment—ranging from data networks to handset telephones—gives it **economies of scope.**

For example, when NTT develops a new kind of telephone, there is no additional cost of transporting it to market, since it can be shipped in the same trucks as the existing phones. Thus the average cost of transporting each kind of phone is reduced.

Economies of scope occur when the addition of a new product reduces the cost of existing products.

In view of the economies of scale and of scope which NTT enjoys, it is not yet clear how successful the new, smaller firms will be in breaking the monopoly of this industrial giant.

KEY POINTS

1. Monopoly means that there is a single seller. This situation may occur when a firm controls something essential to the production or sale of a good—such as a patent, resource, or government license. Or it may occur if a number of firms merge.

2. Another important reason for monopoly is that a firm's costs may fall over such a wide range of output that total market demand can be most inexpensively satisfied by a single firm. This is a *natural monopoly.* Even if there are initially many firms in such an industry, they will tend to be eliminated by competition, with the single large firm that emerges able to undercut any present or future competitors.

3. A monopoly can do something a perfectly competitive firm cannot. Because it faces a demand curve that slopes downward to the right, it can quote the price at which it will sell.

4. Whereas marginal revenue MR for a perfect competitor is the same as price, MR for a monopoly is less than price. That is, a monopoly's MR curve lies below its demand curve. The demand curve represents the marginal benefit of the good to consumers and to society. The lower MR represents the marginal benefit to the monopoly.

5. A monopolist maximizes profit by equating MC with MR, not with price. As a consequence, monopoly results in an inefficiently low output. It also results in a transfer of income from consumers to the monopolist.

6. If the firm is not a natural monopoly—but instead is, say, the result of a merger—a strong case can be made for breaking it up. The government has antitrust laws to break up monopolies, or to prevent such monopolies from being formed in the first place. These laws will be described in Chapter 14.

7. If the firm is a natural monopoly, breaking it up will raise costs. A preferred government policy is to set the maximum price the monopolist can charge. Facing this given price, the monopolist is forced into the price-taking role of the perfect competitor and consequently increases output to a more efficient quantity.

8. A case can sometimes be made for allowing a monopoly to price-discriminate, that is, to charge a higher price to one group than to another. One example is a dentist in a small town who charges a higher price to her wealthy patients. Such discriminatory pricing may be justified if the good or service cannot otherwise be produced.

KEY CONCEPTS

patent
legal monopoly
merger
natural monopoly
oligopoly
market power
price maker
price taker
monopolist's marginal revenue
inefficiency from monopoly
transfer effect of monopoly
marginal cost pricing
discriminating monopoly
dividing the market
economies of scope

PROBLEMS

12-1. Which is closer to being a monopoly, Volkswagen or Rolls Royce? Answer the same question for the producer of pastries in a small town or the producer of the wheat used in them. In each case, explain your answer.

12-2. Consider an industry in which the discovery and development of advanced machinery and technology mean that, as time passes, average costs for a firm tend to drift lower and lower. That is, through time the average cost for an individual firm moves from AC_1 to AC_2 in the diagram below. What do you think would happen in such an industry? Explain why. From the point of view of society as a whole, does the falling cost involve any advantages? Any disadvantages? In your view, how do these compare?

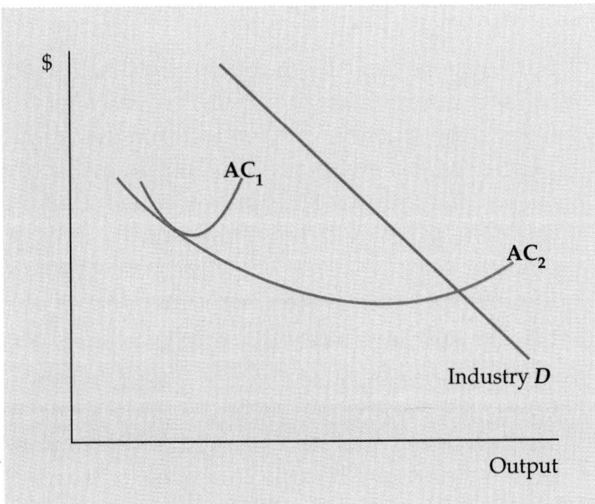

12-3. (a) If the firm with AC_2 in the figure above is not regulated, would you expect all the monopoly profits to go to the firm's owners? If not, who else do you think might eventually capture a share of these profits?

(b) Draw in the marginal cost curve that corresponds to AC_2. Show the best level at which regulated price should be set. Explain why it is best.

12-4. The diagram below provides another way of viewing a monopolist's profit maximization, in addition to the two views set out in Figure 12-4. The TC and TR curves for a monopolist are the same as those for a perfect competitor on page 202, except for one important difference. Because a monopoly faces a downward sloping demand curve, its TR is a curved rather than a straight line. Using that earlier approach, describe how the profit-maximizing output of this monopolist is determined. In particular, show geometrically why MC = MR.

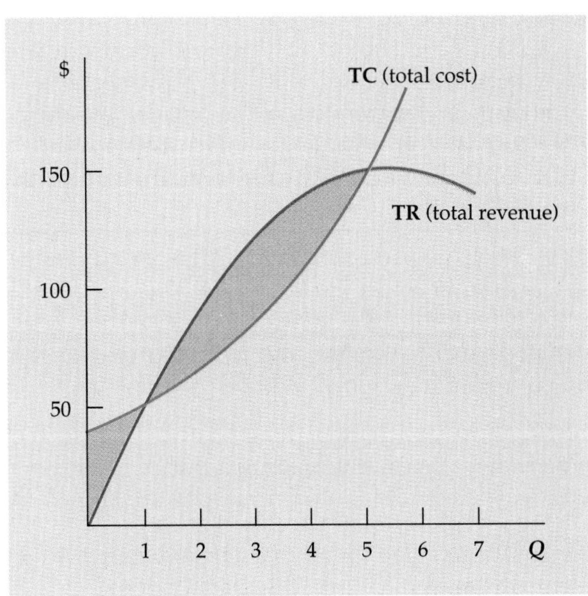

12-5. "Marginal revenue for a monopolist equals the marginal benefit of its product to society." Do you agree or disagree? Explain.

12-6. Given the cost conditions in the diagram below, name the price that would be set by a monopoly that is (a) maximizing its profit, (b) operating as a nonprofit organization, (c) being run by the government at an efficient output. If the prices set in (a) and/or (b) are not efficient, explain why.

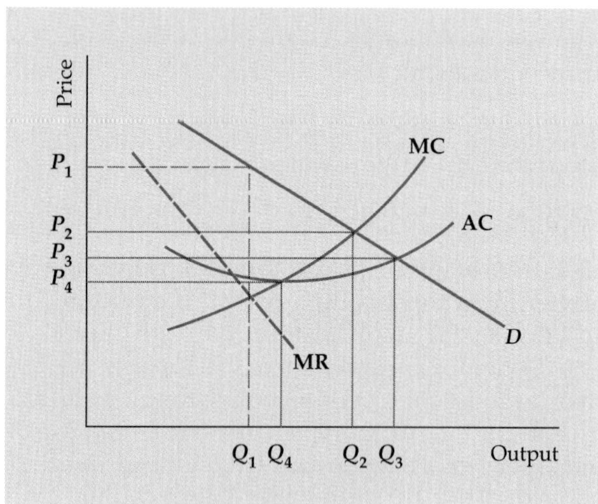

12-7. Does output Q_1 in Figure 12-4*b* yield the monopolist the largest profit per unit of output? Explain your answer.

12-8. Consider the following statement: "Monopolies should be subject to price control. Competitive industries should not. Every owner has a monopoly in the renting of his or her building. Therefore, the government should control rents." Do you agree with this statement in part or in whole? Explain.

12-9. We have seen that the uncontrolled monopoly operating at E_1 in Figure 12-7 is inefficient. Which condition for efficiency in Box 11-1 has been violated? (*Hint:* What is the marginal cost of the uncontrolled monopoly? What is its price?)

12-10. Suppose that the demand and the costs the government faces in providing a public utility service (say, electricity) in a certain city are shown in the following diagram:

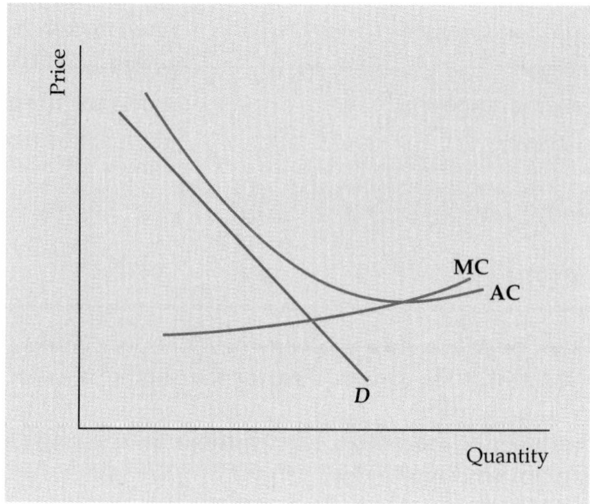

(a) If the government is interested only in maximizing the utility's profit—or minimizing its loss—show the price it will set and how much it will produce and sell. Also show its profit or loss.

(b) Is this output the best from the viewpoint of allocative efficiency? If so, explain why. If not, show what the efficient output is and explain why. What price does the firm set to achieve the efficient output, and what is its profit or loss at that output?

(c) Suppose that this public utility is allowed to set discriminatory prices. It decides to charge the public a higher rate for the initial purchases, whereas, for any additional purchases, it continues to charge the rate it set in question (b). Could the public utility sell an efficient output and still make profits by following a policy of price discrimination?

(d) Do you now see why public utilities are sometimes allowed to set discriminatory rates?

(e) In the section on price discrimination, it was observed that for successful discrimination, a firm must be able to segregate its market and prevent resale among buyers. Would a public utility selling electricity be able to do this?

12-11. Suppose the government owns the two monopolies shown in Figures 12-7 and 12-8. In the interests of efficiency, how should their prices be set? Would each firm operate at a profit or a loss? What government subsidy(ies) would be required? Would two such monopolies taken together necessarily require a subsidy? Explain.

12-12. Evaluate the following policy recommendation: "The sole objective in regulating monopoly price is to eliminate excess profits. And this is easy to do. Just examine the firm's current operations, calculate its average cost (including normal profit), and set price at this level."

APPENDIX

AVERAGE COST PRICING
Public Utility Regulation

Several problems arise when a policy of average cost pricing—outlined in Box 12-2—is put into practice in regulating a **public utility.**

> A ***public utility*** is a firm—typically a natural monopoly—that provides an essential service to the public and is either owned or regulated by the government. Examples include companies that supply natural gas or electricity; they are natural monopolies because of their high fixed costs, in the form of pipelines or transmission lines.

HOW IS AVERAGE COST CALCULATED?

Recall from Figure 12-8 that average cost pricing means setting price that will barely cover average costs, including normal profit. In other words, the objective is to keep the price low enough to prevent monopoly profits but high enough to provide the normal profit that will keep the firm in business. Estimating a fair or normal profit for the owners requires estimating the amount of capital invested, and a fair percentage rate of return for that capital.

1. *What is a fair percentage rate of return on capital invested?* A reasonable answer is, the opportunity cost of capital—the percentage rate of return it could earn in its next best use. Although regulatory agencies have given some consideration to earnings in other sectors of the economy, the rates of return for public utilities have generally not matched rates elsewhere, perhaps because of tradition and a feeling that prices should be kept down to benefit the public. The relatively low rate of return for public utilities has been further depressed by an inflationary squeeze that has raised the costs of inputs to utilities. (Compensating price increases have been allowed, but only after a time lag.) Because of their low rates of return, utilities have had difficulty floating new issues of stock.

It is sometimes argued that this lower return is a reflection of the lower risk in public utility investment. Certainly, there is no risk that the public utility will be driven bankrupt by competitors, for there are no competitors. But a utility may be driven bankrupt by costs that get out of control. Moreover, public utility investment presents its own special kind of risk: the risk that the regulators will not adequately or quickly enough protect the investors' return from being eroded by inflation. Finally, there is another substantial risk in a public utility using nuclear power. At any point, the government or the courts may force the firm to suspend or terminate its operations. Because of all these considerations, public utilities are far from being a risk-free form of investment. Therefore the relatively low rate of return earned on this investment does make it difficult for a utility to float new stock issues.

2. *What is the value of the capital invested (the "rate base")?* Should it be the *original cost* of the machinery and other capital bought by the firm, or the *present replacement cost* (less depreciation in either case)? Because of inflation, this choice makes a lot of difference. The cost of replacing most equipment far exceeds its original cost years ago. Thus far there is no clear consensus among the regulatory agencies on which method to use.

CHAPTER 13
MARKETS BETWEEN MONOPOLY AND PERFECT COMPETITION

People of the same trade seldom meet together, even for merriment and diversion, but the conversation ends in a conspiracy against the public, or in some contrivance to raise prices.
ADAM SMITH, *WEALTH OF NATIONS*

Monopoly represents the clearest form of market power; the monopoly firm is alone in the marketplace and has the power to choose its selling price. However, if we look at such giants of American business as General Motors, IBM, and General Electric, we find that most of them are not monopolists. General Motors competes with Ford, Chrysler, and foreign producers; IBM has to compete with Apple in personal computers and with Digital Equipment in business computers; General Electric competes with Westinghouse in electrical generators, and with Pratt and Whitney in jet engines. Each of these firms—GM, IBM, and GE—is an oligopolist, operating in a market dominated by a *few* sellers. Oligopoly is more significant in the U.S. economy than outright monopoly.

This chapter describes several kinds of market which, like oligopoly, lie in the middle ground between the extremes of monopoly on the one hand and perfect competition on the other.

1. **Monopolistic competition** occurs when a firm has *many competitors* but is nonetheless still able to exercise some *small influence over its price* because it is selling a **differentiated product.** Monopolistic competition is common in retailing and some service sectors. For example, a hair stylist in a large city has many competitors. Even so, she retains some influence over her price. If she raises it by a small amount—perhaps by 25¢ or 50¢—she won't lose much business; few of her customers will be willing to switch to someone with a different style. She is limited in her ability to raise price, however. If she tries to raise it by several dollars, many of her customers will go elsewhere.

2. In contrast, **oligopoly** is a market that is dominated by a few sellers, each with considerable influence over price.

3. Finally, **duopoly** is a market with only two sellers. It is often viewed as a special case of oligopoly, when the number of firms has shrunk to two.

The first line of Table 13-1 sets out the basic characteristics of a perfectly competitive market. This chapter will explain lines B, C, and D, showing how each of the other market forms is similar (in green) or different (in black). Monopolistic competition is the same as perfect competition in some respects: It has a large number of firms and easy

TABLE 13-1 Types of Market Structure

Type of Market	*Number of Firms*	*Type of Product*	*Entry*	*A Firm's Influence over Its Price*	*Does the Firm Worry about the Responses of Its Competition?*	*Examples*
A. Perfect Competition	Many small firms	Standardized	Easy	None (price taker)	No: it is too small	Some agricultural products
B. Monopolistic Competition	Many small firms	Differentiated	Easy	A little	No: it is too small	Some retail trade and services
C. Oligopoly	A few firms	Usually differentiated (through it may be standardized)	Difficult	Considerable (price searcher)	Yes	Autos, computers (for a standardized product: aluminum)
D. Duopoly	Two	Usually differentiated	Difficult	Considerable (price searcher)	Yes, particularly in this case	Some long-distance telephone service
E. Monopoly	One	—	Difficult or impossible	Substantial (price maker unless regulated by government)	The firm has no direct competitors	Local telephone service

entry. However, it is different because of its nonstandardized product and the consequent power of each firm to exercise some influence over its price. Oligopoly and duopoly are different from perfect competition in *all* of the five features shown in Table 13-1.

This chapter begins with the market closest to perfect competition—monopolistic competition—and then moves to markets with fewer and fewer sellers.

MONOPOLISTIC COMPETITION

Because each firm offers a differentiated product and therefore has some influence over its price, it does not face the perfect competitor's perfectly horizontal demand curve. Instead, its demand curve slopes downward to the right. However, because of the existence of many competitors, its control over price is not great. In other words, as Figure 13-1 illustrates, the demand curve facing the individual producer is very elastic, with very little slope.

Even if products are physically identical, they may still be differentiated in other respects. For example, tubes of Crest toothpaste are sold in stores in different locations. Although the products are physically the same, the toothpaste sold in the store closest to the customer is "better" because it is more convenient. As a result, the consumer will be willing to pay a few cents more for it. Thus location gives each store some control over its price; it can charge a few cents more and not lose all its customers. Similarly, a gasoline station with a particularly convenient location can charge more. However, it doesn't have much control over price. If it charges a much higher price, buyers will bypass it to go to one of its less expensive, though less convenient, competitors.

It is relatively easy to get into small-scale retailing; it is not necessary to have a vast pool of funds to buy or rent a single drug store. Where existing firms are making above-normal profits, new

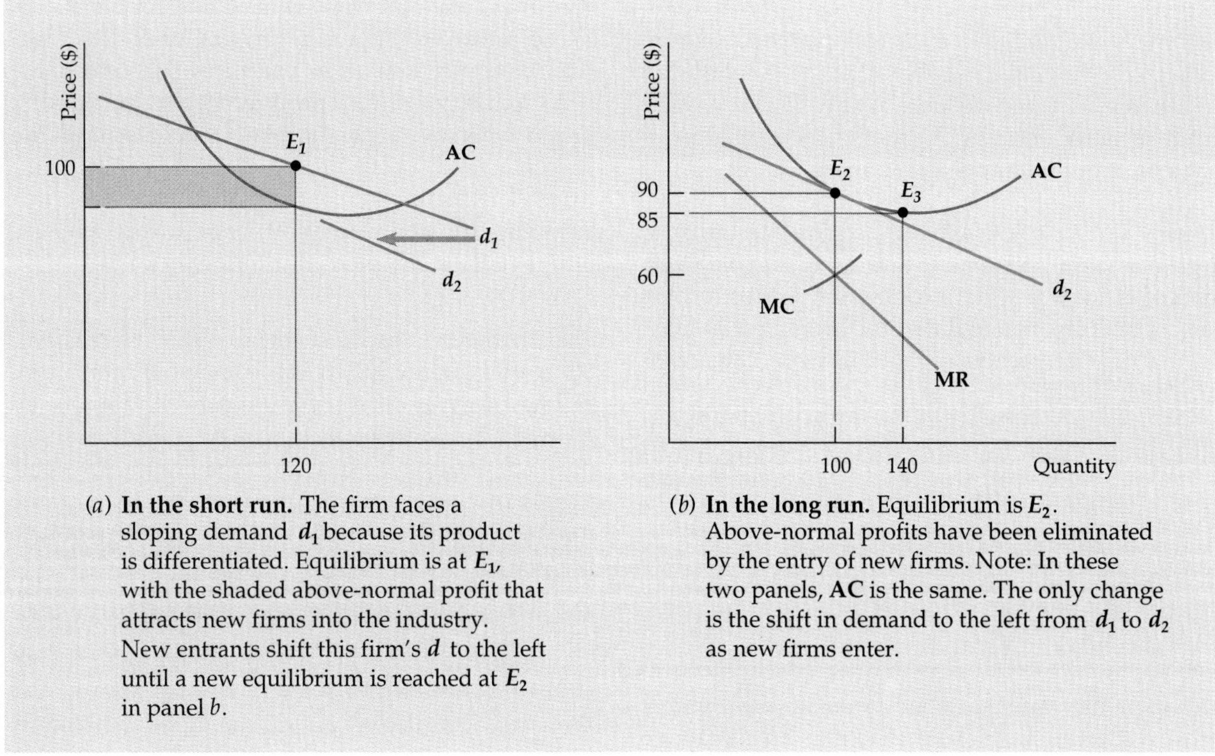

(*a*) **In the short run.** The firm faces a sloping demand d_1 because its product is differentiated. Equilibrium is at E_1, with the shaded above-normal profit that attracts new firms into the industry. New entrants shift this firm's d to the left until a new equilibrium is reached at E_2 in panel *b*.

(*b*) **In the long run.** Equilibrium is E_2. Above-normal profits have been eliminated by the entry of new firms. Note: In these two panels, **AC** is the same. The only change is the shift in demand to the left from d_1 to d_2 as new firms enter.

FIGURE 13-1 Equilibrium for a typical firm in monopolistic competition.

entrants come in, eliminating these excess profits, as illustrated in Figure 13-1. Initially, the typical firm shown in panel *a* is operating at E_1 and earning a profit shown by the shaded area. As new competitors enter and capture some of its sales, however, it gets a smaller share of the total market. The demand curve facing the firm therefore shifts to the left. This process continues until its demand becomes tangent to the average cost curve, as shown in panel *b*. Faced with this new demand curve, the best the firm can do now is to select the point of tangency E_2 where it earns no excess profit. Any other point on the demand curve would leave it operating at a loss. Thus just as free entry eliminates above-normal profits for the typical firm in perfect competition, so free entry also eliminates such profits for the firm in monopolistic competition. In the three decades following the early postwar period, profits in retailing were consistently less than in manufacturing, where firms generally had a greater degree of market power.

In terms of efficiency, how does monopolistic competition rate? At first glance, panel *b* of Figure 13-1 suggests that monopolistic competition is inefficient: At the firm's output of 100 units, MC ($60) is less than price ($90), so this is apparently an inefficient quantity of output. Put another way, it is often claimed that there is "excess capacity," with too many firms in the industry, each producing too few units. Consumer demand could be satisfied at lower cost if there were fewer firms, each producing more—that is, if the typical firm in panel *b* were to move from E_2 to E_3 by increasing its output from 100 to 140 units, thus lowering its average cost to the minimum of $85. If the industry were changed in this way, wouldn't the result be a more efficient allocation of resources?

The answer is, not necessarily. Although cost would be lower, which would be an advantage for society, there would also be a disadvantage. Since there would be fewer firms, consumers would have less choice. For example, a reduction in the number of retail stores would mean that those remaining could sell a larger volume, thus reducing their costs and prices. But it would also mean that some customers would have to travel further to shop. Perhaps the convenience of local stores is worth the slightly higher price we have to pay. Thus it is difficult to criticize strongly the inefficiencies—if any—that arise from monopolistic competition.

In conclusion, monopolistic competition is sufficiently similar to perfect competition—in terms of large numbers, free entry, and a reasonably high level of efficiency—that economists do not recommend government regulation of firms in this market, particularly when regulation itself can introduce inefficiencies.

However, public policy problems can arise in the case of oligopoly, where firms are larger and fewer, and thus typically have greater influence over price.

OLIGOPOLY

Although the large number of small retail stores that exist in a sizable metropolitan area may be monopolistic competitors, if there are only three stores that operate alone in a small, isolated village, they are oligopolists. Similarly, the three U.S. auto companies are oligopolists; each has some influence over price, and each knows that any price change it makes will be noticed by the others, who may well react. For example, if GM cuts its price, Ford and Chrysler may follow suit. Therefore, *before changing its price, each firm must take into account the possible reactions of its competitors.* This is the important new issue raised by oligopoly.

> ***Oligopoly*** is a market that is dominated by a small number of sellers. Each firm has considerable influence over its price, and must take into account the reaction of the others.

MEASURING THE CONCENTRATION OF AN INDUSTRY

The degree to which a few sellers dominate an industry—that is, the concentration of the industry—can be measured in several ways.

The Four-Firm and Eight-Firm Concentration Ratios. These ratios are shown in Figure 13-2. The **four-firm concentration ratio** measures the percentage of an industry's output produced by its four largest firms, whereas the eight-firm ratio measures the percentage of output produced by its eight largest firms. This figure shows that some industries such as autos are dominated by large firms, whereas others such as commercial printing are not.

The Herfindahl-Hirschman Index. The Herfindahl-Hirschman Index (HHI) is a somewhat more complicated way of measuring the concentration of an industry. To understand it, first consider a monopoly—an industry with the maximum possible degree of concentration. One firm has 100% of the market share. To calculate the HHI, this percentage is squared:

$(100)^2 = 10{,}000$, the largest value the index can take

Formally, the Herfindahl-Hirschman Index is constructed by squaring the percentage market share of each firm, and then adding up these numbers. To illustrate further, consider a nearly monopolized industry. One firm has 90% of the market share of the industry, and the only other firm has 10%. In this case, the HHI becomes

$$90^2 + 10^2 = 8{,}200, \text{ still a very high value}$$

Notice that the value of the HHI decreases as the number of firms in the industry increases.

Next, suppose that there are again two firms in the industry, but the first one no longer dominates. Instead, both produce the same amount; their market share is 50% each. When percentage shares are again squared, the HHI becomes

$$50^2 + 50^2 = 5{,}000$$

Thus the HHI also falls as the market shares of the firms become more equal.

Finally, note that, in a perfectly competitive market with 100 firms, each making 1% of total sales, the HHI would be much smaller:

$$1^2 + 1^2 + 1^2 \text{------} + 1^2 = 100$$

The HHI does a good job of taking into account the number of firms in an industry and the degree of equality in their market shares—two

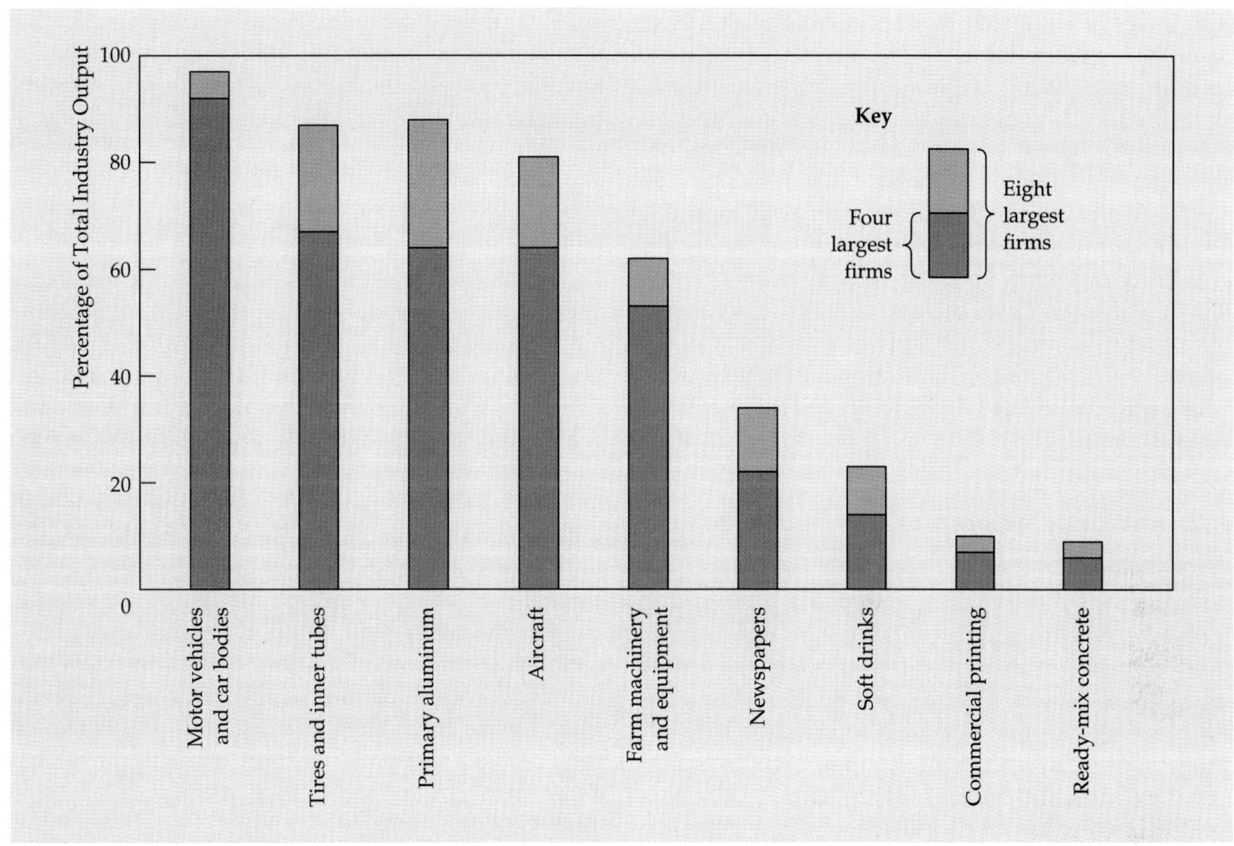

FIGURE 13-2 Concentration ratios showing the importance of the "big four" and "big eight" in selected industries, 1982.

(*Source:* Bureau of the Census, U.S. Department of Commerce, *1986 Census of Manufacturers, Concentration Ratios in Manufacturing,* April 1986.)

important characteristics in any evaluation of the concentration of an industry. Moreover, because this index is based on the shares of *all* firms, it is superior to the four-firm (or eight-firm) concentration ratio, which takes into account only the four (or eight) largest firms. Therefore the HHI is the index that the Justice Department uses in deciding whether an industry is highly concentrated.

Has concentration been increasing or decreasing over time? The answer is: increasing for some industries, decreasing for others. If we look at the *average* for all industries, however, we see little evidence of any dramatic increase or decrease over time. In the words of MIT's Morris Adelman, any change that has occurred seems to have been "at the speed of a glacial drift." For example, over the long period from 1947 to 1972, the four-firm concentration ratio for 167 U.S. manufacturing industries rose, on average, from 41% to 43%. There seems to have been no strong tendency, over the economy as a whole, for large firms to increase their dominance.

Indeed, more recently, the overall competitiveness of the U.S. economy seems to have been getting somewhat greater because of (a) the rise of new industries such as microcomputers, with many small, highly competitive firms; (b) the increasing importance of service industries, where firms are often small; and (c) greater competition from imports. For example, import competition has made the U.S. auto industry more competitive than the high concentration ratio for the domestic industry in Figure 13-2 suggests. Failure to take imports into account limits the validity of any measure of concentration based on domestic output.

The United States is not becoming an increasingly monopolized economy, with oligopoly merely a temporary stop on an inevitable road to monopoly. This then raises the question: Why do a few firms grow so large, while none goes all the way to become a monopolist? In other words, why are there typically several firms in an industry rather than just one?

NATURAL OLIGOPOLY: THE IMPORTANCE OF COST CONDITIONS

Costs are one reason why there may be a few firms in an industry. In many industries, there are economies of scale, with average cost declining as output increases. A plant designed to produce 100,000 cars per year can operate at a much lower average cost than a plant designed to produce 10,000. But costs do not continue to fall forever. If a plant is producing 500,000 units, doubling its output won't significantly reduce costs further. When costs cease to fall, firms no longer have a cost incentive to continue to grow into a monopoly position.

The result is **natural oligopoly.** Panel *b* of Figure 13-3 illustrates how this market form falls somewhere between the extremes of perfect competition and natural monopoly. Note that average costs for an individual firm continue to fall over a considerable range, up to an output of 300 units. (Compare this to perfect competition in panel *a*, where costs stop falling at an output of 10 units.) If existing firms in panel *b* are producing less than 300 units, they have an incentive to expand. However, at an output of 300 units—still far short of satisfying total market demand of 1,000 units—costs stop falling. At this point, existing firms no longer reap a cost advantage by expanding further.

> ***Natural oligopoly*** occurs when the average costs of individual firms fall over a large enough range so that a few firms can produce the total quantity sold at the lowest average cost.

It is not just cost conditions that account for the persistence of oligopoly. Oligopoly represents a balance between the forces that encourage concentration and those that work against it.

OTHER INFLUENCES IN OLIGOPOLISTIC MARKETS

One of the strongest forces working toward larger and larger corporations is the incentive such firms have to acquire market power. The larger a firm becomes by internal growth or by buying its competitors—or by driving them out of business—the greater its power to set price. For this reason, a firm in natural oligopoly, with no further opportunities to cut costs by expanding, may nonetheless still seek to expand in order to push competitors out of the market and thus acquire more power to raise price.

On the other side, the government provides a countervailing force that discourages the development of highly concentrated industries. Specifically, the desire to protect consumers and competitors has led Congress to pass antitrust laws that deter firms from establishing monopoly or near-monopoly positions.

Moreover, product differentiation in many oligopolistic markets also discourages monopolization. For example, Unysis builds computers that are similar but not identical to giant IBM's. McDonnell-Douglas builds planes that are similar but not identical to those of Boeing. By searching for market niches, smaller firms can survive.

Thus oligopoly is often a stable market form because government antitrust policy and product differentiation prevent large firms from driving out their rivals. But what prevents oligopoly from drifting in the other direction, toward more competition, with a large number of new firms entering the market? The answer is that there are often substantial barriers to the entry of new firms.

BARRIERS TO ENTRY

The economies of scale that make an industry a natural oligopoly act as an important barrier to the entry of new firms. For example, in the natural oligopoly shown in Figure 13-3*b*, there are three large firms, each producing 300 units of output.

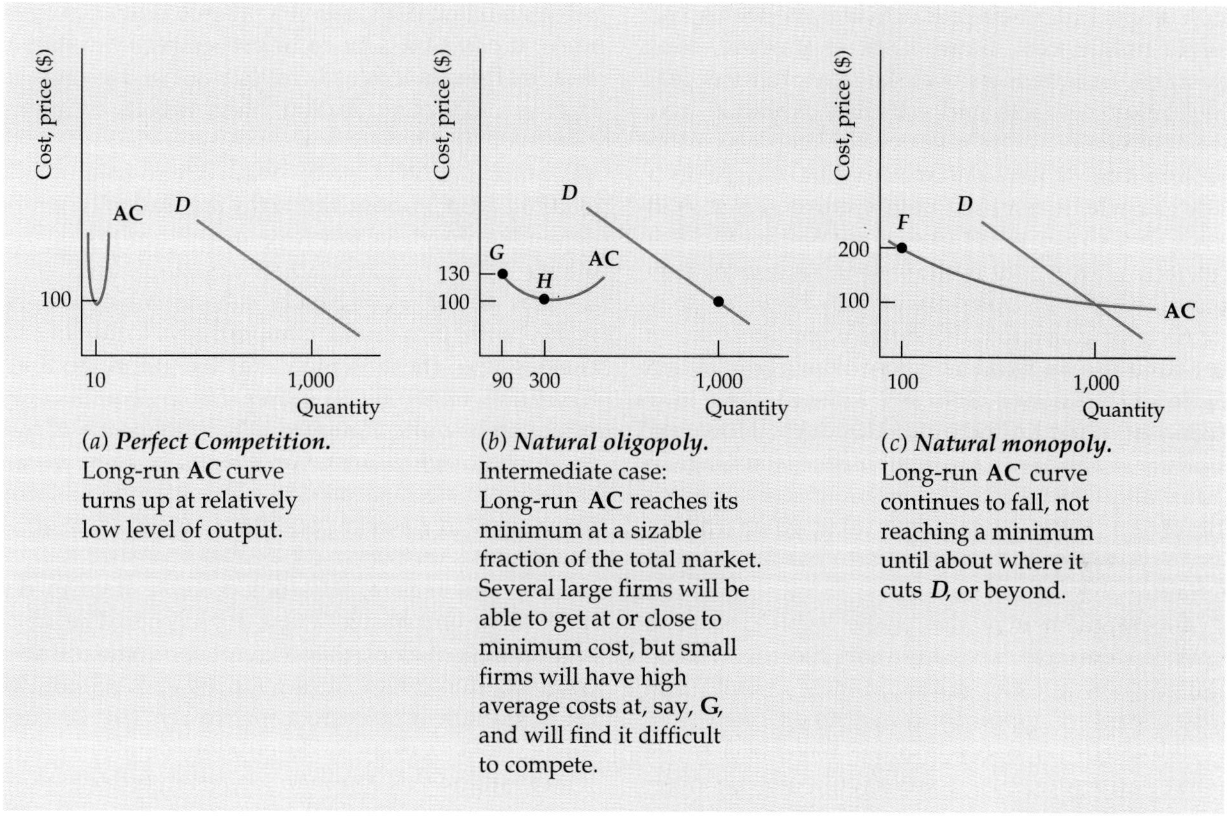

FIGURE 13-3 Natural oligopoly compared with perfect competition and natural monopoly.

Each has far lower costs of $100 per unit than a new, smaller firm producing 90 units of output, with costs at $130 a unit. Because of this difference in costs, it will be easy for existing high-volume producers to undercut the price of a new entrant that is starting up at low volume and higher costs. Therefore new firms may have to enter the industry on a grand scale. It is important for them to have the financial resources—the "deep pockets"—necessary to set up a productive facility large enough to move them quickly into the high-volume, low-cost range of production. For this reason, new competition in oligopolistic markets often comes not only from struggling new firms, but also from giants in other industries. For example, Xerox was faced with new competition when IBM, Kodak, and several Japanese firms entered the market for office copiers.

There are other barriers to entry. For example, it is often very difficult for a new firm to compete with existing firms that produce "name-brand" products that have been widely advertised and accepted by the public in the past.[1] To illustrate, anyone thinking of producing a new type of washing machine must recognize that one problem in entering such an industry will be overcoming the public's acceptance of such brand names as Maytag.

New producers of items such as breakfast foods, soft drinks, or cosmetics may also encounter

[1]In "Industrial Economics: An Overview," *Economic Journal*, September 1988, p. 669, MIT's Richard Schmalensee cites evidence that the more heavily an industry advertises, the more difficult it is for new firms to enter. This article summarizes much of the recent research on the topics covered in this chapter and the next.

difficulty getting their products into the stores and before public view. Stores tend to provide more favorable treatment for well-known products that they know will sell, and established brands may provide retailers with incentives to keep new competitors out. A new entrant may be caught in a vicious circle. It can't sell unless stores give it shelf space, but stores won't give it shelf space until it can prove it can sell. A similar problem faces new manufacturers of microcomputers. How do they get their products into the stores when most stores can comfortably stock no more than eight or ten models? One option is to sell through their own stores, as Tandy (Radio Shack) does. However, Tandy was already in the retail business, selling CB radios and other electronics before it developed its computers. Setting up a new retail chain can be very expensive, and this presents a barrier to small entrants.

Government may also create legal barriers to entry. For example, for many years the government limited entry into the airline business, thereby creating a stable oligopoly for the existing firms.

Although oligopoly is often a stable form of market structure, this point should not be overstated. In the rapidly changing U.S. economy, there are many exceptions. On the one hand, some industries are becoming less concentrated. For example, new "mini-mills" are providing competition to established steel producers, as technological changes have reduced the importance of economies of scale in steel. On the other hand, some other industries have drifted toward a more concentrated form of oligopoly. One illustration is the farm machinery industry, where the four-firm concentration ratio rose from 26 to 53 between 1947 and 1982.

THE OLIGOPOLIST AS A PRICE SEARCHER

Prices are determined quite differently in perfect competition, monopoly, and oligopoly. In perfect competition, price is determined by the impersonal forces of demand and supply. Each firm is a **price taker;** it has no influence over price. In monopoly, the firm is a **price maker.** It is able to choose the price at which it will sell by selecting a point on the market demand curve. In oligopoly, the firm is a **price searcher.** Although it has some influence over price, it can't set a price in the simple way that a monopolist can. Instead, in its pricing decisions it faces a major complication: How will its competitors react? If it reduces price, will they follow? Will its action set off a price war? Where might this lead? In an oligopoly, the firms are mutually interdependent; each is sensitive to the actions of the others.

The world of oligopoly can resemble a chess game, with move and countermove. And, like a chess game, the outcome may be unpredictable. Often the oligopolists' search for an equilibrium price can be quite complex. Oligopoly is one of the most challenging areas of economic theory, because it can't be analyzed using simple models like those used to describe perfect competition or monopoly.

For this reason, it is not possible here to do more than emphasize a few highlights. The next section describes oligopolists who recognize their common interest in raising prices and collude to act as though they were a monopoly. This discussion is followed by a description of oligopolists who abandon this common interest in order to pursue their own individual interests. As a result, the collusive arrangement comes apart.

COLLUSION

In the United States, an agreement to fix prices is against the law. To see why, let's look at the economic effects of a cartel, the most formal type of collusion.

> A ***cartel*** is a formal agreement among firms to set price and share the market.

As a simple example, consider a hypothetical market in which there are three similar firms. Suppose that, while maintaining their separate corporate identities with their own plants and sales forces, they get together to agree on a common price. In their collective interest, what is the best price? The answer: the price that a monopolist would pick—that is, the price that maximizes their combined profits. This price is determined in Figure 13-4 as follows. The three arrows in panel *a* show how the marginal cost curves of the three

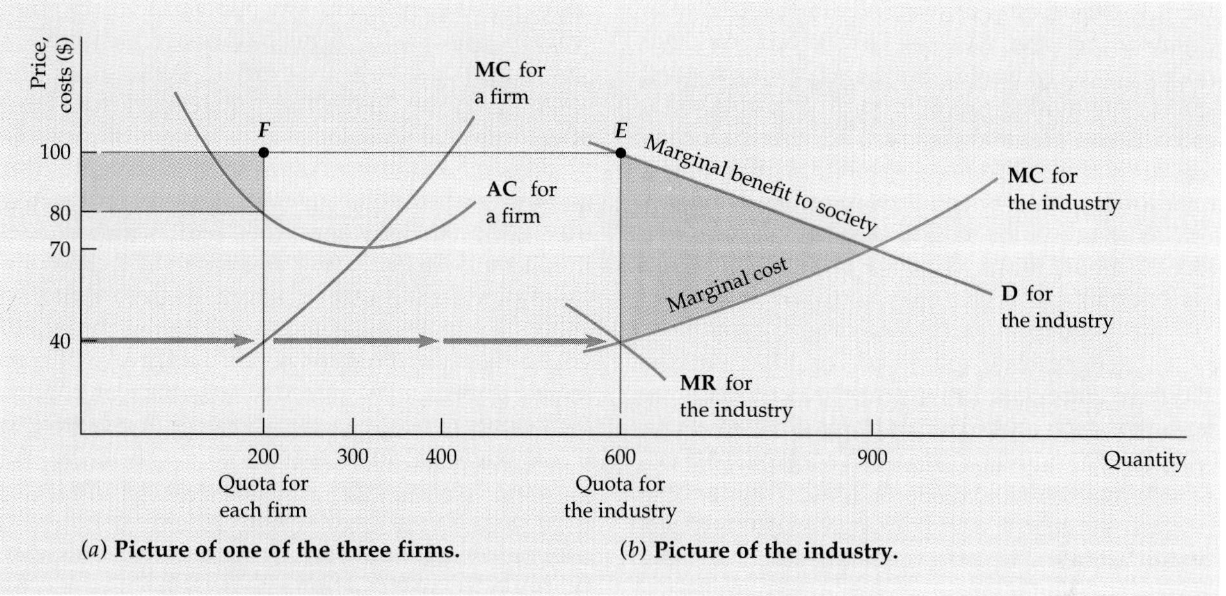

FIGURE 13-4 Collusion by three oligopolists.

In panel *b*, MC for the industry is shown as the horizontal sum of the MC curves for the three individual firms on the left, and MR for the industry is calculated from the industry's demand *D*. The maximization of industry profit requires that output be 600 units, where the industry's MC = MR, and that price be $100. Each of the three firms is therefore allowed a quota of 200 units in panel *a*, where it earns the blue profit area. This arrangement may come apart if individual firms facing the $100 price cannot resist the temptation to cheat by selling more than their 200-unit quota. (Each firm can sell an additional unit for $100, whereas its cost of producing it is only $40.)

individual firms are added horizontally to create MC, the marginal cost curve of the industry in panel *b*. The highest profit for the industry is earned at an output of 600 units, where the industry's MC curve cuts its marginal revenue curve MR. (MR may be calculated from the demand curve for the industry, just as it was for the monopoly in Chapter 12). Point *E* on the demand curve shows that the profit-maximizing output of 600 units can be sold at a price of $100.

Thus the collusive oligopoly can maximize profits by behaving as if it were a monopoly. However, it faces a problem which the monopolist doesn't have to worry about: How is the restricted production of 600 units to be divided among the three firms? The simplest solution is to set a quota of 200 units for each, as shown in panel *a*. Each firm sells at point *F*, where it makes a profit of $4,000, illustrated by the blue area. That is, it sells 200 units at a profit of $20 each, the difference between the selling price of $100 and the average cost of $80.

Although this collusive arrangement benefits the three firms, it is harmful to the economy as a whole. Just as in the case of monopoly, too little is produced, as shown in panel *b*. For an efficient allocation of resources, output should not be 600 units. Instead it should be 900, where the marginal cost to society equals the marginal benefit to society—that is, where the industry's marginal cost curve intersects the demand curve. The red triangle shows the efficiency loss that occurs because collusion, like monopoly, results in too little output. In a cartel, Adam Smith's "invisible hand" fails, as Smith himself recognized in the quotation at the beginning of this chapter.

Participants in a cartel can agree to limit sales in a number of ways, in addition to the equal division just described. For example, in the 1930s, an agreement between General Electric and Westinghouse effectively limited Westinghouse to a small share of the market for light bulbs. (Westinghouse agreed to pay General Electric a 2% royalty for the right to produce GE's improved light bulb, provided Westinghouse confined itself to selling only one-third as many bulbs as GE. If Westinghouse sold more, it would have to pay a prohibitively high royalty of 30%.) Another way to divide the market is to use historical market shares—or, even more simply, geographical areas. For example, in the 1920s two European firms agreed to carve up the market for explosives. Dynamit was allowed exclusive rights in certain continental European markets, in exchange for leaving British Empire markets to Nobel—the same Nobel who became famous for the peace prize.

THE BREAKDOWN OF COLLUSION: THE INCENTIVE TO CHEAT

Market-sharing arrangements tend to be unstable, whether or not the firms have agreed on equal shares. Each firm in the cartel has an incentive to cheat by producing more than its allotted share. Incidentally, although this is "cheating" as viewed by the other members of the cartel, it is still in the public interest, since more production moves the industry to a larger, more efficient output.

To see why firms cheat, note in panel *a* of Figure 13-4 that an individual firm producing 200 units of output could produce another unit at a marginal cost of only $40. If it could sell this unit for the going price of $100 by stealing away a sale from one of its competitors, the firm's profit would increase by $60. Thus it has an incentive to step up sales efforts or to give secret price rebates in order to win customers. Even if a firm grants a 30%, 40%, or even 50% rebate on the selling price of $100, it will still receive more from this sale than its marginal cost.

Thus a cartel has the following problem. The members have a *collective* interest in restricting sales in order to keep the price up. However, each member has an *individual* interest in selling more than its allotted share. If individual interests come to dominate, with firms producing beyond their quotas, industry output in panel *b* will increase beyond 600 units, and there will be a move down the demand curve from *E* to a lower price. In other words, a struggle by firms to increase their market share may destroy the cartel. Because of the strength of the individual interest, cartels have often collapsed after short and stormy histories.

When a cartel breaks down, the struggle over markets may become intense. This is particularly true if the cost advantages of large-scale production have been increasing as a result of technological change. In this case, a natural oligopoly may be evolving into a natural monopoly. In the absence of government intervention, only one firm will ultimately survive. The question is, which one? Each firm wants to be the victor; each has an incentive to try to gain an advantage over its rivals by expanding rapidly to gain the lower costs from large-scale production. Excess production is likely, with firms pushing frantically for sales. The result may be **cutthroat competition**—that is, sales at a price below cost in order to drive rivals out of business. During **price wars,** the prize sometimes goes to the firm with the "deepest pockets" (the largest financial resources), which enable it to sustain heavy short-term losses while it is cutting the throats of its rivals.

LIVING IN A GLOBAL ECONOMY

THE OPEC STORY OF COLLUSION AND CHEATING

The most conspicuous collusive arrangement of recent decades has been the Organization of Petroleum Exporting Countries (OPEC), a loose but initially effective price-fixing association of many of the major oil exporters, including a number of Middle Eastern nations, Indonesia, Nigeria, and Venezuela. The prime objective of OPEC was to raise the price of oil, and in less than a decade—between 1973 and 1982—the price rose from $3 a barrel to $34, as shown in Figure 13-5. The result was far and away the greatest peacetime transfer among nations in history as the OPEC countries gained income at the expense of oil-importing countries. Why was OPEC this successful in the 1970s? And why was it far less successful in the 1980s, when the price of oil fell, at one point dropping below $10?

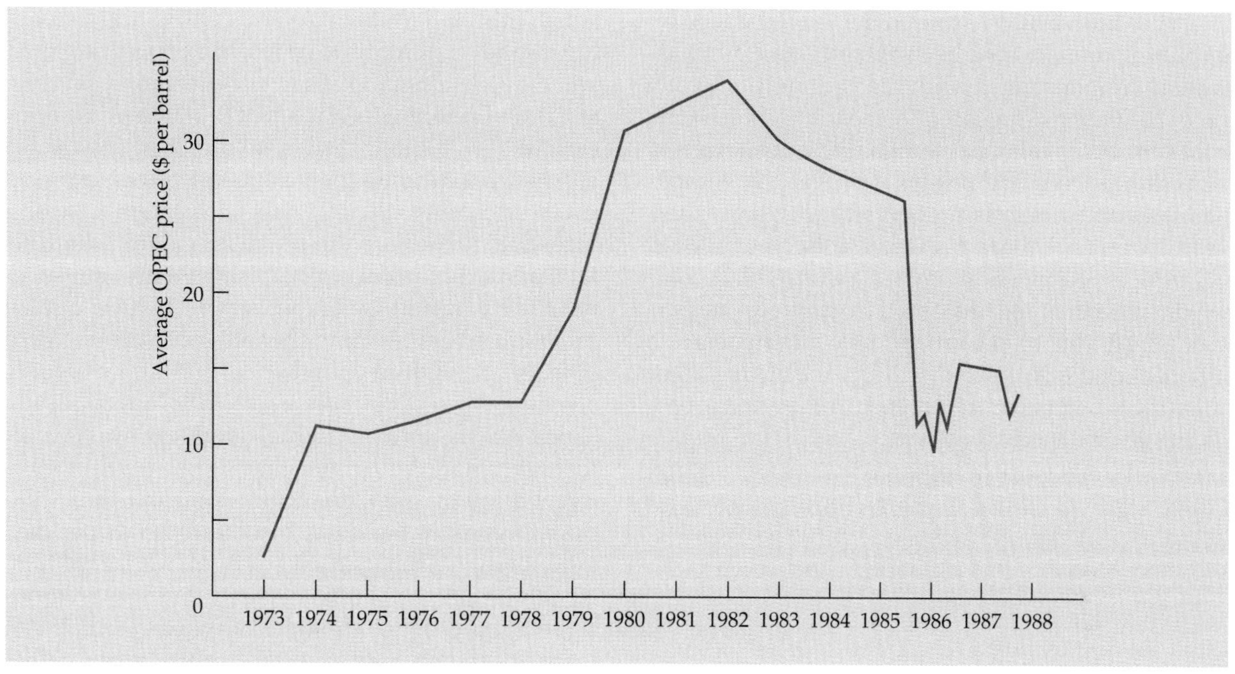

FIGURE 13-5 Oil price on world markets.

There have been two periods of very rapid increases in the price of oil—1973 to 1974 and 1979 to 1980. By the early 1980s, the dollar price of oil had started to decline, and by 1986 it temporarily fell below $10.

THE 1970s WHEN EVERYTHING WENT RIGHT FOR OPEC

OPEC's early success was surprising because, during the 1970s, it did not enforce the formal production quotas on its members that a cartel typically requires to maintain high price. Instead, its success in raising and maintaining price was due to a number of very favorable special conditions.

1. During the 1970s, the United States and a number of other oil-importing countries imposed controls that kept their domestic prices below the high world price that OPEC was setting. Thus U.S. consumers were saved from having to pay the full OPEC price. But precisely because they didn't have to pay this high price, they did not cut back their purchases as much as they would have otherwise. In other words, energy policies in the United States and elsewhere made the demand for OPEC oil less elastic—that is, less sensitive to an increase in price. This meant that as OPEC raised its price, it did not suffer a big loss in sales.

2. At the same time, the demand for OPEC oil by all countries was expanding. That is, the demand curve facing OPEC was shifting to the right. A dramatic example occurred during the Iranian revolution in 1979, when oil users made large purchases to increase their inventories in order to insure themselves against a future disruption in supply.

3. Because demand was inelastic and shifting to the right, OPEC was under very little pressure to enforce production quotas during the 1970s. Nevertheless, for noneconomic reasons, the Arab countries put an embargo on sales to the United States and other countries supporting Israel in the 1973 Yom Kippur War. As a result, OPEC's oil exports fell by about 25%. This helped make OPEC's 1973 price increase stick.

4. OPEC was further able to control oil sales because of the practices of the large international oil companies. They acted as market-stabilizing agents for OPEC, by lifting and selling only the amount of oil that could be sold at the high OPEC price.

Why didn't those companies such as Exxon encourage price cutting by switching their purchases away from a country with the high official OPEC price to a country prepared to cheat by lowering its price? (Some of this did happen, but not enough to break the price.) One reason was that the companies wanted to maintain good relations with their OPEC suppliers in order to ensure that they would still be able to buy oil in any future crisis. A second reason was that the major oil companies had no strong incentive to encourage price cutting, since a higher world price set by OPEC meant a higher price for the companies on the oil they were producing within the United States.

5. As the dominant supplier in OPEC, Saudi Arabia was prepared to maintain the high price by taking special actions.

THE KEY ROLE OF THE SAUDIS

Whenever it appeared that a substantial oversupply was developing on the world oil market, Saudi Arabia would reduce its own production. Thus the Saudis acted as a "residual supplier," satisfying only the demand that was left unsatisfied by other OPEC suppliers. This Saudi limitation of supply kept the price from falling. (The appendix to this chapter provides a more formal analysis of a market dominated by a residual supplier large enough to maintain price.) Thus during the 1970s, OPEC had one of the characteristics of a cartel: it set price. But it was not a cartel in the sense of enforcing formal production quotas to limit the sales of each member country. Instead, several factors kept price up by keeping production from exceeding demand. One such factor was the willingness of the Saudis to eliminate any excess production by cutting back on their own output. For this reason, some experts downplay OPEC in the 1970s as a traditional cartel and instead emphasize the leadership role played by the Saudis.

FALLING PRICE IN THE 1980s: THE ATTEMPT TO ENFORCE PRODUCTION QUOTAS

Because of the high price of oil during the 1970s, it was not surprising that, by the early 1980s, new sources of supply had developed in Mexico, the North Sea, and elsewhere. Thus OPEC was satisfying a smaller proportion of world demand at a time when world demand itself was declining because of (1) a severe recession, and (2) a change in policies in the United States and other importing nations that allowed their domestic prices to rise to the world level, thus giving consumers a strong incentive to reduce oil purchases. With demand falling short of production, OPEC finally moved to restrict its output by enforcing production quotas on its members. At first, this attempt was not very successful, with a number of OPEC members cheating by selling more than their quotas. Thus Saudi Arabia, as the residual producer, was forced to make more and more cuts in its own output. Eventually, by 1986, the Saudis had cut their production back to less than 2 million barrels per day, even though their capacity was about 10 million. At this point, the Saudis decided that it was better to sell more, even though this would break the price. Moreover, they wanted to show other OPEC producers how costly it would be if these other producers did not abide by their quotas. When the Saudis turned up their production and increased their sales, the price fell below $10 a barrel (Fig. 13-5).

The lesson was apparently not lost on other OPEC producers. Subsequent attempts by OPEC to enforce production quotas, while far from completely successful, were at least successful enough in the 1986–1989 period to keep the price of oil above $10, though still far below the $34 price that had once been reached.

This story leaves four major questions outstanding for the future: (1) How successful will OPEC be in enforcing production quotas? (2) How substantial will the supplies of non-OPEC producers be—supplies that reduce OPEC's dominant role in the world oil market and hence reduce OPEC's ability to hold price up? (3) Will OPEC be able to draw non-OPEC producers—such as Mexico—into its output and price-fixing decisions? (4) Will world demand for oil increase enough to absorb the oil production of OPEC and non-OPEC nations? If this happens, then OPEC will no longer have to restrict its supply in order to keep price up; a cartel will no longer be necessary.

In short, by 1988, OPEC had become a classic example of the three difficult problems a cartel faces. It needs to (1) set a production quota for each member; (2) ensure that each member abides by its quota; and (3) prevent outside producers from expanding production and undercutting the cartel's price.

WHERE CARTELS ARE ILLEGAL, HOW DO OLIGOPOLISTS DETERMINE PRICE?

The OPEC story illustrates how oligopolists can try to avoid price wars by forming a cartel and agreeing on price and market shares. For the OPEC countries, this story has been one of failure as much as success. But oligopolistic firms within the United States, or within many other countries, have an additional problem: such collusion is illegal. Producers may not even be able to discuss prices with their competitors without risking a jail sentence. How, then, do oligopolists reduce the pressure of price competition? How do they avoid price wars and arrive at a reasonably profitable price?

A large number of answers to this question are possible. Indeed, this is what makes oligopoly more complicated and challenging than perfect competition or monopoly. The first possible explanation is that each firm faces a "kinked demand curve." Although this concept is controversial, it provides important insights into how each oligopolist must take the others' responses into account.

THE KINKED DEMAND CURVE

The best way to understand this idea is to put yourself in the position of one of the three large oligopolists in an industry. Suppose that, in assessing how your competitors will react if you change your price, you expect the worst. Then:

1. If you cut your price, competing firms will take this as a challenge. They will not want you to take customers away from them; therefore, they will meet your price cut with a price cut of their own. As a result, you cannot hope to capture a larger share of the market by cutting your price.

2. On the other hand, if you raise your price, your competitors will consider this move a golden opportunity. By keeping their own selling price stable, they will be able to capture a share of your sales.

In short, your competitors behave in a nonsymmetrical way: If you drop your price they will follow you, but if you raise your price they will not.

Figure 13-6 shows how this behavior leads to a kinked demand curve and to price stability. Panel *a* illustrates an industry with three firms of similar size. Each initially has one-third of total sales, with point E_1 showing the initial price and sales of your firm. If you changed price and *if* your competitors were to follow, you would retain your present one-third of the market. Thus you would move along the relatively steep demand curve d_f. (At any price, say P_2, the quantity you would sell on d_f would be one-third of the total industry demand D.)

However, d_f is relevant only if you quote a price *below* the existing price at E_1. If you quote a price *above* this—say P_3—your competitors will *not* follow. Instead, they will stand pat. Because you will now be quoting a higher price than they are, you will lose part of your market to them, as shown by the red arrow *b*.

Therefore if you drop your price below E_1, you face demand d_f; if you raise your price above E_1, you face demand d_n. In other words, the behavior of your competitors presents you with the kinked demand curve shown by the heavy lines.

> The ***kinked demand curve*** shown by the heavy lines in Figure 13-6 is the demand the oligopolistic firm faces *if its competitors follow its price down but not up.*

Faced with this demand curve, how do you maximize profit? The likely answer: Stay at point E_1, where the kink occurs. Thus, you sell Q_1 at the prevailing market price P_1; this maximizes your shaded profit area. By experimenting, you can see that the shaded profit area shrinks if you move either to the left or right of Q_1.

Panel *b* confirms that Q_1 is the profit-maximizing output. This diagram shows the firm's marginal cost curve MC, and its kinked demand curve reproduced from panel *a*. What is MR when the demand curve is kinked? If you start at point *A* and move down the demand curve from *A* to E_1, your corresponding marginal revenue curve is *AF*. But once you get to the kink E_1, you move down the demand curve d_f, with the corresponding marginal revenue curve now being MR_f. Thus the marginal revenue curve is the solid line traced by

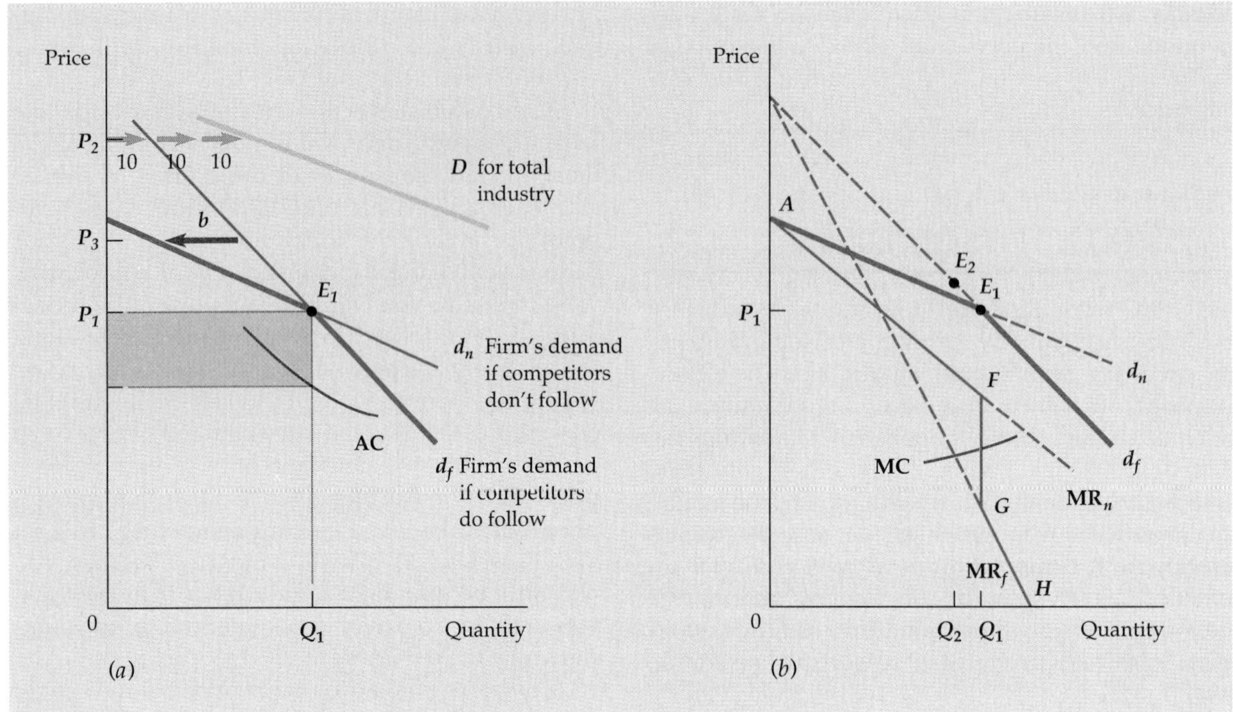

FIGURE 13-6 Stable price and quantity for an oligopolist with a kinked demand curve.

Panel *a*. Suppose you are one of three equally large competitors and your initial position is at E_1. If your competitors were to follow any price change you might make, you would face demand curve d_f. Regardless of the price you might quote, you would retain one-third of the market. But since your competitors will follow you only if you *reduce* price, d_f is relevant only in the heavily lined section below E_1. If you raise price, your competitors will *not* follow and thus will cut into your market share, as shown by the red arrow. Therefore above E_1 you will face demand curve d_n. In short, if your competitors follow your price down but not up, you face the heavy kinked demand curve. In the case shown, you maximize shaded profit by selecting the kink point E_1, selling Q_1 at the prevailing price P_1.

Panel *b*. The heavy kinked demand curve that you face is reproduced from panel *a*. For quantities less than Q_1, the demand curve is AE_1, and the corresponding MR is *AF*. For quantities greater than Q_1, the demand curve is E_1d_f with *GH* being the corresponding MR. Thus MR is *AFGH* which intersects MC at quantity Q_1, with the firm accordingly charging price P_1. Moreover, the firm's quantity and price won't change, even if marginal cost rises all the way up to F or falls all the way down to G.

AF, followed by a sharp drop to *G* and then *GH*. This marginal revenue curve intersects MC at quantity Q_1, the profit-maximizing output already identified in panel *a*. It is now clear why output and price are stable. If marginal cost MC shifts anywhere up to *F*, or shifts anywhere down to *G*, MC and MR will still intersect in the range *FG*. Output will remain at Q_1 and price at P_1, even though there has been a large change in costs.

The idea of a kinked demand curve was first developed in the 1930s. It has had continuing appeal as a way of explaining why oligopoly prices are stable, and in particular, why they often remain firm during recessions when demand declines.

Nevertheless, there are important exceptions. For example, during the severe recessions of 1974 and 1982, auto manufacturers offered rebates—in effect, price reductions—in order to increase their lagging sales. Perhaps they made this offer because they were no longer strong oligopolists. Because of intense competition from imported cars, the big three no longer dominated the market so completely.

The theory of the kinked demand curve is controversial. In the first place, it assumes that the oligopolistic firm knows how its competitors will react if it changes its price. (They will follow its price down but not up.) But often the firm doesn't know this, and has the difficult task of trying to predict its rivals' reactions. This task can't be avoided. If the firm can't make at least an educated guess as to how its competitors will react, it doesn't know what sort of demand and marginal revenue curves it faces. Consequently, it will not be able to maximize its profits.

The second problem with the kinked demand curve is that the theory is incomplete. Although it may explain price stability, it does not explain how price is established in the first place. For example, in Figure 13-6, price remains at P_1 because it started out at P_1 and that is where the kink occurs. But how did price get to be P_1 in the first place? It has no explanation, like the "smile without the cat" in Alice in Wonderland.

The third difficulty with the kinked demand curve is that prices are not nearly as rigid as the theory suggests. As already noted, automobile prices have occasionally fallen, and frequently they have risen. Over the years, the prices of large mainframe computers have been cut many times, even though a few producers dominate the market.

Thus the theory of the kinked demand curve explains too much; it explains something (price stability) that frequently does not exist. Rather than try to explain why oligopoly prices are stable—when often they are not—it makes more sense to ask why oligopoly prices change in a reasonably orderly way. One answer is provided by the theory of price leadership.

PRICE LEADERSHIP

Although overt price collusion is against the law in the United States, firms may be able to change price in an orderly way if one firm takes the initiative and the others follow.

To illustrate price leadership, suppose that you are the price leader in the sense that you are confident that if you change your price, your competitors will follow. Then the demand curve you face is no longer kinked. Instead, in Figure 13-6*b* it is the line d_f *throughout its entire length* because your competitors will follow any price change you may make, either down or up. Moreover, your marginal revenue curve will be the corresponding MR_f, also throughout its entire length. In these circumstances, you will reduce output to Q_2, where $MC = MR_f$, and lead the industry up to a new, higher price at E_2—provided you are correct and the other firms do indeed follow your lead.

If your leadership is assured, the result may approach that of a cartel. As leader, you will select the price at point E_2 at the output where $MC = MR_f$, and your profits are thus maximized. This price should be approximately the one that will maximize profits for the industry as a whole. This is why the other firms may be willing to accept your leadership. The outcome at E_2 is the same monopoly-like solution that would result from collusion. Therefore, although collusion does not formally exist, the result may be similar. Firms arrive at the profit-maximizing price, not by illegally agreeing on it beforehand, but by simply following the leader. This is sometimes called *tacit collusion.*

However, because there is no formal agreement, others may not follow your leadership after all; the problem of "cheating" may be substantial. The leader may find others shaving prices—or providing rebates—in order to increase their market shares. For example, during the first half of this century, giant U.S. Steel sometimes acted as price leader and did not react to under-the-table price cuts by smaller firms. It was better to ignore them than to retaliate and risk leading the whole industry, including U.S. Steel's largest rivals, into a round of price cutting. Consequently, the smaller firms were able to take advantage of U.S. Steel's price umbrella to cut into its markets. In 1910, U.S. Steel held almost half the market, but by the 1950s, its share had fallen to one-third. Thus all the advantages in an industry need not go to the giant. Smaller firms may have a major advantage since they may be able to compete aggressively without provoking competitive responses from the giant.

In practice, it may be quite difficult to identify

any clear pattern of price leadership. There may be no firm that acts consistently as leader; first one company may take the initiative in changing prices and then another. General Motors does not always announce its new model prices first; the initiative is sometimes exercised by Ford. Furthermore, price leadership may be quite tentative. One firm may announce a price increase to see if others follow. If they don't, the price change may be rescinded. This sort of "trial and error" pricing may just be a firm's way of testing whether or not it can in fact act as a price leader.

Finally, even when oligopolists follow a pattern of price leadership, we cannot be certain that they are exerting monopoly power. If costs have generally risen by, say, 10%, an oligopolist may raise price by about 10% in the expectation that others will follow. Price leadership has apparently occurred. Yet the firms may merely be responding to rising costs, rather than exploiting monopoly power at the expense of the public.

FOCAL POINT PRICING

Harvard's Thomas Schelling gives the following noneconomic example to illustrate how independent firms may end up quoting the same price even though there is no price leadership, or any collusion, or even any preexisting price:

> You are to meet someone in New York City. You have not been instructed where to meet; you have no prior understanding with the person on where to meet; and you cannot communicate with each other. You are simply told that you will have to guess where to meet and he is being told the same thing and that you will just have to try to make your guesses coincide. You are told the date but not the hour of this meeting; the two of you must guess the exact minute of the date for the meeting. At what time will you appear at the chosen meeting place?[2]

Of the thousands of possible choices, Schelling discovered that most people selected high noon at the information booth at Grand Central Station. Both are "focal points" because they provide the best guess of what the other person will do. So too with price. A retailer who wants to guess the price that competitors will charge for a new product in the range of, say, \$11.20 to \$12.40 may well select the focal point \$11.98. This price is based on the familiar tradition of "charging \$12 but making it seem like \$11." Thus without any communication whatsoever between firms, this focal point of \$11.98 may become the industry price.

[2]Thomas C. Schelling, *The Strategy of Conflict* (Cambridge, Mass.: Harvard University Press, 1960), p. 56.

COST-PLUS PRICING

Under cost-plus pricing, a firm determines its price by adding a specified markup of, say, 20% to its average cost. Economists have been uncomfortable with this idea because it raises two nagging questions: (1) Why does the firm pick 20% rather than some other figure? (2) Since average cost AC changes with output, how does the firm know its average cost without first knowing its output? In practice, firms may solve this problem by arbitrarily specifying a target output of, say, 85% of capacity. Then their average cost is determined by the height of the AC curve at this specified output. Finally, by adding on their fixed percentage markup, they arrive at a price.

This approach presumes that a firm that prices in this way will be able to sell roughly its target quantity, using the target markup. However, if it is under pressure from price-cutting competitors, it may have little hope of doing so. To prevent its sales from falling, it may have to reduce its markup. Although such a firm may view itself as engaged in fixed-markup (cost-plus) pricing, it may in fact not be doing this. Instead, it may only start with cost-plus as a rule of thumb and may then adjust its price in response to market pressures like any other profit-maximizing firm. Its markup may not be a fixed percentage at all.

NONPRICE COMPETITION

Price is not the only dimension in which oligopolistic firms compete. They also compete in other ways, such as better service, research and development, or advertising. These forms of nonprice competition are often preferred to price competition because there is less risk of starting a price war in which all participants lose. Indeed, firms often compete vigorously in these nonprice dimensions;

there is little evidence that they collude to reduce these expenditures.

ADVERTISING

The firm that advertises has a simple objective: to make people want more of its product. That does not mean, however, that the more advertising the better. Since advertising must be paid for, it also shifts the cost curve up. At some point, the firm will find that enough advertising is enough. Any more advertising will involve a further cost that can no longer be justified by increased sales.

In an oligopoly, an important goal of advertising is to capture the competitor's market. Thus, for example, the primary objective of Ford's advertising is to take sales away from General Motors and other auto companies. For its part, General Motors advertises to take sales away from Ford and the Japanese.

Advertising also increases the total market demand for the product. A monopolistic firm will sometimes advertise, not to take sales away from competitors (since it has none), but instead to increase the demand for its product. For example, AT&T advertised its long-distance phone service, even when it still had a monopoly. Some associations of perfect competitors also advertise to increase total market demand, even though no single producer would find it profitable to do so. For example, milk producers' associations sometimes advertise to encourage people to drink milk.

Although monopolists or perfect competitors may occasionally advertise, the most heavily advertised products lie in the battleground in between—that is, in monopolistic competition, and to an even greater degree in oligopoly. For example, a firm like General Motors may benefit from advertising because it increases the total demand for automobiles—but even more important, because it takes sales away from its rivals.

Is advertising beneficial from the point of view of society as a whole? This is a controversial question. On behalf of their industry, advertising agencies make the following points:

1. Advertising helps the consumer to make better decisions. It informs the public of new products and of improvements in old ones. By informing consumers of what is available, it reduces search costs. For example, advertising may tell consumers where the bargains are, so they can save time and effort in shopping.

2. Advertising helps new producers to compete. By informing the public of a new product, it helps the producer to expand sales and may thereby lower costs.

3. Advertising supports the communications industry. Radio and television are financed by advertising revenues. If we didn't pay for our entertainment this way, we would have to pay for it in some other way. Even the mundane classified ads play a significant role in the support of newspapers.

4. Advertising results in higher quality products. The goodwill built up from past advertising of a brand name may be an asset of great value for a firm—an asset it will be careful not to damage by turning out a shoddy product.

On the other side, critics respond:

1. Most advertising represents a waste. The heaviest advertising takes place in oligopolistic markets where firm *A's* major motive is to steal customers from firm *B*, and *B* advertises to protect itself from losing sales to *A*. After advertising, *A* and *B* may share the market in roughly the same way as before. Little has changed, except that costs have gone up. Consumers pay more for this product merely because it is advertised. Even if firms recognize the waste, they can't opt out, because they would lose market share to competitors.

2. Where advertising is not a self-canceling waste, it can be pernicious, creating frivolous wants, distorting tastes, and increasing the materialism of a materialistic society. (Recall Galbraith's skepticism of the "creation" of wants in Chapter 4.)

3. Advertising that sells products to some people may be offensive to the vast majority. We cannot listen to radio or television without being bombarded with tasteless ads.

4. Advertising may lead to distorted news coverage. It may be difficult for a newspaper to provide a balanced treatment of a labor dispute if it is getting a great deal of advertising revenue from the firms involved but none from the labor union. (However, if a lot of workers buy the paper, the pressures may even out.)

Because it is difficult to compare these conflicting claims, our conclusion is that the statement that advertising involves "all loss" is too extreme, as is the statement that advertising involves "no loss whatsoever."

OTHER NONPRICE WAYS IN WHICH FIRMS COMPETE

A firm can hire a larger sales staff in order to beat the bushes for customers. Or it can spend more on research, development, or design to improve the quality or attractiveness of its product. The typical oligopolistic firm, such as an auto or appliance company, is locked in a struggle to match its competitors' price, advertising, sales force, service, and improvements in design and quality. Little wonder that the world of the oligopolist seems more competitive than that of the farmer, who may operate in a "perfectly competitive" market but who never even thinks of a neighbor as a competitor. We should remember, however, that according to the economist's definition, farming is the more competitive industry, because a single farmer has no influence whatsoever over price.

DUOPOLY: THE INSIGHTS OF GAME THEORY

This chapter began with a description of monopolistic competition where there are many firms. This was followed by a description of oligopoly where there are only a few. We now continue this pattern of moving toward markets with fewer and fewer firms, and consider **duopoly,** a market with only two firms. This is a special case of oligopoly, in which each firm is concerned with the response of only a single competitor. As a special case of oligopoly, duopoly may sometimes be analyzed using the models developed for oligopoly. For example, duopolists may engage in tacit collusion, perhaps with one of the firms acting as price leader. Or a duopolist may face a kinked demand curve.

Another framework for studying duopoly—and some broader oligopoly problems as well—is the theory of games, developed by mathematician John von Neumann and economist Oscar Morgenstern. While this theory can, as its name suggests, be applied to poker and other games, it also has much more serious applications, for example, in military strategy. Its economic application to duopoly can best be introduced by a noneconomic example that is easy to understand.

THE PRISONERS' DILEMMA

Two thieves, Blake and Reid, have been caught robbing a bank, a crime they have committed many times before. In two separate and isolated jail cells, they are each given a choice: "Each of you can be jailed for two years for the job you were caught doing last night. But if one of you confesses to the whole *series* of robberies, your sentence will be reduced to one year, with your accomplice being put away for 8 years. He is being given the same deal, and the same incentive to confess on you. If you both confess, you both get 5 years. You each have an hour to decide."

In terms of **game theory,** the choices facing each thief are set out in the **payoff matrix** of all possible outcomes in Table 13-2. Each outcome for Reid is shown in red, and each outcome for Blake is shown in blue. It is evident that the best *collective* outcome for both is not to confess (cell I). Each, however, is under great pressure to confess. For example, Reid can see an advantage in confessing no matter what Blake may do. If Blake doesn't confess, then the outcome will be in the top half of this matrix (that is, in cell I or II). In this case Reid's confession would move the outcome from cell I to cell II, thus reducing his sentence from two years to one. On the other hand, if Blake *does* confess— and the outcome is therefore in the lower half of this table—then Reid's confession will move the outcome from cell III to cell IV, reducing his sentence from eight years to five. Thus, Reid is likely to confess. Blake, facing exactly the same choice, is also likely to confess. If both confess, the outcome is in cell IV; both serve five years instead of the two they would have served if they had both held out.

An exception may occur if they have foreseen this problem and have a prearranged agreement not to confess. But this is not enough. Each must trust the other to hold to that agreement regardless of pressure. Thus a key consideration influencing the strategy of each is information, or lack of it, about how the other will ultimately behave (as opposed to just promise) under this sort of duress.

TABLE 13-2 Payoff Matrix in Prisoner's Dilemma

		Reid's choices	
		don't confess	*confess*
Blake's choices	don't confess	I 2 years (Reid) 2 Years (Blake)	II 1 year (Reid) 8 Years (Blake)
	confess	III 8 years (Reid) 1 year (Blake)	IV 5 years (Reid) 5 years (Blake)

DUOPOLY PRICING

A similar dilemma may face two firms, Bluechip and Redpath, selecting their price. The **payoff matrix** shown in Table 13-3 is in fact exactly the same as the payoff matrix in Table 13-2, except that it shows the dollar losses facing two competing duopoly firms in a short-run recession in which there is no hope of either firm making a profit. All that either can do is minimize its loss.

Cell I shows the $2 million loss each will suffer if they both hold their price at the higher $12 level. Cell IV shows the much greater $5 million loss that each will suffer if they both cut their price to $10. The other two cells show the incentive each firm has to cut its price—exactly the same sort of incentive that the two prisoners had to confess. This example shows how, in a duopoly market just as in the oligopoly market studied earlier, it is in the firms' *collective* interest to collude by holding up price, but it is in the *individual* interest of each firm to cut price.

If this "game" is to be played only once, and the two firms do not have an agreement to quote a $12 price (or, even if they do, they can't trust each other), then it is very likely that they will engage in price competition. The equilibrium will be cell IV

TABLE 13-3 Hypothetical Payoff Matrix in Duopoly Pricing

		Redpath's choices	
		$12 price	*$10 price*
Bluechip's choices	$12 price	I $2 million loss (Redpath) $2 million loss (Bluechip)	II $1 million loss (Redpath) $8 million loss (Bluechip)
	$10 price	III $8 million loss (Redpath) $1 million loss (Bluechip)	IV $5 million loss (Redpath) $5 million loss (Bluechip)

for exactly the same reason as it was for the two prisoners who didn't trust each other.[3]

On the other hand, suppose this "game" is to be repeated, as is typically the case in business. Firms set their price, but they can then change it in the "next play of the game." There is still some incentive to cut price, and as a consequence the equilibrium may continue to be in cell IV. However, there is now an increased chance of a collusive, high-price outcome in cell I. Each firm may now use a "stand-pat" strategy of setting its price at $12 and only cutting it if the other firm does. True, Bluechip risks taking a greater loss in the first period when it is vulnerable to price cutting by Redpath. But offsetting this risk is the possible high reward if Redpath also follows this "stand-pat" strategy and this higher price therefore does "stick." In this case the outcome will be to their mutual advantage, in cell I rather than IV. But why should competitor Redpath also stand pat? The answer is, for precisely the same reason that Bluechip does; the numbers in Table 13-3 and hence the incentives are exactly the same for both firms.

This analysis suggests that several issues are important to the duopolist trying to figure out a pricing strategy:

1. Is the decision a "game" that takes place once and for all, or does it recur?

2. How much can each firm trust the other—or, more broadly, how much information does each firm have about the other? This is important even in a recurring game. For example, if you know your competitor can't be trusted and will be cutting price immediately, you should also start off by cutting your price and thus avoid the first-period loss you will otherwise face.

3. In a repeated game, how long is each time period? For example, how long does it take for your competitor to realize you are cheating by cutting your price to $10 in violation of a tacit understanding to hold it at $12? The more rapidly your competitor can detect your cheating and respond by also cutting price, the less incentive you have to cheat. On the other hand, if you can escape detection completely, you have a much stronger incentive to cheat because your competitor won't realize and therefore won't retaliate. To prevent detection, or at least delay it, oligopolists may be secretive about their price reductions.

4. Once your competitor has detected your cheating, how long does it take to retaliate? If you are cutting price, then your competitor may retaliate immediately with a similar price cut. On the other hand, if you are competing by increased advertising or research and development, your competitor cannot retaliate immediately; it takes time to launch these efforts. This is another reason why firms often prefer advertising and other forms of nonprice competition to price competition.

5. How difficult is it to reach an outcome based on tacit collusion in the first place? Bear in mind that a collusive outcome such as the one shown in cell I of Table 13-3 may be in the collective interests of the two firms, but not in the interests of society. For this reason the Congress has enacted antitrust laws that outlaw overt collusion and any flow of information between firms that would make tacit collusion easier—as we will see in the next chapter.

In summary, game theory sheds additional light on some of the points encountered earlier in this chapter, such as the critical question of how competitors may react to a change in a firm's price. It also adds new insights on how two firms may be able to engage in tacit collusion; an example was the selection of the high-price outcome in cell I in the repeated game in Table 13-3.

Although game theory has been used to illustrate duopoly, the market to which it can most obviously and simply be applied, it can also bring an increased understanding to other forms of oligopoly where there are more than two competitors. The challenge here is to include such complications in order to make these games more realistic without making the games too complicated to solve. Moreover, even if they are solvable in theory, they may not be in practice; in that respect, they are like chess. However, even theoretical solutions—in economics or chess—may provide insights that can sharpen decisions in the simpler games humans play.

[3]Cell IV represents a Nash equilibrium. In such an equilibrium, each firm has made its best choice, on the assumption that the other firm sticks to its existing strategy. No other cell is a Nash equilibrium. For example, cell III is not, because Redpath has a better strategy, namely, cut its price and move to cell IV.

DON'T JUST COUNT NUMBERS: THE CONCEPT OF CONTESTABLE MARKETS

When one observes a market in which there is only a single firm, there is a natural tendency to conclude that it is a monopoly, with all the problems that it raises, including high price and restricted output.

However, even though a firm is technically a monopoly—in the sense that it is a single seller—it may not be able to *behave* like one by raising its price and restricting its output. In this case, the difficult policy problems of monopoly may not arise.

For example, consider a route that only one airline is now flying. It may appear that this airline has monopoly power. But in fact it may not, if it is operating in a contestable market. In such a case, any attempt by the airline to exercise monopoly power by raising its price will result in a profit that will attract another airline into flying this route. That is, another airline will "contest" this market. This potential competition forces the airline to behave like a competitor, even though it is a single seller. The moral is this. In analyzing any market—and in particular, in analyzing what appears to be a monopoly—don't just count the number of actual sellers. Emphasis must also be placed on freedom of entry—that is, on the potential new sellers. How contestable is the market?

Airline routes have been cited as examples of contestable markets, provided there are no problems in acquiring landing rights, and so forth, and an airline can therefore easily shift planes in and out of routes. Note that, for entry to be free, exit must also be free. Just as entry into a nightclub isn't free if you know you have to pay to get out, entry into an industry isn't free if a firm knows it faces losses if it has to leave.

A ***contestable market*** is one in which there is free entry and exit. Even if there is only one, or a small number of firms, they must act like perfect competitors. They are not free to raise price.

Another example of a contestable market might be a small town with only two or three contractors building houses. If they can restrict the entry of new competitors in some way—for example, by getting special zoning restrictions or acquiring all the available land—an oligopoly model with long-run profits may be the best way to describe their behavior. But if they can't restrict entry and local construction workers can start to build houses, there may be enough potential competition to keep the two or three existing firms from raising their prices in an attempt to earn above-normal profits. Similarly, the only carpenter in a village may not be able to charge high prices because this will simply cause somebody else to take up carpentry. In contrast, people can't simply "take up" medicine; they must go to medical school and be licensed. Thus the doctor has more market power than the carpenter. Once again, we see the importance of ease of entry. It is not only existing competition, but also potential competition that matters.

KEY POINTS

1. Monopolistic competition occurs when there are many small firms with differentiated products and no barriers to entry—such as patents or economies of large-scale production. Because each firm is selling a differentiated product, it has some small control over price. It faces a slightly sloping demand curve rather than the completely flat demand facing a perfect competitor. Because of free entry, above-normal profits disappear in the long run.

2. Price *could* be reduced below the level that occurs in monopolistic competition, but only at the cost of providing consumers with less choice. Therefore, little case can be made for government regulation.

3. When an industry is dominated by only a few firms and there are barriers to the entry of new competitors, the result is oligopoly. In an oligopoly, there is an incentive for firms to collude so that they can act like a monopolist in raising price and restricting output. Such monopoly-like behavior would lead to an inefficient allocation of resources. One deterrent to such collusive behavior is the difficulty of establishing and enforcing the production quotas or market-sharing that is typically required to maintain a high price. Even more important are the legal prohibitions against collusion in the United States.

4. An important example of a collusive agreement is the Organization of Petroleum Exporting Countries (OPEC). Between 1973 and 1982, OPEC increased the world price of oil more than 12-fold. The result was the greatest peacetime transfer of wealth in history. OPEC was remarkable because for very special reasons it did not have to enforce formal production quotas during the 1970s when it was raising price. One reason was that Saudi Arabia kept the price up by acting as a residual producer, satisfying only the demand for oil that was left unsatisfied by other OPEC producers.

5. During the 1980s, the Saudis became unwilling to continue as the residual producer, because it left them producing such a small amount of oil. When the Saudis expanded their production, the price of oil fell. This increased the pressure on OPEC to establish and enforce production quotas. By 1989, it wasn't clear how successful these efforts would be.

6. Antitrust laws prohibit American firms from engaging in overt collusion. Nevertheless, some forms of tacit collusion—such as price leadership—are difficult to prosecute and may allow oligopolists to exercise some degree of monopoly-like power.

7. Oligopolists often prefer to compete in ways other than cutting price. They may try to capture sales from rivals by extensive advertising campaigns, or by expenditures on research to develop better products.

8. Duopoly is a market in which there are two sellers. Game theory is one method of analyzing the pricing policy of duopolists—or, by extension, the policy of several oligopolists. It highlights a basic issue that arises when there are only two, or a very few, large firms: Before a firm changes its price, it should take into account how its competitors may react.

9. In analyzing any market, counting the number of competitors is not enough. One must also examine the freedom of entry; is the market "contestable"? If it is, even a single producer may have little monopoly power.

KEY CONCEPTS

monopolistic competition
differentiated product
four-firm concentration ratio
Herfindahl-Hirschman index
natural oligopoly
price searcher
collusion
cartel
cutthroat competition
price war
Organization of Petroleum Exporting Countries (OPEC)
kinked demand curve
price leadership
tacit collusion
focal point pricing
cost-plus, or markup, pricing
nonprice competition
duopoly
prisoner's dilemma
game theory
payoff matrix
repeated game
contestable market

PROBLEMS

13-1. If there are only four large firms in your industry, explain why collusion would be in your economic interest as a producer. Explain how consumers of your product would be affected. Describe the problems involved in arranging a collusive agreement and making it stick. Would the agreement be legal?

13-2. **(a)** Derive the four-firm concentration ratio and the Herfindahl-Hirschman Index for

(i) A monopoly.

(ii) An industry in which there are three equal-sized firms.

(iii) An industry with three firms, one

with 50% of the market and two with 25% each.

(b) In your view, does the four-firm concentration ratio or the Herfindahl-Hirschman index do a better job of describing the degree of industry concentration? Explain your answer, using as an illustration your calculations in part (a).

13-3. What are the benefits and costs of advertising to (a) the firm, and (b) society? On balance, do you think that advertising is beneficial or damaging to society?

13-4. (a) Both manufacturers of cigarettes and producers of perfume advertise. Do you think waste is involved in either case? In one more than the other? Discuss the possible benefits and damage from advertising each product.

(b) Cigarette producers claim that advertising doesn't increase the sales of cigarettes but only redistributes these sales among producers. If this is so, how would a government ban on cigarette advertising affect the output of the whole industry? How would it affect its costs? Its profits? Would a national cigarette manufacturer be likely to oppose such a ban?

13-5. At one time, lawyers who cut their fees below the level allowed by their state bar association could be disbarred. How would you evaluate this regulation from an economic point of view? If you were a lawyer, how would you view it?

13-6. What do you think would happen to the world price of oil if

(a) OPEC countries were able to enforce a tighter quota system?

(b) Non-OPEC producers were to reduce their production?

(c) Non-OPEC producers in the North Sea were to cut price by $5 a barrel?

(d) Large new deposits of oil were discovered off the California coast?

(e) Large new deposits of oil were discovered off the Saudi Arabian coast?

(f) Saudi Arabia were to withdraw from OPEC?

(g) There were major developments in nuclear technology, with fusion power expected to become a major source of energy by 2010?

(h) The U.S. government were to impose an additional tax of $1 per gallon on gasoline?

13-7. In trying to get Blake and Reid (Table 13-2) to confess, should the police try to get each to think that the other (a) has confessed, or (b) has not confessed? Why?

13-8. Use your imagination to construct a payoff matrix illustrating the game that will result in a duopoly if each firm has two possible strategies: (a) continue as is; (b) market a new product it has just discovered that takes a much longer time to wear out.

13-9. Table 13-4 shows the situation faced by Bluechip and Redpath, the two firms in Table 13-3, in a later year of prosperity. Each figure now represents profit rather than loss. Explain the conditions under which they might jointly maximize profit. Explain why they might engage in price competition.

TABLE 13-4 Profit Matrix in Duopoly

		Redpath	
		$14 price	*$11 price*
Bluechip	$12 price	I Redpath: $10 million Bluechip: $8 million	II Redpath: $14 million Bluechip: $2 million
	$10 price	III Redpath: $3 million Bluechip: $11 million	IV Redpath: $4 million Bluechip: $3 million

APPENDIX

A MARKET WITH ELEMENTS OF BOTH COMPETITION AND MONOPOLY

One of the markets in the broad range between monopoly and perfect competition is the market shown in Figure 13-7 which has elements of both. Many small firms act as perfect competitors by taking price as given, and one large firm acts like a monopolist by determining price.

In panel *a*, *D* represents total market demand, while *S* represents the marginal cost and hence the supply of the small producers who act as perfectly competitive price takers. If they were the only firms, this industry would be perfectly competitive, with equilibrium at E_0 and price P_0.

But they are not the only firms. In this industry there is also the very large firm shown in panel *b* which can produce a huge quantity at a relatively low price as shown by its MC curve. It is large enough that it can influence price. What price should it quote?

It can't select a price at P_0 or above, because at this price all market demand is already satisfied by the existing firms. This raises the important question: What is the demand for the large firm's output? The answer is: demand curve *d* in panel *b*, that is, the market demand *D* in panel *a* that is left unsatisfied by the small firms. For example, at price P_2, the difference between *D* and *S* is the short arrow in panel *a*. This is the market demand *D* that is not satisfied by *S*, the supply of the small firms. It is the large firm's demand and is therefore reproduced as the short arrow in panel *b*. The long arrow at price P_1 is derived in the same way. The collection of all such arrows defines the large firm's demand curve *d*.

Since it faces a sloping demand *d*, the large firm—just like a monopoly—can select the best point on that curve, which is at *R*, where its MC equals its MR. Consequently, it will quote price P_1 and sell quantity *Q* shown by the long arrow. The resulting equilibrium for the industry is shown in panel *a* at E_1. The large producer has set price at P_1, and the small firms—as price takers—respond according to their supply curve *S*, by producing the quantity Q_2 shown by the gray arrow. This, along with the (long-arrow) output of the large firm, just satisfies total market demand *D*.

Note how this analysis blends elements of competition and monopoly. On the one hand, a large number of small firms take market price as given; they represent the competitive element. At the same time, there is also a large firm which, though technically not a monopoly, nonetheless in one important respect *acts* like one. Rather than take market price as given, it sets price by selecting the profit-maximizing point on its sloping demand curve. But in another respect this large firm is not like a monopoly: Demand *d* which it faces depends not only on how much consumers want to buy, but *also* on how much its competitors sell. Thus, like a monopoly, it must keep its eye on the consumer, but unlike a monopoly, it must also keep an eye on its competitors. If you refer to it as a monopoly, you will be quickly corrected, since it is not the only seller. In fact, it is severely restricted in its actions by competing firms. (Consider how much higher it could raise the price if its competitors did not exist and it could operate on total market demand *D* rather than just on its own *d*.)

One example of this type of market might be oil, if all OPEC members except Saudi Arabia were to ignore their production quotas completely. In this situation, Saudi Arabia would be the large residual producer, satisfying the demand left unsatisfied by the other OPEC countries. As the dominant producer, it would determine the price, whereas the other OPEC members would take that price as given and produce like perfect competitors, without being restricted by their quotas.

Of course, this model does not perfectly describe the real world of OPEC. Although other OPEC members sometimes do ignore their quotas,

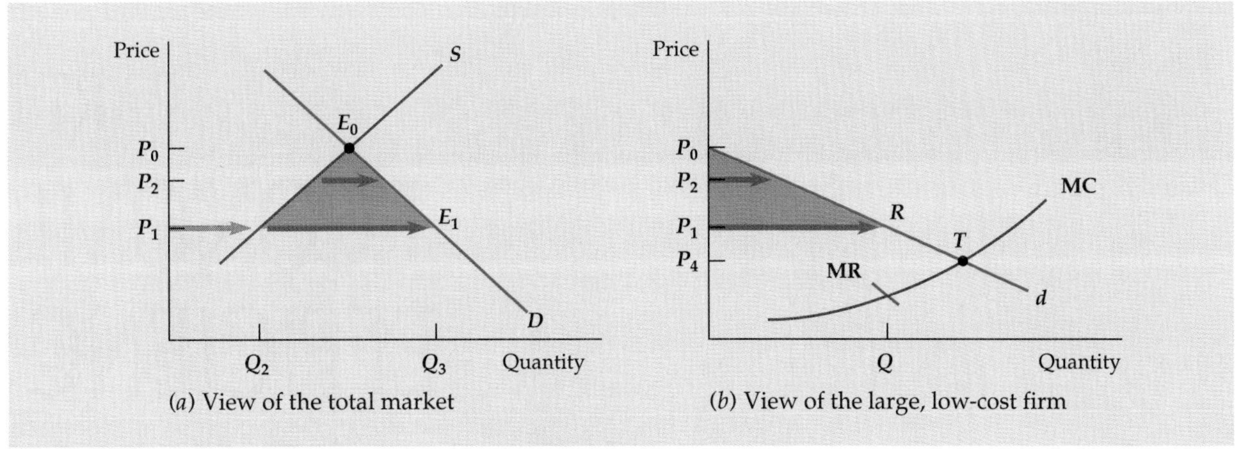

FIGURE 13-7 A market with elements of both competition and monopoly.
The large firm in panel *b* faces residual demand *d*—that is, the demand left unsatisfied by the large number of small competing firms in panel *a*. For example, at price P_2, the demand left unsatisfied by the small firms in panel *a* is given by the short arrow, which then helps to make up the large firm's demand *d* in panel *b*. The large firm now acts like a monopolist in maximizing its profit at point *R* and quotes price P_1. Each of the competing price-taking firms in panel *a* then takes P_1 as given. Together they supply Q_2. With the large firm producing Q_2Q_3 (that is, *Q* in panel *b*), the equilibrium for the industry is at E_1 in panel *a*. The presence of the dominant firm reduces price from P_0 to P_1 because this firm can produce such a large quantity at a very low cost.

at other times they abide by them (more or less). If they all abide by them, then the outcome will be a collusive cartel. The real world of OPEC seems to fall somewhere between the cartel model and the residual producer model in Figure 13-7, with the degree of discipline of OPEC members in abiding by their quotas determining which model is more relevant. During the 1970s, the residual producer model had considerable relevance because formal quotas were not being enforced and the Saudis' sales were covering demand left unsatisfied by other OPEC producers. Because of expanding world demand *D*, the residual demand *d* left for the Saudis remained substantial.

The situation changed in the 1980s. Shrinking world demand *D* for OPEC oil meant that the residual demand *d* facing the Saudis kept shifting to the left, leaving the Saudis with shrinking sales. When they responded by increasing their production and price fell dramatically, there was some evidence that other OPEC members became more willing to exercise discipline in abiding by quotas. The cartel model seemed to become more relevant.

One final observation on Figure 13-7: One might expect that if a large, dominant firm with monopoly power enters an industry, price will rise. But this isn't necessarily so, if that dominant firm has low costs. To see why, note that if the large producer is not in the industry, then the price in Figure 13-7*a* is P_0. But when that producer does come into the industry, the price falls to P_1. In this case, the entry of a firm with monopoly influence into a perfectly competitive industry *lowers,* rather than raises, price. The reason is that the large, low-cost firm adds greatly to the quantity that the industry can supply at a low price. (Note in our example how the MC curve for the large firm in panel *b* indicates that its costs remain low over a wide range of output, in comparison with the costs of the small firms, as reflected in the *S* curve in panel *a*.) This introduces an important theme of the next chapter. Before judging against the entry of a dominantly large firm into an industry, one must consider how costs are affected.

PART IV

ECONOMIC EFFICIENCY

Issues of Our Time

Part 3 has raised a number of questions:

- When do free markets work well, and when do they work badly?
- When they work badly, can the government improve them?
- If so, what are the most efficient ways?

In Part 4, these questions will be addressed in a study of several broad areas where the government has been intervening in the economy, by

- Regulating business (Chapter 14).
- Providing support for farmers (Chapter 15).
- Imposing environment, health, and safety standards (Chapter 16).
- Influencing our use of natural resources (Chapter 17).
- Providing "public goods" that a free market cannot deliver (Chapter 18).
- Influencing our international trade (Chapters 19 and 20).

CHAPTER 14

HOW MUCH SHOULD THE GOVERNMENT REGULATE BUSINESS?

Th' trusts . . . are heejous monsthers built up be th' enlightened intherprise iv th' men that have done so much to advance progress in our beloved country. . . . On wan hand I wud stamp thim undher fut; on th' other hand not so fast.

PETER FINLEY DONNE'S CHARACTERIZATION OF THEODORE ROOSEVELT

John D. Rockefeller's Standard Oil was a good customer of the railroads—so good that, when Rockefeller told the railroads what he wanted, they listened. Rockefeller wanted a lot. He not only wanted the railroads to give Standard Oil discounts on its own shipments; he also wanted the railroads to give Standard Oil "drawbacks"—that is, payments on all the shipments by *rival* oil firms. When the railroads agreed, Standard Oil was on the fast track to wealth and power. During the 1870s, the group of companies it led increased its oil refining capacity from 10% to 90% of the U.S. total.

In 1882, the partially independent companies that made up the Standard Oil group formed the Standard Oil Trust, into which each of the participating firms put a controlling share of its common stock. These firms thereby came under centralized management and were better able to act as a single firm. The trust then did what one might expect of a firm with monopoly power: It closed down a number of its refineries in order to restrict its output and raise its price. It was not surprising that trusts became a target of U.S. lawmakers.

This chapter will examine U.S. antitrust laws and other methods used to regulate business. These regulations can be divided into two broad categories.

1. Antitrust laws to prevent firms from reducing competition by such acts as collusion or cutthroat pricing.

2. Regulatory controls over an industry's price and conditions of entry. Within this broad category, two quite different kinds of regulation should be distinguished:

> **(a)** Regulation of a natural monopoly such as a power company. Since this form of regulation has already been studied in Chapter 12 (see, for example, Box 12-2) here we will concentrate on the second kind.
>
> **(b)** Regulation of naturally more competitive industries such as trucking and the airlines.

During the 1970s, there was a growing concern that the government was regulating too much. Accordingly, during the late years of the Carter presidency, and especially during the Reagan years in the 1980s, the growth in government regulation was in some cases reversed. Specifically, antitrust enforcement was relaxed, as was regulation of the airlines and trucking. By 1989, the question had become: Was the government regulating too little?

In analyzing government regulation in this chapter, we begin with a description of antitrust policy.

U.S. ANTITRUST LAWS

Because of the complexity of U.S. antitrust laws, it is not feasible to do more than note the most important ones.

THE SHERMAN ANTITRUST ACT (1890)

In response to the growing concentration of industry—and in particular, to the growth of giant trusts like Standard Oil—Congress passed the Sherman Act in 1890. It was direct and to the point. "Every contract, combination in the form of a trust or otherwise, or conspiracy in restraint of trade" was declared illegal. It was likewise illegal to "monopolize, or attempt to monopolize, or combine or conspire . . . to monopolize" trade.

Teddy Roosevelt became the first "trust-busting" president. The surge of legal activity during his presidency led to the breakup of Standard Oil and the American Tobacco Company in 1911. Even today, these two judgments are sometimes cited as a highwater mark in antitrust enforcement.

THE CLAYTON ACT (1914)

The Clayton Act spelled out some of the missing details of the Sherman Act. Among its provisions, the Clayton Act prohibits the following, if they "substantially lessen competition":

1. **Interlocking directorates,** which exist when a director sits on the board of two or more competing firms.

2. **Tying contracts,** which require a firm's customers to buy other items in its line in order to get the ones they really want. A firm with a particularly appealing product may be able to use such contracts to monopolize the sale of its other products.

3. The **takeover** by corporation *A* of corporation *B* by the purchase of *B's* common stock. However, this prohibition was evaded by some firms that purchased the physical assets of the other company instead. This loophole was not closed until the Celler-Kefauver Antimerger Act in 1950.

THE FEDERAL TRADE COMMISSION ACT (1914)

The Federal Trade Commission (FTC) is a five-member board set up in 1914 to prosecute "unfair methods of competition." Although it can issue cease-and-desist orders when it finds unfair competition, the law does not define what "unfair" means, and the courts have made it clear that they, and not the FTC, will pass judgment on this question. Nevertheless, the FTC still has a role in deciding whether agreements among firms will be permitted. For example, it was the FTC that approved the 1983 agreement between GM and Toyota to produce cars in California. In addition, the FTC has responsibility for curbing misleading advertising and misrepresentation of products.

These three acts—the Sherman Act, the Clayton Act, and the Federal Trade Commission Act—form the cornerstones of antitrust policy.

THE OTHER SIDE: LEGISLATION THAT TENDS TO REDUCE COMPETITION RATHER THAN INCREASE IT

Antitrust laws have often been designed not so much to protect the consumer as to protect small producers from predatory competition. But by placing the interests of small producers above those of consumers, such laws have often discouraged, rather than encouraged, competition. Two of the most prominent examples have been:

1. **The Robinson-Patman Act (1936)**—sometimes called the Chain Store Law—was designed to protect small firms in an industry from larger competitors. In the words of cosponsor Wright Patman, the act's objective was to "give the little business fellows a square deal" by curbing price cutting by large discount and chain stores. It was designed to prevent large stores from buying from suppliers at quantity discounts, unless such discounts were justified on the basis of actual cost economies. It also prohibited stores from selling to the public "at

unreasonably low prices." Its major effect was to impede, though not prevent, the efficient development of retail trade.

2. **The Miller-Tydings Act (1937)** exempted fair trade contracts from antitrust laws when such contracts were permitted by state law. Under a fair trade contract, the manufacturer of a name-brand good could fix the price that retail stores charged the public. During the 1960s and 1970s, manufacturers found it increasingly difficult to enforce such contracts, and under heavy public attack, the fair trade exemption was ended.

THE KEY ROLE OF ENFORCEMENT AGENCIES AND THE COURTS

An effective antitrust policy requires not only a good set of laws. It also requires government agencies, such as the Justice Department and the FTC to enforce these laws, as well as court judgments to uphold them.

Government Enforcement of the Laws. If the Justice Department ignores collusion or other conspiracies in restraint of trade, then these practices will continue. On the other hand, if it prosecutes offenders, the laws become a more effective deterrent.

Presidents have had widely differing views about how tough the government should be in dealing with business. Under Teddy Roosevelt, the first "trust-busting" president, the Justice Department aggressively took firms to court. In contrast, the Reagan administration preferred a low-keyed approach, setting guidelines for merging firms in the hope that court action would not be necessary.

Court Judgments. If the government does decide to take firms to court for violating the antitrust laws, then the question is: How will the court decide? Antitrust history has been marked by big swings in attitude, not just by presidents, but by the courts as well.

At an early stage, in its 1920 judgment in favor of giant U.S. Steel, the Supreme Court confirmed a "rule of reason": Being large or having monopoly power was, of itself, not to be judged illegal. Violations of the law occurred only if large firms *exercised* their monopoly power by engaging in unreasonable actions in restraint of trade, and "benevolent" U.S. Steel was not doing this. However, standards change. In the Alcoa case in 1945, the Court held that, even if a firm's actions might be otherwise reasonable, these actions were nevertheless illegal if they just helped the firm to maintain a monopoly position. For example, one reasonable business policy is to expand plant capacity in anticipation of increased demand, in order to be better able to serve customers. The Court decided, however, that such increases in capacity represented a violation by Alcoa, since they tended to block out potential new firms:

> Alcoa insists that it never excluded competitors; but we can think of no more effective exclusion than progressively to embrace each new opportunity as it opens, and to face every newcomer with new capacity already geared into a great organization, having the advantage of experience, trade connections and the elite of personnel.

The permissive U.S. Steel decision in 1920 at the one extreme, and the much tougher Alcoa decision in 1945 at the other, illustrate how the courts have interpreted the antitrust laws in a wide variety of ways.

SPECIAL ANTITRUST PROBLEMS

Two difficult issues must be faced by the authorities in making and enforcing antitrust laws. The first arises in an industry where there is a special kind of price *cutting;* in contrast, the second arises in an industry engaged in unjustified price *increases*.

1. PREVENTING CUTTHROAT PRICING DESIGNED TO ELIMINATE COMPETITORS

The government can take action against a "predatory" firm that is lowering its price in order to drive its competitors out of business. A low price may be in the consumers' interest in the short run, but it will not be in the long run if the firm succeeds in establishing a monopoly position and then raises price above its original level. A second reason for opposing cutthroat pricing is to protect small firms from unfair competition from the giants in their industry.

Cutthroat competition—sometimes called *predatory pricing*—is pricing below cost in order to drive competitors out of business.

In practice, however, it is difficult to draw a line between "cutthroat" pricing and healthy, vigorous competition. It might seem like a simple matter to calculate cost and forbid any sales at a price below this. But in fact, calculating cost is very difficult, particularly for a large firm producing many goods. It is not clear how fixed costs (overhead) should be allocated among its various products. Furthermore, it isn't even clear that pricing below cost *should* be forbidden, since this isn't necessarily an attempt to eliminate competitors. In the early 1980s, GM, Ford, and Chrysler all suffered large losses—that is, they priced below average costs. However, GM and Ford weren't trying to "cut Chrysler's throat." Rather, they were frantically trying to sell cars in the face of stiff Japanese competition and a domestic recession. Because of such real-world complexities, it is very difficult even to identify—let alone control—cutthroat competition.

2. PREVENTING COLLUSION THAT WOULD RAISE PRICE

The government may encounter a major problem in preventing firms from colluding to raise price: It may be difficult to prove that collusion has actually taken place. True, there may be exceptional cases where collusion has clearly occurred. For example, competitors may get together with the specific intention of fixing price and splitting up the market. In such cases, they can be sent to jail for their efforts (Box 14-1). But what action should be taken in more complex cases, where oligopolists with a common interest arrive at the same high price without even so much as a wink or a nod because all firms follow a price leader? Certainly, quoting the current market price cannot be judged illegal. If a firm's price "meets the competition," how can it be condemned? After all, that's exactly what farmers and other perfectly competitive producers do; they sell at the going market price. If everybody sells at the same price, this does not *prove* collusion.

A further complication is that collusion isn't necessarily bad. For example, allowing automobile firms to collude on research could mean a more rapid development of pollution-control and safety equipment. But there is a valid concern with even this type of collusion—the concern that firms which begin by reasonably colluding on research may eventually engage in unjustified collusion on price.

While the government faces difficult problems when firms collude, what should its policy be when firms go one step further and merge?

MERGERS

There are three kinds of mergers—horizontal mergers, vertical mergers, and conglomerate mergers.

The merger that, in the language of Section 7 of the Clayton Act, is most likely to "substantially lessen competition or tend to create a monopoly," is a **horizontal merger**—that is, a combination of firms which previously competed against each other in the same market. However, a **vertical merger**—in which firm *A* merges with one of its suppliers—may also suppress competition by making it difficult for other suppliers to sell to firm *A*.

In the third type of merger—a **conglomerate merger**—a firm joins another in a completely different activity. For example, several decades ago International Telephone and Telegraph (ITT) grew into a huge conglomerate by acquiring firms in unrelated activities: Sheraton (hotels), Avis (car rental), Grinnel (automatic fire sprinklers), Continental Baking, Hartford Fire Insurance, and many others.

A *horizontal merger* is a union of firms in the same competing activity.

A *vertical merger* is a union of a firm and its supplier.

A *conglomerate merger* is a union of firms in unrelated activities.

Conglomerate mergers are generally far less damaging to competition than vertical or horizontal mergers. For example, if Avis had been taken over by Hertz in a horizontal merger, the creation of the resulting giant rent-a-car company could

BOX 14–1 *The Great Electrical Equipment Conspiracy and Other Misdeeds*

The classic case of price fixing occurred three decades ago, when the manufacturers of heavy electrical equipment illegally conspired to set prices, thereby raising the cost of almost every power-generating station built in the United States. Senior officials from General Electric, Westinghouse, and 27 other firms ended up in court. Two million dollars in fines were eventually paid, and seven executives each spent 30 days in jail. Moreover, they faced an even greater personal cost. Almost as soon as the Justice Department began its investigation, the salary of one GE vice president was cut from $127,000 to $40,000. While he was recovering from that shock, he was fined $4,000 and sent to prison for 30 days. When he got out, GE eased him out of the company altogether. Here is how *The Wall Street Journal* (January 10, 1961) described the conspiracy in a passage that strangely echoes the words of Adam Smith, written over two centuries ago and quoted at the beginning of Chapter 13.

> Many of the meetings took place at the conventions of the National Electrical Manufacturers Association and other trade groups. Rather typically, after a conventional and perfectly lawful meeting of some kind, certain members would adjourn for a rump session and a few drinks in someone's suite. It seemed natural enough that mutual business problems would be discussed—specifications, for example—and like as not prices would come up. In time it was easy enough to drift from general talk about prices into what should be done about them—and finally into separate meetings to fix them for everyone's mutual benefit.

One scheme they used was a form of bidding cartel. The firms agreed in advance on a complicated system in which each firm knew from the phase of the moon whether it should bid low or high on a contract. Thus each firm waited for its turn to be the winning low bidder. When its turn came, it knew that it would have no competition, so it could set its "low" bid substantially above the bid it would have otherwise made.

More recently, bid rigging has also been used on a much wider scale by U.S. road builders to raise prices by up to 20% on highway construction. The resulting extra cost to taxpayers who have had to foot the bill has run as high as several hundreds of millions of dollars per year. This action triggered the largest single antitrust investigation in U.S. history. Between 1979 and 1983, federal prosecutors in 20 states obtained 400 criminal convictions with 141 jail sentences and fines totaling about $50 million. It should be emphasized that the targets in this case were many small firms, rather than giants of U.S. industry, like the electrical equipment manufacturers.

Even more surprising was the following report of an apparent attempt by American Airlines' Robert Crandall to fix price in a phone call to Braniff Chairman Howard Putnam. This excerpt—taped by Putnam without telling Crandall—picks up a discussion of how difficult it was for the two airlines to make a profit when they were both flying the same routes and cutting prices.

> *Crandall:*. . . there's no reason I can see, all right, to put both our companies out of business.
>
> *Putnam:* But if you're going to overlay a route of American's on top of. . . every route that Braniff has—I can't just sit here and allow you to bury us without giving our best effort.
>
> *Crandall:* Oh, sure, but Eastern and Delta do the same thing in Atlanta and have for years.
>
> *Putnam:* Do you have a suggestion for me?
>
> *Crandall:* Yes, I have a suggestion for you. Raise your [expletive] fares 20%. I'll raise mine the next morning.
>
> *Putnam:* Robert, we. . . .
>
> *Crandall:* You'll make more money and I will too.
>
> *Putnam:* We can't talk about pricing.
>
> *Crandall:* Oh [expletive] Howard. We can talk about any [expletive] thing we want to talk about.

In this case, no price fixing actually occurred because Putnam didn't take the bait. However, if he had, the tape could have sent them both to jail.

have reduced competition in that business. But when Avis was taken over by ITT in a conglomerate merger, no rent-a-car giant was created; Avis remained essentially the same size.

Between 1950 and 1980, the antitrust authorities exercised a substantial degree of restraint over vertical and horizontal mergers but were much more relaxed in allowing conglomerate mergers, since these were less likely to damage competition. The result was successive waves of conglomerate mergers. After 1980, restraints on vertical and horizontal mergers were also relaxed, as were restraints on joint ventures. Thus, in the example noted earlier, the government decided not to contest the joint venture of GM and Toyota to build small cars in California. This operation helped GM overcome its weakness in small cars, but it was also open to criticism because it was a cooperative arrangement between the two largest auto companies in the world.

Hereafter, we will concentrate on the merger that is potentially very damaging to competition—the horizontal "Avis-Hertz" type of merger of two firms in the same market.

POSSIBLE DISADVANTAGES OF A MERGER TO SOCIETY

Several problems may arise if two or more firms merge into a larger firm:

1. If the resulting firm is sufficiently large and immune from competition, it may be free from pressure to innovate and to keep costs down. For example, its managers may be able to engage in such forms of "wasteful corporate consumption" as holding conventions in exotic distant locations and hiring incompetent relatives and friends.

2. Very large firms may be tempted to exercise political influence. For example, International Telephone and Telegraph (ITT) became involved in schemes to influence a presidential election in Chile.

3. Firms large enough to exercise market power create the classic problem of monopoly. They may restrict production in order to raise price.

On the other hand, big isn't *necessarily* bad.

POSSIBLE BENEFITS FROM A MERGER

When a merger creates a new, larger firm, there may be benefits based on economies of scale. If such economies do exist, the newly expanded firm may be able to operate at substantially lower cost.

Economies of Scale. Figure 14-1 illustrates the tradeoff between a major advantage of a merger (economies of scale) and disadvantage of a merger (exercise of market power). Initially, suppose that there are two firms with each operating at R, selling q_1 at price P_1. This price is just high enough to cover q_1R, the average cost AC of each of the two firms. With price just barely covering average cost, each firm operates with a zero profit at R, while the industry operates at E_1.

If these two firms merge, the monopoly power of the new, larger firm allows it to increase its price from P_1 to P_2 by reducing the industry output from Q_1 to Q_2. (Output for the industry is shown in capital letters, and output for the firm in small letters.) Whereas the output of the industry is reduced, the output produced by the single remaining firm has increased from q_1 to q_2. This larger output by the individual firm lowers average cost from the height of R to S. Consumers lose area 1 + 2 because of the price increase, while the producing firm—which had zero profit before—now gains area 1 + 3 in profit. (Its price per unit is the height of E_2, while its cost per unit is the height of S. Therefore its per-unit profit is E_2S. Since it earns this profit on each of its Q_2 units of output, its total profit is area 1 + 3.) Because the producer gains 1 + 3 while consumers lose 1 + 2, area 1 is a transfer to the producer from consumers, whereas area 3 is a gain to society and area 2 is a loss. Specifically, area 2 is a loss to society because the new firm has used its new monopoly power to raise price by reducing the quantity sold to consumers from Q_1 to Q_2. Area 3 is a gain to society because of economies of scale; the average cost of producing this good has been reduced from the height of R to the height of S. In this example, the benefits from economies of scale exceed the losses from the exercise of market power, although in other cases the reverse could be true.

Thus, if there are economies of scale, the government should take them into account before making a decision on a merger. In particular, if the firm is the natural monopoly shown in this example, with a falling AC curve that allows the total quantity sold to be produced at lowest cost by a monopoly firm, then preventing monopoly will keep costs high. In terms of just the issues illustrated in this diagram, it is difficult to justify government opposition to this merger. (Note that in this natural monopoly, price competition would lead to the same result; price cutting and cost cutting would drive one firm out of business, with the other emerging as a monopolist at new equilibrium E_2.

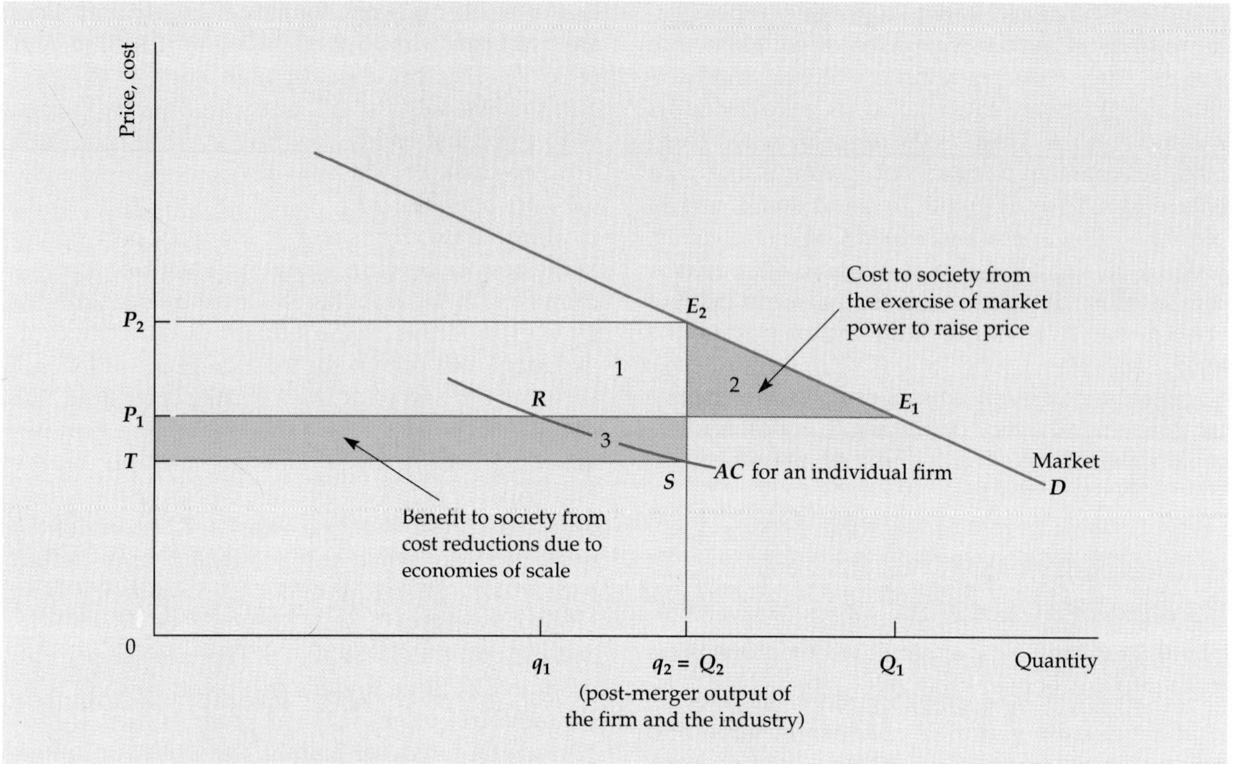

FIGURE 14-1 A key tradeoff in evaluating a merger.
Before the merger there are two firms, each producing q_1 at point R and earning no profit. Industry equilibrium is at E_1. *After* the merger, the new monopoly operates at E_2, selling Q_2 units at price P_2 and earning a profit of 1 + 3. However, consumers facing the price increase lose 1 + 2. Therefore, on balance, society as a whole loses 2 because the new monopoly has raised price and gains 3 because economies of scale have reduced the costs of production. (1 is a transfer from consumers to producers.)

Indeed, a merger in a natural monopoly may be viewed by the firms involved as a less costly way than price competition of getting to a monopoly outcome.)

Rather than blocking a merger, a better approach by the government in this case might be to allow the industry to monopolize and thus lower its costs while at the same time preventing the new monopoly firm from abusing its market power by raising price. The government might prevent price increases by regulating price—as, say, in Figure 12-7—or by easing restrictions on imports, with foreign competition then preventing a price increase. This approach would allow (blue) economies of scale benefits to be realized from the merger, while controlling (red) market-power losses.

In the more typical case in which there are several—say, six—firms in an industry and two are considering a merger, any benefits from cost reduction should again be taken into account. How would this advantage compare to the disadvantage of having a less competitive industry with only five rather than six firms?

This simple principle that costs should be considered in evaluating a merger has not always been recognized by the courts in antitrust judgments. Most notably, in the Alcoa case of 1945, Judge Learned Hand implied that costs should *not* be taken into account when he stated that the purpose of the antitrust laws is to "perpetuate and preserve, for its own sake and, *in spite of possible cost*, an organization of industry in small units which can effectively compete with each other." (Italics added.)

Another Advantage of Large Size: Research and Development. Because of their very large sales, big firms can finance large research and development (R&D) projects that are too large for small firms to undertake. These expenditures benefit not only the big firms that are thereby able to develop profitable new products, but also society as a whole as these new products become available. In his classic defense of large firms, Joseph Schumpeter wrote:

> As soon as we go into details and inquire into the individual items in which progress was most conspicuous, the trail leads not to the doors of those firms that work under conditions of comparatively free competition but precisely to the doors of the large concerns—which, as in the case of agricultural machinery, also account for much of the progress in the competitive sector—and a shocking suspicion dawns upon us that big business may have had more to do with creating that standard of life than keep it down.[1]

Although large firms are able to afford heavy R&D expenditures and are often the source of innovation, their role should not be exaggerated. Many innovations come not from firms that are already large, but from firms that are small or medium-sized and are seeking to become large. For example, the personal computer was introduced by upstarts like Apple, not by the giants of the computer industry. The oxygen furnace for producing steel was invented not by a giant U.S. firm, but by a small Austrian firm that was less than one-third the size of a single plant of U.S. Steel.

In fact, studies have shown that the highest payoff from R&D expenditures comes not from the largest firms in an industry, but rather from the next tier of firms that are almost as large. This finding has led to the recommendation that mergers be made easier among smaller firms than among the largest firms in an industry. A further justification for this policy is that smaller firms are more likely to acquire benefits from economies of scale than are the largest firms, which may have already come closer to capturing all available economies of scale. Moreover, a merger of smaller firms may *increase* competition in an industry, if it creates a new large firm that can more effectively compete with the existing giants.

[1]Joseph Schumpeter, *Capitalism, Socialism and Democracy* (New York: Harper, 1942), 3d ed., p. 82.

THREE STEPS IN JUDGING A MERGER

A merger involves conflicting interests. For example, in any takeover of a target firm by an acquiring firm, the interests of the two firms may be in conflict—although not necessarily so (Box 14-2). Moreover, other firms that have to compete with the new, larger firm will have a different interest, as will the consuming public. Thus, from an overall social viewpoint, any specific merger may or may not be justified. Here the prime concern is to evaluate a merger from the social point of view, drawing together a number of the issues considered in the last two chapters. In order to work through the complications, the process used by the Department of Justice to decide on whether or not to allow or oppose a merger is simplified into a three-step procedure.[2]

Before these steps are described, a preliminary question must be addressed: How is the market to be defined? The answer to this is important because it determines how many competing firms there are. To illustrate, suppose that there are two producers of salt and many producers of other seasonings. If the two salt producers are seeking to merge, they will argue for a broad definition of their market as "salt and seasonings." Under this definition, they have a lot of competitors.

On the other hand, in opposing this merger, the

[2]For more detail on the decision process that has actually been used since 1984 by the U.S. Department of Justice, see Steven C. Salop, "Symposium on Mergers and Antitrust," *Journal of Economic Perspectives*, Fall 1987, pp. 6–10; and, in the same journal, Franklin M. Fisher, "Horizontal Mergers: Triage and Treatment," pp. 23–40. According to both Salop and Fisher, most economists would agree that the Department of Justice procedure is a reasonable way to organize the analysis. The three-step process described in this section—a simplified version of the Department of Justice procedure—draws heavily on the Salop and Fisher articles cited above.

BOX 14–2 *Takeovers*

Following a wave of increasingly large takeovers, all records were smashed in 1988 when Kohlberg, Kravis and Roberts bought out R.J.R. Nabisco for over $24 billion. That dramatic act sent out a strong signal: size is no longer a defense against a takeover. With this acquisition, KKR had to assume a mountain of debt. Why have companies been willing to pay out that kind of money and take on that kind of debt? The answer is: There have been strong incentives for doing so. Should the government change those incentives?

THE MARKET FOR CORPORATE CONTROL

One view of takeovers is that they represent the normal working of a "market for corporate control," in which alternative management teams compete for the right to manage the nation's corporate assets—specifically, the assets of potential target firms. The management team that will pay the highest price for the target firm's assets—that is, for the target firm's common stock—is the team that will acquire these assets. The winning management team can afford to pay a high price for the stock—say, $70 rather than the current $50—because it believes it can earn a higher return on those assets by reorganizing and managing them more efficiently. This increased efficiency represents a benefit to society as a whole because it increases the nation's productivity and income.

Skeptics reply that the gains from takeovers do not necessarily come from increased efficiency. Some may come from losers in the takeover game. While winners and losers will be examined in detail later, we begin by considering how a takeover will affect the stockholders of the target firm and the acquiring firm.

THE EFFECTS ON THE ACQUIRING FIRM AND THE TARGET FIRM

To set the stage, first note that a takeover may increase efficiency in several ways. If one airline company purchases another, the new higher-volume company may be able to achieve economies of scale because it can integrate its flights and fly planes with more passengers. Moreover, there may be economies of scale in R&D or in management. For example, the acquiring firm may be able to use its underutilized management talent in running the new business.

An acquiring firm may benefit further if the target firm can be bought for a bargain, perhaps because market sentiment has temporarily depressed the price of its stock. One example was the 1984 purchase of Gulf by Socal (Standard Oil of California). Gulf shares were so depressed that they were selling for less than the value of Gulf's oil reserves. Thus it was cheaper for Socal to buy the whole Gulf company than to drill for new reserves.

Our observations so far suggest that benefits from a takeover are likely to go to the acquiring firm. But strangely, this isn't so; there is very little observed increase *on average* in the value of the stock of the acquiring firm after a takeover. True, some takeovers are very profitable because they occur at a bargain price or they result in higher-than-expected earnings. However, others are a disaster because of an inflated purchase price or because of a badly miscalculated "fit" between the two firms. One such disaster was noted earlier: the takeover by Texaco of Getty Oil which ended up in court and eventually cost Texaco $3 billion in damages.

While, on average, takeovers do not bring big gains to the shareholders of acquiring firms, they do bring large benefits to the shareholders of the target firms, in the form of the high premium price they receive for their stock. (Historically, this price premium has averaged over 30% and recently about 50%. In the case of R.J.R. Nabisco, it was almost 100%.) Thus competition among acquiring firms in the market for corporate control bids up the price of the stock of target firms until almost all the gains from takeovers go to the owners of target firms. Therefore one game in the stock market is to try to identify a takeover and buy the stock, not of the acquiring company, but of the target firm before it actually receives a takeover bid. Ivan Boesky made a fortune doing this, but ended up in jail for using illegal inside information provided by specialists who were helping companies design their takeover bids.

STOCKHOLDERS VERSUS MANAGERS: THE PRINCIPAL/AGENT PROBLEM

Although the stockholders of a target firm may welcome a takeover bid that raises the price of their stock, a quite different view may be taken by management—the president, vice presidents, and so on, who run the target firm. Even though they may benefit as shareholders, *in their role as managers* they may oppose a takeover for fear of losing their jobs in the corporate reorganization that follows. Thus, in their own personal interest, they may resist a takeover that is in the interest of the stockholders they represent.* This is one example of the "principal/agent" problem: How do principals (in this case, the stockholders) ensure that their agents (the firm's managers) act in their interests?**

One answer is for the stockholders to provide the firm's managers with a "golden parachute," a large financial settlement if the firm is taken over and they are then fired or decide to "bail out." These parachutes are controversial, because they can be a way for executives to gain millions of dollars at the expense of stockholders. However, they may be a bargain for stockholders if they reduce management's opposition to a takeover bid.

If the managers of a target firm agree, the takeover is a "friendly" one. But if they are opposed and the takeover becomes "hostile," they can use defensive actions against the raider, sometimes called a "shark" or "black knight."

GREENMAIL, WHITE KNIGHTS, POISON PILLS, AND OTHER FORMS OF SHARK REPELLANT

When the managers of a target firm realize that a block of its stock has been accumulated by a shark, they may offer to buy back that block at a premium price above its current market value. This "payoff in the face of a threat" is called **greenmail.** Its cost falls on the other shareholders in the target firm who don't get paid off and are left with a company of diminished value. Thus greenmail enables top executives to save their jobs by using shareholders' money to pay off the shark. A takeover bid that might have *benefitted* the target firm's stockholders has been thwarted by managers using greenmail at great *expense* to the stockholders. Sometimes infuriated shareholders sue the managers.

Other ways that managers may resist a shark include:

- Adopt a Pac-Man strategy of eating it before it eats you. For example, if company *A* is trying to take over company *B*, then *B* may retaliate by purchasing *A's* stock in an attempt to take over *A*.
- Find a "white knight"—a "friendly" firm with compatible goals that is invited to take over the target firm to prevent it from falling into unfriendly hands.
- Swallow a "poison pill" to make the firm indigestible for a shark. For example, the target's managers may incur a lot of debt to buy a highly risky third firm. When the target thus makes itself fat and ugly, the shark may lose its appetite. Or the target's management may allow its stockholders to acquire more stock at a bargain price, thereby making it more difficult for the shark to accumulate a controlling share of the stock.

LEVERAGED BUYOUTS (LBOs) AND BREAKUP ARTISTS

Leveraged buyouts occur when an acquiring firm or group of firms borrows heavily to buy the stock of a target firm such as R.J.R. Nabisco. That particular deal was of interest not only because it was by far the largest takeover in history, but also because the bidding was opened by a group led by some of the managers of R.J.R. Nabisco, including then-president Ross Johnson.

Johnson argued that he was just getting stockholders a higher price for their shares; and, in fact, these shares almost doubled before the bidding was over. Critics countered that the deal was designed to provide Johnson with enormous personal gain. Had his bid succeeded, Johnson's own multimillion dollar stake in the new company would have immediately increased by about 10 times, with a *further 10-fold increase* possible over the next five years. Johnson was also criticized for "attacking the company from the inside, using insider information." This case illustrated a problem of increasing interest to economists—namely, a "principal/agent problem with asymmetrical information," since the agent (Johnson) had more information about the company than the principals (the stockholders).

In many LBOs, the new owners are referred to as breakup artists, because they have to sell off many of the firm's assets piece by piece in order to reduce their staggering debt. Such "borrowing to break up a company" may often be profitable, but it is highly risky because most of the firm's earnings initially have to go into paying interest on

BOX 14–2 *Takeovers (continued)*

the large debt load. If sales fall in a recession or if interest rates rise, earnings may no longer be sufficient to cover these interest payments. Although relatively few of the new LBOs had gone bankrupt by 1988, it wasn't clear what may happen when they are tested by their first recession.

CONCLUSIONS: WINNERS, LOSERS, AND THE INTEREST OF SOCIETY AS A WHOLE

The big benefits from a takeover go to the target firm's stockholders who receive a higher price for their stock. (Stockholders of acquiring firms are not, on average, big winners or losers.) Benefits also go to the lawyers and investment bankers who provide advice. These benefits would reflect an efficiency gain for society, if there were no losers.

But there are losers. One is typically the U.S. Treasury. Because an additional slice of the target firm's earnings now has to go to pay interest on heavy new debts, it never shows up as corporate profits that can be taxed. (Avoiding tax is one of the incentives for takeovers. It's also an incentive for a firm that is *not* being taken over to increase its debt.) Bondholders in the target firm also frequently lose because a takeover leaves them with bonds in a more heavily indebted and therefore riskier company. When the first takeover bid for R.J.R. Nabisco was announced, the value of the company's outstanding bonds fell 20%.

Employees of the target company who are fired in the corporate reorganization also lose as their human capital (expertise in the firm's operations) disappears. A new management without ties to employees or communities will find it easier to fire loyal employees of long standing. This may be one of the reasons why a new management can get higher earnings out of the firm's assets. This does not happen without cost, however.

The degree to which these losses offset the gains from a takeover is controversial, and a matter of judgment. In cases where gains do exceed losses, the resulting net gain reflects an increase in efficiency, resulting from the more effective organization of assets. Moreover, efficiency may increase not only in the firms that are actually taken over; it may also increase in many firms that are not taken over but have been forced to reorganize to improve their performance in the face of just a *threatened* takeover. (Of course, in some cases the threat of a takeover may reduce efficiency, if the threatened firm defends itself by taking on a lot of debt or some other form of poison pill.)

While the issues discussed so far have led a number of analysts to conclude that takeovers have, on balance, often been beneficial, this judgment must be tempered by several broad concerns about the recent takeover wave.

1. To avoid becoming takeover targets, are managers becoming so preoccupied with increasing the earnings on their assets in the short run that they may damage their earnings in the long run?

2. Are acquiring firms trying to capture monopoly positions by taking over rivals? There is little evidence that recent takeovers have led to greater industrial concentration. Whereas some takeovers make firms larger, breakup artists split up other firms into smaller pieces.

3. Are takeovers being financed by too much debt? Takeovers are one of the reasons why the nation's nonfinancial corporate debt, which in the previous 20 years had remained a remarkably stable 33% to 35% of GNP, increased from 33% to 42% of GNP between 1981 and 1988. Because the corporate sector is more highly leveraged, it could be more vulnerable to bankruptcies in the next recession. In turn, this effect could spill over, damaging banks and other financial institutions that have been supplying funds, and thus leading to a financial crisis.

These concerns have raised two questions. (1) Should the government impose tougher restrictions on the financing of takeovers, in order to reduce the financial risk? (2) Should the corporate tax be changed so that it no longer encourages increased debt in firms that are being taken over, *and* in firms that are not?

---

*Sometimes managers resist in the stockholders' interest. For example, their resistance may encourage further bidding and a higher final price for the stock; or it may be that the takeover deal is simply a bad one.

**There is often a principal/agent problem in an acquiring firm as well. Even though it may not be in their stockholders' interest, the managers of an acquiring company may take over a target because, as managers of the new larger corporation, their influence, reputation, and salaries will increase. Moreover, with their egos on the line, they may get carried away in the bidding and pay too much for the target firm.

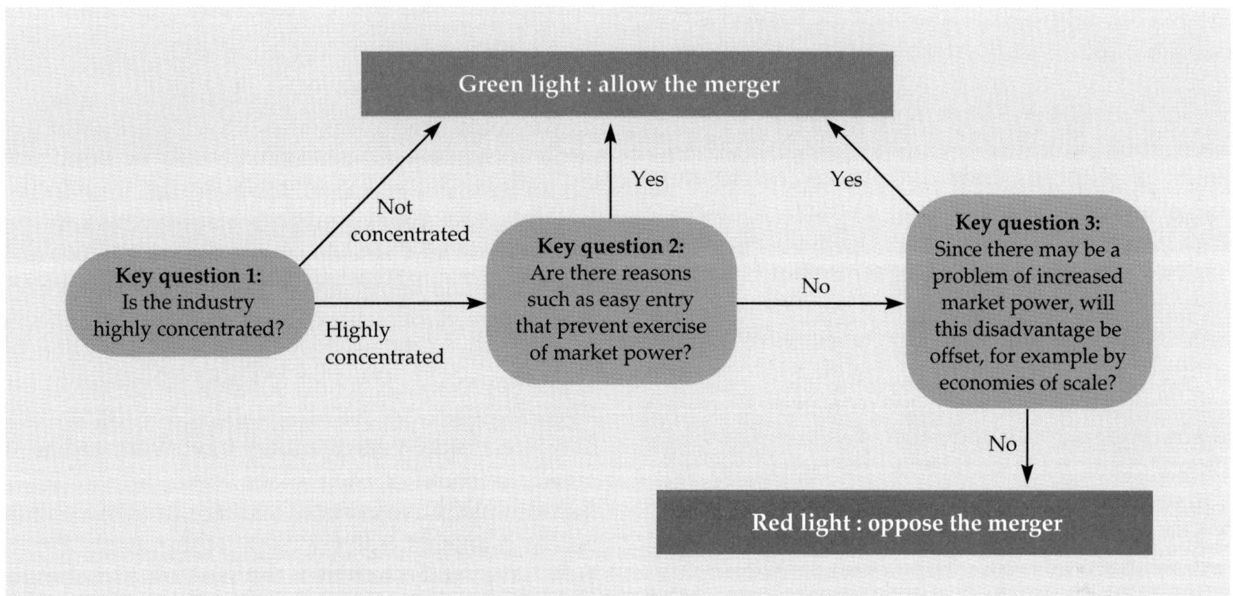

FIGURE 14-2 Step-by-step procedure for deciding whether or not a merger should be allowed.

government may argue for a narrow definition of their market as "salt only." Under this definition, the merger of these two firms would lead to a complete monopolization of the market. Thus the definition of the market may be critical in setting the stage for the Justice Department's step-by-step evaluation of a merger shown in Figure 14-2.

STEP 1: HOW CONCENTRATED IS THE INDUSTRY?

As noted in Chapter 13, the concentration of an industry has traditionally been measured by the four-firm concentration ratio (Fig. 13-2). However, the Department of Justice has now replaced this measure with the Herfindahl-Hirschman Index (HHI) which takes account of *all* firms rather than just the four largest. Recall that the HHI ranges in value from near zero for an industry with a very large number of firms to a maximum value of 10,000 for a completely monopolized industry. If an industry is expected to have an HHI of 1,000 or less after the proposed merger, then this industry is judged "not concentrated" and the merger is automatically approved. In other words, an HHI of less than 1,000 is a safe haven that protects merging firms from antitrust action. But if the industry is expected to have an HHI of over 1,800, the industry is judged to be too highly concentrated for the merger to be automatically approved, and the authorities move on to step 2. (In the range 1,000 to 1,800, the government studies the concentration of the industry in more detail, before deciding whether to proceed.)

STEP 2: WILL THE MERGED FIRM FACE STRONG COMPETITION?

In addressing this question, two of the influences that we should take into account are foreign competition and freedom of entry by new firms.

Foreign Competition. In those industries that are now subject to intense competition from abroad, large U.S. corporations are far less objectionable than they would be in an isolated U.S. economy for two reasons: (1) U.S. producers may be unable to compete with imports unless they are large enough to capture economies of scale in production and R&D. With the flood of Japanese auto imports in recent years, no one is any longer talking about breaking up General Motors. (2) Because of competition from imports, the market power of U.S. giants is reduced. They are not as free to raise prices since they risk losing markets to foreign firms.

The real question then is: *How* should foreign competition be taken into account? Should one look at the amount that Toyota actually exports to the United States or at Toyota's worldwide capacity (as an indicator of how competitive Toyota might possibly become)? On the other hand, if foreign firms have a quantity restriction on their U.S. sales, perhaps even these limited sales should not be counted. After all, doesn't a quantity restriction neutralize foreign firms from being effective competitors, since they can't increase their sales and thus deter U.S. firms from raising their price?

Potential Entrants. Here the analysis draws on the theory of contestable markets from the previous chapter. If there is free entry, then even a monopoly firm, such as the only airline on a certain route, may face strong potential competition. It may be unable to exercise market power since this would attract new firms that would compete away any profits. Thus free entry prevents monopoly abuse. If two airlines were flying such a route, then their merger would not create market power even though it would create a monopoly.

If there are such competitive pressures that prevent large firms from exercising market power, then the government may be able to drop its opposition to a merger, even in a highly concentrated industry. The merger may then be allowed, as shown in the center section of Figure 14-2. But if such pressures do not exist—for example, if airlines are not free to enter, but are blocked by the need to obtain costly landing rights—then it is likely that the newly merged firm *will* be able to exercise some market power. In that case, the analysis moves on to the third and final question: How will the costs to society of such an exercise of market power compare to the possible benefits of having a larger firm, such as the benefits from economies of scale? That is, the basic tradeoff illustrated earlier in Figure 14-1 must now be addressed.

STEP 3: ARE THE BENEFITS FROM LARGER SIZE IMPORTANT ENOUGH TO OFFSET ANY EXERCISE OF MARKET POWER?

Lower costs from economies of scale are an obvious source of benefit that may be cited by firms trying to justify a merger. However, the authorities must be very skeptical of such claims. Government officials are at a disadvantage in assessing economies of scale because the merging firms have so much more information about their costs. Furthermore, these firms may provide biased evidence. They may offer clear and concrete information on how increased size reduces some of their costs, but they are unlikely to mention how increased size may *raise* some of their other costs—for example, the administrative costs of setting up a whole new tier of management. For this reason some observers have suggested that the government should take a tough stance. They contend that the burden of proof of economies of scale should be on the firms that wish to merge. This is particularly important when the merged firm will have substantial market power.

If large enough benefits from increased firm size can be established, then the merger is given the green light. If not, it is opposed.

MERGER POLICY: FURTHER OBSERVATIONS

There are often other considerations that should also be taken into account. For example, the authorities will want to see if there have been any previous antitrust violations by either of the merging firms, as an important possible clue to "What's *really* going on in this industry?" However, Figure 14-2 does highlight most of the important questions. Moreover, it has another attractive feature: It can be applied by those with quite different philosophical views. An administration that wishes to be "tough on mergers" can use a relatively demanding standard in answering each of the key questions. For example, it can set a different threshold level for concentration in question 1, thereby making it less likely that a merger will get a green light at this early stage. Alternatively, a laissez-faire, hands-off administration can use a less demanding standard in addressing those questions. In short, while most agree that this three-step procedure asks the right questions, there is great disagreement on the answers.

BREAKING UP AN EXISTING FIRM TO MAKE AN INDUSTRY MORE COMPETITIVE: AT&T

If a case can be made for blocking a merger that will create a large firm, then a similar case might be made for breaking up a large firm that already exists. The problem is that it is much more difficult to break up an existing large firm than to block a new one.

Just how difficult a breakup may be was illustrated in the case of AT&T (American Telephone and Telegraph), a huge company that had monopoly power in some phone services, and had assets greater than those of Exxon, Mobil, and General Motors combined. In 1974, the Justice Department sued AT&T to force it to divest itself of Western Electric, its manufacturer of telephone equipment. The government held that Western Electric's association with AT&T gave it a clear advantage in selling its products and partially excluded other manufacturers of telephone equipment from the marketplace. Because of the death of the first judge and other serious delays, the case didn't go to trial until 1981. Since both AT&T and the government wished to reduce the uncertainty surrounding the future of the company, they reached an out-of-court settlement in 1982 to split up AT&T, not into two companies, but into eight.

Seven of the new companies—with names like Pacific Telesis and Bell Atlantic—now provide local phone service to a separate region of the country. As a local monopoly, each continues to have its rates regulated. The eighth company—the new, leaner AT&T—still retains Western Electric to produce telephone equipment, along with divisions that provide research and long-distance service. In this breakup, the government largely achieved its goal: Western Electric no longer has an inside track but now has to compete with manufacturers like General Electric and Northern Telecom in selling telephone equipment to the seven regional phone companies. An AT&T executive described the breakup as the "largest corporate event in history, like taking apart a 747 and putting it back together while it is still in the air."

Deregulation caused a major realignment of telephone rates. Previously, AT&T had kept local rates low, in effect subsidizing local service with its very profitable long-distance service. With the breakup of the company, such subsidization could no longer continue. Local rates went up, while long-distance rates came down—partly because AT&T faced greater competition. Technological improvements such as earth satellites and fiberglass lines also contributed to the reduction in long-distance rates.

Because the old AT&T had been one of the world's most efficient telephone systems, breaking it up was a rejection of the guideline "If it works, don't fix it." It's not clear whether the new system works better than the old. The jury is still out.

ANTITRUST POLICY: CONCLUDING REMARKS

In the face of the need to balance the complex considerations of market power, tacit collusion, economies of scale, and the other issues that monopoly and oligopoly raise, it is too much to hope for a simple solution. Perfect competition is the perfect answer only in textbooks. In the real world, we must settle for **workable competition,** by which we gain many of the advantages of large-scale business but curb its more flagrant abuses. Harvard's Richard Caves has compared antitrust laws with traffic laws. Drivers can usually get away with 38 miles an hour in a 35-mph zone; the police are there to catch the speeder who goes 45 or 50. The fact that we might get caught makes most of us drive a little more slowly. Similarly, the electrical machinery and road construction cases described in Box 14-1 remind business executives that there is a jail cell awaiting the flagrant offender; they are likely to be more careful as a result.

Fear of prosecution by the government is not the only discipline a business faces. A firm may also be sued by a competitor that has been damaged by anticompetitive practices. In such a civil antitrust suit, the court may award the injured party up to *three times* the amount of the damage. For example, after the electrical equipment executives were sentenced to jail for criminal price fixing, their companies were also taken to court in almost 2,000 *civil* suits. As a consequence, they had to pay about $500 million in damages. Obviously, this treble damage clause acts as a deterrent to antitrust violations.

By and large, the antitrust laws make industries more competitive. Now let's turn to other forms of government intervention that have sometimes made industries *less* competitive.

REGULATION OF ENTRY

In the airlines it appears that the prime obstacle to efficiency has been regulation itself, and the most creative thing a regulator can do is remove his or her body from the market entryway.

ALFRED KAHN,
FORMER CHAIRMAN OF THE CIVIL AERONAUTICS BOARD

In Chapter 12, we examined in detail the case for government regulation of the price of a natural monopoly, such as an electric company. Such regulation can force the single firm to act in a more competitive way—indeed, more like a perfect competitor facing a given market price. However, the government may also regulate a naturally more competitive industry, such as the airline or trucking industry. Government regulation in this case may allow firms to act in a *less* competitive way. For example, regulation may reduce competition by blocking the entry of potential new firms. Therefore it is no surprise that this form of regulation is often welcomed by the firms that are already in the industry. (See Box 14-3.)

DEREGULATION OF TRUCKING

The Interstate Commerce Commission (ICC) used to restrict the entry of new firms into the trucking industry. Government regulations prohibited trucks from carrying certain items. For example, one company was permitted to carry empty ginger ale bottles but no empty cola or root beer bottles. Another was allowed to haul 5-gallon cans but not 2-gallon cans. Such regulations caused inefficiency and were in direct conflict with the government's desire to conserve fuel.

The ICC therefore began to relax its regulations, and in 1980 Congress enacted legislation to remove many of the regulations altogether. Increased competition led to a reduction in shipping rates and an increase in efficiency. Thousands of new firms entered the industry. In the subsequent shakeout, hundreds went bankrupt, including some sizable firms. Wages also came under pressure, because the high earnings in this industry could no longer be passed along in the form of a high price. In this case, deregulation often hurt the existing firms that had been exercising market power. However, it provided benefits to new firms wishing to enter, as well as to the users of trucking services who enjoyed lower prices.

AIRLINE DEREGULATION

Until 1978, the Civil Aeronautics Board (CAB) regulated airline ticket prices and the routes serviced by each airline. By controlling routes, the CAB controlled the entry of new competitors. In the four decades prior to 1978, the CAB turned down *every* request by new carriers to serve long-distance "trunk" routes between major cities. This led to the charge that the CAB was regulating the industry more in the interests of the regulated firms than of the general public. In effect, the regulatory agency had taken on some of the responsibilities of a cartel manager by restricting entry, setting price, and dividing up the market (the routes each airline serviced). Moreover, this special kind of "public cartel" administered by the government offered the firms two advantages not available to a private cartel: (1) They were immune from prosecution under the antitrust laws. (2) There wasn't the problem of cheating that arises in a private cartel; the government prohibited new entrants and low prices.

At the same time, regulations limited the profits of the airlines in several ways. One of the most important was the CAB requirement that forced airlines to service smaller cities, even at a loss. Thus regulation resulted in **cross-subsidization**—that is, one group of passengers being subsidized by another. Specifically, small-city travelers, who got service they would not have otherwise enjoyed, were subsidized by travelers on trunk lines who paid more for their tickets. One of the chief arguments of those who supported regulation was that it provided small-city passengers with convenient and safe service that would be dropped if regulation were to end.

Deregulation. In 1978, Congress passed the Airline Deregulation Act, which allowed new airlines to service any routes they judged profitable, provided

BOX 14–3 The Parable of the Parking Lots

Producers have a natural interest to narrow the market and raise the price.

ADAM SMITH

Henry Manne, dean of the law school of George Mason University, tells a simple parable to illustrate the problems of government regulation which protects existing firms by blocking the entry of new firms.*

Once upon a time in a city not far away, thousands of people would crowd into the domed football stadium on a Saturday afternoon. The problem of parking was initially solved by a number of big commercial parking lots whose owners formed the Association of Professional Parking Lot Employers (APPLE).

As time passed and crowds grew, every plumber, lawyer, and schoolteacher who owned a house in the neighborhood went into the parking business on Saturday afternoon, and cars appeared in every driveway and on most lawns. Members of APPLE viewed the entry of these "amateurs" into their business with no great enthusiasm, especially since some were charging a lower fee. Stories began to circulate about their fly-by-night methods and the dents they had put in two cars (although, on investigation, it was discovered that denting was an equally serious problem in the commercial lots).

At a meeting of all members of APPLE, emotions and applause ran high as one speaker after another pointed out—in some cases, in a very statesmanlike way—that parking should be viewed, not as a business, but as a profession governed by professional standards. In particular, cutthroat price competition with amateurs should be regarded as unethical. The one concrete proposal, quickly adopted, was that APPLE members should contribute $1 per parking spot "to improve their public image, and put their case before the proper authorities."

No accounting was ever made of this money, but it must have been spent wisely, since within a few months the city council passed an ordinance to regulate industry price and to require that anyone parking cars must be licensed. However, it turned out to be difficult for an independent house owner to get a license; it required passing a special driving test to be "professionally administered" by APPLE, a $27,000 investment in parking facilities, and $500,000 in liability insurance. Because every commercial lot found its costs consequently increasing by 20 percent, the city council approved a 20 percent increase in parking fees. (Within a year, APPLE had requested that the city council guarantee the liability insurance, so that people would have no fear of parking in commercial lots. One argument put forward by an APPLE spokesman was that this idea was similar in its intent to the proposal for the government to set up an insurance scheme for stockbrokers.)

On the next football afternoon, a funny thing happened on the way to the stadium. Since police were out in large numbers to enforce the ordinance, driveways and lawns were empty and long lines of cars were backed up waiting to get into each commercial lot. The snarl was even worse after the game. Some people simply gave up waiting for their cars and had to return to retrieve them the next day. (There was even a rumor that one car was never found.) In response, APPLE decided to go ahead with a "statistical-logistic study of the whole socioeconomic situation" by two computer science professors at the local university. Their report cited the archaic methods of the industry and pointed out that what each firm needed was fewer quill pens and more time on a computer.

As the parking lots began to computerize their operations, it became quite clear that in the face of these rising costs, a further increase in parking fees was required. The increase was quickly approved by city councilors relieved that, in the modernization of the industry, they had finally found a solution. Unfortunately, it was no solution after all. The problem, it turned out, was not so much deciding which car should be moved where, as actually moving it—and that continued to be done by attendants who had become surly and uncooperative because of the pressures they were facing.

Relief, however, did appear in two forms. First, many people got so fed up with the hassle that they started watching the game on television. Second, small boys who lived in the houses closest to the stadium went into the car wash business on Saturday afternoon. They charged $10, but it was worth the price, since they guaranteed a top-quality job. (In fact, they guaranteed that they would spend at least two hours on it.) And they always had as many cars as they could handle, even on rainy days—in fact, especially on rainy days.

---

*"The Parable of the Parking Lots," *Public Interest*, no. 23 (Spring 1971), pp. 10–15. Abbreviated with the author's permission.

they met safety standards. That is, airlines were freed of regulations over entry and pricing, but not over safety. With this new, freer entry, major changes began to occur.

1. Increased competition made more discount fares available to the public. In 1976, 15% of travelers flew on discount fares, but by 1987 this figure had increased to 90%. The price of discount fares also fell. In response to the greater availability and lower price of discount fares, airline travel increased greatly—by a full 40% in the first year of deregulation alone. The Council of Economic Advisers has estimated that deregulation has provided the traveling public with more than $11 billion per year of benefits in the form of more flying at lower prices.[3]

2. Increased competition and freedom from regulation also made the airlines more efficient. They were now free to reallocate their aircraft between routes. For example, the major airlines no longer had to fly their big jets almost empty out of the small cities that they had previously been forced to service. In many cases they dropped these routes.

3. This change didn't mean the end of service to these cities, since new airlines usually moved in to take up the slack. Because the new airlines used smaller aircraft, they could offer more frequent service. Thus even the public in the small cities—expected by many to be big losers—enjoyed the benefit of more frequent flights (admittedly in smaller planes). Moreover, once they got to big-city connecting points, they became the big-city passengers who won hands down. These passengers received the greatest cut in discount fares, and because of the heavier airline travel, they enjoyed more frequent service on large aircraft.

4. This restructuring of the industry, along with the freer entry of new firms, led predictably to an increased number of airlines: Between 1978 and 1988, 200 new firms entered the industry. In the subsequent shakeup, some failed, some merged and others grew on their own, so that by 1987 there were 78 certified airlines compared to 36 before deregulation.

The fear that smaller commuter airlines wouldn't be able to compete with the giants was unfounded. True, their costs per passenger mile were higher, but only because they were flying shorter routes. If the giants came in to compete on these routes, their costs rose to the same level.

5. With increased travel, the skies and airports became more congested, causing increased delays. The government was slow to take action to reduce this problem. Suggested solutions included peak-load pricing, under which airports would charge a higher landing fee in rush hours as an incentive for private planes and other small aircraft to fly at less congested times. In 1988, there was still no such incentive; for example, at Washington's congested National Airport, a private plane could still land, even at peak periods, for only $6. If these fees could instead be adjusted to equate supply and demand, they would allow the market to work, ensuring that delays would be reduced and that the airlines landing planes during rush hours would be those that placed the highest value on that right.

Other suggestions for "letting the market work" to limit airport congestion included auctioning off landing slots, or allocating slots to airlines and allowing them to buy or rent such slots from each other. In all such cases, a market price would develop for the right to land at a certain time.

6. As airlines were flying more flights over big cities, the resulting congestion led to more near misses and concerns about safety. It became clear that, while other forms of regulation were being relaxed, safety regulation should *not* be. In any case, there was no evidence that the airlines were becoming less safe, even though they faced increased competition and greater congestion. In fact, Figure 14-3 shows that the accident rate continued to fall after deregulation, at least until 1987. Indeed, it was even possible to argue that airline deregulation had made the total travel by Americans *safer.* An estimated 800 U.S. lives were saved per year because, as deregulation brought lower fares, Americans traveled more by air (where there are only 0.3 deaths per billion passenger miles) and less in autos which are about 100 times as dangerous!

---

[3]*Economic Report of the President, 1988,* p. 199. This section draws heavily on this source.

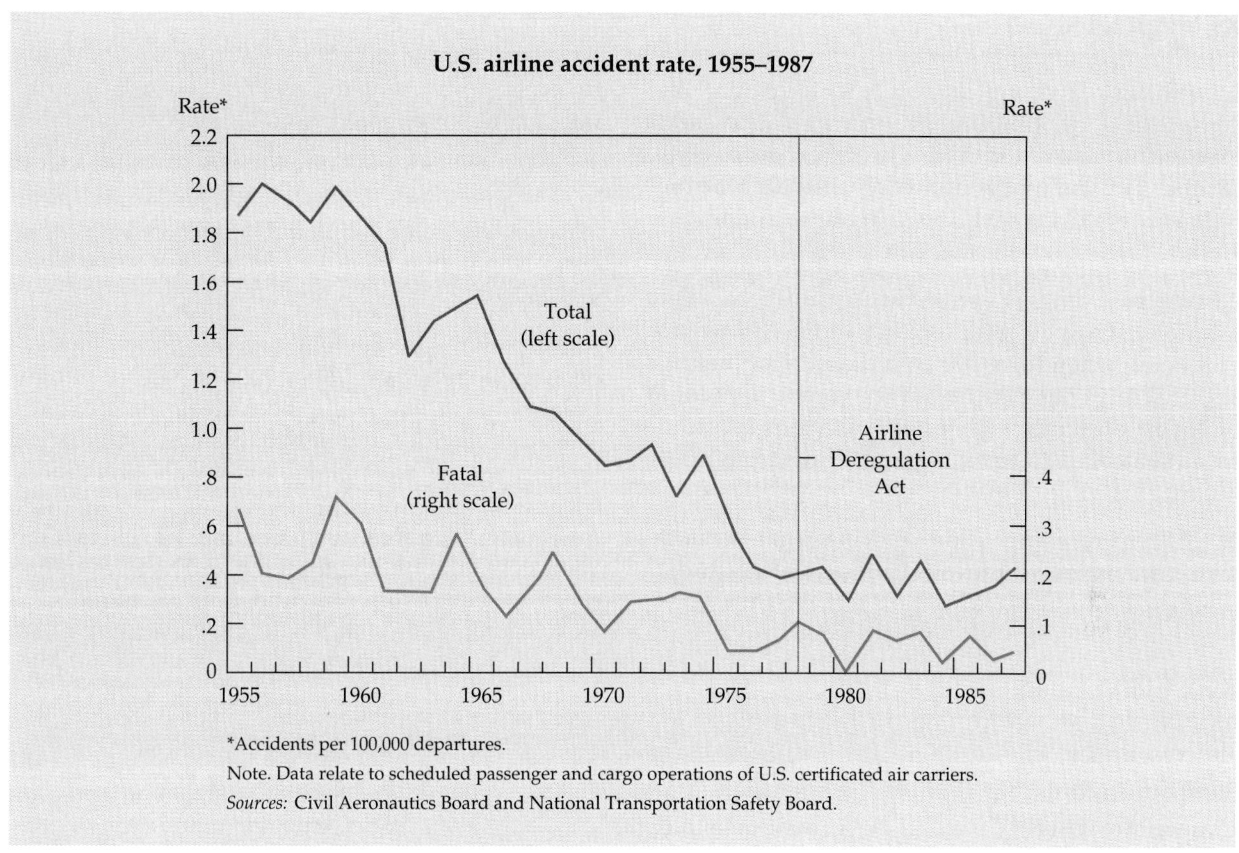

FIGURE 14-3 U.S. airline accident rate, 1955–1987.

To sum up: By letting the market work, deregulation brought substantial advantages. The congestion problem it raised could be reduced by letting the market work even better in the allocation of airport slots.

LIVING IN A GLOBAL ECONOMY

AIRLINE TRAVEL IN EUROPE

Passengers flying from New York to London are often bemused—or angered—to find that a further short hop onto the continent costs even more than their transatlantic flight. One reason is that many European airlines are not private but are state-owned, and deregulation of routes in Europe has seriously lagged deregulation of international and U.S. domestic flights. Remaining European regulations have, in some ways, made that industry resemble the U.S. system prior to its deregulation.

Changes are occurring, however. In 1988 the European Community began to introduce easier entry and more competition into airline routes on which service had previously been limited to only one carrier from each country. Travelers planning a European trip in the future will find European prices high. But in airline travel, they may find that fares are at least moving in the right direction—down.

KEY POINTS

1. Antitrust laws are designed to keep markets competitive by limiting the accumulation and exercise of market power. The three main laws in the government's antitrust arsenal are the Sherman Antitrust Act, the Clayton Act, and the Federal Trade Commission Act.

2. Antitrust laws raise difficult questions. For example, when is price cutting unfair? How do you know when firms are colluding? Nonetheless, antitrust laws have improved the competitive tone of American business, because violations can lead to jail sentences, to fines, or to civil suits from competitors for triple damages.

3. To protect competition, the government may take legal action to prevent collusion or cutthroat pricing. It can also take action to break up large firms, or to prevent the merger of existing firms into a new, larger enterprise.

4. There are substantial benefits and costs to society of mergers. Recently, mergers have been allowed unless the industry is highly concentrated, entry is not free, and economies of scale are not substantial.

5. Although government regulation has always been an appropriate policy to deal with a natural monopoly, it was less satisfactory in naturally more competitive industries such as trucking or the airlines. In such cases, the regulatory agency became a legal way of "cartelizing" the industry by raising its price and dividing up its market. With deregulation, the trucking and airlines industry became more efficient, and their prices fell.

KEY CONCEPTS

antitrust policy
Sherman Antitrust Act (1890)
Clayton Act (1914)
Federal Trade Commission Act (1914)
cutthroat competition
collusion
horizontal merger
vertical merger
conglomerate merger
workable competition
treble damage clause
price-entry regulation
cross-subsidization
deregulation

PROBLEMS

14-1. It sounds like a good idea to forbid any firm from predatory price cutting—that is, pricing to drive its competitors out of business. However, consider the two examples below. In each case, do you think that the price-cutting action should be judged illegal (as it sometimes has been)?

(a) An efficient firm with lower cost than any of its competitors charges a lower price and thus drives the less efficient firms out of business. This is an example of how our competitive system works: The more efficient take business away from the less efficient. Do you think this is a good system? If the less efficient are not driven out of business, what happens to the cost of producing goods?

(b) In a natural monopoly with economies of scale, the large expanding firm finds its costs are falling; hence it lowers its price and drives its small competitors out of business.

Do you see now why enforcing antitrust laws is difficult?

14-2. Which of the following agreements among firms in an industry do you judge desirable? Undesirable? (a) An agreement to reduce output by 10% to end a glut on the market; (b) an agreement to quote the same price; (c) an agreement by the railroads to lay the same width of track.

14-3. In 1962, the Supreme Court disallowed a merger between the Brown Shoe Company and T. R. Kinney, under which shoe manufacturer Brown would have become a major supplier to Kinney's retail shoe stores. The merger was of interest because (1) both firms manufactured shoes, and (2) both firms had retail shoe stores. Which form or forms of merger took place: (a) horizontal, (b) vertical, or (c) conglomerate? Explain your answer.

14-4. Will firms prefer to monopolize their industry through a merger or through a cutthroat price war that drives one firm out of business? Which will consumers prefer?

***14-5.** Does government encourage or discourage takeovers with (a) its tax laws? (b) its antitrust laws? Explain your answer.

14-6. Suppose that, for the last 10 years, a government agency has been regulating the prices of hotel rooms, thus preventing price competition among the big companies like Hilton and Sheraton. Also suppose that in return, these companies have maintained hotels in many smaller cities. Suppose the government is now considering an end to this regulation. (a) As an adviser to this industry, draw up a brief on how dangerous this action would be. (b) Now, switch roles and criticize the brief. In your view, which is the stronger case? Do you think this example is similar to airline regulation? Why or why not?

14-7. To understand cross-subsidization better, consider a simplified example in which there are two individuals: *A* lives in a large city, *B* in a small one. Draw a diagram showing what the demand curve of each individual for airline services might look like.

> **(a)** Suppose that in the initial regulated situation, *A* gets airline service at price P_1, while *B* gets no service. Show the consumer surplus—if any—for each individual.
>
> **(b)** Suppose the following policy of cross-subsidization is introduced. *A* is forced to pay a price above initial price P_1—and has consumer surplus reduced—in order to allow *B* for the first time to have airline service and thereby enjoy a consumer surplus. Show how this policy may provide a collective benefit, that is, an increase in the combined consumer surplus of both individuals taken together.

Does this example support the return of airline regulation? Explain.

14-8. In what respects would an auction of airport landing rights be the same as allocating landing rights to airlines and letting them sell them to each other? In what respects would the two proposals differ?

CHAPTER 15
WHY IS AGRICULTURE A TROUBLED SECTOR?

"When sorrows come, they come not single spies,
But in battalions."

SHAKESPEARE, *HAMLET*

In 1930, the average U.S. farm family produced enough to feed itself and four other families. By 1988, it was producing enough to feed itself and 50 other families. American farmers were among the world's most productive. By this standard, U.S. farming was a tremendous success. Why then were so many farmers in such trouble?

A dramatic illustration of the difficulties faced by U.S. farmers occurred in the first half of the 1980s. While the severe recession of 1981–1982 hit both the farm and nonfarm sectors, the U.S. farm community did not share in the subsequent recovery in the rest of the U.S. economy. Many farmers faced large operating losses and drastic reductions in the value of their land. Those who had borrowed heavily during the 1970s faced a nearly impossible task; it often seemed that no matter how efficiently they produced, they were unable to generate enough income to pay their bills. Many tried to hold on by earning off-farm income, which became more important than farm income in the support of farm families. Some farmers went bankrupt, and as they did, so did some of their banks. At the same time, producers of farm machinery also suffered. Between 1979 and 1986, sales of farm tractors fell by more than 50%. Finally, when signs of a farm recovery did develop in the second half of the 1980s, it was, to a substantial degree, due to an increase in government subsidies.

INTRODUCTION

In any study of agriculture, several perplexing questions arise. Why has the cost of government programs to assist farmers been rising, when the number of farm families has been falling? How can an agricultural sector that has often set the world standard for efficiency be taking a beating in world export markets—especially when the government has been heavily subsidizing U.S. export sales? Why does the farmer, who obviously benefits as an individual from a good crop, suffer if there are good crops nationwide and worldwide?

There is one set of questions that is most perplexing: Why are agricultural problems so difficult to solve? Why have we been grappling with them since the Civil War? Why do they continue, even though the government has been devoting large sums in an attempt to find solutions?

In this chapter, it will be shown that one of the keys to a better understanding of agriculture is to recognize that this sector, more than any other, is characterized by perfectly competitive markets in which productivity improvements result in increased supply and therefore lower price. It is this bountiful supply of food at a relatively low price that generates such benefits to the U.S. public and such problems for U.S. farmers.

This chapter examines the causes of farm problems in detail and evaluates the policies the government has introduced in response. First, however, let's recall an important message from the last chapter. Although government intervention may be justified in a natural monopoly, it may create serious problems in a naturally competitive industry. Because agriculture is a naturally competitive industry, it is not surprising that government intervention has raised problems, regardless of how good the intentions of the government may have been.

One form of intervention has been a guarantee to farmers that the price they will receive for some of their products will not fall below a specified level. Why has the government made this guarantee to farmers but not to producers of industrial goods? One reason is the special set of problems that agriculture has historically had to face.

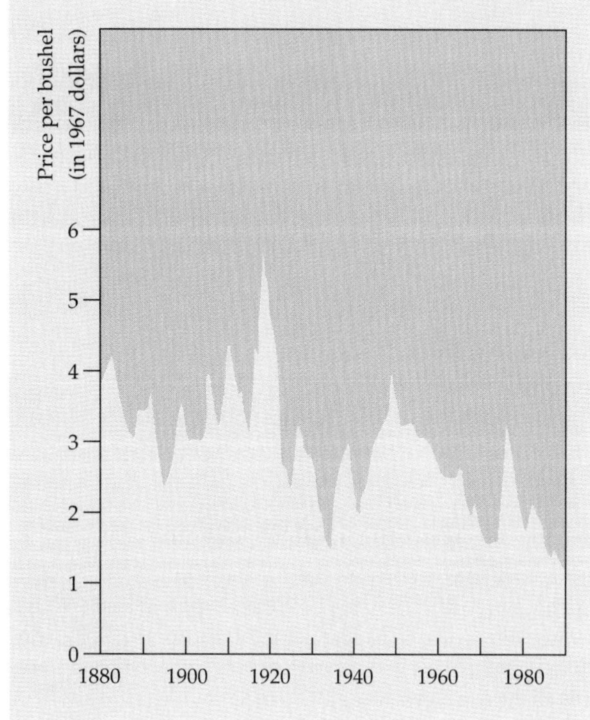

FIGURE 15-1 Instability and downward trend in the real price of wheat, 1880–1988.

In the last century, the real price of wheat has been unstable in the short run and trending down in the long run. (*Source:* U.S. Department of Agriculture, *Agricultural Outlook*, April 1988, p. 2.)

THE PROBLEMS OF AGRICULTURE

Two of the problems of agriculture are that prices have been *unstable in the short run*, with severe fluctuations up and down; and they have shown a *long-run tendency to fall* compared to the price of other goods. Both of these problems have existed for over a century, as the wheat price in Figure 15-1 illustrates. A third problem is a new one: a decline in export sales. The fourth problem—a growing debt burden—became, by some measures, more serious in the 1980s than at any time in this century.

The crisis facing the U.S. farmer in the early 1980s arose because all of these problems converged at once. Each is serious enough to be considered in detail.

1. YEAR-TO-YEAR PRICE INSTABILITY

Prices are unstable because the markets for many agricultural products are perfectly competitive, and demand and supply are inelastic in the short run. Demand for farm products is inelastic because people need to eat no matter what happens to the price of food. Supply is inelastic in the short run for products that are perishable or for crops that are already planted where it is too late for farmers to respond much to a change in price.

The result is shown in Figure 15-2. In a normal year with demand D and supply S_1, equilibrium is at E_1 with price P_1. If there is a poor crop, supply shifts to S_2 and price increases all the way up to P_2 because of the inelasticity of demand. However, with a bumper crop, supply shifts to S_3, equilibrium moves to E_3, and price falls all the way down to P_3. Worse yet for farmers, the inelasticity of demand means that their income falls. Specifically, it is reduced from the rectangle enclosed to the southwest of E_1 to the smaller rectangle to the southwest of E_3. (See Fig. 6-2.) This answers one of the perplexing questions posed in the introduction

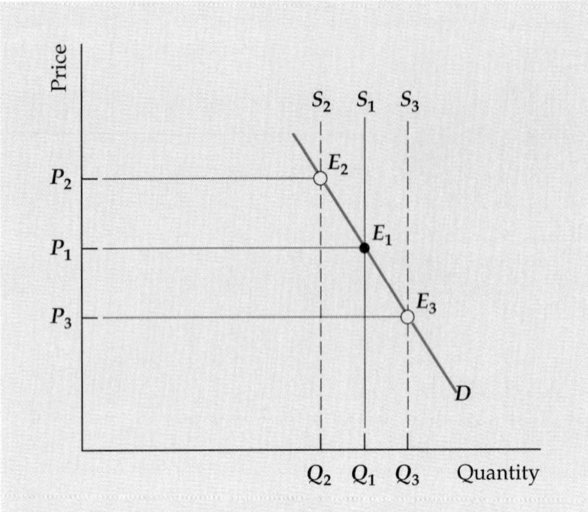

FIGURE 15-2 Short-run instability of farm price.

In a normal year, inelastic demand D and supply S_1 result in equilibrium at E_1. If there is a poor crop, supply shifts to S_2 and, because of inelastic demand, price increases from P_1 all the way up to P_2. If there is a bumper crop, supply shifts to S_3 and price falls all the way down to P_3.

to this chapter: A farmer who will obviously benefit as an individual from a good crop may nonetheless suffer if everyone has a good crop because it may dramatically reduce price.

2. LONG-RUN DOWNWARD TREND IN PRICE

The second farm problem is best understood by considering our economic history. If we go back far enough, farming was more important than all other economic activities combined, and a majority of the population worked on the soil. With old-fashioned techniques of agricultural production, an individual family could produce little more than enough for itself.

With improvements in agricultural methods and technology, productivity increased. A typical farm family could produce more and more food: enough for two families, then three, then four, and so on. As that happened, the number of people required on the farm to produce food fell to a smaller and smaller fraction of the population. The effects of this decline have reached far beyond agriculture. In fact, one of the essential requirements of our industrial development has been the ability of farmers to produce much more food than they consume. Without this capability, the labor force necessary for a developing industry would never have been released from the task of grubbing a bare living from the soil. It was no accident that the Industrial Revolution in Britain in the eighteenth century was preceded by a revolution in agricultural productivity. That agricultural revolution has continued ever since.

This huge increase in agricultural productivity has been a mixed blessing for the farmers who have achieved it. In panel *a* of Figure 15-3, E_1 represents the initial equilibrium in an earlier period, at the intersection of supply S_1 and demand D_1. Over many decades, D has been shifting to the right from D_1 to D_2 because of (1) the increase in the total food-consuming population and (2) the rising income of that population. The effects of rising income have been fairly small, however. Although consumers purchase more of almost everything as their incomes rise, their expenditures on food rise less rapidly than their expenditures on many other goods. With rising incomes, people may double the clothes they acquire and triple the vacations they take, but they do not consume much more food. After all, how much more can anyone eat? Thus the income elasticity of demand for food is low—that is, food purchases respond weakly to an increase in income, and the demand curve shifts very little to the right.

On the other hand, over these same decades rapid improvements in farm productivity have led to an even greater shift in supply, as illustrated by the shift from S_1 to S_2 in panel *a* of Figure 15-3. With supply shifting to the right more rapidly than demand, equilibrium has moved from E_1 to E_2 where price is lower. However, as price falls, farmers—and even more important, their children—leave the farm to pursue more highly paid careers in the city. Because they do, the proportion of the population on the farm falls. This outflow of people from the farm means that there is a less rapid increase in farm output than would otherwise occur. In other words, agricultural supply S_2 shifts less rapidly to the right. In turn, this means a less severe price reduction.

This, in a nutshell, is the history of American agriculture. Because productivity has outrun demand, the proportion of the population on the farm has fallen. By becoming more and more productive, American farmers are doing a great service to

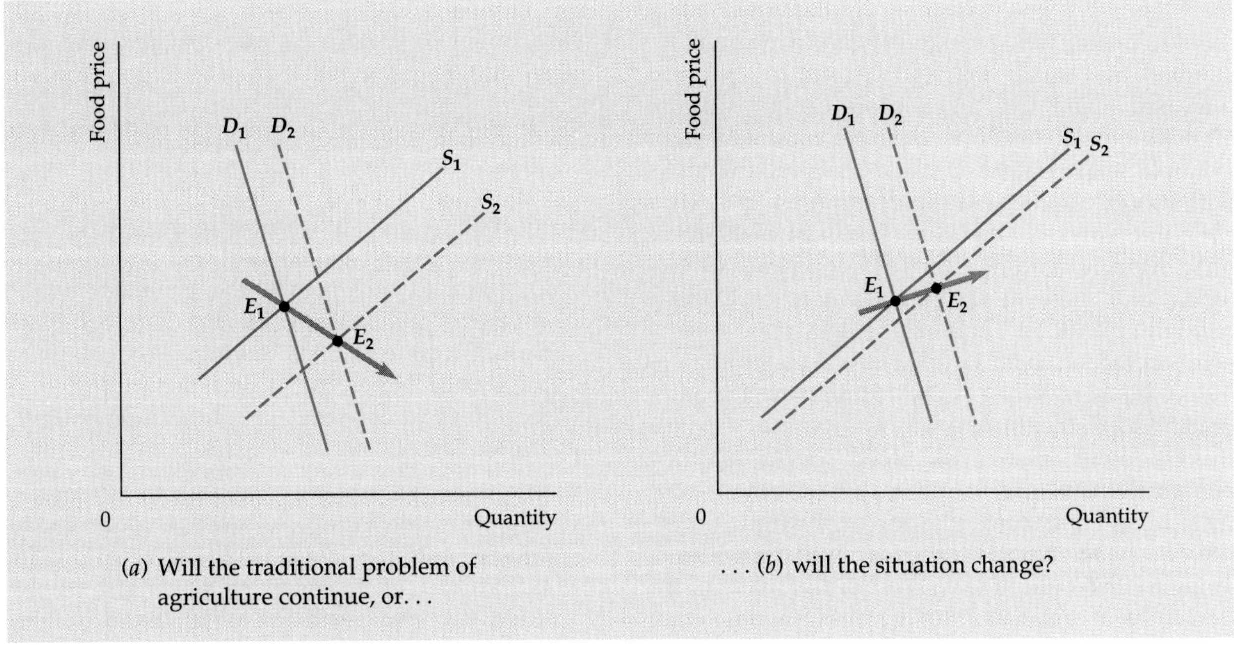

FIGURE 15-3 The long-run trend in agriculture.

The classic problem of agriculture in part *a* has been that supply has shifted to the right more rapidly than demand. Hence price has fallen. This situation may repeat itself in the future, or it may, as some people predict, change to the situation shown in part *b*. There, shifts in supply do not keep pace with shifts in demand and price rises.

the public in terms of providing large quantities of food at a very low price. However, their very success has meant that farmers are producing themselves—or their neighbors—out of jobs.

Will past trends continue or will the future bring food scarcity and higher price? A number of observers contend that, although the problem in the past has usually been an oversupply of food that has depressed price, this situation will not persist. Instead, they predict a chronic food shortage.

As an omen of things to come, they cite our experience in the early 1970s when, as a result of crop failures in the Soviet Union and other countries, there was a world shortage of agricultural goods and prices rose rapidly. For example, the price of wheat more than doubled. The American farmer responded to this high price by expanding export sales. America again became "the world's breadbasket"—the source of food supply to a world suffering from a severe shortage.

Are such periods of scarcity and high price just an early warning of a new era of food shortage rather than surplus? Specifically, will the traditional problem of supply outrunning demand and downward pressure on price shown in panel *a* of Figure 15-3 be replaced by the new situation shown in panel *b*, where supply shifts less than demand and food prices rise?

Some of the reasons put forward for expecting food supply to lag behind demand are not very convincing. For example, it is claimed that we are facing a food crisis because the world is running out of land. In fact, studies indicate quite the contrary. Only about half of the world's arable land is now being used, and much of the unused acreage has good agricultural potential, especially the productive land that has been idled by government programs. Moreover, it is not clear that we will need more land. Recent advances in technology have allowed us to increase output by expanding our use of other inputs—such as fertilizer—rather than land. For example, over a recent period of three decades, U.S. acreage of land in peanuts remained the same, but our output of peanuts increased about five times. More capital can also increase output, without requiring more land. For example, experiments indicate that milking cows with robots can increase their output by 15%. Thus the same cows on the same land can yield more milk. More important, new developments in biotechnology, such as the development of disease-resistant plants and animals, will increase output even further. If such developments materialize as expected, there may be little requirement for additional land in the future.

The other reasons why food supply may lag behind demand are not as easy to dismiss. First, there is the continuing question of how much damage the heavy use of fertilizers and pesticides is doing to the environment. There is a problem of the depletion of ground-water because so much has been drawn off for irrigation purposes. The deforestation of many areas has interfered with a steady supply of water and has damaged soil conditions. Finally, some observers believe that an unfavorable trend in the world's climate has been one of the causes of crop failures in foreign countries.

To decide whether the future situation will be the one shown in panel *a* or panel *b* of Figure 15-3 requires projecting not only world food supply, but also demand. This projection requires an answer to the difficult question: Will the rapid population increase in the developing countries continue, or will these countries begin to experience the lower birth rates observed in the industrialized parts of the world? Or will birth rates fall even lower as a result of government restrictions on family size such as the Chinese policy of one child per couple?

It is impossible to predict whether, in the next century, we will face a continuing surplus in agriculture or a severe world scarcity. All we can say for sure is that by the late 1980s, the major agricultural problem facing governments in both North America and Europe was not food scarcity. Quite the contrary, the problem was oversupply in world markets. For the U.S. farmer, this problem appeared in the form of falling export sales.

3. DECLINE IN EXPORT MARKETS

Figure 15-4 shows the boom in U.S. agricultural exports during the 1970s, resulting in part from crop failures and food shortages abroad. By the 1980s, however, conditions had changed, and U.S. export sales began to fall. Two of the reasons were:

(a) The European Community, traditionally a large market for U.S. food products, had a Common Agricultural Policy (CAP) designed to achieve self-sufficiency. In fact, CAP had moved Europe well beyond this point, so that Europe had now joined the United States as another "breadbasket for the world." Thus Europe was not only buying less food from the United States, but it was also selling more food in third countries in competition with the United States.

(b) Americans not only faced increased competition from the Europeans in third country markets. In addition, these traditional markets for U.S. exports were shrinking as a result of productivity improvements that were moving these countries closer to self-sufficiency. For example, China had adopted agricultural reforms, moving toward freer markets in farm products. As farmers were given an increased opportunity and incentive to sell, they responded with dramatic increases in output. Thus agricultural reform in foreign countries reduced the demand for U.S. exports. Moreover, the question arose as to whether the Soviet Union would respond to this success in other countries by introducing stronger market incentives for its own farmers, in which case its history of crop failures and consequent large demand for imported food might be reversed.

Figure 15-4 shows not only how these developments adversely affected U.S. exports, but also how sensitive U.S. farm income had become to export performance. Note how the fall in exports (in blue) in the 1980s led to a widening gap (in red) between farm income and city income.

The last two diagrams provide another important message. We have seen that the problem of supply outrunning demand in Figure 15-3 has led to a relatively low price for agricultural products. In turn, these low prices have meant relatively low incomes for farmers, as the red income gap in Figure 15-4 illustrates. This is not the result of any general principle. It doesn't *necessarily* follow that low prices lead to low incomes. In fact, it is possible to have low prices and *high* incomes, as the

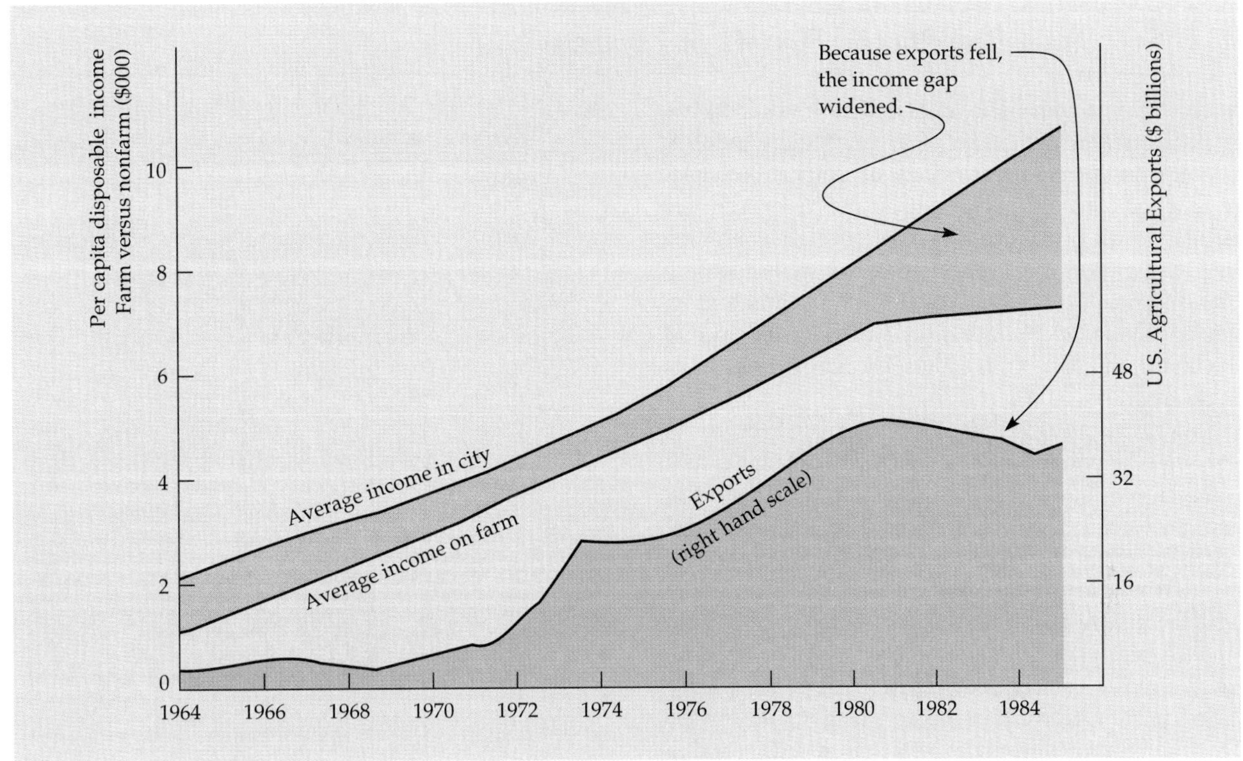

FIGURE 15-4 The farm versus nonfarm income gap and agricultural exports.
As exports decreased after 1981, farm income fell even farther behind city income. Between 1985 and 1987, exports fell again to less than $30 billion. *Source: Economic Report of the President*, 1986 and 1989.

story of IBM in Box 15-1 illustrates. Indeed, IBM has been selling more and more powerful computing power at lower and lower prices. Yet at IBM there has been a rapid increase in the incomes of labor, management, and stockholders alike.

Agriculture illustrates the other possibility, where low prices *have* led to relatively low incomes, on average. Of course, what is true of average income is not true of all incomes. Although many farms generate low incomes, a number of large, highly productive farms generate very high incomes.

Another reason why average farm income was so disappointing was the heavy burden of debt many farmers were carrying.

4. THE DEBT BURDEN

By the mid-1980s, U.S. farmers were over $200 billion in debt, an amount equal to the foreign debt of Mexico and Brazil combined. The burden which this debt imposed on farmers is shown in Figure 15-6. Much of this debt was incurred during the 1970s, when the general inflation was accompanied by a rapid increase in land prices. Expecting the inflation to continue, many farmers borrowed heavily to buy more land. This further increased the demand for land and contributed to the escalation in land values in the late 1970s, shown in Figure 15-7. Farmers who borrowed at this time to buy land paid unrealistically high prices and incurred debt that would have been very difficult to service, even if conditions had not changed.

Conditions did change, however. As world food prices and export sales fell, many U.S. farms that had been prosperous in the 1970s began to suffer losses in the 1980s. Moreover, interest rates rose rapidly in the early 1980s, and this added to the burden of debt. High interest rates also added to the squeeze on heavily indebted third world coun-

BOX 15-1 *Is a Falling Price the Sign of a Sick Industry?*

In some cases, a falling price does indicate a sick industry. In other cases, it is the sign of a very healthy industry indeed. With the rapid development of computer technology, IBM and other computer manufacturers have been able not only to cut prices, but also to increase their incomes. Thus what matters is not simply prices, but the relationship between prices and productivity. In fact, the health of an industry is affected by three major variables—the price of its outputs, the price of its inputs, and the increase in its productivity.

For American agriculture, the relationship between the first two—the price of outputs and the price of inputs such as machinery—has long been a matter of concern, at least since the early 1930s, when farm prices plummeted while machinery prices remained more stable. During the Second World War, the price of farm products rose sharply. By 1950, the picture had again changed, as the price of farm products began to fall. As a result, the ratio of prices farmers received to the prices they paid—that is, the **parity ratio** shown in Figure 15-5—began a long-run downward trend, interrupted only briefly by the prosperous period in the 1970s.

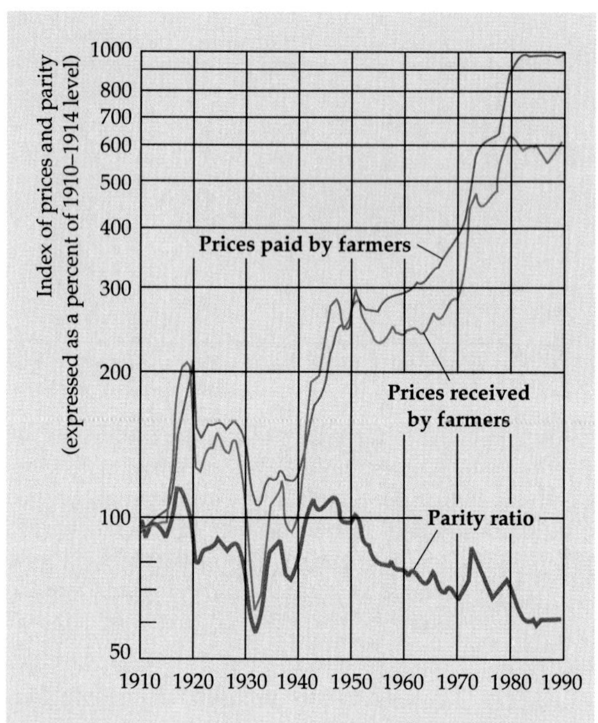

FIGURE 15-5 The parity ratio, 1910 to mid–1989.
The farm parity ratio, which nosedived during the depression in the early 1930s, recovered during the 1940s to above 100, its original level during the base period of 1900–1914. However, since then it has been on a downtrend.

The ***parity ratio*** is the ratio of prices received by farmers divided by the prices paid by farmers.

In conclusion, there has been downward pressure on farm income because of the falling relative price of farm outputs compared to inputs, as shown in the falling parity ratio. To explain farm income more completely, however, we must also look at the important third factor: the increase in productivity, which has raised income. *On balance,* what has been the combined effect of all three pressures on farm income? The answer is an unfavorable effect overall. Although there are many highly productive farmers who earn high incomes, the *average* farmer has a low income relative to incomes elsewhere, and that gap has recently been widening.

tries. As a consequence, they were forced to cut back their purchases of U.S. agricultural exports. Thus high interest rates contributed in an indirect, as well as a direct, way to the malaise of U.S. agriculture.

Those farmers who had to watch the value of their land fall below the amount of their debt found it difficult to escape. They could no longer sell their land even to repay their debt, let alone recapture the downpayment they had made. In addition, falling land prices put the banks in a squeeze as well. They could no longer recapture the full value of some of the loans they had made to farmers, even by foreclosing and auctioning off

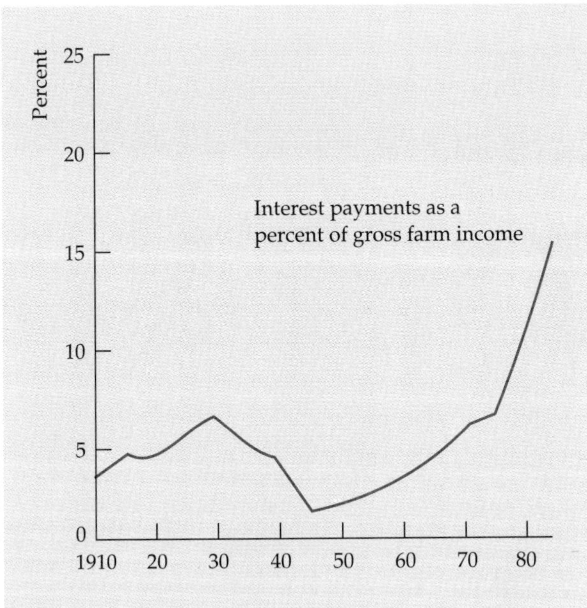

FIGURE 15-6 The burden of farm debt, 1910–1984.

Source: Alden C. Manchester, *Agriculture's Links with U.S. and World Economies,* Agriculture Information Bulletin No. 496, U.S. Department of Agriculture, 1985, p. 32.

the farmers' land and other assets. As a result, an increasing number of agricultural banks went bankrupt, and the crisis on the farm spilled over into America's towns and cities.

Farmers who owned their land outright were not trapped in this way, but all farmers found their incomes seriously affected by the fall in export markets and the softness of agricultural prices. This increased the pressure on the government to increase its aid to farmers.

GOVERNMENT POLICIES TO RAISE FARM PRICES

Each of the panels in Figure 15-8 shows a policy that the U.S. government has used to raise price. Supply and demand are identical in each of these diagrams, and, before any government action, equilibrium is at E_1. Farm income is equal to the rectangle to the southwest of E_1—that is, price P_1 times quantity Q_1.

POLICY 1. PRICE SUPPORT

In panel *a* the government supports the price at the higher level P_2. Farmers respond to this price incentive by moving up their supply curve from E_1 to E_2. At the same time, consumers are discouraged by this higher price and move back up their demand curve from E_1 to E_3. Thus at this higher price there is an excess supply of E_3E_2, which must be purchased by the government if it is to keep the price from falling below P_2. The cost of this government purchase to the taxpayer is the shaded rectangle—that is, the quantity of bushels the government must buy (the base of the rectangle) times the price P_2 it must pay for each bushel (the height of the rectangle). Although this policy imposes a cost on consumers facing a higher price and on taxpayers, it provides a benefit to farmers, because it increases farm income from the original rectangle to the southwest of E_1 to the larger rectangle to the southwest of E_2. That is, farmers now receive price P_2 on the Q_2 bushels they sell. (In actual practice, the government has used a complicated loan scheme, but it has had essentially the same effects as the price support shown here).

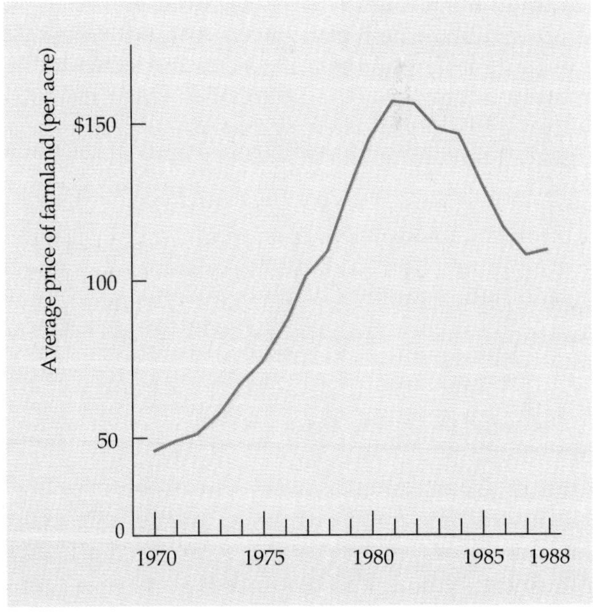

FIGURE 15-7 Price of U.S. farm land, 1970–1988.

The price of U.S. farm land tripled between 1970 and 1981. Since then it has fallen about one-third. *Source: Economic Report of the President,* 1989, p. 421.

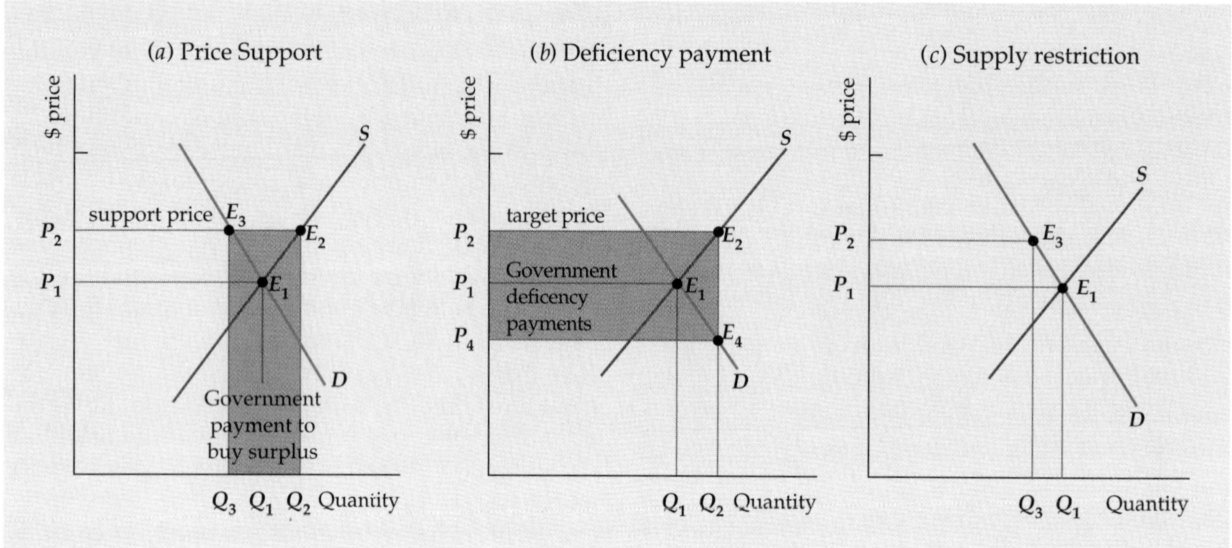

FIGURE 15-8 Three policies the government uses to assist farmers, with the shaded areas showing the cost to taxpayers.

Original equilibrium is at E_1. All three policies raise the price farmers will receive from P_1 to P_2 per bushel.

In panel *a*, the government supports the price at P_2. Consumers move up their demand curve from E_1 to E_3, whereas producers move up their supply curve from E_1 to E_2. The difference between the amount produced at E_2 and the amount consumed at E_3 must be purchased by the government, at a cost shown by the shaded area.

In panel *b*, the government still guarantees farmers price P_2, so they again move up their supply curve from E_1 to E_2 producing Q_2. But here the government does not support the price, and quantity Q_2 can be sold only if the price falls to P_4. The government pays farmers a deficiency payment P_2P_4 on each bushel—that is, the difference between the price P_2 that they have been guaranteed and the price P_4 they are receiving from the market. The total deficiency payment farmers receive for their Q_2 bushels is the shaded area.

In panel *c*, the government restricts output from Q_1 to Q_3, which raises price to P_2.

Although all three policies raise price to P_2, farmers will prefer panel *a* or *b* since they receive a higher income (the area to the southwest of E_2, rather than the smaller area to the southwest of E_3 in panel *c*).

POLICY 2. DEFICIENCY PAYMENT

Panel *b* shows an alternative government policy that is of equal benefit to the farmer. In this case, the government again guarantees the same price P_2 to farmers, although in this case it is called a "target price" rather than a support price. Farmers again move up their supply curve from E_1 to E_2 and produce Q_2. However, in this case the government makes no attempt to maintain the market price at P_2 by buying up the surplus. Instead, it lets the market price "find its own level." Because Q_2 is coming onto the market, price falls to P_4. (Point E_4 on the demand curve indicates that large quantity Q_2 will be purchased by the public only at low price P_4.) This policy is quite different from the previous one from the point of view of consumers who benefit from a *lower* price P_4.

Farmers are guaranteed P_2 per bushel by the government, but they are receiving only P_4 per bushel from the market. Therefore the government must provide a "deficiency payment" or subsidy to farmers of P_2P_4 for each bushel they sell. Multiplying this by Q_2, the number of bushels sold, yields the shaded area—the total subsidy paid by the government to farmers.

Either of the policies can be expensive. A price support requires the government to purchase surplus stocks of the commodity, whereas a deficiency payment requires the government to make payments to farmers. However, the government has a less expensive third option—a restriction of supply.

POLICY 3. RESTRICTION OF SUPPLY

The third option, in panel *c*, is to raise price to the same level P_2 by restricting production from Q_1 to Q_3. Point E_3 on the demand curve shows that when Q_3 is produced, it will be purchased at a price of P_2. Thus equilibrium moves from E_1 to E_3. Consumers are hurt by the high price P_2 that they have to pay. On the other hand, farmers receive this high price because the government, like a private monopolist, has restricted output. (Although a government supply restriction does raise price, it may not raise it as far as a profit-maximizing monopolist would.)

Government supply restrictions have appeared in several forms. For example, there have been acreage limitations in grains. "Marketing orders" in milk and some fruits and vegetables have been used to restrict the quantity sold in a specific geographic area.

COMBINED PROGRAMS

Sometimes the three programs above have been used in combination. For example, for some grains the government has instituted both a price support, which it has maintained by purchasing any surplus, *and* an even higher target price. The difference between the target price and the support price has been covered by a deficiency payment to farmers. (See Problem 15-6.) In order to qualify for these benefits, farmers have sometimes been required to restrict their supply by reducing their planted acreage. Farmers willing to make *further* cuts in their planted acreage have been paid cash or the equivalent for doing so.

Clearly, an understanding of each of the three policies outlined in Figure 15-8 is required to analyze the complex combinations that the government sometimes uses.

EVALUATION OF GOVERNMENT PROGRAMS: EFFICIENCY EFFECTS

A price support (panel *a* of Fig. 15-8) or a deficiency payment (panel *b*) results in "too much" being produced—that is, Q_2 rather than the efficient, perfectly competitive Q_1. On the other hand, the supply restriction shown in panel *c* results in "too little" being produced—that is, Q_3 rather than the efficient Q_1. (See Fig. 11-3.)

The Council of Economic Advisers has estimated efficiency losses for five products, shown in Figure 15-9. In each case, the first column shows the cost to taxpayers who make direct payments to farmers and/or the cost to consumers who have to pay a higher price. This exceeds the benefit in the second column to farmers who receive the higher price or direct payments from the government. The remaining "excess cost" is the efficiency loss shown in the third column.

In terms of efficiency, the overall judgment on these programs is unfavorable. Nonetheless, there is an important possible exception. A price support program may *increase* efficiency in a market in which price is fluctuating year to year and the government is not trying to raise average price, but is *only stabilizing* price. That is, the government is not only buying during years of plenty to keep the price from falling, but is also selling during years of shortage to keep the price from rising. Hence it is operating a "buffer stock" which it adds to in years of plenty and draws from in years of shortage. By preventing shortages, such a program could increase efficiency, as detailed in Box 15-2. It should be emphasized that this favorable effect occurs only if a support program is used just to stabilize price. This is often not the case. Even when these programs are designed to stabilize price, they typically are used to raise price as well.

EQUITY EFFECTS

The standard defense of farm programs is that they are equitable because they transfer income to relatively poor farmers from taxpayers/consumers

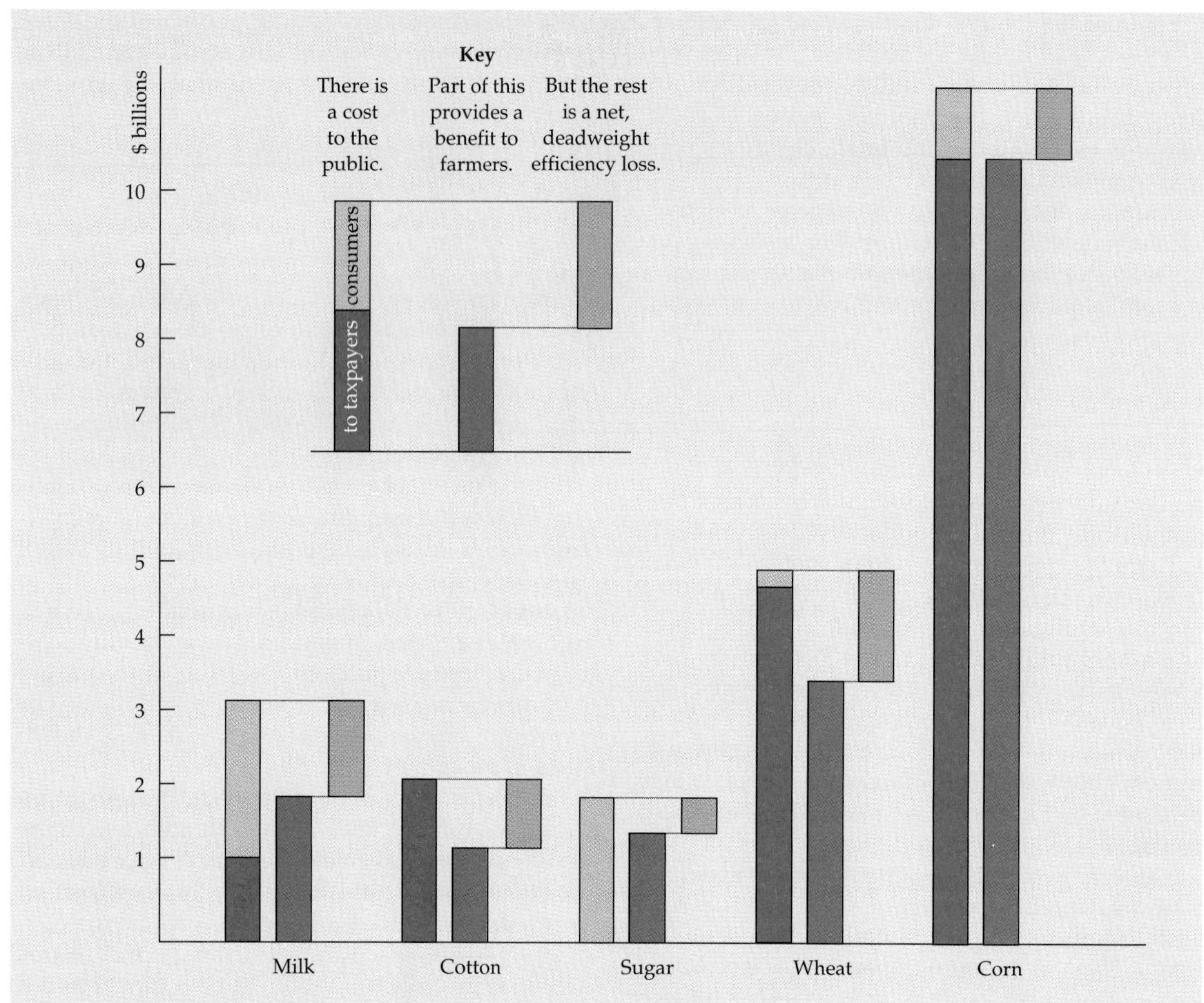

FIGURE 15-9 Annual gains and losses from agricultural assistance policies of the U.S. government.

Source: Averages of estimates in *Economic Report of the President, 1987*, p. 159.

who typically have higher average incomes. Recall from Figure 15-4 that, *on average*, farm income is indeed low, being substantially below nonfarm income. The problem is that, within this average, there are many farmers with high incomes. Moreover, it is these individuals who receive the largest income transfers, rather than the relatively poor farmers who most need assistance.

To illustrate, Figure 15-10 compares small farms on the left with large farms on the right. The first point on the brown line shows the large number of U.S. farms that are very small, with less than $10,000 of sales. Indeed, there are almost as many farms in this category as in all the others combined. On average, these farmers operate at a loss and survive by earning off-farm income. Their almost invisible gray bar indicates that they receive almost no direct government assistance.

On the other hand, on the right of this diagram there are relatively few big farms, but they receive

BOX 15–2 *How Government Price Stabilization Could Increase Efficiency*

And let them gather all the food of those good years that come, and lay up corn under the hand of Pharaoh, and let them keep food in the cities.

And that food shall be for store to the land against the seven years of famine, which shall be in the land of Egypt; that the land perish not through the famine.

GENESIS 41: 35–36

In some years there is a good crop, and in some years a bad one. When crops are good, there is a plentiful supply and price is low. When crops are poor, small supply drives the price up. Thus, without government intervention, the price of wheat could rise by 50% in a year of drought and fall by 50% in a year of plenty. In those circumstances, government stabilization of price can also stabilize consumption.

To see why, note that in the years of plenty when the government price support keeps price from falling, the government has to buy up a surplus and thus adds to its buffer stock. (See panel *a* of Figure 15-8.) On the other hand, in years of scarcity, the government prevents the price from skyrocketing by selling off some of its buffer stock. Thus to prevent price from fluctuating, the government takes wheat off the market in periods of plenty (when it can be easily spared) and returns it to the market in periods of scarcity when it has a much higher value. The public benefits—that is, there is an efficiency gain.

Note that this argument is similar to the one in Figure 11-7 on page 186 which shows that successful speculation by private investors can also increase efficiency by reducing fluctuations in price and consumption. Who can do the better job of stabilizing price—the government or private speculators? To some degree, the answer depends on whether the government can predict average future price as well as speculators can. If it can, a government price support may be the better way to stabilize price. The reason is that a government guarantee to farmers at planting time of the price they will eventually receive is the best way to induce the right production response. Private speculators cannot provide such a guarantee.

However, many doubt that the government can predict as well as private speculators. After all, those in government are good at winning elections, whereas private speculators are good at predicting future price. (Those who aren't lose money and go out of business.) Moreover, those in government may adjust their predictions in response to political pressure. If they do so, they may raise prices rather than just stabilizing them.

If the government succeeds in only stabilizing price by setting the support price at the average of the fluctuating free-market price, it will sell as much in years of scarcity as it buys in years of plenty. It will not accumulate a growing surplus over time.

On the other hand, if the government *is* accumulating an ever-growing surplus (or if it is keeping its surplus from growing by letting some rot or by otherwise disposing of it at a loss) it is no longer just stabilizing price. It is now also raising it and thereby encouraging farmers to produce "too much." In this case there *is* an efficiency loss.

How can the public determine whether a government price support program is only stabilizing price, rather than inefficiently raising average price? Although there is no sure-fire way of answering this question, here's an important clue. If the government surplus is not growing beyond the buffer stock amount necessary to cover future crop failures (and the surplus is not rotting or being disposed of at a loss), then price supports have been stabilizing farm price rather than raising it. In contrast, if the government is having to deal with an unwanted surplus, then price supports have been raising average price.

Unfortunately, in most years, North American and European countries are having to deal with an unwanted surplus. Thus, in practice, a policy of stabilizing price has been turned into an inefficient policy of raising price.

very large benefits from the government. For example, in 1985 each of the 31,000 largest farms on the right received an average of almost $40,000 from the government. Indeed, some received more than $1 million, and the crown prince of Liechtenstein, as a partner in a Texas rice farm, received a subsidy of over $2 million. Such abuses led to limits on the benefits going to any individual. However, some farmers evaded this regulation by establishing several farm corporations, each of which drew subsidies from the government.

Thus critics charge that farm programs may be

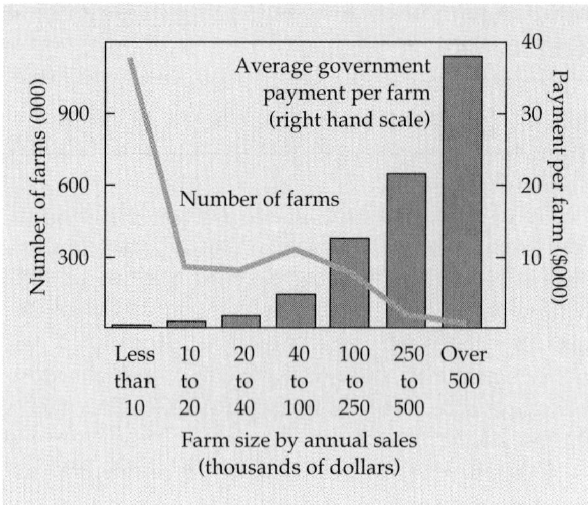

FIGURE 15-10 Number of farms, and average direct government payment per farm, by sales class, 1985.
Source: Economic Report of the President, 1986, p. 132, and *1987,* p. 156.

transferring income to farmers, but, by and large, the wrong farmers are getting it. It is easy to see why. Since farm programs pay farmers according to how much they produce, the big producers get the big subsidies. If the government wants to cure farm poverty, shouldn't it put its subsidy on each poor farmer rather than on each bushel of, say, wheat? (Although reform in this direction is frequently recommended, it is not entirely trouble-free. As Chapter 25 will show, direct payments to those with low incomes can create problems, too.)

A second concern about the equity of farm programs is that most of the benefits may be ultimately captured by landowners rather than by those who operate the farms. How is this possible? The process, described in detail on pages 275 to 276 below, can be sketched out as follows. When the government raises the price of a product such as wheat, the land on which wheat is grown becomes more valuable and can be sold for a higher price. Higher priced land means that the farmer has to pay more to buy it or rent it. Thus farmers who rent or buy land to grow crops may get little benefit. Although they receive higher revenue because government policies are raising price, they also face higher land cost. The benefits go instead to the owners of the land when the government program was introduced, since this policy raised the value of their land. Often farmers *are* landowners, of course, and in such cases they benefit. But they benefit largely because they are landowners, not because they are farmers.

High-priced farmland makes it difficult, if not impossible, to end farm assistance policies suddenly. To see why, consider those individuals who do raise the necessary funds to get into farming by borrowing heavily on a large mortgage. They will be able to earn a living—and make those big mortgage payments—only if the government price support program continues. So these farmers of *necessity* become strong supporters of the government program. Without it, agricultural prices would fall, and they would no longer be able to make their mortgage payments. In short, when government support programs are introduced, they tend to benefit one group—those who initially own the land. If these initial owners sell it, they become "out-of-reach." For example, if they have retired to Florida on the proceeds of their land sale, they cannot be damaged if the farm support program is then ended. Instead, the damage falls on the *new* owners.

This is not an argument that price supports should be set in stone and never reduced. Instead, it is a warning that subsidizing the price of wheat and other farm products may have quite different effects from those intended. Such subsidies may benefit farm owners rather than farmers and, once introduced, may be difficult to end.

LOOKING TO THE FUTURE

The fall in the U.S. dollar from its high level in the mid-1980s has made U.S. agricultural products more competitive in world markets. Moreover, a highly productive U.S. agriculture now stands ready to cover any world food shortage that may develop. If such a shortage were to occur, it would, by raising world price, "solve" many of the perplexing problems facing U.S. agriculture. It would raise farm income and provide U.S. farmers with the satisfaction of playing the role they have traditionally wanted—of providing a breadbasket for a hungry world. In such a situation, the role of the government would be reduced. The government could phase out acreage limitations and other supply restraints. It would no longer have to finance support prices and target prices, because they would become irrelevant once the world market price, in response to scarcity, rose above them. In short, shortages in the rest of the world would bring on a new golden age for U.S. agriculture.

But there is little sign of this happening. While there are still pockets of starvation—and while one has to recognize the possibility of future crop failures due to unpredictable weather conditions—the world as a whole seems to be moving in the opposite direction. Even high-population countries such as China and India have been moving toward self-sufficiency. Indeed, China has become the world's largest wheat producer. Typically, world markets have been characterized not by shortages, but by oversupply, as illustrated by the huge government accumulation of stocks of grain, shown in Figure 15-11.

U.S. farmers face other problems as well. Because heavy application of fertilizer, pesticides, and other chemicals has been contributing to the nation's water pollution problems, the government may impose new requirements on farmers to comply with antipollution and conservation guidelines. Such measures would add to farm costs. But perhaps the most important problem confronting the U.S. farmer has been the "subsidy war" between the United States and the European Community (EC) which has imposed a heavy cost on the U.S. Treasury and has deprived American farmers of some of their traditional export markets.

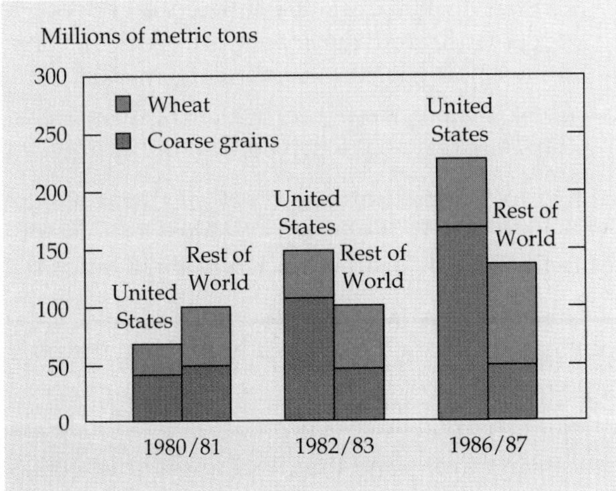

FIGURE 15-11 Carryover stocks of coarse grains and wheat.

Source: Economic Report of the President, 1987, p. 160.

LIVING IN A GLOBAL ECONOMY

THE SUBSIDY WAR IN FARM PRODUCTS

To understand how the subsidy war began, note that once any country *A* has domestic price supports, it finds itself under pressure to introduce two trade policies:

1. *Restrict imports by imposing quotas or tariffs.* Without such a policy, foreign food producers could freely sell their products in *A* at *A's* artificially high support price. Consequently, they would benefit at the expense of *A's* taxpayers who provide the funds to support the price.

2. *Subsidize exports.* Specifically, *A's* government will be under pressure to get rid of the mounting surpluses it has been purchasing in order to support prices. It may try to do so by selling in foreign markets, even though the price is low. The difference between *A's* high domestic price and the lower export price is an export subsidy.

Both the United States and the EC have used these two policies. As applied by the EC, these policies have severely damaged U.S. farmers in two ways. First, the EC's import restrictions have been a major cause of reduced U.S. exports to Europe. Second, the EC's export subsidies have been an important reason why the Europeans have been able to capture sales from the United States in its traditional third country markets. In these markets, Europeans have sold food for a small fraction of its support price within Europe, with the difference, as already noted, being an export subsidy. By the late 1980s, the losses to U.S. farmers had become so substantial that the United States announced that it would increase American export subsidies by whatever amount might be necessary to retain its third-country sales. Thus began the subsidy war, or 'international food fight,' between the United States and Europe. To protect their own sales, other exporting countries were under pressure to follow suit.

This war proved to be very damaging, as the treasuries of the exporting countries had to bear an increased burden of subsidy payments. A recent World Bank study estimates that all subsidies and import restrictions have been costing consumers and taxpayers in about 20 developed countries roughly $150 billion a year, while providing only about $50 billion of benefits to their farmers. The $100 billion difference has represented the deadweight efficiency loss plus the benefit to importing countries such as the Soviet Union that have been buying the subsidized exports at bargain prices.

There has been a less obvious, but possibly much more important, form of damage. Protectionism and subsidy wars have been a major source of friction between the United States and Europe. Failure to resolve agricultural disputes may make it difficult to achieve much progress in liberalizing industrial trade. Thus the agricultural subsidy war may impose major costs on both agricultural *and* industrial trade. This has led the United States to propose that all countries end agricultural export subsidies.

Although such a drastic solution is unlikely, there is some hope of moving at least some distance in this direction. Hence it is still of interest to ask whether in a world without subsidies, the U.S. farmer could compete. The answer, in most agricultural products, is yes. With its plentiful fertile land and high productivity, the United States is one of the world's lowest cost sources of food and could easily compete against Germany and other higher cost countries in Europe.

It is a challenge that many U.S. farmers would welcome.

KEY POINTS

1. Agricultural prices are unstable in the short run because agriculture is perfectly competitive and short-run supply and demand are inelastic.

2. In the long run, the demand for food has been expanding (shifting to the right) relatively slowly. One reason is that the public's expenditure on food doesn't rise very much as incomes increase. At the same time, supply has been expanding more rapidly, due to dramatic improvements in farmers' productivity. As a result, agricultural prices have followed a long-run downward trend relative to other prices—in particular, relative to the prices farmers have to pay for their inputs.

3. The U.S. farmer has suffered losses in traditional export markets because these countries are becoming more self-sufficient, and because Europe has gone beyond self-sufficiency to become a competitor in these markets.

4. In the 1980s, many U.S. farmers operated under a heavy burden of debt because of their earlier purchases of land at inflated prices.

5. To keep the price the farmer receives from falling, the government has used the following policies, sometimes in combination:

> **(a)** A price support policy of purchasing farm products to prevent their price from falling below a specified level.
>
> **(b)** A deficiency payment made directly to farmers to make up the difference between a target price and the lower price they receive from selling their products on the market.
>
> **(c)** A supply restriction which raises price in the same way that a private monopoly does.

6. A price support or deficiency payment results in an inefficiently large output, whereas a supply restriction results in an inefficiently small output.

7. Farm policies that raise the price of food typically benefit the rich farmer far more than the poor farmer.

8. The U.S./European subsidy war has benefited farmers in Europe and the United States, as well as consumers in countries buying the subsidized exports. But it has imposed a heavy burden on taxpayers in Europe and the United States.

KEY CONCEPTS

parity
farm debt burden
price support
deficiency payment
target price
supply restriction
marketing orders
export subsidy
subsidy war

PROBLEMS

15-1. How were U.S. land prices affected by inflation in the late 1970s and by high interest rates in the early 1980s?

15-2. How might marketing orders in agricultural products be defended by using the theory of the second best? (For a review of that theory, see Box 12-1.) Do you think that, on balance, this argument justifies this policy?

15-3. The British Columbia Milk Board sells milk at a price more than 10% above the free-market level. The board has also made it illegal to sell reconstituted milk—that is, powdered milk mixed with water and fresh milk. The reason given for this action is to protect the consumer from an inferior product. Yet, in tests, consumers cannot distinguish this milk from fresh milk, and it would cost much less. Is the marketing board protecting consumers or some other group?

15-4. If the United States imports a commodity, is it possible for the government to introduce a price support without restricting those imports?

15-5. In 1982, there was good weather and a bountiful grain harvest. Show the effect of this on price support programs in Figure 15-8*a*.

***15-6.** Suppose the government introduces a price support program that raises price. Suppose further that the government also guarantees an even higher target price for farmers, by providing a deficiency payment equal to the difference between the target price and the support price. Add a fourth panel to Figure 15-8 to illustrate this combined policy.

CHAPTER 16

GOVERNMENT REGULATIONS TO PROTECT OUR QUALITY OF LIFE

The difference between inefficient and efficient . . . policies to control pollution can mean scores, perhaps hundreds, of billions of dollars released for other useful purposes over the next several decades.

ALLEN V. KNEESE AND CHARLES L. SCHULTZE

Like the ancient mariner, a captain sails the high seas, searching for a spot to dump a barge full of garbage. Meanwhile, the past dumping of chemicals has made Times Beach, Missouri, a ghost town. Its 2,000 inhabitants have left, its houses are boarded up, and the wind whistles through its empty streets. In Bhopal, India, a leak in a Union Carbide plant released toxic gases that killed almost 3,000 people. In the following year, a leak in another Union Carbide plant sent 135 people to hospital in West Virginia. Americans sweating out the unusually hot summer of 1988 were wondering: Is this an early warning of damage the human race may be doing to its atmosphere by burning so much fossil fuel?

True, some of these problems are not new; for decades the air in large cities has been polluted. However, environmental threats have now become more serious. One reason has been the development of more than 4 million synthetic chemicals. Many are very useful, such as the modern herbicides and fertilizers that contribute to agricultural productivity. The problem is that some of their side effects are not benevolent. For example, the chemical that leaked at Bhopal was used to produce an insecticide that becomes relatively harmless to humans a few days after it is sprayed on crops. But when accidentally released at the wrong time, it is lethal.

To deal with such problems, the Environmental Protection Agency (EPA) has been set up to restrict pollution of our water, soil, and air. Analyzing the policies of this agency is the first topic covered in this chapter. This is followed by a description of how other government agencies listed in Table 16-1

TABLE 16-1 Selected Agencies Designed to Improve the Quality of Life

Agency		*Year Established*
CPSC	Consumer Products Safety Commission	1972
EPA	Environmental Protection Agency	1970
FAA	Federal Aviation Administration	1958
FDA	Food and Drug Administration	1931
OSHA	Occupational Safety and Health Administration	1971

monitor safety and health in the workplace and prevent the sale of unsafe products to consumers. Why are these agencies necessary? Because the public places such a high value on our quality of life, why won't a free market deliver what the public wants? If government intervention is to be undertaken, what is the most efficient form?

MEASURES TO CONTROL POLLUTION

In order to reduce pollution, Congress has passed laws such as the Water Pollution Control Act, the Clean Air Act, and the Toxic Substances Control Act. These laws provide for

1. Limits, to be enforced by the EPA, on the pollutants a firm may discharge into the water, air, or earth.

2. Limits on the pollutants that may be discharged by a product, such as the exhaust emissions discharged by automobiles.

3. Subsidies to municipalities for building waste disposal plants and tax reductions to firms installing pollution-control equipment.

4. Special taxes on oil and chemical companies to create a Superfund to finance the cleanup of old chemical and oil dumps.

The results have been substantial, with some kinds of pollution reduced by an estimated quarter to a half. There are now boutiques in Cleveland along the Cuyahoga, a river that used to be so contaminated with oil and debris that it twice caught fire. As local residents say: "If you don't believe the Cuyahoga was that bad, you should have taken a walk on it." The Great Lakes are cleaner and clearer, and the fish are returning. In Maine, salmon have come back to the Penobscot River. But these tales tell only half the story. The EPA is to be judged not only by the improvements it has brought to the environment, but also by its successes in keeping the environment from getting worse. It is important to recognize that pollution will be a continuing problem because it will never be possible to eliminate it completely. Even if U.S. industry were to be brought to a standstill by the closing of every plant that did any polluting whatsoever, pollutants from millions of country barnyards and city streets would still wash into our streams. Because it is not possible to eliminate pollution, the realistic questions are:

> How far should pollution be cut back?
>
> What costs should we be willing to bear?

POLLUTION: THE EXPENSIVE JOB OF CONTROL

No matter how the cleanup is initially financed, the public eventually bears the burden in one of the following ways.

1. Taxpayers bear the cost not only of subsidizing waste disposal plants and pollution-control equipment, but also of operating the agencies such as the EPA which set the cleanup regulations.

2. Business firms face costs in complying with the regulations, such as the costs of installing pollution controls or using cleaner, more expensive fuel. Eventually, these costs are passed on to the firms' wage earners or shareholders, or on to the public which has to pay a higher price for the firms' products.

3. Alternatively, to the degree that firms cover their costs of reducing pollution by investing less in capital equipment, our growth of productivity and output is reduced. In this case, the opportunity cost of controlling pollution is slower growth. Therefore the public pays in the future.

Because it is so costly to control pollution, it is important to use the least expensive methods. Unfortunately, the method initially used by the EPA was an inefficient and costly one.[1] However, more recently the EPA has been moving toward a less expensive policy. In this chapter, these policies will be compared. (An extremely costly policy—and one that is sometimes recommended, though never used—is described in Box 16-1.)

To set the stage, consider why government intervention is necessary in the first place. Why

---

[1]For more on the cost of the EPA's original pollution controls, see T. H. Tietenberg, "Uncommon Sense: The Program to Reform Pollution Control Policy," in Leonard W. Weiss and Michael W. Klass, eds., *Regulatory Reform: What Actually Happened* (Boston: Little, Brown, 1986), pp. 286–289. This source is drawn on heavily in this chapter.

BOX 16-1 *Why Not Control Pollution by Ending Economic Growth?*

Industrial growth generally means more industrial waste. Therefore why not deal with the pollution problem by stopping industrial growth? The answer is that it would be a very inefficient policy. Stopping growth would only *stop the increase* in pollution; it would not reduce *existing* pollution. Thus, as a way of reducing pollution, a nongrowth policy would be inferior to our present policies, which have allowed us to reduce some kinds of pollution even though the economy has been *growing*. To have achieved such a reduction in pollution simply by limiting GNP would have required not zero growth but instead a reduction in GNP.

Thus, as a means of reducing pollution, limiting output would be extraordinarily expensive, yet ineffective. It would be like killing a rat by burning your house down. Even if you cure the problem, the side effects are appalling. It is better by far to find a cure specifically designed to deal with the problem. If the problem is a rat, get a trap. If the problem is pollution, find a policy that directly reduces it.

does the private market fail? Why can't we count on Adam Smith's "invisible hand" to protect the quality of life?

POLLUTION: AN EXTERNAL COST

Because of pollution, *private and social costs differ.* To understand why, consider a pulp and paper factory located on a river. The costs of paper to society include not only the private or *internal costs* faced by the pulp and paper firm—such as the costs of labor and raw materials—but also the cost to those who live downstream and must put up with the wastes that the firm releases into the river. Although the pulp and paper firm has to pay for its internal costs, any cost downstream is *external* to its operation, since this cost is borne by others.

> ***Internal*** or ***private costs*** are the costs incurred by those who actually produce or consume a good.
>
> ***External costs***—also known as ***cost spillovers***—are costs borne by others. Pollution is an example.

Consider a simple illustration. Suppose that each unit of a product is treated with an ounce of a fluid that is then released as a waste into a river. Suppose also that each of these ounces of fluid then imposes a constant damage to those downstream. Then each unit of output imposes a constant external pollution cost, shown as the short red arrow in Figure 16-1. When it is added to the internal cost borne by producers (the brown arrow MC), the result is the tall arrow MC_S, the marginal cost of this good to society. MC_S is a constant height above MC because of our assumption of a constant external cost for each unit of output.

> ***Marginal social cost*** is the sum of (1) marginal private cost, plus (2) marginal external cost.

External costs cause a *misallocation of resources, even if markets are perfectly competitive.* Figure 16-2 shows why. MC and MC_S are reproduced from Figure 16-1, and demand *D* represents this good's marginal benefit—both private and social. S_1 shows what firms are willing to supply. This curve

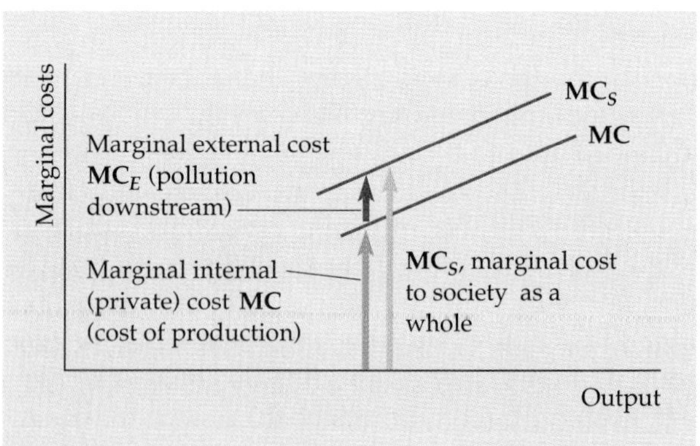

FIGURE 16-1 With pollution, private and social costs differ.

The marginal cost to society of a good, shown by the tall arrow MC_S, includes both the marginal *internal* cost to the producing firm and the marginal *external* cost not borne by the producing firm.

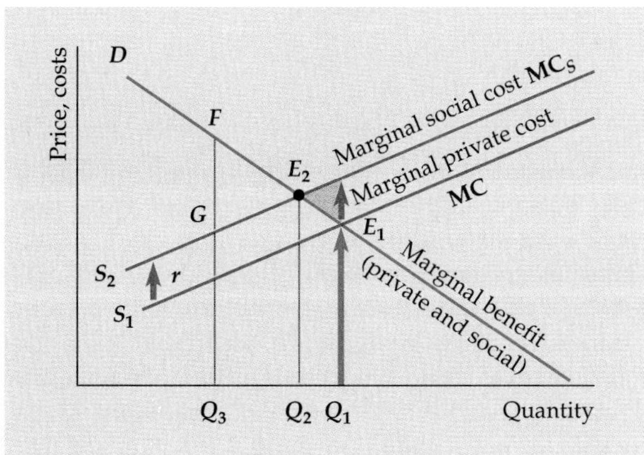

FIGURE 16-2 Free-market efficiency loss when there is an external cost.

Before government intervention, industry supply is S_1, reflecting only the private internal costs facing sellers. This supply equals demand at E_1, with inefficient output Q_1 because marginal social cost exceeds benefit. Thus the last unit Q_1 is not worth producing; its benefit, shown by the blue arrow under the demand curve, is less than its cost to society (the blue arrow plus the red arrow under the MC_S curve). The efficiency loss is the sum of all such red arrows—that is, the red triangle. *After the tax r,* producers are forced to face both the internal and external costs, so that their supply curve shifts up from S_1 to S_2. D and S_2 now yield an equilibrium at E_2, with output Q_2. This is efficient because marginal social cost and benefit are equal.

measures internal private costs—the only costs that the firms making supply decisions have to face. With demand D and supply S_1, the perfectly competitive equilibrium is E_1.

For society, E_1 is not an efficient outcome, because it equalizes marginal social benefit and marginal *private* cost only. An efficient solution requires that marginal social benefit be equal to marginal *social* cost MC_S. This occurs at E_2, at the smaller output Q_2. Thus, in a perfectly competitive market, firms produce too much of a polluting good—Q_1 rather than the efficient amount Q_2. It is efficient to cut back production of this good and use the resources to produce something else instead.

To confirm that Q_1 is an inefficient output, note that the benefit from the last unit produced is the blue arrow under the demand curve. However, its cost is even greater, because it includes both its private cost (this same arrow) and its external cost (shown by the red arrow). Hence, this red arrow represents the net loss in producing this last unit Q_1. Since there is a similar loss in the production of each of the other "excess" units between Q_2 and Q_1, the total efficiency loss is measured by the red triangle.

It is to eliminate this efficiency loss that government intervention is justified.

CONTROLLING POLLUTION: THE SIMPLE CASE

A relatively simple way for the government to increase efficiency in Figure 16-2 is to levy a per-unit tax r on producers equal to the marginal external cost (the red arrow on the left). Such a tax imposes a cost on producers equal to the cost of their pollution on others. Thus the tax "internalizes" the externality: The producer is forced to face the external cost just like the internal cost. As a result of the tax, the supply curve shifts up from S_1 to S_2. To confirm, recall that supply reflects marginal cost, which has risen by the amount of the tax that must be paid. The new equilibrium is at E_2, where demand and new supply S_2 intersect. The new output of Q_2 is efficient because marginal benefit equals marginal *social* cost. Finally, the efficiency gain from this tax policy is the red triangle, the original efficiency loss that has now been eliminated. In brief, as a result of this tax, society gets a benefit that the market would otherwise not deliver—cleaner water.

Several other ways have been suggested for reducing pollution. One is discussed in Box 16-2. Another is to set a limit on the output of polluting firms.

Such a limit may or may not help to solve the problem. In fact, if the limit is set at the wrong quantity, it may even be worse than doing nothing at all. For example, suppose output is limited to Q_3. As an exercise (Problem 16-1) you can show that too little will be produced, and there will be a loss to society of triangle FE_2G. Because this loss exceeds the original loss, the cure in this case is worse than the original problem. Rather than imposing an arbitrary limit on output, a better approach—if the cost of pollution can be estimated—is to impose a tax equal to this cost. Then the correct degree of pressure will be applied to the mar-

BOX 16–2 The Possible Role of Property Rights in Dealing with Pollution

Why not reduce water pollution by providing those living downstream with the property right to clean water? Suppose, for example, that they can sue or charge any polluting firm an amount that compensates them for any damage they incur. Specifically, suppose in Figure 16-2 that those living downstream can charge firms r per unit of pollution that these firms emit. Polluting firms are now in the same position as they were when the government imposed a tax of r; the only difference is that they are now paying this "tax" to the residents downstream instead of to the government. In either case they have the same incentive to reduce their output from Q_1 to Q_2, where inefficiency has been eliminated. It seems that proper assignment of property rights over the water might be one way to deal with the pollution problem.

In a famous article on "The Problem of Social Cost" (*Journal of Law and Economics*, October 1960), Ronald Coase of the University of Chicago put this argument forward and went one step further. He argued that, strictly from the point of view of economic efficiency, *it does not matter who holds the property rights.* In our example, it does not matter whether those downstream have the property rights and are compensated r per unit by the upstream polluting firms, or whether the upstream firms have the property rights. True, if the upstream firms have the rights, they are free to dump waste into the river. However, those living downstream will be willing to pay them r for each unit that pollution is reduced, and the upstream firms will therefore find it profitable to cut back their pollution.*

Thus, according to Coase, a problem such as pollution arises because there is something valuable—in this case, clean water—over which there are no property rights. Consequently, there is no market; that is, clean water can't be bought and sold. Create property rights, and you create a market that makes it possible for Adam Smith's invisible hand to work to reduce or eliminate inefficiency. Some other form of government intervention is not necessary. All the government needs to do is to establish a market and then let it work.

It is enlightening to consider this analysis from another point of view. The problem with pollution is that something that used to be in unlimited supply—clean water—has now become scarce. Unless someone owns it and charges for its use, it will be used in wasteful ways; for example, the water will be used to carry off pollutants and the river will become a public sewer. On the other hand, if someone does own the water and charges for it, its price will act as a monitoring device to direct it into its most productive uses.

The conclusion that property rights and free bargaining may eliminate inefficiency is a very interesting one. This conclusion follows—subject to a number of important reservations considered below—because the existence of inefficiency means that the two parties collectively lose. It is therefore in their collective interest to get together and make a deal to eliminate this inefficiency.

Making such deals involves problems—or "transactions costs." How do a thousand residents on a river and

ket to push it back from the initial output Q_1 to the efficient Q_2.

CONTROLLING POLLUTION: A MORE COMPLEX CASE

In practice, policymakers face a number of complications. First, in any particular airspace like that of Los Angeles, or any particular body of water, like Lake Erie, the problem is not just a single polluting industry, as shown in Figure 16-2, but many. Second, pollution and output are not locked together in the fixed way assumed in Figure 16-2, in which each additional unit of output generates a constant amount of pollution. In the more typical case, the amount of pollution may vary. A good may be produced with a large amount of pollution if wastes are dumped without restriction into the water or air. However, if wastes are treated, or if cleaner fuels are used, there will be less pollution.

Consider a firm that begins to treat its wastes, or uses cleaner but more expensive fuels. This firm the hundreds of polluting firms upstream organize themselves to make and receive payments? To illustrate, suppose the property rights to the water are owned by the polluting upstream firms. How do downstream residents get together to pay these firms to reduce their pollution? Specifically, how do the downstream residents keep some of their members from becoming "free riders," that is, people who are happy to have a payment made—and their pollution thereby reduced—but who won't contribute themselves?**

Another problem is: How do downstream residents know which firms are polluting the river and which are not? If the downstream residents do reach an agreement with the polluting firms, how do they know that these firms do indeed reduce their pollution? Even attempting to solve these problems may involve substantial transactions costs.

For this reason, the existence of property rights and free bargaining would not always lead to an efficient result. Even if it did, the question of equity would not be resolved: Who should pay the fee necessary to achieve efficiency and who should receive it? Specifically, should the upstream firms be paying the downstream residents to compensate them for the pollution they suffer, or should the downstream residents by paying the firms to get them to reduce the pollution? Nonetheless, Coase's ideas are important because they help us to understand more clearly why externalities are a problem, and how it may be possible to deal with them in a wide variety of ways.

*Those living downstream will be willing to pay this r per unit because this is what pollution costs them; r is therefore what they would be willing to pay to get rid of a unit. Moreover, since the polluting firms receive a payment of r per unit for reducing pollution, they will cut back to Q_2—for the same reason that they cut back that far in the face of the government's r per-unit tax. (It doesn't matter whether firms are paid r per unit for cutting back or are taxed r per unit if they do not cut back. In either case they have the same incentive to cut back.)

**These problems may be far less serious if the property rights are held not by the upstream firms but by the downstream residents, and if the payment (fine) to be paid to them by the upstream firms is set by the courts. Polluting firms would then respond to this fine just as they did to the tax in Figure 16-2. In fact, this policy is effectively the same as the pollution tax in that earlier diagram—except for one important respect. The residents downstream, rather than the government, receive the payment from the polluting firms. This sounds very equitable: The people downstream who are hurt by pollution are compensated for it. Unfortunately, this policy provides an example of why the objectives of equity and efficiency are often in conflict. This very equitable solution introduces a different source of inefficiency. Because of the compensation people receive if they locate downstream, more decide to do so, and the pollution they consequently absorb represents a loss to society. In their location decision, people should take pollution into account and—other things equal—locate away from the river. But they won't take pollution into account if they are fully compensated for it by the polluting firms. Thus too many people locate downstream, and there is an efficiency loss.

reduces pollution, but at a cost. This cost of reducing pollution for all firms in a locality is shown in Figure 16-3 as the curve MCR. (R stands for reducing pollution.) It is drawn by first graphing point Q_1, the amount of pollution that will occur if it is not restricted in any way. As pollution is cut back, firms move to the left up the MCR curve. At first, cleanup costs are low as the easy battles are won; the least expensive ways of reducing pollution are used first. For example, pollution unit Q_2 can be eliminated at the low cost shown by the short arrow. However, the more pollution is reduced, the higher becomes the cost of further cleanup. That is, the MCR curve becomes higher and higher as firms move to the left in this diagram.

Until the last few decades, there were few restrictions on pollution. As a result, firms generally dumped pollutants rather than going to the expense of treating them. The result was heavy pollution at Q_1. Some of our lakes and rivers became open sewers.

To prevent such contamination, suppose the government wishes to reduce pollution dramatically. Specifically, suppose it wants to cut pollution in half—from Q_1 to Q_3. Consider three policies that might be used.

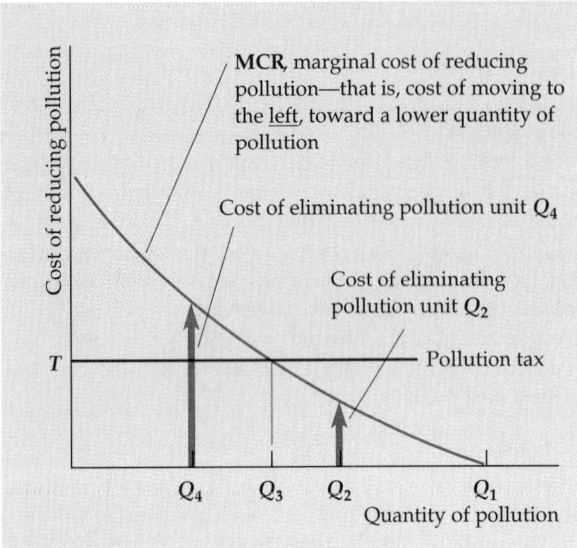

FIGURE 16-3 The cost of reducing pollution and the effect of a tax.

If no controls were imposed, the amount of pollution would be Q_1. Moving back to the left along MCR, we see the cost of reducing pollution by one more unit—for example, by installing pollution-control equipment. Thus if pollution has been restricted all the way back to Q_4, reducing pollution by another unit will be at the very high cost shown by the tall arrow.

If pollution tax T is imposed, firms voluntarily reduce pollution from Q_1 to Q_3. Firms to the right of Q_3 will stop polluting, because this costs less (for example, the short arrow) than the cost of paying the tax T. But firms to the left of Q_3 continue to pollute and pay the tax T, because this costs less than reducing pollution (the tall arrow).

OPTION 1. A POLLUTION TAX

Assume that the government levies an *effluent fee*—that is, a tax on each unit of pollution discharged into the environment. Specifically, in Figure 16-3, suppose that tax T is charged for each unit of pollution. Then firms eliminate pollution in the right-hand tail of the MCR curve, where it costs less to stop polluting (for example, the short arrow) than to continue to pollute and pay the tax T. However, pollution is reduced only to Q_3, where the tax line intersects MCR. To the left of this point, the costs of reducing pollution (the tall arrow) are higher than the tax T. Thus, in this range, firms pay the tax and continue to pollute.

OPTION 2. COMMAND-AND-CONTROL: A PHYSICAL LIMIT ON THE POLLUTION BY EACH FIRM

Why go to all the trouble of setting the pollution tax in Figure 16-3 when pollution could be cut by the same amount to Q_3 by a simple, direct control—specifically, by requiring every firm to cut its emissions by half? The answer is that, although this approach would achieve the same reduction in pollution, it would involve heavier cleanup costs.

The reason is that firms do not all face the same costs in reducing pollution. With a tax, pollution is cut back by firms that can do so *at the lowest cost*—that is, by firms to the right of Q_3. Firms to the left of Q_3 continue to pollute. However, if all firms are required to cut their pollution in half, firms to the left of Q_3 must now also participate—at the high cost illustrated by the tall arrow.

Therefore the advantage of a *pollution tax* is that it "lets the market work." With firms reacting to the tax, pollution is reduced by those firms that can do so in the least expensive way. As a result, society devotes fewer real resources to the cleanup task. The savings can be substantial. Recent estimates suggest that a pollution tax could cost society 70% to 80% less than a policy of requiring all firms to reduce pollution by the same fraction.

Which of these two policies have governments used? The answer is surprising. Instead of letting the market work with some form of pollution tax, governments initially relied on a command-and-control policy that set physical limits on pollution for individual firms. Although this policy was reasonable enough for radioactive wastes or other materials so toxic that an outright ban was required, in other cases this policy involved unnecessarily large cleanup costs.

Since 1977, the authorities have sometimes used a third approach that sets physical limits on pollution but also, like a tax, "lets the market work."

OPTION 3. PHYSICAL LIMITS ON POLLUTION WITH TRADE ALLOWED IN EMISSIONS PERMITS

Under this third option, the authorities set a specific limit on the amount of pollution that each firm is permitted. For example, in Figure 16-3, each firm is given permits to pollute just half as much as in the past. Thus far, this alternative is just like option 2. But now a twist is added to let the market work. If a firm to the right of Q_3 eliminates *all* its pollution—rather than just half—it ends up with an "emissions permit" that it can use at another location or sell to a firm to the left of Q_3. It can be shown that if the firms in Figure 16-3 are perfectly competitive, these permits will sell for price T. Therefore firms have exactly the same incentive T to clean up as under option 1, and the result is exactly the same pattern of low-cost cleanup. Specifically, firms to the right of Q_3 gain by selling their permits for T and cleaning up pollution at the low cost shown by the short arrow. Firms to the left of Q_3 find it cheaper to buy permits costing T and continue to pollute rather than clean up at the high cost shown by the tall arrow.[2] Pollution is thereby reduced by those firms to the right of Q_3 which can do so at the lowest cost. Therefore 1 and 3 are equally low-cost options and are superior to option 2. It is only under option 2, which requires all firms to reduce pollution by a fixed amount, that cleanup involves higher costs, because some of it must be undertaken by firms to the left of Q_3.

The general principle is this:

> **Pollution can be reduced at lower cost if the government enlists the power of the market. It can change incentives by imposing a tax or by introducing marketable emissions permits, and then letting private firms respond. The firms themselves know best what their costs are and accordingly are best able to select the response that will minimize those costs.**

Our basic conclusion, then, is this. Because the command-and-control option 2 does not use the market, it is more costly than the tax option 1 or the emissions-trading option 3, both of which do use the market. In comparing options 1 and 3, which is preferable?

HOW DOES TAX OPTION 1 COMPARE TO OPTION 3 (EMISSIONS TRADING)?

Here are some of the important considerations in comparing these two options:

1. If the major concern is to avoid too much pollution, then emissions permits may be preferred to a tax. One reason is that, in a period of inflation, a $1 tax becomes a weaker and weaker deterrent. If such a tax is to remain fully effective, it must be adjusted upward with inflation. However, with emissions trading, inflation raises no such problem; the government can achieve the appropriate reduction in pollution by fixing the number of emission permits.

2. Businesses prefer emissions trading because it costs less than a tax. They can do some polluting free, whereas under a tax they must pay for *any* polluting they do. If they can eliminate their pollution at low cost, they can sell their emissions permits for a profit. A tax offers no such opportunity.

On the other hand, here are two of the reasons why emissions trading has been criticized.

1. It has raised problems of equity. Why should businesses that have polluted in the past be granted valuable emission permits, some of which they may sell? In other words, why should some firms be allowed to profit from their past pollution—especially firms that may have been slow to comply with previous cleanup policies? Isn't the tax option preferred because it penalizes—rather than rewards—past polluters? Why should new entrants into an industry have to buy emissions permits when existing polluters are given permits free? Won't existing firms favor emissions trading because it deters free entry and increases their market power? Note that if emissions trading were changed so that the government were to *sell* all emissions permits at auction rather than granting them free to past polluters, then these problems would disappear.

2. The "free-market benefits" of emissions trading have been reduced by the slow development of a market for emissions permits. True, there are now brokers who buy and sell these permits, and hundreds of transactions have taken place; but the market does not yet work very well.

---

[2]Why is T the equilibrium price for permits? At this price Q_3 is the quantity of permits firms want. This is exactly equal to the Q_3 of permits the government supplies.

For more detail on the tax versus emissions trading debate and other pollution-control issues, see Wallace Oates' testimony in December 1987 before the House Ways and Means Committee on H.R. 2497, the Sulphur and Nitrogen Emissions Tax Act of 1987.

BOX 16–3 *Pollution Control: Problems and Perspective*

In Figure 16-3, the target amount of pollution is assumed to be Q_3. In fact, it is not a simple task to determine the target amount.

HOW FAR SHOULD POLLUTION BE REDUCED?

In Figure 16-4 we reproduce MCR from Figure 16-3 and also show MCP, the marginal cost of pollution to society. These two curves should not be confused. MCR is the cost of *reducing* pollution—for example, the cost of pollution-control equipment. On the other hand, MCP is the cost of *having* pollution—that is, the cost to us of foul air and contaminated water. As long as there is only a small amount of pollution—at, say, Q_4—the marginal cost of having this pollution (the height of MCP) is low. The first units of waste that are dumped into a stream generally break down and are absorbed by the environment. Similarly, the smoke from a campfire in a deserted area has no perceptible effect on the air. However, as pollution builds up, additional emissions become increasingly noxious and damaging; that is, as we move to the right in this diagram, the MCP curve rises.

With these two curves, the best target is to reduce pollution to point Q_3, where MCP = MCR. Any other quantity is less desirable, as we can illustrate with the case in which pollution is left completely uncontrolled and consequently reaches Q_1. For all units of pollution to the right of Q_3, MCP is greater than MCR, so it is a mistake to let this pollution continue. To evaluate the social cost of this mistake, consider one unit of this excess pollution, say, unit Q_2. The cost of eliminating this unit of pollution is the height of the MCR curve, as shown by the light red arrow. This is less than the cost of letting this pollution continue (the height of the MCP curve, as shown by both red arrows). Therefore the net cost of allowing this unit to continue is the dark red arrow. If we sum the similar costs on all such units through the range Q_3 to Q_1, the result is the triangular red area—the loss to society from allowing pollution to continue at its uncontrolled level of Q_1 rather than limiting it to Q_3.

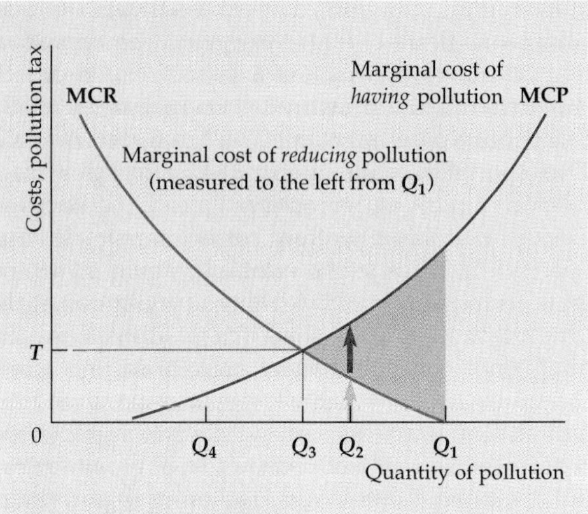

FIGURE 16-4 Efficiency loss from leaving pollution uncontrolled.

MCR is reproduced from Figure 16-3. We also show MCP, the environmental cost of additional units of pollution. The best target is to restrict pollution to Q_3, where MCR = MCP.

On the other hand, a policy of cutting pollution back to the left of Q_3 also causes a loss. For example, if pollution is reduced to Q_4, the environmental cost imposed by the last unit is just the height of the MCP curve above Q_4. However, this last unit is exceedingly costly to eliminate (the height of the MCR curve). Eliminating it is therefore a mistake. We conclude that the best target, Q_3, can be found only by taking into account both the cost of having pollution (MCP) and the cost of removing it (MCR).

Unfortunately, in practice it is not that easy to estimate the target Q_3 because of the difficulties in estimating MCP and MCR. For example, in trying to estimate the marginal cost of pollution MCP, we simply do not know with any precision how dangerous many pollutants really are. Furthermore, there are many pollutants, and the damage that any one pollutant does may depend on the presence of other types. For example, asbestos in the air is more likely to cause cancer when other pollutants are present or when people smoke.

POLLUTION IN HISTORICAL PERSPECTIVE

Why are we so concerned now with pollution, whereas a few decades ago we were almost totally unconcerned? Is the problem worse, or have we just awakened? If it is getting worse, what can we expect 20 or 30 years from now?

Figure 16-5 illustrates how the MCR curve shifts to the right as the economy grows. MCR_{1960} cuts the baseline at Q_{1960}, the level of pollution that would have occurred had it been left completely unrestricted at that early date. Similarly, the other MCR curves indicate uncontrolled pollution levels Q_{1990} and Q_{2020} at those later dates. The red triangle marked 1990 shows the loss from a policy of leaving pollution uncontrolled at that time. It is defined just like the red triangle in Figure 16-4.

Now consider our situation in 1960. At that time, there were fewer factories clustered along any river and fewer cars spewing fumes into the air. Therefore pollution was less severe. The result of leaving pollution uncontrolled was the relatively small loss shown as the red triangle marked 1960. In those days, people did not think much about this problem.

Now let us look ahead to the future, to the year 2020. If industrial activity keeps growing, unrestricted pollution will grow to Q_{2020} and the loss from failing to deal with it will be the very large red triangle 2020. There are several reasons why this loss builds up so rapidly. First, as output grows, so too does the unrestricted pollution level, from Q_{1960} to Q_{1990} to Q_{2020}. Second, pollution may grow even faster, because more powerful chemicals and other materials may be used as technology changes. Thus MCR shifts rapidly to the right.

We emphasize that Figure 16-5 is not a prediction of the future; it is merely a picture of what the future would have looked like if we had not taken action—or what it will look like *if* we give up our efforts to control pollution. In this respect, pollution is similar to the public health problem in the nineteenth century. With the increase in urban population, lack of adequate sanitation produced a growing health problem that could equally well have been described by a diagram like Figure 16-5. The response to this challenge was the public health programs that prevented the "prophecy" in such a diagram from coming true. Similarly, pollution-control legislation can help to ensure that the prophecy in Figure 16-5 does not come true.

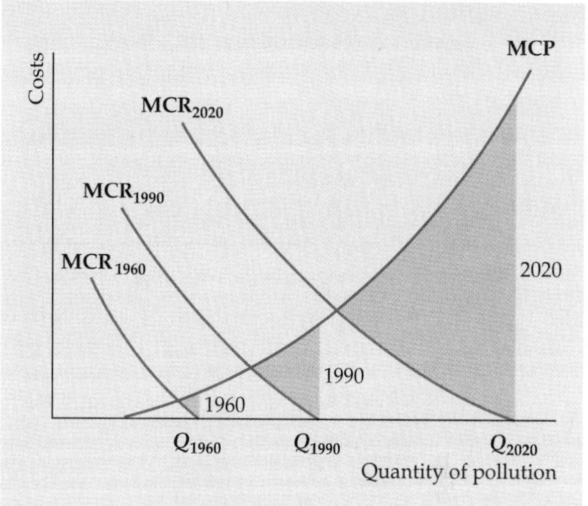

FIGURE 16-5 Pollution in perspective.
Without controls, unrestricted pollution would have increased (with growing GNP) from Q_{1960} to Q_{1990}, and eventually to Q_{2020}. The loss to society of leaving pollution unchecked in each of these years would have been the rapidly growing set of triangles marked 1960, 1990, and 2020.

To this point, it has been assumed that the government has set as its target a reduction in pollution by one-half, to Q_3. Why not by one-third, or three-quarters, or some other figure? Box 16-3 describes how the target should be set.

AN ALTERNATIVE POLICY? SUBSIDIZING POLLUTION-CONTROL EQUIPMENT

To supplement its other efforts, the federal government has provided large grants to municipalities that install waste treatment plants. It has also provided subsidies in the form of tax reductions to firms that install pollution-control equipment. How effective are such subsidies?

In the first place, such subsidies are effective only if the equipment that is installed does a good job of reducing pollution. One of the problems has been that, after the government has subsidized the new installation, it has sometimes paid little or no attention to how efficiently it has been operated—that is, how effectively it has reduced pollution. In some cases, the municipalities that have been subsidized to install expensive equipment have not even been able to cover its operating costs, and the equipment has no longer been used at all.

The second problem is that this form of subsidy puts all the emphasis on *end-of-pipe treatment*—that is, on the reduction of pollution as it is about to be discharged into the environment. However, if a subsidy is justified for end-of-pipe treatment, it should be similarly justified for *any* reduction in pollution, regardless of how it may be achieved—for example, by the use of less powerful chemicals or cleaner fuels. Such alternatives may be far less costly. For instance, at a cost of only $1 million, the 3M Company introduced a less polluting process that saved the company over $10 million in waste disposal and other costs.

It may be concluded, therefore, that an end-of-pipe subsidy is too narrowly focused. Firms may not use the lowest cost method to control pollution but instead may switch to the end-of-pipe method solely because it is subsidized. The correct principle is simple: It is better to tell firms what to do than to give them detailed instructions on how to do it. A regulation made as far back as 1700 B.C. illustrates this principle. Hammurabi, king of Babylonia, set a very simple building code. If a house collapsed and killed an occupant, the builder was put to death. All details for meeting this regulation were left to the builder.

An even narrower approach that raises a new set of problems is the requirement that a *specific kind* of end-of-pipe equipment must be installed. For example, some coal-burning plants are required to install "scrubbers" to clean the smoke they emit. This diverts them from the less costly solution of using cleaner coal; as long as the government requires scrubbers, there is no incentive to use the more expensive, cleaner fuel. Moreover, scrubbers generate sludge. Thus reducing air pollution in this way can create water pollution.

PROTECTING THE ENVIRONMENT: THE PAST RECORD AND FUTURE CHALLENGES

The original command-and-control policy has been partly replaced with emissions trading and a number of interesting variations on this theme. For example, a firm with dozens of discharge points such as smokestacks may be enclosed in an imaginary **bubble.** The government regulates only the amount of emissions coming from the bubble; it makes no attempt to regulate emissions from each discharge point. The firm is therefore able to increase its emissions at one discharge point provided it has an equivalent reduction or **offset** at the others.

Despite such progress, a number of serious problems remain. The inefficient, high-cost command-and-control policy is still frequently used. Furthermore, air and water standards are often established with little regard for the cost of reducing pollution. Indeed, in some cases the courts have interpreted the law as *prohibiting* the EPA from even considering costs when setting standards. Instead, the EPA concentrates on what is technologically possible with existing pollution-control knowledge, and some of these measures are very expensive. Furthermore, the Clean Air Act, as amended, is designed to "protect and enhance" the quality of the nation's air. This is a worthy objective, except that the legislation has been interpreted to mean that the air should not be allowed to deteriorate significantly *anywhere*. Consequently, even the states with the cleanest air have encountered problems attracting new firms. True, growth can still occur in these states by the entry of new firms that have purchased emissions permits from other firms or from state or municipal governments that have been able to reduce pollution. Nonetheless, the fixed limit on emissions in the cleanest areas has blocked one avenue for reducing the overall pollution problem, namely, shifting firms from overloaded, highly polluted areas where their emissions are particularly damaging, into regions with low pollution levels where their emissions could be partially "washed away" by natural processes.

One of the problems is that the EPA has become an embattled agency. It is under pressure from environmentalists because it is too lenient, and it is under fire from business because it is too harsh. One thing is certain. As the EPA continues to impose limits on business, there will be continued conflict between the two. This is another reason for the government to impose fewer of its own regulations and rely more on the marketplace— that is, replace detailed regulations with a market-oriented system of incentives that requires business to worry about the details. In other words, the government should be spending more of its effort in designing and building "better dams to control pollution" (such as tax or marketable permit systems) and less on "putting a regulatory finger into every leak." However, the biggest advantage of relying on the marketplace is that it allows pollution to be reduced at lower cost. This point can be put a different way: It will allow us to use any given percentage of GNP to make far greater reductions in pollution. This is of critical importance, because we are likely to face escalating costs of reducing pollution in the future.

In these criticisms of the government for not always using the most effective pollution-control method, it is important to keep perspective. Certainly, control should be improved, but not relaxed. A question that should be kept in mind is, "Where would we be without an agency such as the EPA?" The answer is: Back in Figure 16-5.

RECYCLING

One of the most promising ways to deal with pollution is to recycle wastes rather than dump them into the environment. Beer cans do not deface the landscape if they are reprocessed and used again. Wastes that are recycled into the production process do not foul our rivers.

Figure 16-6 illustrates the benefits from recycling by using the concept of *material balances.* On the left, production draws in the materials it requires. Included are both new materials drawn up through "pipe" *a* and recycled materials returned to the production process through pipe *c*. These materials pass through the production/consumption process and reappear in different form as "total materials out" on the right side of the diagram. Some of these leftover materials—such as chemical wastes—are the result of production.

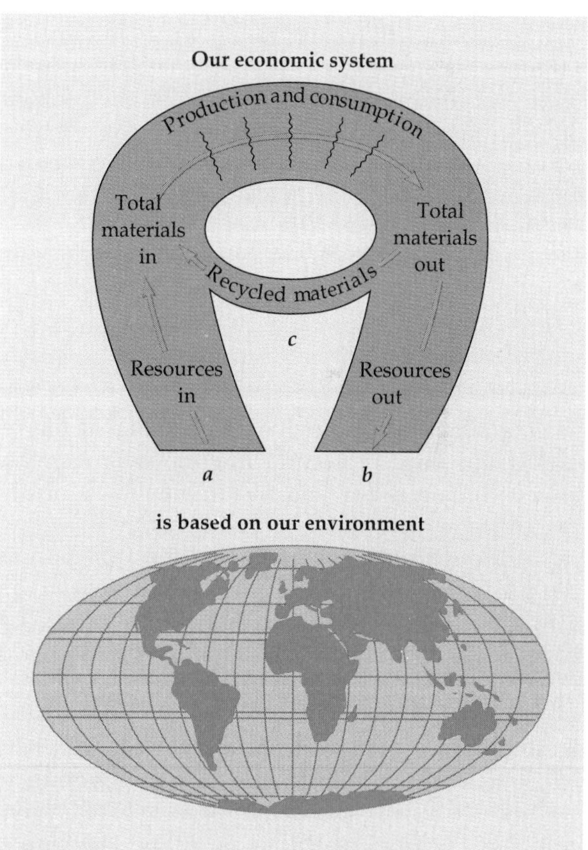

FIGURE 16-6 Recycling and the environment.

The economic system extracts resources through pipe *a* from the environment and also returns residuals back to it through pipe *b*. Recycling—that is, diverting materials from pipe *b* to pipe *c*—provides two benefits: (1) it reduces environmental damage through pipe *b*, and (2) it reduces the depletion of natural resources through pipe *a*.

Others—like beer cans—are residuals from consumption.

This figure provides a framework for thinking about two important issues:

1. As our economic system expands, strains on the environment increase, both because more resources are drawn up through pipe *a* and because more pollutants are dumped back into the environment through pipe *b*.

2. The pollution problem can be reduced by more recycling, that is, by directing more of the leftover material on the right into pipe *c* rather than pipe *b*. Moreover, any success on this score will provide a further benefit. The more our production/consumption requirements on the left can be satisfied by materials recycled through pipe *c*, the fewer natural resources will have to be drawn from the environment through pipe *a*. In brief, recycling helps to solve two important problems at once: the problem of controlling pollution and the problem of conserving natural resources. In the next chapter we will turn to a detailed analysis of the conservation of natural resources.

SAFE JOBS AND SAFE PRODUCTS

Maintaining and improving our quality of life requires not only protecting our environment, but also enforcing safety and health standards on the places we work and the products we buy.

Although most employers are concerned about the conditions under which their labor force works, even the most conscientious may be tempted to cut corners if threatened with bankruptcy. One way they may cut corners is to allow their workplaces to become less safe. Similarly, faced with possible bankruptcy, an airline might allow its safety standards to deteriorate in the absence of government controls; or a drug company might release a product—its "last hope"—before its testing is completed. If cutting corners is perceived to be the only way to survive, a firm may be prepared to run risks with public health and safety. Government intervention to prevent this is therefore justified, as it is in the case of pollution, because an unregulated free market will fail to do the job.

At first glance, this seems like a problem of externalities, just as in the case of pollution. Doesn't a firm selling products to consumers take account of only its own costs but not the risks its customers will face? In hiring labor, doesn't a firm take account of only its own private costs, but not the risk that its employees face in its workplace? A bit of reflection, however, makes it clear that these are not simple examples of externalities after all. The reason is that the workers and customers are parties to these transactions and can therefore force the firms to take risks into account. Thus customers and workers can provide themselves with some protection. They are not innocent bystanders, like those downstream or downwind who have pollutants dumped on them.[3] For example, workers can refuse to take a risky job of handling chemicals unless the employer compensates for the risk by paying a higher wage. Employers then have a market incentive to improve safety, because if they don't, they will have to pay a higher wage rate. Thus they may respond, for example, by installing machines to handle the chemicals. Similarly, airline customers can protect themselves by refusing to fly on an airline with a bad safety record. This will provide the airline with a market incentive to maintain high safety standards. Since workers and customers can thus protect themselves, surely the market doesn't fail.

Or does it? The answer is that insofar as workers and customers *can* protect themselves, the free market does not fail. But since they can't protect themselves fully, it does fail to some degree. To illustrate, consider how much employees can protect themselves in the workplace and how much they cannot.

SAFETY AND HEALTH IN THE WORKPLACE

Evidence indicates that workers who take risky jobs do indeed partly protect themselves by hold-

[3]In the case of airline travel, those on the ground who are killed by a crash *are* innocent bystanders. This is an externality and may provide some justification for government intervention. Hereafter we keep the analysis simple by avoiding such complications.

ing out for a higher wage. However, they don't protect themselves completely.[4] The most plausible explanation is that frequently the risks in these jobs are not fully understood. The high turnover rate in risky jobs provides support for this view. Workers don't fully understand the risks when they take these jobs; when they do find out, many conclude that the risk premium in their wage is insufficient, and so they leave.

When people being hired don't have full information on risk, employers can pay a wage differential that falls short of covering risk. In that case, employers make hiring decisions without fully taking into account all costs, including the risks to their employees. The result is too much of this activity—that is, too much hiring in risky jobs. The reason is not an externality, as in the case of innocent bystanders suffering from pollution. Instead, the problem is that workers who are parties to the hiring transaction have inadequate information about risk.

In this case, a justification for government interference in the marketplace is to improve the information available to workers. For example, the Occupational Safety and Health Administration (OSHA) requires firms to label chemicals that are dangerous to handle. In addition, OSHA takes direct action to reduce risk. For example, it requires firms to install safety devices on machinery and to follow a number of other health and safety standards in the workplace.

SAFETY AND HEALTH IN CONSUMER PRODUCTS

Lack of information may also prevent a free market from working efficiently in the provision of consumer goods and services. It's all very well to say that, in the long run, the public will turn away from an airline once they realize it is unsafe as a result of a series of crashes. The problem is that this information doesn't become available until there is a serious loss of life. In this case, the main problem is again inadequate information. Specifically, information is just too expensive to acquire because it involves loss of life—and this justifies safety regulations imposed by the Federal Aviation Administration (FAA). A similar case can be made for the monitoring of new drugs by the Food and Drug Administration (FDA). The public does not have information on which drugs are a health threat. By the time people recognize the risks, the damage has already been done.

An example was thalidomide, which was banned in the United States. In a number of European countries where it was not banned, it caused birth defects. Although the danger in this case became evident in nine months, for some carcinogens the danger may not show up for decades. Hence there is a strong case for FDA testing of drugs rather than allowing the market to deal with the problem over decades of serious damage to health. Even in the long run, the public might not discover the effects of some drugs without an agency such as the FDA. The reason is that identifying the effects may require controlled experiments or some other form of careful statistical analysis.

Although the FDA reduces the information problem, it doesn't eliminate it. The reason is that even FDA testing involves *some* delay. Indeed, for some drugs there has been a serious delay of five to seven years before full approval has been given. The reason is that people in such an agency often develop a defensive "siege" mentality. They are faced with two conflicting objectives: (1) Get a drug out as quickly as possible so that it can begin to save lives, but (2) delay its release for enough safety testing to ensure that it won't *take* lives. Faced with this choice, regulators often delay. They will be criticized less for delaying too long—and failing to save lives—than they will be for releasing a drug too soon, in which case its fatal effects may raise a political storm.

The FDA has recognized the cost of unnecessary delay and as a consequence has set up a "fast

---

[4]Estimating the degree to which workers cover their risks by negotiating a higher wage is complicated by the fact that the government program of Workers' Compensation covers workers for part of the risk they face. Although this factor complicates the analysis, it doesn't alter our broad conclusions. See W. Kip Viscusi and Michael J. Moore, "Workers' Compensation: Wage Effects, Benefit Inadequacies and the Value of Health Losses," *Review of Economics and Statistics*, May 1987, p. 260.

track" for promising drugs in the battle against particularly threatening diseases such as AIDS and cancer.

LACK OF INFORMATION: MORE SERIOUS FOR HEALTH THAN SAFETY

Ignorance is a greater problem with health risks such as radiation than with safety risks that are obvious, such as inadequate protection for a worker operating a buzz saw. In the case of safety, the public finds out as soon as accidents happen. In the area of health, it may be decades before people subjected to radiation develop cancer. Moreover, the longer the delays in contracting a disease, the more difficult it becomes for the public to identify the cause. Is the cancer that is now developing a result of that radiation 20 years ago, or a result of the thousands of other things that have occurred since?

Because it is more difficult for the public to identify health risks than accident risks, it is appropriate for government control agencies to place more emphasis on risks to health. OSHA is now moving in that direction.[5]

HOW EFFECTIVE ARE THESE AGENCIES?

Initially, OSHA was not very effective in reducing accident and illness rates. Although there is some evidence that it may have recently become more effective, its performance is still disappointing. The standard explanation is that firms often do not comply with its regulations, for two reasons.

1. The penalties for violation have never been adequate, and they decreased in the early years of the Reagan administration. By 1984, the average penalty was only one-third as high as in 1979.

2. OSHA has the resources to inspect less than 1% of firms each year, because workplaces are spread out all across the nation. In contrast, the FDA or the Consumer Products Safety Commission (CPSC) can check out the products sold by hundreds of firms by simply taking one trip to the drug store or supermarket. It is no surprise that these agencies get far more compliance.

Because OSHA fines are both low and unlikely, the "expected" penalty for an OSHA violation is only about 57 cents per worker for first offenders. Even for repeat violators, it is still far less than the costs of complying, such as the cost of installing safety devices on machinery. This very low expected penalty not only explains why firms often ignore OSHA regulations. It also shows that, in inducing worker safety, OSHA is less important than market pressures on employers—in particular, wage premiums that workers require in dangerous jobs.

Although there is a high rate of compliance with CPSC standards such as safety caps on aspirin bottles, these standards have not substantially reduced accidents. One explanation is that they may have a "lulling effect." As the risks of accidents decrease, parents may become less careful and more likely to leave medicines within the reach of small children.

In brief, the benefits of quality-of-life regulations have been mixed: disappointing in some of the OSHA and CPSC regulations, but substantial in other cases, such as the FDA ban on thalidomide.

EVALUATING A REGULATION: DOES IT PASS THE BENEFIT-COST TEST?

By now it is clear that a regulation cannot be justified simply because it has a desirable objective such as improving safety. It must also be effective in achieving that objective. Specifically, it should pass a **benefit-cost** test to ensure that it provides benefits sufficient to more than offset its costs, including the costs of administering the regulation and the cost to business of complying.

> ***Benefit-cost analysis*** is an estimate of the benefits and costs of a policy and a comparison of the two. A ***benefit-cost test*** is the requirement that the benefits of a policy exceed its costs.

Examples of regulations that pass the benefit-cost test include the controls on airline safety imposed by the FDA. However, there have been other

---

[5] For more on informational and other problems that lead to market failure, see W. Kip Viscusi, "Reforming OSHA Regulation of Workplace Risks," in Weiss and Klass, eds., *Regulatory Reform*, especially pp. 244–-245.

regulations that may not have passed this test; in such cases there may have been too much regulation. One possible example was the banning of saccharin, a very mild carcinogen. Under the law, the FDA has been required to ban artificial carcinogens, *regardless* of the overall costs and benefits. The benefit of this ban was to reduce cancer. But its cost included the increase in heart disease of overweight people who were driven back to sugar. (At the time, saccharin was the only available substitute for sugar.) Thus the ban on saccharin may have saved some lives from cancer but cost others from overweight; the net effects were unclear.

WHY BENEFIT-COST ANALYSIS IS NOT THE LAST WORD

Benefit-cost analysis is not easy. For example, suppose that, with great difficulty, it has been estimated that the cost of a certain regulation will be $10 million, and its benefit will be the saving of 20 lives. Before these two figures can be compared, it is necessary to put a dollar value on the human lives that will be saved. But how can *that* be done? Box 16-4 provides some suggestions, along with the reasons why such estimates cannot be very accurate. Thus the benefits and costs of regulations protecting human life cannot be compared in a very precise way.

Fortunately, however, it may still be possible to identify a desirable policy change, even when only fragmentary evidence is available.

THE IMPORTANCE OF CONSISTENCY

OSHA has imposed an arsenic standard that is very costly. Furthermore, it deals with risks so remote that it is extremely unlikely to save many lives. Consequently, it costs an estimated $70 million *for each life it saves.* Clearly, it makes no sense to impose this regulation when there is an alternative way of saving lives—the elimination of railroad crossings— that would cost only $100,000 per life.

Note that in this case we can arrive at an important conclusion—even though we have information only on the *cost* of saving a life, but none whatsoever on the *benefit* of saving a life. Specifically, we can conclude that government policy is inconsistent. It does not make sense to engage in any activity—saving lives or anything else—in an exceedingly expensive way (at $70 million a life) when one can achieve the same objective at far less cost ($100,000 a life).

Moreover, if we have even the roughest sort of estimate of the benefit of saving a life—for example, if we know that this benefit falls anywhere in the broad $330,000 to $5 million range cited in Box 16-4—we can make an even stronger recommendation: Not only should the regulation on arsenic standards be abolished; in addition, a regulation should be imposed to eliminate railroad crossings. This switch will save far more lives at the same cost. This example illustrates how it may be possible to make good judgments and eliminate at least some regulatory inconsistency even though estimates of benefits and costs are very imprecise.

The problem of regulatory inconsistency goes far deeper than this. Agencies have often been established with objectives that are in direct conflict. For example, in pursuing its goal of protecting the environment, the EPA encouraged the conversion of the nation's power plants from coal to less polluting fuels such as natural gas. However, in pursuing its goal of conserving scarce forms of energy, the Federal Energy Administration reversed the EPA's guidelines and urged the conversion from gas back to coal because coal is our most plentiful energy source.

CONCLUDING OBSERVATIONS

The quality-of-life regulation considered in this chapter is quite different from the price-entry regulation in Chapter 14, for two reasons.

1. Price-entry regulation is imposed on a single industry, such as trucking, but often quality-of-life regulations to protect safety and health and limit pollution are imposed economywide on *all* industries.

2. Price-entry regulation has typically been supported by the firms being regulated because it promotes their interests. On the other hand, quality-of-life regulation is often opposed by regulated firms because it raises their costs. However, there may be an important exception. Firms may support quality-of-life regulation, if it reduces the

BOX 16–4 *The Eternal Puzzle: What is a Human Life Worth?*

Thief (holding a gun): "Your money or your life." Jack Benny (pausing): " . . . I'm thinking. . . I'm thinking."

The simple answer to the question in the title is: Any life is worth an infinite amount. The miner trapped underground has a life that is priceless. Yet, we don't value our own lives this way. Were lives to have infinite value, safety concerns would dominate all others. We would live as close as possible to our work and never drive a car, let alone take a trip to earn something as trivial as a few thousand dollars.

Society doesn't place an infinite value on a life either. For example, lives can be saved by installing crash barriers down the middle of roads. Yet we don't have them on every country road. We simply aren't willing to spend the billions of dollars they would cost. This then raises the critical question, "How much *are* we willing to spend to save a human life?" This is really just a recasting of the original question: "What is a human life worth?" However, this new question is one that everyone—including even those who philosophically refuse to place a money value on a human life—will recognize should be asked if a sensible decision is to be made on, say, whether or not a crash barrier should be built.

Why not then just ask people: "What would you be willing to pay to save *your* life?" We wouldn't be able to get a sensible reply to this question because almost everyone would say, "An infinite amount if I could get my hands on it." However, we *can* estimate how much some people value their lives by observing those who actually "put their lives on the line." Thus we may ask, for example: "How much more than the average wage must be paid to induce a worker to take a high-risk job like that of a lumberjack?"

Although this is probably the most promising way of evaluating a human life,* several difficulties remain. For example: (1) This estimate includes only the valuation of the person's *own* life. But isn't an additional value placed on this life by family and friends?** (2) The higher wage paid in high-risk jobs indicates only how the workers who actually take these jobs value their lives. But isn't this far less than the valuation of the vast majority of the population who won't take such risky jobs because they value their lives more highly? (3) How much of the higher wage is compensation for the risk of death, and how much is for the risk of injury? The higher wage compensates for both, but only the risk of death is being considered here. (4) These estimates are meaningful only if the people taking these jobs understand the risks they are taking; and we've already seen that, because of inadequate information, they tend to underestimate these risks.

Studies that examine how workers act in risky situations provide estimates of the value of a life that range all the way from about $100,000 to over $10 million.*** However, almost all fall in the range of $330,000 to just over $5 million. The imprecision of this sort of estimation clearly illustrates how difficult it is to place a value on a human life.

*It is certainly an improvement over one of the methods that has frequently been used in legal judgments—namely, evaluate a life by asking: "How much would the individual have earned over the rest of his or her lifetime?" This yields a poor measure because it implies that the value of the life of a disabled person is zero.

**In "Families and the Economic Risks to Life," *American Economic Review*, March 1988, pp. 255–260, Maureen L. Cropper and Frances G. Sussman review previous studies of this question and consider why people seem to put a higher value on their own lives if they have loved dependents than if they do not.

***For a review of such estimates, see Alan E. Dillingham, "The Influence of Risk Variable Definition on Value of Life Estimates," *Economic Inquiry*, April 1985, pp. 277–294. He also notes that an alternative method used to estimate the value of a life (or more precisely, how much people are willing to pay to save their own lives) is to examine how much they are willing to pay for consumer goods like auto air bags and fire detectors that reduce the risk to their lives. See also Martin J. Bailey, *Reducing Risks to Life* (Washington, D.C.: American Enterprise Institute, 1980), p. 26.

competition they face by driving small firms out of their industry or by preventing new firms from entering.

For example, small firms may be driven out of an industry if they are unable to afford the safety or antipollution equipment that is required and can be easily purchased by their larger competitors. Or new firms may, as noted earlier, face a barrier to entering an industry if they have to purchase emissions permits to pollute and are therefore unable to compete with the existing firms that have received these permits from the government free. In such cases, regulation may have an anticompetitive outcome.[6] It should be reemphasized that, to prevent this outcome, an auction of emissions permits open to existing firms *and* potential new entrants is preferable to granting these permits to existing firms free.

In a world in which environmental problems are becoming more serious and more clearly understood, quality-of-life regulation is likely to become more and more important. In the design of such regulation, its potential side effects—for example, on the degree of competition in an industry—should always be kept in mind. This is not an argument against regulation, but rather an appeal for its proper design.

LIVING IN A GLOBAL ECONOMY

WHO WILL DEAL WITH THE GARBAGE?

In 1987, a group of Italian businesses paid a Nigerian $100 a month to store 8,000 drums of what they called a "safe industrial chemical" on his property. Within a year, the drums had rusted through and were leaking polychlorinated biphenyl (PCB), a powerful carcinogen. The Nigerian government arrested all those involved whom it could reach and put them on trial for their lives.

Suppose, however, that the garbage isn't transported by people who can be arrested but is airborne? Acid rain from coal-burning power plants in the Ohio Valley is borne by prevailing west-to-east winds and falls on upper New York State and New England, where it is harmful to trees and fish. Preventing this dumping can only be done through the U.S. political process, and this has been very difficult—especially since it is not clear how much of the acidity in northeastern lakes is due to power plants, and how much is due to automobile emissions and natural causes.

The same winds carry acid rain across national boundaries—for example, those in Western Europe. International pollution raises a particularly vexing problem. For example, how can the Germans induce the French to reduce their discharges into the air when the French will bear the costs, but the Germans will get much of the benefits? Similarly, how can the Dutch induce the Germans to reduce their discharges into the Rhine River?

Carbon dioxide may raise an even greater international problem. If present fears are confirmed that the burning of fossil fuels (oil, coal, and natural gas) is causing an increase in the "greenhouse effect," the earth's average temperature may increase by several degrees in the next few decades. This in turn could cause increased drought and other damaging changes in the world's weather. To prevent this outcome, a massive conversion may be necessary from fossil fuels to other forms of energy. Huge reforestation projects may also be necessary to replace the tropical forests that are now being cut down—forests that have helped to keep the greenhouse effect under control in the past.

Such actions would require an international agreement of unprecedented scope, along with a mechanism for ensuring against cheating. In economic terms, this move could be viewed as creating a cartel in the collective interests of all its members. It would be a "good cartel" because it would also be acting in the interests of the world as a whole. (Compare this with one such as OPEC which acts in the interests of its own members but *not* in the interests of the world as a whole.) The cartel would have to have strong enforcement powers because there would be an incentive to cheat; as long as all other countries are cleaning up the world's atmosphere, a small country might try to save costs by avoiding its cleanup responsibilities.

It is far from clear how such an agreement could be negotiated. This may become one of the major challenges facing the human race in the future.

[6]For more on the potentially anticompetitive nature of regulation, see Ann P. Bartel and Lacy Glenn Thomas, "Predation Through Regulation: The Wage and Profit Effects of OSHA and EPA," *Journal of Law and Economics,* October 1987, pp. 239–264.

KEY POINTS

1. Three important ways of protecting the quality of life are the EPA's controls over pollution, OSHA's enforcement of safety and health standards in the workplace, and the prevention of the sale of dangerous products by the FAA, FDA, and CPSC.

2. Pollution is an example of an external cost—a cost that is borne not by the buyer or seller of a product, but by a third party.

3. Since the EPA was established in 1970, it has imposed limits on the physical amounts of pollutants that firms can release into our air or water. However, there are two alternative market-oriented systems of control that are more efficient: (a) a tax on polluters or (b) marketable emissions permits. Both are designed to encourage the reduction in pollution by those firms that can do so at the lowest cost. The EPA has recently been turning to more market-oriented systems.

4. Either a marketable permit system or a tax is superior to another government policy that has been used: subsidizing firms or municipalities for installing certain types of equipment that reduce pollution. Because such an "end-of-pipe" subsidy is too narrow an approach to the problem, opportunities to reduce pollution in less costly ways may be missed.

5. Recycling wastes from production or consumption back into the production process helps solve two problems. First, less polluting waste is dumped into the environment. Second, fewer natural resources need to be extracted from the environment to support our present production and consumption levels.

6. Whereas EPA regulations are justified because pollution is an external cost, regulations by OSHA and consumer protection agencies are justified because workers and consumers cannot quickly, accurately, and inexpensively acquire information about safety and health risks.

7. A regulation should not be imposed simply because it is pursuing a desirable goal. Instead, any regulation should pass a benefit-cost test. However, estimating benefits and costs is often difficult. Nonetheless, regulatory policy can often be improved with only fragmentary estimates.

8. One of the most difficult future challenges will be to create a "good cartel" whereby each country will act to reduce pollution in the collective interest of improving the environment of all countries. Strong controls will be necessary to prevent member countries from cheating, that is, to prevent countries from cutting corners as they impose costly cleanup measures.

KEY CONCEPTS

internal (private) cost
external cost
social cost
inefficiency of a free market
optimal amount of pollution
internalizing an externality
pollution tax, or effluent fee
tradeable emission permits
bubbles
offsets
end-of-pipe treatment
recycling
inadequate information
benefit-cost analysis
regulatory inconsistency

PROBLEMS

16-1. Is output Q_3 in Figure 16-2 efficient? If not, explain why, showing the triangular efficiency loss.

16-2. Critically evaluate the following statements:

(a) "Pollution taxes are immoral. Once a firm has paid its tax, it has a license to pollute. No one should have this license."

(b) "Imposing a physical limit on the emission of a pollutant is like saying that you can do just so much of a bad thing and pay no penalty, but the moment you step over this line you will pay a large penalty."

(c) "There is no point in insisting on crystal-clear discharges into a river as muddy as the Mississippi."

(d) "Whereas a tax discourages a polluting activity, a subsidy to install pollution-control equipment does not. Therefore a subsidy should not be used."

16-3. Because monopoly is inefficient, the two parties are collectively worse off. Why then don't they make a deal to avoid it? Specifically, why don't buyers compensate the monopoly firm to get it to stop acting like a monopolist, that is, to get it to lower its price and increase its output? (*Hint:* See the discussion of transactions costs in Box 16-2.)

16-4. Redraw Figure 16-4 to illustrate the two special cases in which a pollution tax is not appropriate: (a) where pollution is no problem and (b) where pollution is so costly that it should be banned outright. (An example would be a lethal chemical that takes almost forever to decay.)

16-5. We have seen that the target rate of pollution is not zero. Do you think that the target rate of crime should be zero? In other words, do you think we should expand crime prevention and hire police until the crime rate is driven to zero?

16-6. If a tax is to be imposed on pollution, should it be the same in the desert as in heavily populated areas? Explain your answer.

16-7. In a free market, the public can refuse to fly on an airline that has had a series of crashes. Why can't the public conclude that the airline is unsafe after *one* crash? Does this illustrate the difficulty the public may face in acquiring information? Explain your answer.

16-8. Should a driver who is careless and runs into a railroad train be able to sue the automaker for producing a car that is "an unreasonable safety risk" because it didn't protect him? Should he be able to sue the auto company if he has bumped into another car at very slow speed and his engine has exploded as a consequence? If your answer differs in these two cases, how do you draw the line?

16-9. At a cost of $70 million, how many lives can be saved by eliminating railroad crossings? By imposing OSHA's arsenic standard? Explain to your member of Congress who believes that life is sacred and should be saved in every possible way, why you believe that the arsenic standard should, or should not, be imposed.

CHAPTER 17
NATURAL RESOURCES
Are We Using Them at the Right Rate?

The . . . economy of the future might be called the "spaceman economy," in which the earth has become a single space ship, without unlimited reservoirs of anything.

KENNETH BOULDING

At about the time the price of oil began its rapid rise, a group of researchers at the Massachusetts Institute of Technology (MIT) developed a computer model to analyze the long-run outlook for natural resources. They came to an alarming conclusion:

> If the present growth trends in world population, industrialization, pollution, food production, and resource depletion continue unchanged, the limits to growth on this planet will be reached sometime within the next one hundred years. The most probable result will be a rather sudden and uncontrollable decline in both population and industrial capacity.[1]

Because of their grim predictions, the MIT group quickly became known as the "doomsday" theorists. They were overly pessimistic. It is of course true that, *if* all present trends continue indefinitely, we—or our descendants—will indeed face doom sooner or later. However, it is not necessary to have a complicated computer model to show this outcome. There are many simple illustrations that will do. For example, if we project from a period in which the fruit fly population is growing, in a relatively few years the earth will be buried miles deep in fruit flies. Any such projection provides an illustration, not of good economics or biology, but of the mathematical magic of mechanically compounding a rate of growth.[2]

It is far more challenging and relevant to ask: Why will the population of fruit flies eventually stop growing at a constant rate? What major changes in our present economic and social system will take place to alter existing trends and prevent a future doomsday? One important answer: If a resource comes to be in critically short supply, its price will rise. This in turn will have a number of consequences studied in this chapter. For example, it will encourage conservation and stimulate the

[1]Donella H. Meadows et al., *The Limits to Growth* (New York: Universe Books, 1972), p. 30.

[2]To confirm the magic of compound growth, consider this: We will give you a million dollars, if you will give us just 1 cent today, 2 cents tomorrow, 4 cents the next day, and so on for just 1 month.

development of substitutes. To illustrate, an increase in the price of base metals will speed up the development of plastic and ceramic substitutes. Thus the projection of present trends is unlikely to be nearly as useful in telling us what will happen in the future as in telling us which resources will become scarce. Where will conservation have to occur? Where will consumption have to be reduced and substitutes be developed?

This chapter will also address a number of related questions:

- What is the most efficient rate at which to use resources?
- Under what circumstances might the free market permit a too rapid use of resources?
- If resources are being used too rapidly, what, if anything, can the government do? Specifically, how can the government assist the market forces that can help us to conserve?
- What are the relationships among the goals of economic growth, a healthy environment, and the conservation of resources?

WHERE ARE CONSERVATION PROBLEMS MOST LIKELY TO ARISE?

Some raw materials are much more likely to cause future problems than are others. What characteristics should we consider, if we are trying to anticipate problems?

1. WHAT IS THE SUPPLY/DEMAND RELATIONSHIP?

The oil problem came to the fore in the early 1970s because the balance between supply and demand was upset. Demand was rising with the worldwide economic boom. The growth in oil discoveries was tapering off, raising doubts that the long-run supply would be adequate to permit the continuation of past patterns of heavy use. Furthermore, supply was temporarily disrupted by export restrictions imposed by a number of oil-exporting nations.

Although oil is a good example of a resource where supply fell short of demand (at least during part of the 1970s), there are other natural resources that are so plentiful that it is hard to imagine such a problem arising. For example, computer chips are made of silicon, which comes from sand. We don't need to worry about a shortage of silicon. Conservation is not a problem for sand as it could be for oil.

2. ARE USERS HEAVILY DEPENDENT ON THE RESOURCE?

Oil has frequently dominated the headlines in the past two decades because users have become so dependent on it; it is difficult to do without it. If gasoline becomes scarce, there may be lines at the pumps—as there were in 1979. The problem affects us in a direct and obvious way.

On the other hand, we can imagine some raw materials running out without hardly anyone noticing or caring. Consider, for example, a rare clay used to make a pigment for artists' paints. If it runs out, artists may have trouble reproducing exactly that hue, but few people will notice.

3. WHEN THE RESOURCE IS USED, DOES IT DISAPPEAR?

Oil has another characteristic: when it is used, it is burned up; the resulting gasses dissipate into the atmosphere. In contrast, when iron ore or copper is used, its scrap can be recycled. Thus we don't have to worry about running out of copper or steel in the same way as oil.

The next two questions are very important, and a substantial part of this chapter will be devoted to analyzing them.

4. IS THE RESOURCE RENEWABLE OR NONRENEWABLE?

Even if the units of a resource that we use are destroyed, nature may restore them. For example, fish are used up when they are eaten. However, new fish hatch and grow. Fish are thus a *renewable* resource. So are trees. In contrast, oil, copper, or iron ore is a *nonrenewable* resource. There is only a finite amount in the ground; no more is being created. If we use these resources at a constant rate, then sooner or later the resources in the ground will be completely depleted. The need for conservation is therefore more obvious for a nonrenewable resource such as oil than for a renewable resource such as fish—although in practice, measures to conserve may be required in either case.

5. IS THE RESOURCE COMMON PROPERTY OR PRIVATELY OWNED?

Even if a resource is renewable, it may have to be conserved. For example, too many fish may be caught, and a species thereby endangered. The reason is that nobody owns the oceans, rivers, and lakes, nor the fish that swim there. Fish are thus a *common-property resource.* Consequently, fishing-boat captains pay little attention to conservation. As individuals, they have inadequate incentive to reduce their catch, even if the result would be more fish in the future. This will be of little benefit to them because someone else is likely to catch the extra fish that they leave in the water.

Timber is also a renewable resource, but, unlike fish, it is often *privately owned.* Owners cutting trees *do* have an incentive to conserve. They will benefit in the future because they will own the extra trees they leave standing today.

This chapter begins with a detailed demonstration of why a free market does a far less satisfactory job of conserving a common-property resource such as fish than a privately owned resource such as timber. This will be followed by an analysis of the conservation of a nonrenewable resource such as base metals. Finally, attention is directed to oil, a nonrenewable resource that has raised a wide range of special conservation issues.

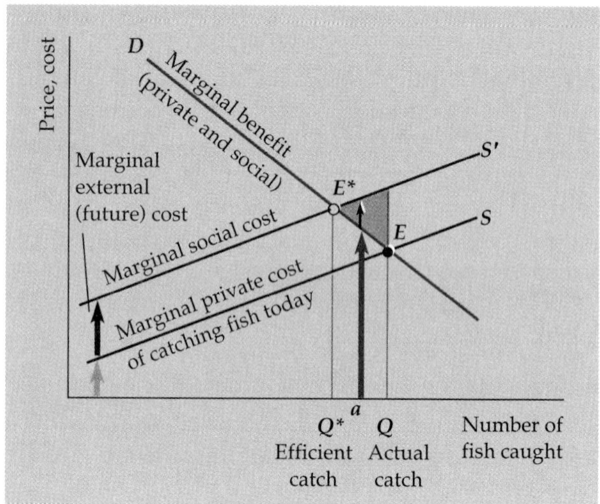

FIGURE 17-1 Market for a common-property resource: fish.

S', the marginal social cost of fishing today, includes the pink arrow representing marginal private cost, such as labor and mending nets, *plus* the red arrow above it representing external cost because there will be fewer fish available in the future. Efficiency requires an outcome at E^*, where marginal benefit is equal to marginal social cost. However, those who fish take into account only their marginal private cost and ignore the external future cost. Therefore their supply curve is S and the *actual* outcome is at equilibrium E, where $S = D$. The result is an inefficiently large catch Q, with an efficiency loss shown by the red triangle.

THE DIFFICULTY IN CONSERVING A COMMON-PROPERTY RESOURCE: FISH

The problem of overfishing is illustrated in Figure 17-1. D is the market demand for fish. The height of this curve, as usual, reflects the marginal benefit of these fish to the consuming public. S is the supply of fish, with the height of this curve reflecting the marginal cost faced by those who catch the fish. This includes costs such as the expense of hiring crews and mending nets, shown by the pink arrow on the left. S does not take into account another important cost, shown by the red arrow. This is the external cost of fishing. The more fish are caught today, the fewer will be available for those who fish in the future.

WHY A FREE MARKET FAILS TO CONSERVE

Individual boat captains who fish today do not take the second, external cost into account, because any fish an individual boat catches today will not perceptibly affect the number it will be able to catch in the future. Each captain therefore has an incentive to respond to supply curve S, taking no account of how fishing today affects the future fish population. The result is an equilibrium at E where $D = S$, and the catch is Q. However, this outcome is not efficient. Instead, the efficient equilibrium is at E^*, with a smaller catch Q^*, where marginal social benefit D equals marginal social cost S'. The efficiency loss from the overfishing that occurs at E is shown as the familiar red triangle. To confirm, consider *a,* one of the "excess" fish caught. The blue arrow under the demand curve is the marginal benefit of catching *a,* whereas its marginal cost—including the external cost of reduced future catches—is this same arrow *plus* the black arrow above it. Hence the net loss from catching this fish is the black arrow, and the sum of the losses on all the other "excess" fish caught over the range Q^*Q is the red triangle. In short, this triangle shows the efficiency loss from overfishing because conservation concerns about the future fish population are ignored.

Similar problems arise for other common-property resources. For example, the commonly owned pastures, or commons, that existed many years ago were often overgrazed.

Note how the problem of overfishing or overgrazing is analytically similar to the problem of pollution graphed on page 281. In each case, decision-makers do not take the external cost into account. In the case of pollution, the external cost is the damage to those who live downstream or downwind. In the case of fishing, the external cost is the damage to those in the future who have less of the resource available. (For more detail on how fishing today may reduce future catches, see Box 17-1.)

MEASURES TO INDUCE CONSERVATION

Three approaches may be used to provide better conservation of a common-property resource. That is, there are three ways to reduce the catch in Figure 17-1 from the inefficient overfishing quantity Q to the efficient quantity Q^* and thus eliminate the triangular efficiency loss.

To keep the analysis simple, we consider the problem of conserving fish in our inland lakes and rivers, thus setting aside the more difficult issue of ocean fishing. First, however, some of the complications raised by ocean fishing should at least be noted. If a government provides foreign fishing boats with free, unrestricted access to the ocean waters off its coast, this will undermine any conservation efforts by its own people. Therefore recent attempts by a number of countries to extend control of the waters off their coasts—and thus control foreign fishing—should be judged not only in terms of the obvious issue of whether domestic or foreign fishing boats will get this year's catch, but also in terms of the more subtle issue of whether this policy is designed to conserve the resource. (The difficult task of conservation is complicated by the fact that fish swim. No matter how carefully a nation may protect them, they may be caught outside its waters.)

Now let's turn to the simpler question: How can fish in our inland lakes and rivers be conserved?

1. *Place Limits on the Catch.* The government may limit the catch directly by restricting the number of fish each person or fishing boat captain can take. In some cases, limits have been imposed on the number of nets or the type of equipment that can be used.

Unfortunately, it is not clear how much such restrictions may actually reduce the size of the catch. Thus in Figure 17-1, there is no way of pinpointing whether the catch will be reduced from Q to more or less than the desired target Q^*. This is an important issue because—just as in the case of pollution—a restriction that is too severe may be worse than no restriction at all. Moreover, even if a government restriction on, say, nets *were* to reduce the catch to exactly the desired target Q^*, it would be an expensive way of doing it. The reason is that labor would be wasted because each person would be able to use only a restricted number of nets. As a result, more people than necessary would be engaged in fishing. The same problem arises if each individual or fishing boat is limited in the number of fish it can keep: Too much labor or too many boats are expended in the effort. Of course, this objection applies to commercial fishing rather than sports fishing where the whole point is to pass time in a pleasant way.

The problem with this first approach to conservation is that it does not use the market mechanism. However, the next two approaches do.

2. *Impose a Tax or a Fishing Fee.* The government could deal with the externality by using a tax similar to the one suggested for controlling pollution in the previous chapter: Impose a tax equal to the external cost. Tax those who catch fish today according to the damage they do to future catches.

BOX 17–1 The Maximum Sustainable Yield

The statement that "the more we fish today, the less there will be to catch in the future" is sometimes true but sometimes not. To make it more precise, first note that in certain circumstances, fishing today may have a disastrous effect on future catches; in other cases, it may have little or no effect at all. As an example of a disaster, suppose the fish population is so reduced that it can barely survive. Reducing that population further by fishing today may, like shooting passenger pigeons, extinguish the species and reduce *all* future catches to zero. At the other extreme, the fish population may be so large that it cannot grow further. There are no additional natural food sources to sustain it, and for every fish that is hatched, another must die. Then fishing today will have little effect on the fish population and therefore on future catches. If we don't prevent the fish population from growing by catching some, it will be prevented from growing by lack of food.

These two cases, and the many other possibilities, are illustrated in Figure 17-2. This diagram shows how the *growth* in a fish population on the vertical axis depends on the *size* of the population on the horizontal axis. Point D indicates that the maximum size of the population is 10 million fish. This is the point at which there are so many fish that their population cannot increase further: For each new fish, an existing one will die. If there is no fishing, the fish population will grow toward this number but not beyond. To confirm this, note that at any point to the left of D, such as K, the fish population will grow (by the height of K). As a result, the population will be greater in the next period, causing a movement to the right, which will continue as long as the curve lies above the axis. But once D is reached, there is no further increase in the number of fish.

There is no reason why a hungry human race should be particularly interested in this "no fishing" solution. There is little satisfaction in knowing that the sea is as full of fish as it can possibly get. Instead, consider a point like C that does involve fishing. Here the fish population is $X_c = 2$ million and is increasing by $Y_c = 1^1/_3$ million fish per year. At this point, we can take out the natural increase of $1^1/_3$ million fish year after year without reducing the 2 million population. Hence this curve is known as the **sustainable yield curve.**

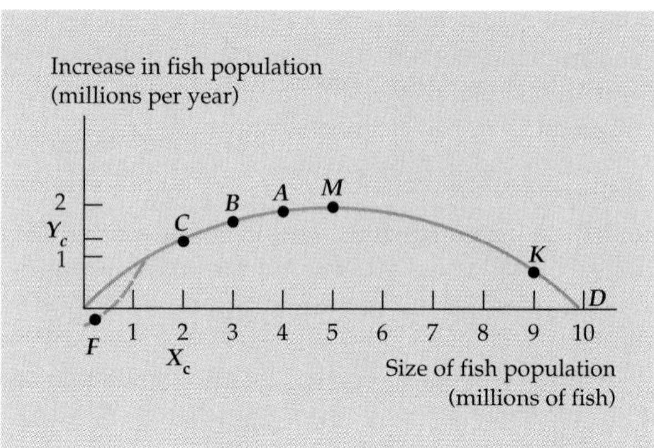

FIGURE 17-2 Sustainable yield curve.

At point C, the population of fish on the horizontal axis is 2 million and will increase by $1^1/_3$ million per year, measured up the vertical axis. Therefore $1^1/_3$ million is the sustainable yield; it is the number of fish that can be caught each year and still leave the population constant at 2 million. As we move to the right along this curve, it rises at first: the larger the fish population, the greater its natural increase. However, this increase reaches a maximum at M, where a fish population of 5 million generates a "maximum sustainable yield" of 2 million, the largest number that can be caught per year and still leave the fish population intact.

In other words, tax them or charge them a fishing fee equal to the marginal external cost shown by the red arrow in Figure 17-1. This will raise their supply curve from S to S', thereby internalizing the externality. That is, this tax will force decision-makers to take into account the external as well as the internal costs of their actions. Accordingly, it will result in an efficient catch Q^*, where D intersects the new supply curve S'. There is, of course, the problem that arises whenever the government tries to internalize an external cost: Can the external cost of fishing—in this case, the reduction in future catches—be estimated accurately?

3. *Create Property Rights.* There may be an even simpler way of achieving efficiency. In certain circumstances, a common property resource may be transformed into private property. For example, a large common pasture may be divided into 50 smaller fields, with one given to each of the fami-

The highest point *M* on this sustainable yield curve is the maximum sustainable yield. This is the maximum number of fish (in this case, 2 million) that can be caught on a continuing basis without depleting the parent stock. To harvest fish at this maximum rate requires a parent population of 5 million, measured along the horizontal axis. A reasonable conservation objective is to prevent the resource from falling below this quantity of 5 million.

Sustainable yield is the amount of a renewable resource (such as fish) that can be harvested while still leaving the population constant.

Now consider the situation long ago, before large-scale commercial fishing. This is illustrated by a point like *K*, with the ocean almost as full of fish as it could get. As human population and our demands on the seas increased, the fish population was reduced by heavy commercial fishing; there was a move to the left in this diagram. However, as long as the fish population still remained above 5 million (that is, to the right of the maximum sustainable yield at *M*), there was no conservation problem. As we harvested more, the fish population fell, but it became more able to regenerate itself. That is, the natural increase—as shown by the height of the curve—became greater as we moved from *K* toward *M*. It is only at point *M*, where the fish population is only 5 million, that we encounter the conservation problem. If at this point we continue to harvest more than the natural increase, we will continue to reduce the fish population. But now, with each such decline, the fish population becomes less able to regenerate itself. That is, each movement to the left leads to a lower point on the yield curve, closer to the point where the fish population can barely survive. If we do not limit catches, we may risk extinguishing a whole species, just as we extinguished the passenger pigeon.

Exterminating a species of fish is not just a theoretical possibility. This almost happened with herring in 1969 as a result of the development of larger, more efficient fishing boats. Moreover, the introduction of sonar for chasing down whales has meant that some types of whale would face extinction if there were no controls over whaling.

To understand fully the dangers of overfishing, suppose the yield curve is the dashed curve on the left in Figure 17-2. In this case, heavy fishing may do irreversible damage to the species. This will occur, for example, if we have fished the population down to a quarter-million fish and are consequently at point *F*. There are still some fish, but they cannot find other fish to spawn. There is no longer a natural increase. Instead, there is a natural decrease in population: *F* lies below the horizontal axis. If we reach a point like *F*, the population will eventually die out on its own even if we stop fishing altogether. The first rule of conservation should be to prevent such irreversible disasters.

To sum up: As a first approximation, conservation measures should be taken to prevent the population from falling below the one that provides the maximum sustainable yield M. For plentiful species where unrestricted catches occur far to the right at a point such as K, there is no need to limit catches.

Complications may mean that the best target is actually somewhat to the right or left of M. For example, the target is pulled to the right by the fact that, as the fish population gets larger, the fish become easier and cheaper to find. However, because there are other influences that pull in the opposite direction, a target of M is a reasonable first approximation.

lies that previously used the commons. Once these fields have been fenced, each family will have an incentive not to overgraze its particular field.

It is not as easy to create property rights in the case of fish, but in some cases it may be possible. For example, where fish are drawn from a number of small lakes, the fishing right to each separate lake might be sold to an individual, who will then have an incentive to limit the fishing in that lake.

To see how creating private ownership may result in desirable conservation, consider the case of timber, much of which is already privately owned.

A PRIVATELY OWNED RESOURCE: TIMBER

The market for timber is illustrated in Figure 17-3, with curve *S* representing the supply curve. Con-

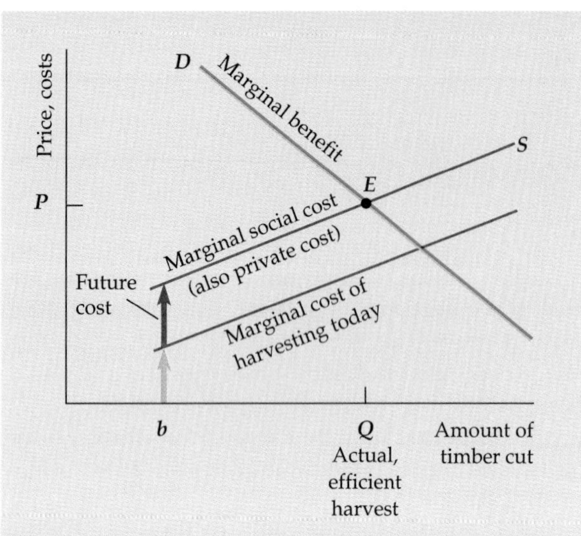

FIGURE 17-3 Market for a privately owned natural resource: timber.

This is the same as the earlier example in Figure 17-1, except that the resource is now privately owned. In assessing what their harvesting today costs them, the private owners *do* include the red arrow of marginal future cost. Thus their supply is *S*, and equilibrium is at *E*, with an efficient harvest of *Q*.

sider a single unit of output, *b*. The height of the supply curve *S* shows the price required to induce the owner to cut and sell that unit today. This price, sometimes known as the *reservation price,* covers two costs:

1. The direct cost of harvesting the timber—the wages of lumberjacks, the cost of hauling, etc., shown by the light arrow—plus

2. The cost to the owner because less timber will be left to cut in the future. This is shown by the dark arrow.

> The ***reservation*** price of a privately owned resource includes both the cost of harvesting or extracting the resource today *and* the amount necessary to compensate the owner for the reduction in the resource available in the future. In other words, it is the height of supply curve *S* in Figure 17-3.

For more details on reservation price, see Box 17-2.

Observe that Figure 17-3 is very similar to Figure 17-1. In each diagram, there are two curves that slope upward to the right. The lower curve represents the direct cost of production—the harvesting cost of cutting the trees or catching the fish. Moreover, in each diagram the vertical distance between the two curves is a reflection of the conservation problem. It measures the cost of having fewer trees or fish available in the future.

There is, however, one big difference between the two diagrams. In the case of a common property resource such as fish in Figure 17-1, producers take into account only the direct costs of catching the fish today. Therefore their supply curve is the lower curve, and the result is a socially inefficient output. Future costs are ignored and there is inadequate conservation. In contrast, timber owners in Figure 17-3 do conserve. They do take into account the red arrow that measures the marginal cost of having fewer trees in the future. This is an *internal cost* to the owners. Therefore their supply curve is the upper curve. For a privately owned resource such as timber, equilibrium is at *E* and output is the socially efficient quantity. There is adequate conservation.

In some other respects, private ownership may not be efficient. For example, if a single firm were to buy up all the timber land, it would be able to exercise monopoly power. That is, it would be able to raise price above *P* by reducing the quantity harvested to even less than *Q*. The result may be a "conserving monopolist," who uses exaggerated fears about conservation as a defense for overcharging the public. Although this diagram doesn't cover all issues, it does show how a privately owned resource in a *perfectly competitive* industry can lead to the efficient rate of production.

THE PROBLEM OF THE MYOPIC OWNER

Thus far it has been assumed that private owners of a resource take into account its future value. They do not shortsightedly consider only the present. However, if they do suffer from myopia and fail to see the full implications of their present harvests on the amount of timber available in the

BOX 17–2 *What Influences the Reservation Price of a Privately Owned Resource?*

The major influences on reservation price include:

1. The **expected future price** of the natural resource. The greater the expected price of timber next year, the greater the incentive to leave timber standing "in the bank," so to speak. Therefore the higher will be the reservation price that owners will require before allowing their timber to be cut today.

2. The **expected future cost of harvesting** the resource. The higher the expected cost of cutting the timber next year, the less incentive the owners will have to leave the timber standing, and the lower will be their reservation price.

3. The **rate of growth** of the forest. If the forest has become fully mature, the owners will acquire no more timber by letting it stand for another year. Some trees may be harvested without substantial adverse effects on future harvests. Therefore the reservation price will be low.

For simplicity, we have assumed that the owner's decision is only whether to cut the timber this year or next year. But, of course, the problem is the more complex one of finding the efficient pattern of harvesting over the next *n* years. If the owner is engaged in replanting the forest—rather than simply letting it grow up itself—this is another important cost to be taken into account.

future, they will ignore or underestimate the dark arrow of future costs in Figure 17-3. Consequently, their supply curve will lie below *S*, and the harvesting of the resource will be more than the efficient quantity *Q*. In this case, private ownership does not provide adequate conservation.

An extreme example of this problem of myopia is aging owners who don't look into the future beyond a few years simply because they don't expect to live longer. If their philosophy is "Clear-cut the trees now and enjoy the income; who cares about ten years hence?" it's no surprise that they fail to adequately conserve. However, aging owners do not necessarily cause excessive harvesting. They do not, for example, if their objective is to pass on an asset of high value to their heirs. Even if they have no heirs and their only concern is to get their money out quickly, they have a better option than excessive harvesting: Sell the forest outright to someone younger with a long-term view who would thus be willing to pay far more for the forest than the older person could ever hope to get from clear-cutting it.

Hereafter, we avoid such complications and assume that resources are privately owned, with the owners having neither myopia nor monopoly power.

CONSERVATION OF NONRENEWABLE RESOURCES[3]

The fish and timber resources studied so far are both renewable. We now turn to nonrenewable resources such as oil and base metals.

As a highly simplified example, suppose there is a limited quantity of a metal that will be completely replaced in two years by a cheaper and better plastic substitute that is now being developed. Conservation requires that we do not use up all this metal this year but instead use it up over the next two years in the most efficient way. (Because

---

[3]*Note to instructors.* This section on nonrenewable resources is slightly more demanding. However, it can be skipped without loss of continuity. It is based on Harold Hotelling's classic article that inspired the study of natural resource economics more than half a century ago: "Economics of Exhaustible Resources," *Journal of Political Economy*, April 1931, pp. 137–175. For a summary of some of the research that this article has stimulated, see Shantayanan Devarajan and Anthony C. Fisher, "Hotelling's 'Economics of Exhaustible Resources': Fifty Years Later," *Journal of Economic Literature*, March 1981, pp. 65–73.

cheaper plastic will then become available, there is no need to save any metal beyond this date).

In a perfectly competitive market, what will be the quantity used up this year and next year?

HOW THE MARKET CONSERVES THE RESOURCE

The equilibrium price and quantity in the two years is shown in Figure 17-4. The resource prices P_1 and P_2 in the two years will be determined so that the following two conditions are met:

1. The quantities used in the two years will add up to the total available quantity Q, that is, $Q_1 + Q_2 = Q$. In other words, the holders of the resource will sell it off in the two years, because it will be worth less thereafter, once the cheaper substitute becomes available.

2. Price P_2 will be higher than P_1 by a gap AB equal to the interest rate. Thus, if the interest rate is 8%, P_2 should be 8% higher than P_1.

Why wouldn't there be the same price of, say, $100 per unit in the two years? The answer is that in this case holders of the resource would want to sell it all in the first year, earn interest of 8% on the $100 proceeds, and thus have $108 in the second year. This is better than holding it until the second year and selling it for $100 then. Note that the incentive for selling it all in the first year is the interest rate that can be earned. With resource holders trying to sell it all in the first year, the large supply then forces the price down. A new equilibrium is reached when the first-year price falls below the second-year price by the amount of the interest rate. Then and only then will the "interest rate incentive" to sell it all in the first year disappear and supplies become available to satisfy the demand in *both* years.

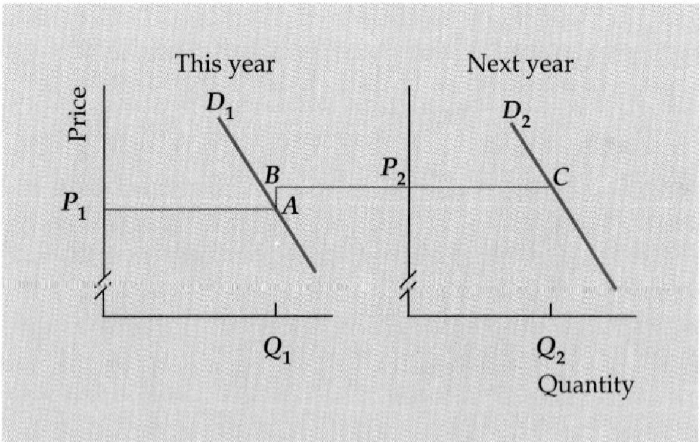

FIGURE 17-4 Efficient pricing pattern for a nonrenewable resource over two years.

Efficient pricing requires that the gap AB between prices in the two years be equal to the interest rate. Efficiency also requires that the amount of the resource used up ($Q_1 + Q_2$) be equal to the total quantity available.

It should be emphasized that, because price is lower this year, the quantity Q_1 that the owners can sell now is greater than the Q_2 they can sell next year (assuming, as in Figure 17-4, that "other things are equal," that is, D_1 is the same as D_2).

DYNAMIC EFFICIENCY IN A PERFECTLY COMPETITIVE MARKET FOR A RESOURCE

The price pattern described so far—low this year, higher next—results in the efficient allocation of the resource over time, with the resource being used in both years but more heavily this year than the next (assuming that the demand curves in the two years are the same). Although the efficiency of this outcome is too complicated to prove in an introductory book, it can be intuitively confirmed by noting that, from society's point of view, it is better for more of the resource to be used this year than next. The reason is that, say, an iron ore resource can be used to produce steel for capital equipment that will allow us to be more productive next year. Consequently, we can produce more by putting some of this resource to productive use right away than by holding it and not using it until next year. The lower price this year does indeed result in a greater amount Q_1 of this resource being used this year than next (Q_2).

To sum up the message of Figure 17-4: Conservation doesn't mean to stop using any of the resource at all. This solution would be the same as not having any of the resource. There is no point in holding a valuable resource until its value disappears because it has been replaced by a substitute. Instead, conservation means using a resource in the efficient pattern over time. This is what occurs under perfect competition in Figure 17-4. Other things equal, some of the resource is used this year and some the next, with more used this year. This method is efficient because of the productivity of the resource in capital investment. This is an example of how perfect competition results in **dynamic efficiency.**

Dynamic efficiency occurs when an economic activity (such as the use of a resource) takes place at the best rate, that is, the *best pattern* over time (as in Figure 17-4).

The key to the efficient pattern of prices is the interest rate. This is not surprising since the interest rate is a measure of how much more society can produce by using a resource this year rather than next (a point developed in more detail in Chapter 23).

Again, it should be emphasized that no claim can be made that the efficient price pattern in Figure 17-4 will necessarily prevail. In fact, it may not. For example, if the supply of this resource is controlled by a small number of producers they may, like any other oligopolists, use their market power to set prices above the perfectly competitive levels P_1 and P_2. Higher prices will mean that some of this resource will not be used up by the end of year 2, when it will be displaced by substitutes. Nonetheless, the oligopolists may still have maximized profits because of the increased price on the amount they actually *do* sell. This is just an extension of our conclusion in Chapter 13 that it may be profitable for colluding oligopolists to raise price, even though they sell less as a consequence.

WHY THE REAL WORLD IS MORE COMPLICATED

In Figure 17-4, it has been assumed that the resource will be completely replaced by a substitute in two years. Figure 17-5 extends this analysis to the case in which the resource is replaced after a longer period—specifically, after year 4. This does not necessarily mean that a substitute eliminates all demand in succeeding years. There is still demand for the metal in year 5, namely, D_5. However, this demand lies below P_5; the inexpensive substitute has pushed the demand curve for this metal below the price line P', so none is used thereafter.

MARKET FORCES THAT PROMOTE CONSERVATION AND OTHER FORMS OF ADJUSTMENT

As time passes in Figure 17-5 and the resource becomes more and more scarce, its price rises. This change triggers several kinds of adjustment.

1. *Substitution in Consumption and Production.* As resource prices rise, people are encouraged to use less. For example, as the price of oil increases, people turn down their thermostats and use more insulation. This kind of adjustment is illustrated in Figure 17-5, where price rises in year 2 while other things remain constant (D_2 is identical to D_1). The

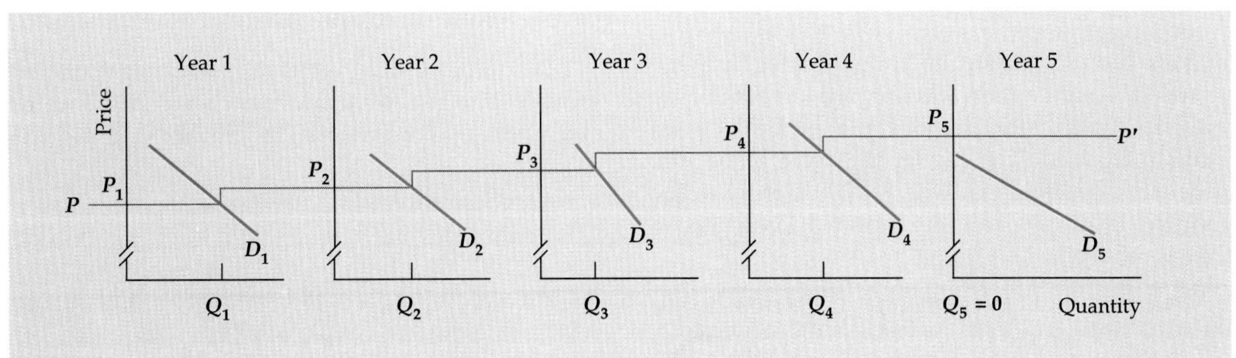

FIGURE 17-5 Efficient pricing pattern for a nonrenewable resource over a longer period.

This figure extends Figure 17-4. Determining the efficient, perfectly competitive pattern of price and resource use over time may be viewed as fitting a "price staircase" PP' to the demand curves, with the restriction that $Q_1 + Q_2 + Q_3 \ldots$ be equal to the total fixed available quantity of the resource. As before, the height of each step in this staircase is the interest rate.

higher price pushes users of this resource in year 2 up their demand curve to the left. As a result, this resource is conserved; the smaller amount Q_2 is used rather than Q_1.

2. *Intensified Search for the Resource.* As the price of a resource rises, there is an incentive to find more of it by increased search. True, for a nonrenewable resource in finite supply, this cannot be a permanent solution; some day there will be no more left to find. For many such resources, however, that day is far in the future. Indeed, for many resources, we are now discovering reserves at least as fast as we are using them. An example cited by MIT's Morris Adelman is oil, often regarded as a resource in critical supply, with U.S. oil fields on the wane. In 1945, there were 20 billion barrels of reserves in the United States (excluding Alaska). In the next four decades, 100 billion were used and 100 billion discovered, so that in the late 1980s reserves still totaled 20 billion. Reserves were being found about as fast as they were being used. This wasn't the result of any great new discovery, such as occurred elsewhere in Alaska. Instead, it was from small discoveries and the expansion of existing fields. For example, the Kern River oil field in California, discovered in 1899, had remaining reserves estimated at 54 million barrels in 1942. From then until 1985 it produced 730 million barrels. Yet at the end of that time it had reserves of 900 million. Reserves were being found faster than they were being pumped out.[4]

Although some experts view this pattern as unlikely to continue in the United States, it is expected in many other less mature oil-producing countries, where for decades more oil has been found than used. The higher the price of oil, the more intense this search will be. When more of the resource is discovered, the upward pressure on price is relieved.

3. *Discovery and Development of Substitutes.* To illustrate, the discovery of optical fibers made of glass has displaced copper in communications systems. This change could not have been predicted 20 years ago. Even though we can't precisely predict future technology, we can expect that more innovations will displace copper in even more uses in the future.

4. *Reductions in Population Growth.* As resources become scarce and expensive, market pressures discourage population growth. For example, as cities become more crowded, one resource that increases in price is land. As housing and other costs rise as a consequence, it becomes more expensive to bring up children, and this may influence the typical couple's decision on family size. Moreover, the population growth rate may also fall for other reasons that have less to do with economics. In the highly industrialized countries, birthrates have recently been dropping as a result of (a) changing social attitudes toward the family and children, and (b) the development of birth control methods. True, much of the world's population remains in the less developed countries, where the rate of increase is still high. Reasons for this continued high rate include a decline in death rates because of better medical treatment, religious or social objections to birth control, and poverty. (Parents who are too poor to afford insurance view children as a way of providing for their old age.) However, these influences are likely to weaken. Living standards are rising, and death rates cannot be expected to fall as rapidly in the future as in the past. Moreover, in some of the less developed countries, governments have introduced measures to reduce family size.

Resource use is affected not only by population growth, but also by growth in per capita income and GNP—in other words, by growth in our ability to produce.

RESOURCES, THE ENVIRONMENT, AND ECONOMIC GROWTH

In earlier chapters, several arguments in favor of growth in per capita GNP were considered. For example:

1. Growth makes it easier to solve the poverty problem. An across-the-board increase in income lifts many families out of poverty; it is a "rising

[4]Morris A. Adelman, "Are We Heading Towards Another Energy Crisis?" Speech to the National Press Club, Sept. 29, 1987, published by the *MIT Center for Energy Policy Research.*

tide that lifts all boats." On the other hand, if there is no growth, any attempt to solve the poverty problem by transferring income to the very poor will require that someone else's income actually declines.

2. Growth increases not only our own future income, but also the income of our children.

On the other hand, there are disadvantages of growth: Increased production depletes our resources and increases the pollution in our environment. Do these unfavorable effects justify slowing growth—or, as some suggest, setting a target growth rate of zero? Earlier, we argued that a no-growth policy would be a costly and ineffective way to attack the pollution problem, because it would only prevent pollution from growing but would not cut it back. There are similar reasons for being skeptical of a no-growth policy to conserve our resources. Many of our resources are not as scarce as is frequently claimed. Even if they were to become scarce, a costly no-growth policy would be inferior to policies designed specifically to deal with the problem—such as removing any impediments to the discovery and development of substitutes.

A no-growth policy would therefore involve great cost and would not directly attack the problem of resource scarcity. Even if we were to end growth completely, we would still need to use resources, and we might seriously deplete them—especially common property resources where the market does not work to promote conservation. In short, a policy of slowing growth is not specific enough to cure any single problem like resource depletion, pollution, or congestion.

Finally, in assessing the growth-versus-antigrowth debate, it is helpful to ask: Would the arguments now used against growth have applied equally well a hundred years ago? If so, has the growth over the past century been a mistake? Some people argue that, if it were possible, the clock should be turned back. Most would disagree, however. In comparing the past with the present, don't forget the simple things that are taken for granted today. Before deciding in favor of the idyllic pastoral life of a few centuries ago, consider what it would be like to live in a world with less medical care, food, and the other things we now view as essential.

LIVING IN A GLOBAL ECONOMY

U.S. POLICY AND THE WORLD PRICE OF OIL

Any discussion of scarce natural resources would be incomplete without some reference to the resource problem that has been an important issue in public policy over the last two decades: oil. Recall that the world price of oil rose from less than $3 a barrel in 1973 to more than $30 in 1982. Although the $3 price in 1973 may have been insufficient to induce adequate world conservation, by the 1980s such a case could no longer be made. The problem was no longer the classic one of ensuring a high enough price to encourage conservation. That problem had already been more than solved by the huge price increases. Instead, the problem was an entirely different one. It was the problem of the dependence of the United States—and many other countries—on foreign oil supplies that could be disrupted at any time. Indeed, in 1988 the risk of a supply disruption became painfully evident, as warring Iran and Iraq attacked oil tankers in the Persian Gulf.

When the international price of oil skyrocketed in 1973–1974 and 1979–1980, one of the most important policy decisions the U.S. government had to face was whether or not to intervene to prevent the domestic U.S. price of oil from rising as rapidly. Specifically, the U.S. government considered two options:

1. Adopt a hands-off policy, letting the price of domestic oil within the United States rise as fast as the world price.

2. Control the domestic price of oil to keep it *below* the world price.

Initially, the government chose option 2, keeping the domestic price from rising as fast as the world price. However, in mid-1979, the Carter administration began to shift to option 1; it began a program of decontrol that was scheduled to be completed by October 1981. When President Reagan entered office, he moved the timetable forward and abolished price controls on oil in early 1981. Thus both presidents ultimately judged that keeping the domestic oil price below the world price was a mistake.

This was not the first—nor is it likely to be the last—occasion for the government to be tempted to keep a domestic price below a rapidly rising world price. The next time it may be the price of oil again or the price of some other commodity. Accordingly, in Figure 17-6 it is instructive to examine the problems such a policy raises.

IMPLICATIONS OF KEEPING THE DOMESTIC PRICE BELOW THE WORLD PRICE

Without government intervention, the U.S. price would be the same as world price P_w. (As long as the government doesn't interfere and oil can be freely bought and sold on the world market for P_w, U.S. buyers won't pay more for it, and U.S. producers won't sell it for less.) At price P_w, U.S. consumers would purchase at point *C* and oil firms would produce at *B*, with the difference *BC* being imported. Now consider the effect of government controls that kept the U.S. price below P_w, at P_1. (Actual U.S. policy was more complicated, but it had essentially the same effects as the simple price ceiling P_1.)

Consumers responded to lower price P_1 by moving from point *C* to *F*. Thus price control resulted in an increase of *CJ* in consumption. In other words, price control discouraged conservation. In addition, the lower price induced domestic producers to move from point *B* to *A*, thereby resulting in *HB* less of production. The triangular efficiency losses *CJF* from increased consumption and *HBA* from reduced production are detailed in Figure 17-6. With greater U.S. consumption and less production, the "energy gap" between the two that had to be covered by imports increased from *BC* to *AF*. Therefore this policy *increased* the dependence of the United States on unreliable foreign supplies.

Furthermore, the large U.S. import purchases were an important component of the demand for world oil and helped to keep the world price high during the 1970s. Paradoxically, the use of controls in an attempt to keep the U.S. *domestic* price *down* helped to keep the *world* price up.

In sum, the price controls

1. weakened the incentives to conserve oil,
2. reduced domestic production,
3. stimulated larger imports, and thereby
4. added to upward pressures on the world price of oil.

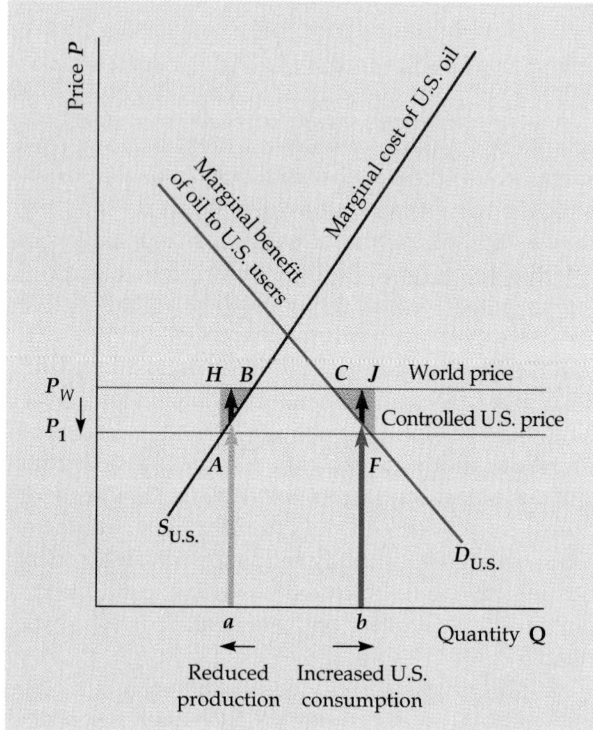

FIGURE 17-6 The effects of keeping the domestic U.S. price of oil (P_1) below the world price P_w.

The lower price reduced U.S. oil production by *HB*, and this had to be satisfied by imports. Each of these barrels, such as *a*, cost more to import (P_w) than it previously cost when produced domestically (the height of the pink arrow below the supply curve). The result was a loss on this barrel equal to the red arrow, and a loss on all such barrels over the relevant range *HB* equal to the triangular efficiency loss *HBA*. This was the efficiency loss from importing oil rather than producing it domestically at lower cost.

At the same time, the lower price increased domestic consumption by *CJ*, and this also had to be satisfied by increased imports. Each of these barrels, such as *b*, cost more to import (P_w) than the benefit it provided to consumers (the blue arrow below the demand curve). The result was a loss on this barrel equal to the red arrow, and a loss on all such barrels over the relevant range *CJ* equal to the triangular efficiency loss *CJF*. This efficiency loss occurred because the new oil imports cost more (P_w) than the benefit consumers got from them.

With all these disadvantages,[5] why did the government follow this policy? The answer is that it wanted to soften the "oil price shock" on consumers by keeping the U.S. price below the skyrocketing world price. At the same time, U.S. producers were hurt because the price they received was less than it would have otherwise been. Therefore this policy benefited consumers at the expense of producers; in other words, it transferred income from producers to consumers. Many viewed this transfer as equitable because it was small compared to the transfer in the opposite direction—from consumers to producers—that was taking place during the 1970s because the world price of oil was rising so rapidly.

Nevertheless, the problems with this policy were severe enough that both Presidents Carter and Reagan phased out oil price controls. Efficiency was increased as the distorting effects on U.S. production and consumption were removed. It is true that the oil industry initially benefited at the consumers' expense as the price ceilings were removed and the domestic price rose to the world price. In the longer term, however, this higher domestic price reduced the U.S. demand for imported oil, and thus helped drive down the world price—and with it, the U.S. domestic price. During the 1980s, the price facing U.S. producers and consumers actually *fell*.

SHOULD THE U.S. PRICE OF OIL BE PUSHED ABOVE THE WORLD PRICE?

Since allowing the domestic price to rise to the world price helped to reduce the world price, why not go one step further? Specifically, why not push the domestic price *above* the world price? In this paradoxical world, wouldn't this lower the world price even further? The answer is, yes. By encouraging U.S. production and reducing U.S. consumption, this policy would reduce the U.S. purchase of imports, which in turn would reduce the world price.

There are other arguments in favor of such a policy. Some economists—including James Tobin of Yale—have argued that the true cost to Americans of imported oil *exceeds the price we pay for it*. Two of the points they make have been noted in our introduction, where we recognized that oil involves special problems:

1. High risk is involved in large U.S. imports of oil, because the international oil market could be disrupted by conflicts in the Middle East. A sudden rise in price or an interruption of supply could cause a recession. It is true that, after increasing in the 1970s, U.S. imports of oil fell in the early 1980s as price controls were removed. However, by 1988, the U.S. Energy Information Administration was projecting that U.S. imports would increase to one-half of U.S. consumption by 1995. The reason is an expected fall in U.S. production as oil becomes more expensive to find and extract here.

2. The more dependent we and our allies are on imported oil, the greater is the danger we will become militarily involved, at great cost, in the Middle East.

These two risks can be viewed as costs we have to bear because we import large quantities of oil. Such risk-related costs should be added to the world price P_w that we have to pay for oil in order to arrive at its true cost. According to this argument, efficiency requires that the domestic U.S. price should fully reflect this cost and therefore be above P_w. (Efficiency requires that the domestic price faced by consumers and producers provides a clear message to them of *all* the costs of a good.) Therefore oil should be taxed to raise its price above P_w. Such a tax would also have the beneficial side effect of raising revenue, thereby reducing the deficit in the government's budget.

What form might this tax take? Two specific proposals have been a tariff on oil imports or a tax on domestic gasoline sales. The best estimate is that a 25 cent per gallon tax on gasoline would reduce the U.S. fiscal deficit by $25 billion a year and the

---

[5]The government attempted to deal with some of these disadvantages. For example, the reduction in domestic production was in fact less than *HB* in Figure 17-6 because the government used a two-price system within the United States. Although producers only received a low price for oil from "old" wells, they received a higher price for "new" oil from recently drilled wells. This gave producers more incentive to drill for new oil than Figure 17-6 implies.

amount of imported oil by 5 to 10% by 1995. But such a tax would be regressive, taking a smaller percentage of the income of the rich than the poor, and it would be politically unpopular with U.S. drivers who make up almost the entire voting public.

Another proposal to reduce our dependence on foreign oil is to develop other forms of energy.

CONSERVING OIL BY DEVELOPING SUBSTITUTE FORMS OF ENERGY

Our dependence on foreign oil may be reduced by the use of substitute forms of energy such as hydroelectricity, solar heating, or gasahol (a liquid fuel produced from vegetation). Although there is a wide variety of such alternative forms of energy, we will now consider three of the most prominent substitutes—natural gas, coal, and nuclear power. Each of these, especially coal and nuclear power, raises concerns about the environment. The important question is: What are the cheapest sources of energy when both costs of production *and* external costs to the environment are taken into account?

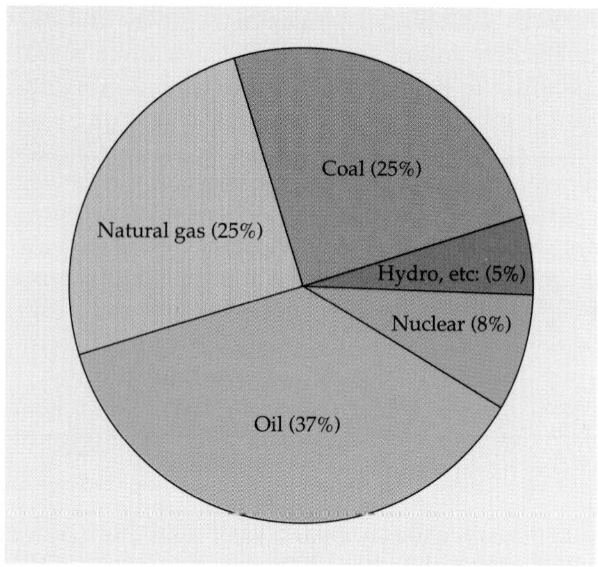

FIGURE 17-7 Forms of energy as a percentage of U.S. consumption.

NATURAL GAS

Next to oil, natural gas and coal are the largest American sources of energy; each accounts for about a quarter of U.S. consumption (Fig. 17-7). Compared to nuclear power, natural gas involves no waste disposal problem and much less safety risk. Compared to coal, its extraction from the ground does little damage to the environment. Although, as a fossil fuel, its burning involves a cost to the atmosphere, this cost is less than that for coal or oil because gas burns more cleanly.

Like oil, gas was subject to heavy government controls during the 1970s; as a consequence, gas discovery and extraction were discouraged. The resulting shortage of gas during the winters of 1977 and 1978 resulted in hardship and millions of dollars worth of lost industrial production.

The higher price for gas that came with decontrol stimulated production; in 1980, for the first time in years, new gas finds were as great as the amount of gas used. Most geologists believe that the natural gas fields under the United States or its continental shelf are substantial enough to satisfy U.S. requirements into the next century. Some say almost to the end of that century.

COAL: THE CONFLICT BETWEEN ENERGY AND THE ENVIRONMENT

The United States is the Saudi Arabia of coal, holding about 28% of the world's coal reserves. In comparison, the United States holds less than 10% of the world's natural gas and 5% of the world's oil reserves. At present rates of consumption, there is enough coal in the United States to last about 600 years. Yet the role of coal in satisfying U.S. energy requirements declined from 75% in 1920 to about 25% in the early 1960s, where it remains. Coal failed to make a comeback even in the 1970s and early 1980s when oil prices were very high.

An important deterrent to a greater use of coal has been its environmental cost. Strip-mining leaves land scarred and mining companies facing the high cost of repairing the landscape. On the other hand, mining coal deep underground raises safety concerns and the risk of black lung disease. When coal is burned, it releases gasses that create acid rain and may have a damaging greenhouse effect on the atmosphere.

The conflict between energy and the environment has been serious enough for coal, but it has been even more serious for nuclear power.

NUCLEAR POWER

In the search for substitutes for oil, the recent decades have been a time of disappointed expectations, but nowhere more so than in nuclear power. In the 1950s, advocates of nuclear power suggested that it would become so cheap that meters would become obsolete; people would be able to use as much electricity as they wanted for one low monthly fee. By 1974, nuclear power was hailed as the key to reduce U.S. dependence on foreign oil. Yet, we now realize, that was the year in which growth of the industry virtually ceased. Orders for new nuclear plants almost completely collapsed in the face of unexpectedly high plant costs, tough regulations, and public opposition which became stronger after the Three Mile Island (3MI) accident in Pennsylvania in 1979 and the Chernobyl disaster in the Soviet Union in 1986.

In spite of the 3MI experience, the U.S. industry believes that it has a good safety record. Nuclear power has exposed the public to much less radiation than an equivalent use of coal, since coal contains traces of radioactive materials that are released into the atmosphere when it is burned. Moreover, while lives have been lost in accidents in coal mines and on offshore oil drilling rigs, there have been no fatal accidents in commercial U.S. nuclear plants. Consequently, the debate on safety has been less concentrated on the past than on questions for the future: What is the chance of a catastrophic accident, perhaps worse than Chernobyl? Will a worldwide use of nuclear power contribute to the proliferation of nuclear weapons? What will we do with nuclear wastes which remain radioactively "hot" for thousands of years?

The nuclear industry is now suffering battle fatigue from fighting critics and vocal "not-in-my-backyard" groups opposed to nuclear plants or waste disposal units planned anywhere near their own communities. The debate has become so heated and time consuming that, even if it were possible to get a nuclear plant into operation, it would take 12 to 14 years of time and escalating costs to do so. Time is money—big money. At a 12% interest rate, a $1 billion cost grows over 12 years to over $4 billion—and even then this investment still may not have earned a nickel of income. Moreover, with nuclear power, it's far from guaranteed that an investment will *ever* earn income. By 1988, the completed but unused $5 billion plant at Seabrook was threatening to drive New Hampshire's power company into bankruptcy, and the $5 billion Shoreham plant on Long Island was about to be broken up for scrap.

One uncertain hope for the future is *nuclear fusion*. This process, which simulates the sun by joining together hydrogen atoms, is expected to generate less than 1% as much radioactive waste as the current *nuclear fission* technology, which splits uranium and other atoms apart. In theory, fusion could provide an unlimited supply of cheap energy forever, with no risk that it could get out of control. (If a fusion reactor malfunctions, it automatically shuts down; in contrast, a fission reactor may melt down.) The question is: How soon will fusion reactors be developed? As this book went to press, the prediction was "in about 40 years." But that was the same 40-year prediction that was made as far back as 1960. Scientists may be chasing a receding goal. As rapidly as they make progress, they discover that it's a longer and more difficult task than they anticipated.

A fusion breakthrough could essentially solve the problem of *clean energy*, but it cannot be counted on. Thus efforts to clean up existing dirty sources of energy will continue, as will the search for new sources of clean energy—such as the import of hydroelectricity from Canada under the 1989 U.S./Canada free trade agreement. Although hydroelectricity will satisfy only a small part of the U.S. requirement, it is clean energy.

KEY POINTS

1. In extracting common-property resources such as fish which are publicly owned, fishing boat captains take no account of how this year's harvest will affect future harvests. The result is an efficiency loss: Too much is harvested today.

2. In an attempt to solve this problem by reducing the current catch of fish, the government may impose various restrictions, such as fishing licenses or off-season limits on fishing.

3. Another way to reduce the harvest to an efficient level is to establish property rights. This is a possibility if the fish are located in inland lakes. Once the resource becomes privately owned, its supply will reflect not only the current cost of harvesting it, but also the amount necessary to compensate the owner for the adverse effect of present harvests on the future stock.

4. Special problems arise when a resource is nonrenewable. As it becomes scarcer, its price rises. This encourages conservation and stimulates the search for new reserves and substitutes.

5. The policy of keeping the domestic U.S. oil price below the world price led to two kinds of efficiency loss: (1) It reduced conservation efforts by U.S. oil users and (2) it discouraged production by domestic U.S. producers. By increasing U.S. oil imports, it also increased the world price of oil.

6. A case can be made for raising the U.S. domestic price above the world price. This would discourage oil imports and thus reduce dependence on Middle Eastern oil supplies.

7. Important current substitutes for oil include coal, natural gas, and nuclear fission. The problem with all of these energy sources is that they do damage to the environment or pose safety risks. The search for cleaner and safer substitutes, such as nuclear fusion, will continue.

KEY CONCEPTS

common-property resource
privately owned resource
reservation price
creation of property rights
renewable resource
nonrenewable resource
dynamic efficiency
producer myopia
nuclear fusion versus fission

PROBLEMS

17-1. Suppose 50 boats are fishing in a lake, into which other boats cannot get access. Would there be any reason for the government to allow the boat owners to sign an agreement restricting the amount each catches? Is it possible that restricting the catch, which began as a conservation measure, may become a means of exercising market power? Explain.

17-2. The problem of efficient timing in cutting timber is illustrated in Figure 17-8. For example, point *A* indicates that if we wait 15 years before cutting again, an acre will yield 10 units of timber. Which point represents a forest in which there is no longer any timber growth? Would you cut timber every 15, 30, or 66 years? Explain. (Assume that the direct costs of cutting and replanting are negligible.)

17-3. Explain why a "myopic monopolist" might sell an inefficiently large or inefficiently small amount of a resource.

17-4. "If we use a resource at a constant rate—no matter how small—we will eventually run out. Therefore, there is an almost insoluble conservation problem. The only solution is to have a zero rate of consumption, which will mean that the resource lasts forever." Comment critically on this quotation.

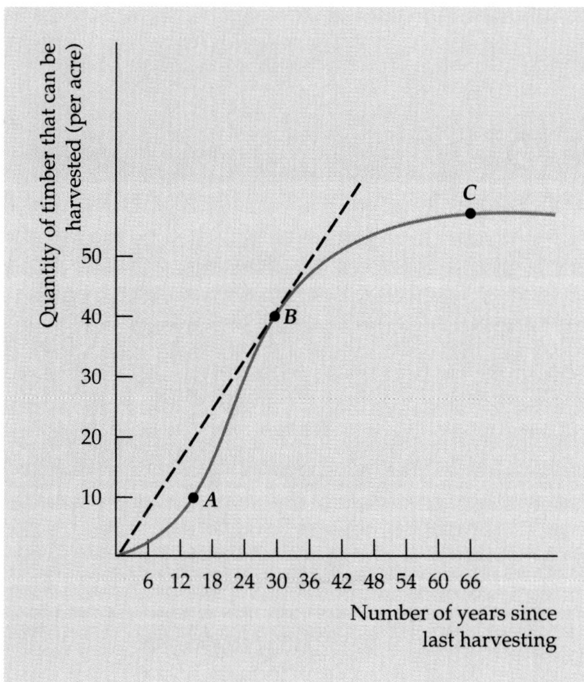

FIGURE 17-8

17-5. Using Figure 17-5, explain how conservation measures may be taken too far. Specifically, explain why it would be inefficient to cut back consumption one unit below Q_1 in year 1 in order to conserve that unit for use in year 5.

17-6. Explain what happens to the price staircase in Figure 17-5 if (a) existing deposits of the resource turn out to be less plentiful than expected; (b) there is an unexpected increase in demand for this resource.

17-7. In 1865, Doomsday forecasters predicted that economic growth couldn't continue far into the future because the world would run out of coal, the prime source of energy at that time.

(a) If you had lived then, how would you have evaluated this claim?

(b) Knowing what you do now about U.S. reserves and the way coal has been replaced as an energy source, what would you say about any attempt to use this 1865 argument to apply restrictions on oil production today?

17-8. "The lower world price of oil benefits the U.S. in many ways, but it also increases our imports and thus makes us more dependent on foreign supplies." Do you agree? Explain.

CHAPTER 18
PUBLIC GOODS AND PUBLIC CHOICE

Government is a contrivance of human wisdom to provide for human wants.
EDMUND BURKE

A lighthouse stands at the edge of the rocks, throwing out a beacon to warn ships against disaster. For the ship's captain, crew, and passengers, it provides a lifesaving service. Yet even with a role this important, that beam of light cannot be delivered by a free market. Instead, it must be provided by the government.

This is the paradox that will be resolved in this chapter: Why can't such an essential service be provided by the same free market that manages to deliver millions of other products, including such trivial services as psychiatric advice for dogs and cats? What is so special about a lighthouse? Similarly, what is so special about some of the other services the government provides? For example, the government hires the police that patrol our streets. It appoints the judges that preside over our courts. It trains the soldiers who protect us, and it purchases the military equipment they use. Why does a free market fail in such cases, leaving these goods and services to be delivered by the government?

In the study of such products, it will become evident that externalities are once again the key. However, the kind of externalities that are important now are not external *costs* such as pollution, but rather **external benefits** such as the benefits neighbors get when a homeowner hires a gardener, or the services provided by a lighthouse to ships' captains who had nothing to do with its purchase or sale.

An ***external benefit*** of a good or service is a benefit enjoyed by someone other than those who produce or purchase it.

This chapter will not only show that external benefits resolve the paradox posed by the lighthouse and other goods and services that can't be provided by a free market. It will also show that external benefits may be important in less dramatic cases where products *can* be provided by a free market. An example is vaccinations which provide both an internal benefit to purchasers who are protected from the disease and an external benefit to others who are also less likely to get the disease. Here a free market does not fail outright. It can provide such services but in an inefficiently small quantity. In this case, externalities may justify government intervention to encourage the market to deliver more. This is the simpler case, and it will be considered first. It will be followed by an analysis of cases like the lighthouse where externalities dominate, and the only way these "public goods" can be produced is by the government.

The second major topic in this chapter—public choice—examines the special set of problems that arise when the government does produce goods or services. A whole new set of questions arise, such as, "How does the government decide what the public really wants?"

EXTERNAL BENEFITS: A FREE MARKET PROVIDES TOO LITTLE OUTPUT

If there are any external or spillover effects, whether they be harmful or beneficial, the free market cannot be expected to allocate economic resources efficiently. For example, because the good in Figure 16-2 on p. 281 had an external cost, a free, perfectly competitive market resulted in too much output. Accordingly, we might guess that, if a good has an external benefit, a free market will result in too little output.

Figure 18-1 confirms that this guess is correct. The supporting argument can be stated briefly because it parallels the analysis of external costs. The key is to recognize that, instead of the external costs that had to be added to the *supply* curve in Figure 16-2, there are now external benefits that have to be added to the *demand* curve. Specifically, to get the marginal social benefit MB_S in Figure 18-1, we must take the private benefit to the purchaser (MB) as shown by the height of the demand curve and add to it the marginal external benefit shown by the arrow. For example, in the case of vaccinations, both the private benefit MB to those who acquire them and the external benefit to others who become less likely to pick up the disease must be added to calculate the social benefit (MB_S) of the shots.

If this marginal social benefit MB_S is equated to the marginal cost MC, the result is an efficient outcome at E_2. However, in the absence of government interference, a free competitive market will reach equilibrium at E_1 instead, where marginal cost is equal to marginal *private* benefit. (This is the only benefit taken into account by those buying the vaccinations; thus it is their demand curve and is marked D_1.) With equilibrium at E_1 rather than E_2, the free market generates too little output—specifically, Q_1 rather than Q_2, with the resulting efficiency loss shown in red.

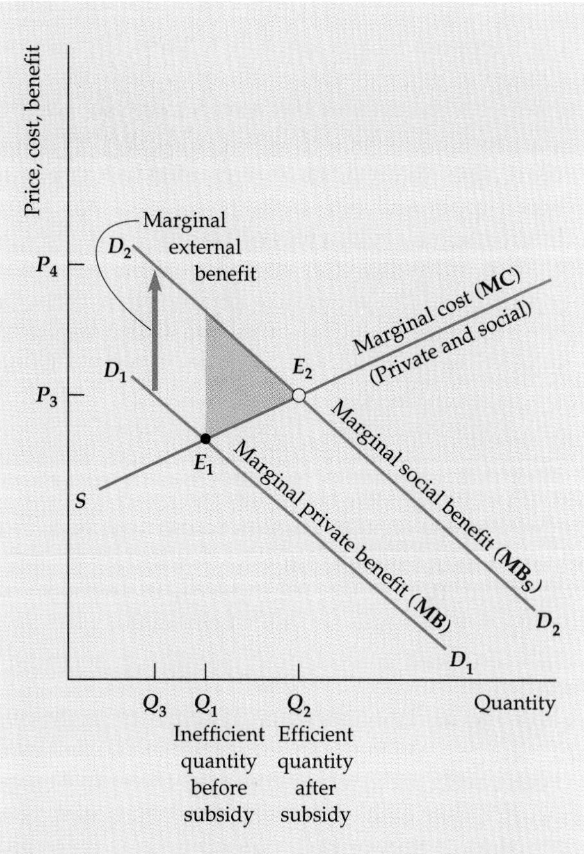

FIGURE 18-1 Efficiency loss for a product with an external benefit, such as vaccinations.

The height of the market demand D_1 shows the marginal internal benefit to those who get vaccinations because they are protected from the disease. The blue arrow shows the external benefit to others because the disease isn't passed on to them. The sum of these two benefits is the marginal social benefit MB_S. Free-market equilibrium is at E_1, where marginal cost S is equal to D_1, the marginal *private* benefit (the only benefit taken into account by those who make the decision to get vaccinations). The result is that too little is produced at Q_1. To confirm, all units of output between Q_1 and Q_2 have a benefit (the height of MB_S) that would exceed their cost (the height of MC). With this net benefit, they should be produced. Because they are not, there is a net loss shown by the red triangle.

ONE SOLUTION: A SUBSIDY

One way of getting to the efficient equilibrium E_2 is to provide buyers with a per-unit subsidy equal to the external benefit arrow, thereby shifting the demand curve up from D_1 to D_2. (Demand shifts in this way because, for example, the individual initially prepared to pay only P_3 for unit Q_3 is now prepared to pay P_4—that is, the original P_3 plus the subsidy received from the government shown by the arrow.) With this shift in demand, a competitive market does the rest. Its new equilibrium is at E_2, where supply and new demand D_2 intersect. Thus efficient output Q_2 is achieved.

Such an increase in efficiency alone does not necessarily justify a subsidy or any other form of government intervention. One must also examine the administrative costs of that intervention. Thus, for example, the government does not subsidize each homeowner for hiring a gardener, even though an attractive garden provides an external benefit to neighbors. The efficiency gains from such government intervention aren't sufficient to cover the costs of administering such a widespread subsidy program. On the other hand, in the case of many vaccinations, the efficiency gains do outweigh the costs of administration, and a subsidy is justified.[1]

In Figure 18-1 efficiency is achieved by subsidizing a product with an external benefit, just as a product with an external cost was taxed in Figure 16-2. In either case, the government *internalizes the externality*. In Figure 16-2, polluting firms that paid the tax were made to "feel internally" the external damage they were causing, so they did less. On the other hand, buyers in Figure 18-1 receive a subsidy that allows them to *enjoy internally* the external benefit they provide; thus this product is encouraged. In either the tax or subsidy case, private firms or individuals act appropriately because they take external effects into account.

Externalities may sometimes be internalized even without government action, but simply as a result of private market forces.

PRIVATE MARKET TRANSACTIONS THAT INTERNALIZE AN EXTERNALITY

One example of this type of transaction is provided by the private real estate firm that purchases a whole block of houses in a rundown neighborhood. Its renovation expenditure on each house raises the value of that house and also provides a spillover benefit by raising the value of the other houses in the block as well. Once the firm has renovated all the houses in the block, it can capture both the internal and external benefits. Specifically, when it sells each house, it will enjoy two types of price increase: (1) the price increase because that particular house has been renovated and (2) the additional price increase because the neighborhood has improved as a result of the renovations to the other houses. Thus, although the firm may not be able to make a profit by purchasing and renovating a single house, it may be able to do so if it purchases and renovates the whole block, simply because it is able to capture the spillover effects.

As another example, if a firm constructs a ski lift on a mountain, it will be able to sell tow tickets. These receipts will be an internal benefit to the firm. At the same time, the ski lift will also generate an external benefit in the form of greater pleasure for those eating at a nearby restaurant who enjoy watching people ski. The internal benefit to the ski lift company from ticket sales may be insufficient to justify constructing the lift. Suppose, however, that the firm can buy the restaurant and, once the ski lift is built, start charging customers more. It thereby captures (internalizes) the external benefit it creates. It now becomes profitable to build the lift. The nation's output of ski lift services is no longer too low. It has now been increased to an efficient quantity because external benefits have been internalized. They are now being realized by the new, larger firm.

This analysis suggests another approach to externalities: Allow firms to merge into large enough units so that decision-makers will take such spillovers into account. However, this approach raises a conflict for policymakers. Although a case can be made for allowing mergers that internalize externalities, mergers to accumulate market power may not be desirable. The problem is that mergers often do both.

PUBLIC GOODS AS A WAY OF DEALING WITH EXTERNALITIES

Now let's pursue the issue of positive externalities further by considering a flood-control dam in a riv-

[1]In order to avoid the paperwork and other administrative costs of subsidizing children's vaccinations one at a time, the government often provides them free. This is just another way of subsidizing vaccinations to encourage people to acquire more.

er valley. If a single farm family were to build such a dam, it would enjoy an internal benefit because its own crops and buildings would be protected from floods. However, this internal benefit would be small compared with the enormous cost of constructing the dam. As a result, no individual farmer builds it—even though its construction might be easily justified by the large external flood-control benefits it would provide for the thousands of other farmers in the valley.

If the dam is to be built at all, it will have to be built by the government. Thus we come to the idea of a **public good.**

PUBLIC GOODS

The simplest definition of a public good is "anything the government provides." However, this definition is too broad for our purposes, for two reasons: (1) It includes all sorts of welfare payments such as free food or cash that are designed to transfer income from one group to another. Such policies are deferred to Chapter 25. (2) "Anything the government provides" also includes all sorts of activities that *could* be undertaken by private firms but are provided by the government instead. Examples include public bus systems, state colleges, and public electricity-generating plants such as those operated by the Tennessee Valley Authority. Thus we use a narrower definition of a public good—namely, a good such as a flood control dam that cannot be provided by private firms.

Because the idea of external benefits is important to the definition of a public good, let's look more closely at two previous examples. The first is hiring a gardener. Most of the benefits are internal; that is, they go to the family that hires the gardener to work on its own property. Therefore the private market works, at least to some degree: Individuals do have gardening done, although the quantity is less than the efficient amount.

Compare this example with our example of a flood-control dam in a river valley. There are two important differences in this case. First, as already noted, a free market will not work at all. No dam will be built because no individual farmer will do it. The reason is that the internal benefits of flood control to that individual would be small compared to the large cost of building a dam. Most of the benefits would be external—the protection from floods provided to other farmers in the river valley. Because no individual farmer will do it, any dam that is built will have to be constructed by the government. The second difference is more subtle: Once the government has built the dam, *an individual farmer's benefit from it will be the same as if he had built the dam himself.* In other words, he cannot be excluded from enjoying its benefits; technically, its benefits are described as *nonexcludable.* Indeed, many economists use this as their definition of a public good: It provides an individual with a benefit that does not depend on whether or not that person is the actual purchaser. Another illustration is the lighthouse. Once it is built, no sailor can be excluded from using its services. All sailors are protected from the rocks whether or not they helped to pay for the lighthouse.

Another characteristic of a public good is that it provides an *inexhaustible benefit.* When you use the light from the lighthouse, the amount available for others is still there undiminished. You haven't used it up. When one farmer uses the flood-control service of a dam, its flood-control benefits remain undiminished for other farmers to enjoy. Compare this to a private good, such as a hamburger. When you use it, it disappears; it is exhausted. Even when you buy a private service such as an appointment with your doctor, it is temporarily exhausted; the doctor you are seeing cannot see someone else at the same time.

> A ***public good*** provides a nonexcludable benefit that is available to everyone, regardless of who pays for it. Its benefit is also inexhaustible; when one person enjoys it, the amount of benefit it provides to others is not diminished.

Note that, whereas a flood-control dam is a public good, some kinds of dams are not. For example, a dam used to generate electricity may be built by a private firm. The reason is that electricity can be made available only to those who pay for it, so a private firm can sell it.

The distinction between a public good and an ordinary private good is shown in Figures 18-2 and 18-3. A private good is illustrated in Figure 18-2. The first two panels show the marginal benefit (demand) of two individual consumers. Each con-

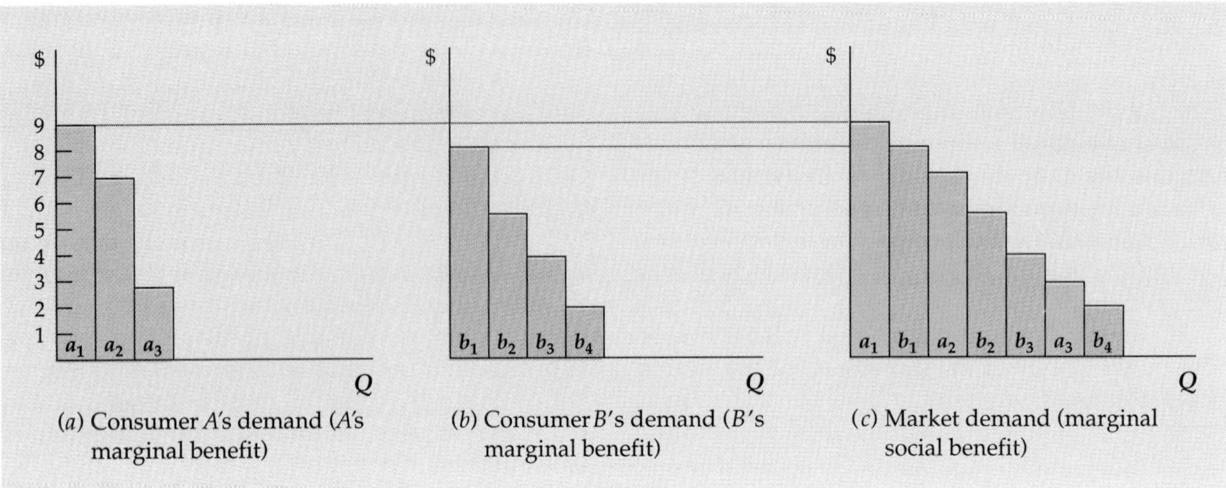

FIGURE 18-2 A private good.
Individual demands in panels *a* and *b* are horizontally summed to get market demand in panel *c*. (At a price of $9, *A* buys one unit. If the price falls to $8, *B* also buys a unit. If the price falls to $7, *A* buys a second unit, and so on.) For such a private good with no external benefits, the market demand curve in part *c* represents marginal social benefit.

sumer would have to purchase and acquire the good in order to realize this benefit from it. As we saw in Figure 7-1, a horizontal summation of the individual demands (marginal benefits) in panels *a* and *b* provides the total market demand in panel *c* (the marginal social benefit).

In contrast, Figure 18-3 shows a public good, where all individuals can benefit from each unit produced. For example, consumer *A* gets benefit a_1 from the first unit. At the same time, this first unit also provides consumer *B* with benefit b_1. Because both individuals benefit from the first unit—both can, for example, see the warning beam from the same lighthouse—the benefit provided by this first unit is a_1 *plus* b_1, as shown in panel *c*. For such a public good, marginal social benefit (MB_S) is found by *vertically* adding the individual benefits—in contrast to the horizontal addition for a private good.

It is important to recognize that the resulting marginal social benefit curve (MB_S) in Figure 18-3 is *not* a demand curve. Nobody would buy the first unit if its price were $a_1 + b_1$. However, if it can be produced at this cost or less, the first unit (for example, the first dam) should be produced. Finally, note that Figures 18-2 and 18-3 present only the two extreme cases: a "pure" private good, which provides benefit only to the purchaser, and a "pure" public good, which provides each individual with a level of benefit that does not depend at all on who purchases the good. There are, of course, many intermediate cases where a good provides benefit to the purchaser and to others, but where the level of benefit for each individual *does* depend on who purchases the good. (If I purchase it, I'll get more benefit from it than if you purchase it.) Such intermediate cases were illustrated earlier in the examples of gardening and vaccinations.

PROBLEMS IN EVALUATING THE BENEFITS OF A PUBLIC GOOD

Suppose that panel *c* of Figure 18-3 shows the benefits of building a system of flood-control dams on a river. Suppose further that the cost of the first dam would be C. Because this is less than its benefit $a_1 + b_1$, this dam should be built. Let us now examine in more detail our earlier claim that this public good can be provided only by the government. Why can't it be provided by private enterprise instead? After all, since the two farmers value it at $a_1 + b_1$, why doesn't some entrepreneur collect this amount from them and build the dam? (The

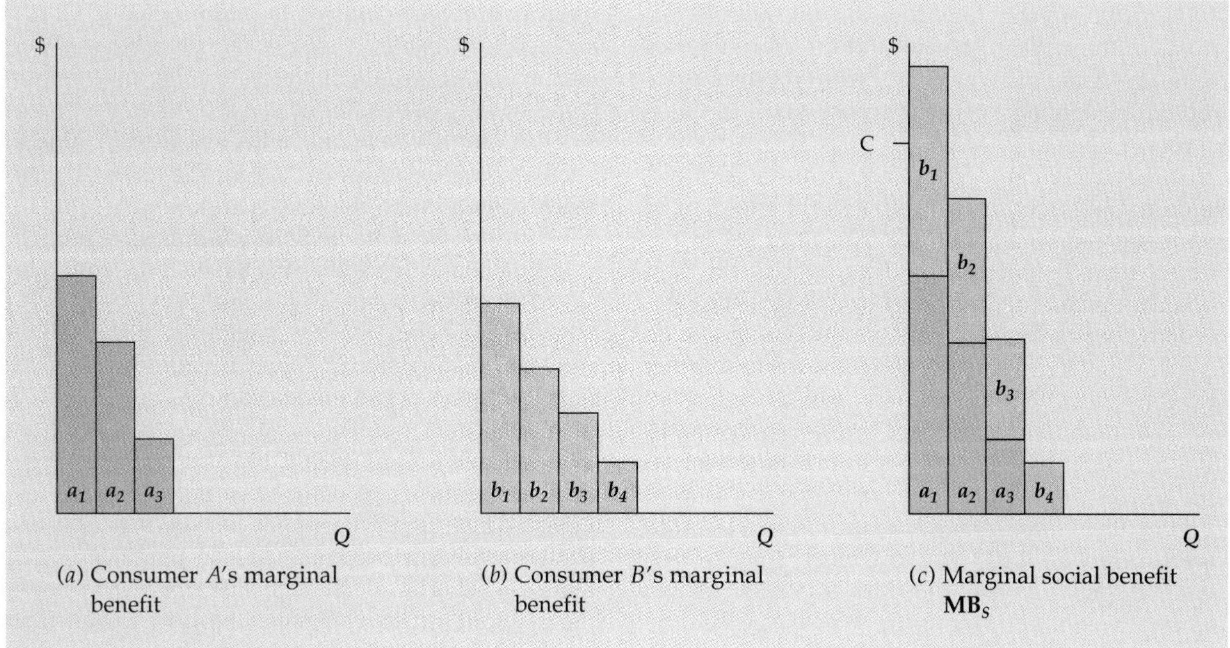

FIGURE 18-3 A public good.

The individual marginal benefits in panels *a* and *b* are *vertically* summed to get the marginal social benefit in panel *c*. Thus b_1 is stacked on top of a_1 to show that both consumers get a benefit from the first unit.

entrepreneur would be collecting more than the cost of the dam and therefore could pocket a profit.)

To answer this question, note that any public good has a very large number of consumers. In our example, the two farmers *A* and *B* represent thousands of farmers in the valley. Thus MB_S is the vertical sum, not just of two individual marginal benefit curves but instead of thousands of them—with each individual curve being relatively insignificant. Now suppose that you are one of these individuals and the private entrepreneur who is promoting this project asks you for your valuation of the dam. Specifically, how much would you be willing to pay for its construction?

What would you reply? Clearly, you would have a strong incentive to understate your benefit, because you realize that it is very unlikely that your answer will influence the decision on whether the dam is built. You will either get a dam or not, depending on how the thousands of other farmers in the valley respond. All your reply will do is determine the amount that you will be contributing—and it's in your interest to minimize this. So you reply that you believe a flood-control system is exactly what this valley needs, and you believe your neighbors will value it very highly. However, it will provide little value for you; you personally are willing to pay very little for it.

If the dam is built—as you secretly hope—it will cost you very little. Yet you cannot be excluded from enjoying its services. If the dam prevents a flood, your buildings and land will be protected. You become a **free rider,** enjoying the benefits while paying little of the costs. The problem, of course, is that you will not be the only one with an incentive to ride free. Every other individual in the valley also has exactly the same incentive, so that the entrepreneur gets a seriously biased response from everyone.

A *free rider* is someone who cannot be excluded from enjoying the benefits of a project but who pays nothing (or pays a disproportionately small amount) to cover its costs.

Accordingly, the dam does not get built by the private entrepreneur. It is natural therefore to turn to the government, which can solve the free-rider problem by forcing everyone to pay taxes to build the dam.

Although it can collect enough taxes to build the dam, the government still faces the problem of evaluating the benefits of the dam in order to decide whether or not it should be built in the first place. In evaluating the benefits, the government, just like the private entrepreneur, encounters problems. It cannot simply ask people how highly they value the dam. If it were to ask you, and you believe that the government will build the dam without noticeably increasing your taxes, it will be in your interest to *overstate* your valuation in order to increase the chance that the dam will be built. Therefore, even though you previously told the private entrepreneur that the dam is worth almost nothing to you, you now turn around and tell the government it is worth $1 million to you since you know you won't actually have to pay the $1 million. In short, estimates by individuals of what the dam is worth are unreliable, regardless of who is collecting them.[2]

Another approach is to forget about canvassing people for their views and instead estimate benefits of the dam in some other way. For example, by examining past records, the government can estimate the value of the crops that are likely to be saved from floods. Such benefits can then be compared with the estimated cost of the dam.

There are, however, two potential problems with such **benefit-cost analysis.** First, unless it is treated with care, it may be used simply as an economic justification for projects which the government has already decided to build for political reasons. For example, a dam may have been promised to a key group of voters in the last election campaign. A politically motivated official who has to evaluate this dam and who wants to be able to back up the government's promise may (1) estimate construction costs on the low side and (2) keep adding benefits until the dam is justified. For example, such benefits might include the lives saved by flood control. Although any lives saved are an important benefit, a wide range of values can be placed on them, as has already been seen in the discussion of the evaluation of a human life in Box 16-4.

Another reason why it may be difficult to get an accurate estimate is that the engineers who expect to construct the dam may also be the ones who evaluate its benefits. They may be tempted to estimate the benefits on the high side in order to justify the dam and, in so doing, create future income and employment for themselves.

THE ENVIRONMENT AS A PUBLIC GOOD

This discussion of public goods can be tied into the analysis of environmental and resource protection in the last two chapters. There we concluded that, in a private market without government intervention, decisions by private firms may seriously damage the environment or deplete resources such as fish. The government may limit such damage with taxes, regulations, or the creation of property rights.

Suppose, however, that the environment is deteriorating of its own accord; no firm or individual is at fault in any way. For example, suppose that a species of wildlife is dying off in the wilderness. In this case, the proper approach is to recognize that the preservation of this species is a public good, just like the construction of a dam. Because no individual values the species highly enough to incur the cost of personally preserving it, the private market generally won't deliver. Although private conservation organizations may act, the ultimate decision on whether to save the species—and how much to spend on the effort—may rest with the government. If the government does act, everyone can enjoy the resulting benefits.

[2]Devising ways to get a better evaluation of public goods has become an important area of inquiry. One imaginative suggestion is to inform people that they will be taxed, but only if their individual valuation tips the scale in favor of building the dam. For such an individual, the tax would be the cost of the dam minus the sum of everyone else's valuation. Putting the question this way makes it less likely that people will provide a wildly inaccurate evaluation. In particular, it would prevent you from making your wild overestimate of a million dollars. Think about it: The more you exaggerate, the more likely it is that your answer will tip the scales in favor of the dam and you will be taxed. In addition, the more you exaggerate, the higher your tax bill could be.

How large would these benefits be? This question is not easy to answer. Although most people would put some value on the preservation of a wildlife species, it is very difficult to say how much. As Harvard's Richard Caves has put it: "How highly should we value wombats, if they are so far from civilization that no one will ever see them, let alone eat them?" One answer is that we may place some value on them, even though we may never see them, just as we may place a value on an air-conditioning system, even though we may not actually turn it on this year. This phenomenon is described as **option demand**—the desire to have an option, whether or not we exercise it. We may want to keep open the option of seeing a species, or drawing on it for, say, medical research, even though we may never in fact exercise this option. Similarly, we may have an option demand for public parks which we may or may not actually visit. Option demand should be taken into account in the evaluation of environmental benefits.

PUBLIC CHOICE: PROBLEMS WITH GOVERNMENT DECISION-MAKING

In the last six chapters we have seen that private decision-making often has serious flaws; in the face of private market failure, the government may be justified in intervening in the economy. However, this argument is incomplete unless we recognize that government intervention may itself fail, because government decision-making also has its own special set of flaws.

1. THE DIFFICULTY IN REVERSING A PUBLIC EXPENDITURE

When Coca-Cola announced a new formula, only to see its sales slip, it reconsidered its decision and brought back Coca-Cola Classic. The reason is that a private company like Coca-Cola would sooner admit its mistake than lose market share; business executives will admit their mistakes to save their jobs. This is not so in the public sector, where admitting mistakes may cost politicians their jobs. For example, if a government drops an expenditure that it introduced earlier, the opposition party may be able to use this "admission of error" to defeat the government in the next election. Furthermore, the taxpayer bears the cost of government expenditures, whether wise or foolish; politicians do not personally pick up the tab. This also makes them less likely to admit a mistake and reverse an expenditure decision. Thus there may be too much production of public goods.

2. VOTING POLITICALLY FOR PRODUCTS IS NOT SPECIFIC ENOUGH

The Coca-Cola example suggests another important difference between public and private decision-making. When you buy a particular item, you register a clear vote for its production. However, in the public sector, you vote for a dam—at least in theory—by voting for a candidate committed to building it. Unfortunately, in practice it is not this simple. In fact, you may not get to vote on this issue at all. The reason is that, in an election, you vote for a candidate who advocates a whole set of policies. Like most other voters, you may vote for this candidate because of some other completely unrelated issue, such as foreign policy, or even personality. It is therefore quite possible that the voters who have elected a candidate promising a dam don't really want the dam at all. Instead, they may be supporting this candidate *despite* his or her support for the dam.

Although the issue is not quite this simple—the public can also express its preferences via campaign contributions, lobbying, and so on—it is nonetheless true that the political process is a relatively poor method for the public to express its preferences on detailed questions. The public does not vote often enough and specifically enough to provide a clear message to the government of who wants what. Compare this situation with the private market, where communication is much more effective. Each day millions of messages on millions of products are communicated to producers by consumers when they buy—or do not buy—those products.

3. SHORT-RUN, CRISIS-ORIENTED DECISION-MAKING

The desire to be reelected leads politicians to favor policies with costs that are hidden, and benefits that are obvious and will be realized quickly, before the next election. Why should they promote policies that the public won't understand, or policies that will provide benefits after the next election—and thus may help to reelect their successors? One reason why elected officials may take this limited short-run view is that a busy public cannot be adequately informed about the hundreds of issues on which the officials must decide. They therefore tend to put off tough, long-run decisions, and when they finally do take action, it is often in response to a crisis.

When officials make decisions that provide short-run benefits at the expense of long-run costs, this is very expensive for future generations who get no vote on this issue. In this sense, no process—not even a democratic one—can ever be a perfectly representative one in which both the present and future generations who will be affected get to vote.

4. THE INCENTIVE FOR POLITICIANS TO SUPPORT SPECIAL-INTEREST GROUPS

The diffuse and inchoate consumer interest has been no match for the sharply focused, articulate and well-financed efforts of producer groups.

WALTER W. HELLER

In making decisions, our elected representatives have a number of motives. For example, they may honestly be trying to promote the public interest. Frequently, their desire to serve the public is their reason for entering politics in the first place. Once they enter politics, however, they can't accomplish anything without being elected. Thus, of necessity, all politicians—no matter how noble—must be concerned with getting elected or reelected. One of the best ways to get reelected is to gain the backing of organized constituencies—or "special-interest" groups—who are able to deliver votes and/or financial support. In turn, the best way to get such backing is to support programs that are of great interest to such groups but of far less concern to the public that has to pay. The special interest of most people is their job—the goods or services they are producing; the source of our income is of intense interest to each of us. Politicians therefore pay particular attention to people as producers rather than as consumers.

Even for a politician who is prepared to support the public interest, it's not always clear what that may be.

PROBLEMS IN DEFINING THE PUBLIC INTEREST

Majority rule is a basic principle of democracy. Can't we use this simple and well-accepted principle to determine what is in the public interest? Unfortunately, we often cannot—for several reasons.

1. THE PROBLEM OF THE OPPRESSIVE MAJORITY

Under majority rule, if 51% of the public want a certain policy they can get it. It doesn't matter how small they value the benefit—as long as they get some benefit. Nor does it matter how heavy the cost of this policy may be to the minority. Hence it is possible for majority rule to leave society as a whole worse off, with the benefits to the majority falling short of the costs imposed on the minority.

As an illustration, consider the following modified version of an example suggested by Gordon Tullock of George Mason University. There are 100 farmers in a community. Each requires a small connecting road to get access to a main highway. It is in the interests of 51 of these farmers to vote to have access roads put into their own farms only, using taxes collected from all 100 farmers. However, this will involve a loss to society if the 49 losers who don't get roads suffer a great deal from the tax they have to pay, while the 51 winners who do get roads get a benefit that barely exceeds the tax they pay. Therefore majority rule may be defective. Like private decision-making, it may result in inefficiency—an overall loss to society.[3]

Is there a better voting procedure than majority rule? The answer is that there are a lot of alternatives, but each has some weakness or another. For example, one could avoid the problem of the oppressive majority by requiring unanimous consent; then no policy could hurt anyone. But this rule is hopeless. By providing a veto to each individual, it paralyzes the government. Any policy

[3]Majority rule can be inefficient, not only because such undesirable policies *are* introduced, but also because *desirable* policies are *not* introduced. For example, a desirable policy that benefits the minority a great deal may be rejected if it hurts the majority even slightly.

that damaged even one voter would be vetoed. Rather than searching for a voting system that might conceivably be better than majority rule, a more common and reasonable approach is to protect minorities from an oppressive majority with a constitution, either written or unwritten.

Our example of the oppressive majority illustrates two additional points: (1) The government can redistribute income without transferring any cash. Suppose the 51 farmers who get roads receive more benefits than we have so far assumed. Specifically, suppose their net benefits are roughly equal to the loss borne by the minority. In this case, the minority pays taxes to help finance projects that benefit the majority. The majority receives a large transfer from the minority—even though no cash transfer takes place between the two. (2) Members of a minority have a strong incentive to try to break down the existing majority coalition in order to form a new ruling coalition including themselves. For example, the 49 excluded farmers are likely to try to get 2 farmers to leave the present majority and join them. Then the newly formed coalition can turn the tables on the 49 who were in a majority but now find themselves out of power. Of course, the new coalition may then come under the same pressure from outsiders as the old; there may be a cycle of changing coalition patterns.

2. THE VOTING PARADOX: WHY MAJORITY RULE MAY LEAD TO NO CLEAR WINNER

Consider a population of only three individuals faced with a choice among three options, A, B, and C. Table 18-1 shows how each individual ranks each of these options. For example, the first column tells us that individual I prefers option A to option B, and B to C. Which of these options is the will of the majority?

If these individuals choose first between options A and B, a majority (individuals I and III) will vote for A. With A the choice so far, the only remaining question is how it compares with C. In voting between A and C, the majority (individuals II and III) prefer C. So C is the final choice, reflecting the apparent will of the majority.

Now, suppose instead that these individuals vote first between B and C. In this case, C is immediately rejected because individuals I and II prefer B. Thus the preference of the majority isn't clear at all. C may be the final choice or immediately rejected, depending on how the voting is set up.

Consequently, in a world in which individual preferences differ, an important determinant of the final choice may be the political process itself (in this example, the political decision on which options will be voted on first). The individual who sets a committee's agenda or controls its voting procedure may therefore be able to control the result.[4]

3. LOGROLLING

Logrolling occurs when several members of Congress agree: "You vote for my policy, and I'll vote for yours." Table 18-2 shows how it works in a simple case with three voters.

The first row in this table indicates that policy A provides a benefit of 3 to individual I, and a cost of 2 to each of the other two voters.

In a simple majority vote, policies A and B are both defeated; individuals II and III vote against policy A, and I and III vote against B. However, I

[4]This voting paradox, first described over a century ago, was extended by Kenneth Arrow in *Social Choice and Individual Values* (New York: John Wiley, 1951).

TABLE 18-1 The Voting paradox: Preferences of Three Individuals for options A, B, and C

	Individual		
Choice	*I*	*II*	*III*
First choice	A	B	C
Second choice	B	C	A
Last choice	C	A	B

TABLE 18-2 Logrolling: Benefits (+) or Costs (–) of Each Policy to Each Individual

Choice	*Individual* I	*II*	*III*
Policy A	+3	–2	–2
Policy B	–2	+3	–2
Net effect on each individual if *both* policies are passed because of logrolling:	+1	+1	–4

and II have an incentive to get together first and agree to have II vote for I's pet policy A, if I will vote for II's pet policy B. Because of this logrolling agreement, both policies pass. As shown in the bottom row of this table, individuals I and II both benefit. Indeed, that was the reason why they engaged in logrolling in the first place. However, III loses by even more than the combined gains of I and II. Thus logrolling hurts the community overall, even though it benefits the groups who engage in it—in our example, individuals I and II.

This is the classical example of logrolling, but there is another possibility. Change the two entries of +3 in Table 18-2 to +5. As before, in the absence of logrolling, neither policy will pass. Logrolling occurs again for exactly the same reason as before, and once again I and II benefit while III loses. The difference this time is that the combined gain of I and II exceeds III's loss. Thus logrolling results in a net overall benefit for this community. Therefore logrolling isn't necessarily bad. In some cases, it may be the only way to achieve a socially desirable result. Observe that, in this example, logrolling overcomes the problem of the oppressive majority. Specifically, it prevents the majority of II and III from blocking desirable policy A.

THE PROBLEMS OF GOVERNING WITH A BUREAUCRACY

Suppose the public interest on a specific issue is clearly defined, Congress has voted for it, and the president has approved. Even in these favorable circumstances, problems may arise because this policy must be introduced and enforced by the appropriate government department—for example, the Department of the Interior or the Department of Health and Human Resources. Each of these departments is a "bureau." That is, it receives its income from a granting agency (Congress) rather than as a private firm does—from the sale of a product in the marketplace.[5]

DIFFICULTIES IN CONTROLLING A BUREAU'S PERFORMANCE AND COST

The government bureau typically is a monopolist in the provision of its service to the public. Indeed, the reason the government may have taken over this activity may be that it is a natural monopoly. For precisely this reason it is difficult for Congress to judge its performance: There is no equivalent private agency providing the same service with which the government bureau might be compared. Another difficulty is that a bureau's output can't be measured. Thus, for example, the Department of Agriculture can't be judged, like a private firm, on the number of bushels of wheat it produces because it doesn't produce any. (This problem reaches right down through the ranks of a bureau. Difficulties in measuring output make it difficult for senior members in a bureau to evaluate the productivity of their juniors.)

This difficulty in evaluating performance is

[5]Departments of large private firms may develop many of the characteristics of a bureaucracy. If they do, the difference between the operation of a government department and a business is reduced.

only one of the reasons why a bureau's costs are hard to control. Another reason is that a bureau's officials sometimes feel under pressure at the end of the year to inflate costs by spending any remaining funds in their budget. If they don't, their budget may be cut the next year. Then there are the problems of bureaucratic waste that apply year round and that arise because a bureau is in a different situation than a private firm under pressure to sell its product in the marketplace. The private firm has great incentives to cut costs. These incentives come in the form of both a carrot (the desire to make profits) and a stick (the fear of bankruptcy if costs aren't kept in line). On the other hand, a bureau need not fear going broke. It is therefore under far less pressure to keep its costs down. Moreover, because officials in a bureau are not spending their own money, they may lose track of what it is worth. They simply don't "pay attention" in the same way that entrepreneurs do when they have their own money on the line. The result is great waste in, for example, the world's largest bureau: the Pentagon, which at one time paid $91 for screws available in any hardware store for 3 cents.

Unfortunately, waste sometimes occurs not only in the Pentagon's purchases, but also in its sales. For example, in 1983, the Pentagon sold $1.6 billion worth of surplus items for $89 million—less than 6 cents on the dollar. Many of these items were, at the same time, being purchased at full price by other Pentagon officials unaware that the Pentagon was already overstocked and was selling them off at a huge discount.

In the absence of a profit motive, what incentives are there in a bureau? Government officials tend to substitute two other objectives: (1) the public interest, at least as they perceive it, and (2) their own interest, including establishing a public reputation, accumulating the power and perquisites of office, and—often most important—increasing the size of the bureau.

THE TENDENCY FOR A BUREAU TO EXPAND

There are several reasons why the head of a bureau might try to increase its size. By increasing the number of employees, the official will seem to have more responsibility and thus may gain prestige. More employees may also mean more echelons of management—just as in a private firm—and therefore more jobs at the top. This in turn means improved prospects for promotion. Government officials may also seek more funds in order to serve the public or their constituents better. For example, the more funds going to the Department of Agriculture, the more benefits it can provide to the nation's farmers. The more its constituents are thereby satisfied, the more they will put pressure on Congress if any attempts are made to cut the bureau's budget.

MONOPOLY INEFFICIENCY: PUBLIC VERSUS PRIVATE

Both a private monopoly and a monopolized public activity may operate in a technically inefficient way—that is, with unnecessarily high cost. One reason is that both have less incentive than a competitive firm to keep costs down. Moreover, both monopolies can also result in allocative inefficiency—that is, the wrong amount of output. However, this kind of inefficiency appears in two different forms. On the one hand, a private monopoly produces too little output and therefore employs too few resources. On the other hand, a public monopoly—a bureau—has natural tendencies to expand. Consequently, it often tends to employ too many resources.[6]

THE PUBLIC VERSUS THE PRIVATE SECTOR: A REVIEW OF MICROECONOMIC MARKETS

This chapter concludes with a comparison of the various kinds of private markets described in earlier chapters, ranging from perfect competition through monopoly. These markets are then com-

[6]In the view of John Kenneth Galbraith, government is too small; compared to a private business, it provides too few goods and services. One reason is that the sales of privately produced goods, such as autos, are increased by advertising. However, publicly supplied goods, such as roads, are generally not advertised. Therefore we overspend on autos but underspend on roads.

pared to the market for a public good. Although a complete comparison is beyond the scope of this book, these markets can be better understood by answering the following important question. In each market, how does the cost curve of a single producer compare to its total market demand curve?

In Figure 18-4, this question is answered for four types of markets (panels *a* through *d*); the final panel shows public goods, for comparison. In each of the first four cases (starting with perfect competition in panel *a*), the type of market depends heavily on how long the firm's average costs continue to fall. To highlight this point, we have assumed that the four products shown are similar in all other respects. For example, total market demand is exactly the same for each, and the average cost *AC* of each reaches a minimum at the same height, *C*. The only difference in these four products is that, as we move from left to right from panel to panel, *AC* reaches a minimum at an increasingly large output. Thus, in panel *a, AC* reaches a minimum at a very small output Q_1, whereas in panel *d, AC* reaches the same minimum height *C* at such a large output—that is, so far to the right—that it cannot even be shown in the diagram.

In the case of perfect competition in panel *a*, market demand can be satisfied at minimum cost by a large number of producers. There is little role to be played by the government, because this market is generally efficient when left to its own devices. (We assume here that there are no complications, such as important externalities.)

Panel *b* illustrates the case of natural oligopoly, where market demand can be satisfied at minimum cost by just a few firms. In such a market, a strong case can be made for the vigorous enforcement of antitrust laws to prevent collusion or the merger of these firms into a monopoly.

In the case of natural monopoly in panel *c*, market demand can be satisfied at lower cost by one firm than by more than one. Here, the application of antitrust legislation to split up a single firm makes little sense, because the split would raise costs. A preferred approach is to relax import restrictions, with foreign competition to then preventing the firm from charging a high monopoly price; at the same time, the firm would be able to

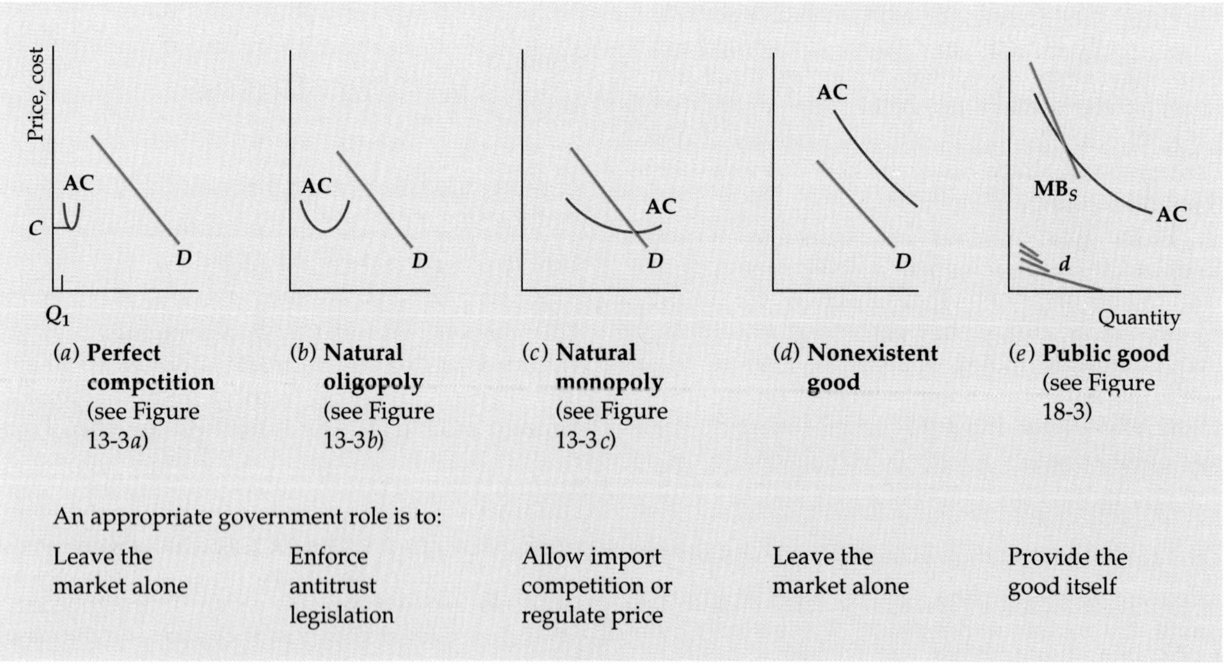

FIGURE 18-4 The relationship of the costs of a single producer and total market demand.

gain the cost advantages of large-scale production. If foreign competition does not exist, then an alternative is price regulation.

In panel *d* costs have outrun demand. At no point do *D* and *AC* overlap, that is, at no point does *D* lie above *AC*. Therefore there is no single price a firm can charge and still cover its costs. The product will not even appear on the market.[7]

Finally, consider panel *e*, which shows a public good. In this case, the good is not produced by private firms; there is no standard market demand *D* (as the horizontal sum of individual demands *d*). However, the marginal social benefit MB_S of this good does exist. It is the vertical sum of the individual demand curves. If the MB_S curve overlaps (that is, lies above) the *AC* curve, it is in the public interest for the government to provide this good.

We conclude by noting that, in some cases, government intervention in the marketplace is not justified. However, in other circumstances, when there is private market failure, a case can be made for such intervention. However, our earlier word of warning should be repeated. Even in cases of private market failure, it should not be assumed that government intervention is a simple, fool-proof solution; it may also fail. Recall, for example, the difficulties that arise in bureaucratic decision-making, and the problems the government encounters in reversing a bad decision or in controlling its costs. Just because government intervention *could* increase efficiency does not mean that it necessarily *will*. The government may improve things, or it may make them worse.

Now that we have completed the discussion of public goods, where one of the strongest cases can be made for government intervention, we will turn in the next chapter to international trade, in which the case for government intervention is far weaker. In fact, economists have historically been extremely critical of government interference in this area.

[7]An exception occurs in the case of the discriminating monopolist. If the gap between *D* and *AC* is small enough, a discriminating monopolist such as the dentist in Figure 12-9 may be able to cover her costs if she is able to charge different prices to different buyers. In this special case, the product does appear on the market, and its production can be justified by the benefits it provides to a public that would otherwise have to do without.

KEY POINTS

1. If a good provides an external benefit, a perfectly competitive market will provide less than the efficient quantity of output. The government can induce the expansion of output to the efficient quantity by subsidizing buyers of this good by the amount of the external benefit. This policy "internalizes the externality" because buyers then personally enjoy not only the benefit the good provides to themselves, but also an amount equal to the benefit it provides to others.

2. No individual farmer would consider building a flood-control dam, because of its high cost and because the internal benefits to that farmer would be trivial compared to the external benefits that would go to thousands of neighboring farmers. This, then, is the general idea of a public good: It is a good that will not be produced by the private market; if it is to exist at all, it must be produced by the government.

3. A more precise definition of a public good is that it provides inexhaustible benefits that can be enjoyed by everyone, regardless of who pays for it. For example, once a flood-control dam has been built, no one can be excluded from enjoying its flood-control services.

4. Building such a dam will be justified if its cost is less than the sum of its benefits to all the public.

5. In practice, there may be major problems in evaluating these benefits. Even if people have a clear idea in their own minds of what the benefits would be, they are unlikely to tell any government official (or, for that matter, any private entrepreneur). Therefore the alternative approach of benefit-cost analysis is often used. For example, the benefit of flood control is estimated by looking at past records of how often floods have occurred and the damage they have done to crops.

6. There are two important ways to protect the environment. When it is being damaged by, say, polluting firms, the proper approach is to use one of the policies described in Chapter 16, such as a tax or a system of marketable emission permits. On the other hand, when the environment is deteriorating of its own accord—for example, if a wildlife species is becoming extinct—the preservation of the environment may be viewed as a public good. Thus government protection of the environment is justified if the costs of this protection are less than the benefits it provides to all individuals in society.

7. When the government intervenes in the economy, a number of problems arise. For example, reversing an error is more difficult for the government than for private firms because politicians fear losing votes if they admit mistakes.

8. By watching what the public buys, private firms can get a clearcut indication of what the public wants. But when the public votes for a candidate who has promised to, say, build a dam, it's not clear whether or not the public wants the dam. It may have voted for the candidate for foreign policy or other reasons.

9. Politicians often make economic decisions, not so much in the interests of the general public, as in the interests of their specific constituency (or some special interest group within that constituency). Moreover, they tend to favor policies with a payoff that is obvious and will be realized quickly—in particular, before the next election.

10. There are problems in defining the public interest, because a majority vote may lead to no clear winning policy. In addition, a majority vote may, by oppressing a minority, lead to an overall loss to society.

11. There is a natural tendency for a bureau and its budget to expand. One reason is that a bureau is typically not under the same cost-cutting pressures as a private firm that must sell its output on a competitive market.

KEY CONCEPTS

external benefit
internalizing an external benefit
nonexcludable benefit
inexhaustible benefit
public good
free rider
benefit-cost analysis
option demand
oppressive majority
voting paradox
logrolling
bureau

PROBLEMS

18-1. If a freeway is to be built into a city, discuss the benefits and costs that you think should be estimated. Explain why preparing such estimates might be a difficult task.

18-2. Do you think national defense is a public good? Why? Would estimating its benefits be difficult? Why?

18-3. Suppose you are working for a government in the tropics and a proposal is being considered to spray malarial mosquitoes. A critic states that, if such an expenditure were justified, a private entrepreneur would already have seized this opportunity. What position would you take?

18-4. Equilibrium E_1 in Figure 18-1 is inefficient. Which, if any, of the efficiency conditions in Box 11-1 is violated?

18-5. "Since a public good provides a benefit that is nonexcludable, the supplier cannot charge for it. Its price will therefore be zero. That raises no problems because, in terms of efficiency, its price *should* be zero. The reason is that, because it is a public good, its benefits are nonexhaustible. For example, the light from a lighthouse is nonexhaustible, so the marginal cost MC to the government of providing this light to one more user is zero. Since efficiency requires that price = MC, the efficient price is zero." Do you agree or not? Explain why.

18-6. Suppose that, instead of the per-unit subsidy to the buyer equal to the arrow in Figure 18-1, the government provides exactly the same subsidy to the seller. Show the effect. Does this subsidy increase output to the efficient quantity? How does this policy compare with the policy of subsidizing the buyer?

18-7. Construct an example, along the lines of Table 18-2, to show how logrolling may result in two policies that are neutral, that is, that leave the community with neither an overall benefit nor loss.

CHAPTER 19
WHAT ARE THE GAINS FROM INTERNATIONAL TRADE?

Instructed ships shall sail to quick commerce
By which remotest regions are allied
Which makes one city of the universe
Where some may gain and all may be supplied.
JOHN DRYDEN (1632 1700)

Economic gains come from **specialization.** One of the reasons for the high material standard of living in the United States is our high degree of specialization. Steel is produced near the coal fields of Pennsylvania, wheat is grown in the midwestern states, and citrus fruits are produced in California and Florida. By such specialization, we are able to increase our total output of goods.

Just as specialization and trade within the United States increase output and efficiency, so too do specialization and trade between the United States and other countries. There are four reasons. The first two are new, while the last two have already been noted in Chapter 3:

- Increased competition.
- Greater availability of products.
- Economies of scale.
- Comparative advantage.

Each of these reasons will be described in turn, with comparative advantage left to the end, so that this very important benefit from trade can be examined in detail.

In the great debate on trade policy—free trade versus protection—the gains from trade discussed in this chapter represent the case for free trade. The arguments for tariffs or other trade restrictions will be discussed in the next chapter.

Before describing the gains from trade, we begin with a brief description of the pattern of U.S. trade. Which countries are our best export customers? From which do we make the largest import purchases?

WITH WHOM DO WE TRADE? WHAT DO WE TRADE?

The first column of Table 19-1 shows that Canada and Japan are the two most important U.S. trading partners, by a wide margin. One reason why Canada ranks first is that distance and therefore transport costs—natural deterrents to trade—are at a minimum in U.S. trade with Canada. In the future, these close ties will become even closer. In 1989, the United States and Canada entered a free trade agreement, which will lead to a gradual elim-

TABLE 19-1 U. S. Merchandise Trade in 1988 (excluding military, in billions of dollars)

With whom do we trade?		*What do we trade?*	
Exports: U. S. sales to		Exports	
Canada	73.1	Agricultural products	38.3
Japan	37.2	Chemicals, excluding medicinals	25.3
Mexico	20.7	Metals and related products	20.4
U. K.	18.1	Civilian aircraft and parts	20.5
West Germany	14.1	Motor vehicles and parts	33.1
Taiwan	11.9	Consumer goods, except food and autos	23.8
South Korea	10.7	Computers and parts	21.7
Other Asian countries	37.1	Other machinery	68.0
Latin America (except Mexico)	23.2	All others	68.8
Africa	5.5		
Eastern Europe	3.8		
All others	64.5		
Total	319.9	Total	319.9
Imports: U. S. purchases from		Imports	
Canada	84.1	Food, feed and beverages	24.8
Japan	89.8	Petroleum and products	39.2
Mexico	23.3	Chemicals, excluding medicinals	12.4
U. K.	17.8	Metals and related products	35.0
West Germany	26.3	Civilian aircraft and parts	7.5
Taiwan	24.9	Motor vehicles and parts	87.9
South Korea	20.1	Consumer goods, except food and autos	96.3
Other Asian countries	55.9	Computers and parts	18.4
Latin America (except Mexico)	28.1	Other machinery	74.9
Africa	9.3	All others	50.0
Eastern Europe	2.2		
All others	64.6		
Total	446.4	Total	446.4

Source: U. S. Department of Commerce, *Survey of Current Business,* March 1989, pp. 41–44.

ination of tariffs between the two countries by 1998. After Canada and Japan, the most important U.S. trading partners are Mexico, the United Kingdom, West Germany, Taiwan and South Korea.

The right-hand side of the table indicates that the United States trades a wide variety of goods. Exports include such diverse items as grain from Iowa and aircraft from Seattle. Imports include both primary materials essential to American industry and highly manufactured goods. For a nation on wheels, autos and oil account for an important part of our trade, although oil no longer plays as important a role in U.S. imports as it did a decade ago.

BENEFITS FROM TRADE: INCREASED COMPETITION

Consider the monopoly firm illustrated in Figure 19-1*a*. Initially, without international trade, this firm has the domestic market all to itself. If it is not subject to government regulation, it will be able to set a monopoly price. Panel *b* illustrates what happens when trade is opened up. The potential demand facing the American producer is much larger, as shown by the total world demand curve. Therefore the American firm is now able to go after foreign markets as well as the domestic market.

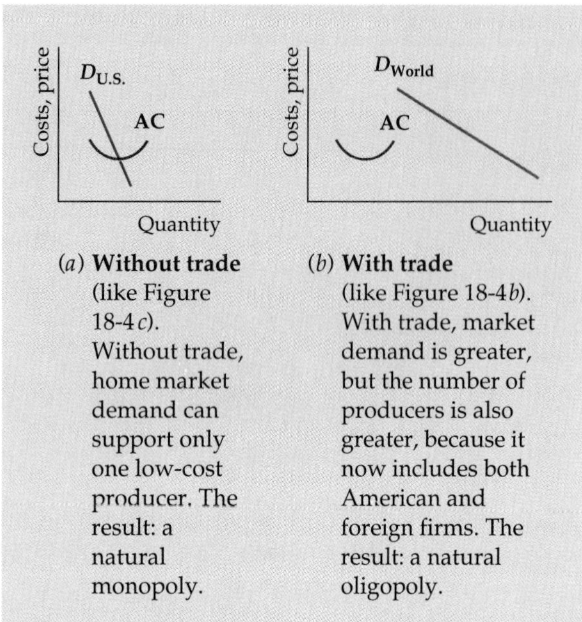

(*a*) **Without trade** (like Figure 18-4*c*). Without trade, home market demand can support only one low-cost producer. The result: a natural monopoly.

(*b*) **With trade** (like Figure 18-4*b*). With trade, market demand is greater, but the number of producers is also greater, because it now includes both American and foreign firms. The result: a natural oligopoly.

FIGURE 19-1 How international trade breaks down monopoly power.

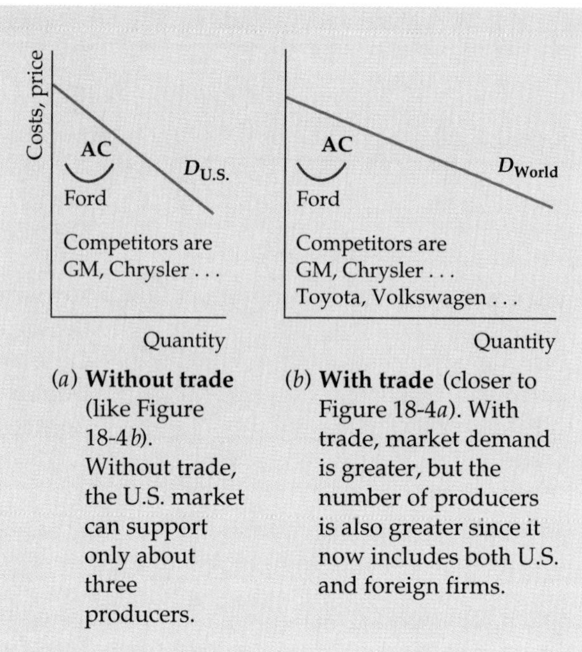

(*a*) **Without trade** (like Figure 18-4*b*). Without trade, the U.S. market can support only about three producers.

(*b*) **With trade** (closer to Figure 18-4*a*). With trade, market demand is greater, but the number of producers is also greater since it now includes both U.S. and foreign firms.

FIGURE 19-2 How international trade makes an oligopoly more competitive.

However, it is no longer able to take the U.S. market for granted, because it faces stiff competition here from foreign producers. Thus foreign trade can transform a natural monopoly in the domestic market in panel *a* into a natural oligopoly in the world market in panel *b*. In the process, this firm's monopoly control of the U.S. market is broken, and its ability to exercise market power (charge a high price) is reduced. As shown earlier, a lower more competitive price results in an improved allocation of resources, with a corresponding efficiency gain. Moreover, if the firm's previous monopoly position has allowed it to operate in a technically inefficient way at a point above its AC curve, increased competition may force it to reduce its costs, thus driving the firm down closer to its AC curve. Therefore there may also be a gain in *technical* efficiency.

Similarly, if a market is originally a natural oligopoly, international trade can make it substantially more competitive. For example, consider the U.S. firm in Figure 19-2 which, before trade, has about one-third of the domestic U.S. market. After trade is opened up in panel *b*, this firm will have a much smaller fraction of the market because the market is now the whole world. Again, increased competition will tend to keep costs and price down, with U.S. consumers benefiting. Furthermore, there may be other gains if domestic producers are forced to compete in nonprice ways, such as making improvements in quality or design. For example, the U.S. automobile industry has been pressured into producing higher quality cars as a result of foreign competition.

BENEFITS FROM TRADE: MORE PRODUCTS BECOME AVAILABLE

Because of trade, Americans can purchase existing foreign goods such as bananas, rare minerals and Japanese silks that might otherwise not be available in the United States.

Trade makes *new* goods available as well. Panel *a* in Figure 19-3 illustrates such a good. Demand is too low in the U.S. economy for this good to be profitably produced. However, when the foreign market becomes available, demand becomes large enough to cover average costs and make it profitable to produce this good. An example is Boeing, which exports more than half of its output of commercial aircraft. Without exports, Boeing might never have produced the 747 jumbo jet in the first place; it would have had difficulty covering the enormous design and tooling costs. With exports, its costs could be covered.

What is true in the United States is also true in other countries. Trade allows them to produce new goods as well. Therefore Americans benefit from a greater variety of goods—not just new goods produced in the United States such as 747s, but new goods such as the Airbus, which other countries are able to produce because they too can sell in the huge world market. Thus a major benefit of trade is greater variety for U.S. consumers—and also for U.S. producers buying raw materials and other inputs.

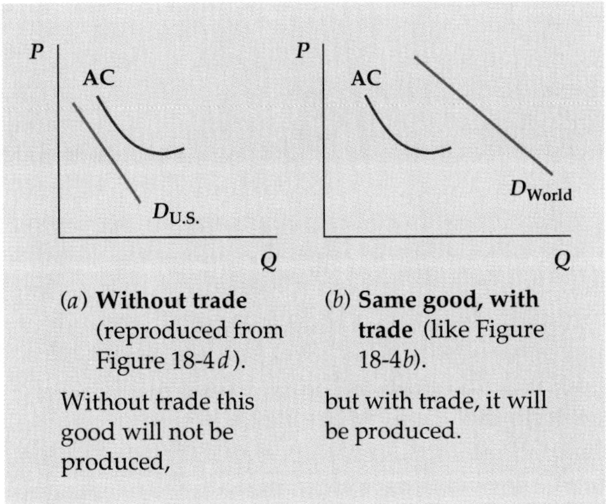

FIGURE 19-3 How international trade may create new products.

The AC curves in these two figures are identical, but because of trade, the demand curve in part *b* is much farther to the right.

BENEFITS FROM TRADE: ECONOMIES OF SCALE

When there are **economies of scale,** trade can lead to more efficient production. For example, with the elimination of tariff barriers within the European Community (EC), a manufacturer in any member country can sell freely to buyers in all member countries. This allows European producers to manufacture goods such as household appliances in much larger volume. In industries with economies of scale, this larger volume means lower cost, which in turn makes it possible for these products to be sold at a lower price. This increase in efficiency from economies of scale is beneficial to buyers, not only in the countries where these goods are produced, but also in the other European countries where these goods can be purchased tariff-free.

GAINS FROM TRADE: COMPARATIVE ADVANTAGE

Even if the above reasons for trade did not exist, there would still be the strong traditional argument that remains valid in any case: the benefit from comparative advantage.

The basic idea behind this concept has already been introduced in Chapter 3. Even though the lawyer cited there may be more skillful (that is, may have an absolute advantage) in both law and gardening, she does not do both. Absolute advantage does *not* determine what she does. Instead, she concentrates on law, the activity in which she has a comparative advantage. By specializing in this way, she can acquire more gardening service than if she were to take the time to do it herself. It is comparative advantage that determines what she does.

Internationally, the idea is exactly the same. Even though the United States may be better—that is, have an absolute advantage—in producing both aircraft and radios, it may be in our interest to concentrate on aircraft and other products in which we have a comparative advantage and leave radios to other countries. By specializing in aircraft, we may be able to acquire more radios by trading for them rather than by producing them ourselves.

The idea of comparative advantage was developed in the early nineteenth century by David Ricardo, an English economist, financier, and member of Parliament. In his simplified illustration, markets are perfectly competitive, there are no transport costs, all production costs are constant, and the only input is labor. He also assumed that there are only two countries (we will call them America and Britain) producing two goods (food and clothing).

ABSOLUTE ADVANTAGE

As a preliminary, Table 19-2 shows the case in which each country has an *absolute advantage* in the production of one good. In the first column, note that a clothing worker in Britain can outproduce a worker in America (4 to 3), so Britain has an absolute advantage in clothing. Similarly, in the second column, America has an absolute advantage in food, because an American worker can outproduce a British worker (2 to 1). The most efficient allocation of resources is to have America specialize in food and Britain in clothing, as the calculations at the bottom of Table 19-2 confirm.

Thus far, each country specializes in the good in which it has an absolute advantage. But this is not always so. The key to specialization is *comparative advantage* rather than absolute advantage.

COMPARATIVE ADVANTAGE

Table 19-3 illustrates the case in which one country, America, has an absolute advantage in the production of *both* goods. An American worker outproduces a British worker in both clothing (6 to 4) and food (3 to 1). Nonetheless, America—like the lawyer of Chapter 3—will not try to satisfy its require-

TABLE 19-2 Illustration of Absolute Advantage Hypothetical Output per Worker in Britain and America

	Clothing	*Food*
America	*3 units*	*2 units*
Britain	*4 units*	*1 unit*

In the first column, Britain has an absolute advantage in clothing production because a worker can produce 4 units compared with only 3 in America. In the second column, America has an absolute advantage in food, because a worker here can produce 2 units, compared with only 1 in Britain. Both countries together can produce more total output when America specializes in food and Britain specializes in clothing.

To confirm, suppose specialization has not occurred; in other words, suppose that each country is initially producing both goods. Now suppose that they begin to specialize—America in food, Britain in clothing. Therefore, a worker in America is switched out of clothing and into food production. At the same time, a worker in Britain is switched in the opposite direction (out of food and into clothing). As a result of these two switches:

	Clothing output changes by	Food output changes by
In America	−3	+2
In Britain	+4	−1
Therefore, net world output changes by	+1	+1

TABLE 19-3 Illustration of Comparative Advantage Hypothetical Output per Worker in Britain and America

	Clothing	*Food*
America	*6 units*	*3 units*
Britain	*4 units*	*1 unit*

In the bottom row, one British worker can produce either 4 units of clothing or 1 unit of food. Thus, the opportunity cost of 1 unit of food in Britain is 4 units of clothing. In the row above, an American worker can produce either 6 units of clothing or 3 of food. The opportunity cost of food in America is therefore 6/3 = 2 units of clothing. [Notice how we calculate this opportunity cost by taking the ratio of the figures in the American row, just as we calculated the British cost (4/1) from the figures in the British row.] Since the opportunity cost of food in America is less than in Britain, America has a comparative advantage in food and specializes in this good.

To confirm that this specialization will increase total world output, again suppose that each country is initially producing both goods. Now suppose they begin to specialize: America switches one worker out of clothing and into food, and Britain switches two workers out of food and into clothing. Then:

	Clothing output changes by	Food output changes by
In America	−6	+3
In Britain	+8	−2
Therefore, net world output changes by	+2	+1

ments by producing both goods itself. Its production is not determined by absolute advantage. Instead, America will specialize in its product of comparative advantage and buy the other from Britain.

To see why, the first step is to calculate the opportunity cost of food in each country. First, in Britain: The second row of Table 19-3 shows that a British worker who is now producing one unit of food could instead be producing four units of clothing. In other words, in Britain *the opportunity cost of one unit of food is four units of clothing*. Because prices reflect costs in a perfectly competitive economy, these two goods exchange in Britain for the same 1:4 ratio; that is, in the absence of international trade, one unit of food will exchange in Britain for four units of clothing.

On the other hand, what is the opportunity cost of food in America? The first row of Table 19-3 shows that an American worker who is producing three units of food could instead be producing six units of clothing. In other words, in America the opportunity cost of a unit of food is 6/3 = 2 units of clothing. Consequently, the two goods would exchange in America at this 1:2 ratio; that is, before trade, one unit of food will exchange in America for two units of clothing.

Because the opportunity cost of food in America is less (two units of clothing versus four in Britain), America has a **comparative advantage** in food. By definition:

> **A country has a *comparative advantage* in the good that it can produce relatively cheaply—that is, at lower opportunity cost than its trading partner.**

A similar set of calculations, again using the figures in Table 19-3, shows that in clothing, Britain has a lower opportunity cost and hence a comparative advantage.[1] In this simple case of only two countries and two goods, if one country (America) has a comparative advantage in one good (food), then the other country (Britain) *must* have a comparative advantage in the other (clothing).

Gains from Trade. Both countries benefit if they specialize in their product of comparative advantage and trade for the other at any price ratio between the 1:2 price ratio that would prevail in an isolated America and the 1:4 in Britain. Suppose this price ratio—often called the *terms of trade*—is 1:3; that is, one unit of food exchanges internationally for three units of clothing. This price ratio depends not only on the cost conditions described here, but also on demand in these two countries. For example, the more strongly the British demand food—the U.S. export good—the higher the price of food will be.

Faced with an international price ratio of 1:3 (one unit of food exchanging for three units of clothing), America can benefit by specializing in its product of comparative advantage, food, and trading to satisfy its clothing needs. Specifically, for each American worker taken out of clothing production, America loses six units of clothing. However, that worker instead now produces three units of food, which can then be traded (at the 1:3 international price ratio) for nine units of clothing—for a clear gain of three units of clothing.

Similarly, Britain also gains by specializing in its product of comparative advantage—clothing—and trading it for food. In switching a worker from food to clothing production, Britain loses one unit of food. However, that worker produces four units of clothing instead. This output can be traded (at the 1:3 international price ratio) for $4/3 = 1^1/_3$ units of food—for a gain of 1/3 of a unit of food.

To sum up, both countries gain from trade. America benefits by specializing in food (its comparative advantage) and trading for clothing. At the same time Britain benefits by specializing in clothing (its comparative advantage) and trading for food. The reason why there are gains from trade is that the ratios in the two rows of Table 19-3 (namely, 6/3 and 4/1) are different. If these ratios (that is, opportunity costs) were the same, there would be no comparative advantage and no gain from trade.

Comparative advantage thus leads to gains from trade. However, why does comparative advantage exist? Why does America have a compara-

---

[1]Specifically, the opportunity cost of clothing in Britain is only 1/4 of a unit of food, that is, 1/4 of a unit of food must be given up to acquire 1 unit of clothing. In America, the opportunity cost of clothing is higher: 3/6 = 1/2 unit of food. With its lower opportunity cost of clothing, Europe has a comparative advantage in clothing.

BOX 19–1 *Wages and Trade*

In the example presented in Table 19-3, an important question arises: Will wages be higher in America or Europe? The answer is, in America, because labor is more productive here. (Remember, America has an absolute advantage in the production of *both* goods.) Because they *can produce* more goods, American workers can be *paid* "more goods," that is, a higher real wage. Moreover, Americans will have a higher real income whether or not the two countries trade. What trade and specialization make possible is an increase in real income in both countries.

tive advantage in wheat? One important reason is our large endowment of highly productive land, especially in the Midwest. Similarly, the reason why Saudi Arabia specializes in oil is its huge endowment of this resource. On the other hand, a country like India, with its huge pool of unskilled labor, tends to have a comparative advantage in activities that require a great deal of labor. Comparative advantage depends not only on such resource endowments, but also on skills and technology. For example, our highly developed technology gives us a comparative advantage in producing items such as large aircraft and high-speed computers.

Diagrammatic Illustration. The gain to the United States from trade may be illustrated in another way. Figure 19-4 shows the American production

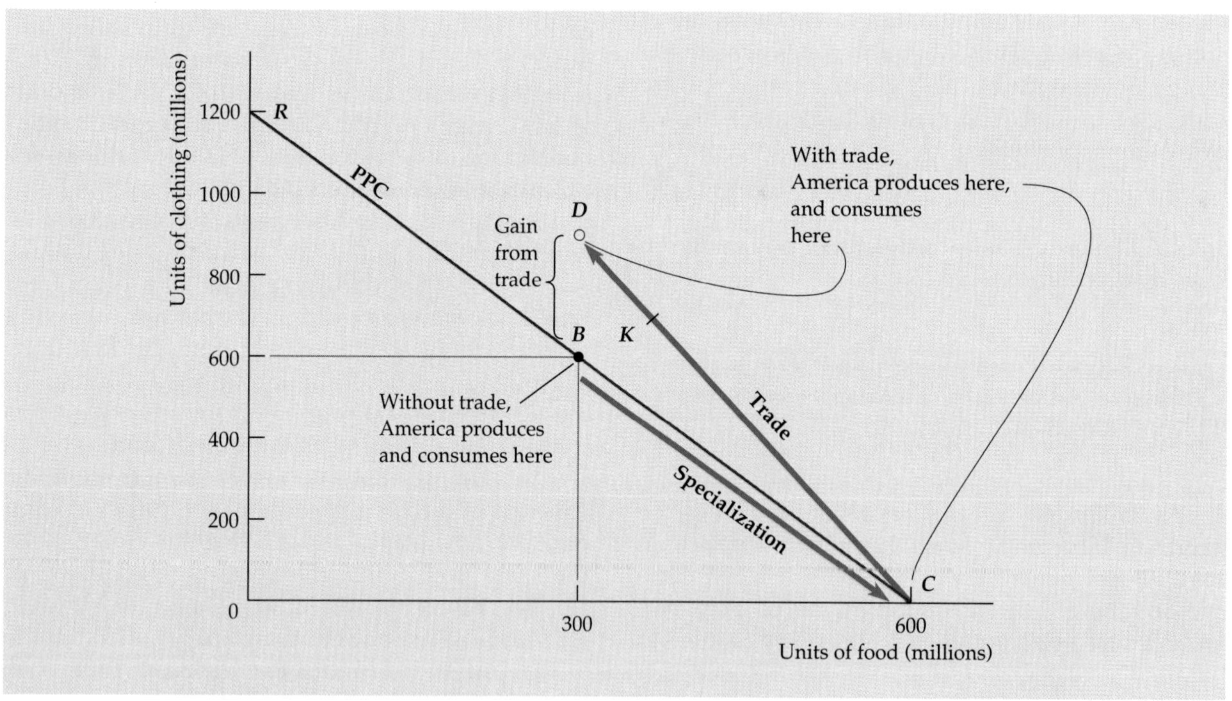

FIGURE 19-4 Gain from trade.

Without trade, Americans produce and consume at point *B*. When trade is opened, Americans can (1) specialize in food by shifting production from *B* to *C* and (2) move from *C* to *D* by trading 300 million units of food for 900 million units of clothing at the prevailing 1:3 international price ratio. The American gain from trade is the 300 million extra units of clothing acquired in the move from *B* to *D*.

possibilities curve (PPC), derived from the U.S. figures in the first row of Table 19-3, assuming that there are 200 million workers in America. For example, if they all work at producing clothing, each of the 200 million workers produces six units, for a total of 1,200 million units of clothing, as shown at point *R*. Alternatively, if they all work at producing food (three units each), they will produce 600 million units of food and no clothing at point *C*. Finally, if half the workers produce food and half clothing, the 100 million workers in clothing produce 600 million units (six units each), while the other 100 million workers in food produce 300 million units at point *B*. In this simple Ricardian example, the constant figures in the first row of Table 19-3 ensure that the production possibilities curve *RC* is a straight line: The opportunity cost of food in America remains constant as we move down this curve. No matter how much food America may be producing, it must give up two units of clothing to produce one more unit of food.

Before trade, America will produce and consume at a point on the production possibilities curve, such as *B*. With trade, America can benefit by the following two steps:

1. *Specialize.* Shift production along the specialization arrow from *B* to *C* in Figure 19-4; that is, produce 300 million more units of food by giving up 600 million units of clothing. Thus America concentrates on food, the good in which it has a comparative advantage.
2. *Trade.* Trade these 300 million additional units of food at the 1:3 international price ratio for 900 million units of clothing. That is, move along the trade arrow from C to *D*.

As a result of this specialization and trade, America's consumption can rise from point *B* to point *D*. In other words, there are 300 million more units of clothing available for consumption. This is America's *real income gain*—or efficiency gain—from trade. Of course, America might move along the trade arrow from *C*, not all the way to *D*, but instead just to *K*. As an exercise, you can confirm that, in this case, America would consume more of both clothing *and* food, and the gain from trade would be the additional units of each consumed.

Trade with Increasing Opportunity Costs. Panel *a* of Figure 19-5 shows that a gain from trade exists even when opportunity costs are not constant, that is, in the frequent case when the country's production possibilities curve is not a straight line. This diagram also shows that, although trade induces a country to specialize, it will often not specialize completely. America moves from *B* to *C*, but not all the way to complete specialization at *F*. Indeed, this is a frequently observed pattern of trade. America not only specializes in and exports its product of comparative advantage—in this case, food. It also produces other goods as well—in this example, it produces *some* clothing at point *C*.[2]

TRADE AND TECHNOLOGICAL CHANGE: THEIR SIMILARITIES

Panel *a* of Figure 19-5 has shown how trade allows a country to consume at a point such as *D* that is beyond its production possibilities curve (PPC). True, *production* is always limited by a country's

[2]Why doesn't America specialize completely, by moving from *B*, not just to *C* but all the way to *F*? The answer is that America would then be trading along the arrow at *F*, and this doesn't allow it to reach the high consumption point *D* that can be achieved by specializing just to *C* and trading along the higher arrow. For exactly the same reason that *F* is inferior to *C*, any other point on the production possibilities curve is also inferior to *C*. Therefore tangency point *C* is best.

Figure 19-5*a* can be used to show how demand also influences specialization and trade. (This elementary treatment emphasizes the other side of the coin—the importance of costs, as reflected in the production possibilities curve. But demand is important too.) Suppose that in both countries there is an increase in the demand for food. As a consequence, its price rises. As a result, a given quantity of food can buy more clothing. In other words, the trade arrow becomes steeper. Consequently, it is no longer tangent to the production possibilities curve at point *C* but is instead tangent at a point to the right, say *G*. *G* is therefore the best production point for this country. Thus this country specializes even more, by moving from *B*, not just to *C* but to *G*. (And, of course, from point *G*, it trades up to the northwest along its new, steeper trade arrow, to a consumption point even better than *D*.) To sum up, in response to increased demand for its export, this country's production pattern changes. By producing even more of its export, it specializes to an even greater degree than before.

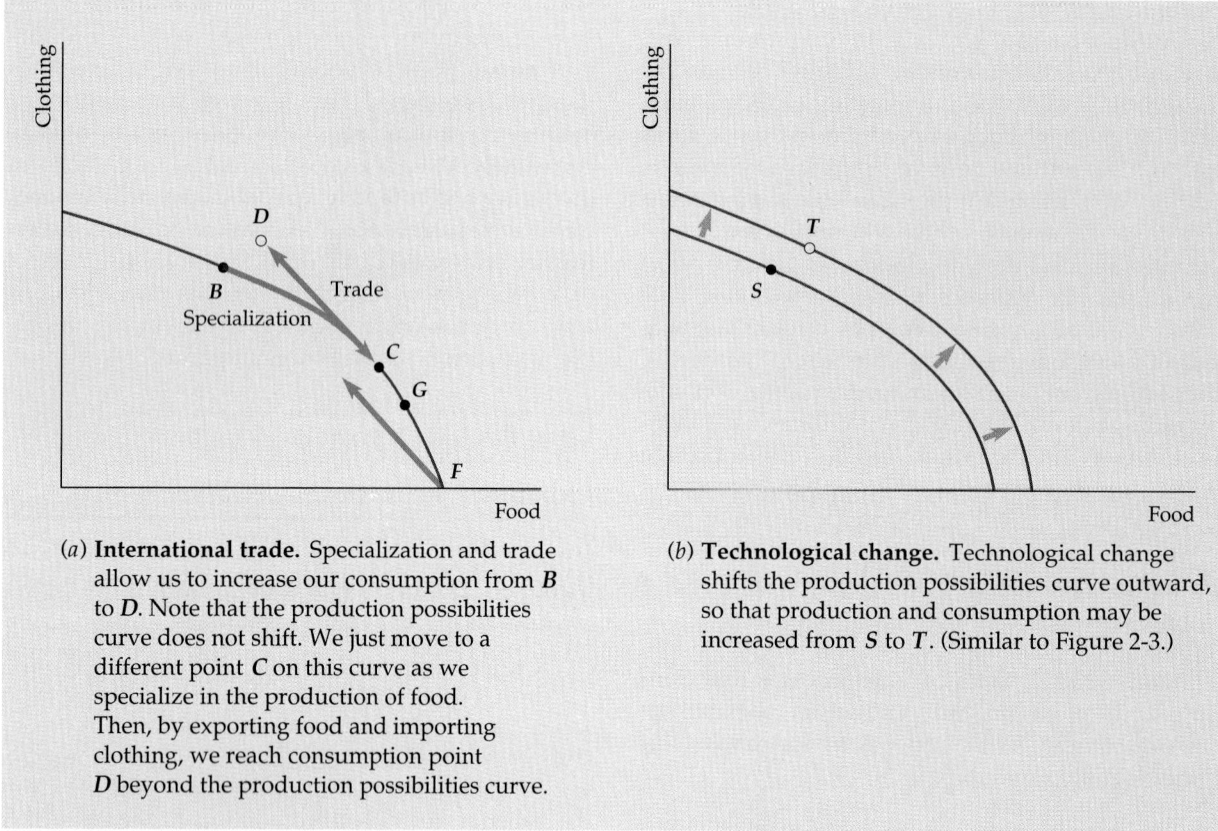

(*a*) **International trade.** Specialization and trade allow us to increase our consumption from ***B*** to ***D***. Note that the production possibilities curve does not shift. We just move to a different point ***C*** on this curve as we specialize in the production of food. Then, by exporting food and importing clothing, we reach consumption point ***D*** beyond the production possibilities curve.

(*b*) **Technological change.** Technological change shifts the production possibilities curve outward, so that production and consumption may be increased from ***S*** to ***T***. (Similar to Figure 2-3.)

FIGURE 19-5 Both trade and technological change allow us to increase consumption.

PPC, but consumption can be greater because of the gain from trade. In other words, international trade is the way for a country to break out of its production limitation and reach a point of consumption beyond it.

Panel *b* shows how technological change has the same effect of allowing a country to move from a point on its PPC such as *S* to a higher point of consumption *T*. But it does so by shifting the PPC outward.

Trade and technological change are alike in another significant respect. Although they generally provide a benefit to the nation as a whole, they do not necessarily benefit *every* group within the nation. Thus there are often groups that object vehemently to trade or to technological change. For example, during the period of rapid technological change at the beginning of the Industrial Revolution, textile workers feared that the new machinery being introduced would eliminate their jobs. Indeed, some workers did lose their jobs, even though machinery has ultimately made possible jobs with much higher productivity and pay. The fear of job loss led some workers to throw their wooden shoes—*sabots*, in French—into the machinery; hence, the word *sabotage* was coined.

Similarly, international trade may displace textile workers if production is shifted from textiles—where some markets have been lost to imports—to computers or wheat, where the United States exports because of its comparative advantage. Once again, those who are harmed may strongly object. In this case, they need not throw their shoes into the machinery; restrictions on imports are the way to seek protection. Note that trade restrictions and sabotage are similar in one respect. Both prevent a general improvement in the standard of living in order to protect a specific group.

The temporary unemployment that follows either trade or technological change is indeed a problem, but it is frequently exaggerated, particularly when the overall economy is prosperous. Workers displaced by technological change usually, but not always, get new jobs fairly quickly, as do workers displaced by imports. For example, when the European Community opened up trade among countries on a very large scale, temporary unemployment was less than expected. (Of course, this problem would have been more serious if the European Community had been formed during a period of severe recession when jobs would have been much harder to find.)

Although there are striking similarities between trade and technological change, there is an important difference. Technological change is permanent. Once the production possibilities curve shifts outward in panel *b* of Figure 19-5, it doesn't shift back. In contrast, a trade gain is not necessarily permanent. If trade is cut back because of the imposition of high tariffs, the gains from trade will be reduced; the country in panel *a* will move from *D* back toward *B*.

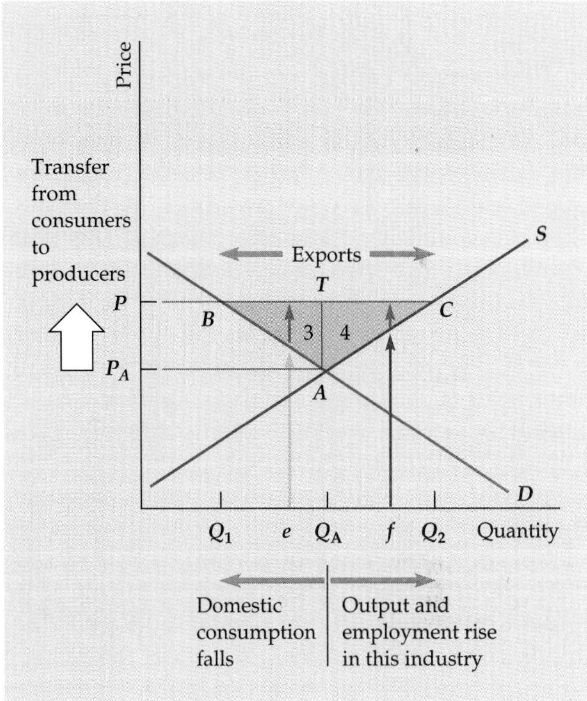

FIGURE 19-6 Detailed effects of the export of an individual good: wheat.

With trade, domestic price increases from P_A to P with Q_1Q_2 exported. In part, these exports come from reduced consumption (Q_1Q_A); the net gain on these units is area 3. The other part of these exports comes from increased production (Q_AQ_2); the net gain on these units is area 4. Thus the total efficiency gain from exporting is the entire blue area.

GAINS FROM TRADE: ILLUSTRATION USING DEMAND AND SUPPLY

Although in many respects the analysis above is the best way to illustrate the gains from trade, it is oversimplified in one way: It is a "two-good model" that lumps all American exports into a single food category and all imports into a single clothing category. In contrast, the supply and demand analysis that will now be developed can be used to examine an individual export and an individual import.

EFFICIENCY GAIN ON AN EXPORT

Figure 19-6 shows the demand and supply curves for an export, such as wheat. Without trade, equilibrium in the domestic market is at point *A*, where the nation's supply and demand intersect. Thus quantity Q_A is produced at price P_A. At the same time, the price in the rest of the world is at the higher level *P*, reflecting the higher costs of producing wheat in foreign countries.

When trade is opened, U.S. producers discover that they can sell abroad at this higher price *P*, and they begin to do so. Moreover, because they can sell at *P* abroad, they are unwilling to sell at any lower price in the home market. As a result, the domestic price rises to the world level *P*. (The domestic price won't rise quite this much if exporters incur transport costs. However, we continue to ignore complications of this kind.)

American producers, earning this more attractive price *P*, expand their output. Specifically, they move up their supply curve from *A* to *C*, increasing their output from Q_A to Q_2. But, of course, consumers view this higher price quite differently. They move back up their demand curve from *A* to *B*, thereby reducing their consumption from Q_A to Q_1. In short, Q_2 is now produced and Q_1 is consumed, with the difference (Q_1Q_2) being exported. Thus exports come (1) partly from increased production, and (2) partly from reduced domestic consumption.

To understand these two effects in detail, first consider *e*, one of the units of reduced consumption. The height of the demand curve—the light blue arrow—was the marginal benefit from consuming this unit; in other words, it is the loss because this unit is no longer consumed. This unit is now being exported instead, providing a gain equal to the export price *P*, as shown by the sum of the light blue arrow plus the dark blue arrow above it. Hence, the net gain from exporting it, rather than consuming it, is the dark blue arrow. The sum of all such arrows throughout the relevant range Q_1Q_A is the shaded triangle 3. This is the efficiency gain from switching goods from consumption to a more highly valued use, namely, export.

Next consider *f*, one of the units of increased production for export. The cost of producing it is the red arrow under the supply curve. (Recall that supply reflects marginal cost.) However, the benefit from producing it is the export price *P* received for it, which is the red arrow plus the blue arrow above it. Therefore the net gain from producing it for export is the blue arrow. The sum of all such arrows through the relevant range Q_AQ_2 is the shaded triangle 4. This is the efficiency gain from expanding production for export.

The total gain from exporting is shown as the sum of both these effects, that is, the total shaded area in Figure 19-6. In simple terms, this gain indicates that wheat can be sold to foreigners for more than the cost of producing it, or more than is lost by switching some of it away from domestic consumption.

Of course, this shaded area will represent an efficiency *loss* if producers who are already exporting are no longer allowed to do so, either because of an export restriction imposed by this country or an import restriction imposed by a trading partner. This shows how interference in a competitive world market may be damaging, in the same way that we have seen that interference in a competitive home market may be damaging.

EFFICIENCY GAIN ON AN IMPORT

A parallel analysis illustrates the gain from importing a specific item. Figure 19-7 shows the domestic supply and demand curves for an import-competing product like woolens. Without trade, equilibrium in the domestic market is at point *A*, with price P_A and quantity Q_A produced and consumed. At the same time, the price in the rest of the world is at the lower level *P*, reflecting the lower costs of production there.

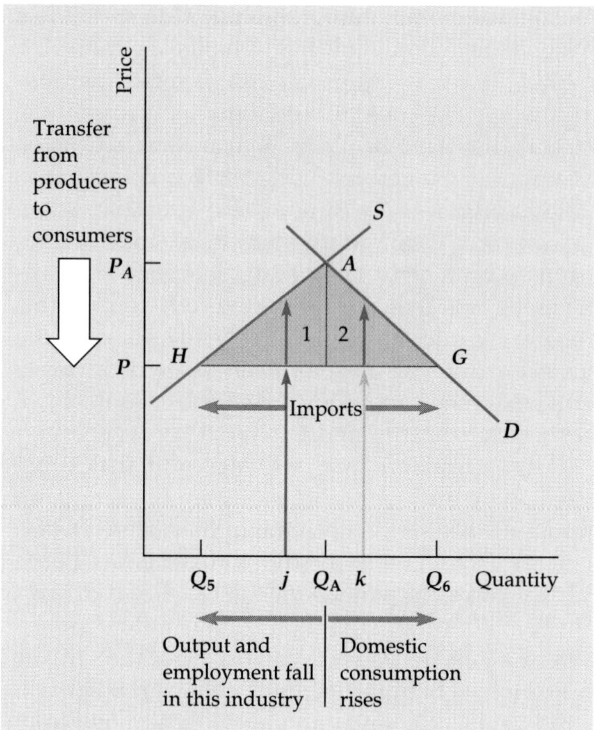

FIGURE 19-7 Detailed effects of the import of an individual good: woolens.

With trade, price decreases from P_A to *P*, with *HG* imported. This reduces home production by Q_AQ_5; the net gain on these units is area 1. Imports also result in increased consumption of Q_AQ_6; the net gain on these units is area 2. Thus the total efficiency gain from importing this good is the entire blue area.

When trade is opened, U.S. consumers can buy imported woolens at this lower price *P*. Because they are unwilling to buy from American producers at higher price P_A, the domestic price falls to the world level *P*. At this lower price, U.S. consumers increase their purchases; they move down their demand curve from *A* to *G*, increasing their consumption from Q_A to Q_6. At the same time, domestic producers respond to lower price *P* by moving back down their supply curve from *A* to *H*, thereby reducing their output from Q_A to Q_5. In short, Q_5 is now produced in the United States, whereas Q_6 is consumed. The difference (Q_5Q_6) is the amount imported. Thus U.S. imports result in both decreased production and increased consumption.

First, consider *j*, one of the units of decreased production. The cost of importing it is the price *P* that must be paid for it, shown as the red arrow. But because it is being imported, we save the cost of producing it ourselves, which is the red arrow plus the blue arrow above it—that is, its marginal cost as given by the height of the supply curve. Hence the net gain from importing it, rather than producing it more expensively at home, is the blue arrow. The sum of all such arrows over the relevant range Q_5Q_A is shaded triangle 1. This is the efficiency gain from allowing imports to displace higher cost domestic production.

Finally, consider *k*, one of the units of increased consumption. Its cost is the import price *P* shown by the pink arrow. However, the consumer values it as this arrow plus the blue arrow above it—that is, its marginal benefit given by the height of the demand curve. Therefore the net benefit from this unit of increased consumption is that blue arrow, and the sum of all such benefits is the shaded triangle 2. This is the efficiency gain from allowing consumption to expand in response to a bargain international price.

The total efficiency gain from imports on both accounts is the whole shaded area in Figure 19-7. In simplest terms, this area shows that we can benefit by buying a low-cost import because it allows us to cut back our own inefficient high-cost production and also allows us to increase our consumption of a bargain-priced good.

WINNERS AND LOSERS FROM INTERNATIONAL TRADE

Although trade leads to an overall gain in efficiency, it is important to emphasize again that not all groups benefit. For example, in Figure 19-6, trade brings an increase in the price of wheat. As a result, wheat farmers gain while consumers lose. This transfer is shown by the wide arrow to the left of the diagram. On the other hand, the import in Figure 19-7 results in the opposite sort of transfer. Because it lowers price, consumers benefit while producers lose.

The benefits and losses to each group as a result of imports are shown more precisely in the alternative analysis set out in Figure 19-8.[3] Each panel reproduces the domestic supply and demand curves for woolens from Figure 19-7. The gain to the nation's consumers from a lower price is shown by the blue area in panel *a* enclosed to the left of the demand curve. At the same time, producers receive a lower price and lose sales to imports. As a result, producers lose red area 5 in panel *b* enclosed to the left of the supply curve.[4] Because this red loss also appears as a blue gain in panel *a*, it is a transfer from the producers who lose it in panel *b* to the consumers who receive it in panel *a*. (This technique of identifying a transfer is important because it can be used on a wide variety of problems; for example, see Problem 19-8.) At the same time, area 6 in panel *a* is a blue gain that is *not* offset by a red loss. This net gain of area 6 is reproduced in panel *c*. This is, of course, exactly the same blue efficiency gain that appeared in the preceding diagram.[5] Finally, in any such analysis, it is important to repeat an earlier warning. In concluding that there will be a net gain, we have assumed that the consumers' valuation of a $1 increase in income is roughly the same as the producers' valuation of a $1 reduction in income—or at least that they are sufficiently similar so that our conclusions are not upset.

---

[3]*Note to instructors:* Most of the analysis of transfer and efficiency effects in the balance of this book will be limited to diagrams like Figure 19-7. For those who wish to supplement these illustrations with diagrams similar to those that will now be developed in Figure 19-8, see the Instructor's Resource Guide.

[4]For a review of how consumers are affected by a price change, see Figure 7-4. For a review of how producers are affected, see Figure 10-9.

[5]The analysis shown in Figure 19-8 can also be used to explain Figure 19-6 more fully. Specifically, as price rises in Figure 19-6, (i) consumers lose area $PBAP_A$, (ii) producers gain $PCAP_A$, and thus (iii) the net effects are a transfer of $PBAP_A$ from consumers to producers, and an efficiency gain of *ABC*.

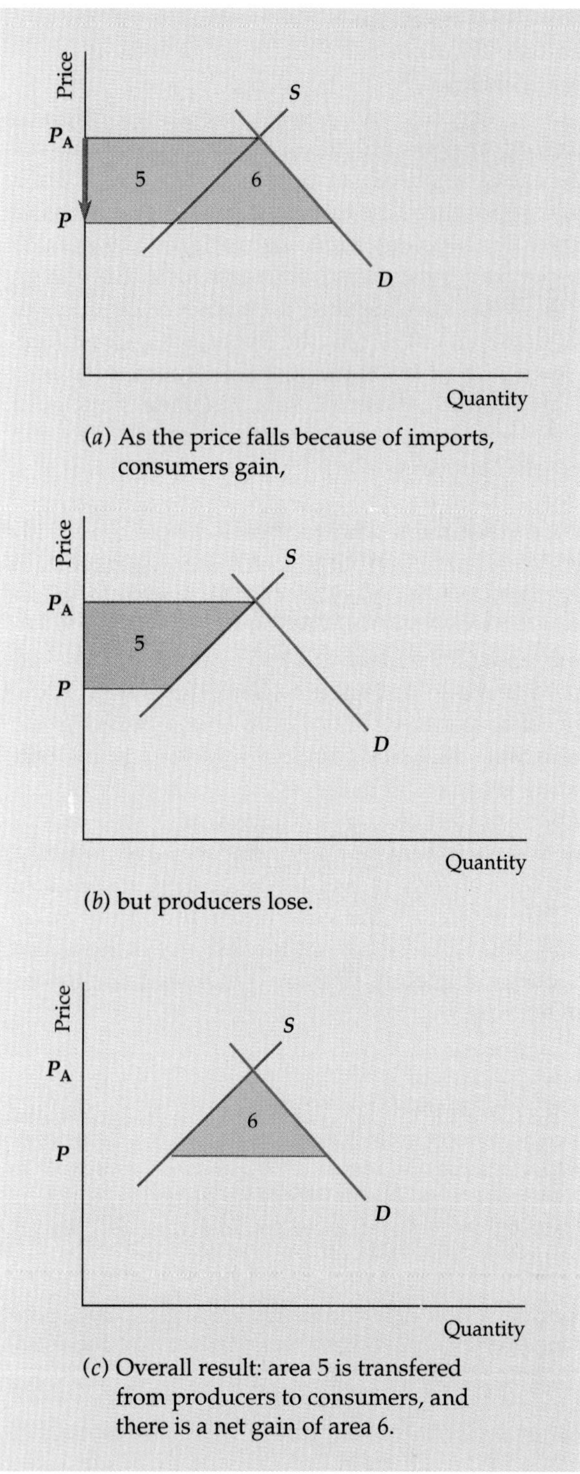

(*a*) As the price falls because of imports, consumers gain,

(*b*) but producers lose.

(*c*) Overall result: area 5 is transfered from producers to consumers, and there is a net gain of area 6.

FIGURE 19-8 Detailed effects of an import of woolens (an alternative to Fig. 19-7).

As a current example of how imports affect various groups in the United States, consider our imports of textiles from the Far East. The effect on American textile producers is clear. They are damaged because these imports depress the domestic price of textiles and reduce their sales. At the same time, it is clear to American consumers that they benefit from a lower textile price. What is not always clear in public debate is the net effect on the nation as a whole. Figure 19-8 suggests that the overall effect is favorable, because consumers gain more than producers lose.

Finally, note that whereas output and employment fall in import-competing industries (Fig. 19-7), they rise in export industries (Fig. 19-6). When both of these effects are taken into account, there is no reason to expect either a large increase or decrease in employment as a result of trade—although unemployment may rise during the adjustment period. Let us repeat that the purpose of international trade—like technological change—is not to increase employment. It is to increase efficiency and therefore real income. A more efficient economy will be better able to generate high income jobs in the future.

KEY POINTS

1. In this chapter, a strong case has been made for international trade; the next chapter will deal with the case for tariffs and other restraints on trade.

2. There are four major sources of benefit from trade: (a) greater competition, (b) greater availability of goods, (c) economies of scale, and (d) comparative advantage.

3. When trade is opened, countries specialize in certain products, increasing their output of these goods. If there are economies of scale, costs fall as a result of this increase in output.

4. Even if costs do not fall with rising output, trade will be beneficial if countries specialize in the goods in which they have a comparative advantage, that is, in those products in which they are relatively most efficient. We saw this not only in the Ricardian case where cost is constant, but also even in cases such as the one shown in Figure 19-5 where opportunity cost rises as output increases (that is, the production possibilities curve bows outward).

5. Because trade lowers the prices of goods we import and raises the prices of goods we export, it hurts some while benefiting others. Consumers of imports benefit, whereas consumers of exported goods are harmed. To some degree, but not completely, these are the same people, so that these effects partly cancel out. In addition, producers of exports benefit, whereas producers of import-competing goods are hurt. This provides an incentive for firms producing both to specialize by increasing their production of exports and decreasing their production of import-competing goods.

6. In many respects international trade is similar to technological change. Both increase real income by allowing a nation to consume more. Trade allows a country to consume beyond its production possibilities curve, whereas technological change shifts the production possibilities curve out. Trade and technological change can cause the same sort of short-run unemployment until workers who have lost their jobs shift to new, more productive employment.

KEY CONCEPTS

specialization
increased competition because of trade
economies of scale due to trade
greater variety
absolute advantage
comparative advantage
opportunity cost
gain from trade
trade compared to technological change
efficiency and transfer effects

PROBLEMS

19-1. "Foreign competition makes an industry more competitive." Should this result be viewed as an advantage or a disadvantage by (a) consumers of this good? (b) producers of the good? (c) the nation as a whole?

19-2. Suppose that there are economies of scale in the production of both X and Y. If Europe specializes in one and America in the other, is it possible for both countries to benefit? Explain your answer. Does this answer still hold if the cost curves for each good are identical in the two countries? (*Hint:* Review the discussion of economies of scale in Chapter 3.)

19-3. Explain the efficiency gains or losses in the United States if each state were to impose high barriers against its imports from the other states.

19-4. Return to Table 19-2, where costs are constant. (a) Change the "northwest" number 3 to 5. Does Europe now have an absolute advantage in either good? A comparative advantage in either? Draw a diagram like Figure 19-4 to show the potential American gain from trade, again assuming that there are 200 million workers in the United States and that the international price ratio is 3:1. (b) Now change that same northwest number to 8. Which country now has a comparative advantage in food? In clothing? Are there potential gains from trade? Explain your answer.

19-5. Figure 19-9 shows the situation of Britain corresponding to the American situation in Figure 19-5*a*.

(a) When trade is opened, what happens to British production?

(b) How much of each good does Britain export or import?

(c) Are there any lines or curves in this diagram that must be similar to those that appear in Figure 19-5*a*?

(d) Does Britain gain from trade? If so, how much?

19-6. "Economists say that international trade and technological change are similar—but they are wrong. Technological change increases our real income by making us more productive. Trade does not." Evaluate this statement.

19-7. This problem looks ahead to Chapter 20. Suppose two trading countries become involved in a trade war, with each imposing such heavy restrictions on imports that trade between the two is eventually cut off altogether. Use Figure 19-9 and panel *a* of Figure 19-5 to show the gains or losses each would suffer. Is a trade war a "zero-sum game" (what one country wins, the other loses)? Or is it like any other kind of war, with both sides losing?

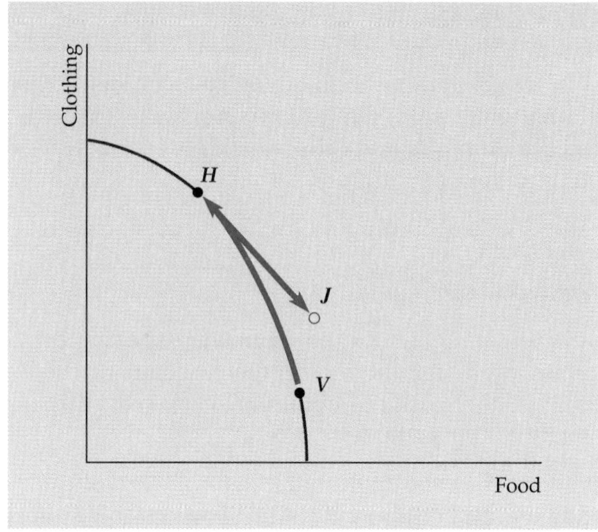

FIGURE 19-9

19-8. To see how the analysis of Figure 19-8 can be applied to an entirely different problem, consider the government price support policy for agriculture set out in Figure 15-8*a*.

(a) Use a series of colored diagrams like the panels in Figure 19-8 to show how each of the following three groups benefits or loses: consumers, producers, and U.S. taxpayers. (How much of the taxpayers' money does the Treasury pay out on the program?) By comparing these effects, indicate the transfers that take place, and in a final diagram show the net, overall efficiency effect of this policy.

(b) Confirm this efficiency effect by noting how this policy affects output and then applying the analysis of Figure 11-3.

CHAPTER 20
INTERNATIONAL TRADE
Policy Debates

Park your Japanese car in Tokyo.
DETROIT BUMPER STICKER

Our interest will be to throw open the doors of commerce, and to knock off its shackles, giving freedom to all persons for the vent of whatever they may choose to bring into our ports, and asking the same in theirs.
THOMAS JEFFERSON

Japanese barriers against rice imports are so severe that the price to Japanese consumers is more than *six times* the world price. In Europe, import restrictions and agricultural price supports are so high that when the Europeans came to sell their butter surplus on the world market in 1987, the best they could do was to sell it to the Soviet Union at a *discount of 93%* below its European cost. Although the United States has been calling for an end to such practices, it has still been pursuing similar, though less blatant, policies itself. In a world moving toward a global economy in which many governments are committed to a policy of freer trade, at least on paper, how could such trade-distorting policies have developed and survived? Given the potential gains from trade described in the last chapter, why does virtually every nation still restrict its imports with barriers such as *tariffs* (taxes imposed on imported goods as they enter a country) or *quotas* (limits on the number of units that can be imported)?

Since the 1930s, tariffs have been substantially reduced. By 1989, U.S. tariffs had been slashed to only a tenth of the remarkably high level they had temporarily reached during the depression of the 1930s. However, the negotiations to achieve this have been long and arduous, and substantial tariffs still remain. Moreover, as tariffs have been reduced, *nontariff barriers* such as quotas have become more important.

This chapter sets out the arguments—some fallacious, some with an element of truth—that have been used to defend trade barriers. It also describes various attempts to reduce these barriers. These include not only the multilateral negotiations to reduce the trade barriers of all countries, but also negotiations to eliminate trade barriers among a selected group of countries. Prominent examples include the European Community and the more recent free trade agreement between the United States and Canada. The final sections will describe the special issues raised by trade with Japan and the controversial role of multinational corporations in moving the world toward a global economy.

ARGUMENTS FOR TARIFFS AND OTHER FORMS OF PROTECTION

In an attempt to counter the strong case for international trade set out in the last chapter, advocates of protection have put forward a number of arguments.

1. AN INDUSTRY MAY BE ESSENTIAL FOR NATIONAL DEFENSE.

Two centuries ago, Adam Smith argued that in the interest of national security, a country should be willing to protect its defense industries even if such protection involves an economic cost—that is, even if foreign countries have a comparative advantage in producing military equipment. Consider an extreme example. Even in the unlikely event that the Soviet Union agreed to sell us tanks more cheaply than we could produce them ourselves, we wouldn't buy. Obviously, we don't want to ever find ourselves, in a time of crisis, dependent on the Soviet Union for our supply of tanks or spare parts. Therefore we buy from American manufacturers instead. We provide them with this protection because a defense industry is considered essential.

However, in protecting our defense industries, several questions arise: Where do we draw the line? Do we protect just our tank and military aircraft industries, or do we go one step beyond and protect our electronic chip industry because it provides an essential component for military equipment? Should the Pentagon help to revive the U.S. television industry, since high-definition television screens will be used in a wide range of weapons systems? Do we take yet another step and protect the textile industry, which produces military uniforms? Although the defense argument makes sense in some cases, it can be taken too far, since almost every industry makes some indirect contribution to national defense.

Although we don't want trade in weapons with the Soviet Union, it does make sense to engage in trade in weapons with our allies. This allows us all to gain economies of scale, which are often very important in weapons production. However, in spite of the potential cost savings, the North Atlantic Treaty Organization (NATO) has had only limited success in promoting standardization and international procurement of weapons. The major reason is that each national defense industry lobbies hard to make sure that weapons are bought at home.

2. PEOPLE VOTE FOR THEIR PRESENT JOBS.

Increased international trade can mean that some jobs are lost in industries whose sales fall because of competition from imports. However, new jobs are created in export industries. The problem is that people are more concerned about the present jobs they may lose than the possibility of new jobs in an export industry. (After all, who knows for sure who will actually get these new export-based jobs?) Accordingly, workers who don't want to take risks vote against increased trade; that is, they vote for the tariffs and other trade restrictions that protect their current jobs. As a consequence, too much attention may be paid to the employment that is lost from increased imports, and not enough to the employment that is gained from increased exports. Even if we focus just on the import side, remember from Chapter 19 that the losses to producers from increased imports are more than offset by gains to the consuming public. By pointing this out, why can't a politician sell the idea of allowing imports in more freely?

The answer is that individuals tend to think and vote as producers, not consumers. To illustrate why, suppose that the import is shirts. There may be large benefits to consumers as a group from lower priced shirts. But this gain is distributed widely among millions of purchasers, with each benefiting by such a small amount that nobody is likely to switch votes on this account. On the producers' side, however, things are different. Here, fewer individuals are affected by increased shirt imports, but the effect on each individual—whether in management or labor—is much greater. For people in this industry, the possible loss of jobs and profits will be important enough to determine how they vote; they become "single issue" voters. In brief, producers vote for politicians who will protect their jobs with a tariff, whereas consumers scatter their votes around on a whole variety of issues, with only a few voting against the tariff.

Therefore the interest of consumers in freer trade may be inadequately represented. (For problems that arise when a policy ignores consumers, see Box 20-1.)

A further, related reason why shirt producers may be able to exert strong political pressure is that they are not spread out all over the United States, as consumers are. Instead, they are concentrated in a few states or congressional districts. For members of Congress representing such districts, one very good way of getting political support may be to push for import restrictions on shirts. If they do, they will gain many votes from shirt producers, while losing very few from consumers. Moreover, this is not just a political sleight of hand. From the narrow point of view of *just the shirt-producing districts,* there may be a net *cost* from tariff-free imports of shirts. The reason is that such districts would bear much of the cost of this policy; costs fall on shirt producers who are concentrated in these districts. At the same time, these districts would receive little of the benefit; instead, these benefits go mostly to consumers who live in other states. Thus, although gains from tariff-free imports of shirts would exceed losses for the United States as a whole, losses may exceed gains in these districts.

Accordingly, it is no great surprise if the members of Congress from shirt-producing districts go to Washington committed to restricting imports of shirts. When they get there, they meet other members with similar problems: They too may be seeking protection for the goods produced in their own districts. The result can be logrolling. The members from shirt-producing districts agree to vote to protect the products of other districts, in return for the promise of other members to vote for restrictions on shirt imports.

The result is continuous pressure in Congress for protection for industries that compete with imports. When imports on a wide variety of goods are restricted, the shirt-producing district may well be damaged after all because of the higher prices of a wide range of imported goods. However, the members of Congress from these districts may still be popular locally because they are remembered for their conspicuous support for protection of the shirt industry, rather than for their less obvious support for protection of other goods.

Thus it is no surprise that some 200 years after the case for free trade was clearly stated by Adam Smith and David Ricardo, protection lives on. In fact, there would be even more severe trade restrictions except for two influences: (1) Producers in export industries have a strong interest in international trade and recognize that foreigners won't buy our exports unless we buy imports from them. Thus a concerted, producer-led lobby for freer trade may partially offset the protectionist lobbies. (2) The president is elected by all the people and represents the country as a whole. Most presidents have supported international initiatives to reduce trade barriers.

Although the two explanations for protection

BOX 20–1 *What Happens If the Consumer Is Forgotten: Bastiat's Negative Railway*

The absurdity of ignoring the interests of the consumer has never been more eloquently stated than by the French economist Frederick Bastiat (1801–1850):*

> It has been proposed that the railway from Paris to Madrid should have a break at Bordeaux, for if goods and passengers are forced to stop at that town, profits will accrue to bargemen, pedlars, commissionaires, hotel-keepers, etc. But if Bordeaux has a right to profit by a gap in the line of railway, and if such profit is considered in the public interest, then Angouleme, Poitiers, Tours, Orleans, nay, more, all the intermediate places, Ruffec, Chatellerault, etc., should also demand gaps, as being for the general interest. For the more these breaks in the line are multiplied, the greater will be the increase of consignments, commissions, transshipments, etc., along the whole extent of the railway. In this way, we shall succeed in having a line of railway composed of successive gaps, which we may call a Negative Railway.

---

*Abridged from Frederick Bastiat, *Economic Sophisms* (Edinburgh: Oliver and Boyd, Ltd., 1873), pp. 80–81.

just cited include substantial military and political considerations, the rest of the arguments more heavily emphasize economics. The first three that follow are fallacious, but the rest have at least partial validity.

3. "BUY AMERICAN BECAUSE IT KEEPS OUR MONEY AT HOME."

This argument is sometimes expanded to: "If I buy an imported radio, I get the radio, and foreigners get the dollars. But if I buy a radio made in the United States instead, I get the radio and the dollars stay here." The problem with this argument is that it fails to recognize that foreigners sell to us not just to accumulate dollars, but instead to use those dollars to buy things from us, such as machinery and food. In other words, when we import radios, we ultimately give up machinery and food, not dollars. Similarly, if we buy radios at home, we also give up machinery and food. (Some of our own resources have to be diverted from producing machinery and food to producing radios.) Thus the key question is: Which way of acquiring radios—by importing them or producing them ourselves—will cost us less machinery and food? The answer was given in Chapter 19: Radios will cost us less in terms of foregone machinery and food if we import them, provided, of course, that foreigners have a comparative advantage in radios, and we have a comparative advantage in machinery and food.[1]

4. "WE CAN'T COMPETE WITH CHEAP FOREIGN LABOR."

To clarify this issue, it is important first to ask: Why is labor more expensive in the United States? The answer is that wages are higher in America than in most foreign countries because labor here is more productive; it can produce more goods per hour. Thus it can be "paid more goods"—that is, its real wage is higher than elsewhere (as explained in Box 19-1). When we take into account both our higher wages and our higher productivity, we find that we can compete internationally in some goods but not others. Although we cannot compete with cheap labor in other countries in products in which they have a comparative advantage, we can compete in products of our comparative advantage, in which our higher labor productivity more than offsets our higher wage. These are the products on which we should be concentrating. (For more on the argument that we will be unable to compete, see Box 20-2.)

5. "TARIFFS SHOULD BE TAILORED TO EQUALIZE COSTS AT HOME AND ABROAD."

Suppose that the U.S. cost of producing a specific good were 50% higher than foreign costs. Then, according to the proposal for a "tailored tariff," U.S. producers should be protected with a 50% tariff to allow them to compete on an equal basis with imports.

This recommendation may sound plausible, but it misses the whole point of international trade. Gains from trade are based on cost differences between countries; the United States imports bananas or radios precisely because they can be produced more cheaply abroad than at home. Eliminate cost differences and you eliminate the incentive to trade; and when you eliminate this, trade disappears. If we were to follow this recommendation to its logical conclusion, we would no longer be importing cheap bananas; instead, we would be producing them very expensively at home in greenhouses, with the costs of cheap imports from Central America being equalized by an extremely high tariff. In other words, to the degree that we were successful in the well-nigh impossible task of tailoring tariffs to make costs precisely equal at home and abroad, we would lose the gains from trade we now enjoy. In a word: All that tailored tariffs would do would be to strangle trade.

Now let's turn to the arguments for protection that contain at least some element of truth.

[1]Chapter 19 of the companion volume, *Economics, 4e*, deals with the situation in which American imports from foreign countries are substantially greater than foreign purchases from the United States. In this case, the argument in this section is no longer so clear-cut; there may be a lag of months or years between our imports and foreign purchases of our goods. Nevertheless, our main point is still valid: The ultimate purpose of other countries in selling goods to the United States is to acquire the dollars to buy goods from us, either now or in the future.

BOX 20–2 *The Petition of the Candlemakers*

Sometimes the argument that we can't compete with cheap foreign labor appears in the slightly different form: "We can't compete with cheap foreign products." This idea has never been more effectively criticized than by Frederick Bastiat over a hundred years ago, in a satirical description of an appeal by French candlemakers for protection against unfair competition:*

> We are subjected to the intolerable competition of a foreign rival, who enjoys, it would seem, such superior facilities for the production of light, that he is enabled to inundate our national market at so exceedingly reduced a price, that, the moment he makes his appearance, he draws off all custom from us; and thus an important branch of French industry, with all its innumerable ramifications, is suddenly reduced to a state of complete stagnation. This rival is no other than the sun.
>
> Our petition is, that it would please your honorable body to pass a law whereby shall be directed the shutting up of all windows, dormers, skylights, shutters, curtains, in a word, all openings, holes, chinks, and fissures through which the light of the sun is used to penetrate into our dwellings, to the prejudice of the profitable manufactures which we flatter ourselves we have been enabled to bestow upon the country; which country cannot, therefore, without ingratitude, leave us now to struggle unprotected through so unequal a contest.
>
> Does it not argue the greatest inconsistency to check as you do the importation of coal, iron, cheese, and goods of foreign manufacture, merely because their price approaches zero, while at the same time you freely admit, and without limitation, the light of the sun, whose price is during the whole day *at zero?*

*Abridged from Frederick Bastiat, *Economic Sophisms*, pp. 56–60.

6. "IF WE BUY STEEL FROM PITTSBURGH RATHER THAN JAPAN, EMPLOYMENT WILL RISE IN PITTSBURGH RATHER THAN IN JAPAN."

This statement may be true, particularly if there is large-scale unemployment in Pittsburgh. Why, then, does it not provide a very strong case for restricting trade, ranking in importance with the efficiency argument for free trade in the previous chapter? Why shouldn't import restrictions be used to raise and maintain U.S. employment? There are two reasons.

> **a.** *If we protect an industry's employment by import restrictions, how can we keep producers from raising their price?* If the government becomes committed to providing an industry with whatever trade barrier it needs to protect it from losing sales and employment to foreign firms, this removes a very important restraint on the industry. If it can raise its price without fear of losing sales, it may well decide to do so.

The U.S. auto industry provides an instructive example. In 1981, the U.S. government pressured the Japanese into imposing "voluntary" restraints on their auto exports to the United States. The resulting reduction in foreign competition imposed a high cost on the U.S. public. According to Wharton Econometric Forecasting Associates, the International Trade Commission, and the Federal Trade Commission, these voluntary export restraints (VERs) on Japanese cars led to increases of about $950 in the price of cars in 1981–1982. By 1985, these restrictions were saving about 45,000 jobs but at an estimated cost to U.S. car buyers of from *$90,000 to $240,000 per year for each job saved.*

Because these restrictions decreased competition from the Japanese and led to increased sales and profits to the U.S. auto companies, these firms were not only able to pay their labor force increased wages; they were also able to pay their executives large bonuses. This raised the question: Why should other U.S. workers earning lower wages be asked to subsidize U.S. autoworkers and auto executives by paying higher prices for cars?

Accordingly, in 1985 the U.S. government eased its pressure on Japan to continue its export restraints to the United States, and for the first time these restraints really *did* become voluntary. The problem was: Why shouldn't the Japanese continue them? The United States had shown the Japanese how to cartelize their export sales—that is, how to force each of the Japanese companies to reduce its U.S. sales and thereby raise price in the U.S. market. Why should the Japanese companies start an uncontrolled expansion of their U.S. sales and thus turn the lucrative U.S. market into an extension of the extremely competitive Japanese home market where they were earning almost no profit?

b. *If our employment is protected by import restraints, won't our trading partners retaliate by imposing their own protection against imports from us?* To see why this might indeed happen, suppose we restrict specialty steel imports so that American purchases are switched from Europe to Pittsburgh. This is often called a **beggar-my-neighbor policy** because we would be trying to solve our unemployment problem by shifting it onto the Europeans. The problem with this policy is that the Europeans may respond by restricting their imports of our goods and thus shift the unemployment problem back onto us.

In periods of worldwide recession, all countries are tempted to initiate a beggar-my-neighbor policy of increased protection; it is tempting for each of them for exactly the same reason that it is tempting for us. If all countries attempt to solve unemployment this way, the result will be a general disruption of trade. Unemployment may consequently rise, not fall. For example, the highly protective Smoot-Hawley Tariff of 1930, combined with foreign retaliation, contributed to the severity of the worldwide depression of the 1930s. Between 1930 and 1933 the trade of 75 countries was reduced by more than half.[2] The recognition that trade restrictions made the Great Depression worse has weakened the political pressures for protection.

If there is large-scale domestic unemployment, the appropriate policies are the domestic monetary and fiscal policies discussed in Parts 3 and 5 of the companion volume, not mutually destructive beggar-my-neighbor trade restrictions.

[2]For detail on the contracting spiral of world trade, and other policy issues described in this chapter, see *Economic Report of the President, 1988,* Chapter 4, especially p. 148. This chapter also draws on *Economic Report of the President, 1987,* Chapter 4.

7. "RESTRICTING TRADE WILL DIVERSIFY A NATION'S ECONOMY."

This statement is true. Just as trade leads a country to specialize, so trade restrictions lead to the opposite: diversification. Isn't it a good thing for a country to diversify, to avoid putting all its eggs in one basket? The answer is, perhaps. But for countries, like individuals, the benefits from specialization often more than offset the risks. (The risk of a future oversupply of lawyers or doctors does not prevent individuals from specializing in such a career. Their expected gains outweigh the risks.) At the national level, an example of a high degree of specialization is Ghana's dependence on exports of cocoa, a product with a fluctuating price. It is true that Ghana's risks could be reduced by diversification, and this could be encouraged by protecting new industries. However, even for a country like Ghana, the argument must be balanced against the advantages of specialization—the gains from trade. Moreover, fluctuations in cocoa price work both ways. There is the risk that price may fall, but there is also the possibility that price may rise, with great benefit to the exporting country.

Finally, for an advanced industrial country such as the United States, policies to diversify the economy are hard to justify. No matter how freely we may trade and specialize, our activities are still likely to remain remarkably diversified.

Just as it has been argued that a country should not become too dependent on an export, it has also been argued that a country should not become too dependent on an import.

8. "RESTRICTING AN IMPORT REDUCES OUR VULNERABILITY TO A CUTOFF IN FOREIGN SUPPLIES."

Oil has been cited earlier as an example of the risks we face if we become highly dependent on an import whose supply is suddenly reduced or cut off. A serious reduction in imported oil due to, say, political instability in the Middle East—the source of a large share of the world-traded supply—would create severe adjustment problems for U.S. industry and auto owners. One way of reducing this risk is to restrict oil imports so that we become less dependent on them. However, even in this most sensitive product, the argument for import restrictions is not conclusive. During the 1950s and

1960s we limited oil imports when the world price was only $2 per barrel, in order to reduce our dependence on foreign supplies. What was the result? Because of the import restrictions, the domestic U.S. oil price rose. In response, U.S. producers pumped more domestic oil, leaving less in the ground. As a result, we became more dependent on foreign oil, thereby increasing our problem when the price rose later to over $30 a barrel. In other words, an attempt to use protection to reduce our vulnerability today may *increase* our vulnerability tomorrow.

Furthermore, it is difficult to think of another product to which the vulnerability argument might apply. For example, we import a lot of textiles from Asia, but there is no risk that they will be cut off. Even if they were, we could continue to get supplies from Europe or produce more textiles at home. Or we could easily cut back on our purchases, using our existing clothing longer. In contrast, it is difficult to reduce our consumption of oil quickly.

9. "RESTRICTING IMPORTS MAY REDUCE THE PRICE WE HAVE TO PAY FOR THEM."

This argument has also been applied to oil and to other products where the United States purchases a substantial portion of the world-traded supply. The idea is this: If the United States were to restrict its imports of oil, and thus buy less on the world market, the world demand for oil would decrease and the price of oil would fall. Thus by restricting this import, the United States would be able to acquire oil at a lower price.[3] This is sometimes referred to as improving our **terms of trade**—that is, reducing the price of what we buy compared to the price of what we sell.

> A nation's ***terms of trade*** is the price of what it sells compared to the price of what it buys.

Although the United States is large enough to affect world price by such a restriction on its import purchases, this policy has limited applicability. True, it would succeed if applied to our import of oil, much of which comes from OPEC countries; or if applied to coffee, much of which comes from Brazil. However, it would not succeed if applied to products supplied by many of our other trading partners. The reason is that they, like the United States, are large enough buyers in world markets that they too can play the same game. For example, if we restricted our imports of products which we purchase heavily from Europe in order to reduce their price, the natural reaction of the Europeans would be to restrict their purchases from us, thus driving down the price of our exports. With the price of both our imports and exports depressed, it is far from clear that we would benefit on balance. The only certainty is that the volume of both European and U.S. exports would be reduced. Both sides would be likely to lose.

10. "A COUNTRY NEEDS TO PROTECT ITS INFANT INDUSTRIES."

A country may not be able to compete with other nations in an industry with economies of scale until this industry is well established and operating at high volume and low cost. This may be the case even in an industry in which the country will eventually have a comparative advantage and be able to produce very cheaply. The question that arises is: Shouldn't such an industry be protected from being wiped out by tough foreign competition during the delicate period of its infancy?

The infant industry argument has historically attracted some of the strongest support for protection. It was influential in the United States and Germany in the nineteenth century and in Latin America during this century. However, it raises problems.

a. *How do you know that the only advantage of the foreign countries is that their industry is already established?* For example, if a country is thinking of protecting an infant watch industry, how does it know that the only advantage of the Swiss and Japanese is that their industry is already established? Maybe they enjoy some basic advantage in watchmaking. If so, a watchmaking industry established elsewhere may never be able to compete.

---

[3]Although the United States as a *nation* would pay less to oil-exporting nations such as Saudi Arabia, the price paid *by oil buyers within the United States* would rise because they would not only have to pay the amount the Saudis get, but also the tariff that would go to the U.S. government. (It would be in response to this higher price that U.S. buyers would reduce their oil purchases.)

b. *When does an infant subsidy become an old-age pension?* Industries that receive protection as infants never seem to grow up but instead continue to lobby for tariffs. Such industries can become a real problem. Once established, they employ many people who vote; protection continues to go to them rather than to the real infants who have not yet hired a large enough labor force to give them voting clout.[4]

11. "PROTECTION CAN BE USED TO ENGINEER A COMPARATIVE ADVANTAGE."

The traditional example of comparative advantage begins with differences in costs. In the example in Chapter 19, the United States was simply assumed to have a comparative advantage in food, and Europe in clothing. Critics point out that, although some differences in costs depend on gifts of nature such as the wheat-growing capacity of the U.S. plains or the oil-producing wells of the Middle East, comparative advantage can often be created or "engineered." For example, a country can encourage the accumulation of capital and thus acquire a comparative advantage in an industry that requires plentiful capital. Alternatively, a country may develop a comparative advantage in high-tech industries by subsidizing education and research—or by providing its high-tech industries with protection. Such protection may help these industries attract engineers and scientists, and thus lay the foundation for future strength.

Note that this argument for protection is a variation on the infant-industry theme. In either case, proponents view protection as a way to develop new industries with a comparative advantage in the future. Consequently, this argument is subject to the same criticisms as the infant-industry argument.

12. "INDUSTRIES WITH POSITIVE EXTERNALITIES SHOULD BE PROTECTED."

High-tech firms often provide benefits not only to their own employees and stockholders, but also to the public at large. As an example of such a positive externality, consider AT&T. Its Bell Labs developed the transistor, but only a small part of the benefits have gone to AT&T employees and stockholders. The broad public has benefited greatly as transistors have improved the quality of computers, audio equipment, automobiles, and even inexpensive watches. Because a free market will result in "too little" output from high-tech industries with positive externalities, protection should be used—so the argument goes—to encourage them.

However, the existence of positive externalities does not make a compelling case for protection of high-tech industries. In a rapidly changing industry, protection can have unforeseen consequences. For example, in 1986, the United States pressured Japan into raising the prices and limiting exports of computer chips sold in the United States. This encouraged U.S. production of chips, but by raising costs and creating shortages of chips, it weakened the competitive position of the U.S. computer industry that uses chips.

Furthermore, protection of high-tech industries, like protection in general, may lead to **retaliation.** It can split the world up into small, inefficient national markets. If the government wants to encourage the chip industry, it should do so with a domestic policy that will not trigger retaliation and will not raise the price of chips, and therefore not discourage the computer industry. An example of such a policy might be government assistance for the education and training of technicians or engineers, or possibly the relaxation of antitrust laws to permit joint research and design. In fact, U.S. antitrust laws have been relaxed to permit joint research projects.

13. "A THREAT TO RESTRICT OUR IMPORTS WILL FORCE OTHER COUNTRIES TO LOWER THEIR BARRIERS TO OUR EXPORTS."

If the Japanese, for example, won't ease their restrictions on our goods, why can't we threaten restrictions on their goods and thereby persuade them to lower their barriers? This policy, which is sometimes called **aggressive reciprocity** or **fair trade,** is a tit-for-tat strategy that might work.

At the same time, threats may become a prescription for a trade war if each country views the other as having more severe trade restrictions, and thus feels justified in using fair trade to increase its

[4]A third question is, If such an industry will eventually be a profitable one, why shouldn't its owners cover any initial losses out of their future profits? One possible answer is that capital markets may not work very well. As a result, firms may be unable to raise the capital necessary to get them through the initial period of losses.

own protection. Countries almost always do hold the view that they are fairer than their trading partners; fairness is often in the eye of the beholder. For example, for decades the United States and Europe have protected their agricultural industries with a whole series of restrictions. Each thinks the other is more protective. If each uses protection to force the other to behave in a "fair" way, protection may escalate.

Recently the United States has experimented with aggressive reciprocity in the form of the "super-301" provision in the 1988 trade legislation. Under this law, Congress requires the U.S. administration to designate which countries systematically restrict U.S. access to their markets; and if these restrictions are not removed in negotiation, the U.S. government is to retaliate by introducing new trade barriers against the offending countries. When the United States designated Japan, Brazil and India in 1989, there was an international outcry, not just from these three countries, but from others as well. They not only feared that they might be next in line, but were also concerned that the judgment on what was, or was not, "fair trade" was being made unilaterally—that is, by the United States alone. The fear was that this could seriously weaken the international trading system, including U.S. trade relations not only with the three designated countries, but with other countries as well.

Thus, while it is possible that aggressive reciprocity may open up foreign markets, there is also a substantial risk that it may close them further.

FREE TRADE VERSUS PROTECTION: A SUMMARY

This discussion shows that a policy should not be judged by counting up the number of arguments for and against. There are only a few arguments for free trade, but they are very impressive, such as the real income gains from comparative advantage and economies of scale.

On the other hand, there is a whole battery of arguments for protection. Some are downright illogical—for example, the argument that tariffs should be tailored to equalize costs between countries. Those that do make some sense—like the infant-industry argument or the use of protection to stimulate high-tech industries—lose their attraction if other countries retaliate by protecting their industries, too. In this case, the world economy becomes less efficient as it is split up into small national markets.

For a large country such as the United States, a major move toward protection would be particularly likely to cause retaliation. The United States is so large that other countries could scarcely fail to notice its protective policies which often severely damage them. U.S. leadership has been essential for the encouraging—although uneven—move toward more open trade. In the words of MIT's Paul Krugman, "Free trade can serve as a focal point on which countries can agree to avoid trade wars. It can also serve as a simple principle with which to resist pressures of special-interest politics."[5]

Free trade means the elimination of not only tariffs, but also a whole set of other trade restrictions known as nontariff barriers.

NONTARIFF BARRIERS (NTBs)

Here are a few of the most important nontariff barriers.

QUOTAS AND OTHER QUANTITATIVE RESTRAINTS

One highly publicized example of a quantitative restraint was cited earlier: the voluntary export restraint (VER) in autos that the United States negotiated with Japan in 1981–1985. This Japanese limitation of its exports to the United States meant, of course, that the quantity of U.S. auto imports from Japan was restricted.

Alternatively the United States may itself impose a quantitative limit—that is, a quota—on its imports. An example is the U.S. quota on the importation of sugar.

Under certain conditions, a quantitative restraint may be equivalent to a tariff (as shown in the appendix). For example, in 1988 restraints on U.S. imports of textiles and apparel were roughly as restrictive as a very high 50% tariff. Other highly

[5]"Is Free Trade Passe?" *Journal of Economic Perspectives*, Fall 1987, p. 143. This article evaluates some of the more recent arguments for protection.

developed countries also restrict their imports of textiles and clothing. This policy has been particularly damaging to the less developed countries with a comparative advantage in these products. According to some experts, this damage more than offsets the benefits these countries receive from reduced tariff rates on their exports to highly developed countries.

HEALTH OR QUALITY STANDARDS

Countries may impose NTBs in the form of stiff quality or health standards that may be difficult for imports to satisfy. If such standards lead to an improvement in the nation's health, they may be justified even though they have the unfortunate side effect of restricting trade. On the other hand, if they have little effect on the nation's health, they may be just a way of reducing imports. For example, the Japanese at one time prevented the import of Perrier (a natural sparkling water from France) by requiring that it be boiled. Some European nations have "health" restrictions against low-alcohol foreign beers, even though they make drinkers *less* inebriated. It is often difficult to answer the key question: Is a health standard imposed to protect health or to protect domestic industries? For example, in 1989 the European Community banned imports of U.S. beef that had been fed growth hormones, on the ground that this beef was a health hazard. The U.S. government argued that the meat was safe and that the EC was using health regulations as a pretext to protect their domestic beef industry. In cases like this, it is not easy to sort out how much of the health concern is valid and how much is an excuse for protection.

BUREAUCRACY AND RED TAPE

A country may impose other NTBs, such as complex and costly customs procedures, in order to discourage or delay imports. For example, in 1982 the French were determined to discourage imports of Japanese video cassette recorders (VCRs). They therefore required that all imported VCRs be cleared through the tiny customs office at Poitiers, an inland town far from any main port—ironically, the same small town used about 150 years ago by Frederick Bastiat to illustrate how ridiculous protection could become (Box 20-1).

Negotiating down tariffs and NTBs has been a long and difficult process, which is still far from complete.

TRADE LIBERALIZATION

Figure 20-1 illustrates how U.S. tariffs have been reduced from a peak they reached in 1930 with the Smoot-Hawley Tariff. While substantial progress has been made, keep in mind that Figure 20-1 describes only tariffs, but not NTBs. Thus it does not adequately show how high the cost of protection still remains for the United States.

MULTILATERAL NEGOTIATIONS: THE GENERAL AGREEMENT ON TARIFFS AND TRADE (GATT)

An important event in the history of trade liberalization occurred in 1947, when the United States and 22 other nations signed the General Agreement on Tariffs and Trade. This has since provided a forum in which all participating countries have negotiated lower trade barriers. In 1967, the **Kennedy Round** of negotiations cut existing tariffs on average by about one-third. Following this major success, a new set of negotiations were begun during the 1970s to liberalize trade further—the **Tokyo Round.** This agreement cut tariffs, on average, by another third and eliminated them on civilian aircraft.

Subsequently, there was a period in which the world drifted slowly back toward more protectionism. Accordingly, in his state-of-the-union message in January 1985, President Reagan called for a further round to negotiate down trade barriers. The resulting **Uruguay Round** of negotiations began in 1986.

Although these Rounds of negotiations in the GATT have led to **multilateral agreements** in which many countries have participated, there have also been **plurilateral agreements** in which only a few countries have participated and **bilateral agreements** between two countries.

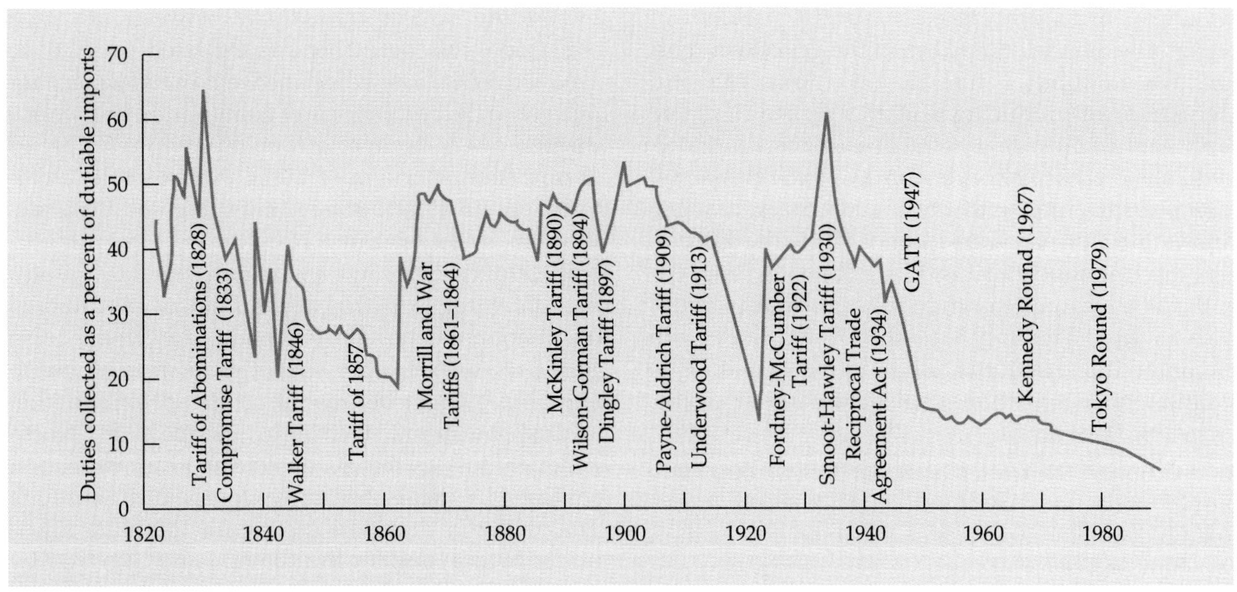

FIGURE 20-1 Average U.S. tariff rates.

The United States has had high tariffs during some periods and low tariffs during others. Since 1930, the trend has been down, so that U.S. tariffs now average less than 5%. Nontariff barriers, not shown here, have now become the most important impediments to trade. (*Source: Statistical Abstract of the United States.*)

In a ***multilateral agreement,*** many countries participate.

In a ***plurilateral agreement,*** several countries participate.

In a ***bilateral agreement,*** two countries participate.

A PLURILATERAL AGREEMENT: THE EUROPEAN COMMUNITY

In the late 1950s, West Germany, France, Italy, Holland, Belgium, and Luxembourg (later joined by Britain and several other countries) agreed to form a common market. Its provisions included tariff-free trade among the member nations and a common set of import barriers against goods coming into the European Community (EC) from other countries. The eventual objective was to create a barrier-free European market like the United States in which goods, services, people, and capital could move without restriction. But while many of the barriers between European countries were being removed, some remained—and new ones were being created. Thus in 1988, the EC announced that it would be taking action by 1992 to remove remaining restrictions and create the truly common market which its founders had originally sought.

One of the reasons why the EC was created was the desire of the member countries to make it impossible for France and Germany to go to war again; thus they eventually wanted to move some distance toward political union. They also had a strong economic motive: to gain the benefits of freer trade among themselves. Since its formation, the EC countries have made substantial economic progress, although it is difficult to assess how much has been due to the formation of the EC and how much has been due to other causes. It is also difficult to assess how the EC has affected outside countries like the United States. On the one hand, by inducing more rapid European growth, it has made Europe a better potential customer for U.S. exports. On the other, the formation of the EC has raised two problems for an "outsider" like the United States:

1. Because the United States is not an EC member,

American firms now face the special problem of being outsiders in competing in the European market. For example, before the EC, American and German firms producing machinery faced the same tariff barriers in selling in the French market. However, since the creation of the EC, U.S. firms still face a tariff going into the French market, while competing German firms do not. Thus the EC creates discrimination against U.S. exports in France—and, for the same reason, in other European countries as well. The only way the United States can eliminate this discrimination is by participating in multilateral negotiations that eliminate all tariffs, including the French.

2. Although the United States and other outsiders would face this discrimination even if European barriers to imports had remained constant, in fact European barriers against agricultural imports were increased. As noted earlier, this policy has been very costly to the United States because it has further discouraged U.S. export sales to Europe. Moreover, higher European barriers to imports have been one of the policies that have raised the price of food within Europe and thus generated European overproduction which has been sold at much lower prices in third countries. The butter sale to the Soviet Union cited at the beginning of the chapter was an extreme example. Such European exports have reduced U.S. export sales to third countries. EC protection has therefore made it difficult for U.S. farmers to sell, not only in Europe, but also in other traditional export markets.

BILATERAL AGREEMENTS

The cornerstone of U.S. policy since 1947 has been, and still remains, the multilateral approach. Even so, the United States has recently participated in several bilateral agreements. In 1985, the United States signed a bilateral free trade agreement with Israel. In addition, the United States signed a "Framework Agreement" with Mexico in 1987 to reduce disputes and attempt to liberalize trade between the two countries in the future.

However, the most significant U.S. bilateral agreement has been the 1989 free trade agreement with Canada noted earlier, which will eliminate essentially all tariffs and many other trade barriers between the two countries by 1998. Because their trade is so large—indeed, even before 1989 it was by far the largest trade flow between any two countries—this agreement is expected to provide great benefits from comparative advantage, economies of scale, and increased competition in the production of goods. In addition, it provides for broad trade liberalization in services. For example, architects will be able to freely move and sell their services in either country. It is hoped that this liberalization of trade in services will provide a useful precedent for the Uruguay Round of multilateral negotiations. The U.S./Canada agreement also puts pressure on other countries to support multilateral free trade because it creates discrimination against outsiders trying to compete in North America (just as the EC has created discrimination against U.S. firms trying to compete in Europe). The only way outsiders can escape this discrimination is by pressing for multilateral tariff removal by all countries.

Bilateral or plurilateral agreements are not the final objective. They would leave us in a world in which we would be insiders in some trade agreements but outsiders (at considerable cost) from others. This world would be inferior to one in which all countries would be insiders in one broad multilateral free trade agreement.

THE SPECIAL PROBLEM OF U.S.-JAPANESE TRADE RELATIONS

In addition to making the Kennedy and Tokyo Round tariff cuts required by the GATT, Japan has recently been making further reductions in its tariffs and some of its more obvious NTBs. Nonetheless, there are still quotas on Japanese food imports that dramatically raise the price that the Japanese have to pay. In addition, a myriad of less formal and visible NTBs protect Japanese industrial products. For example, auto imports are subject to a zealous inspection, with legendary stories of cars being taken apart; and the Japanese have restricted imports of skis on the mysterious ground that Japanese snow is somehow different.

The consequent difficulties that foreign firms have faced in selling in the Japanese market have been a continuing source of friction. Recently U.S. complaints became even more vocal. In 1987, U.S. merchandise imports from Japan were more than three times the value of U.S. exports to Japan. In

1988, the difference in the two was reduced; but even then, U.S. imports from Japan were almost $90 billion, while U.S. exports to Japan were just over $37 billion.

In a complex world in which trade is flowing in all directions among all countries, there is no reason why the export and import flows between two countries should be equal. However, the difference in this case was so large that it raised a political problem. It was a major reason why Congress included the super-301 provision in the 1988 trade legislation (p. 355). The question was: Would a frustrated U.S. Congress take further action aimed at Japan?

THE MULTINATIONAL CORPORATION (MNC)

By assisting in the international transfer of capital and technology, **multinational corporations** have become prime agents in moving the world toward a global economy.

> ***Multinational corporations*** are firms that have their head office in one country and subsidiaries in other countries. One example of an American MNC is Ford Motor Company, which has subsidiary companies in Britain, Canada, West Germany, and elsewhere. Other countries have their multinationals too, such as Royal Dutch Shell, which is controlled by the Dutch and British.

Why does a company become a multinational? Some firms go abroad to acquire raw materials. A good example is an oil company that has gone to the Middle East to find oil. But there are other important reasons as well. Once an American firm has developed a new product for the domestic market at great research and development costs, it will want to sell the product worldwide. Moreover, an American company that has decided to sell its product in, say, Europe may also decide to produce it there, if this is cheaper than producing it in the United States and exporting it over the European tariff wall.

A U.S. firm may also go abroad in search of lower wages. For example, it may go to Korea or Taiwan to produce goods requiring a great deal of labor. As a result, American labor unions have complained that the multinationals are "exporting American jobs." In particular, labor has asked why U.S. MNCs should be allowed to transfer their technological know-how abroad, especially when some of it has been developed with the assistance of government funds provided by U.S. taxpayers. When U.S. firms set up manufacturing operations abroad, doesn't this make it easier for foreign firms to copy their technology?

Multinational companies reply that you can't stop foreign competitors from copying your products. You can't prevent the spread of new technology. The most you can hope for, by keeping your technology at home, is to prolong the normal copying time, but not by much. If U.S. firms don't have subsidiaries abroad to produce their goods, these goods are likely to be produced abroad by foreign firms. Furthermore, subsidiaries of U.S. firms in foreign countries may create jobs in the United States. For example, a General Motors subsidiary that assembles cars in Canada buys auto engines and transmissions produced in the United States, thus creating U.S. jobs. About one-fourth of all U.S. exports go to foreign subsidiaries of U.S. firms.

Because of the resources which MNCs have at their disposal to set up new factories anywhere in the world, they may make it easier for countries to get established quickly in their activities of comparative advantage. By making specialization easier, MNCs help increase world income.

However, the growth of multinational corporations has raised problems, mostly for the host countries in which the MNCs have subsidiaries. For example, there is some concern that a large multinational may be able to acquire monopoly power in the host country's market. (On the other hand, the entry of a multinational may reduce the market power of an existing domestic monopolist.) Host countries are also concerned that they may become too dependent on foreign technology. They fear that their political independence may be eroded because decisions important for a host country may not be made there at all, but may instead be made in London, New York, or Tokyo in the head offices of a MNC. Worse yet, such decisions may be made by the parent company's government. Europeans resented President Reagan's decision to prohibit U.S. subsidiaries in Western Europe from selling the Soviet Union equipment for a pipeline that would send natural gas to Western Europe. European countries viewed this U.S. action as unwarranted interference, and the policy was dropped.

Host governments may also be concerned that MNCs may try to put pressure on them by threatening to pull their subsidiaries out and relocate them in another country. In addition, the reputation of multinationals has not been improved by the isolated instances in which they have made payoffs in an attempt to secure foreign contracts. Such scandals have touched a member of the Dutch royal family and a former prime minister of Japan. Finally, the image of multinationals was severely damaged by the Bhopal accident in India, where poisonous fumes from a subsidiary of Union Carbide killed over 2,500 people in the worst industrial disaster in history.

Although multinationals make a substantial contribution to world economic growth, they can raise serious problems—problems that may be particularly difficult to resolve because they extend across national borders.

KEY POINTS

1. Trade restrictions such as tariffs or quotas result in an efficiency loss. The gains from trade described in Chapter 19 are eroded as trade is reduced.

2. Trade restrictions on a good also transfer income from consumers to producers. One reason why countries have trade restrictions is that producers generally have more political power than consumers.

3. Athough many statements on the long list of economic arguments for protection are fallacious, some have a degree of validity. Protecting a defense industry may be justified on military grounds. A less developed country, now exporting only a natural resource, may protect a domestic industry in order to diversify its economy, thus reducing its economic risks. An even stronger case can be made if that industry is a "promising infant," that is, an industry of comparative advantage if only it can become established. The problem is that assistance to infants can evolve into an old-age pension.

4. The United States, as a large buyer, might impose a tariff on an imported good to reduce the demand and hence the world price that has to be paid for the good. This is the *terms-of-trade* argument. However, because other countries are likely to retaliate by imposing their tariffs on our goods, this is not a very strong argument for protection except, perhaps, in the special case of oil.

5. The same risk of foreign retaliation arises if a country imposes a tariff to try to ease its unemployment problem. Because this tariff would shift its unemployment problem to its trading partners, their likely reaction would be to impose their own tariffs, thus shifting the unemployment problem back onto the first country—in particular, onto its export industries.

6. Since the signing of the GATT agreement in 1947, the United States has emphasized multilateral trade liberalization with all countries. In the meantime the European Community has formed a common market that liberalizes trade among the countries in Europe. In 1985, the United States signed a bilateral agreement with Israel, and in 1989 entered a comprehensive free trade agreement with its largest trading partner, Canada.

7. Multinational corporations transmit technology across national borders. Because of their ability to set up new plants quickly, they may make it easier for countries to develop their activities of comparative advantage. For example, multinationals often allocate labor-intensive activities to low-wage countries.

KEY CONCEPTS

tariff
quota
a tariff tailored to equalize costs
voluntary export restraints (VERs)
beggar-my-neighbor policy
diversification versus specialization
terms of trade
retaliation
infant-industry protection
aggressive reciprocity
nontariff barriers (NTBs)
General Agreement on Tariffs and Trade (GATT)
Kennedy Round
Tokyo Round
Uruguay Round
multilateral, plurilateral, and bilateral agreements
European Community (EC)
U.S./Canada free trade agreement
multinational corporations (MNCs)
subsidiaries
host countries

PROBLEMS

20-1. (a) If you don't know the answer to this question, you should be able to guess it. When Japanese companies faced quotas (specifically, voluntary export restraints) on the number of cars they could ship into the U.S. market, did they concentrate on sending stripped down, inexpensive models or higher priced models loaded with extras? Why? Did these quotas drive the Japanese "up-market?" Twenty years ago they were known as producers of inexpensive cars. What has happened to their reputation?

> ***(b)** When VERs on Japanese exports were saving an estimated 44,000 jobs at a cost to the U.S. public between $90,000 and $240,000 per job, was a Pareto improvement possible? Assume that there are only two groups: the auto workers and the car-buying public. (*Hint:* Would autoworkers prefer to keep their jobs in the auto industry or to receive, say, $80,000 each?)

20-2. In 1988, merchandise exports were equal to less than 7% of U.S. GNP. They are more important for a number of other countries, where they account for even higher proportions of GNP—for example, more than 20% in Britain and Sweden.

> **(a)** Which of the three countries trades most in absolute terms, that is, which country has the largest number of dollars-worth of trade?

> **(b)** If the United States were, like Europe, split up into several countries, what would happen to the export/GNP ratio of each of these countries?

20-3. The following statement was made earlier in this chapter: "In activities of our comparative advantage, our higher productivity more than offsets our higher wage." Along these same lines, what statement would you make about activities in which a low-wage foreign country has a comparative advantage?

20-4. "The higher the tariff on an import, the more revenue the government collects." Is this statement necessarily true? Explain.

20-5. (a) Following Figure 19-8, show the effect of a "prohibitive" U.S. tariff that completely eliminates our import of a good.

> **(b)** Using a similar diagram, explain the effects of a foreign tariff that prevents us from exporting a good.

20-6. "Transport costs are like tariffs. Both deter trade. If either were reduced, countries would reap increased benefits from trade. Raising tariffs is much the same as going back to shipping goods in old, expensive clipper ships." Do you agree? Why or why not? (*Hint:* Don't forget that the government collects revenues from tariffs.)

20-7. Foreign industries seeking protection from

U.S. goods sometimes argue: "Even though our wages are low, we can't compete with American firms, because their labor is more productive." Are they always right? Explain.

20-8. Explain why you agree or disagree with the following statement: "Because trade between countries provides benefits, a nation will benefit from an open border in goods. The same principle applies to fishing. Each nation should have an open border here as well. It should not have territorial rights, since they are just a way of protecting its domestic fishing industry."

20-9. "The United States has created a comparative advantage in industries requiring a great deal of physical capital by accumulating a large amount of it. Why not create a comparative advantage in high-tech industries requiring a great deal of human capital by accumulating a lot of it—through protection of high-tech industries?" Evaluate this statement.

APPENDIX

THE EFFECTS OF A TARIFF OR QUOTA THAT REDUCES IMPORTS

Figure 20-2 illustrates the effects of a tariff imposed by a country that is not large enough to affect the world price.

First, consider what happens if the tariff is so high that it eliminates trade altogether. Equilibrium occurs at point *A*, where the domestic demand *D* and supply *S* intersect. Next, consider what happens with free trade. At the world price P_w, consumers buy at point *J*, while domestic producers supply at point *H*. Imports are *HJ*, the difference between domestic consumption and production.

Finally, consider the intermediate case of a tariff that reduces, but does not eliminate, trade in this product. The tariff *t* is added to the world price P_w, giving a new domestic price of P_t. Consumers respond to this price by moving to point *K*, which is, as expected, between free trade point *J* and no-trade point *A*. At the same time, domestic producers move to point *R* on their supply curve. Imports are *RK*, the difference between domestic consumption and domestic production.

The effects of tariff *t* on all parties are shown in panels *b*, *c*, and *d*. As the U.S. domestic price rises from P_w to P_t, consumers lose the red area enclosed to the left of the demand curve in panel *b*, whereas producers benefit by blue area 3 enclosed to the left of the supply curve in panel *c*. However, there is now another effect, not encountered before, that is shown as area 4. This is the benefit to U.S. taxpayers because the U.S. Treasury is now collecting tariff revenue. A tariff *RF* is collected on each of the *RK* units imported for a total revenue of area 4.

Because the two blue benefits in panel *c* also cover parts of the red loss in panel *b*, they are transfers. Specifically, area 4 is a transfer from consumers who pay a higher price, to the Treasury that collects the duty, whereas area 3 is a transfer from consumers to producers. However, some of the red loss in panel *b* is not canceled out by blue gains in panel *c*. This balance is the net efficiency loss to society, shown as the two red triangles in panel *d*.[6]

Thus a tariff results in efficiency losses and a transfer from consumers to producers, as well as a transfer from consumers to taxpayers.

EFFECTS OF A QUOTA

Trade may be restricted by a tariff or by a nontariff barrier (NTB) such as a quota. Such a restriction limits the number of units of a good that can be imported and has many effects similar to a tariff. For example, panel *a* of Figure 20-2 shows that a tariff *t* raises price in the U.S. market from P_w to P_t and thus reduces imports from *HJ* to *RK*. Another way to reduce imports by the same amount would be simply to prohibit any imports in excess of *RK*; in other words, impose a quota of *RK*. If the government does this, the new equilibrium will again be at point *K*, just as it was with the tariff. (To con-

[6]These two efficiency effects are marked 1 and 2 because they correspond to the two triangular efficiency effects first encountered in Figure 19-7. (Red is used here to show the efficiency losses when trade is restricted, whereas in earlier Figure 19-7 trade was being opened up, and the resulting gains were shown in blue.) As an exercise, you should be able to confirm that triangle 1 in Figure 20-2*d* is the efficiency loss that results because inexpensive imports have been replaced by higher cost domestic production, and triangle 2 is the efficiency loss that results because consumers have been prevented from purchasing this good at the lowest possible price.

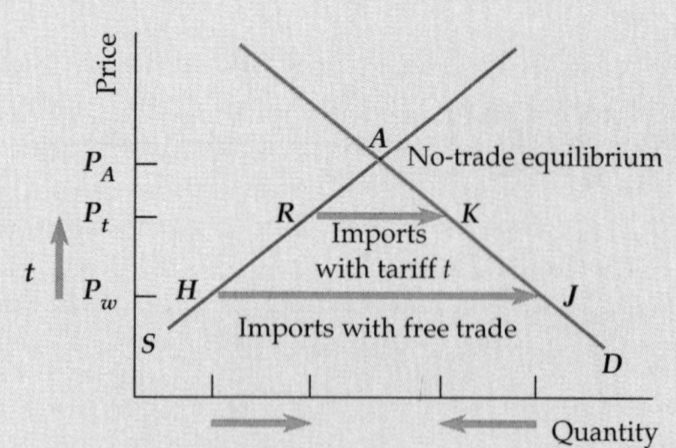

(*a*) The domestic American supply is *S*. Under free trade, there is assumed to be a completely elastic world supply at price P_w. Therefore, the total supply on the American market— from both domestic and foreign sources—is ***SHJ***. This intersects American demand ***D*** at point ***J***, the free-trade equilibrium where there are imports of ***HJ***. Thus the U.S. domestic price is the same as the world price P_w. However, when tariff ***t*** is imposed, the world supply shifts up by this same amount ***t***. (Foreign suppliers now require their original P_w, plus an amount ***t*** to compensate them for the tariff they must pay at the U.S. border.) With this upward shift in foreign supply, the total supply on the American market—from both domestic and foreign sources—becomes ***SRK***. This intersects American demand ***D*** at point ***K***, which is the new equilibrium under the tariff. Thus the domestic U.S. price has been raised by the amount of the tariff to P_t.

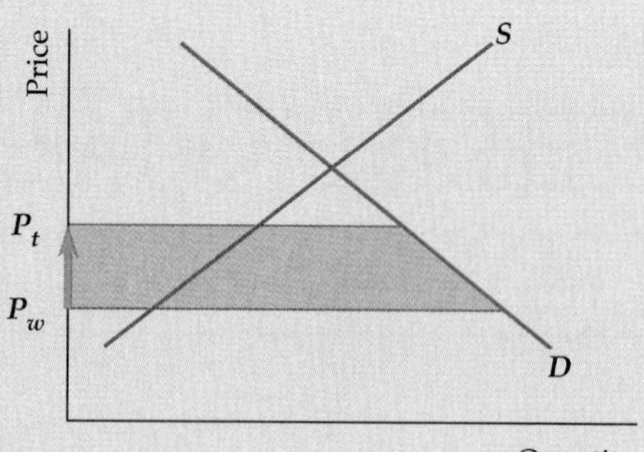

(*b*) Because price rises, consumers lose.

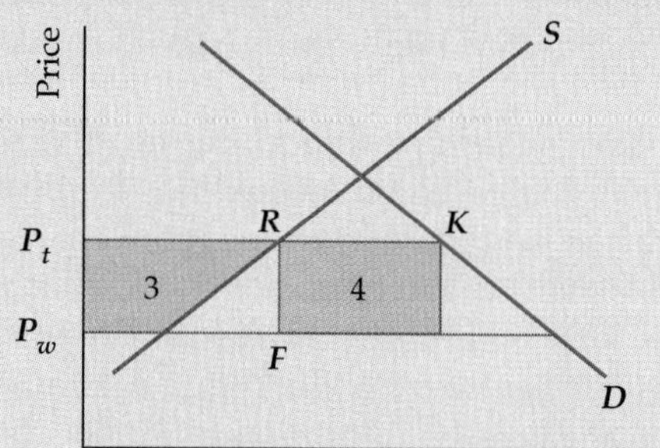

(*c*) But producers gain 3 and the Treasury gains 4. As a result there is a transfer 3 from consumers to producers, and a transfer 4 from consumers to the Treasury.

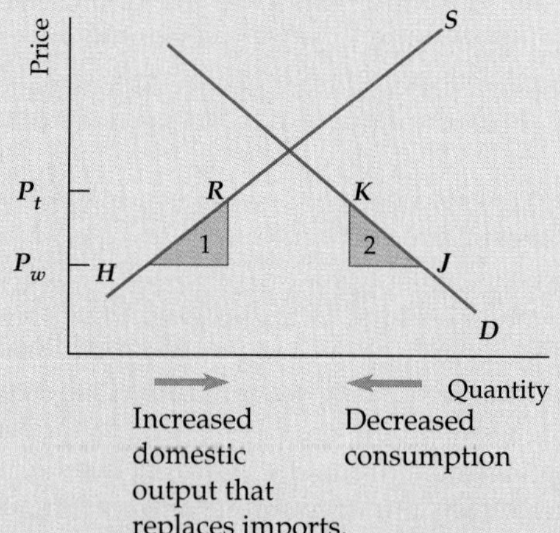

(*d*) There are also efficiency losses 1 + 2.

FIGURE 20-2 Effects of a tariff.

firm, K is where demand D is equal to supply, including both the domestic supply at point R plus the foreign supply RK.)

A quota of RK is sometimes referred to as "the quota equivalent of tariff t."[7] It distorts domestic price and leads to the same inefficiency in resource allocation as tariff t. Specifically, by making the good scarce, it raises price in the U.S. market and so induces high-cost domestic production and decreased consumption. However, there is one big difference. With a tariff, the U.S. Treasury collects revenues (area 4 in panel c of Figure 20-2). *But with a quota, no such revenues are collected.* As a result, this amount goes not to the Treasury but instead to whoever is lucky enough to acquire the import quota rights—that is, to whoever is able to (1) acquire the good on the world market at cost P_w, (2) ship it into the United States, and (3) sell it there at a price P_t. If the U.S. government grants quota rights, or import licenses, to American importers, this windfall income 4 goes to these U.S. importers rather than to the Treasury. However, if the quota rights end up in the hands of the foreign firms that sell this good in the U.S. market, *this income goes to them rather than to the U.S. Treasury.* Consequently, this is a loss to the United States, and this sort of quota becomes a much more costly protectionist device for America than a tariff. Isn't there some way to ensure against this loss to the United States? One answer would be for the U.S. government to auction off the import licenses. Because the total revenue raised by the U.S. Treasury from this sale would be roughly area 4, such a quota would have effects similar to those of the tariff shown in Figure 20-2.

A 1984 proposal for U.S. steel quotas provided a concrete example of how costly such a trade restriction might be on the country imposing it. According to estimates by the Congressional Budget Office,[8] efficiency losses similar to areas 1 and 2 in panel d of Figure 20-2 would have run as high as \$1.1 billion in the first five years of the quota. Even so, this would have been only half as large as the \$2.2 billion loss to the United States—area 4 in panel b—which would have represented a transfer from U.S. buyers to foreign firms. This windfall to foreign firms might have been reinvested, making them even more difficult to compete against in the future.

This raises serious questions about the U.S. policy of pressing hard to get certain countries to agree to impose voluntary export restraints, that is, "voluntary" limits on their exports to the United States. In terms of this analysis, any such VER can be viewed as having the same effect as a U.S. import quota with rights being held by foreign firms. As a result of these restraints, we have lost area 4 to the foreign firms exporting to us, as well as efficiency losses 1 and 2 that follow from any form of protection.

Figure 20-2 clearly shows one reason why foreign countries agree when the United States presses them to impose voluntary export restraints on their sales. Their exporters benefit (by area 4 in Fig. 20-2) because they hold the valuable rights that allow them to sell at an inflated price in the U.S. market. This bonanza to foreign producers provided by area 4 has been illustrated in Hong Kong, where there has been a thriving market for the rights to export clothing to the United States. At times, these rights have sold for as much as 10% or more of the value of the clothing. Some Hong Kong exporters have found that it has been more profitable to sell these rights than to produce the goods. They have closed down their factories and lived off the proceeds from the sale of the rights.

[7]Figure 20-2, with its demand and supply curves, assumes perfect competition. Tariffs and quotas are not as easily compared in more complicated situations in which imperfect competition prevails.

[8]*The Effects of Import Quotas on the Steel Industry,* July 1984, p. 45.

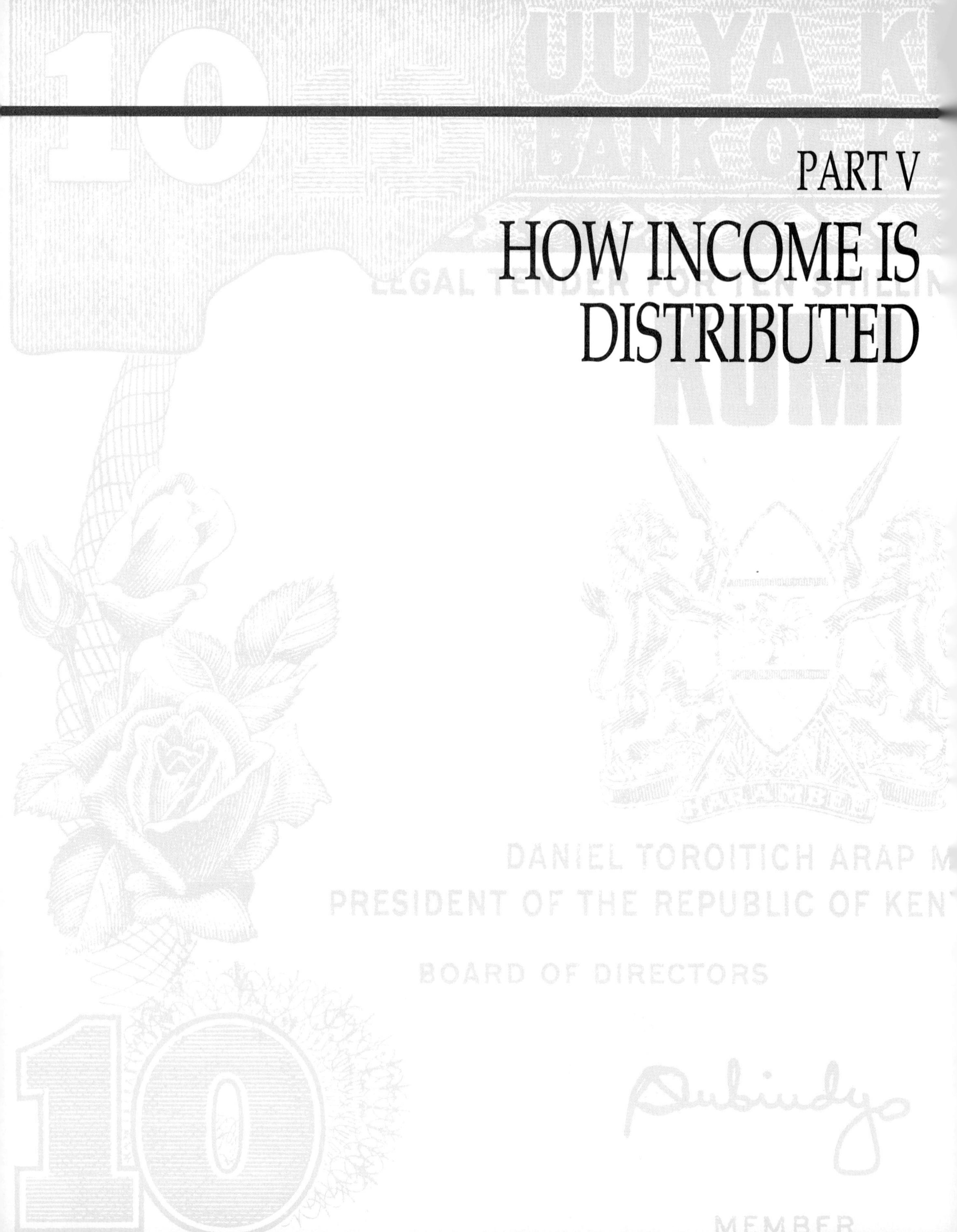

PART V

HOW INCOME IS DISTRIBUTED

For whom is the nation's output produced? Why does the heavyweight champion earn millions of dollars for every fight, while the nurse who may have to save his life earns only a few thousand a year? These and other related questions will be studied in the remaining chapters:

- Markets for labor (Chapters 21 and 22).
- Markets for capital and land (Chapter 23).
- The inequality that results from the operation of these markets (Chapter 24).
- Government policies to reduce inequality (Chapter 25).
- The Marxist critique (Chapter 26).

Markets for labor, capital and land are often like the markets for wheat and autos studied earlier, and will be analyzed using similar tools. When a price changes, there is an *equity effect*—that is, a transfer between buyers and sellers—and an *efficiency effect*. The Box on the next page shows why both must be considered.

Why Both Efficiency and Equity Should Be Considered

This box reviews conclusions from Parts 3 and 4 that provide an important focus for Part 5. Whether or not you embark on this detailed review, you should at least look at Figures 1 and 2 to get the general idea of their message:

- Figure 1 shows two policies with exactly the same equity effects (transfers) shown by the white arrows. However, the two policies have completely different efficiency effects. One results in a red efficiency loss, while the other results in a blue efficiency gain.
- Figure 2 shows two policies with exactly the same efficiency effects (blue gains) but completely different transfers (arrows).

Clearly, any analysis that examines only the efficiency effect of a policy—or only its transfer effect—may provide a seriously misleading picture. Both effects should be considered.

TAXING A GOOD THAT POLLUTES AND ONE THAT DOES NOT

Panel *a* of Figure 1 shows the effect of a commodity tax on a good that creates no pollution or any other externality. Panel *b* shows a similar tax applied to a good that does pollute. Otherwise, these two panels are identical. In both panels, the tax generates exactly the same set of transfers, shown by the broad white arrows. The transfers are identical because, in both cases, the tax shifts supply from S_1 to S_2 and equilibrium from E_1 to E_2. In each case, consumers lose because the price they pay rises from P_1 to P_2, and producers lose because the price they receive (after paying the tax) falls from P_1 to P_3. (Producers actually receive P_2, but out of this they must pay the tax of P_2P_3.) But while consumers and producers lose, the U.S. Treasury gains in the form of increased tax receipts. Thus, in each panel, the broad upward arrow shows the transfer from consumers to the Treasury, and the arrow pointing down shows the transfer from producers to the Treasury.

Although transfers are the same in these two panels, the effects on efficiency are quite different. Without pollution in panel *a,* the tax causes a red efficiency loss. However, in the face of pollution in panel *b,* this same tax causes a blue efficiency gain (provided that the tax is equal to the marginal cost that pollution imposes on society). The reason is simple. In either case, the tax reduces output from Q_1 to Q_2. If there is no pollution (panel *a*), this output reduction moves the economy *away from* the efficient output at Q_1, and this results in an efficiency loss. However, when pollution exists (panel *b*), the free market results in too much output at Q_1; the efficient output is at Q_2. By moving the economy toward this point, the tax generates an efficiency gain.

There is another way of seeing why this policy improves efficiency in panel *b* but not in panel *a.* When the production of a good generates pollution (panel *b*), the tax provides a benefit that does not exist in panel *a*—the benefit to the public of having a polluting activity curtailed.

These two panels contain an important message. In two sets of circumstances, a policy can have identical transfer effects but quite different efficiency effects.

FIGURE 1 Transfers the same, efficiency effects different.

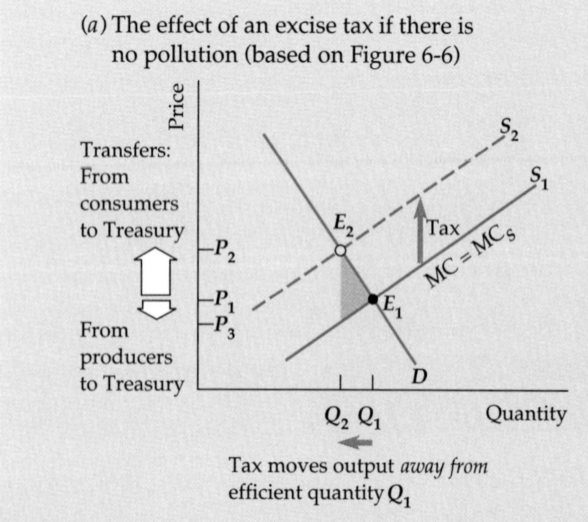

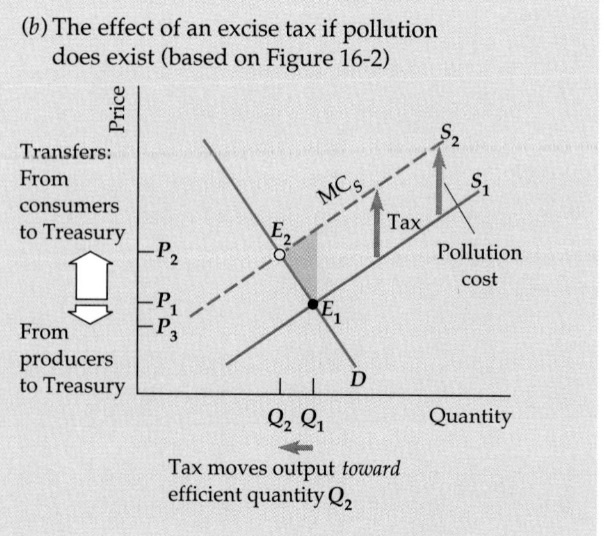

THE PROBLEM OF MONOPOLY

Figure 2 illustrates two ways to increase monopoly output and thus efficiency. In panel *a*, the monopoly is regulated, with a price ceiling set at P_2 where marginal cost intersects demand (Figure 12-7). This forces the monopoly down its demand curve from its initial equilibrium E_1 to E_2. Its output is therefore increased from Q_1 to the efficient quantity Q_2. The result is the blue efficiency gain. The reduced price causes a transfer from the monopoly to consumers shown by the white arrow.

In panel *b*, exactly the same efficiency gain is achieved by allowing the monopoly complete pricing freedom—including the freedom to charge different prices on different units. Suppose the monopoly is able to divide up its market and thus engage in price discrimination, just like the monopolist in Figure 12-9. However, where that earlier dentist monopolist could divide the market into just two segments and thus quote only two prices, suppose that this present monopoly is in a sufficiently strong position to quote a different price *on each unit sold*. In other words, in dealing with the very first buyer, this monopoly refuses to sell even one unit unless it receives the maximum price that this buyer is prepared to pay, namely, the thin arrow *a*. The monopoly then turns to the next buyer and similarly extracts *b*, the maximum price that the second purchaser is willing to pay. Thus the monopoly continues to work its way down its demand curve, exercising the ultimate degree of market power by squeezing every last nickel from every buyer along the way. Thus it extracts the entire amount of consumer surplus from buyers. Moreover, by pricing each unit all the way up to its demand curve, the monopoly converts its demand curve into a marginal revenue curve. For example, price *b* on the monopoly's demand curve is also a point on its marginal revenue curve because its additional revenue from selling the second unit is *b*.

Such a monopoly will not stop at E_1, since its marginal revenue Q_1E_1 is still greater than its marginal cost Q_1W. Instead, it will move all the way to *F*, where its marginal cost MC does equal its marginal revenue *D*. Thus in panel *b* the monopoly increases its output from Q_1 to Q_2, the same efficient quantity shown in panel *a*. Hence, there is exactly the same blue gain in efficiency in the two panels.

However, the transfers are different. In panel *a*, consumers gain and the monopolist loses. In panel *b*, the monopolist gains at consumers' expense; this transfer, shown by the white arrow, is the average of the price increases which the monopoly is now charging its original customers.

Panel *b* also illustrates why monopoly profit may be a poor measure of how much monopoly reduces efficiency. Price discrimination increases the monopoly's profit in panel *b*; but this *increases* rather than decreases efficiency.

To sum up: Any economic policy can have both a transfer and an efficiency effect. If only one of these is examined, part of the total picture will be missed. For example, if we were to look only at the transfer effects of the two policies in Figure 1, we would conclude that there was no difference between the two. However, we would miss their different effects on efficiency. Or, if we were to look only at the efficiency effects of the two policies in Figure 2, we would conclude that they were the same. But we would miss their completely different transfer effects.

FIGURE 2 Efficiency effects the same, transfers different.

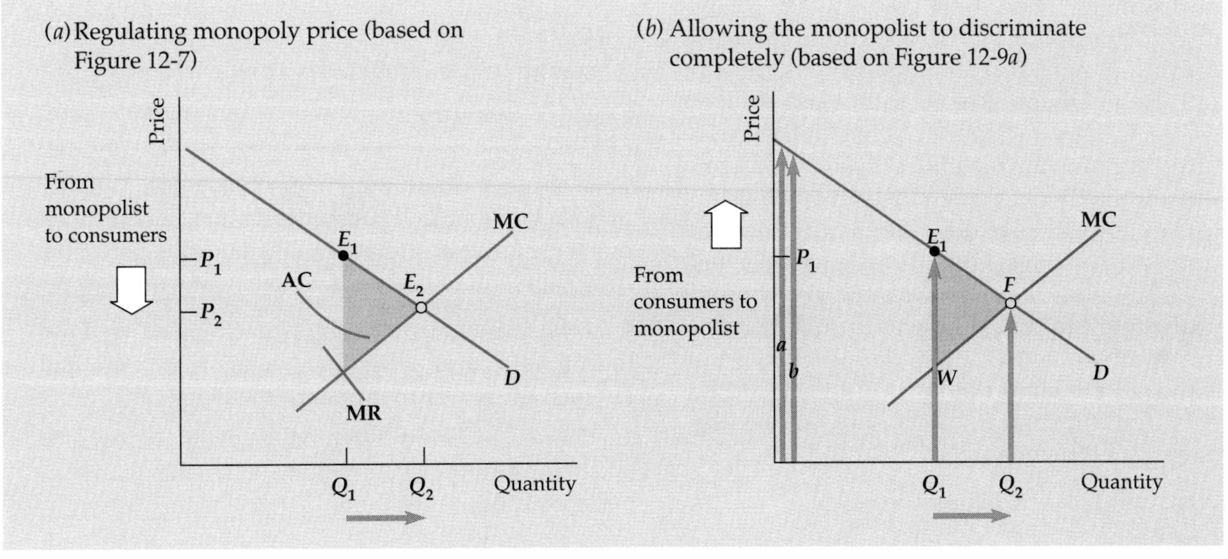

CHAPTER 21
WAGES IN A PERFECTLY COMPETITIVE ECONOMY

In a thriving town the people who have great . . . [capital] to employ, frequently cannot get the number of workmen they want, and therefore bid against one another in order to get as many as they can which raises the wages of labor, and lowers the profits of [capital].

ADAM SMITH, *WEALTH OF NATIONS*

The wage rate is the price of labor, and the market for labor is somewhat similar to the market for a good, such as wheat or machinery. Of course, these two markets are far from being completely the same. Labor is not just a commodity; labor involves people, which makes a big difference. For example, if manufacturers wish to abuse their machines, that is pretty much their own business; the cost will come when the machines wear out quickly, and no case can be made for government intervention. This is not so in the labor market. If an employer abuses workers by putting them in jobs where there are major health risks, government intervention to set standards *is* justified. As another example, some business executives have peculiar quirks about their products. In the early days of the automobile, Henry Ford's attitude was, "You can have any color of car you want—so long as it is black." No question of public policy arose; Ford paid for his views with lost sales when competitors were willing to give buyers their choice of colors. In contrast, personal quirks in the market for labor can be pernicious. If an employer just doesn't like some racial groups, the government may reasonably intervene to enforce nondiscrimination. Machines have no rights, but workers do.

Although the labor market is different in these respects from other markets, it may still be analyzed in much the same way.

- What affects labor demand?
- What affects labor supply?
- When is a free labor market efficient, and when is it not? (An economy cannot be efficient overall, unless it has both efficient product markets—as explained in Chapter 11—and efficient markets for labor and other factors.)
- Can the government intervene in the labor market to transfer income to labor, just as it sometimes intervenes in a product market to transfer income from one group to another?
- When the government does intervene, what effect does its intervention have on efficiency?

A PERFECTLY COMPETITIVE LABOR MARKET

This chapter deals with a perfectly competitive market for labor in a specific industry. Such a labor market has characteristics similar to a perfectly competitive market for a product:

1. There are so many buyers of labor service (employers) and sellers (workers) that none has any market power to influence the wage rate.

2. Labor is standardized. All workers are equally skillful and equally productive in the industry being studied.

3. Workers are mobile. They are not prevented from moving from one job to another.

Because labor markets are typically more complicated than this, each of these simplifying assumptions will eventually be relaxed. The next chapter relaxes the first assumption—that nobody has the market power to influence the wage rate. What happens when workers form a labor union in order to acquire market power and raise wages? Or when employers have market power and are therefore able to keep wages down? Chapter 23 relaxes the second assumption—that all workers are equally productive. What happens to wage patterns when some workers are better educated or more skillful than others? Finally, Chapter 24 relaxes the third assumption that labor is mobile. What happens when employers prevent minorities from taking certain jobs and limit them instead to low-productivity, low-income jobs?

The initial task in this chapter is to describe a perfectly competitive market in which all three assumptions do hold. To do so, first consider the question: What determines the demand for labor? Although the main focus of this chapter is on the labor market in a specific *industry* (such as furniture), let's first set the stage by examining the labor demand by a single *firm*—an individual producer of furniture.

THE DEMAND FOR LABOR

In the United States, the **real wage rate per hour** is now about six times as high as in 1900. It has increased because of rising labor productivity.

> The *real wage rate* is the nominal (or dollar) wage rate adjusted for inflation. The statement that the real wage is six times as high now as in 1900 means that the hourly wage will now buy six times as many goods and services as it did in 1900.

To describe the concept of labor productivity more precisely and to examine its central role in determining the demand for labor, consider the firm in Table 21-1 with a given stock of plant and machinery.

THE VALUE OF THE MARGINAL PRODUCT OF LABOR

The first two columns of Table 21-1 illustrate how this firm can increase its physical output (col. 2) by hiring more labor (col. 1).[1] In column 3, the **marginal physical product of labor** is the increase in total product in column 2 as each additional worker is hired. For example, hiring the second worker increases output from 5 to 12 units in column 2. Thus the marginal physical product of that second worker is 7 units, shown in column 3.

> *The marginal physical product (MPP) of labor* is the additional number of units of output a firm can produce because it has one more unit of labor.

The firm is even more interested in how its revenue increases as it hires each additional worker. This is called its **marginal revenue product of labor.**

> *The marginal revenue product (MRP) of labor* is the amount the firm's revenue increases because it has one more unit of labor.

The marginal revenue product for the firm in Table 21-1 is calculated in the last column, on the assumption that this firm is selling its output in a perfectly competitive market in which it cannot influence price. Specifically, the price of its output remains $20 per unit in column 4 no matter how many units it sells. In this case, the additional revenue from hiring the second worker is $140—that is, the seven additional units that the second worker produces times the $20 price of each unit. Observe that, in this example, each marginal revenue product in the last column is the marginal physical product in column 3 times the $20 price—that is, it is the **value of the marginal product of labor.**

[1]These figures are taken from the last row of the firm's production function in Table 9-1 on p. 136.

In this example and throughout this chapter, we assume for simplicity that labor is the only variable input. In practice, a firm generally uses other variable inputs too—for example, parts, electricity and heating.

Value of the marginal product (VMP) = marginal physical product x product price.

If the firm's output is sold in a perfectly competitive market,

VMP = marginal revenue product

To repeat: As long as perfect competition exists in the product market with product price being constant—as assumed here—the firm's marginal revenue product is the same as the value of its marginal product. However, if the product is sold in an imperfect market, with the prices in column 4 consequently changing rather than being constant, then MRP and VMP are not the same. (An example is given in Problem 21-3.)

How many units of labor will the firm hire? To answer this question, first take the marginal revenue product figures in the last column of Table 21-1 and graph them as the heavy line in Figure 21-1. If the daily wage paid to each worker is the $60 shown by the red line, this firm will stop hiring when it has employed four workers. (The fifth won't be hired because that worker would provide only $40 of additional revenue but would be paid a wage of $60.) Note that, in deciding how much labor to hire, the firm uses a familiar guideline. It hires labor up to the point where its marginal benefit (the marginal revenue product of labor) is equal to its marginal cost (the wage rate).

In a perfectly competitive labor market, the profit-maximizing firm hires labor to the point where the marginal revenue product (MRP) of labor equals the wage rate (*W*), that is, where

$$MRP = W \qquad (21\text{-}1)$$

As we have seen, MRP = VMP when the firm sells its output in a perfectly competitive market, as assumed here. In this case, conclusion (21-1) can be restated:

If its labor market *and* output market are perfectly competitive, the profit-maximizing firm will hire labor to the point where the value of the marginal product (VMP) equals the wage rate (*W*), that is, where

$$VMP = W \qquad (21\text{-}2)$$

TABLE 21-1 Marginal Physical Product, Marginal Revenue Product, and Value of the Marginal Product of Labor†

(1) *Number of Workers*	(2) *Total Physical Product*	(3) *Marginal Physical Product, MPP (change in column 2 because one more worker is hired)*	(4) *Price per Unit of Product*	(5) *Marginal Revenue Product, MRP Also VMP, the value of the marginal product, if output sold in perfect competition* (5) = (3) × (4)
0	0			
1	5	5	$20	$100
2	12	7	$20	$140
3	18	6	$20	$120
4	21	3	$20	$ 60
5	23	2	$20	$ 40

In this hypothetical example, marginal physical product falls, provided that more than two workers are hired (col. 3). Thus beyond the second worker there are diminishing returns to labor.

†Shown for a hypothetical firm with a given capital stock and selling in a competitive market at a constant price.

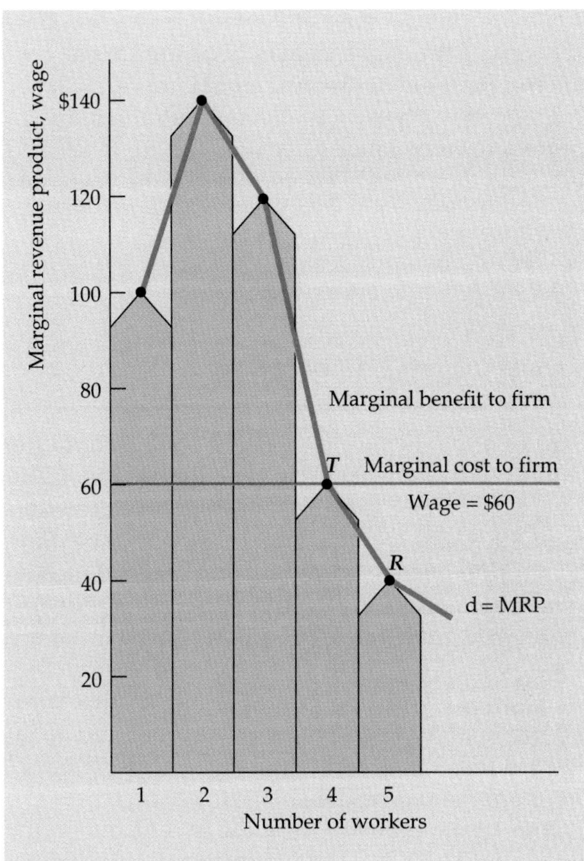

FIGURE 21-1 A firm's demand for labor is the marginal revenue product of labor (col. 5 of Table 21-1).

The points on the MRP curve represent points on the firm's demand curve. For example, point *T* on the MRP curve is also on the demand curve because at a wage rate of $60 the firm hires four workers.

What is true of labor is also true of any other factor.

If all factor and output markets are perfectly competitive, the profit-maximizing firm hires each factor of production to the point where the value of its marginal product (VMP) equals the price (or wage) of the factor. (21-3)

THE DEMAND CURVE FOR LABOR

The next question is: What is the firm's **demand curve for labor?** The answer is, its marginal revenue product curve. To see why, note that point *T* on the firm's MRP curve is also a point on its demand curve (since, at a $60 wage, the firm hires four workers). Similarly, other points such as *R* on this MRP curve are also points on the firm's demand curve. (At a $40 wage, the firm would hire five workers.) With points on the MRP curve representing points on the labor demand curve, the two curves coincide. Accordingly, the MRP curve in Figure 21-1 is labeled the demand curve for labor *d*.

A set of arrows, such as those shown in Figure 21-1, can be visualized as being enclosed beneath the demand curve for labor. Each arrow shows the marginal benefit to the firm that hires another worker—that is, the marginal revenue product.

Finally, you should now work through Problem 21-1 to see how the firm's income is divided between the wages it pays to labor and the amount it has left over to pay interest, profit, and rent to other factors of production. This will be a useful introduction to our discussion later in this chapter of how income is divided.

WHAT CAUSES A SHIFT IN THE DEMAND FOR LABOR?

Another way of asking this question is: What causes a shift in the marginal revenue product schedule in column 5 of Table 21-1? There are two reasons. First, labor may become more productive, that is, the marginal physical product of labor in column 3 may increase. Second, there may be a change in the price of the firm's output in column 4. For example, if this price rises from $20 to $30, all the marginal revenue product figures in column 5 will correspondingly rise, causing the demand for labor to shift upward to d_2 in Figure 21-2. Examples of such a shift in demand include the increased demand for carpenters resulting from an increase in the demand for—and price of—houses, and the increased demand for farm labor following an increase in the price of wheat. Both of these examples illustrate the **derived demand** for labor. Labor is demanded, not for its own sake directly, but for the goods and services it produces.

Derived demand exists when a good or service is demanded because of its usefulness in producing some other good or service. Thus, there is a derived demand for labor to produce cars and for land to grow wheat.

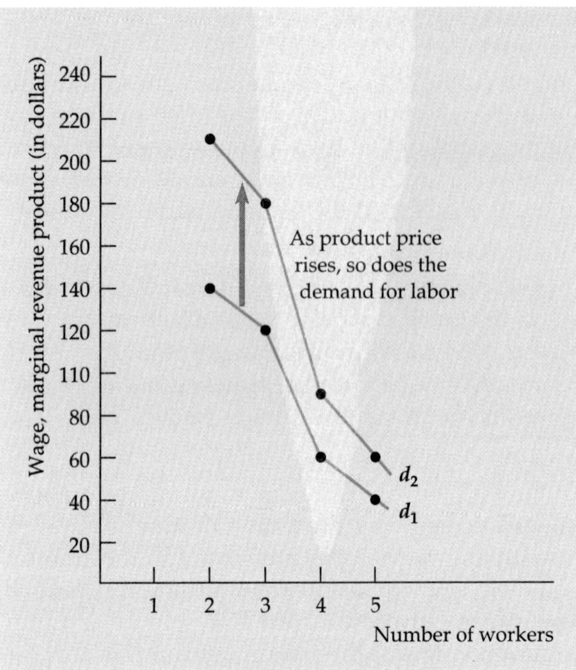

FIGURE 21-2 The firm's derived demand for labor.

d_1 is the marginal revenue product of labor when product price is $20. (It is calculated in col. 5 of Table 21-1 and has already appeared as d in Fig. 21-1.) d_2 is the marginal revenue product of labor if product price rises to $30. (This is a recalculation of col. 5 in Table 21-1, with $30 replacing $20 in col. 4.)

THE LABOR MARKET FOR AN INDUSTRY

Now let us turn from the demand for labor by a firm (*d*) to the demand for labor by an industry (*D*). In a perfectly competitive economy, the industry's demand for labor is the horizontal sum of the demands by the individual firms[2] in somewhat the same way that the market demand for a good (Fig. 7-1) is the sum of the demands of individual consumers. Such an industry demand curve for labor *D* is shown in Figure 21-3, along with the industry supply curve of labor *S*, which will be described later. Together, *S* and *D* determine *W*, the wage rate for the industry.

[2]In fact, the industry's demand for labor is not exactly the horizontal sum of the demands by the individual firms. To see why, note that if the wage rate falls, each firm hires more workers, as shown by the individual labor demand curves. This increased hiring results in increased industry output, which depresses the price of that output. In turn, this reduced output price shifts the labor demand curve of each individual firm. (Remember, each of these curves is drawn on the assumption that the output price does not change.)

In short, the individual demand curves that are being summed do not remain fixed. Because this problem is ignored, the statements made from now on will be only approximations. (There are many other such complications in economics.)

THE DEMAND FOR LABOR AND THE DIVISION OF INCOME

A major topic in the rest of this book is how the nation's income is divided or "distributed." The marginal revenue product of labor curve (the demand for labor) can throw light on this issue. Specifically, the income going to labor and the income going to other factors of production in an industry can be read from the MRP curve shown in Figure 21-4.

To see how, suppose equilibrium in this labor market is at *E*, with wage *W* (reproduced from Figure 21-3). What is the industry's total revenue? The employment of the first worker increases the revenue of the industry by *a*, the first arrow on the left in Figure 21-4. That is, the marginal revenue

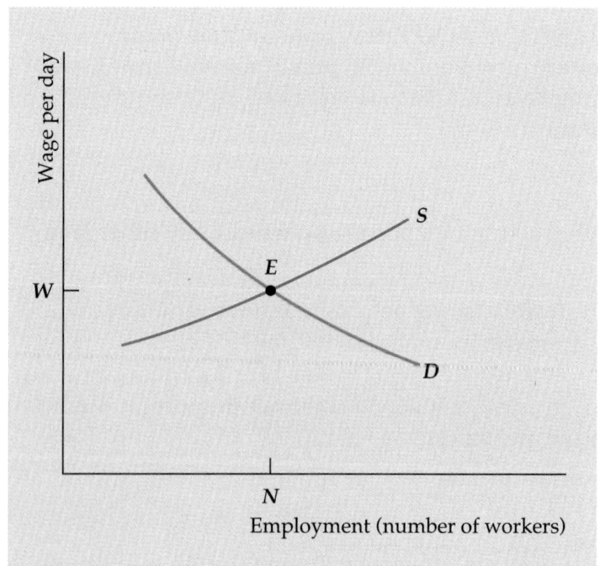

FIGURE 21-3 Determination of an industry's wage rate.

In a perfectly competitive labor market, the wage rate *W* is determined by the intersection of the demand and supply curves for labor.

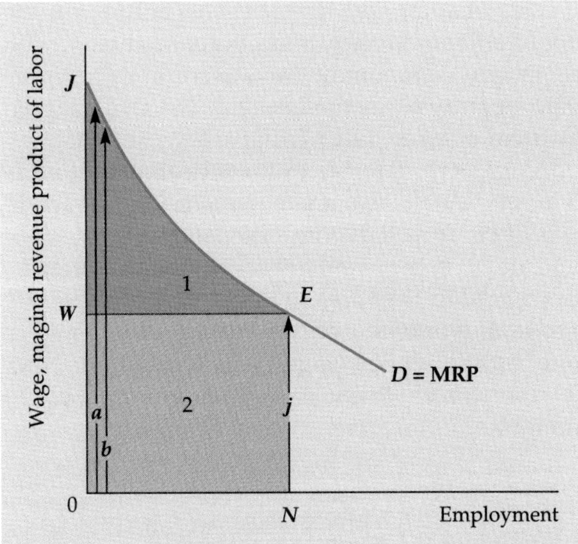

FIGURE 21-4 An industry's demand curve for labor and the distribution of income.

Total income earned by all factors of production is area 1 + 2. Of this, area 2 is paid to labor and area 1 goes to other factors of production.

product of the first worker is *a*. The second worker adds *b*, and so on to the last worker, who adds *j*. The total revenue of the industry is the sum of all these arrows—that is, shaded areas 1 + 2.

What part of this total revenue goes to labor? The answer is area 2, since wage *W* is paid to the *N* workers employed. Thus, if the labor market is competitive, the industry's revenue is distributed as follows:

Labor receives income equal to the wage rate times the number of workers employed. This labor income is the rectangle to the southwest of the equilibrium point on the demand curve for labor.

After labor is paid area 2, area 1 remains. This is what is left for other factors of production: interest and profit to capital, rent to land, and so on. Thus:

After labor is paid, all other factors of production together receive the triangular area enclosed to the northwest of the equilibrium point on the demand curve for labor.

AN INDUSTRY'S SUPPLY OF LABOR IN A PERFECTLY COMPETITIVE ECONOMY

The labor supply for an industry, first shown in Figure 21-3, is examined in more detail in Figure 21-5. As the wage rate rises from W_1 to W_2, the labor supplied to this industry increases from N_1 to N_2; workers are drawn in from other industries by this increasingly attractive wage rate. As a specific example, the labor supply curve for this industry—say, the furniture industry—tells us that when the wage rate rises to W_3, worker *h* is drawn into this industry.

In order to persuade this worker to move, the wage rate W_3 must be high enough to cover the individual's **transfer price.** Specifically, the wage must be high enough to compensate the worker for

1. The wage paid in the industry from which the worker is moving, say, the textile industry.
2. Moving costs, both financial and psychological.
3. Differences in the pleasantness of working conditions in the new industry (furniture) compared to the old industry (textiles).

Item 2—moving costs—may be substantial. For example, those who have to move their families to another state may agree with Benjamin Franklin

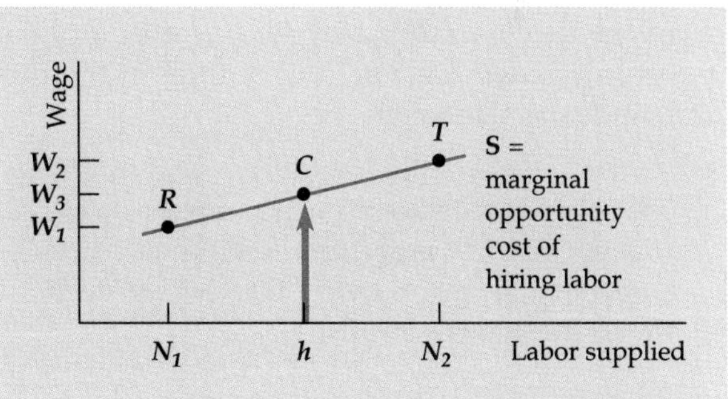

FIGURE 21-5 Supply of labor for the furniture industry.

The upward sloping supply curve for labor shows how an increase in the wage paid by the furniture industry increases the number of workers seeking jobs there. In a perfectly competitive economy, the height of the supply curve at any point like C reflects the opportunity cost of hiring another worker *h* in the furniture industry—that is, the value of the worker's marginal product in the previous job in the textile industry. Thus the supply curve for labor reflects the opportunity cost of hiring one more worker, just as the supply curve for a product reflects the cost of producing one more unit of output.

that "Three moves is as bad as a fire." On the other hand, moving costs may be zero for the worker who is moving from a textile factory to take a job at a furniture factory next door. Item 3—differences in working conditions—may be either positive or negative. If the new job in furniture is not as pleasant as the old job in textiles, a higher wage will be needed to induce the worker to move. If, on the other hand, the new job in furniture is more pleasant, the worker may be willing to come for a lower wage than in the old textile job.

The ***transfer price*** necessary to induce a worker to move includes not only the worker's previous wage rate, but also moving costs and differences in working conditions.

Items 2 and 3 will be taken into account later. For the moment, we consider only the first item, which is usually the most important. The wage in the textile industry which the worker is leaving was also the value of the worker's marginal product there. (Remember from conclusion 21-2 that, in the perfectly competitive economy we are studying, the wage in *any* industry is equal to the value of the worker's marginal product there.) The arrow at *h* represents the value of this worker's output in the alternative activity of producing textiles. It is what society loses when this worker leaves the textile industry. In other words, it is the **opportunity cost** of having this worker in the furniture industry. Therefore:

The height of an industry's supply curve for labor will, in a perfectly competitive economy, measure the opportunity cost to society of having another worker hired in this industry.

This conclusion leads us to the appropriate way to view a supply curve for labor:

A labor supply curve for any industry *A* should be visualized with a whole set of arrows beneath it, with each representing the value of the marginal product of that worker in alternative industry *B*. Thus each arrow represents the opportunity cost of labor in industry *A*.

This chapter and the next concentrate on the supply of labor facing an individual industry, with the supply of labor for the economy as a whole being dealt with in the appendix to this chapter. However, note in passing that when the economy-wide supply of labor is examined, the question is no longer "As the wage rate rises, how many workers will be attracted from other industries?" since there are no "other industries." Instead, other questions come to the fore, such as "If the wage rate rises, will workers sacrifice some leisure to work more? Will a higher wage induce people to enter the labor force? Will it encourage more people to immigrate?"

THE INVISIBLE HAND IN A PERFECTLY COMPETITIVE ECONOMY

Does Adam Smith's invisible hand work in factor markets as it did in product markets? In a perfectly competitive economy, will market prices result in an efficient allocation of labor?

Panel *a* in Figure 21-6 illustrates the labor market for an industry in a perfectly competitive economy. The quantity of employment is N_1 and the wage is W_1. This is efficient because it satisfies the fundamental criterion. For any activity—in this case, hiring labor—the *marginal benefit to society* must equal the *marginal cost to society*. The two are equal in panel *a* because demand reflects the marginal benefit of labor (that is, the value of its marginal product in this industry), whereas supply reflects labor's marginal cost (that is, the value of its marginal product elsewhere). The efficiency of this result is perhaps most clearly seen by showing in panels *b* and *c* that any other solution is inefficient.

For example, consider the industry in panel *b* where, for some reason, employment is greater than N_1. Specifically, suppose it is N_2. Let *f* represent one of the units of "excess employment." The benefit from employing this worker here is the value of this worker's marginal product (which hereafter will be abbreviated to "marginal productivity"). This is shown graphically as the blue arrow under the labor demand curve. However, the cost of employing this worker is this worker's marginal productivity in an alternative activity, shown by the height of the supply curve, that is,

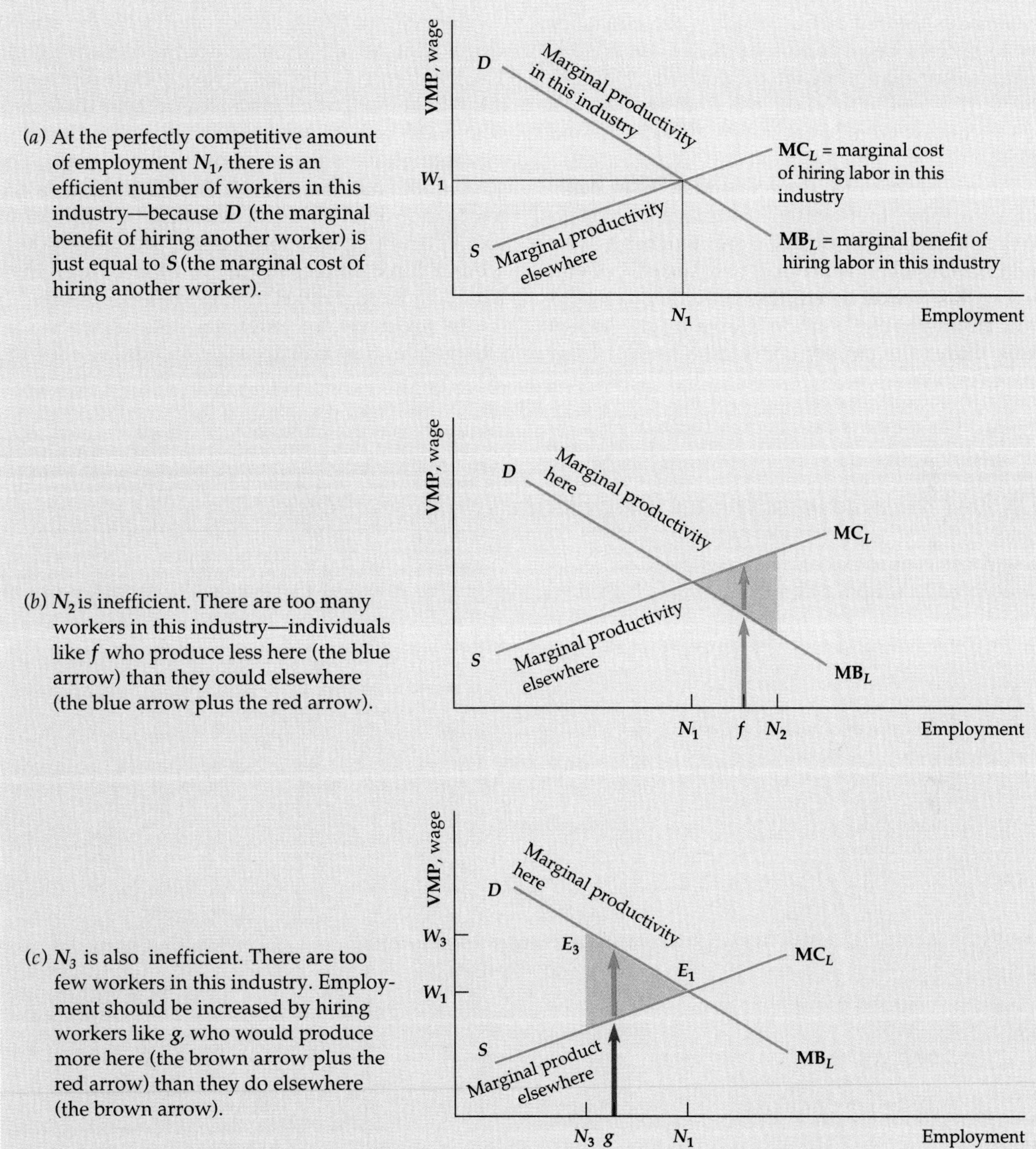

FIGURE 21-6 Why the labor market is efficient in a perfectly competitive economy.

the blue arrow plus the red arrow above it. The difference is the red arrow, which is the efficiency loss to society because this worker is in this industry rather than a higher productivity job elsewhere. The total efficiency loss to society for all such excess workers in the range N_1N_2 is the red triangle.

On the other hand, at employment N_3 in panel *c*, there are too few workers in this industry. To confirm this point, consider one worker *g* who might be employed here but is not. The cost of employing this worker here is the worker's productivity in an alternative activity, shown by the brown arrow under the supply curve. The benefit from employing this worker here is this individual's productivity in this industry, shown by the brown arrow plus the red arrow under the demand curve. The difference is the red arrow, which represents this worker's greater productivity here than elsewhere; this greater productivity here is lost because this individual is not employed here. Finally, the sum of all such losses over the range N_3N_1 is the red triangle which shows the total efficiency loss to society. In brief, this loss occurs because workers are not hired in this industry, even though they would be more productive here than elsewhere.

In summary, an efficiency loss occurs if employment in this industry is greater or less than the

BOX 21–1 *Does an Invisible Hand Bring Efficiency to the Labor Market?*

The earlier analysis of the product market in Figure 11-2 is now extended to a factor market in Figure 21-7. If all individual employers and employees make decisions that are in their own self-interest, the result will be efficient, as long as

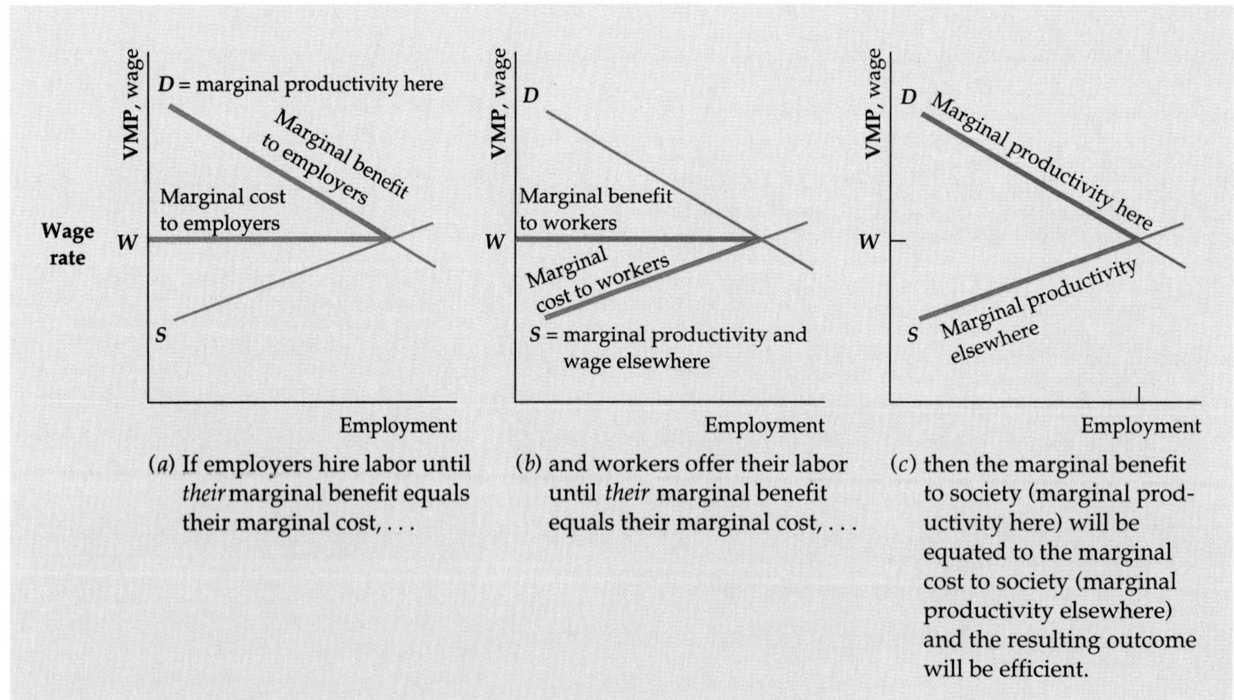

FIGURE 21-7 How the pursuit of private benefit in a perfectly competitive economy results in the efficient employment of labor. (Compare with Fig. 11-2.)

perfectly competitive quantity N_1 in panel *a*. (Further detail on this point is provided in Box 21-1.) This analysis confirms the clear analogy between the labor market, where perfect competition generates an efficient level of employment in each industry, and the product market in Chapter 11, where perfect competition generates efficient output.

SOME COMPLICATIONS

As always, we can make no claim that perfect competition necessarily results in the best of all possible worlds. It satisfies only one of society's important objectives: the elimination of deadweight inefficiency. However, it does not address the question: How fair is the resulting distribution of income between labor and other factors of production? This important and difficult question is left to Chapter 24.

Moreover, in practice there may be a number of departures from the very simple, perfectly competitive model described here. For example, there may be external spillover costs or benefits. Externalities may arise in a labor market just as in a product market. To illustrate, the public in a large city may receive an external benefit when musicians are

perfect competition prevails throughout the economy. In panel *a*, employers in this industry maximize their profit by hiring labor up to the point where their marginal benefit from doing so (the marginal productivity of labor in this industry) is equal to their marginal cost of hiring labor—that is, the wage they have to pay. In panel *b*, workers pursue *their* self-interest by offering their labor services up to the point where their marginal benefit (the wage they can earn here) is equal to their marginal cost of offering their services—that is, the wage they could earn elsewhere (their opportunity cost). The result in panel *c* is an efficient one for society, made possible by the key role played by a competitive wage rate. It is the employers' reaction to this wage in panel *a* and the workers' reaction to this same wage in panel *b* that ensure in panel *c* that the marginal productivity of labor will be the same in this industry and elsewhere. Therefore the nation's output cannot be increased by shifting labor either into or out of this industry. In short, as long as no single individual or firm on either side of the market can influence W, it is the key in orchestrating the actions of employers and employees in an efficient way.

In Figure 21-7, it has been assumed that the height of the supply curve for labor reflects the marginal productivity of labor in other industries. That is, it reflects only item 1 cited earlier, the wage paid in the job the worker is leaving. But what about items 2 and 3 which also determine the height of the supply curve; namely, the costs of moving and the pleasantness of the job? Do they upset the conclusion that a competitive market is efficient? The answer is no, because if a worker has to relocate in another city in order to get a new job, resources must be used in moving the worker's furniture and other possessions. From the point of view of society, it is not efficient for the worker to move unless that individual's marginal productivity (and wage) in the new industry is sufficiently higher to cover the costs of the move. But it must be; otherwise the worker won't move. Accordingly, the operation of the market leads to an efficient result.

Likewise, complication 3 does not cause inefficiency. Suppose that the new job is more attractive, and therefore the worker moves even though the wage and marginal productivity in the new job are somewhat less than in the old. Because this worker is producing less here, this seems to be an undesirable move. But that is not so. For economic welfare, we should count more than the goods and services produced. It is also important for people to enjoy their jobs. If the pleasantness of the new job at least compensates for the worker's lower wage, no loss of efficiency occurs. And this will be the case: The pleasantness of the new job must compensate for the lower wage—otherwise the worker won't move. Once again, the efficiency of a perfectly competitive market is confirmed.

hired for the local symphony orchestra, because musicians may make an indirect contribution to the cultural life of the community merely by living there—in addition, of course, to the direct benefit they provide whenever they play in a concert. This external benefit will mean that a free, perfectly competitive market will result in "too little hiring of musicians"—just as external benefits lead to too little production of a good.

Now consider how the labor market may depart from the competitive outcome if the government imposes a minimum wage.

THE MINIMUM WAGE

The Fair Labor Standards Act of 1938 set a minimum wage of 25 cents an hour, covering 43% of the nonagricultural labor force. By early 1989, the minimum wage had been increased 13 times, and its coverage more than doubled. Some workers do not receive the minimum wage because their industries are still not included; even in those that are, some firms do not comply with this law, because there are inadequate penalties for breaking it. By 1989, the minimum wage had become a heated issue because it had not been raised since 1981 and had therefore been eroded by inflation. It was still \$3.35 an hour, even though the average U.S. wage had increased by more than 32%, from \$7.25 to \$9.60. Congress wanted the rate raised to \$4.55 to compensate for inflation. President Bush opposed any increase above \$4.25.

To analyze the minimum wage in the United States where some industries are covered by it and some are not, consider two cases. (1) Suppose the minimum wage is applied to only one industry; and (2) suppose it is applied to all industries. The U.S. economy is between these two polar cases.

CASE 1: ONLY ONE INDUSTRY IS COVERED BY THE MINIMUM WAGE.

This case can be described in panel *c* of Figure 21-6. Suppose that there is initially a perfectly competitive, free-market wage of W_1, where supply equals demand for labor. Then the government imposes a minimum wage W_3, above W_1. Because of the higher wage, employers hire fewer workers. Equilibrium moves back up the demand curve from E_1 to E_3, with the number of workers employed falling from N_1 to N_3. As a result, there is the red efficiency loss because too few workers are hired in this industry.

Why then does the government introduce this policy? The answer is to provide a fairer, equitable wage and thus help to solve the poverty problem. In fact, this policy can indeed be expected to redistribute income—but not necessarily in the way intended, since some workers lose while others gain. The winners are the N_3 workers who still have a job in this industry and who enjoy a wage increase from W_1 to W_3. The losers are the N_3N_1 workers who lose their jobs in this industry or are not hired in the first place. They are left in lower productivity jobs paying lower wages elsewhere.

CASE 2: ALL INDUSTRIES ARE COVERED BY THE MINIMUM WAGE.

The result in this case is the same in many respects. The winners are those who retain their jobs, whereas the losers are those who do not. There is now one important difference, however. Those who lose their jobs do not get jobs elsewhere. Because the whole economy is covered, there are no other jobs for them to get. Because they become unemployed, they lose far more than they do in case 1. Moreover, the overall efficiency loss to the economy is greater because their lost output is no longer partially offset by their output in other, lower productivity jobs. They don't get another job. The result is a large gap between the income of those who still have a job (whose wage has increased) and those who no longer have a job (whose wage has disappeared).

Since much, but not all, of U.S. employment is subject to the minimum wage, the world in which we live lies somewhere between case 1 and case 2. It is likely that some workers who lose their jobs because of a minimum wage will get lower productivity jobs elsewhere, but some will not. For those who obtain jobs elsewhere, there is an efficiency loss because they produce less. For those who remain unemployed, there is an even greater efficiency loss because they produce nothing.

THE MINIMUM WAGE AND TEENAGE UNEMPLOYMENT

Who are the workers who lose their jobs? The answer is often teenagers. Because they lack work experience and seniority, they tend to be the "last hired, first fired." Consequently, their unemployment rate is more than double the national average. *Minority* teenagers get the worst of both worlds; their unemployment rate is more than four times the national average. The University of Michigan's Charles Brown estimates that an increase in the minimum wage to $4.55 would result in 150,000 fewer jobs for teenagers over three years, with black teenagers suffering most.

One way to reduce the teenage unemployment problem is to institute a "two-tiered system," with a lower minimum wage for teenagers than for adults. Numerous such proposals have come before Congress. Indeed, since 1961 employers in higher education, retailing, and other services have been allowed to pay students 15% less than the minimum wage for part-time or summer work.[3] In 1989, President Bush proposed a lower minimum wage for new workers—many of whom are teenagers—during a six-month training period. Such proposals for a two-tiered minimum wage have been opposed by labor unions on the grounds that they are not fair. Employers might lay off adults with families to support in order to hire teenagers at a lower wage.

THE MINIMUM WAGE: CONCLUDING OBSERVATIONS

The minimum wage can affect not only the wage of the unskilled, but it can also have a "ripple effect" in raising the wage of skilled workers who are above the minimum. The reason is that employers have sometimes regarded it as only fair to maintain a gap between the two wage levels, and workers have tried hard to maintain this gap by bargaining for increases in skilled wages whenever the minimum wage has been increased.

On the other hand, there are several reasons for believing that the minimum wage is less important than is often supposed.

1. *It has not been very effective in reducing inequality.* The reason is that it has raised the income, not just of the working poor, but of the non-poor as well. One estimate indicates that less than 20% of the benefits from an increased minimum wage would go to households living below the poverty line for a family of four. At the same time, over 60% of the benefits would go to households with incomes at least double the poverty level. (In many such cases, it would be teenage children still holding jobs who would benefit.)

2. *The minimum wage may be less damaging to efficiency than Figure 21-6c suggests.* It is true that, in perfect competition, the minimum wage does lead to the efficiency loss shown in that diagram. However, in the imperfectly competitive labor markets described in the next chapter, it may lead to an efficiency gain.

3. *There are fewer clear winners and clear losers than the standard analysis implies.* It is frequently difficult to distinguish between the winners who get the minimum wage jobs and the losers who do not. The reason is that, in minimum wage jobs, there is a high turnover rate (according to one estimate, over 12% *per month*). Therefore workers share these jobs to some extent. Accordingly, many individuals are both part-time winners (when they have one of the minimum wage jobs) *and* part-time losers (when they do not). This means that the concern about clear losers who end up without any jobs at all is sometimes exaggerated. It also means that there are fewer clear winners. Moreover, even for a "winner" who still has a job and has gotten a wage increase, part of this increase may be an illusion if employers who have to pay the higher wage cover this additional cost by cutting back on other benefits to labor such as on-the-job training.

---

[3]The source for figures cited here, and for a description of a special minimum wage, is Albert Rees, "An Essay on Youth Joblessness," *Journal of Economic Literature,* June 1986, especially pp. 615 and 624. See also Charles Brown, "Minimum Wage Laws: Are they Overrated?" *Journal of Economic Perspectives,* Summer 1988.

KEY POINTS

1. In a perfectly competitive labor market, a firm will hire workers until the marginal revenue product (MRP) of labor equals the wage rate. Thus the demand for labor reflects MRP. If output markets are also perfectly competitive, MRP equals the value of the marginal product (VMP). Therefore the demand for labor also reflects VMP.

2. The demand for labor in an industry, say, textiles, may shift because of an increase in the price of textiles. Thus the demand for labor is "derived" from the demand for textiles. The demand for labor may also shift because labor becomes more productive.

3. The supply of labor for an industry reflects the opportunity cost of hiring more workers, which is their marginal productivity elsewhere (that is, the value of their marginal product in other industries). The supply of labor also depends on other factors, such as the pleasantness of the job and costs of moving.

4. Adam Smith's invisible hand works to allocate labor in the most efficient way in a perfectly competitive economy. If all market participants (employers and employees) pursue their individual economic gain, the result is an efficient solution for society as a whole.

5. If labor markets are perfectly competitive, the introduction of a minimum wage above the existing wage level will result in an efficiency loss. It will benefit workers who retain their jobs but hurt workers who become unemployed.

6. However, if labor markets are not perfectly competitive, then a minimum wage may result in an efficiency gain, rather than a loss, as the next chapter will demonstrate.

KEY CONCEPTS

real wage
marginal physical product of labor (MPP)
marginal revenue product of labor (MRP)
value of marginal product of labor (VMP)
demand for labor
derived demand
supply of labor
opportunity cost of labor
transfer price
labor market efficiency
minimum wage

PROBLEMS

21-1. In Figure 21-1 we concluded that, at a $60 wage, the firm hires four workers.

> **(a)** What, then, is its total revenue? (Use the data in Table 21-1.) What is its total wage bill? How much of its total revenue remains after its wages have been paid; that is, how much does the firm have left over for interest, rent, and profit for its other factors of production?
>
> **(b)** In that diagram, show the areas that represent (i) the firm's total revenue; (ii) the part of this revenue that it pays to labor; and (iii) the part that is left for other factors of production.

21-2. The curve in Figure 21-1 showing the firm's marginal revenue product is drawn on the assumption of a given $20 price for the firm's output. But now suppose that, because of decreased consumer demand for this output, its price falls to $15. Show graphically what happens to the firm's MRP curve. What happens to its demand for labor curve? Does the firm change its employment? If so, by how much? Is this a further illustration of how "producers dance to the consumers' tune"?

21-3. In this chapter, perfectly competitive labor and product markets have been assumed. To see why imperfect competition in product markets is important, return to Table 21-1, but now make the assumption that the firm has influence over its price. Specifically, assume that the figures reading down column 4 are $24, $23, $22, $21, and $20. Now, MRP in column 5 does not equal the value of the marginal product (VMP). Confirm this by calculating MRP and VMP.

21-4. Because of a special commonwealth association, Puerto Rico has many close economic ties with the United States. What do you think of the idea of Puerto Ricans introducing the U.S. minimum wage on their island? In answering this question keep this in mind: Because of low labor productivity and a rapidly growing labor supply, Puerto Ricans have historically had a wage rate substantially lower than in the continental United States.

Would such a common minimum wage result in a more severe unemployment problem in Puerto Rico or in the continental United States? In your view, should the Puerto Ricans have a minimum wage below the U.S. level? What do you think of the idea of setting a minimum wage in Puerto Rico low enough so that it will not cause any unemployment there? If it were set at this level, would it achieve the objective of raising wages?

21-5. Would a minimum wage be more likely to raise the total income of labor if the elasticity of demand for labor were low rather than high? Explain your answer.

21-6. "The wage rate acts as a screening device that determines where scarce labor will be employed and where it will not be." Illustrate this idea, using an argument parallel to the one used in Figure 11-5. Use the example of labor that is hired to build apartment buildings but is no longer hired to hoe field corn.

APPENDIX
THE ECONOMYWIDE SUPPLY OF LABOR

As a rough first approximation, the supply of labor for the economy as a whole—rather than for just one industry—is sometimes viewed as a vertical line, reflecting the given labor force in the whole economy. Because it is vertical, the quantity of labor that will be supplied is independent of the wage rate. However, there are two reasons why the supply curve may not be completely vertical after all. That is, there are two reasons why the total amount of labor supplied by the present population may change if the wage changes.

(a) The labor participation rate may change; that is, there may be a change in the proportion of the population in the labor market.

(b) There may be a change in the average number of hours worked by the existing labor force.

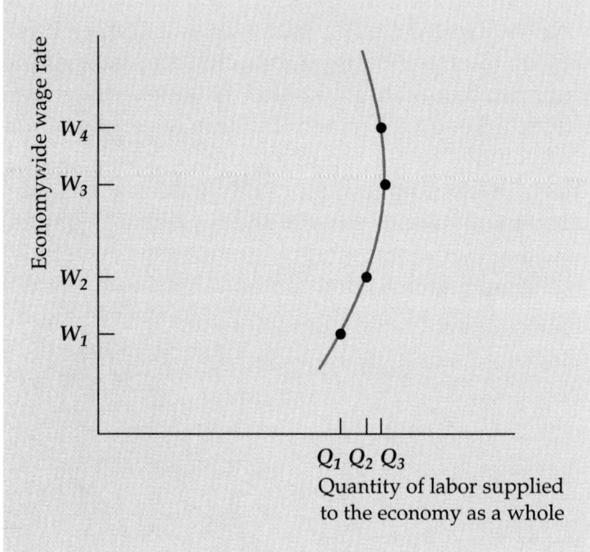

FIGURE 21-8 The supply of labor in the economy as a whole, rather than just in a single industry.

At low wage W_1, an increase in the wage to W_2 results in an increase in the quantity of labor supplied from Q_1 to Q_2. However, at some higher wage rate (W_3) workers achieve a high enough income level that they can afford to take part of any further increase in income in the form of leisure. Accordingly, they work less; the labor supply curve is backward-bending.

Although a wage increase is likely to change the quantity of labor supplied, it is not clear whether it will increase it or decrease it. This is because a wage increase exerts two conflicting pressures:

1. *The substitution effect.* Because the reward for work (the wage rate) has increased relative to the reward from leisure, people have an incentive to substitute, working more and taking less leisure.

2. *The income effect.* This effect works in the opposite direction. A higher wage means higher income and thus allows workers to acquire more of everything they want: not only more goods, but also more leisure. In acquiring more leisure, they work less. (The income and substitution effects were explained in the appendix to Chapter 7.)

Which of these two conflicting effects dominates? We cannot be sure. As Figure 21-8 is drawn, the two are exactly balanced at wage W_3, where the quantity of labor supplied is at a maximum. If the initial wage is lower than this, the substitution effect dominates. As the wage rate rises from, say, W_1 to W_2, people increase the amount they work from Q_1 to Q_2. On the other hand, at a wage above W_3, the income effect dominates. Workers have now reached a high enough wage that they can say: "Let's use any further increase not only to buy more goods, but also to buy more leisure." In other words, an increase in the wage rate induces them to work less. Specifically, if the wage rate rises from W_3 to W_4, they reduce the quantity of labor they supply. In this range, the labor supply curve is described as "backward bending."

CHAPTER 22
WAGES IN IMPERFECTLY COMPETITIVE LABOR MARKETS

You must offer the American working man bread and butter in the here and now, instead of pie in the sky in the sweet bye and bye.

THE PHILOSOPHY OF EARLY LABOR LEADER SAMUEL GOMPERS
(AS DESCRIBED BY CHARLES KILLINGWORTH)

Like Rodney Dangerfield, baseball players sometimes "don't get no respect." Ted Turner, owner of the Atlanta Braves, has been quoted as saying, "I don't understand why grown men play this game anyhow. They ought to be lawyers or garbage men. Games should be left for kids." By 1990, players could laugh about these comments all the way to the bank. It was no longer unusual for a star to get over $2 million a year. Twenty years before, things were different. Players got only a small fraction of their present-day salaries. This chapter will show why.

The broad objective of this chapter is to describe departures from perfect competition in labor markets. Specifically, it covers:

- Imperfect competition on the supply side of the labor market, when unions acquire the market power to bargain for a higher wage.
- Imperfect competition on the demand side, when employers acquire the market power to keep wages down.
- Imperfect competition on both sides of the market, in the special circumstances of bilateral monopoly.
- The effect of strikes and measures to prevent or resolve them.
- A review of why wage differences exist.

LABOR UNIONS: THE BENEFITS TO LABOR OF COLLECTIVE ACTION

A union is established so that workers—the suppliers of labor—can bargain with "one voice." They collectively negotiate for higher wages rather than take the wage rate as given. Once they form a union, the labor market is no longer perfectly competitive, because they exercise market power in order to influence price (their wage).

In addition to bargaining for higher wages, unions have other important roles as well, such as helping workers to maintain their stake in their jobs and providing them with a collective voice in setting the conditions of their employment.[1] With the backing of unions, workers are protected from arbitrary dismissal or changes in the "rules of the game" by management. Because of these assurances, workers get a stake in their jobs and are able to commit themselves to an occupation more completely than they could in an impersonal, perfectly competitive market with "no memory and no future."

[1]This chapter, in particular the discussion of labor's voice, draws heavily on Richard B. Freeman and James L. Medoff, *What Do Unions Do?* (New York: Basic Books, 1984).

COLLECTIVE BARGAINING

Workers in a union who speak with a collective voice overcome three disadvantages of standing alone: (1) A single worker may have difficulty even getting management to listen to a grievance, let alone negotiate to remove it. (2) Management may retaliate personally against an individual who is complaining, but it generally cannot against workers acting collectively. (3) Even if an individual could negotiate a change, it is unlikely to be worth the effort, because most of the benefits would go to other workers. In this sense, the resolution of a labor grievance is a public good; all workers benefit, regardless of who bargains for it. Therefore bargaining is undertaken collectively—by a union.

> ***Collective bargaining*** is any negotiation between a union and management over wages, fringe benefits, hiring policies, job security, or working conditions.

HOW UNIONS RAISE WAGES

In addition to raising wages by negotiating higher pay rates, unions may attempt to raise wages indirectly by negotiating other terms of employment. For example, unions may:

1. Negotiate a shorter work week and early retirement. Such changes reduce the supply of labor and thus put upward pressure on wages.

2. Negotiate with employers to hire only union members, and then limit union membership by imposing barriers to entry such as high initiation fees or long periods of apprenticeship. This approach also restricts the supply of labor and thus raises wage rates.

In such negotiations, a union may, of course, have other objectives than just raising wages. For example, a shorter work week may be desired for its own sake, and apprenticeship may be a way of screening bumbling amateurs out of dangerous occupations. Not surprisingly, motives are sometimes mixed. The charge has been made that the American Medical Association—the association of U.S. doctors—used to act like a union. Before its change in policy about 25 years ago, the association used its power to limit the number of medical schools and the number of students admitted to these schools. Although the stated reason for this tough policy was to improve the quality of medical service, it also restricted the supply of graduating doctors and thus increased the incomes of the members of the association.

OTHER OBJECTIVES OF UNIONS

Unions also try to negotiate reasonably pleasant physical conditions and establish **seniority rules** to protect those who have been on the job longest and who have the most to lose if they are discharged.

> ***Seniority rules*** typically ensure that those who have been longest on the job will be laid off last and rehired first.

Without seniority rules, older workers might be in a vulnerable position. Because of their declining productivity, they might be the first to be laid off.

Unions also seek to negotiate job security, sometimes even in preference to a wage increase. For example, in 1984 the United Auto Workers (UAW) successfully negotiated to get General Motors to agree to spend up to $1 billion to keep displaced workers on its payroll. Moreover, in its 1987 negotiations with Ford and GM, the UAW allowed the companies to relax some union work rules (and thereby introduce Japanese-style production innovations) in exchange for a guarantee that current workers would not lose their jobs for any reason except reduced car sales.

Protecting jobs is a way of introducing compassion into an often impersonal economic system. However, it may be far from the best way to do it, especially if it goes beyond ensuring jobs for those individuals who now have them, to ensuring that *their jobs will continue* even after they have retired or gone elsewhere. For example, when an industry gets long-term protection from imports, it is not just the workers at that time whose jobs are protected. The jobs themselves continue to exist as long as protection remains. When new people, perhaps now studying in high school, take these low-productivity jobs, the cost, in terms of reduced efficiency, can extend far into the future. (For more on the relation between compassion and efficiency, see Box 22-1.)

BOX 22–1 *The Conflicting Objectives of Compassion and Efficiency*

Two centuries ago, at the beginning of the Industrial Revolution in Britain, labor-saving machinery was introduced into the textile industry. Displaced workers in those days had much bleaker prospects than today: It was harder to find another job. Without a job, a worker's family faced severe malnutrition, or worse. Consequently, there were riots in which workers (the Luddites) broke into the factories and destroyed the new labor-saving machines. While recognizing their plight, we might ask: What if they had succeeded? What if labor-saving machinery had been banned and primitive handcrafting jobs guaranteed? If the Luddites and their heirs had been successful in thwarting technological change, wouldn't our situation today be very much like theirs two centuries ago? If so, what progress would we have made against the problem that concerned them most: poverty?

Although labor-saving machinery may create transitional unemployment, it creates far better jobs in the long run. When bulldozers are introduced, whole armies of workers with shovels lose their jobs. But in the long run, this is beneficial not only for society but also, in most cases, for the workers who initially lose their jobs. This is not only true of the ditchdiggers who get high-productivity and high-paying jobs driving the bulldozers. It is also true of other ditchdiggers who get high-productivity jobs in new, growing industries such as electronics and aircraft. These jobs exist because the introduction of bulldozers and other machines increases our ability to produce and therefore raises our income and purchasing power. This in turn means that we can afford to buy products that did not exist before.

In brief, society benefits because the labor force is engaged in more productive activities than ditchdigging. Because machines now perform menial jobs, we produce more. The resulting increase in our income allows us to afford more compassion—that is, we are able to ensure people against the extremes of poverty that had to be faced in earlier, less productive eras. The point is a simple one: In protecting people against severe economic adversity, it is important not to use methods that thwart progress by locking in inefficiency.

WILL UNIONS SEEK BROADER AREAS OF INFLUENCE?

Will unions seek a voice in the nation's boardrooms? West Germany is experimenting with *codetermination* which provides labor with the same number of seats as management on the board of directors, with the owners making the decision in the event of a tie. In the United States, Douglas Fraser, UAW president in 1980, became the first union leader to get a seat on the board of a major U.S. corporation—Chrysler. This was not so much the result of a change in any underlying philosophy of management-labor relations as an act of desperation to save a near-bankrupt company: The UAW got a seat on Chrysler's board in exchange for deferring several hundred million dollars in wages and benefits. Pan American and a number of other companies also introduced this innovation. Although such experiments may have improved communications between labor and management, some rank-and-file workers fear that their leaders may begin to think like managers and soften their demands for higher wages and better working conditions.

Unions, with their wide variety of objectives, faced a long struggle in becoming established in the United States.

LABOR UNIONS: THEIR HISTORICAL DEVELOPMENT

Trade unionism is not socialism. It is the capitalism of the proletariat.

GEORGE BERNARD SHAW

The beginning of the American union movement dates back to an era in which a relatively powerless labor force lived in poverty, or near it. In the last third of the nineteenth century, the Knights of Labor emerged, hoping to become the one great organization that might speak for all labor. Like the labor movement in England and a number of other European countries, the organization sought to make labor a unified force for radical political change.

However, American workers have never been sympathetic to such an overt political objective. The Knights disappeared, to be replaced in the 1880s by the American Federation of Labor (AFL), led by Samuel Gompers and devoted to the bread-and-butter issues of improving wages and working conditions, rather than a "pie-in-the-sky" political class struggle.

The bread-and-butter approach remains an important characteristic of American labor. While unions sometimes support Democratic candidates, they often remain uncommitted and sometimes support Republicans. Thus American labor has not followed the common pattern in Britain and some other European countries of formal, close association with one political party.

There are two kinds of unions in the United States:

1. **Industrial unions,** such as the United Auto Workers, which draw on all workers in a specific industry or group of industries, regardless of the workers' skills.

2. **Craft unions,** such as the plumbers' or carpenters' unions, which draw their members from any industry, provided the workers have a common skill.

The history of American unions can be divided into the three periods sketched in Figure 22-1: (1) an initial low-membership period until the mid-1930s, (2) rapid growth for the next decade, and (3) a period of decline since World War II.

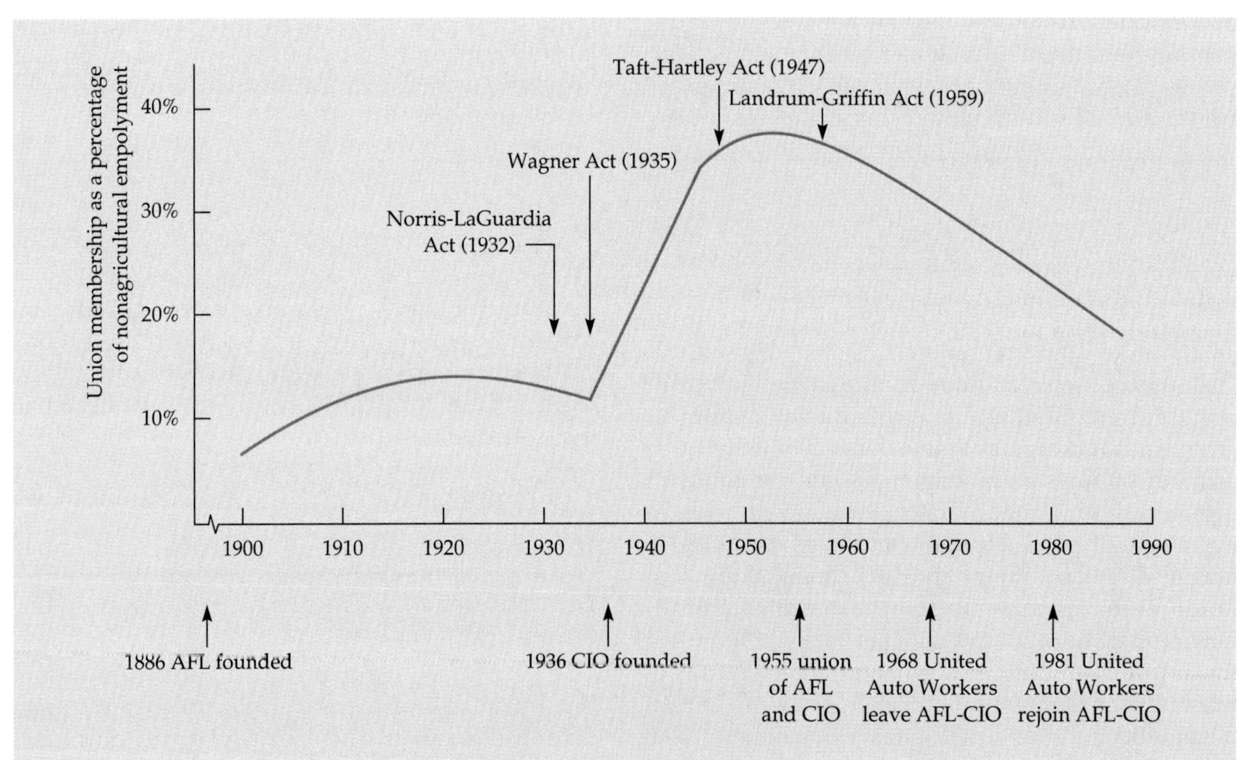

FIGURE 22-1 Major trends in U.S. union membership, 1900–1986.

American union membership remained low until the mid-1930s, then rose rapidly until the end of World War II. After a postwar decade of little or no growth, union membership has fallen as a proportion of the labor force. (*Sources:* These data are only approximations. They are based on U.S. Department of Labor figures and data in the two articles by R. B. Freeman and M. W. Reder in the *Journal of Economic Perspectives,* Spring 1988, pp. 63–110. The Freeman and Reder articles are drawn on heavily throughout this chapter.)

THE PERIOD BEFORE THE GREAT DEPRESSION

Until the early 1930s, unions developed in a hostile climate. On the one hand, business executives strongly resisted any attempts to unionize their firms and would frequently retaliate against pro-union workers by firing them and then blacklisting them with other potential employers. They would also sometimes use so-called yellow-dog contracts which specified that a worker getting a job had first to sign a commitment not to join a union.

An important question was how the courts would treat labor–management disputes. In particular, in light of the Sherman and Clayton antitrust acts, would the courts view unions as restraints on trade? Judgments either for or against unions seemed possible. On the one hand, a union could be viewed as a restraint on trade, since it is a combination of workers seeking to raise wages, just as a collusive oligopoly is a combination of sellers seeking to raise price. On the other hand, the Clayton Act seemed to exclude unions by stating that "labor is not an article of commerce." By and large, the courts' judgments during this early period did not favor labor.

For several reasons, union growth was thwarted during the 1920s and early 1930s. The AFL lost ground because it remained firmly committed to the idea of craft unionism on which it was founded. Therefore it did not adequately appeal to the increasing number of unskilled workers in mass-production industries, such as steel and autos. Moreover, there was growth in employer resistance to unionism. Employers introduced paternalistic schemes providing labor with relatively generous benefits in an attempt to demonstrate that workers would do better without a union. As a result of growing court hostility toward unions, employers were allowed to use injunctions (court orders) to prevent unions from picketing, striking, or pursuing almost any other activity judged threatening to business. Sometimes the courts issued injunctions without even hearing the union case.

THE PERIOD OF RAPID UNION GROWTH: THE EARLY 1930s TO 1945

In the depths of the depression in the 1930s, Congress passed several laws that improved the climate for unions. The first was the Norris-LaGuardia Act of 1932 which limited employers' use of what had become a prime weapon in the struggle against unions: the injunction. Court intervention in a labor dispute was to be limited to protecting property and preventing violence.

In 1935, the Wagner Act (the National Labor Relations Act) moved the government from a position of neutrality to one that favored labor. This act had three key provisions:

1. It declared the legal right of workers to form unions.

2. It prohibited employers from using a number of unfair labor practices, such as firing or blacklisting pro-union workers.

3. It established the National Labor Relations Board (NLRB) to control unfair labor practices by employers and to resolve disputes among unions. For example, the NLRB is empowered to hold elections in which workers decide which of two or more competing unions will represent them.

The Wagner Act achieved its objective of removing barriers to the growth of unions. During the decade that followed, the proportion of the labor force that belonged to unions almost tripled. There was another important reason for this growth. In 1936, several union leaders, led by John L. Lewis, split away from the AFL because of its concentration on craft unions. They formed the Congress of Industrial Organizations (CIO), a collection of industrial unions. Between 1936 and 1945, the CIO had great success in unionizing the auto, steel, and other mass-production industries. (In 1955, the two unions resolved their differences and rejoined forces in the new AFL-CIO.)

THE PERIOD SINCE WORLD WAR II

After a period of little growth in the first postwar decade, the percentage of workers in unions has steadily declined. Reasons cited include the relative decline in employment in heavy industry, where union membership has been most heavily concentrated, and the shift in industrial jobs to the south, where unionism is weaker than in the north.

The popularity of unions began to decline during World War II when unions may have overplayed their hand. During the early years of the war, unions had added muscle in the form of a rapidly increasing membership. By 1944 they were flexing that muscle in a series of strikes that were viewed by many as damaging to the war effort. The feeling that unions were becoming too powerful contributed to the passage of the Taft-Hartley Act in the face of stiff union opposition.

The Taft-Hartley Act (1947). Just as the Wagner Act 12 years earlier had dealt with unfair employer practices, the Taft-Hartley Act now attempted to outlaw unfair union practices. For example, it prohibited **closed shops** in industries engaged in interstate commerce. (Since only union members could be hired in a closed shop, it provided a union with veto power over who could be hired.) The Taft Hartley Act also prohibited jurisdictional strikes—strikes arising from conflicts between unions over whose members will do specific jobs. It also forbade the "checkoff" of union dues unless workers agree to it in writing. (With a checkoff, employers collect dues for the union by deducting them from workers' paychecks.) In addition, the Taft-Hartley Act included provisions to increase the financial responsibility of union leaders. For example, it required pension funds to be kept separate from other union funds, and it required union leaders to provide both their own membership and the National Labor Relations Board with detailed information on how union funds were to be spent. The act also contained a provision to delay strikes that "imperil the national health or safety." Specifically, the U.S. president was empowered to seek a court injunction in such circumstances to require strikers to return to work for an 80-day cooling-off period.

The most controversial provision of the Taft-Hartley Act is its famous section 14(b). This recognizes the right of states to enact **right-to-work laws** that make the **closed shop** and the **union shop** illegal. In states with such laws, workers cannot be required to join a union. By 1963, 20 states—more than half in the south—had passed right-to-work laws. Union leaders consider section 14(b) to be overtly antiunion. They argue that, if membership in a union is not compulsory, workers can be free riders, participating in the benefits provided by a union without being members. Moreover, if many workers choose not to be members, it weakens the union's bargaining position.

A ***closed shop*** means that a firm can hire only workers who are already union members.

A ***union shop*** permits the hiring of nonunion members but requires workers who are not yet members to join the union within a specified period, such as 30 days.

A ***right-to-work law*** outlaws the closed shop and the union shop in favor of the *open shop,* in which there cannot be a requirement to join a union.

Although the precise impact of right-to-work laws is still controversial, one estimate suggests that union membership has been reduced by 5 or 10% in states that have enacted these laws.[2]

The Landrum-Griffin Act (1959). The Landrum-Griffin Act was passed by a Congress that was concerned over union corruption and wished to increase the restraints on union leaders. Among other stipulations, union officials were prohibited from borrowing more than $2,000 of union funds, the embezzlement of union funds became a federal offense, and restrictions were placed on ex-convicts seeking union offices. This act also sought to make union decisions more democratic by strengthening the power of members to challenge their leaders through the ballot box. It required regularly scheduled elections of union officers by secret ballot, with every member being eligible to vote. A member's right to participate in union meetings was also guaranteed, and any member was given the right to sue a union that tried to withhold any of these privileges.

It is difficult to judge how effective this legislation has been in limiting union corruption, but it is clear that it has not completely solved the problem. For example, in the Teamsters, the largest and most powerful union in the United States, four recent presidents have been in trouble with the law. Three spent time in jail, and charges against the fourth were dropped because he was dying. U.S. workers have found that their labor leader, as well as their boss, may end up in jail. (A sample of white-collar crime by management was provided back in Box 14-1).

---

[2]David T. Ellwood and Glenn Fine, "The Impact of Right-to-Work laws on Union Organizing," *Journal of Political Economy,* April 1987, pp. 250-273.

THE 1980s: UNIONS UNDER PRESSURE

During the 1980s unions came under a great deal of pressure. In August 1981, in response to an illegal strike by air-traffic controllers, President Reagan fired the striking workers. In a number of industries, unions have been unable to prevent a decline in real wages. In the airline industry, deregulation has meant a much more competitive environment. To survive, the airline companies have put pressure on employees to accept lower wages. In an extreme case, Texas Air declared bankruptcy in order to nullify its union contract and pay its workers less. In the construction industry, some unions were forced to accept lower real wages during the severe recession of 1981–1982. In autos and steel, the unions made substantial wage concessions in the early 1980s because of intense foreign competition. A number of unions found their bargaining power weakened when firms threatened to move to the less unionized Sunbelt or abroad. Between 1982 and 1984, over one-third of nongovernment workers under major newly negotiated union contracts accepted a wage freeze or cut.[3]

Management opposition to unions has become stronger. By 1980, the number of charges of unfair labor practices against management had reached a level three times as high as the pre-1970 average. Moreover, in 1980, the National Labor Relations Board judged that 15,000 workers had been illegally fired for union activities; the penalty for those who were caught was not high enough to discourage the practice. As an example of how embattled and defensive the unions had become, some of the members of the United Food and Commercial Workers International Union took a 25% cut in hourly wages, while others lost their jobs altogether and were replaced by nonunion workers at a 50% lower wage. Economic pressures forced a number of unions to accept such two-tiered wage contracts under which new workers could be hired at substantially lower wages than old workers. As the economic recovery continued into the late 1980s, wage concessions became less frequent. However, it wasn't clear that the unions would be able to recapture their earlier position of power.

[3]Daniel J.B. Mitchell, "Shifting Norms in Wage Determination," in *Brookings Papers on Economic Activity 2* (1985), pp. 576–577.

LABOR UNIONS: THE EXERCISE OF MARKET POWER

While the fortunes of U.S. workers—union and nonunion alike—have ebbed and flowed, statistical studies indicate that unions have succeeded in their major task of raising wages. Union members earn an average of 10% to 25% more than nonunion workers in comparable activities. However, some of this higher wage can be explained by the fact that union workers are different; for example, unionized firms are able to hire more productive workers who could be earning a higher wage, whether or not they were in a union. This means that, for workers with the same productivity and other characteristics, a union is able to raise wages by an estimated average of about 10 to 15%.[4]

EFFECTS OF A HIGHER UNION WAGE: A FIRST APPROXIMATION

Figure 22-2 illustrates a perfectly competitive labor market, with equilibrium at E_1. Employers have no market power and take the wage rate as given. Workers have no market power and also take the wage rate as given.

Now suppose that the workers who supply labor form a union that raises the wage rate from, say, \$10 to \$12 per hour. The enforcement of this higher wage requires "union discipline"; members must not be allowed to offer their labor services for less than \$12. Faced with this wage, employers react by moving up their demand curve from E_1 to E_2. Because the union has raised wages, employment is reduced from N_1 to N_2.

[4]See H. Gregg Lewis, *Union Relative Wage Effects: A Survey* (Chicago: University of Chicago Press, 1986), Ch. 9; and Gopa Chowdhury and Stephen Nickell, "Hourly Earnings in the United States," *Journal of Labor Economics*, January 1985, p. 62. In addition, Peter Linneman and Michael L. Wachter provide evidence of how widely the 1984 union versus nonunion wage dfferential varied among industries in "Rising Union Premiums and the Declining Boundaries Among Noncompeting Groups," *American Economic Review Proceedings*, May 1986, pp. 105, 106.

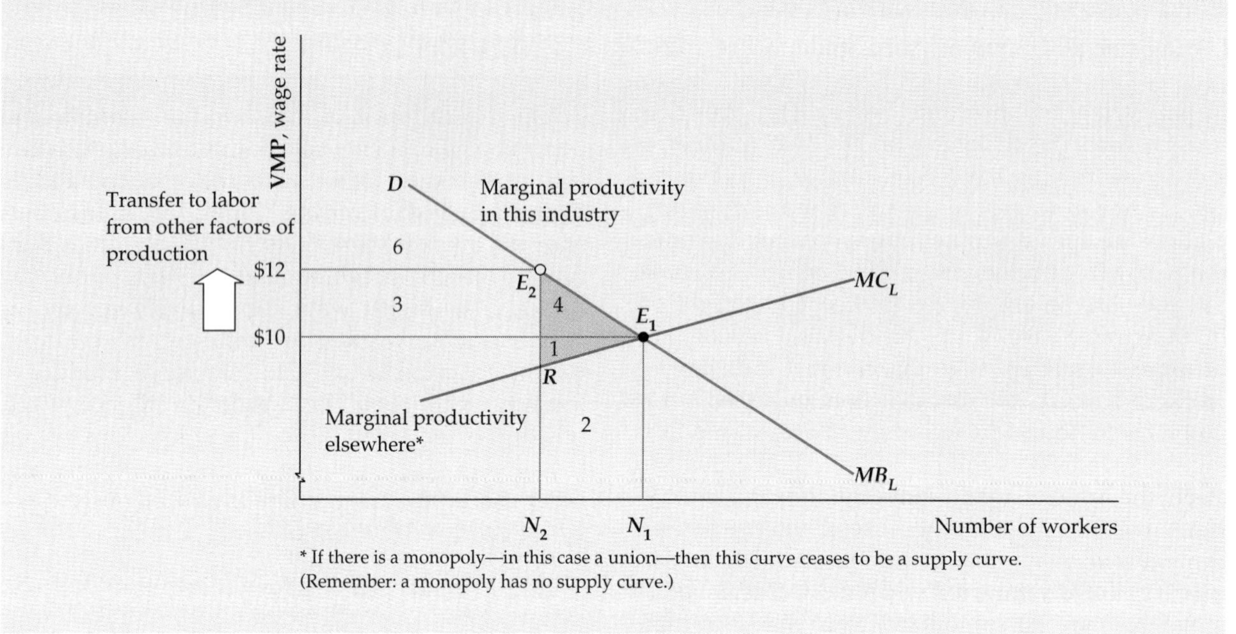

FIGURE 22-2 The effects of unionizing an industry in a previously competitive labor market.

When a union is formed and raises the wage rate from \$10 to \$12, equilibrium moves from the perfectly competitive point E_1 to E_2; that is, employers respond by reducing employment from N_1 to N_2. The result of "too little employment," first described in Figure 21-6*c*, is the red efficiency loss 4 + 1. This arises because N_2N_1 workers don't have jobs in this industry where their productivity would be high, as shown by the height of the demand curve *D*. Instead they have to take jobs elsewhere with lower productivity shown by the height of the marginal cost for labor curve MC_L. The higher wage also results in a transfer to labor from other factors of production, as shown by the arrow on the left.

Transfer Effects. Capital and other nonlabor factors of production lose area 3 + 4. (As explained back in Figure 21-4, they earned 6 + 3 + 4 at initial equilibrium E_1. After the union is formed and equilibrium moves to E_2, they earn only area 6, for a net loss of 3 + 4.) Of this loss, 3 is a transfer to the N_2 workers who retain their jobs in this industry and enjoy a wage increase of \$2. This is the reason why they formed a union: to acquire area 3 of income that the owners of capital and other factors of production would otherwise receive. However, while these N_2 workers in the industry gain, there is a loss to the workers between N_2 and N_1 who would like to work in this industry but who must instead take lower productivity, lower wage jobs elsewhere.

Efficiency Effect. The standard deadweight efficiency loss is shown by the red triangle. This loss occurs because employment has been reduced from its perfectly competitive, efficient amount at N_1 to N_2. Displaced workers have had to move elsewhere, to industries where their productivity is lower, and the nation's output is consequently reduced.

Figure 22-2 illustrates the similarity of the markets for labor and goods. Specifically, note how a union's monopolization of a labor market in Figure 22-2 is similar to the monopolization of a product market in Figure 12-5 except, of course, that the union's actions affect the wage and employment of labor rather than the price and quantity of a product.[5]

HOW UNIONS INCREASE EFFICIENCY

A union may also have favorable effects on efficiency.[6]

1. Unions may set up grievance procedures and improve the morale of the work force, thus improving communication between workers and management.

2. By providing workers with a collective voice, a union makes it possible for them to improve their working conditions rather than quitting. Because unions reduce quit-rates and labor turnover, there is less disruption in the workplace.

3. If market power is held by employers on the other side of the market, then the formation of a union may be a counterbalance that increases efficiency.

[5]There is an important reason why monopoly cannot be analyzed in a labor market in exactly the same way as in a product market. In a product market, a monopoly firm will take into account any loss of sales (reduction in output) that results from its high price. However, in a labor market, it is not clear how fully a union will take into account any reduced employment that results from its high wage—especially if the industry is growing and the high wage reduces only the number of new workers coming into the industry, rather than the number of current union members. This difficulty prevents us from applying the standard analysis of monopoly to determine precisely how high the union will try to push up the wage rate.

[6]For evidence that unions may increase efficiency, perhaps by raising the performance of management, see Robert N. Mefford, "The Effect of Unions on Productivity in a Multinational Manufacturing Firm," *Industrial and Labor Relations Review,* October 1986, p. 114. For a more skeptical view, see Barry T. Hirsch and John T. Addison, *Economic Analysis of Labor Unions—New Approaches and Evidence* (Boston: George Allen and Unwin, 1986).

MONOPSONY: MARKET POWER ON THE EMPLOYERS' SIDE OF THE LABOR MARKET

Employers typically quote the wage rate they will pay. In doing so, they frequently do not act like perfect competitors who take a market wage as given. Instead, they exercise a degree of market power. In particular, any firm that employs a large fraction of a local labor force may influence the wage rate, or even be able to set it.

To analyze this situation in Figure 22-3, initially assume a perfectly competitive labor market with equilibrium at E_1. But now, instead of introducing monopoly (a single seller, in the form of a union), introduce *monopsony*—a single buyer, in the form of a single employer of labor. What happens if this single employer quotes a lower wage rate, while workers on the other side of the market act as perfect competitors, taking the wage rate as given? Specifically, suppose that the employer quotes a wage of W_2, which is well below the perfectly competitive wage of W_1. In response to wage W_2, some workers leave the industry for other jobs that are now more attractive. In other words, the workers in this industry move down their supply curve from E_1 to a new equilibrium at E_2. The result is the red triangular efficiency loss because employment at N_2 is less than the perfectly competitive amount at N_1. Workers being paid W_2 are getting less than their marginal benefit to society (the height of G).

At the same time, the reduction in the wage paid by the employer results in the transfer shown by the white arrow. This transfer is from workers who receive the lower wage, to other factors of production who benefit because there is more of the firm's income left for them. (Further details on how a monopsonist may lower wages are given in Box 22-2.)

Here we see another example of how Adam Smith's invisible hand may go astray. The monopsonistic employer's pursuit of private benefit does not lead to public benefit. Quite the contrary: It leads to the triangular efficiency loss in Figure 22-3.

In reality, there are few cases in which monopsony occurs in its pure form with only one buyer.

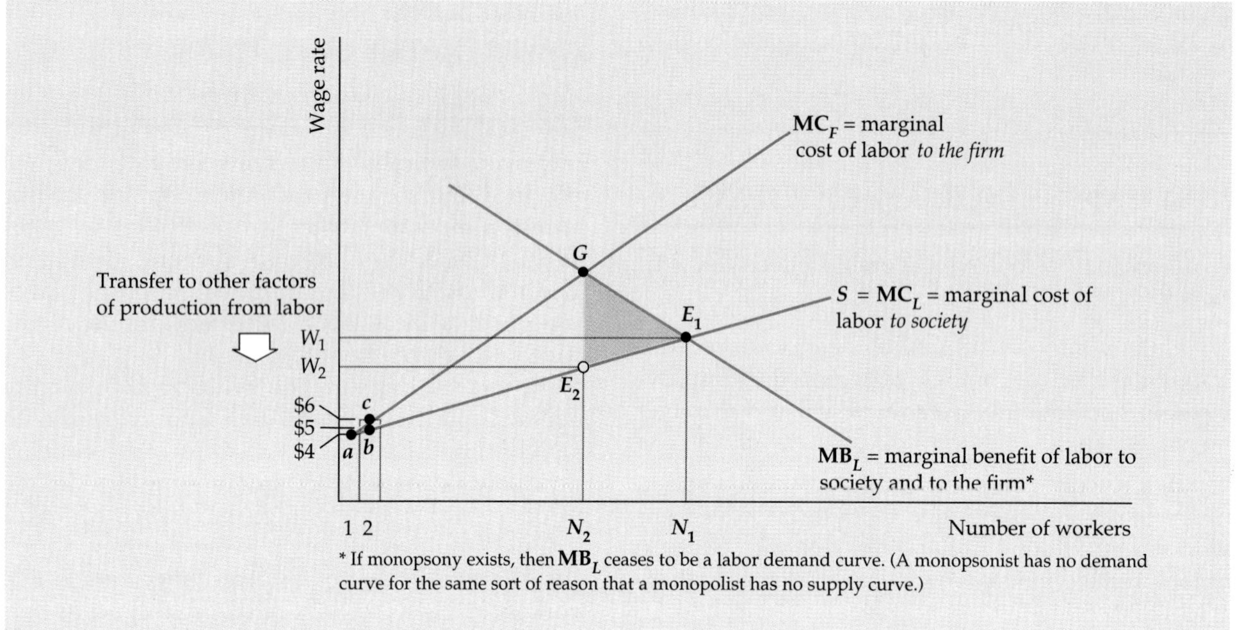

FIGURE 22-3 Effects when a perfectly competitive labor market is monopsonized.

When a monopsony is formed, equilibrium moves from the perfectly competitive point E_1 to E_2. (Because the monopsonist quotes lower wage W_2, fewer workers offer their labor services and employment falls from N_1 to N_2.) Because too few workers are employed in this industry, there is the efficiency loss shown by the red triangle. The lower wage also results in a transfer from labor to other factors of production, as shown by the white arrow.

One-company towns and coal mines have been cited as examples, but they are very rare. There is more likely to be a small group of employers, that is, an oligopsony with a few buyers. Although each firm has some latitude in quoting a wage rate, it is influenced by the wages quoted by competing firms. On the one hand, competition among these firms may leave each with very little influence over the wage it can quote. In this case, the wage may be close to the competitive level W_1. On the other hand, if the few oligopsonists collude, perhaps in some covert way, they may together lower the wage rate well below W_1 toward the W_2 that a monopsonist would choose.

Although monopsony rarely occurs in its pure form, with only one buyer, there has been a notable example: the monopsony power a baseball club used to have in buying the services of its players.

MONOPSONY AND BASEBALL SALARIES

Before 1976, a "reserve clause" made each major league baseball team a monopsony, because a player could not sign a contract with any other team. This meant that the typical star was paid less than his value to the club. However, beginning in 1976, a player in certain circumstances could become a free agent and negotiate with other clubs.

Figure 22-4 shows what happened to a few of the players who became free agents. These before-and-after comparisons showing how much free agency raised salaries indicate the remarkable way that the monopsony power of the reserve clause had previously depressed salaries. Since 1976 confirming evidence has continued to accumulate. In 1980, the baseball world was astonished when the New York Yankees signed free agent Dave Winfield

BOX 22–2 *How Far Does a Monopsonist Try to Reduce the Wage Rate?*

To choose the wage rate that will maximize its profits, the monopsony firm first calculates its marginal cost of hiring labor MC_F from the supply of labor *S*. This calculation is illustrated in the lower left-hand corner of Figure 22-3: From the *S* curve we see that the firm must pay $4 an hour at point *a* to hire one worker and $5 an hour at point *b* to hire two. However, the firm's marginal cost MC_F of hiring the second worker is not $5 but $6—the $5 x 2 = $10 it costs to hire the two workers less the $4 it costs to hire one. Thus MC_F, the marginal cost of labor to the monopsony firm, lies above the supply curve of labor *S*.

To maximize profit, this firm hires labor to point *G*, where its marginal cost of hiring labor MC_F is equal to MB_L, the marginal benefit it receives from hiring labor. With its desired employment thus being N_2, what is the lowest wage it can quote? The answer is W_2. At this wage rate, the labor supply curve *S* indicates that just exactly the desired number of workers N_2 will offer their services to this firm.

Finally, Figure 22-3 provides another view of why a red efficiency loss arises from an employment level of N_2: The private firm equates the marginal benefit of labor MB_L not to *society's* marginal cost MC_L, but instead to *its own* marginal cost MC_F. Since the marginal benefit and cost of labor to society are not equated, the outcome is not efficient.

As a final note, consider the monopsony firm that has already used its market power to depress the wage rate of its entire labor force from W_1 to W_2. It may go one step further and reduce even more the wage paid to a specific subset of its workers, such as a minority group. The firm may discriminate in this way for the same reason that the dentist who was a monopolist in a small town discriminated by charging different fees. In either case, discrimination is a way of increasing profit. However, in other respects, the two cases are different. The action of the dentist who discriminated between patients on the basis of their income was efficient since it left everyone better off. It also was equitable because it made incomes (after dental expenses) more equal. On the other hand, discrimination based on race or sex cannot be justified, since it *reduces* efficiency, (as we will confirm later), makes incomes *less* equal, and is objectionable for noneconomic reasons.

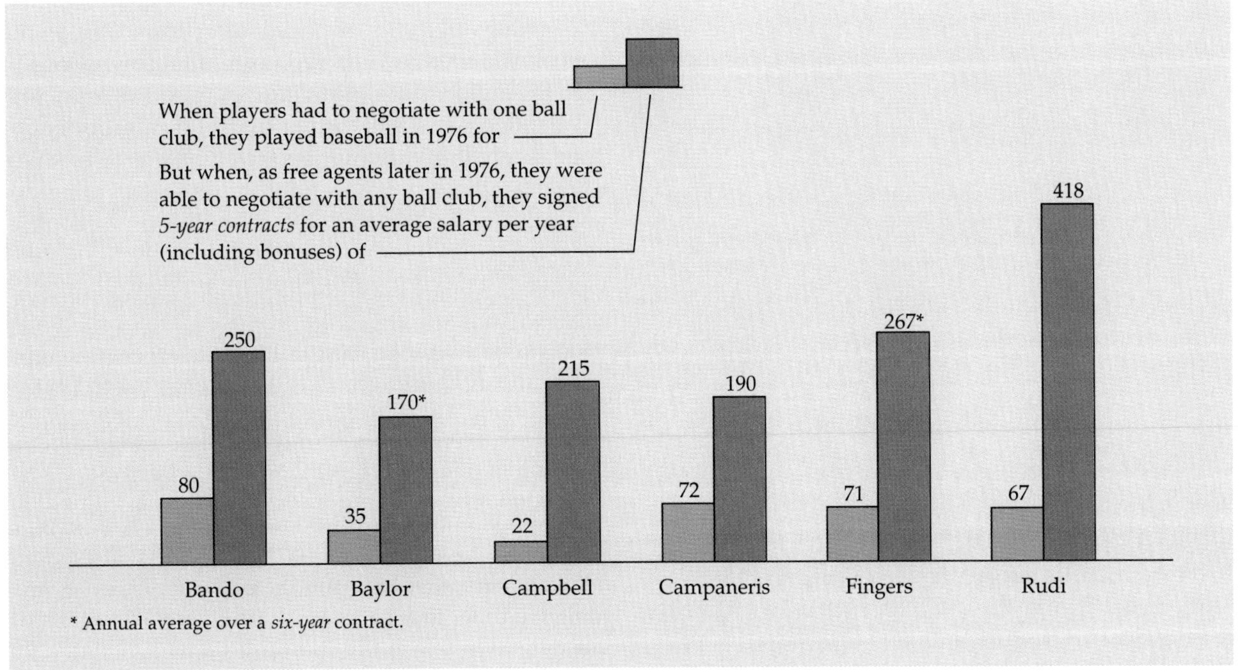

FIGURE 22-4 How monopsony (the reserve clause) depressed baseball salaries. (Figures in $000s, rounded)

for an estimated $1.5 million to $2 million per year for 10 years. Compare this with his $350,000 salary in San Diego the previous year before his escape, as a free agent, from the monopsony power of the reserve clause. To get some idea of Winfield's "before-and-after" situation, just increase the height of both bars for Baylor in Figure 22-4 by *ten times*. But even these numbers are no longer surprising; by 1990, salaries of over $2 million per year are no longer uncommon. (Whereas recent before-and-after salary figures confirm the importance of free agency in raising salaries, they don't do nearly as accurate a job as Figure 22-4 in estimating its precise effect. The reason is that free agency now raises salaries both before and after it happens; owners today often increase the pay of players well before they become free agents in order to reduce their incentive to choose this option.)

THE EFFECTS OF UNIONS RECONSIDERED

Suppose that the monopsony firm in Figure 22-5 has lowered the wage rate from the $10 competitive level to $8, and perfectly competitive workers have taken this wage rate as given. At this lower wage, fewer workers have been offering their labor services to this industry. Therefore employment has been reduced from N to N_1—that is, equilibrium has moved from E to E_1—with a consequent efficiency loss of areas 1 + 2. If a union is now formed and raises the wage rate from $8 to $9—moving the equilibrium from E_1 to E_2—the efficiency loss is reduced from areas 1 + 2 to just area 2. In other words, the formation of this union results in an efficiency *gain* of area 1. Thus a union that reduced efficiency in a perfectly competitive labor market *increases* efficiency in the monopsonized labor market in Figure 22-5.[7] Of course, the union in this diagram also benefits union members by recapturing some of the income previously lost to the monopsonist.

If the union gets very strong and pushes the wage up beyond $10 toward $12, equilibrium will shift away from E toward E_3, and efficiency will once again be reduced.

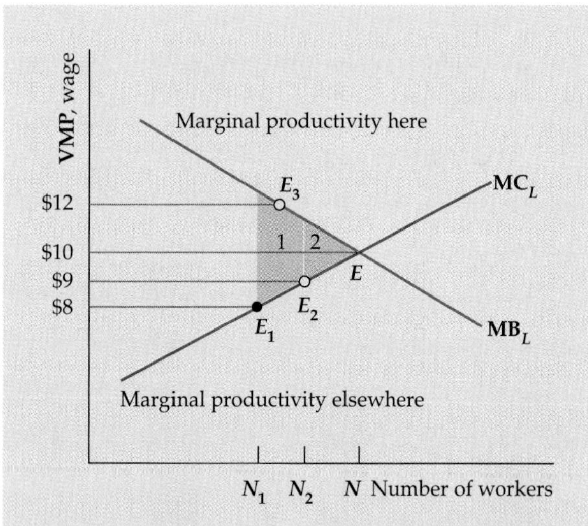

FIGURE 22-5 How inefficiency may be reduced if a union raises wages in a monopsonized labor market.

Before the union, the monopsonist set the wage rate at $8. With equilibrium at E_1, there was an efficiency loss of 1 + 2. When the union is formed, it raises the wage to $9. Equilibrium moves from E_1 to E_2, some employment is restored, and the efficiency loss is reduced to area 2. Consequently, the union increases efficiency by area 1.

BILATERAL MONOPOLY IN A LABOR MARKET

When both sides have market power as in Figure 22-5, they push in opposite directions. While the employer tries to keep the wage rate down close to $8, the union tries to push it up close to, say, $12. The outcome in this case of **bilateral monopoly** depends on the bargaining power of the two sides. An examination of the two curves in this diagram will not indicate precisely where the final solution will be.

[7] This diagram can be used to illustrate another example of the theory of the second best, first encountered in Box 12-1. If there is only a single firm in a small town, it will be able to exercise monopsony influence over the wage rate, driving it down toward $8. The economist's "first-best" efficient solution—with perfect competition on both sides of the market—is simply not possible, no matter how desirable it might be. However, there is a good second-best solution—namely, for workers to form a union in order to raise wages. If they roughly counterbalance the power that the monopsonist already enjoys on the other side of the market, the outcome may be close to the perfectly competitive $10 price and efficient employment of N.

Bilateral monopoly is a market in which there is only one buyer and one seller.

WHICH SIDE HAS THE STRONGER BARGAINING POSITION?

To see the importance of bargaining power, suppose that there is only one company in a mining town and that it faces an ineffective union representing only a few workers. In this case, the company will be in a good position to keep the wage low. On the other hand, if there is a single, strong union facing a number of employers, the union will have the stronger bargaining position.

An outcome close to the efficient outcome E requires that the market power of the two sides be in rough balance. If labor has all the market power, the outcome will be the inefficient E_3. If management has all the market power, the outcome will be the inefficient E_1.

REPRISE: THE MINIMUM WAGE

If the government is setting a minimum wage or raising the wage rate in any other way, it will be reducing efficiency if the labor market is already at the perfectly competitive equilibrium E. However, if the labor market is monopsonized at, say equilibrium E_1, a minimum wage above this level will increase efficiency.

STRIKES

In any wage negotiation, an important influence strengthening the bargaining position of either side is its ability to outlast the other in a long strike. For example, the credibility of a strike threat by a union depends in part on the size of its strike fund. If this has been depleted by earlier strikes, the union is in a weak position. The company can play a strong hand, making a low offer near $8 in Figure 22-5 and sticking close to it, with the knowledge that the union cannot afford to strike. Another influence that may weaken a union's bargaining position is the existence of widespread unemployment in the economy which makes workers very uncertain about the alternative jobs they can get, and thus makes them less willing to strike.

On the other hand, a company will be in a weak bargaining position if it cannot afford a strike. This may be the case for several reasons:

1. A strike may be very costly to a capital-intensive firm that must face high overhead costs whether or not the strike occurs. An example is an airline with a fleet of very expensive aircraft that would be left idle on the runway.
2. A construction company that has to pay heavy penalties for delay in completing a project may be forced to capitulate to a strike threat by the union.
3. A strike may cost a firm a lot in terms of lost sales. This may be particularly important in a period of prosperity when the firm has high sales. It may also be important for a firm producing a perishable good or service. Such a firm may be in a weak bargaining position because sales and profits lost during a strike may be lost forever. (The term *perishable* is used broadly, applying not only to physically perishable goods such as fruit, but also to goods that go out of date, like yesterday's newspaper.)

Of course, firms producing goods that are not perishable are in a much stronger position—especially if these firms have accumulated large inventories and can consequently keep selling right through a strike. It is no accident that before critical wage negotiations, companies try to build up inventories, just as unions try to build up strike funds.

It is also no surprise that a strike becomes less likely if both sides have been financially weakened by a long and costly strike during the previous contract negotiation.

THE COST OF A STRIKE

Strikes are costly to both sides: to labor in the form of lost wages, and to management in the form of lost sales and profits. For example, suppose that, in the absence of a strike, the wage is W in Figure 22-6, with employment N. In this case a strike that temporarily reduces employment to zero imposes a cost in terms of lost output valued at areas 1 + 2. Labor loses income 1—that is, its wage W times employment N—while the income lost by other factors is the remaining area 2.

Since both parties face a substantial loss in the

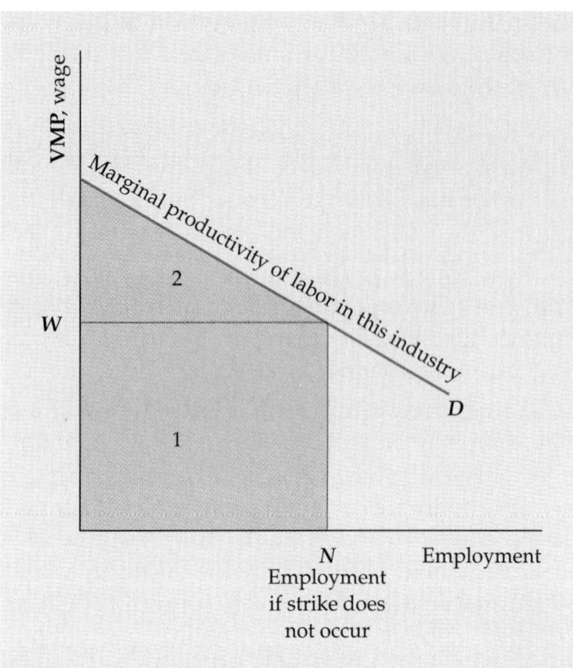

FIGURE 22-6 Short-run cost of a strike to labor and other factors of production.

Without a strike, the value of total output in this industry is area 1 + 2. Labor earns area 1, and other factors of production earn 2. If a strike does occur, both of these incomes are lost. (The cost may be less if the firm is able to anticipate the strike and increase its output and inventories beforehand, or if some of the production lost during the strike can be made up afterwards.)

event of a strike, it is often assumed that when a strike does occur, it is the result of an error in judgment by at least one of the conflicting parties. However, this need not be the case, as shown in Figure 22-7.

LABOR–MANAGEMENT NEGOTIATIONS TO AVOID STRIKES

Case *a* in Figure 22-7 illustrates the outcome of most labor negotiations: Both sides find a wage to agree on and thus avoid a strike. The range of wages management is willing to pay (arrow *M*) and the range of wages labor is willing to take (arrow *L*) overlap through the shaded range $W_1 W_2$. Any wage rate in this "contract zone" is acceptable to both parties. (Remember that here the term *wage* means total compensation, including fringe benefits and improvements in working conditions.)

Negotiations typically begin with labor demanding W_4 and management offering W_3. To the public, it appears that they are far apart and there is little hope of an agreement. However, as the negotiations proceed, both sides compromise, trading one claim against another. Often neither party will officially concede anything. Instead, each simply remains silent on a claim made by the other, and a "trade" is thereafter mutually recognized. Thus management moves up its arrow *M* and labor moves down its arrow *L*, until they reach a point of agreement at, say, W_5. In settling on this, management's negotiating team claims success; labor has been negotiated all the way down from its original demand of W_4. The union also claims success; it has negotiated management all the way up from its original offer of W_3.

With many labor negotiations following this pattern, why do strikes occur?

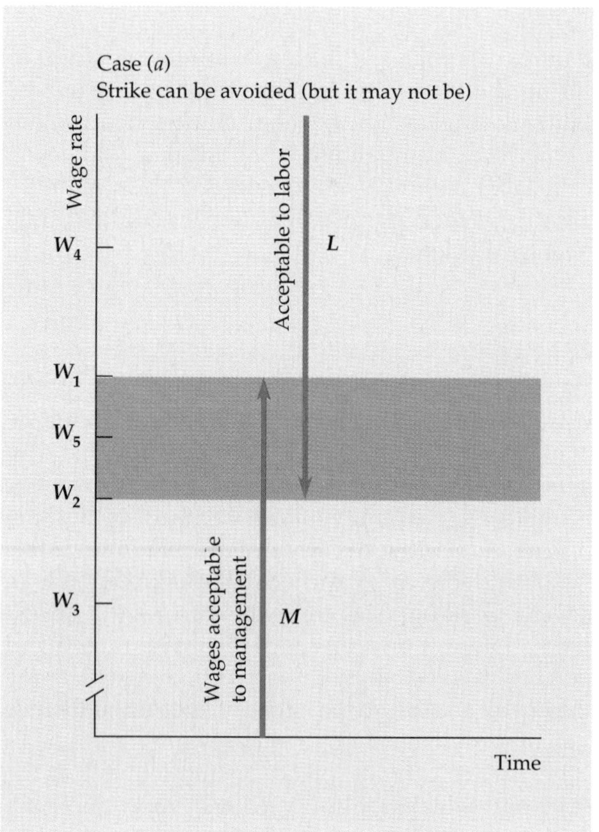

FIGURE 22-7 Most strikes may be avoided. . .

CAUSES OF A STRIKE

A strike may occur even when there is a contract zone of mutually acceptable wage rates (as in panel *a*), for several reasons.

1. *One or both of the parties may have inept negotiators who engage in poor bargaining strategy.* For example, suppose that management's initial offer is far below W_3—in fact, so low that labor views it as an insult. The anger that results may sour the negotiations enough to cause an unnecessary strike. An alternative bargaining error by management may be to make an initial offer that is too *generous.* Specifically, suppose management initially offers W_1 and states that this is its final, best possible offer (which it is; note that W_1 is right at the top of arrow *M*). The problem is that the union leaders may not believe it. They may view it as a standard opening offer and attempt to negotiate it up. When this attempt fails, a strike occurs because wage W_1 cannot be accepted by the union. It will look foolish to its members if it has gone through weeks or months of negotiations and has been unable to budge the company. Management seems to have dictated the wage from the beginning, and all that the union has done is to make concessions. Why do the workers need such a union? Thus, although management has been very generous in offering W_1, it has inadvertently caused a strike because it has not "played the negotiating game." It has not followed the cardinal rule of "giving the other side a ladder to climb down."

More generally, the problem of inept negotiating has been described by Lloyd Reynolds of Yale University as follows:[8]

[8]*Labor Economics and Labor Relations,* 7th ed., (Englewood Cliffs, N.J.: Prentice-Hall Inc., 1978), p. 447.

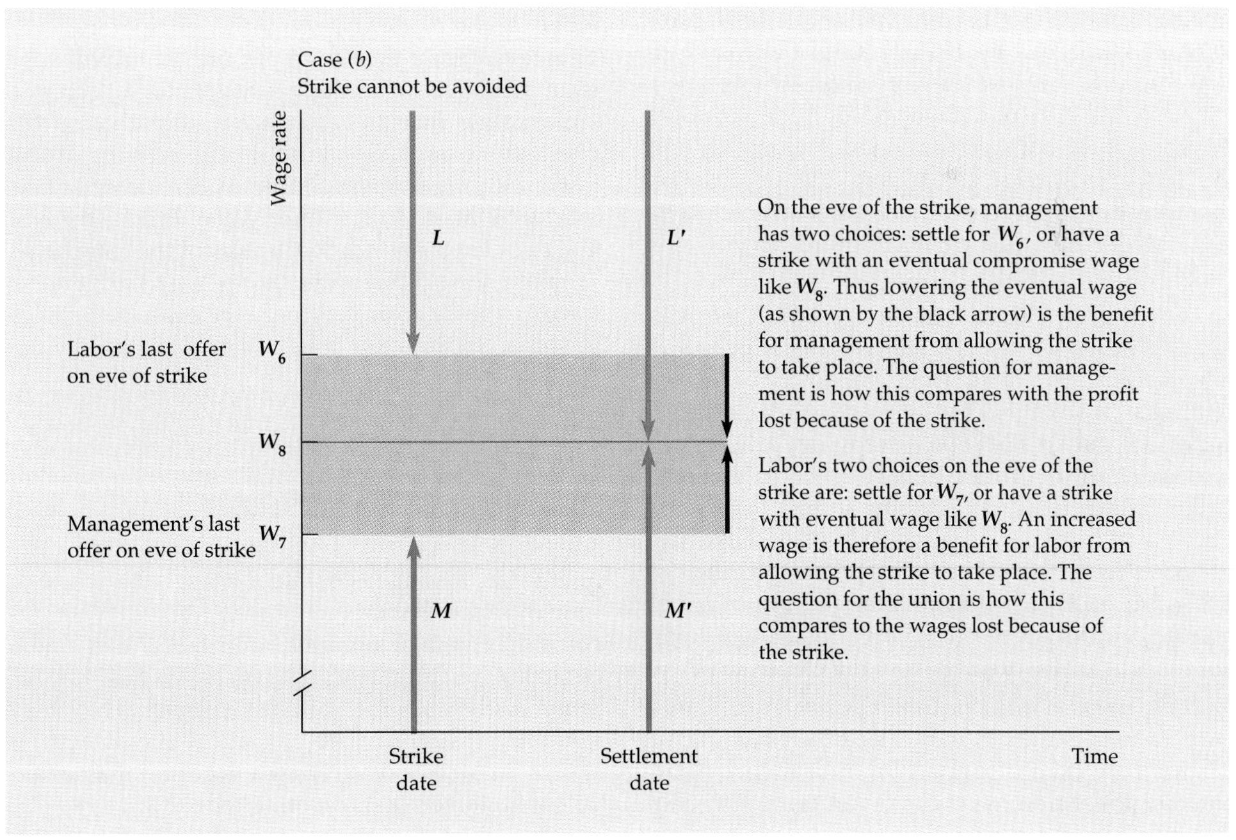

. . . but some may not.

Negotiators may stake out firm positions from which it is later difficult to retreat, may misread the signals from the other side, or may be unable to surmount the tactical difficulties of graceful concession.

Although economic forces set the background and help to define the limits W_1W_2 within which the negotiated wage will fall, collective bargaining has some of the characteristics of a poker game: The wage negotiated is very much the product of the bargaining skills of the participants. Without minimal skills, there may be no bargain at all.

2. *One or both of the parties may be irrational.* To illustrate, a strike may occur if labor is irrational and holds out for a wage of W_4, even though it knows that management can't pay more than W_1.

3. *One side may lack information.* Even though the negotiators are expert *and* rational, a strike may still occur because of *"asymmetric information"*—that is, one side knows something the other does not. For example, even though management knows that its best offer is W_1, labor may not know this, since it has far less information about how profitable the firm may be. If labor holds out for W_4, a strike occurs. Such a strike can also be viewed as a way that one side (or both) acquires information. In this case, when management doesn't accept W_4 and the strike continues, labor gains the information that the firm is not as profitable as it seemed to be and therefore cannot after all afford to pay this wage.

4. *Either side may want a strike to establish its credibility.* When one side threatens a strike in future negotiations, the other side will know it is not bluffing. Credibility is very important for each side because it may make it possible to get satisfactory settlements in the future simply by threatening to strike, rather than by actually striking. This explains why strikes are less likely if a strike has occurred in the previous contract negotiation. In this case, each side knows that the other is not bluffing and is prepared to strike. Each side may also be financially drained from the earlier strike.

5. *One party has an extraneous objective.* A company may want a strike as a means of weakening or destroying workers' support for their union. Alternatively, the union may want a strike in the belief that it will improve labor solidarity and morale.

All the above are possible reasons for a strike even though a contract zone does exist, as in panel *a* of Figure 22-7. This then leaves the final reason for a strike:

6. *A positive contract zone does not exist.* This possibility is illustrated in case *b* in Figure 22-7. Here a strike cannot be avoided because the positions (arrows) of the two parties do not overlap. On the eve of the strike, there is no wage that is acceptable to both. Each party would rather have a strike than agree to the other side's last offer.

The longer the strike goes on, the farther the two parties move to the right in this diagram, and the more likely it is that each side will modify its previous strong position—that is, the more likely it is that the two arrows L' and M' will approach each other. Workers on the picket lines increasingly feel the financial pinch of lost wages. Similarly, management sees its losses mount. Both recognize that the other does, in fact, mean business. Thus L' and M' eventually meet and the strike is settled, at a compromise wage such as W_8. Precisely because W_8 is a compromise wage, it is more attractive for each side than its opponent's last offer before the strike, as the black arrows on the far right indicate. Thus eventually achieving a more attractive wage is an incentive for a rational negotiator to accept a strike rather than to capitulate to the other on the eve of the strike. (Of course, before arriving at this favorable judgment on a strike, each side must take into account its losses during the strike—the lost wages of labor and the lost profits of the company.)

Sometimes, one side "loses a strike" and is forced to settle at or very near the prestrike offer of the other. In this case, it has made a mistake by not settling earlier.

SPILLOVER COSTS OF A STRIKE

Although strikes do occur, they are not very frequent. On average, less than 1% of the working time of unionized labor is lost in strikes. When account is taken of nonunionized labor, this figure becomes much smaller. However, strikes may be more costly than the statistics suggest. They may not only result in lost output in the industries where the strikes occur; they may also inflict external, or spillover, costs on other industries.

To illustrate, suppose that when the tire industry is on strike the value of the lost output and income in that industry is shown as area 3 in Figure

22-8*a;* this is exactly the same as areas 1 + 2 in Figure 22-6. The loss may not end here. As tire supplies are depleted, auto production may be delayed or dislocated. This disruption involves a cost to the auto industry and inconvenience to the car-buying public. Because these costs are not incurred by buyers or sellers of labor in the tire industry, they are external spillover costs of the strike and are shown as area 4. Specifically, when worker *k* becomes unemployed there is a loss of this individual's output of tires, as shown by the lower arrow. However, there is a further cost, shown by the arrow above, because of the dislocation in the auto industry, where car production is delayed because of the shortage of tires. In short, if a strike occurs in the industry, it will involve both internal cost 3 to the industry plus external cost 4 elsewhere in the economy.

Panel *b* shows that the situation could be worse. If auto companies are eventually forced to shut down, the value of the lost output in the auto industry and the inconvenience to the public—shown as area 4—may be very large indeed. An example of a strike with a substantial external cost occurred in Californian canneries. Lost income in these factories represented only a small part of the total cost. Far more important was the loss of farm output: Tomatoes, peaches and apricots were left to rot because the canning factories were closed down. Clearly, strikes in some industries will cause much larger external costs than strikes in others. In industries producing luxuries or durable goods (say, perfumes or home appliances) the public can "temporarily make do," and little external cost is incurred. On the other hand, a nurses' strike can have costs far beyond the lost income to the nurses and hospitals, since it may be damaging to public health.[9]

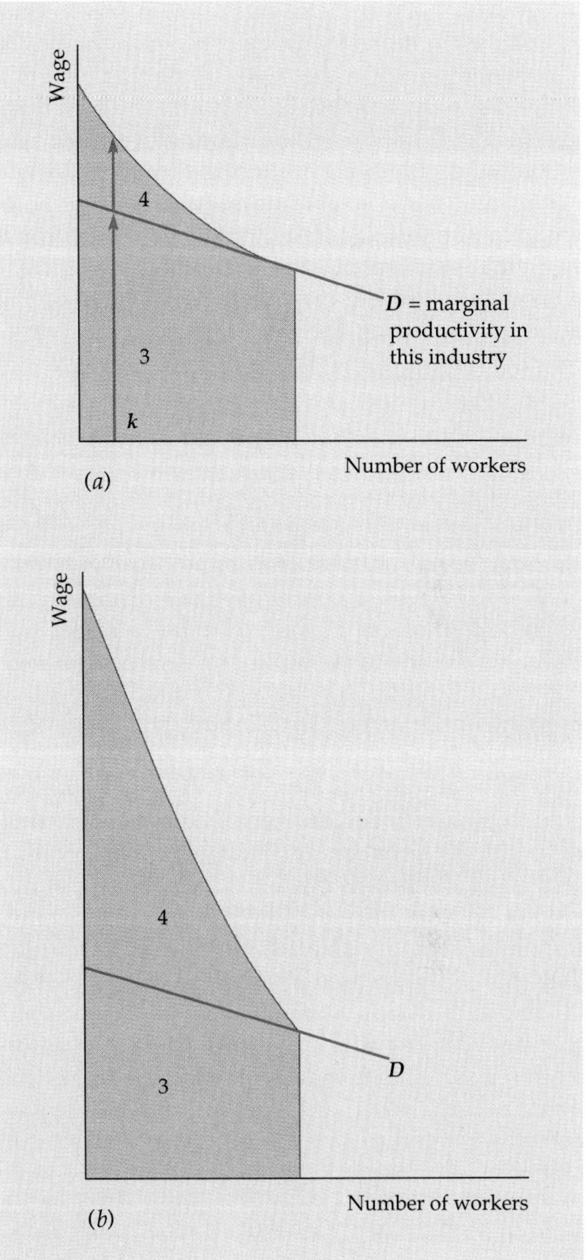

FIGURE 22-8 Spillover cost of a strike.

(*a*) When a strike occurs in tire production, the internal cost to the industry is area 3. This is the value of the lost output of tires and reflects the loss of profits to the tire companies (the buyers of labor) and loss of wages to tire workers (the sellers of labor). Area 4 is the additional external cost to the auto industry, where production is dislocated because tire supplies have dried up.

(*b*) If the shortage of tires becomes so severe that auto companies have to lay off workers, spillover cost 4 from the strike may become much more severe.

---

[9]Strikes may impose external costs not only on other industries and on the general public, but also on unions that are not on strike. One example is a "wildcat strike," in which a small group of workers walks off the job, even though their union has opposed this action because it will leave the rest of the union members idle. Such wildcat strikes are uncommon in the United States, but they are more frequent in some other countries like Britain, where they have contributed to the decline of several important industries. Such strikes can be more disruptive than a full-scale strike that follows a breakdown in union–management contract negotiations. Wildcat strikes may be the result of unions that are too weak to prevent their members from taking such action.

Although the general public often has a stake in a strike decision in a specific industry, the public is not represented in the negotiations that lead to a strike. Its attitude is often: "While labor and management in this industry are fighting over how area 3 is to be divided, we are losing area 4. It doesn't matter whether it is labor or management, or both, who are responsible for this strike; we in the broader public are the big losers. Something is very wrong. True, strikes may play a role in resolving disputes by forcing the two sides to compromise. But isn't there some far less damaging way of doing this?"

LAST RESORT PROCEDURES TO RESOLVE DISPUTES WITHOUT STRIKES

As noted earlier, the Taft-Hartley Act empowers the president to seek a court injunction imposing an 80-day "cooling-off period" to delay a strike that threatens the national health or safety. Although this provides time for labor and management to negotiate a settlement, a strike may still occur after the 80-day period.

One method to assist deadlocked negotiations is to appoint a **mediator**—an impartial third party to study the situation and suggest a compromise settlement. Although mediators' recommendations are not binding, they may help to resolve disputes insofar as they are able to (1) discover a solution that the two contending parties have overlooked; (2) find out who is bluffing and who is not, thus reducing the risk of a strike because lack of information has led one side to miscalculate the true position of the other; or (3) provide a means of saving face for parties that are otherwise locked into highly publicized positions from which there is no graceful retreat. For example, a union can go back to its members and say: "We didn't capitulate to the company. We had no choice but to accept the recommendation of an impartial third party." Thus the two sides may be able to achieve a settlement because each is able to shift the responsibility (blame) onto the mediator.

A more forceful technique to resolve a dispute is **arbitration** with a *binding* decision by an impartial third party. Conventional arbitration has been criticized because it often leads arbitrators to "split the difference," in an attempt to appear impartial. Thus, critics charge, an arbitrator may be less concerned with the objective facts than with finding a decision that both parties will accept and that will thus strengthen the arbitrator's reputation. Another criticism is that knowledge by the two conflicting parties that arbitration can be used can have "chilling" effects on the negotiations leading up to it. Each party becomes reluctant to make any prior concession, because any such concession would automatically reduce its award when the arbitrator eventually comes in and "splits the difference."

One solution is **final-offer arbitration,** under which the arbitrator is forced to accept, *without compromise,* the final offer of *one* of the parties. This provides a strong incentive for each party to come up with a reasonable final offer; the more reasonable, the more likely it is to be accepted by the arbitrator. One study has found an interesting pattern: Labor's final offer is more often accepted than management's, but there is an even smaller average increase in wages than under conventional arbitration.[10] One explanation is that risk-averse unions don't gamble but make a very reasonable final offer.

DISPUTES INVOLVING GOVERNMENT EMPLOYEES

The most damaging strikes are usually those with large external costs, and these costs—illustrated in panel *b* of Figure 22-8—are often particularly large in the public sector. When subway workers go on strike, area 3—the lost income of these workers and the transit authority—is typically far less than area 4—the spillover cost of tying up the city's economic activity. Serious spillover costs similarly result from a strike of garbage collectors or firefighters.

Public service employees sometimes argue that,

---

[10]See Orley Ashenfelter and David E. Bloom, "Models of Arbitrator Behavior: Theory and Evidence," *American Economic Review*, March 1984, pp. 111–124. This section on strikes and the next section on public service disputes also draw on Beth Hayes, "Unions and Strikes with Asymmetric Information," *Journal of Labor Economics,* January 1984, pp. 57–83; and Richard B. Freeman, "Unionism Comes to the Public Sector," *Journal of Economic Literature,* March 1986, pp. 41–86.

if they don't have a union, the government can use its monopsony power in setting their wage rate. They must accept whatever take-it-or-leave-it contract the government offers. Accordingly, membership in public service unions increased rapidly during the 1960s and 1970s from just over 10% to roughly 35% of public servants. Moreover, there was little decline in the early 1980s, when unions in the private sector were shrinking. By that time, the American Federation of State, County and Municipal Employees (AFSCME) had become the largest union affiliated with the AFL-CIO.

Disputes in the public sector raise a number of special problems.

1. Whereas a strike in the private sector puts pressure on employers to settle because of the income they will lose, a strike in the public sector puts pressure on the employers (the government) because of the votes it may lose from an irate public suffering from the suspension of some essential service.

2. A government may find it easier than a private employer to raise the funds necessary to pay a higher wage. For example, the government may borrow or increase taxes. (However, recent taxpayer revolts have made tax increases much more difficult in some states.) Another way a government may be able to avoid a strike is to provide a generous increase in pensions, a relatively painless measure because it commits a future—rather than the present—government to pay employees when they retire. Thus it has appeal to politicians whose major concern is to win the next election. New York City proved how painful the long-run consequences of such a policy may be. By 1975, "the chickens had finally come home to roost." Wage and pension commitments—combined with other major problems, such as large welfare expenditures—drove the city to the brink of bankruptcy, where it was saved only by a period of austerity.

3. In private industry, strikers may drive a firm out of business and find that their jobs have disappeared. There is far less restraint of this kind on public servants. Even though, in the extreme case, a strike costs the government an election, firefighters and the police will still have jobs. With little risk of substantial job loss, a public service union is in a strong bargaining position.

4. Public employees and their dependents may become a significant percentage of the voting population. This weakens the resistance of elected officials to their demands.

Most strikes of public servants are illegal. In a number of cases the president and state governors have broken illegal strikes. As noted, President Reagan fired air-traffic controllers who went out on an illegal strike. Nonetheless, about one state in five has legalized strikes for some public servants. The question, "Should they be allowed to strike?" remains a pressing one. Many legislators, in passing antistrike laws, believe that they should not. If trash collectors go on strike, pollution may threaten public health. If firefighters or the police go on strike, people may die in fires or be victimized by criminals. In the face of such strike threats, a government may feel almost forced to meet labor demands. Surely no group of individuals should hold this sort of power over the public.

However, many government workers argue that, if they are not allowed to strike, they have no weapon to ensure that the government will take their demands seriously. What alternative mechanism do they have for achieving a fair wage? Will compulsory arbitration be enough? One approach is to provide civil servants with salaries equal to those in comparable private sector jobs. However this provides neither a simple nor a complete solution. One difficulty is in defining what is meant by a "comparable" private sector job. Another problem is in determining what downward adjustment, if any, should be made to government salaries because of attractive pensions and a greater degree of job security.

WAGE DIFFERENCES: WHY DO THEY EXIST?

The question "Why do wage differences exist?" can now be answered by drawing together points made in this and previous chapters.

1. First, there may be **dynamic differentials** in wage rates. For example, if there is a large increase in the demand for construction workers in Alaska, their wages will rise above wages earned elsewhere; a dynamic differential is created. Eventually, this higher Alaskan wage will attract workers from other parts of the country, and this wage will

settle back toward the wage level elsewhere; the dynamic differential declines. Such differentials are only temporary; the speed with which they disappear depends on the mobility of the labor force.

A ***dynamic wage differential*** arises because of changing demand or supply conditions in the labor market. It declines over time as labor moves out of jobs with relatively low wages and into those that pay a relatively high wage.

2. Some of the Alaskan wage differential may not disappear over time. To some degree wages may remain higher in Alaska to compensate for some disadvantage of working there, such as the colder climate. Similar **compensating wage differentials** may arise in jobs offering less security or less pleasant working conditions.

Compensating wage differentials result if labor views some jobs as less attractive than others. Employers have to pay a higher wage to fill the unattractive jobs.

For example, boring jobs, or jobs with high stress or risk to human life, pay higher wages.

3. Some wage differences reflect monopsony or monopoly power. Thus workers in a small town facing a monopsony employer may receive a low wage. On the other hand, workers who are exercising market power through a union tend to get higher wages. A particularly high wage may be received by workers who are not only able to exercise market power in their own labor market through a strong union, but who are also employed by a firm with monopoly influence over its product market. For example, workers at General Motors have been able to earn a high wage, not only because of the strength of the UAW, but also because they work for a company that has been able to earn oligopoly profits in the car market. In short, this union has been able to negotiate wage increases out of GM's oligopoly profits in the car market. This was confirmed between 1980 and 1982, when the auto companies' oligopoly power was reduced by competition from imported cars. Combined with the effects of recession, this resulted not only in losses for the car companies, but also pressure on the UAW to give up some wage increases won in earlier negotiations. The companies were no longer earning oligopoly profits that could be shared with labor.

Similarly, a union may be able to negotiate wage increases out of the excess profits earned by firms because they are in a regulated industry. For example, an estimated 65% to 75% of such profits earned by the regulated trucking industry were captured by the union, and lost again once the industry was deregulated.[11]

4. The more capital a firm has per worker, the more likely it is that workers will be able to negotiate higher wages. For example, the more huge jets an airline has sitting idle at great cost, the more willing it may be to concede a few cents on a labor contract.

The last two points provide some explanation of why workers often get a higher wage simply because of the industry they are in. For example, wages are much higher in the chemical industry than in the textile industry. Moreover, this seems to hold true, regardless of the job. Both janitors and highly skilled machine operators get more if they are in the chemical industry than if they are in textiles.

5. Barriers to entry—another departure from perfect competition—may result in wage differentials. For example, long apprenticeship requirements that keep new entrants out of a labor market may keep wages up. Discrimination that keeps women or minorities out of a white male labor market will result in wage differentials by raising the wages of white males and lowering the wages of others.

6. Some companies use a strategy of paying a higher wage in order to have their choice of the most productive workers. If they succeed, their

[11]Nancy L. Rose, "Labor Rent Sharing and Regulation: Evidence from the Trucking Industry," *Journal of Political Economy,* December 1987, pp. 1146–1178. In "Work Disutility and Compensating Differentials: Estimation of Factors in the Link Between Wages and Firm Size," *Review of Economics and Statistics,* February 1986, pp. 67–73, L. F. Dunn finds evidence that labor may capture some of the excess profits of larger firms.

costs may not be higher. However, workers who get a job there do receive a higher income.

7. Finally, wage differences exist because people have different talents, education, and training. This is a major topic in the next chapter.

LIVING IN A GLOBAL ECONOMY

UNION MEMBERSHIP IN OTHER COUNTRIES

Figure 22-9 shows that the rapid decline in union membership that took place in the United States between 1970 and 1985 did not occur elsewhere. True, there was a decline in Japan, but it was at a much slower rate; and in 16 other comparisons (of which a few of the important ones are shown here) union membership rose or did not substantially decline. This was even true in the United Kingdom where union membership in 1985 was essentially the same as in 1970. However, early in that comparison period there was an increase, but it was offset by a subsequent decline after the Thatcher government came into office.

Analysts have been particularly puzzled by the difference in the Canadian and U.S. experience. Although the two countries have many of the same firms and unions, membership in unions increased in Canada while it was decreasing in the United States.

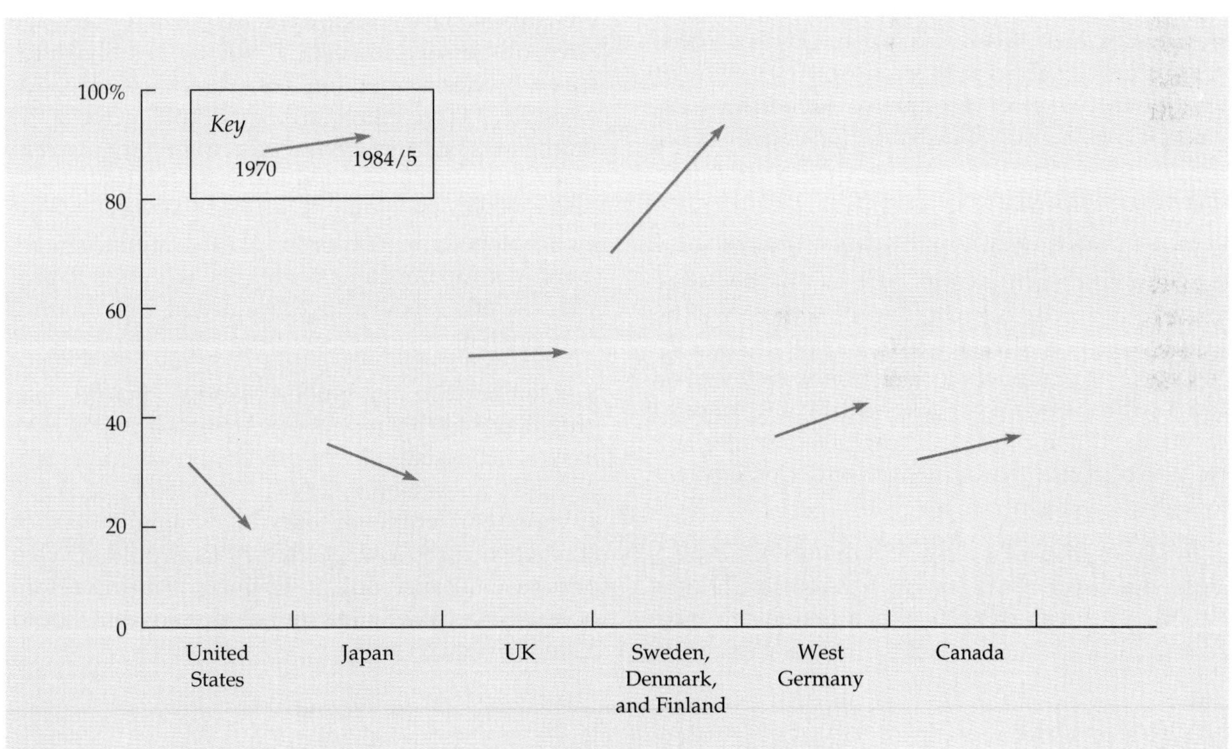

FIGURE 22-9 Percentage of nonagricultural workers who were union members in selected countries, 1970 and 1985. (*Source:* Richard B. Freeman, "Contraction and Expansion: the Divergence of Private Sector and Public Sector Unionism in the United States," *Journal of Economic Perspectives*, Spring 1988, p. 69).

KEY POINTS

1. Labor markets are often imperfect. Workers form unions to exercise monopoly power on the supply side of the market. On the other side of the market, employers may exercise monopsony power. Examples include a government that hires public service employees, and a private firm that is the only major employer in a small town.

2. Unions provide labor with a collective voice. In collective bargaining, unions promote the interests of their workers by pressing for such improvements as (a) better working conditions, (b) seniority rules to protect long-time workers, and (c) higher wages.

3. If a union is formed in a perfectly competitive labor market without externalities and uses its market power to raise the wage rate, there is an overall efficiency loss. The reason is that some workers are not hired in this industry even though they would be more productive here than elsewhere. There is also a transfer: By raising the wage rate, the union transfers income to labor from other factors of production.

4. On the other side of the market, if employers acquire monopsony power and lower the wage below its perfectly competitive level, there will be the same sort of efficiency loss. But while the efficiency effects of monopoly and monopsony will be similar, their transfer effects will be in opposite directions. When a monopsonist lowers wages, the transfer is from labor to other factors of production.

5. If a labor market is already monopsonized by a single employer, it no longer necessarily follows that efficiency will be reduced if a union is formed to raise the wage rate. In fact, if the union's market power is used only to offset the market power of the employer, efficiency will be increased.

6. A union may increase efficiency in other ways, too. By providing workers with a collective voice, it may improve their performance and reduce costly turnover of the labor force. A union may increase productivity by improving morale and communication between labor and management.

7. Bilateral monopoly occurs when market power exists on both sides of the market: Unions with monopoly power bargain with employers with monopsony power. The wage that results will fall between the high wage an unopposed union would seek and the low wage an unopposed monopsonist would offer. But, within these limits, it is impossible to predict precisely where the wage rate will be set. However, it will be heavily influenced by the bargaining power of each side. For example, a large union strike fund will increase the union's bargaining power, whereas a large inventory of finished goods will increase the bargaining power of management. Bargaining is also affected by the negotiating expertise of labor and management. An incompetent negotiator who won't provide the other side with a face-saving compromise may prevent an agreement from being reached.

8. Membership in public service unions has grown rapidly in recent years. Such a union may have a strong bargaining position, particularly if it provides an essential service. To avoid a strike, a government employer may be willing to tax or borrow to meet a wage claim that would drive a private employer out of business. An important policy issue is whether public employees should have the right to strike.

KEY CONCEPTS

industrial union
craft union
collective bargaining
seniority rules
codetermination
closed shop
union shop
open shop
right-to-work law
transfer and efficiency effects of a union
transfer and efficiency effects of monopsony
bilateral monopoly
spillover costs of a strike
mediation
arbitration
final-offer arbitration
dynamic wage differential
compensating wage differential

PROBLEMS

22-1. Before deregulation, the Civil Aeronautics Board allowed the airlines to charge high fares, with some of the resulting profit being absorbed by high wage and salary payments. In such circumstances, would you expect that the deregulation that has made the airlines more competitive in setting their fares has affected their labor contracts as well? If so, how? What, in fact, did happen to the wages and salaries of employees when the airlines were deregulated?

22-2. "Monopsony in the labor market may have exactly the same effect on efficiency as a union." Is this possible? Explain. Would the transfer effects be the same in the two cases? (If you have studied Figure 2 on page 369, show how the two cases in the present example can involve identical efficiency effects but entirely different transfer effects.)

22-3. In the case of monopsony, which efficiency condition in Figure 21-7 has been violated? Explain.

22-4. In Figure 22-5, suppose that the initial wage rate in a unionized labor market is $12. If employers form a bargaining association and successfully negotiate a lower wage rate, show how efficiency is affected. Consider two cases: What happens if the association negotiates the wage down to $9? Down to $8?

22-5. Do you think that, as capital accumulates, the bargaining power of workers vis-à-vis management increases or decreases? Which workers can more effectively threaten to strike: Workers who would be leaving bulldozers idle? Or workers who would be laying down their shovels?

22-6. Which union in each of the following pairs has the greater bargaining power? In each case, explain why. (a) A union of workers on the New York subway or a union of workers who build the trains. (b) A firefighters' union or a public school teachers' union. (c) A public school teachers' union or a university professors' union.

22-7. "Tying wage increases in the public sector to wage increases in private industry will not necessarily equalize wages. All it will do is keep them the same if they start out equal. If public sector wages are initially less than private sector wages, tying wages in this way only guarantees that inequities will be preserved." Do you agree? Do you think it is fair to pay both public and private employees the same wage if public employees have greater job security? If not, explain why, and give an estimate of the differential you consider fair.

22-8. Use a diagram to show how the theory of the second best applies to labor forming a union in a market that is already monopsonized.

CHAPTER 23
OTHER INCOMES

Buy land. They ain't making any more of the stuff.
WILL ROGERS

For the average American, an education brings a higher income. In 1986, Americans with only an elementary school education earned a median income of $9,000; those with a high school diploma earned $20,000; and those with four or more years of college earned $33,000. The higher average income of university graduates is a return to their greater natural ability and to the investment in their education made by themselves, their families, and American taxpayers. As you are spending time and money today to get an education and thus increase your productivity and income in the future, you are making an investment in *human capital,* just as a business invests in machinery and other form of *physical capital.* Either represents an expenditure today that is expected to pay off in the future.

The previous two chapters have focused on the income of labor. The spotlight now turns to the incomes of other factors of production, that is, the income of capital—both physical and human—and the income of land.

The first broad topic is the income earned from physical capital such as plant and machinery. This income comes in two forms. First, **interest** income is received by those who provide **debt capital,** that is, those who lend money to firms—or to others—to finance the purchase of machinery or the construction of new buildings. (One way to lend money to a firm is to buy its bonds. Another way is to lend money to a bank or other financial intermediary which in turn lends it to the firm.) Second, **profits** are earned by those who own **equity capital,** that is, those who own small firms outright or who own shares of a corporation's stock. Although the individual who buys stocks and bonds may view them quite differently, in this chapter their similarity is emphasized. Both represent a way in which people can contribute to the expansion of the nation's physical capital and receive income in return.

INTEREST: THE RETURN TO DEBT CAPITAL

To begin, suppose that firms finance investment only by borrowing. Borrowing takes place in the market for loanable funds, where lenders who supply funds come together with borrowers who demand funds. Like a competitive commodity market, a perfectly competitive market for loans can be studied with demand and supply curves.

HOW THE DEMAND AND SUPPLY OF LOANS DETERMINES THE INTEREST RATE

Figure 23-1 shows the demand curve for loans by firms seeking the funds to finance investment projects—for example, funds to acquire new machinery. (People who need loans to buy cars or furni-

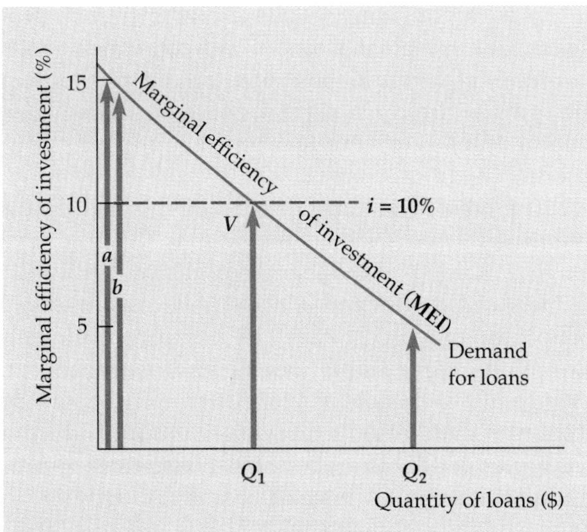

FIGURE 23-1 The marginal efficiency of investment and the demand for loans.

Investment opportunities are ranked in order, starting on the left with those yielding the highest return. The resulting MEI schedule is also the demand for loans. For example, if the interest rate is 10%, firms will demand Q_1 of loans. They keep borrowing to point V, where the marginal benefit of borrowing (the MEI schedule) is equal to the marginal cost of borrowing (the interest rate).

ture also participate in this market, but such complications are avoided in this simple introduction.) Just as the demand for labor depends on the productivity of labor, so too the demand for loans to buy, say, machinery depends on how productive that machinery will be—that is, on the *marginal efficiency of investment* (*MEI*) shown in this diagram. Arrow *a* on the far left represents the investment with the highest return (MEI) of 15%. To illustrate, suppose a machine costs $100,000 and lasts only one year. If this machine generates enough sales to cover labor, materials, etc., and leave $115,000 in addition, it repays the firm for its initial $100,000 investment and provides a $15,000 return on that investment. When expressed as a percentage (15% on the $100,000 investment), this return is called the marginal efficiency of investment.

The next most attractive investment is project *b*, which provides a return of just less than 15%. When all investment projects are ordered in this way, starting with those yielding the highest return and moving down to the right to projects with lower yields, the result is the marginal efficiency of investment curve (MEI). This curve also represents the demand for investment loans. For example, if the interest rate is the 10% shown, then Q_1 of loans will be demanded. Firms will wish to invest in all the high-return opportunities to the left of V. For example, project *a* will return enough (15%) to pay the 10% interest, and leave something over to add to profits. On the other hand, projects to the right of V will be rejected because their returns would not be enough even to cover the interest cost.

Recall from Equation (21-1) on p. 372 that firms hire labor to the point where its price (the wage rate) is equal to its marginal revenue product. Similarly, Figure 23-1 shows how firms acquire capital to the point where its price (the interest rate) equals the marginal efficiency of investment. In the process, the market works to direct financial capital to the nation's most productive investment projects. Those yielding high returns to the left of V get funds. Low-return projects to the right of V do not get funds.

In Figure 23-2, the demand for investment loans (MEI) is reproduced from Figure 23-1. This diagram also shows the other important influence on investment—the supply of funds by lenders. This supply indicates how much businesses and households are willing to provide at various interest rates.[1] For example, the 4% interest rate that would just barely induce individual f to save and lend reflects how highly he or she values this money in its alternative use—current consumption. Individuals who value current consumption more highly won't be induced to save and lend until the interest rate rises above 4%. Therefore they appear further to the right in this supply schedule. They are often described as having a stronger **time preference.**

> ***Time preference*** is the preference for consuming now rather than in the future.

[1]Here, a number of macroeconomic complications are assumed away, such as the role of financial institutions in moving funds from savers to investors, and in particular the effects of the banking system on the supply of loans. These complications are studied in Chapters 11, 12 and 17 of the companion volume.

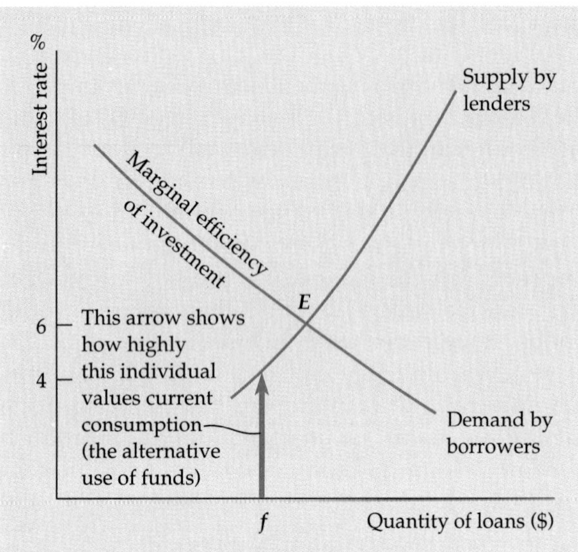

FIGURE 23-2 The market for loans.

The demand for loans is reproduced from Figure 23-1. The supply of loans depends on time preference—that is, on how highly lenders value income in its alternative use, consumption. The equilibrium is at *E* with a 6% interest rate.

In a perfectly competitive market for investment funds, equilibrium is at *E*, where demand and supply intersect. In this example, the equilibrium rate of interest is 6%.

It is important to emphasize that this 6% interest rate reflects the height of the demand curve at *E*. In other words, the rate of return on investment (the marginal efficiency of investment) is equal to the interest rate, in this case 6%. $1 worth of goods today can be invested to produce $1.06 of goods next year. In short, investment converts present goods into a larger amount of future goods.

Through investment, present goods can be exchanged for a larger amount of future goods. Thus present goods are worth more than future goods, with the interest rate telling us how much more.

ROUNDABOUT PRODUCTION, WITH INTEREST AS THE REWARD FOR WAITING

Investment is often described as *roundabout or indirect production*. Rather than using resources today to produce consumer goods directly, society produces an even greater amount of consumer goods indirectly by a roundabout method. First, resources are used to produce capital goods, and then this capital is used to produce even more consumer goods.

The greater quantity of consumer goods that is eventually produced in this way is the incentive for undertaking roundabout production. However, roundabout production is not possible unless some people are prepared to *wait*, by deferring their consumption today; that is, people must be willing to save. This is necessary in order to release the resources that would otherwise go into producing consumer goods, and allow these resources to produce capital goods instead. For their decision to defer consumption—to wait before enjoying their income—savers receive an interest return. Thus the interest rate can be viewed as a reward to savers for waiting, just as the wage rate is a reward to labor for its time and effort.

RISK AND OTHER INFLUENCES ON THE INTEREST RATE

Although only one interest rate is shown in Figure 23-2, in fact at any point in time there are many rates of interest. A very large and financially sound corporation will be able to borrow funds at a low interest rate, since lenders view this loan as relatively *risk-free*. But a company in shaky financial condition will have to pay a higher interest rate to compensate lenders for the greater risk that the loan will not be repaid. Thus the interest rate shown in Figure 23-2 may be viewed as the "base rate of interest" that applies to a risk-free loan; as such, it is the best simple measure of the marginal efficiency of investment. Even though this base rate remains the focus of attention, it should be kept in mind that there is a whole array of interest rates on loans of varying risk.

Interest rates also reflect the expectation of inflation. (This macroeconomic issue is dealt with in Chapter 15 of the companion volume. For simplicity, a noninflationary world is described here.) In addition, interest rates today depend on the length of term of the loans and the expectation of future changes in interest rates. To illustrate, suppose interest rates today are expected to rise next year because of an increase in the demand for loans by business. In this case, lenders will now be reluctant to lend money for a long period of, say, 5 or 10 years. They will prefer instead to lend their money for a short period of, say, a year, at which time they will get it back, and can then lend it out again at the expected higher interest rate. Thus lenders now increase their supply of short-term, one-year loans, and this lowers the price (the interest rate) on these loans. At the same time, lenders now decrease their supply of longer term, 5- or 10-year loans, raising the interest rate on these loans. Therefore the expectation of a future increase in interest rates will cause today's long-term interest rate to rise relative to today's short-term interest rate.

As noted in earlier chapters, an important question in product or labor markets is: What happens if the government intervenes to impose some restriction on price? This is also an important question in the capital market—that is, in the market for loans.

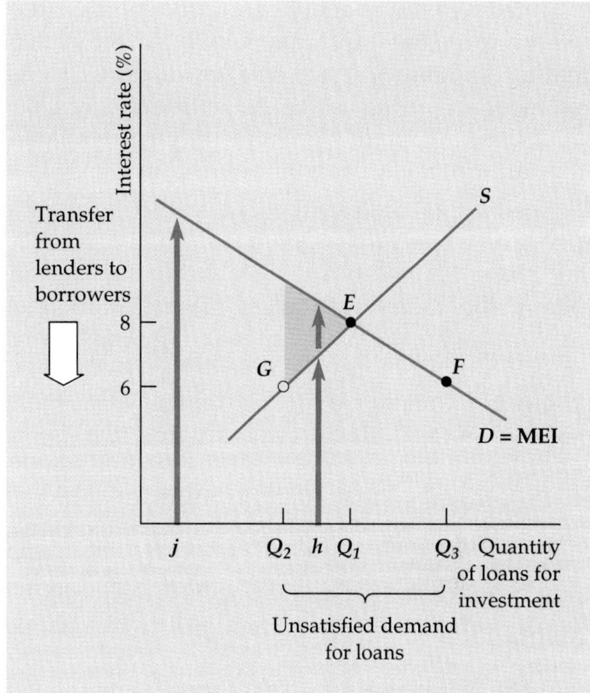

FIGURE 23-3 Effects of an interest rate ceiling.

Before the interest rate ceiling, equilibrium is at *E*, with Q_1 of investment funds loaned out at an 8% interest rate. When a ceiling of 6% is imposed, borrowers attracted by the lower rate try to move down their demand curve from *E* to *F* and seek Q_3 of loans. However, only Q_2 of loans are available because lenders, discouraged by the reduced interest return, move down their supply curve from *E* to *G*. Thus loans are reduced from Q_1 to Q_2, and there is Q_2Q_3 unsatisfied demand for loans. There is an efficiency loss because economically justified investment projects like *h* in the range Q_2Q_1 cannot be undertaken because of lack of funds. This is a loss because the cost of project *h* would have been only the tall red arrow under the supply curve (the 7% cost to the lender of having to reduce consumption), whereas the benefit of project *h* would have been both red arrows under the demand curve (that is, the return of almost 9% on this investment). Thus the net loss because this particular project is canceled is the short red arrow. The efficiency loss from all such cancellations in the relevant range Q_2Q_1 is the red triangle. (This assumes that projects like *h* are the ones to be knocked out as funds are rationed. But if higher productivity projects like *j* are knocked out instead, the efficiency loss is even greater.)

The wide arrow on the left shows the transfer from lenders to those borrowers lucky enough to get the bargain funds.

EFFECTS OF AN INTEREST RATE CEILING

Figure 23-3 shows what happens in a perfectly competitive capital market when the government intervenes to impose a ceiling on the price of money, that is, a ceiling on the interest rate that can be charged by banks and other lenders. Original equilibrium before the ceiling is at *E*, with an 8% interest rate. When the government sets a ceiling below this rate, say, at 6%, the market no longer clears. There is a shortage of funds of *GF*, representing unsatisfied investors who would like to borrow at this low interest rate but who cannot find loans.

One of the arguments in favor of an interest rate ceiling is that it will reduce the burden of interest payments on relatively poor individuals and small firms. The lower interest rate does result in a transfer (shown by the white arrow) from lenders to borrowers—but *only to those borrowers lucky enough to get loans*. However, there is no guarantee that this redistribution will "help the poor," since it is the poor who are most likely to be turned down for loans. If you had $100,000 to lend, would you lend it to the wealthy or to the poor? Thus it is often the well-to-do who get the bargain loans to finance their big homes and business ventures.

Moreover, the interest rate ceiling has two unfavorable effects on efficiency.

1. It reduces the quantity of loanable funds available for investment from the initial, perfectly competitive amount Q_1 to the smaller quantity Q_2. As expected, the result is the red efficiency loss because there are too few investment funds available, as detailed in the caption to this diagram.

2. Inefficiency occurs not only because the quantity of investment funds is reduced, but also because the wrong borrowers may get the limited funds. Because the interest rate ceiling makes the demand for loans Q_3 greater than the supply Q_2, the limited supply of funds must be rationed in some way. Whatever rationing method bankers may use, there will be a second efficiency loss unless the Q_2 of available funds are rationed out to exactly the right set of borrowers—that is, those borrowers like *j* to the left of Q_2, who have the investment projects with the highest productivity (MEI). In other words, the projects that are knocked out must be the low-productivity projects like *h* in the range Q_2Q_1. But suppose this isn't the case. Suppose, for example, that high-productivity project *j* on the left is the one that is knocked out, not *h*. (The borrower for *h* may have been more persuasive to a banker who is rationing loans.) There is now this second efficiency loss, because an even more productive investment (*j* rather than *h*) is knocked out. (Moreover, as illustrated in Problem 23-3, this rationing inefficiency may be even worse, since there are now borrowers with even less productive projects in the range Q_1Q_3 who now, for the first time, apply for loans, and some may get them. If they do, higher productivity investments will lose out. Why do these borrowers apply, when they didn't originally? The answer is that the artificially lower interest rate has made their projects profitable for the first time.)

This second source of inefficiency—above and beyond the red triangle in Figure 23-3—may be summarized as follows. In an unrestricted, perfectly competitive capital market, the interest rate is a price that allocates funds to the most productive investment projects. When the government intervenes to set an interest rate ceiling, some other allocating device must be used, and there is then a risk that the wrong set of projects will get the funds. In the rationing process, high-productivity projects may lose out to those with low productivity.

This is just another illustration of the general problem that applies to any form of price fixing, such as the earlier example of rent control. Not only does rent control result in fewer apartments for rent. In addition, the apartments that do exist may be used inefficiently because the wrong people get them. For example, a retired couple may continue to hang on to a choice New York apartment even though they now spend 9 months a year in Florida, and would give it up if they had to pay the higher free-market rent.

Thus, if we wish to transfer income from the rich to the poor, regulating a market price like apartment rents or the interest rate may be an unwise way to do it. In the first place, an interest ceiling may be an ineffective form of transfer because it may not move income from the rich to the poor at all. Instead it may, to some degree, benefit the rich who get the scarce loans and hurt the poor who do not. Moreover, an interest ceiling may have damaging effects on efficiency. Isn't it better for the government to do any transferring directly, by taxing the rich and subsidizing the poor? The answer is yes, provided the government can do so without incurring large efficiency losses of a different sort—an issue to be addressed in Chapter 25.

NORMAL PROFIT: A RETURN TO EQUITY CAPITAL

Thus far (Fig. 23-2), all funds for investment projects have gone through the market for loanable funds. However, a firm may also raise funds by selling its stock. This is called equity finance, because those who buy the stock obtain a share of the equity (ownership) and future profits of the firm.

Chapter 9 drew a distinction between two kinds of profit: **Normal profit** reflects opportunity cost—the return necessary to induce and hold funds in one activity rather than another. **Above-normal profit** is any additional profit above this. Above-normal profit will be described later in this chapter. For now, let us consider normal profit.

For those who provide equity funds, what is their normal profit; that is, what is the opportunity cost of these funds? The answer is the return the funds could earn in their best alternative use. An alternative to buying stock is to buy interest-bearing securities such as government bonds. Thus normal profit can be viewed as the base, no-risk rate of interest *plus* an appropriate premium for risk—a risk that may be substantial in a world of uncertainty in which the entire amount that is put into the ownership of a firm may be wiped out. [Profit is sometimes described as a reward for risk-taking. However, it is more than this, since it must also include a base rate of return needed to attract funds away from no-risk, interest-bearing alternatives.]

Figure 23-2 can now be recast in the more general form shown in Figure 23-4, which represents the total market for investment funds. Now *D* includes the total demand by business for investment funds, whether these funds are raised by borrowing or by the sale of stock, and *S* is the corresponding supply. The resulting equilibrium *Q* is the quantity of both debt and equity funds provided by savers to those who invest.

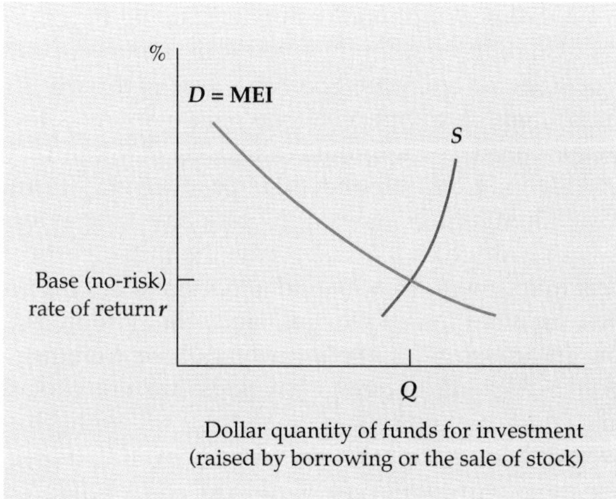

FIGURE 23-4 The market for investment funds (a generalization of Fig. 23-2).

Whereas Figure 23-2 showed only borrowing, this diagram shows two ways that business may raise funds—by borrowing or by the sale of stock. *D* is the demand for funds to finance new investment, whereas *S* is the corresponding supply of funds. In equilibrium, the base rate of return, in the absence of risk, would be *r*. However, in a risky world, the rate any specific business must actually pay for the funds it raises will be *r* plus an appropriate amount to compensate the lender for risk.

FACTOR PRICES AND THE ALLOCATION OF SCARCE RESOURCES

Just as price acts as the screening mechanism for deciding who will consume a good and who will not (Fig. 11-5), so a factor price acts as a screening device to determine how a scarce resource will be used.

HOW FACTOR PRICES DETERMINE THE ECONOMYWIDE USE OF SCARCE FACTORS

The wage rate acts as a screen to determine the particular activities in which society's scarce labor will be employed. In a competitive, fully employed economy, the wage rate rises as productivity increases. This conveys a clear message to those producers who can no longer afford the higher wage. The message is: "Society can no longer afford to have its scarce labor employed in your activity. There are now too many other, more productive pursuits." This may seem harsh, but it is the sign of economic progress. Think back, for a moment, to all the things labor used to do but no longer does. At the current high wage rate, it doesn't pay to hire workers to hoe field corn, as in the "good old days." Household servants have almost vanished.

Similarly, the interest rate is a market price that acts as a screen to determine in which particular projects investment will take place. When that screening device is replaced by another—such as the rationing that occurs when an interest rate ceiling is imposed—investment funds are less likely to go to the most productive projects.

HOW FACTOR PRICES INFLUENCE DECISIONS BY INDIVIDUAL FIRMS

In its decision making, a firm must address several issues. On the one hand, it must decide how much labor and how much capital equipment it will use. At the same time, it must also decide which goods to produce and how much of each. To illustrate, suppose the wage rate rises. The firm responds by using less labor and more capital; that is, it substitutes capital for labor because labor has become more expensive. Because of the higher wage, the firm may also reduce the output of its final products, especially those requiring a great deal of labor.

As a further example of how factor and product decisions are interrelated, suppose there is an increase in the price of one of the firm's products. In response, the firm will increase its output of this good by hiring more factors of production and/or by shifting production away from one of its other outputs. In short, the firm's decisions on what to produce and the amount of factors to employ are not separate decisions. Instead, they are all elements of one overall decision.

THE RETURN TO INVESTMENT IN HUMAN CAPITAL

Income is earned not only by investment in machinery and other physical capital, but also by investment in human capital—the acquisition of skills, training, and education.[2] In many respects, an investment in human capital is similar to an investment in physical capital. Current consumption is reduced in the expectation of higher future income and consumption. The best illustration is the example cited earlier. Students give up the income they could make if they were not busy studying; they live frugally in the hope that an education will pay off in higher income after graduation. Similarly, apprentices may be willing to work for abnormally low wages if they are receiving training that is likely to lead to a better job.

Because of human capital, everyone in the labor force is not equally productive; thus our earlier assumption that all workers are similar is now being relaxed. In fact, the quality of labor depends on the amount of education, skill, and experience that various individuals have acquired. Some have a lot of human capital, others very little. Frequently, their incomes reflect this difference. Three-quarters of the national income is paid in the form of wages and salaries, but wages and salaries include not only a basic payment for the time and effort of unskilled labor, but also a return on the human capital that skilled workers have acquired.

Who pays for the investment in human capital? In the case of higher education, much of the investment is undertaken by the individuals who pay university fees and spend their time studying instead of earning an income. However, governments also invest: Federal, state, and local governments all help to finance education. One justification for such subsidies is that they are *equitable* because they provide everyone—regardless of family background or income—with an educational opportunity. Another justification is that these subsidies are *efficient*, because education provides not only a benefit to those who acquire it, but also external benefits to others in society as well. For example, if a highly educated doctor discovers a new vaccine, it may not only increase the discoverer's own income, but will also generate benefits far beyond this for the general public, which now has protection from a disease. In the face of such external benefits, the unaided free market will provide an inefficiently low investment in human capital. The government subsidizes this investment to increase it to a more efficient level.

On-the-job apprenticeship or training in industry also represents an investment in human capital. There are several ways the initial cost of this investment may be covered. Workers may accept a low wage during the apprenticeship period when they are learning the job and their productivity is still low. Alternatively, employers may pay apprentices a higher wage and thereby bear the initial costs of this investment. However, this option raises a serious problem for employers, since they are investing in an asset—in the form of skill or training—which they do not own. Workers are not slaves, and they can always quit and go to work elsewhere, taking the training with them. (Of course, the ease with which they can do so depends on how specific their expertise is to the company that trained them.) This is another reason why there may be underinvestment in human capital: Employers may not invest as heavily in training programs as they would if workers would guarantee to stay on the job and thus allow employers to "get their investment back."

Even though our investment in human capital may be inadequate, it is still very large, substantially exceeding the nation's investment in physical capital such as machinery. Improving the "machinery in our heads" is more important than improv-

[2]For a sample of early work in this field, see Gary S. Becker, *Human Capital: A Theoretical and Empirical Analysis, with Special Reference to Education*, 2d ed. (New York: National Bureau of Economic Research, 1975) and Jacob Mincer, *Schooling Experience and Earning* (New York: National Bureau of Economic Research, 1974).

ing the machinery in our factories. How much does this cost? In 1987, about $100 billion was devoted to worker training, not including on-the-job efforts to improve skills, and $500 billion was devoted to formal education. (These figures include both the direct bills for schools and other forms of education paid by governments and students, and, almost as important, the indirect cost of lost output by those who were learning rather than at work.) In total, this far exceeded the $450 billion gross private investment in plant and equipment.

MEASURING THE RETURN TO HUMAN CAPITAL: WHAT IS A COLLEGE EDUCATION WORTH?

A college education is costly. Two of the most important costs are illustrated in Figure 23-5, which shows the income pattern of those with a college degree and those without.

The first cost is the income foregone during the actual period of study. This cost can be visualized as a set of arrows like *a*, one for each year spent in college. But that's not the only sacrifice college students make. Even after their education is complete, their average incomes at first are below the incomes of people without a degree who have four years of experience and seniority instead. This cost to college students is the set of postcollege arrows like *b*. However, this income disadvantage disappears fairly quickly. By point *F* in their mid-twenties, college graduates have caught up. Arrow *c* shows that, by their late thirties, they have gone well ahead—and their advantage widens.

Thus the costs and benefits of a college education can be summed up:

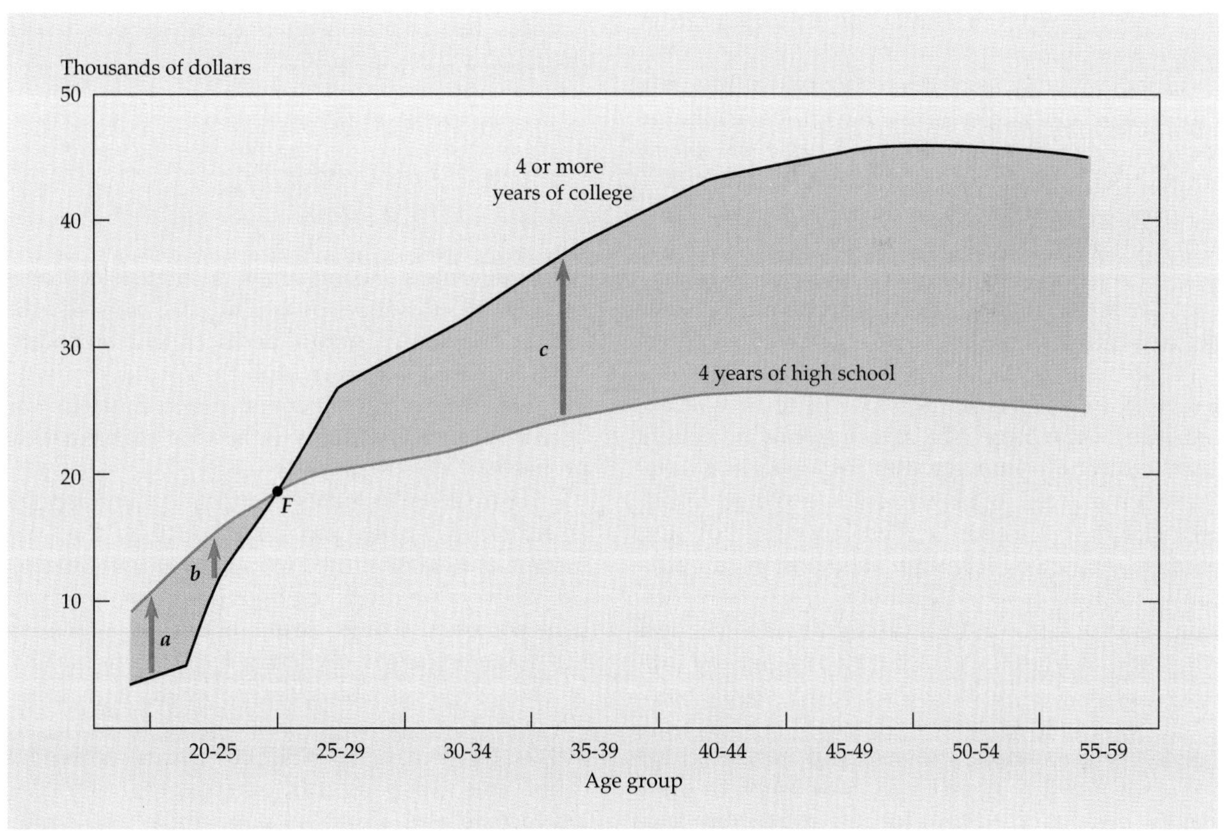

FIGURE 23-5 Lifetime profile of people's incomes, with and without a college education.

Average annual earnings of male, year-round, full-time workers, 1984–1985 in 1985 dollars. (*Source: Economic Report of the President, 1988,* p. 172. Estimates prior to age 27 are by authors, based on earlier studies.)

1. The costs include both (a) the income foregone during college and the later "catchup period," shown as the red area in this diagram, and (b) a set of costs not shown in this diagram, including tuition.

2. The benefits are in the form of a higher income later, as shown by the blue area. Over a lifetime, this difference is more than $600,000 (at 1985 prices) for the average graduate.

By comparing these initial costs and eventual benefits, we can calculate the percentage return on a college education in much the same way as the return on physical capital such as machinery. Recent estimates place this rate of return on human capital at 8 to 10% on a college education. This compares favorably with the historic rate of return on physical capital but is not quite as high as the 10 to 13% rate of return on a high school education. (For those going on to a Ph.D, the estimated rate of return is only 2%.)

Such calculations of the return on college education raise special problems. First, these estimates may be *too high.* Some of the income of college graduates is due, not to their education, but to other factors. For example, on average they are more able, persistent, and hard-working. But don't forget: What is true *on average* is not true of *all individuals.* There are some individuals without a college degree who are more able than some with a degree.

There is also a reason why estimates of the return to a college education may be too *low.* These estimates don't take into account another benefit from education—namely, the fact that it is consumption as well as investment. People go to college not just to earn higher incomes, but also because they enjoy learning. Furthermore, an education often leads to more attractive, safe, and challenging jobs. For example, even if the income were the same, it would be more interesting and less risky to design a building than to put up the steel. Then, too, jobs may come with what the British call "perks." For example, expense-paid business trips are often fun. The question is, how much of these special benefits are offset by the greater pressure facing those at the top?

A further problem with estimated rates of return to higher education is that they represent a *private return* to those acquiring the education. The rate of return to *society as a whole* may be quite different.

WHY THE PRIVATE AND SOCIAL RATES OF RETURN TO EDUCATION DIFFER

To estimate the social return to investment in higher education, the estimated private rate of return should ideally be adjusted as follows:

1. Adjust the private return *down* to take account of government subsidies to higher education. These are costs of the investment to society but not to the private individuals being educated. Because private individuals do not take these costs into account, they are not included in the calculation of private rates of return. However, they should be taken into account in calculating the rate of return to society.

2. Adjust the private rate of return *up* to take account of any external benefits, such as the spillover benefit from the education of the doctor who discovers a new vaccine.

THE COMPLEX NATURE OF WAGES AND SALARIES

An individual's income may be higher not only because of education or training. It may also be higher because of some specific talent or ability. Magic Johnson was born with the natural ability to become a basketball superstar. Albert Einstein was born with a special talent for solving mathematical problems.

Figure 23-6 illustrates this idea. An initial point of reference is provided on the left by the base income of $18,000 earned by a worker with no special talent or training. The remaining three individuals work for a large firm. Individual A has an MBA and five years experience. He earns $40,000 income which is also what he could earn in an alternative occupation. (This figure includes the $18,000 base wage plus a $22,000 return on his education and experience.) In other words, $40,000 is his income and also his opportunity cost. Individual B has exactly the same education and experience as A, and the same $40,000 opportunity cost. However, her income is another $25,000 higher because she has a special flair for solving the prob-

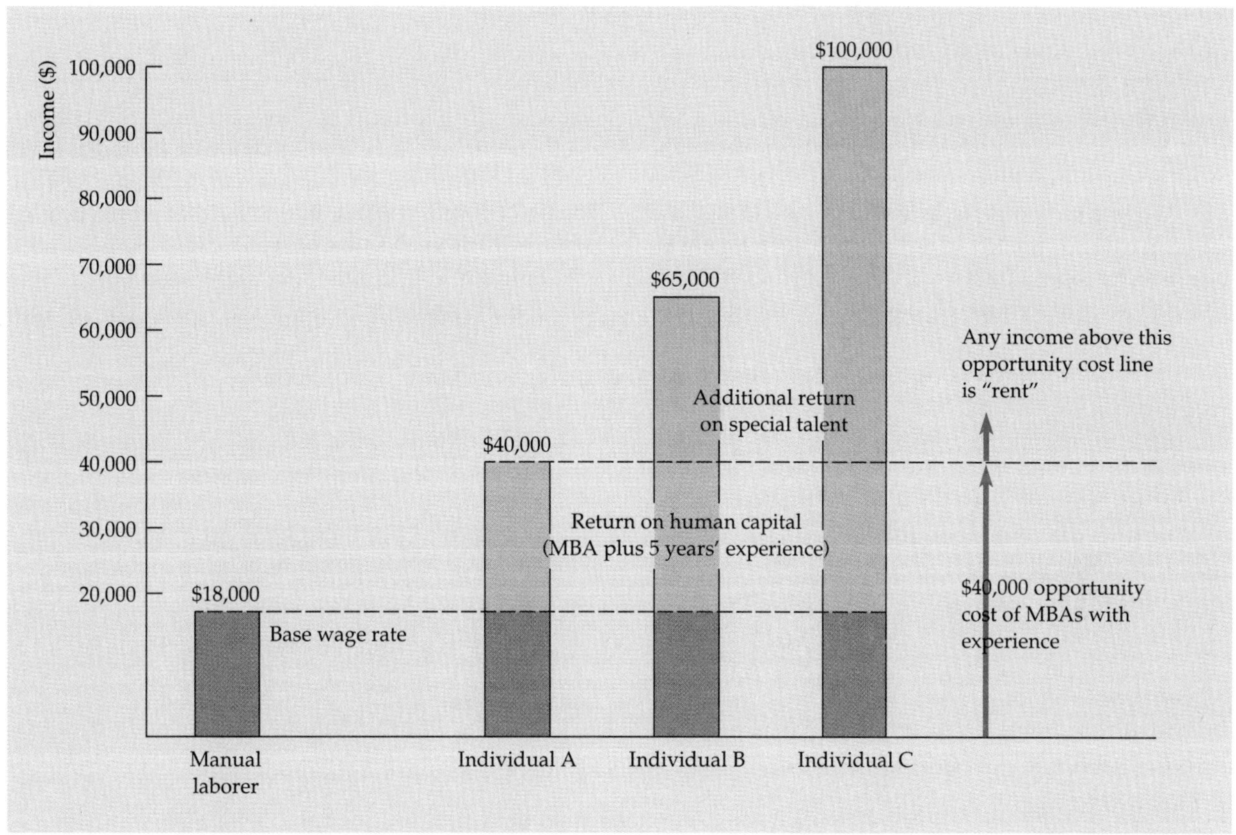

FIGURE 23-6 Dividing income into its components.
Individuals A, B, and C have the same qualifications—an MBA plus five years experience—and the same $40,000 opportunity cost. Any surplus income above this is rent. Thus A earns no rent, B earns $25,000 rent, and C—with the greatest natural talent for the job—earns $60,000 rent.

lems encountered by this firm. Finally, individual C has exactly the same education, experience, and opportunity cost as A and B. But he has an even more incisive mind in dealing with this firm's problems. Consequently, his income is a hefty $100,000.

Three components of income can be distinguished:

1. The $18,000 base income for unskilled work.
2. The additional $22,000 of income that these individuals could earn in other jobs because of their education and experience.

The first two components represent opportunity cost. The last one does not:

3. Additional returns to those with special talents.

This final item falls under the *economists' broad definition of rent*.

Rent is the return to any factor of production in excess of its opportunity cost.

Thus rent is the gap between what a factor *is* earning and what it *could* earn elsewhere. There are two reasons why an individual's income might include a very large rent component: (1) The income he or she is earning may be very high, or (2) what he or she could earn elsewhere is low. Here the focus continues to be on the first reason; the second is considered in Box 23-1.

BOX 23–1 Rent and Opportunity Cost

Rent is the difference between what a factor is earning and what it could earn elsewhere (its opportunity cost). The three business executives in Figure 23-6 had the same $40,000 opportunity cost but different incomes, so they had different rents. Differences in rent can also occur if individuals have the same income but different opportunity costs. This is illustrated in Figure 23-7*a* which shows a labor market where all individuals have the same salary *Y*. However, their opportunity costs differ, as shown by the height of the labor supply curve *S*. For example, individuals *f* and *g* have the two different opportunity costs shown by the two red arrows. Therefore their rents differ.

Specifically, individual *f* has barely been attracted into this industry by income *Y*, since this is what she can earn

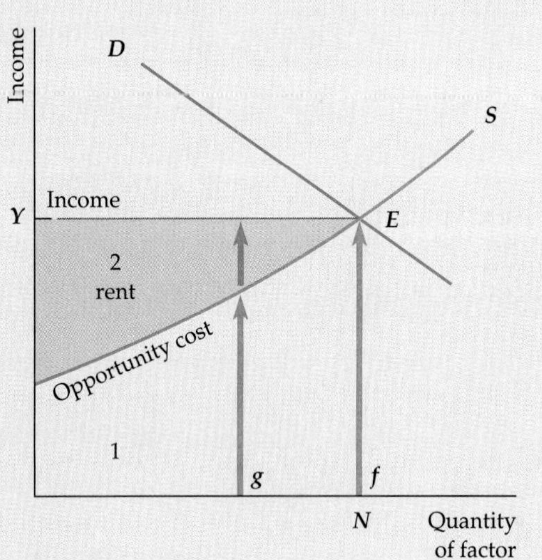

(*a*) All individuals in this panel earn the same income **Y**, but they have different opportunity costs, as given by the height of the curve **S**. The difference between their income and opportunity cost is rent. For individual **g**, this is the blue arrow, while for individuals **f** it is zero. For all individuals, it is the blue area.

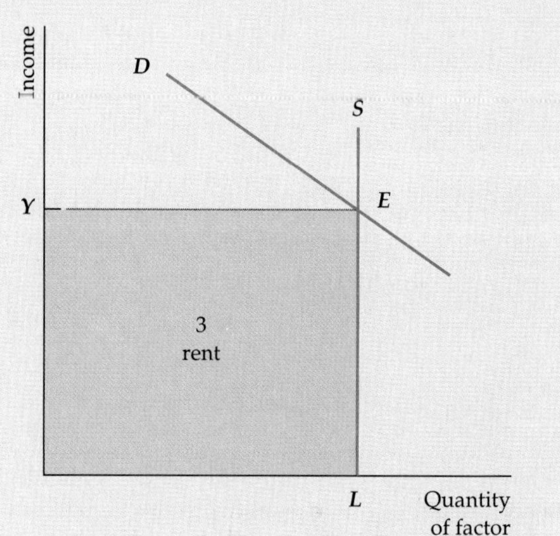

(*b*) None of the plots of land in this panel has any other use. All plots have zero opportunity cost, and their supply is completely inelastic. Therefore, their entire income 3 is rent.

FIGURE 23-7 Rents depend on alternative uses.

RENT

What do Placido Domingo, Steffi Graf, and an acre of Iowa farmland have in common? The answer is: They all are like business executive C in Figure 23-6. They all earn an economic rent because of their superior quality. Domingo has an exceptional voice. Graf plays outstanding tennis. An acre of Iowa land yields unusual quantities of corn.

RENT ON AGRICULTURAL LAND, BASED ON DIFFERENCES IN QUALITY

Figure 23-9 shows three plots of land with no

elsewhere (her opportunity cost). Because there is no difference between her income and her opportunity cost, she earns no rent.

The situation for individual *g* is different. His lower opportunity cost (potential income elsewhere) is shown by the shorter red arrow. The difference between this and his actual income *Y* is the blue arrow. This is his rent. If the similar red arrows representing the rents of other workers are also taken into account, the result is blue triangle 2 representing the rent earned by all workers in this industry.

To sum up this example: The *N* workers, all earning salary *Y*, have a total salary income of areas 1 + 2. Of this, area 1 is their opportunity cost, while area 2 is their rent. The income of any other factor of production can similarly be divided into the two components of opportunity cost and rent.

Panel *b* shows rent on land with a completely inelastic supply; it can't be used for anything but agriculture. In other words, quantity *L* will be supplied no matter what its price may be. Because this land can't earn anything in any other use, its opportunity cost is zero, and all its income 3 is rent.

However, rent must be more complicated than this, since this analysis assumes that all individuals have the same income *Y*, and often they do not. Therefore, to complete this discussion of rent, consider Figure 23-8, which shows a case where *both* income and opportunity cost differ between two professional basketball players. This diagram illustrates how an individual can earn rent because (1) he's very good at what he's doing, therefore his income is higher; or (2) he's bad at anything else, therefore his opportunity cost is lower. Washington is a better basketball player than teammate McTavish, and his higher income reflects this. If they had the same opportunity costs—that is, the same ability to earn income elsewhere—Washington would have a higher rent. But they don't have the same opportunity costs. Whereas Washington could play pro football instead for $100,000 a year, McTavish has no other talent than basketball. His opportunity cost is the bare $18,000 that he could earn in unskilled manual labor. Because his opportunity cost is so low, almost all McTavish's income is rent. Indeed, for this reason there's a larger rent component in his small income than in Washington's large income.

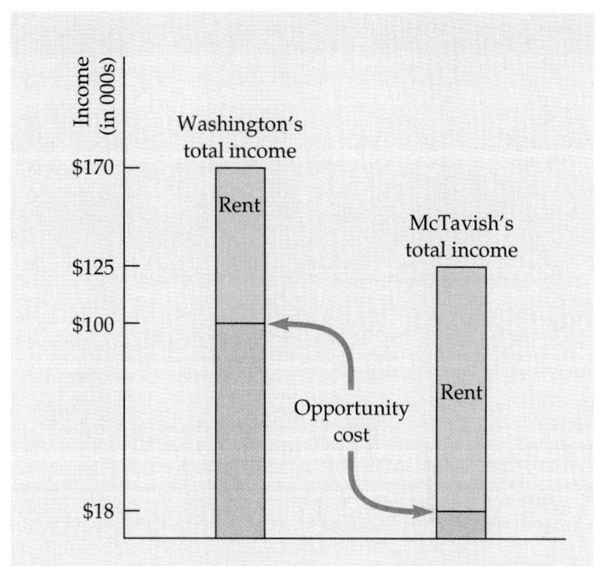

FIGURE 23-8 Rent depends on income and opportunity cost.

Washington has more basketball talent and earns a higher salary. If the red opportunity costs of the players were the same, Washington would earn the higher rent. But their opportunity costs are not the same. In fact, McTavish's is so much lower that rent makes up a larger part of his income than Washington's.

alternative use but to grow a crop. In other words, their opportunity cost is zero. It therefore follows from the preceding definition that any income they earn is rent. In this special case, the economist's and the public's definition of rent coincide: It is the income earned by land.

Relatively poor land C has such low productivity that with a $3 price of wheat, it has just been brought into cultivation. The value of the wheat it produces is barely sufficient to cover the costs of fertilizer, machinery, the farmer's time, and other inputs. Therefore it earns no rent. Land B is more fertile soil that grows enough wheat per acre to pay for other inputs and leave $60 per acre; that is, its

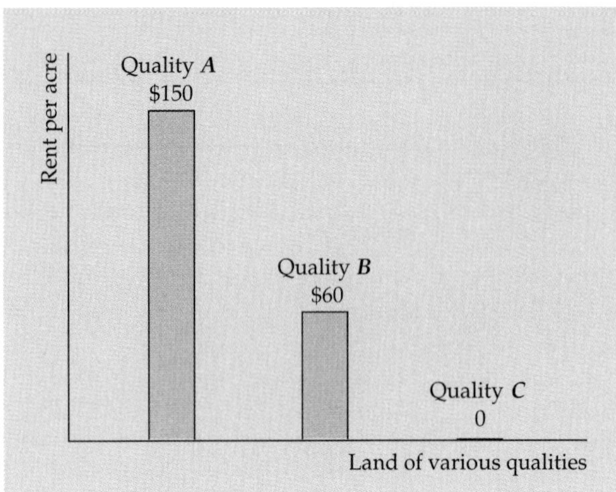

FIGURE 23-9 Rent based on differences in quality of land (based on wheat price of $3 per bushel).

Marginal land C, which is just barely fertile enough to cultivate, earns no rent. High-productivity land A earns the highest rent.

rent is $60 per acre. Land A is even more productive and earns a rent of $150.

Of course, the rent on these plots of land depends on the price of wheat. Suppose that crop failures elsewhere in the world push the price of wheat up from the initial $3 a bushel (in Fig. 23-9) to $4. The result is shown in Figure 23-10. Land C, which previously did not earn rent, now does, and the rents earned by plots A and B increase. Land D is now the marginal land, which has just been brought into cultivation and is earning zero rent.

ANOTHER EXAMPLE OF RENT: THE INCOME FROM MINERAL DEPOSITS

Mineral deposits, like any other gifts of nature in the earth, are included in the economists' broad definition of land, and, like farmland, they earn an economic rent. To confirm this, reinterpret Figures 23-9 and 23-10 as follows. Mineral deposit A is a rich vein of ore, easy to reach. Mineral deposit B is also a rich vein of ore but difficult to reach and extract. Deposit C is of poorer quality and so difficult to reach that initially in Figure 23-9 it is barely being mined. Figure 23-10 then shows how an increase in the price of ore increases the rent earned on each of these deposits and induces the mining of low-yield deposit D for the first time.

RENT ON LAND BECAUSE OF ITS LOCATION

Land may yield economic rent not only because of its fertility but also because of its location. To illustrate, land A in Figure 23-11 is in the prime business district of a city and can be used in a highly productive way. A business might wish to locate there for a variety of reasons. It might want to be close to suppliers and competitors so that it can easily keep up with new developments and innovations in the industry. Or it might wish to have access to the large labor pool that exists in this area of high-density population. Or it might wish to be close to the population center in order to reduce the cost of transporting its product to market.

For all these reasons, location A earns a rent. Land B is less attractive since it is not in this prime district, and it earns a smaller rent. Finally, land C earns no rent because it is even farther away and therefore involves even higher costs of inconvenience and transportation.

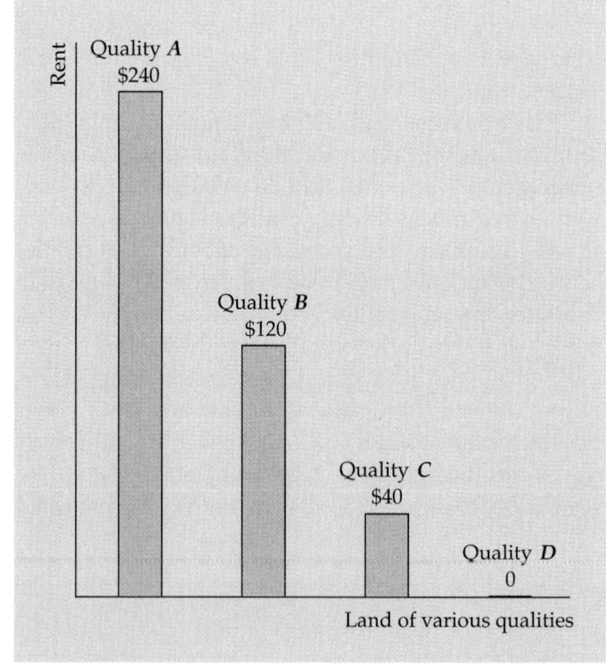

FIGURE 23-10 How rents increase when the price of wheat increases.

This figure is the same as Figure 23-9 except that the price of wheat has risen from $3 to $4 per bushel. Because of this increased price, all existing plots of land earn greater income—that is, greater rent. Moreover, less productive plot D has just barely been brought into cultivation by this higher price.

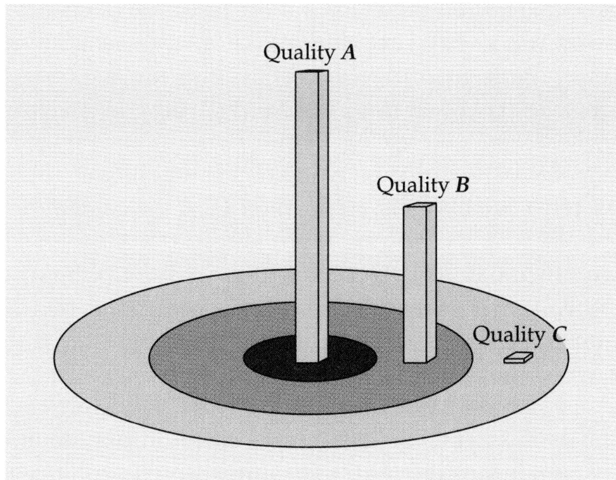

FIGURE 23-11 Rent based on differences in location.

Compare with Figure 23-9. Because of its greater convenience and lower transport costs, land A earns a higher rent than land B. Land C, in a relatively poor location, earns no rent.

Note that, although the heights of the blocks have been drawn to reflect rents, they also reflect land values. (The greater the rent a plot of land will earn, the higher its price.) The heights of these blocks also provide some rough indication of where the tallest buildings will be constructed. Office space becomes more and more expensive to construct as a building gets higher and higher. Consequently, if land is cheap, firms buy more land and construct low buildings. But if land is expensive enough, they conserve it by building up. Therefore buildings tend to be tallest in the prime, most expensive locations.

ABOVE-NORMAL PROFIT AS A RENT

Because above-normal profit is a return above opportunity cost, it is, by definition, a rent. The most obvious illustration occurs in the case of monopoly. For example, the blue area of above-normal profit in Figure 12-4 is a *monopoly rent.* It exists because entry by new firms into the industry is restricted. Therefore it is a rent on whatever restricts entry. For example, it may be rent on a government license that is granted to one firm (or a few) that blocks out other potential competitors. Or it may be rent on a patented product that other firms cannot copy.

HOW RENTS ARE CAPITALIZED

If land plots A and B back in Figure 23-9 are put up for sale, A will command a higher price because of the higher rent it can earn. But can't we be more precise about how the value of land is determined?

If you had the money and were interested in buying plot B, how much would you be willing to pay for it? Suppose that, as an alternative, you can purchase bonds instead and earn a rate of return of, say, 6%. Because the rent of land B is $60 per year, you should be willing to pay about $1,000 for it. This gives you the same 6% rate of return on your land (a $60 return on $1,000) as on the alternative of buying bonds. Moreover, the competition of other potential buyers who feel the same way will ensure that the price of land B will settle at about $1,000—if the rent on B is expected to remain at $60 per year.

Now if the rent on land B doubles in Figure 23-10 to $120, potential buyers will be attracted by this higher income it can earn, and will begin to bid up the price of this land. This process will continue until the price of this land roughly doubles to $2,000, where its rate of return will again be the same 6% as before—that is, a $120 return on $2,000. To describe this process, economists say that *an increase in rent is capitalized in the value of the land.*

In practice, there are complications. In particular, the price of land is affected not only by present rents but by expected future rents too. If a single year's rent increases by 20%, the price of land may increase by more than 20% if people expect rents to continue to rise.[3]

Other economic rents—as well as those on land—may also be capitalized. The number of taxis in Boston is limited, since each must have a medallion. Because this requirement makes taxis scarce, the fares collected by each taxi are greater. This higher income (rent) becomes capitalized in the value of a medallion. By 1989, the price of a medallion had risen to $95,000, many times the cost of even the most expensive cab. Thus someone

[3]Further detail on how an income flow (such as rent or interest) is capitalized in the value of an asset (such as land or a bond) is given in Box 12-1 of the companion volume. The "capitalization of an income flow" is just another way of saying "the calculation of the present value of an income flow."

who wants to own and operate a cab in Boston may be able to do reasonably well once he gets into the business. But how does he raise the money to get started in the first place?

Taxi medallions raise another question. Rather than let the medallion owners benefit from the city's policy of restricting the number of cabs, would it not have been better for Boston to auction off the rights to operate cabs for a year at a time? Then the city would have been able to collect the rents. Moreover, individual drivers could now enter the industry far more easily. They would have to buy only the right to operate a cab for a year rather than the far more expensive medallion, which represents the right to operate a cab permanently. Desirable as such an auction system might be, it would raise a problem: The government cannot switch from the present medallion system to an auction of annual permits without inflicting a loss on present owners of medallions, some of whom may have recently gone heavily into debt to buy a $95,000 medallion. (This is similar to a problem with agricultural price supports. They cannot be lowered without inflicting a loss on present owners of land.) Note that this problem of capital loss to present owners of medallions would never have arisen if the government had introduced an annual auction rather than the present medallion system when a limit on the number of taxis was first introduced in 1934.

TAXING RENT

Rent is a natural target for taxation. About a century ago, Henry George built a powerful single-tax movement on the idea that nothing should be taxed but land rents. (His book *Progress and Poverty* sold millions of copies, and he was almost elected mayor of New York.) Why, asked George, shouldn't the government tax land rents, since they represent a pure windfall? Owners obviously don't produce the land, nor do they work for their rental incomes. Instead, they just hold the land and become wealthy from "unearned increments" as the population increases and rents rise. George argued that the land rents belong to the public as a whole and should be taxed away from the owners and used for public purposes.

George's case was based not only on equity but also on efficiency. A levy on land rents is one of the few taxes that need not distort resource allocation. Even if half the rent on land is taxed away, it will still remain in cultivation. What else can the owner do with it? (Even marginal land earning a zero rent will still barely remain in cultivation. Since its rent is zero, its tax will be zero, and it will be left unaffected.) Because the quantity of land in use will not be affected by the tax, there is no reason to expect an efficiency loss. Compare this with a tax on any other factor of production. For example, a tax on capital can affect the incentive to invest and thus reduce the quantity of capital in use.

However, George's proposal to tax land rent raises two serious difficulties—in addition to the obvious problem that, as a single tax, it would not raise nearly enough money to cover today's large government expenditures. First, if present owners paid the current high price when they bought their land, rents are not a windfall to them at all but just a reasonable return on their large initial expenditure. (Why tax those who have just bought land and not those who have just bought bonds instead? Both may be receiving the same return of, say, 6%.) The only windfall is to the previous owners who sold the land for a high price. But they may now be living in Bermuda, beyond the reach of the taxing authority. Second, in practice it may be impossible to separate the rent on land from the return to buildings. If you tax a landowner's income, you will be taxing both. But the return to buildings—or to any other improvements on the land—is not a return to the land itself. Instead, it is a return to capital, and it cannot be taxed without causing distortion and inefficiency. For example, a tax on the returns from apartments will reduce the quantity of apartments and thus lead to an efficiency loss.

LIVING IN A GLOBAL ECONOMY

FOREIGN INVESTMENT IN THE UNITED STATES

Between 1984 and 1988, foreign investment in the United States exceeded U.S. investment in foreign countries by $650 billion. In the process, foreigners acquired a wide range of U.S. assets including U.S. Treasury bills and bonds, corporate stocks and bonds, and commercial real estate. On these assets, foreigners are now earning interest, profit, and rent.

One reason for this heavy investment was the high rate of saving in a number of foreign countries, particularly Japan, where gross private saving has been as high as 25 to 30% of GNP, a much larger figure than in the United States. This huge supply of loanable funds in Japan has kept its supply curve in Figure 23-2 far to the right, and interest rates low there. This has led the Japanese to invest in U.S. bonds in order to earn a higher interest return. The huge Japanese savings are also used to buy up all sorts of Japanese assets, thus driving up their prices. Consequently, real estate is worth up to ten times as much per acre in downtown Tokyo as in Manhattan, and the total value of real estate in Japan—a nation smaller than some U.S. states—is greater than the value of all the real estate in the United States. Therefore, to the Japanese, it isn't just U.S. bonds that are a bargain. So too are U.S. real estate, factories, and other assets, and the Japanese have been buying them on a large scale. Moreover, it is not just the highly visible Japanese who are investing heavily in the United States. So too are Canadians and British. In 1986–1987, British direct investment in the United States was more than double that of Japan.

FOREIGN INVESTMENT IN THEORY

Figure 23-12 analyzes foreign investment in the United States. Consider first the situation **without foreign investment.** As in Figure 23-4, D is the U.S. demand for investment funds and S is the U.S. domestic supply. S is drawn well to the left in this diagram, because of the relatively small amount of U.S. savings. Equilibrium is at E_1 with a rate of interest of i_1. (To simplify, the rate of interest i on borrowed capital is used to represent the rate of return on the broader concept of both borrowed capital and equity capital.)

With foreign investment, the supply of funds for investment in the United States increases, that is, shifts to the right from S to S_T, where S_T includes both domestic savings S *and* foreign investment. Thus equilibrium is at E_2, where S_T intersects D. Total investment in the United States is increased from Q_1 to Q_2, and the rate of return on investment in the United States is reduced from i_1 to i_2.

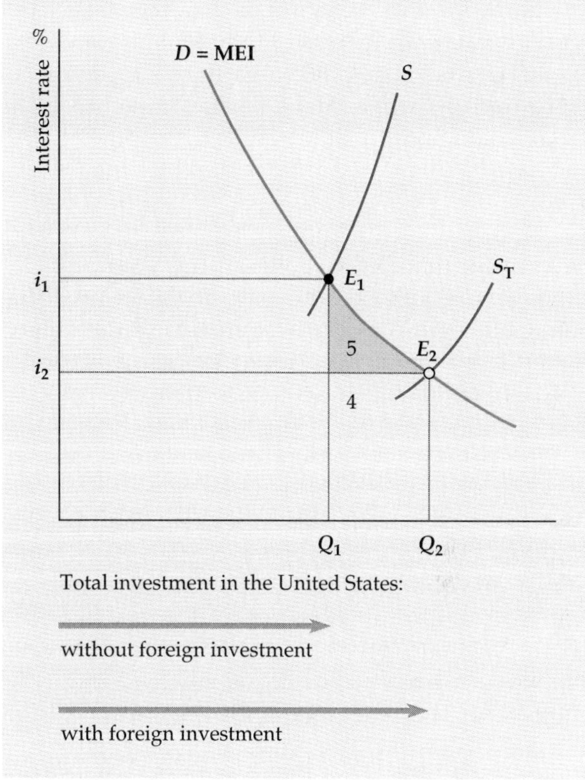

FIGURE 23-12 The effects of foreign investment in the United States.

Without foreign investment, equilibrium in the United States is at E_1 where demand for investment funds D is equal to domestic savings S. With foreign investment, the supply of funds in the United States is increased, that is, it shifts to the right from S to S_T, and equilibrium is at E_2. Total investment in the United States increases from Q_1 to Q_2. Area 5 is a net benefit to the United States because it is the difference between the cost of foreign funds (area 4) and the greater productivity (4 + 5) of these funds when invested in the United States.

Foreign investment provides a net benefit because it increases the total investment in the United States by Q_1Q_2. Because the productivity of this investment is given by the height of the D = MEI curve, the total benefit from this increased investment is area 4 + 5. However, its cost to the United States is the area 4 that must be paid to foreign investors; this is the Q_1Q_2 of funds that they provide times the rate of interest i_2 that they earn on these funds. As a result, there is a net benefit to Americans of area 5—the benefit that comes from using relatively inexpensive foreign funds to make higher return investments in the United States.

Some of this benefit goes to the U.S. labor force, because an increase in the amount of capital in the United States increases the productivity of labor and the wage rate. To paraphrase the quote from Adam Smith that introduced Chapter 21: "An increased amount of capital will bid up the price of labor."

Finally, there is another benefit from foreign investment that is not shown in this diagram. U.S. taxpayers benefit because part of the income that foreigners earn on their investments in the United States doesn't go to these foreigners at all; instead it goes as a tax payment to the U.S. Treasury.

SOME COMPLICATIONS IN PRACTICE

The above analysis describes a country that imports, but does not export, capital. The United States does both. Although it is a large net importer, it is also an exporter. U.S. firms like IBM that design and develop a new product may get a high return from producing it in, say, Europe, so they do so. The benefit these firms get from exporting capital is the higher productivity they get when they invest these funds in Europe rather than adding to their investments in the United States.

A second complication is that the analysis in Figure 23-12 applies most clearly in a world in which there are no domestic distortions. However, such distortions have existed in the United States. For example, the U.S. supply of funds has been reduced by a tax system that provides disincentives to save. A further complication is that there has been a large demand for funds by the U.S. government to finance its deficits. This, along with buoyant business opportunities to invest, has led to a heavy U.S. demand for funds. Without foreign investment, this small supply and large demand for funds would have resulted in a very high interest rate (such as i_1 in Figure 23-12) and a low amount of investment (Q_1). However, because foreign investment *has* taken place, the interest rate in the United States has been at the lower level i_2, and investment has been the greater amount Q_2. By making up for the shortfall in U.S. savings, foreign funds have played an important role in sustaining investment in the United States.

Although economists recognize that foreign investment has been beneficial in filling the gap created by the low U.S. saving rate, many believe that this issue should not have become so prominent in the first place. Rather than blocking out foreign investment with the benefits it provides, they propose changes in U.S. tax laws so that these laws would no longer discourage U.S. saving. (Such a change was begun in the tax reform in 1986.) They also recommend reducing government deficits as a further way of reducing the U.S. requirement for foreign capital. Indeed, such changes might move the United States from its present status of being a large net importer of capital, to become, once again, a net exporter to the rest of the world.

KEY POINTS

1. Those who have saved to provide funds for business to invest in physical capital, such as plant and equipment, receive income in the form of interest or profit.

2. In a perfectly competitive market for loanable funds, the interest rate is determined by demand and supply. Demand reflects the productivity of investment (the marginal efficiency of investment). Supply reflects how highly savers value funds in their alternative use—consumption.

3. Because capital is productive, present goods can be exchanged for even more future goods. Therefore present goods are worth more than future goods. The interest rate indicates how much more.

4. The interest rate also acts as a screening device that allocates funds to the most productive investment projects. A government ceiling that lowers the interest rate below its perfectly competitive level can result in two kinds of efficiency loss: (1) The total amount of funds available for investment is reduced, and (2) the limited funds that do go to investment are allocated to the wrong set of projects. Even though this policy may be designed to benefit poor individuals or small businesses, it only helps those who are still able to borrow.

5. Income is earned not only on machinery and other forms of physical capital, but also on human capital—that is, on skills, training, and education. The individuals who own the human capital are not the only ones who bear the cost of the investment in human capital. Governments also invest by subsidizing education, and businesses invest in training programs.

6. Economists define rent as the return to any factor of production above its opportunity cost. Those with superior talents in any occupation, whether it be business or basketball, earn a rent.

7. Land also earns a rent, with the most fertile plots earning the largest rent. If the price of farm products increases, rents rise and new plots of land are brought into cultivation. Rent is also earned on land because of its location.

8. Mineral deposits also earn rents, with the richest, most accessible deposits earning the highest rents.

9. The higher the rent earned by an asset such as a plot of land, the higher its value; thus rents are "capitalized."

10. Foreign investment can be beneficial because the productivity of this investment exceeds its cost, and foreign investors pay taxes to the U.S. Treasury.

KEY CONCEPTS

physical and human capital
marginal efficiency of investment (MEI)
roundabout production
time preference
base (risk-free) rate of interest
private versus social return to education
economists' broad definition of rent
rent on land due to fertility
rent on land due to location
monopoly rent
capitalization of rent

PROBLEMS

23-1. To review Chapters 21, 22, and 23, explain why wages and salaries are higher in the United States than in most other countries. Why are our other forms of income also higher?

23-2. "If the marginal efficiency of all investment projects is zero, then the interest rate will be zero." Draw a diagram similar to Figure 23-2 to show this case.

23-3. (a) Using a three-panel diagram like Figure 10-5, show how the interest rate acts as a monitoring device to determine which investments will be undertaken and which individuals will provide the saving.

(b) Just as the return to projects j and h are shown in Figure 23-3, also show the return to a project (call it g), in the range Q_1Q_3. Now suppose that h is knocked out by g when the 6% interest rate ceiling is imposed. What is the additional efficiency loss because this happens? Is it also possible, as banks ration funds, for project j to lose out to g? How could this happen? If it does happen, what is the additional efficiency loss?

(c) Use a diagram like Figure 23-3 to show how rent control results in an efficiency loss even without any "rationing errors"; and a further efficiency loss if rationing errors do occur.

23-4. If expectations change, with borrowers and lenders expecting that interest rates will fall in the future, what is likely to happen to the interest rate on long-term bonds today?

23-5. Why might a firm pay a very high salary to attract an executive from a competing firm?

23-6. In the sport or entertainment field of your choice, draw a diagram to show the rents earned by (a) the superstar, (b) the star, and (c) the marginal player.

23-7. The public's idea of rent does not coincide with the economist's definition. How are the two concepts different? Give an example of (a) a return which an economist considers rent, but the public does not; (b) a return which the public considers rent, but the economist does not; and (c) a return which both consider rent.

23-8. Do you think that rent is an important or an insignificant part of the income of: (a) Robert Redford, (b) an elevator operator, (c) a textile worker?

23-9. Are these statements true or false? "An increase in the price of oil not only stimulates the search for oil. It also brings previously uneconomic sources of oil into production. But it does not affect rent on existing oil fields." If any of these statements is false, correct it.

23-10. Suppose that all the agricultural land within 100 miles of Kansas City is equally fertile. Suppose, too, that all corn must be sold in Kansas City and that the cost of transporting it there depends only on distance. What pattern of land rent would you expect over this area?

23-11. **(a)** Suppose Boston imposed its taxi restriction by allowing only a restricted set of individuals to drive cabs. Would rents be generated in this case? If so, who would earn these rents?

> **(b)** At present, there are 1,525 taxi medallions in Boston, the same number that existed in 1934 when the system was established. How do you think the present owners view recent proposals to increase that number as the population increases? What would such an increase do to the value of their medallions?
>
> **(c)** If there were an annual auction of taxi permits by Boston, how would cab drivers view an increase in the number of permits?

23-12. When Dave Winfield decided to play baseball, he turned down offers to play pro football (where, let's suppose, he might now be working for \$100,000 a year) and basketball (for \$500,000 a year). Divide his current income of about \$2 million a year into rent and opportunity cost.

CHAPTER 24
INCOME INEQUALITY

When Babe Ruth was told that he earned more than the President, he replied: "I had a better year than he did."

By 1990, Babe Ruth's successors were having very good years. New York Yankee outfielder Dave Winfield—with his $2 million a year contract—was not the only rich baseball player. A number of others had also reached this income level, which was rapidly becoming the symbol of superstar status. With players in basketball and hockey earning the same—or more—one could only wonder: Should an athlete earn ten times as much as the president of the United States? Should a disc jockey earn five times as much as a violinist with a symphony orchestra? Should a television newscaster earn almost three times as much as the chairman of the Board of NBC?

This chapter will address four main questions.

- Why do incomes differ?
- How great is this inequality, overall?
- What is a fair distribution of income? Is it the income distribution that results from the free play of market forces? Or an equal income for all? Or some compromise between the two?
- What are the effects of discrimination against a minority, one of the major causes of income inequality?

REVIEW: WHY DO INCOMES DIFFER?

A number of reasons for differences in wage rates have already been described in earlier chapters. For example, a construction worker in a dangerous job typically earns a higher wage to compensate for the risks. Workers often receive a higher wage if they belong to a union.

In addition to wages, there are the other forms of income described in the last chapter—such as rent, interest payments, and dividends—which help to explain why some individuals have higher incomes than others.

First, income differences arise because of differences in *wealth.* Those who own stocks, bonds, and other forms of property often receive very large incomes from them. There are great differences in wealth in the United States. The richest 1% of the U.S. population holds more than 20% of the nation's wealth, while the poorest 25% holds almost no wealth at all.

Some people earn a high income because they have a lot of wealth in the form of *human capital.* For example, a surgeon's high income provides compensation for the years of foregone income and hard study necessary to accumulate human capital. In this case, higher income may also be partly a rent on greater-than-average innate talent. Of course, other individuals have gifts of quite a different sort; star athletes and entertainers also earn very large rents.

Family background explains some income differences. America is still a land of opportunity where someone from a poor family can achieve prominence and success. Michael Blumenthal, who arrived in America as a penniless immigrant, became Secretary of the Treasury and the Chairman of Unisys, one of the largest U.S. computer firms. However, for the overwhelming majority with less talent, coming from the "right family" does help, especially if parents provide not only a silver spoon but also practical advice and inspiration.

Income differences may also arise because some people work harder than others. For example, a specific doctor's income may be lower because of a personal decision to sacrifice income in order to get more leisure. An example is the doctor with a clinic at the base of a mountain who skis in the morning and sets broken bones in the afternoon. On the other hand, many doctors work very long hours, and this helps to explain their high incomes.

Some income differences may be the result of differences in *health*, or just plain *luck*. An example is the star quarterback who is injured and must give up football and the large income that goes with it.

Just as bad luck can lower income, good luck can raise it. One form of good luck is "being the right person at the right time," like the second-string quarterback who is headed nowhere but suddenly gets a chance to step into the injured star's shoes. If this leads to a high-income career, some—but certainly not all—of this success is attributable to luck.

Finally, those in a minority group may face a lower income because of *discrimination*, a problem considered later in this chapter.

Of all the causes of income differences, can we say which is most important? In a surprising early study, Jacob Mincer of Columbia University concluded that the answer was: human capital. He found that differences in human capital explained roughly 60% of the differences in American incomes.[1]

HOW MUCH INCOME INEQUALITY IS THERE?

It's the rich whot gets the gryvy,
It's the poor whot gets the blime.

ENGLISH BALLAD, WORLD WAR II

Are wide differences in individual incomes the exception or the rule? How much inequality is there in the United States?

In 1986, the median U.S. income was about $30,000, with half the households receiving more and half less. However, the lowest fifth on the income scale received less than $15,000. On the other hand, the highest fifth received more than $50,000.

This unequal distribution is described in another way in panel *a* of Table 24-1 which shows, for example, that the lowest income fifth of U.S. households received only 4.7% of the nation's income, after taxes and transfers. These figures can

[1]This study covered white urban males. See Jacob Mincer, *Education, Experimental Income and Human Behavior* (New York: McGraw-Hill, 1975), p. 73.

TABLE 24-1 Estimated Income Distribution of U. S. Households, after Taxes and Transfers, 1986

(a) Income Distribution		*(b) Cumulative Income Distribution*		
Households	*Share of Total Income*	*Households*	*Share of Total Income*	*Point in Figure24-1*
Lowest 20%	gets 4.7%	First 20%	gets 4.7%	*H*
Second 20	gets 10.6	First 40	gets 4.7 + 10.6 = 15.3%	*J*
Third 20	gets 16.0	First 60	gets 15.3 + 16.0 = 31.3	*K*
Fourth 20	gets 23.0	First 80	gets 31.3 + 23.0 = 54.3	*L*
Highest 20	gets 45.7	Total	gets 54.3 + 45.7 = 100.0	*M*

Source: U. S. Bureau of the Census, *Current Population Reports*, Series P-60, No. 164-RD-1, *Measuring the Effect of Benefits and Taxes on Income and Poverty: 1986*, Washington, D. C., 1988, p. 5.

be used to derive a **Lorenz curve.** The first step in drawing such a curve is to rearrange the data in panel *a* of Table 24-1 into cumulative form in panel *b*. For example, in the second row, the poorest 40% of the households earn 15.3% of the nation's income. (This number is the sum of the first two numbers in panel *a*.) This 15.3% is then plotted in Figure 24-1 as point *J*, along with other points that

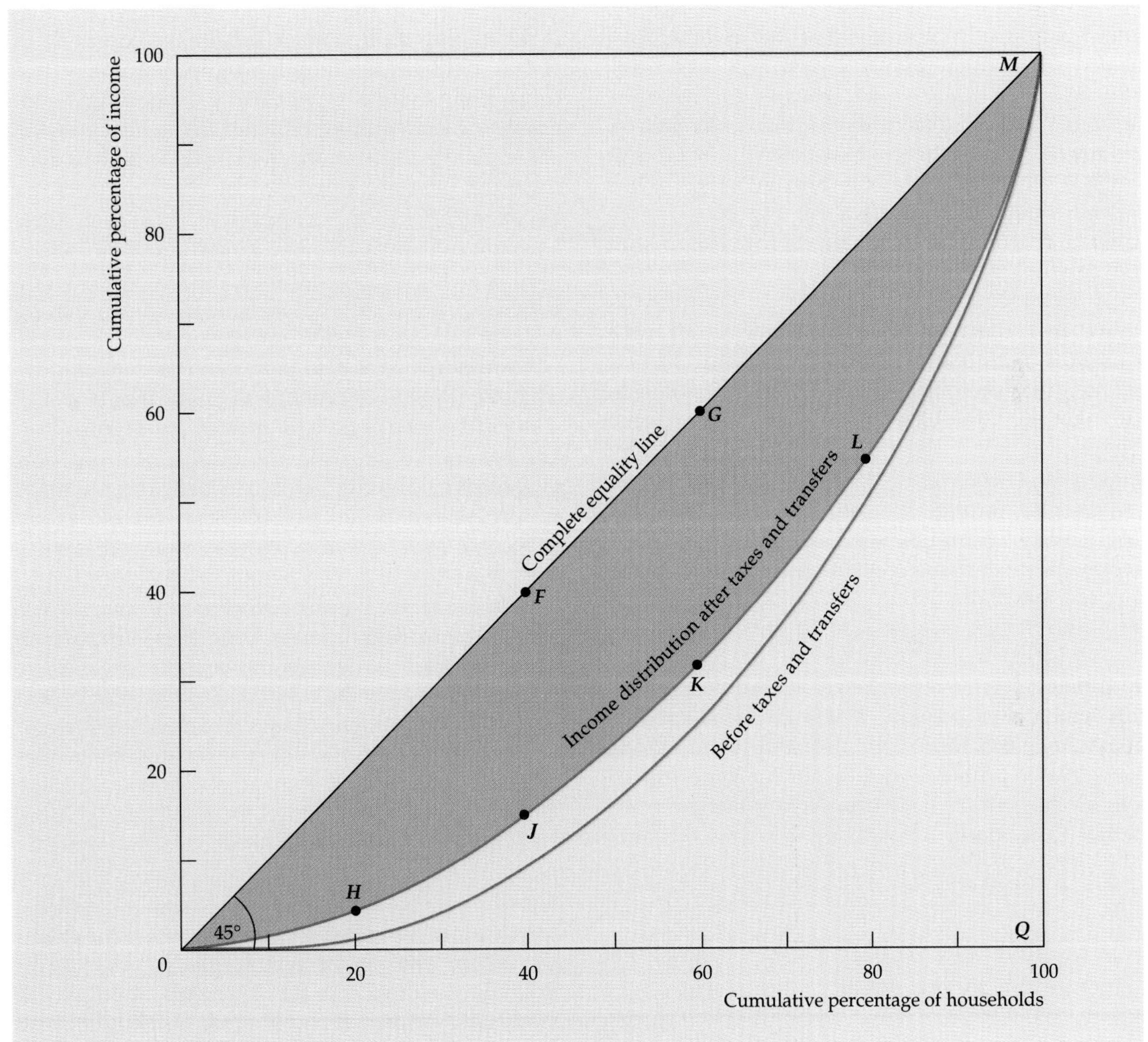

FIGURE 24-1 Lorenz curves showing 1986 U.S. income distribution before and after taxes and transfers.

If every household had exactly the same income, the American income distribution would follow the 45° "complete equality" line. The actual income distribution (after taxes and transfers) is shown by the curve that lies below this—with the shaded area between the two showing the amount of income inequality. If there were no government policies to transfer income from the rich to poor, there would be an even greater bow of income inequality, as shown by the brown curve. (*Source:* See Table 24-1.)

are similarly calculated. The result is the Lorenz curve of U.S. income.

To get some idea of how much inequality this curve represents, consider what this Lorenz curve would look like if all households received exactly the same income. In this case, point *F* would be observed instead of point *J:* The "lowest" 40% of the households would receive 40% of the income. And instead of point *K,* point *G* would be observed, with 60% of the households receiving 60% of the income. When all points like *F* and *G* are joined, the result is the complete equality line *OFGM,* which is the 45° straight line from the origin. Thus income inequality is shown by the bow in the Lorenz curve, that is, by the size of the shaded slice between the curve and the 45° line.

In fact, inequality is not as serious a problem as Figure 24-1 suggests. One reason: Even if each household were earning exactly the same *lifetime* income, the Lorenz curve would still not coincide with that 45° line. One would still observe some "inequality slice." The reason is that, during any single year, there would be observations of young households starting out with low incomes and observations of middle-aged households in their income prime earning, on average, more than twice as much. Inequality would still be observed in that year, *even though each household would have exactly the same lifetime income pattern.*

Nonetheless, even when such influences are fully taken into account, a substantial degree of inequality exists. Moreover, inequality would be an even greater problem were it not for government policies that reduce it by transferring income from the rich to the poor.

GOVERNMENT POLICIES TO REDUCE INEQUALITY

While the green curve in Figure 24-1 shows the U.S. income distribution after taxes and transfers, the brown curve shows the income distribution *before* taxes and transfers—that is, the income distribution just as it was earned. It has an even larger inequality bow. The lowest income fifth of U.S. households earns only 1.1% of the nation's income, whereas the highest fifth earns almost half.

The government policies that reduce income inequality from the brown curve to the green curve in Figure 24-1 include taxation which concentrates more heavily on the rich, and expenditure programs such as social security, unemployment insurance, and food stamps which raise the relative income of those who are poor. One surprise is that most of this reduction in inequality comes from government expenditure programs rather than from taxes. These government expenditure programs, described in more detail in the next chapter, are transfers to the poor both *in cash* and *in kind.* Included in the category of in-kind transfers are goods such as food, and services such as medical assistance. Claims that the government is ineffective in changing the nation's income distribution have frequently been based on calculations that do not take in-kind transfers into account.

Although taxes also play a role in reducing inequality, it is by an amount so small that it would scarcely be perceptible if plotted in Figure 24-1. The reason is that taxes are, on balance, not very progressive. Although it is true that income taxes are progressive (with the percentage tax rate rising as income rises), other taxes are somewhat regressive.

On the face of it, the message in Figure 24-1 is clear. Government transfer programs—in particular, expenditure programs rather than taxes—have been effective in reducing inequality in the United States. But why haven't they been *more* effective? Why does so much inequality remain? One answer to this question is this: It is quite true that transfers to the poor directly reduce inequality by shifting the Lorenz curve up (as illustrated, for example, by the shift from the brown to the green curve in Figure 24-1). But *indirectly,* these transfers shift the brown curve down, *increasing* inequality. For example, the income guarantee provided by the unemployment insurance program makes unemployed people less desperate to get a job quickly, because they can at least survive without one. Although this guarantee provides an important social benefit in the form of a safety net, at the same time it does allow some relatively poor people to earn less. Thus inequality is increased, with the brown curve having a bigger bow than it would otherwise have. In short, transfers to the poor have two conflicting effects on income inequality. Indirectly, they increase inequality by shifting the brown Lorenz curve down, giving it a bigger bow. But directly they reduce inequality by shifting the Lorenz curve up. The reason why transfers aren't more effective is that, to some degree, these effects cancel each other out.

While the government has been transferring income from the rich to the poor, another important transfer has been occurring.

TRANSFERS FROM YOUNG TO OLD

An increasing transfer has been taking place from the young generation to the old. One reason has been the increasing cost of Social Security which transfers income from the younger generation that pays taxes to support this program to the older generation that receives benefits. Rising real estate prices have also transferred income from young to old, as young families now have to pay much higher prices to buy houses from the older generation selling them. While headlines asking whether the elderly are now "consuming their children" are exaggerated, the traditional experience of "doing better than your parents" may have been reversed. 19-year-olds who observed their parents' standard of living when they left home to go to work in 1962 were able, on average, to substantially improve on that within the next decade. However, the reverse was true, on average, for 19-year-olds leaving home in 1973. They were *not* able to attain their parents' standard of living within 10 years.

IS THE MIDDLE CLASS SHRINKING?

Everyone has heard the story of the middle-class worker who has recently lost a high-wage job in manufacturing and has had to take a lower paying service job in retailing. Is this just an isolated example, or has it become a problem for the U.S. economy as a whole? Is the lower income group expanding at the expense of a shrinking middle class?

There are two conflicting views on this question. But first, consider the facts that are not in dispute. Manufacturing—one of the most important sources of income for the middle-income group—has not been creating large numbers of new jobs. One reason has been the contraction of highly paid union jobs in heavy industries such as autos and steel. (Between 1967 and 1987, employment in durable goods manufacturing fell slightly, as did overall employment in manufacturing.) While some middle-income jobs have been created outside of manufacturing, job creation over the entire middle-income group between 1979 and 1984 was somewhat (though not dramatically) less than in the previous seven years.

However, from here on, there is disagreement. Some economists point to the workers who have been pushed out of middle-income jobs in manufacturing into low-income jobs, such as nonunionized jobs in service industries like fast food. In contrast, others point to the people who have left middle-income jobs to go into even higher paying jobs. Although service employment has increased at the expense of manufacturing, many service jobs offer high incomes, such as jobs in finance and computer programming.

A more fundamental issue is this: While manufacturing employment fell slightly in the two decades from 1967 to 1987, manufacturing output rose 69% because of increased efficiency.[2] Was this bad? Wasn't it a reflection of increased productivity just like in agriculture, where increased productivity has also led to increased output with fewer workers?

Now let's turn from the question "What *is* the income distribution?" to "What *should* the income distribution be?" Is there such a thing as a "fair" or "equitable" distribution?

---

[2]During the same period, real GNP also rose 69%. Thus manufacturing remained the same share of real GNP. See *Economic Report of the President, 1989*, pp. 321, 356.

For an optomistic view of U.S. manufacturing, see Marvin Kosters and Murray Ross, "A Shrinking Middle Class?" *Public Interest*, Winter 1988, pp. 3–27. For a pessimistic view, see Barry Bluestone and Bennett Harrison, *The Great American Job Machine: The Proliferation of Low-Wage Employment in the U.S. Economy* (Washington, D.C.: Joint Economic Committee of the U.S. Congress, 1986).

WHAT IS AN EQUITABLE DISTRIBUTION OF INCOME?

See how the fates their gifts allot,
For A is happy—B is not.
Yet B is worthy, I dare say,
Of more prosperity than A!

If I were fortune—which I'm not—
B should enjoy A's happy lot,
And A should die in miserie—
That is, assuming I am B.

GILBERT AND SULLIVAN
THE MIKADO

A search for an equitable or just distribution of income for society leads into treacherous intellectual terrain, from which some of the world's noted philosophers have been unable to escape with reputations intact. Although it is not possible to arrive at a definitive answer, some of the important issues can be identified.

To begin, two important points made earlier should be reemphasized:

1. Equity and equality are not necessarily the same. The Lorenz curve throws light only on the question of equality: How equal are incomes? This is a positive question—an empirical question that can be answered by looking at the facts and examining how much each American household earns. On the other hand, the question of equity is not what incomes are, but rather what they *should be.* This is a normative question requiring judgment. What income distribution is fair and just? On this ethical issue, people are not unanimous. Some judge that equity is equality—that it is fair for everyone to receive the same income. On the other hand, some believe that equity is not equality; for example, the individual who works harder or more effectively should be paid more.

> ***Equal*** means "of the same size." ***Equitable*** means "fair." The two are not necessarily the same.

2. Government policy cannot be designed just to achieve equity—that is, a fair division of the nation's income pie. Instead it must also take into account other, often conflicting goals such as efficiency—increasing the size of that pie. However, to sharpen the idea of equity, suppose for now that this is the only concern. *On grounds of equity alone,* what is the best distribution of income?

Of the many possible answers, consider three: first, the distribution that results from the free play of the economic marketplace; second, a completely equal distribution of income; and third, some compromise between the two.

IS THE FREE MARKET'S DISTRIBUTION OF INCOME EQUITABLE?

Whatever is, is right.

ALEXANDER POPE

Few would agree that whatever is, is necessarily right. The free market does not do an entirely satisfactory job of distributing income. Consider a monopolist who makes a fortune by successfully cornering the supply of a good, selling some at a very high price and letting the unsold balance rot. In these and other less extreme cases of monopoly it is very difficult to argue that the free market leads to a fair, equitable outcome.

The free-market distribution of income raises problems not only when markets are monopolized, but also when they are perfectly competitive. Such markets will, under certain conditions (no externalities, etc.), allocate factors of production in an efficient way that will maximize the nation's total income. In the process, they determine a set of prices of both goods and factors of production—the wages of labor, rents on land, and so on. Thus they both maximize the nation's income pie and determine how it will be divided. But they do not necessarily divide the pie up in a fair, equitable way. Remember: While the size of the pie is maximized, *it still goes to those who have the income to pay for it.* Output in a competitive market economy may include luxuries for the rich and too few necessities for the disabled and others who are poor through no fault of their own.

Even strong supporters of the free market, while championing its efficiencies, are still in favor of aid for those who are destitute. This point is important enough to repeat: The demonstrable virtues of a free, perfectly competitive market have to do with its efficiency, not its equity.

Perhaps the best illustration is this. In a perfectly competitive economy, rents on land efficiently direct the nation's scarce land into its most productive uses; if rents are forced below the competitive level, land may be used in wasteful ways. However, the payment of competitive rents to those who own the land does not necessarily result in a fair distribution of income. To illustrate, consider an extreme example of land that has been inherited by the idle rich. Why should they earn an income many times that of the able and hardworking people whom they hire to manage and work this land?

EQUALITY AS A TARGET

The idea of complete equality has an immediate appeal (see Box 24-1). Since everyone has certain other rights, such as the right to vote and equality before the law, why should each of us not have an equal share of the nation's product—the right of equal income? In other words, since everyone has an equal vote to cast in elections, why shouldn't everyone have equal "dollar votes" to spend in the marketplace? In practice, it would be prohibitively costly to give everyone this right: An equal division of the pie would greatly shrink its size. The reason—to be examined in detail in the next chapter—is that guaranteeing people an income reduces their incentive to work, and they produce less. When they do, the nation's output—its available income pie—is reduced.

Even if this problem did not exist, there would be others. For example, how is equality to be defined? One way is to define it, most simply, as "equal money incomes." But this answer is not satisfactory because people work different numbers of hours. Those who decide on shorter working hours are taking some of their potential income in the form of leisure rather than cash. Therefore income should be defined more broadly to include both income taken in the form of cash and "income" taken in the form of leisure. Fairness requires that an individual who takes a lot of income in one form—leisure—should get less in the other form—cash. Similarly, those whose work is dangerous should be paid higher money wages to compensate them for the risk. According to this approach, the overall economic position (rather than just money income) should be equalized.

Unfortunately, this broader approach raises as many problems as it solves. If the overall position of individuals is to be equalized, those who have unpleasant jobs should be paid high enough wages to compensate them, and those whose jobs are fun should accordingly be paid less. But what should people be paid in a job like teaching which some find extremely rewarding, while others find boring. Should those who like teaching be paid less than those who don't, in order to make them equal? Quite apart from the practical problem of determining how much each teacher likes the job—in a situation in which they would all have an incentive to lie—this broad approach would lead to an unsatisfactory result: People would be paid for hating their jobs. Since those who love teaching generally make the best teachers, this would mean that the best teachers would be paid the least. Surely this would not be fair.

Worse yet, bored, dissatisfied teachers often don't work so hard; they take "leisure on the job." Would it be fair to pay them a premium salary, when those taking a lot of leisure at home would receive low pay?

Therefore the search for fairness does not lead to complete equality. Complete equality seems to be no more appropriate as a target than the free-market determination of income. How about some compromise between the two?

A COMPROMISE BETWEEN THE FREE MARKET AND COMPLETE EQUALITY

It is easy to conclude that neither the free market nor complete equality provides an adequate guiding principle. What is far more difficult is to say where, in the broad range in between, society should aim. There is no clear answer. But here are some suggestive ideas.

Make it a fair race, . . . Suppose the economy is viewed as a race, in which each runner's income is determined by his or her finish. The egalitarian view that "justice is equality of income" implies that all rewards should be equalized at the end of the race. Give everyone a bronze medal—no golds, and no booby prizes. As the Dodo in *Alice in*

BOX 24–1 Rawls on Equality

Harvard philosophy professor John Rawls has argued that income equality is a desirable goal—except in special circumstances. His analysis starts in a promising way. A consensus on the fair distribution of income is difficult to achieve because everyone has a special ax to grind. Those with high incomes favor a system in which inequality is allowed because it lets them keep their higher income. Those with low incomes are likely to advocate equality because it will improve their position. Rawls therefore suggests that, to get an objective view, people must be removed from their present situation and placed in an original position where they decide what the distribution of income should be, without knowing the specific place they themselves will eventually take in this distribution. What income distribution will they choose?

Here are the essentials of Rawls' argument. The typical person in the original position will think something like this: "Whatever income distribution is chosen, with my luck, chances are that I'll end up at the bottom. So I'll vote for the income distribution that will leave me, the lowest one on the totem pole, as well off as possible." Since everyone is similarly situated in the original position, Rawls argues that all will reason in the same way. He concludes that a consensus will develop in favor of an equal distribution of income—unless there is an unequal distribution that leaves everyone better off. This is what Rawls calls the **difference principle.***

While Rawls' approach will generally lead to equality, there are circumstances in which it will not. To illustrate, we use two extreme examples, but the argument applies in less extreme cases as well. For the first example, suppose people in the original position choose between the two income distributions shown in Table 24-2. Option A represents complete equality, with everyone's annual income at $5,000. Now suppose it is possible to move to option B, where everyone's income is $10,000 except for the last individual, whose income is $5,100. (Suppose that this move is possible because there was previously a very high tax aimed at equalizing income. When the tax is removed, people respond by working more.) Because everyone benefits, Rawlsian logic leads to a move from A to B—a move **away from equality.**** Most people would agree with such a move. Thus far, Rawls' theory is not controversial. In the circumstances shown in Table 24-2, Rawls, like almost everyone else, would allow inequality.

Table 24-3 illustrates the second, more likely situation, with options A and C. As before, the move away from equality (in this case, from A to C) benefits almost everyone by $5,000. But now we recognize that any such substantial change is likely to leave at least one person worse off. (Note in the last column how the income of the last individual is reduced by $100.) In this case, Rawls argues that people in an original position would choose option A. With their pessimistic view that they would end up at the bottom of the totem pole, they would focus on the figures in the last column and prefer A with its $5,000 income to C with its $4,900 income. Thus, according to Rawls, people would choose equality.

It is here, when he puts forward a strong argument in favor of equality, that Rawls' theory is open to criticism. Ask yourself: If you were in Rawls' original position, without knowledge of where you would eventually end up, which option would you choose? Would you join the consensus Rawls expects in favor of option A? Most people would find C difficult to resist. The minuscule risk of being $100 worse off seems trivial in comparison with the near certainty of being $5,000 better off. This seems to be a risk well worth taking. Indeed, those who would select Rawls' option A are those who would avoid risk at almost any cost. How in the world would you find anyone so risk-averse? Observe that the risk you would be taking in choosing income distribution C rather than A would be the same as your risk at the race track or the stock exchange if you were to bet $100 for a chance to win $5,000, with odds in your favor of 240 million to 1. Why those odds? There are 240 million people in the United States. In moving from option A to C, they would all "win" $5,000—except for the one who would lose $100. With such odds, who in the world would turn down such a bet?

Try an experiment to see the difficulty with Rawls' argument. Change the number in the southwest corner of Table 24-3 to $100,000. No matter how high this number may be, Rawls' argument still leads to the choice of equality (option A). Would this be your choice? If so, would you choose option A or C if the number were even higher, say, $1 million? Or $1 billion? Won't you eventually come

TABLE 24-2 When Rawls' Theory Leads to Inequality: An Example

	Income of All Individuals But One	*Income of Last Individual*
Option A (equality)	$ 5,000	$5,000
Option B (inequality)	$10,000	$5,100†

†Option B chosen because everyone is better off

TABLE 24-3 When Rawls' Theory Leads to Equality: An Example

	Income of All Individuals But One	*Income of Last Individual*
Option A (equality)	$ 5,000	$5,000†
Option C (inequality)	$10,000	$4,900

†Option A chosen because a move to C would damage the last individual

around to option C and give up voting in a Rawlsian way?

Because people in an original position would not necessarily vote for equality option A over C, Rawls does not make a convincing case for equality. The difficulty is that his argument is based on the assumption that people's only concern is with what is happening in the last column in those two tables—that is, with that last, poorest individual. Specifically, the choice is based on *maximizing* the *minimum* income; hence, this is often referred to as the *maximin* criterion. But why should we completely ignore the vast majority and be totally preoccupied with that last individual?

In a later reconsideration of the maximin criterion,*** Rawls concluded that, although he still viewed it as attractive, "a deeper investigation. . . may show that some other conception of justice is more reasonable. In any case, the idea that economists may find most useful. . . is that of the original position. This perspective. . . may prove illuminating for economic theory."

*In his *Theory of Justice* (Cambridge, Mass.: Harvard University Press, 1971), p. 63, Rawls was concerned with more than income: "All social values—liberty and opportunity, income and wealth, and the bases of self-respect—are to be distributed equally unless an unequal distribution of any, or all, of these values is to everyone's advantage."

While we consider the lowest income individual in our examples, Rawls' focus is on a typical individual in the lowest income group. But this does not seriously affect his conclusion or our evaluation of it.

**Envy is not taken into account: It is assumed that nobody's happiness is reduced by the knowledge that someone else has become richer.

***See John Rawls, "Some Reasons for the Maximin Criterion," *American Economic Review*, May 1974, pp. 141-146.

Advocates of income equality were immediately attracted to Rawls' theory because it seemed to provide a firmer foundation for equality than the traditional argument. According to the earlier argument, equality is a desirable goal because it would maximize the total utility of all individuals in society. However, this conclusion requires that all individuals have the same capacity to enjoy income. (If this assumption does not hold, we can improve the outcome by moving away from complete equality, by transferring some income away from those who are less able to enjoy it, to those who are more able to enjoy it.) Unfortunately, there is no way we can confirm or deny the assumption that people enjoy income equally. Remember, there is no way to measure people's heads to compare the satisfaction they get from $1 of income.

Therefore this traditional argument does not provide convincing support for income equality. Nor, as we have seen in this box, does Rawls' theory. Like the older theory, it has a weak link—in this case the assumption that the only concern is for the lowest person on the totem pole. Moreover, many of those who believe in equality became less enthusiastic about Rawls' theory when they discovered that it allows for a very substantial degree of inequality—as we have seen in Table 24-2 and as Rawls himself has emphasized. (Rawls, "Some Reasons for the Maximin Criterion," p. 145.)

Wonderland put it, "Everybody has won, and all must have prizes."

An alternative view is that the government's only responsibility is to ensure that the race is fair. Disadvantages should be eliminated: No one should start with a 50-yard handicap because of being a woman, or a black, or the child of parents who are not influential. In this race, everyone has a right, but it is the right of equality of opportunity, not equality of reward. In brief, everyone should have the right to an equal start—but not to an equal finish.

Although the idea of equal opportunity is appealing, it too is difficult to define. Buried in any definition of a fair race is a judgment on which advantages are unfair and should be removed, and which advantages should not. Advantages of race, color, and ethnic background clearly should be removed. But what should we do about advantages arising from differences in natural ability? Should an individual in the economic race be penalized for natural business talent so that all may start equal? Does it make any more sense to do this than to penalize a marathon runner for strong legs? If we were to embark on such a penalty or handicap system, we would end up in the world of Kurt Vonnegut's Handicapper General, who weighs down naturally talented ballerinas with bags of birdshot (Box 24-2). In such a world, nobody would come close to breaking the 4-minute mile; the economy would fall far short of its potential.

. . . but modify the rewards. It is quite possible to have a fair race, yet still have a bad system of rewards. For example, suppose the winner were to be given a million dollars and the loser were to be thrown, Roman style, to the lions. Believing in a fair economic race does not prevent us from modifying its rewards—in other words, using taxes and transfer payments to reduce the income differences that result.

This idea of a fair race and a modified system of rewards that reduces but does not eliminate income inequality is an appealing principle. But again, the idea is not as simple as it sounds. Is not an individual's economic life less like a standard race than like a relay race? Moreover, a relay race with no beginning or end? The race you run depends on the start you get, in terms of your whole background, including your family wealth. A first reaction is that it should not be like this. To keep the race fair, everyone should be started off equally, without any advantage of inherited wealth. Should the government therefore tax away all inheritances and, for the same reason, gifts?

This is a difficult proposal to defend, even on equity grounds. Consider two men with equal incomes. One spends it all. The other wishes to save in order to pass wealth on to his children. Is it fair to impose a tax that prohibits him from doing so? Is not charity a virtue? What can one say of a society that prevents gifts to family or friends?

CONCLUSIONS: CAN WE PIN DOWN THE IDEA OF EQUITY?

Unfortunately, the answer is no. The only conclusions of this chapter are both negative. Equity is not complete equality of income, nor is it the income distribution that the free market generates. Instead, equity seems to be somewhere between. Thus it may be concluded that, in terms of equity considerations alone, society should move from a free-market distribution some distance, but not the whole way, toward equalizing incomes.

In practice, government policies have equalized incomes to some extent, as Figure 24-1 illustrated. Some argue that this equalization has gone too far; others argue, not far enough. The question of how the nation's income should be distributed is likely to remain an issue of continuing debate.

As this debate continues, it is essential to remember that a move toward equalizing income will often impose an efficiency cost by shrinking the national income pie. Because of this efficiency cost, it is desirable to stop short of the degree of equality that would be chosen if equity were the sole objective.

Whereas many policies do involve a conflict between the objectives of equity and efficiency, there are exceptions. Some policies can improve both. It is important that the search for such policies continue. This chapter concludes with an important example—ending discrimination in the labor market.

BOX 24-2 *Kurt Vonnegut on Why Only Horses and Golfers Should Be Handicapped**

The year was 2081, and everybody was finally equal. They weren't only equal before God and the law. They were equal every which way. Nobody was smarter than anybody else. Nobody was better looking than anybody else. Nobody was stronger or quicker than anybody else. All this equality was due to the 211th, 212th, and 213th Amendments to the Constitution, and to the unceasing vigilance of agents of the United States Handicapper General. . . .

George Bergeron, whose intelligence was way above normal, had a little mental handicap radio in his ear. He was required by law to wear it at all times. It was tuned to a government transmitter. Every twenty seconds or so, the transmitter would send out some sharp noise to keep people like George from taking unfair advantage of their brains. . . .

On the television screen were ballerinas. . . . They weren't really very good—no better than anybody else would have been anyway. They were burdened with sash-weights and bags of birdshot and their faces were masked, so that no one, seeing a free and graceful gesture or a pretty face, would feel like something the cat drug in. George was toying with the vague notion that maybe dancers shouldn't be handicapped. But he didn't get very far with it before another noise in his ear radio scattered his thoughts. . . . George began to think glimmeringly about his abnormal son who was now in jail, about Harrison, but a twenty-one-gun salute in his head stopped that. "Boy!" said Hazel, "that was a doozy, wasn't it?" It was such a doozy that George was white and trembling, and tears stood on the rims of his red eyes. Two of the eight ballerinas had collapsed to the studio floor, were holding their temples. . . .

The television program was suddenly interrupted for a news bulletin. It wasn't clear at first as to what the bulletin was about, since the announcer, like all announcers, had a serious speech impediment. For about half a minute, and in a state of high excitement, the announcer tried to say, "Ladies and gentlemen—"

He finally gave up, handed the bulletin to a ballerina to read. . . . "That's all right—" Hazel said of the announcer, "he tried. That's the big thing. He tried to do the best he could with what God gave him. He should get a nice raise for trying so hard."

"Ladies and gentlemen—" said the ballerina, . . . "Harrison Bergeron, age fourteen. . . has just escaped from jail, where he was held on suspicion of plotting to overthrow the government. He is a genius and an athlete, is underhandicapped, and should be regarded as extremely dangerous."

A police photograph of Harrison Bergeron was flashed on the screen. . . . Harrison's appearance was Halloween and hardware. Nobody had ever born heavier handicaps. . . . Instead of a little ear radio for a mental handicap, he wore a tremendous pair of earphones, and spectacles with thick wavy lenses. The spectacles were intended to make him not only half blind, but to give him whanging headaches besides.

Scrap metal was hung all over him. Ordinarily, there was a certain symmetry, a military neatness to the handicaps issued to strong people, but Harrison looked like a walking junkyard.

*Abridgment of "Harrison Bergeron" from *Welcome to the Monkey House* by Kurt Vonnegut, Jr. Copyright 1961 by Kurt Vonnegut, Jr. Originally published in *Fantasy and Science Fiction.* Reprinted by permission of Delacorte Press/Seymour Lawrence.

DISCRIMINATION IN THE LABOR MARKET

What happens if employers favor one group for the better positions, and offer only inferior jobs to minorities with equal skill and training? While demand and supply curves for labor will now be used to answer these questions, it must be recognized that this economic framework alone cannot deal with the other social, moral, and political effects of discrimination. Moreover, our supply and demand analysis will not cover the even greater problem that arises when some individuals in a minority group are offered *no* jobs because of discrimination. In this case, the minority group suffers even greater damage.

To set the stage, the left panel in part *a* of Figure 24-2 shows the situation in an economy in which there is no discrimination. This panel describes the labor market for the economy as a whole rather than for a single industry; discrimina-

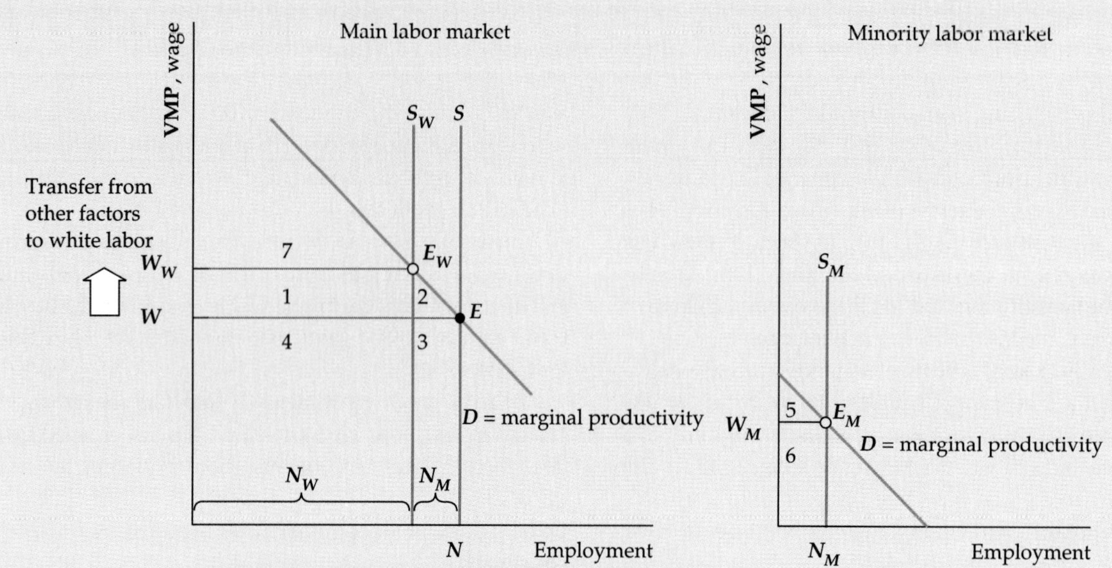

(*a*) **How discrimination affects wages and incomes.**
In a color-blind market *without discrimination*, equilibrium is at E in the left panel. The wage received by all workers is W, with N_W white and N_M minority workers employed. *With discrimination* minorities are forced into the ghetto market on the right, where equilibrium is E_M. Thus minority wages fall from W to W_M and the wage income of minority workers falls from area 3 to area 6. Meanwhile, the forced departure of minorities from the main labor market on the left reduces labor supply there from N to N_W, thus raising wages of whites from W to W_W, and raising the wage income of white workers by area 1 (that is, from area 4 to area 4 + 1).

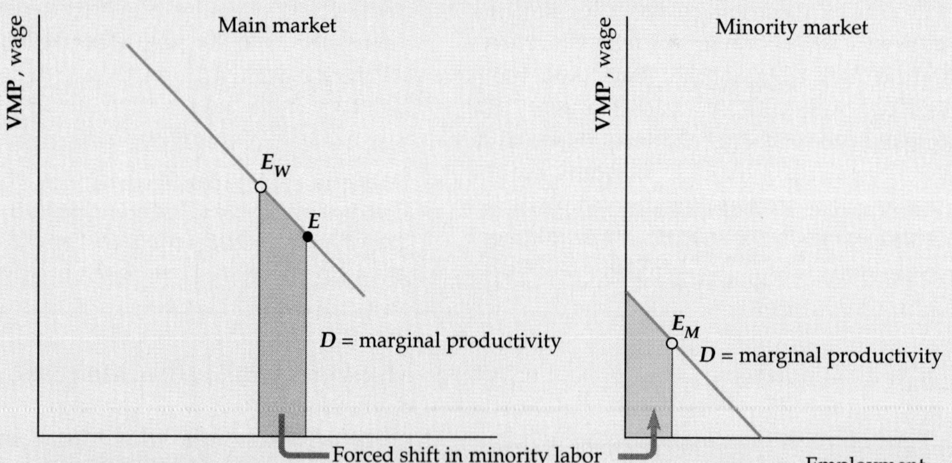

(*b*) **The efficiency effects of discrimination**
As a result of the forced departure of minority labor from this main labor market, there is lost output of the red area under the demand curve. This is more than . . . the output (blue area) produced by minority labor when it is hired in this low-productivity market. The efficiency loss is the difference in these two areas—the reduced output of minority labor because it is shifted from high to low productivity jobs.

FIGURE 24-2. Discrimination in the labor market.

tion is an economywide problem. Thus the demand curve D includes the demands of all hiring firms in the economy. As a first approximation, assume that the number of workers in the economy as a whole is given, with the supply curve of labor consequently being vertical.

In the labor market shown here, wage W is paid to N workers—N_W whites and N_M workers from a minority group. No distinction is made between them; for example, in hiring workers, employers are "color-blind."

What happens if discrimination is introduced into this market? Specifically, consider the case of segregated employment where employers no longer hire minorities to do the same jobs as whites in the main labor market but hire them instead only for deadend jobs in which their marginal productivity is low.

In this case, there is a *dual labor market*—that is, there are two quite separate labor markets, as shown in the top two panels of Figure 24-2. In the "whites only" panel on the left, discrimination that excludes minorities shifts supply from S to S_W, and the wage rate rises from W to W_W. In the minority labor market on the right, demand for labor D is low, reflecting the fact that the only jobs available are low-productivity tasks. Supply in this market is S_M. The wage rate is W_M, substantially less than the wage W that minorities received before discrimination.

A dual labor market exists when there is a low-wage, secondary market, and there are noneconomic barriers such as discrimination that prevent workers in the secondary market from getting jobs in the other, higher wage, primary market.

The effects of such discrimination on each group and on the overall efficiency of the economy may be summarized:

1. Minority workers lose. Because their wage rate is depressed from W to W_M, their total wage income falls from area 3 to area 6. They may also suffer higher unemployment, which does not show up in this diagram.

2. White workers gain. Because their wage rate rises from W to W_W, their total wage income increases by area 1.

3. Owners of other factors of production lose. Specifically, the income earned by capital and other nonlabor factors of production in the main labor market decreases by areas 1 + 2. (According to Fig. 21-4, their income before discrimination was area 7 + 1 + 2, but afterward it is only area 7.) Of this, area 1 is a transfer from other factors to the white workers who receive the wage increase.

This suggests that discrimination is not in the interest of employers because it depresses their profits (included in area 7). In other words, employers have an economic incentive not to discriminate. This incentive acts as a market pressure that tends to reduce discrimination. Another way to view this point is to note that there is a profit opportunity for employers who do not discriminate: They can increase their profit by hiring minorities at their low prevailing wage and putting them in high-productivity jobs in the main labor market.

Yet despite this market pressure, discrimination continues. One reason is that economics is not a controlling influence over long-standing prejudices of employers. A second explanation is that employers may simply be responding to discriminatory pressure from their customers. A firm may not hire a minority sales representative if its customers are prejudiced against buying from minorities. Although black players dominate professional basketball, it has been estimated that NBA teams pay a 20% higher salary to whites of equal ability. The reason is that a white player raises home attendance by 8,000 to 13,000 fans per season.[3] In such cases, the problem is still prejudice, but it may be prejudice of the fans rather than just the owners.

4. There may be little effect on whites overall. Because nonlabor factors of production (like capital) are owned mostly by whites, there may be little effect on all whites taken together. True, white wage earners gain area 1, but this is just a transfer from other white-owned factors. The loss 2 incurred by other factors may be roughly offset by new income 5 earned in the minority market.

5. There is an efficiency loss. When attention is turned from the transfer effects to the efficiency effects shown in the lower part b of this diagram, it is evident that the total product of the economy falls. Because minority workers are forced out of the main labor market, the value of output there

[3]Lawrence M. Kahn and Peter D. Sherer, "Racial Differences in Professional Basketball Players' Compensation," *Journal of Labor Economics*, January 1988, p. 40.

falls by the red area.[4] This is only partially offset by the new blue output produced in the segregated market. The difference is the reduced total output of the economy, that is, the efficiency loss that results from discrimination.

6. This efficiency loss is borne primarily by minorities. Because there is little net effect on whites, minorities suffer most—perhaps all—the efficiency loss from discrimination. To confirm this, notice that the reduction in minority income from area 3 to 6 in the two panels in part *a* is essentially the same as the efficiency loss (the difference between the red area and the blue area in the panels below).

In conclusion, note how ending discrimination will increase both equity *and* efficiency; there is no conflict between goals here. Such a policy is equitable because it prevents individuals from being excluded from higher income jobs simply because they are from a minority group. It is efficient because it eliminates the efficiency loss from discrimination shown in this diagram.

MEASURING THE EFFECTS OF RACIAL DISCRIMINATION

In an analysis in the *Review of Economics and Statistics* (May 1988, pp. 236–243), Jeremiah Cotton of the University of Massachusetts has used a more complicated model to answer a question raised in Figure 24-2. How large a gap between white and black wages has been created by discrimination in hiring decisions by employers? In a sample taken from the U.S. Census, black male wages in 1980 were $1.44 less than white male wages ($6.04 versus $7.48). About half of this differential ($0.71) could be attributed to skill differences—due at least in part to the inadequate access to education that blacks have faced in the past. The other half could be attributed to discrimination by employers (the difference between W_W and W_M in Fig. 24-2).

RELATED PROBLEMS

Discrimination appears in other forms and raises other thorny issues.

1. *Housing.* Minorities are victims of discrimination not only in the labor market, but also in the market for housing. This restricts their entry into certain neighborhoods and therefore restricts the access of their children to the educational facilities provided there. With less education, their children encounter difficulty when they come to seek jobs. In short, minorities may get stuck in low-productivity, low-wage jobs either because they are discriminated against by employers (as in Fig. 24-2) *or* because they have lower qualifications as a result of other forms of discrimination, such as discrimination in the housing market, which may leave them with less access to a good education. (Housing discrimination is examined in more detail in Box 24-3.)

2. *Discrimination against women.* Figure 24-2 may be applied to some forms of discrimination that women face. (Although women are not a minority in the population, they are a minority in the labor force.)

The problem of discrimination against women has become more important as women have been entering the labor force in larger numbers. Increasingly, women are facing the challenge of a career. Although some have chosen to work because tastes have changed, others have been forced into a career because of the increased breakup—or risk of breakup—of their households.

Figure 24-3 shows how women's earnings have lagged behind men's. Note how the gap increased in the 1960s and 1970s as women with less work experience—and in some cases with less education—entered the work force. Recently, as both these problems have been reduced, the earnings gap has been narrowing. This process seems likely to continue, because the wage gap is far smaller for younger women who suffer from fewer educational disadvantages.

Although about half of the earnings gap is attributable to differences in experience and education, half still remains to be explained. One explanation is discrimination against women. But how is this possible, when the 1964 Civil Rights Act prohibits sex discrimination in hiring and promotion, while the 1963 Equal Pay Act guarantees "equal pay for equal work"—that is, men and women in the same job must be paid the same salary? One answer is that discrimination is still possible when men and women have *different jobs.* To illustrate,

[4]This area can be visualized as a whole set of vertical bars, each representing the marginal productivity that is lost when a minority worker is forced out of this market and there is one less worker employed there.

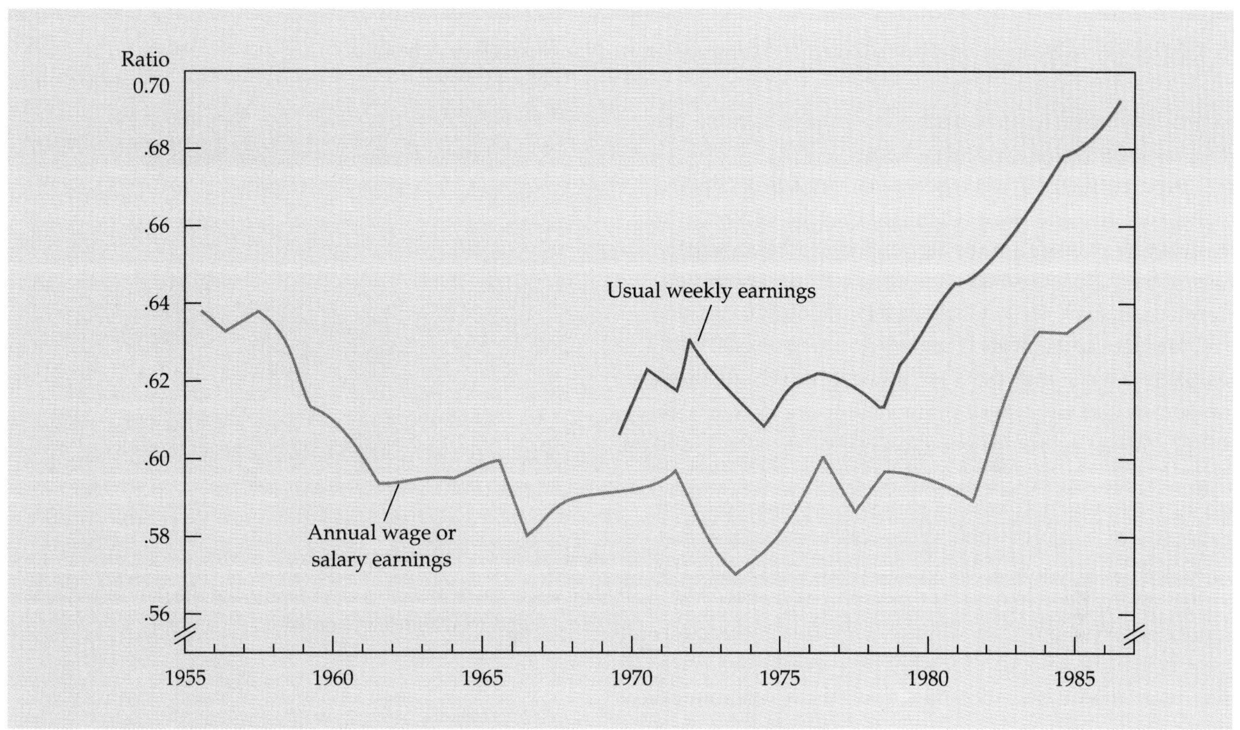

FIGURE 24-3 Ratio of female to male earnings for full-time workers, 1955–1986.

Source: Economic Report of the President, 1987, p. 221. This is the basic source in our discussion of sex discrimination.

suppose the government succeeds in getting men and women paid exactly the same salary of, say, $16,000 a year in nursing. Suppose further that the government also succeeds in getting both men and women paid exactly the same salary of, say, $24,000 a year as electricians. Isn't there still a problem? After all, most nurses are women, while most electricians are men. Aren't women underpaid if their whole profession of nursing is underpaid? Isn't there discrimination unless you ensure that people get the same pay not only for the same job, but also for different jobs of *comparable worth,* like being nurses and electricians?

In recent years, the idea of equal pay for jobs of comparable worth has been a subject of controversy. To determine whether these two jobs do have equal worth—or that one has more worth than the other—one must address questions like: Which job is more demanding physically and mentally? Which job requires greater qualifications, knowledge, skill, and responsibility? Which involves more hazard or unpleasantness? And so on. When all jobs are rated in this way and a female-dominated job like nursing and a male-dominated job like electrical repairing get the same rating—that is, are judged to have comparable worth—then the lower pay in nursing indicates sex discrimination. Salaries in this job should be raised. So say the proponents of comparable worth.

Opponents see difficulties in putting the concept of comparable worth into practice. They ask: How can one possibly evaluate or trade off the greater risks required in washing windows in a skyscraper with the greater academic qualifications required in teaching school? A job that 10% of the population views as pleasant may be viewed by others as downright unpleasant. In this case, should rating points be added or subtracted? Isn't the best way to answer this question to look at workers' willingness to take such jobs, which will

BOX 24–3 *Discrimination Against Minorities in the Housing Market*

Figure 24-4 illustrates how discrimination can increase the price minorities have to pay for a house.

Suppose there is segregation, with minorities in the central core area and whites in the suburbs. Any increase in the white population can be accommodated by an expansion of new housing into the surrounding countryside. However, an expansion of the minority population encounters resistance at the white boundary, for two reasons. First, real estate agents often don't tell minority buyers about all the houses that are available. For example, a 1981 Boston survey indicated that black buyers were told about 30% fewer houses for sale than were white buyers.* Second, whites may be reluctant to rent or sell to minorities. This resistance to minority expansion raises the price that minorities have to pay to the point where whites near the border are finally willing to rent or sell to minorities. Thus minorities pay more than whites—with the difference in price being the amount that whites require to overcome their reluctance to deal with minorities. (How can a house owner sell to someone in a minority at a higher price than to a white? The answer is that the owner quotes a price above the market value and accepts a lower bid if it is made by the white, but not if it is made by the person from the minority.)

Exceptions to this pattern may occur. For example, prices in the white area next to the minority core area may even temporarily fall, if real estate agents stampede whites into selling quickly. In the past, agents tried to do this by the now illegal practice of "blockbusting." This practice involved selling one or two houses in an all-white block to minorities and then using high-pressure tactics on the remaining whites to try to frighten them into quick sales "while there is still time." The incentive for this practice was the commission that agents made from the rapid turnover of homes.

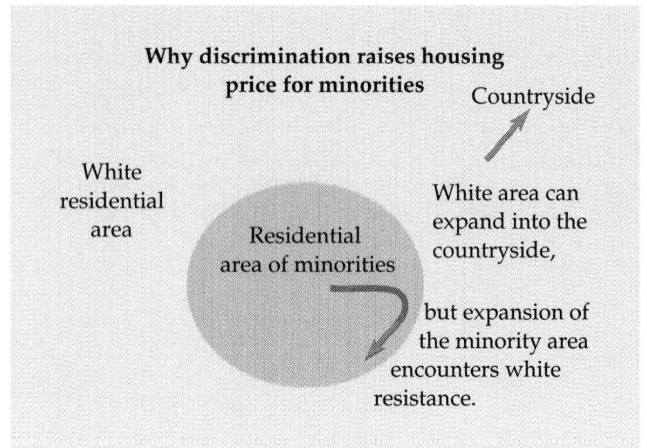

FIGURE 24-4 Housing discrimination.
The white residential area can expand, but the minority area is surrounded by white neighborhoods.

*John Yinger, "Measuring Racial Discrimination with Fair Housing Audits: Caught in the Act," *American Economic Review*, December 1986, p. 881. This discussion of housing also draws on Edwin Mills and Bruce Hamilton, *Urban Economics*, 3d ed. (Glenview, Ill.: Scott Foresman, 1984).

be reflected in supply conditions and therefore the wage rate? Do we really want the government overriding labor markets?

In particular, if the government is involved in determining wages on the basis of comparable worth rather than market forces, how will the economy adjust when there is a shortage of one kind of labor and an oversupply of another—a problem normally solved by a change in market wage rates? Will government interference result in the sort of imbalance of supply and demand that has marked government interference in the housing market? In this case, will the losers be the women who can't get jobs because the government has raised the female wage? (This problem of unemployment need not occur in government jobs, where the first applications of comparable worth occurred.) Finally, this policy may be of limited success in closing the wage gap, insofar as it only forces individual employers to equalize their wages. To take an extreme example, if one firm employs only electricians, while another employs only nurses, then imposing this policy *on each firm* won't raise nursing salaries at all.[5] In short, opponents of

[5]For more detail on this problem, see George Johnson and Gary Solon, "Estimates of the Direct Effect of Comparable Worth Policy," *American Economic Review*, December 1986, pp. 1117–11257.

comparable worth argue that it would either be ineffective or would lead to a great deal of government interference based on the arbitrary and subjective judgment of those who rank jobs.

In rebuttal, proponents argue that continuing to rely on the market would allow discrimination to continue, and that is unacceptable.

Even if employers today are completely color-blind and do not discriminate, a problem remains.

HUMAN CAPITAL AND DISCRIMINATION

The problem of low income for a minority may reflect more than present discrimination by employers. It may also be the result of the past inability of the minority to acquire human capital. The members of such a group may be caught in a vicious circle. Past discrimination has meant that they have been receiving lower wages. Consequently, they have been unable to help their children cover the expenses of higher education. As a result, their children remain at a disadvantage. They have more difficulty in getting jobs and are paid lower wages—*even* if employers today are color-blind and don't discriminate.

One way of breaking this vicious circle is to ensure equal educational opportunity. To make up for past discrimination, special efforts have been made under affirmative action programs to get minorities into universities, training programs and positions where they can accumulate human capital.

KEY POINTS

1. Large differences exist in the incomes of individual Americans. Some have high incomes because of their wealth, human capital, native talent, family background, or just plain luck.

2. There is a great deal of inequality in the U.S. income distribution before taxes and transfers. The poorest 20% receive about 1% of the nation's income, while the highest 20% get about half.

3. Some of this inequality is eliminated by taxes and by government transfer expenditures that benefit the poor. Taxes do much less equalizing than government transfer payments.

4. Equality is a question of fact: How equal are incomes? On the other hand, equity is a matter of judgment: What pattern of incomes is fair? A strong case can be made that neither a completely equal distribution of incomes nor the unequal free-market distribution is equitable, and that the target should be somewhere between.

5. Although it is very difficult to be more precise than this, some rough guidelines have been suggested. For example, the "economic race" should be fair, with everyone given an equal opportunity. However, equal opportunity need not result in equal reward. Even if everyone could be given an equal start, there is no reason to expect that all will finish in a tie. Some will get greater rewards than others. A responsibility of the government is to modify rewards—that is, to reduce income inequality by taxes and transfer payments.

6. Even if we could determine an equitable income distribution, it does not follow that the government should continue to redistribute income up to this point. The reason is that the act of redistributing income—changing the division of the national pie—affects the incentive to work and hence the size of that pie. Therefore a compromise should be selected between the conflicting objectives of equity and efficiency.

7. There are a few policies, such as ending discrimination, that are both equitable and efficient, so no conflict arises.

8. Discrimination against minorities by employers hiring labor will result in an efficiency loss that is borne primarily by minorities who are segregated into low-wage, low-productivity jobs. Although white workers benefit, it may be largely at the expense of white owners of other factors of production.

9. To reduce sex discrimination by employers, women are guaranteed equal pay for equal work by the Equal Pay Act. It is more difficult to identify and deal with discrimination when men and women hold different jobs. One proposal is to pay women the same as men in jobs of comparable worth.

10. Even if present employers do not discriminate, a problem may still exist because of past discrimination. The reason is that minorities in the past have not had equal access to educational opportunities.

KEY CONCEPTS

cumulative income distribution (Lorenz curve)
difference between equity and equality
difference between equalizing opportunity and equalizing reward
dual labor market
human capital and discrimination
comparable worth

PROBLEMS

24-1. Mark McCormack is, in his own words, an "engineer of careers." His company grosses millions of dollars by charging a 15% to 40% agent's fee for managing hundreds of tennis stars and golfers. Do you think McCormack's large income is the result of (a) only luck, (b) luck and other reasons, or (c) just other reasons? If you answer (b) or (c), explain what the other reasons might be.

24-2. Explain how the marketplace generates a rental income for those with high reputation, just as for those with great skill.

24-3. Explain why you agree or disagree with the following statement: "Free-market prices of factors of production help to maximize the total national income pie and also divide it in an equitable way."

24-4. This question is based on Box 24-1. Is the following statement true or false? If true, explain it. If false, correct it:

> Rawls' maximin principle is to maximize the minimum possible income. However, this is the preference only of people who are unwilling to risk any of their income in the hope of acquiring more. Many people are not like this, including all those individuals who bet a small part of their income at the races or Monte Carlo in the hope of winning more.

24-5. In 1899, John Bates Clark wrote in the *Distribution of Wealth* that "free competition tends to give to labor what labor creates (that is, the value of the marginal product of labor), to capitalists what capital creates (that is, the marginal product of capital), and to entrepreneurs what the coordinating function creates." This sounds as though everyone gets what he or she deserves; that is, free competition distributes income in an equitable way. Do you agree? In your view, what does a free competitive market do well and what does it do not so well?

24-6. The efficiency loss illustrated in Figure 24-2 can be viewed as the result of splitting the labor market into minority and white segments with different productivity in each. Explain why a similar efficiency loss occurs, at least to some degree, in the U.S. labor market because of its geographical divisions. (Because workers find it difficult and costly to move, they often stay in low-wage and low-productivity areas rather than move into higher productivity areas.) Is it therefore true that barriers to labor mobility impose a cost on the economy? Do you see why a policy of increasing labor mobility raises the efficiency of the economy even if it doesn't reduce unemployment? (In fact, it may also provide an additional benefit by reducing unemployment.)

CHAPTER 25
GOVERNMENT POLICIES TO REDUCE INEQUALITY
Can We Solve the Poverty Problem?

If a free society cannot help the many who are poor, it cannot save the few who are rich.
JOHN F. KENNEDY

Although Americans differ on the question of how far the government should go in reducing income inequality in general, there is one specific issue on which the overwhelming majority agree: Nobody should starve, nor should children grow up in abject poverty. Yet, in 1987, poverty was still a fact of life for about 1 in 10 American families. You can confirm the grinding effect of poverty by driving from a wealthy suburb of any large American city into a depressed core area. In the United States, overall wealth stands in stark contrast to the poverty faced by those who are insufficiently fed, housed, and clothed.

This chapter is a study of the poor—the individuals who appeared in the bottom left-hand corner of the Lorenz income curve in the last chapter. Who are the poor? Why are they poor? What programs has the government introduced to fight the war on poverty? Do these programs help solve the poverty problem? Can the faults in these programs be cured? If so, how?

POVERTY

The economic definition of poverty is "inadequate income." But this does not mean that poverty is strictly an economic condition. It is often also a state of mind, a condition in which the individual feels helpless. Poverty raises the chicken-or-egg question: Are people unable to cope because they are poor, or are they poor because they are unable to cope? The answer is, partly both.

> Poverty exists when people have inadequate income to buy the necessities of life. In 1988, a family of four fell below the poverty line if it had an income of less than $12,075.

HOW THE POVERTY LINE IS DEFINED

Those who calculate the poverty line recognize food as the first essential and calculate the minimum cost of a nutritious diet. Here judgment is very important, because as little as $200 or $300, spent on just the right combination of things like soybeans, orange juice, and liver, will provide a medically balanced diet for one person for a year. Moreover, this menu will be healthier than the present diet of some wealthy Americans. But who would eat it? Consequently, a reasonably appetizing—though certainly not luxurious—diet is used instead to calculate essential expenditures on food.

Since past studies have shown that the average family spends about one-third of its income on food, the cost of this diet is multiplied by 3 to arrive at the official poverty line. This figure is then adjusted for family size—$12,075 for a family of four, $14,290 for a family of five, and so on.

To take account of inflation, the poverty line is adjusted upward each year. Furthermore, it rises over the long term because our concept of poverty keeps changing. The 1988 poverty income of $12,075 would have been regarded in colonial times as a very handsome income indeed—even after full adjustment for inflation. In fact, it would still have been considered a good income as late as the 1930s. When President Roosevelt spoke at that time of one-third of the nation living in poverty, he was using a poverty line that was far lower, and that would buy far less, than the poverty income today. Thus upward adjustments in the definition of poverty do occur. But beware: If the definition of poverty is made too flexible, the concept becomes meaningless. If, for example, poverty were defined as the income of the bottom one-tenth of the population, there would be no hope of eliminating it. By definition, 1 in 10 Americans would *always* be poor, no matter how much everyone's income might increase. And the statement that 1 American family in 10 was living in poverty would tell us absolutely nothing about the seriousness of the problem or about our success in curing it.

WHO ARE THE POOR?

Poverty is more likely to occur in some groups than in others. For example, someone with less than eight years of education is more likely to be poor than someone who has finished high school; and completion of a college education almost—but not quite—provides a guarantee against poverty. People living in the core of a big city are more likely to be poor than those living in its suburbs. Part of the reason is that many of those in the core who have been able to raise their income above the poverty level have used this income to move to the suburbs. However, poverty is not limited to centers of big cities. Many of the poor live on farms or in small towns or cities.

Figure 25-1 shows some of the other faces of poverty. A black is almost three times as likely to be poor as a white.[1] The picture is little better for those of Spanish origin. Persons in single-parent families are far more likely to be poor than those living in a home with both parents. Half of those in black, single-parent families are below the poverty line.

The two categories of elderly in Figure 25-1 show that poverty is a smaller problem for them today than it used to be. In 1970, the elderly were more likely to be poor than the public at large. Now they are less likely to be poor. One reason has been an improvement in pensions, including social security. As the situation of the elderly has improved, attention has been increasingly directed to the poor in the growing number of single-parent households with young children.

[1]However, there are more poor whites than poor blacks. Without reading further, can you see why? The answer is: There are more poor whites because most of the population is white.

THE WAR ON POVERTY

In the mid-1960s, President Johnson declared a war on poverty. Within the next two decades, antipoverty programs such as Aid for Families with Dependent Children and food stamps grew by more than twelve times in dollar terms, and about four times after adjustment for inflation. When the public thinks of programs to fight poverty, these are two that often come to mind. These outlays relieve the *symptoms* of poverty. They make it more bearable without providing much hope that the problem will be cured—that is, that the poor will be able to increase their earnings. A more promising long-run approach is to attack the *causes* of poverty. For example, one of the causes of poverty is inadequate human capital; assistance for education and training can help cure this. (Although it is usually more promising to attack the causes of a problem than its symptoms, this is not always the case. In extreme cases of "clinical" poverty, where individuals have such serious physical or mental handicaps that no amount of training will allow them to earn a living, straight support programs are often a more effective form of assistance.)

POLICIES TO REDUCE THE CAUSES OF POVERTY

Lack of human capital is only one of the many reasons why people live in poverty. Other important causes include discrimination and cyclical unemployment that leaves people without a job. What

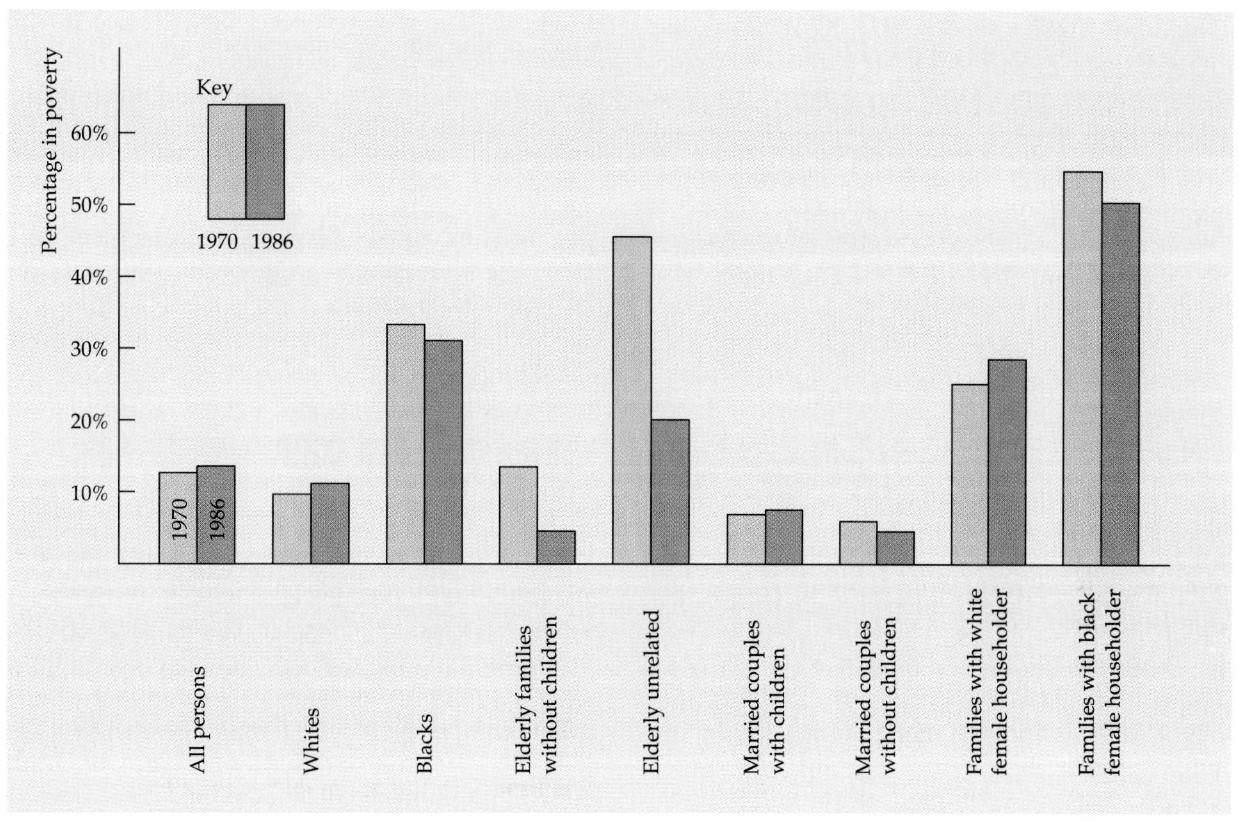

FIGURE 25-1 Incidence of poverty, 1970 and 1986.
Source: Economic Report of the President, 1988, p. 282; and *Trends in Family Income: 1970-1986* (Washington, D.C.: Congressional Budget Office, 1988), p. 31.

policies are there to deal with these causes of poverty?

SUBSIDIZED INVESTMENT IN HUMAN CAPITAL

Federal, state, and local governments subsidize education in various ways. The provision of free elementary and secondary schooling is the most important. However, there are also other programs—in particular, the Jobs Training Partnership Act (JTPA, enacted in 1982) which assists companies in training workers for jobs tailored to local needs.

ANTIDISCRIMINATION POLICIES

As noted earlier, the Equal Pay Act (1963) mandates equal pay for equal work; the Civil Rights Act (1964) outlaws discrimination in hiring, firing, and other employment practices; and affirmative action programs are designed to help compensate for past discrimination.

DEALING WITH UNEMPLOYMENT AND DISABILITY

The government attempts to reduce the problem of unemployment by macroeconomic policies designed to restore the economy to a high level of output. But what can be done about permanent disability which cannot be cured once it has happened? It is then too late to deal with the cause. However, it is not too late to deal with the causes of *future* disabling accidents, some of which can be prevented. This is the task of the Occupational Safety and Health Administration (1971).

POLICIES TO REDUCE THE SYMPTOMS OF POVERTY: GOVERNMENT PROGRAMS TO MAINTAIN INCOMES

Even if it is not possible to cure a disease, it is very important to provide the patient with relief from the symptoms. There are several programs that reduce the symptoms of poverty by helping families to stay above the poverty line.

SOCIAL INSURANCE PROGRAMS

Social insurance programs to protect the elderly and the unemployed were not designed specifically to deal with the poverty problem; people need not be poor to receive benefits. Nonetheless, such programs play a key role in keeping people from falling into poverty.

1. *Unemployment Insurance* (UI, 1935) provides temporary assistance to people who have lost their jobs. This deals with a symptom of poverty by limiting the drop in income. Thus the government uses UI to attack a symptom of poverty, while at the same time it uses macroeconomic policies to fight a cause of poverty (unemployment).

2. *Social Security* (1935) is by far the most important income maintenance program. The government collects contributions from both employers and employees and from self-employed individuals. In turn, these contributions are paid out in retirement, disability, and other benefits that totaled almost $220 billion in 1988.

3. *Medicare* (1965) is a health insurance program that provides medical services for the elderly. In 1988, it paid out $79 billion in benefits.

A major reason why poverty has been reduced so much among the elderly is that they have been receiving increasingly large benefits from Social Security and Medicare.

WELFARE PROGRAMS TARGETED ON THE POOR

Although the welfare programs shown in Table 25-1 are much smaller than Social Security or Medicare, they have been designed specifically to combat poverty, and they are paid only to the poor.

1. *Aid to Families with Dependent Children (AFDC).* This program provides cash grants to poor families with dependent children. Until recently, such grants were given only to families headed by a single parent because of desertion, divorce, or death. AFDC is administered by state and local governments, with financial support from the federal government.

2. *Medicaid.* This health insurance program is similar to Medicare except that it provides medical services for those with low incomes. Some of the problems encountered in providing medical care are discussed in Box 25-1.

TABLE 25-1 Selected Welfare Programs

	Year Enacted	*Estimated Expenditures, 1990 (in $ billions)*
Cash		
Aid to Families with Dependent Children (AFDC)	1935	17.3
In Kind		
Medicaid	1965	37.4
Food Stamps and School Lunch Subsidies	1964	20.6
Housing Assistance	1937	16.2

Source: Budget of the United States Government, Fiscal Year, 1990 (Washington: Government Printing Office, 1989), pp. 5–117, 5–129, 5–138.

BOX 25–1 The Rising Cost of Health Care

It is widely recognized that the quality of medical services in the United States is as good as anywhere in the world—at least for those who can afford it. However, it has become *very* costly. Americans are now spending well over 10% of GNP on health care. Although the government provides medical services to the elderly (Medicare) and the poor (Medicaid), it does not provide such services for the rest of the population. An important reason is that broader coverage would add to the bill the government would have to pay for medical services—a bill that has been rising rapidly.

One reason why such a large proportion of the nation's GNP is devoted to health care is that medical research has now made it possible to save lives in a variety of new ways. If an attempt were made to capture all of these opportunities, the cost would become prohibitive.

Therefore society must have some way of deciding at what point its lifesaving efforts will be limited—that is, at what point funds that could save lives will be cut off. Which patients will be the lucky ones who will live because they get access to the limited number of lifesaving machines and treatments that society can afford?

No one likes to make this life-and-death decision on "who will get a seat in the lifeboat" and who will not. For this reason, there are a number of alternative ways of making this decision.

1. **Delay.** In 1984 the British National Health Service provided about 110 free heart transplants. But because of a waiting list of up to a year, most of those in line simply died.

2. **Set an age limit.** Unofficially, heart transplants are given only to Americans less than 50 years of age.

3. **Use chance.** Decide on who will live and die in some sort of doomsday lottery. However, this makes no sense at all, because an Einstein may lose out to a suicidal derelict who places no value on his own life.

Because these methods are unsatisfactory or inadequate, the life-or-death decision frequently has to be made by doctors on the spot—or administrators or committees allocating funds. It is not an easy decision. The difficulty in putting a value on a life has been described in an earlier chapter. However, the task of saying that one *particular* life is worth more than another—and therefore is the one that should be saved—is even more difficult. Therefore, whenever possible, those making such decisions understandably argue: Instead of choosing between two lives, let's save them both—if there is any conceivable way that the cost can be covered. This, then, is one reason why there is persistent upward pressure on costs.

Another reason is that, with such a substantial share of medical bills paid for by Medicare, Medicaid, and private insurance schemes, there is inadequate pressure to cut costs. Patients have little incentive to seek out low-cost treatment; when your health is at stake you don't go bargain hunting, especially when an insurance company is paying the tab.

In the eyes of the critics, a more efficient and less costly system of health care would require that individuals pay more of the cost. True, it may not be appropriate to allow money to make the life-or-death decision on who will get lifesaving care and who will not; that is, it may not be desirable to put "seats on the lifeboat" up for sale. Nonetheless, it may still be possible to use money in far more limited ways to provide an incentive for people to seek out low-cost care. One way might be to have insurance schemes with larger "deductible" clauses that require patients to pay part of the cost of treatment. This would make patients more cost-conscious, and competition would be stimulated among doctors and hospitals.

A final reason why medical costs are rising is that some doctors and hospitals have been defrauding the plans. A Senate committee investigating the cost of Medicaid found that some doctors would carry out complete physical examinations—with the whole battery of laboratory tests—on essentially healthy people who came to their offices with a minor complaint. Through referrals, a group of specialist doctors may "ping-pong" patients back and forth among themselves. Medicaid patients getting a doctor's appointment have sometimes been told to bring their children too, so that Medicaid can be charged for an office visit for each. The vast majority of physicians, of course, have not wasted time and money in such "medifraud." However, according to the Department of Health and Human Resources, there are enough doctors who have engaged in these practices that the costs of Medicare and Medicaid have been raised by a substantial amount.

On the question "Should Medicare coverage be broadened?" opponents point to the high cost and to problems such as medifraud. Those in favor of broader coverage argue that it would be desirable on equity grounds, in particular for those families—more than 1 in 10—who do not have private health insurance or access to government assistance and who may be wiped out by a serious illness.

3. *Food stamps.* The government provides the poor with food stamps, which they can exchange for food.

4. *Public housing.* The federal government subsidizes local governments to acquire housing and rent it to low-income tenants, who pay 25% of their income in rent, with the federal government paying the rest. (For other housing subsidies, see Box 25-2.)

It is worth emphasizing that while AFDC provides cash benefits, the other three programs—Medicaid, food stamps, and public housing—provide benefits in kind.

> ***Benefits in kind*** are payments, not of cash, but of some good such as food, or some service such as medical care.

From 1965 to 1975 both cash and in-kind programs grew. But after 1975, cash programs were cut back, while in-kind programs continued to expand, especially until 1980. By that time, in-kind payments had become the most important part of the welfare package.[2]

ASSESSING THE PRESENT WELFARE PACKAGE

In spending large sums, is the United States making substantial headway against the poverty problem? Figure 25-1 suggests that between 1970 and

[2]For more detail on social insurance and welfare expenditures—including both cash and in-kind payments—see Gary Burtless,"Public Spending for the Poor: Trends, Prospects and Economic Limits," in Sheldon Danziger and Daniel Weinberg, *Fighting Poverty: What Works and What Doesn't* (Cambridge, Mass.: Harvard University Press, 1986). This chapter draws heavily on this book and on Isabel V. Sawhill, "Poverty in the U.S.: Why Is It So Persistent?" *Journal of Economic Literature,* September 1988, pp. 1073–1119.

BOX 25–2 Housing Subsidies: Who Benefits?

Many voters believe that better housing is an important social goal—better housing for the poor and better housing for the average citizen, too. Of the numerous incentives for housing, the most notable is a provision that allows home owners to reduce the income tax they have to pay. (In calculating their taxable income, they can deduct property taxes and most interest payments on their mortgages.) The idea is to encourage people to own their own homes. Partly as a consequence, the United States now has the highest rate of owner-occupied housing in the world. Far from being an antipoverty program, this policy benefits the average home owner more than the poor who own small homes or none at all.

Another government housing policy is urban renewal, which is designed to improve slum housing, revitalize downtown business areas, and attract middle-class residents from the suburbs back into the big cities. This program provides federal subsidies to local governments to tear down central city slums and rebuild these core areas. This policy has generated heated controversy: While its supporters view it as the last hope of saving the big cities, its critics point out that, initially at least, it resulted in more dwellings being torn down than constructed. As a consequence, the central city poor found that their housing supply was shrinking. Another reason for the shrinkage was the success of this program in its important objective of attracting the middle class back from the suburbs. Thus more of the new available space was occupied by the nonpoor. To ensure that the poor will be better accommodated, attempts have been made to guarantee that any renewal program includes specified amounts of low-income housing.

1986, the answer was no—except for the elderly. Figure 25-2 shows a longer period. Between 1930 and 1970, great progress was made. By recent poverty standards, one in two Americans was poor in 1930; by 1947, the figure was one in three; and by 1970, it had fallen to one in eight. In particular, the 1960s brought a rapid reduction in poverty because of declining unemployment and a large expansion of income maintenance programs, including both welfare programs aimed at the poor and other pro-

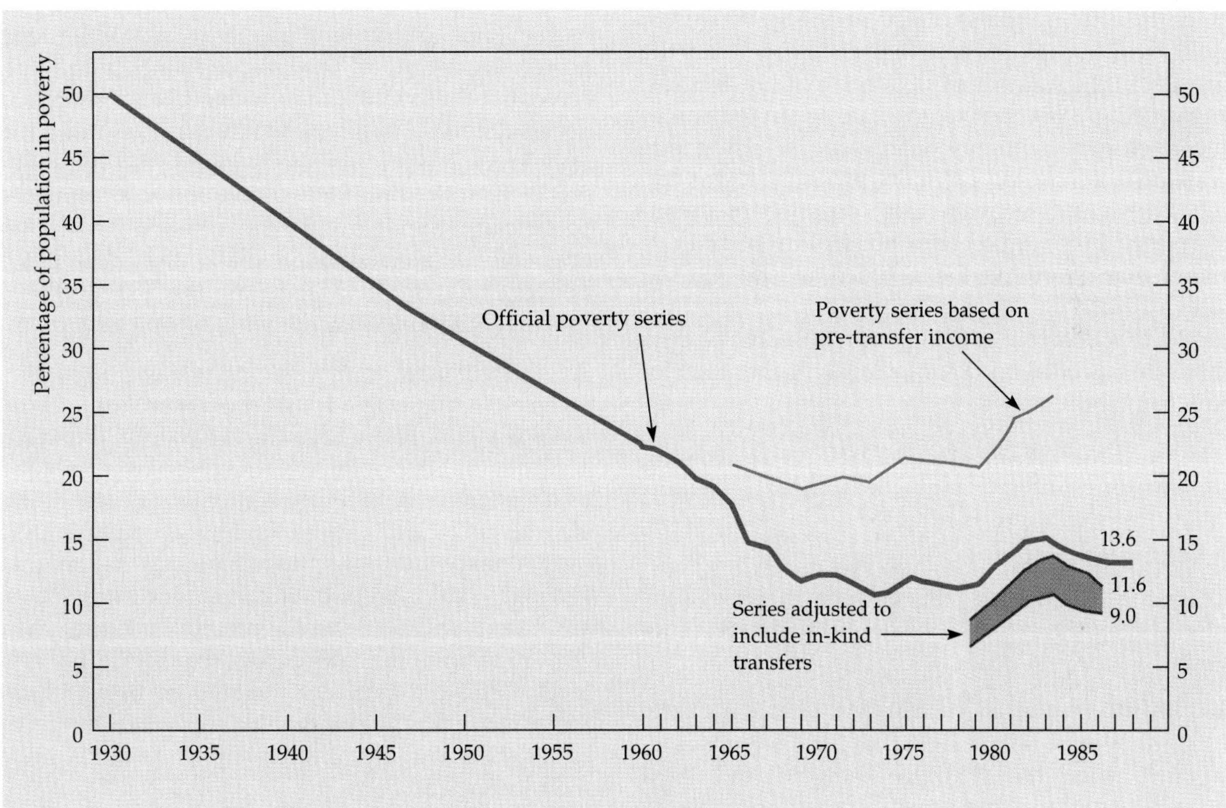

FIGURE 25-2 How the poverty rate has been changing over time.

By recent poverty standards, the percentage of the population in poverty followed a downward long-term trend until the early 1970s. However, in the early 1980s there was an increase in the incidence of poverty, followed by another decrease. (*Sources:* Trend lines only from 1929 to 1947, and from 1947 to 1960. The 1929 figure reflects the fact that the average real income in 1929 was about the same as the poverty level in the mid-1970s. The 1947 figure is from the *Economic Report of the President, 1964.* The before-transfer series from 1965–1983 is taken from Sheldon Danziger and Daniel Weinberg, *Fighting Poverty: What Works and What Doesn't* (Cambridge, Mass.: Harvard University Press, 1986), p. 54. The official poverty series since 1960 is from U.S. Bureau of the Census, Current Population Reports, Series P-60, No. 161, *Money Income and Poverty Status in the United States, 1987* (Washington, D.C.: 1988), p. 9. Poverty series after in-kind transfers is taken from U.S. Bureau of the Census, Technical Paper 57, *Estimating Poverty Including the Value of Non-cash Benefits, 1986* (Washington, D.C.: 1987), p. 5.)

grams such as social security, which are aimed at the whole population but still greatly assist the poor.

In 1973, the official poverty rate stopped falling, and the rest of that decade brought no further reduction. From 1979 to 1983, the poverty rate increased because of the tightening of income maintenance programs and the high unemployment that occurred during the most severe recession since the 1930s. The increase in the poverty rate was also due to long-term trends, such as the growth in the number of single-parent households. However, in 1984 the poverty rate began to drop as the unemployment rate decreased. A "rising tide was lifting all boats." Or, more precisely, it was lifting *some* boats; recovery from a period of unemployment helps those who are in the labor force rather than those like the disabled and the elderly, who are not.[3]

In this description so far, only the official poverty rate has been used. Unfortunately, that calculation has serious flaws.

WHY THE OFFICIAL POVERTY RATE IS TOO HIGH

There are two reasons why poverty is not as serious as the official poverty rate in Figure 25-2 suggests.

1. *In-kind income is ignored.* The official poverty rate—shown in purple—does not include income-in-kind, such as Medicare benefits and food stamps, which in some cases are sufficient to lift some of the poor above the poverty line. When these benefits are taken into account, the poverty rate is lowered to the shaded band in Figure 25-2. This band is defined by an upper and lower estimate. The lower estimate (9% in 1986) takes account of in-kind payments at their full market value. However, this raises a problem. For some people, housing or medical benefits have a high enough value to raise their income above the poverty level—even though they may still be destitute because they haven't got the cash to buy other necessities. The conclusion is that this frequently quoted 9% poverty rate is too low because it does not include such people, even though they are actually living in poverty.

This 9% figure can be appropriately adjusted by recognizing that such people would prefer cash rather than some of the in-kind benefits they receive. In other words, their in-kind benefits should be valued at a lower price. When this is done (no easy task), in-kind income is lower, and the number of people in poverty is consequently higher—specifically, the 11.6% figure for 1986 at the top edge of the shaded band. Note that this 11.6% poverty rate is still well below the 13.6% official rate that ignores in-kind benefits completely.

2. *In the official poverty rate calculations, some nonpoor people with only a temporary income loss are erroneously placed below the poverty line.* To illustrate, consider those people who have enjoyed a good past income and have used it to accumulate assets such as furniture, a car, a savings account, and so on (items which, of course, are not taken into account in calculating their current income). If they are faced with temporary unemployment, their current income may fall below the official poverty level. Officially, they are counted as being below the poverty line, even though they may be living better than that by temporarily drawing on, say, their savings accounts.

Even though poverty may not be as serious as the official figure suggests, progress in reducing it since 1970 has been disappointing. The reason is that the welfare programs designed to cure poverty have sometimes been ineffective.

PROBLEMS WITH THE PRESENT WELFARE SYSTEM

Critics charge that the present welfare system is complicated, unfair, and does not encourage people to escape from poverty.

Perverse incentives. It is difficult to design a welfare system without creating perverse incentives. For

[3]For more detail on the boats that are lifted by a rising tide and those that are not, and the reasons why a rising tide may be less effective in the future than in the past, see Sheldon Danziger and Peter Gottschalk, "Do Rising Tides Lift All Boats? The Impact of Secular and Cyclical Changes on Poverty," *American Economic Review, Proceedings,* May 1986, pp. 405–410.

example, until recently a mother was unable to qualify in some states for Aid to Families with Dependent Children if an able-bodied man was living in the home. Although this provision was designed to provide an incentive for able-bodied fathers to go to work, it sometimes encouraged them to desert their families instead, on the grounds that the simplest way for them to support their dependents was to leave and thus allow their families to qualify for AFDC. In addressing the problem, the 1988 welfare reform has allowed families with two unemployed parents to qualify for AFDC provided one is willing to work for 16 hours a week in a government or community-service job.

To illustrate another perverse incentive, consider the public housing program, which requires families to pay 25% of their income in rent. This means that, for every $1 more they earn in income, they must pay 25 cents more in rent because the government reduces their subsidy by this amount. By itself, this effect on the incentive to work may not be very important. However, other forms of assistance are also reduced as a family's income rises. When the effect of all these reductions is taken into account, the accumulated impact on the incentive to work may be substantial. The poor may well wonder: "Why go to work to earn an additional $1,000 of income, if it means that our housing subsidy will be reduced by $250, and our other forms of assistance will be reduced by, say, another $450—for a total reduction of $700? It's as though we had to pay a $700 tax on this $1,000 of additional income." Such a family is paying an **implicit tax** of 70% on its additional income. In some cases, the implicit tax exceeds 100%. For such families, going to work *lowers* their income.

The ***implicit tax*** built into a welfare program is calculated by examining all the ***benefits lost*** when a family earns another $1 of income. (If its benefits are reduced by 46 cents, the implicit tax is 46%.)

Complexity and Inequity. Because some families qualify for more welfare programs than do other equally poor families, this complex system cannot be viewed as equitable. Poor families who can draw on several programs may be lifted not only to the cutoff poverty level but somewhat above it, whereas other families are left substantially below it. In some cases, welfare recipients end up with more income than some of the workers who pay taxes to support them, and it is no surprise that these workers sometimes become vocal critics of welfare.

The poor sometimes feel that the administrators of these programs hold far too much arbitrary power over them, and are thus able to subject them to hassles and humiliation. In turn, some administrators view the programs as a nearly hopeless tangle. In view of these problems, why not replace the whole checkered pattern of policies with a single, universal program that treats poor families equitably?

Two such universal programs have been proposed—a guaranteed minimum income and a negative income tax. Although these proposals have serious flaws and are unlikely to be introduced in a comprehensive way in the near future, some of their features have been incorporated in other welfare policies. They are worth studying for this reason and because they so clearly illustrate the fundamental problems that a government faces when it introduces policies to reduce poverty.

GUARANTEED MINIMUM INCOME: A CURE FOR THE POVERTY PROBLEM?

Why not eliminate poverty in one stroke by setting a *minimum income* at the poverty level? If any family's income were to fall below this level, the government would cover the shortfall with a direct grant. What would this cost? If we add up the shortfall in income of all families below the poverty line, the total would only be about 1% or 2% of GNP. Since this would not be a large sum and would replace other costly welfare expenditures, why not end poverty this way?

Unfortunately, it is not that easy.

INEFFICIENCIES IN A SUBSIDY PROGRAM

The problem is this. A program that raises the income of the poor by $10 billion costs far more than $10 billion. Waste occurs because such a program has several adverse effects on incentives.

Disincentives for those paying for the subsidy. The first adverse incentive applies to those who pay the higher taxes necessary to finance this scheme. The heavier the tax rate, the more likely it is that a taxpayer will ask, "Why am I working so hard when the government gets such a large slice of what I earn?" By reducing the reward for working, higher taxes can have a negative effect on the incentive to work. Higher tax rates also encourage those with high incomes to hire accountants or lawyers in a socially unproductive effort to find loopholes to reduce their tax payments.

Disincentives for those receiving the subsidy. Figure 25-3 shows what happens to families at the bottom of the income scale who receive the subsidy. (For simplicity, any taxes now paid by these families are ignored, and a "round figure" of $10,000 is used for the poverty line.) Families are plotted along the horizontal axis according to how much income they originally earn. Thus family *h* with a $8,000 earned income is plotted at point *Q* along the horizontal axis. Income after the implementation of this policy is measured up the vertical axis. If no subsidy were paid to family *h*, its "income after" would also be $8,000, as shown by the green arrow. In other words, family *h* would be at point *F* on the 45° line, where its before and after incomes are equal. Hence this 45° line may be called the "same-before-and-after" line, or just the "no-subsidy" line.

However, the minimum income program does pay family *h* a subsidy—specifically, the $2,000 blue arrow *FK* that is necessary to raise its income to the poverty line of $10,000. Since the income of any other family below the poverty line is similarly subsidized up to this $10,000 level, the "income after subsidy" line is *CAB*. Shaded triangle 1 represents the shortfall that the government must fill at a cost of 1% or 2% of GNP—*provided people continue to work and earn as much after the subsidy as before.*

The problem is that, because they are being subsidized, some people will *not* work as hard as before. For example, the father of family *h* may realize: "If I don't work at all, the government will still guarantee us the same $10,000; so why should I work?" If he stops working, that $8,000 of income he earned disappears. The position of that family on the horizontal axis therefore shifts all the way to the left, from situation *h* to situation *g*. At this point, nothing is being earned, that family has become totally unproductive, and it must be subsidized by the full $10,000. Therefore, in order to raise this family's income by the original $2,000 shortfall, the government ends up paying $10,000. This example illustrates what Arthur Okun referred to as transferring income "with a leaky bucket."[4] Although $10,000 has been spent to increase the income of a poor family, it has increased their income by only $2,000. The other $8,000 has "leaked away" because the family has stopped working. In other words, the "transfer bucket" in this hypothet-

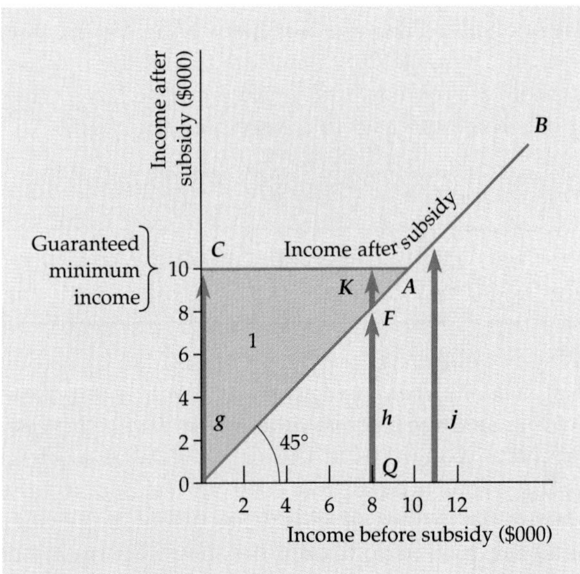

FIGURE 25-3 Possible disincentive effects of a guaranteed $10,000 minimum income.

The 45° line *OAB* is the no-subsidy line. For example, at point *F* on this line, family *h* which earns $8,000 (measured left to right) ends up with $8,000 (measured up). On the other hand, blue line *CAB* shows income after the subsidy. Family *h* is paid the $2,000 subsidy necessary to raise it to the guaranteed $10,000 level. But this program erodes the incentive to work: Because *h's* income will remain at the same $10,000 level whether or not a parent is working, the parent may stop working. The family moves to *g*, thus receiving a $10,000 subsidy.

---

[4]Arthur Okun, *Equality and Efficiency: The Big Trade Off* (Washington, D.C.: Brookings Institution, 1975). This has become a classic reference for the problems encountered in transferring income.

ical example has an 80% leak. Note that this $8,000 leakage, shown by the green arrow at *h*, is the efficiency loss from this policy. The original income this family produced was that $8,000, but this is now lost to society because no one in the family any longer works.

Disincentives that apply to the nonpoor. Disincentive effects may apply not only to poor families like *h*, but also to nonpoor families like *j* with incomes *above* the $10,000 support level. For example, consider the father in family *j* who has been earning $11,000 in a boring job. The subsidy program may now offer a tempting option: Go fishing instead and receive a $10,000 income from the government. If this happens, family *j* also shifts to the far left into position g, where it too qualifies for the full $10,000 subsidy. Thus the government has to subsidize not only those with initial incomes below the $10,000 poverty level, but *also* some with incomes above the poverty line for whom this program was never intended. This is a further reason why the cost of this subsidy program may far exceed the initial income shortfall that it set about to cure.

Moreover, when a family like *j* goes on the subsidy program, the overall efficiency loss to society is particularly severe. It is the $11,000 arrow of lost income at *j* because someone who used to work has now gone fishing.

The reason why this policy is so inefficient is that the portion *CA* of the "income after subsidy" line is completely horizontal, leaving the poor *no* incentive to work; that is, they face an implicit tax of 100%. They have nothing to show for any additional $1 they earn, because their subsidy is reduced by the same $1. Since their income is fixed at $10,000 whether or not they work, why should they?

Critics charge that, in terms of its antiwork incentives, the present U.S. welfare system is quite close to this simple subsidy scheme. In some instances, the present system exacts an implicit tax of less than 100%, but in some special cases the implicit tax is more. In such cases, individuals are better off financially if they do not have a job. Thus their incentive is not to get a job but to *avoid* a job. However, it should be emphasized that the present system—with its wide variety of programs—cannot be fully described by any such simple diagram.

CONFLICTING VIEWS ON WELFARE

Figure 25-3 illustrates why some observers view welfare as a *cure* for the poverty problem while others view it as a *cause* of this problem.

IS POVERTY CURED OR CAUSED BY WELFARE?

Those who argue that welfare programs reduce poverty point to individuals who are disabled or just cannot cope. Because they are unable to succeed economically, they initially start at *g* in Figure 25-3. A welfare program that pays them the $10,000 benefit shown lifts them up to the poverty line. Poverty is reduced with no adverse effects on efficiency.

On the other hand, welfare critics point to the individuals who start out at *h* or *j* and respond to welfare by shifting toward *g*. According to this view, welfare payments provide potentially productive people with an incentive to stop producing—to stop earning the green arrow of income at *h* or *j* and instead go on welfare at *g*. In such cases, welfare creates a social problem. Society has to subsidize these families, and they come to accept a poverty-line income. Moreover, if the income-support level is set below the poverty line, then these families may resign themselves to a permanent state of poverty.

In practice, a welfare system has both effects: It solves the poverty problem for some people who start at *g*, and it creates a problem by inducing some of the people who start at *h* or *j* to move toward *g*. In the U.S. system, what is the relative importance of these two effects? In particular, how much does welfare erode the incentive to work?

MEASURING THE LEAK IN THE BUCKET

Welfare programs seem to erode the incentive to work less than Figure 25-3 might suggest. Many families at *h* or *j* *don't* stop working; they don't move to the left. Their (green arrow) productivity is not lost. Moreover, those who are disabled or can't work for some other reason start at *g* and stay there; for them, there is no leak in the bucket at all. Welfare can't reduce their productivity because they don't produce anything in the first place. Thus the Okun transfer bucket is not completely shot through with holes. Nonetheless, available evidence suggests that a substantial leak does exist. For $1 of welfare expenditure, an estimated 25 cents leaks away because welfare recipients work less.

As noted above, there is another leak in the transfer bucket because taxes must be collected to finance the welfare expenditure, and this encourages the search for loopholes and reduces the incentive to work of those who are taxed. Estimates of this leak—often called the *excess cost of taxation*—vary widely but suggest a figure of about 30%. This means that there is a leak on both the taxation and expenditure ends of roughly 50%. When the administrative costs of running a welfare program are considered, the picture is one of a bucket with a leak of somewhat more than 50%.[5]

Figure 25-4 illustrates how a number of smaller leaks can combine to give a total rate of leakage of 50%. Begin at line 2 where we suppose that the government collects $100 in taxes; with $10 in administrative costs, $90 is left to be distributed to the poor. The problem is that roughly 25% of this (about $25) leaks away. It does not raise the income of the poor at all; it just replaces their lost income because they work less. (An example was the $8,000 of lost income in Fig. 25-3 when family *h* moved to *g*.) Thus the income of the poor is increased by only $90 – $25 = $65. Finally, the top of this diagram shows that when the government raises the original $100 in taxes, this imposes a $30 excess cost on the economy because, for example, those who are taxed work less. When this $30 of excess cost is added to the $100 of taxes, it is costing the American public $130 to provide a net benefit of $65 to the poor. It is in this sense that there is a 50% leak. (Note that a 50% leak does *not* mean that the government raises $100 in taxes but only delivers $50 to the poor.)

Such a large leak does not mean that welfare expenditures should necessarily be cut back because of the waste in the transfer process. To take an extreme example: Nobody objects to providing a starving child with $1 of milk, even though the cost to society, all things considered, may be $2. However, it does illustrate that solving the poverty problem is a more expensive task than was once assumed.

NONECONOMIC BENEFITS AND COSTS

It is no surprise that economists focus on the economic effects of welfare programs, such as "How much does the bucket leak?" But such programs have effects that go beyond economics.

On the positive side, welfare programs are society's way of stating its commitment to the less fortunate. By contributing to a humane society, a welfare program can have social gains that go beyond the benefits to the welfare recipients themselves.

There is also a negative side. Critics suggest that our welfare system has unintended social costs. For example, some have argued that there is a "welfare trap." Welfare tends to be addictive, inducing those who are on it to stay on. Moreover, children in a family receiving welfare may in turn grow up to depend on welfare rather than work as the source of their support. Thus welfare may be creating a welfare-dependent society.[6]

Other questions critics have raised about welfare include: Does welfare destroy pride and self-respect? Being the breadwinner may be one of the few sources of pride and self-respect for those with low-paying, no-promise jobs. If welfare provides as adequately for their families as they can, does it make them feel like so much excess baggage and destroy their self-respect? Why should they stay at home? And when some leave, new single-parent families are created, and the poverty problem is made worse.

---

[5]For more detail on estimates of the leaks in the transfer bucket, see Gary T. Burtless and Robert H. Haveman. "Taxes and Transfers: How Much Economic Loss?" *Challenge*, March-April 1987. These authors cite evidence that welfare recipients work less, not so much because they work fewer hours, but because they leave their jobs. In "Labor Supply Response to Welfare Programs: A Dynamic Analysis," *Journal of Labor Economics*, 1986, pp. 93, 94, Daniel M. Blau and Philip K. Robins provide confirming evidence of this "increased exit effect." They also find even stronger evidence of a "slower entry effect"—that is, the unemployed take longer to get a new job if they are on welfare.

[6]This view has been challenged by Mark W. Plant in "An Empirical Analysis of Welfare Dependence," *American Economic Review*, September 1984. For detail on how welfare may provide an incentive for the creation of female-headed families, see Frank S. Levy and Richard C. Michel, "Work for Welfare: How Much Good Will It Do?" *American Economic Review, Proceedings*, May 1986, pp. 402–403.

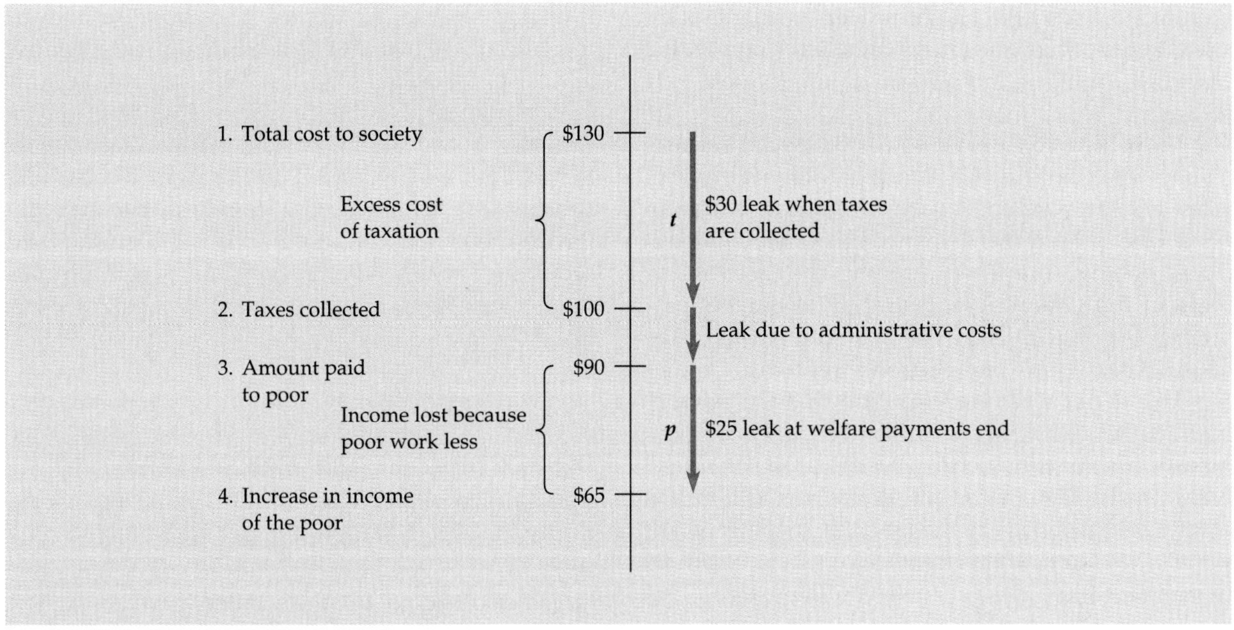

FIGURE 25-4 Leaks in the transfer bucket.

This diagram provides a rough consensus of many estimates that vary widely because there are so many ways the government can raise taxes and spend the proceeds. In estimating arrow *t*, the leak at the taxation end, Charles Stuart's simulations 1 and 6 in Table 2 of "Welfare Costs per Dollar of Additional Tax Revenue in the United States," *American Economic Review*, June 1984, lead to estimates of this leak that range from 7% to 53%, with 30% to 40% being, in his judgment, the most likely range. In Table 3 of "General Equilibrium Computations of the Marginal Welfare Costs of Taxes in the United States," *American Economic Review*, March 1985, Charles L. Ballard, John B. Shoven, and John Whalley provide estimates of this leak that range between 17% and 56%, with their best estimate being roughly 33%. In the *National Bureau of Economic Research Reporter*, Spring 1983, Jerry Housman estimates this leak to be 28%. Thus we conclude that leak *t* on the taxation end is about $30.

The leak *p* of 25%—or roughly $25—on the welfare payments end (because welfare recipients work less) is from Sheldon Danziger et al., "How Income Transfer Programs Affect Work, Savings and the Income Distribution: A Critical Review," *Journal of Economic Literature*, September 1981, pp. 975–1028.

THE KEY TRADEOFF: EQUITY VERSUS EFFICIENCY

It all seemed so simple. As we look back over the microeconomic half of this book, the following message seemed to be emerging: Where product or factor markets are inefficient, the government should intervene to increase efficiency. For example, it should intervene to tax polluters or to regulate monopoly price. This intervention is particularly desirable if it also has favorable equity effects—for example, if it benefits a low-income, disadvantaged group. Then there are no conflicts, and the appropriate policy choice is a simple one. An illustration is eliminating discrimination in the labor market. This policy increases efficiency and also transfers income to those who have faced disadvantages because of their race or sex. However, such cases are the exception rather than the rule; most policies do involve a conflict between equity and efficiency. Thus the attempt to achieve equity by intervening in product or factor markets often leads to inefficiency. To achieve equity, we should therefore rely on direct government transfers rather than inefficient interventions into factor or product markets—like the imposition of an interest rate ceiling.

Unfortunately, it's not so easy after all, because of one weak link in this argument. Direct government transfers may not be very efficient either. In particular, government spending on the poor reduces national output by eroding the incentive to work of both the recipients and the taxpayers providing the funds. Thus the tradeoff between the objectives of equity and efficiency remains.

This is not a recommendation that the government continue to transfer income by the inefficient market interventions criticized in earlier chapters. Not only are they inefficient. Worse yet, as a means of achieving equity by raising the income of the poor, they are often ineffective. Rent controls designed to help the poor may not have this effect in the long run because of the damage these controls do to the housing stock. An interest rate ceiling designed to help poor borrowers will not have this effect if poor borrowers are the ones who are no longer able to acquire funds. Price supports on grain designed to help poor farmers may have little effect if most of the grain is produced, not by poor farmers, but instead by large, wealthy farmers.

The message remains: The way to reduce poverty is not by inefficient and often ineffective interventions into factor or product markets. Instead, it is by direct government policies to aid the poor. But is there a better way to make these transfers than the simple tax and subsidy programs discussed so far? In particular, is it possible to find policies that are not only *equitable* but also *efficient*—that is, policies that do less damage to the incentive to work?

THE NEGATIVE INCOME TAX: CAN EQUITY AND EFFICIENCY BE COMBINED?

Figure 25-3 showed how the incentive for low-income people to work might be completely destroyed by a program with an implicit tax of 100%. In contrast, the negative income tax (NIT) proposal would guarantee the same minimum income of $10,000, but still maintain the incentive to work. To understand the NIT, put the guaranteed minimum income in Figure 25-3 back on the drawing board at the bottom left-hand corner of Figure 25-5 and extend it to the right to also take account of higher-income families that pay the government a tax. The 45° line *OQB* now represents the "no-subsidy, no-tax" line, where families would be if the government neither subsidized nor taxed them.

DESIGN OF A NEGATIVE INCOME TAX

Rather than subsidizing incomes just up to the $10,000 level *CA* by filling gap 1 as in Figure 25-3, suppose the government instead pays subsidies (*negative taxes*) to fill the shaded gap 1 + 2 + 3, thereby bringing incomes up to the heavy line *CQ*. (Beyond an income of $20,000, a family pays "positive" taxes to the government, as shown by the red area 4.) Because the "income-after-tax" line *CQH* slopes upward, people have an incentive to work. The more income they earn (the more they move to the right in this diagram), the more income they keep (the higher they rise on line *CQ*). However, this program must replace *all* existing welfare programs, such as food stamps. If some of these subsidies remain, the poor may get a higher income from these subsidies and the NIT than from working, and therefore quit work.

In addition to increasing efficiency by encouraging work, proponents argue that the NIT is equitable because it (1) guarantees a minimum income for all, (2) replaces the wide variety of existing welfare programs with one consistent policy that treats all alike, and (3) leaves those who work with a higher income than those who do not.

However, this program would apparently be very expensive, since the subsidy is now area 1 *plus* areas 2 and 3. Specifically, there is now an even greater subsidy (areas 1 + 2) to poor families earning less than $10,000, and there is *also* a subsidy 3 to *nonpoor* families with incomes all the way up to $20,000. Of course, families earning even higher incomes (say, $26,000) do pay a tax (the $3,000 red arrow *t*). Although after-tax-and-subsidy line *CQH* need not have a constant slope, it does in this

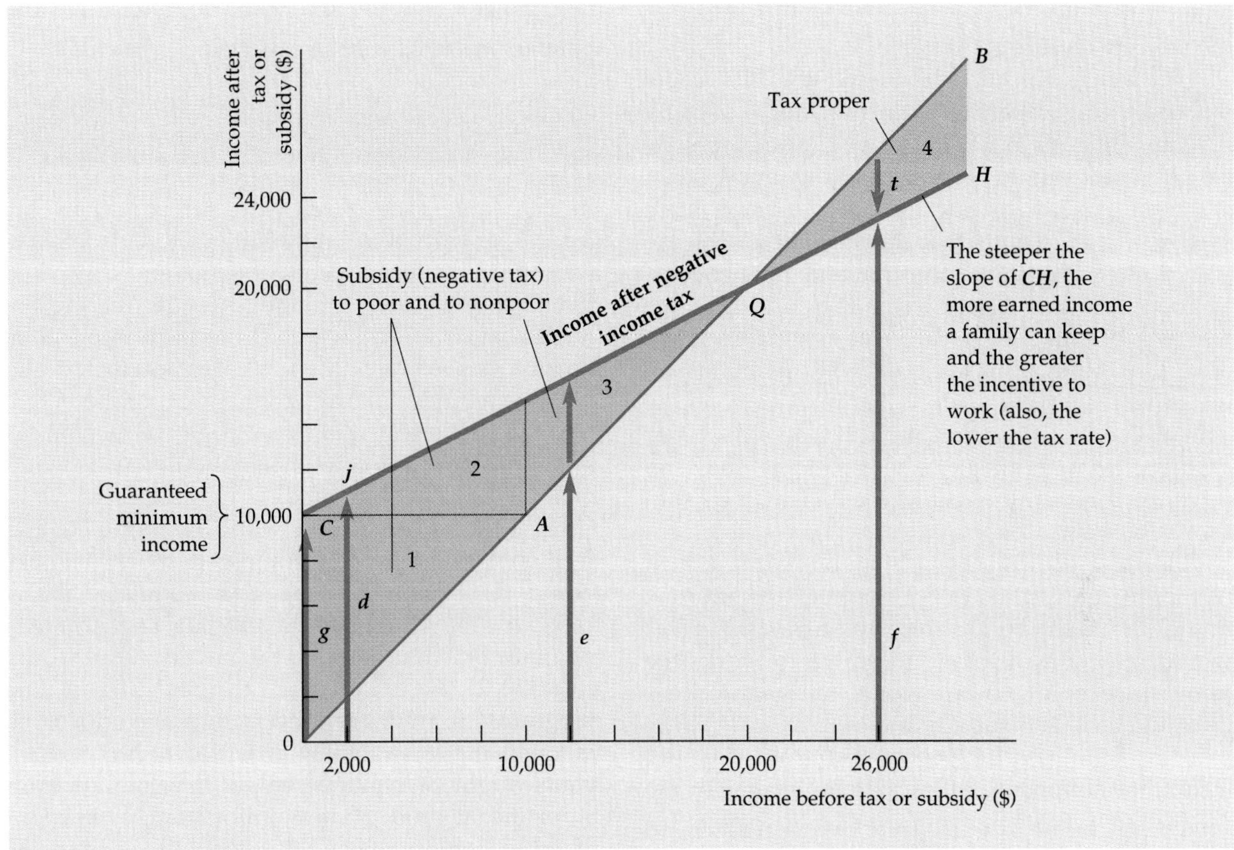

FIGURE 25-5 A negative income tax (compare with Fig. 25-3).

Family *g* with zero earned income is paid the full grant of $10,000. How much should family *d* with $2,000 of earned income be subsidized? If the same mistake is made as in Figure 25-3 and its income is raised only to $10,000 (by a $8,000 grant), that family will have no incentive to keep working to earn that $2,000. To provide an incentive to work, this family is granted $9,000 instead (arrow *d*), thus bringing its total up to $11,000 at point *j*. If the program continues in this way, always providing a $1,000 incentive for families to earn an additional $2,000 of income, families with increasing income move up heavy line *CQ* to cutoff point *Q*, where no subsidy is paid. Moreover, if families are allowed to keep half of any additional income they earn, their incomes in excess of this level can be taxed down, as shown by red area 4. For example, family *f* with a $26,000 income pays the $3,000 tax *t*. At the same time, blue area 1 + 2 + 3 shows how any family with an income below $20,000 is subsidized—that is, "taxed in reverse." Hence the name: negative income tax.

simple example, where any family, whether rich or poor, keeps half of any additional income it earns.

The NIT is expensive not only because it adds new areas of subsidy 2 + 3, but also because the treasury loses the taxes previously collected from nonpoor families with incomes between $10,000 and $20,000; they are now subsidized instead. Moreover, this antipoverty program would also reduce the taxes paid by at least some families with incomes *above* $20,000.[7] Benefiting such families who are far from poor was scarcely the objective

[7]To confirm this statement, consider a family with income just barely over $20,000. In Figure 23-5, it pays a minuscule tax that is less than the tax it used to pay.

when this policy was set up to raise all families to the poverty level of $10,000!

All things considered, doesn't the NIT come out badly in comparison with the simple subsidy scheme in Figure 25-3? The answer is: not necessarily, because it should be a far less leaky bucket than a simple subsidy scheme (or our present welfare system). The reason is that the subsidies in Figure 25-3 destroy the work incentive and thus encourage people to move to the left in Figure 25-3, where they will produce less and receive even more subsidies. On the other hand, the NIT maintains an incentive for people to work and thus move to the *right* in Figure 25-5. Accordingly, it may reduce—or perhaps even eliminate—the subsidies they receive. As a result, the cost of the NIT may be substantially less.

The cost of this scheme may be reduced even further by modifications. For example, the after-tax line *CQH* might be lowered by, say, $2,000. This would maintain the same incentive to work (the same slope of *CQH*) but would substantially reduce the cost (the subsidy area 1 + 2 + 3). Moreover, by shifting critical point *Q* to the left, it would mean that nonpoor families with an income in the $16,000 to $20,000 range would now pay a tax rather than receive a subsidy. However, one problem would remain: Those at *C* doing no work would now receive less than the $10,000 poverty-line income.

This problem might be reduced by providing a guaranteed $10,000 income to those who are aged, infirm, or disabled and *cannot* work. If these people can be clearly identified, guaranteeing them a minimum income would result in no inefficiency; it would not reduce the amount they work, because they can't work in any case. It would also be equitable, because it would provide an adequate safety net for those who cannot do without it. Such a policy of identifying a specific needy group is called **tagging.** In practice, it is difficult to identify exactly who should be tagged as unable to work; it is often difficult to determine who is disabled. While people don't blind themselves to get welfare, some may exaggerate back pain in order to qualify.

Although these problems have not been completely resolved, the NIT nonetheless has appeared to be a promising approach—at least in theory. Unfortunately, in cases where it has been tested, it has not performed as well as expected.

THE NEGATIVE INCOME TAX EXPERIMENTS

In four large-scale experiments supported by the federal government, randomly selected families were put on a negative income tax and compared to a "control group" of families under the present welfare system. The results have been interesting, because this is one of the few cases in which it was possible to undertake an economic experiment.

The first effect was that a negative income tax specifically designed to encourage people to work more led instead to modest reductions in work effort. Men reduced their work by about 7% and women by about 17% compared to the control group. Consequently, it has been estimated that a U.S.-wide NIT that would provide a guaranteed minimum income equal to the poverty level would cost $20 to $60 billion more than existing welfare programs. Second, the concern by some critics that much of the extra money provided to NIT participants might be squandered on frivolous, immoral, or illegal products was unfounded, as patterns of consumption remained essentially unchanged. Third, almost all of the reduced work time by the young went into increased schooling. (Others put much of their reduced work time into leisure.) The NIT therefore did have a positive effect on the accumulation of human capital. Fourth, preliminary results indicated that a NIT increased marriage breakups by 40 to 60%, but when more complete results became available, this estimate was reduced to only 5%, with the significance of this small figure being debatable.[8]

In summary, the experimental results did not establish that the negative income tax—so promising on the drawing board—is the hoped-for "solution" to the welfare problem, and other welfare proposals have come to the fore. The reason for studying the NIT is that it so clearly highlights the

---

[8]These results of the NIT experiments are taken from Alicia H. Munnell (ed.), *Lessons from the Income Maintenance Experiments* (Federal Reserve Bank of Boston and Brookings Institution, 1987), Ch. 1.

issues that must be addressed in any broad attack on the welfare problem.

WORK FOR WELFARE?

The analysis in this chapter has identified a major problem with any income support program: How can people on welfare be induced to work more rather than less? A current proposal that addresses this problem is **workfare.** This provides welfare payments to those who work but not to those who don't (with exceptions, of course, for those who can't work).

WAGE SUBSIDIES

One way of paying people according to the amount of work they do is some form of wage subsidy. By raising take-home pay, a wage subsidy would not only increase the incentive to work, but also help to reduce several welfare-related problems. By channeling the family's income through the employed worker's paycheck, it would eliminate the incentive for the creation of single-parent families and thus help to break the cycle of welfare dependence. It would also increase the worker's pride in having a job and supporting a family. Moreover, a wage subsidy that replaces existing welfare programs would also increase the father's fear of severe financial distress for his family if he were to walk out. This should make it more likely that fathers would stay with their families.

As an example, consider one specific recent proposal. Instead of raising the minimum wage to a new level W, use this same wage W as a **target wage.** Employers would then pay whatever the lower market wage might be, while the government would make up any shortfall between that market wage and the higher target wage. Because employers' labor costs would not rise, this policy would avoid the major disadvantage of a minimum wage—namely, the tendency of a minimum wage to raise labor costs and thus induce firms to employ less labor. This target wage would also be a form of welfare that would encourage people to work more, rather than less, because their welfare payment would increase as they work more. This proposal would be equitable because it would reduce poverty. At the same time, it would be efficient because it would encourage rather than discourage work.

Welfare still leaves two other pressing questions. First, what can be done to assist women who are caring for their children on their own and who therefore cannot work? Expanded child-care facilities may make it possible for them to get into the job market, and various programs have been introduced at the local level to assist them in their job search.

The other question is how to ensure that children are supported by their absentee fathers rather than the taxpayers. This means a further tightening up of child-support payments. The policy of a target wage provides one way of ensuring that at least some fathers comply. When paying fathers a wage subsidy, the government can first deduct their child-support payments.

1988 WELFARE LEGISLATION: A MOVE TOWARDS WORKFARE

The concept of workfare is a key element in the welfare law passed by Congress in 1988. Most welfare recipients with children over the age of three are required to participate in work, education, or training programs in order to qualify for assistance. To encourage parents to do this, the states must maintain child-care assistance for as much as a year after a job is found. This legislation also includes measures to provide greater assurance that absentee parents will make child-support payments.[9]

[9]For further suggestions to reduce poverty, see Alice Rivlin (ed.), *Economic Choices 1984* (Washington, D.C.: Brookings Institution, 1984.) For more detail on workfare, see Frank S. Levy and Richard C. Michel, "Work for Welfare: How Much Good Will It Do?", *American Economic Review, Proceedings,* May, 1986, pp. 399–404; and Michael Wiseman, "How Workfare Really Works," *Public Interest,* Fall 1987, pp. 36–47.

LIVING IN A GLOBAL ECONOMY

POVERTY IN THE UNITED STATES COMPARED TO OTHER COUNTRIES

Figure 25-6 shows how U.S. children and working-age adults face higher poverty rates than their counterparts in several other developed countries. It is only the U.S. elderly who do better, at least compared to Norway and especially the United Kingdom.

Sweden has a low poverty rate across-the-board; the comprehensive Swedish welfare system has apparently been quite successful in reducing poverty. Canada also has low rates across-the-board, although not as low as Sweden. For the other countries—Norway, West Germany and the United Kingdom—the results are more uneven, with a relatively large percentage of the elderly remaining in poverty. (Since the 1979–81 period on which this figure is based, the rate of poverty among the elderly in the United States has fallen from 16% to less than 13%.)

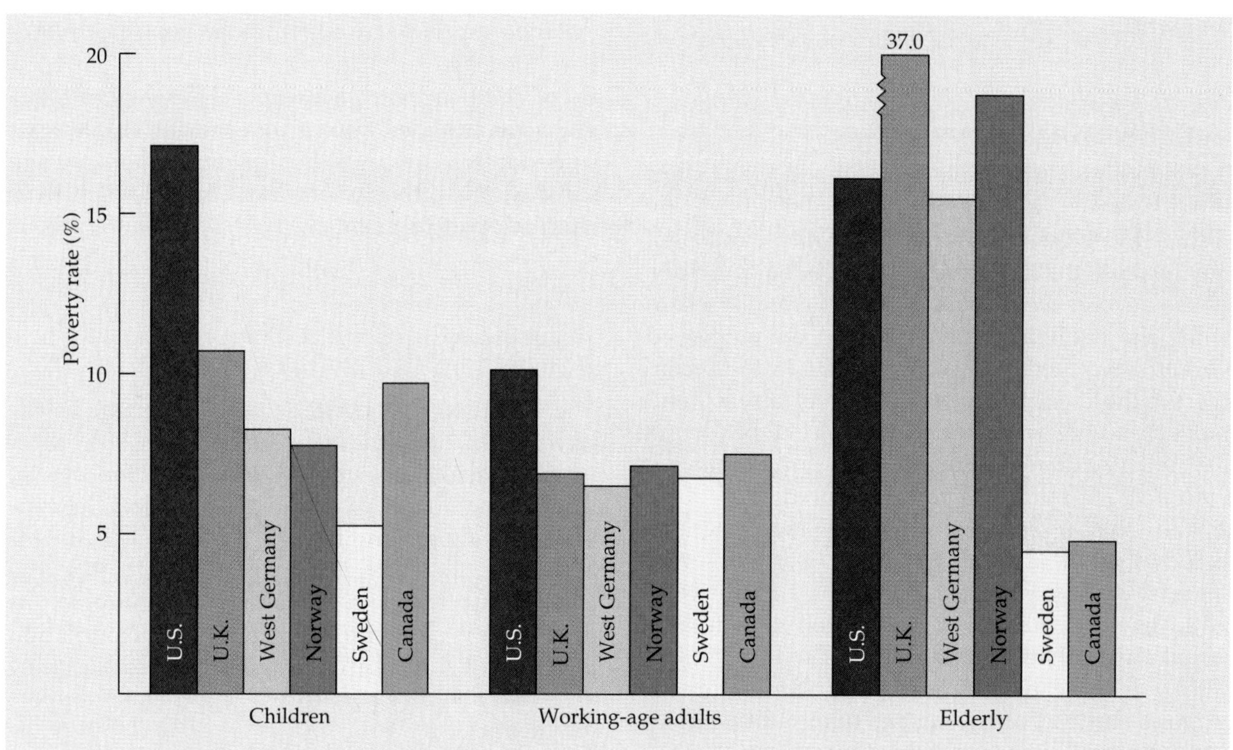

FIGURE 25-6 International poverty rates, 1979–1981.

Source: Gary Burtless, "Inequality in America: Where Do We Stand?" *Brookings Review*, Summer 1987, p. 14. Figures refer to percentage with disposable income below the U.S. poverty line.

KEY POINTS

1. Poverty is defined as inadequate income to buy the necessities of life. A specific poverty-line figure is determined by calculating the minimum cost of a nutritious and barely appealing diet and multiplying that figure by 3. In 1988 the poverty line for a family of four was $12,075. In that year, about one in ten American families was living in poverty.

2. Blacks are more likely to be poor than whites. The less an individual is educated, the greater the risk of poverty. The problem exists in cities, towns, and farms, with the areas least affected being the suburbs of big cities. Poverty is a particularly serious problem in fatherless families. However, the poverty problem facing the elderly has become far less serious.

3. In the long run, the most promising government antipoverty policies are those that deal with the causes rather than the symptoms of poverty. Policies to reduce the causes of poverty include eliminating discrimination against minorities and subsidizing investment in human capital, including both education and on-the-job training.

4. Government income maintenance programs include social security and unemployment insurance, which are paid to poor and nonpoor alike. But there are also many programs, like Aid to Families with Dependent Children, food stamps, and certain housing subsidies that provide benefits only to the poor. The problem with programs aimed at the poor is that when the poor earn more income, they often face an implicit tax in the form of a reduction in the subsidies they receive. This implicit tax reduces their incentive to work, thus lowering the nation's output.

5. The package of present programs is not only inefficient; it is also inequitable. Some of the poor are not lifted up to the poverty line, whereas others who qualify under several programs are lifted above it—indeed, in some cases, even above the income earned by some of the people who pay taxes to support the antipoverty programs.

6. Why not, then, replace this present system with a single policy that would lift all the poor up to the same minimum income level? One answer is that the poor, with their incomes thus guaranteed, would have little or no economic incentive to work, and the nation's output would be reduced. Thus the conflict between equity and efficiency persists: As the national pie is carved up more equally by raising the income of the poor, the total size of that pie is reduced.

7. One policy that addresses the problem of inadequate work incentives, at least in theory, is the negative income tax. Under this policy, families would be allowed to keep part of any additional income they earn. This would leave them with an incentive to work. Unfortunately, in experiments so far, the negative income tax has been a disappointment. People tend to work less rather than more.

8. In 1988, Congress moved toward a system of workfare, which requires that people work in order to qualify for welfare.

KEY CONCEPTS

poverty line
causes of poverty
symptoms of poverty
Social Security
unemployment insurance
Medicare
Aid to Families with Dependent Children (AFDC)
Medicaid
food stamps
public housing
benefits in kind versus in cash
perverse incentives
implicit tax in a welfare system
guaranteed minimum income
leak in the transfer bucket
negative income tax
tagging
workfare
wage subsidy
target wage

PROBLEMS

25-1. What is meant by an implicit tax rate of 90%? Of 105%? What is the effect of each of these tax rates?

25-2. Review the efficiency losses from the income redistribution policy in Figure 25-3. What is the efficiency loss if this subsidy induces the income earner of family *h* to go fishing? The income earner of family *j*? What is the efficiency loss if the income earner of family *j* takes one day off each week to go fishing? What is the efficiency loss from subsidizing a family like *g* that originally earned no income?

If the minimum income level were set at $12,000, rather than $10,000, would the efficiency loss be greater or smaller?

25-3. "Government transfer programs affect the Lorenz curve of income (Fig. 24-1) and the poverty rate (Fig. 25-2)." Do you agree? If not, why not? If so, how?

25-4. "Health and wealth tend to go together—though not always. The reasons are that the wealthier tend to be healthier, and the healthier tend to be wealthier." Do you agree? Explain.

25-5. Research by Stanford's John Shoven indicates that every person born in 1920 who took up smoking saved the social security system $20,000. (All smokers have saved the system hundreds of billions of dollars.) How is this possible?

25-6. Do the following policies raise a conflict between equity and efficiency?

(a) Eliminating discrimination against women in the labor market.

(b) Reducing taxes on the wealthy.

25-7. In Figure 25-5, the incentive to work is the $1,000 a family can keep out of each additional $2,000 it earns. Now suppose that the amount it can keep is reduced from $1,000 to $600.

(a) Redraw Figure 25-5 to take this into account, assuming that the guaranteed minimum income stays at $10,000.

(b) What has happened to the incentive to work?

(c) What has happened to the implicit tax in this welfare proposal?

(d) Are your answers to (b) and (c) related in any way? If so, how?

(e) What has happened to the total amount of subsidy the government must pay? (Be careful.)

(f) Has this transfer bucket become more or less leaky?

(g) Now regraph this policy, making one further change. Set the guaranteed minimum income at $8,000 rather than $10,000. Again answer questions (b), (c), and (e). What are the pros and cons of the two policies you have graphed?

25-8. Suppose you are designing a negative income tax. Graph your answers to each of the following questions:

(a) What do you consider a reasonable minimum family income (*OC* in Fig. 25-5)?

(b) What do you consider to be the maximum reasonable implicit tax rate? How does the slope of *CQ* in your diagram compare with *CQ* in Figure 25-5?

(c) From your answers to (a) and (b), calculate the break-even level of income (like the $20,000 at *Q* in Fig. 25-5).

(d) Do you think the tax on families to the right of the break-even point *Q* should be greater or smaller than the implicit tax on families to the left of *Q*?

(e) Explain the possible "public finance problem" in your scheme. In other words, do you think your scheme would make it difficult for the government to collect enough taxes from those to the right of *Q* to cover the costs of subsidizing those to the left of *Q*—and cover other government costs as well? As real incomes rise, would this public finance problem become more serious, or less?

25-9. "Just as a tax on a good discourages its production and consumption, so too a tax on income discourages people from earning income. In short, taxation discourages the activity being taxed. Unless the activity should be discouraged (like pollution), there is an efficiency loss." Do you agree or disagree? Explain.

CHAPTER 26
MARXISM AND MARXIST ECONOMIES

In proportion as capital accumulates, the lot of the laborer, be his payment high or low, must grow worse.

KARL MARX, *DAS KAPITAL*

The events of late October 1917 have become known as the "10 days that shook the world." When Nikolai Lenin, a disciple of Karl Marx, seized power in Russia, it became the first country to put Marx's ideas into practice. Within 35 years, about a third of the world's population was living under Marxist governments. Why did Marx's ideas have such an appeal? How have they worked out in practice in the Soviet Union and China? Why have these two countries been recently moving away from the ideas of Marx and Lenin? Finally, what problems arise when a country moves away from a Marxist system toward freer markets?

THE THEORY OF KARL MARX

The capitalist gets rich. . . at the same rate as he squeezes out the labor power of others, and then forces on the laborer abstinence from all life's enjoyments.

KARL MARX, *DAS KAPITAL*

Karl Marx wrote in response to what he viewed as serious failures of the free-market system. One major criticism was that a free market does not distribute income in an equitable way because of the income payments that go to capitalists, that is, the private owners of factories and other forms of physical capital. A second criticism of capitalism by Marxists has been that the economic and political power held by capitalists limits the government in its attempts to achieve a more equal and just society. Furthermore, a capitalist economy can suffer periodic crises and depressions. Indeed, Marx believed that crises would become ever more severe, eventually causing the collapse of the capitalist system. Marxists contend that the solution is to replace our system with one that is fundamentally different—specifically, a system in which (1) capital is owned by the workers and used on behalf of all the people; and (2) government planning is used to prevent depressions.

When Marx criticized the free market over a century ago, he drew on two theories that had already been accepted by many orthodox economists: (1) **the labor theory of value,** and (2) the theory that wages tend toward a socially defined **subsistence level.** According to the labor theory of value, the value of any good is determined by the amount of labor that goes into producing it. (But the reader should be aware that, as Marx recognized, this value must include both the labor time directly required to produce the good and the labor time spent on, or "congealed in," the machinery used to produce the good.) Marx then asked: With labor being the source of all value, does it receive the total value of the nation's output in return for its effort? His answer was no: All that labor receives is a low wage representing only a fraction of what is produced. The rest is **surplus value** that goes to the employer or capitalist (the owner of the capital equipment that labor uses). Marx concluded that this surplus value should go to labor. Because it does not, the working class is exploited.

SURPLUS VALUE AND THE CLASS STRUGGLE

According to Marx, the exploitation of the **proletariat** (workers) by the **bourgeoisie** (capitalists) results in a **class struggle.** He urged workers to organize themselves to fight this struggle. In his words, "Let the ruling classes tremble at a Communist revolution. The proletarians have nothing to lose but their chains. They have a world to win. Working men of all countries, unite!"[1] In his view, the capitalist class would continue to accumulate more and more capital and use it to exploit labor more and more. Thus there would be "an accumulation of misery, corresponding to the accumulation of capital." Marx's cure was a revolution—which he viewed as inevitable[2]—in which the workers would seize power and abolish the ownership of capital by individuals: "By despotic inroads on the rights of property, workers would centralize all instruments of production in the hands of the State." Finally, after this new socialist system has been firmly established, the state will wither away, leaving Marx's ideal communist society.

Socialism is an economic system in which the "means of production" (capital equipment, buildings, and land) are owned by the state.[3]

In Marxist countries like the Soviet Union, ***communism*** means an ideal system in which all means of production and other forms of property are no longer owned by individuals or the state, but instead are owned by the community as a whole; all members of the community share in its work and income. The Soviet Union makes no claim to have achieved communism. Rather, it claims to be working "through socialism towards communism."

In the West, communism has a quite different meaning. It refers to the present economic and political system of countries like the Soviet Union.

HOW THE CRITIC HAS BEEN CRITICIZED

Marx's critics have pointed out that a number of his predictions have proven false. First, there is no evidence that a socialist state will "wither away." After 75 years, the Soviet state is not disappearing. Many view this prediction of a disappearing state as one of the most curious ideas in the history of political and economic thought. Second, crises in the capitalist system have not become progressively more severe. Indeed, only one event in this century could be called a crisis—the Great Depression of the 1930s. Third, as capital has accumulated, there has not been the accumulation of misery that Marx predicted. Quite the contrary: Misery has been reduced and for good reason. Over the long run, the accumulation of capital has raised the

---

[1]The source of quotes in this paragraph is Karl Marx and Friedrich Engels, *Manifesto of the Communist Party* (Peking: Foreign Languages Press, 1975), pp. 59, 77. Note that Marx went far beyond an analysis of economic forces to suggest what should be done to change them. In taking such a normative approach, Marx and the Marxists strongly dispute the view of some economists that a positive, "value-free" economic analysis is possible.

[2]If this revolution is the inevitable result of an historical process governed by unchangeable economic laws—as Marx believed—what's the point of exhorting workers to struggle hard to achieve it? One possible answer is that even an inevitable event may be speeded up.

[3]"Socialism" has become an emotion-laden word that is now used loosely in a wide variety of meanings. To the American millionaire, it is a plot to deprive the wealthy of their hard-earned fortunes. To the Swedish politician, it means a mixed economic system, combining substantially free markets and a large degree of private ownership with a highly developed social welfare system. To Nobel prizewinner Friedrich Hayek, it represents a loss of freedom by the individual to the state and thus is a step along "the road to serfdom." To the British Fabian socialist, it means the gradual evolution to a more humane economy, with a more equal distribution of income. With such disagreement over the meaning of socialism, it is little wonder people have difficulty debating its virtues and vices.

demand for labor and thus has raised, rather than lowered, the wage rate. To cite an earlier example, workers who drive bulldozers are paid more than workers who use shovels. Although many Marxists concede that workers' income has indeed risen in absolute terms, they reinterpret Marx's prediction to mean that workers would become poorer, not in any absolute sense, but relative to other classes in society. Even this weaker claim is difficult to support with historical data.

Another way in which Marxists have reinterpreted Marx is to argue that, although capitalists may have been unable to exploit labor in Europe and North America to the degree that Marx predicted, they have succeeded in exploiting labor in the less developed countries (LDCs), which have become today's economically subjugated proletariat. Sometimes, this argument is put very simply: "We are rich. They are poor. Therefore, we must have become rich by making them poor." This conclusion does not follow, because it is based on the invalid *zero-sum assumption*—that the LDCs lose what we gain, and vice versa. Our trade with the LDCs is not a zero-sum game. As we saw in our earlier discussion of comparative advantage, both parties typically gain from trade. Our foreign investment in the LDCs is not a zero-sum game either because it typically provides not only profits to foreign investors, but also benefits to the LDCs when foreign investors bid up wages and pay out part of their profits in taxes to LDC governments. Foreign capital, far from exploiting the LDCs, has been one of the important reasons why a number of areas such as Singapore have been able to grow out of their former LDC status.

In brief, Marx's prediction that workers would become poorer has proven false. Nonetheless, it is true that workers are paid less than what the nation produces. We have referred to the gap between the two as *payments to other factors of production;* Marx called it *surplus value.* In particular, he focused his attack on the payments to owners of capital. Was he justified in dismissing these payments as simply the exploitation of labor?

HOW ARE CAPITAL COSTS TO BE COVERED?

As already noted, part of the cost of capital is the payment for the labor time spent on producing machinery. As Marx recognized, this is an appropriate payment to labor; therefore it is not surplus value. However, Marx did regard as surplus value the interest and profit paid to those who provide the funds to finance investment. But remember: Investment requires that someone, somewhere, defers consumption. In our system, interest is a reward to those who voluntarily defer consumption.

The Marxist contention is that it is precisely these interest and profit payments that make our system inequitable. Moreover, Marxists maintain, it is possible to set up a system in which investment occurs, even though there is no interest rate to act as an incentive to get the public to provide the necessary funds. The way to ensure that investment takes place is for the state to impose taxes high enough not only to cover current government expenditures, but also to provide the funds for investment. Under such a system, the ownership of capital is held by the state on behalf of the people, rather than by capitalists.

Such a Marxist solution raises two new problems:

1. Raising investment funds by involuntary saving—that is, by taxes—may "hurt" more than our system of voluntary saving. Under our system, people can save when it is most convenient, and they need not save when it is difficult to do so. Under a Marxist system, they are forced to save throughout their taxpaying lives. Taxes must be paid, no matter how much they hurt.

2. Investment decisions made by government officials in a communist state may be far less flexible and innovative than decisions made by the owners of capital in a free-market system.

INVESTMENT DECISIONS

In communist countries, **investment targets** for each sector are typically set out in a **five-year plan,** with **one-year plans** used to fill in short-term details. To illustrate the practical problems which planners face in setting targets, first consider what happens in our economy when more investment is required. Specifically, suppose there is a major new discovery of, say, a base metal. To finance its development, the companies that have made the discovery increase their borrowing (or issue new stock) and the interest rate rises slightly. In response, marginal investments elsewhere in the nation are cut back. Funds for this development thereby come from all over the country, as a result of a large number of individuals and firms reacting to a rise in the market interest rate.

In comparison, what occurs in a communist country when there is such a discovery and investment targets have just been set, say, a month before? Do the planners sit down and go through the planning process all over again? For a big enough discovery, they might. For less significant events, however, they can't be continuously rewriting their plans. Although one-year plans provide them with more flexibility than is sometimes supposed, their investment targets still tend to get "locked in." Thus adjustment to unexpected changes is much more cumbersome than in a free-market economy, where markets are continuously responding to change.

Any society must have a mechanism to determine which investments are undertaken and which are not. In our economy, the interest rate and expected profits are such a mechanism. They are used to direct funds toward high-return investments, and away from those with low returns. Although this system is far from perfect, it does provide a framework within which to make choices. Recognizing this advantage, central planners now quietly make their interest-like calculations after all. (Nevertheless, blunders still occur. A contributing factor in Poland's economic difficulties was the construction of a steel mill in a location that was poor from an economic point of view, but was the home town of the Communist party secretary. It is true that politicians anywhere may thus "feather their own nest." However, this problem is potentially more serious in a Marxist economy, in which most capital is owned by the state and controlled by government officials.)

THE ROLE OF PROFIT

Recall that *normal profit* is a return to a firm's capital equal to the return that could be earned elsewhere. *Above-normal profit* is any additional return above this; in a free-market economy, it goes to those who take risks—in particular, to entrepreneurs. Is this justified? To throw light on this issue, consider two kinds of above-normal profit—**monopoly profit** and **profit from a successful innovation.**

Above-normal Monopoly Profit. Many non-Marxist economists would agree that above-normal monopoly profit should be reduced or eliminated by "trustbusting" or regulation. However, Marxists charge that we are naive if we believe that we can effectively deal with monopoly in our present economic and political system. The reason, Marxists argue, is that in our system, monopolists can make campaign contributions in order to translate their economic power (money) into political power (votes). This power then allows them to thwart antimonopoly action. In short, our elected officials are too often committed to the interests of the rich and powerful rather than to the interests of the public. Thus, Marxists contend, the only effective way to deal with this problem is to change the system and prevent the accumulation of wealth that makes such political corruption possible.

There is an element of truth in this criticism—more, perhaps, than we would like to admit. But the question is one of alternatives. If a system is to be set up based on the "public interest," how is that elusive concept to be defined? What better way is there to determine it than by elections (with appropriate restrictions on campaign contributions)? If there are no elections and one party has the monopoly of power, what protection is there against the abuse of that power? It is scarcely satisfactory to say that the elections we have between two or more contending parties are unnecessary in a Marxist state because the Communist party represents the interests of the workers. In establishing their Solidarity union, Polish workers made it clear that they didn't believe that their government, run by the Communist party, represented their interests.

Above-normal Profit from Innovation. In our system, various kinds of innovation may allow a firm to earn an above-normal profit. For example, a firm may develop a new cost-cutting technique or a product that better satisfies consumers. True, in the long run, such above-normal profit may disappear as competing firms follow suit. Nonetheless, this profit still provides the incentive for businesses to innovate by cutting costs and by responding to changing consumer tastes. In short, the opportunity for profit is what makes our system go; it determines what will be produced and how. We tax away part of profits but not all; some incentive to innovate must be left.

An Alternative to Profits? Many Marxists maintain that, although the profit system may have worked well enough in our early stages of development,[4] it is no longer satisfactory. The whole incentive system should be changed and the economy directed in some other way. Precisely how, of course, is the big question.

This question is not answered by Marx's recommendation: "From each according to his ability; to each according to his need." This guideline sounds fine in theory, but in practice it is impractical. If individuals define their own needs, the sum will always outrun a nation's ability to produce. Alternatively, if needs are defined by someone else, who is to decide? And how does that person decide who needs what? The Soviets, supposedly in a transition stage to communism, modified this guideline to: "From each according to his ability; to each according to his work." However, the Soviet system of incentives has not delivered the goods. A major theme of the rest of this chapter will be the Soviets' search for a new incentive system.

[4]In the *Communist Manifesto,* Marx and Engels expressed admiration for the growth generated by capitalism, which in the preceding 100 years "created more massive and colossal productive forces than have all preceding generations together."

THE COMMAND ECONOMY OF THE SOVIET UNION

Russia is a riddle wrapped in a mystery inside an enigma.
WINSTON CHURCHILL

The first sustained attempt to put Marx's philosophy into practice occurred in the Soviet Union. The Soviet economy was set up to be different from a free-market economy in two major respects: (1) Productive assets are predominantly owned by the state rather than by individuals, and (2) many production decisions are made on the command of a central authority. Our discussion of each of these differences is summarized in Table 26-1. For now, we describe the Soviet system as it has existed in the past, deferring until later the recent attempts to change that system, which may or may not succeed.

PUBLIC VERSUS PRIVATE OWNERSHIP

In the United States, the basic pattern is private ownership—with some exceptions, such as school buildings and public works like the Tennessee Valley Authority. In contrast, the basic pattern in the Soviet Union has been public ownership, with some exceptions. For example, an increasing number of retail and wholesale businesses have become

TABLE 26-1 How the Soviet System of Public Ownership and Central Planning Has Differed from Our System

Basic Issues	*Soviet System*	*Modified Free-Market System*
1. Is ownership of productive assets held by the state or by private individuals?	State ownership—with some exceptions; for example, in parts of agriculture and retail trade	Private ownership—with exceptions like the post office, some utilities, and some transport systems
2. How are prices and outputs determined?	Largely by central planning agency	Largely in individual markets, in response to profit motive
3. How much freedom of choice do consumers have?	In theory, free choice in spending income; but in practice, items of desired style, size, etc., have been difficult to obtain	Essentially free choice in spending income, with producers more responsive to a wide variety of tastes

privately owned. In addition, many houses in cities and virtually all houses on farms are privately owned. Moreover, each family working on a collective farm can use a small plot of land and the livestock and equipment to go with it. Finally, of course, personal assets like clothing and household tools are privately owned.

Otherwise, assets in the Soviet Union have been predominantly owned by the state. These assets include the *means of production* such as factories and machinery which, in Marx's view, were used by capitalists to exploit labor.

CENTRAL PLANNING IN THE SOVIET ECONOMY

The second big difference between the two systems lies in how they answer the question: What will be produced? In our economy most such decisions are made by individual producers responding to a profit incentive. (But not all: A number of our production decisions, such as the number of new schools or military aircraft, are made by federal, state, or local governments.) In contrast, most decisions on what will be produced in the Soviet Union have been made *by command*, by a central state planning agency.

Soviet planning has worked as follows. The first step is for the government to decide on the desired rate of growth over the coming five-year period, and the investment necessary for that growth. Within this broad framework of a five-year plan, a more detailed plan is drawn up for each year, specifying **output targets** throughout the economy. Government planners do not choose the targets in a completely arbitrary way. Rather, the targets are the result of an elaborate set of consultations, in which each firm and industry suggests amendments to its targets. Nonetheless, the targets are eventually set by the planners, and each plant manager has a specific quota to fulfill. The manager faces an array of incentives (bonuses, promotions, etc.) to reach or exceed the quota.

Profits exist in the Soviet Union and can be calculated just as in our economy. However, profits do not provide the same sort of incentive as in our system because most go to the state. Moreover, profits are calculated from output and input prices that are set by planners, and hence are not closely related to demand and supply conditions. Because profits do not provide the same information or the same incentive to produce as in our system, they do not play the same key role in allocating resources. An example is the decision sometimes made by central planners to contract an activity that is profitable in order to expand one that is not—a pattern exactly the opposite of the normal pattern in our system.

The surprising thing about such a highly complicated planning system is not that it sometimes works badly, but that it works at all. Consider the problem that arises whenever the planners increase the target for steel to be used in building bridges. Because steel production requires machinery, the machinery target also has to be increased. But because machinery production requires steel, the steel target has to be increased again. In turn, this results in a second-round increase in the machinery target, and so on, and on. Because steel is an input for machinery production and machinery is an input for steel production, it is impossible to set one target without regard to the other. This example illustrates only the simplest possible "loop" in the economic system. In reality, a complex economy like that of the Soviet Union is made up of a myriad set of much more complicated loops, with the output of one industry being used directly or indirectly as an input of many of the others. Thus a target cannot be set in isolation.

In theory, mathematical models should allow the Soviets to "get the plan right"—that is, to come up with a consistent set of outputs. However, as the Soviet economy, like all others, has become more complex it has become more and more difficult to avoid major mistakes. A further problem is this: While Soviet central planning *requires* more information, planners get *less* because managers of enterprises are often less interested in providing honest information than in passing on information that they want their superiors to believe. In contrast, in a free-market economy, market information such as changing price is quickly and automatically available.

When mistakes are made, *bottlenecks* occur. What happens if the production of steel is inadequate to meet the needs of the machinery industry and other steel-using industries? What can be done by a plant manager desperate to acquire steel? The response has often been to dispatch a *tolkach* (fixer), cognac and rubles in hand, to acquire steel with the appropriate bribe. Although bribery occurs in any economy, the difference is that this and similar forms of "fixing" are often quietly condoned in the Soviet Union because of the role they play in making the Soviet economy operate. Without such emergency measures, quotas would be even more difficult to achieve. Thus in the Soviet Union, a market economy has been replaced by a *central-command quota system* and by a *second economy* which fills the inevitable cracks in the quota system. Black markets also exist in goods stolen from the state. In such a system, there is no clear line between what is silently tolerated and what is punished. An executive of GUM (a large department store in Moscow) was unable to make this distinction and was executed for "excessive" operations in the second economy.

A second way in which bottleneck problems are reduced—but not eliminated—is for Soviet planners, faced with a shortage, to simply let consumers do without. If steel is in short supply, it will be used to produce defense equipment and industrial machinery rather than home refrigerators. With this set of priorities, it is no surprise that Soviet performance has been better in heavy industry than in consumer goods and housing.

THE POSITION OF THE SOVIET CONSUMER

Consumers have been the forgotten people in the Soviet system, not only because they are forced to shoulder a special burden when bottlenecks develop, but also because they have to sacrifice current consumption to finance the heavy investment the government undertakes.

Soviet planners have two principal ways to divert production away from consumption. First is the planning process, which gives priority to investment rather than consumption and has often resulted in shortages of consumer goods. The second method is a tax on consumer goods that accounts, on average, for about one-third of their price. This tax has helped to finance investment and has taken income out of the hands of consumers, thus reducing their purchasing power. Consequently, shortages of consumer goods have been reduced, though not avoided.

There is yet another cost in the Soviet command economy that consumers have had to bear. To understand it, consider again the Soviet plant manager whose major concern is to produce a given quota of, say, nails. If planners set the quota in terms of kilograms, the manager can most easily satisfy it by producing a relatively small number of large nails. (Visitors often wonder why so many things seem "heavy" in the Soviet Union. One reason is that many quotas are expressed in kilograms. Thus an easy way to achieve a quota is to build weight into the product. As one would expect, the Soviet Union is the world's largest producer of steel.)

On the other hand, suppose that the quota of nails is defined as a certain number. In this case, the manager produces mostly small ones. Again, the resulting nail production does not satisfy the consumer, who wants a selection of various kinds. Of course, the consumer may be able to make a wrong-sized nail do in a pinch. But what does a person with big feet do if shoe producers meet their quotas by concentrating on small sizes? The inadequate quality, as well as quantity, of goods and other problems facing the consumer (Box 26-1) have remained major weaknesses of the Soviet system. The problem is that the consumer has not been king; the "customer" whom producers have been most concerned about has been the central authority to which they report.

HOW MUCH CAN THE SOVIET CONSUMER BUY?

Feeding a family requires more than twice as many hours of work in Moscow as in Paris or Washington. In 1982, the purchase of a color television required over 700 hours of labor time in Moscow compared with 106 in Paris or 65 in Washington. A small car required 53 months of work in Moscow versus 8 months in Paris or 5 in Washington.

It has been argued that such comparisons are not entirely fair, since the Soviet Union started from so far behind and has had some success in catching up. Moreover, the lot of Soviet citizens is not as bad as the above comparisons sound because government subsidies provide Soviet citizens with bargain housing and free medical care. While this reduces the gap in living standards, it would be even more significant if Soviet citizens were able to acquire more of these services. Unfortunately, because of a housing scarcity, the average Soviet urban dweller doesn't get much housing—only

BOX 26–1 A Shopper's Guide to the Soviet Union*

Shopping in the Soviet Union is often a lottery. The stores seem well stocked but typically with inferior or out-of-fashion items that nobody wants. When attractive goods arrive they are quickly snapped up. Long lines immediately form as passersby queue up, sometimes without even asking what's on sale. (They find that out later; sometimes nobody in the last 20 or 30 yards of a lineup will yet know.) When you get to the head of the line, chances are you may have to deal with rude salesclerks who know that you will buy anyway, and who may be getting even for the frustrations they face in doing their own shopping. But you disregard all this unpleasantness in order to buy for yourself, your friends, your parents, and your cousins.

Buying this way involves a lot of luck and good management. Shoppers know by heart the sizes and color preferences of relatives and friends; they carry a lot of cash, because credit cards and checks aren't used, and one never knows where lightning will strike next. To be ready, women carry a bag called an *avoska* (derived from the Russian word for "maybe"). Soviet citizens have been known to line up through a freezing December night just to get on an 18-month-long waiting list to buy a car and have viewed themselves as lucky when they succeeded. Thus the efficiency loss in this centrally planned system is substantial, not only because consumers often get inferior products, but also because consumers waste time in queues. In the early 1980s, the Soviet press estimated that the public was spending 30 billion hours in line per year—a waste equal to having 15 million unemployed. Despite strenuous efforts to improve the delivery of consumer goods, queues in 1989 were even longer.

*This box draws heavily on Hedrick Smith, *The Russians* (New York: Quadrangle-New York Times Book Co., 1976), Chapter 2.

about one-third the average for an American family or one-half the average in Western Europe.

Although there is still a substantial shortfall in average Soviet income compared to incomes in Europe or North America, one might at least expect that a Marxist government would have reduced or eliminated income inequality *within* the Soviet Union. However, the Soviets have had only limited success in this objective.

INCOME INEQUALITY WITHIN THE SOVIET UNION

All animals are equal. But some are more equal than others.

GEORGE ORWELL

Figure 26-1 shows that there is less inequality in the Soviet Union than in the United States—but not less than in some market economies such as Sweden and the Netherlands. This is surprising since the Soviets have an economic system devoted to reducing inequality by keeping ownership of most capital in the hands of the state rather than in the hands of individuals.

It should be emphasized that such estimates are, at best, not very precise. On the one hand, income inequality in the Soviet Union may be less than Figure 26-1 suggests, because of housing and medical subsidies. On the other hand, Soviet inequality may be greater, because those who are privileged and receive a higher income are also far better able to spend it. While the average Soviet citizen stands in line for inferior products, the privileged are able to spend their incomes in special stores stocked with higher quality products.

Higher incomes and other privileges have been the incentives that the Soviets have provided to encourage people to increase production. Thus scientists receive a much higher income than clerks, and skilled workers earn more than unskilled workers. As a result, human capital is a significant source of income difference in the Soviet Union, just as in the United States. Moreover, the return in the Soviet Union to one important form of human capital—education—increases as individuals get more and more of it, unlike the situation in the United States.[5] Because of the importance of

[5]Paul R. Gregory and Janet E. Kohlhase, "The Earnings of Soviet Workers: Evidence from the Soviet Interview Project," *Review of Economics and Statistics*, February 1988, pp. 23–35.

human capital, a socialist policy that deals only with physical capital (by putting it in the hands of the state) hasn't made the Soviet economy any more egalitarian than some market economies. This raises two questions: Is the appeal of socialism to those who believe in equalizing incomes becoming less strong than in Marx's day? Is the distinction between workers and capitalists that Marxists make in calling for a class struggle in, say, the United States now beginning to break down as workers become "capitalists" because of their increasing amounts of human capital?

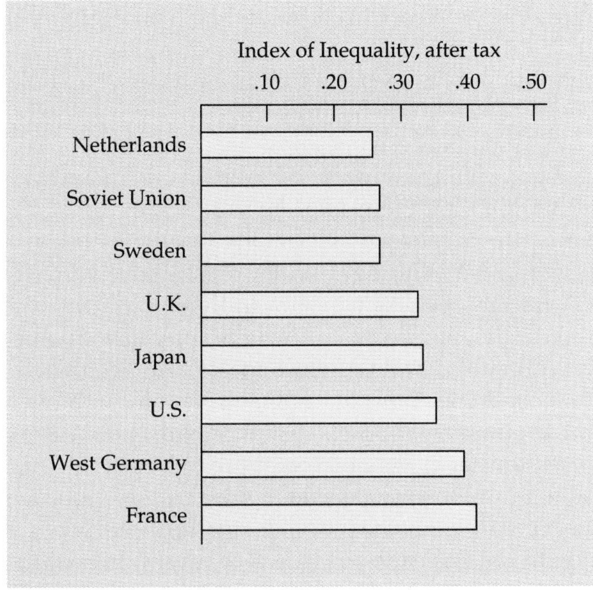

FIGURE 26-1 Index of Inequality, Selected Countries.
Each index of inequality (known as a "Gini Coefficient") is the area of inequality within the bow of the Lorenz curve, divided by the total area *OMQ* in Figure 24-1. For example, the area in the bow of the Lorenz curve for the Netherlands is 26% of the area of triangle *OMQ*. (Actually, the U.S. Lorenz curve used for these calculations is neither of the ones shown in Figure 24-1, but instead is a post-tax curve that lies between the two.)
Sources: Lars Osberg, *Economic Inequality in the United States* (Armonk, N. Y.: M. E. Sharpe, 1984), p. 27; Abram Bergson, "Income Inequality Under Soviet Socialism," *Journal of Economic Literature*, September 1984, p. 1092; and Timothy Smeeding et al., "Patterns of Income and Poverty: The Economic Status of the Young and the Old in Six Countries," paper for the Urban Institute, February 1987. The U.S. figure is based on data from the early 1980s, while the other estimates are based on data from about a decade earlier. While more recent international comparisons are not strictly comparable and cover fewer countries, they remain consistent with the view that the general pattern has not recently changed in a dramatic way, although the U. S. and West German positions may have switched.

THE INTERPLAY OF ECONOMIC AND POLITICAL SYSTEMS

The Soviet system of rule by a single party is quite consistent with Marx's prediction that the overthrow of the capitalist system would be followed by a "dictatorship of the proletariat." One of the interesting questions is whether a centrally planned economy like the Soviet system would work at all with the degree of political freedom we enjoy. The more economic commands are issued by a central authority, the more dictatorial a system generally becomes.

This is an important issue, because a major Soviet criticism of our system—one that contains an element of truth—is that economic power corrupts political institutions. But if the Soviets' alternative economic system leads to an even worse form of government, what sort of cure is that?

Rather than "withering away" as Marx and Engels predicted, the socialist state in the Soviet Union has given enormous political power to its leaders without providing adequate means for controlling them. Specifically, it provided inadequate restraints against the ruthless exercise of power by a ruler like Joseph Stalin. The majority of Marxists now view Stalin as an aberration that no better reflects true Marxism than the Holy Wars reflected Christianity. Nonetheless, the principal point remains: There were in fact no controls in the Soviet system to prevent Stalin from rising to the top and, worse yet, from staying there. Even when there is substantial liberalization—as has occurred under Gorbachev in the past few years—power remains heavily concentrated in the hands of one man. Indeed, General Secretary Gorbachev has been quicker than his predecessors to consolidate his power by placing his supporters in key party positions.

Nonetheless, Gorbachev has allowed the beginnings of democratic reform. The first exciting election in Soviet history took place in 1989. Voters had a choice among candidates and about 20 prominent party leaders went down to defeat. But the reforms were limited; that election pitted communist against communist. Gorbachev still dismissed the idea of a multiparty democracy as "rubbish." The Communist Party recognized no legitimate competing party.

However, powerful non-communist groups have developed in Poland and Hungary. In Poland the interplay of economic and political events has been particularly intense. The suppression of the Solidarity Union in the early 1980s was followed by widespread resentment and economic stagnation. Faced with an intractable economic problem, the Polish government recognized Solidarity and in 1989 permitted it to compete with the Communist Party in the most free and open election in Eastern Europe in recent history. The response of the people was clear; they overwhelmingly voted for Solidarity candidates over Communist ones. By prior agreement, Solidarity was not allowed to contest the majority of seats in the Sejm (lower house of parliament); the majority was reserved for the ruling coalition of the Communist Party. It appeared that the Communists would remain in power. However, the moment of truth came with astonishing speed. With the outright rejection of the Communist Party at the polls, the non-communist parties defected from their coalition with the Communists and threw their support to Solidarity. The Communist president called on Solidarity to form a government. For the first time in history, a Communist Party recognized the right of the people to vote it out of office.

BETTER MACROECONOMIC BALANCE?

The Soviets seem to have been able to do a better job of curing unemployment than we have. However, while they have faced less **overt unemployment,** they have had a greater problem with **disguised unemployment**—that is, workers on the job who seem to be producing something but who are in fact contributing little or nothing to the national product. An earlier example was the labor used to produce undersized shoes that are never worn. Although this may appear to be productive employment, it is, in fact, wasted effort.

An oft-cited failure in the U.S. economy was Ford's decision in the 1950s to introduce the Edsel, an automobile that sold very poorly. Its failure represented a loss not only to Ford, but also to the nation as a whole because resources were wasted in the development of this car. In the Soviet Union, such a failure would not have occurred. Instead, the public would have bought the Edsel. It might not have been quite what they wanted, but they would not have had much choice. In the United States, an incorrect decision results in a loss to producers and short-run unemployment in an industry; both of these can be identified and evaluated. On the other hand, a similarly erroneous decision in the Soviet Union results in a loss to consumers that may not be as obvious and as easy to measure, but may be just as real. This suggests an important question to keep in mind when comparing the Soviet and American systems: Do Edsel-type goods that the public does not like still exist in the Soviet Union, or are they disappearing?

Which is the worse problem—the Soviets' disguised unemployment or our overt unemployment? Our problem may be less damaging in the long run because it is obvious to all. Therefore a government is brought under pressure to reduce it. (There may be less pressure in the Soviet Union to reduce disguised unemployment, precisely because it is disguised and therefore may go unrecognized.) A second consideration is that a system with overt unemployment allows rapid growth following a recession, as the unemployed are put back to work. When growth slows in the Soviet Union—as it has in recent years—no pool of unemployed labor is created to fuel a rapid recovery; everyone already has a job.

In some respects, however, the Soviet problem of disguised unemployment may be less damaging than ours: The workers are at least on the job and hence feel productive, even though they are not. Therefore its psychological and social effects are less serious. One might also argue that the Soviets' disguised unemployment is more equitable than our overt unemployment because in the Soviet system, the big winners are those at the bottom of the economic ladder who would be unemployed in other countries but who get jobs in the Soviet Union. The Soviet losers are those at all levels on the ladder—the poor and rich alike who get inferior products.

GROWTH IN THE SOVIET UNION

One might expect high rates of growth in the Soviet economy for three reasons: (1) It has been operating at high levels of employment; (2) its planners have been choosing high growth at the expense of current consumption by devoting a large percentage of Soviet GNP to investment; and (3) the Soviets have been "playing catch up." As the Japanese illustrated when they were less advanced than the United States, it is far easier and less costly to be able to copy technology from more advanced countries than to have to develop it yourself.

Figure 26-2 shows that the Soviet Union grew more rapidly than the United States from 1950 to 1970. As a consequence, the Soviet economy climbed from one quarter the size of the U.S. economy in 1928 to more than one half by the 1970s. Just when many observers were predicting that the Soviets would close the gap completely, this catch-up process ceased, as Soviet growth rates fell to the U.S. level. Then in the 1980s, Soviet growth rates fell even more.

A number of reasons have been cited for slow Soviet growth.

1. *Industrial Inefficiency.* The Soviet economy has suffered from the inefficiencies that come from central planning. For example, planners suffering from an "edifice complex" have put too much emphasis on building new plants rather than replacing equipment in existing ones. In addition, Soviet productivity has been damaged by restrictions on labor mobility. Particularly damaging has been the **soft budget restraint** facing Soviet firms. Whereas free-market firms must cut costs and be efficient in every way possible because they typically face a **hard budget restraint** (which, if violated, will drive them bankrupt), the same has not been true in the Soviet Union. If Soviet firms violate their soft budget restraint by continually running losses, they don't go bankrupt. Instead, they are just forced to go to the government for assistance. The resulting insulation from market pressures that has allowed Soviet manufacturers to produce, say, undersized shoes, has led to shortages not only in consumer goods but also in capital goods. The result has been a stretch-out of investment projects—from a normal 3 or 4 years to 10 years or longer. Thus the large volume of Soviet capital formation has yielded a disappointing payoff in terms of growth.

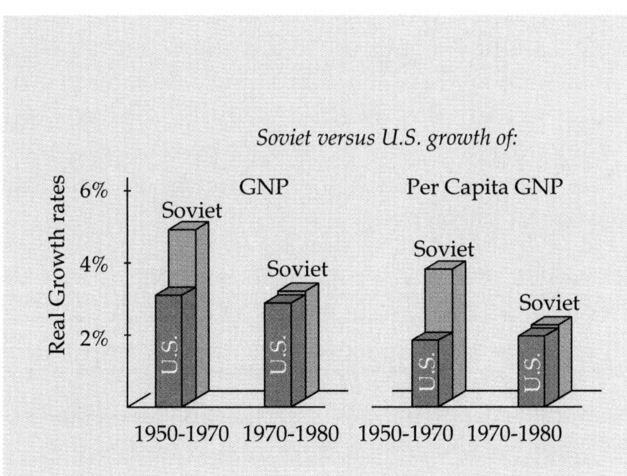

FIGURE 26-2 Comparison of Soviet and U.S. growth rates, 1950–1980.

(*Sources:* Gur Ofer, "Soviet Economic Growth: 1928–1985," *Journal of Economic Literature*, December 1987, pp. 1767–1833. Our discussion of growth draws heavily from this source and from Padma Desai, "Soviet Growth Retardation," *American Economic Review, Proceedings*, May 1986, pp. 175–180.)

2. *Disappointing Development and Adaptation of New Technology.* Socialist theoreticians hoped that a command economy could lead to better technological performance, because one central agency could sponsor, finance, direct, and diffuse new technology. The experience has been the opposite—with some exceptions, such as oceanography, polar research, and theoretical mathematics in which the Soviets are among the world leaders. In the United States, new technology is often developed by people willing to take a huge risk and work 18-hours for days on end to develop a company to sell their new idea. In contrast, the Soviet economy rewards caution and conformity rather than risk-taking. Plant managers often resist experimenting with promising but risky new techniques. Indeed, they may even resist *proven* risk-free innovations because introducing them would temporarily reduce their production and make their quotas more difficult to achieve. Whenever you compare planning and free-market systems in the future, ask: Which of their technological innovations are we using? Which of ours are they using?

An important area in which Soviet technology has lagged is computers. Despite the Soviets' theoretical contributions to computer development and their ability to produce the large-scale computers necessary to put astronauts into space, they have missed out on some of the early stages of the small computer revolution. The problem was not just inadequate technology, but also a planning mistake that took years to correct. In the 1970s, central planners in Moscow decided against the production of personal computers, leaving the Soviet Union far behind in small computer production throughout the 1980s. By 1988, there were only about 200,000 personal computers in the Soviet Union. One of the first actions of Soviet leader Mikhail Gorbachev in 1985 was to introduce a crash program to make high school students familiar with computers.

3. *Isolation from the World Economy.* Socialist planners in the Soviet Union, or in any other country, develop a natural resistance to opening their economy to international trade. One reason is that planning is far more difficult in an economy that is open to the winds of international trade than one that is not. Because Soviet industry has not been subject to international competition, Soviet firms often turn out low-quality goods at a high price.

4. *Agricultural Failure.* Nowhere has Soviet failure been more obvious than in agriculture—an area in which individual initiative, rather than central command, is essential for success. Despite the fact that the Soviets have poured into agriculture about a quarter of their total investment—about five times the percentage in the United States—their agricultural productivity remains low. One explanation is that, as agriculture has become more dependent on chemical fertilizers, harvests have been increasingly damaged by shortages of these fertilizers owing to the inefficiency of the chemical industry. Another problem has been the lack of incentive for individuals to work or innovate on the large Soviet collective farms, which, on average, have 500 laborers working on 25,000 acres. The result is farm productivity which is less than 20% of the U.S. level. As much as a quarter to a third of the nation's total agricultural output is produced on the minuscule 2% of the Soviet farmland that is privately operated, where individuals are rewarded for hard work and initiative. Soviet leaders have often attributed poor harvests to the weather, but grain was exported from these same lands before the First World War, and the weather doesn't raise the same problems on adjacent privately owned plots of land. Some critics quip that, between 1917 and 1990, the Soviet Union has announced a poor harvest due to bad weather 72 times.

5. *Military Expenditures.* A great deal of Soviet industrial capacity has been devoted to the production of military hardware rather than to the research, development, and investment that can generate more rapid growth. The arms race has imposed a greater burden on the Soviet economy than on the larger U.S. economy.

6. *Morale and Incentive Problems.* There have been reports that limited incentives to work have led to low morale, alcoholism, and absenteeism in the USSR. The lack of work incentives seems strange inasmuch as the authorities have introduced a number of incentives for individual workers that appear to be similar to—and sometimes may even exceed—those available to American workers. Not only are Russian workers paid higher wages in some occupations than in others; in addition, high piecework rates (that is, payments according to the number of units produced) are more common as an incentive in the Soviet Union than in the United States. Often the most productive workers are granted tangible rewards, such as free government-financed holidays.

One explanation of why these incentives have not been more successful is that, after so many years of being told to restrain consumption today in order to enjoy a higher standard of living in the future, Soviet citizens have become cynical. Although their paychecks are guaranteed, the goods they can buy continue to be disappointing and often unavailable. The damaging effect of this on work incentives is illustrated by the Soviet quip: "They pretend to pay us, and we pretend to work."

Hebrew University's Gur Ofer has summed up the Soviet problems:

> Command replaces initiative and entrepreneurship, discipline replaces innovation, and a rigid bureaucratic organization . . . that encompasses the entire production sector . . . replaces the more flexible market. . . . Mistakes, when made, are . . . huge and . . . difficult to correct.

When Gorbachev came to power in 1985, he announced a broad set of economic reforms. He was motivated not only by the disappointing Soviet performance, but also by a challenge from the East:

By introducing reforms into their economy, the Chinese had roughly doubled their growth rate.[6]

CHINA

For the first three decades after the 1949 victory of the Communist party in the Civil War, China's economy was dominated by central, Soviet-style planning. Under Chairman Mao, China embarked on two nationwide campaigns—the "Great Leap Forward" of the late 1950s which unsuccessfully attempted to encourage small-scale industrial production, and the "Cultural Revolution," which was aimed at ensuring ideological purity, but in the process severely damaged the economy and almost destroyed the educational system. Following Mao's death in 1976, Deng and the other new Chinese leaders—some of them survivors from Mao's purges—put less emphasis on ideological purity. Indeed, the official *Peoples' Daily* conceded that Marxism might no longer solve all of China's problems. By 1978, the Chinese were willing to experiment and, if it worked, call it socialism. They saw that China was falling far behind not only Japan, but also Taiwan and Hong Kong, whose market economies were generating per capita incomes exceeding those in China by *20 and 35 times,* respectively.

Chinese economic reform began with the introduction of freer markets in agriculture. This policy was so successful that the Chinese began to extend reform to industry, particularly in the region close to Hong Kong.

[6]Dwight Perkins, "Reforming China's Economic System," *Journal of Economic Literature,* June 1988, p. 627. This source is used throughout the discussion of China. This chapter also draws on the experience of the Soviet Union as described in Gur Ofer (1987) and Padma Desai (1986) cited in Figure 26-2, and Vladimir V. Popov, *Perestroika: An Insider's View,* (Toronto: C.D. Howe Institute, Trade Monitor, July, 1989.) Popov is a Senior Research Fellow at the Institute of the U.S.A. and Canada in Moscow. This chapter also draws on the Hungarian experience with reform; see János Kornai, "The Hungarian Reform Process," *Journal of Economic Literature,* December 1986, pp. 1687–1737.

PROBLEMS ENCOUNTERED IN REFORMING MARXIST ECONOMIES

No attempt will be made to provide a complete description of the reforms that have recently been introduced in China and the Soviet Union, for they are subject to change and may indeed be reversed at any time. Instead, it is of more interest to use the experience of these two countries, and of Hungary and other Eastern European states that have experimented with reforms from an even earlier date, to illustrate the key issues that must be addressed by any Communist or Marxist country seeking to move its economy away from a bureaucratic command system and toward the market.

THE KEY ECONOMIC QUESTIONS

1. *Are soft budget restraints being replaced by hard ones?* In other words, are firms that don't cut costs and satisfy buyers going bankrupt? Although the Chinese announced a bankruptcy with great fanfare in 1986, it wasn't clear that this threat would be maintained. Bankruptcies can mean unemployment. Could the Chinese break the iron rice bowl system that guaranteed workers a job for life, regardless of their productivity? By 1988, a few workers with chronic histories of absenteeism were being fired, and a small number of Chinese lifetime labor contracts were being replaced by contracts that ran for only three years and thus allowed layoffs.

2. *Will government planners still set prices, or will they be allowed to change in response to demand and supply?* Even if prices are bureaucratically set, technical efficiency (eliminating waste) can still be achieved. However, to achieve both technical efficiency *and* allocative efficiency (production of the right amount of each good), prices must be determined by the market in response to supply and demand.

3. *Are the reformers willing to open up the economy to foreign competition?* Foreign competition is desirable because of the gains from trade, including improvement in the quality of domestic products. (Buyers can quickly tell if the domestically produced good is inferior to an import and can then insist on higher quality.) The Chinese have applied for admission to the General Agreement on Tariffs and Trade. However, neither China nor the Soviet Union yet seems prepared to face much foreign competition.

4. *How much private ownership will be allowed?* To improve incentives, both countries have allowed some private ownership, provided firms are "small" (with the definition of small being frequently revised). In the Soviet Union there is an additional restriction: An individual must work in a private firm (a "cooperative") to own even part of it. However, this restriction does not resolve the conflict between private ownership and Marxism. The reason is that, as the firm grows and the owners hire workers, the owners earn a "surplus value" above the wages they pay. This contradicts an important tenet of Marxism, since Marx viewed surplus value as the exploitation of labor.

5. *Will Marxism be compromised even more by allowing foreign ownership?* To acquire benefits from foreign firms (the new technology they bring in, plus the wages and taxes they pay) the Chinese have allowed in some foreign companies such as Volkswagen. They have made a special effort to attract foreign investors into the seaboard provinces in China by allowing them to acquire land on a 70-year lease. However, foreign investment has been a story not only of success, but also of failure, in part because of the Chinese system of two currencies—one that is convertible into other currencies (such as dollars and yen) and one that is not. Some foreign firms selling in China and receiving non-convertible currency have been unable to get enough dollars or other currencies to buy critical imported components. The Chinese have used this system to pressure foreign firms into buying components made in China, but instead it has sometimes induced firms to stay out of China altogether.

6. *Should agriculture or industry be reformed first?* The Chinese reforms began with new incentives in agriculture in 1979. Once peasants had produced their quota for the government, they were allowed to sell the rest on the open market and keep the proceeds. As a result, the rate of growth of agricultural output increased from 4.3% in 1971–1978 to 13.0% in 1982–1986. In contrast, the Soviets first emphasized industry, where reform is more complicated and takes more time.

Agricultural reform is easier for several reasons: (a) The farm family can be the decision-making unit, and it automatically faces a hard budget constraint. It *must* respond to prices and cut costs because the government will not bail it out; thus it is automatically subjected to the discipline of the marketplace. (b) There are so many farm families that this sector is highly competitive and thus raises no problems of monopoly. (3) Farmers often produce their output almost from scratch, without purchasing many inputs. In contrast, industrial firms draw on complex patterns of inputs from each other. Thus industrial reform is more difficult.

7. Can a means be developed for controlling aggregate demand, and thus inflation? In 1989, the Soviets ran a fiscal deficit more than four times the U.S. deficit (as a percentage of GNP). It was financed mainly by printing money. This added to inflationary pressure, and so long as prices were controlled, led to the more severe shortages and longer queues noted above. As price controls are removed, it becomes particularly important to deal effectively with such inflationary pressure.

8. *Can partial reform work, or should reform be across the board?* Because reform implies substantial restructuring of the economy (*perestroika,* as the Russians call it), *a phased-in process* may be less painful. Thus by the late 1980s, the Chinese had allowed some prices to fluctuate in response to market demand and supply, whereas others remained bureaucratically set. However, it is easy to think of circumstances in which such a phased-in reform could be disastrous. For example, even a highly efficient firm may go bankrupt if the price of its output remains fixed while the prices of its inputs are allowed to rise. Thus it has been argued that, if some prices are to be set free, all of them should be. In an exaggerated analogy, piecemeal economic reform is likened to piecemeal switching of traffic from the right lane to the left—trucks this year, cars next. Yugoslavia, with an inflation rate that reached 120% in 1987, is sometimes cited as an unsuccessful attempt to mix market forces and bureaucratic command. In practice, some sort of phase-in probably can't be avoided because of the massive short-run dislocation costs of any immediate across-the-board reform. However, it is essential that reformers recognize and try to avoid the special problems a phase-in may create.

9. Will it be possible to develop the institutions that freer markets require? For example, will it be possible to establish an adequate judicial system for resolving conflicts such as broken contracts? The lack of such a system has been a major flaw in Marxist countries in the past; it was assumed that civil courts were unnecessary because Marxism would eliminate all conflicts.

10. Can the government regulations necessary in a free-market system be developed? For example, once output targets and price controls are removed, other forms of regulation—such as pollution controls and antitrust laws—became essential. If they don't exist, a monopoly can seize the opportunity to raise its price and produce too little, and a polluting firm will produce too much.

Economic reform will not be easy, especially because these economic difficulties will be complicated by strong political pressures.

THE POLITICAL ECONOMY OF REFORM

As the public comes to enjoy more economic freedom, how much political freedom will it demand? That was the question facing the Chinese government in the spring of 1989, when students gathered in Tiananmen Square to demonstrate for democracy, and against the failures of the one-party system. After days of indecision, the government declared martial law. Tanks and troops were brought into action, and many demonstrators were killed. The core support for the demonstration came from students at Chinese universities; the desire for economic reforms may have been a contributing factor.

In the Soviet Union, Gorbachev went some distance toward satisfying the desire for political freedom when he permitted voters some choice among candidates—although not between parties. Some experts judge that Gorbachev's motive in making this radical political change was to get the broad public support necessary to prevent his economic reforms from being sabotaged by bureaucrats who were losing their influence. It appeared that Gorbachev was engaged in a complex and risky strategy—as the leader of the government and leader of the opposition at the same time.

Political reform is, of course, a major objective in its own right. Moreover, it may play an important role in encouraging the cooperation and hard effort by the public that are necessary to make economic reform successful. At the same time, there is a paradox. Once a country does get political reform and has a more democratic system, economic reform may in one sense become more difficult. To see why, note that in our democratic society, getting rid of just one bureaucratically fixed price—rent control—is almost impossible. The public and its elected representatives will often not put up with the short-term pain (in the form of temporary increases in rent) in order to acquire the long-term gain (from a more plentiful supply of housing). In contrast, economic reform in a country like the Soviet Union or China means the removal of fixed prices *throughout the economy*—that is, the removal of price controls not just on housing, but on a whole multitude of goods. In an economy where many goods are in short supply, this means that prices will increase temporarily until expanding supplies (along with appropriate aggregate demand policies) bring them under control—in a new more efficient relative pattern that eliminates shortages. This is the long term gain. But if the people were able to express their views in a democratic way, would they put up with this increase in the cost of living, along with other forms of short-term pain such as the new risk of unemployment and a greater degree of income inequality? (Greater income inequality seems likely because wealth would accrue to those who, like the Chinese peasants of the 1980s, become the successful new suppliers in shortage-prone markets.)[7] Moreover, the bureaucrats who would be losing their influence and jobs might become strong and articulate opponents of reform in any political campaign on this issue. Although it is conceivable that the Soviets would, in a democratic election, vote for economic reform, there is a good chance they would turn it down because of the short-run pain it would inflict.

---

[7]Because entrepreneurs can become very wealthy very fast when opportunities open up for the first time, some experts argue that inequality may increase as a result. However in "Reforming China's Economic System," p. 639, Dwight Perkins argues that it is not at all clear that this happened during the early Chinese reforms, since the benefits of these reforms were so widely shared.

FINAL OBSERVATIONS

Like other systems, Marxism must be judged, not on what it promises, but on what it delivers. How well does it solve the basic economic problem of transforming resources to satisfy human wants? As you evaluate this issue for yourself in the future, remember that the standard criticism of communism—conceded now by many Soviets, Chinese, and Eastern Europeans—is that it does not do a good job of satisfying these wants. Also remember another basic criticism that applies both to Marxist economies and to our own: They do a far better job of satisfying the wants of the privileged than of the poor.

Another criticism that also applies to our own free-market economy is that large corporations often exercise too much economic and political power—power that should be exercised by the government on behalf of the people. However, if a Marxist country cures this problem by keeping economic power (including the ownership of capital) in the hands of the government, is too much power then held by the state? Lane Kirkland, president of the AFL-CIO, has expressed American labor's reservations about dealing with a powerful state:

> We on the whole prefer to negotiate with private companies that have roughly equivalent bargaining power than with government corporations that control the courts, the police, the army, the navy, and the hydrogen bomb.

KEY POINTS

1. Most of the physical capital in our free-market system is owned by individuals; under communism it is owned by the state. The theoretical appeal of communism is that it eliminates one of the major causes of inequality in our system: the power and income enjoyed by those who own capital.

2. The two major economic characteristics of the system that exists in the Soviet Union today are (a) physical capital is owned publicly rather than privately and (b) investment, output levels, and prices are determined by a central planning authority.

3. One of the advantages of Soviet economywide central planning is that industry output targets can be set at a level that keeps unemployment low. There are disadvantages, too. Central planning results in a great accumulation of power in the hands of the central political authorities. The more such power is centralized, the greater the risk that this power will be abused. A key question is: Could a Soviet-style command economy be run without political dictatorship?

4. A further problem with economywide planning is that it is extremely difficult to administer, and therefore it often results in bottlenecks and other inefficiencies. Accordingly, central planning tends to result in higher levels of disguised unemployment, with workers engaged in unproductive activities such as producing goods that poorly satisfy consumer tastes.

5. Although the Soviet economy grew faster than the U.S. economy between 1950 and 1970, Soviet growth has slowed down since, and the Soviets are no longer closing the income gap with the United States. Reasons for this slowdown in Soviet growth include inefficiencies from being subject only to a soft budget restraint; a poor technological performance because of inadequate rewards for risk-taking; continued failure in agriculture; and a heavy burden of military expenditures.

6. China successfully introduced agricultural reform in the late 1970s and a decade later began to reform industry as well.

7. As the Chinese and Soviets began to reform their economies, they faced a set of perplexing questions. Should they allow bankruptcies, with their adverse effect on employment? Should they allow all prices to fluctuate, or should they proceed in a less ambitious way by freeing prices a few sectors at a time? Should they allow foreign competition in order to force their domestic producers to sell higher quality goods at lower prices? How much private ownership, including foreign ownership, should be allowed? How can inflation be controlled when prices are no longer fixed, in markets that are often in chronic short supply?

KEY CONCEPTS

capitalists
labor theory of value
subsistence level of wages
surplus value
proletariat
bourgeoisie
class struggle
socialism
communism
five-year plan
one-year plan
output target
overt versus disguised unemployment
soft budget restraint

PROBLEMS

26-1. (a) What did Marx mean by "surplus value"? Does it include some, all, or none of the costs of capital that must be paid by firms undertaking investment?

> **(b)** Do privately owned cooperatives in the Soviet Union that require all owners to also be workers avoid the problem of surplus value? Would cooperatives that require all *workers* to be *owners* solve this problem? Would such a system be feasible?

26-2. What are the two forms of unemployment? Which is worse in the Soviet system? Which is worse in our system? Explain.

26-3. "Because many workers are hostile to capital, they oppose a rapid accumulation of it—either by a firm or by the nation as a whole. Thus they fail to understand their own interest, which is to be working with more, rather than less, capital." Do you agree? Explain.

26-4. Give a concrete example to show how a bottleneck may occur in a centrally planned economy.

26-5. Do we acquire more new technology from the Japanese, British, and Germans, or from the Russians and Czechs? Why?

26-6. "In an unrestricted free market, a stupid, shiftless individual who has inherited a great deal of valuable land can charge a high rent, and through the diligent pursuit of idleness, become very wealthy—indeed, far wealthier than the intelligent, hardworking person who rents the land. Something is wrong." Explain why you agree or disagree.

Now consider three alternative solutions to this problem, carefully criticizing each:

> **(a)** Put a ceiling on rent. This solution would transfer income from landlords to tenants.
>
> **(b)** Charge the maximum rent but have the land owned by the state, with all income going to the state.
>
> **(c)** Let the shiftless owner continue to own the land and charge a maximum rent. But place a heavy percentage tax on his income.

Which solution is closest to the socialist blueprint? Which is closest to our modified free-market system?

26-7. "Although socialism and communism promise less, they deliver more." Explain why you agree or disagree.

GLOSSARY

(Not all these terms appear in this book. Some appear in the companion volume, Macroeconomics, and some are included because they occur frequently in readings or lectures. Page numbers provide the primary references for the terms. For additional references, see the index.)

ability to pay principle. The view that taxes should be levied according to the means of the various taxpayers, as measured by their incomes and/or wealth. Compare with *benefit principle.* (p. 73)

absolute advantage. A country (or region or individual) has an absolute advantage in the production of a good or service if it can produce that good or service with fewer resources than other countries (or regions or individuals). See also *comparative advantage.* (pp. 41, 336)

accelerationist. One who believes that an attempt to keep the unemployment rate low by expansive demand policies will cause more and more rapid inflation, and that a steady inflation will cause the unemployment rate to return to its natural or equilibrium rate.

accelerator. The theory that investment depends on the change in sales.

accommodative monetary policy. (1) A monetary policy that allows the money stock to change in response to changes in the demand for loans. (2) A monetary policy that increases aggregate demand when wages and other costs increase, in order to prevent an increase in unemployment in the face of cost-push forces.

accounts payable. Debts to suppliers of goods or services. (p. 133)

accounts receivable. Amounts due from customers. (p. 133)

action lag. The time interval between the recognition that adjustments in aggregate demand policies are desirable and the time when policies are actually changed.

actual investment. Investment as it appears in the GNP accounts; investment including undesired inventory accumulation.

adaptive expectations. Expectations that depend on past and/or present observations. Contrast with *rational expectations.*

adjustable peg system. A system in which countries peg (fix) exchange rates but retain the right to change them in the event of fundamental disequilibrium. (In the adjustable peg system of 1945–1973, countries generally fixed the prices of their currencies in terms of the U.S. dollar.)

adjustable-rate mortgage. A mortgage whose interest rate is adjusted periodically in response to changes in a market rate of interest.

ad valorem tax. A tax collected as a percentage of the price or value of a good.

aggregate demand. Total quantity of goods and services that would be bought at various average price levels.

aggregate expenditures. Total quantity of goods and services that would be bought at various levels of national income or national product. Total quantity of goods and services demanded as a function of national income or product.

aggregate supply. (1) Total quantity of goods and services that would be offered for sale at various average price levels. (2) Potential GNP.

allocative efficiency. Production of the best combination of goods with the lowest cost combination of inputs. (p. 11)

annually balanced budget principle. The view that government expenditures should be limited each year to no more than government receipts during that year.

antitrust laws. Laws designed to control monopoly power and practices. Examples: Sherman Act, 1890: Clayton Act, 1914. (p. 243)

appreciation of a currency. In a flexible exchange-rate system, a rise in the price of a currency in terms of another currency or currencies.

arbitrage. A set of transactions aimed at making a profit from inconsistent prices.

arbitration. Settlement of differences between a union and management by an impartial third party (the arbitrator) whose decisions are binding. (p. 402)

arc elasticity of demand. The elasticity of demand between two points on a demand curve, calculated by the midpoint formula. (p. 86)

asset. Something that is owned.

automatic stabilizer. A feature built into the economy that reduces the amplitude of fluctuations, *without any policy change being made* (in contrast to a *discretionary policy action*). For example, tax collections tend to fall during a recession and rise during a boom, slowing the change in disposable incomes and aggregate demand. Thus they are an automatic fiscal stabilizer. Interest rates tend to fall during a recession and rise during a boom because of changes in the demand for funds. These changes in interest rates tend to stabilize investment demand. Thus they are an automatic monetary stabilizer.

average cost pricing. Setting the price where the average-cost curve (including normal profit) intersects the demand curve. (p. 205)

average fixed cost. Fixed cost divided by the number of units of output.

average product. Total product divided by the number of units of the variable input used.

average propensity to consume. Consumption divided by disposable income.

average propensity to save. Saving divided by disposable income.

average revenue. Total revenue divided by the number of units sold. Where there is a single price, this price equals average revenue.

average total cost. Total cost divided by the number of units of output.

average variable cost. Variable cost divided by the number of units produced.

balanced budget. (1) A budget with revenues equal to expenditures. (2) More loosely (but more commonly), a budget with revenues equal to or greater than expenditures. (p. 70)

balanced budget multiplier. The change in equilibrium national product divided by the change in government spending when this spending is financed by an equivalent change in taxes.

balance of payments. (1) The accounts showing transactions between residents of one country and the rest of the world. (2) The summary figure calculated from balance-of-payments credits less balance-of-payments debits, with official reserve transactions excluded from the calculation.

balance-of-payments accounts. A statement of a country's transactions with other countries.

balance-of-payments surplus (deficit). A positive (negative) balance of payments.

balance of trade (or balance on merchandise account). The value of exports of goods minus the value of imports of goods.

balance sheet. The statement of a firm's financial position at a particular time, showing its assets, liabilities, and net worth. (p. 132)

band. The range within which an exchange rate could move without the government's being committed to intervene in exchange markets to prevent further movement. Under the adjustable peg system, governments were obliged to keep exchange rates from moving outside a band (of 1% either side of parity).

bank rate. The rate of interest charged by the central bank on loans to commercial banks or other institutions. The discount rate.

bank reserve. Bank holding of currency and reserve deposits in the Federal Reserve.

bank run. A situation in which many owners of bank deposits attempt to make withdrawals because of their fear that the bank will be unable to meet its obligations.

bankruptcy. (1) A situation in which a firm (or individual) has legally been declared unable to pay its debts. (2) More loosely, a situation in which a firm (or individual) is unable to pay its debts.

barrier to entry. An impediment that makes it difficult or impossible for a new firm to enter an industry. Examples: patents, economies of scale, accepted brand names. (p. 220)

barter. The exchange of one good or service for another without the use of money. (p. 36)

base year. The reference year, given the value of 100 when constructing a price index or other time series.

beggar-thy-neighbor policy (or beggar-my-neighbor policy). A policy aimed at shifting an unemployment problem to another country. Example: an increase in tariffs. (p. 352)

benefit-cost analysis. The calculation and comparison of the benefits and costs of a program or project. (p. 292)

benefit in kind. Payment, not of cash, but of some good (like food) or service (like medical care). (p. 450)

benefit principle. The view that taxes should be levied in proportion to the benefits that the various taxpayers receive from government expenditures. Compare with *ability to pay principle.* (p. 72)

bilateral monopoly. A market structure involving a single seller (monopolist) and a single buyer (monopsonist). (p. 397)

bill. See *Treasury bill.*

blacklist. A list of workers who are not to be given jobs because of union activity or other behavior considered objectionable by employers. (p. 389)

black market. A market in which sales take place at a price above the legal maximum. (p. 60)

block grant. Grant that may be used in a broad area (such as education) and need not be spent on specific programs (such as reading programs for the handicapped).

bond. A written commitment to pay a scheduled series of interest payments plus the face value (principal) at a specified maturity date. (p. 124)

book value. The book value of a stock is its net worth per share. (It is calculated by dividing the net worth of the firm by the number of its shares outstanding.) (p. 134)

bourgeoisie. (1) In Marxist doctrine, capitalists as a social class. (2) The middle class. (3) More narrowly, shopkeepers. (p. 466)

boycott. A concerted refusal to buy (buyer's boycott) or sell (seller's boycott). A campaign to discourage people from doing business with a particular firm.

break-even point. (1) The lowest point on the average total cost curve. If price is at this height, revenues are just equal to costs, and therefore economic profit is zero. (p. 163) (2) The level of disposable income at which consumption just equals disposable income, and therefore saving is zero.

broker. One who acts on behalf of a buyer or seller. (p. 128)

budget deficit. The amount by which budgetary outlays exceed revenues. (p. 70)

budget line (or income line or price line). The line on a diagram that shows the various combinations of commodities that can be bought with a given income at a given set of prices. (p. 115)

budget surplus. The amount by which budgetary revenues exceed outlays. (p. 70)

built-in stabilizer. See *automatic stabilizer.*

burden of tax. The amount of the tax ultimately paid by different individuals or groups. (For example, how much does a cigarette tax raise the price paid by buyers, and how much does it lower the net price received by sellers?) The incidence of the tax. (p. 93)

business cycle. The more or less regular upward and downward movement of economic activity over a period of years. A cycle has four phases: recession, trough, expansion, and peak.

capital. (1) Real capital: buildings, equipment, and other materials used in the production process that have themselves been produced in the past. (p. 26) (2) Financial capital: either funds available for acquiring real capital *or* financial assets such as bonds or common stock. (p. 26) (3) Human capital: the education, training, and experience that make human beings more productive. (pp. 27, 414)

capital account. In international economics, changes between countries in the ownership of assets.

capital consumption allowance. Depreciation, with adjustments for the effects of inflation on the measurement of capital. Loosely, depreciation.

capital gain. The increase in the value of an asset over time.

capitalism. A system in which individuals and privately owned firms are permitted to own large amounts of capital, and decisions are made primarily in private markets, with relatively little government interference. (p. 47)

capitalized value. The present value of the income stream that an asset is expected to produce.

capital market. A market in which financial instruments such as stocks and bonds are bought and sold.

capital-output ratio. The value of capital divided by the value of the annual output produced with this capital.

capital stock. The total quantity of capital.

cartel. A formal agreement among firms to set price and share the market. (p. 222)

categorical grant. A federal grant to a state or local government for a specific program. Such a grant generally requires the recipient government to pay part of the cost of the program.

cease-and-desist order. An order from a court or government agency to an individual or company to stop a specified action. (p. 243)

central bank. A banker's bank, whose major responsibility is the control of the money supply. A central bank also generally performs other functions, such as check clearing and the inspection of commercial banks.

central planning. Centralized direction of the resources of the economy, with the objective of fulfilling national goals. In a centrally planned economy, the government owns most of the capital. (p. 47)

certificate of deposit (CD). A marketable time deposit.

ceteris paribus. "Other things unchanged." In demand-and-supply analysis, it is common to make the *ceteris paribus* assumption, that is, to assume that none of the determinants of the quality demanded or supplied is allowed to change, with the sole exception of price. (p. 52) We may also speak of how income affects the quantity demanded, *ceteris paribus*—that is, if nothing but income changes.

check clearing. The transfer of checks from the bank in which they were deposited to the bank on which they were written, with the net amounts due to or from each bank being calculated.

checking deposit. A deposit against which an order to pay (that is, a check) may be written.

checking deposit multiplier. The increase in checking deposits divided by the increase in bank reserves.

checkoff. The deduction of union dues from workers' pay by an employer, who then remits the dues to the union. (p. 390)

circular flow of payments. The flow of payments from businesses to households in exchange for labor and other productive services and the return flow of payments from households to businesses in exchange for goods and services. (p. 39)

classical economics. (1) In Keynesian economics, the accepted body of macroeconomic doctrine prior to the publication of Keynes' *General Theory.* According to classical economics, a market economy tends toward an equilibrium with full employment; a market economy tends to be stable if monetary conditions are stable; and changes in the quantity of money are the major cause of changes in aggregate demand. (2) The accepted view, prior to about 1870, that value depends on the cost of production. [In the late nineteenth century, this was replaced with the "neoclassical" view that value depends on both costs of production (supply) and utility (demand).]

class struggle. In Marxist economics, the struggle for control between the proletariat and the bourgeoisie. (p. 466)

clean float. A situation in which exchange rates are determined by market forces, without intervention by central banks or governments.

clearing of checks. See *check clearing.*

closed economy. An economy with no international transactions.

closed shop. A business that hires only workers who are already union members. Compare with *union shop* and *right-to-work law.* (p. 390)

cobweb cycle. A switching back and forth between a situation of high production and low price and one of low production and high price. A cobweb cycle can occur if there are long lags in production and if producers erroneously assume that price this year is a good indicator of price next year.

coincidence of wants. This exists when *A* is willing to offer what *B* wants, while *B* is willing to offer what *A* wants. (p. 37)

collective bargaining. Negotiations between a union and management over wages, fringe benefits, hiring policies, or working conditions. (p. 386)

collective goods. Goods that, by their very nature, provide benefits to a large group of people.

collusion. An agreement among sellers regarding prices and/or market shares. The agreement may be explicit or tacit. (p. 222)

commercial bank. A privately owned, profit-seeking institution that accepts demand and savings deposits, makes loans, and acquires other earning assets (particularly bonds and shorter term debt instruments).

commons. Land that is open for use by all or by a large group. Example: commonly owned pastureland.

common stock. Each share of common stock represents part ownership in a corporation. (p. 121)

communism. (1) In Marxist theory, the ultimate stage of historical development in which (a) all are expected to work and no one lives by owning capital, (b) exploitation has been eliminated and there is a classless society, and (c) the state has withered away. (2) A common alternative usage: the economic and political systems of the People's Republic of China, the Soviet Union, and other countries in which a Communist party is in power. (p. 466)

company union. A union dominated by the employer.

comparable. Of equal value, requiring equivalent effort, responsibility, training, and skills. The *comparable worth issue* is the question of whether employers should be required to pay women as much as men working in different but comparable jobs. Comparable worth—also sometimes known as *pay equity*—takes the anti-discrimination idea beyond the requirement that people be paid the same amount for doing the same job. (p. 441)

comparative advantage. A nation (or city or individual) has a comparative advantage in a good or service if it can produce the good or service at a lower opportunity cost than its trading partner. (p. 337)

compensating wage differential. Wage difference that may result if labor views a job as less attractive than an alternative. (Employers have to pay a higher wage to fill the unattractive job.) (p. 404)

competition. See *perfect competition.*

competitive devaluations. A round of exchange-rate devaluations in which each of a number of countries tries to gain a competitive advantage by devaluing its currency. (Not all can be successful; each must fail to the extent that other countries also devalue.)

complementary goals. Goals such that the achievement of one helps in the achievement of the other. (Contrast with *conflicting goals.*) (p. 13)

complementary goods, or complements in consumption. Goods such that the rise in the price of one causes a leftward shift in the demand curve for the other. (Contrast with *substitute.*) (p. 53)

complements in production. Goods such that the rise in the price of one causes a rightward shift in the supply curve of the other. Joint products. (p. 55)

concentration ratio. Usually, the fraction of an industry's total output produced by the four largest firms. (Sometimes a different number of firms—such as eight—is chosen in calculating concentration ratios, and sometimes a different measure of size—such as sales or assets—is chosen.) (p. 218)

conflicting goals. Goals such that working toward one makes it more difficult to achieve the other. (p. 16)

conglomerate merger. See *merger.*

consent decree. An agreement whereby a defendant, without admitting guilt, undertakes to desist from certain actions and abide by other conditions laid down in the decree.

conspicuous consumption. Consumption whose purpose is to impress others. A term originated by Thorstein Veblen (1857–1929).

constant dollars. A series is measured in constant dollars if it is measured at the prices existing in a specified base year. Such a series has been adjusted to remove the effects of inflation or deflation. Contrast with *current dollars.*

constant returns (to scale). Occurs when an increase of $x\%$ in all inputs causes output to increase by the same $x\%$. (p. 146)

consumer price index (CPI). A weighted average of the prices of goods and services commonly purchased by families in urban areas, as calculated by the U.S. Bureau of Labor Statistics. (p. 93)

consumer surplus. The net benefit that consumers get from being able to purchase a good at the prevailing price; the difference between the maximum amounts that consumers would be willing to pay and what they actually do pay. It is estimated as the triangular area under the demand curve and above the market price. (p. 105)

consumption. (1) The purchase of consumer goods and services. (2) The act of using goods and services to satisfy wants. (3) The using up of goods (as in capital consumption allowances).

consumption function. (1) The relationship between consumer expenditures and disposable income. (2) More broadly, the relationship between consumer expenditures and the factors that determine these expenditures.

contestable market. A market with only one or a few producers, whose market power is nevertheless severely limited by the ease with which additional producers may enter. (p. 235)

convergence hypothesis. The proposition that the differences between communistic and capitalistic societies is decreasing.

convertible bond. A bond that can be exchanged for common stock under specified terms and prior to a specified date, at the option of the bondholder.

cornering a market. Buying and accumulating enough of a commodity to become the single (or at least dominant) owner, and thus acquire the power to resell at a higher price. (p. 187)

corporation. An association of stockholders with a government charter that grants certain legal powers, privileges, and liabilities separate from those of the individual stockholder-owners. The major advantages of the corporate form of business organization are limited liability for the owners, continuity, and relative ease of raising capital for expansion. (p. 121)

correlation. The tendency of two variables (like income and consumption) to move together.

cost-benefit analysis. The calculation and comparison of the benefits and costs of a program or project. Also called *benefit-cost analysis.* (p. 292)

cost-push inflation. Inflation caused principally by increasing costs—in the form of higher prices for labor, materials, and other inputs—rather than by rising demand. (p. 232) Contrast with *demand-pull inflation.*

countercyclical policy. (1) Policy that reduces fluctuations in economic activity. (2) Policy whose objective is to reduce fluctuations in economic activity.

countervailing power. Power in one group which has grown as a reaction to power in another group. For example, a big labor union may develop to balance the bargaining power of a big corporation. The term was originated by Harvard's John Kenneth Galbraith.

craft union. A labor union whose members have a particular craft (skill or occupation). Examples: an electricians' union or a plumbers' union. Contrast with *industrial union.* (p. 388)

crawling peg system. An international financial system in which par values would be changed frequently, by small amounts, in order to avoid large changes at a later date.

credit crunch. Severe credit rationing, where demand for loans substantially exceeds the available supply.

credit instrument. A written promise to pay at some future date.

credit rationing. Allocation of available funds among borrowers when the demand for loans exceeds the supply at the prevailing interest rate.

creeping inflation. A slow but persistent upward movement of the average level of prices (not more than 2% or 3% per annum).

cross-section data. Observations taken at the same time. Example: the consumption of different income classes in the United States in 1986.

crowding out. A reduction in private investment demand caused when an expansive fiscal policy results in higher interest rates.

currency. (1) Coins and paper money (dollar bills). (2) In international economics, a national money, such as the dollar or the yen.

current account surplus. The amount by which a country's export of goods and services is greater than the combined sum of its imports of goods and services plus its net unilateral transfers to foreign countries.

current dollars. A series (like GNP) is measured in current dollars if each observation is measured at the prices that prevailed at the time. Such a series reflects both real changes in GNP *and* inflation (or deflation). Contrast with *constant dollars.*

current liabilities. Debts that are due for payment within a year.

customs union. An agreement among nations to eliminate trade barriers (tariffs, quotas, etc.) among themselves and to adopt common tariffs on imports from nonmember countries. Example: the European Economic Community.

cutthroat competition. Selling at a price below cost, with the objective of driving competitors out of the market (at which time prices may be raised and monopoly profits reaped). (p. 224)

cyclically balanced budget. A budget whose receipts over a whole business cycle are at least equal to its expenditures over the same cycle. Unlike an annually balanced budget, a cyclically balanced budget permits the use of countercyclical fiscal policies. Surpluses during prosperity may be used to cover deficits during recessions.

cyclical unemployment. Unemployment caused by a general downturn in the economy.

deadweight loss. A loss of allocative efficiency, owing to the wrong pattern of production or the wrong combination of inputs. (p. 178)

debasement of currency. (1) Reduction of the quantity of precious metal in coins. (p. 40) (2) More broadly, a substantial decrease in the purchasing power of money.

debt. The amount owed. (p. 70)

debt instrument. A written commitment to repay borrowed funds.

declining industry. An industry whose firms make less than normal profits. (Firms will therefore leave the industry.)

decreasing returns (to scale). Occurs if an $x\%$ increase in all inputs results in an increase of output of less than $x\%$.

deficiency payment. The government's payment of the difference between the market price and its target price. (p. 270)

deficit. A *budget deficit* is the amount by which government expenditures exceed government revenues. (p. 70) A *trade deficit* is the amount by which imports exceed exports.

deflation. (1) A decline in the average level of prices; the opposite of inflation. (p. 9) (2) The removal of the effects of inflation from a series of observations by dividing each observation with a price index. The derivation of a constant-dollar series from a current-dollar series.

deflationary bias. Exists in a system if, on average, monetary and fiscal authorities are constrained from allowing aggregate demand to increase as rapidly as productive capacity. (The classical gold standard was criticized on the ground that it created a deflationary bias.)

deflationary gap. See *recessionary gap.*

deindustrialization. A reduction in the size of the manufacturing sector, usually as a result of competition from imports.

demand. A schedule or curve showing how much of a good or service would be demanded at various possible prices, *ceteris paribus.* (p. 50)

demand deposit. A bank deposit withdrawable on demand and transferable by check.

demand management policy. A change in monetary and/or fiscal policy aimed at affecting aggregate demand.

demand-pull inflation. Inflation caused by excess aggregate demand. Contrast with *cost-push inflation.*

demand schedule. A table showing the quantities of a good or service that buyers would be willing and able to purchase at various market prices, *ceteris paribus.* (p. 50)

demand shift. A movement of the demand curve to the right or left as a result of a change in income or any other determinant of the quantity demand (with the sole exception of the price of the good). (p. 52)

demand shifter. Anything except its own price that affects the quantity of a good demanded. (p. 53)

depletion allowance. A deduction, equal to a percentage of sales, that certain extractive industries are permitted in calculating taxable profits.

depreciation. (1) The loss in the value of physical capital owing to wear and obsolescence. (2) The estimate of such loss in business or economic accounts. (3) The amount that tax laws allow businesses to count as a cost of using plant or equipment.

depreciation of a currency. A decline in the value of a floating currency measured in terms of another currency or currencies.

depression. An extended period of very high unemployment and much excess capacity. (There is no generally accepted, precise numerical definition of a depression. This text suggests that a depression requires unemployment rates of 10% or more for two years or more.) (p. 7)

derived demand. The demand for an input that depends on the demand for the product or products it is used to make. For example, the demand for flour is derived from the demand for bread. (p. 374)

desired investment. (Also known as *investment demand* or *planned investment.*) This is the amount of new plant, equipment, and housing acquired during the year, plus additions to inventories that businesses wanted to acquire. Actual investment less undesired inventory accumulation.

devaluation. In international economics, a reduction of the par value of a currency.

dictatorship of the proletariat. In Marxist economics, the state after a revolution has eliminated the capitalist class and power has fallen into the hands of the proletariat. (p. 473)

differentiated products. Similar products that retain some distinctive difference(s); close but not perfect substitutes. Examples: Ford and Chevrolet automobiles, different brands of toothpaste. (p. 216)

diminishing returns, law of eventually. See *law of eventually diminishing returns.*

dirty float. See *floating (or flexible) exchange rate.*

discounting. The process by which the present value of one or more future payments is calculated, using an interest rate. (See *present value.*) (2) In central banking, lending by the central bank to a commercial bank or other financial institution.

discount rate. (1) In central banking, the rate of interest charged by the central bank on loans to commercial banks or other institutions. (2) The interest rate used to calculate present value.

discouraged worker. Someone who wants a job but is no longer looking because work is believed to be unavailable. A discouraged worker is not included in either the labor force or the number of unemployed.

discretionary policy. Policy that is periodically changed in the light of changing conditions. The term is usually applied to monetary or fiscal policies that are adjusted with the objectives of high employment and stable prices. Contrast with *monetary rule.*

diseconomies of scale. Occur when an increase of x% in all inputs results in an increase in output of less than x%. (p. 145)

disposable (personal) income. Income that households have left after the payment of taxes. It is divided among consumption expenditures, the payment of interest on consumer debt, and saving.

dissaving. Negative saving.

dividend. The part of a corporation's profits paid out to its shareholders.

division of labor. The breaking up of a productive process into different tasks, each done by a different worker (for example, on an automobile assembly line).

dollar standard. An international system in which many international transactions take place in dollars and many countries hold sizable factions of their reserves in dollars. Also, other currencies may be pegged to the dollar.

double-entry bookkeeping. An accounting system in which each transaction results in equal entries on both sides. When double-entry bookkeeping is used, the two sides of the accounts must balance.

double taxation. The taxation of corporate dividends twice—once as part of the profits of the corporation, and once as the income of the dividend recipient. (p. 122)

dual labor market. A double labor market, where workers in one market are excluded from taking jobs in the other market. (p. 439)

dumping. The sale of a good at a lower price in a foreign market than in the home market—a form of price discrimination.

duopoly. A market in which there are only two sellers. (p. 233)

duty. A tax on an imported good as it enters the country. (pp. 5, 348)

dynamic efficiency. Efficient change in an economy, particularly the most efficient use of resources, the best rate of technological change, and the most efficient rate of growth. (pp. 180, 307)

dynamic wage differential. A wage difference that arises because of changing demand or supply conditions in the labor market. It tends to disappear over time as labor moves out of relatively low-wage jobs and into those that pay a relatively high wage. (p. 404)

econometrics. The application of statistical methods to economic problems.

economic efficiency. See *allocative efficiency; dynamic efficiency;* and *technological (or technical) efficiency.*

economic integration. The elimination of tariffs and other barriers between nations. The partial or complete unification of the economies of different countries.

economic problem. The need to make choices because our resources are scarce while our wants are virtually unlimited. (p. 25)

economic profit. Above-normal profit. Profit in excess of the amount needed to keep capital in the industry. (p. 149)

economic rent. The return to a factor of production in excess of its opportunity cost. (p. 417)

economics. (1) The study of the allocation of scarce resources to satisfy alternative, competing human wants. (p. 25) (2) The study of how people acquire material necessities and comforts, the problems they encounter in doing so, and how these problems can be reduced.

economies (diseconomies) of scale. Occur when an increase of $x\%$ in all inputs results in an increase in output of more (less) than $x\%$. (p. 43)

economies of scope. Occur when the addition of a new product reduces the cost of existing products. (p. 210)

economize. To achieve a specific benefit at the lowest cost in terms of the resources used. (p. 25) To make the most of limited resources. To be careful in spending.

economy. (1) A set of interrelated production and consumption activities. (2) The act of reducing the cost of achieving a goal.

efficiency. The goal of getting the most out of our productive efforts. See also *allocative efficiency; dynamic efficiency;* and *technological efficiency.* (p. 10)

effluent charge. A tax or other levy on a polluting activity based on the quantity of pollution discharged. (p. 284)

elastic demand. Demand with an elasticity whose absolute value exceeds 1. A fall in price causes an increase in total expenditure on the product in question, because the percentage change in quantity demanded is greater than the percentage change in price. (pp. 85–88)

elasticity of demand. The price elasticity of demand is

$$\frac{\text{Percentage change in quantity demanded}}{\text{Percentage change in price}}$$

Similarly, the income elasticity of demand is

$$\frac{\text{Percentage change in quantity demanded}}{\text{Percentage change in income}}$$

The unmodified term "elasticity" usually applies to price elasticity. (pp. 84–99)

elasticity of supply. The (price) elasticity of supply is

$$\frac{\text{Percentage change in quantity supplied}}{\text{Percentage change in price}}$$

(p. 91)

elastic supply. Supply with an elasticity of more than 1. A supply curve which, if extended in a straight line, would meet the vertical axis. (p. 91)

emission fee. See *effluent charge.*

employer of last resort. The government acts as the employer of last resort if it provides jobs for all those who are willing and able to work but cannot find jobs in the private sector.

employment rate. The percentage of the labor force employed.

endogenous variable. A variable explained within a theory.

Engel's laws. Regularities between income and consumer expenditures observed by nineteenth-century statistician Ernst Engel. Most important is the decrease in the percentage of income spent on food as income rises.

entrepreneur. One who organizes and manages production. One who innovates and bears risks. (p. 27)

envelope curve. A curve that encloses, by just touching, a series of other curves. For example, the long-run average-cost curve is the envelope of all the short-run average-cost curves (each of which shows costs, given a particular stock of fixed capital). (p. 144)

equation of exchange. MV = PQ.

equilibrium. A situation in which there is no tendency to change. (p. 51)

equity. (1) Ownership, or amount owned. (p. 134) (2) Fairness. (p. 11)

escalator clause. A provision in a contract or law whereby a price, wage, or other monetary quantity is increased at the same rate as a specified price index (usually the consumer price index).

estate tax. A tax on property owned at the time of death.

Eurodollars. Deposits in European banks that are denominated in U.S. dollars.

ex ante. Planned or desired (as contrasted to actual or *ex post*). Example: *ex ante* investment.

excess burden of a tax. The decrease in efficiency that results when people change their behavior to reduce their tax payments. Distinguish from *primary burden of a tax.* (p. 172)

excess demand. The amount by which the quantity demanded exceeds the quantity supplied at the existing price. A shortage. (p. 52)

excess reserves. Reserves held by a bank in excess of the legally required amount.

excess supply. The amount by which the quantity supplied exceeds the quantity demanded at the existing price. A surplus. (p. 52)

exchange rate. The price of one national currency in terms of another.

exchange-rate appreciation (depreciation). See *appreciation (depreciation) of a currency.*

excise tax. A tax on the sale of a particular good. An *ad valorem tax* is collected as a percentage of the price of the good. A *specific tax* is a fixed number of cents or dollars on each unit of the good. (p. 93)

exclusion principle. The basis for distinguishing between public and nonpublic goods. If those who do not pay for a good can be excluded from enjoying it, then it is not a public good. (p. 319)

exogenous variable. A variable not explained within a theory; its value is taken as given. Example: investment in the simple Keynesian theory.

expansion. The phase of the business cycle when output and employment are increasing.

export (E). Good or service sold to foreign nationals.

export of capital. Acquisition of foreign assets.

ex post. Actual (as contrasted to desired or *ex ante*). Example: *ex post* investment.

external benefit. Benefit enjoyed by someone other than the buyers or sellers of a product; a spillover benefit. (p. 316)

external cost. Cost borne by someone other than the buyers or sellers of a product; a spillover cost. Example: pollution. (p. 76)

externality. An adverse or beneficial side effect of production or consumption. Also known as a *spillover* or *third-party effect.* (p. 76)

externally held public debt. Government securities held by foreigners.

Fabian socialism. Form of socialism founded in Great Britain in the late nineteenth century, advocating gradual and evolutionary movement toward socialism within a democratic political system.

face value. The stated amount of a loan or bond. The amount that must be paid, in addition to interest, when the bond comes due. The principal.

factor mobility. Ease with which factors can be moved from one use to another.

factor of production. Resource used to produce a good or service. Land, labor, and capital are the three basic categories of factors. (p. 26)

fair return. Return to which a regulated public utility should be entitled.

fallacy of composition. The unwarranted conclusion that a proposition which is true of a single sector or market is necessarily true for the economy as a whole.

featherbedding. (1) Commonly: Make-work rules designed to increase the number of workers or the number of hours on a particular job. (2) As defined in the Taft-Hartley Act: Payment for work not actually performed.

federal funds rate. The interest rate on very short term (usually overnight) loans between banks.

Federal Reserve Bank interest rate. The rate of interest charged by the Federal Reserve on loans to commercial banks or other institutions. The discount rate.

fiat money. Paper money that is neither backed by nor convertible into precious metals but is nevertheless legal tender. Money that is money solely because the government says it is.

final product. A good or service purchased by the ultimate user, and not intended for resale or further processing.

financial capital. Financial assets such as bank accounts, bonds, and common stock. Funds available for acquiring real capital. Distinguish from *real capital*, such as buildings or equipment. (p. 26)

financial instrument. A legal document representing claims or ownership. Examples: bonds; Treasury bills.

financial intermediary. An institution that issues financial obligations (such as checking deposits) in order to acquire funds from the public. The institution then pools these funds and provides them in larger amounts to businesses, governments, or individuals. Examples: commercial banks; savings and loan associations; insurance companies.

financial investment. The acquisition of financial capital, such as bonds or common stock. Distinguish from *real investment*—the accumulation of real capital, such as buildings or equipment. (p. 26)

financial market. A market in which financial instruments (stocks, bonds, etc.) are bought and sold. (p. 125)

fine-tuning. An attempt to smooth out mild fluctuations in the economy by frequent adjustments in monetary and/or fiscal policies.

firm. A business organization that produces goods and/or services. A firm may own one or more plants. (p. 49)

fiscal dividend. A budget surplus, measured at the full-employment national product, that is generated by the growth of the productive capacity of the economy. (This term was most commonly used during the 1960s.)

fiscal drag. The tendency for rising tax collections to impede the healthy growth of aggregate demand that is needed for the achievement and maintenance of full employment. (This term was most commonly used during the 1960s.)

fiscal policy. The adjustment of tax rates or government spending in order to affect aggregate demand. *Pure fiscal policy* is a change in government spending or tax rates, unaccompanied by any change in the rate of growth of the money stock. (p. 305)

fiscal year. A twelve-month period selected as the year for accounting purposes.

Fisher equation. The equation of exchange: $MV = PQ$.

fixed asset. A durable good, expected to last at least a year.

fixed cost. A cost that does not vary with output.

fixed exchange rate. An exchange rate that is held within a narrow band by the monetary authorities or by the operation of the gold standard.

fixed factor. A factor whose quantity cannot be changed in the short run.

flat tax. A tax with only one rate applying to all income. A proportional tax.

floating (or flexible) exchange rate. An exchange rate that is not pegged by monetary authorities but is allowed to change in response to changing demand or supply conditions. If governments and central banks withdraw completely from the exchange markets, the float is *clean.* (That is, the exchange rate is *freely flexible.*) A float is *dirty* when governments or central banks intervene in exchange markets by buying or selling foreign currencies in order to influence exchange rates.

focal point pricing. Occurs when independent firms quote the same price even though they do not explicitly collude. They are led by convention, rules of thumb, or similar thinking to the same price. Example: $39.95 for a pair of shoes. (p. 230)

forced saving. A situation in which households lose control of their income, which is directed into saving even though they would have preferred to consume it. This can occur if the monetary authorities provide financial resources for investment, creating inflation that reduces the purchasing power of households' incomes (and therefore reduces their consumption). Alternatively, forced saving occurs if taxes are used for investment projects (such as dams).

foreign exchange. The currency of another country.

foreign exchange market. A market in which one national currency is bought in exchange for another national currency.

foreign exchange reserves. Foreign currencies held by the government or central bank.

forward price. A price established in a contract to be executed at a specified time in the future (such as three months from now). See also *futures market.*

fractional-reserve banking. A banking system in which banks keep reserves (generally in the form of currency or deposits in the central bank) equal to only a fraction of their deposit liabilities.

freedom of entry. The absence of barriers that make it difficult or impossible for a new firm to enter an industry. (p. 158)

free enterprise economy. An economy in which individuals are permitted to own large amounts of capital, and decisions are made primarily in private markets, with relatively little government interference. (p. 47)

free good. A good or service whose price is zero, because at that price the quantity supplied is at least as great as the quantity demanded.

free market economy. An economy in which the major questions "What?" "How?" and "For whom?" are answered by the actions of individuals and firms in the marketplace rather than by the government. (p. 47)

free rider. Someone who cannot be excluded from enjoying the benefits of a project, but who pays nothing or pays a disproportionately small share to cover its costs. (p. 321)

free trade. A situation in which no tariffs or other barriers exist on trade between countries.

free-trade area (or free-trade association). A group of countries that agree to eliminate trade barriers (tariffs, quotas, etc.) among themselves, while each retains the right to set its own tariffs on imports from nonmember countries. Compare with *customs union.* (p. 44)

frictional unemployment. Temporary unemployment associated with adjustments in a changing, dynamic economy. It arises for a number of reasons. For example, some new entrants into the labor force take time to find jobs, some with jobs quit to look for better ones, and others are temporarily unemployed by such disturbances as bad weather.

front-loaded debt. A debt on which the payments, measured in constant dollars, are greater at the beginning than at the end of the repayment period.

full employment. (1) A situation in which the unemployment rate is brought down as low as possible, without causing an increase in the rate of inflation. (2) A situation in which there is no unemployment attributable to insufficient aggregate demand, that is, in which all unemployment is due to frictional or structural causes. See also *natural rate of unemployment.*

full-employment budget (or high-employment budget). The size that the government's surplus (or deficit) would be with existing spending programs and tax rates, if the economy were at full employment. Full-employment government receipts (that is, the receipts that would be obtained with present tax rates if the economy were at full employment) minus full-employment government expenditures (that is, actual expenditures less expenditures directly associated with unemployment in excess of the full-employment level).

full-employment GNP. The GNP that would exist if full employment were consistently maintained. Potential GNP.

full-line forcing. See *tying contract.*

fundamental disequilibrium (in international economics). A term used but not defined in the articles of agreement of the International Monetary Fund. The general idea is that a fundamental disequilibrium exists when an international payments imbalance cannot be eliminated without increasing trade restrictions or imposing unduly restrictive aggregate demand policies.

futures market. A market in which contracts are undertaken today at prices specified today for fulfillment at some specified future time. For example, a futures sale of wheat involves the commitment to deliver wheat, say three months from today at a price set now.

gain from trade. Increase in real income that results from specialization and trade. (p. 338).

game theory. Theory dealing with conflict, in which alternative strategies are formally analyzed. Sometimes used in the analysis of oligopoly. (p. 231)

general equilibrium. Situation in which all markets are in equilibrium simultaneously.

general equilibrium analysis. Analysis taking into account interactions among markets.

general glut. Occurs when excess supply is a general phenomenon. The quantity of goods and services that producers are willing to supply greatly exceeds the quantity buyers are willing and able to purchase.

general inflation. An increase in all prices (including wages) by the same percentage, leaving relative prices unchanged.

general price level. Price level as measured by a broad average, such as the consumer price index or the GNP deflator.

Giffen good. A good whose demand curve slopes upward to the right. (p. 118)

Gini coefficient. A measure of inequality derived from the Lorenz curve. It is the "bow" area (in Fig. 38-1 on p. 429) between the curve and the diagonal line divided by the entire area beneath the diagonal line. It can range from zero (if there is no inequality and the Lorenz curve corresponds to the diagonal line) to one (if there is complete inequality and the Lorenz curve runs along the horizontal axis).

GNP (price) deflator. Current-dollar GNP divided by constant dollar GNP, times 100. Measure of the change in prices of the goods and services included in GNP.

GNP gap. Amount by which actual GNP falls short of potential GNP.

gold certificate. Certificate issued by the U.S. Treasury to the Federal Reserve, backed 100% by Treasury holdings of gold.

gold exchange standard. International system in which most countries keep their currencies pegged to, and convertible into, another currency that in turn is pegged to and convertible into gold.

gold point. Under the old gold standard, an exchange rate at which an arbitrager can barely cover the costs of shipping, handling, and insuring gold.

gold standard. System in which the monetary unit is defined in terms of gold, the monetary authorities buy and sell gold freely at that price, gold acts as the ultimate bank reserve, and gold may be freely exported or imported. If central banks follow the "rule of the gold standard game," they allow changes in gold to be reflected in changes in the money stock.

gold sterilization. Occurs when the central bank takes steps to cancel out the automatic effects of the gold flow on the country's money supply (that is, when the "rule of the gold standard game" is broken).

good. Tangible commodity, such as wheat, a shirt, or an automobile. (p. 26)

graduated-payment mortgage. A mortgage on which the money payments rise as time passes, in order to reduce front loading. If the money payments rise rapidly enough to keep real payments constant, then the mortgage is *fully* graduated.

greenmail. The premium over the market price that a firm pays to purchase its stock from a holder who is threatening to take over the company or engage in a proxy fight. (p. 251)

Gresham's law. Crudely, "Bad money drives out good." More precisely: If there are two types of money whose values in exchange are equal while their values in another use (like consumption) are different, the more valuable item will be retained for its other use while the less valuable item will continue to circulate as money. (p. 40)

gross domestic product (GDP). U.S. GDP = U.S. GNP *less* U.S. income from American investments in foreign countries *plus* income earned by foreigners on investments in the United States.

gross national product (GNP). Personal consumption expenditures plus government purchases of goods and services plus gross private domestic investment plus net exports of goods and services. The total product of the nation, excluding double counting.

gross private domestic investment (I_g). Expenditures for new plant, equipment, and new residential buildings, plus the change in inventories.

growth. An increase in the productive capacity of an economy; an outward shift of the production possibilities curve. (p. 30)

Herfindahl-Hirschman index. A measure of concentration. Specifically, the sum of the squared percentage market shares of each of the firms. (p. 218)

high-employment GNP. The GNP that would exist if a high rate of employment were consistently maintained. Potential GNP.

holding company. A company that holds a controlling interest in the stock of one or more other companies.

horizontal merger. See *merger.*

human capital. Education and training that make human beings more productive. (pp. 27, 414)

hyperinflation. Very rapid inflation, at a rate of 1,000% per year or more. (p. 10)

hysteresis. The property of not returning to the original state when a disturbance is removed.

identification problem. The difficulty of determining the effect of variable *a* alone on variable *b* when *b* can also be affected by variables *c, d,* and so on.

impact lag. The time interval between policy changes and the time when the major effects of the policy changes occur.

imperfect competition. A market in which any buyer or seller is able to have a noticeable effect on price. (p. 48)

implicit (or imputed) cost. The opportunity cost of using an input that is already owned by the producer. (p. 148)

implicit GNP deflator. See *GNP (price) deflator.*

implicit tax. A tax built into a welfare program. The benefits a family or individual loses when another $1 of income is earned. For example, if benefits are reduced by 46¢, the implicit tax is 46%. (p. 453)

import (M). Good or service acquired from foreign nationals.

import of capital. Sale of assets to foreign nationals.

import quota. A restriction on the quantity of a good that may be imported.

incidence of a tax. The amount of the tax ultimately paid by different individuals or groups. (For example, how much does a cigarette tax raise the price paid by buyers, and how much does it lower the net price received by sellers?) (p. 93)

income-consumption line. The line or curve traced out by the points of tangency between an indifference map and a series of parallel budget (income) lines. It shows how a consumer responds to a changing income when relative prices remain constant.

income effect. Change in the quantity of a good demanded as a result of a change in real income with no change in relative prices. (p. 117)

income elasticity of demand. See *elasticity of demand.*

income line. See *budget line.*

incomes policy. A government policy (such as wage-price guideposts or wage and price controls) aimed at restraining the rate of increase in money wages and other money incomes. The purpose is to reduce the rate of inflation.

income statement. An accounting statement that summarizes a firm's revenues, costs, and income taxes over a given period of time (usually a year). A profit-and-loss statement. (p. 132)

increasing returns to scale. Occurs when an increase of $x\%$ in all inputs results in an increase in output of more than $x\%$. Economies of scale. (p. 146)

incremental cost. The term that business executives frequently use instead of "marginal cost."

incremental revenue. The term that business executives frequently use instead of "marginal revenue."

index. A series of numbers, showing how an average (of prices, or wages, or some other economic measure) changes through time. Each of these numbers is called an index number. By convention, the index number for the base year is set at 100.

indexation. The inclusion of an *escalator clause* in a contract or law. An increase in the wage rate, tax brackets, or other dollar measure by the same proportion as the increase in the average level of prices.

indifference curve. A curve joining all points among which the consumer is indifferent. (p. 113)

indifference map. A series of indifference curves, each representing a different level of satisfaction or utility. (p. 114)

indirect tax. A tax that is thought to be passed on to others, and not borne by the one who originally pays it. Examples: sales taxes; excise taxes; import duties.

induced investment. Additional investment demand that results from an increase in national product.

industrial union. A union open to all workers in an industry, regardless of their skill. Example: the United Auto Workers. Contrast with *craft union.* (p. 388)

industry. The producers of a single good or service (or closely similar goods or services). (p. 49)

inelastic demand. Demand with an elasticity whose absolute value is less than 1. A fall in price causes a fall in total expenditure on the product in question, because the percentage change in quantity demanded is less than the percentage change in price. (pp. 85–88)

inelastic supply. Supply with an elasticity of less than 1. A supply curve which, if extended in a straight line, would meet the horizontal axis. (p. 91)

infant-industry argument for protection. The proposition that new domestic industries with economies of scale or large requirements of human capital need protection from foreign producers until they can become established. (p. 353)

inferior good. A good for which the quantity demand decreases as income rises, *ceteris paribus.* (p. 53).

inflation. A rise in the average level of prices. (p. 9)

inflationary gap. The vertical distance by which the aggregate expenditures line is above the 45° line at the full-employment quantity of national product. The opposite of a recessionary gap.

infrastructure. Basic facilities such as roads, power plants, and telephone systems.

inheritance tax. Tax imposed on property received from a person who has died.

injection. Expenditure for a GNP component other than consumption. Example: investment or government expenditures for goods and services.

injunction. Court order to refrain from certain practices or requiring certain action. (p. 389)

innovation. A change in products or in the techniques of production.

inputs. Materials and services used in the process of production.

interest. Payment for the use of money.

interest rate. Interest as a percentage per annum of the amount borrowed.

interlocking directorate. Situation in which one or more directors of a company sit on the boards of directors of one or more other companies that are competitors, suppliers, or customers of the first company. (p. 243)

intermediate good or intermediate product. A product intended for resale or further processing.

internal cost. Costs incurred by those who actually produce (or consume) a good. Contrast with *external cost.*

internalization. A process that results in a firm or individual being penalized (or rewarded) for an external cost (or benefit) of its actions. (p. 318)

international adjustment mechanism. Any set of forces that tends to reduce surpluses or deficits in the balance of payments.

international liquidity. The total amount of international reserves (foreign exchange, special drawing rights, etc.) held by the various nations.

inventories. Stocks of raw materials, intermediate products, and finished goods held by producers or marketing organizations.

investment. (1) Accumulation of capital. Unless otherwise specified, economists use the term "investment" to mean *real* investment (the accumulation of real capital such as machinery or buildings) rather than financial investment (such as the acquisition of bonds). (p. 28) See also *gross private domestic investment* and *net private domestic investment.*

investment bank. A firm that markets common stocks, bonds, and other securities.

investment demand. (Also known as *desired investment* or *planned investment*). This is the amount of new plant, equipment, and housing acquired during the year, plus additions to inventories that businesses wanted to acquire. Actual investment less undesired inventory accumulation.

investment good. A capital good; plant, equipment, or inventory.

investment, private domestic. See *gross private domestic investment* and *net private domestic investment.*

investment tax credit. A provision at one time in the tax code providing a reduction in taxes to those who acquire capital goods.

invisible. An intangible; a service (as contrasted with a good).

"invisible hand." Adam Smith's phrase expressing the idea that the pursuit of self-interest by individuals will lead to a desirable outcome for society as a whole. (p. 5)

iron law of wages. The view, commonly held in the nineteenth century, that the human propensity to reproduce causes a tendency for the supply of labor to outrun the productive capacity of the economy and the demand for labor. As a consequence, an iron law of nature was at work to drive wages down to the subsistence level. (Any excess population at that wage would die from starvation, pestilence, or war.)

jawbone. To persuade; to attempt to persuade, perhaps using threats.

joint products. Goods such that the rise in the price of one causes a rightward shift in the supply curve of the other. Complements in production. Products produced together. Examples: meat and hides. (p. 55)

joint profit maximization. Formal or informal cooperation by oligopolists to pick the price that yields the most profit for the group. (p. 223)

jurisdictional dispute. Dispute between unions over whose workers will be permitted to perform a certain task. (p. 390)

key currency. A national currency commonly used by foreigners in international transactions and by foreign monetary authorities when intervening in exchange markets. Examples: the U.S. dollar, and, historically, the British pound.

Keynesian economics. The major macroeconomic propositions put forward by John Maynard Keynes in *The General Theory of Employment, Interest and Money (1936),* namely: A market economy may reach an equilibrium with large-scale unemployment; steps to stimulate aggregate demand can cure a depression; and fiscal policies are the best way to control aggregate demand. Contrast with *classical economics.*

kinked demand curve. A demand curve that an oligopoly firm faces if its competitors follow any price cut it makes but do not follow any of its price increase. The kink in such a demand curve occurs at the existing price. (p. 227)

L. M3 + U.S. savings bonds + short-term Treasury securities + short-term marketable securities issued by corporations; liquid assets.

labor. The physical and mental contributions of people to production. (p. 26)

labor force. The number of people employed plus those actively seeking work.

labor-intensive product. A good whose production uses a relatively large quantity of labor and a relatively small quantity of other resources.

labor participation rate. See *participation rate.*

labor productivity. See *productivity of labor.*

labor theory of value. Strictly, the proposition that the sole source of value is labor (including labor "congealed" in capital). Loosely, the proposition that labor is the principal source of value. (p. 465)

labor union. See *union.*

Laffer curve. A curve showing how tax revenues change as the tax rate changes.

laissez faire. Strictly translated, "let do." More loosely, "leave it alone." An expression used by the French physiocrats and later by Adam Smith, meaning the absence of government intervention in markets. (p. 5)

land. A term used broadly by economists to include not only arable land, but also the other gifts of nature (such as minerals) that come with the land. (p. 26)

law of diminishing marginal utility. As a consumer gets more and more of a good, the marginal utility of that good will (eventually) decrease. (p. 103)

law of eventually diminishing returns. If technology is unchanged, then the use of more and more units of a variable input, together with one or more fixed inputs, must eventually lead to a declining marginal product of the variable input. (p. 141)

leading indicator. A time series that reaches a turning point (peak or trough) before the economy as a whole.

legal tender. The item or items that creditors must accept in payment of debts.

leakage. (1) A withdrawal of potential spending from the circular flow of income and expenditures; saving, taxes, and imports. (2) A withdrawal from the banking system that reduces the potential expansion of the money stock.

leakages-injections approach. The determination of equilibrium national product by finding the size of the product at which leakages are equal to injections.

legal tender. An item that creditors must, by law, accept in payment of a debt.

leverage. The ratio of debt to net worth. (p. 126)

leveraged buyout. The purchase of a corporation, financed in such a way as to increase leverage—that is, by borrowing. (p. 251)

liability. (1) What is owed. (2) The amount that can be lost by the owners of a business if that business goes bankrupt. (p. 121)

life-cycle hypothesis. The proposition that consumption depends on expected lifetime income (as contrasted with the early Keynesian view that consumption depends on current income).

limited liability. The amount an owner-shareholder of a corporation can lose in the event of bankruptcy. This is limited to the amount paid to purchase shares of the corporation. (p. 121)

limited partnership. An organization that avoids the corporate disadvantage of double taxation, while providing the corporate advantage of limited liability to some of its owners. (p. 122)

line of credit. Commitment by a bank or other lender to stand ready to lend up to a specified amount to a customer on request. (p. 126)

liquid asset. An asset that can be sold on short notice, at a predictable price, with little cost or bother.

liquidity. Ease with which an asset can be sold on short notice, at a predictable price, with little cost. (p. 125)

liquidity preference. The demand for money—that is, the willingness to hold money as a function of the interest rate.

liquidity preference theory of the interest rate. The theory put forward by J. M. Keynes that the interest rate is determined by the willingness to hold money (liquidity preference) and the supply of money (that is, the stock of money in existence). Contrast with *loanable funds theory of interest.*

liquidity trap. In Keynesian theory, the situation in which individuals and businesses are willing to hold all their additional financial assets in the form of money—rather than bonds or other debt instruments—at the existing interest rate. In such circumstances, the creation of additional money by the central bank cannot depress the interest rate further, and monetary policy cannot be effectively used to stimulate aggregate demand. (All additional money created is caught in the liquidity trap and is held as idle balances.) In geometric terms, the liquidity trap exists where the liquidity preference curve (the demand for money) is horizontal.

loanable funds theory of interest. The theory that the interest rate is determined by the demand for and the supply of funds in the market for bonds and other forms of debt. Contrast with *the liquidity preference theory of interest.*

lockout. Temporary closing of a factory or other place of business in order to deprive workers of their jobs. A bargaining tool sometimes used in labor disputes; the employer's equivalent of a strike.

logarithmic (or log or ratio) scale. A scale in which equal proportional changes are shown as equal distances. For example, the distance from 100 to 200 is equal to the distance from 200 to 400. (Each involves a doubling.) (p. 20)

long run. (1) A period long enough for prices and wages to adjust to their equilibrium levels. (2) A period long enough for equilibrium to be reached. (3) A period of time long enough for the quantity of all inputs, including capital, to be adjusted to the desired level. (p. 135) (4) Any extended period.

long-run Phillips curve. The curve (or line) traced out by the possible points of long-run equilibrium, that is, the points where people have adjusted completely to the prevailing rate of inflation.

long-run production function. A table showing various combinations of inputs and the maximum output that can be produced with each combination. For a simple firm with only two inputs (labor and capital), the production function can be shown by a two-dimensional table. (p. 152)

Lorenz curve. A curve showing cumulative percentages of income or wealth. For example, a point on a Lorenz curve might show the percentage of income received by the poorest half of the families. (The cumulative percentage of income is shown on the vertical axis. The family with the lowest income is counted first, and then other families are successively added in the order of their incomes. The cumulative percentage of families is on the horizontal axis). Such a curve can be used to measure inequality; if all families have the same income, the Lorenz curve traces out a diagonal line. See also *Gini coefficient.* (p. 429)

lump-sum tax. A tax of a constant amount. The revenues from such a tax do not change when income changes.

M1. The narrowly defined money stock; currency (paper money plus coins) plus checking deposits plus travelers' checks held by the public (that is, excluding holdings of currency, etc., by the federal government, the Federal Reserve, and commercial banks).

M2. A more broadly defined money stock; M1 plus noncheckable savings deposits plus small time deposits plus money market mutual fund accounts.

M3. An even more broadly defined money stock; M2 plus large time deposits.

macroeconomics. The study of the overall aggregates of the economy, such as total employment, the unemployment rate, national product, and the rate of inflation.

Malthusian problem. The tendency for population to outstrip productive capacity, particularly the capacity to produce food. This is the supposed consequence of a tendency for population to grow geometrically (1, 2, 4, 8, etc.) while the means of subsistence grows arithmetically (1, 2, 3, 4, etc.). The pressure of population will tend to depress the wage rate to the subsistence level and keep it there, with the excess population being eliminated by war, pestilence, or starvation. A problem described by Thomas Malthus in his *Essay on the Principle of Population* (1798).

managed float. A dirty float. *See floating (or flexible) exchange rate.*

marginal. The term commonly used by economists to mean "additional." For example, *marginal cost* is the additional cost when one more unit is produced; *marginal revenue* is the addition to revenue when one more unit is sold; and *marginal utility* is the utility or satisfaction received from consuming one more unit of a good or service.

marginal cost pricing. Setting price at the level where marginal cost intersects the demand curve. (p. 205)

marginal efficiency of investment. The schedule or curve relating desired investment to the rate of interest. The investment demand curve.

marginal physical product. The additional output when one more unit of an input is used (with all other inputs being held constant). For example, the *marginal physical product of labor* (often abbreviated to the *marginal product of labor*) is the additional output when one more unit of labor is used. (p. 141)

marginal product. (1) Strictly, the marginal physical product. (2) Sometimes, the value of the marginal physical product. (p. 141)

marginal propensity to consume (MPC). The change in consumption expenditures divided by the change in disposable income.

marginal propensity to import. The change in imports of goods and services divided by the change in GNP.

marginal propensity to save (MPS). The change in saving divided by the change in disposable income. 1 – MPC.

marginal rate of substitution. The slope of the indifference curve. The ratio of the marginal utilities of two goods. (p. 114)

marginal revenue product. The additional revenue when the firm uses one additional unit of an input (with all other inputs being held constant). (p. 372)

marginal tax rate. The fraction of additional income paid in taxes. (p. 69)

marginal utility. The satisfaction an individual receives from consuming one additional unit of good or service. (p. 103)

margin call. The requirement by a lender who holds stocks (or bonds) as security that more money be put up or the stocks (or bonds) will be sold. A margin call may be issued when the price of the stocks (or bonds) declines, making the stocks (or bonds) less adequate as security for the loan.

margin requirement. The minimum percentage that purchasers of stocks or bonds must put up in their own money. For example, if the margin requirement on stock is 60%, the buyer must put up at least 60% of the price in his or her own money and can borrow no more than 40% from a bank or stockbroker.

market. An institution in which purchases and sales are made. (p. 46)

market economy. See *free market economy.*

market failure. The failure of market forces to bring about the best allocation of resources. For example, when production of a good generates pollution, too many resources tend to go into the production of that good and not enough into the production of alternative goods and services.

market mechanism. The system whereby prices and the interaction of demand and supply help to answer the major economic questions "What will be produced?" "How?" and "For whom?" (p. 59)

market power. The ability of a single firm or individual to influence the market price of a good or service. (p. 48)

market-power inflation. See *cost-push inflation.*

market share. Percentage of an industry's sales accounted for by a single firm.

market structure. Characteristics that affect the behavior of firms in a market, such as the number of firms, the possibility of collusion, the degree of product differentiation, and the ease of entry.

Marxist economy. An economy in which most of the capital is owned by the government. (Individuals may, of course, own small capital goods, such as hoes or hammers, but the major forms of capital—factories and heavy machinery—are owned by the state.) Political power is in the hands of a party pledging allegiance to the doctrines of Karl Marx.

measure of economic welfare (MEW). A comprehensive measure of economic well-being. Per capita real national product is adjusted to take into account leisure, pollution, and other such influences on welfare.

median. The item in the middle (that is, half of all items are above the median and half are below).

medium of exchange. Money; any item that is generally acceptable in exchange for goods or services; any item that is commonly used in buying goods or services. (p. 39)

member bank. A bank that belongs to the Federal Reserve System.

mercantilism. The theory that national prosperity can be promoted by a positive balance of trade and the accumulation of precious metals.

merchandise account surplus. The excess of merchandise exports over merchandise imports.

merger. The bringing together of two or more firms under common control through purchase, exchange of common stock, or other means. *A horizontal merger* brings together competing firms. *A vertical merger* brings together firms that are each others' suppliers or customers. *A conglomerate merger* brings together firms that are not related in any of these ways. (p. 245)

merit good. A good or service that the government considers particularly desirable and that it therefore encourages by subsidy or regulation—such as the regulation that children must go to school to get the merit good of education. (p. 76)

microeconomics. The study of individual units within the economy—such as households, firms, and industries—and their interrelationships. The study of the allocation of resources and the distribution of income. (p. 81)

midpoint formula. The elasticity formula that uses the average of price and average of quantity, rather than either end point. (p. 86)

military-industrial complex. The combined political power exerted by military officers and defense industries; those with a vested interest in military spending. (In his farewell address, President Eisenhower warned against the military-industrial complex.)

minimum efficient scale. The output at which the average total cost curve reaches its minimum and becomes level. (p. 146)

minimum wage. The lowest wage that an employer may legally pay for an hour's work. (p. 378)

mint parity. The exchange rate calculated from the official prices of gold in two countries under the gold standard.

mixed economy. An economy in which the private market and the government share the decisions as to what will be produced, how, and for whom.

model. The essential features of an economy or economic problem, explained in terms of diagrams, equations, or words—or some combination of these.

monetarism. A body of thought that has its roots in classical economics and that rejects much of the teaching of Keynes' *General Theory.* According to monetarists, the most important determinant of aggregate demand is the quantity of money; the economy is basically stable if monetary growth is stable; and the authorities should follow a monetary rule, aiming for a steady growth of the money stock. Many monetarists also believe that the effects of fiscal policy on aggregate demand are weak (unless accompanied by changes in the quantity of money), that the government plays too active a role in the economy, and that the long-run Phillips curve is vertical.

monetary base. Currency held by the general public and by commercial banks plus the deposits of commercial banks in the Federal Reserve.

monetary policy. Central bank policies aimed at changing the rate of growth of the money stock or of interest rates. Example: open market operations or changes in required reserve ratios.

monetary rule. The rule, proposed by monetarists, that the central bank should aim for a steady rate of growth of the money stock.

money. Any item commonly used in buying goods or services. Frequently, M1.

money illusion. Strictly defined, people have money illusion if their behavior changes in the event of a proportional change in prices, money incomes, and assets and liabilities measured in money terms. More loosely, people have money illusion if their behavior changes when there is a proportional change in prices and money incomes.

money income. Income measured in dollars (or, in another country, income measured in the currency of that country).

money market. The market for short-term debt instruments.

money multiplier. The number of dollars by which the money stock can increase as a result of a $1 increase in the reserves of commercial banks.

money stock (or supply). Narrowly, M1. More broadly and less commonly, M2 or M3.

monopolistic competition. A market structure with many firms selling a differentiated product, with low barriers to entry. Individual firms have some small influence over price. (p. 215)

monopoly. (1) A market in which there is only a single seller. (pp. 48, 192) (2) The single seller in such a market. A *natural monopoly* occurs when the average total cost of a single firm falls over such an extended range that one firm can produce the total quantity sold at a lower average cost than could two or more firms. (p. 194)

monopoly rent. Above-normal profit of a monopoly. (p. 421)

monopsony. A market in which there is only one buyer. (p. 393)

moral hazard. Any tendency for those who are protected (for example, by guarantees or insurance) to behave less carefully because they are protected. (p. 184)

moral suasion. Appeals or pressure by the Federal Reserve Board intended to influence the behavior of commercial banks.

most-favored-nation clause. A clause in a trade agreement that commits a country to impose no greater barriers (tariffs, etc.) on imports from a second country than it imposes on imports from any other country.

multinational corporation. A corporation that carries on business (either directly or through subsidiaries) in more than one country.

multiplier. The change in equilibrium real national product divided by the change in desired investment (or in government expenditures or exports). In the simplest economy (with a marginal tax rate of zero and no imports), the multiplier is 1 ÷ (the marginal propensity to save). See also *checking deposit multiplier.*

municipals. Bonds or shorter term securities issued by municipal governments.

Nash equilibrium. Equilibrium that exists when each firm has made its best choice, on the assumption that the other firms stick to their existing strategies.

national bank. A commercial bank chartered by the national government.

national debt. (1) The outstanding debt of the federal government. (2) The outstanding federal government debt excluding that held by federal government trust funds. (3) The outstanding federal government debt excluding that held by federal government trust funds and the 12 Federal Reserve Banks.

national income. The sum of all income of a nation, derived from providing the factors of production. It includes wages and salaries, rents, interest, and profits.

national product. The money value of the goods and services produced by a nation during a specific time period, such as a year. See *gross national product* and *net national product.*

natural monopoly. See *monopoly.*

natural oligopoly. See *oligopoly.*

natural rate of interest. The equilibrium rate of interest; the rate of interest consistent with a stable price level.

natural rate of unemployment. The equilibrium rate of unemployment that exists when people have adjusted completely to the existing rate of inflation. The rate of unemployment to which the economy tends when those making labor and other contracts correctly anticipate the rate of inflation. The rate of unemployment consistent with a stable rate of inflation.

near money. A highly liquid asset that can be quickly and easily converted into money. Examples: a savings deposit or a Treasury bill.

negative income tax. A reverse income tax whereby the government makes payments to individuals and families with low incomes. (The lower the income, the greater the payment from the government.) (p. 458)

negotiable order of withdrawal (NOW). A check-like order to pay funds from an interest-bearing savings deposit.

neocolonialism. The domination of the economy of a nation by the business firms or government of another nation or nations.

net exports. Exports minus imports.

net national product (NNP). Personal consumption expenditures plus government purchases of goods and services plus net private domestic investment plus net exports of goods and services. GNP minus capital consumption allowances.

net private domestic investment (I_n). Gross (private domestic) investment minus capital consumption allowances.

net worth. Total assets less total liabilities. The value of ownership. (p. 132)

neutrality of money. Occurs when a change in the quantity of money affects only the price level without affecting relative prices or the distribution of income.

neutrality of taxes. (1) A situation in which taxes do not affect relative prices, and therefore disturb market forces as little as possible. (p. 72) (2) The absence of an excess burden of taxes.

New Left. Radical economists; Marxists of the 1960s and 1970s.

nominal. Measured in money terms. Current dollar as contrasted to constant dollar or real.

noncompeting groups. Groups of workers that do not compete with each other for jobs because their training or skills are different.

nonprice competition. Competition by means other than price. Example: advertising or product differentiation. (p. 230)

nontariff barrier (NTB). Government-imposed impediment to trade other than tariffs. Example: an import quota.

normal good. A good for which the quantity demanded rises as income rises, *ceteris paribus.* Contrast with an *inferior good.* (p. 53)

normal profit. The opportunity cost of capital and/or entrepreneurship. (Normal profit is considered a cost by economists but not by business accountants.) (p. 148)

normative statement. A statement about what should be. (p. 33) Contrast with a *positive statement.*

NOW account. A savings account against which a negotiable order of withdrawal (a check) may be written.

official settlements surplus. The balance-of-payments surplus of a country acquiring net international reserves (that is, a country whose international reserves are increasing more rapidly than foreign countries' reserve claims on it).

Okun's law. The observation that a change of 2% to 3% in real GNP (compared with its long-run trend) has been associated with a 1% change in the opposite direction in the unemployment rate. (Named after Arthur M. Okun.) (p. *110*)

old age, survivors, and disability insurance. Social security.

oligopoly. A market that is dominated by a few sellers; they may sell either a standardized or differentiated product. (p. 48) A **natural oligopoly** occurs when the average total costs of individual firms fall over a large enough range that a few firms can produce the total quantity sold at the lowest average cost. (p. 220) (Compare with *natural monopoly.*)

oligopsony. A market in which there are only a few buyers.

open economy. An economy that has transactions with foreign nations.

open market operation. The purchase (or sale) of government (or other) securities by the central bank on the open market (that is, not directly from the issuer of the security). A purchase of securities causes an increase in bank deposits; a sale causes a decrease.

open shop. A business that may hire workers who are not (and need not become) union members. Contrast with *closed shop* and *union shop.* (p. 390)

opportunity cost. (1) The alternative that must be foregone when something is produced. (p. 29) (2) The amount that an input could earn in its best alternative use. (p. 147)

optimal purchase rule. A rule for maximizing the utility from a given income, by choosing the consumption pattern in such a way as to equalize the ratio of marginal utility to price for all goods and services purchased. (p. 108)

output gap. The amount by which output falls short of the potential or full-employment level. The GNP gap.

panic. A rush for safety, historically marked by a switch out of bank deposits into currency and out of paper currency into gold. A run on banks. A *stock market panic* occurs when there is a rush to sell and stock prices collapse. (p. 128)

paradox of thrift. The paradoxical situation, pointed out by Keynes, whereby an increase in the desire to save can result in a decrease in the equilibrium quantity of saving.

paradox of value. The apparent contradiction, pointed out by Adam Smith, when an essential (such as water) has a low price while a nonessential (such as a diamond) has a high price. (p. 107)

Pareto improvement. Making one person better off without making anyone else worse off. (Named after Vilfredo Pareto, 1848–1923.) (p. 179)

Pareto optimum. A situation in which it is impossible to make any Pareto improvement. That is, it is impossible to make any individual better off without making someone else worse off. (p. 179)

parity price. The price of a farm product (such as wheat) that would allow a farmer to exchange it for the same quantity of nonfarm goods as in the 1910–1914 base period. (A concept of fair price used in American agricultural policy since the Agricultural Adjustment Act of 1933.) (p. 268)

partial equilibrium analysis. Analysis of a particular market or set of markets, ignoring feedback from other markets.

participation rate. Number of people in the civilian labor force as a percentage of the civilian population of working age.

partnership. An unincorporated business owned by two or more people. (p. 119)

par value of a currency. Up to 1971, under the IMF adjustable peg system, the par value was the official price of a currency specified in terms of the U.S. dollar or gold.

patent. Exclusive right, granted by the government to an inventor, to use an invention for a specified time period. (Such a right can be licensed or sold by the patent holder.)

payoff matrix. A grid showing the various possible outcomes when two or more individuals are engaged in a cooperative or competitive activity. (p. 233)

payroll tax. A tax levied on wages and salaries, or on wages and salaries up to a specified limit. Example: social security tax.

peak. The month of greatest economic activity prior to the onset of a recession; one of the four phases of the business cycle.

peak-load pricing. Setting the price for a good or service higher during periods of heavy demand than at other times. The purpose is to encourage buyers to choose nonpeak periods and/or to raise more revenue. Examples: electricity; weekend ski tow.

pegged. Fixed by the authorities, at least temporarily. Examples: pegged interest rates (1941–1951); pegged exchange rates (1945–1973).

penalty rate. A discount rate kept consistently above a short-term market rate of interest (such as the rate on Treasury bills).

perfect competition. A market with many buyers and many sellers, with no single buyer or seller having any (noticeable) influence over price. That is, every buyer and every seller is a *price taker.* (For detailed characteristics of perfect competition, see p. 158.)

permanent income. Normal income; income that is thought to be normal.

permanent-income hypothesis. The proposition that the principal determinant of consumption is permanent income (rather than current income).

perpetuity (or "perp"). A bond with no maturity date that pays interest forever.

personal consumption expenditures. See *consumption.*

personal income. Income received by households in return for productive services, and from transfers.

personal saving. (1) Loosely but commonly, disposable personal income less consumption expenditures. (2) More strictly, disposable personal income less consumption expenditures less payment of interest on consumer debt.

petrodollars. Liquid U.S. dollar assets held by oil-exporting nations, representing revenues received from the export of oil.

Phillips curve. The curve tracing out the relationship between the unemployment rate (on the horizontal axis) and the inflation rate or the rate of change of money wages (on the vertical axis). The *long-run Phillips curve* is the curve (or line) tracing out the relationship between the unemployment rate and the inflation rate when the inflation rate is stable and correctly anticipated.

planned investment. Desired investment; investment demand; *ex ante* investment.

plant. A physical establishment where production takes place. (p. 49)

policy dilemma. Occurs when a policy that helps to solve one problem makes another worse.

political business cycle. A business cycle caused by actions of politicians designed to increase their chances of reelection.

positive statement. A statement about what is (or was) or about how something works. (p. 33) Contrast with a *normative statement.*

potential output (or potential GNP). The GNP that would exist if a high rate of employment were consistently maintained.

poverty. A condition that exists when people have inadequate income to buy the necessities of life. (p. 11)

poverty level (or poverty standard). An estimate of the income needed to avoid poverty. In 1988 it was $12,075 for a family of four. (p. 11)

precautionary demand for money. The amount of money that households and businesses want to hold to protect themselves against unforeseen events.

preferred stock. A stock that is given preference over common stock when dividends are paid. That is, specified dividends must be paid on preferred stock before any dividend is paid on common stock.

premature inflation. Inflation that occurs before the economy reaches full employment.

present value. The value now of a future receipt or receipts, calculated using the interest rate, i. The present value (PV) of $X to be received n years hence is $\$X \div (1 + i)^n$.

price ceiling. The legally established maximum price.

price discrimination. The sale of the same good or service at different prices to different customers or in different markets, provided the price differences are not justified by cost differences such as differences in transportation costs. (p. 205)

price-earnings ratio. The ratio of the price of a stock to the annual (after-tax) earnings per share of the stock.

price elasticity of demand (supply). See *elasticity of demand (supply).*

price floor. (1) The price at which the government undertakes to buy all surpluses, thus preventing any further decline in price. (2) The legally established minimum price.

price index. A weighted average of prices, as a percentage of prices existing in a base year.

price leadership. A method by which oligopolistic firms establish similar prices without overt collusion. One firm (the price leader) announces a new price, expecting that the other firm or firms will follow. (p. 229)

price line. See *budget line.*

price maker. A monopolist (or monopsonist) who is able to set price because there are no competitors. (p. 196).

price mechanism. See *market mechanism.*

price parity. See *parity price.*

price searcher. A seller (or buyer) who is able to influence price, and who has competitors whose responses can affect the profit-maximizing price. An oligopolist (or oligopsonist). (p. 222)

price support. A commitment by the government to buy surpluses at a given price (the support price) in order to prevent the price from falling below that figure. (p. 269)

price system. See *market mechanism.*

price taker. A seller or buyer who is unable to affect the price and whose market decision is limited to the quantity to be sold or bought at the existing market price. A seller or buyer in a perfectly competitive market. (p. 196)

price-wage flexibility. The ease with which prices and wages rise or fall (especially fall) in the event of changing demand and supply. Contrast with *price-wage stickiness.*

price-wage stickiness. The resistance of prices and wages to a movement, particularly in a downward direction.

primary burden of a tax. The amount of tax collected. Compare with *excess burden of a tax.* (p. 172)

prime rate of interest. (1) a bank's publicly announced interest rate on short-term loans. (2) Historically, the interest rate charged by banks on loans to their most creditworthy customers.

prisoners' dilemma. The dilemma as to whether or not you should confess, when a confederate may implicate you. The dilemma arises when a person who confesses receives a smaller penalty than a person who is implicated by a confederate. (p. 233)

private domestic investment. The production of private (nongovernmental) capital during a time period, including (1) plant and equipment, (2) residential buildings, and (3) additions to inventories.

privatization. The sale of government-owned businesses and assets to private firms or individuals. (p. 77)

procyclical policy. A policy that increases the amplitude of business fluctuations. ("Procyclical" refers to results, not intentions.)

producer surplus. Net benefit that producers get from being able to sell a good at the existing price. Returns to capital, entrepreneurship, workers, and others in the productive process in excess of their opportunity costs. Economic rent. Measured by the area left of the supply curve and below the existing price. (p. 171)

product differentiation. See *differentiated products.*

production function. The relationship showing the maximum output that can be produced with various combinations of inputs. (p. 140)

production possibilities curve. A curve showing the alternative combinations of outputs that can be produced if all productive resources are used. The boundary of attainable combinations of outputs. (p. 27)

productivity. Output per unit of input.

productivity of labor. The *average* productivity of labor is total output divided by the units of labor input. The *marginal* productivity of labor is the additional output when one more unit of labor is added, while all other factors are held constant. (p. 141)

profit. In economics, return to capital and/or entrepreneurship over and above normal profit. (p. 149) In business accounting, revenues minus costs. (p. 148) Also sometimes used to mean profit after the payment of corporate income taxes. (p. 134)

profit-and-loss statement. An accounting statement that summarizes a firm's revenues, costs, and income taxes over a given period of time (usually a year). An income statement. (p. 134)

progressive tax. A tax that takes a larger percentage of income as income rises. (p. 69)

proletariat. Karl Marx's term for the working class, especially the industrial working class. (p. 466)

proportional tax. A tax that takes the same percentage of income regardless of the level of income. (p. 69)

proprietors' income. The income of unincorporated firms.

prospectus. A statement of the financial condition and prospects of a corporation, presented when new securities are about to be issued.

protectionism. The advocacy or use of high or higher tariffs to protect domestic producers from foreign competition.

protective tariff. A tariff intended to protect domestic producers from foreign competition (as contrasted with a *revenue tariff,* intended as a source of revenue for the government).

proxy. A temporary written transfer of voting rights at a shareholders' meeting.

proxy fight. A struggle between competing groups in a corporation to obtain a majority vote (and therefore control of the corporation) by collecting proxies of shareholders.

public debt. See *national debt.*

public good. See *pure public good.*

public utility. A firm that is the sole supplier of an essential good or service in an area and is owned or regulated by the government. (p. 214)

pump priming. Short-term increases in government expenditures aimed at generating an upward momentum of the economy toward full employment.

purchasing power of money. The value of money in buying goods and services. The change in the purchasing power of money is measured by the change in the fraction 1 ÷ the price index. *General purchasing power* is something that can be used to buy any of the goods and services offered for sale; money. (p. 37)

purchasing-power parity theory. The theory that changes in exchange rates reflect and compensate for differences in the rate of inflation in different countries, leaving real exchange rates stable.

pure fiscal policy. A change in government spending or tax rates, unaccompanied by any change in the rate of growth of the money stock.

pure public good. A good (or service) with inexhaustible benefits that people cannot be excluded from enjoying, regardless of who pays for the good. (p. 319)

qualitative controls. In monetary policy, controls that affect the supply of funds to specific markets, such as the stock market; selective controls. Contrast with *quantitative controls.*

quantitative controls. In monetary policy, controls that affect the total supply of funds and the total quantity of money in an economy.

quantity theory (of money). The proposition that velocity is reasonably stable and that a change in the quantity of money will therefore cause nominal national product to change by approximately the same percentage.

quota. A numerical limit. Example: a limit on the amount of a good that may be imported.

random sample. A sample chosen from a larger group in such a way that every member of the group has an equal chance of being chosen.

rate base. Allowable capital of a public utility, to which the regulatory agency applies the allowable rate of return.

rate of exchange. The price of one national currency in terms of another.

rate of interest. Interest as a percentage per annum of the amount borrowed.

rate of return. (1) Annual profit as a percentage of net worth. (2) Additional annual revenue from the sale of goods or services produced by plant or equipment, less depreciation and operating costs such as labor and materials, expressed as a percentage of the value of the plant or equipment.

rational expectations. The best forecasts that can be made with available information, including information on (1) what the authorities are doing, and (2) how the economy works. If expectations are rational, people may make mistakes, but they do not make *systematic* mistakes. Their errors are random.

rationing. (1) A method for allocating a good (or service) when the quantity demand exceeds the quantity supplied at the existing price. (2) More loosely, any method for allocating a scarce resource or good. In this sense, we may speak of the market *rationing by price.*

ratio (or logarithmic) scale. A scale in which equal proportional changes are shown as equal distances. For example, the distance from 100 to 200 is equal to the distance from 200 to 400. (Each involves a doubling.) (p. 20)

Reaganomics. The economic program of President Reagan, including (1) tax cuts, (2) restraint in domestic spending, (3) increases in defense spending, and (4) less regulation. (p. 70)

real. Measured in quantity terms; adjusted to remove the effects of inflation.

real capital. Buildings, equipment, and other materials used in production, which have themselves been produced in the past. Buildings, equipment, and inventories.

real exchange rate. The nominal exchange rate adjusted for differences in inflation.

real wage. The quantity of goods and services that a money wage will buy; the money wage adjusted for inflation.

recession. A decline in output, income, employment, and trade, usually lasting six months to a year and marked by widespread contractions in many sectors of the economy. (p. 9)

recessionary gap. The vertical distance by which the aggregate expenditures line is below the 45° line at the full-employment quantity of national product.

recognition lag. The time interval between the beginning of a problem and the time when the problem is recognized.

regression analysis. A statistical calculation of the relationship between two or more variables.

regressive tax. A tax that takes a smaller percentage of income as income rises. (p. 69)

rent. (1) In economics, any payment to a factor of production in excess of its opportunity cost. (p. 417) (2) A payment by the user of land to the owner. (3) Payments by users to the owners of land, buildings, or equipment.

replacement-cost depreciation. Depreciation based on the current replacement cost of buildings and equipment rather than their original acquisition cost.

required reserve ratio. The fraction of deposit liabilities that a bank must keep in reserves.

required reserves. The reserves that a bank legally must keep. For members of the Federal Reserve System, these reserves are held in the form of currency or deposits with a Federal Reserve Bank.

rescheduling of debt. The renegotiation of the terms of the debt, to give the debtor more time to repay, sometimes including a reduction in the interest rate.

reservation price of a resource. The cost of harvesting the resource today plus the amount necessary to compensate for the reduction in the quantity of the resource available in the future. (p. 304)

reserves. See *required reserves* and *foreign exchange reserves.*

resources. Basic inputs used in the production of goods and services, namely, labor, land, and capital. (p. 26)

restrictive agreement. Agreement among companies to restrain competition through practices such as price fixing or market sharing.

retail price maintenance. Practice whereby a manufacturer sets the minimum retail price of a product, thereby eliminating price competition among retailers of that product.

return to capital. See *rate of return.*

revaluation of a currency. An increase in the par value of the currency.

revenue sharing. Grant by the federal government to a state or local government. *General revenue sharing* involves grants whose use is (practically) unrestricted.

revenue tariff. A tariff intended to provide revenues for the government (as contrasted with a *protective tariff,* intended to protect domestic producers from foreign competition).

Ricardian equivalence theorem. The theorem that the path of consumption will be the same, whether the government finances its spending by taxes or by issuing debt.

right-to-work law. State law making it illegal to require union membership as a condition of employment. State prohibition of closed shops and union shops. (p. 390)

risk premium. The difference between the yields on two grades of bonds (or other securities) because of differences in their risk. The additional interest or yield needed to compensate the holder of bonds (or other securities) for risk. (p. 127)

roundabout production. The production of capital goods and the use of these capital goods in the production of consumer goods. The production of goods in more than one stage.

rule of the gold standard game. The understanding that each country would permit its money stock to change in the same direction as the change in its gold stock. That is, if a country's gold stock were to rise, it should allow its money supply to increase, and vice versa.

rule of 70. A rule that tells approximately how many years it will take for something to double in size if it is growing at a compound rate. For example, a deposit earning 2% interest approximately doubles in $70 \div 2 = 35$ years. In general, a deposit earning x% interest will double in about $70 \div x$ years.

run. A rush to switch into safer assets. Example: a *run on banks.*

satisficing theory. The theory that firms do not try to maximize profits but rather aim for reasonable target levels of profits, sales, and other measures of performance.

saving. (1) Loosely but commonly, disposable personal income less consumption expenditures. (2) More strictly, disposable personal income less consumption expenditures less payment of interest on consumer debt. (3) National saving—that is, personal saving plus business saving plus government saving.

saving function. (1) The relationship between personal saving and disposable income. (2) More broadly, the relationship between personal saving and the factors (like disposable income) that determine saving.

Say's law. The discredited view that supply in the aggregate creates its own demand (regardless of the general price level).

scarcity. (1) The inability to satisfy all wants because they exceed what we can produce with our available resources. (p. 27) (2) A shortage—that is, the amount by which quantity supplied is less than quantity demanded at the existing price. (p. 52)

SDRs. See *special drawing rights.*

seasonal adjustment. The removal of regular seasonal movements from a time series.

secondary boycott. Boycott against a firm to discourage it from doing business with a second firm, in order to exert pressure on the second firm (which may be in a strong position to withstand other forms of pressure).

secondary reserves. Bank holdings of liquid assets (Treasury bills, etc.) that can readily be converted into primary reserves (currency or reserve deposits).

second best, theory of the. The theory of how to get the best results in remaining markets when one or more markets have defects about which nothing can be done. (p. 203)

secular stagnation. A situation of inadequate aggregate demand extending over many years. Consequently, large-scale unemployment persists, and it may even become increasingly severe. (This was considered a major problem half a century ago.)

secular trend. The trend in economic activity over an extended period of years.

selective controls. In monetary policy, controls that affect the supply of funds to specific markets, such as the stock market; qualitative controls.

sell short. See *short sale.*

seniority rules. Rules giving preference to those who have been longest on the job. Individuals with seniority are typically the last to be discharged or laid off, and the first to be rehired. (p. 386)

shortage. (1) The amount by which quantity supplied is less than quantity demanded at the existing price; the opposite of a surplus. (2) Any deficiency. (p. 52)

short run. (1) The period before the price level has adjusted to its equilibrium. (2) The period in which the quantity of plant and equipment cannot change. (3) The time period before equilibrium can be reestablished. (4) Any brief time period.

short-run production function. The table showing the relationship between the amount of variable factors used and the amount of output that can be produced, in a situation where the quantity of capital is constant. For the simple case of a firm with just two inputs—capital and one variable factor—the short-run production function is one row in the long-run production function. (pp. 140, 152)

short sale. A contract to sell something at a later date for a price specified now.

shutdown point. The lowest point on the average variable cost curve. If the price is lower than this point, the firm will shut down. (p. 164)

single-tax proposal. The proposal of Henry George (1839–1897) that all taxes be eliminated except one on land. (George argued that all returns to land represent an unearned surplus.) (p. 422)

slope. The vertical rise in a function divided by the horizontal run. (p. 23)

snake. An agreement among some Western European countries to keep their currencies within a narrow band of fluctuation (the snake). Prior to 1973, they allowed their currencies to move jointly in a wide band with respect to the dollar. (This was called the *snake in the tunnel.*) Since 1973, the snake has not been tied to the dollar.

socialism. An economic system in which the means of production (capital equipment, buildings, and land) are owned by the state. (p. 466)

soil bank program. A government program under which the government pays farmers to take land out of production (in order to reduce crop surpluses).

sole proprietorship. A business owned by an individual person. Contrast with *partnership* and *corporation.* (p. 119)

special drawing rights (SDRs). Bookkeeping accounts created by the International Monetary Fund to increase the quantity of international reserves held by national governments. SDRs can be used to cover balance-of-payments deficits.

specific tax. A fixed number of cents or dollars of tax on each unit of the good. Contrast with *ad valorem tax.*

speculation. The purchase (or sale) of an asset in the hope of making a profit from a rise (fall) in its price. (p. 185)

speculative demand for money. The schedule or curve showing how the rate of interest affects the amount of assets that firms and households are willing to hold in the form of money, rather than in bonds or other interest-bearing securities.

speculator. Anyone who buys or sells an asset in the hope of profiting from a change in its price. (p. 185)

spillover. See *externality.*

stagflation. The coexistence of a high rate of unemployment (stagnation) and inflation.

standard of value. The item (money) in which the prices of goods and services are measured.

state bank. A commercial bank chartered by a state government.

sterilization of gold. See *gold sterilization.*

store of value. An asset that may be used to store wealth through time; an asset that may be used to finance future purchases.

structural budget (or high-employment budget). The size that the government's surplus (or deficit) would be with existing spending programs and tax rates, if the economy were at full employment. Full-employment government receipts (that is, the receipts that would be obtained with present tax rates if the economy were at full employment) minus full-employment government expenditures (that is, actual expenditures less expenditures directly associated with unemployment in excess of the full-employment level).

structural unemployment. Unemployment resulting from a mismatch between the skills or location of the labor force and the skills or location required by employers. Unemployment resulting from a changing location or composition of jobs.

subchapter S corporation. A corporation treated in the tax code as if it were a partnership. Advantage: It avoids double taxation. (p. 122)

subsidy. A negative tax.

subsistence wage. Minimum living wage. A wage below which population will decline because of starvation or disease.

substitute, or substitute in consumption. A good or service that satisfies similar needs. Two commodities are substitutes if a rise in the price of one causes a rightward shift in the demand curve for the other. (p. 53)

substitute in production. A good or service whose production uses the same inputs. Two commodities are substitutes if a rise in the price of one causes a leftward shift in the supply curve of the other. (p. 55)

substitution effect. The change in the quantity of a good demanded because of a change in its price when the real income effect of the change in price has been eliminated. That is, a change in the quantity demanded as a result of a movement along a single indifference curve. See also *income effect.* (p. 117)

sunspot theory. The theory put forward in the late nineteenth century that cycles in sunspot activity cause cycles in agricultural production and hence cycles in business activity.

supply. The schedule or curve showing the quantities of a good or service that sellers would be willing and able to sell at various prices, *ceteris paribus.* (p. 51)

supply of money. See *money stock.*

supply schedule. A table showing the quantities of a good or service that sellers would be willing and able to sell at various prices, *ceteris paribus.* (p. 51)

supply shift. A movement of the supply curve of a good (or service) to the right or left as a result of a change in the price of inputs or any other determinant of the quantity supplied (except the price of the good or service itself). (p. 54)

supply shifter. Anything that affects the quantity of a good or service supplied except its own price. (p. 55)

supply shock. A sudden and unexpected change in the price or availability of inputs that can push costs and the supply curve upward.

supply side. The view that it is supply factors—such as the quantity of capital and the willingness to work—that are the principal constraints to growth. According to this view, a lack of aggregate demand is not the main constraint.

surplus. (1) The amount by which quantity supplied exceeds quantity demanded at the existing price. (p. 52) (2) A *budget surplus:* an excess of government revenues over expenditures. (p. 70) (3) Any excess or amount left over. Contrast with *shortage.*

surplus value. In Marxist economics, the amount by which the value of a worker's output exceeds the wage; a measure of capitalist exploitation. (p. 466)

sustainable yield. The amount of a renewable resource (like fish) that can be harvested while still leaving the population constant. (p. 303)

sympathy strike. A strike by a union that does not have a dispute with its own employer but rather is trying to strengthen the bargaining position of another striking union.

syndicate. An association of investment bankers to market a large block of securities.

tacit collusion. The adoption of a common policy by sellers without explicit agreement. (p. 229)

takeoff. The achievement of the situation of sustained growth, in which capital can be accumulated without depressing the standard of living below its existing level.

target price. Agricultural price guaranteed to farmers by the government. (If the market price falls short of the target price, the government pays farmers the difference.)

tariff. (1) A tax on an imported good; a duty. (2) A schedule or list of duties.

tax-based incomes policy (TIP). An incomes policy backed up with tax penalties on violators or tax incentives for those who cooperate.

tax credit. A subtraction from the tax payable.

tax deduction. A subtraction from taxable income. Suppose an individual pays $1,000 in interest on a home mortgage. This $1,000 can be deducted from taxable income. For someone in the 28% tax bracket, this results in a $280 reduction in taxes.

tax incidence. See *incidence of a tax.*

tax neutrality. (1) A situation in which taxes do not affect relative prices. (2) A situation in which the excess burden of taxes is zero. (p. 72)

tax shifting. Occurs when the initial taxpayer transfers all or part of a tax to others. (For example, a firm that is taxed may charge a higher price.) (p. 93)

technological (or technical) efficiency. Providing the maximum output with the available resources and technology, while working at a reasonable pace. The avoidance of wasted motion and sloppy management. (p. 10)

terms of trade. The average price of goods sold divided by the average price of goods bought. (p. 353)

theory of games. See *game theory.*

theory of public choice. Theory of how government spending decisions are made and how they should be made.

third world. Countries that are neither in the "first" world (the high-income countries of Western Europe and North America, plus a few others such as Japan) nor in the "second" world (the countries of Eastern Europe). Low-income countries.

time preference. The desire to have goods now rather than in the future. The amount by which goods now are preferred over goods in the future. (p. 409)

time series. A set of observations taken in successive time periods. Examples: GNP in 1988, in 1989, in 1990, etc. (p. 18)

TIP. See *tax-based incomes policy.*

total cost. The sum of fixed costs and variable costs.

total revenue. Total receipts from the sale of a product. Where there is a single price, that price times the quantity sold.

transactions demand for money. The amount of money that firms and individuals want to cover the time between the receipt of income and the making of expenditures.

transfer payment. A payment, usually made by the government to private individuals, that does not result from current productive activity and is not compensation for services rendered. (p. 67)

transfer price. The price necessary to attract a factor of production. (p. 376)

Treasury bill. A short-term (less than a year, often three months) debt of the U.S. Treasury. It carries no explicit interest payment; a purchaser gains by buying a bill for less than its face value.

trough. The month of lowest economic activity prior to the beginning of a recovery; one of the four phases of the business cycle.

turnover tax. A tax on goods or services (whether they are intermediate or final products) whenever they are sold.

turning point. The trough or peak of a business cycle.

tying contract. Contract that requires the purchaser to buy another item or items in a seller's line of products in order to get the one that is really wanted. (p. 243)

underemployed. (1) Workers who can find only part-time work when they want full-time work. (2) Workers who are being paid full time but are not kept busy because of low demand for output.

underground economy. Economic activity unobserved by tax collectors and government statisticians.

underwrite. To guarantee that a new issue of stock will all be sold. (An investment banker who underwrites stock but is unable to sell it all must buy the remainder.)

undesired inventory accumulation. Actual inventory accumulation less desired inventory accumulation.

undistributed corporate profits. After-tax corporate profits less dividends paid.

unemployment. The condition of people who are willing to work but cannot find jobs. More generally, the condition of any underutilized resource.

unemployment rate. The percentage of the labor force unemployed.

union. An association of workers, formed to negotiate over wages, fringe benefits, and working conditions. (p. 385)

union shop. A business where all nonunion workers must join the union soon after they are employed. Compare with *closed shop* and *right-to-work law.* (p. 390)

unit elasticity. Elasticity of 1. If a demand curve has unit elasticity, total revenue remains unchanged as price changes. (The demand curve is a rectangular hyperbola.) If a supply curve has unit elasticity, it is a straight line that would, if extended, go through the origin. (pp. 85, 91)

unlimited liability. Responsibility for debts without limit. (p. 121)

utility. The ability to satisfy wants. (p. 103)

value added. Value of the product sold less the cost of intermediate products bought from outside suppliers.

variable cost. Any cost that increases as output increases.

variable rate mortgage. A mortgage whose interest rate is adjusted periodically in response to changes in a market rate of interest.

velocity of money. The average number of times per year that the average dollar in the money stock is spent. There are two principal ways of calculating velocity. (1) *Income velocity* is the number of times the average dollar is spent on final products (that is, GNP ÷ M). (2) *Transaction velocity* is the number of times the average dollar is spent on *any* transaction (including those for intermediate goods and financial assets). That is, total spending ÷ M.

vertical merger. See *merger.*

vicious circle of inflation and depreciation. The tendency for inflation to cause a depreciation of the currency, which can lead to more inflation and more depreciation.

vicious circle of poverty. The interrelationships that make it difficult to escape from poverty. For example, a poor country has difficulty saving and investing.

virtuous circle. The tendency for a lower-than-average rate of inflation to cause an appreciation of the currency, which can help to keep inflation.

wage-price spiral. A tendency for inflation to lead to higher nominal wages, which can lead to even more inflation.

workable competition. A compromise that limits monopoly power while allowing firms to become big enough to reap the economies of scale. A practical alternative to the often unattainable goal of perfect competition. (p. 255)

yellow-dog contract. Contract in which an employee agrees not to become a member of a union. (p. 389)

yield. The annual rate of discount that would make the present value of a stream of future payments equal to the price or present value of an asset. The *rate of return.*

zero-base budgeting. A budgeting technique that requires items to be justified anew "from the ground up," without regard to how much has been spent on them in the past.

INDEX